*Special Edition*

# Using Corel WordPerfect 7

*Special Edition*

# Using Corel WordPerfect 7

Written by Gordon McComb with

*Laura Acklen • Read Gilgen • Diane Koers • Gabrielle Nemes
Judy Petersen • Gary J. Pickavet • Robert P. Raleigh*

# Special Edition Using Corel WordPerfect 7

Copyright© 1996 by Que® Corporation.

All rights reserved. Printed in the United States of America. No part of this book may be used or reproduced in any form or by any means, or stored in a database or retrieval system, without prior written permission of the publisher except in the case of brief quotations embodied in critical articles and reviews. Making copies of any part of this book for any purpose other than your own personal use is a violation of United States copyright laws. For information, address Que Corporation, 201 W. 103rd Street, Indianapolis, IN, 46290. You may reach Que's direct sales line by calling 1-800-428-5331.

Library of Congress Catalog No.: 95-72575

ISBN: 0-7897-0140-5

This book is sold *as is*, without warranty of any kind, either express or implied, respecting the contents of this book, including but not limited to implied warranties for the book's quality, performance, merchantability, or fitness for any particular purpose. Neither Que Corporation nor its dealers or distributors shall be liable to the purchaser or any other person or entity with respect to any liability, loss, or damage caused or alleged to have been caused directly or indirectly by this book.

98 97 96    6 5 4 3 2 1

Interpretation of the printing code: the rightmost double-digit number is the year of the book's printing; the rightmost single-digit number, the number of the book's printing. For example, a printing code of 96-1 shows that the first printing of the book occurred in 1996.

All terms mentioned in this book that are known to be trademarks or service marks have been appropriately capitalized. Que cannot attest to the accuracy of this information. Use of a term in this book should not be regarded as affecting the validity of any trademark or service mark.

Screen reproductions in this book were created using Collage Plus from Inner Media, Inc., Hollis, NH.

# Credits

**PRESIDENT**
Roland Elgey

**VICE PRESIDENT AND PUBLISHER**
Marie Butler-Knight

**PUBLISHING DIRECTOR**
David W. Solomon

**EDITORIAL SERVICES DIRECTOR**
Elizabeth Keaffaber

**MANAGING EDITOR**
Michael Cunningham

**DIRECTOR OF MARKETING**
Lynn E. Zingraf

**ACQUISITIONS EDITOR**
Deborah F. Abshier

**PRODUCT DIRECTORS**
Lisa D. Wagner
Jan Snyder

**PRODUCT MARKETING MANAGER**
Kim Margolius

**ASSISTANT PRODUCT MARKETING MANAGER**
Christy Miller

**TECHNICAL EDITORS**
Rick Brown
Rebecca Campbell
Jeff Hall
Robert Hartley
Mitch Milam
Gabrielle Nemes
Jan Snyder

**PRODUCTION EDITORS**
Lisa M. Gebken
Lynn Northrup

**TECHNICAL SPECIALIST**
Nadeem Muhammed

**ACQUISITIONS COORDINATORS**
Carmen Krikorian
Tracy M. Williams

**OPERATIONS COORDINATOR**
Patty Brooks

**BOOK DESIGNER**
Ruth Harvey

**COVER DESIGNER**
Dan Armstrong

**PRODUCTION TEAM**
Stephen Adams, Marcia Brizendine, Jerry Cole, Chad Dressler, CJ East, Joan Evan, DiMonique Ford, Trey Frank, Jason Hand, Kay Hoskin, Damon Jordan, Clint Lahnen, Bob LaRoche, Michelle Lee, Darlena Murray, Ryan Oldfather, Casey Price, Kaylene Riemen, Laura Robbins, Bobbi Satterfield, Julie Searls, Kelly Warner, Paul Wilson, Donna Wright, Jeff Yesh, Jody York

**INDEXERS**
Chris Barrick
Ginny Bess

Composed in *Century Old Style* and *Franklin Gothic* by Que Corporation.

# About the Authors

**Gordon McComb** has written 45 books and more than 1,000 magazine articles. His specialties are Windows, word processing, and office automation. Gordon is the author of Que's best-selling *I Hate Windows*, and is a contributing author to Que's *Using WordPerfect 6 for DOS, Special Edition* and *Using WordPerfect 6.1 for Windows, Special Edition*. His book *WordPerfect 5.1 Macros and Templates* won *PC Magazine's* Editors' Choice Award, as well as an award for Best Product Specific book from the Computer Press Association.

**Laura Acklen** is an independent author and instructor in Austin, Texas. She has been training and supporting computer users in DOS and Windows products since 1986. Laura is the author of Que's *WordPerfect 6.0 SureSteps* and co-author of *Oops! WordPerfect… What To Do When Things Go Wrong*. She is also a contributing author of *Using WordPerfect Version 6 for Windows, Special Edition*, and the revision author for *Windows QuickStart, 3.11 Edition*. Her most recent projects include Que's *First Look at Windows 95* and Que Education's *Windows 3.1 Essentials*, *WordPerfect 6.1 for Windows Essentials*, and *Windows 95 Essentials*. Laura is also enjoying her second year as a contributing editor for *WordPerfect for Windows* Magazine.

**Read Gilgen** is director of Learning Support Services at the University of Wisconsin, Madison. He holds a Ph.D. in Latin American Literature. Read's professional interests include support of higher education, especially foreign language education. He has taught and written extensively on DOS and WordPerfect. He is author of Que's *WordPerfect for Windows Hot Tips*, and contributing author to Que's *Using WordPerfect for Windows, Special Edition*, and a frequent contributor to *WordPerfect for Windows* Magazine.

**Diane Koers** owns and operates All Business Service, a software training and consulting company formed in 1988 that serves the central Indiana area. Her area of expertise has long been in the word processing, spreadsheet, and graphics area of computing, as well as providing training and support for several popular accounting packages. Diane's authoring experience includes developing and writing software training manuals for her clients' use.

**Gabrielle Nemes** is an owner of MicroTutor Training Services and a principal in MicroPoint Incorporated, both computer and technical training firms located in the greater Seattle, Wash. area. Specializing in law firm automation, Gabrielle has been a WordPerfect certified instructor since 1989 and is a Novell Select Partner, writing custom WordPerfect macro applications and technical training manuals. Gabrielle is the author of Que's *10 Minute Guide to Microsoft Exchange* and a contributing author to Que's *Killer WordPerfect 6 Utilities*. She has also served as a technical editor for several books for Que.

**Judy Petersen** provides software training and support through a retail facility for the more popular word processing and spreadsheet programs. In her own business, Judy is a computer software consultant and trainer for businesses and individuals in the Tallahassee, Fla. area and provides abstracts of titles for firms performing environmental audits of real property throughout the southeastern U. S. She has been a contributing author of Que's *Using WordPerfect Version 6 for Windows, Special Edition, Using WordPerfect 6.1 for Windows, Using PC Tools 8.0* and *Using PC Tools for Windows, Killer WordPerfect 6 Utilities*, as well as revision author for Que's *Computer User's Dictionary*, 5th Edition. She recently co-authored Sams' *Windows 95 Unleashed*.

**Gary J. Pickavet** is the assistant superintendent for Business and Data Processing Services for the Santa Barbara County Education Office. His wife Marilyn, daughter Debbie, and son Gary Jr. know his Que projects are truly family projects. Their patience, support, and understanding through the late hours helped make this book possible. Gary has used WordPerfect extensively since version 3.0. As an author, he contributed to the Que books *Using WordPerfect Version 6 for Windows, Special Edition, Using WordPerfect for DOS, Upgrading to Windows 3.1*, and *Killer Windows Utilities*. He has also served as technical editor for several books for Que.

**Robert Raleigh** is a freelance writer and multimedia developer. In his six years at WordPerfect Corporation, Robert documented WordPerfect features in manuals and online help systems. He has also written numerous articles for *WordPerfect Magazine* and the *PerfectOffice Newsletter*. He specializes in multimedia design and typography. Robert currently plies his trade at the foot of the beautiful Wasatch mountain range in Salt Lake City, Utah.

# Acknowledgments

Que Corporation would like to offer a special thanks to several people who worked extra hard to make this book the best possible.

Acquisitions editor Debbie Abshier worked tirelessly with the book's eight authors, coordinating their writing schedules in accordance with the timing of Corel's WordPerfect beta releases.

Product developers Lisa Wagner and Jan Snyder spent countless hours shooting figures and comparing text to the final product before shipping. With the substantial revisions made to the latest WordPerfect product, Jan's technical expertise in tying together the various technical editor's comments was vital to ensure the most accurate book possible.

Production editor Lisa Gebken did her best not only to set deadlines for the book's authors, but to meet her own.

Special thanks to Robert Hartley and Kathy Ivens, who jumped in part way through the project and helped with the technical editing. Their assistance in acquiring updated versions of WordPerfect, as well as answering questions over the phone and via e-mail, is greatly appreciated. Also, kudos to Sue Plumley, who added her expertise in shooting figures and completing some eleventh-hour tech editing.

# We'd Like To Hear from You!

As part of our continuing effort to produce books of the highest possible quality, Que would like to hear your comments. To stay competitive, we really want you, as a computer book reader and user, to let us know what you like or dislike most about this book or other Que products.

You can mail comments, ideas, or suggestions for improving future editions to the address below, or send us a fax at (317) 581-4663. For the online inclined, Macmillan Computer Publishing has a forum on CompuServe (type **GO QUEBOOKS** at any prompt) through which our staff and authors are available for questions and comments. The address of our Internet site is **http://www.mcp.com** (World Wide Web).

In addition to exploring our forum, please feel free to contact me personally to discuss your opinions of this book: I'm **74404,3307** on CompuServe, and I'm **lwagner@que.mcp.com** on the Internet.

Thanks in advance—your comments will help us to continue publishing the best books available on computer topics in today's market.

Lisa D. Wagner
Product Director
Que Corporation
201 W. 103rd Street
Indianapolis, Indiana 46290
USA

# Contents at a Glance

Introduction  1

## I | Basic Tasks

1 Getting Started  11
2 Creating and Saving a Document  55
3 Retrieving and Editing Documents  81
4 Formatting Text  121
5 Formatting Pages and Documents  155
6 Using Writing Tools  207
7 Integrating Text and Graphics  249
8 Basic Output: Printing, Faxing, and E-Mail  277

## II | Automating Your Work

9 Customizing WordPerfect  299
10 Using Styles  333
11 Using Templates  363
12 Creating Macros  387
13 Working with Toolbars  413

## III | Specialized Procedures

14 Working with Text Columns  433
15 Organizing Documents with Outlining  461
16 Working with Tables  495
17 Creating and Modifying Charts with WP Draw  535
18 Importing Data and Working with Other Programs  559
19 Assembling Documents with Merge and Sort  587

## IV | Professional Output

20 Using Fonts and Special Characters  633
21 Using Advanced Graphics Techniques  657
22 Using WordPerfect Draw and TextArt  683
23 Desktop Publishing with WordPerfect  723
24 Using the Equation Editor  759

## V  Large Documents

25  Using Footnotes and Endnotes   801
26  Assembling Document References   823
27  Working with Large and Multi-Part Documents   869
28  Using WordPerfect with the Corel WordPerfect Suite   899

## VI  Techniques from the Pros

29  Advanced File Management   917
30  Advanced Macro Techniques   949
31  Advanced Tables   981
32  Interactive Documents   1021
33  Publishing Documents on the World Wide Web   1041

## VII  Appendixes

A  Installing and Setting Up WordPerfect 7   1075
B  Making the Transition to WordPerfect 7   1091

## VIII  Indexes

Action Index   1121
Index of Common Problems   1125
Index   1135

# Table of Contents

**Introduction** 1

    WordPerfect 7 Enhancements 2

    Who Should Use This Book? 4

    How This Book Is Organized 4

    Where To Find Help 6

    How To Use This Book 6

    Conventions Used in This Book 7

## I | Basic Tasks

### 1 Getting Started 11

    Starting and Exiting WordPerfect 12

    Using the WordPerfect 7 Interface 14

        Using the Keyboard 14

        Using the Mouse 14

    Understanding the Editing Screen 16

        Windows 95 Controls 17

        The WordPerfect Title Bar 20

        The Pull-Down Menus 20

        QuickMenus 21

        The Toolbar 22

        The Power Bar 23

        The Status Bar 24

        The Ruler Bar 25

        Guidelines 25

        The Scroll Bars 26

        Previous and Next Page Buttons 27

        Feature Bars 27

        View Modes 28

        Hide Bars 30

    Using Dialog Boxes 31

        Moving Around in a Dialog Box 32

        Understanding Dialog Box Elements 33

        Using QuickSpots 39

Understanding What You Don't See   41
    Reveal Codes   41
    Show Spaces, Tabs, and Hard Returns   42
    Templates   43
Working with Multiple Documents   43
    Arranging Documents On-Screen   44
    Switching Between Documents   44
    Tiling or Cascading Documents   44
Using Help   45
    The Help Menu   47
    The WordPerfect Help Dialog Box   48
    Help's Glossary Terms and Hints   52
    Navigating the Help System   53

## 2 Creating and Saving a Document   55

Understanding WordPerfect's Built-in Settings   56

Entering Text in WordPerfect   56
    Inserting Blank Lines   59
    Creating a Sample Letter   59

Moving Through the Document   61
    Moving with the Mouse   61
    Moving with the Keyboard   63
    Moving the Insertion Point with Go To   64
    Completing the Sample Letter   66

Adding Text Within a Document   67

Using Typeover   67

Using Cancel (Esc)   68

Printing an On-Screen Document   68

Saving a Document to Disk   70

Saving a Document with a Different Name or File Format   75

Closing Documents   77

Opening New Document Windows   78

Exiting WordPerfect   79

## 3  Retrieving and Editing Documents    81

Opening Files    82
    Opening a File    82
    Using Insert File To Combine Files    85

Revising and Editing Text    86
    Inserting and Overwriting Text    86
    Deleting Text    87
    Restoring Deleted Text    88

Using WordPerfect's Undo and Redo Features    89

Understanding WordPerfect's Hidden Codes    91
    Working with Reveal Codes    93
    Closing the Reveal Codes Window    94
    Editing in the Reveal Codes Window    95
    Changing the Size of the Current Reveal Codes Window    96
    Customizing Reveal Codes to Meet Your Needs    97

Selecting Text    99
    Highlighting a Selection    99
    Canceling a Highlighted Selection    104
    Transferring Selected Text to Another Location    104
    Deleting and Undeleting a Selection    109
    Saving a Selection to a File    109
    Enhancing Text by Using Block Selections    109
    Converting the Case of a Selection    110

Using Find and Replace    111
    Finding Words and Phrases    111
    Choosing Search Criteria    113
    Finding and Replacing Words and Phrases    113
    Understanding Find and Replace Options    115
    Finding and Replacing Word Forms    117
    Finding and Replacing Formatting Codes    118

## 4  Formatting Text    121

Using WordPerfect's Text-Formatting Tools    122
    WordPerfect's Default Text Format Settings    122
    The Format Menu    123
    The QuickMenu    123

　　　　　　The Toolbar, Power Bar, and Ruler Bar   124
　　　　　　Paragraph QuickSpot   125
　　　　　　Using the Keyboard   125
　　　　　　QuickFormat   125
　　　　　　Auto Code Placement   126

　　　　Formatting Characters   126
　　　　　　Changing Character Appearance and Size   126
　　　　　　Changing Character Attributes with the Power Bar   130

　　　　Formatting Lines and Paragraphs   130
　　　　　　Centering and Flush Right   131
　　　　　　Controlling Line Spacing and Line Height   132
　　　　　　Setting Margins   135
　　　　　　Using Indent and Back Tab   137
　　　　　　Setting and Using Tabs   138
　　　　　　Formatting Text with QuickFormat   144
　　　　　　Customizing Formatting Options   145

　　　　Using Justification   147

　　　　Using Hyphenation   148
　　　　　　Splitting Words with Hyphens   148
　　　　　　Preventing Hyphenation   149
　　　　　　Using Automatic Hyphenation   150
　　　　　　Choosing a Hyphenation Point   150
　　　　　　Removing Hyphenation from a Document   151
　　　　　　Customizing the Hyphenation Prompt   152

## 5  Formatting Pages and Documents   155

　　　　Creating Separate Pages   156
　　　　　　Inserting Page Breaks   156
　　　　　　Forcing New Pages   157

　　　　Centering Pages   158

　　　　Keeping Text Together   159
　　　　　　Block Protect   159
　　　　　　Conditional End of Page   160
　　　　　　Prevent Widows and Orphans   161

　　　　Working with Facing Pages   162

　　　　Numbering Pages   163
　　　　　　Choosing a Page Number Position   163
　　　　　　Choosing a Page Number Format   164

Customizing the Page Number Appearance   165
Changing the Current Page Number   168
Incrementing Page Numbers   169
Inserting a Page Number   170
Counting Document Pages   172
Suppressing Page Numbering   172

Using Headers and Footers   173
Creating a Header or Footer   173
Editing Headers and Footers   176
Using Page Numbers in Headers and Footers   176
Suppressing Headers and Footers   177
Discontinuing Headers and Footers   178
Using Other Features with Headers and Footers   178

Selecting Page Size and Type   179
Choosing a Different Page Size   179
Creating Custom Page Definitions   180
Creating a New Page Definition   180
Editing and Deleting Page Definitions   181
Customizing Page Size   182
Considering Other Page Size Factors   183

Using Subdivide Page   184

Using Delay Codes   185

Using the Make It Fit Expert Feature   187

Working with Envelopes   188
Addressing an Envelope   188
Creating New Envelope Definitions   189
Setting Envelope Options   190
Editing and Deleting Envelope Definitions   190

Working with Labels   191
Choosing a Label Definition   191
Using Labels   192
Creating Custom Label Definitions   192
Editing and Deleting Label Definitions   193
Understanding Label Customizing Options   194
Creating Custom Label Files   195

Using Advance To Place Text   196

Setting the Document Initial Font   197

Creating the Initial Codes Style   199

Setting Up the Redline Method   200

Using Document Summaries   201
    Creating a Summary on Save/Exit   204
    Using Document Summary Options   204
    Customizing the Document Summary Fields   205

# 6 Using Writing Tools   207

Using Spell Checker   208
    Starting Spell Checker   209
    Spell Checking the Document   210
    Looking Up a Word   216
    Using Spell-As-You-Go   217
    Customizing Spell Checker   217
    Working with Main and User Word Lists   220

Using Grammatik   224
    Running Grammatik   225
    Customizing Grammatik for the Current Document   228
    Working with Writing Styles   229
    Displaying Parse Tree and Parts of Speech Diagrams   230
    Getting Statistical Information   231

Using the Thesaurus   232
    Looking Up a Word in the Thesaurus   232
    Understanding the Thesaurus Window   233
    Replacing a Word   234
    Looking Up Reference Words   235

Working with Other Languages   235
    Using the Language Feature   236
    Using the Language Resource File   237

Using QuickCorrect   238

Using SmartQuotes   239

Checking Document Information   240

Using Other Writing Tools   241
    Using Document Comments   241
    Using Hidden Text   244
    Using Abbreviations   245
    Inserting the File Name   247

## 7 Integrating Text and Graphics  249

Using Graphics Lines  250
  Using Horizontal Lines  250
  Using Vertical Lines  251
  Customizing Lines Using the Mouse  252
  Deleting Lines  253

Using Graphics Borders  255
  Using Paragraph Borders  256
  Adding Paragraph Fill  257
  Adding a Page Border  258
  Adding a Column Border  259
  Turning Off a Border  260
  Deleting a Border  261

Using Graphics Boxes  262
  Understanding Graphics Box Styles  262
  Creating a Graphics Box  268
  Moving a Graphics Box  269
  Resizing a Graphics Box  270
  Deleting a Graphics Box  271
  Using a Graphics Box in a Letter  271

Using Watermarks  272
  Using a Text Watermark  272
  Using Images as Watermarks  273
  Creating a Watermark  275

## 8 Basic Output: Printing, Faxing, and E-Mail  277

Using Basic Printing Skills  278
  Selecting a Printer  278
  Using Zoom and View To See the Printed Output  279
  Printing: The Basics  280
  Printing Multiple Copies  281
  Canceling a Print Job  281

Printing Specific Document Pages  283
  Printing the Current Page  283
  Printing Multiple Pages  283
  Printing Odd or Even Numbered Pages  285

Using Printing Options  286
    Printing Selected Text  286
    Printing Booklets  286
    Printing Documents with Graphics or Color  286
    Printing the Document Summary  287
    Using Custom Print Settings  287

Controlling the Printer and Print Jobs  289
    Controlling Print Jobs from WordPerfect  289
    Controlling Print Jobs Using Windows  290

Selecting and Setting Up Your Printer  290
    Understanding Printer Drivers  291
    Selecting and Configuring Your Printer  291
    Adding Fonts for Your Printer  292

Using Other Forms of Output  293
    Printing on a Network  293
    Printing to a File  294
    Faxing from WordPerfect 7  294
    Using Novell GroupWise or Other E-Mail Programs  295

# II  Automating Your Work

## 9  Customizing WordPerfect  299

Customizing the Display  300
    Document Display  300
    Show Formatting Symbols  303
    View/Zoom Display  304
    Reveal Codes Display  305
    Ruler Bar Display  306
    Merge Codes Display  306

Customizing Environment Options  306
    User Information  307
    Language  307
    Beep Options  308
    Save Workspace  308
    Menu Display Options  308
    Formatting Options  309
    Automatically Select Words  310

    Set QuickMark on Save   310
    Activate Hypertext   310
    Reformat Documents for Default Printer on Open   311
    Code Page   311

Customizing File Preferences   312
    Documents/Backup Files   315
    Templates   316
        Labels   318

Customizing Document Summaries   319
    Subject Search Text   319
    Default Descriptive Type   319
    Create Summary on Save/Exit   320
    Use Descriptive Names   320

Customizing Convert Options   320

Customizing Window Features   321
    Toolbars   321
    The Power Bar   322
    The Status Bar   322
    The Pull-Down Menus   324

Creating and Customizing Keyboards   324
    Selecting Another Keyboard   325
    Creating, Copying, and Editing Keyboards   325
    Making Keyboard Assignments   327
    Deleting and Renaming Keyboards   331

## 10  Using Styles   333

Understanding Styles   334
    Benefits of Using Styles   335
    Styles Versus Macros   335

Considering Types of Styles   336
    Document, Paragraph, and Character Styles   336
    Initial Style   338
    System Styles   338
    Template Styles   338
    Outline Styles   339
    Graphics Styles   339

Creating Styles  340
   Working with a Document or a Template  340
   Bringing Up the Style List Dialog Box  341
   Creating a QuickStyle  341
   Creating a Style Through the Style List Dialog Box  343
Editing Styles  344
   Displaying Style Names  345
   Deleting a Style  346
   Copying and Modifying a Style Definition  347
   Copying Text, Graphics, and Formatting onto the Clipboard  348
   Bringing Up the Styles Editor  348
   Editing a Style Definition  349
   Editing Styles Editor Contents  350
Using Styles Together  350
   Nesting Styles  351
   Chaining Styles  351
Using Styles  352
   Inserting Styles  353
   Using Power Bar Buttons  353
   Applying Document Styles  354
   Applying Paragraph Styles  354
   Applying Character Styles  355
Working with Styles from Other Files  355
   Using System Styles  356
   Using Templates  356
   Saving Styles to Another File  356
   Retrieving Styles from Another Document or Template  357
Examining Some Styles in Use  358
   Letterhead Document Style  358
   Quotation Character Style  359
   Border Text Paragraph Style  360
   Q&A Linked Paragraph Styles  360

## 11 Using Templates  363

Understanding Templates  364
   Comparing Templates to Macros, Merges, and Styles  366
   Applying Templates to Documents  368

Using the Template Feature Bar   369
Using the Templates Provided with WordPerfect for Windows   370
Working with Templates   373
    Editing a Template   374
    Creating a New Template   375
    Deleting Templates You No Longer Need   378
    Creating New Template Groups   378
Using Objects in Templates   378
    Adding an Object to a Template   379
    Copying Existing Objects from Other Templates   380
    Removing Objects from the Current Template   381
Associating Features and Events   381
    Associating to a Feature   382
    Associating Macros to Triggers   383
    Planning for Embedded Macros   384
Using the Letter Expert   384
Using WordPerfect's Other Template Experts   385

## 12   Creating Macros   387

Creating a Macro   388
    Important Considerations   389
    Steps To Record a Macro   390
    A Practical Application Using Macros   391

Playing a Macro   392

Re-Recording a Macro   393

Understanding Where Macros Are Recorded   394
    The Current Template Location Option   394
    The Default Template Location Option   395

Understanding Macro File Names   395
    Unless Noted Otherwise, Macros Use the WCM Extension   396
    All Macros Use Only Valid Windows 95 File Names   396

Creating Instant Play Macros   397
    Renaming a Previously Recorded Macro for Ctrl+Key Playback   397
    Ctrl+Key and Shift+Ctrl+Key Combinations Already in Use   398
    Playing Macros in Other Ways   399

Stopping a Macro   399
    Stopping a Macro During Recording   400
    Stopping a Macro During Playback   400
Using the Macros that Come with WordPerfect   400
Using Macros for Writing and Editing Tasks   401
    A Macro To Transpose Two Characters   402
    A Macro To Write a Memo   403
Using Macros for Common Formatting Tasks   404
Playing Macros Using Other Methods   405
    Assigning a Macro to a Keyboard Layout   405
    Adding a Macro to a Toolbar   408
Managing Macro Files   409
    Creating a Folder for Macros   410
    Moving Files into the MACROS Folder   410
    Specifying the Macros Folder in Location of Files   410
    Giving Macros Descriptive File Names   411
    Deleting Macros You No Longer Need   412

## 13 Working with Toolbars   413

Why Use the Toolbar and Power Bar?   414

Hiding and Viewing the Toolbar   415

Switching Between Toolbars   415

Examining the Toolbar and Power Bar Icons   416

Working with the Toolbar   417
    Positioning the Toolbar On-Screen   417
    Working with Large Toolbars   418
    Changing the Button Style   419

Customizing a Toolbar   420
    Moving Toolbar Buttons   421
    Assigning Program Features to Buttons   421
    Assigning a Text Script to a Button   422
    Assigning Macros to Buttons   423
    Customizing a Button's Text and Picture   424

Customizing the Power Bar   426
    Hiding and Viewing the Power Bar   427
    Customizing Power Bar Button Faces   427
    Adding, Moving, and Deleting Power Bar Buttons   428

## III  Specialized Procedures

### 14  Working with Text Columns  433

    The Types of Columns  434

    Newspaper Columns  436
        Defining Newspaper Columns Using the Power Bar  436
        Defining Newspaper Columns Using the Columns Dialog Box  438
        Defining Newspaper Columns with Custom Widths  440
        Working with Columnar Text  442

    Balanced Newspaper Columns  445

    Parallel Columns  446
        Defining Parallel Columns  448
        Typing Text in Parallel Columns  448
        Adding Space Between Rows in Parallel Columns  450
        Editing Parallel Columns  451
        Moving Parallel Columns  451

    Changing the Appearance of Columns  452
        Changing Column Widths Using the Ruler  452
        Changing Column Widths Using the Column Guidelines  454
        Adding Borders, Fills, or Shadows to Columns  455

### 15  Organizing Documents with Outlining  461

    Understanding What Outlines Can Do  462

    Using Bullets & Numbers  462
        Creating a Simple List with Bullets & Numbers  463
        Making Fewer Keystrokes with Bullets & Numbers  465
        Understanding the Bullets & Numbers Styles  465

    Introducing Outlines  469

    Introducing the Outline Feature Bar  471

    Creating an Outline  473
        Creating Simple Numbered and Bulleted Outlines  475
        Creating Incrementing Numbers in Normal Text  477

    Displaying and Editing an Outline  477
        Hiding and Showing Families and Levels  478
        Editing Outline Text  481

    Modifying an Outline's Structure  481

Adjusting Levels   481
Changing To and From Body Text   482
Copying, Cutting, and Pasting Families   482
Renumbering an Outline   484
Changing an Outline's Definition   485

Introducing Outline Styles   486
Using the Define Outline Dialog Box   487
Editing and Creating Outline Definitions   489
Saving Your Definitions   494

## 16 Working with Tables   495

Understanding Tables   496

Creating a Table   498
Converting Tabular Columns to Tables   500
Moving Within a Table   501
Entering Text   502
Adding Rows to a Table   503
Selecting Text and Cells   503
Deleting Text from Cells   504
Cutting, Copying, and Pasting Text   505
Using the Tables QuickMenu   506
Using the Table Edit QuickSpot   507
Deleting, Cutting, or Copying a Table   507
Saving and Printing a Table   508

Editing the Table Structure   509
Tools for Editing a Table   509
Changing Column Widths   510
Changing the Table Size   513
Joining Cells   514
Splitting Cells   515
Changing Row Height   516
Creating Header Rows   517

Formatting Table Text   518
Understanding Formatting Precedence   518
Accessing the Table Format Dialog Box   519
Formatting Columns   519
Formatting Cells   521
Formatting the Entire Table   522

Changing Table Lines, Borders, and Fills   524
   Using SpeedFormat   524
   Changing Lines   525
   Turning Off Cell Lines   526
   Using Table Cell Guides   526
   Understanding Default Line Styles   527
   Changing Borders   528
   Changing Fills   528

Adding Other Enhancements to a Table   529
   Adding Graphics to a Table   529
   Adding Rotated Text   530
   Adding Text Attributes in Cells   531
   Adding Text with Different Attributes   531

Exploring Other Uses for Tables   532
   Creating Phone Message Forms   532
   Creating Forms for Electronic Fill-In   532

## 17 Creating and Modifying Charts with WP Draw   535

Understanding Chart Basics   536

Understanding How Data Affects a Chart   537

Understanding the Chart Types   538

Creating the Chart   541
   Touring the WP Draw Interface   543
   Moving Between the Chart and the Rest of the Document   544

Changing the Underlying Data   544
   Formatting Data   546
   Widening and Narrowing Columns   546
   Removing or Adding Columns and Rows   547

Changing the Appearance of the Chart   548
   Adding Titles   548
   Including a Legend   549
   Using Labels   550
   Changing Chart Types   551
   Making Other Changes   552
   Making Changes to a Series   554
   Making Changes to Individual Chart Types   557

Placing the Chart in the Document   558

## 18 Importing Data and Working with Other Programs  559

Understanding the Conversion Process  560

Setting File Preferences for Imported Files  561
- Setting Preferences for ASCII Delimited Text Files  562
- Setting Preferences for Metafiles  562
- Setting Preferences for Code Pages and Other Options  563

Importing and Working with Word Processing Data  564
- Importing Documents with WordPerfect's Convert Feature  564
- Exporting Documents with WordPerfect's Convert Feature  568
- Converting Documents to an Intermediate Format  569
- Importing Documents with the Clipboard  570
- Importing Documents with DDE  572

Importing and Working with Spreadsheet/Database Data  573
- Copying Spreadsheet/Database Data  573
- Copying and Linking Spreadsheet/Database Data  577
- Handling Special Spreadsheet/Database Conditions  578
- Importing Spreadsheet Data with DDE  580
- Importing Spreadsheet Data with OLE  580
- Exporting Spreadsheet/Database Data  581

Importing and Working with Graphics Data and Other Types of Data  581
- Creating a DDE Link to Data in Another Program  582
- Creating an OLE Link to Data in Another Program  583

## 19 Assembling Documents with Merge and Sort  587

Using Merge  588

Performing a Simple Merge  588
- Creating the Data File  588
- Creating the Form File  591
- Creating Envelopes  593
- Performing the Merge  595

Understanding Data Files  596
- Understanding Records and Fields  596
- Understanding the Types of Data Files  597
- Understanding Field Names  598
- Using the Quick Data Entry Dialog Box  598
- Entering Data Directly in an Existing Data File  600

Editing the Data File Structure 601
Understanding the Merge Feature Bar 602

Understanding Form Files 604
Using the Merge Feature Bar for Form Files 604
Associating Form and Data Files 605
Understanding Merge Codes 607
Controlling Merge Codes Display 609
Understanding the Keyboard Code 609

Understanding the Merge Process 611
Understanding the Perform Merge Dialog Box 611
Creating Envelopes and Labels 617

Examining Advanced Merge Topics 618
Working with User Input 619
Using Data Files from Other Sources 622
Merging into Tables 623

Using Sort 624
Understanding Sort Record Types 625
Understanding Sort Keys 626
Using Multiple Keys to Sort and Select Records 628

# IV | Professional Output

## 20 Using Fonts and Special Characters 633

Understanding Windows Font Management 634

Installing TrueType Fonts 636

Installing WordPerfect's TrueType Fonts 639

Accessing Special Characters 640
WordPerfect Characters 644
Compose 644
Overstrike 645

Font Mapping 648
Understanding AFC Attributes 648
Editing Automatic Font Changes 650
Editing Display Font Mapping 651

Working with Multiple Languages 653
Entering a WordPerfect Language Code 653

Using Foreign Language Keyboards   655
Working with Character Maps   656

## 21  Using Advanced Graphics Techniques   657

Inserting a Drop Cap   658

Customizing Lines   658
- Changing Line Style   659
- Changing Line Thickness   660
- Setting Line Color   661
- Customizing Horizontal Lines   662
- Customizing Vertical Lines   664

Customizing Borders   666
- Setting Spacing   666
- Changing Color   667
- Changing Corners   668
- Adding a Drop Shadow   668
- Adding Fill   669

Customizing Graphics Boxes   669
- Choosing a Box Style   670
- Choosing Contents   671
- Creating a Caption   672
- Choosing Position Options   673
- Choosing Size Options   674
- Editing Border and Fill   675
- Adjusting Text Wrap   675

Retrieving a Graphics Image   676

Editing a Graphics Image   677
- Rotating Images   678
- Moving an Image   679
- Scaling an Image   679
- Changing Colors   680
- Changing Contrast   681
- Changing Brightness   681
- Setting Fill   681
- Mirroring Images   682
- Using the Image Settings Dialog Box   682

Creating Graphics with Drag To Create   682

## 22 Using WordPerfect Draw and TextArt  683

Starting WP Draw  684
    Creating a New Drawing  684
    Editing an Existing Graphic  685
    Updating Your Document  685

Exploring WP Draw  686
    Glancing at the Pull-Down Menus  686
    Using WP Drawing Tools  687
    Viewing the Tool Palette  689
    Viewing the Ruler and Grid  689

Creating Shapes  690
    Using the Drawing Tools  691
    Using the Mouse and Keyboard To Draw  692

Drawing a Shape  693
    Drawing a Line  694
    Drawing Lines, Polygons, Curves, and Closed Curves  694
    Drawing Rectangles, Arcs, and Ellipses  695
    Drawing Squares and Circles  697
    Drawing Freehand  697
    Drawing Arrows  698

Retrieving and Positioning Clip Art  700

Inserting a Chart into Your Drawing  702

Editing a Figure  703
    Selecting an Item  703
    Deleting an Item  704
    Moving an Item  704
    Copying an Item  705
    Changing the Size and Shape  706

Changing the Shape Attributes  707
    Applying Color  707
    Using the Color Palettes  707
    Using More Options To Change Colors  708
    Filling Solids  709
    Changing the Line or Border Pattern  710

Using Text in WP Draw  712
    Adding Text to the Drawing  712

Using Common Text Features   713
    Wrapping Text Around an Object   714

Scanning or Capturing an Image into WP Draw   715
    Selecting the Image Source   715
    Acquiring the Image   716

Adding the Drawing to Your WordPerfect Document   716

Using TextArt   717
    Understanding the Tools   717
    Saving TextArt   720
    Using TextArt   720

## 23 Desktop Publishing with WordPerfect   723

A Word About Using WordPerfect for Desktop Publishing   724

Designing Successful Publications   725

Planning the Page   729
    Determining Page Margins   729
    Incorporating Columns   731

Refining the Page   736
    Aligning Text   737
    Using Line Spacing   739

Choosing Fonts   740
    Using Typefaces and Attributes   741
    Using Type Sizes   742
    Using Typographical Controls   745

Using Color   750
    Using Color with Text   751
    Using Color with Graphics   753
    Creating a Color Document   756

## 24 Using the Equation Editor   759

Understanding the Equation Editor   760

Starting the Equation Editor   760

Examining the Equation Editor  762
Creating a Simple Equation  764
    Creating Proper Spacing in an Equation  764
    Creating a Simple Fraction  766
    Creating Superscripts and Subscripts  767
Editing Equations  768
Reviewing Key Concepts  768
    Defining Terms  769
    Understanding Syntax  771
Working with the Equation Editor Features  773
    Using the Editing Pane  773
    Using an Equation Keyboard  774
    Using the Equation Palettes  774
    Using WordPerfect Characters  776
    Altering the Equation Display  776
    Using the Equation Toolbar  777
Using Functions and Commands
To Create Equations  778
    Using Functions in the Equation Editor  779
    Using FUNC, BOLD, and ITAL to Format Equations  781
    Using a Backslash (\) To Format Literals  782
    Forming Fractions with the OVER, LEFT, and RIGHT Commands  783
    Creating Sums and Integrals  785
    Creating Roots  787
    Using the Matrix Commands  787
    Creating Multiline Expressions with STACK and STACKALIGN  790
    Using Other Commands and Symbols  791
Changing Equation Box Options  792
    Numbering Equations  794
    Embedding Equations in Text  794
    Changing the Equation Font  795
Saving and Retrieving Equation Files  796

# V  Large Documents

### 25  Using Footnotes and Endnotes   801

Using Footnotes   802
  Inserting Footnotes   803
  Editing Footnotes   808
  Copying Footnotes   809
  Moving Footnotes   810
  Deleting Footnotes   811
  Setting a New Footnote Number   811
  Using Footnote Options   812

Using Endnotes   817
  Inserting Endnotes   818
  Editing and Manipulating Endnotes   818
  Using Endnote Options   818
  Placing Endnotes   819

Converting Footnotes to Endnotes and Endnotes to Footnotes   820

### 26  Assembling Document References   823

Keeping Track of Document Revisions   824
  Highlighting for Emphasis   824
  Revising Routed Documents   826
  Automatically Marking Revisions Using Compare Document   829
  Purging Marked Changes from a Saved Document   834

Creating Lists   834
  Marking Text for Lists   835
  Defining a List   837
  Using Generate To Create and Update Document References   842

Creating a Table of Contents   843
  Marking Text for a Table of Contents   843
  Defining a Table of Contents   845

Creating a Table of Authorities   848
  Marking Text for a Table of Authorities   850
  Defining a Table of Authorities   854

Creating an Index   858

Marking Text for an Index   859
Defining an Index   862

Using Automatic Cross-Referencing   865
Marking References and Targets   866
Marking References to Footnotes and Endnotes   868

## 27  Working with Large and Multi-Part Documents   869

Creating Master Documents and Subdocuments   870
Creating Subdocuments   871
Building a Master Document   872
Adding, Deleting, and Moving Subdocuments   876

Creating Subdocuments Within Subdocuments   877

Expanding a Master Document   878

Saving a Master Document   881

Condensing a Master Document   882

Creating a Table of Contents, List, Index, or Table of Authorities   884
Marking Text for the Table of Contents   884
Defining the Tables of Contents   885
Generating Tables, Lists, and Indexes   886

Using Styles with Master Documents   887
Using Open Styles To Begin Subdocuments   888
Using Paragraph and Character Styles To Format Headings   889

Inserting Page Numbering Codes   890
Inserting a New Page Number   891
Inserting Chapter Codes   891

Using Headers and Footers with Master Documents   892

Adding Footnotes and Endnotes   893
Numbering Footnotes   893
Placing Endnotes   893

Using Cross-References   894

Using Search, Replace, and Spell Check in a Master Document   894

Printing a Master Document   895
Printing the Entire Document   895
Printing Selected Pages or Chapters   895

## 28 Using WordPerfect with the Corel WordPerfect Suite  899

Using the Address Book  900
  Creating an Address Book  900
  Renaming an Address Book  901
  Deleting an Address Book  901
  Adding an Address to the Address Book  902
  Editing an Address Book Entry  904
  Deleting an Address Book Entry  905
  Inserting an Address into a WordPerfect Document  905

Choosing To Paste, Link, or Embed  906

Using Quattro Pro with WordPerfect  906
  Importing a Spreadsheet from Quattro Pro  907
  Converting Spreadsheet Formulas  908

Using Presentations with WordPerfect  908
  Linking a Presentations Chart  909
  Inserting a Presentations Drawing  910
  Exporting a WordPerfect Outline for a Presentations Slide Show  910

Using CorelFLOW  911

Publishing a WordPerfect Document to Envoy  912

Using QuickTasks  913

One for All and All for One  914

# VI  Techniques from the Pros

## 29 Advanced File Management  917

Using the File Management Tools  918
  Copying and Moving Files  918
  Renaming Files  920
  Deleting Files  920
  Changing File Attributes  921
  Opening a File as a Copy  922
  Printing a File  923
  Working with More Than One File  923
  Creating, Renaming, and Removing Folders  923

Customizing the File/Folder List Display  925

Arranging Files and Folders in the List Box   926
Switching to Tree View   928

Finding Files   928
Listing Files by Type   929
Creating a Partial Listing Using DOS Wildcard Characters   930
Using QuickFinder To Search for Files   931

Using the FAVORITES Folder   937
Opening the FAVORITES Folder   937
Adding Shortcuts to the FAVORITES Folder   938
Deleting Shortcuts From the FAVORITES Folder   938

Using the QuickFinder Manager   939
Starting the QuickFinder Manager   939
Creating a Standard Fast Search   940
Creating a Custom Fast Search   942
Editing a Fast Search   943
Updating a Fast Search   944
Displaying Fast Search Information   944
Setting Preferences in the QuickFinder Manager   945

## 30  Advanced Macro Techniques   949

Understanding Macro Storage   950
Opening a Macro Stored in a Template   950
Opening a Macro File   950
Printing a Macro File   951

Using the Macro Feature Bar   952

Introducing the WordPerfect Macro Language   953
Recording a Sample Macro   953
Examining the TESTMAC Macro   954
Using Two Kinds of Commands   955
Comparing Product Commands Versus the
WordPerfect 5.1 Macro Model   956

Understanding the Syntax of Macro Commands   957

Getting To Know the WordPerfect Macro Language   959
Understanding Variables   959
System Variables   960
Commands That Ask for User Input   961
Commands That Make Decisions   963

Commands That Control the Flow of a Macro   966
Commands That Run Other Macros   969
Other Useful Commands   971
Dialog Box Commands   974
The Macro Command Inserter   975
Useful Product Function Commands   975

Extending Your Macro Programming Skills   977

## 31 Advanced Tables   981

Creating and Using Tables: The Next Step   982
    Using the Tables Toolbar, QuickMenu, and Table Edit Tools   982
    Positioning Tables   983
    Placing Tables Side by Side   984
    Splitting Tables   984
    Joining Tables   985
    Creating Forms with Irregular Columns   985
    Merging and Sorting Data in Tables   986
    Importing a Spreadsheet to a Table   986

Using Custom Table Styles   988
    Creating Your Own Table SpeedFormat Styles   988
    Using Alternating Fills for Rows or Columns   988

Customizing Table Lines and Borders   990
    Customizing Lines   990
    Customizing Table Borders   992
    Customizing Cell and Table Shading   993

Using Basic Math and Formulas in Tables   995
    Understanding Spreadsheets   996
    Designing a Spreadsheet   996
    Adding Spreadsheet Capabilities to a Table   997
    Formatting Numeric Data   999
    Forcing Text Mode for Cells that Contain Numbers   1001
    Creating Formulas   1001
    Copying Formulas   1003
    Using Functions in Formulas   1004
    Modifying, Deleting, and Calculating Cells and Formulas   1005
    Locking Table Cells   1005

Designing More Complex Tables: The Grade-Tracking Table  1006
    Understanding Functions  1007
    Using a Function  1008
    Using Formulas with Absolute References  1008
    Using the *SUM()* Function To Create a Total Points Formula  1009
    Creating the Percent Formula and a Percent Format  1010
    Using the *IF()* Function To Calculate the Letter Grade  1010

Using Names To Create a Report Card Table  1011
    Creating the Form  1011
    Creating Names in Tables  1012
    Using Names in Tables  1013

Using Floating Cells To Create a Mortgage Loan Approval Letter  1014
    Understanding and Creating Floating Cells  1014
    Using Calendar Math in a Floating Cell  1015
    Using the *PMT()* Function To Calculate a Loan Payment  1016
    Simplifying Data Entry in a Floating Cell Letter  1018

Using QuickFill To Simplify Data Entry  1019
    Understanding QuickFill  1019
    Using QuickFill To Enter the Days of the Week  1020
    Filling In the Dates of the Month  1020
    Other Uses for QuickFill  1020

## 32 Interactive Documents  1021

Understanding Hypertext  1022

Working with WordPerfect's Hypertext Feature  1023

Creating an Interactive Report  1024
    Designing Your Hypertext Document  1025
    Marking a Hypertext Target with a Bookmark  1027
    Linking Text Within a Document  1028
    Editing Hypertext Links  1030
    Linking Documents with Hypertext  1030
    Linking Hypertext to Macros  1031
    Changing the Style of Hypertext Buttons  1032
    Activating a Document with Hypertext  1033

Creating a Link to a Web Page  1033

Navigating a Hypertext Document   1034
   Jumping and Returning in an Active Hypertext Document   1034
   Jumping and Returning in an Inactive Hypertext Document   1035
   Jumping and Returning Between Documents   1035
   Jumping to Web Pages   1036
   Running Macros with Hypertext   1036

Embedding Sound in a Document   1037
   Using WordPerfect with a Sound Board   1037
   Linking Sound Files to a Document   1037
   Exploring the Sound Clips Feature   1039
   Playing a Sound Clip   1040

## 33 Publishing Documents on the World Wide Web   1041

What is the World Wide Web?   1042
   What is a Web Page?   1042
   Learning Web Terminology   1043

WordPerfect's Internet Publisher   1044

The Basics of Creating an HTML Document   1045
   Converting Standard WordPerfect Documents into HTML Documents   1047
   HTML Document Title   1049
   Creating Body Text   1050
   Adding Headings   1050
   Adding Formatting   1053

Address Blocks   1054
   Creating Bullets and Lists   1054
   Using Color   1056
   Setting Alignment   1057

Adding Graphics   1058
   Understanding Graphic Formats   1058
   Using Graphic Lines   1059
   Adding Special Characters   1060

Creating Links   1061
   Creating Bookmarks   1062
   Creating Hypertext Links   1063

Editing A Hyperlink   1065
Editing the Appearance of a Button   1065
Linking Graphic Images   1066

Finishing Your Document   1066

Publishing to HTML   1067
Getting Your Page Published   1068
Finding a Service Provider   1069
Registering Your URL   1069

Marketing Your Page   1070
Webcrawler, Yahoo, and Other Search Programs   1070
Locating Newsgroups   1070

Final Notes   1070

The Next Step—Forms   1071

# VII  Appendixes

## A  Installing and Setting Up WordPerfect 7   1075

Choosing What To Install   1076

Installing WordPerfect for Windows   1076
Preparing for Your Installation   1077
Installing WordPerfect 7   1078
Choosing Standard Installation   1082
Choosing Other Installation Types   1084
Choosing Custom Installation   1084
Installing Other Suite Programs   1086
Installing WordPerfect Only from CD-ROM or from Disks   1086
Installing Printer Drivers   1087
Installing Fonts   1087

Updating and Adding onto WordPerfect   1088

Using WordPerfect Startup Switches   1088

Uninstalling WordPerfect   1090

## B  Making the Transition to WordPerfect 7   1091

Why Make the Switch?   1092
Do You Have a Choice?   1092

Advantages 1092
Costs 1092

New (and Improved or Relocated) Features in WordPerfect 7 1093
Address Book 1094
Ask the PerfectExpert 1094
Corel 1094
Document Review 1095
Flush Right with Dot Leaders 1095
Guidelines 1095
Help Online 1095
Highlight 1095
Internet Publisher 1096
Print 1096
QuickCorrect 1096
QuickFonts 1097
OLE Server 1097
QuickOpen 1097
QuickSpots 1097
Relocated Features 1097
Shadow Pointer 1098
Show Me 1098
Spell As You Go 1098
Tab Icons 1099
Tables 1099
Workflow 1099
Writing Tools 1099

What Did I Miss in WordPerfect 6.1 for Windows? 1099
Drop Cap 1099
Find/Replace 1100
Grammatik 1100
Graphics 1100
Integration with Other Programs 1100
Macro Dialog Editor 1101
Make It Fit 1101
Outline 1101
Performance 1101
QuickCorrect 1102
QuickFormat 1102
Spell Check 1102

Tables   1102
TextArt   1102
Thesaurus   1103
Templates   1103
Toolbar   1103
Undo   1103
Upgrade Help   1103
Uninstall   1104
Window Tile   1104
WP Draw   1104

If I Didn't Upgrade to WordPerfect 6.0 for Windows, What Did I Miss?   1104

Abbreviations   1104
Bookmarks   1104
Borders   1105
Coaches   1105
Comments   1105
Delay Codes   1105
Document Summary   1105
Envelope   1106
File Management   1106
Floating Cells   1106
Fonts   1106
Graphics   1106
Hidden Text   1107
Hypertext   1107
Interface Bars   1107
Keyboard   1108
Labels   1108
Merge   1108
Mouse   1108
Outlines   1109
Page Mode   1109
Printing   1109
QuickFinder/Kickoff   1109
QuickFormat   1109
QuickMenus   1110
Repeat   1110
Reveal Codes   1110

Revertible Codes 1110
Show Codes 1111
Sound 1111
Speller 1111
Spreadsheet Features 1111
Subdivide Pages 1112
Templates 1112
TextArt 1112
Watermarks 1112
WP Characters 1113
WP Draw 1113

If I Didn't Upgrade to WordPerfect 5.2 for Windows, What Did I Miss? 1113
Auto Code Placement (and Replacement) 1113
Document Conversion 1114
Dynamic Data Exchange (DDE) Links 1114
Fonts 1114
Grammatik 1114
Graphics 1114
Macro Language 1114
Multiple Documents 1115
Object Linking and Embedding (OLE) 1115
QuickList 1115
Undo 1115
WP Characters 1115
Zoom 1115

Where Do I Find It in WordPerfect for Windows? 1116

Summary 1117

# VIII | Indexes

## Action Index   1121

## Index of Common Problems   1125

## Index   1135

# Introduction

*by Gordon McComb*

**S**pecial Edition Using Corel WordPerfect 7 pools the talents of a diverse collection of WordPerfect and Windows experts, providing extensive coverage of all WordPerfect's features while combining tutorial steps with reference information. The authors have made this book unique among books about WordPerfect for Windows because this book is a collaboration in the best sense of that word.

Why a collaboration? When you need to accomplish a complex, tough job on a tight schedule, an excellent strategy is to pull together a team of experts, each one specializing in a particular aspect of the overall discipline. The resulting product in a collaborative effort can be superior to even the best efforts of any individual contributor. This book on WordPerfect 7, a collaboration, pools the knowledge of a range of WordPerfect experts—all experts in particular areas or applications.

As software companies adapt their programs to work with graphical user interfaces (GUIs) and as word processors become more complex, powerful, feature-laden, and useful to a diversity of users, the need for in-depth expertise across a range of experience becomes clear. This kind of coverage is unavailable in a single-author book. Only a team of experts can adequately cover a program as advanced, complex, and versatile as WordPerfect 7. ■

# WordPerfect 7 Enhancements

Version 7 is the latest version of WordPerfect, which still ranks as the world's most-used word processor. This version brings many new features and enhancements that promise to make WordPerfect 7 the most versatile and powerful Windows word processor.

If you were a user of earlier versions of WordPerfect for Windows, note the principal added features and enhancements in version 7 which enable you to do the following:

- Use WordPerfect as a "native" application under Windows 95. This means greater speed, access to long file names, and other features of Windows 95 and Windows NT.
- Write and edit documents for the World Wide Web, right inside WordPerfect. The WordPerfect package even includes Netscape Navigator that you can use to browse the Web, upload files to your Web server, and more.
- Write, edit, and distribute documents for editing and review with others in your office. Revision marks can be added on-the-fly for each reviewer.
- Create and expand Abbreviations for frequently used words and phrases.
- Assemble a variety of graphs (for example, pie and bar) with the Chart feature.
- Use the Ask the Perfect Expert feature for a step-by-step guide to complete a task.
- Delay the action of certain codes for a specified number of pages with Delay Codes.
- Choose from additional document summary fields (a total of 51) to customize the summary information.
- Fax documents from within WordPerfect for Windows.
- Insert *floating cells* (single table cells with full spreadsheet capabilities) anywhere in a document.
- Create hidden text to be displayed only when necessary.
- Insert hypertext links to jump to different sections of the document or to another document—even to documents on the World Wide Web!
- Enjoy pushbutton shortcuts using Power Bars, Toolbars, and Feature Bars.
- Search through files with an improved QuickFinder program.
- Edit document text as well as headers, footers, footnotes, and page numbers with Page mode.

- Copy fonts, font attributes, and paragraph styles from one section of text to another with QuickFormat.
- Double-click codes to quickly access the appropriate dialog box where changes can be made.
- Navigate through your computer's hard disk drive or company network using powerful file management features in the Open and Save file dialog boxes.
- Record and attach sound clips, movie files, and other objects to a document.
- Create mini-spreadsheets with more than 100 predefined spreadsheet functions in tables.
- Automatically print pages in booklet format with Subdivide Pages.
- Create and use "boilerplate" documents with the Template feature.
- Assign special effects (color, shapes, shadowing) to text with TextArt.
- Run the upgrade help to help you migrate from earlier versions of WordPerfect, such as WordPerfect for DOS, as well as word processing programs from competing companies
- Run a demonstration "movie"—complete with sound, animation, and background music—for one of almost a dozen commonly used tasks.
- Create and edit graphics images with WP Draw, a scaled-down version of WordPerfect Presentations.
- Automatically insert typographically correct SmartQuotes (curly quotes) when you press the " (quote) key.
- Insert drop caps effortlessly at the beginning of paragraphs.
- Choose from among several dozen premade table formats using WordPerfect's Table Expert.
- Create instant letters using the Letter Expert, which consists of more than two dozen "fill-in-the-blanks" business letters.
- Create and edit graphics "in place" using Windows OLE 2.0 technology. No more switching between WordPerfect and a separate graphics program.
- Undo up to 300 of the most recent editing steps you've made.
- Reformat documents automatically so that the text better fits within a defined number of pages. WordPerfect does all the work!
- Build custom dialog boxes in macros with the Macro Dialog Editor.
- Quickly switch from a competing word processor (such as Microsoft Word) using the Upgrade Advisor.

# Who Should Use This Book?

WordPerfect for Windows is based to some degree on the best-selling WordPerfect for DOS. If you have never used any version of WordPerfect, this book's complete coverage of program features and its mix of step-by-step procedures with reference information, real-world examples, and clear instructions can help you master WordPerfect quickly.

If you're upgrading from WordPerfect 5.2, 6.0, or 6.1 for Windows, this book can help you make the transition to the newest version of WordPerfect for Windows. Appendix B, "Making the Transition to WordPerfect 7," addresses the costs of upgrading, improvements to existing features, new features, changes in menus, and new enhancements.

**NOTE** To ensure your success with WordPerfect 7, you should have a basic understanding of Windows 95. This book assumes that you are familiar with Windows. As you learn about WordPerfect in Chapter 1, you also learn about Windows.

If you are new to Windows, however, you might want to consult any of the following books published by Que Corporation for information on Windows 95's basic operation:

- Special Edition Using Windows 95
- Platinum Edition Using Windows 95
- Using Windows 95
- Windows 95 Installation and Configuration Handbook

# How This Book Is Organized

This book is organized to follow the natural flow of learning and using WordPerfect 7. *Special Edition Using Corel WordPerfect 7* is divided into six parts.

**Part I: Basic Tasks**   Part I introduces you to WordPerfect 7 and explains how to use WordPerfect to accomplish a range of basic word processing tasks as you complete the cycle of document preparation: planning, creating, editing, formatting, printing, and checking the spelling and grammar of documents. In Part I, you also learn how easily you can insert graphic images into WordPerfect.

**Part II: Automating Your Work**  Part II shows you how to take advantage of a number of WordPerfect features to streamline your work. You see how to change default program settings, use styles to automate document formatting, use templates to create forms, use macros to automate repetitive tasks, and use the innovative Toolbar to place frequently used commands and macros on buttons for instant access.

**Part III: Specialized Procedures**  Part III covers more specialized word processing techniques, such as working with text columns, creating tables, organizing documents with collapsible outlining, creating and modifying charts, importing data and working with other programs, and generating mass mailings with Merge and Sort.

**Part IV: Professional Output**  Part IV focuses on high-quality printed output and WordPerfect's capabilities as a desktop publishing system. This part of the book begins with a look at using fonts and special characters; takes you through customizing graphics lines, borders, and boxes and editing graphic images; covers using the WP Draw and TextArt applets to create graphics images; includes a brief primer on page layout, choosing fonts, using color, and advanced printing techniques; and wraps up with the use of the Equation Editor for scientific or mathematical publications.

**Part V: Large Documents**  Part V is especially useful to those who must work with large documents. You see how to annotate documents with footnotes and endnotes, and with document reference tools, such as tables of contents, lists, indexes, tables of authority, and cross-references.

**Part VI: Techniques from the Pros**  Part VI is designed for users who want to gain more expertise with WordPerfect. This section begins with advanced file management techniques using QuickFinder and QuickList; discusses advanced macro commands; provides additional coverage of the Tables feature, particularly the spreadsheet capabilities; provides an explanation and demonstration of the use of hypertext links and sound clips to create interactive business documents; and concludes with coverage of WordPerfect's exciting Web publishing features.

**Part VII: Appendixes**  Appendix A covers installation, program setup, and WordPerfect's start-up options. Appendix B, designed for users of previous versions of WordPerfect for Windows, covers enhancements and new features added to WordPerfect 7.

## Where To Find Help

If you find yourself stymied on a particular point, WordPerfect's built-in Help feature may answer your questions. Help is explained in Chapter 1. In addition, you can turn to this book or WordPerfect's manual and workbook for help.

Additional online help for WordPerfect for Windows 95 is available through an electronic forum on CompuServe Information Service (CIS). WPUSERS is managed by Support Group Inc., an independent group not affiliated with Corel. Official help from Corel for WordPerfect is available in the **WPWIN** forum; help for CorelOffice is available in the **PEROFF** forum. If you need an updated file (a printer driver, for example), look in the **COFILES** forum.

On the Internet you can reach Corel's home page at **http://wwwe.corel.com**. The page includes links to WordPerfect-related resources.

For up-to-date information on WordPerfect 7, try *WordPerfect for Windows Magazine*, an excellent monthly magazine filled with tips, feature articles on WordPerfect, product information, answers to all types of problems, a disk of the month, and other timely and useful information of interest to WordPerfect users. You can subscribe to *WordPerfect for Windows Magazine* at the following address:

*WordPerfect for Windows Magazine*
270 West Center Street
Orem, UT 84057-4637
(801) 228-9626

The **WPMAG** forum on CompuServe provides assistance for articles that appear in *WordPerfect Magazine* and *WordPerfect for Windows Magazine*.

## How To Use This Book

*Special Edition Using Corel WordPerfect 7* is designed to complement the reference manual and workbook that come with WordPerfect. Beginners will find the step-by-step information in this book helpful; experienced users will appreciate the comprehensive coverage and expert advice. After you become proficient with WordPerfect 7, you can use this book as a desktop reference.

Each chapter in this book focuses on a particular WordPerfect operation or set of operations. Overall, the movement of the book is from the steps typical of any document's creation (such as entering text, checking spelling and grammar, and printing) to more specialized topics (such as macros, styles, equations, and integrating text and graphics).

*Special Edition Using Corel WordPerfect 7* distills the real-world experience of many WordPerfect experts, making this book workplace-based and task-oriented.

> **NOTE** Notes help you discover new and useful ways to use WordPerfect. If you want, as you read a chapter, you may skip the text in a note and read it later.

The tips included in the book's margins either point out information often overlooked in the documentation or help you use WordPerfect more efficiently. You will find many of these tips useful or pertinent as you become more comfortable with the software.

> **CAUTION**
> Cautions alert you to potential problems you should avoid. In *Special Edition Using Corel WordPerfect 7*, figure captions do far more than merely label a screen illustration, such as "The Font Dialog Box." They have been designed to provide enough explanation and description to allow some readers to look at the illustration, read the caption, skim the text, and complete a task without having to read an entire section.

### TROUBLESHOOTING

**What do I do if I run into problems?** If you run into trouble, look for the special Troubleshooting sections found throughout the book. These sections highlight many of the more common problems that can occur when using specific features of WordPerfect, and what to do about them. See the Troubleshooting Index near the end of the book for a compilation of the topics found in the Troubleshooting sections.

# Conventions Used in This Book

The conventions used in this book have been established to help you learn how to use the program quickly and easily. The instructions emphasize use of the mouse to access commands, make choices in dialog boxes, and so forth. WordPerfect enables you to use both the keyboard and the mouse to select menu and dialog box items: you can press a letter (or number), or you can select an item by clicking it with the mouse. The letter or number you press appears as underlined.

If you use a mouse with WordPerfect, place the mouse pointer on the relevant menu or dialog box item and click the left mouse button to make your selection. Instructions for navigating in WordPerfect for Windows appear in Chapters 1 and 2.

The following examples show typical command sequences (note that a semicolon is used to set off the alternate function-key interface):

Choose Edit, Go To, or press Ctrl+G.

Choose Format, Font, or press F9. Then choose Bold.

Uppercase letters are used to distinguish file names, macro names, and merge commands, such as HLINE.WCM. In most cases, the keys on the keyboard are represented as they appear on your keyboard (for example, J, Enter, Tab, Ctrl, Insert, and Backspace).

For keystrokes separated by plus signs, such as Speller (Ctrl+F1), hold down the first key (Ctrl in this example) and press the second key (F1 in this example) to invoke the command. When a series of keys is separated by commas, press and release each key in sequence. For example, to move to the beginning of the line before any hidden codes, press Home twice (Home, Home).

WordPerfect also provides a Power Bar and various Toolbars for your convenience. By clicking a button from either the Power Bar or one of the Toolbars, you can execute a command or access a dialog box. Chapters in this book often contain button icons in the margins, indicating which button you can click to perform the task at hand.

Text you are asked to type is shown in **boldface**. On-screen messages and WordPerfect hidden codes are shown in monospaced font: `[Left Tab]`. Special words or phrases defined for the first time appear in *italic* type. ●

# PART I

# Basic Tasks

**1** Getting Started   11

**2** Creating and Saving a Document   55

**3** Retrieving and Editing Documents   81

**4** Formatting Text   121

**5** Formatting Pages and Documents   155

**6** Using Writing Tools   207

**7** Integrating Text and Graphics   249

**8** Basic Output: Printing, Faxing, and E-Mail   277

CHAPTER 1

# Getting Started

*by Steve Schafer and Judy Petersen*

**W**ordPerfect 7 is a powerful word processing program containing many powerful tools; the program is, however, easy to use. WordPerfect can handle any word processing task, from a simple letter to a complex desktop-publishing document such as a newsletter or a book.

This chapter is designed to introduce you to WordPerfect 7 and to its various interfaces. If you are familiar with previous versions of WordPerfect for Windows, you also should read Appendix B, "Making the Transition to WordPerfect 7."

**Starting and exiting WordPerfect**
With Windows 95, starting WordPerfect is easier than ever.

**Using the keyboard and the mouse**
You learn the many ways to use the mouse and the keyboard to move around a document, make choices, select text, and enter information.

**Understanding the editing screen**
You are introduced to the many kinds of on-screen bars and other tools that put WordPerfect's features only a click away.

**Using dialog boxes**
Dialog boxes provide you the opportunity to communicate with WordPerfect; you learn how to use the buttons, boxes, and lists each contains.

**Working with multiple documents**
You learn how to work with several documents open at the same time, transfer data from one document to another, and save several documents as a single workspace.

**Using Help**
Because everyone needs a little help now and then, you tour the WordPerfect Help program.

## Starting and Exiting WordPerfect

Before learning how to be productive with WordPerfect 7, you must learn how to start and exit the program. Installing WordPerfect 7 adds a Corel WordPerfect Suite 7 menu to the Start menu available on the Windows 95 taskbar. Click the Start button and choose Corel WordPerfect Suite 7 to see the menu shown in figure 1.1. If you have installed other parts of the CWP Suite, these apps will also appear on this menu.

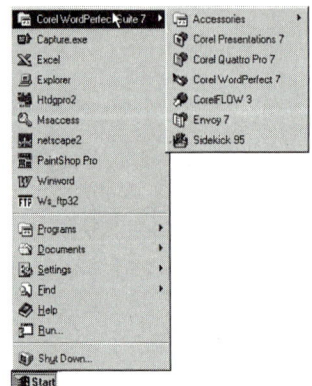

**FIG. 1.1**
The Corel Office 7 menu contains the WordPerfect 7 program icon and the Accessories folder, which contains a suite of Corel Office tools such as the Address Book.

> **NOTE** WordPerfect 7 requires Windows 95. For a full list of system requirements, see Appendix A, "Installing and Setting Up WordPerfect 7."

To start WordPerfect 7, choose it from the Corel Office 7 menu; Windows 95 starts WordPerfect. A Corel WordPerfect 7 copyright screen appears briefly, then WordPerfect displays its main editing screen (see fig. 1.2).

To exit WordPerfect for Windows 95, click the mouse pointer on File in the pull-down menu bar; or press Alt+F. Either method opens the File menu shown in figure 1.3. Then click the mouse pointer on the Exit command in the File menu; or press X.

 To quickly close WordPerfect or any other Windows 95 application, press Alt+F4.

If you have not saved an open document, WordPerfect displays a dialog box similar to the one shown in figure 1.4. If you choose Yes, WordPerfect asks for a file name in which to save the document before exiting. If you choose No, WordPerfect exits without saving the document. Choosing Cancel stops the exit operation, and you return to your document.

Starting and Exiting WordPerfect 13

**FIG. 1.2**
The WordPerfect 7 main editing screen appears when you launch WordPerfect.

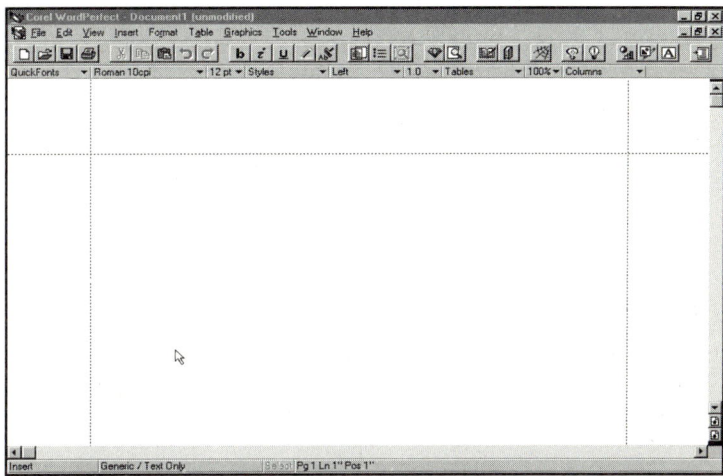

**FIG. 1.3**
The WordPerfect 7 File menu includes commands to open and save your work and to exit WordPerfect.

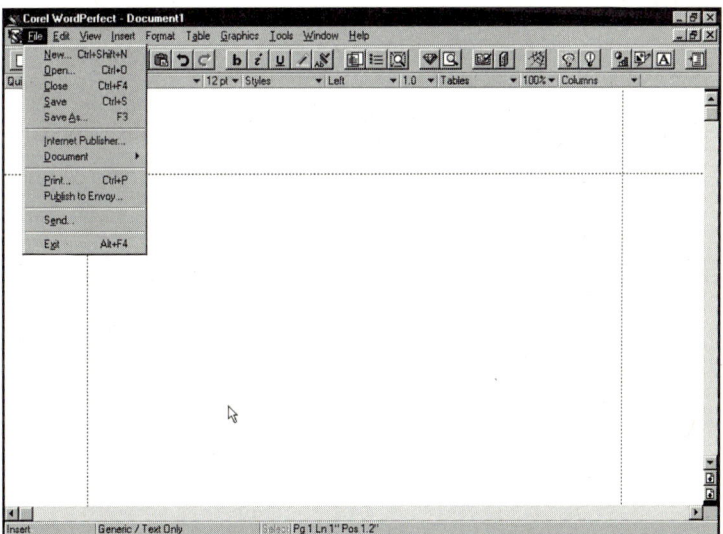

**FIG. 1.4**
The WordPerfect confirmation dialog box enables you to save changes.

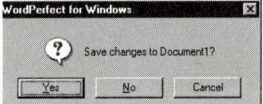

# Using the WordPerfect 7 Interface

This section explains the basics of using the keyboard and mouse to control WordPerfect.

## Using the Keyboard

WordPerfect uses *mnemonics* (clues to jog your memory about which keystrokes to use) for most of its options. To access the pull-down menus, you must press and hold the Alt key as you tap the menu's mnemonic (just as you would press Shift+A to type an uppercase A). To access the File menu, for example, press Alt+F. To choose an option or command, simply press the mnemonic letter in its description. To choose Open from the File menu, for example (after the File menu is open), press O.

> **NOTE** Mnemonics for all options and commands are underlined on-screen and in this book. The F in File, for example, is the mnemonic for the File menu and appears underlined.

WordPerfect also enables you to use the arrow keys to navigate through the pull-down menus and the Tab and Shift+Tab keys to move around in dialog boxes. In menus, a highlight bar appears on the selected item. In dialog boxes, a dotted line outlines the selected item. After you highlight a menu item, you press Enter to choose, or *execute*, that command. The key or keys used to choose selected items in dialog boxes differ by the object selected. See the later section, "Using Dialog Boxes," for more information about how to work with dialog boxes.

WordPerfect 7 also uses the Ctrl key and function keys as shortcut keys to access dialog boxes directly. To open a document, for example, you can either open the File menu (or press Alt+F) and then choose Open (or press O), which takes you to the Open dialog box; or you can press Ctrl+O to bypass the menu system and directly access the Open dialog box. Similarly, you can press F3 to directly access the Save As dialog box instead of choosing File, Save As.

> **NOTE** Shortcut keys appear on the pull-down menus next to the items these keys operate. Ctrl+O, for example, appears next to the Open command on the File menu.

## Using the Mouse

Depending on the manufacturer, a mouse can have two or three buttons. By default, the left button is the *primary mouse button*, and the right is the *secondary mouse button*.

> **TIP** If you prefer another button as your primary mouse button, you can make this change through the Mouse option of the Windows 95 Control Panel.

The *mouse pointer* is either an arrow or an I-beam that moves around the screen as you move the mouse across your desktop or mouse pad. You use the mouse pointer to "point" at on-screen items.

WordPerfect's features are activated and controlled using either the mouse or the keyboard. By using a mouse, actions that otherwise take numerous keystrokes or complex keystroke combinations can be accomplished simply by moving the mouse pointer to a menu choice and clicking a mouse button.

Using the mouse, however, also removes your hand from the keyboard. You may, therefore, find yourself using keyboard commands to format text as you enter it, but switching to the mouse to format existing text.

The three basic mouse operations include the following:

- *Clicking*. Quickly pressing and releasing the primary or secondary mouse button while the pointer is on a menu option, a button, or another selection to activate that item. Clicking the name of a menu causes that menu to appear on-screen, for example, and clicking the Toolbar's Speller button starts WordPerfect's spell-checking feature. Clicking is used to execute a command or an option, or to relocate the insertion point in the text. (The *insertion point* is the thin bar that marks your current position in the text.)
- *Double-clicking*. Quickly pressing and releasing the primary mouse button twice while the pointer is on a menu option, button, or another selection. Double-clicking is primarily used to simultaneously select an item and execute an action. You can double-click a graphic, for example, to access the Edit Graphics Box for that graphic.

> **TIP** With WordPerfect, you can also triple-click to select a sentence or quadruple-click to select a paragraph.

- *Dragging*. Positioning the mouse where you want to start and then holding down the primary mouse button while you move the mouse across your desk or mouse pad. Within a document, you can drag to select blocks of text or to move graphics or other objects. As you drag the object, its position on-screen changes or a dotted line appears to show your progress.

You can use the mouse to quickly move the insertion point from one place in your document to another. Place the mouse pointer over the location where you want the insertion point, and then click. The insertion point moves to the specified location. Using this mouse technique to move from one part of a document to another part visible on-screen often is much quicker than using the arrow keys.

To move to a part of the document not visible on-screen, use the scroll bars or the Page Down and Page Up keys to move from page to page. After you reach the page you want to edit, move the mouse pointer to the text you want to change, and click. The insertion point moves instantly to the specified location.

**T I P**  Using the Go To command makes it easy to move directly to a specific page.

**N O T E**  The mouse pointer assumes different shapes on-screen, depending on its particular task. If you use the mouse to position a graphic box, for example, the pointer becomes a four-headed arrow, then changes to an arrow with a small box attached when you begin dragging the graphic box.

**TROUBLESHOOTING**

**When I use the scroll bars to move through a document and press a cursor key to move to a specific line, the display jumps back to where I began scrolling. What am I doing wrong?** The scroll bars change the part of the document displayed, but do not move the insertion point. To move to a new location in the document, use the scroll bars to go to that location, then use the mouse to click where you want the insertion to appear on-screen.

**When I drag with the mouse to select text, it is difficult to select the exact text I want.** Place the insertion point at the beginning of the text you want to select, then Shift+click at the end of the selection. All of the text is immediately selected.

# Understanding the Editing Screen

With its default settings, the WordPerfect 7 editing screen offers many tools to help with word processing tasks. Many of its screen elements, however, can be customized to further enhance your productivity. Figure 1.2 shows the WordPerfect editing screen in its default state. Figure 1.5 shows the WordPerfect editing screen with many of its graphical tools active.

Understanding the Editing Screen 17

In the following sections, you learn the basics about each element shown in figure 1.5. In following chapters, you learn in detail how to use these elements most effectively.

▶ **See** "Customizing the Display," **p. 300**

## Windows 95 Controls

Because WordPerfect 7 is a fully capable Windows 95 application, it operates in a window. This window is called an *application window*. All WordPerfect operations occur within this window. The WordPerfect application window includes all the controls offered by other Windows 95 programs. Figure 1.5 shows the various control buttons available on the WordPerfect 7 window. These include the Minimize, Maximize, Close, and Control buttons. The following sections explain each button in detail.

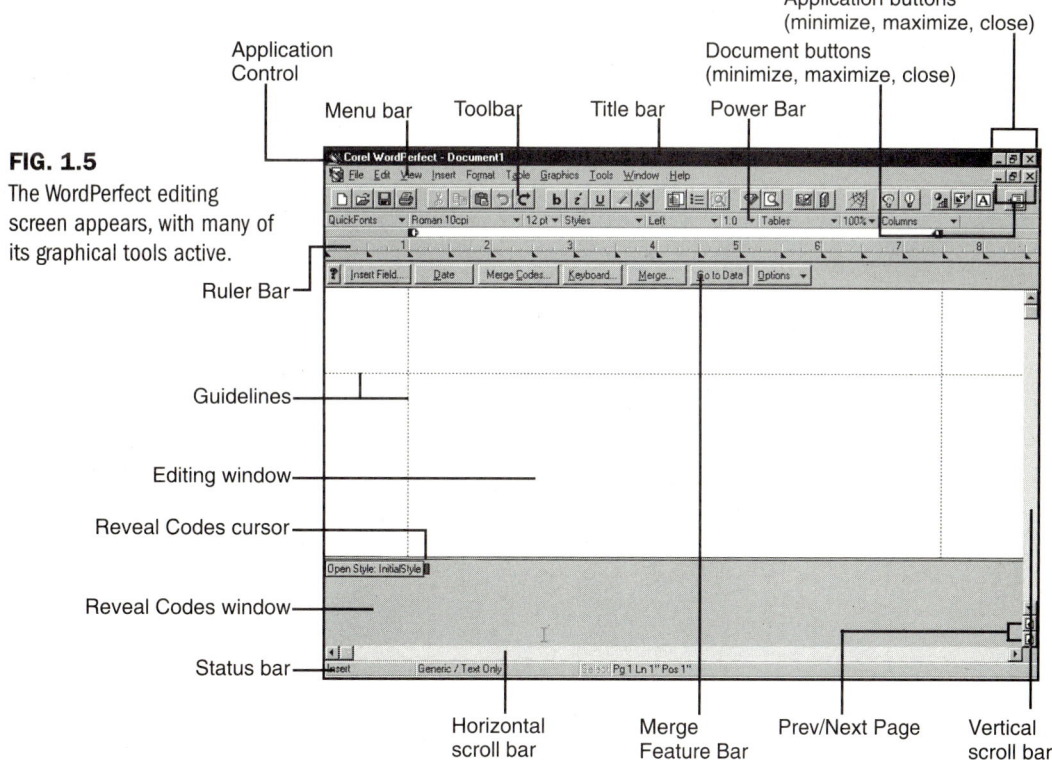

**FIG. 1.5**
The WordPerfect editing screen appears, with many of its graphical tools active.

**Minimize, Maximize, and Close Buttons** The button in the upper-right corner of the window is known as the Close button. Clicking the button closes the active window. If you try to close a document window before saving the document, WordPerfect displays the confirmation dialog box shown earlier in figure 1.4.

To the left of the Close button is the Maximize button. This button functions as a toggle. Click it once, and it maximizes the WordPerfect window, expanding the window to occupy the entire screen. If the window is already full-screen, clicking the button returns the window to its former smaller size.

To the left of the Maximize button is the Minimize button. Clicking this button closes the window but its button continues to display on the Windows 95 taskbar. To restore the minimized window, click its button on the taskbar.

To restore the window with the keyboard, press and hold the Alt then press Tab to display a dialog box containing icons for all open applications (see fig. 1.6). Continue to press Tab to move the selection box to the icon of the program you want to restore, then release the Alt key.

**FIG. 1.6**
Press Alt+Tab to display a window of the icons representing the applications presently open.

**N O T E**   The Minimize, Maximize, and Close buttons can be used only with a mouse. To use the Minimize, Maximize, and Close functions with a keyboard requires using the Application Control menu, described in the following section.

**Application Control Menu**   In the upper-left corner of the application window is the Application Control button. This button is marked with the WordPerfect 7 application icon. To access the Application Control menu, click this button or press Alt+space bar.

The control menu enables you to Ma_x_imize, Mi_n_imize, or _R_estore the WordPerfect 7 window. If WordPerfect is not full-screen, you also can choose _M_ove or _S_ize. After choosing either option, you can use the arrow keys to move the WordPerfect window around the screen or to resize the window. When you are satisfied with the result, press the Enter key to put your change into effect.

You also can close the WordPerfect window (exiting WordPerfect) by choosing _C_lose.

**N O T E**   When an application is running in a window, you can move or size the window using the mouse by simply dragging the application's title bar to move the window to a new location on-screen or dragging the appropriate border to resize the window. You can also drag one of the corners of the application's border to resize it horizontally and vertically at the same time. Release the mouse button to drop the window or border at its new location.

To move the WordPerfect window with the keyboard, press Alt+space bar to open the Application Control menu and choose <u>M</u>ove. Press the arrow key that corresponds to the direction you want to move the window. As you press the arrows, a dotted line shows you the motion of the window. Press Enter to drop the window at its new location.

To resize the window, open the Application Control menu and choose <u>S</u>ize. Press an arrow key to move the pointer to the corresponding side of the window and then use the arrows to move that side. Pressing the left-arrow key, for example, moves the pointer to the left border of the window; pressing the left- or right-arrow key then moves the border left or right. A dotted line shows your progress. Pressing the Enter key stops the sizing process, leaving the window at its new size. Pressing Esc aborts the sizing process, leaving the window at its original size.

**Document Controls**   Each document you work with in WordPerfect 7 is contained in a *document window*. Each document window has its own frame, title bar, Minimize button, Maximize button, Close button, and Control button.

By default, WordPerfect 7 displays a document in a maximized document window; that is, the document window takes up the entire WordPerfect editing window as shown in figure 1.5. When a document is maximized in the editing window, its title bar and frame are the same as those of the application window. The Document Control button and the Minimize, Maximize, and Close buttons are on the menu bar immediately below their respective application controls. If a document window is sized to be smaller than the application window, its border and title bar are separate from those of the application. When a document is minimized, its title bar appears immediately above the status bar in the WordPerfect application window (see fig. 1.7).

**FIG. 1.7**
Each document window includes a Document Control menu. The title bar of three minimized documents appears just above the status bar.

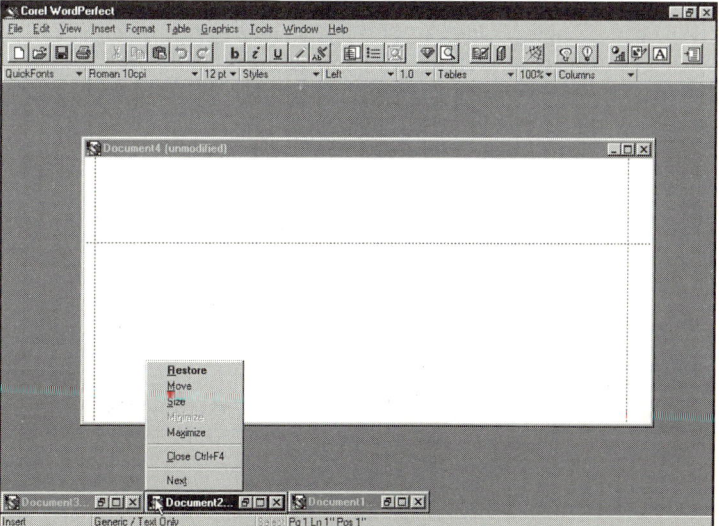

The Document Control menu (see fig. 1.7) operates much like the Application Control menu and contains many of the same menu options. Notable differences include the use of Ctrl+F4 as the shortcut key for Close (instead of Alt+F4) and the inclusion of a Next command. Next switches to the next open document in WordPerfect.

You can open the Document Control menu by clicking the mouse pointer on the Document Control button, or by pressing Alt+- (hyphen).

For more information about the document controls and on editing multiple documents in WordPerfect for Windows 95, see the later section "Working with Multiple Documents."

## The WordPerfect Title Bar

The WordPerfect window title bar (refer to fig. 1.5) serves several purposes. Its primary purpose is to identify the WordPerfect application window. It also displays the current document's name when the document window is maximized.

## The Pull-Down Menus

The pull-down menu bar always appears at the top of the screen. You can access all of WordPerfect's features by using these menus.

To activate one of the menus, press and hold the Alt key while pressing the menu's mnemonic. Pressing Alt+F, for example, activates the File menu. You also can use the mouse to move the mouse pointer to the menu you want and then click the mouse button to activate the menu.

Pressing and releasing the Alt key also activates the pull-down menus, highlighting the Document Control button. You can then use the arrow keys and the Enter key to choose the appropriate menu.

**TIP** Point to any command on a pull-down menu and a QuickTip appears containing a description of the command and its shortcut keystroke, if any.

Take time now to open WordPerfect's menus one at a time and notice the commands contained in each menu. Although you cannot expect to memorize the location of every command, notice that each menu contains a logically grouped set of commands. After you understand the logic behind the grouping of commands in the WordPerfect menus, you can speed through all your writing, editing, and document-formatting tasks.

**NOTE** You can fully customize WordPerfect 7 menus to rearrange items as you prefer—or even to add entirely new menu items. See Chapter 9, "Customizing WordPerfect," for more information.

If a menu command has a shortcut keystroke, the keystroke appears on the right edge of the drop-down menu. When a menu command appears with a triangle on the right margin of the menu, choosing the command displays another menu. Choosing File, Document, for example, causes an additional menu of options to appear.

## QuickMenus

You can use WordPerfect's QuickMenus to help speed customizing the interface and formatting text. *QuickMenus* are pop-up menus that appear after you click the right (or secondary) mouse button while the mouse pointer is at a particular location on-screen. If you click the right mouse button while the mouse pointer is in a document margin, for example, the QuickMenu shown in figure 1.8 appears.

Try clicking the right mouse button while the mouse pointer is on the following elements:

- Between the edge of the page and the left or right margin
- Between the edge of the page and the top or bottom margin
- Document text
- Selected documented text
- A misspelled word that WordPerfect has underlined in red
- A table
- A graphic figure or line, sound clip, or OLE object
- The Toolbar, Power Bar, menu bar, status bar, Ruler Bar, or either of the scroll bars

**FIG. 1.8**
Click the left margin to access a QuickMenu that includes commands to select text, change margins, insert a comment, sound, or subdocument, or change to Outline mode.

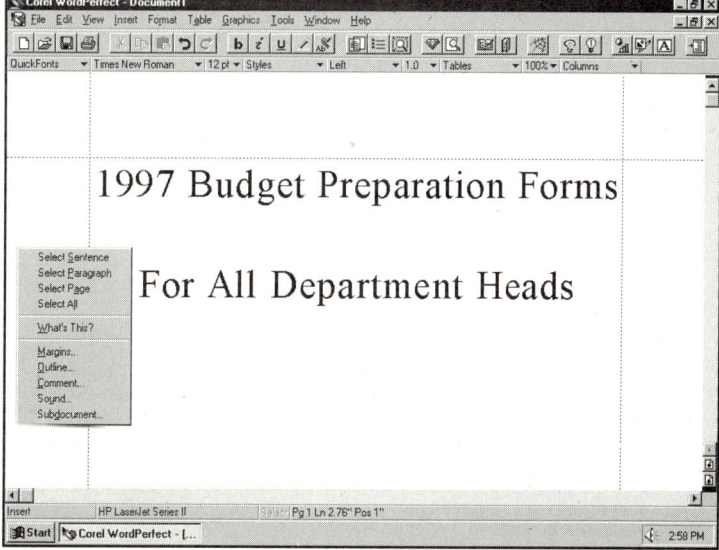

## The Toolbar

By default, the Toolbar appears at the top of the screen between the Power Bar and the pull-down menus. You also can display the Toolbar on the left, right, or bottom of the screen, or in a floating palette that you can position anywhere on-screen. To change the Toolbar's position, choose Edit, Preferences, Toolbar, Options, and then choose Left, Right, Top, Bottom, or Palette, or simply drag the Toolbar to one of these positions.

**TIP** To see more document text when both the Power Bar and Ruler also are active, choose the left or right on-screen position for the Toolbar.

While the mouse pointer is on any of the Toolbar buttons, pause briefly and a QuickTip appears containing the name of the button and a brief explanation of its function (see fig. 1.9). To use any of the buttons, position the insertion point in the document where you want to use the feature, and click the appropriate button.

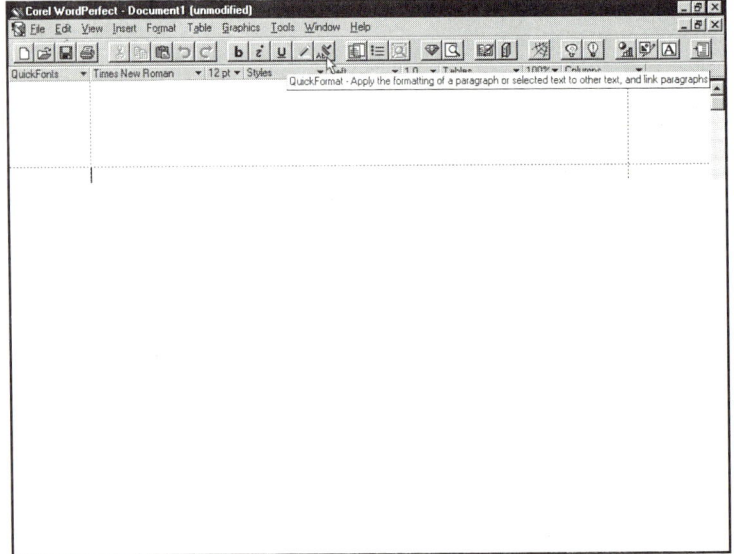

**FIG. 1.9**
When you place the mouse pointer over a button and pause briefly, a QuickTip displays the button name and what task the button performs.

**TIP** To quickly move the Toolbar, place the mouse pointer between, above, or below the Toolbar buttons until the mouse pointer becomes a hand; then drag the Toolbar to a new location on-screen.

WordPerfect provides many Toolbars, each one geared toward a different set of features. You can use one Toolbar when working in a table, for example, another for text formatting, one when you are creating or editing macros, and a fourth when you are creating cross-referencing features. Each Toolbar can also be customized; you can add any feature, command, or macro to the bar as a button. Choose Edit, Preferences, Toolbar, select the Toolbar you want to customize, and then choose Edit to open the Toolbar Editor.

**N O T E** You must use the mouse to access the Toolbar.

Finally, you can hide (or redisplay) the Toolbar by choosing View, Toolbars/Ruler then choose Toolbar to remove the X from its check box.

▶ See "Working with the Toolbar," **p. 417**

▶ See "Switching Between Toolbars," **p. 415**

## The Power Bar

The Power Bar consists of several buttons that give you quick access to commonly used text layout and formatting features. If active, the Power Bar appears near the top of the screen (refer to fig. 1.5).

By using the Power Bar, you can instantly access a drop-down list of options for frequently used text functions, such as a list of font faces or sizes, with a single click of the mouse button. The Power Bar enables you to work quickly without needing to hunt through menus or remember obscure keystroke combinations to accomplish basic tasks.

**TIP** You can hide the Power Bar by choosing View, Toolbars/Ruler, then selecting the Power Bar to remove the X from its check box.

**N O T E** You must use the mouse to access the Power Bar.

While the mouse pointer is on any of the Power Bar buttons, a QuickTip displays a description of its function. To use any of the buttons, position the insertion point in the document where you want to use the feature, click the appropriate button, and choose the option you want from the drop-down list.

**TIP** Point to any button on the Power Bar, and a QuickTip appears containing a brief description of the button function.

The Power Bar can also be customized; you can add several other Power Bar buttons, or any WordPerfect feature, command, or macro. Choose Edit, Preferences, Power Bar to customize the appearance of the Power Bar or choose Edit to open the Toolbar Editor—Power Bar dialog box where you can add and remove buttons.

You can add buttons for some commonly accessed features to the Power Bar.

▶ **See** "Customizing the Power Bar," **p. 426**

## The Status Bar

The status bar appears along the bottom of the WordPerfect window. It informs you of the status of many WordPerfect for Windows 95 features. By default, the status bar displays the following information:

- Whether Insert or Typeover mode is active, or the status of such features as columns, tables, macros, and merge
- The current printer
- Whether any text or codes are selected
- The current page, vertical position, and horizontal position of the insertion point

**TIP** Point to any item on the status bar, and a QuickTip appears containing a description of the item and what happens if it is double-clicked.

The status bar can be configured to show additional—or less—information, as desired. You can move and size any of the items displayed on the status bar as needed. Items that can be added include the current Font, the Caps Lock, Num Lock and Scroll Lock state, the active keyboard definition, and whether Outline is on or off.

In addition to showing information, most items on the status bar can be double-clicked to access related features. On the default status bar, you can double-click the following:

- Insert to change to Typeover
- The printer name to access the Select Printer dialog box
- Select to change to Select mode
- The cursor position to display the Go To dialog box

**NOTE** You must use the mouse to use the status bar items as buttons.

You can choose to display or hide the status bar by choosing View, Toolbars/Ruler, Status Bar. To add or remove buttons on the status bar and customize its appearance, right-click the status bar or choose Edit, then choose Preferences, Status Bar; or use the status bar QuickMenu to quickly access the Status Bar Preferences dialog box.

## The Ruler Bar

If active, the Ruler Bar appears below the Power Bar at the top of the screen (refer to fig. 1.5). The Ruler Bar consists of margin indicators above a ruler with the default measurements (either inches, centimeters, millimeters, points, or WordPerfect units) and markers for all tabs. Each tab stop is represented by a marker that also shows what type of tab is set at that position. You choose to display or hide the Ruler by choosing View, Toolbars/Ruler, then choose Ruler Bar so an X appears in its check box.

The top of the ruler shows the current left and right margins, and small triangles indicate the current paragraph indentations. If the insertion point is currently in a column, text box, or table, this area also shows the margins for the columns, box contents, or cells.

You can use the mouse to move tabs or margins on the Ruler Bar. Drag the tab marker or margin bar to a new location. To remove a tab stop, drag its marker off the ruler. To add a tab, right-click the lowest portion of the Ruler Bar to access the Ruler's QuickMenu and choose the type of tab you want to add, then click the mouse pointer on the ruler where you want to add the tab.

▶ **See** "Setting and Using Tabs," **p. 138**

▶ **See** "Setting Margins," **p. 135**

## Guidelines

The default view of document window includes blue dashed guidelines at the current top, bottom, left, and right margins. When you move the mouse pointer over a guideline, the pointer changes to an arrow with a line, at which time you can drag the guideline to change the margin. As you drag the guideline, a QuickTip appears showing the current margin measurement in decimal inches. Continue to drag the guideline until you see the margin measurement you want in the QuickTip.

> **CAUTION**
> When you use guidelines to set a new margin, before you start dragging be sure the mouse pointer is located on the guideline where you want the margin change to begin.

Guidelines are also available for headers and footers, when you turn columns on, and in tables. When you drag the margin guidelines in columns, the QuickTip shows both the new column margin and the remaining space between the adjacent columns. The QuickTip that appears on the guideline when you change the margins of a column or row in a table displays the width of the column or row on either side of the guideline.

You can turn the WordPerfect guidelines off or on as your needs require. Choose View, Guidelines to display the Guidelines dialog box. Choose Tables, Margins, Columns, or Header/Footer to remove or add a check in the adjacent check box.

## The Scroll Bars

Scroll bars enable you to move quickly through a document that is too long or too wide to fit on-screen. The vertical scroll bar moves up and down through the document, while the horizontal bar moves right and left. By default, WordPerfect displays both a horizontal and a vertical scroll bar. To disable the scroll bars or display them only when needed, choose Edit, Preferences, Display, choose the Document tab and then select either Vertical or Horizontal. You can also set the horizontal scroll bar to Show Always or When Required.

 Use Ctrl+Tab to move to the Document tab using the keyboard.

To use a scroll bar, place the mouse pointer on the scroll arrow that points in the direction you want to move, and click the mouse button to scroll the document one line up or down or one character left or right. (Scroll arrows are located at the top and bottom of the vertical scroll bar and at either end of the horizontal scroll bar.) By holding down the mouse button on a scroll arrow, you continue to scroll through the document until you release the mouse button.

To move quickly from one part of the document to another—for example, to move from the top to the bottom—place the mouse pointer on the scroll box, and then drag the box up or down.

 A QuickTip displays the current page number when you use the scroll bar to scroll vertically through a document.

You also can click anywhere in the gray area between the scroll box and the arrows to move a screen forward or backward (using the vertical scroll bar) or left or right (using the horizontal scroll bar). When the part of the document you want to work with scrolls into view, move the mouse pointer over the document and click to position the insertion point where you want.

There is a fundamental difference between moving around using the scroll bars and moving around with the keyboard. Moving with the keyboard simultaneously moves the insertion point to the new position. The scroll bars enable you to scroll another part of the document into view while the insertion point remains in its original location. You can now click the insertion point in the current screen or return to your original location by pressing a cursor key or character key on the keyboard.

Use the scroll bar QuickMenu to access the Go To and Bookmark features.

**NOTE** You must use the mouse to use the scroll bars.

## Previous and Next Page Buttons

At the bottom of the vertical scroll bar lie two small buttons with a graphic of a page on each of their faces. The top button moves the display one page backward in a document; the bottom button moves it one page forward.

> **CAUTION**
> Like the scroll bars, Previous/Next Page buttons do not move the insertion point; they only change the part of the document displayed on-screen. You must click the document screen to move the insertion point to the visible page.

**NOTE** Previous/Next Page buttons appear only if the vertical scroll bar is displayed.

## Feature Bars

Various features in WordPerfect have their own Feature Bars. (These are bars that contain buttons representing common commands used with that feature.) Different Feature Bars appear on-screen for each feature you use. If you choose to create a template, for example, the Template Feature Bar appears on-screen, as shown in figure 1.10.

You can use the mouse with the Feature Bars to quickly make changes while using various features. WordPerfect includes Feature Bars for the following features:

- Comment
- Cross-Reference
- Delay Codes
- Footnote/Endnote
- Header/Footer
- Hypertext

- Index
- List
- Macro Edit
- Merge Data File
- Merge Form File
- Outline
- Table Formula
- Table of Authorities
- Table of Authorities Full Form
- Table of Contents
- Template
- Watermark

Each Feature Bar is discussed in the chapter in which its specific feature is covered.

**FIG. 1.10**
The Template Feature Bar is activated when you create a new template.

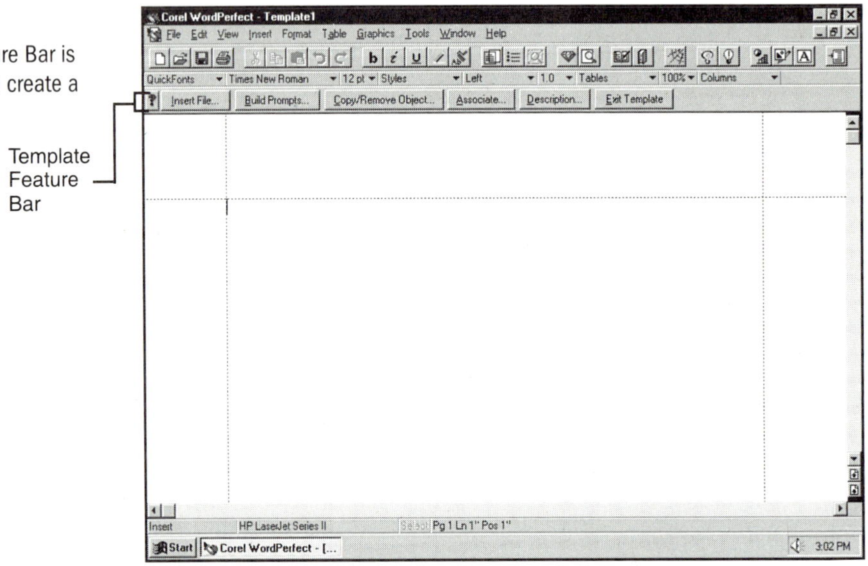

Template Feature Bar

## View Modes

WordPerfect has three View modes that provide different views of your document. These views are all *WYSIWYG* (*What You See Is What You Get*) views, but each displays different elements than its counterparts. You change modes by opening the View menu and choosing Draft, Page, or Two Page, as appropriate.

In Draft and Page modes, you also can control the Zoom—that is, how much of and the size at which the document is displayed.

**Draft Mode**  Draft mode displays your document text close to how it will look when printed, but does not show headers, footers, page numbers, watermarks, and other page formatting features on-screen. Because of this, you can usually work faster in Draft mode and see more of the document content on-screen.

**Page Mode** By default, WordPerfect displays your document in Page mode, its full WYSIWYG mode. While in Page mode, you can see all aspects of a page, including such elements as headers, footers, and watermarks.

> **N O T E** The amount of the page displayed on-screen in Page mode is governed in part by the current Zoom ratio. See the later section "Zoom" for more information.

Because WordPerfect displays all screen elements in this mode, working in Page mode can be slower than working in Draft mode. Page mode also can limit the amount of document text you can view on the screen at one time.

**Two Page Mode** The third view WordPerfect 7 offers is Two Page mode. This mode displays two pages side-by-side on the editing screen, as shown in figure 1.11.

**FIG. 1.11**
Two Page mode is particularly helpful when you want to check the layout of facing pages.

Although you can edit in this mode, you may find it impractical to do so on a textual level. Two Page mode does present the best view of the page as a whole, however, and header, footer, or graphic placements can be fine-tuned at this level.

> **N O T E** Two Page mode does not enable you to choose the Zoom ratio; this mode always displays two pages on-screen, as shown in figure 1.11.

**Zoom**   In Draft or Page mode, you can control the zoom ratio of the document—that is, the size in which the document appears on-screen in relation to its size when printed. You can choose a value between 25 and 400 percent by choosing View, Zoom and then choosing the zoom ratio you want from the Zoom dialog box, as shown in figure 1.12.

 **T I P**   You also can click the Zoom button on the Power Bar and choose the zoom ratio from the list that appears.

**FIG. 1.12**
The Zoom dialog box enables you to customize the size of the document on-screen in relation to its size when printed.

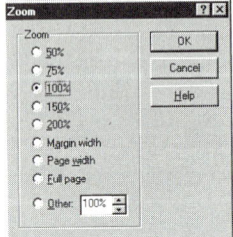

WordPerfect also supports three zoom values determined by the document's page and margin size instead of by a percentage:

- *Margin Width*. Zooms the document so that you can see all the text and graphics between the left and right margins.
- *Page Width*. Displays the entire document between the left and right edges of the page.
- *Full Page*. Shows the complete current page on-screen.

Instead of picking one of the dialog box's preset percentages, you also can set your own value between 25 and 400 percent by choosing Other.

## Hide Bars

To display another full-page view, choose View, Hide Bars; or press Alt+Shift+F5. This feature affects all the various editing bars (Ruler, Button, Power, pull-down menu, and so on), as well as the title bar, but not the Feature Bars. After you choose Hide Bars, WordPerfect zooms the editing window to full-screen size and displays only the document and any active Feature Bars. A document with Hide Bars active is shown in figure 1.13.

**N O T E**   This view is governed by the current zoom ratio. If Zoom is set to 100 percent, for example, the document is shown at 100 percent when you hide the bars.

**FIG. 1.13**
The WordPerfect editing screen shows the Hide Bars feature in its active state. The shaded area shown here—indicating the binding offset—and other document format elements continue to display.

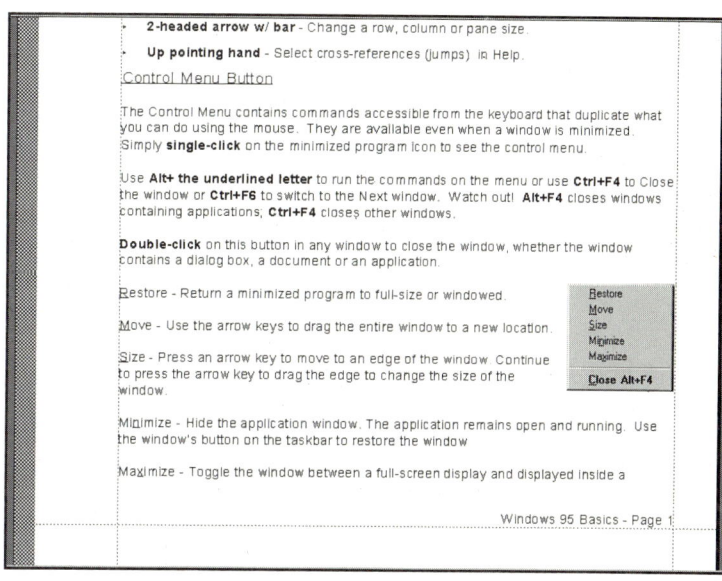

To redisplay the hidden bars, press Esc or Alt+Shift+F5.

 **TROUBLESHOOTING**

**I want to see as much of my document as possible, but I use a lot of commands on the menu bar. Is there a way to view my document this way?** Choose View, Toolbars/Ruler, then Toolbar, Power Bar, and Status Bar to remove the X from the adjacent check box. Remove the scroll bars in the Document tab in the Display Preferences dialog box.

**Why does pressing Alt plus the mnemonic for a button on a Feature Bar not access the button?** To select feature bar buttons using the keyboard, press Alt+Shift plus the mnemonic.

## Using Dialog Boxes

If you choose a menu option that requires additional information before WordPerfect can execute the command, a dialog box appears. The dialog box enables you to provide any additional information needed by WordPerfect to execute the command. The names of menu options that access dialog boxes end in ellipses (...). Because the File, Open command ends in an ellipsis, for example, you know that a dialog box appears after you choose this command.

**NOTE** Some command buttons are found in dialog boxes. The label on these buttons ends in an ellipsis (see fig. 1.14).

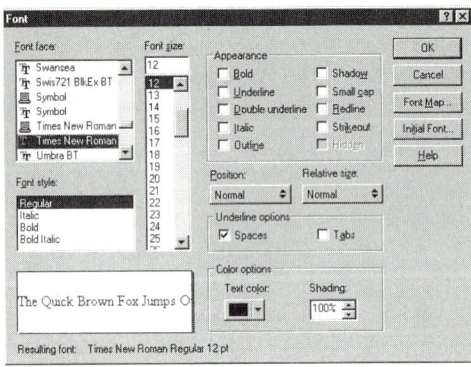

**FIG. 1.14**
The Font dialog box shows several dialog controls, including lists, pop-up lists, check boxes, and command buttons.

Some dialog boxes require you to choose an option box or button or to type any necessary information. Other dialog boxes offer choices in drop-down or pop-up lists. Each of these items is known as a *dialog box control*. Many dialog boxes require the manipulation of several different controls and options. Figure 1.14 shows the Font dialog box, which presents several different types of choices. Additional dialog box features are illustrated in the Files Preferences dialog box shown in figure 1.15.

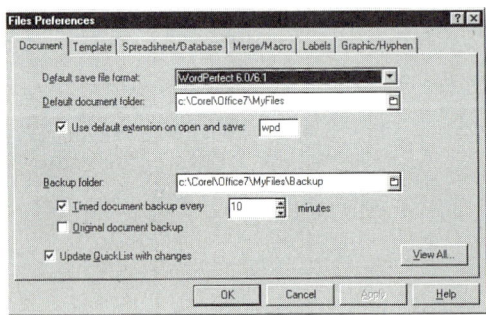

**FIG. 1.15**
The Files Preferences dialog box includes text boxes with lookup buttons and a text box with increment arrows, a drop-down list, check boxes, and command buttons. Choose a different tab from the top of the box to change the dialog box contents.

The various dialog box controls and how to use them are discussed in the following sections.

## Moving Around in a Dialog Box

You can move from section to section in dialog boxes simply by clicking the part of the dialog box in which you need to work. If you prefer using the keyboard, simply press the Alt key and the mnemonic for the option you want to change or the area in which you want to work. To select Bold in the Font dialog box, for example, click the word Bold (or the check box next to it), or press Alt+B (refer to fig. 1.14).

Alternatively, you can use Tab and Shift+Tab to move among the available options in the dialog box. After an item is selected (signified by the dotted line surrounding that item or a highlight bar in lists), the keystroke to activate or change that item varies depending on the control's type. See the following sections about each specific dialog box element for information on how to control that element.

> **NOTE** In Windows 95 terms, a highlighted control is said to have the *focus*. That is, the next action, command, or keystroke affects that object.

Many dialog boxes in WordPerfect 7 include numerous options distributed on several screens, each of which appears when you choose its index tab located just under the dialog box title bar (refer to fig. 1.15).

## Understanding Dialog Box Elements

WordPerfect 7 dialog boxes use several different controls. Each control is discussed individually in the following sections.

**Understanding Buttons** Every dialog box in WordPerfect 7 has at least one button: OK or Close. Either button closes the dialog box and causes the changes you make in the box to take effect. Most dialog boxes also have a Cancel button. You use the Cancel button to leave the dialog box without executing the changes you made.

> **NOTE** Some confirmation dialog boxes do not have an OK or Close button. Instead they have Yes, No, and Cancel buttons.

Other buttons also are available, as shown in the Font dialog box (refer to fig. 1.14). Typically, if you choose a dialog box button with an ellipsis, another dialog box appears. Clicking Initial Font from the Font dialog box, for example, accesses the Document Initial Font dialog box. After you leave the Document Initial Font dialog box, you return to the Font dialog box.

> **TIP** You can right-click options in dialog boxes to display a Help tip that describes what the option controls.

Other buttons in the Font dialog box include an arrow. Clicking the Position or Relative Size accesses a pop-up list of options, while clicking the Text Color button accesses a pop-up list that displays graphically the colors available.

To choose a button, click that button, or use the keyboard to move to the button and then press Enter. If the button has a mnemonic, you can use the mnemonic to activate the button.

**Understanding Text Boxes**   One of the most common dialog controls is the *text box*. The Files Preferences dialog box shown in figure 1.15, for example, contains two text boxes. You select each box by using the mouse or keyboard, and then type information in the provided space.

**TIP**   When you need to see what is behind a dialog box, point to its title bar with the mouse and drag the dialog box to the side of the screen.

After you press Enter or move away from the text box, WordPerfect evaluates your entry and displays the applicable text in the box. If you type **1 1/3** as the measurement for the left margin in the Margins dialog box, for example, WordPerfect displays 1.33.

> **N O T E**   Most text boxes do not accept invalid information. If you type a letter instead of a number in the Left text box, for example, WordPerfect does not display the letter in the text box.

If you use the keyboard to move to a text box that already contains text, WordPerfect selects that text. To replace the text, begin typing. The current entry is deleted and replaced with what you type. To edit an existing entry, use the arrow keys or the mouse to position the insertion point in the text where you want to make a change.

**TIP**   Use Tab and Shift+Tab to move to a text box and simultaneously select the contents of the box.

Most text boxes containing numeric values in WordPerfect 7 use increment and decrement arrows to change the current value by a set amount. The text box where you enter the number of columns in the Columns dialog box (refer to fig. 1.16), for example, displays a set of increment and decrement arrows beside it, or refer to the Shading text box visible in figure 1.14. Clicking the up arrow increases the value in either of these text boxes by 1. Clicking the down arrow decreases the value by 1. The increment and decrement arrows for other features, such as margins or line length, may only change by 0.1 or 0.01 when you click the appropriate arrow.

**Understanding Check Boxes**   *Check boxes* enable you to choose more than one of the offered choices. A check in a check box indicates that the option is active. In the Font dialog box, for example, you can choose several text appearance attributes (refer to fig. 1.14). To make your text bold, italic, and small caps, for example, choose the check box next to each item. You can choose as many or as few of the check boxes as you want. Check boxes act independently of each other.

Check boxes toggle a feature on and off. Clicking the option name or its box or using the keyboard to choose the option alternately displays or clears a check in the check box. When the check appears, the feature is on, or *active*.

> **N O T E** When a check box has the focus, pressing the space bar alternately puts a check in and clears the box.

**Understanding Radio Buttons**   *Radio buttons* (sometimes referred to as *option buttons*) appear as small round dots in the dialog box and always occur in groups. Their operation is similar to that of check boxes, except that you may select only one of the options available in each group. In the Columns dialog box, for example, you can choose Newspaper as the Type of column, but you cannot choose Parallel at the same time (see fig. 1.16). After you choose a radio button, the circle is filled in to indicate that the button is selected.

Radio buttons also are used to control the contents of some dialog boxes. Selecting a different radio button changes the contents of the dialog box accordingly. Such dialog boxes (see fig. 1.16) are used primarily to set up features or functions within WordPerfect.

**FIG. 1.16**
The Columns dialog box contains several radio buttons used to select the type of columns you want to define.

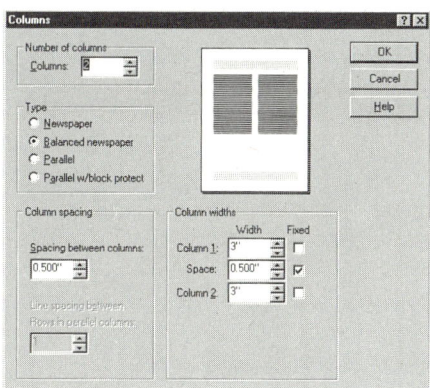

**Understanding Lookup Buttons**   WordPerfect also uses several special buttons to help you input values. These lookup buttons take you to another dialog box or open up a special selection list to help you enter values into text boxes. Lookup buttons are placed next to the text boxes to which they apply; a graphic representing the button's function appears on its face.

The small buttons with a file folder on them in the Files Preferences dialog box (refer to fig. 1.15) open the Select Folder dialog box. Figure 1.17 shows a lookup button you can use to enter a date in a text box.

**N O T E**  The contents of some dialog boxes vary depending on the option(s) chosen. These dialog boxes are used primarily to set up features or functions within WordPerfect.

**Understanding Selection Lists**  If you can choose only from a specific list of choices for one option, a list of all the valid choices is usually provided. Such lists are known as *list boxes*. The Font dialog box, for example, includes three such lists: Font Face, Font Style, and Font Size (refer to fig. 1.14). To choose a different font face in the Font dialog box, first choose Font Face to select the Font Face list, and then choose from among the choices provided.

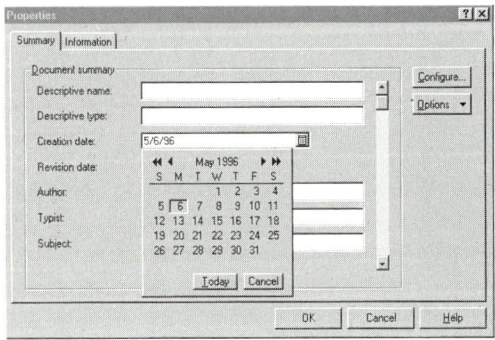

**FIG. 1.17**
Selecting the small calendar graphic next to the Creation Date text box in the document's Properties dialog box opens a calendar dialog box from which you can select a date.

List boxes can contain text options, such as in the Font dialog box, or the choices may be displayed graphically to help you make your choice. When applying a border to a page, the Page Border/Fill dialog box shows a graphic of each available style (see fig. 1.18).

You can select an item from a list by clicking the item or by using the arrow keys to highlight the option you want; you do not need to press Enter to select items in a normal list. After making a selection, the list remains open.

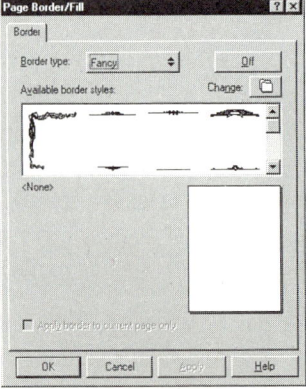

**FIG. 1.18**
The available page borders appear graphically in the list box found in the Page Border/Fill dialog box.

Some lists are contained in drop-down lists. Usually these lists relate to options in which the current value is important, but constantly seeing all the various values that option may contain is not as important. The Save As dialog box, for example, contains two such drop-down lists: Save In and As Type (see fig. 1.19). Pressing the list's mnemonic and then pressing the down arrow, or clicking the downward pointing arrow next to the list, opens that list shown in figure 1.19.

**FIG. 1.19**
The Save As dialog box contains a list box and two drop-down lists. The As Type drop-down list is shown open with the current drive selected.

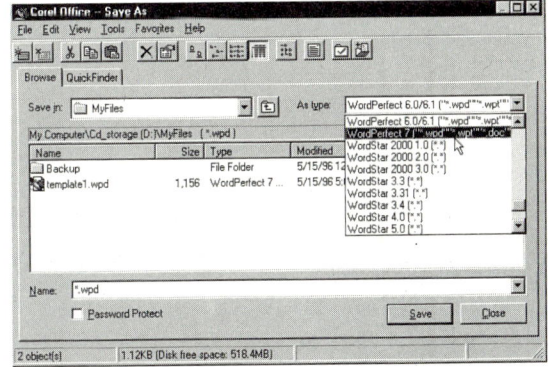

After the list is open, you can select an item by clicking that item or by using the arrow keys to highlight the option you want and pressing Enter. After you make your choice, the list closes.

> **TIP** Double-click a file name in the Save As dialog box to choose the name, save the file, and close the box.

Some text boxes may feature a combination of text box and selection list, such as the Font Size text box in the Font dialog box (refer to fig. 1.14). These text boxes differ from the standard drop-down list, because you can either type in new text or select an option from the supplied items.

**Understanding Pop-up Lists**  One other type of list that WordPerfect offers is the *pop-up list*. Examples of pop-up lists include the Position and Relative Size list in the Font dialog box (see figs. 1.14 and 1.20). Pop-up lists resemble buttons with upward- and downward-pointing arrows on the right side of the button's face. The currently selected item also usually appears on the button's face.

> **NOTE** Some pop-up lists are marked with only a drop-down arrow or triangle and display the name of the feature rather than the currently selected value. The Options button on the Outline Bar, for example, expands into a list of options that lead to dialog boxes that help you to configure the current outline.

**FIG. 1.20**

The Font dialog box contains pop-up lists for Position and Relative Size which is selected in this illustration.

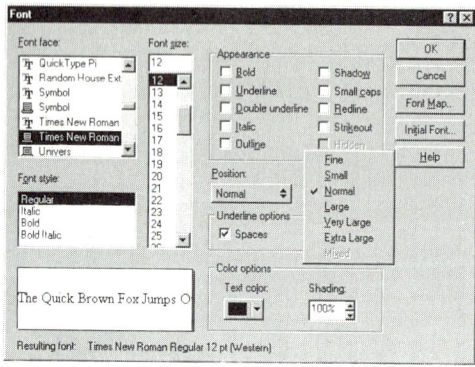

After it is selected, the button expands into a list of items from which you can choose. Choosing Relative Size, for example, opens the pop-up list from which you can choose one of the available sizes (refer to fig. 1.20). After you choose an item, that option reverts to its original button-like state.

*Example-type pop-up lists* display graphic representations of your choices. The Column Border/Fill dialog box in figure 1.21, for example, contains three example pop-ups—Color, Line Style, and Drop Shadow—represented by square buttons. The graphic lists usually are accompanied by lists of equivalent options in text form.

**FIG. 1.21**

The Column Border dialog box contains three example pop-up lists: Color, Line Style (shown open), and Drop Shadow.

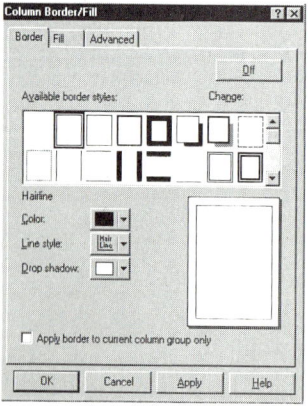

Using the keyboard, press Tab to move the selection to the button and then press the space bar, or click the button with the mouse. After the button is activated, a box showing the graphic equivalent of the various available values appears, with the current value outlined in blue (refer to fig. 1.21). Use the mouse to click the desired value, or use the arrow keys to move to your choice and press Enter. After you make a selection, the button reverts to its former state, displaying the currently selected option on its face.

Using Dialog Boxes | 39

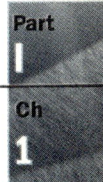

## Using QuickSpots

New to WordPerfect 7 are *QuickSpots*, small buttons that appear next to paragraphs, and within selected images and table cells. When you move the mouse pointer over a paragraph, the Edit Paragraph QuickSpot appears in the margin to the left of the first line of the paragraph (see fig. 1.22). Click the button to display the Paragraph dialog box shown in figure 1.23.

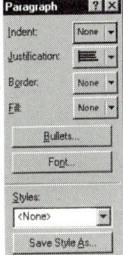

**FIG. 1.22**
An Edit Paragraph QuickSpot appears in the left margin of a paragraph when the mouse pointer is over the paragraph.

**FIG. 1.23**
Click the Edit Paragraph QuickSpot next to a paragraph to display the Paragraph dialog box containing various paragraph formatting commands.

When you select an image, an Edit Box QuickSpot appears within the selection handles, and the small black boxes surround the image in figure 1.24. Click the button with the mouse to display the Edit Box dialog box shown in figure 1.25.

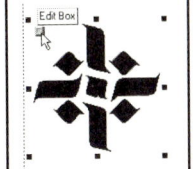

**FIG. 1.24**
When you select an image, a QuickSpot appears. Move the mouse pointer over the QuickSpot to see the Edit Box QuickTip.

**FIG. 1.25**
Click the Edit Box QuickSpot in a graphic to display the Edit Box dialog box containing various Graphics command buttons.

Move the mouse pointer to a cell or over several selected cells in a table, and an Edit Table QuickSpot appears (see fig. 1.26). Click the button to display the Tools dialog box shown in figure 1.27. Use the tools in the dialog box to format individual cells, adjust columns, and insert and delete columns and rows.

**FIG. 1.26**
When you move the mouse pointer to a cell in a table, an Edit Table QuickSpot appears.

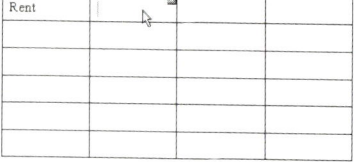

**FIG. 1.27**
Click the Edit Table QuickSpot in a cell to display the Tools dialog box containing command buttons you can use to change the cell lines, join or split cells, and other table formatting tools.

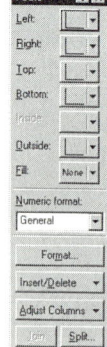

**TROUBLESHOOTING**

**When I am using features for the first time, I often end up opening the wrong dialog box. Can I close a dialog box quickly using the keyboard?** Yes. Just press the Esc key.

**When I click into a text box, I have to delete the contents as well as enter new contents. Is there any way to simplify entering new information?** When you use Tab to move from feature to feature (Shift+Tab to move back), the contents of a text box are highlighted. The selected contents are deleted when you enter new information.

# Understanding What You Don't See

WordPerfect 7, like its DOS predecessors, operates on a clean screen principle. Many formatting codes are inserted while you work on a WordPerfect document, but they do not appear in the editing document.

Likewise, spaces, tabs, and hard returns (from pressing Enter in a document) do not appear in the document text. Occasionally, however, knowing where the formatting codes, spaces, tabs, and hard returns occur in text is helpful. WordPerfect 7, therefore, offers options for displaying these elements.

## Reveal Codes

WordPerfect inserts hidden codes into your document for almost everything it does. These hidden codes may seem complex at first, but you cannot afford to ignore them. These codes indicate margin settings, tabs, carriage returns, indents, and additional information about how your document appears in the editing window.

Hidden codes also contain information about headers, footers, font changes, document comments, and nonprinting notes. Other hidden codes turn certain features on and off. Such codes occur in pairs and show you exactly where the feature is active in the text.

To see the hidden codes in a document, choose View, Reveal Codes, or press Alt+F3. Repeat the procedure to turn off Reveal Codes. Figure 1.28 shows the Reveal Codes window.

If Reveal Codes is active, the document window is split between the editing screen and the Reveal Codes window. A cursor (highlighted block) in the Reveal Codes window shows where the insertion point is in regard to the text and surrounding codes.

**FIG. 1.28**
The Reveal Codes window shows you the codes that WordPerfect uses to format your text.

## Show Spaces, Tabs, and Hard Returns

Along with the formatting codes displayed in the Reveal Codes window, you can choose to show graphic representations of spaces, tabs, hard returns, and more in your document text. Figure 1.29 shows a document displaying spaces, tabs, and hard returns.

**FIG. 1.29**
WordPerfect 7 can show you where spaces, tabs, and hard returns occur in the text.

Choose E̲dit, Pr̲eferences, D̲isplay, Symbols ¶, and then select the items you want to display or hide. To cause the items to appear, you then choose Sho̲w Symbols On New And Current Document so a check appears in the adjacent box.

In addition to the preceding three elements, you also can choose to display I̲ndents, So̲ft Hyphens, and Ce̲nter, F̲lush Right, A̲dvance, and Ce̲nter Page codes.

## Templates

*Templates* play an important role in WordPerfect 7. Templates primarily act as a boilerplate document construction tool, enabling you to build a document from preformatted text. Templates, however, can do much more.

Templates act as containers for WordPerfect tasks. They also can hold styles, macros, abbreviations, Toolbars, menus, and keyboard definitions. By using templates, you can make sure that the tools you need for a specific task are close at hand. You can create a Newsletter template, for example, that contains newsletter styles, macros, Toolbars, and menus. By accessing the Newsletter template, you activate all these specific tools for use on the newsletter.

WordPerfect uses a special template named Standard to define the standard tools available to all templates you create. This template is used as the default to create new documents after you first start WordPerfect.

▶ **See** "Understanding Templates," **p. 363**

# Working with Multiple Documents

WordPerfect enables you to open as many as nine documents at a time—memory permitting. This capability gives you an exceptional amount of freedom in exchanging information between documents. With several documents open, for example, you can move quickly from one document to the next, copying parts of each to create a new document.

WordPerfect loads each document into a document window. The document can be displayed full-screen, in a window, or minimized (refer to the earlier section "Document Controls"). You can move these windows around the screen, and you can open and close each window without affecting the others. By displaying documents in these ways, WordPerfect enables you to accomplish the following tasks:

- Remove a document almost completely from the screen by minimizing it to an icon.
- Move a document window from one location to another.

- Overlap document windows so that you can switch between them by clicking each in turn.
- Position two or more documents side by side so that you can compare files or make it easier to cut and paste data from one to the other.

## Arranging Documents On-Screen

The most common way to work in a WordPerfect document is to maximize its window to occupy the entire editing area. Maximizing the window provides the best view of the entire document. You also can reduce, or minimize, the document window so that it uses only part of the main WordPerfect screen. You minimize a document by clicking the Minimize button or by choosing Mi_n_imize from the Document Control menu. You can return the document to its original size by clicking the Maximize button or by choosing Ma_x_imize from the Document Control menu.

As mentioned in the earlier section, "Application Control Menu," you can size and position the window by using the mouse or the keyboard.

## Switching Between Documents

Although you can have open up to nine documents simultaneously, only one document can be active at a time. You can make changes only to the active document. A document must be active before you can close or save it.

You can click the document you want to make active if you can see any part of its border on-screen.

The active document's title bar is displayed in a color different from the color of the title bars in inactive documents. To work on a document, you first must make it active. To make a document active, choose _W_indow, and press the number corresponding to the document you want active. You can quickly switch to the next document by choosing Nex_t_ from the Document Control menu or by pressing Ctrl+F6 on the keyboard.

## Tiling or Cascading Documents

To help you arrange multiple documents so that you can switch more easily from one to another, WordPerfect enables you to tile or cascade your document windows. *Tiling windows* gives each window the same amount of screen space without overlapping (see fig. 1.30). *Cascading windows* overlaps the windows but leaves each title bar showing (see fig. 1.31). To tile or cascade windows, choose _W_indow, _T_ile Top To Bottom or Tile _S_ide By Side; or _W_indow, _C_ascade, respectively.

**FIG. 1.30**
Documents can be tiled one above the other in the editing window. Tiling is useful if you want to compare two documents or if your work requires that all documents remain visible.

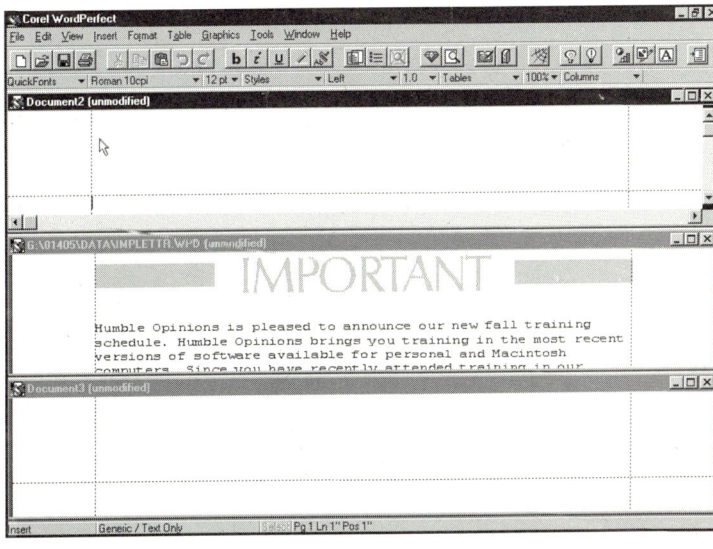

**FIG. 1.31**
Documents can also be cascaded in the editing window. Cascading is useful if you need access to multiple documents but want to see as much of the active document as possible.

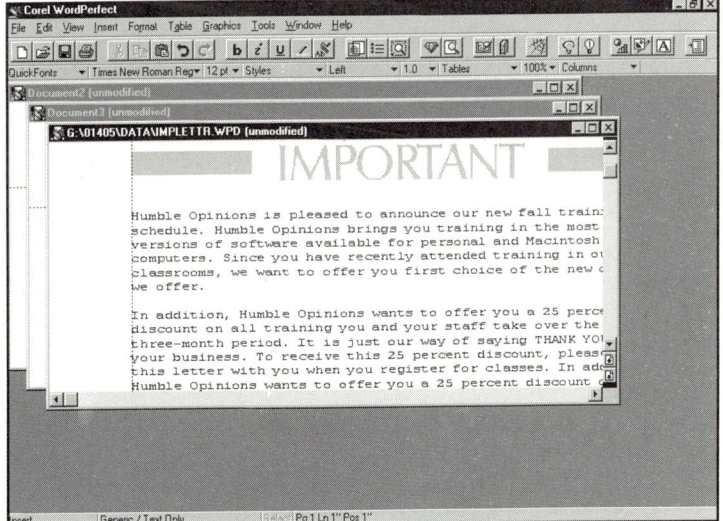

# Using Help

WordPerfect's Help system provides quick, easy access to a large body of explanatory information on WordPerfect, including an automated tutor that walks you through such operations as italicizing, boldfacing, or underlining text, or creating a table of contents.

Except to perform highly technical operations, you may only rarely need to refer to the program's manual; the information available from Help is usually sufficient.

You can access Help from virtually anywhere in the program, either through the Help menu, as shown in figure 1.32, by pressing F1 (Help), or by clicking a Help button when one is available. Help is especially useful if you are in the middle of an operation and do not know exactly how to complete it. Whether you are in a dialog box or adding special formatting to a section of text, you can press F1 to access *context-sensitive help*—that is, help that pertains directly to the current task.

**FIG. 1.32**
The WordPerfect Help menu enables you to select from several common Help features.

You also can obtain help on a specific element on-screen by pressing Shift+F1. The mouse pointer turns into a pointer with a question mark balloon. Position the pointer on the button or other element with which you want help, and click. The Help system displays help specific to that element (see fig. 1.33).

**FIG. 1.33**
Press Shift+F1, then click a feature (such as the QuickFormat button) to display detailed help.

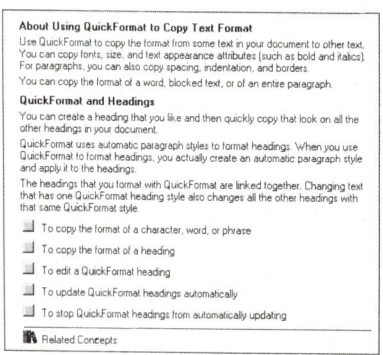

Help anticipates your questions about the program and understands that you may not know the correct terminology to use as you look for answers in an index. For step-by-step instructions on printing a document, for example, you simply choose Help, Ask the PerfectExpert, and then type **set tabs** or a similar request.

WordPerfect's PerfectExpert also offers automated procedures in which WordPerfect instructs you step-by-step on how to perform an operation. The PerfectExpert tells you when to select text, what to do next, how to complete the operation, and how to save your changes and can even walk you through the task in your current document. Consequently, after you complete the task, you have not merely been taught the operation but have actually performed the task in your document.

Help is actually a separate application, run in a separate window from WordPerfect. Help has its own Maximize/Restore, Minimize, and Control Menu buttons and border. You can treat it as any other Windows 95 application, keeping it active so that you can instantly switch to it, or tiling the Help and WordPerfect windows on the desktop so that you can read the Help text as you work.

## The Help Menu

WordPerfect's Help menu contains three different options that provide different levels and functions of help. The Help menu includes the following items:

- *Help Topics*. This option displays the WordPerfect Help dialog box. The first screen lists a handful of common help topics (see fig. 1.34). If the topic displays a book icon, double-click the topic, or highlight it then press Enter, to display more topics.

- *Ask the PerfectExpert*. This option displays a PerfectExpert dialog box in which you can type a phrase or question to locate Help topics about the task you describe (see fig. 1.35).

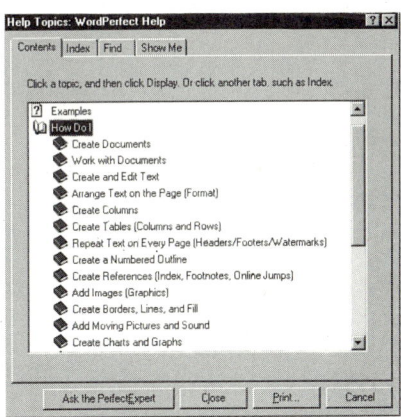

**FIG. 1.34**
The Help Contents screen enables you to select from several specific Help topics. Click the topic you want or press an arrow key to move the highlight bar to the topic and press Enter. The How Do I topic has been expanded to display its contents.

- *Help Online*. This feature enables you to go directly to online WordPerfect Help if you have any online services such as CompuServe, America Online, or an Internet connection and a modem installed in your computer. When you first access Help Online, choose Configure to have WordPerfect locate your online service software and set up access in the Help Online dialog box. Thereafter, you need only choose the service from the Select A Service list. WordPerfect then dials the service and connects you to Corel forums where you can ask questions and find help.

- *Upgrade Expert*. Provides information about WordPerfect features as compared to other word processing applications. Choose your old program in the upper list box, then choose a feature from your former program to see a display of the corresponding WordPerfect menu command, what the feature does, and a graphic illustration. By using the buttons at the bottom of the window, you can obtain even more Help on how to use the feature in WordPerfect.

- *About WordPerfect*. Displays a screen that shows your PIN and Serial numbers, the program and PerfectFit release version information, and the physical memory currently available for your use. You can use this feature to see your registration number when calling WordPerfect Customer Support.

**FIG. 1.35**
Use Ask the PerfectExpert to enter a question or just a word. Click Search to see the results.

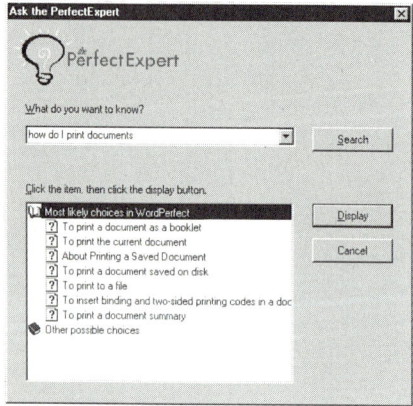

## The WordPerfect Help Dialog Box

Choosing Help, Help Topics opens the WordPerfect Help dialog box which includes tabbed sections that divide the Help program into Contents, Index, Find, and Show Me.

**Contents**  When you first open the WordPerfect Help dialog box, the Contents section appears, offering the following topics:

- *Example*. Displays a screen with seven different document types and an enlargement of the current selection with arrows to each document feature. Click an arrow to learn more about that feature.

- *How Do I*. Provides information on all WordPerfect functions in easily understood terminology. If a task is possible, How Do I can tell you how to do it without the frustration of searching through the manual (or the Help Index) for a feature name which you do not know.

- *What's New Or Changed.* Displays a list of WordPerfect features that can be used to access Help topics and describe how the feature has changed from WordPerfect 6.1 to WordPerfect 7.
- *Troubleshooting.* Presents an extensive list of Help topics that have a troubleshooting topic.
- *Macros.* Provides help on WordPerfect's extensive Macro Language. To use this option, you must have WordPerfect's Online Macro Help file installed. See Appendix A, "Installing and Setting Up WordPerfect 7," for more information on installation.
- *Technical Support.* Provides information on how to obtain technical support in the United States and internationally.
- *Copyright, Trademark, and License.* Information about your license agreement, the WordPerfect trademarks and copyrights, and a list of WordPerfect patents.
- *Using Help.* Lists several topics that explain the various aspects of the Help program, particularly including the effective use of the Find tab.
- *Customizing Help.* Provides topics on changing the Help screen font, creating bookmarks, adding annotations, and other modifications to the way Help works.

**Index**  Select the Index tab and WordPerfect Help displays an alphabetical list of WordPerfect functions you can search by typing a character or word. Type one or more characters in the Type The First Few Letters Of The Word You're Looking For text box, as shown in figure 1.36. The list scrolls to the first word that starts with the text you type.

**FIG. 1.36**
The Index dialog box in the WordPerfect 7 Help system provides an alphabetical list of WordPerfect features and actions. Type **g** as shown, and WordPerfect highlights the first word that begins with "g."

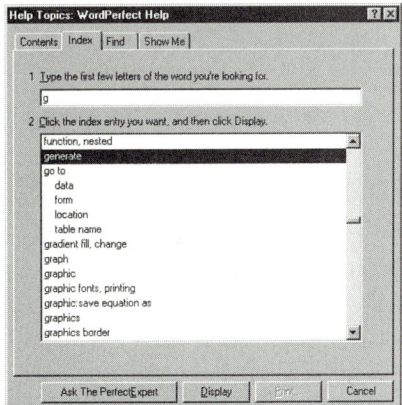

Move the highlight to the topic you want to view and press Enter or double-click the topic with the mouse. When you are ready to return to your document, press Esc or click the Close button.

**TIP** After you have reviewed a topic, you can easily return to the Help dialog box by clicking the Help Topics button.

**Find**  An extremely powerful approach to obtaining help is to use Find to create a word and topic list of everything in the WordPerfect Help program. When you first choose Find, the Find Setup Wizard shown in figure 1.37 appears.

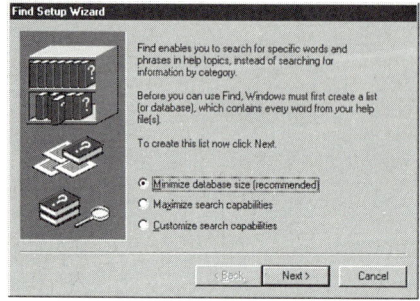

**FIG. 1.37**
In the Find Setup Wizard dialog box, choose the type of list you want WordPerfect to create.

The list, or database, that is created by Find includes all the words in all of the help topics in WordPerfect. WordPerfect suggests you choose to minimize the size of the list. Although you can maximize the database size, most users will find the standard size is sufficient. If you choose to customize the list, you can select parts of the WordPerfect program, such as TextArt, Print System, or PerfectFit, to exclude from one database.

Select which kind of list you want created, then choose Next. If you chose to customize the list, select any WordPerfect components to exclude or include in each screen; choose Next in each screen to continue. To begin building the list, choose Finish. After a few minutes, the completed Find dialog box appears (see fig. 1.38).

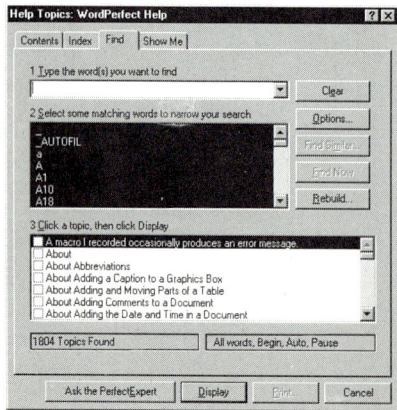

**FIG. 1.38**
In the Find tab, enter words in the Type The Word(s) You Want To Find text box. The list of topics shows the Find results.

Now you can type a word or words to search for and topics that contain what you type in the Click A Topic, Then Click Display list box. As you type a word and press the space bar, the found topics appear in the list box below. Continue entering words, and the list of topics updates each time you press the space bar indicating the end of a word. When you see a likely topic in the list, double-click the topic with the mouse or click the topic, then click Display.

You can type words into the Type The Word(s) You Want To Find text box in any order; WordPerfect automatically searches for topics that contain all the words you type, in any order, anywhere in the topics. If you want to limit or otherwise customize Find, choose Options to open the Find Options dialog box shown in figure 1.39.

**FIG. 1.39**
In Find Options, you can choose how WordPerfect conducts the search for topics, including whether to match parts of a word and when to begin searching.

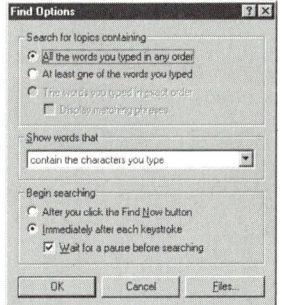

As you enter text, words that match what you type appear in the Select Some Matching Words To Narrow Your Search list box. Watch for a likely word to appear; you can choose the word to display the matching topics in the box below.

When you aren't sure of the exact word or phrase to use, you can enter your best guess, and Find displays a selection of words based on the Find Options settings. An interesting option is the ability to choose what characters to match in the text you type. From the Show Words That drop-down list, you can choose to match the first or last characters of the word, any characters in any order, or all characters.

If Find works very slowly or the suggestions are not enough on point, you can always choose the Rebuild button and customize the word list to exclude some WordPerfect features.

**Show Me**   Selecting the Show Me tab activates the PerfectExpert, the perfect place for some basic how-to help. When a feature is a complete mystery, it often helps to see the feature used. PerfectExpert can do just that for you. Click Play a Demo, or use the arrow keys to move the dotted outline to Play a Demo. From the list box, choose a feature, such as Make It Fit, and view an animated tutorial that both explains and illustrates the features. If you have a sound card, the demo becomes a multimedia presentation that includes background music and verbal instructions.

Perhaps you do understand a feature well enough to know you want to use it but cannot figure exactly how to make it work in your document. Choose Guide Me Through It and select the feature from the adjacent list box. Your PerfectExpert guide then provides a dialog box in which you can indicate whether you want to be led through each step of the task in the current document or for PerfectExpert to do all the work until it reaches a point where you must make a choice.

## Help's Glossary Terms and Hints

Throughout the Help system are glossary terms, which appear in green with a dotted underline. Notice the many dotted underlined items in figure 1.36, which shows a Help selection. The underlined terms `form`, `data source`, `data file`, and `address book` are glossary terms. Use the glossary terms to access a definition of terms and an explanation of how they relate to WordPerfect. To select a glossary term, click the term, or use Tab or Shift+Tab to highlight the term and then press Enter. After you select a glossary term, a small pop-up box appears, offering a definition of the selected term. Click outside the box or press Enter to close the box.

Many Help topics include one or more topic titles at the bottom of the screen that take you further into the feature (see figs. 1.40 and 1.41). Click the adjacent button, and WordPerfect displays the Help topic. Many titles also have a Related Concepts item at the bottom of the window (refer to fig. 1.37). Click the books icon adjacent to Related Concepts to see a list of suggested topics that take you into other similar features.

**FIG. 1.40**
The About Merge Help screen displays glossary terms.

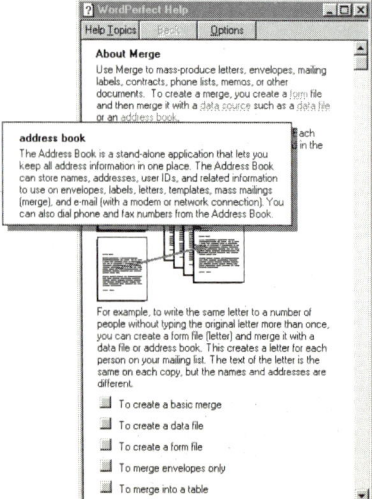

**FIG. 1.41**
The Troubleshooting Toolbar Assignments topic includes an additional topic title as well as Related Topics.

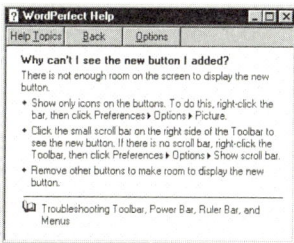

## Navigating the Help System

Along with the jump terms and glossary terms, you can use the buttons at the top of the Help screen to access information. These buttons, which appear on all Help screens, provide rapid movement from one part of the Help system to another. The following list briefly describes each Help button and its use:

- *Help Topics*. Returns to the Contents screen.
- *Back*. Returns to the previous Help screen.
- *Options*. Displays a menu of Help features.

You can use the arrow keys to move from one jump term or glossary term to the next. Use the Page Up and Page Down keys to move from one page of Help information to the next.

The Options menu includes a variety of powerful tools that can help you take full advantage of WordPerfect's Help program:

- *Annotate*. Enables you to add a comment to a Help topic. Click Annotate, and type your comment in the Current Annotation text box. A green paper clip appears next to the topic title. Click the paper clip to review the annotation.
- *Copy*. Copies the contents of the topic to the Windows 95 Clipboard. You can now paste the contents in a document.
- *Print Topic*. Enables you to print the current topic to the current printer. A Print dialog box appears, in which you can choose a different printer or set the number of copies.

- *Font*. Enables you to choose a Small, Normal, or Large size font.
- *Keep Help on Top*. Help topics move to the background when you switch to another application. To perform a task and see a Help topic at the same time, choose Keep Help on Top, then select On Top.
- *Use System Colors*. Enables you to use the Windows 95 default colors even though you have chosen to use another color scheme.
- *Open a File*. Enables you to display the Help file from any application.
- *Exit*. Provides an immediate means of closing Help.
- *Define a Bookmark*. Enables you to add the current topic to a list of bookmarks in the Help system, making it easy to find particular topics at a later time.
- *Display a Bookmark*. Displays the list of Help topics saved as bookmarks. Highlight the one you want to display, then choose OK.
- *Version*. Shows the version number of the current Windows 95 Help program, along with Microsoft and Corel copyright information.

### TROUBLESHOOTING

**How can I use Help to learn the steps for a task when Help disappears every time I click in my document?** Try using the Coach feature found on the WordPerfect Help menu. Select the task you want to apply from the list of coaches, and execute each step in the Coach. The Coach remains visible as you work in your document. When you have completed the task, the changes remain in your document. If you want to refer to another Help feature while working in your document, choose Help, Keep Help On Top, On Top and resize the Help window so it does not block your work.

**How can I keep Help open while I am working with several documents and between applications?** You can minimize the Help program or just click the window visible in the background. Then, press F1 for Help or use Alt+Tab to cycle to Help when you need it again.

CHAPTER 2

# Creating and Saving a Document

*by Gary Pickavet*

In Chapter 1, you learned how to start WordPerfect and were introduced to the major features in Corel WordPerfect 7. You learned about the WordPerfect environment and its graphical user interface. You also learned how to use the Help system to quickly obtain information on a feature. You are now ready to learn how to use WordPerfect to create basic documents.

This chapter provides basic information on how to use WordPerfect to compose documents and safely save them to disk, and how to print documents. ■

- **Understand WordPerfect's built-in settings**

  When you start WordPerfect, many default settings for WordPerfect features enable you to immediately begin writing your thoughts.

- **Create a sample document**

  While creating a sample document, learn how to enter text, insert blank lines, use Typeover, and insert additional text.

- **Move through your documents using the mouse and keyboard**

  Learn how to move the insertion point through a document by using the mouse and keyboard.

- **Print one page or your entire document**

  Learn how to print either the current page or your entire on-screen document.

- **Save your completed document to disk**

  Most of the time, you will want to save the documents you've composed on-screen to a folder on your disk. In this chapter, you learn how.

- **Calling it quits for the day**

  When you exit WordPerfect, you are then prompted to save any documents that have been modified or not previously saved.

## Understanding WordPerfect's Built-in Settings

Even before you start typing, WordPerfect is at work for you. Many features—such as line spacing, tabs, margins, and fonts—are set at initial (or *default*) values when you start the program. For example, all margins are set at one inch, and the line spacing is set at single space. The paper size is assumed to be 8 1/2 × 11-inch letter with a portrait orientation (printing left to right across the small side of the page). Because WordPerfect starts with these default settings, you don't have to make any formatting decisions to start entering text. In subsequent chapters—especially those chapters devoted to formatting, printing, and desktop publishing—you learn how to override the default settings, alter the look of your documents, and create new templates where you can store custom settings to be applied to only certain documents.

Table 2.1 lists a few of WordPerfect's many default settings. Other defaults are covered where appropriate in chapters throughout this book. In addition, WordPerfect enables you to change default settings to suit your needs.

**Table 2.1  Examples of WordPerfect's Built-in Initial Settings**

| Setting | Default Value |
| --- | --- |
| Margins | 1-inch top, bottom, left, and right |
| Line spacing | Single-spaced |
| Page numbering | None |
| Justification | Left |
| Automatic timed backup of files | Automatically backs up files every 10 minutes |
| Paper size | Letter-size paper (8 1/2 × 11 inches) |
| Tabs | Every 1/2 inch |

## Entering Text in WordPerfect

When WordPerfect starts, it displays a clean editing screen and several graphical tools to help you with your primary task: writing your document. These helpful tools include the Toolbar, Power Bar, and status bar, and are described in Chapter 1, "Getting Started." These graphical tools enable you to quickly perform WordPerfect commands or start WordPerfect tools such as the writing tools or the WordPerfect Draw and Chart applications. The status bar provides you with a variety of useful information such as the current

printer, the page number, and the position of the insertion point on the page.
The status bar can be customized to add functions to display additional information such as the current font, date and time, zoom percentage, and caps lock status. As detailed in Chapter 9, all these bars can be extensively modified to enable you to operate at peak efficiency.

▶ **See** "Understanding the Editing Screen," **p. 16**

▶ **See** "Customizing Window Features," **p. 321**

In addition, WordPerfect also provides other graphical tools to help you format documents. These include the following:

- *Guidelines*. Dotted lines that show you where the margins, tables, headers and footers, and columns begin and end.
- *QuickSpots*. Enable you to quickly display the editing options for an object. QuickSpots are small boxes that pop up as you pass the mouse pointer over paragraphs, tables, and graphic boxes. Clicking the QuickSpot pops up a palette of common editing tasks relevant to the object.
- *Shadow cursor*. A faint vertical line that makes it easy to see precisely where the insertion point will be placed in a document.
- *QuickStatus box*. A box that pops up near the mouse pointer and quickly shows you on-screen the effect of dragging to change things such as tabs and margins.

The View menu item enables you to turn the bars and guidelines on and off. If any of the bars are displayed on-screen and you find them distracting, you can turn them off, freeing even more screen space for text. These bars are turned on and off by making selections from the View menu. To turn off the Power Bar, for example, choose View, Toolbars/Ruler. The Toolbars dialog box appears. Click the Power Bar choice to uncheck it and turn off the Power Bar. Click a toolbar with an empty box next to it to display the bar.

 To disable an information dialog box (such as the Hide Bars Information dialog box) from being displayed in the future, choose Disable This Message Permanently at the bottom of the displayed information dialog box.

To turn off all bars, including the vertical and horizontal scroll bars, choose View, Hide Bars, or press Alt+Shift+F5. An information box appears to tell you what will happen if you continue. Click OK to hide the bars and return to the editing window. To bring the bars back, press Esc or again press Alt+Shift+F5, or choose View, Hide Bars. The bars reappear.

To turn guidelines on or off, choose View, Guidelines. The Guidelines dialog box appears. Click each type of guideline to toggle its display on or off. A check mark next to each type of guideline (for example, Tables or Margins) means a guideline appears to graphically show the location for that object.

Think of the WordPerfect editing window as a piece of paper you have just rolled into a typewriter, ready to receive your thoughts. Unlike using a typewriter, using WordPerfect frees you from having to be concerned with the final product of your work when you start typing. You can first devote your energy and time to getting your thoughts down, and then go through the document adding formatting commands for each page and for your text.

▶ **See** "Formatting Text," **p. 121**

▶ **See** "Formatting Pages and Documents," **p. 155**

As you type documents into WordPerfect, remember these important word processing rules:

- Do not stop typing or press Enter at the end of each line. Let WordPerfect wrap the text for you. With a typewriter, you must press Return at the end of each line. With WordPerfect, you press Enter only when you want to end a paragraph or insert blank lines in the document. If WordPerfect cannot fit a word on a line, the program inserts a hidden code called a *soft return* into the document. This code ends the line and wraps the word to the next line. This feature is often called *word wrap*.

- When you let WordPerfect wrap words and determine the end of each line, exciting things happen. If you change the size of the font you are using, WordPerfect automatically reformats the text so that each line still extends from the left to the right margin.

    WordPerfect moves words between lines as necessary so that each line is still full. WordPerfect also reformats your text when you add or delete text in a paragraph, moving words down a line or up a line as necessary.

- Do not indent lines by inserting spaces with the space bar. Always use the Tab key when you want to indent only the first line of a paragraph, or the Indent key (F7) to indent all the lines in the current paragraph.

- Text can be monospaced or spaced proportionally. With monospaced text, every letter, number, space, or any other character is represented by the same amount of space (for example, the letter m takes up the same space as the letter i). Most printers (especially laser printers) print proportionally, which means that smaller letters (like i) are printed in less space than wider letters or numbers (like m). Spaces on a proportional printer take up very little space. The Tab and Indent keys move the insertion point to an exact line position, making it possible to line up text neatly in a document.

## Inserting Blank Lines

Within a paragraph, you don't press the Enter key at the end of each line; instead, you let WordPerfect end each line and move words to the next line if they don't fit on the current line. WordPerfect places a hidden soft return formatting code in the document.

To end a paragraph or insert one or more blank lines, press the Enter key, which causes the program to insert a hidden hard return formatting code at the place where you pressed Enter, and moves the insertion point to the next line. Pressing Enter twice ends the paragraph and places a blank line into the document. Each time you press Enter, WordPerfect places another hard return code into the document and creates a new line.

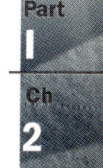

Chapter 3, "Opening and Editing Documents," describes a method of viewing WordPerfect's hidden codes. This feature is called *Reveal Codes*. Even without using the Reveal Codes feature, you can have WordPerfect show you where the hard returns are located in a document—right in the editing window. To view the location of hard returns as well as graphics symbols to represent spaces, tabs, and other formatting codes in the document window, choose View, Show ¶; or press Ctrl+Shift+F3. WordPerfect shows the hard returns in the editing window as a paragraph symbol. Follow the same steps to turn this feature off and hide the paragraph symbols.

▶ **See** "Understanding WordPerfect's Hidden Codes," **p. 91**

## Creating a Sample Letter

To illustrate the concepts introduced up to this point and to get you accustomed to entering text, this section asks you to create a sample letter. Over the course of this chapter, you complete the letter.

First, start WordPerfect as described in Chapter 1. Then type the text in the following paragraph. Don't worry if you make a mistake; just use the Backspace key to erase the mistake and then retype the text. Don't forget to indent the first line of each paragraph by pressing Tab, not by using the space bar. Do not press Enter at the end of each line. Just keep typing and let WordPerfect wrap words as necessary. Press Enter twice at the end of each paragraph to end the paragraph and insert a blank line.

> Thank you for the recent gift you sent me for my birthday. The rhinoceros earrings were perfect. Right after I received them, I attended a fundraising event at the Child's Estate Zoo. The earrings were the hit of the reception. I can't tell you how many people came up to me and commented on how unusual and pretty they thought the earrings were.

Press Enter twice.

> I'm looking forward to seeing you over your spring break. I received the note you sent, telling me about your arrival at our airport on April 5th at 9 a.m. My son Gary and my daughters Debbie and Jessica are really excited about your visit. Remember how much fun we had when we all got together last summer? I have planned several events to keep us all busy for the week. I can't wait to see you! We have so much to catch up on.

Press Enter twice.

> **Sincerely,**

Press Enter five times to insert four blank lines for your signature.

> **Marilyn Boyd**

Figure 2.1 shows the sample letter to this point, with the appropriate spacing. Soft returns are placed in a document by WordPerfect at the end of each line. Hard returns are line breaks that you insert to create additional white space in the document—for example, between paragraphs.

**FIG. 2.1**
This sample letter demonstrates the use of soft and hard returns in a document.

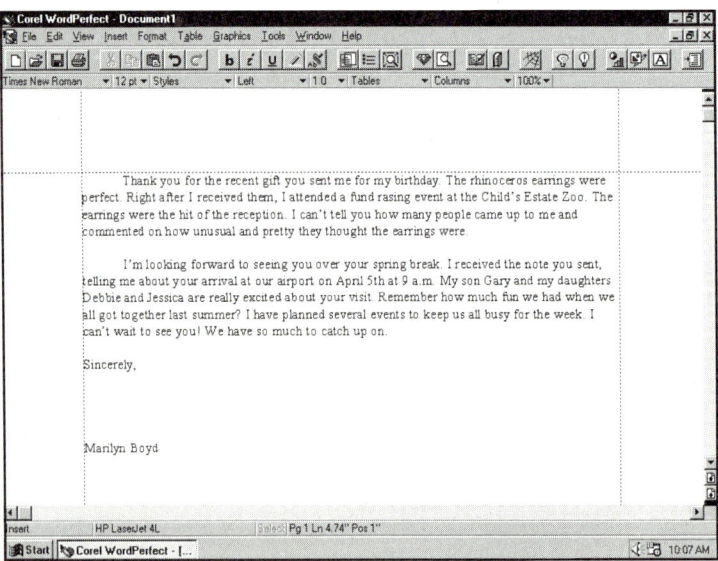

▶ See "Starting and Exiting WordPerfect," **p. 12**

# Moving Through the Document

After you have entered text for a while, you might need to move the insertion point to a different place in the document to insert or delete text. WordPerfect provides a variety of methods for you to move to a different place in your text. You can move the insertion point by using the keyboard or the mouse.

The insertion point can be moved as little as one character at a time or in major increments throughout the document. By using a mouse, you can also use scroll bars to move the insertion point quickly.

If you are not familiar with the basic parts of the WordPerfect screen, see Chapter 1 for details.

▶ **See** "Understanding the Editing Screen," **p. 16**

## Moving with the Mouse

You can use the mouse to move the insertion point quickly to a new location on the current screen or to move through the document. To move the insertion point a short distance, you can probably do so faster by using the keyboard insertion point-movement keys (described in the section "Moving with the Keyboard").

To move the insertion point quickly to a different location on the current screen, follow these steps:

1. Move the mouse pointer to the location on-screen where you want to move the insertion point. (While in the document, the shadow pointer appears and moves through the text, indicating where the insertion point would be placed if you clicked the mouse.)
2. Click the left mouse button. The insertion point moves to the desired location.

By using the scroll bars, you can scroll through the document. The scroll bars normally are shown only when a document extends beyond the boundaries of the screen (although you can set a display preference so that they always appear).

 When you use the mouse to scroll through a document, the insertion point does not move until you stop scrolling. To move the insertion point, move the mouse pointer into the document editing screen, and click the left mouse button.

The steps for using the horizontal scroll bar to scroll the document left to right are similar. To scroll a document with the scroll bars, use these methods:

- You can scroll a document one line at a time by clicking the scroll arrow that points in the desired direction at the end of the scroll bar. A new line of text moves onto the screen, and a line of text at the opposite side of the screen scrolls off the screen. The text that scrolls off is not lost; WordPerfect keeps track of the entire document. To scroll text continuously, click a scroll arrow and hold down the mouse button.

- With the scroll bar, you can scroll a document one screen at a time. If you click the scroll bar between the *scroll box* (the gray square box shown on the scroll bar between the scroll arrow boxes) and the scroll arrow—but not on them—the next screen of the document appears and the current screen of text scrolls off the screen.

- Use the scroll box to scroll to any place in a document. The location of the scroll box on the scroll bar shows you the relative position of the current screen in relation to the entire document. If the scroll box is near the top of the scroll bar, you are near the beginning of the document. To scroll the document quickly to another location in the document, drag the scroll box to the position you want. When you release the mouse button, that portion of the document appears. If you drag the scroll box to the bottom of the scroll bar, for example, the end of the document appears on-screen.

- At the bottom of the vertical scroll bar, you see a pair of icons that both look like a page—one with an up arrow (called the *Previous Page button*) and one with a down arrow (called the *Next Page button*). If you click the Previous Page or Next Page icon, the document is positioned to the top of the current page (if you click the up arrow) or the top of the next page (if you click the down arrow).

- You can also use the Status Bar Preferences option to display the page number on the status bar at the bottom of the screen. When you choose Page in the Status Bar Items box as a Status Bar Preferences option, the page number appears, and an icon of a book appears with left and right arrows on the book's pages. Click the left arrow to go to the top of the previous page. Click the right arrow to go to the top of the next page. Unlike the scroll bars, which do not move the insertion point in the document, clicking the book icon moves the insertion point and places it at the top of the page after the page is displayed on-screen. For information about adding the Page item to the status bar, see Chapter 9.

  ▶ **See** "The Status Bar," **p. 322**

## TROUBLESHOOTING

**I'm left-handed, and I find using the primary and secondary mouse buttons difficult in WordPerfect.** Although WordPerfect doesn't provide an easy way to fix this problem, Windows 95 does. You can switch the button assignments so the primary button is the right button instead of the left button, enabling you to use the index finger on your left hand for the primary button.

To reverse the button assignments for a Microsoft mouse (other mouse control panels work in a similar way), first activate the Start menu and choose Settings, Control Panel. Double-click the mouse icon. A properties sheet appears on which you can control the mouse settings. Choose Button Configuration and then Left-handed or Right-handed as desired.

## Moving with the Keyboard

Most keyboards in recent years have separate insertion point-movement keys and a 10-key number pad. With some keyboards, you use the number pad to move the insertion point. If you must use the number pad for insertion point movement, you can temporarily turn off the Num Lock feature so that when you press an insertion point-movement key (for example, the 4 key doubles as the ← key), a number is not printed. If you turn off Num Lock and want to enter a number with the number pad, hold down the Shift key so that the number is displayed instead of the insertion point being moved.

The WordPerfect directional keys are:

- Home
- Page Up
- Up arrow (↑)
- Left arrow (←)
- End
- Page Down
- Down arrow (↓)
- Right arrow (→)

As you can see in table 2.2, you can use these keys alone or in combination with other control keys (such as Alt and Ctrl) to move quickly and easily throughout the document. When you move through the document by using the keyboard directional keys, the insertion point moves, too.

**NOTE** Table 2.2 is based on the assumption that you are using the default WordPerfect 7 keyboard.

**Table 2.2 Moving the Insertion Point with the Keyboard**

| Movement | Key |
| --- | --- |
| One character left | ← |
| One character right | → |
| One word left | Ctrl+← |
| One word right | Ctrl+→ |
| One line up | ↑ |

*continues*

**Table 2.2 Continued**

| Movement | Key |
|---|---|
| One line down | ↓ |
| Beginning of the preceding paragraph | Ctrl+↑ |
| Beginning of the following paragraph | Ctrl+↓ |
| Beginning of the current line (after codes) | Home |
| Beginning of the current line (before codes) | Home, Home |
| End of the current line | End |
| Top of the editing screen | Page Up |
| Bottom of the editing screen | Page Down |
| First line of preceding page | Alt+Page Up |
| First line of following page | Alt+Page Down |
| Top of the document | Ctrl+Home |
| Bottom of the document | Ctrl+End |

## Moving the Insertion Point with Go To

WordPerfect's Go To command enables you to move great distances in a document very quickly. You can choose Go To from the menus or the keyboard.

**TIP** You can add a Go To button to the Power Bar or Toolbar, or double-click the Combined Position box (the one that displays the page number, line, and position) on the status bar to display the Go To dialog box.

To use the Go To feature, follow these steps:

1. Choose Edit, Go To, or press Ctrl+G. The Go To dialog box appears (see fig. 2.2). This dialog box gives you options to move the insertion point to a specific position, page number, bookmark, table, or cell/range.

2. Move the insertion point to the desired location by choosing from the following options:

**FIG. 2.2**
The Go To dialog box enables you to quickly move to a specific location in a document.

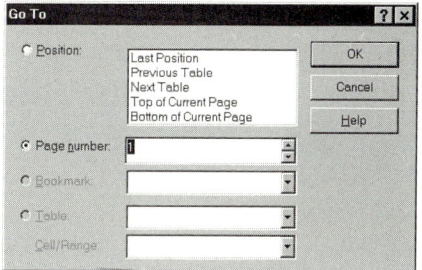

*Position—Last Position.* Moves to the location of the insertion point prior to the current location of the insertion point.

*Position—Previous Table.* Moves to the top of the table prior to the current location of the insertion point.

*Position—Next Table.* Moves to the top of the table following the current location of the insertion point.

*Position—Top of Current Page.* Moves to the top of the current page.

*Position—Bottom of Current Page.* Moves to the bottom of the current page.

*Page Number* (this is the option WordPerfect offers as the default). Moves to a specific page number in the document. Type the desired page number or use the up and down arrows to scroll the page number.

If you have highlighted selected text in your document, several other options are listed in the Position list box. These additional options are:

*Position—Beginning of Selection.* Moves the insertion point to the beginning of the selected text. The text is deselected.

*Position—End of Selection.* Moves the insertion point to the end of the selected text. The text is deselected.

*Position—Reselect Text.* This option reselects the text that was selected when either the Beginning of Selection or End of Selection options are used.

After you have selected and then deselected a portion of your document, the following additional option is available:

*Position—Reselect Last Selection.* Re-highlights the portion of a document that was last selected.

As indicated in the following list, in certain situations other actions are also available in the Go To dialog box:

*Bookmark.* Moves to the location of the selected bookmark. This choice is not available if the document has no bookmarks set. Type the bookmark name or choose the drop-down list arrow to display a list of bookmark names from which to choose.

*Table*. Moves to the selected table. This choice is available if a document contains one or more tables. Type the table name or choose the drop-down list arrow to display a list of table names from which to choose.

*Cell/Range*. Moves to the cell or range within the selected table. Type the cell or range name or choose the drop-down list arrow to display a list of names from which to choose.

▶ **See** "Selecting Text," **p. 99**

## Completing the Sample Letter

Now that you have learned the various methods with which to move the insertion point and scroll your document, you are ready to finish the sample letter by following these steps:

1. Press Ctrl+Home to move the insertion point to the top of the first paragraph of the letter.
2. Press Enter twice.
3. Press Ctrl+Home to again move the insertion point to the top of the document.
4. To enter today's date, choose Insert, Date, Date Text, or press Ctrl+D. WordPerfect inserts the current date, based on your computer's internal clock.
5. Press Enter twice.
6. Type the following name and address. Don't forget to press Enter at the end of each line to insert a hard return and move to the next line.

    **Ms. Alexandria Ferguson**

    **1234 El Camino Real**

    **Winterland, CA 93111**

7. Press Enter twice and type the following salutation:

    **Dear Ali,**

Your screen now shows the completed sample letter (see fig. 2.3).

If the date and time are incorrect, use the DOS DATE and TIME commands to correct them as needed. From Windows, change the date and time by following these steps:

1. Choose Start, Settings, Control Panel. The Control Panel dialog box appears.
2. Double-click the Date/Time icon. The Date/Time Properties dialog box appears.
3. From the Date & Time tab, choose Date or Time as appropriate and make the desired changes.
4. Click OK to apply the changes.

**FIG. 2.3**
The completed sample letter now includes the date and an opening salutation.

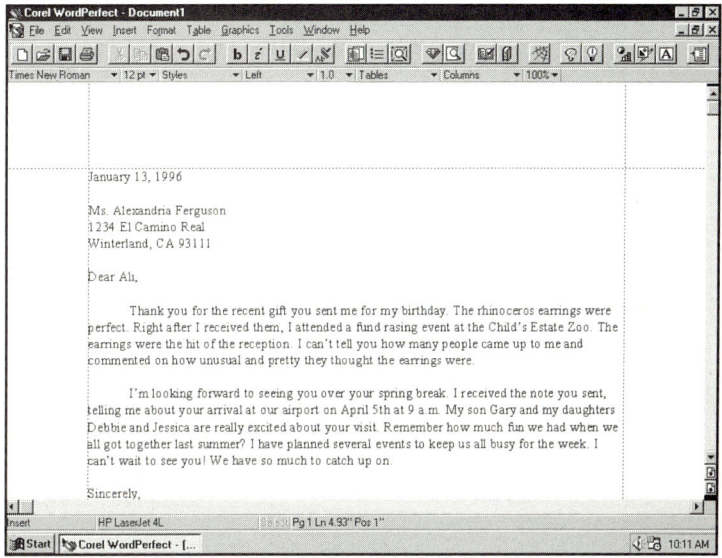

## Adding Text Within a Document

One of the most powerful features of word processing is the capability to move or add text anywhere in a document. With a typewriter, adding text in the middle of a document requires retyping one or more pages. With WordPerfect, you simply move the insertion point to the location in the document where you want to add the text, and type. WordPerfect takes care of adjusting line breaks and page breaks.

Suppose that you want to add a sentence in the second paragraph of the sample letter used in this chapter. To do so, follow these steps:

1. Use the mouse or insertion point-movement keys to move the insertion point to the word I at the beginning of the next-to-last sentence of the second paragraph.
2. Type the following:

   **Don't forget to bring your bathing suit.**

As you type the new text, existing letters are moved to the right, making room for the new text.

## Using Typeover

If you don't want to add new text but just want to type over existing text, you can use the Typeover feature. To turn the Typeover mode on and off, press the Insert key on the keyboard or double-click the General Status display box on the status bar at the bottom left of the screen. When Typeover mode is on, Typeover appears in the General Status box on the status bar at the bottom left of the screen. Instead of moving text to the right to make room for the new text, what you type replaces existing text. When Typeover is off and Insert mode is on, Insert is displayed and existing text is moved to the right to make room for the new text.

 **TIP** If a style is in use at the location of the insertion point, its name is shown in the General Status button, and the Insert/Typeover status is only shown if the status is Typeover.

▶ **See** "Inserting and Overwriting Text," **p. 85**

▶ **See** "The Status Bar," **p. 322**

Typeover mode is useful when making character-for-character replacements, such as changing a misspelled word (for example, changing the word *teh* to *the*).

# Using Cancel (Esc)

To cancel a function-key command or to back out of a menu, use Cancel (Esc).

You can also use Esc to redisplay the bars (for example, the Menu Bar, Power Bar, and status bar) after you have chosen the Hide Bars option on the View menu.

Now that you have composed your document, you might want to print it. In the next section, you learn how to print an on-screen document on your printer.

# Printing an On-Screen Document

You do not have to save your document before you print it (although saving your document before printing is a good idea in case a problem occurs while you are printing that causes your machine to crash). To save your document, see the section "Saving a Document to Disk" later in this chapter.

Although you will be printing only an on-screen document in this section, with WordPerfect you have much flexibility when printing. A document does not have to be on-screen to print. WordPerfect can also print documents directly from disk. (Refer to Chapter 8, "Basic Output: Printing, Faxing, and E-Mail," for more detailed information on printing.) The steps listed in this section are the most basic for printing an on-screen document.

**N O T E** The steps that follow assume that you have already installed and selected a Windows printer driver, as described in Chapter 8.

To print the on-screen document, follow these steps:

1. Decide whether you want to print one page or the entire document. To print just one page, make sure that the insertion point is located somewhere on the desired page.

2. Choose File, Print, press F5, press Ctrl+P, or click the Print icon on the Toolbar. The Print dialog box appears (see fig. 2.4).

**N O T E** If the printer shown in the Current Printer box at the top of the Print dialog box is not the printer you will be using, use the Printer tab and select the correct printer before continuing. For information on selecting printers, see Chapter 8.

**FIG. 2.4**
In the Print dialog box, you can tell WordPerfect how much of your document you want to print by using the options in the Print section.

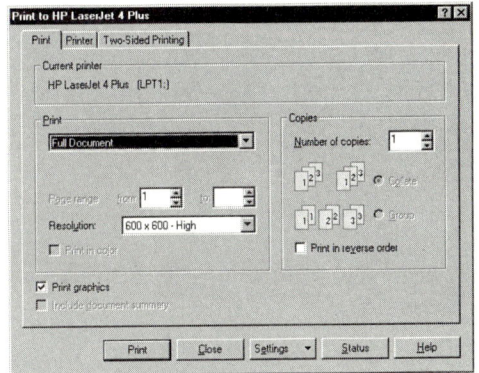

3. Because the sample letter is less than one page, leave the default setting at Full Document. For a document that is more than one page, choose Current Page in the drop-down list to print just one page.
4. Click Print to print the desired selection. You return to the document.

WordPerfect displays the message `Preparing document for printing` on-screen as it prepares to print. If the printer is configured and connected properly, printing begins almost immediately.

Figure 2.5 shows the printed sample letter.

**FIG. 2.5**
Here is the printed sample letter complete with a date, opening and closing salutations, and body text.

---

January 13, 1996

Ms. Alexandria Ferguson
1234 El Camino Real
Winterland, CA 93111

Dear Ali,

Thank you for the recent gift you sent me for my birthday. The rhinoceros earrings were perfect. Right after I received them, I attended a fund raising event at the Child's Estate Zoo. The earrings were the hit of the reception. I can't tell you how many people came up to me and commented on how unusual and pretty they thought the earrings were.

I'm looking forward to seeing you over your spring break. I received the note you sent, telling me about your arrival at our airport on April 5th at 9 a.m. My son Gary and my daughters Debbie and Jessica are really excited about your visit. Remember how much fun we had when we all got together last summer? I have planned several events to keep us all busy for the week. Don't forget to bring your bathing suit. I can't wait to see you! We have so much to catch up on.

Sincerely,


Marilyn Boyd

---

You do not have to wait until the document is printed to continue working in WordPerfect. WordPerfect and Windows print documents in the background, so you can continue your work on the same or a new document while the printing occurs.

> **NOTE** Your document doesn't have to be on-screen to print. You can print a document stored on disk (either a floppy or hard disk) directly from the disk. You can also print selected pages from a document rather than the entire document or a single page. Chapter 8 explores the various print options.

Now that you have composed and printed your document, you may want to save it safely to disk for future use. In the next section, you learn how to save an on-screen document to a disk.

▶ **See** "Selecting and Configuring Your Printer," **p. 291**

▶ **See** "Printing Specific Document Pages," **p. 283**

# Saving a Document to Disk

You often want to keep on disk a copy of the documents you create. If you don't want to save your new document (or changes to an existing document), simply exit WordPerfect without saving. WordPerfect gives you several methods of saving a document as a file on disk.

With the Save or Save As command, you save a copy of the on-screen document to disk. When you use Save or Save As, the document remains on-screen for additional work.

If you have not saved the on-screen document or have made changes since the last time you saved the document, when you use the Close (Ctrl+F4) or Exit command (Alt+F4), a dialog box appears that asks whether you want to save the on-screen document. Choose Cancel to return to the on-screen document. If you answer No, the document is not saved. If you selected Close, the current document window closes and you remain in WordPerfect. If you chose Exit, WordPerfect closes and you return to the Windows Program Manager.

**NOTE** When you close a document, you are telling WordPerfect that you are finished with the on-screen document but don't want to exit WordPerfect. To close a document, choose File, Close, or press Ctrl+F4. A dialog box appears and asks whether you want to save the on-screen document. After you indicate whether you want to save the document, the text is cleared. You are now ready to continue with your next project.

The first time you save a document, WordPerfect prompts you for a file name to assign to your document. The file name is not limited to the older DOS conventions of an eight-character file name and three-character extension. In WordPerfect 7, you can use longer descriptive file names to make it easier to figure out what information is contained in a document. The file name you use must meet Windows 95 conventions.

The file name consists of a primary file name and an optional extension (which can be from one to three characters). If you choose to enter a suffix, the primary file name and suffix must be separated by a period. The length of the entire file name, including the location (for example, drive letter, path, and server name if any) cannot exceed 255 characters. The file name can include spaces.

> **CAUTION**
> The file name cannot contain certain reserved characters, such as the question mark (?), asterisk (*), semicolon (;), colon (:), forward slash (/), backward slash (\), greater-than sign (>), or less-than sign (<). The file name cannot contain certain reserved characters, such as the question mark (?), asterisk (*), semicolon (;), colon (:), forward slash (/), backward slash (\), greater-than sign (>), less-than sign (<), plus sign (+), equal sign (=), left square bracket ([), right square bracket (]), double quotation mark ("), or vertical bar (|).

**NOTE** Although you can use uppercase and lowercase letters in the file name, Windows does not treat them as different for filenaming conventions. For example, you can save a file with the file name Jessica or JESSICA, and Windows remembers and displays the file name exactly as you've typed it. However, Windows considers those two file names identical.

Once you have typed the file name in with the upper- and lowercase characters you want, saving the file with the same name but different case does not change the file name on disk. To rename a file and change its name or the case of the file name, choose File, Rename in the Open dialog box (or Save As dialog box), or use the Windows Explorer.

Windows 95 uses a folder analogy to represent what most DOS users have called directories. Within a *folder*, file names must be unique. For example, if you are working in a folder named DEBBIE'S LETTERS, and have saved a file called LOVE LETTER TO JIMMY, you cannot save a different file also called LOVE LETTER TO JIMMY in that same folder unless you replace the older file with the newer file.

However, you can have a document named LOVE LETTER TO JIMMY in the folder named DEBBIE'S LETTERS and also in a folder named DEBBIE'S LOVE LETTERS. Although both documents are named LOVE LETTER TO JIMMY, they can both exist because they are stored in different folders.

Although Windows enables you to have very long descriptive document names, limit the number of characters to just as many as you need to quickly locate and determine the contents of the document. The long document names can clutter the save and open dialog boxes and because there is much more text to read, can actually make it take longer to locate a document.

If you do not enter a file extension, WordPerfect adds the extension WPD by default. You can customize WordPerfect to use a different default file extension, or to not add a file extension at all.

### CAUTION

When you install WordPerfect 7, Windows is told to associate the file extension WPD with the application WordPerfect 7. When files are displayed with icons, a WordPerfect 7 icon appears next to files with a WPD extension. Double-clicking a document with a WPD extension from the Windows Explorer or My Computer applications will start WordPerfect 7 and automatically open the document.

If you customize WordPerfect to save documents without a file extension or with an extension other than WPD, Windows will not be able to associate the file with the application WordPerfect 7. WordPerfect files without WPD will no longer be displayed with a WordPerfect 7 icon, and WordPerfect 7 will not automatically start when double-clicking the file from the Windows Explorer or My Computer.

Entire chapters in books are written on file management and how to name folders and documents within the folders. In the end, only you can decide on what is a meaningful system for *your* use. The best advice is to keep your system logical and think it through before you start saving files. Then, always organize and save your files in accordance with the system you have chosen to use.

To save the sample letter, follow these steps:

1. With the sample letter on-screen, choose File, Save As; or press F3. The Save As dialog box appears (see fig. 2.6).

The insertion point is placed in the Name text box, where you give the document a name. The characters *.wpd appear in the Name text box and must be replaced with a valid document name. These highlighted characters are replaced when you type a character.

**FIG. 2.6**
The Save As dialog box contains useful information and a variety of option buttons. It also displays the file format type that is used to save the file.

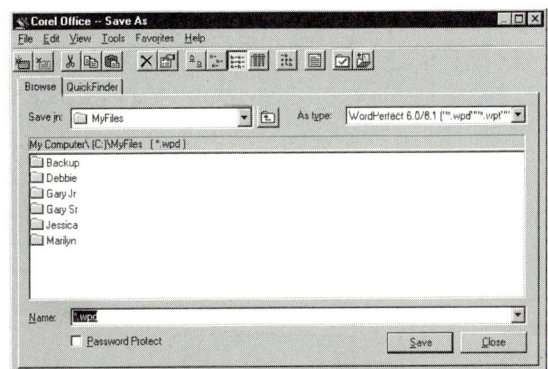

2. To save the file to a drive or folder different from the current drive and folder—shown above the document list box—enter the full path name.

   You can type the new path name in the Name text box, or use the mouse or Tab and arrow keys to highlight a different folder, drive, or server in the Save In drop-down list. If you type a drive and folder in the Name text box instead of actually selecting another drive or folder, the default drive and folder do not change, but the file is saved to the alternate drive and folder as shown in the Name text box.

   The Save As dialog box's View menu provides you with choices that enable you to modify the way the dialog box looks and information is displayed within the box. The Tree View option changes the display to show folders and documents in a hierarchical way. You can click the plus or minus sign to the left of each folder to display or hide folders and files at levels beneath the folder.

   Another choice on the View menu, Preview, enables you to have a Preview area added to the Save As dialog box. The Preview area shows you the contents of each file you highlight and is very helpful if you aren't sure of the contents of a file listed. For more information about using the Preview feature, see Chapter 3.

   The Favorites menu enables you to use the Favorites feature to build shortcut paths to your files and folders. The various options and the Favorites functions are explained in detail in Chapter 29, "Advanced File Management."

3. Type **Sample Letter** as a document name for the sample letter in the Name text box.

4. Click Save or press Enter to save the sample letter.

The default WordPerfect document window name (for example, Document1) that appears on the title bar at the top of the document editing window is replaced by the file name and folder you specify for the document.

To tell WordPerfect the folder you want as the default when you save and open files, follow these steps:

1. Choose Edit, Preferences. The Preferences dialog box appears.
2. Choose Preferences, Files, or double-click the Files icon. The File Preferences dialog box appears. Choose the Document tab if it isn't already selected.
3. Type the desired path in the Default Document Folder text box. Or, use the Browse button to the right of the text box (or press Alt+↑ or Alt+↓) for help with locating the desired folder.
4. To save your change, choose OK and Close until you return to the document. The selected folder can now be used as the beginning point for file open and save functions.

**TIP** You can tell WordPerfect where you want your documents stored as the default or normal location. This location will be used when you open or save files, unless you change it.

After you save your document, subsequent saving of the document is even easier. After making changes to the document, you don't have to type the document name again unless you want to change its name. After you save the document on-screen and give it a name, WordPerfect remembers the name.

To save an already named on-screen document, choose File, Save, or press Ctrl+S. The file is saved with the same name you assigned previously. Because you have already assigned the document a file name, WordPerfect saves the file without stopping to display the Save As dialog box.

As the file is being saved, the mouse pointer changes to an hourglass, showing that WordPerfect is saving the file.

▶ See "Opening a File," **p. 82**

▶ See "Customizing File Preferences," **p. 312**

# Saving a Document with a Different Name or File Format

Unless you specify otherwise, WordPerfect assumes that you want to save files in WordPerfect 6.0/6.1 format. WordPerfect enables you to save files in a variety of other file formats as well, including prior WordPerfect formats. WordPerfect 5.1 cannot read WordPerfect 6.x files unless you have upgraded to WordPerfect 5.1+. So, if you are giving a file to someone who does not have WordPerfect 6.x or 5.1+, you need to save a copy of your file in WordPerfect 5.1 format. WordPerfect also includes many other common file formats, such as various versions of Microsoft Word, MultiMate, and WordStar.

You also might want to save a file under a different name, to a different folder, or to a different disk drive. If you plan to give a copy of a file to someone else, for example, you might want to save the file onto a floppy disk.

When you want to save an existing file under a different name or in a different format, follow these steps:

1. Choose File, Save As, or press F3. The Save As dialog box appears with the document name shown in the Name text box and WordPerfect 6.0/6.1 as the file format in the As Type text box. The insertion point appears in the Name text box.

2. If you want to save the document with a different file name, type a different file name in the Name text box.

    Because the file name is highlighted, typing a character causes the existing entry to disappear. To change only a small part of the existing information, move to the point where you want to make the change by using the arrow keys or the mouse. Then use the Delete key and type new characters as necessary to complete your changes to the information in the Name text box.

    Use the Save In drop-down list box if you want to save the file to a different folder or drive.

3. To save the file with a different file format, choose As Type. A drop-down list appears that shows other file formats (see fig. 2.7). A variety of file formats is available from which you can select, both for WordPerfect and other word processing programs. In figure 2.7, WordPerfect 5.1/5.2 format is highlighted. Use the scroll bar or keyboard arrow keys to move to the desired file format. Double-click your choice or press Enter to select it.

4. When you have the document name, drive, folder, and file format type information the way you want it, choose Save or press Enter to save the file.

**FIG. 2.7**
The Save As dialog box includes an As Type drop-down list of file format options for saving documents in a variety of file formats.

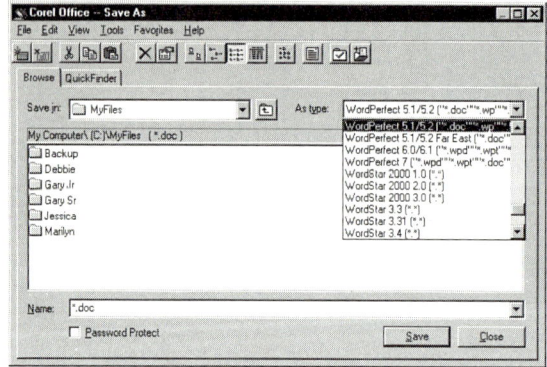

### TROUBLESHOOTING

**I accidentally saved my file with the wrong name (or to the wrong place). What should I do now?** WordPerfect is extremely well-prepared for these kinds of mistakes. Unlike many other programs, WordPerfect enables you to fix problems like this from within WordPerfect. If you've saved the document with the wrong name, simply rename it. If you've saved the document to the wrong location, you can move it.

First, close the document you've saved with the wrong name or location following the instructions in the section "Closing Documents" later in this chapter.

To rename a file or folder, follow these steps:

1. Choose File, and then either Open or Save As.
2. Highlight the file or folder you want to rename. To rename the highlighted file or folder, choose File, Rename, or press F2. A small editing box appears, enabling you to type a new name. Press Enter, and the name is changed. You can also display the small editing box by clicking the file or folder you want to rename, pausing a second, and clicking the item again.
3. If you've saved the file with both the wrong and right names, highlight the wrong file name and press Delete to delete the incorrectly saved document. The Confirm File Delete dialog box appears. Choose Yes to send the document with the wrong file name to the Windows Recycle Bin.
4. Choose Cancel or press Esc to close the Open or Save As dialog box and return to the editing screen.

▶ See "Copying and Moving Files," **p. 918**
▶ See "Renaming Files," **p. 920**

▶ See "Deleting Files," **p. 920**

▶ See "Creating, Renaming, and Removing Folders," **p. 923**

## Closing Documents

When you are finished editing or composing a document, you can close the document and continue editing or composing other documents in WordPerfect. To stay in WordPerfect but close the document you are working on, do the following:

1. Choose File, Close, or press Ctrl+F4. If you have modified the document during the current editing session, a dialog box similar to figure 2.8 appears and asks whether you want to save the on-screen document. If the document has already been assigned a name, the document and folder name are shown. If this document is new and hasn't been saved, the document name appears as Document1.

   If you have not modified the document, WordPerfect does not display a message dialog box—it simply closes the document.

**FIG. 2.8**
The WordPerfect for Windows dialog box appears with the Save changes to <filename> message.

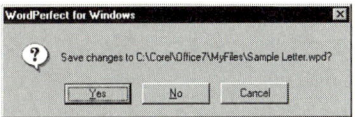

2. Choose Yes to save the file, No to clear the screen without saving the document, or Cancel (Esc) to change your mind and return to the on-screen document.

If you close the last open document, you can continue the WordPerfect session in a new document window. If the document you close is not the last open document, you are switched to one of the current open documents, which you can edit.

**N O T E** WordPerfect has a Close All feature that can be added to the Toolbar or Power Bar. It can also be found on the Utilities Toolbar provided by WordPerfect. When you add the icon and then use this feature, all open document windows are closed. A convenient Close All Documents dialog box appears. This dialog box has a check mark in the Save check box for each modified document. It enables you to indicate whether or not you want to save each file, and to enter the file name you want used for each saved file. To toggle the save option for each document, press Alt+the number next to the Filename text box.

▶ See "Switching Between Toolbars," **p. 415**

▶ See "Customizing a Toolbar," **p. 420**

▶ See "Customizing the Power Bar," **p. 426**

# Opening New Document Windows

WordPerfect enables you to have up to nine document editing windows open at the same time. To open a new document, follow these steps:

1. Choose File, New, press Ctrl+Shift+N, or click the New Document Toolbar icon. The Select New Document dialog box appears (see fig. 2.9). By default, this dialog box highlights the Create A Blank Document choice in the Main group. This creates a new blank document based on the default standard template. WordPerfect has created and provides a variety of templates for your use, or you can create your own templates. From this dialog box, you can also view or edit templates.

**FIG. 2.9**

Make selections from the Select New Document dialog box to create a new document based on a variety of templates.

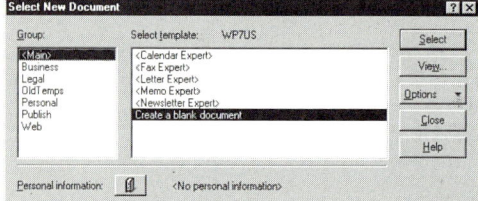

2. To begin a new document based on the standard template, in the Group box choose Main.
3. In the Select Template list box, highlight Create A Blank Document.
4. Click Select or press Enter. A new blank editing screen appears, and you are ready to begin composing your document.

To begin a new document using the settings from a template other than the Standard template, choose the desired template. WordPerfect has created a variety of templates that enable you to quickly create professional looking letters and memos, fax cover sheets, business cards, resumes, and even term papers.

 You can create a new document based on the default template without displaying the New Document dialog box by pressing Ctrl+N. A new document immediately appears.

▶ See "Using the Templates Provided with WordPerfect for Windows," **p. 370**

# Exiting WordPerfect

To exit WordPerfect, optionally saving any open files, follow these steps:

1. Choose File, Exit, or press Alt+F4. WordPerfect prompts you to indicate whether you want to save each open document.

2. Respond Yes if you want WordPerfect to save the file and exit to Windows, No to exit immediately to Windows without saving the file, or Cancel to return to the document without saving the file or exiting WordPerfect. If you have more than one document window open, you are prompted to save each modified document, and then WordPerfect exits to Windows.

If you have made no changes to any open document windows, WordPerfect exits immediately to Windows.

# CHAPTER 3

# Retrieving and Editing Documents

*by Gary Pickavet*

In this chapter, you learn how to retrieve a previously saved document from disk and edit it. If you are new to word processing, this chapter acquaints you with electronic editing. When using a typewriter, editing a document entails retyping one or more pages—even to make a very small change. With WordPerfect's electronic editing features, you can make changes and print corrected pages quickly and easily. After you become accustomed to WordPerfect's editing features, you may wonder how you got along without them!

Preparing a document from beginning to end involves at least three essential steps: creating, editing, and formatting. Chapter 2 covers creating a document. In the next chapter, you learn about WordPerfect's powerful formatting commands. But between creating a document and formatting its appearance, you need to edit the document to make sure it says what you want, the way you want to say it. ■

- **Continue working on a previously saved document**
  
  WordPerfect enables you to open an existing document to work on it whenever you want.

- **View the codes that WordPerfect inserts for all editing**
  
  Learn how to open, close, and use the Reveal Codes window to view and work with WordPerfect's hidden document formatting codes.

- **Use the Select function to select parts of your document**
  
  Learn to select text and perform editing actions to the selection.

- **Move or copy text and graphics**
  
  Learn how to move information between WordPerfect document editing windows or between Windows applications.

- **Find/replace text and codes**
  
  As you work with larger or more complex documents, you see it's easy to find and replace text and codes.

- **Correct your mistakes and reverse your corrections**
  
  Learn how to use Undo to reverse actions and, if you change your mind, use Redo to reverse Undo actions.

# Opening Files

Chapter 2, "Creating and Saving a Document," discusses how to save a file to disk. Normally, you save a file because you want to work on it or refer to it later. For example, you may be composing a document and want to stop for the day. You can save the document, and then reopen it the next day to continue working.

WordPerfect has two commands that copy a document from disk to your screen: File, Open and Insert, File.

The File, Open command copies a previously saved document from disk to a blank editing screen, called the *document window*. The document retains its initial settings, such as margins, justification, font, and file name. If you are already composing a document in a document window, WordPerfect opens another blank window for the file you are opening. The newly opened document becomes the *active document editing window*.

The Insert, File command copies a previously saved document from disk into the current on-screen document at the insertion point. In other words, this command is used to retrieve a previously created document that is already stored on disk and insert it within another document.

## Opening a File

Although you can revise a document created during a current WordPerfect session, you will often want to open and edit an existing, previously saved document. For example, you may have a sales report for the prior quarter on disk that you want to use as a starting point for the current quarterly report. To do this, you open the prior quarterly report file, make the necessary changes, and save the revised report (most likely with a new file name).

To open a file previously saved to disk, follow these steps:

1. Choose File, Open, or press Ctrl+O. The Open dialog box appears (see fig. 3.1).

   **N O T E**  WordPerfect keeps track of the last nine documents you have opened. When you choose File, the names of these files appear near the bottom of the File menu. If the file you want to open is listed, highlight it and press Enter, or click the file name.

**FIG. 3.1**
The Open dialog box gives you several options that control how files are listed and enables you to open a preview area to help you choose the right file.

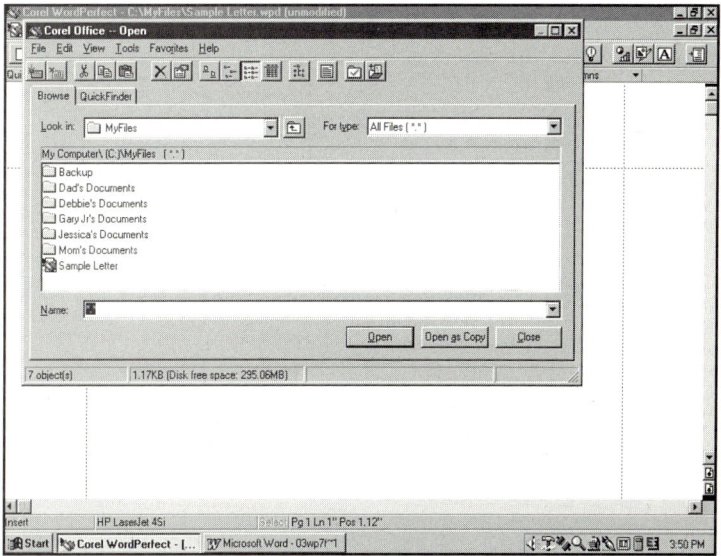

2. After the dialog box opens, you can choose from several actions to open a file:
   - If the file you want to open is in the current default folder, you can type the file name in the Name text box (for example, **Sample Letter.wpd**). Then click OK, or press Enter.
   
     Alternatively, scroll the list of files in the list box until the desired file name is highlighted. Double-click the file name, or press Enter.
   
   - WordPerfect provides several filters so that you can restrict the files listed in the Filename list box. The default is to list All Files (*.*). To change the filter and restrict the files listed, choose For Type. Click the drop-down list button or press the Alt+down-arrow key to display the drop-down list of file type filters. By selecting one of these filters, you can use the file selection mask shown so files of only that type are listed.
   
     For example, when you select Text Files (*.txt), only these files on the disk that end with the extension TXT appear in the list box. Click the filter, or highlight the filter and press Enter. WordPerfect lists only the files that qualify in the list box.
     
     ▶ **See** "Importing and Working with Word Processing Data," **p. 564**
   
   - If the document is on a disk or in a folder other than the current one, you can type the complete path (drive, folder, and document name) in the Name text box—for example, **C:\WPDOCS\1ST Qtr Report.wpd**. If the file you are typing has a WPD extension, typing the extension is optional.

If you don't remember the location of the file you want to open, or don't want to type the complete path, you can use the Look In drop-down list box to move between disk drives (including floppy drives) and folders.

 If you are unsure of the contents of a document listed in the document list box of the Open dialog box, highlight the file name and choose View, Preview, Content to open a file preview area (see fig. 3.2). By choosing Page View instead of Content, entire pages are displayed in the preview area. If WordPerfect cannot view the file (the viewer cannot convert files created by some programs), a message appears. Some document elements, such as headers and footers, are not displayed by the viewer.

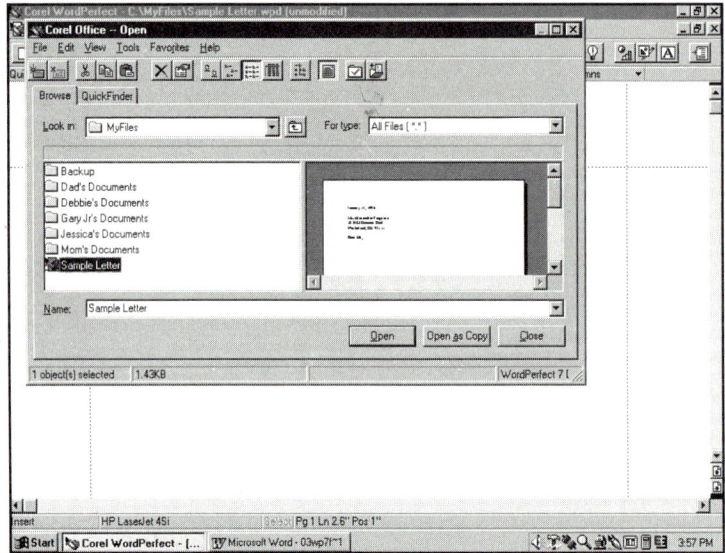

**FIG. 3.2**
The Preview option enables you to look at a document without opening it into a document editing window. As with any window, you can resize the Viewer window to see more of the viewed document.

You can also have WordPerfect open a separate preview window to enable you to see more of the document you want to preview. To do this, from the Open dialog box, choose View, Preview, Use Separate Window. The Previewer window appears with your document displayed.

You can scroll through the document being viewed by using the scroll bars or other scrolling techniques described in Chapter 2, "Creating and Saving a Document."

After you select the viewer window and change the focus to that window (the insertion point moves to the preview window), you can use Find (press F2 or Ctrl+F) to locate characters, a word, or phrase in the viewed document. (For more information about Find, see the section "Using Find and Replace" later in this chapter.)

You can copy one or more lines from the previewed document to the Windows Clipboard to be pasted into WordPerfect or another Windows application. To copy lines to the Clipboard, move the mouse pointer to the first line to be included. Drag the mouse to select the lines of text. Press Ctrl+C to copy the text, or right-click to display the QuickMenu and choose Copy. (For more information about moving text, see the section "Transferring Selected Text to Another Location" later in this chapter.)

If you no longer want to have WordPerfect show a preview of the documents you highlight, choose View, Preview, No Preview to close the file preview area.

**TROUBLESHOOTING**

**I selected a file to view and instead of displaying the file, I see the message No Viewer Available on my screen.** If you see the No Viewer Available message, the conversion file you need was probably not installed during installation. You can quickly install additional conversion files after WordPerfect's initial installation.

▶ **See** "Understanding the Conversion Process," **p. 560**

The Open dialog box also provides the options that enable you to look for text in files, perform DOS functions on files or folders, set up shortcuts to locate your favorite folders or files, or change how files are listed in the Open dialog box. These functions are explained in detail in Chapter 29, "Advanced File Management."

## Using Insert File To Combine Files

You can retrieve a document from disk into the current on-screen document. When you choose Insert, File, WordPerfect copies the requested file from disk into the current on-screen document at the location of the insertion point. WordPerfect ignores the retrieved file's initial codes and file name, and instead uses the initial codes and file name of the on-screen document. Any formatting codes applied to the text that aren't contained in the document's initial codes are inserted into the on-screen document with the inserted document text. If you have already named the on-screen document, that name is used when you save the new combined file.

When you copy the contents of a saved document into the on-screen document, the file on disk is not modified when you save the on-screen document. For example, suppose that you are working on an annual report, named Annual Report, that is on-screen. On disk you have a file called Northern Region Sales with the sales figures from the Northern region. You can copy Northern Region Sales into the Annual Report document by choosing Insert, File. When you save the revised file as **Annual Report**, the original Northern Region Sales document is not modified.

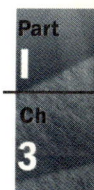

Save your current document before inserting another document into it. That way, if you don't like the results of the file combination, you can simply close the file without saving it, and then reopen the original document and try again.

▶ **See** "Finding Files," **p. 928**

To insert a document into the current document, follow these steps:

1. Move the insertion point in the on-screen document to the location where you want to place the document you are inserting.

2. Choose Insert, File. The Insert File dialog box appears. This dialog box looks similar to the Open File dialog box (refer to fig. 3.1), except that Insert File has an Insert button instead of an Open button.

3. If the file you want to retrieve is in the current default folder, type the file name in the Name text box (for example, **Sample Letter**).

    If the document is on a disk or in a folder other than the current folder, you must type the complete path (drive, folders, and file name) in the Name text box (for example, **C:\WP61\WPDOCS\1ST Qtr Report.wpd**).

    If you don't remember the file name or location of the file you want to insert, you can use the information detailed in step 2 in the preceding section, "Opening a File."

4. Click Insert or press Enter, and WordPerfect copies the file into the current on-screen document at the insertion point's location.

# Revising and Editing Text

The amount of revision each document requires varies greatly. Some people find when they review their documents that very few changes are needed. Others find that a great amount of fine-tuning is required to make the document say just what they want, in just the way they want it said. In some cases, other people review a document, with the author responsible for incorporating the changes into his or her document file. Whatever the reason for editing, WordPerfect enables you to make changes quickly and easily.

## Inserting and Overwriting Text

With a standard typewriter, you cannot insert text into a document without retyping an entire page. Electronic editing with a word processor such as WordPerfect enables you to make corrections quickly to a single character, word, sentence, or entire pages and paragraphs. You simply make the change and reprint any pages that need reprinting.

By default, WordPerfect inserts new text that you type at the location of the insertion point. As you type, existing text after the insertion point is pushed ahead (moves to the right) to make room for the new text. Words move down to new lines as necessary, and pages are reformatted to adjust for the added text.

> **NOTE** If it's not already showing, you can add an Insert Mode item to the status bar that displays `Insert` when in Insert mode and `Typeover` when in Typeover mode.

▶ **See** "Customizing Window Features," **p. 321**

If you want to type over (replace) existing text, you can use the Typeover feature. The Insert key on your keyboard turns Typeover mode on and off; you can also double-click the General Status display box on the status bar at the bottom-left corner of the screen. When Typeover mode is on, `Typeover` is displayed on the status bar at the bottom of the screen. The text that you type replaces existing text instead of pushing it to the right. Typeover mode is useful for making one-for-one replacements, such as changing a misspelled word (for example, changing the word *teh* to *the*). If a style is in use at the location of the insertion point, its name is shown in the status bar, and the Insert/Typeover status is only shown for Typeover mode.

## Deleting Text

WordPerfect makes deleting text easy. You can delete a single character, entire words, sentences, paragraphs, or pages with only a few keystrokes. If you accidentally delete text, you can restore that text with WordPerfect's Undelete and Undo features, covered in the section "Restoring Deleted Text" later in this chapter.

**Deleting a Single Character**  To delete a single character in WordPerfect, use one of these methods:

- Press the Backspace key to delete the character to the left of the insertion point. Use this method when entering text to delete a typing mistake immediately.
- Press the Delete key to delete the character to the right of the insertion point.
- Press the space bar or another character while in Typeover mode to replace the character to the right of the insertion point.

After using each deletion method, determine which method works best for you in each editing situation you encounter.

Pressing the Backspace or Delete key repeats the action, deleting several characters quickly. Using this method, however, often results in deleting more characters than you intend. This requires you to retype accidentally deleted text or to restore all deleted text using Undo or Undelete, and then repeat the deletion. If you need to delete more than a few characters, use one of the deletion techniques described in the following sections.

**Deleting Words and Lines**   To delete a word, place the insertion point anywhere in the word and press Ctrl+Backspace. The word and any spaces or punctuation (up to the next word) are deleted.

To delete text from the insertion point to the end of the current line, press Ctrl+Delete. If the line ends with a soft return code ([SRt]), the text on the next and subsequent lines is reformatted after the deletion occurs. When the line ends with a hard return code ([HRt]), the command does not delete the code, and the text on lines following the hard return code does not change.

To delete an entire line of text in which the insertion point is located anywhere, press Home to move the insertion point to the beginning of the line; then press Ctrl+Delete to delete the line.

**Deleting Other Selections of Text**   In addition to the various methods described in the preceding sections, WordPerfect offers another method of deleting a portion of your document. With the Select function, you can select any portion of your document and delete it. This method of deleting text is described in detail in the section "Deleting and Undeleting a Selection" later in this chapter.

# Restoring Deleted Text

While editing your document, you may accidentally delete text or graphics. If you accidentally delete a few characters or a word, retyping the deleted text is relatively simple, but accidentally deleting larger portions can be very frustrating. WordPerfect offers two useful features to recover and restore deleted text and graphics: Undelete and Undo.

The Undo feature reverses many editing actions, including restoring deleted text and graphics. Undelete is designed for the purpose of restoring deleted text and graphics. Each time you delete something, WordPerfect remembers the deletion and stores the deleted material in case you want to restore it to the document. In fact, WordPerfect remembers the last three deletions made during your current editing session. Because WordPerfect only stores the last three deletions, use the Undelete feature as soon as possible after you make the deletion.

To restore deleted material with Undelete, follow these steps:

1. Position the insertion point where you want the deleted material to be restored.
2. Choose Edit, Undelete, or press Ctrl+Shift+Z.

    A selection of highlighted text appears on the editing screen, displaying the most recently deleted material, and the Undelete dialog box appears (see fig. 3.3).

**FIG. 3.3**
A highlighted block shows deleted text to be restored. WordPerfect remembers the last three deletions and enables you to view and then restore them as desired.

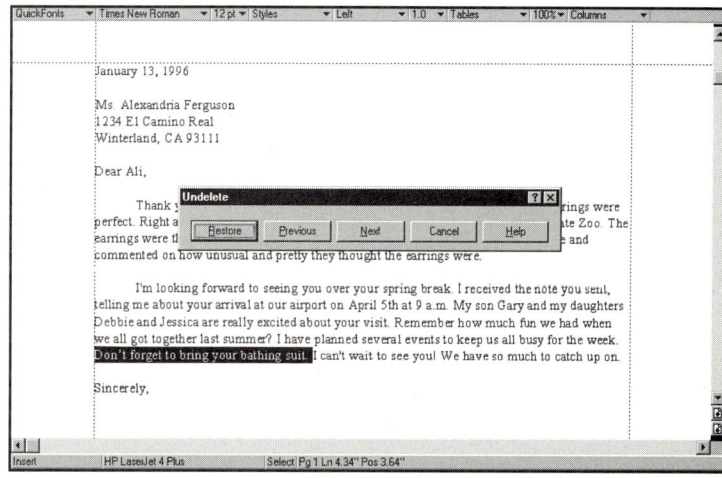

3. Click Restore if the highlighted text is what you want to restore. If there has been more than one deletion and the one displayed is not the one you want to restore, click Next or Previous to examine the other choices of previously deleted text.

   When the text that you want restored appears on-screen, click Restore. If none of the choices are appropriate or you change your mind, choose Cancel.

WordPerfect offers another method for restoring deleted text. Undo reverses up to the last 300 editing actions. When you Undo a deletion, the result is similar to what happens when you restore a deletion with Undelete. Undo, however, restores text at the location from which it was deleted, regardless of the insertion point's location. If you delete a word and then move the insertion point anywhere else in the document, Undo returns to the place of deletion and then restores the word.

 To use Undo, choose Edit, Undo, or press Ctrl+Z.

## Using WordPerfect's Undo and Redo Features

The WordPerfect Undo feature enables you to do much more than simply restore deleted text; it can reverse up to the last 300 editing actions. Likewise, the Redo feature enables you to redo undone editing actions. By default, WordPerfect remembers the last 10 editing actions unless you change the number of undo/redo items in the Undo/Redo Options dialog box. Likewise, the Redo/Undo history is saved with your document unless you change the Undo/Redo Options and tell WordPerfect to do otherwise. You learn how to change the Undo/Redo Options later in this section.

An editing action can be as simple as deleting a word or applying a bold attribute to text. Or, an editing action can be not so simple—like accidentally changing the word *the* to *them* in an entire document. In this case, you can't simply use Find and Replace to change the word *them* back to *the*—the word *them* likely is used properly many places in your document, and those occurrences shouldn't be changed. With WordPerfect's Undo feature, you can reverse both simple and complex editing actions.

Although most editing actions can be undone with the Undo feature, some actions such as saving a document, adjusting the Reveal Codes window, or changing the zoom settings cannot be undone.

To undo the most recent editing action, choose Edit, Undo, or press Ctrl+Z, or click the Undo icon on the Toolbar. The editing action is undone.

As you undo one or more steps, the editing actions are added to the Redo list. If the undone editing action is not what you intended, choose Edit, Redo, press Ctrl+Shift+R, or click the Redo icon on the Toolbar. The undone editing action is reversed.

If you want to undo or redo more than the last editing action, use the Undo/Redo History feature to select the actions to undo or redo.

To undo or redo more than the most recent editing change, follow these steps:

1. Choose Edit, Undo/Redo History. The Undo/Redo History dialog box appears (see fig. 3.4). Editing actions that can be undone are shown in the Undo list on the left half of the screen. Undone editing actions that can now be redone are shown in the Redo list on the right half of the screen. The list of actions are displayed with the most recent editing actions at the top and the least recent actions at the bottom.

**FIG. 3.4**
The Undo/Redo History dialog box has two list boxes that show you the actions you can undo or redo. You can also click the Options button to change how many actions are remembered by WordPerfect and whether or not the Undo/Redo items are saved with the document.

> **CAUTION**
>
> As you undo editing actions, they are moved to the Redo list. After you return to your document and perform another editing action, the actions listed in the Redo list are deleted and cannot be redone.

2. In the Undo list, choose one or more editing actions to be undone or, if you want to redo actions that have been undone, choose from actions listed in the Redo box. When you choose an action below the top item in the Redo or Undo lists, all actions from the selected action to the top of the list also are selected.

WordPerfect normally saves the last 10 editing actions to be undone. To increase this to a larger number, follow these steps:

1. Choose Edit, Undo/Redo History. The Undo/Redo History dialog box appears.
2. Click Options. The Undo/Redo Options dialog box appears.
3. Choose Number Of Undo/Redo Items, and either type a new value or use the increment/decrement arrows to change the value.
4. Click OK and Close to save the changes and return to your document. Changes made in the Undo/Redo Options dialog box remain in effect until you change them again.

When you save your document, WordPerfect normally saves the undo/redo items with the document. This enables you to reverse editing actions even if you save your document and then open it for editing at a later time.

Saving undo/redo items with your document, however, makes the file size larger when it is stored on disk. The higher the number of undo/redo items, the more space the file takes.

If you don't want WordPerfect to save the undo/redo items with your document, follow the preceding steps to display the Undo/Redo Options dialog box. Choose Save Undo/Redo Items With Document to uncheck the option. Unless you turn the option back on, undo/redo items no longer are saved with your current and future documents.

# Understanding WordPerfect's Hidden Codes

When you choose a command such as Underline, you see the results of the action on-screen (text is underlined), but you don't see the hidden codes placed in your document that tell WordPerfect to begin and end underlining. By hiding the codes, WordPerfect keeps the document window uncluttered.

To make certain formatting changes or to make sure that the hidden codes are in the right place, you must display the codes. WordPerfect provides the Reveal Codes window to display hidden codes and make electronic editing easier. WordPerfect uses various hidden codes to control the display of your document. When you are typing text and reach the end of the line, for example, WordPerfect moves text that does not fit on that line to the next line and places a hidden soft return code ([SRt]) at the end of the line to indicate that text was wrapped because the line crossed the right margin. Pressing Enter to end a line rather than allowing WordPerfect to wrap text causes WordPerfect to place a hidden hard return code ([HRt]) in your document.

 Do not stop typing or press Enter at the end of each line. Let WordPerfect wrap the text for you. That way, as you add or delete words to your document, the remainder of the text will adjust automatically for you.

Some codes, such as those that set margins, are single codes placed in your document wherever you choose to set the value of the feature. Text attribute codes, such as bold and underline, are placed into your document in pairs indicating where an attribute is turned on and where it is turned off.

Among the features of WordPerfect are *revertible codes*. When you select text and change its formatting—for example, if you change the font size—WordPerfect places a code at the beginning of the selection to change the formatting and another code at the end of the selection to return the formatting to how it was before the change. These codes point at each other when viewed in the Reveal Codes window.

In WordPerfect 5.1, when the Reveal Codes window is closed and you move the cursor through your text, the cursor pauses one keystroke when you encounter a hidden formatting code. This makes it possible to delete the code. If you deleted the text within the codes, just the formatted character is deleted. A confirmation dialog box appears when you attempt to delete a hidden code at the beginning or end of the text to which the code applies. If you delete the code, the text formatted with the code's attribute becomes unformatted.

By default, WordPerfect 7 does not provide a warning when you delete formatted text or stop on the hidden formatting code when you move the insertion point over it. The hidden formatting codes are deleted after you delete all of the text formatted with the attribute.

You can have WordPerfect 7 emulate the WordPerfect 5.1 cursor movements, including the warning when codes might be deleted. To turn this option on and off, follow these steps:

1. Choose Edit, Preferences. The Preferences dialog box appears.

2. Click Environment. The Environment Preferences dialog box appears.
3. Choose Confirm Deletion Of Codes, Stop Insertion Point At Hidden Codes.

## Working with Reveal Codes

Although you don't need to memorize all of WordPerfect's hidden codes, knowing more about the codes can help you understand how WordPerfect controls and displays text. At times, your screen does not look the way you want it to, and you cannot figure out why. Using the Reveal Codes command to open the Reveal Codes window may provide a quick answer.

In addition, when you need to delete a code, such as bold or underline, it is often easiest to do so by using the Reveal Codes window. When you open the Reveal Codes window, WordPerfect splits the screen, showing the document window in the upper three-quarters and the same text with the hidden codes revealed in the lower quarter (see fig. 3.5). You can change the size of the Reveal Codes window as described in the sections "Changing the Size of the Current Reveal Codes Window" and "Changing the Default Size of the Reveal Codes Window" later in this chapter.

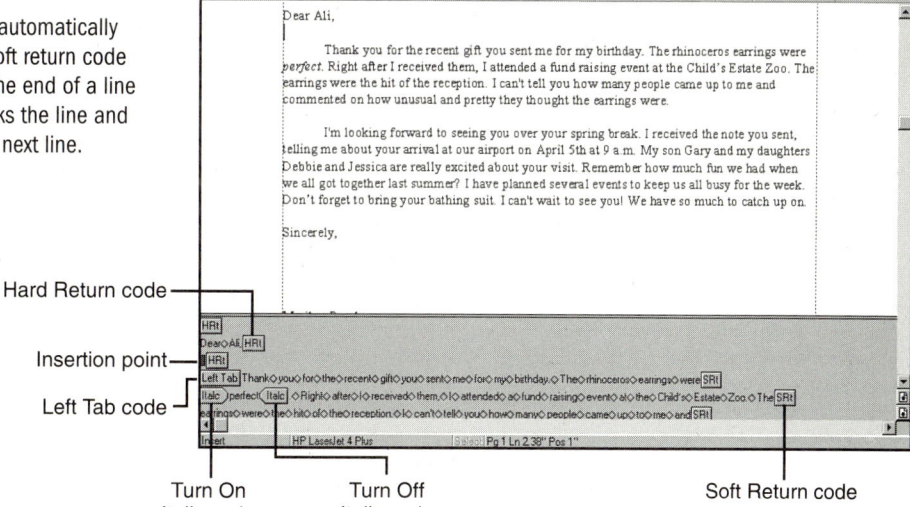

**FIG. 3.5**
WordPerfect automatically places the soft return code ([SRt]) at the end of a line when it breaks the line and wraps to the next line.

Corel ships WordPerfect with the Reveal Codes window closed. You need to experiment by working with documents with the Reveal Codes window open and closed to determine which way you prefer it.

You can open the Reveal Codes window several ways to see your document's hidden codes. Choose the method that works best for you from the following list:

- Choose <u>V</u>iew, Reveal <u>C</u>odes, or press Alt+F3.

- Move the mouse pointer to the heavy black line at the top or bottom of the vertical scroll bar at the right of your screen. The mouse pointer changes to a double-headed arrow. Press and hold the left mouse button. The Reveal Codes dividing line appears horizontally across the document window (see fig. 3.6). Drag the dividing line to the point where the screen is split in the proportion you want; then release the mouse button.

- Move the mouse pointer into the document. Right-click the mouse pointer to display the QuickMenu. Choose Re<u>v</u>eal Codes.

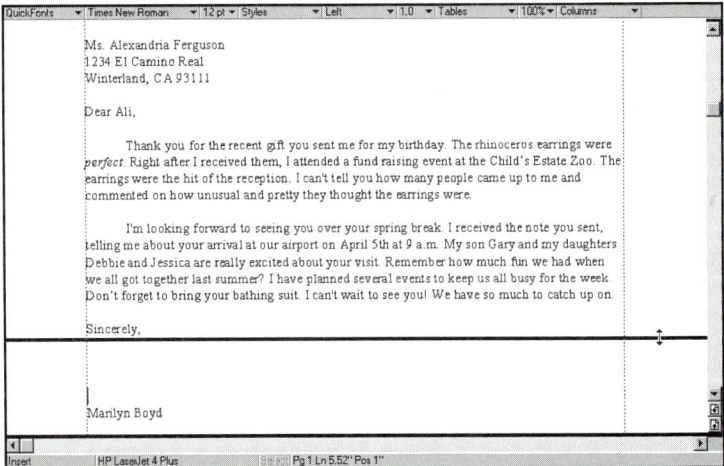

**FIG. 3.6**

The mouse pointer changes to a double-headed arrow and a dividing line appears, enabling you to quickly set the size of the Reveal Codes window.

Unless you exit WordPerfect or change the size of the Reveal Codes window, it remains as you set it for that document. The default size of the Reveal Codes window can be changed for all future documents by using the Display Preferences dialog box. For more information, see the section "Changing the Default Size of the Reveal Codes Window" later in this chapter.

As you move through your document using the mouse or keyboard, the Reveal Codes cursor moves through the Reveal Codes window.

## Closing the Reveal Codes Window

You can close the Reveal Codes window and redisplay the entire document window several ways. From the following list, choose the one that works best for you:

- Choose View, Reveal Codes, or press Alt+F3.
- Move the mouse pointer to the Reveal Codes window and right-click. A QuickMenu appears. Choose Hide Reveal Codes. If you right-click while in the document editing screen, the QuickMenu lists Reveal Codes with a check mark next to it. Choose Reveal Codes to uncheck the option, and the Reveal Codes window closes.
- Move the mouse pointer to the dividing line at the top of the Reveal Codes window. The mouse pointer changes to a double-headed arrow (refer to fig. 3.6). Press and hold the left mouse button. Drag the dividing line to the bottom of the screen and release the mouse button.

After you hide the Reveal Codes window, notice that small, thick black bars reappear at the top and bottom of the vertical scroll bar.

## Editing in the Reveal Codes Window

WordPerfect codes appear as sculptured icons. Among the codes shown earlier in figure 3.5 are hard return ([HRt]), tab indent ([Left Tab]), soft return ([SRt]), and the codes that turn on and off the italic attribute ([Italc]). Notice that attribute codes always appear in pairs; the code that turns on the feature points to the right and the code that turns off the feature points to the left. As you move the mouse pointer over a code in the Reveal Codes window, a dialog box pops up, giving you more information about what the code does. For example, moving the mouse pointer over a [HRt] code displays a QuickStatus box that says Hard Return—End of paragraph.

Being able to see the hidden codes enables you to edit many things in WordPerfect quickly. For example, if you have a section of text that is currently bold and underlined, but you only want it underlined, you simply delete the bold code. This can be done in several ways:

- Place the insertion point just before either of the [Bold] codes in the Reveal Codes window and press Delete.
- Place the insertion point immediately after either of the [Bold] codes and press Backspace.
- Move the mouse pointer to either of the [Bold] codes in the Reveal Codes window. Drag the code out of the Reveal Codes window, and release the mouse button.

The text is no longer bold, but is still underlined. If you delete either the beginning or ending code, its paired code is also deleted, removing the attribute completely.

You can also quickly edit the value of a code, such as a margin code. For example, suppose that a code in your document sets the left margin to 1 1/2 inches. To quickly change

the margin to 2 inches, locate and double-click the [Lft Mar"] code in the Reveal Codes window. The Margins dialog box appears, allowing you to change the value of the margins; in the example, change the left margin to **2.00**, and choose OK.

> **NOTE** You may notice that each new document you create starts with an [Open Style: InitialStyle] code. The document's Initial Style is where you can place codes that you want to apply to the entire document. Formatting codes you place within your document text take precedence over the formatting codes you place in the Initial Codes Style. You cannot delete this code, but you can modify its formatting codes by changing the Initial Codes Style settings.
>
> For information about creating and changing a document's Initial Codes Style, see Chapter 5, "Formatting Pages and Documents."

Working with a document with the Reveal Codes window open is a good way to become familiar with many of the codes WordPerfect places in a document to control its display and printing.

▶ **See** "Creating the Initial Codes Style," **p. 199**
▶ **See** "Creating Styles," **p. 340**

## Changing the Size of the Current Reveal Codes Window

The Reveal Codes window can be distracting at times. For example, when you initially compose a document, you might want to see as much of your text on-screen as possible. You might find that you don't like to leave the Reveal Codes window open because it takes up too much of the screen (on most monitors, it takes up about one-fourth). If so, you can change the size of the Reveal Codes window. You can do so for just the current editing session, or you can change the size for future editing sessions as well.

To quickly change the size of the Reveal Codes window for just the current editing session, move the mouse pointer onto the dividing line at the top of the Reveal Codes window. The mouse pointer changes to a double-headed arrow. Press and hold down the left mouse button, and drag the dividing line of the Reveal Codes window up or down until the location of the line you are moving is positioned where you now want the top of the Reveal Codes window. Release the mouse button, and the Reveal Codes and document windows are resized accordingly.

You can also change the size of the Reveal Codes window for all future documents. This is described later in the section "Changing the Default Size of the Reveal Codes Window."

## Customizing Reveal Codes to Meet Your Needs

WordPerfect enables you to change a variety of options to customize Reveal Codes to fit your preferences. Experiment with different settings until you find ones that you prefer. To open the Display Preferences dialog box and display the Reveal Codes section, follow these steps:

1. Choose Edit, Preferences. The Preferences dialog box appears.
2. Click Display. The Display Preferences dialog box appears.
3. Select the Reveal Codes tab to show the Reveal Codes options (see fig. 3.7).

**FIG. 3.7**
The Display Preferences dialog box shows the Reveal Codes options. This dialog box allows you to change many options that affect how the WordPerfect Reveal Codes feature works.

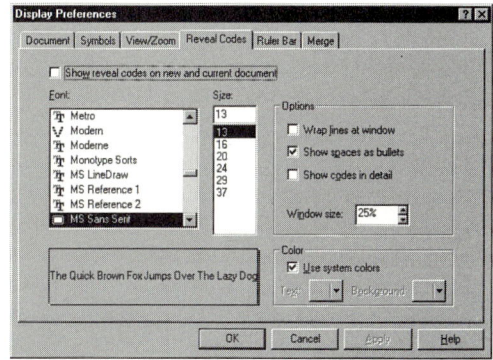

4. Change the Reveal Codes preferences as needed. The options are described in sections immediately following this one.
5. Choose OK and then Close to return to the document window.

> **TIP** You can also reach the Reveal Codes options by right-clicking the mouse in the Reveal Codes window and selecting Preferences from the QuickMenu.

**Automatically Displaying the Reveal Codes Window**  When you first install WordPerfect, the Reveal Codes window is set by default to Hidden. This means that when you start WordPerfect or open a new document, the Reveal Codes window is not displayed.

To automatically show the Reveal Codes window for all future editing sessions and new documents, choose Show Reveal Codes On New And Current Document.

**Changing the Default Reveal Codes Font, Typeface, and Size**  To change the font used in the Reveal Codes window, choose Font. Then choose a font from the font list.

To change the point size of the font, choose Size. Type the desired point size in the text box, or choose a size from the Size list box.

A sample of the highlighted font is displayed in the box at the bottom-left corner of the Display Preferences dialog box.

**Displaying Reveal Codes in Detail**  WordPerfect abbreviates some text-formatting codes that contain much information. For example, if you have set a top margin of 0.5 inches, the abbreviated code appears as `[Top Mar]`. If you want WordPerfect to display all codes as expanded with their values, choose Show Codes In Detail. Now, when you look at the top margin code in the Reveal Codes window, the code appears as `[Top Mar: 0.5"]`.

**Changing the Default Size of the Reveal Codes Window**  To change the number of lines that appear in the Reveal Codes window when you display it for future documents, choose Window Size. Then change the percentage by typing the desired value in the text box or by clicking the increment/decrement arrows. For all new documents, when you open the Reveal Codes window, the size appears as you have entered. To change the size of the Reveal Codes window for the current document, see the section "Changing the Size of the Current Reveal Codes Window" earlier in this chapter.

**Changing the Default Colors of the Reveal Codes Window**  WordPerfect enables you to select alternate colors to the default gray background with black text for the Reveal Codes window.

To change the colors of the Reveal Codes window:

1. Uncheck the Use System Colors option.
2. Choose Text or Background as desired. A palette of colors appears.
3. Choose the desired color by using the mouse or the keyboard arrow keys to move the box that indicates the color to the section of the displayed palette with the color you desire.
4. Press Enter to select the color. You return to the Display Preferences dialog box, and the new Reveal Codes window colors are shown in the sample box at the bottom left corner of the Display Preferences dialog box.

**Changing Other Reveal Codes Preferences**  In addition to those listed in the preceding sections, several other preferences can be set in the Reveal Codes section of the Display Preferences dialog box. The other choices and their effects are as follows:

- *Wrap Lines At Window.* Choose this option to cause WordPerfect to wrap lines in the Reveal Codes window at code breaks so the lines don't run off the right side of the screen. This is the default setting.

■ *Show S<u>p</u>aces As Bullets.* Choose this option to represent each space in your document as a diamond-shaped bullet in the Reveal Codes window. This enables you to see the exact number of spaces between characters. This is also the default setting.

## Selecting Text

One of WordPerfect's powerful electronic editing tools is the capability to use the mouse or keyboard to select a portion of the document. This allows you to perform a variety of functions on only the selected portion of a document. Why work with selections? Often, you want to change the appearance of the document or the arrangement of your thoughts; selection enables you to do so quickly.

A selection can be as small as one character or as large as the entire document. You define what to include in the selection and then choose a WordPerfect function to perform on it.

In addition to applying the common functions described in this chapter to a selection, you can use the selection process with specialized WordPerfect functions, such as Tables, the Speller, and Index.

▶ **See** "Spell Checking the Document," **p. 210**
▶ **See** "Selecting Text and Cells," **p. 503**
▶ **See** "Marking Text for an Index," **p. 859**

### Highlighting a Selection

You must make a selection before any operation can be performed on it. WordPerfect indicates a selection by showing it highlighted on-screen and displaying `Select` in the status bar at the bottom of the screen (see fig. 3.8). The highlighted text shows exactly which portion of your document will change when you choose a function. Graphics and their captions, however, are not highlighted when included in a selection; only text is highlighted.

You can make selections by using either the mouse or the keyboard. Experiment and choose the method you find most comfortable.

> **TIP** Choose <u>V</u>iew, Reveal <u>C</u>odes, or press Alt+F3 to open the window that shows hidden formatting codes.

**FIG. 3.8**
Text is highlighted so you can see exactly what has been selected. After text is selected, most WordPerfect functions will be performed just on the selection.

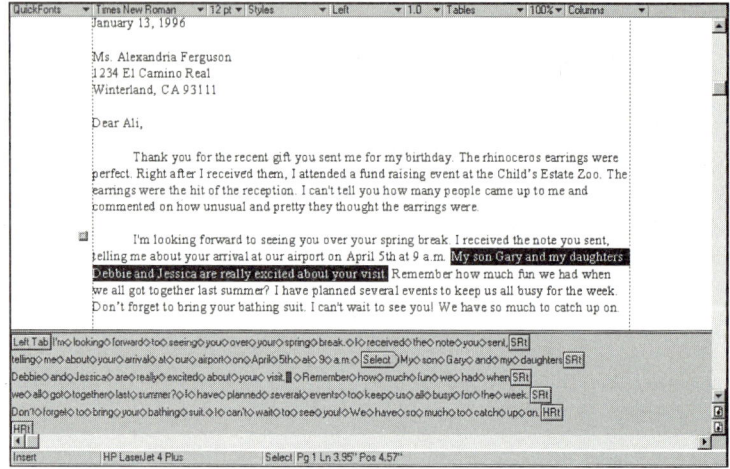

**N O T E** Often you want your selection to include formatting codes. When you make a selection, the code [Select] appears in the Reveal Codes screen indicating where your selection starts (refer to fig. 3.8). Make sure that the formatting codes you want to include in the selection are between [Select] and the end of the selection (shown by the Reveal Codes cursor).

**Using the Mouse To Highlight a Selection** If you have used a mouse with other programs, you should feel right at home with WordPerfect 7. The mouse techniques are similar to techniques in other Windows applications and those for Macintosh computers.

In WordPerfect, selecting a portion of your document with the mouse is quick and easy, as in the following steps:

1. Move the mouse pointer to the left side of the first character you want included in the selection. (In the document window, a shadow cursor guides you in making your selection by showing you exactly where the insertion point will be placed when you click.)

2. Click the left mouse button to move the insertion point to the location of the shadow cursor. This action anchors your selection at that location. The insertion point appears on the left side of the first character to be included in the selection.

**N O T E** If the Reveal Codes window is open at the bottom of the screen, the Reveal Codes cursor represents the insertion point's current location.

3. Hold down the left mouse button and move the mouse pointer to the end of the area you want to select. This process is often referred to as *dragging*. As you select text, it is highlighted on-screen. Release the mouse button when you have everything highlighted that you want to include in the selection.

**N O T E** Keep the left mouse button pressed while dragging the mouse pointer to highlight a selection. If you let go of the mouse button, you can still continue the selection process. Press and hold the Shift key, then press the left mouse button again. Let go of the Shift key but continue to hold the left mouse button, and resume selecting.

Or, you can change the size of the selection by holding down the Shift key and using the insertion point-movement keys. Pressing the left mouse button again without holding down the Shift key cancels the current selection and moves the insertion point to the shadow cursor's location. Likewise, using an insertion point-movement key without holding the Shift key cancels the current selection.

Clicking an object outside the document editing window—for instance, on the vertical scroll bar—will not cancel the selection.

To highlight a selection that extends beyond the portion of the document currently displayed on-screen, continue holding down the mouse button and move the mouse pointer beyond the document window in the direction you want to move. WordPerfect scrolls the document, highlighting text as it scrolls, until you bring the mouse pointer back into the document window. When the desired ending location of the selection appears on-screen, move the mouse pointer to that location and release the mouse button.

To speed your editing, by default WordPerfect highlights full words as you drag the mouse. If you want to highlight less than a full word, hold down the Shift key and use the keyboard arrow keys to highlight one character at a time. Or, to highlight less than a full word at a time, hold down the Alt key while you drag the mouse. If you highlight a selection or words using the mouse and want to expand or reduce the selection, also hold down the Shift key and use the keyboard arrow keys.

If you find that highlighting full words is cumbersome and does not work well with the type of editing you do, you can turn off this feature. WordPerfect then selects by character rather than by words. To change the way WordPerfect selects text as you drag the mouse, follow these steps:

1. Choose Edit, Preferences. The Preferences dialog box appears.

2. Click Environment. The Environment Preferences dialog box appears.
3. Uncheck Automatically Select Words.

You can also use the Find command to extend a selection to a specific word or phrase in your document. See the discussion of the Extend Selection option in the "Understanding Find and Replace Options" section later in this chapter for more information.

If, after you have highlighted a selection, you change your mind about the *amount* of text to select, press Shift while you click the mouse pointer at a new location. The highlighted text area enlarges if you click farther from the anchor point, or reduces if you click closer to the anchor point.

**NOTE** Besides dragging to highlight a selection, you can position the mouse pointer and click to anchor the insertion point where you want the selection to begin. Then move the mouse pointer to the desired ending location of the selection. Press and hold the Shift key and click the left mouse button. This action highlights the selection from the anchored location to the current location of the insertion point. This method is especially useful when highlighting large sections of text.

**CAUTION**
Pressing a keyboard character while a selection is highlighted will automatically delete the selected text and replace it with the character you type. This is a good shortcut for replacing text and saves you the trouble of deleting first. However, a letter pressed unintentionally can be a problem. To remove the unwanted text and bring back the accidentally deleted text, immediately choose Edit, Undo; or press Ctrl+Z.

WordPerfect provides two ways to quickly select a sentence, a paragraph, a page, or an entire document. You can use these methods by selecting from either of the following:

- Choose Edit, Select. Then choose Sentence, Paragraph, or Page; to select the entire document, choose All (or press Ctrl+A).
- Move the mouse pointer to the area between the left margin of your document (where the text ends) and the left side of the screen. When the mouse pointer is moved into this area, the direction of the mouse pointer changes to point up and to the right. (If the arrow points up and to the left, you are not in the correct area.) Right-click to display the QuickMenu. Choose Select Sentence, Select Paragraph, Select Page; to select the entire document, choose Select All.

WordPerfect also provides several mouse shortcuts you can use when highlighting selections. These methods arc shown in table 3.1. Using these shortcuts saves time when you want to highlight entire words, sentences, or paragraphs.

### Table 3.1  Other Mouse Selection Methods

| Selection Action | Result |
| --- | --- |
| Double-click | Selects a word |
| Triple-click | Selects a sentence |
| Quadruple-click | Selects a paragraph |
| Shift-click | Selects from the insertion point to the location of the mouse pointer |

**TROUBLESHOOTING**

**I'm left-handed, and I find using the primary and secondary mouse buttons difficult in WordPerfect.** Although WordPerfect doesn't provide an easy way to fix this problem, Windows does. You can switch the button assignments so the primary button is the right button instead of the left button, enabling you to use the index finger on your left hand for the primary button.

To reverse the button assignments for a Microsoft mouse (other mouse control panels work in a similar way), first activate the Start menu and choose Settings, Control Panel. Double-click the mouse icon. A properties sheet appears on which you can control the mouse settings. Choose Button Configuration and then Left-handed or Right-handed as desired.

**Using the Keyboard To Highlight a Selection**   You can highlight a selection from the keyboard without using a mouse by following these steps:

1. Move the insertion point to the first character you want to include in the selection.
2. Press Shift+→ or Shift+←, depending on the direction in which you want to select.
3. While holding down the Shift key, use the insertion point-movement keys (right arrow, left arrow, up arrow, Page Down, Ctrl+End, and so on) to move to the end of the text you want to select. The common insertion point-movement keys are shown in table 2.2 in Chapter 2, "Creating and Saving a Document."
   ▶ **See** "Moving with the Keyboard," **p. 63**

You can also turn on Select with the Select function key command. The primary difference between using the Select function key command and using a Shift+insertion point movement key combination is that with the former, you don't need to hold down the Shift key while you use insertion point-movement keys to move to the end of the selection.

To use the Select function key command, follow these steps:

1. Move the insertion point to the first character you want to include in the selection.

2. Press Select (F8). Select appears on the status bar at the bottom of the screen. (If the Reveal Codes window is open at the bottom of the screen, the [Select] code appears at the anchor point for the selection.)
3. Use the insertion point-movement keys as needed to move to the end of the information you want to select. As text is selected, it is highlighted on-screen.

## Canceling a Highlighted Selection

After highlighting a selection, you may change your mind and want to cancel it. You can cancel the selection by doing any of the following:

- Click the mouse anywhere in the document window (without holding down the Shift key).
- Move the insertion point with an insertion point-movement key, such as the right-arrow key. (If you started the selection by pressing Select (F8), this does not cancel the selection because the direction keys are being used to change the selection area.)
- Press Select (F8).

## Transferring Selected Text to Another Location

After you highlight a selection, you are ready to perform a WordPerfect operation on that portion of your document. This section deals with using Select to move portions of text between locations in a document, between documents, and between WordPerfect and other applications, such as Windows Notepad. Other sections of this chapter deal with performing other commands on a selection.

As you work with documents, you will find information that you want to move or copy to another location. WordPerfect uses the Cut, Copy, and Append commands to transfer information to the Windows Clipboard. Then you can use the Paste command to place the information elsewhere in the current document or in other Windows applications (or DOS applications running in windows). The current Clipboard information remains unchanged until the next Cut, Copy, or Append operation is performed. If unchanged, the information remains on the Clipboard for the entire Windows session.

To view the contents of the Clipboard, use the Windows Clipboard Viewer. See your Windows manual for more information about the Clipboard and the Clipboard Viewer application. When you exit Windows, any information on the Clipboard is erased.

If you use WordPerfect's drag-and-drop editing feature, described later in the "Drag-and-Drop Editing" section, the text and codes that you move or copy are not passed through the Windows Clipboard; you manipulate them directly on-screen from one location to another, using the mouse.

WordPerfect uses *intelligent* cut and paste. When you cut or paste text, spaces are added or deleted where appropriate.

**Moving or Copying a Selection**   When you finish typing a document, you often find text that you want to place elsewhere in the document. You can move or copy this text easily with WordPerfect's Cut and Paste functions.

▶ **See** "Moving the Insertion Point with Go To," **p. 64**

To move or copy a selection, follow these steps:

1. Select the information (text and/or graphics) that you want to copy.
2. To *move* a selection, choose Edit, Cut, or press Ctrl+X.
   To *copy* a selection, choose Edit, Copy, or press Ctrl+C.

> **TIP**  After selecting the information, right-click to display a QuickMenu. Choose Cut or Copy as desired.

3. Move the insertion point to where you want to place the selection.
4. Choose Edit, Paste, or press Ctrl+V. Alternatively, you can right-click to display a QuickMenu, and then choose Paste.

**Drag-and-Drop Editing**   WordPerfect's drag-and-drop editing feature enables you to visually relocate text and graphics within a document. This technique is more efficient than using Cut and Paste if you are moving or copying the material only a short distance within the same document.

To use the mouse to "pick up" and move or copy a portion of a document, follow these steps:

1. Select what you want to move or copy, and then place the mouse pointer anywhere within the highlighted area.
2. Hold down the left mouse button. To move the selected block, drag the highlighted selection to its new location and "drop" it into place by releasing the mouse button when the insertion point on the modified mouse pointer is where you want the block.

   To copy the highlighted selection, hold down the Ctrl key while dragging the selection to the new location, and then "drop" the copy into place by releasing the mouse button.

> **NOTE**  You can change from a Cut and Paste to a Copy and Paste by pressing the Ctrl key before you let go of the left mouse button. If you have started a Copy and Paste and want to instead Cut and Paste, release the Ctrl key before you release the left mouse button. Notice, however, that the mouse pointer icon changes to indicate that you have changed the type of drag-and-drop procedure.

When you press the mouse button to begin dragging your selected item, the mouse pointer changes to indicate that the drag-and-drop function is occurring, and the insertion point travels with the mouse pointer. The mouse pointer has different icons attached to it to indicate whether the drag-and-drop procedure is a move or a copy. The move procedure has a dotted shadow; the copy procedure has a dotted shadow and a plus (+) sign to the right of the mouse pointer arrow.

**Appending a Selection**   To append a selection to the Clipboard, follow these steps:

1. Select the information (text and/or graphics) that you want to append.
2. Choose <u>E</u>dit, Appen<u>d</u>.

You can now paste the original information plus the newly added information to the location of your choice. The Paste command is described in the earlier section "Moving or Copying a Selection."

> **NOTE**   After you cut or copy a selection to the Clipboard, you can add additional selections of information with the Append function. Because WordPerfect offers no Append command shortcut keys, consider adding the Append command to the Power Bar or Toolbar.

▶ **See** "Customizing Window Features," **p. 321**

**Moving Selected Information Between Windows in WordPerfect**   Moving information between document editing windows in WordPerfect is as easy as moving information within a document. For information about arranging documents on-screen and switching between documents, see Chapter 1, "Getting Started."

To move information between open documents, follow these steps:

1. Open into separate document windows the documents between which you want to move information.
2. Switch to the document from which you want to copy or move information.
3. Select the objects (text and/or graphics) that you want to copy or move.
4. Use the desired Cut, Copy, or Append command, described in the "Transferring Selected Text to Another Location" section earlier in this chapter.
5. Switch to the document into which you want to paste the information. Then move the insertion point to where you want to paste the information.
6. Use the Paste command, described in the "Transferring Selected Text to Another Location" section earlier in this chapter, to retrieve the cut, copied, or appended information from the Clipboard. WordPerfect inserts the information in the document at the insertion point's location.
7. As appropriate, save any modified documents.

You also can use WordPerfect's drag-and-drop editing feature to copy or move information between WordPerfect documents. To do so, follow these steps:

1. Open into separate document windows the documents between which you want to move information. You must be able to see on your screen all the WordPerfect documents you want to copy or move information between.

2. Choose <u>W</u>indow, <u>T</u>ile Top To Bottom. Your open documents will all be visible on your screen. Move and resize the windows as necessary. For more information about moving and resizing document editing windows, see "Understanding the Editing Screen" in Chapter 1.

3. Using the scroll bars, position the documents in each document editing window so that the information you want to move and the location you want to move it to are both visible on-screen.

4. Using the techniques described earlier in the section "Drag-and-Drop Editing," highlight the information you want to copy or move. Then, drag the information moving the mouse pointer from the sending document to the receiving document. When you release the mouse button, the information is placed into the receiving document.

**Transferring Selected Information to Other Windows Applications**   When you choose Cut or Copy in WordPerfect, the information is transferred to the Windows Clipboard, replacing any previous selection. Appended information is added to any existing selection on the Windows Clipboard. This information is available in other Windows applications that use the Clipboard.

Likewise, information cut or copied to the Clipboard in other Windows applications is available to be pasted into WordPerfect. Information that you cut or copy onto the Clipboard stays there until you clear the Clipboard by using the Windows Clipboard Viewer application, cut or copy another piece of information onto the Clipboard, or exit Windows.

To view the contents of the Clipboard, use the Windows Clipboard Viewer application. See your Windows manual for more information about the Clipboard and the Clipboard Viewer application.

**Working with Rectangular Selections**   In WordPerfect, a selection is not limited to continuous text. You can also select text within a defined rectangle. Figure 3.9 shows an example of a rectangular selection.

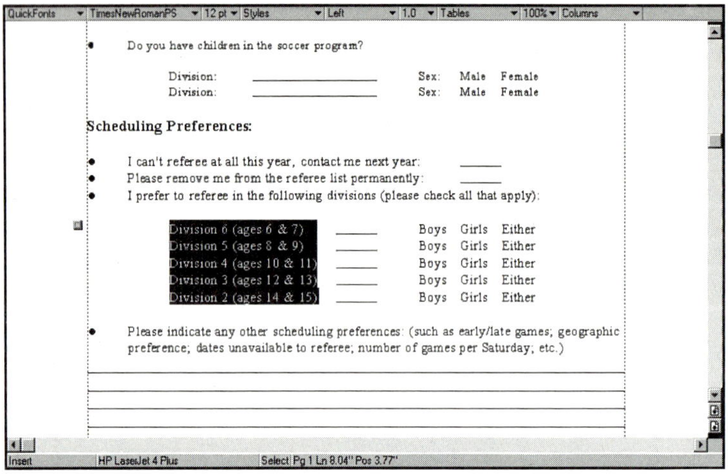

**FIG. 3.9**
When using the Select Rectangle feature, the text you've selected is displayed on screen as a highlighted rectangle.

To highlight a rectangular selection of text, follow these steps:

1. Move the insertion point to the beginning or ending corner of the rectangle you want to select.
2. Move the mouse pointer to the opposite corner and press Shift+click, or press and hold down the left mouse button at the insertion point, drag the mouse pointer to the opposite corner, and then release the mouse button.

**NOTE** At first it appears as if more text is being selected than you want, but after you perform the following step, the highlighted area shrinks to the intended rectangle size, as shown in figure 3.9.

3. Choose Edit, Select, Rectangle. The highlight shrinks to just the rectangle.

You can now cut, copy, or delete the rectangular selection. To place the rectangle in a different location, choose Cut or Copy, then move the insertion point to the desired location and choose Edit, Paste.

**CAUTION**
If you are going to delete or cut the rectangle, make sure that each line ends in a hard return to ensure that the selection is removed without disturbing other text on the page.

## Deleting and Undeleting a Selection

You can delete a highlighted selection by pressing either the Backspace or Delete key. To restore a deleted selection, see "Restoring Deleted Text" earlier in this chapter.

 You cannot retrieve a deleted selection by using the Paste command. Also, you can undelete only the last three deletions.

## Saving a Selection to a File

With the selection feature, you can save a portion of your document to be retrieved into another document later or to be retrieved into a non-Windows application that does not have access to the Windows Clipboard.

To save a selection to a file, follow these steps:

1. Highlight the selection you want to save as a separate file.
2. Choose File, Save As, or press F3. The Save dialog box appears, asking whether you want to save the entire file or your selection.
3. Make sure the Selected Text option is selected, and choose OK. The Save As dialog box appears.
4. If you want to save the file in a folder other than the current folder shown, choose the drive and folder to which you want the file saved.
5. Type a file name in the Name text box.
6. Click Save to save the selection as a file and return to your document.

 You can move selections between WordPerfect documents or to other Windows applications immediately by using the Cut (or Copy) and Paste commands.

## Enhancing Text by Using Block Selections

WordPerfect provides a wide variety of enhancements to change the appearance of your text in the Font dialog box. To access the Font dialog box, choose Format, Font, or press F9. Included on the list of enhancements are Bold, Italic, Underline, Double Underline, Redline, and Strikeout. If you have a color printer, you can even change text color.

▶ **See** "Using WordPerfect's Text-Formatting Tools," **p. 122**
▶ **See** "Accessing Special Characters," **p. 640**

Sometimes you might want to enhance an entire selection of text. To do so, select the text you want to enhance. Then apply an attribute by choosing it from the Font dialog box or, when applicable, by pressing the attribute's shortcut key or key combination.

To apply Bold to a selection, for example, use one of these methods:

- Choose Fo<u>r</u>mat, <u>F</u>ont, or press F9. Then choose <u>B</u>old.
- Press Ctrl+B.
-  Click the Bold button on the Toolbar.

WordPerfect applies the attribute to the selected text and places hidden codes that show where the attribute has been turned on and off.

WordPerfect comes with several ready-made Toolbars. For more information about Toolbars and the Power Bar, see Chapter 13, "Working with Toolbars."

▶ **See** "Why Use the Toolbar and Power Bar?," **p. 414**

**N O T E**  WordPerfect leaves the selection highlighted after each attribute is applied. Therefore, you can apply several attributes to a selection before you deselect the text. You can also apply several attributes to a selection at once by using the Font dialog box. Choose Fo<u>r</u>mat, <u>F</u>ont, or press F9. Then make the desired attribute selections and choose OK to return to your document.

## Converting the Case of a Selection

You can use case to emphasize a point in your document. If you use a printer that doesn't support certain enhancements, you may want to use uppercase letters for emphasis. Or you may find that you have used uppercase letters for a heading in your document and prefer to use a different font with only the first letter of each word an uppercase letter.

You don't need to delete and retype text to change the case. WordPerfect's Convert Case command changes selected text to lowercase, uppercase, or initial caps (where the first letter of each word is uppercase). Notice that when you switch a selection from uppercase to lowercase, certain letters remain capitalized, such as the letter *I* (when occurring by itself) or any character that begins a sentence.

To change the case of a selection, follow these steps:

1. Highlight a selection whose case you want to change.
2. Choose <u>E</u>dit, Con<u>v</u>ert Case.
3. Choose <u>L</u>owercase to convert the selection to lowercase, <u>U</u>ppercase to convert the selection to uppercase, or <u>I</u>nitial Capitals to convert the first letter of each word and single letters to capitals.

The selection remains highlighted so that you can apply additional WordPerfect commands.

You can add a Toolbar button called Case Toggle to the Toolbar. Each time this button is selected, WordPerfect converts the case (one conversion at a time) from Uppercase to Lowercase and then to Uppercase again. You can also add Toolbar buttons for the commands Lowercase, Uppercase, and Initial Capitals. For more information about Toolbars and the Power Bar, see Chapter 13, "Working with Toolbars."

▶ **See** "Customizing a Toolbar," **p. 420**

▶ **See** "Customizing the Power Bar," **p. 426**

# Using Find and Replace

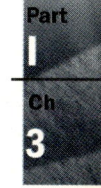

The Find and Replace command enables you to locate text or hidden codes quickly and replace them if desired. A variety of powerful options is available, enabling you to find and replace character strings, whole words, phrases, codes (all or ones with specific values), and fonts and attributes. You can even find and replace word forms. The larger your document, the more efficient you can become by using this command.

Suppose that you are working on an orientation document for new employees in your company. You have changed health insurance carriers and want to change the section of the document that deals with health benefits. When you retrieve the document, the insertion point is on page 1. By using Find, you can quickly locate the words *Health Benefits*, and begin your editing there.

Or suppose that you discover that your boss's name is misspelled throughout the document. You can use Find and Replace to fix that problem in seconds.

You can use Find and Replace with the Select feature. When you use Find and Replace on a selected portion of your document, the operation is performed only within the selection.

## Finding Words and Phrases

Finding a piece of text in a document by visually scanning the document can be very time-consuming and is subject to error. The WordPerfect Find feature, however, accomplishes this task quickly and accurately.

You can begin a search from anywhere in your document. To find all occurrences of the text you are looking for, move the insertion point to the beginning or end of the document before starting the search. Or you can set options so that WordPerfect always begins a search at the top of the document or wraps a search at the end of the document in order to search the complete document before returning to the starting location.

You can search your document from top to bottom, or bottom to top. To find a word or phrase in your document, position the insertion point where you want to begin looking and follow these steps:

1. Choose Edit, Find and Replace, or press Ctrl+F. The Find and Replace Text dialog box appears (see fig. 3.10).

**FIG. 3.10**

The Find and Replace Text dialog box includes a variety of menus that enable you to perform a search more precisely.

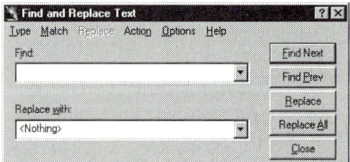

2. Type the text you want to find (up to 80 characters) in the Find text box. This text is called a *search string*.

 If you highlight text before opening the Find and Replace Text dialog box, the selected text is displayed in the Find text box.

3. Click Find Next to search from the location of the insertion point toward the end of the document. Click Find Prev to search from the location of the insertion point toward the beginning of the document.

   WordPerfect enables you to start the search from a location other than the insertion point and to search the entire document even if you are not at the beginning or end of the document.

   To have WordPerfect move to the beginning of the document before it begins searching, choose Options, Begin Find At Top Of Document.

   To have WordPerfect wrap when it gets to the beginning or end of the document and return to the location of the insertion point, thus searching the entire document, choose Options, Wrap At Beg/End Of Document.

When WordPerfect finds the first occurrence of the search string, the program highlights the string. If the word or phrase does not exist in the entire search area, a Find and Replace dialog box displays the search string and the message Not found. Click OK or press Enter to acknowledge the message and close the dialog box.

To find the next occurrence after the insertion point, again choose Find Next or Find Prev; or if you've closed the Find and Replace Text dialog box, press Shift+F2 to find the next occurrence after the insertion point or Alt+F2 to find the next occurrence *before* the insertion point. WordPerfect remembers the search string, so you do not need to retype it.

WordPerfect provides a Find History drop-down list that lists the search items you've previously looked for. To display the drop-down list of find items, click the Find drop-down list button. Alternatively, use the ↑ and ↓ keys to display find items in the Find text box. Choose the desired find item (if necessary, use the scroll bar to display the item).

Unless you specify otherwise, WordPerfect searches in several sections of your document, including headers, footers, comments, graphics box captions, and text boxes. You can choose an option in the Find and Replace Text dialog box to prevent this extended find, as explained in the section "Understanding Find and Replace Options" later in this chapter.

## Choosing Search Criteria

Unless you use wildcard characters (as described in the next paragraph) or the word forms option described later in this chapter, WordPerfect looks for an exact match to the search string. Unless you've specified otherwise, the search is not case-sensitive. For example, searching for **gateway**, **Gateway**, or **GATEWAY** finds gateway, Gateway, and GATEWAY.

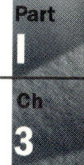

Wildcard characters can assist in your search. You use the wild cards [? (One Char)] and [* (Many Char)] to represent unknown characters in your search. The [? (One Char)] code represents any single character. The [* (Many Char)] code represents one or more characters. For example, searching for **ca[?(One Char)]** finds cat, cab, and car. Searching for **w[*(Many Char)]fall** finds waterfall, but **w[?(One Char)]fall** does not.

You cannot insert wildcard characters by typing them from the keyboard. You must use the Codes option from the Find and Replace Text dialog box. You choose the wildcard codes the same way you do any formatting code. For more information about the Codes option, see the section "Finding and Replacing Formatting Codes" later in this chapter.

You can set options from the Find dialog box to fine-tune the way Find works. For example, you can choose options for case-sensitive searching and searching for whole words only. See the section "Understanding Find and Replace Options" later in this chapter for more information.

## Finding and Replacing Words and Phrases

In addition to finding text, WordPerfect can replace the found text with different text. Or by leaving the Replace With text box empty, you can delete the search string where it occurs in your document. For example, in a lengthy document, you may want to replace the word *waterfall* with *fountain* wherever it occurs. WordPerfect's Replace feature makes this change easy.

> **CAUTION**
> Although a Replace function can be undone, save your document just before doing a search and replace. Then, if something unexpected happens and you cannot undo the undesired replacements, you can simply retrieve the saved file from disk and try again with different find and replace strings.

To find and replace text, follow these steps:

1. Choose Edit, Find and Replace, press Ctrl+F, or press F2. The Find and Replace Text dialog box appears (refer to fig. 3.10).

**TIP** To insert WordPerfect characters in the Find or Replace With text entry boxes, press Ctrl+W to display the WordPerfect Characters dialog box. Select the desired character and choose Insert And Close.

2. Type the text to search for (up to 80 characters) in the Find text box. This text is the search string.

**NOTE** WordPerfect automatically places the last search and replace strings in the Find and Replace With text boxes. In addition, you can click the drop-down list arrow (or press Alt+down arrow while in the text box) and a history list appears showing prior items used for Find and Replace actions.

3. Press Tab to move the insertion point to the Replace With text box.
4. Type the text you want to put in place of the search string. If you just want to remove the search string from your document when found, do not enter anything in the Replace With text box and, if necessary, delete anything in the text box. (If you delete the replacement item, WordPerfect inserts the item `<Nothing>` to indicate you are replacing the found item with nothing, thereby deleting the found item.)

**TIP** To quickly copy text or codes from the Find text entry box to the Replace With text box, highlight the desired text and codes in the Find text box, and press Ctrl+C. Move the insertion point to the Replace With text box and press Ctrl+V to paste the copied information. You can also copy from the document to paste into the Find and Replace dialog box.

5. Choose Find Next to locate the next occurrence of the search string. You can then choose Replace to replace the found text with the contents of your Replace With text box and locate the next occurrence, or choose Find Next to skip this replacement and locate the next occurrence of the search string.

At any point, you can also choose Replace All, and WordPerfect immediately replaces all occurrences of the search string with the contents of the Replace With text box.

When WordPerfect does not find an occurrence of the search string, a Find and Replace dialog box appears stating that the search string is Not Found. Choose OK to continue.

## Understanding Find and Replace Options

WordPerfect provides many options to fine-tune your search to find exactly what you want as quickly as possible. For example, you can choose the direction to search and choose what action should be taken when the end of the document is reached. You can also fine-tune replacement actions, such as limiting the number of items to find and replace. These options are found in menus in the Find Text dialog box.

Choose Type to select from the following options:

- *Text*. This normal search mode enables you to search for individual characters, words, or phrases.
- *Word Forms*. Choose this option to find any form of the word you are looking for. For example, entering **threw** finds threw, throw, and throwing. For more information, see "Finding and Replacing Word Forms" later in this chapter.
- *Specific Codes*. Choose this option to search for WordPerfect formatting codes of a certain value. For more information, see the section "Finding and Replacing Formatting Codes" later in this chapter.

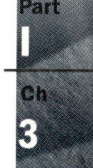

While your cursor is in the Find text box, choose Match to select from the following find options:

- *Whole Word*. Choose this option to find the text you enter only if it is not part of other text. For example, with a normal WordPerfect Find, searching for **fall** finds both fall and waterfall. With this option checked, Find locates only fall.
- *Case*. Choose this option to have WordPerfect match lower- and uppercase letters exactly. With this option checked, for example, **gateway** finds only gateway, and **Gateway** finds only Gateway.
- *Font*. Choose this option to display the Match Font dialog box. In this dialog box, specify various fonts, font sizes, and text attributes. When you make a selection here, WordPerfect only finds the search string you enter if it is in the font, font size, and attributes you have selected.
- *Codes*. Choose this option to find WordPerfect formatting codes. For more information, see the section "Finding and Replacing Formatting Codes" later in this chapter.

While your cursor is in the Replace With text box, choose Replace to select from the following replace options:

- *Case*. Normally, when you enter a lowercase replacement string, WordPerfect uses the first character capitalization of the word being replaced. To force WordPerfect to use the case of the replacement string entered, choose this option. The word `Case Sensitive` appears below the Replace With text box.
- *Font*. Choose this option to display the Replace Font dialog box. From this dialog box, you can choose a font, font style, and font attribute to be applied to the text when replaced.
- *Codes*. This option works the same as the codes option listed earlier in the Match menu.

**N O T E**  Not all the codes listed in the Codes list box from the Match menu are available in the Codes list box from the Replace menu. For example, you can search for a general `[Lft Mar]` code, regardless of its value. But it makes no sense to replace a code with a nonspecific `[Lft Mar]` code. The replacement needs to have a specific value (for example, 2 inches) so you need to use the Type, Specific Codes option to choose a replacement code.

Choose Action to select from the following options:

- *Select Match*. Choose this option, and WordPerfect highlights the search string when it is found. This enables you to immediately perform WordPerfect operations on the selected text. This option is the default that WordPerfect selects each time you start WordPerfect.
- *Position Before*. Choose this option to have WordPerfect position the insertion point immediately before the first item of the search string if it is found.
- *Position After*. Choose this option to have WordPerfect position the insertion point immediately after the last item of the search string if it is found.
- *Extend Selection*. Choose this option to extend a text selection from the location of the insertion point to a specific word, phrase, or code. For example, to select text from the insertion point through the phrase `pay raises`, open the Find and Replace Text dialog box and choose Action, Extend Selection. Type **pay raises** in the text box and choose Find Next. The portion of your document from the insertion point up to and including `pay raises` is highlighted.

Choose Options to select from the following options (Begin Find At Top Of Document and Wrap At Beg/End Of Document are covered in the section "Finding Words and Phrases" earlier in this chapter):

- *Limit Find Within Selection*. This option causes the find to be performed only on the selection you made in the document prior to performing the find.

- *Include Headers, Footers, Etc. In Find.* Choose this option to search for words, phrases, or codes in places other than regular body text. These areas include headers, footers, text boxes, watermarks, footnotes, endnotes, comments, graphics box captions, equations, and tables of authorities full form.
- *Limit Number of Changes.* Choose this option to limit the number of times a word, phrase, or code is replaced. Choosing this option causes the Limit Number of Changes dialog box, in which you enter the limit number, to appear.

Choose Help to display the WordPerfect Help dialog box specific to Finding and Replacing Text and Codes.

## Finding and Replacing Word Forms

In addition to finding specific words, you can use WordPerfect's Word Form option to find all the forms of a word. For example, you can search for the word *threw* and the words *threw, throw,* and *throwing* are all found. WordPerfect selects all the tenses of the root word, for example past and present tense, but does not find other parts of speech (verb, noun, and so on). For example, if you look for the word *run*, you would find *ran* and *running,* but not the noun *runner.*

The real power of working with word forms is apparent when finding and replacing text. Try the following example:

1. Type the following:

   **Jessica said, "I think Debbie is going to the store soon." Gary, realizing the mistake, said, "No, she went to the store an hour ago and has already returned."**

2. Press Ctrl+Home to move the insertion point to the top of the document.
3. Choose Edit, Find and Replace, press Ctrl+F, or press F2. The Find and Replace Text dialog box appears.
4. Type **go** in the Find text box. Type **run** in the Replace With text box.
5. Choose Type, Word Forms. The message `Word Forms of go` will appear under the Find text box and `Word Forms of run` will appear under the Replace With text box.
6. Click Replace All.
7. Choose Close to return to your document. The text now reads:

   ```
   Jessica said, "I think Debbie is running to the store soon." Gary,
   realizing the mistake, said "No, she ran to the store an hour ago and
   has already returned."
   ```

Don't forget to deselect Word Forms if you will be doing subsequent normal searches.

**N O T E** If you choose Replace All and several word forms exist for the replacement word, a Word Form dialog box appears. Choose the desired replacement in the Word Forms list box and then choose Replace to replace this occurrence of the word and locate the next. Choose Use Always to use the selected word form for all subsequent replacements, or Skip to not replace this occurrence of the found word and locate the next.

As you can see, finding and replacing text based on word forms can be a very powerful editing tool.

## Finding and Replacing Formatting Codes

WordPerfect enables you to find or find and replace formatting codes. For example, if you want to find where you set the tabs in your document, you can search for the `[Tab Set]` code. You can search also for specific codes of a certain value. Instead of searching for all `[Lft Mar]` codes, for example, you can search for locations where the left margin is set to 2 inches (`[Lft Mar:2"]`). Additionally, you can change the 2-inch margin to 3 inches by finding and replacing the appropriate hidden codes.

To find and replace hidden codes, follow the general steps described in the preceding sections for finding and replacing text—except that you do not type text in the Find and Replace With text boxes.

To find a code regardless of its value, follow these steps:

1. Choose Edit, Find and Replace, press Ctrl+F, or press F2. The Find and Replace Text dialog box appears (refer to fig. 3.10).

2. Choose Match, Codes. The Codes dialog box appears (see fig. 3.11).

**FIG. 3.11**
The Codes dialog box shows `Tab Set` selected using the highlight bar.

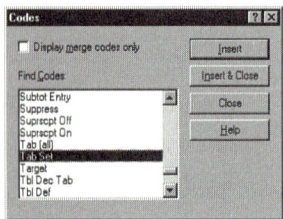

3. Use the scroll arrows to scroll through the list until you highlight the code you want to find, or type the characters of the code. To search for the `[Tab Set]` code, for example, type **Tab S**. As you type the characters, the highlight bar moves closer to your selection.

4. When the desired code is highlighted, click Insert. WordPerfect inserts the code in the Find text box of the Find and Replace Text dialog box. If you have no other codes to select, choose Close. Then continue with the same steps that you use to find text.

To find a code with a specific value, follow these steps:

1. With the Find and Replace Text dialog box open, choose Type, Specific Codes. The Specific Codes dialog box appears.
2. Use the scroll arrows to scroll the list until you highlight the code you want to find, or type the characters of the code.
3. When the desired code is highlighted, choose OK. A Find and Replace dialog box specific to the selected code appears (see fig. 3.12).
4. Enter the value of the code that you want to find in the Find pop-up list (**1.50** in this example), or use the increment/decrement arrows. Continue with the same steps used to find text.

**FIG. 3.12**
The Find and Replace Left Margin dialog box enables you to enter the value of the left margin code you want to find.

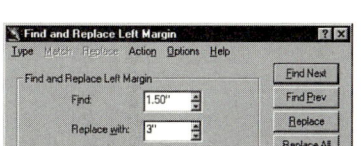

To replace codes with specific values, open the Find and Replace Text dialog box (choose Edit, Find and Replace, or press Ctrl+F, or press F2), and then follow steps 1–4 in the preceding instructions. In step 4, however, type the value to be found and the value to be used as the replacement. Figure 3.12 shows an example of finding one or more left margin codes of 1.5 inches and replacing them with left margin codes of 3 inches. If you want to find codes with a specific value and delete them, check the Replace With Nothing check box.

**NOTE** Not all the codes listed in the Find Codes list box are available in the Replace Codes list box. For example, you can search for a general [Lft Mar] code, regardless of its value. But it makes no sense to replace a code with a nonspecific [Lft Mar] code. The replacement needs to have a specific value (for example, 2 inches) so you need to use the Specific Codes option to choose a replacement code.

Likewise, not all codes appear in the Specific Codes dialog box because many codes—such as bold and underline—do not have variable values.

CHAPTER 4

# Formatting Text

*by George Beinhorn, Cathy Kenny, and Read Gilgen*

**W**ordPerfect's text-formatting features help make documents readable and visually inviting. *Formatting* refers to the way you enhance text and other page elements on the printed page. For example, you can alter the appearance of text by changing the font, line spacing, margins, paragraph spacing, justification, and many other options.

Chapter 5, "Formatting Pages and Documents," describes options for formatting pages. To learn how to apply WordPerfect's font appearance and size controls, see Chapter 20, "Using Fonts and Special Characters." ■

- **Change default formatting settings**
  WordPerfect makes what you say look better through attractively formatted text.

- **Use the Power Bar, Toolbar, Ruler Bar, QuickSpots, and keyboard to perform formatting tasks quickly**
  Using the right tools to format your document helps you work smarter and faster.

- **Set margins, tabs, indents, and back tabs**
  White space around the edges and neatly aligned paragraphs help make your text more readable.

- **Control justification and hyphenation**
  Add a professional look to your documents by eliminating unneeded spaces between words.

# Using WordPerfect's Text-Formatting Tools

WordPerfect sets ready-to-use defaults for formatting text when you install the program. If you prefer other formatting options, you can change your default preferences, or you can override them temporarily by using format codes, as described in this chapter.

The sections that follow describe various ways to access WordPerfect's text-formatting tools. The most basic way to choose text-formatting commands is with the Format menu. However, you can also format text quickly with the mouse or by using keyboard shortcuts. For example, you can click a button on the Toolbar to bold text or format paragraphs with bullets. If you prefer to use the keyboard, you can use keyboard shortcuts, such as Ctrl+B for bold text or Ctrl+Shift+B to format a bulleted paragraph.

For consistency of format, a special button called *QuickFormat* enables you to quickly apply fonts and attributes (boldface, italic, and more) or paragraph styles that you've used elsewhere in a document.

With the mouse and the Power Bar, you can click buttons to change fonts, set tabs, justification, line spacing, and perform other common formatting functions. You can create customized Power Bars and Toolbars to use the mouse to access the commands you use most frequently. You can switch between Toolbars to perform specialized tasks, such as formatting tables or equations. WordPerfect comes with several ready-made Toolbars. For more information about Toolbars and the Power Bar, see Chapter 13, "Working with Toolbars."

## WordPerfect's Default Text Format Settings

When you first install WordPerfect, the following defaults take effect for formatting text: 1-inch margins at the top, bottom, left, and right sides of the page; single-line spacing; and left justified text. Depending on the currently selected printer you installed under Windows, WordPerfect chooses a *default font*—usually a common font such as Courier 10 pitch or Times New Roman Regular 12 point. The currently active font is shown on the Font button on the Power Bar.

 To use formatting commands effectively, you should know how to turn on and work in the Reveal Codes screen, as described in Chapter 3. To turn Reveal Codes on and off, choose <u>V</u>iew, Reveal <u>C</u>odes; or press Alt+F3.

If you change a setting by adding a format code, as described in the various sections of this chapter, that setting overrides the default and remains in effect for the current document only. To learn how to change default settings for all new documents, see Chapter 9, "Customizing WordPerfect."

You can also insert formatting commands with the Document Initial Style feature, described in Chapter 5, "Formatting Pages and Documents," and in Chapter 10, "Using Styles." This feature "hides" codes so that they don't clutter up the Reveal Codes window. You also use this feature so that codes affect an entire document, including headers, footers, and footnotes. To create document initial codes, choose Format, Document, Initial Codes Style. You can override a formatting code contained in a Document Initial style at any time by inserting a manual formatting command.

▶ **See** "Creating the Initial Codes Style," **p. 199**
▶ **See** "Customizing the Display," **p. 300**
▶ **See** "Using Styles," **p. 352**

## The Format Menu

Text-formatting commands are located on the Format menu. You can also choose many text-formatting commands with the Toolbar, Power Bar, and Ruler Bar, or by using keyboard shortcuts as described in corresponding sections of this chapter.

The Format menu provides the following text-formatting commands:

| | |
|---|---|
| Format, Font; or F9 | Format, Columns |
| Format, Line | Format, Margins; or Ctrl+F8 |
| Format, Paragraph | Format, Justification |
| Format, Document | Format, QuickFormat |

## The QuickMenu

Many of the options available on the Format menu can be accessed more quickly on the QuickMenu. Position the mouse point on the document text and click the secondary (right) mouse button to display the QuickMenu, then choose from the options listed (see fig. 4.1).

## Chapter 4 Formatting Text

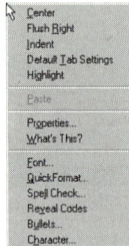

**FIG. 4.1**
Click the text with the secondary (right) mouse button to get WordPerfect's QuickMenus, which provides quick and convenient access to common formatting options.

## The Toolbar, Power Bar, and Ruler Bar

You can change text-formatting settings quickly with the mouse by clicking the Toolbar, Power Bar, and Ruler Bar. The specific steps to perform these operations are described in corresponding sections of this chapter. This section gives basic instructions for using the bars.

Figure 4.2 shows the default WordPerfect 7 Toolbar and Power Bar with text-formatting buttons labeled.

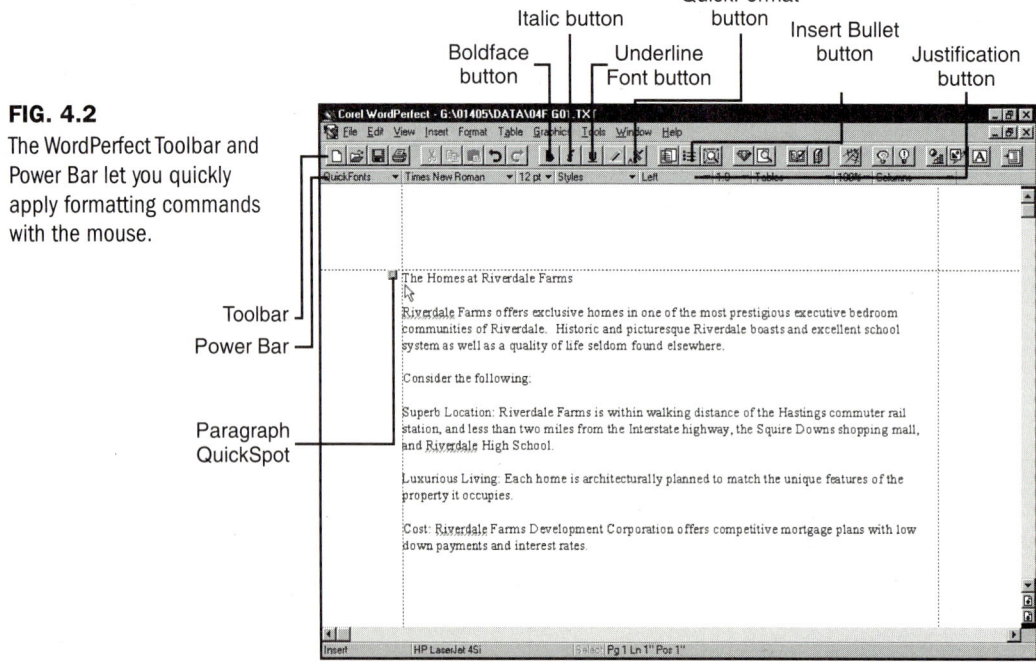

**FIG. 4.2**
The WordPerfect Toolbar and Power Bar let you quickly apply formatting commands with the mouse.

To display or hide any of the bars mentioned here, simply choose View, Toolbars/Ruler. In the Toolbars dialog box, if a bar has a check mark beside it, click that bar to hide it. If no check mark is present, click the bar to display it. Once you turn on a bar, it remains on until you turn it off, even if you exit WordPerfect.

### TROUBLESHOOTING

**I don't seem to have a Toolbar. What happened?** Somewhere along the line, you (or maybe someone using your computer) deselected the Toolbar. To get it back, just choose View, Toolbars/ Ruler, and in the Toolbars dialog box, check the Toolbar (or any other bar) you want to display. The selection remains until you deselect it.

## Paragraph QuickSpot

WordPerfect's QuickSpots give you quick access to common formatting functions. As you move the mouse pointer through your text, you see a small box in the left margin (refer to fig. 4.2). Click this QuickSpot to select the entire paragraph and to display the Paragraph properties dialog box (see fig. 4.3).

**FIG. 4.3**
Clicking the Paragraph QuickSpot gives you the Paragraph properties dialog box where you can change several basic paragraph formats.

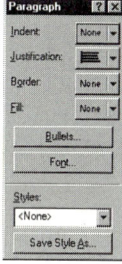

## Using the Keyboard

Don't forget that the keyboard often offers shortcuts to changing text formatting. For example, suppose you want to access the Font dialog box. Rather than moving your hand from the keyboard to the mouse in order to choose the Format menu and then the Font command, you could simply type Alt+R, then F. An even quicker method world be to press F9. Throughout this book, you see many keyboard alternatives which, if used, can save you considerable time.

## QuickFormat

 Notice that the Toolbar includes a button labeled QuickFormat. The QuickFormat tool lets you quickly copy font, attribute, and/or paragraph style formatting from formatted text to other paragraphs or blocks of selected text (see the section "Formatting Text with QuickFormat" later in this chapter.)

## Auto Code Placement

When you choose formatting commands, WordPerfect places hidden codes in the document. To view or hide hidden codes, choose View, Reveal Codes (Alt+F3). For more information on using Reveal Codes, see Chapter 3, "Retrieving and Editing Documents."

WordPerfect automatically repositions certain codes, regardless of where you enter them in a document. This feature is called *Auto Code Placement*. As an example, Auto Code Placement moves codes that affect an entire paragraph—such as left and right margins and justification—to the beginning of the paragraph. Formatting commands that affect an entire page are moved to the top of the page, even if you enter a command in the middle of the page. When you need to find a hidden code, Auto Code Placement ensures that the code is at the top of the document, page, or paragraph.

> **CAUTION**
> Placement of formatting codes is not entirely automatic. Make sure the insertion point is positioned where you want to make a formatting change *before* making the change, otherwise the results may not be what you expect.

▶ **See** "Understanding WordPerfect's Hidden Codes," **p. 91**

# Formatting Characters

You use WordPerfect's character formatting options to turn on character appearance attributes, such as boldface, italic, small caps, and underlining, and to change character size.

You can display any appearance attribute on-screen, but there is a slight chance your printer may not be able to print all character attributes. To be sure, create a test file containing attribute(s) you want to use and print it.

## Changing Character Appearance and Size

You can change character appearance and size attributes with the Font dialog box by following these steps:

1. Select existing text if you want to apply new character attributes to the text; or position the cursor where you want the new attributes to begin.

2. Choose Format, ͟. The Font dialog box appears (see fig. 4.4). Double-clicking the ͟ ͟ on the Power Bar also displays the Font dialog box.

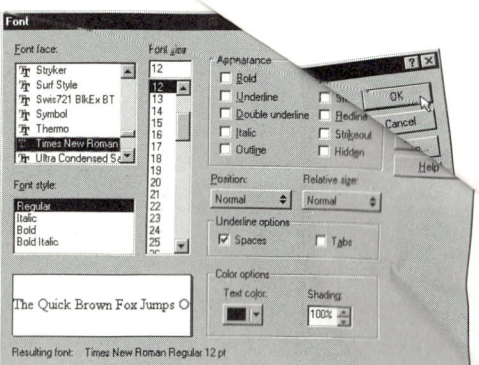

**FIG. 4.4**
In the Font dialog box, choose Windows TrueType fonts or fonts that are supplied with your printer. You can also choose other soft fonts that you've installed on your system from a disk.

3. Choose attributes you want from among the Font Face, Font Size, Font Style, Appearance, Position, Relative Size, Underline Options, and Color Options sections of the dialog box.

   As you make selections, your changes are reflected in the Resulting Font window in the lower-left corner of the dialog box.

4. Choose OK or press Enter to apply the new font attributes and to return to the document screen.

The following list describes the Font dialog box options:

- *Font Face.* Changes the font for selected or new text. Use the arrow keys or mouse to choose a font from the list. Or double-click a font name to select it and return to the document screen. With text selected, WordPerfect encloses the selected text in opening and closing font codes. With no text selected, WordPerfect applies the new font from the insertion point forward, until it encounters another font code.

- *Font Size.* Changes the size of selected or new text. Choose Font Size and use the arrow keys or mouse to choose a font size from the list; or type a font size in the Font Size edit box at the top of the list. Font size is the height of the font measured in *points*, where 72 points equals 1 inch.

- *Font Style.* Displays available variations of the font selected in the Font Face list, such as Regular, Bold, Italic, and Bold Italic. You rarely need to use this option, because you can add bold and italic features to nearly any regular font face. However, some font faces look better when printed using their native style (for example, Bold Italic) rather than a modified Regular style. When you choose a font

...ose OK (or double-click the appearance option from the list) ...nt name] hidden code in the document. This code changes the fo... ce from the insertion point forward. With text selected, WordPerfect... the selected text between opening and closing font codes.

- *Appearance.* ...eck boxes from this section to apply attributes to new or selected text. ...dPerfect encloses the new or selected text in the corresponding character... bute codes.

  The Appearance options are Bold, Underline, Double Underline, Italic, Outline, Shadow, Small Caps, Redline, Strikeout, and Hidden. When you choose one or more attributes, the sample window in the lower-left corner of the dialog box reflects your changes.

  **NOTE** You can apply the most frequently used character appearance attributes to selected or new text with the following keyboard shortcuts:

  | Attribute | Keyboard Shortcut |
  |---|---|
  | Bold | Ctrl+B |
  | Italic | Ctrl+I |
  | Underline | Ctrl+U |

  To return to normal type after applying an attribute, press the right-arrow key to move past the closing attribute code.

  **TIP** You can add bold, italic, or underline attributes to a single word without selecting it first. Simply position the insertion point on the word and use a shortcut key to add the attribute to the entire word.

  Note that Hidden is grayed unless text is selected. You must select text before you can format it as hidden. Hidden text is hidden on-screen by default, and is not printed. To display hidden text for the current document only, choose View, Hidden Text. To turn on the on-screen display of hidden text as a default, choose Edit, Preferences and double-click the Display icon. Then select the Document tab, choose Hidden Text, click OK, and then Close.

- *Position.* Choose this option, and then choose Superscript or Subscript to format selected or new text as superscript or subscript characters. WordPerfect formats superscript and subscript text in characters 60 percent as large as the current font.

- *Relative Size.* Choose this option to quickly change font size to a preset size, relative to the current size of the font at the location of the insertion point. This is particularly useful if you change the document font, because text formatted with the

Relative Size option is always proportionally larger or smaller than the document font. Table 4.1 shows the default size attributes.

**Table 4.1  Size Attributes**

| Font Size Attribute | Size Ratio (in Percent) |
|---|---|
| Fine | 60 |
| Small | 80 |
| Normal | 100 |
| Large | 120 |
| Very Large | 150 |
| Extra Large | 200 |

**N O T E**  If you have more than one position or relative size in the text you have selected, Mixed appears as the selected position or size. Choose a different position or size to make the entire selection the same.

 **TIP**  You can change the default size ration percentages assigned to Fine, Small, Large, Very Large, Extra Large, and Super/Subscript by accessing the Font Size Attribute Ratios dialog box. This dialog box is accessed by playing the SIZEATTR.WCM macro, found in \COREL\OFFICE7\MACROS\WPWIN.

- *Underline Options*. By default, WordPerfect underlines spaces inserted with the space bar when underlining is turned on. Choose Tabs to have WordPerfect also underline spaces inserted with the Tab key, Indent, Flush Right, or Centering commands when underlining is turned on.

- *Color Options*. If your printer supports color, you can choose the color that WordPerfect uses to print selected or new characters. Choose Text Color and click the desired color. If you need extra color control (as in prepress document preparation), you can click the Palette button to define a custom color with the Define Color Palette dialog box. You can set exact color specification using a color wheel, or based on RGB (Red, Green, Blue), HLS (Hue, Luminosity, Saturation), or CMYK (Cyan, Magenta, Yellow, BlacK) models.

Choose Shading and choose a level of shading of the selected color (from 0–100 percent).

 **TIP**  The Shading option is useful for creating artistic effects with large display type—for example, to print a newsletter banner heading with 40 percent gray shaded letters.

## Changing Character Attributes with the Power Bar

You can change the following character attributes quickly by using buttons on the Power Bar:

- *QuickFonts.* Each time you choose a font, WordPerfect places that font's name on the QuickFonts list. When you click the QuickFonts button, each recently used font appears in its actual font face and style. Simply click the font you want to use. If no text is selected, WordPerfect inserts a font code and changes the font until it encounters another font code. With text selected, WordPerfect encloses the selected text in opening and closing font codes.

- *Font.* To change the font, click the Font Face button to drop down a list of available fonts; then click the desired font. If no text is selected, WordPerfect inserts a font code and changes the font until it encounters another font code. With text selected, WordPerfect encloses the selected text in opening and closing font codes. The status line displays the name of the current font. The last four fonts you used appear at the top of this list.

- *Font Size.* Click the Font Size button, and then click a size on the drop-down list. If no text is selected, WordPerfect inserts a font size code and changes the font until it encounters another font code. With text selected, WordPerfect encloses the selected text in opening and closing font size codes.

- *Styles.* Click the Styles button and select a style to apply to selected or new text. WordPerfect inserts the Style opening and closing style codes, using the style name. (If the style is a Document style, there is no closing style code.)

> **TIP** Click the Bold, Italic, and Underline tools in the Toolbar to apply the attribute to new or selected text.

 **See** "Examining the Toolbar and Power Bar Icons," **p. 416**

# Formatting Lines and Paragraphs

You access WordPerfect's line and paragraph formatting commands through the Format menu (see figs. 4.5 and 4.6). You can also insert most formatting codes with the mouse by using the Toolbar, Power Bar, Ruler Bar, QuickMenus, QuickSpots, and the keyboard. The sections that follow give menu, mouse, and keyboard alternatives for choosing formatting commands.

Formatting Lines and Paragraphs

**FIG. 4.5**
The Format and Line menus contain the commands used to format lines in your document.

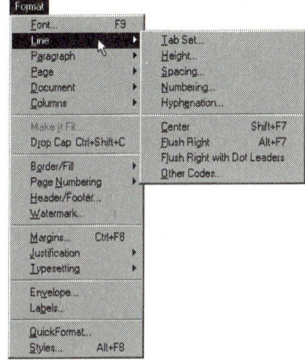

> **NOTE** WordPerfect uses the Format, Line, Other Codes command to access several features not very obviously associated with lines: hard tab codes, dot leaders, and hard spaces.

▶ See "Initial Style," **p. 338**

**FIG. 4.6**
The Format and Paragraph menus provide commands for changing the appearance of paragraphs on a page.

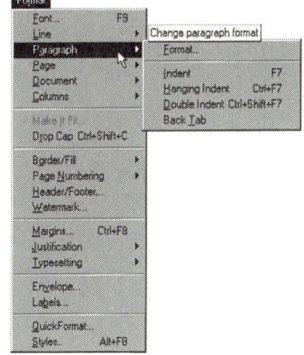

## Centering and Flush Right

One of the more common line formatting tasks is to center or flush-right a line. Flush-right text begins at the right margin and extends "backward" to the left. Centering and flush-right apply to just one line of text at a time; you must insert a new centering or flush-right code at the beginning of each line. Pressing Enter cancels centering or flush-right formatting and returns the insertion point to the left margin.

You can also use the Justification function to tell WordPerfect to continue to format text centered or flush-right even though you press Enter to start a new line. Justification is discussed in the later section, "Using Justification."

To create centered or flush-right text, follow these steps:

1. Position the insertion point at the left end of the line where you want to begin typing centered text, or at the left end of a line of existing text.
2. Choose Fo_r_mat, _L_ine, _C_enter; or press Shift+F7.

    Or, choose Fo_r_mat, _L_ine, F_l_ush Right; or press Alt+F7.

    If you insert the code at the left end of a line of existing text, WordPerfect centers the text or formats it flush-right.
3. If you chose Center or Flush Right on a blank line, type new text and press Enter to turn off centering or flush-right.

You also can align text flush-right or centered using the QuickMenu. First, position the cursor at the line you want to format and then right-click anywhere on the document screen. Select _C_enter or Flush _R_ight from the resulting QuickMenu.

**NOTE** You can combine left, center, and flush-right formatting on the same line. For example, to type your name at the left margin, a report title centered, and the date flush-right at the right margin, type the flush-left text, press Shift+F7 and type the centered title; then press Alt+F7 and enter the flush-right date.

If you choose center or flush-right commands with text selected, WordPerfect inserts a [Just: Center] or [Just: Right] code at the beginning of the selected text and inserts the appropriate "restore justification" code after the [HRt] code at the end of the text. For example, WordPerfect inserts a [Just: Left] code when the text reverts to left justification. The lines of the selected text are formatted centered or flush-right.

If you choose Fo_r_mat, _L_ine, F_l_ush Right with Dot Leaders, you get a series of periods (also known as *dot leaders*) followed by the flush right text.

**TIP** If you choose Center or Flush Right twice (for example, if you press Shift+F7 or Alt+F7 twice), you get centered or flush right text with dot leaders. If you choose Center or Flush Right a third time, you turn off the dot leaders.

## Controlling Line Spacing and Line Height

When you first install WordPerfect, it sets line spacing to single-spacing, and automatically sets the line height to match the currently selected font. You can change these defaults, as described in Chapter 9, "Customizing WordPerfect." Or you can adjust line spacing and line height for part of a document or for the whole document, as described in the following sections. You can also insert formatting codes with Document Initial style, as described earlier in the section "WordPerfect's Default Text Format Settings," and in Chapter 10, "Using Styles."

*Line height* is the distance from the base of one line of text to the base of the next line, and normally depends on the size of the text font being used. Line spacing is based on the line height. For example, if the text is Courier and the line height is .167-inch, then single spacing gives you spacing of .167-inch (six lines per inch), while double spacing gives you spacing of .33-inch (three lines per inch).

You can change the line spacing or line height for existing text by first selecting the text, and then choosing formatting commands. Or you can insert a line spacing or line height code and then begin typing with the new settings in effect. If you apply formatting codes to selected text, WordPerfect inserts a code to restore the preceding value at the end of the selected block. For example, if you change the line height for selected lines, WordPerfect inserts a code at the end of the selected block, returning line height to its previous value.

**Line Spacing**   Line spacing and line height are different functions in WordPerfect. With the Line Spacing command, you can set the space between lines in multiples of the line height that WordPerfect automatically selects or that you select for the currently active font.

With the Line Height command, you can set the spacing of lines much more precisely. Line Height is described in the next section.

To change line spacing, follow these steps:

1. Position the insertion point where you want the change to take effect and choose Format, Line, Spacing. The Line Spacing dialog box appears (see fig. 4.7).

**FIG. 4.7**
Use the Line Spacing dialog box to choose single, double, or even 1 1/2 spacing in your document.

2. Type a number in the Spacing text box, or click the increment and decrement arrows to change spacing in increments of 0.1 line.

   By typing a number in the Spacing text box, you can set spacing in increments of a 100th of a line. You cannot specify line spacing in inches, centimeters, points, and so on. The actual amount of space between lines formatted for single spacing (1.0 in the Spacing box) depends on the current font.

3. Choose OK or press Enter to return to the document window. WordPerfect inserts the appropriate line spacing code.

**Line Height**   WordPerfect automatically chooses a line height that the program designers considered to be readable for the currently active font. For example, for the Courier font, the automatic line height (from the base of one line to the base of the next) is .167-inch (1/6 inch). If you use several type sizes on the same line, WordPerfect sets the line height for the largest font on the line (see fig. 4.8).

You can override WordPerfect's automatic line height settings. This is very useful for precise placement of lines in desktop-publishing documents. If no text is selected, your line height choices take effect from the insertion point forward. If text is selected, they affect only the selected text.

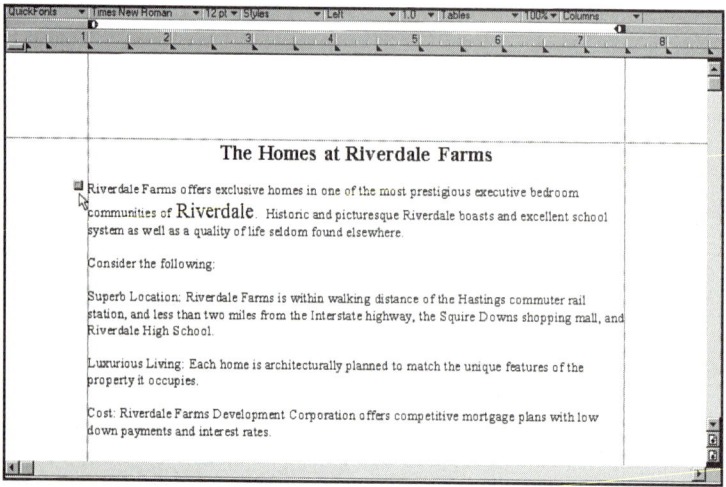

**FIG. 4.8**
The default line heights work fine for most text, but for very long lines or large type, or to squeeze more lines onto a page, you might need to increase line height to keep text readable. You can also decrease line height to squeeze more lines onto a page.

To change line height, follow these steps:

1. Choose Format, Line, Height. The Line Height dialog box appears (see fig. 4.9).

2. Choose Fixed, and type a measurement for line height, or click the increment/decrement arrows to change the setting. Insert the appropriate symbol after the

number to specify the measurement in inches (" or **i**), points (**p**), or centimeters (**cm** or **c**).

3. Choose OK. WordPerfect inserts the line height code and returns to the document screen.

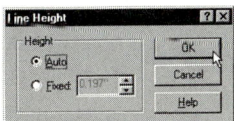

**FIG. 4.9**
Use the Line Height dialog box to set the spacing between lines exactly or to let WordPerfect automatically select the best line spacing.

You can fine-tune line height further by choosing Fo<u>r</u>mat, <u>T</u>ypesetting, <u>W</u>ord/Letterspacing and making changes to the Adjust <u>L</u>eading setting. For complete information, see Chapter 23, "Desktop Publishing with WordPerfect."

You can also change line height with the QuickFormat feature or with a paragraph style.

▶ See "Using Styles," **p. 352**

## Setting Margins

WordPerfect measures margin settings from the edges of the page. When you choose a different paper size, the margins remain the same. When you change to a different font, the margins also remain the same. Margins are measured in inches, unless you change the setting in Preferences (choose <u>E</u>dit, Pr<u>e</u>ferences, Document).

You can change margin settings using the Fo<u>r</u>mat menu, the mouse to drag margin guidelines, or the Ruler Bar.

To set margins using the Format menu, follow these steps:

1. Select text to which you want to apply margin settings. Or, to apply settings to the current and subsequent pages, position the insertion point where you want to make the change and proceed to step 2.

2. Choose Fo<u>r</u>mat, <u>M</u>argins; or press Ctrl+F8. Or, click the top of the Ruler Bar with the right mouse button and choose <u>M</u>argins from the resulting QuickMenu. The Margins dialog box appears (see fig. 4.10).

 **TIP** To specify wide margins for binding left- and right-facing pages, choose <u>F</u>ile, <u>P</u>rint; choose the Two-Sided Printing tab; and specify the <u>P</u>rinting Offset Measurement you want for the left, right, top, or bottom margin.

**FIG. 4.10**
Change the Margin settings in the current document using the Margins dialog box.

3. Type new margin settings in the dialog box or click the increment/decrement arrows to change the settings.

 **TIP** Any time you have to enter a measurement, you can use decimals, fractions, or even other units of measure such as points (72p = 1 inch) or centimeters (2.55c = 1 inch).

4. Click OK to return to the document screen.

WordPerfect inserts the new margin settings in the document. Notice that WordPerfect inserts separate codes for each margin setting you change.

To change margins using the margin guidelines, position the mouse pointer on the margin guideline, and drag the guideline to adjust the margin. You can drag the top or bottom margin guidelines as well as the left or right guidelines as long as you are editing in Page mode (choose View, Page; or Alt+F5).

To change left or right margins using the Ruler Bar, position the mouse pointer on the margin indicator on the Ruler Bar (see fig. 4.11) and drag it to the left or right to adjust the margin setting. Ruler Bar guides can help you determine where the new margins should be located, but to use them you first must choose Edit, Preferences, Display, select the Ruler Bar tab, and choose Show Ruler Bar Guides.

You can also change margins with the QuickFormat feature, or with a paragraph style. For details, see the "Formatting Text with QuickFormat" section later in this chapter.

**NOTE** WordPerfect uses the Document Initial Codes style for determining the margin settings for Headers/Footers. For example, if the Document Initial Codes style contains a left/right margin code of 1.5" for each side, and you have a left/right margin code of 0.75" within the body of the document, WordPerfect still uses the 1.5" setting for the Header/Footer unless you specifically change it. To find out how to create headers and footers, see Chapter 5, "Formatting Pages and Documents."

▶ See "Selecting Page Size and Type," **p. 179**
▶ See "Using Styles," **p. 352**

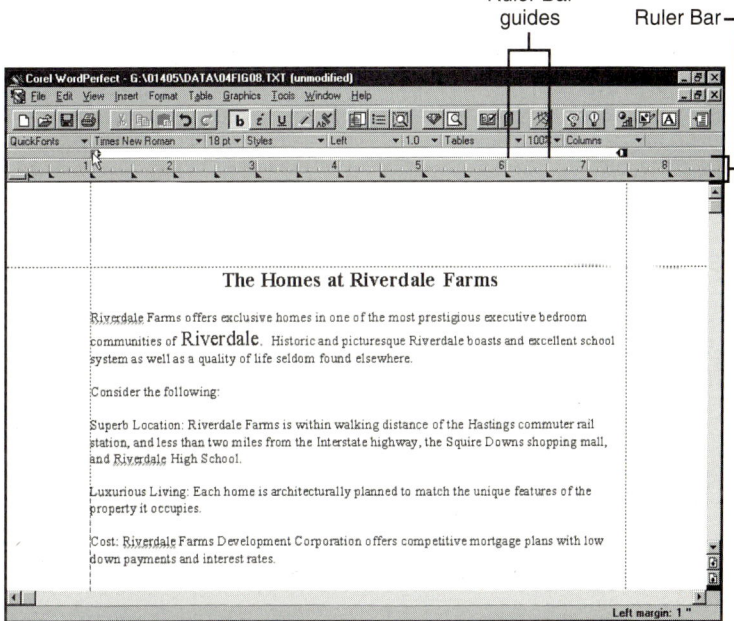

**FIG. 4.11**
Use the Ruler Bar and Ruler Bar guides to change margin settings by dragging the margin indicator.

## Using Indent and Back Tab

You can indent one or more paragraphs to emphasize the text, format a long quotation, or create subordinate levels. You can use the Indent command to indent text quickly, in effect creating a temporary margin without changing the margins. Several related commands—Double Indent, Back Tab, and Hanging Indent—also enable you to change margins temporarily.

 **Indent and Double Indent**   To indent a paragraph to the first tab stop from the left margin, move the insertion point to the beginning of the paragraph and choose Format, Paragraph, Indent; or press F7. Using the mouse, you can choose Indent from the QuickSpot Paragraph properties dialog box, or from the QuickMenu. You can use multiple indents to indent the margin to the corresponding tab stops.

 To indent both left and right margins, move the insertion point to the start of the paragraph and choose Format, Paragraph, Double Indent; or press Ctrl+Shift+F7.

To indent several paragraphs at once, first select the paragraphs, and then follow the steps for indenting or double-indenting a single paragraph. Figure 4.12 shows the effect of various indenting options.

**FIG. 4.12**
When you apply these commands "manually," they override any paragraph style settings for text indents.

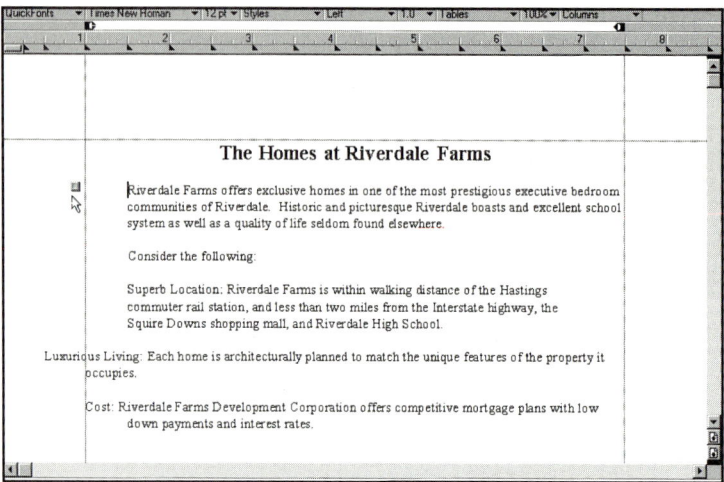

To learn how to set tabs, see the section "Setting and Using Tabs" later in this chapter.

> **CAUTION**
> Don't try to create indents or tabs with the space bar and Enter key. You may get satisfactory results on-screen and even in a printout, but you won't be able to edit the text without a great deal of difficulty.

**Back Tab**   To begin the first line of a paragraph to the left of the current left margin, choose Format, Paragraph, Back Tab; or press Shift+Tab (refer to fig. 4.12). This is sometimes referred to as *releasing the margin*. You can Back Tab only as far to the left as your printer can print.

 **Hanging Indent**   To create a hanging indent, choose Format, Paragraph, Hanging Indent; or press Ctrl+F7.

This command inserts separate Left Indent and Back Tab codes. To delete a hanging indent, you must delete both codes.

You can also create a hanging indent by pressing F7 (Indent), Shift+Tab.

## Setting and Using Tabs

Unlike indents, which affect all text until a hard return is encountered, tabs position text only in the current line (unless Outlining is turned on). To learn more about outlining, see Chapter 15, "Organizing Documents with Outlining."

Tabs are used primarily to indent the first line of a paragraph so that data is organized in tabular columns.

Tab stops determine where WordPerfect positions a tab or an indent code that you insert in the text, and also how text is aligned at a given tab stop.

 **TIP** Don't use Tab when you want to indent an entire paragraph. Instead, use the Indent, Hanging Indent, Double Indent, and Back Tab commands.

**Types of Tabs**   WordPerfect has four types of tabs:

- *Left Align.* Text flows from the tab stop to the right; this alignment is commonly used for ordinary text.
- *Center.* Text centers at the tab stop and extends to right and left from the tab stop.
- *Right Align.* Text flows from the tab stop to the left.
- *Decimal Align.* Text flows from the tab stop to the left until you type the alignment character. After you type the alignment character, text flows to the right from the tab stop. This type of tab is used most commonly to align columns of numbers around decimal points. The default alignment character is a period (or decimal point).

You can use dot leaders with tabs so that a line of dots (dot leaders) connects tab stops. Dot leaders are useful when the space between tabular columns is wide and the reader's eye needs help to associate elements across the gap.

You can create dot leaders with all four types of WordPerfect tab settings: Left, Center, Right, and Decimal. In each case, when you press Tab, WordPerfect moves the insertion point to the next tab setting on the ruler, filling the space from the previous tab setting with dot leader characters.

The default tab stops are left-aligned, every 1/2 inch for 14 inches, from -1 inch to 13 inches.

**NOTE**   Tabs are measured from the left margin, not the left edge of the page. When you create text in columns, tabs are also measured from the left margin of each column, not the left edge of the current page.

**Setting Tabs on the Ruler Bar**   You can quickly set tabs with the Ruler Bar. To move a tab on the ruler, drag it to the new location. As you drag the tab marker, a vertical dotted line extends down through the text (if you have turned on Ruler Bar guides by choosing Edit, Preferences), indicating where the tab will be placed (see fig. 4.13). To place the tab, release the mouse button while the mouse pointer is positioned over the Ruler Bar.

**FIG. 4.13**
Use the Ruler Bar to reposition tab stops, or to add or remove tab stops.

Dotted line indicating where the tab will be placed

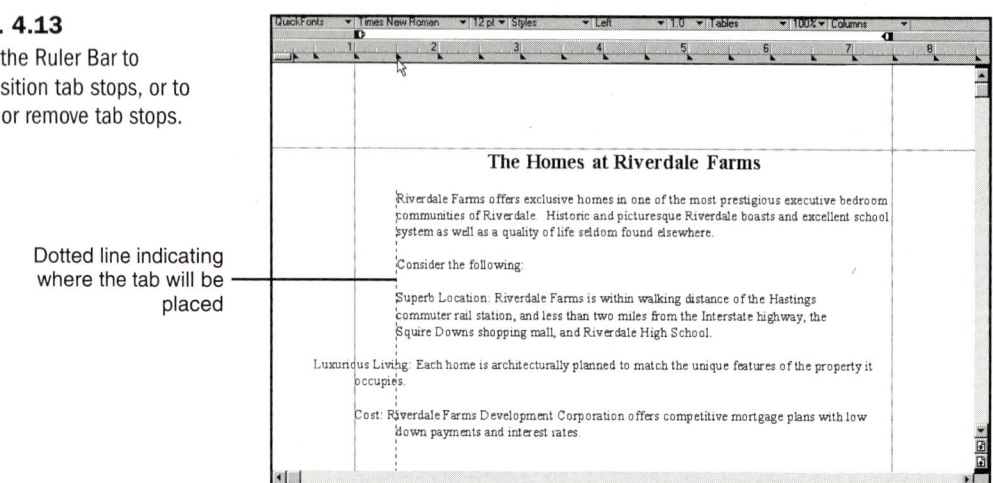

To insert a new left tab with the Ruler Bar, click the Tab area of the ruler beneath the numbered ruler scale. To remove a tab with the Ruler Bar, drag it onto another tab mark, or drag it below the ruler. Dragging a tab mark onto another tab marker replaces the "bottom" tab. If you change your mind about moving or deleting a tab while dragging the tab marker, move the mouse cursor above the Ruler Bar until the tab marker snaps back to its original position, or after releasing the mouse button, use Undo (choose Edit, Undo; or press Ctrl+Z).

To restore default tab settings to the Ruler Bar, choose Format, Line, Tab Set, Default, and click OK.

As you drag a tab mark with the mouse, the status bar shows the position of the tab in 1/16-inch increments. This makes it easier to place tabs at precise intervals. You can place tabs at even more precise intervals of hundredths of an inch by holding down the Shift key while you drag a tab marker. When you drag a tab marker, the status line indicates tab settings in hundredths of an inch. You can turn off the 1/16-inch increments permanently by following the procedure given in the next section.

**Customizing the Ruler Display**   By default, the Ruler Bar does not appear on-screen. To display the Ruler Bar, simply choose View, Toolbars/Ruler, and check the Ruler Bar check box. Selecting this check box turns on the ruler by default for the current and all new WordPerfect documents.

You also can set options that determine how WordPerfect displays the Ruler Bar. To change the Ruler Bar options, follow these steps:

1. Choose Edit, Preferences, and double-click the Display icon. Or, click the right mouse button above the tab line, and then choose Preferences from the resulting QuickMenu.

2. In the Display dialog box, choose the Ruler Bar tab. WordPerfect displays the Ruler Bar options (see fig. 4.14).

**FIG. 4.14**
Choose the Ruler Bar tab in the Display Preferences dialog box to change how the Ruler Bar displays.

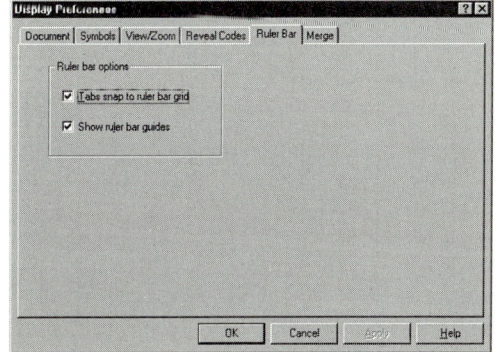

3. Choose Ruler Bar options; then choose OK, then Close to return to the document screen.

 You can also display the Display Preferences dialog box by double-clicking the Ruler Bar above the tab scale.

The following list describes the Ruler display options:

- *Tabs Snap To Ruler Bar Grid.* Displaying the ruler activates invisible gridlines at 1/16 inch, 1/5 centimeter, or the equivalent interval for the unit of measure you choose. With this check box selected, when you move or place a tab, the tab snaps to the gridline nearest your placement. Deselecting this option allows you to place a tab anywhere on the ruler. WordPerfect will not snap the tab setting to the closest gridline.

- *Show Ruler Bar Guides.* When you use the ruler to position tabs, by default a dotted vertical line extends from the bottom of the tab to the bottom of the screen as you use the mouse to move the tab along the ruler. To turn this feature off, deselect the check box.

 To override the grid setting while placing a tab with the ruler grid active, hold down the Shift key while you place the tab.

**Setting Tabs from the Tab Set Dialog Box**  The Tab Set dialog box enables you to set tabs precisely and specify tab options that are not available with the Ruler Bar. To display the Tab Set dialog box, choose Fo_r_mat, _L_ine, and then choose _T_ab Set. Or, click the right mouse button in the Ruler Bar above the ruler line, and then choose _T_ab Set from the resulting QuickMenu. WordPerfect displays the Tab Set dialog box (see fig. 4.15).

**FIG. 4.15**
Use the Tab Set dialog box to position tabs in precise increments as small as 1/1,000 inch.

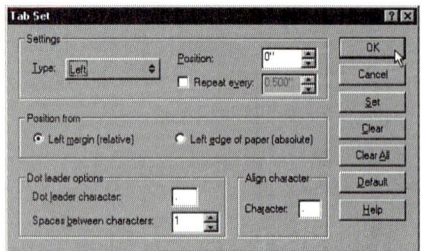

 You can also open the Tab Set dialog box by double-clicking any tab mark.

With the Tab Set dialog box, you can position tabs from -1 to 53.61 inches, relative to the left margin (0 to 54 1/2 inches from the left edge of the paper).

To set a tab with the Tab Set dialog box, follow these steps:

1. Choose _T_ype and select a type from the list: Left, Center, Right, Decimal, Dot Left, Dot Center, Dot Right, or Dot Decimal.

2. Choose _P_osition and type or scroll to a position in inches (") or centimeters (c or cm). You can set a position from -1 to 53.61, but WordPerfect won't insert tabs on or beyond the left edge of the currently selected paper size.

3. To insert tab marks across the ruler at even intervals, choose Repeat E_v_ery and type or scroll to an interval setting. You can specify tab intervals from 0.100 inch to 10 inches.

4. To position tabs from the left margin, choose Left _M_argin (Relative). Or choose Left _E_dge of Paper (Absolute) to measure tabs from the left side of the page.

    If you use columns in a document, choose Left _M_argin (Relative) to create uniform paragraph indents throughout the columns. Tabs will be measured from the left margin of each column. If you change the left or right margins, the tabs shift with the new margins.

5. To change the character used for dot leaders, choose Dot Leader Character and type a character for the dot leaders.

6. To adjust the space between dot leaders, choose Spaces Between Characters and type or scroll to a new number.

7. To change the align character for decimal tabs, choose Character and type the new character.

8. Choose Set to insert the new tab. WordPerfect inserts a new tab mark in the Ruler Bar.

9. Repeat steps 1–8 for each new tab that you want to set.

10. Choose OK to return to the document.

To clear all tab marks from the Ruler Bar, click Clear All from the Tab Set dialog box. To clear a single tab, choose Position and type the tab's position; then click Clear. To restore WordPerfect's default tab settings, click Default.

You can set a maximum of 40 tabs. When you insert evenly spaced tabs, WordPerfect uses all the remaining available tabs.

**Setting Tabs with the QuickMenu**   You can also set tabs by selecting the type of tab you want to create from the QuickMenu. To display the QuickMenu, right-click the lower half of the Ruler Bar (see fig. 4.16). Then, select the type of tab you want to set.

**FIG. 4.16**
Use the Tab QuickMenu to quickly choose a tab type.

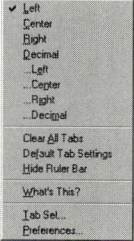

**Inserting Hard Tabs**   When you define new tab settings, WordPerfect reformats the text from that point forward in your document. If you replace a left tab mark with a center tab mark, for example, all the left tab marks at that tab stop become center tabs from that point forward. To restore the preceding tab settings, you must either delete the new tab set code or create a new tab setting with the former tab placement.

You can prevent tabs from changing when you redefine tab settings by using Hard Tabs. Hard Tabs remain constant, even if you later insert a new tab definition above the Hard Tab position.

To insert a Hard Tab, follow these steps:

1. Choose Format, Line.
2. Choose Other Codes. The Other Codes dialog box appears (see fig. 4.17).

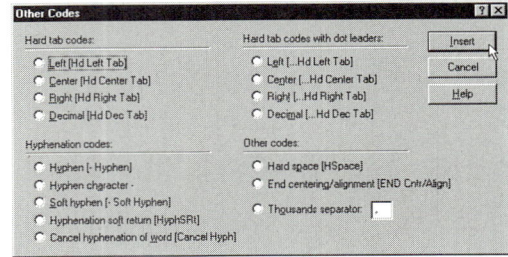

**FIG. 4.17**
Use the Other Codes dialog box to insert Hard Tabs in your document.

3. Choose a hard tab code, and then click Insert to return to the document.

**Changing the Decimal Align Character** *Decimal tabs* are used most often to align columns of numbers at the decimal point. When you press Tab to move to a decimal tab and begin typing, WordPerfect inserts the text to the left until you type the decimal align character (normally a period), and then inserts any further characters to the right.

You can change the decimal align character. For example, colons are often used in descriptive lists, and in some foreign countries, numbers are formatted with commas as the decimal character, instead of periods.

To change the decimal align character, follow these steps:

1. Choose Format, Line, Tab Set. The Tab Set dialog box appears.
2. In the Character text box, type a new decimal align character; then choose OK to return to the document.

# Formatting Text with QuickFormat

QuickFormat enables you to quickly copy fonts and attributes (boldface, italic, and more) or paragraph styles that you've already applied elsewhere in a document to another paragraph or to selected text. To copy formatting with QuickFormat, follow these steps:

1. Move the insertion point into a paragraph that has the format you want to copy; or select the text whose formatting you want to copy.

2. Choose Format, QuickFormat. Alternatively, click the right mouse button in the document text window and choose QuickFormat from the QuickMenu, or click the QuickFormat button on the Toolbar. WordPerfect displays the QuickFormat dialog box (see fig. 4.18).

**FIG. 4.18**
From the QuickFormat dialog box, you can choose to copy the fonts and attributes of a paragraph, the paragraph styles, or both.

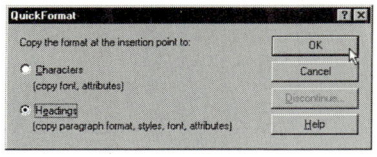

3. In the QuickFormat dialog box, choose Characters to copy only the fonts and attributes of the paragraph that contains the insertion point; or choose Headings to copy the paragraph styles, fonts, and attributes.
4. Choose OK. The mouse pointer becomes a paintbrush.
5. Drag the paintbrush over the text you want to reformat. When you release the mouse button, WordPerfect applies the format to the selected text.

QuickFormat remains in effect until you choose QuickFormat again.

The Headings option in the QuickFormat dialog box copies paragraph styles (margins, for example) as well as character attributes. When you choose this option, the mouse pointer turns into a paint roller, and you apply the style to headings (paragraphs).

Even after you turn the feature off, the QuickFormat styles you use are listed on the Power Bar Styles button as QuickFormat1, QuickFormat2, and so on, and can be applied to selected text just like any other style, unless you choose Discontinue from the QuickFormat dialog box (refer to fig. 4.18).

## Customizing Formatting Options

By default, WordPerfect displays certain indicators on-screen to help you format your document. These include the margin gridlines, Header and Footer gridlines, and Tab setting markers. WordPerfect also can display symbols on-screen to indicate the position of tabs, spaces, and other formatting features. To turn on these display options, follow these steps:

1. Choose Edit, Preferences.
2. Double-click the Display icon and select the Symbols tab. The Display Preferences dialog box appears with the Symbols preferences displayed (see fig. 4.19).
3. To turn on display of formatting symbols, choose the Show Symbols On New And Current Document check box.
4. Choose check boxes for the desired symbols under Symbols To Display; then choose OK and Close to return to the document screen.

The options under Symbols To Display include Space, Hard Return, Tab, Indent, Center, Flush Right, Soft Hyphen, Advance, and Center Page.

**FIG. 4.19**
The Symbols tab in the Display Preferences dialog box enables you to turn on the display of formatting symbols.

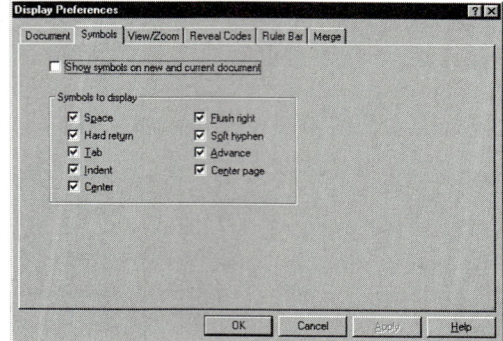

Table 4.2 lists the symbols that WordPerfect displays in the document window for each of these formatting options.

### Table 4.2  Formatting Symbols

| Formatting Command | Symbol |
| --- | --- |
| Space | · |
| Hard Return | ¶ |
| Tab | → |
| Indent | ↔ |
| Center | ↕ |
| Flush Right | →\| |
| Soft Hyphen | – |
| Advance | \|→ |
| Center Page | Page graphic symbol |

These symbols are displayed in both Draft and Page views.

 **TIP** Choose View, Show or press Ctrl+Shift+F3 to toggle the display of these formatting characters.

▶ See "Customizing the Display," **p. 300**

# Using Justification

*Justification* aligns text on the left margin, right margin, both margins, or centered between the margins. Justification affects text alignment until you turn it off or insert a new justification code. These effects are shown in figure 4.20.

**FIG. 4.20**
When you press Enter and type a new line, WordPerfect applies the same justification that was in effect on the preceding line.

All Justification
Left justification (Ctrl+L)
Full justification (Ctrl+J)
Right justification (Ctrl+R)
Center justification (Ctrl+E)

 *Full justification* adjusts the word and letter spacing to format text flush with the left and right margins. This gives text a formal look. To apply full justification, choose Format, Justification, Full; or press Ctrl+J.

 *Left justification,* the default in WordPerfect, is also called *flush left* or *ragged right.* Left justification aligns text with the left margin and leaves the right margin uneven. Left justification, used in most of this book, is considered to be slightly easier to read but less formal than full justification. To apply left justification, choose Format, Justification, Left; or press Ctrl+L.

 *Right justification,* sometimes called *ragged left* or *flush right,* aligns text on the right margin. Right justification is harder to read than left or full justification, and should be used sparingly. It is sometimes used in letterheads. To apply right justification, choose Format, Justification, Right; or press Ctrl+R.

 *Center justification* centers each line between the left and right margins. To apply center justification, choose Format, Justification, Center; or press Ctrl+E.

 When you choose full justification, WordPerfect does not justify lines at the ends of paragraphs that do not extend to the right margin. *Justify All* forces WordPerfect to justify

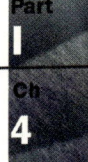

these lines. If a line contains just a few words, WordPerfect justifies the text by increasing the space between words and letters. Some graphic designers use this effect to create a special effect; for example, a company's name may be force-justified between the margins at the top of a letterhead. To apply forced justification, choose Format, Justification, All. There is no quick keystroke for this code.

When using justified or flush-left text, be sure to hyphenate the text to improve the word and letter spacing.

When you apply justification with text selected, WordPerfect justifies the block of text and retains the previous text alignment for text following the selected block.

You can also use the Power Bar to apply justification to lines of text in your document. To do so, click the Justification button in the Power Bar (refer to fig. 4.2), and select the justification setting from the resulting list.

▶ See "Considering Types of Styles," **p. 336**
▶ See "Designing Successful Publications," **p. 725**

### TROUBLESHOOTING

**As I type, the text seems to jump all over the place until I finish a line, then the next line does the same thing.** You probably have Full Justification turned on, so WordPerfect is trying to spread out the line as you type. Choose Left justification while typing, then change to Full Justification if you want to format the document after it is typed.

# Using Hyphenation

The Hyphenation feature splits words that extend beyond the right margin instead of moving them to the next line. Hyphenation can improve the appearance of documents by preventing large spaces at the ends of lines in left-justified text, or between words and letters in full-justified text. WordPerfect can automate hyphenation for you, or you can insert hyphens manually. You can also override WordPerfect's placement of automatic hyphens.

## Splitting Words with Hyphens

You can split words with four different kinds of hyphens, each of which serves a different purpose:

- *Hard hyphen.* This inserts a visible hyphen in a word; for example, "hard-won victories." WordPerfect hyphenates the word if the part after the hyphen extends beyond the hyphenation zone. (The hyphenation zone is explained later in this chapter in the section "Setting the Hyphenation Zone.") You insert a hard hyphen by pressing the hyphen key on the top row of the keyboard or the minus key on the numeric keypad. The hidden code is [-Hyphen].

- *Soft hyphen.* This inserts an invisible hyphen that becomes visible if the word is split at the end of a line. Inserting a soft hyphen enables you to tell WordPerfect where to hyphenate words that may not be included in its hyphenation dictionary. You insert a soft hyphen by pressing Ctrl+Shift+hyphen, or by choosing it from the Other Codes dialog box. (Choose Format, Line, Other Codes.) The hidden code is [- Soft Hyphen].

- *Hyphenation soft return.* This splits a word without a hyphen if a split is required at the end of a line. You insert a hyphenation soft return from the Other Codes dialog box. (Choose Format, Line, Other Codes.) The hidden code is [Hyph SRt].

# Preventing Hyphenation

You may want to prevent WordPerfect from splitting certain words, such as company or product names (DuPont, WordPerfect) or long, hyphenated proper names (Santos-Dumas). WordPerfect has three codes that prevent words from splitting at the end of a line:

- *Cancel hyphenation of word.* This tells WordPerfect to move the entire word to the next line. You insert this code at the beginning of a word, from the Other Codes dialog box. The hidden code is [Cancel Hyph].

- *Hyphen character.* This is a short dash that is ignored during hyphenation—for example, in negative numbers and in subtraction problems. To insert a hyphen character, press the minus key on the numeric keypad, or press Ctrl+hyphen (on the top row of the keyboard). Pressing the hyphen character on the top row of the keyboard inserts a [- Hyphen] code, which is *not* ignored during hyphenation. You can also insert a hyphen character from the Other Codes dialog box. The hidden code is a hyphen [-].

- *Hard space.* This prints as a space but keeps two words together. You enter a hard space from the Other Codes dialog box. The hidden code is [HSpace]. You can also insert a hard space by pressing Ctrl+space.

## Using Automatic Hyphenation

WordPerfect's default mode is Hyphenation Off; words are wrapped to the next line rather than hyphenated. Of course, you can hyphenate words manually, as described earlier in "Splitting Words with Hyphens."

To turn on hyphenation in a document, follow these steps:

1. Choose Format, Line, Hyphenation. The Line Hyphenation dialog box appears (see fig. 4.21).

**FIG. 4.21**
Besides turning hyphenation on, in the Line Hyphenation dialog box, set the size of the hyphenation zone which determines how "ragged" or informal the text will look after hyphenation. The larger the zone, the more ragged the text.

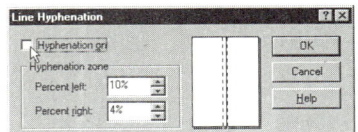

2. Choose Hyphenation On; then choose OK.

WordPerfect places the [Hyph: On] code at the insertion point, where it affects all text that follows it.

**TIP** Left-justified lines look best with the hyphenation zone set to the default 10% Percent Left and 4% Percent Right hyphenation zone settings or larger values.

To turn on hyphenation for the entire document, go to the top of the document (Ctrl+Home) and follow the preceding steps. You can also turn on hyphenation in a Document Initial style. To learn how to use a Document Initial style, see Chapter 5, "Formatting Pages and Documents," and Chapter 10, "Using Styles."

## Choosing a Hyphenation Point

When WordPerfect hyphenates a word, it consults a dictionary file which also contains hyphenation instructions for the words it contains. If the word is in the dictionary, WordPerfect inserts a soft hyphen at the break point nearest the right margin, and splits the word at that point.

If WordPerfect doesn't find the word in its dictionary, it displays the Position Hyphen dialog box and asks you to indicate where you want to put the hyphen.

The word appears with a hyphen initially positioned at the right margin. Use the mouse or arrow keys to place the hyphen where you want to divide the word.

You can position the word break only within the hyphenation zone. After selecting a break point, you can split the word in the following ways:

- To split the word with a hyphen, choose Insert Hyphen. WordPerfect inserts a soft hyphen at the break point and splits the word with a visible hyphen.

- To split the word or phrase without a hyphen, choose Hyphenation SRt. WordPerfect inserts a hyphenation soft return code [Hyph SRt] at the break point and splits the word without a hyphen.

  If you later edit the text and move a word hyphenated with a soft hyphen or a hyphenation soft return away from the hyphenation zone, WordPerfect rejoins the word automatically.

- To break the word or phrase into two distinct elements separated by an ordinary space, choose Insert Space. No hidden code is inserted. The elements subsequently function as if you had typed them as two distinct words.

  The Insert Space option may be most useful when you insert text that abuts another word, and the combined words push across the hyphenation zone. With hyphenation on, WordPerfect treats the inserted text and adjoining word as a single word requiring hyphenation. You cannot continue until you choose one of the options in the Position Hyphen dialog box. By choosing Insert Space, you put a space between elements that will probably end up separated by a space anyway. If the natural break point isn't visible in the window, choose Suspend Hyphenation.

- To keep the word intact with no break, choose Ignore Word. WordPerfect inserts a [Cancel Hyph] code before the word and wraps the word to the next line.

  While scrolling through a document, you may not want to stop to hyphenate words. WordPerfect includes an option to stop hyphenation temporarily.

  ▶ **See** "Formatting Options," **p. 309**

## Removing Hyphenation from a Document

Hyphenation codes that WordPerfect inserts remain embedded in the hyphenated words even after you turn off hyphenation.

You can remove the hyphenation codes from a document manually or automatically. To remove the codes manually, turn on Reveal Codes and delete them individually.

To remove the codes all at once, choose Edit, Find and Replace to replace the codes with nothing, as in the following steps:

1. Press Ctrl+Home to move to the very beginning of the document.
2. Choose Edit, Find and Replace; or press F2 or Ctrl+F. The Find and Replace Text dialog box appears.
3. Choose Match, Codes. The Codes dialog box appears (see fig. 4.22).

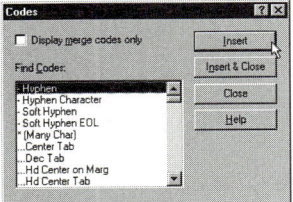

**FIG. 4.22**
The Find Codes list box in the Codes dialog box contains many useful codes that you can replace.

4. Choose Soft Hyphen, and click Insert & Close. WordPerfect places a [- Soft Hyphen] code in the Find box.
5. Choose Replace All. WordPerfect replaces all soft hyphens with nothing.
6. Choose Close to return to the editing screen.

▶ See "Using Find and Replace," p. 111

**TIP** To scroll quickly to the desired item in the Codes dialog box, begin typing the item. WordPerfect jumps to the entry. This "speed scroll" feature is built into all WordPerfect's scrollable list boxes.

## Customizing the Hyphenation Prompt

The hyphenation options available in Environment Preferences establish how much input you can have in hyphenation decisions.

To set hyphenation prompt options, follow these steps:

1. Choose Edit, Preferences.
2. Double-click the Environment icon. The Environment Preferences dialog box appears.
3. Choose Hyphenation Prompt and choose an option from the pop-up menu.
4. Choose OK, Close to return to the document screen.

The following list describes the Hyphenation Prompt options:

- *Always*. WordPerfect prompts you to decide where to place the hyphen in every word that requires hyphenation.
- *Never.* If the word cannot be found in the dictionary, or the dictionary indicates that no hyphenation for the word exists, or the rule-set doesn't indicate a logical place for hyphenation, the word wraps to the next line.
- *When Required.* The word is hyphenated according to the dictionary or the internal rule-set. If the word cannot be found or the rule-set cannot affect a decision, WordPerfect prompts you for a hyphenation point. When Required is the default.

If you choose Never for the Hyphenation Prompt option, WordPerfect hyphenates fewer words, resulting in a more ragged right margin with left justification turned on, or more white space with full justification. If you choose When Required (the default), the internal rule-set asks for hyphenation confirmation more often than the external dictionary would. ●

CHAPTER 5

# Formatting Pages and Documents

*by Judy Petersen*

**W**hether you are writing a letter or a doctoral dissertation, designing a flyer or 20-page newsletter, sending a form letter to all your customers or automating your documents, the formatting features in WordPerfect make it possible for these documents to have a professional appearance. The longer the document, the more important are the features that enhance readability and organization, such as page numbering, headers, and footers.

You need to make decisions about the layout of a document at many levels, including the layout of individual lines of text, paragraphs, entire pages, and the document as a whole. WordPerfect groups these formatting commands in the Format pull-down menu. This chapter focuses on the features that format pages and documents.

A number of WordPerfect features are available to control page layout. Many are features that have previously been available, only with more complex and specialized desktop publishing software. ■

### Center text on a page and keep text together
Create cover pages by centering text from left to right and from the top to bottom of the page.

### Design, create, and edit headers and footers
Design, create, and edit text that appears at the top or bottom of pages.

### Number the pages in your documents
Add and position page numbers on each page.

### Create, edit, and use page definitions for documents, labels, and envelopes
Create, edit, and use different paper and envelope sizes and labels.

### Modify font, redline, and other initial settings
Change some of the default settings WordPerfect provides for your documents.

### Create a database of document summaries
Include information about each document in a summary.

All the features discussed in this chapter place hidden formatting codes in your text. Refer to Chapter 3, "Retrieving and Editing Documents," for more information about hidden codes. These codes provide special information on how to display your text on-screen or how to print the various formatting effects on the page or in your document.

> **NOTE** When formatting a document, consider displaying the Page Toolbar where many of the frequently used page format commands are only a click away. Right-click the current Toolbar to display a menu of available Toolbars, or select the Page Toolbar by choosing P**r**eferences, **T**oolbar.

▶ **See** "Understanding WordPerfect's Hidden Codes," **p. 91**
▶ **See** "Using WordPerfect's Text-Formatting Tools," **p. 122**
▶ **See** "Reveal Codes Display," **p. 305**
▶ **See** "Switching Between Toolbars," **p. 415**

# Creating Separate Pages

WordPerfect automatically divides your document into pages based on the formatting choices you have made. These automatic page breaks are called *soft page breaks*. When you access Reveal Codes, note that each page of text ends with a [SPg] code. If the soft page break falls on the location of a hard return, the hard return code is saved and the new code appears as [HRt-SPg].

A soft page break often occurs at a blank line, such as when a break falls on the hard return between paragraphs. To prevent this blank line from being carried to the top of the next page, but retain it should later editing move the page break location elsewhere, WordPerfect inserts a dormant hard return [Dorm HRt] to save the blank line.

Because it is often necessary to cause a page to break at a specific location or prevent page breaks from dividing text that should be kept together, WordPerfect offers ways to control where pages are divided, as described in the following sections and the later section "Keeping Text Together."

## Inserting Page Breaks

As you edit a document, adding and deleting text and changing formats, WordPerfect recalculates the soft page break locations. To ensure that a page breaks at a specific location, regardless of format changes, use the Page Break feature. Use a page break to end a specific document section and to ensure that the new section starts on the next page. Page breaks also are appropriate to end a cover page, preface, chapter, appendix, or table of contents.

To insert a page break, place the insertion point at the exact location where you want the page to break. Then choose Insert, Page Break; or press Ctrl+Enter. A hard page break code in the Reveal Codes window appears as [HPg]. The only way to override this page break is to delete it.

## Forcing New Pages

Beginning chapters or sections on the right side of facing pages gives a professional appearance to complex documents. The simple way to make sure that this occurs is to insert a page break at the beginning of a chapter or section and then force an odd page number. Forcing an odd page number ensures this right-side placement regardless of later text insertions or deletions.

Forcing a new page is another way to cause a page to break at a specific location. You can force a new page as well as force an odd or even page number.

To use the Force Page command, follow these steps.

1. Choose Format, Page, Force Page. The Force Page dialog box opens (see fig. 5.1).

**FIG. 5.1**
In the Force Page dialog box, you can choose to force a new page or to force an odd or even page number for the current page.

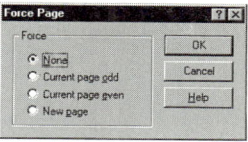

2. From the options in the dialog box, choose New Page to start a new page at the beginning of the current paragraph. Alternatively, choose Current Page Odd or Current Page Even to force the page number to change accordingly.

3. Choose OK or press Enter to return to your document.

If you chose to force a new page, WordPerfect inserts a [Force: New] code in your document at the beginning of the current paragraph. As with hard page breaks, later editing may move the new page to an unacceptable location. To cancel the code, locate and then delete it in the Reveal Codes window.

> **NOTE** This chapter provides you with the actual code text that WordPerfect inserts in your document when you choose a format, although an abbreviated version of the code is displayed unless you choose to display codes in detail as described in the Reveal Codes section in Chapter 9, "Customizing WordPerfect."

When you force an odd or an even page number, WordPerfect places a [Force: Odd] or [Force: Even] code at the top of the current page. If the code changes the current page number, WordPerfect adds a blank page by inserting a [THPg] (*Temporary Hard Page Break*) code before the Force code. Page formatting text—such as headers, footers, and page numbering—prints on the blank page.

## Centering Pages

Centering a page between the top and bottom margins is a quick way to position a small amount of text that stands alone on a page, such as a short memo or list. Centering a page repositions the material in relation to the top and bottom margins only.

> **TIP** To center text properly on a page, the text should not start or end with extra hard returns unless you want to use the resulting blank lines to place the text slightly off-center.

You also can quickly center several sequential pages of a document by using the Current And Subsequent Pages option of the Center command. This feature is helpful, for example, with documents that begin with several individual pages of brief, introductory material.

To center text on the page, follow these steps:

1. Choose Fo_r_mat, _P_age, _C_enter. The Center Page(s) dialog box opens (see fig. 5.2).

**FIG. 5.2**
Choose whether to center a single page, multiple pages, or turn off centering in the Center Page(s) dialog box.

2. In the Center Page(s) dialog box, choose one of the following options:
   - *Current _P_age*. Center only the page where the cursor is located.
   - *Current And _S_ubsequent Pages*. Begin centering all pages beginning at the current cursor location.
   - *_N_o Centering*. End centering of current and subsequent pages.
3. Choose OK or press Enter to return to your document.

The single code [Cntr Cur Pg: On] appears in the Reveal Codes window to center the current page. The code for centering the current and subsequent pages is [Cntr Pgs: On].

The text displays centered on the page in Page mode, but does not appear centered when you are using Draft mode.

 **TIP** Use Center Page to quickly place a short note on letterhead stationery, or for title or cover pages, acknowledgments, and prefaces.

To center a single page of text in a document longer than one page, you must indicate the beginning and the end of the text to be centered. Insert a page break at the end of the centered text if it is the first page of your document. Place a page break at the beginning and the end of the text to be centered if the text is in the middle of a document. (Refer to the "Inserting Page Breaks" section earlier in this chapter for instructions on inserting page breaks.)

▶ **See** "Using Justification," **p. 147**

To cancel centering of a page, delete the code in the Reveal Codes window. To end centering of subsequent pages, place the cursor where you want to end centering and choose No Centering in the Center Page(s) dialog box.

# Keeping Text Together

The capability of word processing software to automate the layout of typed text may well be the most common impetus for purchasing a personal computer. To enhance the capabilities of automated layout, WordPerfect uses standard formatting rules for document layout, controlling the way that automated layout divides pages. You can use the Block Protect, Conditional End Of Page, and Widow/Orphan Protection commands to prevent problems such as section names that dangle at the bottom of a page and page breaks that occur in the middle of a list or table. The following sections cover these commands.

## Block Protect

The Block Protect feature places codes at the beginning and end of a section of text that you want to keep together on the same page. As you edit the protected text, the block expands or shrinks to accommodate your changes.

When WordPerfect encounters a Block Protect code, the program determines whether the entire block of text fits in the space remaining on the present page. If the block doesn't fit, the program inserts a soft page break above the block, which then begins the next page. Block Protect is particularly useful for keeping a list, table, figure and the text that describes it, or a series of numbered paragraphs on the same page.

To protect a block of text, follow these steps:

1. Highlight the block of text you want to protect.

2. Choose Format, Page, Keep Text Together. The Keep Text Together dialog box opens (see fig. 5.3).

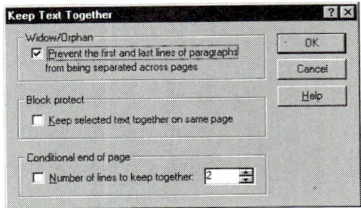

**FIG. 5.3**
In the Keep Text Together dialog box, you can choose to protect a block of text, turn on Widow/Orphan protection, or specify a number of lines to keep together following titles or headings.

3. Choose Keep Selected Text Together On Same Page so a check appears in the check box.
4. Choose OK or press Enter to return to your document.

The paired code that appears in the Reveal Codes window at the beginning and end of the selected text is [Block Pro]. You can remove the protection by deleting either code.

**N O T E** Block Protect is designed to protect a page or less of text. If you add text to a protected block so that the amount of protected text exceeds one page, WordPerfect ignores the Block Protect codes and inserts a soft page break where needed. However, the codes remain around the text. Removing enough text restores the protection. If the text you want to protect contains more than a page of text, try using a smaller font or changing the line spacing to slightly less than one.

## Conditional End of Page

The Conditional End Of Page feature acts to protect a specific number of lines rather than specific text. Use Conditional End Of Page to ensure that titles, headings, and subheadings are not left dangling alone at the bottom of a page. You do so by specifying the number of lines of text to keep together.

To insert a Conditional End Of Page, move the cursor to the beginning of the text you want to protect and follow these steps:

1. Choose Format, Page, Keep Text Together. The Keep Text Together dialog box opens (refer to fig. 5.3).
2. Choose Number Of Lines To Keep Together so a check appears in its check box.

3. In the adjacent text box, enter the number of lines to keep together.
4. Choose OK or press Enter to return to your document.

**NOTE** When using Conditional End Of Page to keep headings together with some of the text that follows, be sure to count the lines between the heading and text and any intervening subheading, as well as enough lines of text. If you triple-space after headings and double-space after subheadings, specify six to eight lines to protect a heading and text, and eight to 10 lines for a heading, subheading, and the text that follows.

The single code [Cond1 EOP: #] appears at the beginning of the protected text in the Reveal Codes window, where # is the number of lines you have chosen to include.

Once the code is inserted, WordPerfect does not permit a page to break within the included lines. If a page would otherwise break within the included lines, WordPerfect inserts the soft page break at the [Cond1 EOP] code. You can always override a Conditional End of Page by inserting a hard page break within the lines the command protects.

## Prevent Widows and Orphans

A heading or subheading dangling at the bottom of a page is not the only time lines appear to be stranded. A single line of a paragraph appearing by itself on the bottom of a page is called an *orphan*. A *widow* is the last line from the end of a paragraph that is pushed to the top of the next page.

To place Widow/Orphan protection in a document, follow these steps:

1. Place the cursor where you want protection to begin, or use Ctrl+Home to move to the beginning of the document.

2. Choose Format, Page, Keep Text Together. The Keep Text Together dialog box opens (refer to fig. 5.3).
3. Choose Prevent The First And Last Lines Of Paragraphs From Being Separated Across Pages so that a check appears in its check box.
4. Choose OK or press Enter to return to your document.

The code appearing in the Reveal Codes window is [Wid/Orph: On].

When Widow/Orphan protection is on, a soft page break cannot be inserted between the first two or last two lines of a paragraph. The two protected lines remain at the bottom of the page or, if located at the end of the paragraph, move to the top of the next page, leaving blank lines at the bottom of the preceding page. Two- and three-line paragraphs move in their entirety.

**TIP** Widow/Orphan protection is used most often to protect an entire document. If you use it regularly, consider including it in a template you create for your preferred document format.

# Working with Facing Pages

WordPerfect provides several commands designed for setting up documents with facing pages. You can place headers and footers on even or odd pages only, offset the printed pages to allow for binding, alternate page-numbering schemes, and force odd or even page numbers.

As you work with commands that place features on odd or even pages, it is easy to confuse odd and even, left and right pages so that you end up superimposing text you mean to place on alternating pages. When choosing an odd or even placement option, try visualizing a printed document bound on the left edge (like this book). When the document is placed on your desk, the top page of the closed document is the first page. When you turn the first page, facing pages are displayed. The second, or even, numbered page is on the left and the third, or odd, numbered page is on the right.

When you use different numbering for the body of a document and individual appendixes, what page do you want to see when you ask for page three? And when labels are pages and you print pages of labels, just exactly what is a page? WordPerfect uses the terms *physical page* and *logical page* to resolve this confusion for the user.

Physical pages are the sides of the actual sheets of page. Logical pages refer to the sides relative to the numbering system used in the document. For example, imagine a book in which the first 10 pages of introductory material have Roman numerals. Those 10 physical pages are logical pages i–x, and the next physical page (11) is logical page 1.

When you work with labels you may have an 8 1/2 × 11-inch sheet covered with 12 labels, for example. The sheet of labels is one physical page, and WordPerfect treats the labels as 12 different logical pages.

When creating Delay codes, for example, the number of pages you specify when setting up a code are the physical pages to skip. The placement of features that you set up to appear on odd or even pages, such as forcing pages or headers and footers, is based on the logical page number. Refer to the sections "Using Delay Codes" and "Using Headers and Footers" later in this chapter for more information.

# Numbering Pages

WordPerfect has the capability of numbering pages automatically, even for complex documents where multiple chapters, introductory parts, and appendixes use different numbering schemes. You can number chapters individually, and opening and closing sections can have different numbering styles, for example.

The page number prints in the top or bottom line of the text area. WordPerfect inserts a blank line to separate the number from the rest of the text. If you use the default 1-inch top and bottom margins for 8 1/2 × 11-inch page and a Courier 10-cpi (characters per inch) font, the text area contains 54 lines. Adding page numbers decreases the number of lines to 52.

In Page mode, page numbers are visible on the page. This makes it easy to immediately preview the page number layout, font, and accompanying text.

To accommodate the most complex of documents, WordPerfect includes five types of page numbers:

- Page and Secondary numbers that increase automatically.
- Chapter and Volume numbers you increase or decrease when appropriate.
- A total pages number that displays the number of pages currently in the document.

In addition, you can number pages with numbers, letters, or Roman numerals. The default page numbering is Arabic numbers that appear at the bottom center of the page.

## Choosing a Page Number Position

There are 10 preset page number positions, including four that place numbers in alternating positions on facing pages. You select the position you want from the Position pop-up menu in the Select Page Numbering Format dialog box.

You can place numbers at the left, center, or right of the top or bottom of the page, and you can alternate page numbers at the outside or inside margins on the top or bottom of facing pages, as in a book. The code inserted at the beginning of the page is [Pg Num Pos: location], which you can see in the Reveal Codes window.

To change the position for page numbers, follow these steps:

1. Choose Format, Page Numbering, Select. The Select Page Numbering Format dialog box shown in figure 5.4 opens.

**FIG. 5.4**
Choose the page number position and page numbering format in the Select Page Numbering Format dialog box; the selection is previewed in the Sample Facing Pages area.

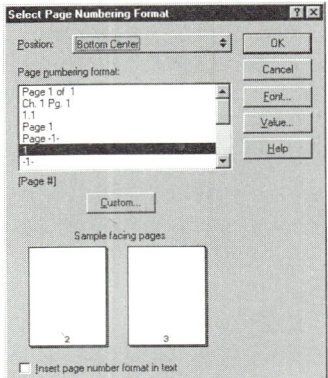

2. Choose one of the following positions from the Position pop-up list:

   | | |
   |---|---|
   | Top Left | Bottom Left |
   | Top Center | Bottom Center |
   | Top Right | Bottom Right |
   | Top Outside Alternating | Bottom Outside Alternating |
   | Top Inside Alternating | Bottom Inside Alternating |

3. Choose OK or press Enter to save the changes and return to your document.

 **TIP** Use alternating numbering when you print a facing-pages document that you plan to staple in the upper corner. If the page is numbered in the upper-right corner, the number on the back of the page may be under the staple.

You access many page-numbering options through the Select Page Numbering Format dialog box. Although the options are discussed here in separate sections, you can choose all the options you want before finally closing the Select Page Numbering Format dialog box.

## Choosing a Page Number Format

WordPerfect can place page numbers in your document using a variety of formats. Preformatted numbering schemes using numbers, lower- or uppercase letters, and lower- or uppercase Roman numerals combined with hyphens and text are available in the Page Numbering Format list box.

To choose a page number format:

1. In the Select Page Numbering Format dialog box (refer to fig. 5.4), choose a page number format from the Page Numbering Format list box.
2. Choose OK or press Enter to save the changes and return to your document.

When you choose a format, the structure of your choice appears just below the list box. If you choose Ch 1. Pg. 1 or 1.1, for example, you see the codes [Chpt #] and [Page #] combined with the appropriate text and punctuation for the format you have selected.

## Customizing the Page Number Appearance

You are not restricted to only the formats in the Page Numbering Format list box. You can create other combinations of number types, add unique text, change the font, use different number styles for each number type (for example, Chapter VII, Page 22), increase or decrease the number or set a new number, and insert page numbering at other locations.

**Changing the Font**   Page numbers appear in the current document default font. To use another font for page numbering, follow these steps:

To change the document font so the features apply automatically to page numbering, choose Format, Document, Initial Font, or add the desired font to the document Initial Codes Style to set up the document format.

1. In the Select Page Numbering Format dialog box, click Font to open the Page Numbering Font dialog box.
2. Choose a typeface and size from the Font Face and Font Size list boxes.
3. Choose Bold, Italic, or Bold Italic from the Font Style list box, or choose one or more of the various styles found in the Appearance section of the Page Numbering Font dialog box.
4. In the Color options section, choose Text Color and press Alt+down arrow or click the down-arrow button and choose a different color for the text from the palette of colors that appears. Click the increment arrows in the Shading text box or type a number to change the intensity of the color of the font.
5. Check the name of the font and view the way it appears in the preview window. When you are satisfied, choose OK to return to the Select Page Numbering Format dialog box.

**Changing Numbering Type**   Five types of page numbers are available with WordPerfect 7. In addition to standard page numbering, you can have another set of page numbers called *secondary numbers*. Journals and newsletters sometimes use two sets of numbers—one that numbers every page consecutively throughout the year, another that numbers the pages in individual issues. You can set up both regular and secondary page numbers in a document and start each with a different number. Either type of page numbers is increased, or incremented, automatically from page to page.

*Chapter* and *volume* numbering are also available. These numbering schemes differ from regular and secondary numbering in that you must instruct WordPerfect when chapter and volume numbers should increase or decrease. You can use volume numbers to number multiple documents and chapter numbers for the sections in each document. Use these with journals and newsletters to provide volume (year) and issue (month) numbers.

If you do not find the preset number type you want, create your own in this matter:

1. From the Select Page Numbering Format dialog box, click Custom to open the Custom Page Numbering dialog box (see fig. 5.5).

**FIG. 5.5**

Choose a page number type and whether to use numbers, letters, or Roman numerals, and create accompanying text in the Custom Page Numbering dialog box. Note the custom number is previewed immediately below the text box where you enter the codes and text.

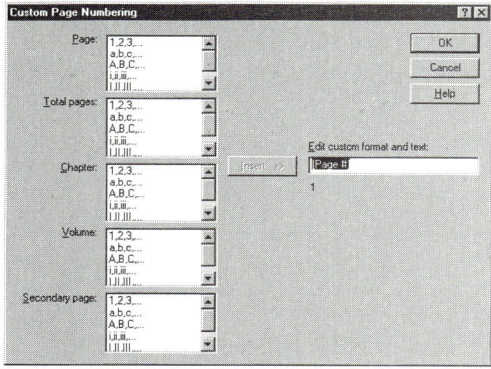

2. Move the mouse I-beam into the Edit Custom Format And Text text box. The text box initially contains the codes for the current page number format selection. Delete the code if you do not want regular page numbering.

3. To use or add another numbering type, move the cursor in the text box to where you want the additional number type to appear in relation to the regular page number.

4. Choose the type you want included in the page number format:

| | |
|---|---|
| Page | [Pg #] |
| Total Pages | [TPgs #] |
| Chapter | [Chp #] |
| Volume | [Vol #] |
| Secondary page | [Spg #] |

5. Click Insert to insert the appropriate code in the text box.

 **TIP** When you choose another number type, a line appears that connects the list box for the number type to the Insert button.

6. Repeat steps 3–5 to add additional page-numbering types. The resulting page number appears just below the text box.
7. When the page number looks the way you want, choose OK or press Enter to return to the Page Numbering dialog box.

In the document, WordPerfect replaces the code with the text and the type(s) of numbering you have chosen. Using more than one numbering type with accompanying text, you can number pages to read Chapter 1, Page 1, or Appendix C, Page II, for example. The style used for the page numbers is also set up in the Page Numbering Options dialog box.

**Changing a Numbering Style** You can number introductory pages, the body, and closing sections of a document differently with the five page-numbering styles available in WordPerfect. In addition to Arabic numbers (1, 2, 3 …), you can use upper- and lowercase Roman numerals (I, II, III … and i, ii, iii …), or upper- and lowercase letters (A, B, C … and a, b, c …).

By default, WordPerfect uses Arabic numerals to number pages. To change the numbering style, follow the previous steps for changing the numbering type. Choose the style of numbering in the list box for each number type before clicking the Insert button.

**Adding Text to Page Numbers** You can number appendixes—for example, A-1, A-2, B-1, B-2, B-3, and so on. Reference manuals often give the section or chapter name before the page number.

You can place up to 49 characters around a page number, including ASCII or WordPerfect characters. These special characters may require more space than standard characters.

To include text with a page number, move the mouse pointer into the Edit Custom Format And Text text box. Type the text to appear on either or both sides of the page number code. Text can precede and follow the page number code. Do not delete the number code if you want text before and after the number.

If you delete the numbering style code, place the cursor where you want the code and insert the code again. WordPerfect inserts the code at the cursor location. To proof your text, right-click the text box to display a QuickMenu that includes the Speller, Thesaurus and Grammatik commands.

The code appears as [Pg Num Fmt: format] in the Reveal Codes window. To change the text in another section of your document, repeat the steps listed in this section.

> **CAUTION**
>
> As you change text or numbering type at several points in your document, proofread the rest of the settings in the dialog box carefully. Your previous settings appear when you reopen the Custom Page Numbering dialog box. As you move from numbering chapters to numbering appendixes, you may need to change more than one option.

## Changing the Current Page Number

Occasionally, you need to begin page numbering other than at page 1, or begin numbering again at 1 later in your document. When introductory, main body, and closing sections use different numbering styles, each section usually starts with page 1.

When you want to leave room in your document for inserts, change the page number to allow for the number of pages to be inserted. For example, if three pages of custom-printed material are to be included after page 6, change the page number for the next WordPerfect document page to 9. If you now add material before page 6, page 9 may not be correct anymore. An option in the Values dialog box—Let Number Change As Pages Are Added Or Deleted—causes WordPerfect to interpret the page number you enter as an interval rather than a fixed number. When additional material is added, the number is adjusted to reflect the new position of the page in the document. If, on the other hand, you want to assure that a new page number you add is not changed, you can choose to Always Keep Number The Same.

Unlike page and secondary numbers, WordPerfect does not automatically increment chapter and volume numbers; rather, you must notify WordPerfect when and how much to change the current number. For instance, if your number format is Appendix [Chpt #], Page [Page #], then at the beginning of each appendix after the first one, you must instruct WordPerfect to increment the chapter number.

To change the number beginning at the current page, follow these steps:

1. In the Select Page Numbering Format dialog box, click Value to open the Values dialog box (see fig. 5.6).
2. Choose the Page (or Chapter, Volume, or Secondary) tab. In the Set Page Number text box, enter the new number to appear on the current page. Alternatively, use the arrow buttons until the number you want appears.

 Use Set Page Number to return to number 1 at the beginning of a preface, appendix, or index.

**FIG. 5.6**
In the Values dialog box, set new page and secondary numbers, and increment chapter and volume numbers.

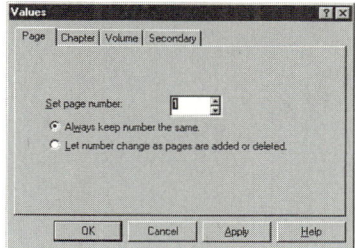

3. Choose whether you want to Al__w__ays Keep Number The Same or use the default __L__et Number Change As Pages Are Added Or Deleted.
4. Repeat steps 2 and 3 to change other numbers in the formatted page number.
5. Choose OK or press Enter to save your changes and return to the Select Page Numbering Format dialog box.

If you include chapter or volume numbers in the page number and use the default to let numbers change, you can cut and paste chapters to change their order so that WordPerfect displays the correct, sequential numbers.

## Incrementing Page Numbers

Although WordPerfect increments page and secondary numbers automatically, you can increment them when you want numbers to increase (or decrease) by a specific amount. As you edit the document to add or remove text, WordPerfect automatically adjusts the page numbering and any increments you have inserted.

To increase or decrease the numbering on the current page, move the cursor to where you want the number to change, such as the beginning of the chapter or volume, and follow these steps:

1. From the Select Page Numbering dialog box, click __V__alue to open the Values dialog box.

 **TIP** To increase or decrease numbering later in a document, you can choose Fo__r__mat, Page __N__umbering, __V__alue/Adjust, then choose the tab for the page-numbering type where you enter the new number.

2. Choose whether you want to Al__w__ays Keep Number The Same or __L__et Number Change As Pages Are Added Or Deleted.
3. Choose OK or press Enter to save the changes and return to the Select Page Numbering Format dialog box.

**NOTE** When you use page numbers in prefatory material and want to set numbering back to 1 when you start body text, be sure to choose Always Keep Number The Same. You can then add more prefatory text and the number that begins the body text does not change.

Alternatively, when you set a different page number to allow for a fixed number of pages to be inserted later, be sure to choose Let Number Change As Pages Are Added Or Deleted. Perhaps at page 10 you plan to add two pages of custom-printed charts so you set the page number on the next page to 13. If you add more text before page 10, the number 13 changes to accommodate the additional text but the interval (here, two pages) is maintained.

Regardless of the numbering style you are using, enter the new number as an Arabic numeral. The numbering style you choose from the Page Numbering Format list box or from the Custom Page Numbering dialog box determines whether an Arabic number, letter, or Roman numeral appears in the document.

## Inserting a Page Number

In addition to using the 10 page number placement options available, you can place a number anywhere else on a single page. You can place a number in a specific location to avoid a header or footer, or in the text where you want to refer to the current page, chapter, or volume number. You can also insert a chapter or volume number directly in chapter or section titles.

▶ **See** "Inserting Page Numbering Codes," **p. 890**

Only the number in the number type(s) currently in use (Arabic, Roman numerals, or letters) appears at the cursor location. You can enter appropriate text before and after the number directly in the document. To insert a regular or secondary page, chapter, or volume number, place the cursor where you want the number to appear and follow these steps:

1. Choose Format, Page Numbering, Insert In Text to display the Insert Number in Text dialog box (see fig. 5.7).

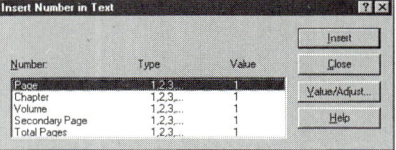

**FIG. 5.7**
In the Insert Number in Text dialog box, choose the type of number you want to insert. Check the values in the Type and Value columns to make sure they are correct before inserting the number.

2. In the Number list box, choose which number you want to insert.
3. To change the number Type or Value from what appears in the list box, click Value/Adjust to display the Value/Adjust Number dialog box (see fig. 5.8).

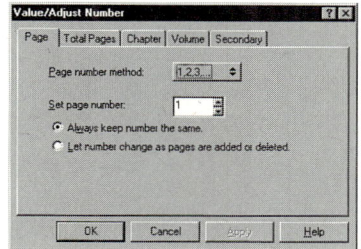

**FIG. 5.8**
Use the Value/Adjust Number dialog box to change a number or its numbering method.

4. Select the appropriate tab, then enter a new number and choose a different numbering method, if desired.
5. Choose OK or press Enter to return to the Insert Number in Text dialog box.

**NOTE** When you use the Total Pages number type or choose the Page X of Y page numbering format, the total number automatically adjusts to reflect the current page total.

6. Click Insert Number In Text to insert the number code in the document text. The dialog box remains open.
7. Click the mouse pointer into your document where you want to insert another number and repeat steps 2–5.
8. When all number codes have been inserted, click Close to return to your document.

If you want to insert a number that includes formatting and text, follow these steps:

1. In the Select Page Numbering Format dialog box, choose the format you want to insert.
2. To change the current number, click Value, select the tab for the type of number, and enter the new page number that you want to insert. (Click OK to return to the Select Page Numbering Format dialog box.)
3. To add text or other number codes, click Custom to open the Custom Page Numbering dialog box.
4. Move the mouse pointer into the Edit Custom Format And Text text box.
5. Type text and insert number codes, as described in the section "Changing Numbering Type" earlier in this chapter, to create the numbering and text you want.
6. When the number and text is satisfactory, choose OK to return to the Select Page Numbering Format dialog box.

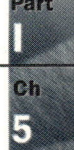

7. Choose Insert Page Number Format In Text so a check appears in the adjacent check box, then choose OK.

## Counting Document Pages

You might find it necessary to occasionally count the pages in the document. To do so, choose Format, Page Numbering, Count Pages to display the Page Count For Total Pages dialog box which displays the current page count. Click Close to return to your document.

**TIP** If you are using a Page X of Y page-numbering format, you can always check the page count by bringing the page number into view.

## Suppressing Page Numbering

The first page of a document does not usually have a page number. On other pages, the page number may interfere with the way a graphic or table is positioned on the page. When this occurs, you can suppress the page number on that page so the number does not appear in the printed version, but still maintains the numbering of subsequent pages in proper order.

**TIP** To end page numbering, choose Format, Page Numbering, Select and choose No Page Numbering from the Position pop-up list.

To suppress numbering on the current page, follow these steps:

1. Choose Format, Page, Suppress. The Suppress dialog box opens.
2. Choose Page Numbering. A check appears in the adjacent check box.

   Alternatively, if centering the number at the bottom of the page solves the placement difficulty, choose Print Page Number At Bottom Center On Current Page.
3. Choose OK or press Enter to close the dialog box and return to the document.

The Suppress code appears as [Suppress: Page Num] in the Reveal Codes window. You can suppress page numbering on any page and as often as necessary.

### TROUBLESHOOTING

**I decided to add text to the plain page number I set up originally. Now the text accompanies the number in part of the document but not the remainder.** When you want to change the appearance of the page-numbering scheme you are using, first return to where you turned on page numbering, either the beginning of the document or the current section.

**I set up page numbering at the bottom of every page. Then I used the Custom command to create the first chapter title in the Edit Custom Format And Text box. When I choose the Insert Page Number Format In Text command, my page numbers change to look like chapter numbering.** The page number created in the Select Page Numbering Format dialog box can be used to create only one page number. You can, however, insert more numbers into the document text. For additional numbers, you must type the accompanying text in the document and use a slightly different procedure to insert the number. To include a chapter number in chapter headings, for example, create the heading in the document; place the cursor where you want the number to display; choose Fo**r**mat, Page **N**umbering, **I**nsert in Text. Choose the number type and click **I**nsert. For subsequent chapters, don't forget to use **V**alue/Adjust to increment the number each time.

# Using Headers and Footers

*Headers* and *footers* are blocks of text that appear at the top or bottom of pages. They can include graphics, page numbers, section title, or any other information about the document. Headers and footers improve the appearance of your work and can provide the reader organizational information at the same time.

WordPerfect enables you to use two headers and two footers on each page, and they can be different on every page. They can appear on only even or odd pages, and you can suppress them where they would conflict with letterhead or figure placement.

Headers and footers start at the edge of the margin and print into the main text area with a blank line added to separate the header or footer from the main text. They can be as long as one page, although that size is not often useful. The headers and footers appear on the WordPerfect screen when in Page mode.

## Creating a Header or Footer

You can create different headers and footers on any page in your document, although they are typically created at the beginning of the document. You may want to create new headers and footers at the beginning of each new chapter.

If you create a header or footer A or B, and one with the same letter is already in effect, the former header or footer is replaced beginning at that page where the next header or footer A or B is created. Headers and footers appear on the page the way they are designed. Designating one as A or B does not determine the order in which each appears on the printed page.

When you create a header or footer, WordPerfect displays the document editing screen, shown in figure 5.9, with guidelines outlining the header or footer. A feature bar is also displayed with command buttons you use to insert page numbers or graphics lines and choose the pages where you want the header or footer to appear. The name of the header or footer appears in the title bar.

 **TIP** To set up document codes for features such as margins and font so the features apply to any header or footer you create, choose Format, Document, Initial Codes Style to set up the document format.

All document default settings are applied to a new header or footer, including the default margins, font typeface, and size and tabs. This is true even if you choose a different font or margins before you create headers or footers. To help you apply formatting appropriate for the current document, the WordPerfect formatting commands and menus are available, although features that cannot be used in a header or footer are grayed.

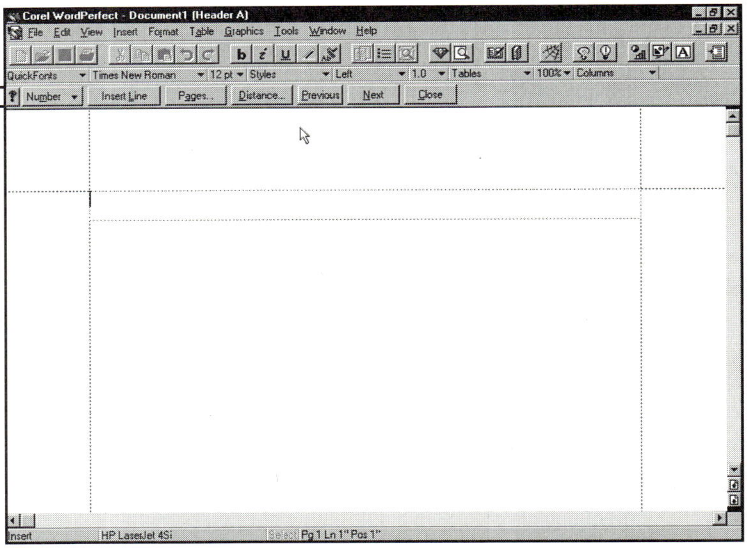

**FIG. 5.9**
The Header Editor includes a feature bar of commands to insert page numbers, add graphics lines, move to the next or preceding header, and close the editor. Guidelines indicate where the header or footer will appear.

Header Feature Bar

The instructions that follow refer to Header A, but are the same as the steps for Header B, or Footer A or B. To create a new header, follow these steps:

1. Choose Format, Header/Footer to open the Headers/Footers dialog box. Here, you can choose whether to create Header A, Header B, Footer A, or Footer B (see fig. 5.10).

**FIG. 5.10**
In the Headers/Footers dialog box, choose which header or footer to create, or which existing header or footer you want to edit or discontinue.

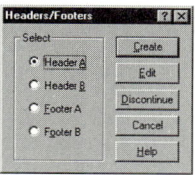

2. Choose Header A, then click Create to open the appropriate editing screen. The header guidelines and the feature bar from the header editing screen appear (refer to fig. 5.9).

3. In the Header editing screen, insert any formatting codes you want. Features that are not available for use in a header or footer are grayed on the menus. Make sure you change the default document settings in the header where appropriate. Do not end a header with a hard return unless you want an extra blank line between the header and the body of the document.

 Choose Insert, File to retrieve boilerplate text saved as a file into a header or footer.

4. By default, the header appears on every page. To change this placement, click Pages from the feature bar to open the Pages dialog box. Then choose Odd Pages if the header is to appear only on odd pages, and Even Pages if you want it only on even pages.

    To include page numbering in the header, refer to the later section, "Using Page Numbers in Headers and Footers."

5. Click Close from the feature bar to remove the feature bar and return to the document, or click the document portion of the screen to work in your document but leave the feature bar displayed.

The following code, for example, appears in the Reveal Codes window:

    [Header A:  Every page, [code]text[code]text..]

Up to three lines of text, including all codes, appears.

If you place two headers on the same page, the headers print in the same location at the top of the page. The same is true for two footers printing at the bottom of the page. Use formatting commands to design headers and footers so the text they contain does not overlap a second header or footer. Try aligning text in one header on the left margin and use flush right to align text on the right margin in the second header. You can also center some of the text, or place text on alternating lines.

While in the header or footer editing screen, right-click the background to display a QuickMenu with several commands, including Paste, Spell Check, Font, Center, Flush Right, and Indent.

## Editing Headers and Footers

You can edit headers and footers as easily as the main body of a document. You can begin the editing process at any point in the document where the header or footer you want to edit is in effect.

To quickly edit a header or footer using the mouse in Page view, click the header or footer text and make the desired changes. WordPerfect activates Editing mode, but the editing window does not appear. Use the commands available on the menu bar, shortcut keystrokes, or the Button and Power Bars.

You cannot perform some tasks, such as adding a page number, by editing the header or footer on the page. As when creating a header or footer, certain menu commands and button faces are grayed while you are in Editing mode. In particular, some of the commands available on the Header or Footer Feature Bar are not available.

To edit a header or footer using the editing screen with the Feature Bar displayed, follow these steps:

1. Choose Format, Header/Footer.
2. Choose the header or footer you want to edit, and then click Edit to display the Header/Footer editing window with the text you entered.
3. Enter any changes, making selections from the Header/Footer Feature Bar as needed.
4. Click Close from the Header/Footer Feature bar to return to your document, or click any part of the document portion of the screen.

 You can display the Reveal Codes window while in the header/footer window. Use it to locate, insert, and delete codes.

## Using Page Numbers in Headers and Footers

When you are working in a header or footer editing window, you can include a page number code by placing the cursor where you want the page number to appear and clicking the Number button from the Header/Footer Feature Bar.

Page numbers are often enhanced with text so they read as Page 24 or - 24 -, for example. To include text with the page number, type the text you want before the page number, insert the page number, and then type any text you want to follow the page number.

With WordPerfect 7, you can easily use Page 24 of 35 pages. Simply choose Page Number for the first number and choose Total Pages for the second number.

**TIP** Another method of inserting Page X of Y numbering is to choose Page X of Y in the Page Numbering Format list of the Select Page Numbering Format dialog box.

When creating a header or footer, all commands on the Format Page menu, including Numbering, are grayed, limiting you to using only the Arabic page-numbering style. You can, however, use four types (Page, Secondary, Chapter, and Volume) of numbering.

There are four ways to remove or override a header or footer:

- Delete it in the Reveal Codes window.
- Replace it by creating another header or footer with the same letter later in the document.
- Suppress a header or footer on any one page by using the procedure in the next section.
- Discontinue it, if the header or footer is not to appear again, as explained in the later section "Discontinuing Headers and Footers."

## Suppressing Headers and Footers

You usually create headers and footers on the first page of a document. However, because headers are often inappropriate when printed on the first page—especially if you use letterhead or chapter headings, and page number footers often start on the second page—you can suppress the printing of headers and footers on a page. You can also suppress headers and footers at the beginning of chapters or elsewhere in a document where you don't want them to appear.

To suppress the header you created in the first section, place the cursor on the page where you want to suppress the header and follow these steps:

1. Choose Format, Page, Suppress. The Suppress dialog box appears.
2. Choose Header A.
3. Choose OK or press Enter to return to the document.

The suppress code appears as [Suppress: Header A] in the Reveal Codes window. When you suppress the printing of a header or footer on one page, it continues to be printed on the following pages. If the header or footer contains a page number, the correct page-numbering sequence is maintained.

## Discontinuing Headers and Footers

To replace a header or footer beginning at a specific point in the document, you simply create a new one and assign it the same letter as the existing one. You can use this method, for example, to have a different header in each chapter.

Discontinue a header/footer when you do not want it to print again and another one does not replace it. To discontinue a header in the index of a report, for example, follow these steps:

1. Choose Fo_r_mat, _H_eader/Footer.
2. Choose Header _A_.
3. Click _D_iscontinue. WordPerfect returns you to the document.

## Using Other Features with Headers and Footers

Headers and footers have an interesting hybrid status in a document. Some WordPerfect features can be used to good advantage in headers and footers; others require an extra step. The following sections describe a few features you may find useful.

**Graphics**   The full range of graphics commands are available from the header or footer window. Choose all or any one or more of the following to enhance your header/footer:

▶ See "Using Graphics Lines," **p. 250**
▶ See "Using Graphics Boxes," **p. 262**

- *Graphics lines.* Click the Insert _L_ine button on the Feature Bar to place a horizontal line into your header or footer. The line goes from margin to margin, and the line height is reduced to match the line thickness. You can also center a short horizontal line above a page number in a footer by choosing _G_raphics, Custom _L_ine. Refer to the instructions in Chapter 7, "Integrating Text and Graphics."
- *Graphics boxes.* Use any of the box styles available in the _G_raphics menu in a header or footer. You can import and link part of a spreadsheet, use any of the WPG figures that come with WordPerfect, or import other graphics. Many of the WPG figures or a company logo can be used effectively in a two-line footer if you size the graphics carefully. Specific instructions for using graphics are given in Chapter 7, "Integrating Text and Graphics."
- *Original drawings and charts.* Use the Draw and Chart utilities available in the _G_raphics menu to create a drawing or chart to include in a header or footer.

**Spell Check**   The Spell Check feature checks headers and footers when you choose to check the entire document, or if you check a page and a header or footer code is on that page. Refer to Chapter 6, "Using Writing Tools," for instructions on how to use Spell Check.

**Search and Replace**   Both the Search and the Replace features automatically search and replace in headers and footers beginning at the cursor location. To include headers and footers created at the beginning of the document, press Ctrl+Home twice to place the cursor before any codes at the top of the document.

If you don't want to return to the beginning of your document before searching, you can cause WordPerfect to wrap the search to find any headers and footers you may have missed. Refer to Chapter 3, "Retrieving and Editing Documents," for instructions on using Search and Replace.

**Cut, Copy, and Paste**   You can cut or copy text or a graphic from a document window or from another header or footer, and then paste the text or graphic into the current header/footer editing window. The reverse is as simple. You can cut or copy the contents of a header or footer in one document and paste the contents into the header/footer window in another document. Right-click the background to display the QuickMenu containing the Paste command. Instructions for selecting text and using Cut, Copy, and Paste are in Chapter 3, "Retrieving and Editing Documents."

# Selecting Page Size and Type

The page size and type options available by default in WordPerfect depend on the printer you select. You can create other sizes and types, such as custom stationery or 5 1/2 × 8 1/2-inch invoices. A specific page size and type is called a *page definition*. The page definitions you can create are limited only by the demands of your task and the capabilities of your printer.

The default page definition selected in the U.S. version of WordPerfect is Letter which is Standard 8 1/2 × 11-inch paper using the default paper feed. This is the page definition used even if no printers have been installed. You can choose any other page definition. The page definition you choose also manages the print job.

## Choosing a Different Page Size

In addition to the Standard 8 1/2 × 11-inch page definition, most printers have several additional page definitions available, such as Legal 8 1/2 × 14-inch continuous and Monarch envelopes. Before you choose a different page size, select the printer you want to use so that the available page definitions appear in the Page Size dialog box. You choose a printer in the Print To *Printer name* dialog box (accessed via the File menu).

After you choose a different page definition, WordPerfect inserts a paper size/type code such as [Paper Sz/Typ: 8.5" x 14", Legal]. You can change the definition at any point in your document by choosing another definition.

To change the current page definition, follow these steps:

1. Choose Format, Page, Page Size. The Page Size dialog box appears (see fig. 5.11).

   The name of the current page definition appears in the Name text box, and the details for the highlighted page size appear at the bottom and right of the box.

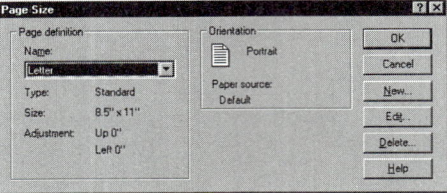

**FIG. 5.11**
The Page Size dialog box provides the page definitions for the active printer and information about the page size, type, adjustment, orientation, and paper source.

2. Highlight the page definition you want to use and choose OK to return to your document.

The versatility of the newest printers on the market means that the list of available page definitions usually exceeds the number that can display at the same time in the Name drop-down list. Use the scroll bar to display more printers. To quickly display the name you want in the list box, type the first few letters of the page name to move the highlight bar to the page definition you want. As you type, the highlight bar moves to the page definition name that begins with the letters you type.

## Creating Custom Page Definitions

Your printer may offer a greater variety of print options than the available page definitions provide. Standard letter-size page definitions are usually available only with portrait and landscape orientation definitions, both with a continuous paper location. You may want to manually feed special letter-size paper for some jobs, or place letterhead in one paper tray and second sheets of your letterhead in a second tray. Each paper location requires a separate page definition. If you cannot find the definition you want in the list provided, you can create definitions for your personal print jobs.

## Creating a New Page Definition

When you want a custom page definition, create a new definition rather than edit a definition provided by WordPerfect, because the changes you make overwrite the original definition. If necessary, you can use the Edit command later to fine-tune page definitions you have created.

You can preset many of the options for your new page size by choosing a similar page definition and then begin creating the new definition. The New Page Size dialog box initially displays all the settings for the page definition active when the dialog box opens.

To create a new page definition, follow these steps:

1. From the Page Size dialog box, click New. The New Page Size dialog box appears (see fig. 5.12).

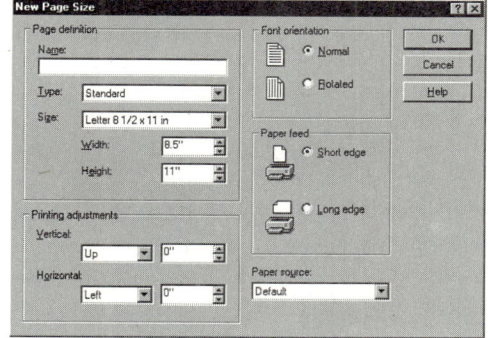

**FIG. 5.12**
Choose page size options in the New Page Size dialog box, including the page orientation and printing adjustment needed, which edge of the paper to feed, and the paper source.

2. Type a unique name for the definition in the Name text box. Right-click the text box to display a QuickMenu that includes text-editing commands.
3. Choose the options you want for the page definition you are creating, as described later in the "Customizing Page Size" section.
4. Choose OK or press Enter to add the definition to the list in the Page Size dialog box.
5. To use the new definition in the current document, press Enter or choose OK.

You do not need to use the new definition immediately. Choosing Cancel to return to the document adds the definition you have created to the Name drop-down list in the Page Size dialog box where you can choose it later when you need it.

**NOTE** The page definition you create is added to the definitions for the current printer driver. When you select another printer driver, your new creation is not available. You must create, or edit, the page definition for every printer driver you want to use with the new page definition.

## Editing and Deleting Page Definitions

To edit a page definition, follow the steps for creating a new definition, except instead of clicking New, highlight the page definition you want to change and click Edit. The Edit

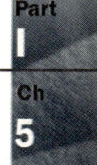

Page Size dialog box initially includes all the choices you made when you created the definition. The options available in the dialog box are described in the following section, "Customizing Page Size."

If you edit a page definition, WordPerfect does not incorporate the changes you make in documents created earlier using that definition. If the document in the active window uses the page definition you are editing, choosing OK to exit the Page Size dialog box replaces the original code.

When you find that you no longer use a page definition, remove it from the Name list by highlighting it in the Page Size dialog box and clicking Delete.

## Customizing Page Size

When creating or editing a page definition, the following options are available in the New Page Size and Edit Page Size dialog boxes (refer to fig. 5.12). The Edit Page Size and the New Page Size dialog boxes both provide the same options for customizing page definitions except that you cannot change the name when editing a page definition.

> **CAUTION**
> Pressing Enter while in the New Page Size or Edit Page Size dialog box closes the box. Do not press Enter when making choices until you have customized all the options you want to change.

- *Name.* Provide a name for the page definition you are creating or edit the current name. Because this name distinguishes one page definition from another, be as clear and descriptive as possible. Type the name in the text box provided and press Tab or choose another option to continue.
- *Type.* Choose this option to display the Type drop-down list. Make your choice from among the popular types in the list, such as Standard, Bond, Cardstock, and Glossy Film; or choose Other.
- *Size.* When you are specifying a page size, initially width appears in the first text box and height in the text box on the right for portrait orientation. If the width you specify is greater than the height, the contents of the text boxes are reversed so the orientation remains the same.
- *Printing adjustments.* By using these options, you can reposition the text on the page if the text does not print according to the margins you set. This printing difficulty is not visible in the document window, so any adjustments you set must be tested by printing a page of text.

Select Vertical and choose from the drop-down list whether to adjust text Up or Down, then specify an amount in the text box to the right. Select Horizontal and choose from the drop-down list whether to adjust text to the Left or Right, then specify an amount in the text box to the right.

- *Font orientation.* You can choose Normal (upright) or Rotated (wide) paper orientation. When you use a landscape orientation with most printers, the short edge of the page feeds into the printer, and the text is printed sideways on the page.

- *Paper feed.* When you use either a portrait or landscape page definition, the Short (narrow) edge of the paper feeds first. If necessary, and if your printer can accommodate wide paper, you can opt to feed the long (wide) edge of the paper first by choosing Long Edge.

- *Paper source.* Paper source describes how the paper feeds to the printer. The Default paper source is continuous feed paper. Use Manual Feed if you want to hand feed letterhead stationery. If your printer can pull paper from several cassettes or sheet feeder bins, the bins or trays are included in the drop-down list when that printer is active.

Choose Paper Source to display the drop-down list and choose the location from the list provided.

## Considering Other Page Size Factors

If you routinely use a page size other than Standard 8 1/2 × 11 inches, you can replace the default definition for all new documents by including your preferred definition in the WP7US template. Refer to Chapter 11, "Using Templates," for instructions on creating and editing templates.

▶ **See** "Selecting and Configuring Your Printer," **p. 291**

▶ **See** "Understanding Windows Font Management," **p. 634**

If you have a printer with multiple paper trays or bins, a frequent print job layout is to specify the bin containing letterhead for the first page of a document, and a second bin containing second sheets for the rest of the document. Choose the letterhead page definition to begin the document; then create a Delay code with a one-page delay to cause WordPerfect to pull paper from the second bin for the remainder of the letter. Learn about Delay codes in the later section "Using Delay Codes."

Some printers make it possible to use a slightly different technique if your printer has only one paper tray. Place the second sheets in the standard paper location and a single page of letterhead in the manual or bypass feed location. When the document prints, the printer pulls the first page from the bypass location and remaining pages from the paper tray. No special page definition is needed.

> **CAUTION**
> Changing page definitions automatically changes the position of soft page breaks in your document. Review your document before printing to be sure that text is still placed on the pages the way you want.

### TROUBLESHOOTING

**I can't find a page size definition that I know I have used before and that my printer can handle. Where did it go?** Page size definitions are part of the printer driver for each printer you have installed. If you created the definition yourself, the new page size is available only with the printer selected at the time you created the definition. The printer with that definition is probably not selected at the moment. Select the appropriate printer or refer to Chapter 8, "Basic Output: Printing, Faxing, and E-Mail," for instructions to select another printer.

# Using Subdivide Page

With the Subdivide Page command, you can subdivide a page into evenly spaced columns and rows of pages. WordPerfect treats the full page as a physical page and the subdivided pages as separate, logical pages. For example, the program numbers each subdivision when you turn on page numbering.

As with labels, when you type on subdivided pages, pressing Ctrl+Enter to insert a hard page break moves the cursor to the next subdivision. The text you type word-wraps within the subdivided page and onto the next subdivision if you enter enough text but do not insert a page break.

To subdivide a page into columns and rows of pages, follow these steps:

1. Choose Format, Page, Subdivide Page. The Subdivide Page dialog box opens (see fig. 5.13).

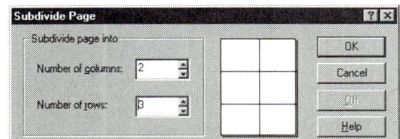

**FIG. 5.13**
As you enter the number of columns and rows in the Subdivide Page dialog box (here 2 by 3), you can preview the results in the page graphic.

2. Enter the number of columns and rows in the text boxes adjacent to Number Of Columns and the Number Of Rows, or click the arrows to increase or decrease the number displayed in each text box.

3. Choose OK or press Enter to return to your document.

When you choose Subdivide Page, WordPerfect uses the current margins for each page. Change the margins you want to use if you have more than a few subdivisions. To illustrate, two columns of subdivided pages use four inches of the page width and height for margins if you do not change the default one-inch margins.

All subsequent pages in your document are subdivided. You may want to subdivide only a single page in your document. To return to full-size pages, move the cursor to the page where you want to restore the original page format, follow the steps to subdivide pages, then choose Off to turn Subdivide Page off.

# Using Delay Codes

Documents longer than one page often require formatting changes after the first page. You may not want headers and footers to begin until after introductory material, such as the table of contents and preface. When printing documents on letterhead, you may want to change to second sheets of letterhead after the first page. These and many other formatting changes can be applied beginning at a specific page in a document by including the codes in a Delay code at the beginning of the document. When you create Delay codes, you specify the number of pages to skip before the format changes take effect. The Delay code appears as [Delay: #].

WordPerfect places a [Delay Codes: codes] code at the top of the page where the delayed formatting takes effect. If you change the current page formatting when the cursor is on the page where you want the change to begin, WordPerfect inserts the codes in a [Delay Codes: codes] code for you.

The # in the Delay code is the number of pages to skip to locate the associated [Delay Codes] code. If a Delay code appears as [Delay: 16], for example, the [Delay Codes] that contains your formatting choices appears at the top of the 17th page (page 1 plus skip 16 equals 17).

If you decide to add more formatting to a page that already has a Delay code, the additional formatting choices you make are added to the single Delay code.

You can manually insert any open code as a Delay code by using the Delay Codes command. *Open codes* are single codes such as page numbering, font, justification, and margins. You can't include typed text or paired codes, such as bold and italics, in a Delay code; these codes and any text you attempt to include are dropped when you close the Define Delay Codes screen.

To create a Delay code, follow these steps:

1. Choose Format, Page, Delay Codes. The Delay Codes dialog box appears.
2. In Number Of Pages To Delay, enter the appropriate number of pages.
3. Choose OK to open the Define Delayed Codes editing screen that contains a feature bar (see fig. 5.14).

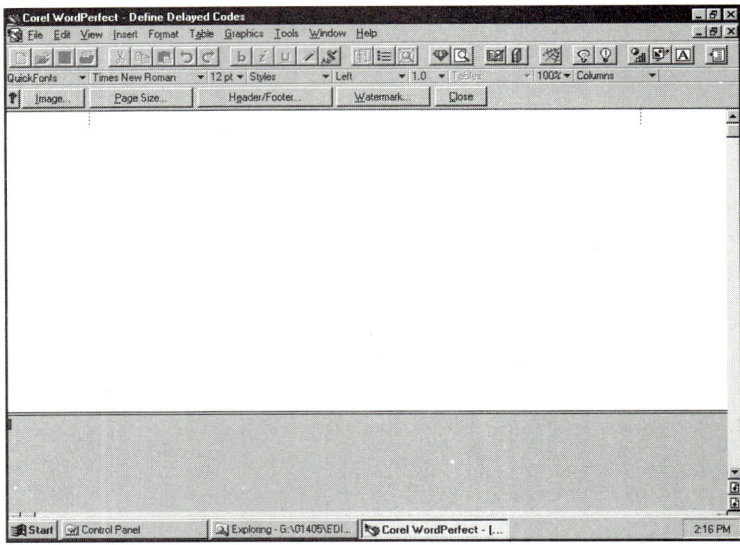

**FIG. 5.14**
The feature bar in the Define Delayed Codes editing screen includes several command buttons you can use to insert Page Size, Header/Footer, and other codes when creating Delay codes.

4. Use any regular WordPerfect commands to create the hidden format codes you want applied to the specified page.
5. Use the command buttons on the feature bar to create headers and footers, a watermark or image, or change page size. Choose the button with a question mark to obtain help or change feature bars.
6. Click Close to return to your document.

The cursor can be anywhere in the document when you create the Delay code. Take into account the current page when you enter the total number of pages to skip. If, for example, your cursor is on the third page when you set up a Delay code, and you request a delay of two pages to place codes on page 5, the Delay code placed at the beginning of the document is [Delay: 4] (first page plus four more). WordPerfect calculates the number of pages to skip based on physical pages rather than page numbers.

# Using the Make It Fit Expert Feature

The Make It Fit Expert command causes WordPerfect to reformat your document so that it fills the number of pages you specify. If the signature block at the end of your letter is at the top of the next page or the newsletter is just a bit too short this month, Make It Fit Expert is the quick solution. Experienced word processor users have traditionally changed the font size and reduced or increased line height minute amounts to adjust document length, but this process often necessitates change after change until the desired result is achieved. Make It Fit Expert saves you the tedious process of adjusting and readjusting line height, font size, and margins to achieve just the right fit.

To have WordPerfect find the best fit for your document, follow these steps:

1. Choose Fo<u>r</u>mat, Make <u>I</u>t Fit to open the Make It Fit Expert dialog box (see fig. 5.15).

**FIG. 5.15**
The Make It Fit Expert dialog box offers several ways to adjust a document to achieve a specific page count.

2. In the <u>D</u>esired Number Of Filled Pages text box, note the current number of pages, then type the number of pages you want the document to fill.

3. Indicate the formatting changes you want WordPerfect to use to achieve the desired fit by choosing one or more of these options:

    <u>L</u>eft Margin    <u>B</u>ottom Margin

    <u>R</u>ight Margin    <u>F</u>ont Size

    <u>T</u>op Margin    L<u>i</u>ne Spacing

4. Click the <u>M</u>ake It Fit button to reformat the document.

> **CAUTION**
>
> Check your entire document very carefully immediately after using the Make It Fit Expert feature to see if the results are satisfactory. If the changes WordPerfect makes do not produce the desired appearance, choose Undo to remove the formatting.

# Working with Envelopes

WordPerfect 7 includes an envelope form that automatically addresses envelopes using the return address you specify and the mailing address in your letter. If you use a standard business letter format where the mailing address is on the left, WordPerfect inserts the mailing address in the envelope form for you.

## Addressing an Envelope

To fill in the mailing address, selection criteria are used to determine what text to select. WordPerfect first checks to determine whether text is currently selected. If not, the program looks on the first page of the document for three to six lines of text where each line ends with a hard return and the last line is followed by two hard returns. If more than one block of text on the first page meets these criteria, the last block is selected. Using standard business letter formats, this ensures that a return address is ignored in favor of the mailing address that follows. Finally, a nonhard end-of-line code, such as the soft return used for word-wrapped text, terminates the search.

To address an envelope after typing a letter, follow these steps:

1. Choose Format, Envelope to open the Envelope dialog box (see fig. 5.16).

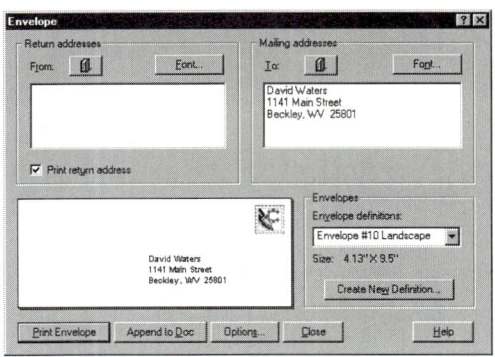

**FIG. 5.16**
The Envelope dialog box displays a preview envelope with the mailing address and ZIP code retrieved by WordPerfect.

2. Choose Envelope Definitions to open a drop-down list of available envelope definitions. Choose the envelope size you want to use.
3. Choose From to place the cursor in the text box, and type the return address.

 **TIP** For envelopes preprinted with a return address, select the Print Return Address check box so the check is removed.

To change the typeface or size of the font used in the return address, click Font to open the Font dialog box, now titled Return Address Font. Refer to Chapter 4, "Formatting Text," and Chapter 20, "Using Fonts and Special Characters," for instructions on choosing options in this dialog box.

 If you have entered the address in your Address Book, click the Address Book button and copy the desired information from the address book. You need to add hard returns to arrange the text in a layout suitable for printing on an envelope.

4. If a mailing address was included in your document and the document used one of the standard business letter formats, WordPerfect extracts the mailing address from the letter and displays it in the Mailing Addresses window automatically. You can edit the address, perhaps adding an **ATTN:** line or other details.

To enter or edit a mailing address, choose To and type the mailing address or edit the available text.

As with the return address, you can change the typeface or size of the font used in the return address by clicking Font to open the Font dialog box, now titled Mailing Address Font. Again, refer to Chapter 4, "Formatting Text," and Chapter 20, "Using Fonts and Special Characters," for instructions on working in this dialog box.

5. To add the envelope to your document, click Append To Doc. If you are ready to print the envelope, click Print Envelope. Otherwise, click Close.

**N O T E**  The envelope uses the current document font to format text. You can use a different font or another size, run a macro, or apply other formatting to the mailing address and return address text. Using a larger font size for the mailing address makes the address easier to read, and the resulting overall envelope appearance is very attractive.

When you do not use a standard business format or you have several mailing addresses in a letter, select the desired address text before opening the Envelope form to have WordPerfect use the selected text as the mailing address. If you have several mailing addresses, create several envelopes by selecting each address in turn. Then print the envelope immediately or append each to the document so all the envelopes print when the document is printed.

## Creating New Envelope Definitions

The envelopes available in the Envelope Definitions drop-down list are the default envelopes for the current printer, plus any envelope definitions you have created for the current printer. Whether you want to create a new envelope definition or edit an existing definition, the now familiar New Page Size dialog box appears. For detailed instructions on entering information and making choices using the commands available in the Page Size dialog box, see the earlier section "Customizing Page Size."

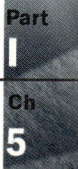

## Setting Envelope Options

In addition to the customizing options described earlier, the position of the return and mailing addresses, whether WordPerfect prints a U.S. POSTNET bar code on the envelope, and where the bar code is printed can be customized by clicking Options in the Envelope dialog box (see fig. 5.17).

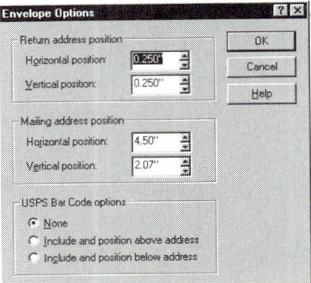

**FIG. 5.17**
In the Envelope Options dialog box, indicate where the mailing and return addresses should be, as measured from the edge of the envelope, and whether to include a POSTNET bar code on the envelope.

To change the position of the return or mailing address, choose the appropriate Horizontal or Vertical position and enter a new value, measured from the edge of the envelope, for both the return address and the mailing address.

To have the ZIP code printed on the envelope in the form of a bar code that can be scanned for automated mail sorting at the post office, indicate whether to include a U.S. POSTNET Bar Code. Choose whether to position the bar code above or below the address so that a dot appears in the adjacent option button. WordPerfect uses the five-, nine-, or 11-digit ZIP code if one is included at the end of the last line of the mailing address. When you are finished, choose OK to return to the Envelope dialog box.

Any changes you make in the Envelope Options dialog box are saved with the current envelope definition. The next time you choose the definitions, the options you entered display in the Envelope Options dialog box as the defaults.

## Editing and Deleting Envelope Definitions

To edit or delete any of the envelope definitions you have created, you must choose Format, Page, Page Size. The name of the envelope definition you created is in the Name drop-down list box. Move the highlight bar to your choice and click Edit. The Edit Page Size dialog box appears. Refer to the instructions for editing and deleting page definitions in the "Editing and Deleting Page Definitions" section earlier in this chapter.

# Working with Labels

WordPerfect 7 includes approximately 190 definitions for standard labels that are readily available at office supply stores. The definitions are stored in a file named WP_WP_US.LAB, which appears at the bottom of the Labels dialog box as the default file. Included in this definition are several popular brand names with identifying label numbers for most of the labels available on the market. The label types range from various styles of address labels to file folder, floppy disk, and name badge labels. Check on the label package for the label name and number. Open the Labels dialog box, choose the matching label definition, and you are ready to go!

## Choosing a Label Definition

To choose a label definition, follow these steps:

**TIP** Begin typing the name of the label to open a search text box and move the highlight bar to the first label beginning with the letters you type.

1. Choose Format, Labels to open the Labels dialog box (see fig. 5.18).

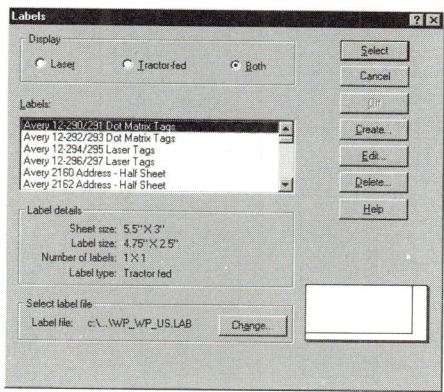

**FIG. 5.18**
The Labels dialog box displays the current label file name, a list of available label definitions, and the label details for the highlighted label definition.

2. Move the highlight bar to the label definition you want to use and click Select.

The list of labels is lengthy. It is easy to make the list more manageable and target the labels you can use. Choose Tractor-Fed or Laser to display only labels suitable for your printer.

## Using Labels

The labels arranged on a full page or a continuous-feed roll are individual logical pages. After you choose the label definition you want to use, begin typing the label information on-screen. When you complete a label, insert a page break by pressing Ctrl+Enter to move to the next label.

Because a label is a document page, only a single label appears in Page mode. When you complete the first label and press Ctrl+Enter, a second blank label appears on the page. You can use all the usual format commands as you create the label. The following information may help you get started:

- When typing several separate lines of text, press Enter at the end of each line.
- When typing a long entry rather than separate lines, the text word wraps within the label.
- You can use the Format, Page, Center command to place the text in the middle of the label.
- Remember that labels are pages. Use Go To to quickly move to a specific label. Choose Edit, Go To, or press Ctrl+G; then type the label number.
- You can change fonts, apply bold and underline, insert graphics, center or right justify the text, and create page or paragraph borders, to name a few possibilities.
- You can include labels in a document. Position the cursor where you want the labels and choose the appropriate label definition. To continue with your regular-text document after the labels are typed, open the Labels dialog box and choose Off to reinstate the original page definition.

## Creating Custom Label Definitions

When you want to create a new labels definition, WordPerfect displays a Create Labels dialog box in which you can specify the size of the page, the size of the labels, all four label margins, and more. To create a new label definition, follow these steps:

 To avoid having to provide all the specifications when you create a new label definition, find an existing definition that is similar to what you want, highlight it in the Labels list box, then choose Create. All the settings for the label you highlighted appear in the Create Labels dialog box.

1. From the Labels dialog box, click Create. The Create Labels dialog box opens (see fig. 5.19).

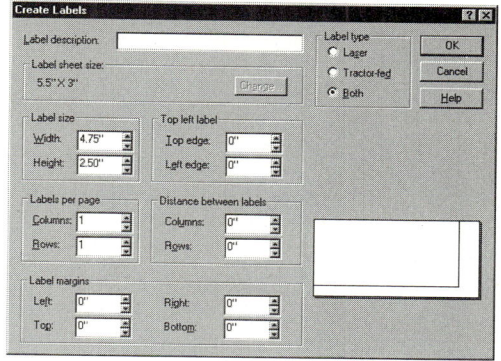

**FIG. 5.19**
Using the Create Labels dialog box, you can customize every aspect of the label spacing with precision. Watch the diagram in the lower-right corner of the dialog box to preview the results of the choices you make.

2. Provide the necessary information in the array of text boxes to set up the label definition for your print job. Refer to the later section, "Understanding Label Customizing Options," for information about the available options.

3. Choose OK or press Enter to add the definition to the list in the Labels dialog box.

4. To use the new label definition immediately, highlight it and click Select.

   To exit without selecting a definition, click Cancel.

If you use the new label definition and find it needs some adjusting, you can edit the definition to incorporate needed changes.

## Editing and Deleting Label Definitions

Because the labels available with WordPerfect all bear the name and number of commercially available labels, avoid editing those definitions. Instead, create a definition as described in the preceding section and give it a name that clearly identifies your personal product. Then edit the definition you have created as needed.

To edit a label definition, follow these steps:

1. From the Labels dialog box, move the highlight bar to the label definition you want to edit and click Edit.

2. Type in the various text boxes the information needed to edit the label definition to suit the needs of your print job. Refer to the next section, "Understanding Label Customizing Options," for information about available options.

3. Choose OK to return to the Labels dialog box. Choose the new label definition to use it immediately, or choose Cancel to return to your document.

If you create label definitions that you no longer need, you can delete them. To delete a label definition, highlight in the Labels dialog box the label definition you want to delete and choose Delete.

## Understanding Label Customizing Options

The Create Labels and Edit Labels dialog boxes offer a variety of options you can customize:

- *Label Description.* Assign the label definition a descriptive name. The name you enter appears in the list box after you save the definition.
- *Label Sheet Size.* For laser printers, page size is usually 8 1/2 × 11 inches. Enter the dimensions of the entire physical page of labels as the label sheet size when working with labels to be printed with a laser printer. Tractor-fed labels are set up by WordPerfect with one row of labels to a page, whether the row contains one or several labels. This arrangement works well, and you should emulate it when designing your own label definitions.

The Change option becomes available when you begin typing a label description. To choose a different label sheet size, choose Change; the Edit Page Size dialog box appears, listing the various page sizes available with WordPerfect. To customize the page size, follow the steps described in the earlier section "Selecting Page Size and Type."

> **CAUTION**
> As you design or edit the sheet of labels, remember that the active printer probably has a small nonprinting area at the edges. Design your labels to allow for this or include text adjustments as described later in this section, or the labels may not print as you planned.

- *Label Size.* Enter the Width and Height of the individual labels. Do not include the space, if any, between labels.
- *Labels Per Page.* Indicate the number of labels in the Columns and Rows on a page.
- *Label Margins.* Indicate the Left, Right, Top, and Bottom margins for the labels. The default is zero.

> **CAUTION**
> If you do not specify margins and a distance between labels, you run the risk of having text on adjacent labels actually touching, or the text may overlap the edge of an adjacent label if the sheet of labels does not feed perfectly.

- *Top Left Label.* Labels may be arranged on a page so that a border remains on all four edges of the page. To adjust for this, specify the location of the top-left corner of the first label. Enter the measurement from the edge of the sheet of labels to the Top Edge and Left Edge of the label in the top-left corner.
- *Distance Between Labels.* Specify any distance between Rows and Columns of labels. The default is zero.
- *Label Type.* Indicate whether the labels are designed to print as Laser or Tractor-Fed labels. If you can print the labels either way, choose Both.

The label definitions you create or edit are saved in the current label file, either the default WP_WP_US.LAB file or a label file that you create.

## Creating Custom Label Files

Rather than hunting through a lengthy list of labels to find your custom creations, you can create a personal label file. Retrieve the file when you want to create a new label definition; then WordPerfect adds the new definition to your file. To create a labels file, follow these steps:

1. From the Labels dialog box, click Change to open the Label File dialog box (see fig. 5.20).
2. Choose Current Folder to change the folder location for the label files. Enter a new folder. To use the Select Labels Location dialog box to browse for the desired folder, click the folder button at the end of the text box or press Alt+↓.

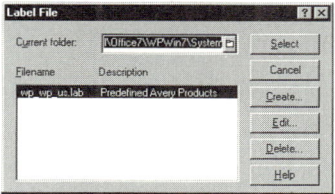

**FIG. 5.20**
The Label File dialog box provides commands for creating and editing label files, and lists the existing label files.

3. Click Create to display the Create Label File dialog box. Type a description of the label file in the Description text box. Type a file name of up to eight characters in the Filename text box. (WordPerfect supplies the extension LAB when you choose OK or press Enter.)
4. Choose OK or press Enter to return to the Label File dialog box.
5. Click Select to open the label file.

When you first select a file you have created, no labels are included in the Labels list box. As you create new label definitions, WordPerfect adds the label definition to the list box for the current label file.

To quickly highlight the file you want, type the first letter of the file name to open a text box and move to the first file that begins with that letter.

You can change either the description or the file name of the label file. Click Edit to open the Edit Label File dialog box where you can edit the file name and description.

If you have created label files and saved them in folders other than the default folder, choose Current Folder and type the folder name in the text box. The default folder for label files is COREL\OFFICE7\WPWIN7\SYSTEM.

When you no longer need a label file that you created, click Delete in the Label File dialog box to remove the file.

## Using Advance To Place Text

The Advance command enables you to place text on the page at a precise location. Frequently used to start letters with a first-page-only allowance for letterhead, Advance can also be the solution for filling in preprinted forms when no typewriter is available. Many users first use the Advance command to superimpose text on a graphic. Advance enables you to ignore line height changes that occur when larger or smaller font sizes are selected.

Advance has two positioning schemes. You can use it to place text at a measured distance—up, down, left, or right—from where WordPerfect inserts the Advance code. WordPerfect refers to this as *relative*. If you edit the preceding text, the position of the code shifts and the effect of the Advance adjusts accordingly.

With the second positioning method, you specify a specific distance from the top or the left edge of the page. This method results in *absolute* placement of the text, regardless of the final location of the Advance code.

To use Advance to place text at a specific location, follow these steps:

1. Place the cursor immediately before the text to be advanced.
2. Choose Format, Typesetting.
3. Click Advance. The Advance dialog box appears (see fig. 5.21).
4. Choose an option button in the Horizontal Position area. The Horizontal Distance text box opens.

**FIG. 5.21**
Choose a vertical or horizontal position in the Advance dialog box, and enter the distance in the corresponding text box.

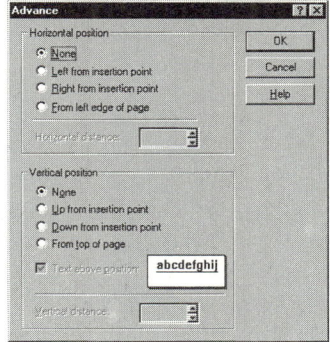

5. Type the distance to move the text left or right from the insertion point, or from the left edge of the page.

6. Choose an option button in the Vertical Position area. The Vertical Distance text box opens.

7. Type the distance to move the text up or down from the insertion point, or from the top edge of the page.

8. Choose OK or press Enter to save the changes and return to your document.

Only one direction of movement is included in an Advance code, although you can specify both directions while in the Advance dialog box so that WordPerfect inserts both codes in your document at the same time.

To use Advance only to allow for letterhead on the first page of a document, enter a measurement down or from the top of the page to indicate where the document should start. If you are using Advance to fill in the blanks in a form, however, you discover that Advance codes that advance text from the top of the page do not result in the text being printed on the form according to the measurements you entered. This is because the measurement indicates where to place the top of the text. When you choose From Top Of Page, the Text Above Position check box becomes active. When a check is in the check box, WordPerfect places the bottom of the text line at the position you entered in the Vertical Distance text box.

# Setting the Document Initial Font

The default font that is used throughout your document is the printer initial font and is set up in the Print to *Printer Name* dialog box. You can change fonts using the Font command at any time in your document when you want to increase or decrease the font size or use a different type face. Any text that is selected when you change the font or the text you type next appears in the new font. The font change does not affect any other text in the document, including header, footer, page number, footnote, and endnote text.

To change the font in headers, footers, page numbers, footnotes, and endnotes, you must either choose a new font when each is created, or you can change the document initial font at any time and from any location in your document. Using the Document Initial Font command to change the font in a document also changes the initial font for text in headers, footers, page numbers, footnotes, and endnotes.

If you find you frequently change the font for documents to the same font, consider changing the printer initial font. You can accomplish this quickly while in the Document Initial Font dialog box.

▶ **See** "Using Printing Options," **p. 286**

To change the initial font used in the active document, follow these steps:

1. Choose Fo<u>r</u>mat, <u>D</u>ocument, Initial <u>F</u>ont. The Document Initial Font dialog box opens.
2. Choose the name of the font you want from the <u>F</u>ont Face list box.
3. Choose the font size from the Font <u>S</u>ize list box or type a number for the size in the text box at the top of the list box.
4. From the F<u>o</u>nt Style list box, choose whether you want the font to be Regular, Bold, Bold Italic, or Italic type.
5. If you want to use the new font as the initial font for all future documents, choose S<u>e</u>t As Printer Initial Font so a check appears in its text box.
6. Check in the preview screen at the bottom of the dialog box to be sure the type appears as you want. Choose OK or press Enter to save the changes and return to your document.

Any font you select while creating your document takes precedence over the document initial font, making the document initial font particularly useful if you have not yet changed fonts in your document. If you have, the initial font change takes effect at the beginning of your document and continues until it encounters a code for a different font name or size.

You also can change the document initial font while in the Font dialog box by clicking Ini<u>t</u>ial Font. Refer to Chapter 20, "Using Fonts and Special Characters," for more about this feature and a full discussion of fonts and how they affect the appearance of your document.

# Creating the Initial Codes Style

You can set up a document's initial codes without those codes appearing individually in the Reveal Codes window. All you have to do is include the codes in the [Open Style: InitialStyle] code that appears at the beginning of every document. If you select codes by choosing Format, Document, Initial Codes Style, the codes you set up take precedence over those in the WP7US template that are used initially in the current document only.

▶ **See** "Considering Types of Styles," **p. 336**

The InitialStyle style can be a very useful tool if you format many of your documents using the same open codes. You might include Widow/Orphan protection, full justification, page-numbering position, and text to accompany the page number as initial codes; every new document you create begins with those settings.

Using Format, Document, Initial Codes Style enables you to add or delete a few codes for more specialized documents, such as changing the page-numbering position or adding a header. These changes affect only the current document.

 To set up the codes you want used initially in every document you create, include the codes in the [Open Style: InitialStyle] code in the WP7US template. Choose Format, Styles to edit the IntialStyle style.

Setting initial codes for a document involves editing the document style called [InitialStyle]. Because this is a system style, few of the options in the Styles Editor are available, simplifying the task if you are unfamiliar with WordPerfect's Styles feature. You can change the descriptive name of the style, close the display of the Reveal Codes window, and choose the codes you want included in the [InitialStyle]. If you have included codes in InitialStyle in the WP7US template, those codes appear in the Styles Editor, and you can edit, rearrange, or delete them as appropriate. WordPerfect 7 includes the Widow/Orphan Protection code in the default InitialStyle.

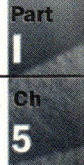

To add codes to the [Open Style: InitialStyle] code for your document, follow these steps:

1. Choose Format, Document, Initial Codes Style to open the Styles Editor shown in figure 5.22.
2. Use the menu bar at the top of the dialog box and keystrokes to choose commands to insert codes for the features you want initially in your document. The codes created appear in the Contents area.
3. Choose OK to save your changes and return to the document.

**FIG. 5.22**

The Styles Editor opens with a rectangular cursor in the Contents area. A limited menu bar is available for choosing commands to insert and edit codes.

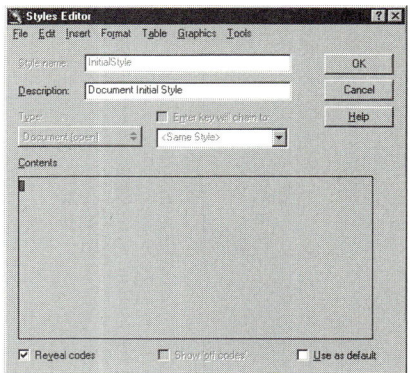

If you want to change the codes you have selected, follow the same steps to open the Styles Editor and make the changes you want. Any codes you insert later in your document take precedence over any contained in the [Open Style: InitialStyle].

To provide a different description for the [InitialStyle] code, choose Description and edit the current description to meet your needs. If you do not want to see the resulting codes as they are inserted, choose Reveal Codes to remove the check from the check box and close the Reveal Codes display in the Styles Editor.

# Setting Up the Redline Method

Redline and Strikeout are special fonts that allow you to edit documents while in WordPerfect by noting suggested additions (Redline) and deletions (Strikeout).

If you have a color monitor, redlined text appears red on-screen. Strikeout shows as a horizontal line (a hyphen) drawn through stricken text with either monitor.

You can select Redline and Strikeout by choosing Format, Font. How to use these fonts as editing tools is discussed further in Chapter 20, "Using Fonts and Special Characters," but the printed appearance of these fonts is an important consideration for formatting documents.

To customize the Redline method to specify how redlined text appears when printed, follow these steps:

1. Choose Format, Document, Redline Method.
2. Choose one of the following four methods for marking Redlined text:
   - *Printer Dependent.* Prints a shaded background with most printers.
   - *Mark Left Margin.* Places a vertical bar (|) in the left margin area alongside your text.

- *Mark Alternating Margins.* Places the vertical bar on either margin, alternating left and right.
- *Mark Right Margin.* Places a vertical bar in the right margin area alongside your text.

3. If you elect to mark text in the margins, the Redline Character box appears. If you want to use a character other than the vertical bar, delete the bar and type in another character.

    If you want to use a WordPerfect character, press Ctrl+W to display the WordPerfect Characters dialog box. Choose the appropriate Character Set, and then in the Characters list box, choose the one you want to use. Finally, choose Insert And Close. Chapter 20, "Using Fonts and Special Characters," provides more information on using the WordPerfect characters.

4. Choose OK or press Enter to return to the document.

Choosing a different Redline method does not change the on-screen display. Because it only affects the way the text appears when you print, you may change the method as often as you want. Your final selection takes precedence over previous selections.

If you are satisfied with the printing results, you can choose Use As Default in the Redline dialog box to change the Redline method for all future documents.

# Using Document Summaries

Creating a document summary enables you to create a database about your documents from which you can obtain information without retrieving individual documents. You can store a substantial amount of information in the document summary. In addition to document creation and revision dates, the typist and author which WordPerfect automatically fills in, text boxes are available for six separate pieces of information about your document; you can configure the summary to add more (see fig. 5.23).

The following list describes the text boxes in the Summary tab of the Properties dialog box:

- *Descriptive Name.* Enables you to enter a name for your document that differs from the name used to save the file. When you save documents using long file names, the long file name displays here if you activate this feature in Edit, Preferences, Summary.
- *Descriptive Type.* Enables you to enter a category to classify your documents into categories such as Letter, Proposal, Contract, or Payroll Report.
- *Creation Date.* Filled in when you create your document. The date appears in the format m/d/yy.

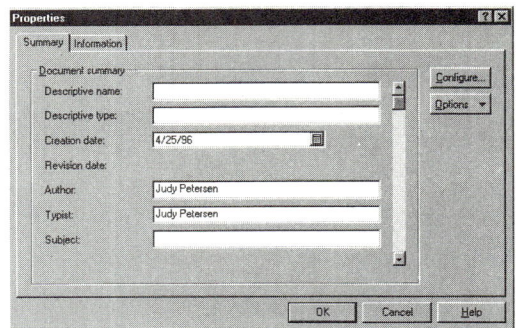

**FIG. 5.23**
The fields initially displayed in the Summary tab of the Properties dialog box depend on whether you specify using descriptive names in the Preferences menu. Click the calendar button or press Alt+↓ in the Creation Date text box to display the calendar shown here.

Click the button at the end of the text box with the calendar icon on its face to open a calendar in which you can choose a creation date. Click the double arrows to change from year to year, or the single arrows to change from month to month; use the arrow keys to move from day to day and week to week; and use Page Up and Page Down to change from month to month. Press Enter or click the desired date to enter it in the text box.

- *Revision Date.* Updated every time you save your document. You cannot enter information in this field.

> **CAUTION**
> The program obtains the Creation Date and Revision Date from the current date and time available in your computer. Check the system date frequently to make sure it is correct.

- *Author.* Enables you to enter text such as the author's name, job title, address, or other information. WordPerfect inserts the name you provide in the Environment Properties dialog box here. Refer to the "Extract Information from Document" section later in this chapter for more information.
- *Typist.* Enables you to enter text including the typist's name, job title, extension number, or other information. The program inserts the name you provide in the Environment Properties dialog box here. Again, refer to the later section "Extract Information from Document."
- *Subject.* Enables you to enter up to 250 characters about the subject matter of your document in the Subject text box. When you choose to extract information,

WordPerfect inserts approximately 250 characters following the default subject text. Refer to the "Extract Information from Document" section later in this chapter for more information.

- *Account.* Enables you to enter up to 160 characters of any information you want in the Account text box. This box provides an additional area for any descriptive information you want to add.

  Use the Account text box to identify a client, customer, or job that may not be apparent in the document summary. You can record an account number, court case number, or case style. This can be a particularly useful box if you regularly prepare routine correspondence to the same individuals about the same subjects on behalf of a different client or job.

- *Keywords.* Searches document summaries for keywords through the Advanced Search feature in File Manager. Use the Keywords text box to enter highly descriptive information about the document that can be useful for a speedy word search.

- *Abstract.* Accepts up to 400 characters of text to describe your document. When you choose to extract information, WordPerfect inserts the first 400 characters (approximately) of your document here. Refer to the later section "Extract Information From Document" for more information on this feature. If the document is a letter, the text inserted includes the recipient's name, address, salutation, and opening paragraph, without hard returns. You can edit freely in the Abstract box, but Copy, Cut, Paste, and Undelete are not available.

> **T I P** Consider listing in the Abstract field the names and descriptions of macros, styles, and other features you have included in the document summary.

By using the text boxes in the Properties dialog box, create a document summary by following these steps:

1. Choose File, Document, Properties to open the Properties dialog box with the Summary tab displayed.
2. Type the information you want included in the text boxes.
3. Choose OK or press Enter to save the summary and return to your document.

## Creating a Summary on Save/Exit

You can have WordPerfect prompt you to fill in the document summary each time you save or exit your document. The program then displays the Properties dialog box for you to fill in, although you can choose Cancel to skip doing so. The Properties dialog box continues to display each time you save or exit until you fill it in.

To be prompted to complete the summary, follow these steps:

1. Choose Edit, Preferences, Summary to open the Document Summary Preferences dialog box.
2. Choose Create Summary On Save/Exit to place a check in the adjacent check box.
3. Choose OK or press Enter; then click Close to return to your document.

If you decide you no longer want document summaries, follow the same steps, choosing Create Summary On Save/Exit to turn the feature off.

## Using Document Summary Options

Several options are available that delete, save, or extract information for you, or print the summary. These options are found on the menu displayed by choosing the Options button from the Summary page of the Properties dialog box.

**TIP** If you do not want to create a document summary for every document, yet you create one fairly often, consider adding the Document Summary button to the Toolbar so you have the option handy, but are not confronted with the dialog box every time you save or exit.

**Print Summary** You might find it useful to have a hard copy of the document summary you create. To print the document summary for the current document you have created, choose Options, Print Summary.

**Delete Summary from Document** The only way to remove a document summary after it is created is to delete it by choosing Options, Delete Summary From Document. You cannot restore a summary after you have deleted it; you must create a new summary for that document. If you have chosen to be prompted to complete a summary, the prompt resumes the next time you save or exit.

**Extract Information from Document** If you choose Options, Extract Information From Document, WordPerfect performs all the following tasks for you:

- Retrieves into their respective text boxes the Author and Typist entries from the last document summary you saved.

- Retrieves approximately 250 characters of text following the Subject text. WordPerfect searches your document for text that identifies the subject of the document and places the text in the Subject box. The default text for the search is RE:. You can change this text if you use other words in your documents to introduce the subject. (Refer to Chapter 9, "Customizing WordPerfect," for instructions to complete this task.)

- Retrieves approximately 800 characters of text at the beginning of the document into the Abstract box. You may want to edit the text included in the Abstract box, because in a letter, for example, this feature extracts the recipient's name and address, salutation, and repeat of the subject with the first words of the letter's body.

**Save Summary as New Document**  You can save document summaries as separate files by choosing Options, Save Summary As New Document. The Save Document Summary dialog box appears, prompting you to type in a file name. The saved file contains the text box label and contents for each entry.

If you enter a file name that already exists, a warning box informs you that a file of that name already exists. Choose Yes if you want to replace the existing file; choose No to return to the Save Document Summary dialog box.

## Customizing the Document Summary Fields

You may want to include information in document summaries other than the fields provided in the default configuration. To change the fields in the Document Summary box, follow these steps:

1. From the Summary page of the Properties dialog box, choose Configure. The Document Summary Configuration dialog box opens (see fig. 5.24).

**FIG. 5.24**
The Document Summary Configuration dialog box enables you to choose and arrange the items of information about your documents to track.

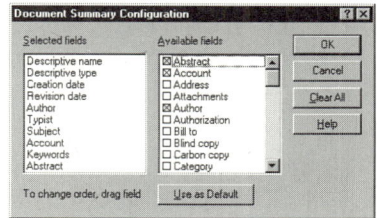

2. Scroll through the Available Fields list box and choose any fields you want to add to the Selected Fields list box; an X appears in the adjacent text box. To remove a field, click it so that the check disappears from the check box.

3. In the Selected Fields list box, drag field names to a new location in the list to change the order in which the fields appear in the Summary page of the Properties dialog box.

4. If it is easier to create your preferred list of fields from scratch, click Clear All to deselect all fields, leaving the Selected Fields list box empty.

5. Choose OK to return to the Properties dialog box.

   ▶ **See** "Customizing Document Summaries," **p. 319**
   ▶ **See** "Using QuickFinder To Search for Files," **p. 931**

The changes you make using Selected Fields apply to the summary for the current document. Click Use As Default if you want to use your design for all future document summaries. ●

CHAPTER 6

# Using Writing Tools

*by Laura Acklen*

**W**riting thoughtful and original material is enough of a challenge without having to worry about typos, bad spelling, or incorrect grammar. Thanks to WordPerfect, you no longer need to juggle a dictionary, thesaurus, and grammatical style book while you type at the keyboard. WordPerfect has these three tools (along with a few other useful features) built into the program to increase your efficiency and accuracy when you write.

WordPerfect's Spell Checker points out misspelled words, duplicate words, and irregular capitalization. Thesaurus provides lists of synonyms and antonyms from which you can select replacements for frequently used words. Grammatik proofreads your document for grammatical accuracy and offers suggestions for improving the readability of the material. Although these three useful tools can find many typos and grammatical errors, they do not replace proofreading. After you use these tools, always review your writing carefully to catch any missed errors.

**Customize Spell Checker**

Work with Spell Checker options and word lists to customize the program for your working environment.

**Proof your document for grammatical errors**

The Grammatik program proofs your document for errors in grammar and style. Like the Spell Checker, Grammatik can be customized for different types of documents.

**Look up words in the Thesaurus**

The Thesaurus makes it easy to select alternate words for overused or ill-suited terms in your documents.

**Correct typos and quotation marks with QuickCorrect**

The QuickCorrect feature fixes common typos while you type; the SmartQuotes feature replaces regular quotation marks with typeset quality quotation marks.

**Accommodate different languages in a document**

The Language feature marks passages in a document so the writing tools for a different language are used to check the text.

WordPerfect's other helpful writing tools include:

- *Document Information*. Provides statistics about your document, such as the number and average length of words and sentences.
- *Languages*. Used to indicate different languages being used in a document.
- *QuickCorrect*. Automatically replaces spelling errors and typos while you type.
- *SmartQuotes*. Replaces the regular single and double straight quotes with typeset-quality paired quotes.
- *Comments*. Used to annotate certain passages without printing or interfering with pagination.
- *Hidden Text*. Used in a document; you can then turn the display of that text on and off.
- *Abbreviations*. Replaces frequently used phrases or complex words; you later can expand the abbreviated words into their full and proper form.
- *Insert File Name*. Enables you to insert the document file name anywhere in the document, including headers and footers, for documentation purposes. Your printed documents then carry a reminder of the file name under which they are stored for your future reference.

If you want to experiment with the writing tools and you don't have any text to work with, type in the following text, complete with the spelling errors and bad grammar:

> **Thank you so very much for your kind lettr about you stay with us at the Kalamar InN from July 3rd thrugh July 13th. I hope you don't mind, but I possted the lettr in the locker room so the the other staff members could see it. YoUr praise is very much apprecated from everyone here and we are all very happy that you enjoyed you're stay. THe entire staff looks forward to your return naxt yeare.**

Notice that when you type **THe**, WordPerfect's QuickCorrect feature automatically changes the text to The. This feature is described later in this chapter in the section "Using QuickCorrect." ∎

# Using Spell Checker

Even the best spellers and typists can benefit from Spell Checker's capability to locate typos, misspellings, and duplicate words. The longer the document you are typing, the greater are your chances of making mistakes.

You can use two different types of dictionaries, or *word lists*, with WordPerfect:

- User word lists
- Main word lists

Spell Checker's own *main* word list, which is included with the program, contains more than 100,000 words. Additional language modules available from WordPerfect and other industry-specific dictionaries (such as legal, medical, or scientific) can be purchased and used with the Spell Checker main word list to provide the most accurate spell check possible. Up to nine main word lists (compatible with WordPerfect 6.1/7.0) can be used together with WordPerfect's main word list to spell check a document.

You use user word lists in conjunction with the main word list(s). There are two user word lists attached to each document: the *default user word list* and the *document user word list*. The default user word list file is called WT61US.UWL on a stand-alone system and on a network, WT*XXXXXX*.UWL where *XXXXXX* represents the user initials and the language code.

The document user word list affects only the document to which it is attached; WordPerfect saves this word list with the document, and the word list does not affect any other document. Within the document user word list, for example, you can add specific terms found in a given document so Spell Checker doesn't stop on those words.

The default user word list, on the other hand, affects all documents. For example, you may add your company name, company address, client names and addresses, and so on. Up to 10 user word lists can be used together with the main word lists to spell check a document.

## Starting Spell Checker

Before you start Spell Checker, save your document. During some operations, the computer is very vulnerable to system problems. For example, you should develop the habit of saving your work before printing, generating, using QuickFinder, or starting any of the writing tools.

**T I P** You can use the QuickMenu to bring up the Spell Checker dialog box. Point in the document editing window and right-click to display the QuickMenu. Choose Spell Check. Or, if you prefer, you can press Ctrl+F1 to begin Spell Checker.

 To start Spell Checker and spell check the on-screen document, click the Spell Checker icon on the Toolbar or choose Tools, Spell Check. The Spell Checker dialog box appears (see fig. 6.1), and Spell Checker starts proofing the document for mistakes. At its default

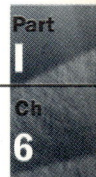

setting, Spell Checker runs through the entire document. Other options for this setting are covered in the later section "Customizing Spell Checker."

> **NOTE** Notice that three writing tools are all integrated into one dialog box: Spell Checker, Grammatik, and Thesaurus. Each writing tool has its own page in the dialog box. To switch to a different page, click the tab (it looks like the tab on a manila folder) at the top of the dialog box.

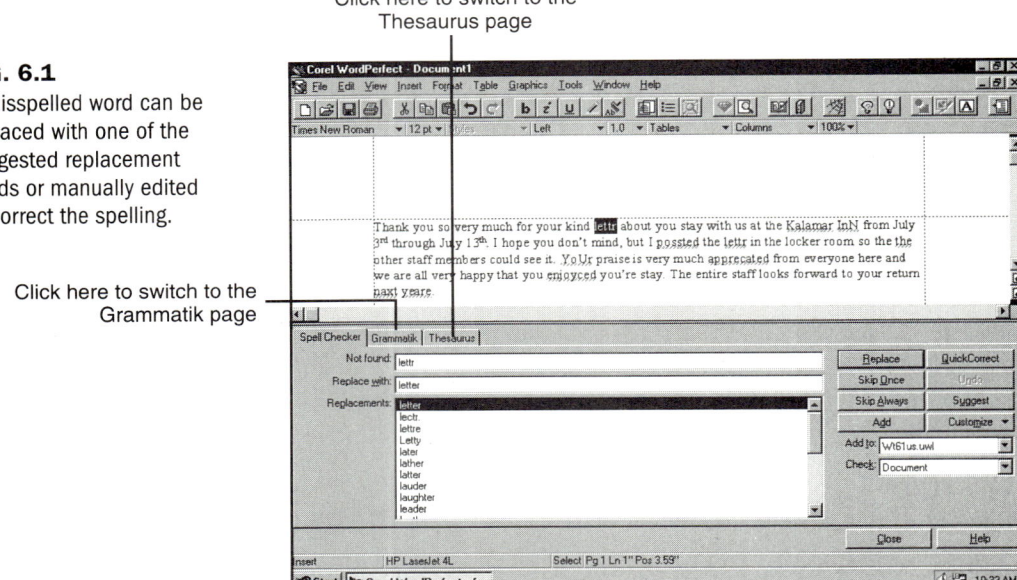

**FIG. 6.1**
A misspelled word can be replaced with one of the suggested replacement words or manually edited to correct the spelling.

## Spell Checking the Document

Spell Checker starts spell checking the document as soon as you open the Spell Checker dialog box. The Spell Checker program compares each word in your document with the words in the user word list(s) first, then with words in the main word list(s). When the program finds a word that doesn't match an entry in the word lists, Spell Checker stops, highlights the word, and gives several options to handle the word. When you are finished working with that word, Spell Checker resumes checking the document.

> **NOTE** You can minimize, rather than close, Spell Checker by clicking the Minimize button (the dash at the top right-hand corner) in the Spell Checker dialog box. This capability offers three advantages:

- Spell Checker is available faster because the program is already loaded.

- You don't have to reset any of the options you specified.
- If you told Spell Checker to make certain replacements (for example, to replace the misspelled word *lettr* with *letter*), Spell Checker remembers and performs those replacements automatically during subsequent spell checks.

**Using Suggested Replacement Words**   When Spell Checker stops on a word that is not in the word lists, it highlights the word and searches the word lists for similar words. Spell Checker then offers these words as suggested replacements for the misspelled word. If you choose one of the suggested words, WordPerfect performs the replacement and resumes spell checking the document.

In the sample text, Spell Checker stops on the word *lettr*, as shown in figure 6.1. Spell Checker highlights the word on-screen so you can quickly discern which word isn't found in the word lists. The questionable word is inserted in the Not Found text box, and a list of suggested replacement words appears in the Replacements list box.

To replace the misspelled word, select the word (which moves the word into the Replace With text box), and click Replace. For the sample text, *letter* is the first suggestion in the list and is already selected, so click Replace to replace *lettr* with *letter* in the text. If you want Spell Checker to automatically replace any other occurrences of the word *lettr*, you can add the word to the QuickCorrect list. See the section "Adding Words to the QuickCorrect Word List" later in this chapter for more information.

> **TIP**  If you prefer, you can double-click a suggested word to use it as a replacement.

**Handling Correctly Spelled Words**   Although Spell Checker's dictionary is extensive, it is not exhaustive. The dictionary does not include all the surnames, street names, and technical jargon, for example, that you may use in a document. WordPerfect's dictionary does include many common proper names and common terms from various professions. The names *Heather* and *Benjamin* are in the dictionary, for example, but the name *Karena* isn't.

In the sample text, Spell Checker stops on the word *Kalamar*, which is spelled correctly, and gives you several options. You can choose Skip Once to tell WordPerfect to skip the word this time but to stop on future occurrences of the word. If you want the program to skip all future occurrences of the word, choose Skip Always. WordPerfect saves the word in a temporary area, and Spell Checker does not stop on the word again in this spell checking session. This temporary area is erased when Spell Checker is closed, so if you start Spell Checker again and spell check the document, Spell Checker stops on the word. In the sample text, choose Skip Always to skip the word *Kalamar*, even if it appears again in the document.

If you frequently use a correctly spelled word that is not included in the WordPerfect main word list, you can add the word to one of the user word lists. For instructions on making this addition, see the sections "Adding Words to the Document User Word List" and "Adding Words to a User Word List" later in this chapter.

**Correcting Irregular Capitalization**   In addition to checking for the correct spelling of a word, the Spell Checker program also checks for irregular capitalization. This type of error occurs when the upper and lowercase letters are combined in a way that doesn't make sense to Spell Checker. The words *THe* and *REaDy*, for example, have irregular capitalization. This type of error can occur if you don't release the Shift key fast enough after capitalizing the first letter of a word. In the sample text, Spell Checker stops on the word InN, as shown in figure 6.2.

**FIG. 6.2**
Spell Checker stops on words with questionable capitalization.

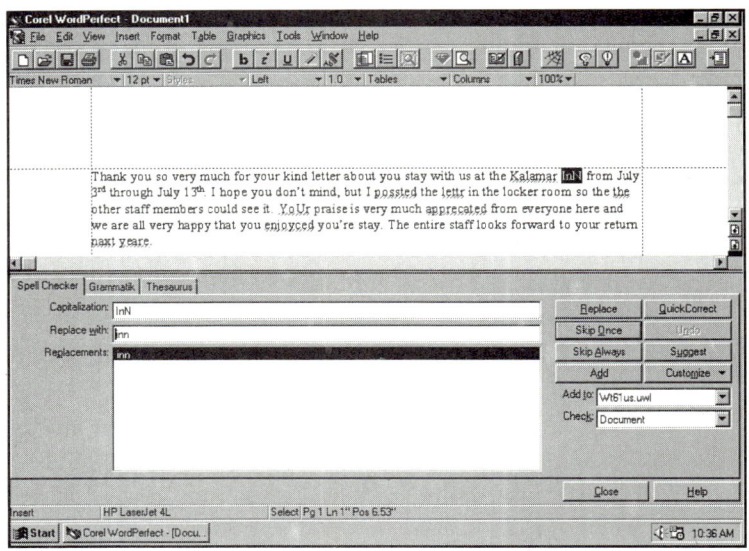

 **TIP**  If the word is not in the dictionary, you must manually type the replacement in the Replace With text box, and click Replace.

Sometimes irregular capitalization is necessary and correct. For example, McDonald and Del'Acour are all words with correct, though irregular, capitalization. Click Skip Once or Skip Always as necessary.

**TIP** You can turn off the option to check words with irregular capitalization by choosing Customize, Check Irregular Capitalization.

The word in the sample text, Inn, is in the main word list, so Spell Checker offers *inn* as a suggested replacement word. inn is the only word in the list, so it is already selected and present in the Replace With text box. The correct capitalization for the word is Inn, so you need to change the text in the Replace With text box. In the Replace With text box, delete the "i," then replace it with "I" so the word Inn is capitalized. Click Replace to replace the incorrectly capitalized word with the correctly capitalized word.

**Skipping Words with Numbers**   In certain types of documents, word and number combinations are common (for example, W4 form or ten-dollar bill). Spell Checker stops on such words, because they rarely are included in the program's dictionaries. You can choose Skip Once or Skip Always, depending on your preference, or you can turn off the option to check words containing numbers by choosing Customize, Check Words with Numbers.

**CAUTION**
Be sure to proofread the document carefully after the spell check if you have Spell Checker ignore words with numbers, because Spell Checker cannot catch typos in those words.

**Eliminating Double Words**   Another important task Spell Checker performs is checking your document for duplicate words. A common duplication that proofreaders often miss is *the the*: the proofreader sees the first *the*, but not the second *the*. Spell Checker does not delete the second occurrence of a word automatically, because in some phrases, duplicate words are grammatically correct.

When Spell Checker finds duplicate words, it stops, highlights both words in the document, and displays the message Duplicate words in the Spell Checker dialog box (see fig. 6.3). A single occurrence of the word appears in the Replace With text box. To delete the second occurrence of the word, click Replace; otherwise, click Skip Once or Skip Always. In the sample text, click Replace to correct the duplicate words *the the*.

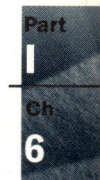

**FIG. 6.3**
Although Spell Checker makes it easy to correct duplicate words, you should do so with caution. In some cases, duplicate words are necessary and grammatically correct.

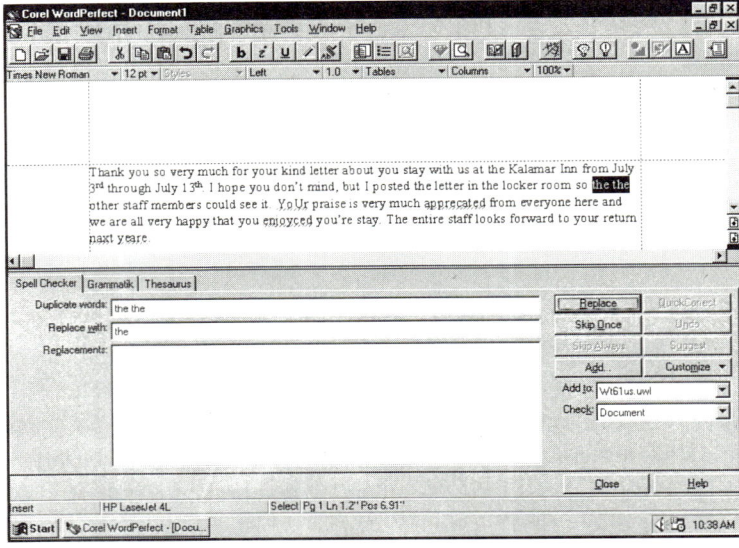

**Editing a Misspelled Word**   Sometimes Spell Checker stops on a word but does not offer any suggested replacements. This situation occurs if the word is not in the word lists, or if the word is so poorly spelled that Spell Checker cannot offer any suggestions. When Spell Checker stops on such a word, you can correct the spelling in one of two ways:

- Type the correctly spelled word in the Replace With text box and click Replace.
- Click the mouse pointer on the misspelled word in the document. Edit the word using the standard editing techniques. After correcting the word, click the Spell Checker dialog box (to make it active again) and click Resume. Spell Checker rechecks the edited word for accuracy; if the word still isn't found in the word lists, Spell Checker stops and highlights the word again. When the word has been replaced with a word found in the word lists, or has been added to a user word list, Spell Checker resumes spell checking the document.

**Adding Words to a User Word List**   Correctly spelled words can be added to the user word lists with the Add option. Subsequent spell checks will not stop on the added words unless they are spelled incorrectly. The word list displayed in the Add To drop-down list is the one to which words are added during a spell check.

The default user word list file is created when the program is installed. On a stand-alone system, the file name is WT61*XX*.UWL, where the *XX* represents the language code. For example, WT61EN.UWL is the English version. On a network, the file name includes user initials (or some other identifier to differentiate it from other users' word list files) and the language code.

To add words to the user word list, click A<u>d</u>d when Spell Checker stops on a word. For example, you can add your name, company name, company address, and other terms that might be common to your documents.

WordPerfect enables you to create separate user word lists for different projects. There is no limit to the number of user word lists you can create. Up to 10 user word lists can be linked together to spell check a given document. To add words to another user word list, select the word list in the Add <u>T</u>o pop-up list. For more information on using user word lists, see the section "Creating and Editing User Word Lists" later in this chapter.

**Adding Words to the Document User Word List**  The document user word list is one that is automatically attached to every document. This word list is saved as a part of the document, and is therefore used only with that document. You should add those words that are only found in this document—for example, technical terms, jargon, or abbreviations.

Words can be edited and deleted from the document user word list as necessary. For more information on using user word lists, see the later section "Creating and Editing User Word Lists."

> **CAUTION**
> 
> If you insert a file into a document, that file's document user word list file is lost. The document user word list file for the original document remains in effect.

**Adding Words to the QuickCorrect Word List**  The QuickCorrect user word list is used to automatically correct typos and spelling errors while you type. If you like, you can add a misspelled word and the correct spelling to the QuickCorrect word list while running Spell Checker.

To add a misspelled word and the correct spelling, wait until Spell Checker stops on the misspelled word, and then place the correct spelling in the Replace <u>W</u>ith text box and click <u>Q</u>uickCorrect. The next time you type the misspelled word, QuickCorrect locates the word in the QuickCorrect word list and substitutes the correctly spelled word automatically.

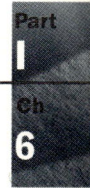

For more information on the QuickCorrect feature, see the section "Using QuickCorrect" later in the chapter.

**Finishing the Spell Check**  When Spell Checker finishes checking the specified text, a Spell Checker message dialog box appears with the message Spell check completed. Close Spell Checker?. Choose <u>Y</u>es to close Spell Checker and return to your document. If you want to be able to quickly access Spell Checker for another function, choose <u>N</u>o.

**TIP** Always save your document after running Spell Checker to save any changes you made during the spell checking process.

To stop a spell check before completion, choose Close. When you choose Close, the Spell Checker program stops, and the dialog box disappears from the screen.

## Looking Up a Word

As you type a document, you can check the spelling of a word by looking it up in Spell Checker. You can type the word phonetically (the way it sounds), or you can type the letters you know are right and use wild cards for the unknown letters.

To look up a word in Spell Checker, start Spell Checker, then begin typing the word in the Replace With text box. As you type, Spell Checker displays a list of possibilities. If you type the phonetic spelling of a word in the Replace With text box and then choose Suggest, Spell Checker performs a phonetic lookup, and then displays a list of suggestions, as shown in figure 6.4.

**FIG. 6.4**
A phonetic lookup on the text receve locates the correct spelling of the word receive.

As you type the word in question, you can use wildcard characters for the letters you are unsure of. The asterisk (*) wildcard character represents an unspecified number of characters in a word; for example, if you type **water\***, Spell Checker suggests *water, water-repellent, water-resistant, water-ski,* and so on. A question mark (?) wildcard character represents a single character in a word; for example, typing **c?p** returns *CPA, CPU,* and *cap* (see fig. 6.5). Clicking Suggest narrows down the list even further. The wildcard characters are helpful if you know only portions of the word you need to look up.

**FIG. 6.5**
You can use both types of wild cards in a word pattern to broaden the list of words.

**N O T E** After looking up suggested words, Spell Checker displays the number of suggestions at the top of the dialog box.

▶ **See** "Creating a Partial Listing Using DOS Wildcard Characters," **p. 930**

## Using Spell-As-You-Go

WordPerfect also has a spell checker that checks your spelling *as you type*. It's called Spell-As-You-Go. When you turn it on, it marks the words it doesn't find in the word lists by underlining the word with red dashes. When you right-click an underlined word, a QuickMenu with suggestions and spell checking options appears, as shown in figure 6.6. You choose a replacement word, add the word to the user word list, skip the word, or start the Spell Checker.

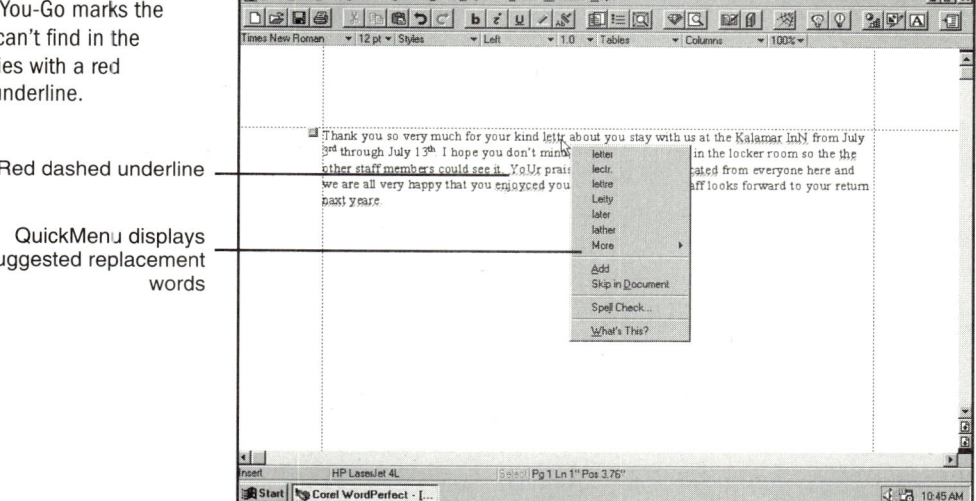

**FIG. 6.6**
Spell-As-You-Go marks the words it can't find in the dictionaries with a red dashed underline.

To turn Spell-As-You-Go on and off, choose Tools, Spell-As-You-Go. A check mark next to Spell-As-You-Go means it's already turned on. Choose Spell-As-You-Go to add or remove the check mark, turning the feature on and off.

## Customizing Spell Checker

Before starting a spell check, you can change some of Spell Checker's options to customize Spell Checker for the session. You can specify what portion of the document is to be checked, which word lists you want Spell Checker to use, and what types of errors you want Spell Checker to find. This section describes how to set the options to meet your needs.

**Specifying What To Check** Spell Checker enables you to run a spell check on a portion of a document; this feature saves time when you don't need to check the entire document. After you start Spell Checker, you can specify which portion of the document you want to check. The Check drop-down list in the Spell Checker dialog box has a list of eight different areas that you can specify within a document. By default, this option is set to Document, meaning Spell Checker checks the entire document. If you have selected a block of text, Spell Checker automatically switches to the Selected Text setting.

To specify the portion of the document to be spell checked, click Check. A drop-down list appears with your choices, as shown in figure 6.7.

**FIG. 6.7**
Spell Checker can be configured to spell check a specific portion of the document as an alternative to spell checking the entire document.

The options on the Check drop-down list provide a great deal of flexibility in determining the extent of your document's spell check. The options are as follows:

- *Document.* Checks the entire document and substructures, including headers, footers, captions, and so on. (This is the default Check menu setting.)
- *Number Of Pages.* Checks a specified number of pages from the current page forward.
- *Page.* Checks the current page.
- *Paragraph.* Checks the paragraph where the insertion point is located.
- *Selected Text.* Checks the selected (highlighted) text.
- *Sentence.* Checks the sentence where the insertion point is located.
- *To End Of Document.* Checks from the insertion point forward to the end of the document.
- *Word.* Checks the word where the insertion point is located.
  - ▶ See "Selecting Text," **p. 99**

**Setting Spell Checker Options** You can alter the default settings for Spell Checker with the items on the Customize menu. Your changes remain in effect until you change them again. Choose Customize to display the pop-up menu of options, as shown in figure 6.8.

**FIG. 6.8**
You can turn off certain elements in Spell Checker and change other settings in the Customize menu.

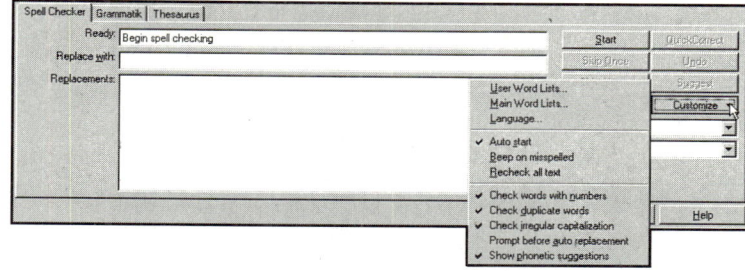

In the Customize menu, the items with a check mark next to them are currently selected (turned on). You can turn a selection off (and back on again) by choosing the item. The first three items have an ellipsis (...) next to them, which means a dialog box follows. See the sections "Working with Main and User Word Lists" and "Working with Other Languages" later in this chapter for more information on the first three menu items.

You use the remaining options as follows:

- *Auto Start*. Automatically starts Spell Checker when you open the Spell Checker dialog box.
- *Beep On Misspelled*. Beeps at you when it finds a spelling error.
- *Recheck All Text*. Checks the entire document each time you run Spell Checker, regardless of what was checked in the previous session.
- *Check Words With Numbers*. Stops on all words that contain numbers and flags them as errors. If your document contains many word/number combinations, you may want to turn off this option.
- *Check Duplicate Words*. Looks for two duplicate words in sequence and suggests that you replace them with a single occurrence of the word.
- *Check Irregular Capitalization*. Looks for capital letters inside a lowercase word and alerts you to the error.
- *Prompt Before Auto Replacement*. Automatically makes any replacements you define in the supplementary dictionaries. Further, if you replace a misspelled word during the spell check, Spell Checker automatically replaces other occurrences of the misspelled word with your replacement word.
- *Show Phonetic Suggestions*. Displays words that sound like the word, as well as words that are spelled like the word, in the Replacements list box.

**Selecting Different Word Lists** The User Word Lists and Main Word Lists items on the Customize menu give you access to the Main Word Lists and User Word List Editor dialog

boxes. The Main Word Lists dialog box is used to specify which main word list files you want to use with Spell Check. The User Word List Editor dialog box is used to create, add, edit, and delete user word list files. See the later section, "Working with Main and User Word Lists," for more information.

## Working with Main and User Word Lists

As stated earlier, you use two types of word lists in WordPerfect: main and user. Spell Checker includes a main word list and two user word lists. Additional word lists can be purchased and used with Spell Checker's main word list. An unlimited number of user word lists can be created and used in conjunction with the main word lists. Main word lists must be created and edited *outside* the of the WordPerfect program; user word lists are created and edited from *within* the WordPerfect program.

> **NOTE** A Spell utility program is available with WordPerfect that enables you to edit Spell Checker's main word list file. You can locate and remove words that you never use to speed up spell checking. You also can create new main word lists and add words to those word lists. The utility can also be used to convert supplementary dictionary files from previous versions of WordPerfect.
>
> The Spell utility is a separate program available when you use the Custom option during the WordPerfect installation. After it is installed to the \COREL\OFFICE7\SHARED\PFIT7\ folder, you can run the Spell utility from Windows 95 by choosing Start, Run, or by double-clicking the filename SPUTL61.EXE in Explorer. Refer to Appendix A, "Installing and Setting Up WordPerfect 7" for more information on installing custom options.

**Using Additional Main Word Lists**   The Spell Checker main word list (named WT61EN.MOR for the English-U.S. version) contains more than 100,000 common words. A variety of industry-specific dictionaries (such as legal, medical, and pharmaceutical) and non-English language dictionaries are available for use with WordPerfect's Spell Checker program. When you install a new dictionary, you add the name of the file to the Main Word Lists list. Adding word lists creates a "chain" of word lists that you can use to spell check a document. The order of the word lists determines the order in which Spell Checker searches through the word lists. The first word list is searched first, the second is searched next, then the third, and so on. You can chain up to 10 main word lists to spell check a document.

To add a main word list, follow these steps:

1. From the Spell Checker dialog box, choose Custo<u>m</u>ize, <u>M</u>ain Word Lists, <u>A</u>dd to display the Open dialog box, as shown in figure 6.9.

**FIG. 6.9**
Main word lists already contain a collection of words and must be created and edited outside of the WordPerfect program. Use the Open dialog box to browse for and select another main word list file.

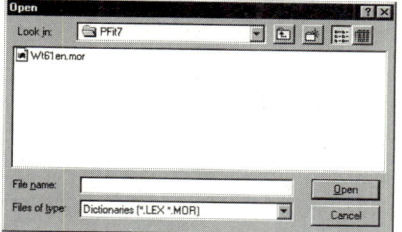

2. Use the Look In drop-down list to select the drive or folder where another word list file is located.
3. Select the main word list file and click Open.

When you close the Open dialog box, the name of the new word list file you selected appears in the Word Lists In Search Order list box. The order of the dictionaries in the list (or chain) determines the order in which Spell Checker uses them during a spell check. You can delete and reinsert file names in the list to change the order in which Spell Checker uses the files. When you delete a word list from the chain, the file itself is not deleted, only the name on the list.

**N O T E** You can greatly reduce the time it takes to spell check a document by optimizing the order of the dictionary files. During a spell check, the Spell Checker program compares each word in the document with the words in the word list files associated with the document.

When Spell Checker locates the word in a word list file, it stops searching for that word and moves on to the next one. Therefore, you should place the dictionary file that contains the words you use the most at the top of the list and the file that contains words you use the least at the bottom of the list.

**Creating and Editing User Word Lists**   You can create additional user word lists and add them to the list of user word list files in the Add To drop-down list of the Spell Checker dialog box. During a spell check, you can add words to any of the user word lists on the list. In addition to adding words to skip, you can set up automatic replacements and suggested alternatives for certain words.

**Creating New User Word Lists**   There is no limit (other than disk space) to the number of user word lists you can create for your projects. You can chain up to 10 user word lists (including the document user word list) to spell check a document.

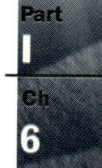

To create a new supplementary dictionary file, follow these steps:

1. From the Spell Checker dialog box, choose Customize, User Word Lists, Add List. The Add User Word List dialog box appears, as shown in figure 6.10.

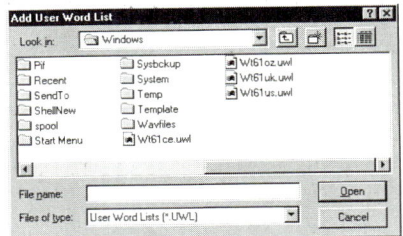

**FIG. 6.10**
A new user word list must be created and named before you can begin adding words to it.

2. The insertion point is already in the File Name text box, where you can type a name for the new user word list file.

**NOTE** WordPerfect automatically assigns a UWL extension to identify the file as a user word list file.

3. Click Open to create the new user word list.

   The name of the new word list file now appears in the Word Lists list box. The order of the dictionaries in the list (or chain) determines the order in which Spell Checker uses them during a spell check. You can delete and reinsert file names in the list to change the order. When you delete a word list file name from the chain, the file itself is not deleted—only the name on the list.

**NOTE** Each user word list name in the Word Lists list box has a check box next to it. You can select and deselect the check box to include or exclude the word list in the chain. This means you can add word lists to the chain, then selectively remove them when necessary.

4. Choose Close to exit the User Word List Editor dialog box and return to the Spell Checker dialog box.

After you close the User Word List Editor dialog box, the new user word list appears on the Add To drop-down list. Select Add To to open the drop-down list where you can select the new user word list. You can now add words to the new word list during a spell check by choosing Add. When the word list is used again, Spell Checker will not stop on the words you added unless they are misspelled in the document.

▶ See "Using Hyphenation," **p. 148**
▶ See "Using Document Summaries," **p. 201**

**Editing User Word Lists**   You can edit the user word lists and add additional words to skip. You can define words that you want Spell Checker to use as automatic replacements for other words within the document. Perhaps you incorrectly type **hte** instead of **the**; Spell Checker can refer to the user word list and automatically correct this error whenever it encounters the misspelling in your document.

In addition, you can assign alternative words for certain words that may be found in the document. For example, firms can establish standards for terminology in their documentation. These standard terms can be listed as alternatives to other terms that might be used.

To edit a user word list file, from the Spell Checker dialog box choose Custo<u>m</u>ize, <u>U</u>ser Word Lists, then select a word list file. In figure 6.11, the Proposals user word list is selected.

The User Word List Editor dialog box offers the following options:

- To add words that you want to skip (unless the word is spelled incorrectly), type the word in the <u>W</u>ord/Phrase text box, then choose <u>A</u>dd Entry.
- To add words to automatically replace other words, type the word to replace in the <u>W</u>ord/Phrase text box. Type the replacement word in the Re<u>p</u>lace With text box.
- To add a list of alternative words for a particular word, type the word to replace in the <u>W</u>ord/Phrase text box. Type the first alternative word in the Re<u>p</u>lace With text box. Repeat this process until you have assigned all the alternative words to the word you want to replace.

**FIG. 6.11**
You can design the user word list files to do some of your spell checking without any user intervention.

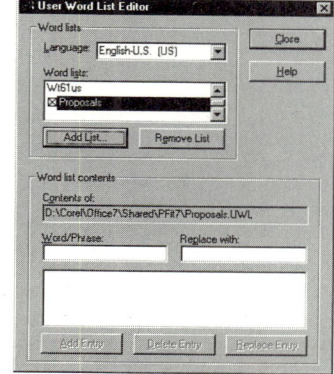

**TROUBLESHOOTING**

**I accidentally added a misspelled word to my user word list.** All user word lists can be edited from within the WordPerfect program. The user word lists, including the document user word list, can be edited through the Customize menu. Choose Customize, User Word Lists, then select the dictionary file that contains the misspelled word. Scroll through the list of entries until you find the misspelled word. Select the misspelled word's entry, then click Delete Entry.

**I accidentally added a misspelled word to the QuickCorrect dictionary.** Because QuickCorrect is a separate feature, you need to use the QuickCorrect dialog box to delete the misspelled word. Choose Tools, QuickCorrect to display the QuickCorrect dialog box. Highlight the misspelled word and click Delete Entry. Choose Close to return to your document.

**I have a misspelled word in my document, but the Spell Checker program doesn't stop on it.** Believe it or not, it may be a valid word in the dictionary. However, you can have Spell Checker suggest replacement words if you select the word, and then start Spell Checker. You may have to click Suggest if you don't see the correct word right away.

# Using Grammatik

The Spell Checker program is a useful tool for catching typos and misspelled words, but it cannot recognize a typo that happens to be a word found in the word lists. Spell Checker sees no error, for example, if you mistakenly type **their** for **there**, or **trial** instead of **trail**. Grammatik is a built-in grammar checker that checks your document for correct grammar, style, punctuation, and word usage, and thus catches many of the errors that pass by the Spell Checker unnoticed.

Similar to any of the writing tools in this chapter, Grammatik can't replace a human editor. Grammatik does not understand poetic or literary license or the intentional bending of rules to make a point. It cannot listen to a sentence to hear how it sounds. Grammatik doesn't find every error, and may even stop on correct phrases. If you set Grammatik to check a document in the Formal Memo or Letter Writing style, for example, Grammatik alerts you to every sentence that contains more than 35 words. You may not want (or need) to shorten every sentence that's more than 35 words. Long sentences can be difficult to read and understand, however, so this Grammatik feature offers you the opportunity to shorten the sentences when appropriate. Grammatik points out areas in your writing that you can consider changing to improve readability.

## Running Grammatik

Before you start Grammatik, save your document. Therefore, if you decide not to keep any changes made by Grammatik, you have a copy of your original document.

 **TIP** If you prefer using shortcut keys, you can press Alt+Shift+F1 to start Grammatik.

To start Grammatik, choose Tools, Grammatik. The Grammatik dialog box appears, as shown in figure 6.12. Notice how similar this dialog box is to the Spell Checker dialog box you used earlier. Three writing tools share a common dialog box: Spell Checker, Grammatik, and Thesaurus. Clicking a tab switches to a different page of the dialog box. Because you chose Grammatik from the Writing Tools menu, the Grammatik page is active.

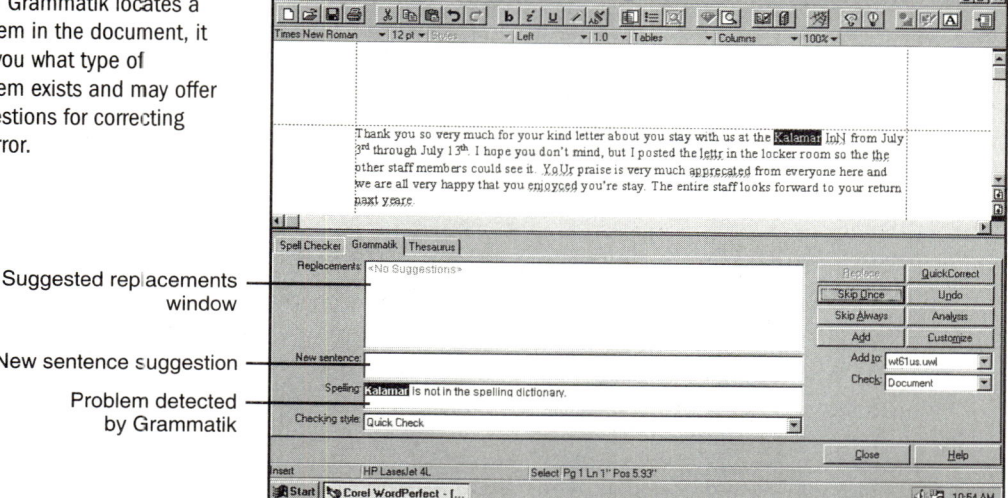

**FIG. 6.12**
When Grammatik locates a problem in the document, it tells you what type of problem exists and may offer suggestions for correcting the error.

Suggested replacements window

New sentence suggestion

Problem detected by Grammatik

As with the Spell Checker, Grammatik starts checking the document for errors as soon as the dialog box is opened. By default, Grammatik is set to perform a Quick Check on the entire document for grammar, mechanics, style, and spelling errors with a general writing style of standard formality. Later in this chapter, in the section "Customizing Grammatik for the Current Document," you learn how to change these settings.

The rules by which Grammatik checks your document are organized into *rule classes*. Grammatik recognizes 67 different rule classes for the checking styles. Rule classes have been established for grammatical style errors such as Sentence Variety, Passive Voice, Split Infinitive, Double Negative, Incomplete Sentence, Run-On Sentence, Ellipsis, Split Words, and Unbalanced Parentheses and Brackets.

When Grammatik encounters a grammatical error in your document, the program stops and highlights the text in question (see fig. 6.12). In the Grammatik dialog box, the program identifies the rule class and offers suggestions for correcting the problem. In some cases, Grammatik suggests replacement words or punctuation marks. You can choose one of the suggested replacements, edit the text to correct a mistake, or skip the problem and continue checking.

**Moving Past a Problem**   Grammatik follows a strict set of grammatical rules when checking your document for problems. Many good writers, however, often bend grammatical rules to make a point. To Grammatik, any word not in the program's word list is a misspelled word. In the sample text shown in figure 6.12, Grammatik stops on the word *Kalamar*—the correct spelling of the inn's name—and identifies it as a misspelled word. Because this word is correctly spelled, you don't want to change it. If Grammatik identifies a problem that you don't want to change, you have three options:

- Click Skip Once to skip the word and go to the next error. Grammatik skips this single occurrence; if Grammatik encounters the word again, it will stop on it.
- Click Skip Always if you don't want Grammatik to stop on the word again during this session.
- Click Add to add the word to the Grammatik dictionary.

**Editing a Problem**   In many cases, to correct a grammatical problem you must edit the document to reword a phrase or to delete extraneous words. For example, Grammatik may advise against using passive voice, in which case you can revise the phrase to use active voice.

The next problem Grammatik finds in the document is in the date format used in `July 3rd` and `13th` (see fig. 6.13). Take the advice offered by Grammatik and edit the two dates to read `July 3` and `July 13`.

Follow these steps to edit the sample text:

1. Click the highlighted text to move the pointer into the document window.
2. Make your correction. In this case, delete the `rd` and `th` after the dates.
3. Click Resume in the Grammatik dialog box to resume checking the document.

## Using Grammatik

**FIG. 6.13**
Grammatik suggests that you use cardinal numbers in the letter.

**Replacing a Word** Grammatik offers suggested replacements for words and punctuation marks whenever possible. In the sample text shown in figure 6.14, Grammatik stops on the word you're, which is used incorrectly in the third sentence. Grammatik identifies the problem as a homonym, describes why the program believes the word is incorrect, and offers a suggested replacement word. To replace a word (or punctuation mark), select the correct replacement and click Replace. Because the suggested replacement word is correct in this case, all you have to do is click Replace.

**FIG. 6.14**
You can choose a suggested replacement word and have Grammatik insert the replacement in the document.

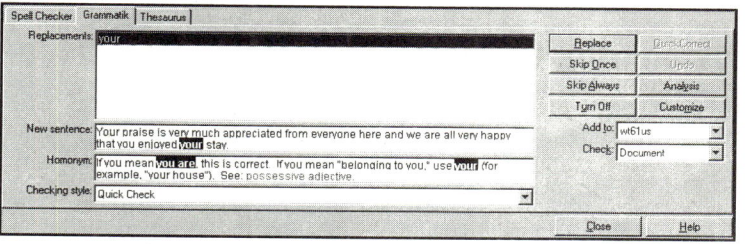

**Using the Undo Option** If you make a correction to a problem and later change your mind, you can use the Undo option to reverse the last action taken by Grammatik. To undo an action on your document, click Undo.

> **CAUTION**
> Remember, when you use the Undo option, you can only reverse the very last action taken.

**Disabling a Rule Class** If you want to disable checking for a particular rule class, choose Turn Off. This change is temporary; it only affects the current Grammatik session. You can repeat this action to disable as many rule classes as necessary.

**Getting Help** Grammatical rules are quite complex, and most of us need explanations and examples to understand them. The Grammatik program has a comprehensive Help system to help you understand the program and to assist you in your writing.

The Grammatik Help system provides explanations and examples for all rule classes. If you want more information about the rule class of a problem upon which Grammatik has stopped, move the mouse pointer over the rule class name. The mouse pointer changes to a pointer with a large question mark attached. When you see this mouse pointer, click the mouse button to display a list of help topics on that rule class. Choose a help topic from the list to display the information. Alternatively, you can click <u>H</u>elp for general help on Grammatik.

**TIP** In some cases, a term in the explanation window is shown in a different color, usually green (refer to fig. 6.14). You can click this term to display a Help screen explaining the term.

The Help system includes information on the types of problems that Grammatik identifies, explanations and examples of rule classes, advice on improving your writing, a glossary of grammatical terms, and instructions on using Grammatik commands. The Help system also includes an option that displays the parts of speech being used in a document; this information can help you understand the problems that Grammatik identifies.

## Customizing Grammatik for the Current Document

Grammatik enables you to change many of its settings to better meet your specific needs. The Cust<u>o</u>mize menu contains options that affect the current and future Grammatik sessions. The Cust<u>o</u>mize menu options are as follows:

- *<u>C</u>hecking Styles*. Select and edit the 10 predefined styles.
- *<u>T</u>urn On Rules*. Displays a list of the rules you have turned off during this session. You can turn a rule back on by selecting it.
- *Sa<u>v</u>e Rules*. If you turn off rules during a grammar check, you can save the turned off rules as a new writing style.
- *<u>U</u>ser Word Lists*. Opens the User Word List Editor dialog box so you can add and remove words from the user word lists. See the section "Editing User Word Lists" earlier in the chapter for more information.
- *<u>L</u>anguage*. Opens the Language dialog box where you can select which language you want to use for this session.
- *Auto <u>S</u>tart*. Automatically starts checking the document when you open the Grammatik dialog box. (This option is selected by default.)
- *Prompt Before <u>A</u>uto Replacement*. Grammatik prompts you when a word or phrase that should be replaced by a word in the user word lists is found and waits for you to confirm the replacement. (QuickCorrect must be turned on to use this feature.)

- *Suggest Spelling Replacements.* Grammatik suggests alternate spellings for a word. (This option is selected by default.)
- *Check Headers, Footers, Footnotes in WordPerfect.* Includes headers, footers and footnotes text in the grammar check.

## Working with Writing Styles

Different types of documents must conform to different grammatical rules and require different levels of formality. To accommodate these differences, Grammatik recognizes 10 predefined writing styles:

- Quick Check (the default writing style)
- Spelling Plus
- Very Strict
- Formal Memo or Letter
- Informal Memo or Letter
- Technical or Scientific
- Documentation or Speech
- Student Composition
- Advertising
- Fiction

Each writing style has a preset formality level, which you can change when you edit the writing style.

To edit a writing style, choose Customize, Checking Styles to display the Checking Styles dialog box, as shown in figure 6.15.

**FIG. 6.15**
You can select another writing style in the Checking Styles dialog box.

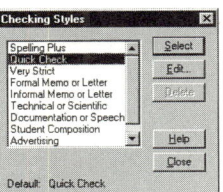

To edit a writing style, select the writing style, then click Edit to display the Edit Checking Styles dialog box (see fig. 6.16). This dialog box has a list of rule classes, a series of threshold settings, three formality levels, and a section where an example of each rule class is displayed. You use Rule Classes check boxes to turn the rule classes on and off (scroll through the list if necessary). The right side of the dialog box is reserved for Maximum Allowed settings. These settings specify what conditions have to be met for Grammatik to identify a particular problem. For example, sentences containing more than 99 words are identified as long sentences. You can select and change each of these five settings to accommodate your specific requirements.

**FIG. 6.16**
Use the Edit Checking Styles dialog box to modify writing styles.

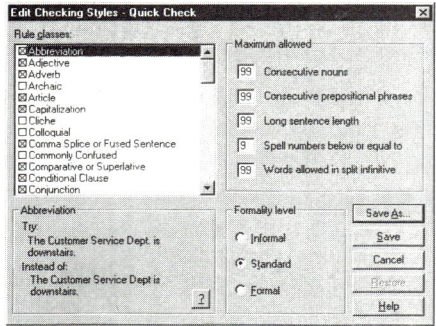

If you want to change the formality level for a writing style, choose a formality level of Informal, Standard, or Formal. The Standard formality level is adequate for most business correspondence, and a level of Informal might be used for personal letters. The bottom-left side of the dialog box is reserved for an example of the selected rule class.

The changes that are made to the writing style can be saved to the selected checking style or to a custom checking style. If you opt to save changes to an existing checking style, those changes are permanent. The checking style is shown with an asterisk next to it in the Checking Style dialog box so you can identify a style that has been modified. Fortunately, you can use the Restore option in the Edit Checking Styles dialog box to restore the default settings for a modified style.

## Displaying Parse Tree and Parts of Speech Diagrams

For those times when you can't figure out why Grammatik has flagged something as an error, use the Parse Tree and Parts of Speech diagrams to help you identify the different components of the sentence. The Parse Tree diagram appears if a group of words has been identified as a clause, and, if so, what type of clause. To display the Parse Tree, choose Analysis, Parse Tree. Figure 6.17 shows the Parse Tree for a sentence in the sample document.

**FIG. 6.17**
The Parse Tree diagram identifies the clauses in a sentence.

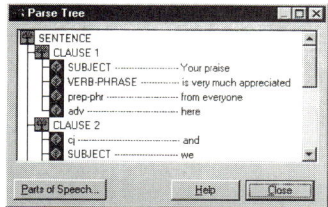

The Parts of Speech diagram identifies each word as a noun, pronoun, adjective, verb, adverb, or some other part of speech. Choose Analysis, Parts of Speech to see the Parts of Speech diagram. Figure 6.18 shows the Parts of Speech diagram for a sentence in the sample document.

**FIG. 6.18**
The Parts of Speech diagram identifies each word as a noun, pronoun, verb, adverb, adjective, or some other part of speech.

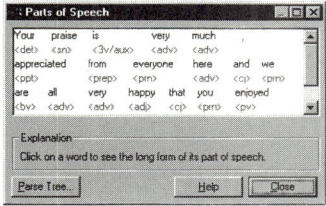

## Getting Statistical Information

Grammatik can compile a list of statistics about your document by running a statistics check. To run a statistics check, choose Analysis, Basic Counts. When Grammatik finishes the check, it produces a Basic Counts dialog box with counts and averages (see fig. 6.19).

**FIG. 6.19**
Grammatik can calculate statistics on the different elements of your document's text.

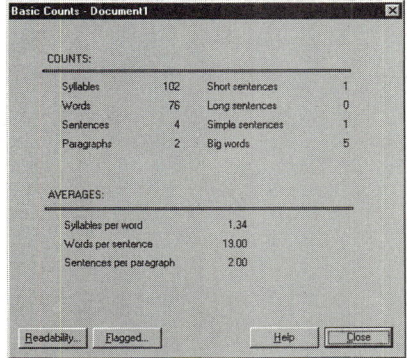

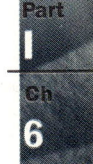

Click Readability to generate a readability score. This information can help you determine the length and complexity of the document. For example, a document with an average sentence length of 25 words is harder to read than one with an average sentence length of 15 words because the sentences are longer and more difficult to follow. Click Flagged to view a list of the potential errors that were found in the document.

**TROUBLESHOOTING**

**I made some changes to one of the writing styles, but I can't seem to save the change.** Any of the 10 writing styles can be modified, but you must be sure you choose Save or Save As before you exit the dialog box. If you choose Save, the changes are saved to the selected writing style. If you choose Save As, you can specify another name for the writing style. A modified writing style is shown with an asterisk (*) next to it in the Checking Styles dialog box.

**Grammatik always stops on my company name and flags it as a spelling error. How can I tell Grammatik that the name is spelled correctly so it won't stop on it again?** Just as you can in Spell Checker, you can add correctly spelled words to the user word list so Grammatik no longer flags the word as a spelling error (unless, of course, the word is misspelled). Click Add the next time Grammatik stops on your company name to add it to the selected user word list.

**Grammatik is constantly flagging long sentences in my documents. Is there any way I can change this?** Each checking style has its own threshold settings in the Maximum Allowed section of the Edit Checking Styles dialog box. You can increase the number of words in the Long Sentence Length (maximum of 99) text box to change the threshold setting for long sentences.

# Using the Thesaurus

A thesaurus helps you find the right words to express your thoughts. Some thoughts and ideas are more complex than others, and most ideas can be expressed in a number of ways. Using the right words enables you to convey exactly the message you want to get across to the reader.

The WordPerfect Thesaurus searches for and displays *synonyms* (words with the same or similar meanings) and *antonyms* (words with opposite meanings) for a word found in your document. You also can type in a new word for the Thesaurus to look up. The Thesaurus displays a list of words from which you can choose a replacement for the word in the text.

Because the Thesaurus is a separate Windows application, you can start the Thesaurus without running WordPerfect first. You cannot use the WordPerfect Thesaurus in another Windows application, but you can copy a word to the Windows Clipboard and then paste it into the Thesaurus.

## Looking Up a Word in the Thesaurus

You can start the Thesaurus from a blank screen, or with the insertion point on the word you want to look up. In the sample text, position the insertion point on the word `kind`.

To start the Thesaurus, choose Tools, Thesaurus. The Thesaurus dialog box appears on-screen with a list of synonyms for the word kind (see fig. 6.20).

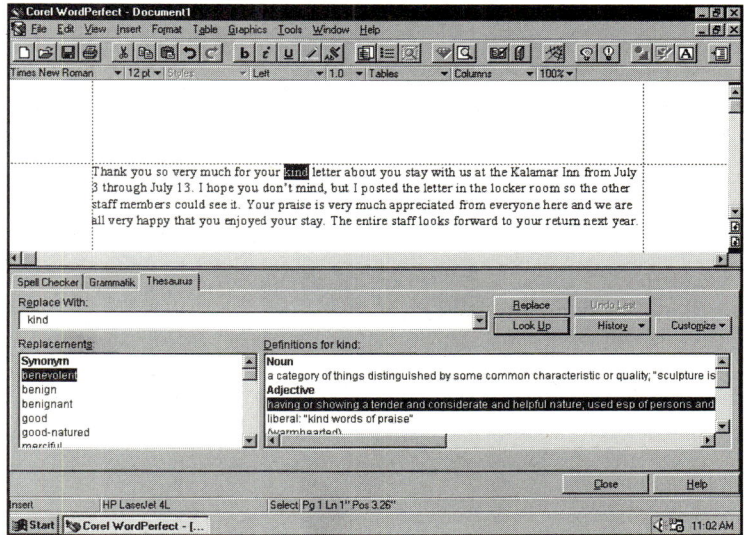

**FIG. 6.20**
The Thesaurus window displays a list of synonyms for a word. Definitions appear if that feature is installed.

## Understanding the Thesaurus Window

When you look up a word, the Thesaurus produces a list of related words, synonyms, and antonyms for that word. The Thesaurus lists the word in the Replace With text box and displays a list of related words, synonyms, and antonyms in the Replacements list box. If all the suggested replacement words cannot fit in the list box, use the scroll bar to scroll through the list.

If you have installed the new Thesaurus Definition feature, the definitions of the suggested replacement words appear in the Definitions For list box. If this list box is not available in your dialog box, you can install the feature by running the Custom installation of WordPerfect 7. See Appendix A, "Installing and Setting Up WordPerfect 7" for details on running Setup for the Custom installation.

> **NOTE** If you look up a word that is not in the Thesaurus, the program cannot provide a list of references. When this situation occurs, the Thesaurus displays a message at the bottom of the screen indicating that no concepts could be found for the word. The insertion point remains in the Insert text box so you immediately can enter another word for the Thesaurus to look up.
>
> You can try looking up the root of the word the Thesaurus could not locate (for example, *success* instead of *successfully*), or you can move on to the next word you want to look up.

Double-click any word in the Replacements list box (or select a word and click Look Up) to look up additional references for the word. Looking up additional references can help you in your search for the right word or phrase.

**TIP** You can enlarge the Thesaurus dialog box to display more words and definitions at one time. Position the mouse pointer over the upper border of the dialog box. When the pointer becomes a double-headed arrow, drag the border up toward the document window and then release the mouse button when the dialog box is the size you want.

## Replacing a Word

You easily can replace a word in your document with a word from a Thesaurus reference list. If the Thesaurus reference word is an exact replacement, select the word to insert it into the Replace With text box, and then click Replace.

**NOTE** If you have not selected a word in your document, the dialog box elements have different labels. The text box is labeled Insert, and the Replace button is labeled Insert, suggesting that you are inserting a new word into your document, not replacing an existing word. You can type a word in the Insert text box or select a suggested word from the list box which, places it in the text box. Click the Insert button to insert the word into your document at the insertion point.

Suppose that you look up the word *assigning*. The Thesaurus produces the reference lists shown in figure 6.21. The program produces a list of synonyms for the word `assign`. One of the words in the list is `distribute`. You want to use this reference word, but not in its current form; you want to use `distributing`. Select the word `distribute` to move it to the Replace With (or Insert) text box. Notice how the Thesaurus automatically changes `distribute` to `distributing`, so the form of the replacement word matches the form of the word you are replacing. Click Replace (or Insert) to replace `assigning` with `distributing`.

**TIP** If, despite the best efforts of the Thesaurus, you have to edit a word before inserting it in the document, type text in the Replace With text box to make your changes, then click Replace.

**FIG. 6.21**
Thesaurus automatically adjusts the reference word `distribute` to `distributing`, so it matches the original word `assigning`.

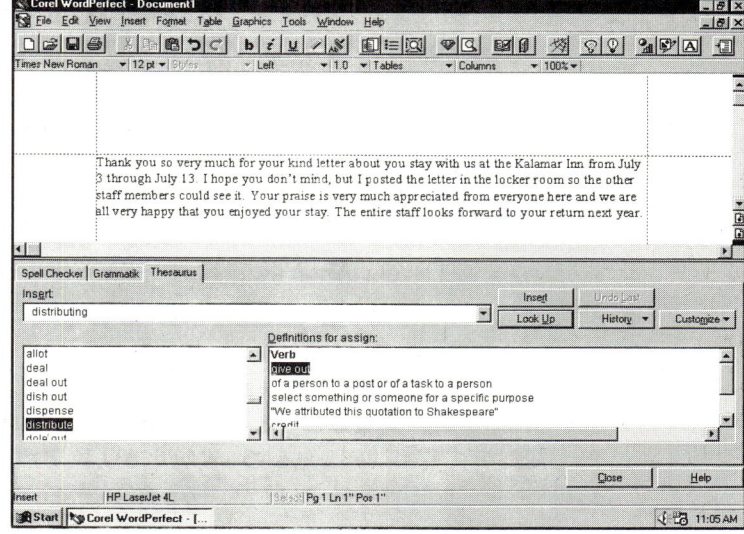

## Looking Up Reference Words

If the list of reference words does not contain the word you want to use, you can select any of the words in the reference list to look up additional references. You can use either of the following methods to look up a word:

- Select the word to move it into the Replace With text box. Press Enter to look up the word.
- Double-click the word.

When you have looked up several words in Thesaurus, you may want to review the words you have looked up, or you may want to go back to a previous word and look up references for it again. Click History to see a list of words that you have looked up since starting the current Thesaurus session. If you want to look up one of the words again, select the word. Thesaurus displays the word and lists its reference words in the list box.

# Working with Other Languages

Writing in different languages involves more than being able to enter, display, and print non-English characters. You also need to be able to correct the spelling, look up terms in

the Thesaurus, and check the grammar, in addition to using the proper date conventions and currency symbols. WordPerfect supports multiple languages in several ways:

- You can buy WordPerfect for a particular language. The menus, prompts, and other messages are in that language, as are the dictionaries that come with WordPerfect.

- You can mark a section of the document as being in one of the more than 30 languages supported by WordPerfect. Language modules containing additional files can be used in conjunction with Spell Checker, Thesaurus, Grammatik, Document Properties, and Hyphenation features.

- A Language Resource File, included with the program, inserts dates in the customary style of the selected language and performs sorts based on that alphabet. If you use the footnote-continued messages, they are printed in the new language. You can edit the Language Resource File to change what is printed for the continued message used when footnotes are carried over to the next page, for the currency symbols, and for the spelling of the days of the week and months of the year used in the Date feature.

**NOTE** If you select text before selecting a language, WordPerfect inserts a code at the beginning of the text to change to the new language, and inserts another code at the end of the text to change back to the original language. Otherwise, a single language code is inserted at the insertion point position in the document.

## Using the Language Feature

You use the Language feature to specify the new language, which in turn tells WordPerfect which language module should be used with the writing tools. You can change languages as often as necessary in a document, or you can specify one language for the entire document.

Most language modules contain a separate dictionary for Spell Checker, Thesaurus, and Hyphenation features. Some modules also include files that can be used with Grammatik and Document Properties. When you run Spell Checker, Thesaurus, or Grammatik, the program checks for the appropriate language module. If the module is not available, WordPerfect displays an error message. In response to the message, you can attempt to locate the necessary files or skip the language section during checking.

To change the language in the document, follow these steps:

1. Position the insertion point where you want to change the language or select the text you want affected.

2. Choose Tools, Language to open the Language dialog box, as shown in figure 6.22.
3. Scroll through the list and select the appropriate language.

**FIG. 6.22**
Language codes placed in the document affect the date format and the currency symbols used in tables. If the Language code is placed in the Initial Codes Style area, it also affects the footnote-continued messages, Grammatik, and Sort.

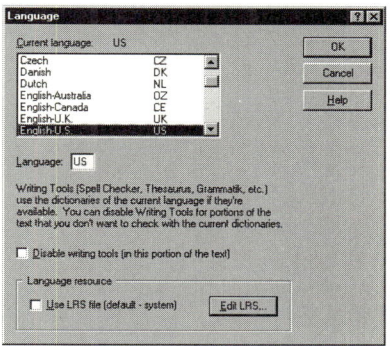

Language codes can also be used to skip sections of a document when using the writing tools. This may be necessary if the appropriate language module is not available or if the sections contain technical references or unusual grammatical styles that are not recognized in the current language.

## Using the Language Resource File

The Language feature can also be used to change the conventions used for the Date, Sort, Footnote, and Tables features to those of another language. A Language Resource File is included with the program for this purpose, so an additional language module is not necessary. The Language Resource File is edited by choosing Edit LRS in the Language dialog box. In the Language Resource Database Properties dialog box that appears, choose a language from the drop-down list and then click a tab to choose the property you want to edit. After changing properties for the language, click OK to return to the Language dialog box.

The Language Resource File contains the correct spelling for the days of the week and months in the year, in addition to the proper date format for many languages. (For example, in U.S. English, the correct format for a date is February 5, 1996; in French, the date should appear as 5 février 1996.) There are also options to modify sort conventions and adjust currency symbols for the chosen language. Finally, the continued messages used with footnotes and other miscellanous items are included on the Miscellaneous page for each language.

Select the Use LRS File check box if you want WordPerfect to use the Language Resource File (LRS) settings instead of the Windows 95 Regional Settings (set in the Control Panel).

You also can disable the writing tools for a selceted block of text by selecting the Disable Writing Tools check box. For example, you may want to disable Spell Checker and Grammatik for a paragraph written in another language to prevent these tools from flagging each word as misspelled.

▶ **See** "Understanding Data Files from Other Sources," **p. 596**

## Using QuickCorrect

The QuickCorrect feature automatically corrects common mistakes while you type. QuickCorrect cleans up extra spaces between words, fixes capitalization errors, corrects common spelling mistakes, and substitutes WordPerfect characters for special symbols. QuickCorrect also replaces regular quotation marks with typeset quality quote marks (see the next section, "Using SmartQuotes," for more information).

Choose Tools, QuickCorrect to display the QuickCorrect dialog box, which displays an extensive list of substitutions that are already defined for you (see fig. 6.23). Scroll through the list to get an idea of the type of substitutions that will be made. When you type a word that matches a word in the Replace list, WordPerfect substitutes the word in the With list as soon as you press the space bar. If you don't want QuickCorrect to make these substitutions while you type, deselect the Replace Words as You Type check box.

**FIG. 6.23**
QuickCorrect comes with a long list of substitutions that will be made as you type.

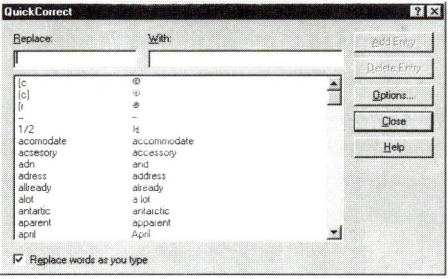

You can add additional combinations with the Add Entry option. Simply type words that you misspell or mistype, or an abbreviation that you want to expand as you type in the Replace text box. Type the replacement in the With text box, and then choose Add Entry. (See the section titled "Using Abbreviations" later in this chapter for more information on the Abbreviations feature, which can also be used to expand abbreviations in your documents.)

As you recall, you can add misspelled words and their correct spelling to the QuickCorrect word list with the QuickCorrect option in the Spell Checker dialog box. If necessary, you can delete an entry from the list with the Delete Entry option.

Click Options to display the QuickCorrect Options dialog box, which allows you to specify the type of corrections you want made (see fig. 6.24). The Sentence Corrections options are all turned on by default. To disable a particular correction, select the option to remove the check mark in the check box. The default End Of Sentence Corrections is set to None. You can select to have a single space changed to a double space or vice versa—a double space changed into a single space. The changes made in this menu are permanent, so they stay in effect until you change them again.

**FIG. 6.24**
The QuickCorrect Options dialog box displays all the corrections you can have QuickCorrect make for you.

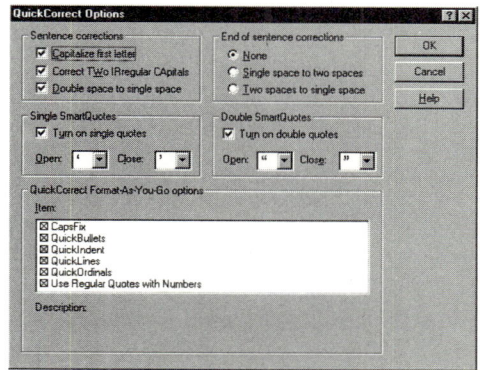

**NOTE** You can use the Replace Words as You Type option to turn off QuickCorrect if you prefer not to use it on a particular document.

# Using SmartQuotes

The SmartQuotes feature automatically replaces the straight single and double quote marks you type in using the keys on the keyboard (for example, ' or ") with typeset-quality quote marks. Options for the SmartQuotes feature are found in the QuickCorrect Options dialog box. To display the QuickCorrect Options dialog box, choose Tools, QuickCorrect, Options.

In the Single SmartQuotes section, make sure the Turn on Single Quotes option is selected (refer to fig. 6.24), and then select the quote mark you want to use in the Open and Close drop-down lists. In the Double SmartQuotes section, make sure the Turn on Double Quotes option is selected, and then select the quote mark you want to use in the Open and Close drop-down lists.

You also have the option of deleting the character shown in either of the Open and Close drop-down lists and using a WordPerfect character instead. Just press Ctrl+W, select a character, and then choose Insert And Close for each quote you want to change. The Use

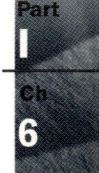

Regular Quotes With Numbers option (in the QuickCorrect Format-As-You-Go options section) can be turned off if you don't want the straight quote mark used after numbers.

# Checking Document Information

Submission requirements often limit grant proposals, research papers, and other projects to a specific number of words or pages. WordPerfect can check your document and compile an impressive list of statistics, including a word count.

To gather information on your document, choose File, Document, Properties to open the Properties dialog box. Click the Information tab to switch to the Information page of the dialog box, as shown in figure 6.25.

**FIG. 6.25**
The Information page of the Properties dialog box provides important information on the length and readability of a document.

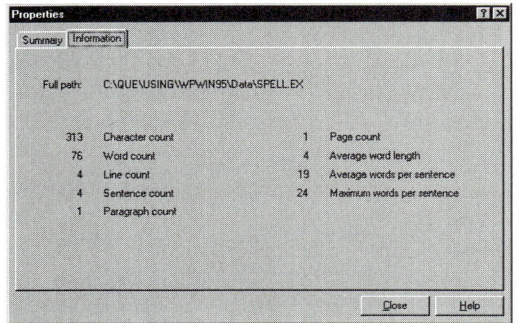

The Information page shows a list of figure counts for characters (excluding spaces, returns, and codes), words, lines (including blank lines), sentences, paragraphs, and pages in the body of your document. Document Information also calculates the average word length, average words per sentence, and the maximum words per sentence (the longest sentence in the document). This information can give you a general idea of the complexity of your writing.

When you are finished looking at the information, choose Close to close the dialog box. You can compile a new set of statistics at any time during the creation and modification of a document.

> **CAUTION**
> Counts may not be accurate if your document contains section titles (just a few words without punctuation preceding a paragraph), which are counted as paragraphs, or footnotes and endnotes, whose note numbers are counted as words.

# Using Other Writing Tools

This section covers other types of tools that can be used while you are writing. You can use Document Comments to insert comments, suggestions, or directions in a document. The Hidden Text feature enables you to insert hidden text into a document, and then choose to display and print the text as necessary. You can use Abbreviations to reduce repetitive typing of long or complex phrases. Finally, an Insert Filename feature enables you to insert the file name (with or without the path name) anywhere in a document for reference purposes.

## Using Document Comments

Most people are familiar with the sticky notes that office workers use to attach comments to documents. The electronic equivalent of these sticky notes is the Comment feature in WordPerfect.

As a writing tool, comments can be quite useful. If you use the sticky notes, you can imagine how you can use document comments. Consider the following uses:

-  Store an idea as a comment then return to the comment later to develop the idea.
-  Create a comment to remind yourself (or someone else) to come back and check a statement's accuracy.
-  Place instructions inside comments throughout on-screen forms to eliminate the need for printed instructions on how to use the form.

**Creating a Comment**  To create a comment, follow these steps:

1. Position the insertion point where you want the comment to appear.
2. Choose Insert, Comment, Create. The Document Comment window appears and displays the Document Comment Feature Bar (see fig. 6.26).
3. Type the text of the comment. You can use different fonts and font enhancements just as you would in the document.

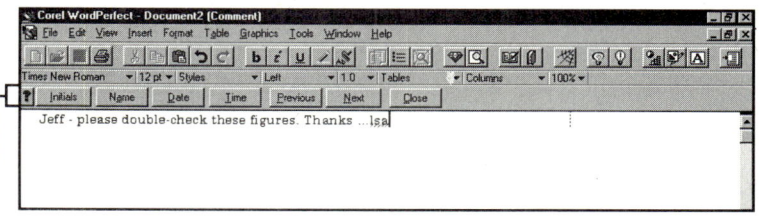

**FIG. 6.26**
The Document Comment Feature Bar enables you to create and edit comments.

Document Comment Feature Bar

Use the feature bar in the Document Comment window to insert your N<u>a</u>me and <u>I</u>nitials (provided they are specified in the Environment Preferences menu), current <u>D</u>ate, and <u>T</u>ime. You also can move to the <u>N</u>ext or <u>P</u>revious comments in the document.

4. Choose <u>C</u>lose to insert the comment in the document.

WordPerfect inserts a comment icon, which represents the comment, in the left margin of the document (see fig. 6.27).

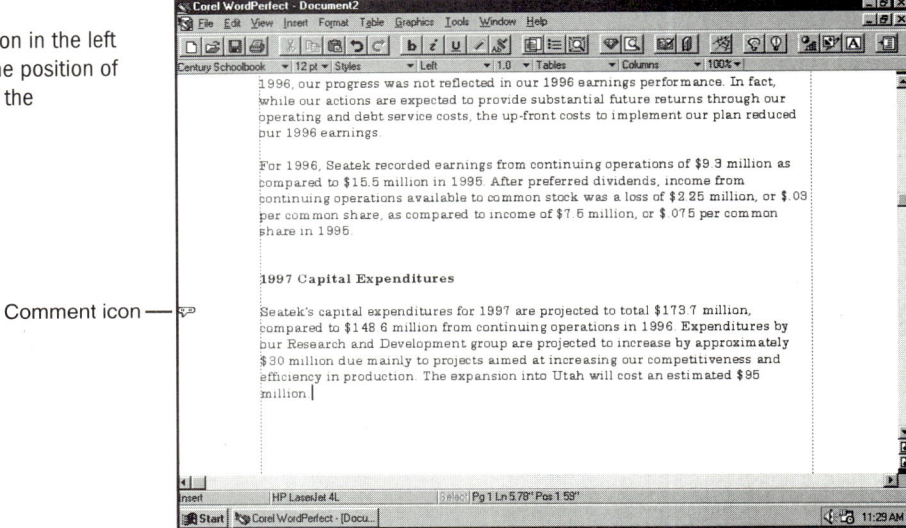

**FIG. 6.27**

The comment icon in the left margin marks the position of the comment in the document.

> **NOTE** The comment icon can only be seen in Page or Two Page View mode. If you use the Draft View mode, comment text shows up on-screen with a shaded background.

If you have supplied your initials in the User Info for Comments and Summary area of the P<u>r</u>eferences, <u>E</u>nvironment menu, they are displayed in the comment icon. In addition, if you specified a User Co<u>l</u>or in the User Info For Comments and Summary section, the comment icon and the comment itself are displayed in that color.

To view a comment, click the comment icon. To hide the comment, click the comment or somewhere in the document window.

> **NOTE** It may be necessary to use the horizontal scroll bar to scroll the screen over to the right until you can see the comment icon in the left margin.

**Editing and Deleting Comments**   The comment text is contained in a code (see fig. 6.28) that you can move or delete as necessary. If changes are necessary, you edit comments in the Document Comments window. You can use either of the following methods to edit a comment:

- Position the insertion point on the line with the comment icon. Choose Insert, Comment, Edit.
- Double-click the comment icon.
- Right-click the comment icon, then choose Edit from the QuickMenu.

Make the necessary changes; choose Close from the Comment Feature Bar to close the Document Comment window and insert the revised comment in the document.

**FIG. 6.28**
Document comment text is contained in a comment code.

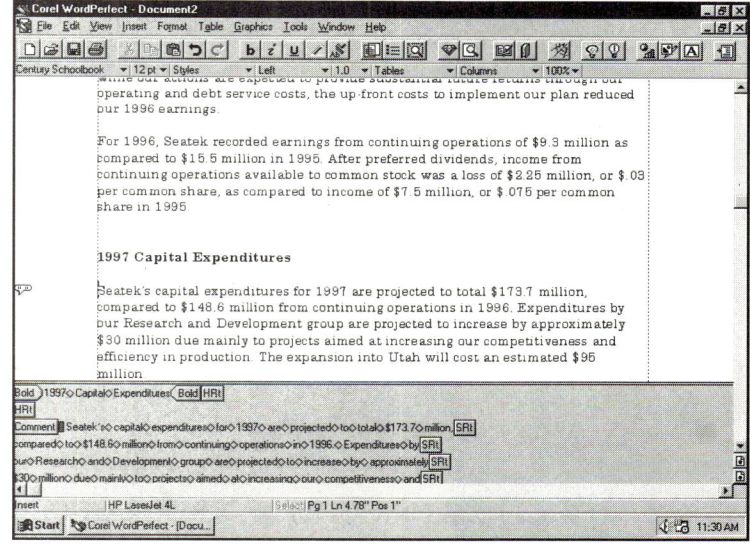

To delete a comment, position the insertion point at the beginning of the line with the comment icon. Turn on the Reveal Codes screen (choose View, Reveal Codes), locate the Comment code, and delete the code.

▶ **See** "Editing in the Reveal Codes Window," **p. 95**

You can move a comment to another place in the document by deleting it and restoring it. To accomplish this task, locate the Comment code in the Reveal Codes screen, delete the code, reposition the insertion point, and restore the code (choose Edit, Undelete, Restore).

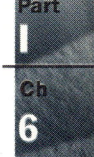

If you want to remove all comments from a document, use the Find and Replace feature. Follow these steps to remove all comments from a document:

1. Position the cursor at the top of the document.
2. Choose Edit, Find and Replace to open the Find and Replace Text dialog box.
3. Choose Match, Codes to display a list of codes for which you can search.
4. In the Codes dialog box, scroll down the list until you find Comment.
5. Select Comment; then choose Insert to insert the Comment code in the Find text box.

   Leave the Replace With text box blank (<Nothing>), so the code will be replaced with nothing.
6. Choose Replace All to replace all comment codes with nothing. This action deletes the comment from the document.

**Converting Comments to Text and Text to Comments**  One of the major advantages of using document comments is that they do not print with the rest of the document. In some situations, however, you may want to print the comment text with the rest of the document. To satisfy this need, you can convert comments to regular document text. If you later want to convert the text back to comments, you easily can do so in WordPerfect.

To convert a comment to text, position the insertion point at the beginning of the line where the comment icon appears; choose Insert, Comment, Convert To Text.

To convert text to a comment, select the text you want to place in the comment; choose Insert, Comment, Create.

## Using Hidden Text

Hidden Text is one of the features that was introduced in WordPerfect 6.0 for Windows. You can use hidden text to enter notes to yourself or to include text that you want to appear in some, but not all, copies of the document. If you are creating a test, for example, you can use hidden text to print the answers on the teacher's copy but not on the student copies.

Unlike comments, which do not print unless you convert them to text, you display hidden text to make it printable. You can turn on and off the display of hidden text by choosing View, Hidden Text.

Follow these steps to insert hidden text:

1. Before you create hidden text, turn on the display of hidden text by choosing View, Hidden Text (a check mark indicates the option is on).

2. Choose Fo**r**mat, **F**ont; or press F9. Then place a check mark in the Hidd**e**n check box (in the Appearance section).
3. Type the text you want to hide.
4. Choose Fo**r**mat, **F**ont. Then choose Hidd**e**n again to remove the check mark and turn off the attribute.

You easily can change existing text to hidden text by using the following steps:

1. Select the text you want to hide.
2. Choose Fo**r**mat, **F**ont; or press F9.
3. Choose Hidd**e**n.

Follow these steps to delete hidden text:

1. Turn off the display of hidden text.
2. Turn on Reveal Codes and locate the hidden code.
3. Delete the code.

Because the hidden text was not displayed, the text is deleted with the code.

Follow these steps to convert hidden text to regular document text:

1. Turn on the display of hidden text.
2. Turn on Reveal Codes and delete the hidden code.

Because the hidden text is currently displayed, the hidden text is converted to normal document text.

> **NOTE** You must display hidden text if you want to include it in page counts, QuickFinder searches, or if you want to check it with any of the writing tools (Spell Checker, Grammatik, Thesaurus, or Document Information).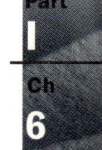

## Using Abbreviations

Abbreviations simplify the insertion of frequently used words and phrases. You assign a short abbreviation to a phrase, use the abbreviation when typing the document, and then expand the abbreviation later. If you must frequently type your company name in a document, for example, you can assign a short abbreviation to your company name. When you type the document, you can type the abbreviation in place of your company name. You can then press Ctrl+A to expand the abbreviation into the full company name.

Follow these steps to create an abbreviation:

1. Select the text for which you want to create an abbreviation.
2. Choose Insert, Abbreviations. The Abbreviations dialog box appears, as shown in figure 6.29.

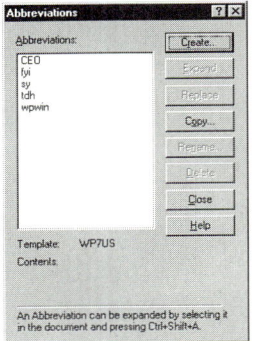

**FIG. 6.29**
The Abbreviations dialog box enables you to create abbreviations that save time and help reduce typing errors within your documents.

3. Choose Create to display the Create Abbreviation dialog box.
4. Type a name for the selected information in the Abbreviation Name text box.
5. Choose OK, and then Close to return to the document.

**N O T E** Abbreviations are case-sensitive. This attribute enables you to use within the same document, for example, the abbreviation "lc" for "last chance" and "LC" for "Lindsey contract."

You can expand a typed abbreviation at any time. To expand an abbreviation, position the insertion point anywhere in the abbreviation. Choose Insert, Abbreviations, Expand; or press Ctrl+Shift+A. WordPerfect includes a macro that expands all the abbreviations in the document at one time. To run the macro, choose Tools, Macro, Play. Select the EXPNDALL macro file and click Play.

You easily can change the information associated with a particular abbreviation. To replace an abbreviation, select the text you now want associated with the abbreviation. Choose Insert, Abbreviations, Replace. For example, if your company name has changed, you will want to update the abbreviation with the new name.

WordPerfect saves abbreviations to the particular template in which you are working. You can set up different abbreviations for different templates. For example, you may have a set of abbreviations for an expense report template and another set for a sales proposal template.

▶ **See** "Using Templates," **p. 364**

If you want to copy an abbreviation to another template, use the following steps:

1. Choose Insert, Abbreviations to display the Abbreviations dialog box.
2. Highlight the abbreviation in the Abbreviations dialog box and click Copy. The Copy Abbreviation dialog box appears.
3. Choose Select Abbreviation To Copy and highlight the abbreviation.
4. Choose Template to Copy To and select a template from the drop-down list; then click Copy.

## Inserting the File Name

Inserting the file name in a printed document can help you and others who use your printed document find the document's file in the computer system. Many users include the file name in a document header or footer, or on the line just above the author/typist initials. You can insert the file name alone, or you can insert both the path and the file name. The *path* is the location of the file on the system; for example, in the path and filename

    C:\NEWACCTS\TAYLOR\WELCOME LETTER

C:\NEWACCTS\TAYLOR is the path, and WELCOME LETTER is the file name.

To insert the file name anywhere in your document, position the insertion point where you want the file name to appear. Choose Insert, Other; then choose Filename if you want to insert just the file name; or choose Path and Filename if you want to insert the path with the file name.

At the insertion point, WordPerfect inserts a code that represents the current path and file name. If you rename the file or save it to a different location, WordPerfect automatically updates the file and path names to show the new path or file name.

You can insert the code for the file name or path and file name even if the document has not been saved (and named) yet. When you name the document, WordPerfect automatically inserts the name wherever you have placed file name codes in the document.

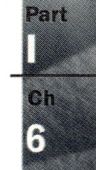

**TROUBLESHOOTING**

**I want to create hidden text, but when I choose F̲ormat, F̲ont, hidden text is dimmed. Why can't I use it?** To create or view hidden text, make sure Hidden Text is selected on the V̲iew menu.

**I inserted the file name in my document. Why doesn't it appear?** You inserted the file name before saving the document. As soon as the file is saved, the file name appears.

▶ **See** "Saving a Document to Disk," **p. 70**

▶ **See** "Understanding WordPerfect's Hidden Codes," **p. 91**

▶ **See** "Customizing Environment Options," **p. 306**

CHAPTER 7

# Integrating Text and Graphics

*by Sue Plumley and Gordon McComb*

▬ **Use horizontal and vertical lines**
Enhance the look of and separate the sections of your document with horizontal and vertical lines.

▬ **Use paragraph and page borders**
You learn how borders for paragraphs and pages allow you to enhance and accent your documents.

▬ **Understand the types of graphics boxes**
WordPerfect has several pre-defined graphics box styles. You explore the different types and their use.

▬ **Create, size, and move a graphics box**
Graphics boxes can be placed anywhere on a page. You learn how in this chapter.

**I***t starts with text*. In previous chapters, you learned to create, edit, and format text in documents, such as letters and memos. The way you assemble the words on the page defines the message of your document.

*It gets better with graphics*. With just a sprinkling of graphics, such as lines, borders, and images, you can greatly enhance the message of your document, without adding more words. Graphics emphasize important items, separate sections of text, and make the text more interesting to look at.

You use graphics lines, borders, and images to enhance your text. A page consisting entirely of text can be monotonous and cause the reader to lose interest in the message. A page containing lines or images, on the other hand, attracts the reader and supports the text. Use graphics, for example, to attract attention to an important announcement in a letter or to dress up a memo.

WordPerfect enables you to add a variety of graphics lines, borders, and images to your documents. You can create horizontal and vertical lines, paragraph and page borders, and boxes that hold text or images. This chapter introduces you to adding basic lines, borders, and images to your document.

Chapter 21, "Using Advanced Graphics Techniques," delves deeper into using and customizing WordPerfect's graphics capabilities. ■

# Using Graphics Lines

Use graphics lines in your documents to add emphasis, separate text, or dress up the page. You can use lines in most documents, such as letters, memos, newsletters, brochures, and reports. WordPerfect for Windows enables you to create various styles, thicknesses, and lengths of lines and to easily change line position, spacing, and color.

> **NOTE** Make sure that all graphics complement the message and add to the overall comprehension of the message. Unorganized use and placement of graphics confuses the reader. For more information on using WordPerfect for Windows as a serious desktop publishing tool, see Chapter 23, "Desktop Publishing with WordPerfect." ■

WordPerfect enables you to add horizontal and vertical lines to the page by using the Graphics menu, a keyboard shortcut, or the Graphics Toolbar; WordPerfect inserts the line at the position of the insertion point. After you insert a line, you can easily move the line on the page and resize the line by using the mouse. This section introduces creating horizontal and vertical lines, and moving and sizing lines using the mouse; for more information about customizing lines, see Chapter 21, "Using Advanced Graphics Techniques."

## Using Horizontal Lines

You can use horizontal lines to guide the reader's eye from page to page, to border pages or paragraphs, or to emphasize important text. You can use horizontal lines, for example, in a memo above and below the heading to make it stand out or to separate the banner lines and the message of the memo. Figure 7.1 illustrates a memo that uses horizontal lines to separate text and add flair to your document.

> **NOTE** If the Toolbar is not already shown on-screen, choose View, Toolbars/Ruler, select WordPerfect 7 Toolbar, and click OK. Once the Toolbar is displayed, right-click anywhere over the Toolbar; a list of available Toolbars appears in the QuickMenu. Find the one that says Graphics, and click it with the left mouse button. ■

**FIG. 7.1**
Horizontal lines separate text and attract attention to the memo. A shortcut for creating a horizontal line is to use the Horizontal Line button on the Graphics Toolbar.

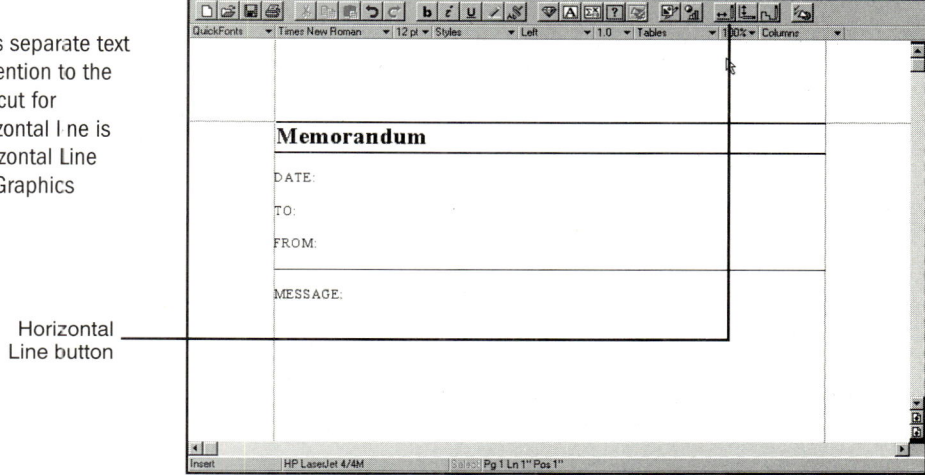

Horizontal Line button

Try creating horizontal lines on a practice document; use a document created previously, or create a new document using the memo in figure 7.1 as a guide. After you create and format the text in the document, add horizontal lines by following these steps:

1. Position the insertion point.

2. Choose Graphics, Horizontal Line; or press Ctrl+F11. The default settings of the line are horizontal extending the length between the left and right margins, single line style, black, and with no spacing above or below the line.

3. Reposition the insertion point and insert another horizontal line.

**N O T E**  To avoid crowding the text, create horizontal lines on a blank line—a line containing only a paragraph return (press Enter to make the hard return). Placing graphics lines on a blank line provides space between the text and the graphic. Alternatively, you can place the line on the same line as the text.

## Using Vertical Lines

You can also create vertical lines in documents to separate text, emphasize text, or dress up the page. For example, use a vertical line to emphasize left text alignment in a business letter or use short vertical lines to draw attention to important items in a report. Figure 7.2 illustrates a business letter with a vertical line near the left margin.

**FIG. 7.2**
Use a vertical line to dress up or emphasize the text. Use the Vertical Line button in the Graphics Toolbar as a quick and easy shortcut for creating vertical lines.

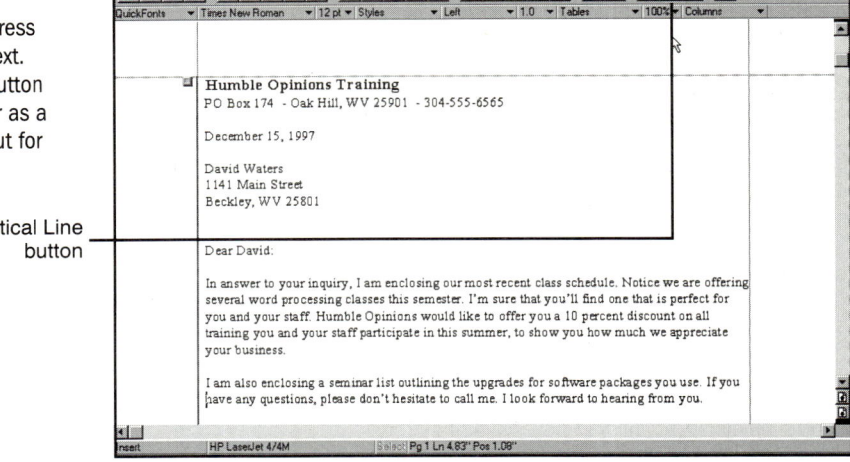

Vertical Line button

To create a vertical line in a document, use a letter you already created, or create a new one using figure 7.2 as a guide. After creating and formatting the text, follow these steps to add the vertical line:

1. Position the insertion point, preferably in front of all text.

2. Choose Graphics, Vertical Line; or press Ctrl+Shift+F11. The vertical line appears. The default line is a single style vertical line, positioned at the insertion point where your cursor was located and extending from the top to the bottom margins.

## Customizing Lines Using the Mouse

WordPerfect enables you to alter the length, thickness, and position of a line by using the mouse or a dialog box. Using the mouse to customize lines is quick and easy, although not as precise as using the dialog box. This chapter covers using the mouse to customize graphics lines. For more information about using the dialog box to customize lines, see Chapter 21, "Using Advanced Graphics Techniques."

▶ **See** "Formatting Lines and Paragraphs," **p. 130**
▶ **See** "Customizing Lines," **p. 658**

> **N O T E**  Add consistency to your document by using the same line style and thickness throughout the document. Occasionally, you may want to use two line styles—such as thick and thin, or thick-thin and thin-thick—but using more than two line styles can distract the reader and make the document look unprofessional.

To use the mouse to customize horizontal or vertical lines, open a document—such as the memo you created previously—and follow these steps:

1. Use the mouse to select the line (see fig. 7.3). Click the line to select it.

**FIG. 7.3**
When you select a line, small black boxes called *handles* appear at the ends and in the middle of the line. Use the handles to resize the line.

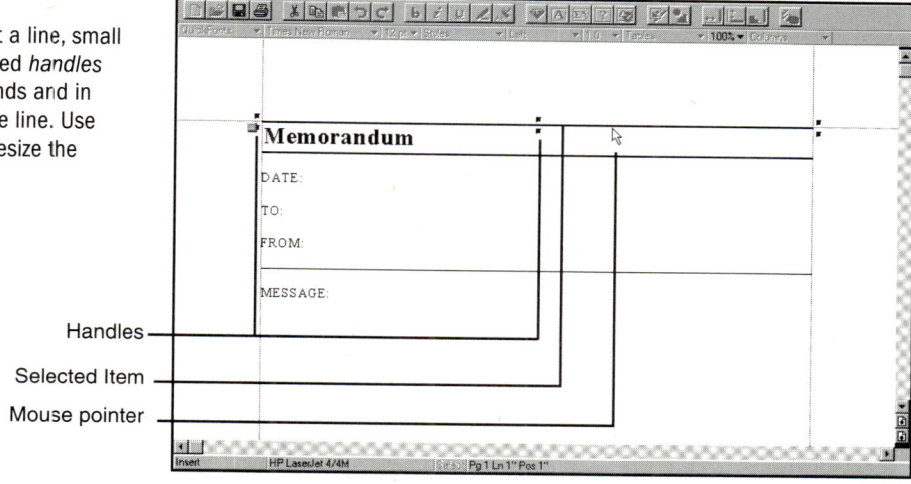

2. Position the mouse arrow on the bottom-right handle; the mouse arrow changes to a diagonal double-headed arrow. Click and drag the handle towards the center of the line to shorten the line length. Be careful not to move the mouse up or down while dragging, or you will thicken the line.

 **TIP** It takes a little time to get used to positioning the mouse pointer just right so that you get the double arrow; with practice, however, you'll have no problem.

3. Position the mouse so you have a vertical double-headed arrow on the bottom-middle handle; click and drag the arrow down 1/4 inch to make the line thicker.
4. Position the mouse arrow on the line; move the line to any position on the page by clicking and dragging the line to its new position.

## Deleting Lines

You can easily delete lines in WordPerfect by deleting the code that represents the line, selecting the line with the mouse and pressing the Delete key (see fig. 7.4), or by using the QuickMenu displayed by right-clicking while your mouse arrow is over the line.

**FIG. 7.4**
Use the mouse to change the length and width of the line by first selecting the line and then manipulating the handles; you can also use the mouse to move the line.

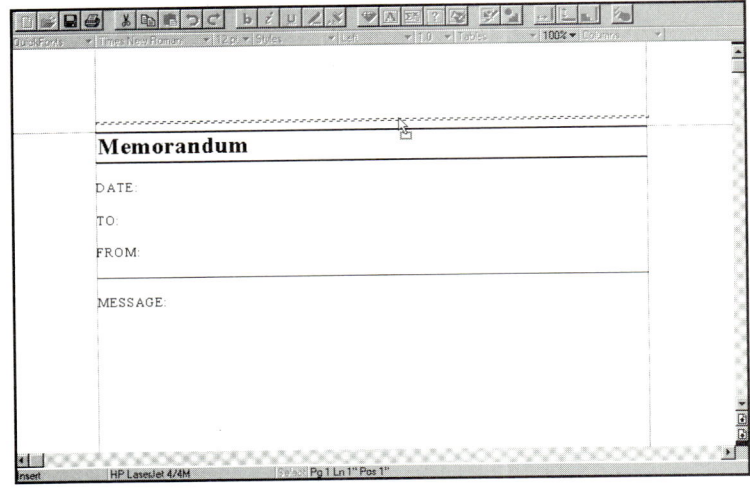

 **T I P** If you accidentally delete the wrong line, press the Undo keyboard shortcut Ctrl+Z to reverse the action or choose Edit, Undo.

To delete a line using the right mouse button menu, follow these steps:

1. Point the mouse at the line to be deleted. The mouse pointer changes to a right-facing arrow.
2. Click the right mouse button; the QuickMenu appears (see fig. 7.5).

**FIG. 7.5**
Delete a line quickly by right-clicking while pointing to a graphic. You can also cut or copy the line, or edit the line using the Edit Graphics Line dialog box.

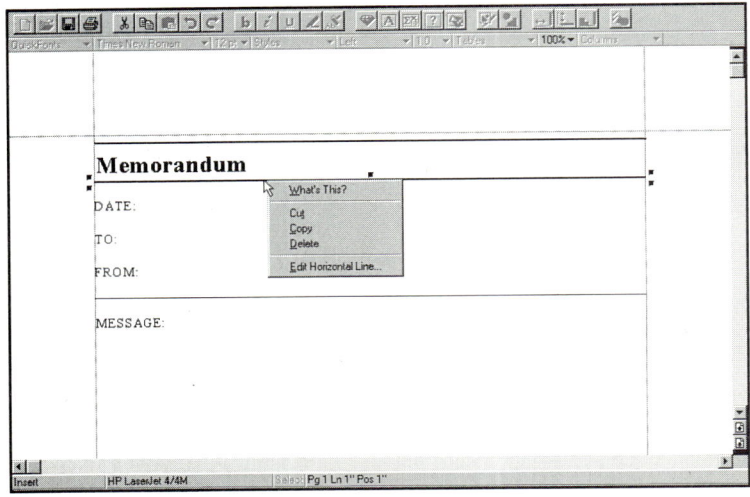

3. Click Delete.

# Using Graphics Borders

A *graphics border* is a box that surrounds text to emphasize your message, separate text, or add pizzazz to the page. You can use a paragraph border to attract attention to one particular paragraph of text in a letter, for example, or you can add a page border to each page of a report to guide the reader and create consistency within the report. Figure 7.6 illustrates an advertising letter that uses both a page border and a paragraph border.

**TIP** You can use a variety of line styles and thicknesses with page and paragraph borders. For more information about customizing border lines, see Chapter 21, "Using Advanced Graphics Techniques."

**NOTE** In WordPerfect, graphics borders contain text on a page or text in a paragraph. In addition, you can use borders—actually graphics boxes—to contain images. For more information about graphics boxes, see the section "Using Graphics Boxes" later in this chapter.

**FIG. 7.6**
The page border dresses up the page and makes it more interesting to look at. The paragraph border emphasizes the text announcing a discount to the customer.

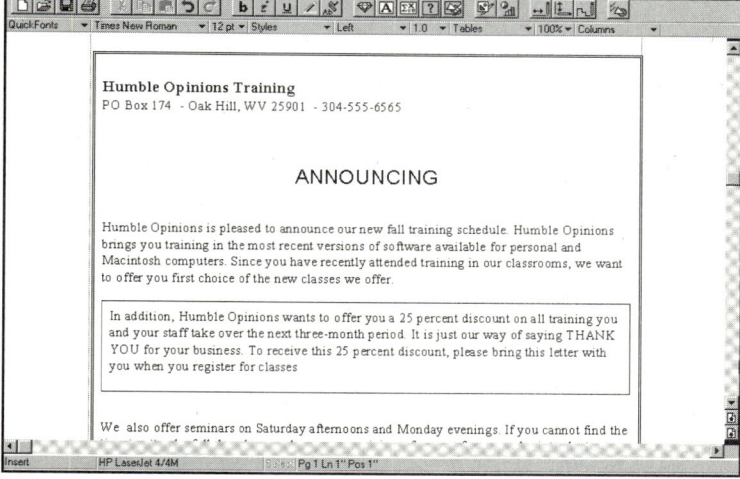

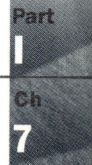

## Using Paragraph Borders

A *paragraph border* is a frame, or box, that surrounds only the selected text. WordPerfect defines a *paragraph* as any amount of text followed by a hard return. When you select a paragraph border, your cursor may be located anywhere within the paragraph.

To add a paragraph border around multiple paragraphs, simply select the paragraphs then select the paragraph border you desire. Any additional paragraphs added inside this multi-paragraph border will cause the border to expand to accommodate the new paragraphs.

▶ **See** "Understanding WordPerfect's Hidden Codes," **p. 91**

▶ **See** "Customizing a Toolbar," **p. 420**

**N O T E**  A paragraph border extends from the right margin to the left margin.

You can create paragraph borders in two different ways with WordPerfect:

- Position the insertion point and create the border. If Apply Border To Current Paragraph Only is selected, all paragraphs from the current paragraph to the bottom of the document are surrounded by a single paragraph border. Otherwise, only the current paragraph will contain a border.
- Select specific paragraphs and create the border; the paragraphs are surrounded by a border.

 **TIP** Generally, use single or thin lines for paragraph borders; you don't want to overwhelm the text with a thick or double-lined border.

To add a paragraph border to a document, open a document previously created, or begin a new document using the one in figure 7.6 as a guide. After you format the text, follow these steps to create the paragraph border:

1. Select the paragraph of text to which you want to apply a border.
2. Choose Format, Border Fill. A cascading menu appears.
3. Click Paragraph. The Paragraph Border/Fill dialog box appears with the Border tab in the foreground (see fig. 7.7).
4. Choose the style of border you want to use by clicking the style. Use the vertical scroll bar on the Available Border Styles list box to view more border styles.
5. Choose OK to accept the border style and close the dialog box. WordPerfect returns to the document with the appropriate border style surrounding the text.

**FIG. 7.7**
The Paragraph Border/Fill dialog box displays plenty of border styles so you can find one to fit your needs.

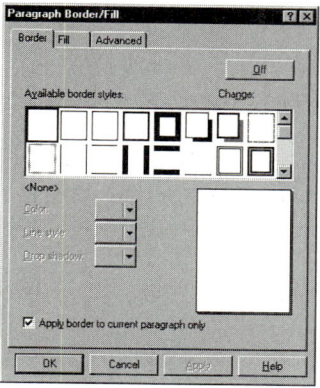

## Adding Paragraph Fill

Often, you will want to include a fill or shade to the paragraph border to emphasize the text even more. WordPerfect makes it easy to add fill to a paragraph, whether the paragraph has a border or not.

If you have a border around three paragraphs and place the cursor in the third paragraph and add fill, that paragraph is separated from the other two with a new border.

In addition, the fill doesn't begin at the insertion point location. If the insertion point is in the middle of a paragraph, the fill begins at the beginning of that paragraph. Specifying a fill style without first selecting the paragraph will result in the paragragh being filled as if it had been selected.

 **TIP** Never add more than a 30 percent shade to black text; fill that is too dark makes the text difficult to read.

To apply fill to a paragraph of text, follow these steps:

1. Select the text.
2. Choose Fo_r_mat, B_o_rder Fill, Pa_r_agraph. The Paragraph Border/Fill dialog box appears.
3. Click the Fill tab to display the available fill styles (see fig. 7.8), then click the appropriate fill for the border. Choose OK. WordPerfect returns to the document.

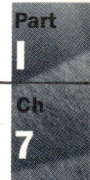

**FIG. 7.8**
Even though WordPerfect provides various fill styles for a border, be careful to choose a fill that enables you to read the text easily.

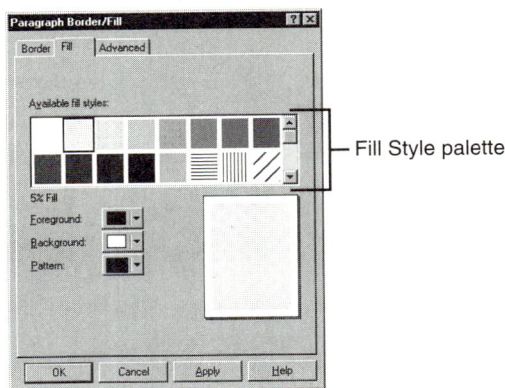

Fill Style palette

## Adding a Page Border

Use a page border to add pizzazz to any document—such as letters, newsletters, menus, reports, and flyers. Normally, you repeat the page border—same line style, thickness, and so on—on all pages of a document. You may not want a page border on some pages, however—a page of a report containing several tables, images, or spreadsheets, for example. In that case, you can turn off the border for a particular page; see "Turning Off a Border" later in this chapter. Usually, try to be consistent with borders throughout a document.

> **N O T E** When using a page border, you can use a heavier border than the single line you use for paragraph borders, as long as you allow plenty of white space. *White space* is the breathing room in the margins, between paragraphs, below headlines, and so on that helps to balance heavy lines.

A page border extends from the top to the bottom margin and from the right to the left margin. When you create a page border in WordPerfect, when using Line styles, the program automatically allows space between the text and the border so that the text is not crowded or difficult to read. Selecting a Fancy page border style could cause text to be overwritten, depending on the border selected.

> **T I P** To set page margins, choose Format, Margins; or press Ctrl+F8.

For this exercise, use any letter or memo document you have created, or create a new document using figure 7.6 as a guide. After the text is formatted, add the page border by following these steps:

1. Choose Format, Border/Fill, Page. The Page Border/Fill dialog box appears (see fig. 7.9).
2. Choose the type of border you want from the Border Type button. Options include Fancy or Line, and the border styles change appropriately.
3. Preview the border style by clicking the scroll bar beside the Available Border Styles list. Click one of the styles to preview it in the Preview box below the list.
4. Choose OK when you find the border style you want to use. You then return to the document.

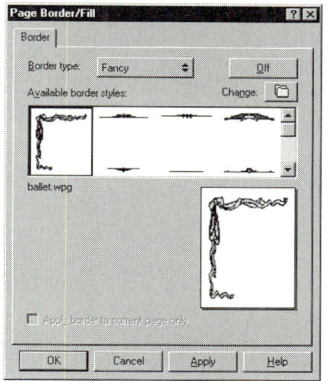

**FIG. 7.9**
Click the appropriate Border square to select the border style for the document. If you've installed other graphics, you can choose Change to move to the folder they're found in.

## Adding a Column Border

Column borders are very similar to paragraph borders covered earlier in the section "Using Paragraph Borders," but have slightly different properties. Here are a few things you need to know when working with column borders:

- Selecting a column border while your insertion point is anywhere in the column will apply that border to the entire column definition. In fact, the Column Border code is actually placed following the Column Definition code.
- Borders and fills occupy the entire width of the column group, including the space between columns.
- Because columns have spacing around the outside of the column group, you may find your vertical borders resting outside the margin of the page.
- Like paragraph borders, the length of the column borders is limited to the text inside the column. For example, if you want to have a column border occupy the entire page but only have a few paragraphs of text, you need to pad the remaining space with hard returns to allow the border to extend down the page.

- If you are in the last column of a column group and insert a manual column break, you are returned to the left margin and a new column starts, as normal. When using column borders, this action causes the previous border to cease and new borders of the same type to begin.
- The Apply To Current Column Group Only causes the current column group to receive the new border style. The other column groups remain as they are.
- If you create a new column group from an existing column group, the properties of that group are inherited by the new column group.

To add a border to a column group, perform these steps:

1. Position your cursor anywhere in the column group.
2. Choose Format, Border Fill. A cascading menu appears.
3. Click Column. The Column Border/Fill dialog box appears.
4. Click the Border tab, and choose the style of border you want to use by clicking the style. Use the vertical scroll bar on the Available Border Styles list box to view more border styles.
5. Choose OK to accept the change and close the dialog box. WordPerfect returns to the document with the appropriate border style surrounding the text.

 Most of the available border styles deal with surrounding the column text on all sides, with the exception of two. The last two rows of the border styles list each have an entry with a vertical bar in the middle of the image. This bar simulates a vertical bar appearing in the column break of a column group. You may be familiar with this technique, as many magazines and newsletters often use such as line to visually break up columns.

## Turning Off a Border

As mentioned in "Adding a Page Border," sometimes you might not want a border on a particular page—for example, on a page that contains a complicated graph or a large image. You can turn the page border off on any page in your document by using the Page Border/Fill dialog box. You can, in addition, turn off a paragraph border if you decide not to use it.

▶ **See** "Selecting Page Size and Type," **p. 179**
▶ **See** "Customizing Borders," **p. 666**

Before turning off a paragraph border, position the cursor anywhere in the paragraph for which you want to turn off the border. If you're turning off a page border, position the insertion point on the page containing the border you want to turn off. To turn off a border, follow these steps:

1. Choose Format, Border/Fill, and then either Page or Paragraph.
2. In the Page or Paragraph Border/Fill dialog box, choose the command button labeled Off.

## Deleting a Border

You can delete a page or paragraph border in WordPerfect by deleting the code that represents the border. To practice deleting a border code, use a document you created previously and follow these steps:

**TIP** When you delete a border containing the fill, both the border and the fill are deleted.

1. Choose View, Reveal Codes; or press Alt+F3.
2. Position the cursor in front of the Page or Paragraph Border code.
3. Press Delete.

### TROUBLESHOOTING

**I can't delete a graphics line by pressing Backspace or Delete.** This is the way WordPerfect works. Normally, when you press the Backspace (or Delete) key, WordPerfect skips over the codes for graphics lines. This applies to both vertical and horizontal graphics lines.

If you want to delete the graphics line, first turn on Reveal Codes by choosing View, Reveal Codes. Now, you can use the Backspace and Delete keys to delete the codes for graphics lines. These codes appear as [Graph Line] in Reveal Codes.

**When I turn off the paragraph border, WordPerfect removes the paragraph border completely.** WordPerfect turns off the paragraph border in the current paragraph. The *current paragraph* is defined as the one that contains the flashing insertion point (or cursor). If you are finished writing the text you want in a paragraph border, make sure that you press Enter first. This inserts an extra blank paragraph. You can now turn the paragraph border off by choosing Format, Border/Fill, Paragraph, Off.

**When I print my document, I can't see the text inside a paragraph that has a filled border.** Exercise care when using a background fill inside a paragraph border. The more solid the fill pattern, the harder it is to see the text when you view or print the document. Depending on your printer, text within a filled pattern may be easier or harder to see than on-screen. You must experiment with your printer to find the optimal background fill pattern. A good fill pattern to start with is 5 percent, which means the fill pattern is 5 percent gray.

# Using Graphics Boxes

A *graphics box* is a box that holds images or text—such as clip art, drawings, callouts, text files, equations, tables, and spreadsheets. Graphics boxes are different from borders in that a graphics box holds text or images that you can change and move with the box; you add a graphics box and its contents to a document, and then adjust the contents of the document to make room for the box. A border, on the other hand, is an added ornamental frame that surrounds text already in your document.

 To format the text in a graphic box, select the text and choose Fo*r*mat, *F*ont, *L*ine, or Pa*r*agraph.

Adding graphics boxes to your documents illustrates the text, draws attention to the message, and adds interest to the document. Images, for example, help the reader understand the text; text callouts attract the reader's attention to the text. WordPerfect enables you to add several types of graphics boxes to your documents, each with a style and purpose of its own.

## Understanding Graphics Box Styles

WordPerfect supplies eleven graphics box styles you can use in your documents. Each graphics box style is designed to work best with one particular type of image or text—for example, the figure box style looks good with an image in a document. Any box, however, can hold any type of image, text, table, equation, and so on. The box style is simply a suggestion for the box's use.

Each box style has specific defaults; however, you can change the characteristics of any box. The primary box style defaults are defined by the box's line style and position. *Line style* refers to the width and type of line used as a border for the box—thick, single, none, and so on.

*Positioning* refers to how the box is anchored—to what element on the page the box is attached. A box can be attached, or *anchored*, to a page, paragraph, or character. A box anchored to the page means that its location is relative to the top and left edges of that page. A box anchored to a paragraph moves with the text in the paragraph to which it is attached. Finally, a box attached to a character acts just like any other character in the paragraph—it moves within the line left to right, and within the paragraph up and down, whenever text is edited around the box.

You can always view the current anchoring of a box by passing the mouse over it, clicking its QuickSpot button and looking at the Attach To pop-up list. The pop-up control box that appears specifies the Anchor, which is typically paragraph. (Click the X in the upper-right corner to close the box when you're finished looking at it.) You can always determine which paragraph, page, or character the box is attached to by clicking and dragging it. An attachment line appears, indicating the current anchor of the box (see fig. 7.10).

**FIG. 7.10**
The attachment line visually shows you the current anchor for a graphic box. You can display the attachment line by clicking and dragging the box. The attachment line is only available for boxes attached to Paragraphs.

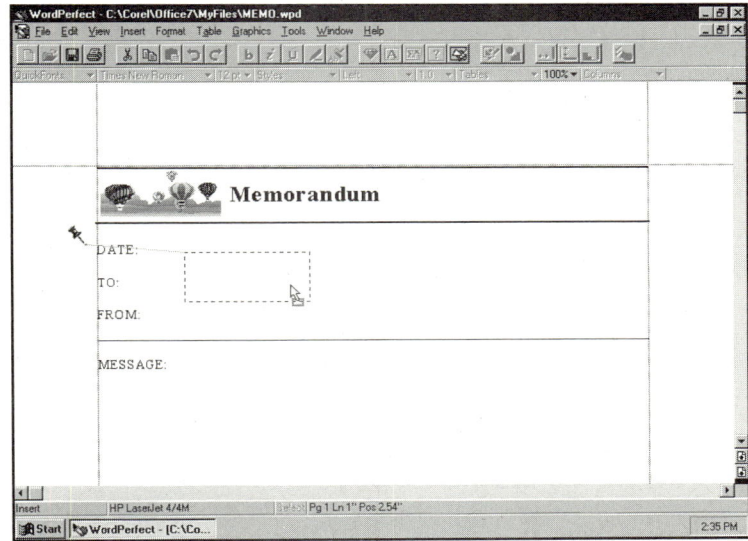

**NOTE** You can customize any box; see Chapter 21 for more information.

The following list describes each graphics box style and the default line styles:

- *Image Box*. No border, anchored to the page. Positioned at the top and right margins of the document. Holds charts, clip art drawings, or WPG files.
- *Figure Box*. Single line, anchored to the paragraph; generally holds clip art, charts, drawings, or WPG files (see fig. 7.11).
- *Text Box*. Thick line on top and bottom, anchored to a paragraph; normally holds text such as a callout, announcement, or imported text files (see fig. 7.12).

■ *Equation Box.* No border or fill, anchored to a paragraph; holds mathematical or scientific equations or text (see fig. 7.13).

**FIG. 7.11**
Images are any graphic art, created with a program like CorelDRAW! or Windows Paint, inserted into WordPerfect. Shown here is a graphics box with one of the many clip art images that come with WordPerfect.

**FIG. 7.12**
When using a text box for a callout, announcement, and so on, you normally don't use a caption; however, you can add one, if necessary, to identify the author or origin of the text.

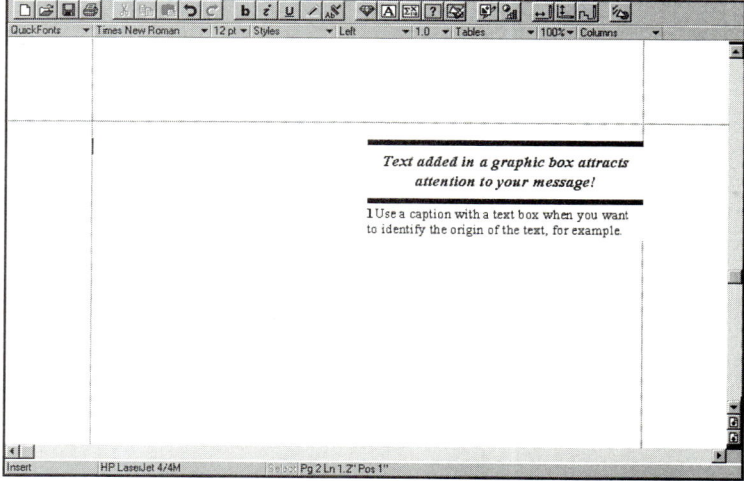

**FIG. 7.13**
As with any graphics box, you can resize and move an Equation Box so that it best suits your document.

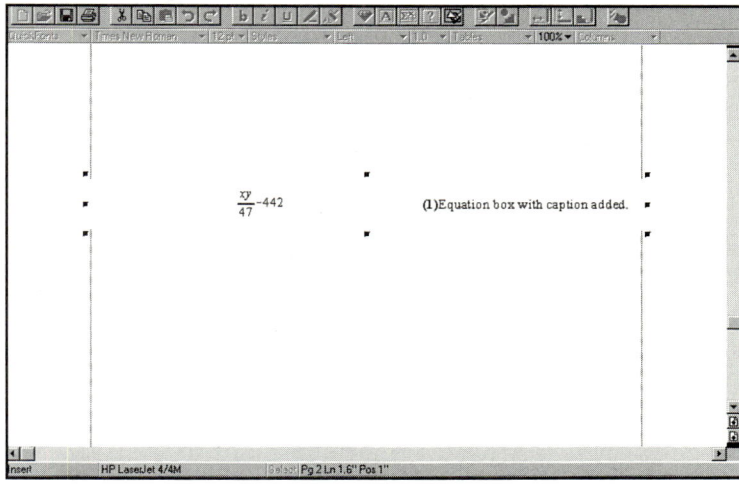

- *Table Box.* Thick line on top and bottom, anchored to a paragraph; normally holds a table (see fig. 7.14).

**FIG. 7.14**
You can format text in any graphics box just as you would text in your document; you can change font, alignment, indents, set tabs, and so on.

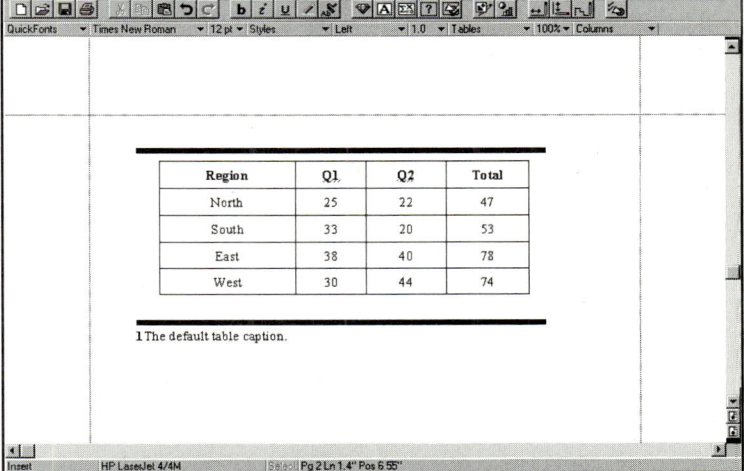

■ *User Box.* No border or fill, anchored to a paragraph; perfect for contour text wraparound images (see fig. 7.15).

**FIG. 7.15**
The User graphics box may be the one you use most of the time; it's easier to start with the user's defaults and customize the box to suit your purposes.

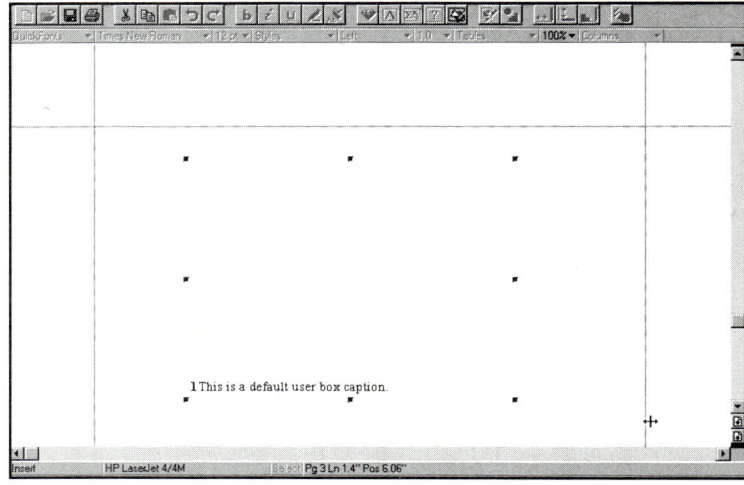

■ *Button Box.* Single-line border with Button Fill, anchored to a character; can contain images or text (see fig. 7.16).

**FIG. 7.16**
Use a Button box within a paragraph to illustrate a keystroke, icon, or other symbol; you can add text or an image to a Button box.

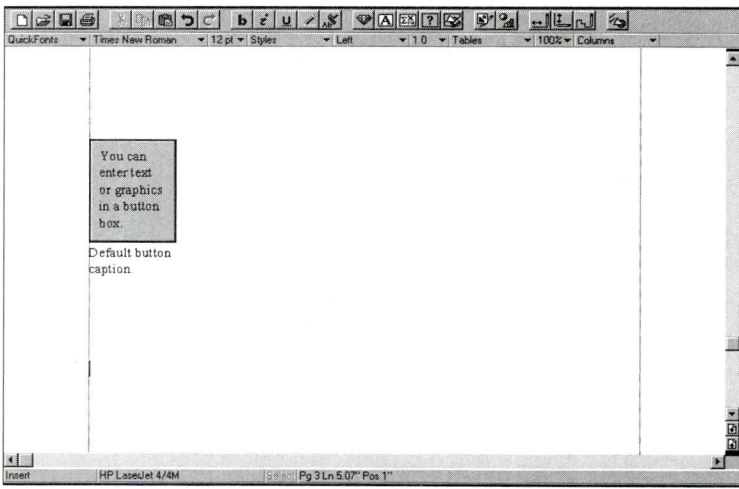

■ *Watermark Box.* No border or fill, anchored to the page; contains images or text screened so that it creates a background for the document (see fig. 7.17).

**FIG. 7.17**
A Watermark box screens the logo, clip art, or other image in the background of the page; you can enter text over the image or use a contour text wrap.

■ *Inline Equation.* No border or fill, anchored to a character; contains an equation for placement within a paragraph of text—treated like a character (see fig. 7.18).

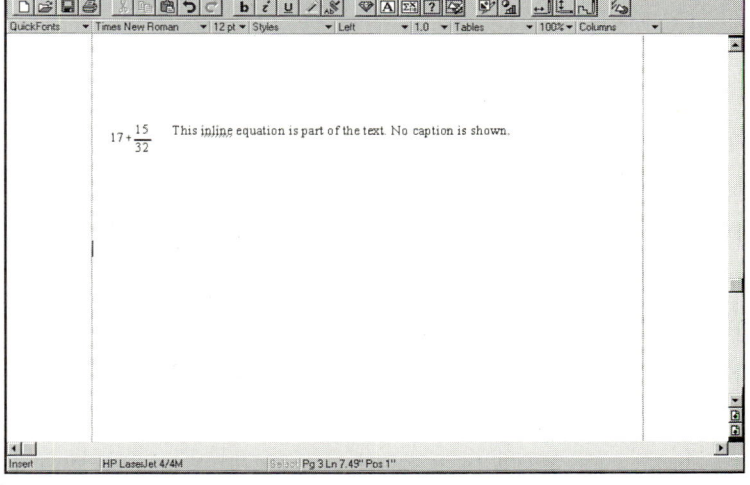

**FIG. 7.18**
You can create a caption for an Inline graphics box, but because the Inline box is a character within the paragraph, the caption fits into a small area that makes reading it nearly impossible.

■ *Ole 2.0 Box.* No border or fill; anchored to a character. For use with OLE objects.

■ *Inline Text.* No border or fill, anchored to a character; contains an equation for placement within a paragraph of text—treated like a character. Similar to the Inline Equation style.

WordPerfect makes it easy to create any box style and add any contents you want to the box. After you create the box, you can change the box style, border, fill, content, position, size, and text wrap options. This section shows you how to create a graphics box, and how to move, resize, and delete a box using the mouse. For more information about other customization options, see Chapter 21, "Using Advanced Graphics Techniques."

## Creating a Graphics Box

You can create a graphics box by using the Graphics Toolbar or the Graphics menu. After you create the box, you can move, resize, and delete the box by using the mouse. To create a simple figure box, for example, follow these steps:

1. Choose Graphics, Image. The Insert Image dialog box appears (see fig. 7.19).

While in the Insert Image dialog box, choose a graphic file, then click the Preview button on the Toolbar to preview the graphic before you insert it in your document.

**FIG. 7.19**
Choose one of WordPerfect's clip art images, or choose a different file type—such as EPS, PCX, PIC, BMP, or TIF—from your own store of graphics images.

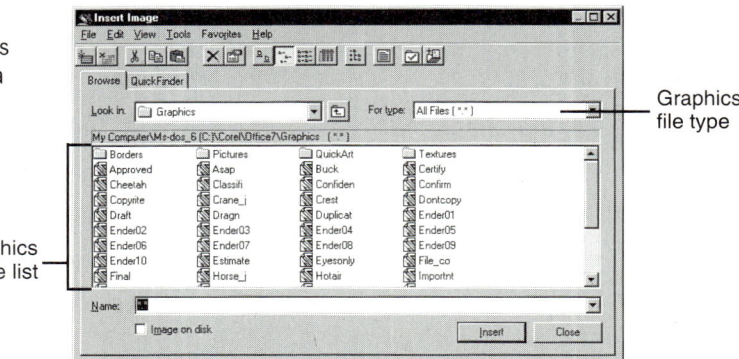

2. Select one of the listed images.
3. Choose Insert or press Enter to close the dialog box and return to the document (see fig. 7.20).

 You can double-click the image file name as a shortcut to choose the image and close the dialog box.

**FIG. 7.20**
When you position the mouse cursor over the graphics box, a four-headed arrow appears; click and drag the arrow to reposition the graphic.

Handles

Mouse cursor

See Chapters 21 and 22 for information about creating other types of graphics boxes.

To perform any alterations to the graphics box—move, resize, or delete, for example—you must first select the graphics box. To select the box, click the mouse cursor on the box. Eight small black handles—or boxes—appear on the corners and in the center of each border line (refer to fig. 7.20). To deselect a box, click the mouse anywhere on the page other than in the graphics box.

## Moving a Graphics Box

You can easily move the graphics box by dragging it to a new position with the mouse. When you position the mouse cursor over the graphics box—anywhere but on a small black handle—you can move the box around your document. To move the graphics box, follow these steps:

 **TIP** When you drag the graphics box, the box appears with a dashed line for the border so that you can easily move it to a new location.

1. Select the graphics box if the sizing handles are not showing.
2. Position the mouse cursor over the box until you see a four-headed arrow.
3. Drag the mouse and the box to its new location.
4. Release the mouse button.

▶ **See** "Customizing Graphics Boxes," **p. 669**
▶ **See** "Retrieving and Positioning Clip Art," **p. 700**

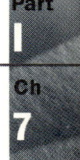

## Resizing a Graphics Box

You can resize a graphics box by using the mouse or a dialog box. For more information about using a dialog box to edit a graphics box, see Chapter 21, "Using Advanced Graphics Techniques."

Use the sizing handles to resize the graphics box with the mouse. If you use one of the four corner handles to resize the box, the box and the image resize proportionally—both in height and width. If you use only one handle located in the middle of each border line, the box enlarges but the figure does not enlarge proportionally. To correct this problem, enlarge the other side of the box proportionally.

To use the mouse to resize the graphics box, follow these steps:

1. Click the mouse on the graphics box if the sizing handles are not showing.

 You see the dashed border of the figure box when you drag the mouse, indicating the new size of the graphics box.

 If you have trouble getting the double-headed arrow, move the mouse cursor slowly back and forth over the handle until the arrow appears.

2. Move the mouse cursor over one of the handles until a double-headed arrow appears. Drag the handle to resize the graphics box (see fig. 7.21).

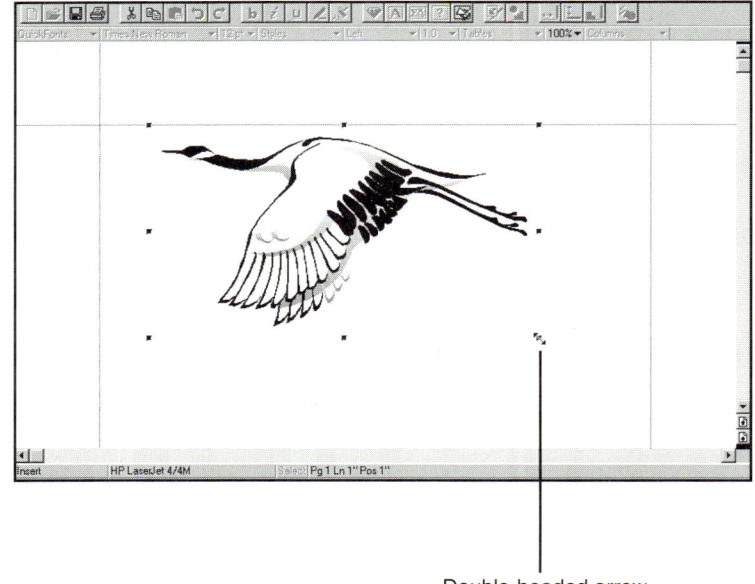

**FIG. 7.21**
When resizing a graphics box, notice that a dash appears surrounding the box. This line indicates the position and size the box will be when you release the mouse button to stop the sizing operation.

Double-headed arrow

## Deleting a Graphics Box

It's easy to delete a graphics box and image by using the mouse. Alternatively, you can use Reveal Codes and delete the graphics box code; but this method is much easier. To delete a graphics box, follow these steps:

1. Select the graphics box to be deleted.
2. Press the Delete key.

## Using a Graphics Box in a Letter

Thus far you have learned how to create, resize, move, and delete graphics boxes, but not how to apply a box to a document. It's easy to add graphics to your documents in WordPerfect. Figure 7.22 illustrates an advertising letter with two graphics boxes: a Text box and a Figure box.

The following instructions review creating a Figure box. The Text box in the figure has been customized—the border has been changed and fill has been added.

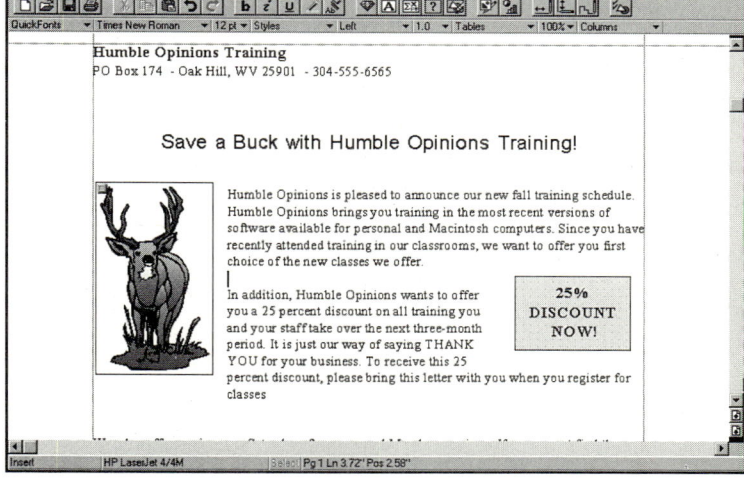

**FIG. 7.22**
Notice that both the graphics boxes and the page border use a single-line style to create consistency; the 10 percent fill added to the Text box attracts the attention of the reader.

**TIP** The graphics box attaches to the paragraph in which the insertion point is located. You can easily attach—or anchor—the graphics box to another paragraph by moving the box to a new position.

For this exercise, use a document you already created or create a new document by using figure 7.23 as a guide. After you enter and format the text, follow these steps to insert the Figure box:

1. Position the insertion point at the point you want the first graphic to appear—at the beginning of the paragraph.

2. Choose Graphics, Image. The Insert Image dialog box appears.
3. Select the graphics image and choose Insert or double-click the mouse on the image name to close the dialog box and return to the document.
4. Using the mouse, resize and move the graphic.

# Using Watermarks

A *watermark* is a custom graphic box that contains either text or graphics but prints in the background. The contents of the Watermark box screens lightly so that text you enter in the foreground is readable.

There are many ways you can use watermarks. You can dress up a letter to a customer with your company logo or a screened border; add clip art in the background of fliers, newsletters, or brochures; add screened text to the background of notices, memos, reports, letters, and so on. You can use any of WordPerfect's watermark files; create your own images or text to use as watermarks; or use images and text from other applications.

## Using a Text Watermark

Most of WordPerfect's watermark files (CONFIDEN.WPG, ASAP.WPG, and so on) consist of text and a few have screened lines, arrows, rectangles, and such. Following is a list of some of the text watermarks included in WordPerfect:

| | | |
|---|---|---|
| A.S.A.P. | Draft | Proof |
| Classified | Duplicate | Proposal |
| Confidential | Estimate | Reply Requested |
| Confirmation | File Copy | Thank You |
| Copyrighted Material | Past Due | |

You can use WordPerfect's Watermark text or create your own. For more information about creating text in a graphics box, see Chapter 21, "Using Advanced Graphics

Techniques." Figure 7.23 illustrates one of WordPerfect's watermarks (IMPORTANT.WPG) in a notice to employees.

**FIG. 7.23**
Although the text in this figure does not overlap the watermark, it very well could. The watermark is screened lightly in the background.

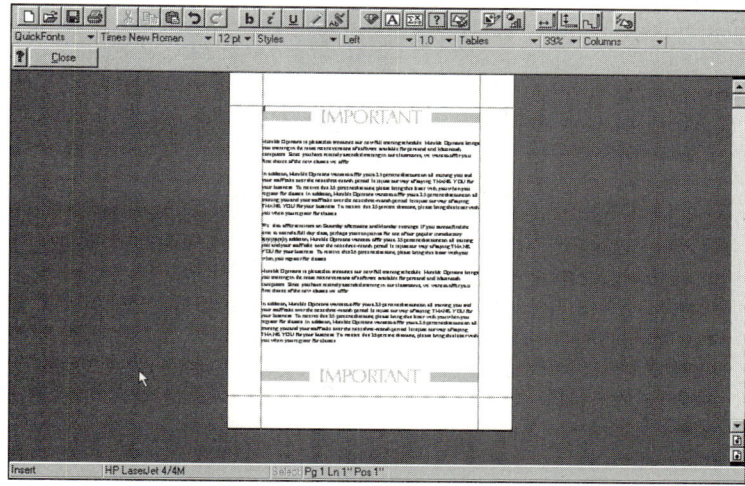

## Using Images as Watermarks

Try using other WordPerfect images as watermarks. Many of the borders are excellent as watermarks; use borders with a p in the file name for portrait (BORD03P.WPG, for example). You also can use any of the WPG images in WordPerfect's GRAPHICS folder. Figure 7.24 illustrates one of WordPerfect's image files—CRANE_J.WPG—used as a watermark in a bank report.

Figure 7.25 illustrates a small watermark added to a letterhead. You can size and position the image within the graphics box. For more information, see Chapter 22, "Using WordPerfect Draw and TextArt."

> **NOTE** When using watermarks, all editing options are available to you on the graphics editing screen. You can add a caption, reposition the contents of the screen, change the size and position of the graphics box, add a border, use the toolbox, and wrap text. For more information on the graphics editing screen, see Chapter 21, "Using Advanced Graphics Techniques."

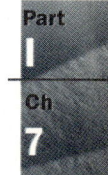

**FIG. 7.24**

In addition to using WordPerfect images, you can use clip art, scanned art, drawings from other programs including Presentations and TextArt, and text in a Watermark Graphics box.

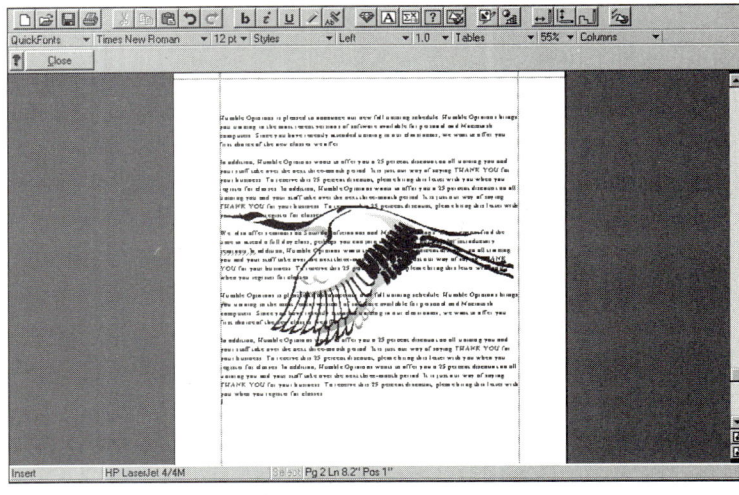

**FIG. 7.25**

This company logo was created with WordPerfect's TextArt, saved as a BMP file, and imported to the Watermark Graphics box.

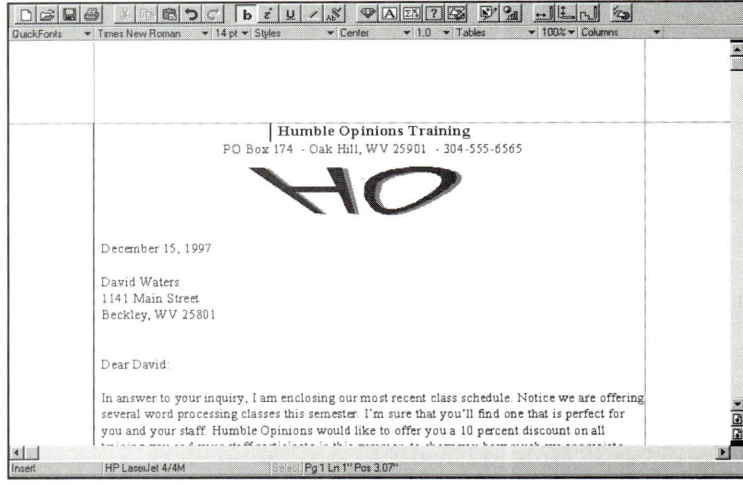

### TROUBLESHOOTING

**I created the wrong type of graphics box by mistake and want to change the box type.**
WordPerfect enables you to easily change the type of an existing graphics box, with little regard to what's inside the box. For example, you can change a figure box (that contains a graphics image) to a text box. Changing the box type can come in handy when you want to use the default style of another box, or if you accidentally create the wrong type of box in the first place.

To change the box type, right-click over the graphics box. Choose Style from the QuickMenu. The Box Style dialog box appears. Choose a new style from the Style list box and then choose OK.

## Creating a Watermark

Before creating a watermark, enter all text and format it. When the watermark appears on-screen, text editing slows considerably. To add a watermark to a document, follow these steps:

1. Choose Graphics, Custom Box. The Custom Box dialog box appears.
2. In the Style Name list box, choose Watermark and choose OK. Right-click over the empty graphic box that was inserted, and Content from the QuickMenu that appears. The Box Content dialog box appears (see fig. 7.26).

**FIG. 7.26**
The Box Content dialog box enables you to choose various images and to position those images within the watermark box.

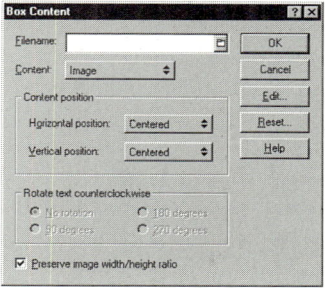

3. Click the file icon next to the Filename text box. The Insert Image dialog box appears (see fig. 7.27).
4. Choose any of the images to use for a watermark.
5. Choose Select; this selects the image and returns you to the Box Content dialog box.
6. Choose OK to return to the document.

**FIG. 7.27**
In the Insert Image dialog box, you can view each watermark before you open it, thus saving time and energy. To view each WPG file, click the Preview button, and select the files you want to look at. Continue to select files in the file list until you find one you like.

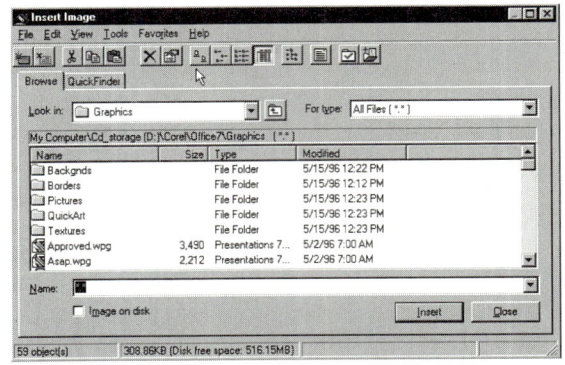

CHAPTER 8

# Basic Output: Printing, Faxing, and E-Mail

*by Rick Hellewell and Read Gilgen*

The paperless office isn't with us quite yet. In fact, printed output is the end objective of nearly every WordPerfect document you create. In this chapter, you learn how to print great-looking documents, whether you use a dot matrix printer or the latest in color laser printer technology. You also learn how to select and set up your printer definitions, and to output your documents via fax or e-mail. ■

### Setting up WordPerfect 7 for your printer
Learn how to hook up and use WordPerfect 7 with your printer.

### Using basic printing skills
Increase your working knowledge of printing with WordPerfect, including using Zoom to preview your document and printing specific pages.

### Control print jobs
Learn how to cancel a print job and various other printing tasks.

### Faxing from within WordPerfect, and sending documents via electronic mail
By using WordPerfect, you can communicate with the world via fax and e-mail.

# Using Basic Printing Skills

Certain basic printing procedures apply to nearly all of the documents you print. In this section, you learn to select the correct printer, preview your document before printing, print one or more copies of your document, and cancel printing when something goes wrong.

## Selecting a Printer

WordPerfect is a WYSIWYG (*What You See Is What You Get*) program. However, in order to truly see on-screen what your document will look like, WordPerfect has to know what printer you are planning to use so it can display the proper fonts and print attributes.

To select a printer, follow these steps:

1. Choose <u>F</u>ile, <u>P</u>rint to display the Print dialog box (see fig. 8.1). The options you see in this dialog box may vary, depending on your printer's features.

**FIG. 8.1**
Use the Print dialog box to select a printer definition and to specify the part of the document you want to print, along with the number of copies and the print quality of the text.

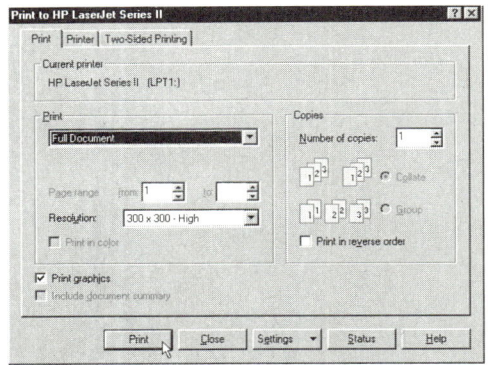

2. In the Current Printer section of the dialog box, WordPerfect displays the current printer. If the printer name displayed is the printer you will be using, press Esc and continue to the next section.

3. If the printer is not correct, click the Printer tab (see fig. 8.2), which shows the current default Windows printer and a drop-down list of other installed printers. These are printers that you (or someone else) set up when you installed Windows.

4. Click the printer to which you want to print.

5. Click <u>C</u>lose to close the Print dialog box. The printer you have selected appears on the status bar at the bottom of your WordPerfect screen.

## Using Basic Printing Skills

**FIG. 8.2**
Use the Name drop-down list in the Printer tab of the Print dialog box to select the printer to which you intend to print your document. The choice of printer determines in part how your document will appear on-screen.

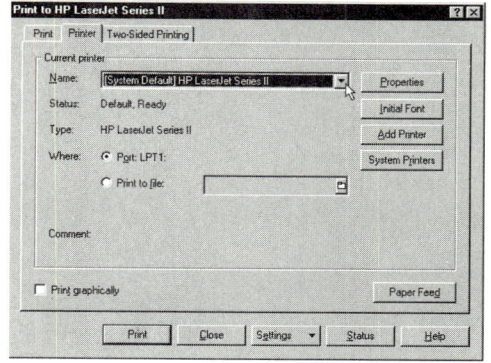

Now you can create or format your document, knowing that the fonts and other formatting you see on-screen will match what your printer can print. See "Selecting and Configuring Your Printer" later in this chapter for more information on selecting a printer definition.

## Using Zoom and View To See the Printed Output

Because WordPerfect 7 is a WYSIWYG program, the text on-screen accurately represents what you get when you print the document. You see the fonts, sizes of characters, and character attributes (such as italic) on-screen as those parameters are selected. You also see graphics elements on-screen, such as pictures and lines. Seeing your document correctly before you print reduces printing errors, thus saving you time (and also saving trees).

To see how everything in your document will print, you first should choose View, Page; or press Alt+F5. This enables you to see not only the text, but also any headers, footers, page numbers, or footnotes you might have. If you click Draft, you see everything except what would appear in the margins. Two Page enables you to see two facing pages side by side.

Now you also can use WordPerfect's Zoom feature to reduce or enlarge the size of the document on your screen to see more of the document, or to see more detail.

 You can view the document in varying sizes by changing the zoom percentage; choose View, Zoom. This displays the Zoom dialog box (see fig. 8.3). You specify the *zoom percentage*, or a percentage of the actual size of the printed document. For example, if you select a zoom percentage of 100 percent, your document appears full-size on-screen. If you choose 90% (by typing it in the Other edit box), you see more of the document because the type and page are smaller.

**FIG. 8.3**
The Zoom dialog box lets you select how the document is sized on-screen. The percentage values indicate the size of the document on-screen relative to the actual printed output.

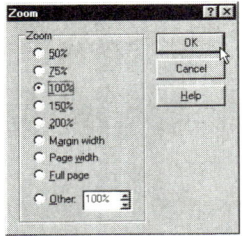

The Zoom dialog box has several preset percentages: 5̲0%, 7̲5%, 1̲00%, 15̲0%, and 2̲00%. Other settings are:

- *Ma̲rgin Width.* The full width of the text is displayed on-screen, with the left margin at the left edge of the screen, and the right margin at the right edge of the screen.
- *Page W̲idth.* Shows the width of the page on-screen, including the left and right margin areas.
- *F̲ull Page.* The full page is displayed on-screen, including the top, bottom, left, and right margins.
- *Other.* With this option, you can enter any percentage value, or use the up- or down-arrows to increment or decrement the value 5 percent at a time. The available range is 25 to 400 percent.

You can use the Zoom settings to display the area of the document at the size you need. If you want to see the whole page, choose the F̲ull Page zoom. Some of the text in Full Page zoom may not be readable, depending on the resolution of your screen and the size of the text. While you are entering or changing text, you may want to choose the Page W̲idth or Ma̲rgin Width zoom.

Switch between F̲ull Page view of your document and the zoom percentage you're using for editing by clicking the Page/Zoom Full button on the Toolbar.

## Printing: The Basics

You have selected the proper printer and viewed your document to determine that it's ready to be printed. In most cases, you now can print the current document in its entirety. You can start the printing process in one of several ways:

- Choose F̲ile, P̲rint.
- Press F5.
- Press Ctrl+P.

- Click the Print button on the Toolbar.

Each of these choices displays the Print dialog box (refer to fig. 8.1).

You can change each setting in the Print dialog box according to your needs. In most cases, however, the default settings shown in figure 8.1 are suitable. To send the entire document to the printer, using the default settings, simply click the Print button. This prints one copy of the entire document with high-quality text and any graphics in the document. The document prints to the current printer.

 If you know you want to print your entire document using the current print settings, you can press Ctrl+Shift–P to bypass the Print dialog box altogether and send your document to the printer.

## Printing Multiple Copies

Use the Copies section of the Print dialog box to specify the number of copies to print and how those copies are generated. Specify the number of copies in the Number Of Copies box. You can enter the value or use the increment or decrement arrows to set the number of copies.

Having specified more than one copy of the document, you now can choose the order in which the copies will print: as a group or collated. These options are in the following list, using a value $x$ you have specified in the Number Of Copies box:

- *Collate*. The entire document prints once, and then reprints until $x$ copies are printed. This results in $x$ collated sets of printed copies.

- *Group*. Each page of the document prints $x$ times, resulting in $x$ copies of page 1, then $x$ copies of page 2, and so on. This setting has no effect when printing with a dot matrix printer.

 If you have a laser printer, your copies will print faster if you choose the Group option, especially if printing tables or graphics. The Group option lets WordPerfect generate the first copy which the printer duplicates as fast as it can. The Collate option requires WordPerfect to generate each copy of each page before the printer can print it.

## Canceling a Print Job

Each time you tell WordPerfect to print something, you create a *print job*. Nearly everyone, at some time or another, begins a print job and then immediately realizes they don't want to print just yet, or have mistakenly printed the wrong thing. Fortunately, WordPerfect lets you cancel your print job.

If you are printing a single page on a fast printer (for example, a laser printer), you might just as well continue printing because you may not be quick enough to cancel the print job. If you want to cancel printing several pages, you can try the following:

1. Choose File, Print; or press F5.
2. In the Print dialog box, click Status. WordPerfect displays the Print Status and History dialog box (see fig. 8.4).
3. Click the print job you want to cancel (usually at the top of the list).
4. Choose Document, Cancel Printing to abort the print job. Alternatively, you can right-click the document you want to cancel, and choose Cancel from the QuickMenu.

**FIG. 8.4**
Use the Print Status and History dialog box to monitor the status of a print job or to cancel it.

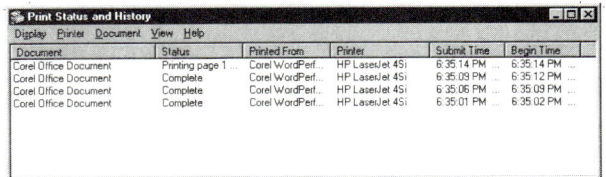

For more information on controlling your print jobs, see "Controlling the Printer and Print Jobs" later in this chapter.

### TROUBLESHOOTING

**I chose Print from the Print dialog box, but nothing happened.** First make sure you have selected the proper printer. Also, make sure your printer is online. Usually, if a printer is not available or is offline, you get an error message telling you so. However, if you are connected to a network, selecting the wrong printer might send your print job to someone else's printer.

**When I try to print a document, everything comes out garbled, with wrong letters and fonts.** Correct printing depends on a complex interaction between the printer and WordPerfect. Sometimes either can get confused, resulting in improper printing. When this happens, you should try exiting WordPerfect (and even Windows if necessary), and turning off the printer to clear up the confusion. Turn on the printer and restart WordPerfect (and Windows), and try printing again. In most cases, this corrects the problem, especially if printing was working properly before the problem occurred. If not, check to make sure your printer cable is connected correctly, and if that fails, have your printer serviced.

# Printing Specific Document Pages

Most of the printing you do follows the pattern described in the preceding section. However, WordPerfect also enables you to print only specific pages of your document. For example, you may often need to print just a portion of a document because you made a change that affected only one page, to check graphics or text placement, or to proofread.

## Printing the Current Page

The easiest way to print a single page of a large document is to use the Print dialog box to print just the current page. To do this:

1. Position your cursor anywhere on the page you want to print. Current Page refers to the location of the cursor.

2. Access the Print dialog box (choose File, Print; or press F5).
3. Choose Current Page from the drop-down list in the Print section.
4. Click the Print button.

 Although the drop-down list of printing options does not show mnemonic keystrokes, you still can type the first letter of each listed item along with the Alt key to access that item from the keyboard. For example, to print the current page, using just the keyboard, type Alt+F, P, C, Enter (choose File, Print, Current Page, Print).

## Printing Multiple Pages

WordPerfect lets you print a portion of the document by specifying a range of pages to print. From the Print dialog box, choose Multiple Pages from the Print drop-down list. Then specify the Page Range you want to print in the From and the To counter boxes. Click the Print button to print the pages you specified.

If you need to print various non-sequential pages, choose Advanced Multiple from the drop-down list of Print options. After you click the Edit button, WordPerfect displays the Advanced Multiple Pages dialog box shown in figure 8.5. After filling in the values, choose OK, then click Print to print the pages you specified.

Printing multiple pages by specifying a range in the Advanced Multiple Pages dialog box is much faster than moving to the desired page, choosing File, Print, Current Page, Print, and then repeating those steps to print the next page.

**FIG. 8.5**
The Advanced Multiple Pages dialog box is used to print specific pages from the document or file by specifying exact page ranges.

You can specify in the Page(s)/Label(s) edit box which pages you want to print:

- Print individual pages by separating the page numbers with commas or spaces, as in **3,15,23** or **3 15 23** to print pages 3, 15, and 23.
- Print a group of pages by separating the pages with a hyphen, as in **4-8** to print pages 4 through 8.
- Print all pages starting with a specific page number by typing a hyphen after the number, such as **3-** to print all pages starting with page 3.
- Print all pages up to a specific page number by typing a hyphen before the page number, such as **-15** to print the pages up to and including page 15.
- You can combine page ranges by separating them with commas or spaces: **2-5,10-12** or **2-5 10-12** prints pages 2 through 5, and pages 10 through 12.

WordPerfect allows you to format page numbers with Roman numerals, using the Page Numbering command (see Chapter 5, "Formatting Pages and Documents," for information on setting page numbering). You can specify a range for such pages in the Multiple Pages dialog box. For example, to print pages 4 through 9 of a document preface that you numbered with Roman numerals, specify **iv-ix** as the page range.

> **CAUTION**
> When using the Advanced Multiple Pages dialog box, make sure that you specify the pages in numerical order. If you specify a page range of **12-15 4**, only pages 12 through 15 print because page 4 comes before page 12 in the document. However, if an inserted code sets the page number to 4 somewhere after page 15, that page 4 which comes later does print.

If you print a document that is divided into chapters or volumes, be sure to specify the chapter or volume number. For example, if you have four chapters that are 20 pages each, and specify **13-17** as the page range, only pages 13 through 17 of Chapter 1 print. To print specific pages of a chapter or volume, put a colon between the chapter or volume number and the page number, as in **4:10-14** to print pages 10 through 14 of Chapter 4.

The Advanced Multiple Pages dialog box lets you specify ranges for secondary pages, chapters, or volumes. Use the Secondary Pages, Chapters, or Volumes choices if you have divided your document into these page types. When you specify volume and chapter settings, remember that volumes have priority, followed by chapters, secondary pages, and pages. If you specify a volume of 4, and pages of 3 through 12, only pages 3 through 12 in Volume 4 print. Chapter 5, "Formatting Pages and Documents," covers the use of these page types.

## Printing Odd or Even Numbered Pages

Normally, all the pages that you specify in the page range print. You can print just the odd or even numbered pages by choosing the Two-Sided Printing tab in the Print dialog box, as shown in figure 8.6. This is useful for printing double-sided documents on a printer that can only print on one side of the page.

**FIG. 8.6**
Use the Two-Sided Printing tab in the Print dialog box to print odd or even pages, along with other formatting and output options.

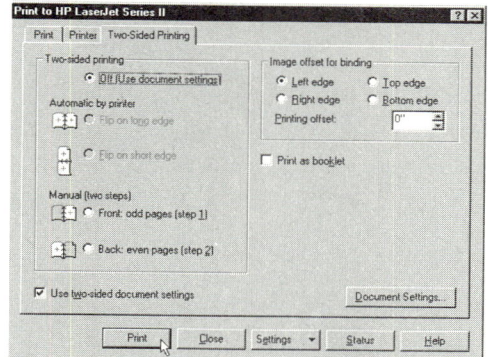

**NOTE** You can print a double-sided document on a printer only capable of single-side printing. Or you can print a document so that you can bind and fold the pages as a booklet.

To print double-sided documents on a printer with only single-side printing capability, first print all the odd pages by choosing Front: Odd Pages (Step 1), and then click the Print button. After all pages have printed, reload the printed pages into the printer and repeat the preceding steps, choosing Back: Even Pages (Step 2) to print the even pages.

You have to determine how to reload the printed pages in your printer so that the pages print properly. To figure this out, create a four-page document with the page numbers on each page. Print the odd pages, reload the paper, and print the even pages. If the pages are not in the proper order (page 2 on the reverse of page 1), you need to print the even pages in reverse order by choosing the Print In Reverse Order check box in the

Two-Sided Printing tab of the Print dialog box. In each test, make sure that you reload the paper the same way.

# Using Printing Options

WordPerfect's printing options enable you to print as much or little of your document as you want. You also can print your most complex documents just the way you want them.

## Printing Selected Text

If you have selected a block of text, choosing File, Print (or one of the other ways discussed earlier in this chapter) displays the Print dialog box with the Selected Text option showing in the Print drop-down list. Click the Print button to print the selected block of text. Printing blocks of text is useful when you need to see text that spans a page boundary or need to print only a part of the text on a page.

The selected text prints on a page in the same position that it occupies in the document. So if you select a paragraph at the bottom of a page, the text prints at the bottom of a page. If you select text across a page boundary, the text is printed on different pages in the same locations as it appears in the document. Printing selected text allows you to check the placement of the text, without having to print the entire page or document.

## Printing Booklets

The Print As Booklet check box in the Two-Sided Printing tab of the Print dialog box allows you to print your document as a booklet. You should set up the subdivided pages and other formatting commands as described in Chapter 5, "Formatting Pages and Documents." When the document has printed, you can staple the pages together into a booklet without having to rearrange the pages. Dialog boxes tell you which pages to insert into the printer so that the text in the completed booklet is in the correct order.

## Printing Documents with Graphics or Color

WordPerfect enables you to specify the print quality of the text and graphics, how color text or graphics print, and whether graphics print with the document.

The print quality is determined by the Resolution setting. The actual print quality depends on the capabilities of your printer and is expressed in dots-per-inch. For example, the HP LaserJet II offers resolutions of $300 \times 300$, $150 \times 150$, and $75 \times 75$, while the Epson LQ1500 offers only $180 \times 180$ or $180 \times 120$. Resolution generally has no effect on laser printer text printing, but it does for laser printer graphics printing. Resolution may have an effect on text printing on dot matrix printers.

The Print In Color setting (on the Print tab of the Print dialog box) determines whether colored text or graphics print in full-color or in black. This option is available only if your printer has color printing capability.

WordPerfect 7 has full support for color printing if you have a color printer. You can place colored text or graphics in your document even without having a color printer. If your printer does not support color, the Print In Color option is not checked, and WordPerfect prints colored text or graphics as shades of gray.

You can deselect the Print In Color check box even when you do have a color printer. This is useful for draft copies of your document, because it usually takes longer to print a document with colors than one without colors.

The Print Graphics check box is available in case you don't want to print any graphics in your document. This is useful for proofreading documents without being distracted by graphics, and may also result in faster printing, especially on a dot matrix printer.

## Printing the Document Summary

The document summary is a special page of your document that you create in the Document Properties dialog box by choosing File, Document, Properties. In that dialog box, if you choose Options, Print Summary, the document summary alone is printed. If you want to print the document summary along with some or all of the rest of the document, select Include Document Summary in the Print dialog box. The document summary prints first, followed by the rest of the document or pages that you specified. The document summary does not print if you have not created it, or if only the author name has been entered in the Document Summary dialog box. The document summary is explained in Chapter 5, "Formatting Pages and Documents."

## Using Custom Print Settings

Although you often customize your printing procedure for a specific printing task, sometimes you also use a customized procedure over and over again. WordPerfect lets you save customized settings so that you can recall them quickly when needed.

Suppose, for example, you have a standard report that requires four copies of the last page to go to the accounting department. Follow these steps to save and use a custom print setup:

1. From the Print dialog box, make the various setup changes you need to print exactly what you want (for example, change Number Of Copies to 4, use Multiple Pages to specify the exact page(s) you want, and choose Group order of printing).
2. Without printing yet, click Settings, and from the pop-up menu choose Named Settings.
3. In the Edit Named Settings dialog box that appears (see fig. 8.7), type the name of the setting (for example, **Accounting Report**) and click Add.

**FIG. 8.7**
You can create custom print settings and save them to use again later.

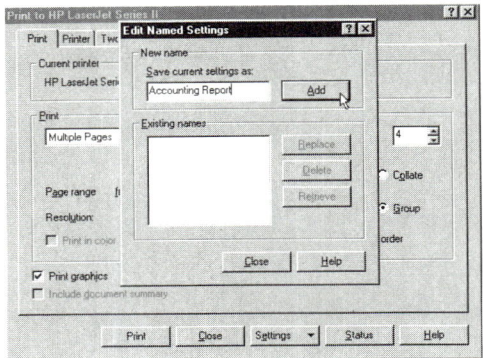

4. Choose Close, and then close the Print dialog box.

Now, whenever you want to print four copies of the designated page of the document (in fact, of any document), follow these steps:

1. Go to the Print dialog box (choose File, Print; or press F5).
2. Click Settings.
3. At the bottom of the drop-down menu is a list of the named settings you have created. Choose the setting you want to use (for example, Accounting Report).
4. Click the Print button.

 **TROUBLESHOOTING**

**When I print a document with graphics, the graphics don't look good even though I'm using a high-quality laser printer.** The problem may be that you don't have the best print resolution selected. Make sure you choose Print, Resolution and set the resolution to the highest possible setting in the Print dialog box (for example, 300 × 300).

**I'm trying to print envelopes, but my printer won't print them, and I get an error message on my printer's display.** If you have a separate envelope bin on your laser printer, you won't have this problem (unless, of course, the bin is empty). On a single-bin laser printer, WordPerfect assumes you will feed an envelope through the manual feed (top of the tray). If you insert the envelope in the manual feed before you print the envelope, you can avoid the error message. If you insert the envelope after you get the message, usually you can press the printer's On Line button (or an equivalent button) to continue printing the envelope.

# Controlling the Printer and Print Jobs

Both WordPerfect and Windows enable you to check the status of any current print jobs and to control multiple print jobs.

## Controlling Print Jobs from WordPerfect

When you print a document or file, WordPerfect prepares the document for printing, then hands it off to Windows which then takes charge of sending the information to the printer and allows you to return to work in WordPerfect. You can check the progress of the print job by clicking Status in the Print dialog box. The Print Status and History dialog box appears (see fig. 8.8) and shows you information about current and past print jobs, including the following:

**FIG. 8.8**
The Print Status and History dialog box enables you to cancel or prioritize waiting print jobs.

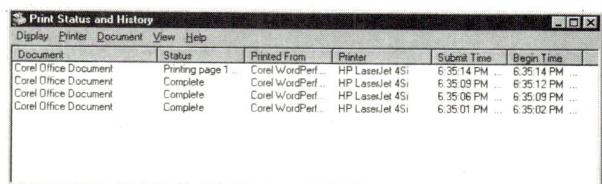

- The name of the current document being printed and a list of previously printed documents. If the documents were saved prior to printing, their names are also listed.
- The current status of the print job, such as `Printing page 1`.
- The source of the document, such as `Corel WordPerfect`.
- The printer to which the document was or is being directed.
- The time you submitted the print job.
- The time the print job was actually printed.

To cancel or pause a print job, simply click the job, choose Document, and then choose Cancel Printing or Pause Printing. To remove the job from the list, choose Document, Remove.

To sort the print jobs by Begin Time, by Document source, and so on, simply click the column button at the top of the corresponding column.

And finally, if your list of past printing jobs is too extensive and you want to see only the current print jobs, choose Display, Hide Completed Jobs.

### Controlling Print Jobs Using Windows

Each installed printer in Windows 95 has its own print job listing, which is nearly the same as the WordPerfect Print Status and History dialog box, although the WordPerfect listing is a bit easier to access.

To use the Windows 95 Print Job listing for the printer to which you sent your document, access the Windows 95 taskbar and double-click the printer icon located near the current time. If there is no printer icon, the print job is probably completed. Alternatively, you can access the taskbar, click the Start button, and then choose Settings, Printers. In the Printers dialog box that appears, double-click the printer you're currently using; the control box for that printer appears (see fig. 8.9).

**FIG. 8.9**
The Windows Control dialog box for your current printer lets you pause, cancel, or remove waiting print jobs.

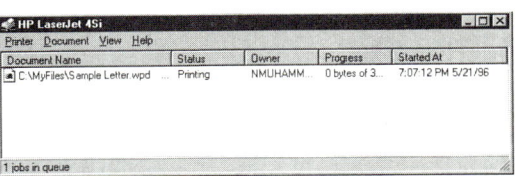

In this dialog box, click the print job you want to change and choose Document or Printer to Pause or Cancel the print job. You also use this dialog box to monitor the progress of any jobs not yet completed.

> **NOTE** Canceling print jobs is most useful for long documents, since by the time you figure out where everything is, a short document (one or two pages) will have already printed. Just promise yourself to be more careful next time before sending a print job off to the printer.

# Selecting and Setting Up Your Printer

Whether what you print turns out right or not depends largely on whether you selected the right printer, and whether it has been set up correctly.

## Understanding Printer Drivers

When you installed Windows, you also selected your printer, and although you may not realize it, you also set up your Windows printer drivers.

Your printer is controlled by a *printer driver* (a file) that contains special commands used to perform various functions. As an example, when you make a word boldface, the printer driver is responsible for sending out the special commands to tell the printer that the next word needs to be printed in bold, rather than normal. These printer commands can be very complex. The printer driver is responsible for translating the text that you type on-screen into commands that the printer uses to print your masterpiece.

In a network or office environment, you might need to print some of your documents on one printer, and others on some other printer. For that reason, you might have more than one printer driver installed in your version of Windows. Because the exact fonts and layout may be slightly different for each printer driver, you should select the intended printer before you complete your document. When you create and save a WordPerfect document, information about the printer driver you have selected is saved along with the document.

**NOTE** In the past, WordPerfect supplied its own printer drivers to complement those provided by Windows so that Windows and DOS WordPerfect users could share printer drivers. In WordPerfect 7, only Windows printer drivers are available.

## Selecting and Configuring Your Printer

When you have multiple printers installed, you can select the current or target printer by accessing the Print dialog box and choosing the Printer tab (see fig. 8.10).

**FIG. 8.10**
The Printer tab in the Print dialog box enables you to choose the current printer.

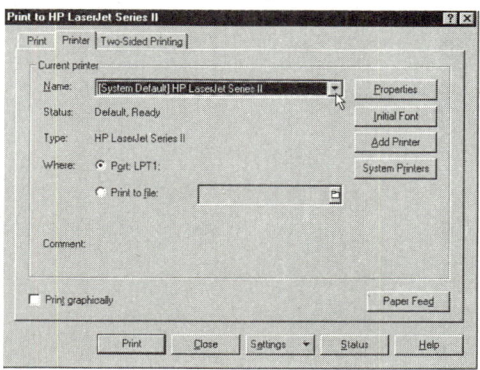

The Current Printer section displays the currently selected printer name, whether it is ready to print, what type driver it is using, and which port or connection is being used to send information to the printer.

To select a different printer, click the Name drop-down arrow button. All installed printers are listed, including those that print to a fax device, and those that publish documents to special electronic readers such as Envoy. Click the printer driver you want, and WordPerfect displays the selected printer in the Name edit box. The buttons on the right side of the dialog box offer you these options:

- *Properties.* View or change various settings for the selected printer, including default paper sizes, installed fonts, graphics quality, hardware setup, and more. (See your Windows documentation for more information on setting up Windows printer drivers.)

- *Initial Font.* Select the base font that is used for the current and all subsequent documents created with the printer definition selected. Selecting this option displays the Printer Initial Font dialog box, in which you can choose the font face, style, and size values to be used as defaults for the current printer. Chapter 20, "Using Fonts and Special Characters," contains detailed information on using fonts in your documents.

- *Add Printer.* This takes you to the Windows Install Wizard which guides you through the steps of installing a new printer for all of your Windows applications. You might need your Windows setup disks or CD to complete this operation.

- *System Printers.* Although you can change printer properties using the Properties button, clicking System Printers takes you to the Windows Printer dialog box where you can delete the printer driver, rename it, monitor print jobs for that printer, or also change that printer's properties.

**CAUTION**
Deleting a Windows printer driver makes that printer unavailable to all other Windows programs, regardless of whether they still need access to that printer.

- *Paper Feed.* If you have a sheet feeder, use this option to select it. Otherwise, you have the choice of indicating that the paper lines up on the left, center, or right side of the paper feed opening.

## Adding Fonts for Your Printer

Each printer that you add comes with the default fonts installed for that printer. If you purchase additional font cartridges or soft fonts, you should add those fonts to your printer definition. There are two different locations you use to add fonts, depending on whether they are printer specific (for example, Hewlett Packard's cartridges or PCL fonts), or whether they can be used by all Windows printers and applications (for example, TrueType fonts).

- For printer-specific fonts, go to the Print dialog box, choose the Print tab, and click Properties to access the printer's Properties dialog box. Next, choose the Font tab. The resulting dialog box differs for each printer because some allow cartridges or specialized fonts, while others simply offer options for using pre-installed fonts. Consult your printer's documentation for more information.

- To add Windows-based fonts to your Windows printer drivers, access the FONT folder in the Windows Control Panel. Fonts installed in this manner are available for all Windows applications, not just for WordPerfect. Chapter 20, "Using Fonts and Special Characters," contains detailed information about installing and selecting fonts.

# Using Other Forms of Output

While most people print documents to their own dot matrix or laser printer, some print to network printers or simply send their documents via fax or electronic mail.

## Printing on a Network

If you or your network administrator have previously installed a network printer, you can select it from the Printer tab of the Print dialog box. WordPerfect prepares the document for the printer, hands it off to Windows, which in turn sends the print job to the network printer. You can choose File, Print, Status to see the progress of the print job until it passes to the network queue. You or your network administrator can then use your network's printer queue program to look at print jobs that are waiting in the network printer queue.

To add a network printer to the list of available printers, access the PRINTERS folder in the Windows Control Panel, add a new printer or select an existing printer, right-click the printer icon, and choose Properties. In the Details tab of the printer's Properties dialog box, you can add a network port by browsing your network until you find the printer connection that matches the printer you have selected. The network printer is now available for all your Windows applications, not just WordPerfect.

You may want to set up several different available network printers, each to a different printer queue. You can then select the appropriate network printer as needed from the Printer tab of the Print dialog box.

## Printing to a File

Sometimes you might want to print to a file because that printer is not connected to your system. By printing to a file, all the printer commands are stored in the file along with the text. You can then take the file to a system that is connected to that type of printer, and "print" it to the printer (as covered later in this section), even if that system doesn't have WordPerfect 7.

For instance, if you need to work on a PostScript-formatted document, you don't need to have a PostScript printer connected to your computer. Just install a PostScript printer driver, and print the document to a file. Then take the file to a computer that is connected to a PostScript printer. Installing a PostScript printer driver and using it with your PostScript document is much easier than trying to format the document with different printer drivers.

To set up printing to a file, select the desired target printer from the Printer tab of the Print dialog box. Then click the Print To File option button, type the name and path of the file you intend to create, and click Print.

> **CAUTION**
> After printing to a file, be sure to select the Port option button and the actual printer you're connected to before printing again, or the next print job will also go to the same file on disk.

After the document has printed, use the Open File dialog box (choose File, Open; or Ctrl+O) to copy the file to a floppy disk. Then take the disk to another computer, and use the DOS COPY command to print the file. For example, if you call the print file PRNFILE.DOC on the A drive, and the computer's printer is connected to the LPT1 port, you type this command at the DOS prompt:

**COPY A:PRNFILE.DOC /B LPT1:**

The document then prints on the printer, just as if you used WordPerfect and were connected to that printer. The /B parameter ensures that the entire file prints.

## Faxing from WordPerfect 7

WordPerfect also has the capability to fax documents when the following conditions are met:

- A fax board is installed in your computer or connected to your network.
- A Windows-based fax program is installed on your computer (so that the fax "printer" driver is available from the Printer tab of the Print dialog box).

To fax a document, follow these steps:

1. With the document that you want to fax in the active window, choose File, Print; or press F5. If you want to fax a block of text, first select the text and then choose File, Print; or press F5.

2. Make sure that the fax printer is shown as the current printer in the Print dialog box. Choose the Printer tab to select your fax printer driver, if it is not the current printer. (See "Selecting a Printer" earlier in this chapter for information on how to select a printer.)

3. Specify the portion of the current document to fax by choosing Current Page or Multiple Pages, or leave Full Document selected to fax the entire document.

4. Click Print to fax the document. The document is *rasterized*—converted to a faxable format—and then handed off to your fax driver for faxing.

5. Your Windows fax program may display a dialog box for the fax destination information. If not, switch to your Windows fax program with Alt+Tab.

6. Fill in the destination information in the fax program's dialog box, and then send the fax. Figure 8.11 shows the dialog box for the WinFax fax program.

**FIG. 8.11**
The WinFax program "prints" to a fax/modem. Your fax dialog box may be different, but should include most of the same information.

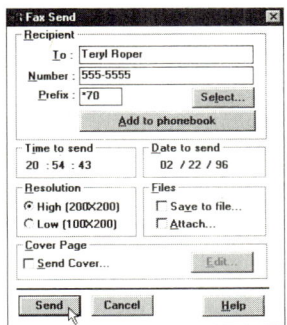

After the document is sent to the fax driver, you can use the fax program's commands to learn the status of the fax, to look at the send or receive log, or to cancel the fax before it is sent.

## Using Novell GroupWise or Other E-Mail Programs

If you are connected to a network, WordPerfect can send mail to others on your network through Novell GroupWise 4.1. The program also supports any mail system that uses the MAPI or CMC standards. Products with a "Designed for Windows 95" logo should support CMC mail enabling. (See your mail program documentation for information on what standards it uses.) If your mail program is supported, when you choose the File menu, the Send option appears. If not, the Send option does not appear.

When you want to mail the current document, simply choose File, Send. Windows opens up your mail program, and the document appears as an attachment to a mail message. For example, if you have Novell GroupWise 4.1 for Windows, choosing Send automatically takes you to the Mail To dialog box which is used to prepare and send a copy of the current document as an attached file to your mail message (see fig. 8.12). Fill in the From, To, Subject, and Message boxes. The current document is saved as a temporary file and attached to the message. You can attach other files and sound objects to your mail message. When you have completed the items in the Mail To dialog box, click the Send button to send the message.

**FIG. 8.12**
If you use Novell GroupWise 4.1 or another compatible mail program such as Microsoft Mail, cc:Mail, and so on, you can choose File, Send to mail documents directly from WordPerfect as attachments to mail messages.

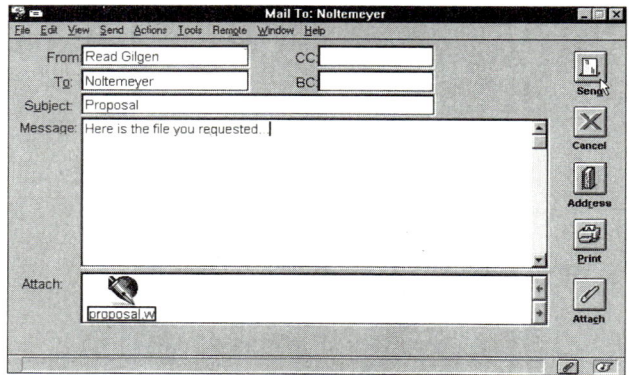

For more information about using Novell GroupWise 4.1 for Windows or any other compatible mail program, see the program manual or contact your network support staff. ●

PART **II**

# Automating Your Work

- **9** Customizing WordPerfect 299
- **10** Using Styles 333
- **11** Using Templates 363
- **12** Creating Macros 387
- **13** Working with Toolbars 413

# Chapter 9

# Customizing WordPerfect

*by Judy Petersen*

Customizing options in WordPerfect enables you to set up WordPerfect's features to match your most frequent needs. In a specific document, you can make these changes using the regular WordPerfect menu options. Or you can use the Preferences options to customize how the feature works for all new documents.

You can customize these options and more using the Preferences feature. The changes you make in Preferences remain in effect until you change them again.

When you choose Edit, Preferences, the features you can customize are displayed as icons in a dialog box that works like a Windows program group (see fig. 9.1), with the addition of a menu bar with the Preferences command. Click the icon for the option you want, or choose from the Preferences pull-down menu. ■

- **Displaying on-screen elements**
  You can decide what WordPerfect screen elements are displayed, where they are positioned, and even what commands each offers you.

- **Saving all open documents simultaneously**
  If you save documents as a workspace, the documents are opened automatically when you next start WordPerfect.

- **The location of files, default file extensions, and backing up your work**
  Manage your files better by telling WordPerfect where your files are saved, using file extensions that identify your files, and protecting valuable documents by having WordPerfect simplify backing up your work regularly.

- **Document summaries**
  Store identifying information about your documents that you can search to help locate documents.

# Customizing the Display

By using Display Preferences, you can customize the way various features such as hidden text and graphics are displayed in the document window, and set options for Zoom and the default view, Reveal Codes window, Ruler Bar, and merge code display.

When you choose <u>D</u>isplay from the Preferences dialog box or pull-down menu, the Display Preferences dialog box shown in figure 9.2 opens with the Document tab selected.

**FIG. 9.1**
To configure a feature, choose the icon for the feature or display the Preferences pull-down menu in the Preferences dialog box.

**FIG. 9.2**
To use the Display Preferences dialog box, choose an option so WordPerfect changes the Display Preferences dialog box to show the specific options you can customize for that option.

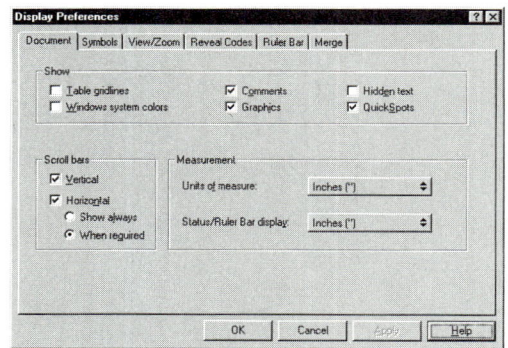

**N O T E** When working in the Display Preferences dialog box, each time you choose an option from the tabs at the top of the dialog box, the choices for that option appear in the remainder of the box. Each of these displays is illustrated later in this chapter in sections describing the options. When you have made your choices in one configuration of the Display Preferences dialog box, choose OK to open up the Preferences dialog box again. If you want to make further configuration choices to the display, do not choose OK. Rather, choose another option tab. Continue choosing other option tabs until you have indicated your preferences for all six options. Then choose OK to exit the dialog box.

## Document Display

With the Document tab selected, you can customize the document window to change the text color; show or suppress the display of comments, graphics, and hidden text; add or remove scroll bars; change the way measurements are stated; and change the appearance of dialog boxes.

**Show** The options in the Show section of the dialog box control the color of document text, and whether document features such as cell guides, graphic images, comments, hidden text, and QuickSpots are visible in the document window. Choose as many of the options as you want to use by clicking the option or pressing Alt plus its mnemonic key. When a check appears in the option's check box, the feature is selected. Choose the option again to toggle it off.

The following six options are available in the Show area:

- *Table Gridlines*. When you use the Tables feature to create a project such as an organizational chart where some of the cell lines are removed by choosing None for line style, it can be difficult to determine where the cursor is located in the table. Choose this option to display cell guides. Any removed cell lines appear as dotted lines.

- *Windows System Colors*. The default color for text used by WordPerfect in document windows is black. If you have changed the Windows 95 default colors, choose Windows System Colors to place a check in its check box.

**TIP** Change the text color in Windows 95 using the Appearance tab in Display Properties, available in the Control Panel.

**NOTE** In addition to text color, you can customize the colors for the active and inactive window title bar, the button faces and shadows, and other elements that make up a window, or select one of the many color schemes provided with Windows 95. The color scheme you create or choose in the Color dialog box controls the appearance of WordPerfect 7.

- *Comments*. You can add nonprinting comments to documents to remind you or others of printing instructions or other information about the document. The presence of these comments are, by default, displayed in the document window as an icon at the left edge of the screen at the comment location. If you use comments to add information you do not want viewed to a document, choose Comments to suppress the display of the icon. The comment code is visible in the Reveal Codes window, but there is no other indication of its existence. Refer to Chapter 6, "Using Writing Tools," for more information about the Comments feature.

- *Graphics*. A major reason for the popularity of the graphical user interface is the display along with text of all document graphics such as lines and figures. When you are working with older systems, in large documents, or editing a document, the display of graphics can slow the screen refresh rate. Graphics images appear by default. To speed your work, suppress the display of graphics by choosing Graph<u>i</u>cs to remove the check from the adjacent check box.

**N O T E** To quickly turn the display of graphics back on to preview a document, choose <u>V</u>iew, <u>G</u>raphics. If hidden text display is turned off, you can view the hidden text in the Reveal Codes window, or choose <u>V</u>iew, Hidden Te<u>x</u>t to see the hidden text displayed in the document.

- *Hidd<u>e</u>n Text*. Hidden text is not available in WordPerfect 7 by default. To enable the use of hidden text, choose Hidd<u>e</u>n Text. The Hidden Text option becomes available in the Font dialog box. Refer to Chapter 6, "Using Writing Tools," for more information about using and displaying hidden text.

- *Quick<u>S</u>pots*. An innovative feature of WordPerfect 7 for Windows is the appearance of QuickSpots that, when selected, displays a highly customized dialog box of options. The small button that follows your mouse pointer as you move from paragraph to paragraph is a QuickSpot. Click it to display a dialog box of options such as Font, Styles, Border, and Justification that apply to paragraphs. After you try out the variety of QuickSpots available, you may find they are not useful for the work you commonly perform. If so, choose Quick<u>S</u>pots so the feature does not appear.

  ▶ **See** "QuickSpots," **p. 39**
  ▶ **See** "Using Hidden Text," **p. 244**

**Scroll Bars**   A vertical scroll bar appears by default in the document window. A horizontal scroll bar appears when the document layout causes a portion of the document to not be visible on-screen. This can happen when you use landscape orientation or a wide paper size. You can choose from the following options in the Scroll Bars group to customize the display of scroll bars:

- *<u>V</u>ertical*. You can turn on or off the display of the vertical scroll bar.

- *Horizo<u>n</u>tal*. You can turn on or off the display of the horizontal scroll bar. When you choose Horizo<u>n</u>tal, the display of the scroll bar can be configured. Choose Show A<u>l</u>ways to display the horizontal scroll bar all the time. Or choose When Re<u>q</u>uired to display horizontal scroll bar only if document features extend past the right edge of the document window.

**Measurement**   When you install WordPerfect, the program is set to display all measurements in decimal inches. This is reflected in the Ln and Pos information in the status bar, the format of the Ruler Bar, and wherever you enter measurements, such as margins and line height. You can change the way measurements are displayed in dialog boxes and have the status bar display measurements in another format. This is a handy way to use points to enter measurements when creating a newsletter, and yet have the status bar and Ruler Bar use the more familiar inches format.

To change the way measurements are displayed, choose either Units Of Measure or Status/Ruler Bar Display in the Measurement group of the Display Preferences dialog box (refer to fig. 9.2) to open the pop-up menu. From the menu, choose one of the units of measurement listed in the following table.

 **TIP** Working with 1,200ths of an inch allows you to specify very small increments, and the amounts can be easy to calculate (600 = 1/2-inch; 1,200 = 1/10-inch).

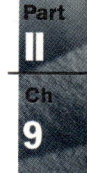

| WordPerfect Unit | Description |
| --- | --- |
| Inches (") | 8.50" |
| Inches (i) | 8.50i |
| Centimeters (c) | 1/100th of a meter |
| Millimeters (m) | 1/1,000th of a meter |
| Points (p) | In WordPerfect, there are 72 points per inch rather than 72.27 |
| 1200ths of an inch (w) | 300w is 1/4" |

WordPerfect calculates measurements to six decimal places, although only three decimal places are displayed in any numeric text box.

Regardless of the measurement unit you have selected, you can enter measurements in any format and WordPerfect converts the measurement for you. If you enter an amount in centimeters followed by a c (for example, 2.75c) when working in inches, WordPerfect converts the centimeters to inches. Better still, if you use a standard ruler to measure a margin or binding offset, you can enter the measurement using fractions of an inch (for example, **1 3/16**) and WordPerfect converts the entry to the decimal equivalent.

**NOTE** The line and column measurement system used by WordPerfect in version 4.2 for DOS and earlier is not available in WordPerfect.

## Show Formatting Symbols

The Symbols tab in the Display Preferences dialog box causes WordPerfect to display symbols in place of spaces, as well as hard returns, tabs, indents, or codes for center, flush right, soft hyphen, advance, or center page, every time you start WordPerfect. This feature is turned off by default. Enabling the display of symbols can help you locate incorrect codes and understand how portions of the document were formatted to create a specific appearance.

▶ **See** "View Modes," **p. 28**

By default, all the symbols are selected. Choose Sho<u>w</u> Symbols On New And Current Document to enable the display of all selected symbols. You can choose individual features (spaces, hard returns, and so on) to toggle each on or off.

 To debug a WordPerfect document formatting problem, try displaying symbols.

 A quick way to turn on or off the display of symbols is to choose <u>V</u>iew, <u>S</u>how ¶ or press Ctrl+Shift+F3.

The steps for customizing the display of symbols used for each formatting code and ideas on using this feature in your work are discussed in the section "Customizing Formatting Options" in Chapter 4, "Formatting Text."

## View/Zoom Display

By default, the document window display is in Page mode. By using Page mode, you can see and edit headers, footers, page numbers, and other features on the page. Two-page mode is available, which is most useful as a Print Preview mode. WYSIWYG (What You See Is What You Get) is used in all modes but in Draft mode; margins, headers, footers, and similar features are not displayed. To use View/Zoom to change the default view and to specify the default zoom percentage for all documents, complete the following steps:

▶ **See** "Show Spaces, Tabs, and Hard Returns," **p. 42**

1. From the Display Preferences dialog box, choose View/Zoom to display the Default View and Default Zoom options in the Display Preferences dialog box (see fig. 9.3).

**FIG. 9.3**
View/Zoom options include Draft, Page, or Two Page view in the document window, a list of Default Zoom percentages, and a text box where you can enter a custom percentage.

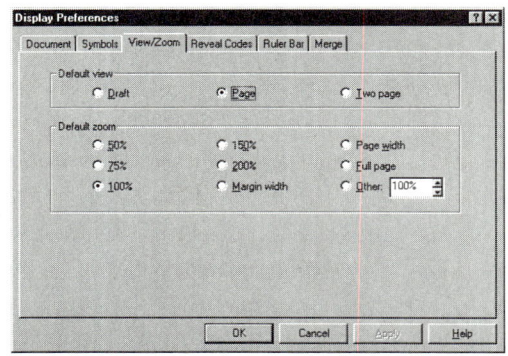

2. To change the default document window view mode for all documents, choose Draft, Page, or Two Page. A dot appears in the option button next to your selection.
3. Choose one of the predefined Zoom percentages, or enter your preference in the Other text box (from 25 to 400 percent). Using the mouse, you can click the adjacent increment or decrement arrows to change the amount in increments of five.

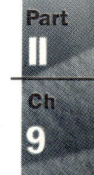

Alternatively, choose a page display format:

- *Margin Width*. Displays the text aligned on the left edge of the screen. The number of lines displayed depends on the font being used, but is about 22 lines for a 12-point font.

 Displaying documents using Margin Width view maximizes the size of the text and leaves page numbering, headers, and footers on-screen, but eliminates the large white space of the page margins.

- *Page Width*. The text is centered on-screen with the page margin width visible on the left and right edges. About 28 lines of text are visible when using a 12-point font.
- *Full Page*. The entire page is visible. This is equivalent to a print preview of a single page.

For information on using the different screen display modes and the effect of the Zoom options on each mode, refer to Chapter 1, "Getting Started."

**NOTE** The selections you make in Display Preferences and the View menu only change the way you look at your document on-screen. The document itself is not affected.

## Reveal Codes Display

By using the Reveal Codes tab in the Display Preferences dialog box, you can customize the text font, background and text color, window size, and other options for the Reveal Codes window. It is easy, for example, to change the background color from gray to one that contrasts with the gray codes, making the codes easier to locate.

▶ **See** "Customizing Reveal Codes To Meet Your Needs," **p. 97**

## Ruler Bar Display

WordPerfect includes a Ruler Bar you can choose to display at the top of the document window. The Ruler Bar shows the placement and type of tab stops, the current margins, and, if the cursor is in a table or columns, the margins of the columns or table columns. By choosing Ruler Bar in the Display Preferences dialog box, you see several options for customizing the way the Ruler Bar functions. Refer to Chapter 4, "Formatting Text," to learn how to customize the ruler display. Chapter 4 also discusses the tab features and using the ruler to set tabs.

## Merge Codes Display

When working with merge documents, WordPerfect displays abbreviated merge codes in the document window. You may prefer to display merge codes as markers, or you can hide them completely. Choose Merge in the Display Preferences dialog box to display the available Merge Code options and choose one of the following:

- Display Merge Codes (the default setting)
- Display Merge Codes As Markers (red diamond bullets)
- Hide Merge Codes
    - ▶ See "Customizing Formatting Options," **p. 145**
    - ▶ See "Using Other Writing Tools," **p. 241**
    - ▶ See "Understanding Merge Codes," **p. 609**

# Customizing Environment Options

In the Environment Preferences dialog box, you can change your personal user information, decide when WordPerfect should beep, change the way menus are displayed, indicate when WordPerfect should prompt for confirmation of actions, set Save options, turn on Hypertext capability, and choose Code Page options. Choose Environment from the Preferences dialog box or the pull-down menu to display the Environment Preferences dialog box shown in figure 9.4.

> **NOTE** If you are a regular WordPerfect user and want to immediately set up document backup protection, the backup options can now be found by choosing Files in the Preferences dialog box to display the Document tab in the File Preferences dialog box.

**FIG. 9.4**
Provide your name and initials; set beep, formatting, menu, and save options; and open the Code Page dialog box from the Environment Preferences dialog box.

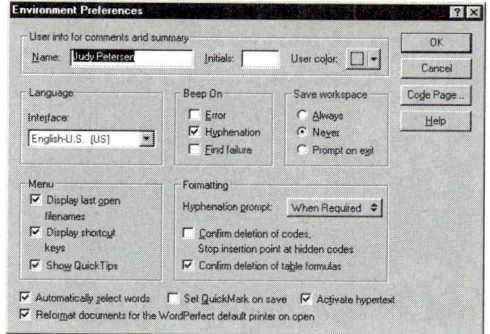

## User Information

The User Info For Comments And Summary section of the Environment Preferences dialog box enables you to display your initials in a box of your personal color to indicate document comments you insert, and to provide your name to be included in the Typist and Author fields in document summaries you create. If you have set up a network name or a name for connecting to the Internet, WordPerfect may retrieve that name automatically.

To configure or edit user information options, follow these steps:

1. Choose Name, and enter your name in the text box.
2. Choose Initials, and enter your initials in the text box.
3. Choose User Color, and choose a color from the color palette using either of these methods:

   - With the mouse, choose User Color to open the color palette. Click the color you want to use.
   - With the keyboard, press Alt+l to choose User Color. Press the space bar to open the color palette. Using the arrow keys, move the box-shaped cursor to the color you want. Press Enter to return to the dialog box.

Refer to Chapter 6, "Using Writing Tools," for information on how to add your initials to a comment, and to Chapter 5, "Formatting Pages and Documents," for instructions on creating document summaries.

## Language

WordPerfect is used in offices and homes throughout the world, as evidenced by the astonishing number of languages in which it is written. If you purchase another language version of WordPerfect, choose Interface and select the language you want from the pop-up list.

## Beep Options

You can change the events that cause your computer's beep, or you can eliminate all sound effects. The default configuration is to only beep when prompted for a hyphenation decision. To change the beep, choose one or more of the following options to place or remove the check from the adjacent check boxes:

▶ **See** "Using Document Summaries," **p. 201**
▶ **See** "Using Document Comments," **p. 241**

- *Error.* Beeps when WordPerfect displays an error message.
- *Hyphenation.* Beeps when WordPerfect prompts for a hyphenation decision. Hyphenation beep is the only one selected by default.
- *Find Failure.* Beeps when a search fails to find a match.

## Save Workspace

With the advent of software that enables the user to have more than one document open at the same time, it is common to have several related documents open simultaneously. By using the Save Workspace options, you can save all the currently open documents as a workspace. The next time you start WordPerfect, you can open all the related documents at once. Following are the options for Save Workspace:

- *Always.* WordPerfect automatically saves the workspace every time you exit.
- *Never.* WordPerfect does not save the workspace when you exit. This is the default setting.
- *Prompt On Exit.* A dialog box prompt appears when you exit, in which you can choose to save the workspace.

## Menu Display Options

You can configure what is displayed with the pull-down menus. By default, WordPerfect shows keyboard shortcut keys for commands on the menus and includes a list of most recently opened files at the bottom of the File menu. WordPerfect also shows a help prompt called QuickTips for all menu commands and Power Bar, Toolbar, and status bar buttons. These options are available in the Environment Preferences dialog box (refer to fig. 9.4) for you to customize, as follows:

- *Display Last Open Filenames.* When you choose this option, the names of the last four open files are listed at the end of the File menu. The file names remain on the menu when you close WordPerfect. To quickly retrieve a file on the list, press the number by the file name to retrieve the file.

- *Display Shortcut Keys.* The default for pull-down menus is to display any keyboard shortcut keys next to the menu command. Choose this option to turn off this feature.
- *Show QuickTips.* When you move the mouse pointer over the Toolbar and Power Bar buttons, available menu selections, or the status bar buttons and pause, a brief explanation of the command or button feature appears. To turn off this feature, choose Show QuickTips.

## Formatting Options

In the Formatting section of the Environment Preferences dialog box, you can customize the action taken when a hyphenation question arises and whether you must confirm the deletion of formatting codes or of formulas in tables.

**Hyphenation Prompts**   You can customize the circumstances under which WordPerfect asks you for hyphenation decisions. WordPerfect uses a dictionary with hyphenation rules to decide how to hyphenate a word.

▶ **See** "Customizing the Hyphenation Prompt," **p. 152**

**Confirmation Deletion Options**   By using the WordPerfect default settings, you can navigate through your document to delete, move, and otherwise rearrange codes with little difficulty. If you prefer to protect the codes you have inserted and the formulas you have entered in tables, two options are available in the Environment Preferences dialog box:

- *Confirm Deletion Of Codes, Stop Insertion Point At Hidden Codes.* When you turn on this option, WordPerfect stops at every code you try to delete and displays a confirmation dialog box that names the type of code and provides Yes and No buttons. If you are editing with the Reveal Codes window open, the codes are deleted and no confirmation prompt appears.
- *Confirm Deletion Of Table Formulas.* Choose this option to guard against accidentally typing text over the formulas you have created in tables or floating cells. Again, when this option is selected, a confirmation dialog box appears, asking whether you want to overwrite the formula already in the cell.

See Chapter 16, "Working with Tables," for information about entering and deleting table formulas, and Chapter 4, "Formatting Text," for instructions on inserting and deleting format codes.

## Automatically Select Words

The I-beam mouse pointer is particularly helpful when you are trying to click the insertion point into place between small, thin, proportionally spaced characters. Unfortunately, you can still sometimes miss the first or last letter of a word when selecting several words.

When you select more than one word of text with the mouse, WordPerfect automatically extends the selection to include entire words. To see how this works, try using the mouse to select several words. You can see the reverse video highlight jump to the end of the current word as you move from word to word. Similarly, try selecting several words, beginning in the middle of the first word.

This feature does not apply to selecting text when you use the keyboard. Although the Automatically Select Words option can be of benefit when you are first learning to work with the mouse, not everyone will find it helpful. To turn off the feature, choose Automatically Select Words to remove the check mark from the adjacent box.

## Set QuickMark on Save

When you save a document you need to further work with, you can configure WordPerfect to place a special bookmark, called the QuickMark, at the cursor location every time the document is saved. When you later retrieve the document, choose Insert, Bookmark, Find QuickMark or press Ctrl+Q to move the cursor to its previous location. To turn on this feature, choose Set QuickMark On Save to place a check in the adjacent check box.

 If you save a workspace and have activated Set QuickMark On Save, launching WordPerfect retrieves all files in the workspace with the insertion point at the QuickMark in each file.

## Activate Hypertext

You can highlight text or insert buttons, called *hypertext links*, in your document that are linked to other locations in the same or another document or to a macro. To use hypertext, the feature must be active, which is the WordPerfect default setting. To turn off hypertext, choose Activate Hypertext from the bottom of the Environment Preferences dialog box to remove the check from the adjacent check box.

▶ **See** "Understanding Hypertext," **p. 1022**

If hypertext is not active and you are working with a document containing hypertext links, when you choose Tools, Hypertext/Web Links, WordPerfect displays a Hypertext Bar that includes an Activate button. Using this method to reactivate hypertext does not restore the Activate Hypertext option in the Environment Preferences dialog box.

## Reformat Documents for Default Printer on Open

You can have any number of printer drivers installed in WordPerfect, even though some of those printers may never be attached to your computer. This feature enables you to create files designed to be printed on a printer at a different location, at another computer or office, using printer-specific formatting such as the font selection.

If you installed fonts or set up cartridge fonts in each printer driver, you can use these driver files to create documents at home that are ready to print when you return to the office if you have the printer drivers on your home computer. You can apply the fonts when you create the document by choosing the appropriate printer driver, even though you don't have the fonts on your computer. When you finally print the job, the fonts and the printer must be available. Refer to Chapter 8, "Basic Output: Printing, Faxing, and E-Mail," for information on setting up printers and installing fonts.

When you create documents using a variety of printer drivers, you usually want to retrieve your documents formatted for the printer you used when you created the document. However, when you retrieve a document, WordPerfect reformats the document for the currently selected (default) printer. Because many documents are faxed today rather than printed as hard copy, users commonly have at least two drivers: one for the printer and another for the fax machine or card. If the last document was faxed, the next document you retrieve will be reformatted for the fax driver.

To turn off this feature so that WordPerfect retrieves the printer driver that was current when the document was saved, choose Reformat Documents For The WordPerfect Default Printer On Open to remove the check in the check box.

▶ **See** "Understanding Printer Drivers," **p. 291**

## Code Page

When you install DOS on your computer, the operating system includes character sets for almost 20 different international languages. The character sets are designated by a three- or four-digit-code page number. WordPerfect and DOS use the ASCII (or U.S. IBM) character set for the basic text characters, some symbols, Greek letters, and simple line drawings used in your documents. WordPerfect also provides its own graphical characters that can be inserted using the WordPerfect character set. Windows uses its own code pages that differ from those used by DOS.

By using the code page defaults for the DOS and Windows code pages, you can copy data freely from spreadsheets to WordPerfect. This is true even though the character numbers are different for the DOS and Windows U.S. character sets. The paragraph symbol (¶), for example, is character 20 in the ASCII character set, but is character 187 if you want to display it in an Excel spreadsheet using the =CHAR() function.

The Code Page option enables you to choose a different character set, or code page, when creating, importing, or outputting documents created using a different language. To change the code page, choose Co_de Page to display the Codes Page Preferences dialog box. To change the _DOS code page or the _Windows code page, choose the language you want from the pop-up menu that appears when you make your choice.

Change the _Input File Code Page if a source file uses a language other than those specified for the DOS or Windows code page. Change the _Output File Code Page to export a file to another language format. Otherwise, input and output files use the DOS and Windows page codes as the default.

### TROUBLESHOOTING

**When I try to edit my work by selecting text, beginning in the middle of a word, with the mouse, WordPerfect selects the entire word and extends the selection to the end of the next word even though I only want to change the first character. What is wrong with my mouse?** By default, WordPerfect selects whole words when you select using the mouse. The feature, Automatically _Select Words, can be turned off in the Environment Preferences dialog box. Selecting entire words does not happen when you select using the keyboard or the keyboard and mouse in combination.

**I opened a document that was created to print on my new color printer. My page breaks have shifted, and the tabular tables do not line up in columns any more.** When you open a document in WordPerfect, it is reformatted to use the printer that was active when you chose the Open command. The active printer is the printer that was last used. Different printers handle fonts differently, changing the text layout on the page. To be sure that the printer selection that was saved with the document is selected when you next open the document, choose Refor_mat Documents For The WordPerfect Default Printer On Open to turn this feature off.

# Customizing File Preferences

As you continue to add programs on your computer, hard disk management becomes more important. WordPerfect offers disk management support by enabling you to have separate folders for documents, backup files, printer files, and others. You can also specify supplemental folders for use with network installations.

The folders used by WordPerfect are created at installation. Refer to Appendix A, "Installing and Setting Up WordPerfect 7," for information on how you can specify the folders using the custom installation feature. You can change the default folders at any time in the Files Preferences dialog box for the specific file type. When you choose _Files from the

Customizing File Preferences | 313

Preferences dialog box, the Files Preferences dialog box appears, with tabs for an array of file types (see fig. 9.5).

You can specify a different folder for each of the 10 file types in the Files Preferences dialog box. If you use WordPerfect on a network, you can access files on your personal hard drive as well as files that are shared by everyone using the network. Use the Supplemental folder options to enter the path used to access network files for all file types except the hyphenation files.

The default for all files types is to update the Favorites feature with new folder locations or file extensions you provide. For instructions on creating and using the Favorites feature, see Chapter 29, "Advanced File Management." If you choose not to use Favorites, you can select this option to turn it off.

**FIG. 9.5**
The Files Preferences dialog box displays the options for the default and supplemental spreadsheet and database files.

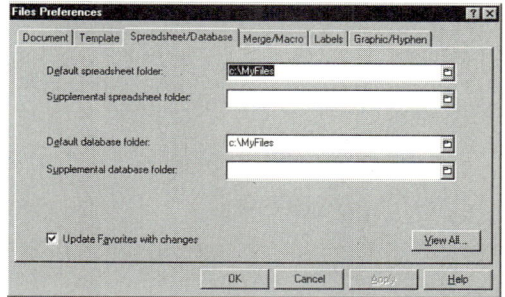

To change a folder for a specific file type, follow these steps:

1. Choose Files from the Preferences dialog box. The Files Preferences dialog box appears.

2. Choose the tab for the file type you want to customize. Figure 9.5 shows the Files Preferences dialog box for Spreadsheet/Database files.

3. Choose Default Spreadsheet folder, and enter the path for the folder where WordPerfect will find spreadsheet files, or click the Folder list button at the right of the text box to choose the folder from the Select Default spreadsheet folder dialog box.

 **TIP** To select the list button with the keyboard, select the desired option, and press Alt+down arrow.

4. Choose Supplemental Spreadsheet folder, and enter the path for the folder location for spreadsheet files to be shared on a network, or choose the folder list button at the right of the text box to choose the folder from the Select Supplemental Spreadsheet folder dialog box.

5. Repeat steps 3 and 4 to enter the default and supplemental database folders.
6. Choose Update F̲avorites With Changes to remove the check from its check box if you do not want the F̲avorites updated automatically.
7. Repeat steps 2–6 to customize the file preferences for other file types.
8. When you have finished changing folders, choose V̲iew All to view the results in the View File Location Preferences dialog box (see fig. 9.6). Choose C̲lose or press Enter to exit the dialog box.
9. Choose OK or press Enter to return to the Preferences dialog box.

**FIG. 9.6**
The View File Location Preferences dialog box lists the information you have provided for the various file preferences, including default file names.

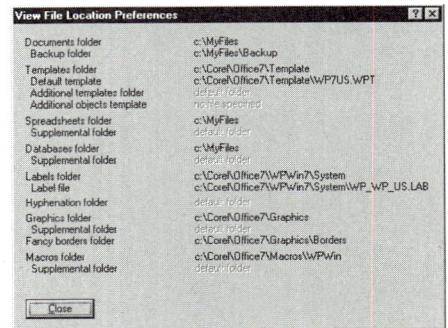

To browse for the folder you want to use, click the folder list button at the end of one of the Files Preferences text boxes folder to open a dialog box in which you can select a default folder (see fig. 9.7).

 To select the list button with the keyboard, select the desired option, and press Alt+down arrow.

**FIG. 9.7**
In the Select Default Document Folder dialog box, scroll through the list of folders or the Favorites to find the folder you want.

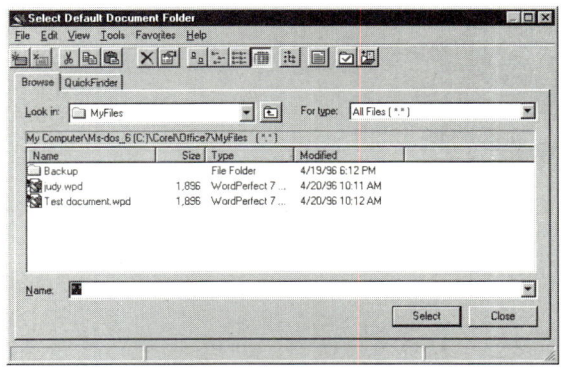

Information for customizing files preferences options for Spreadsheet/Database, Merge/Macro, and Graphic/Hyphen is available in the chapters where these features are discussed. However, in addition to file location information, the Document, Template, and Labels tabs also include options for creating document backups, default file names, and default file extensions. The following sections describe these three tabs in more detail.

▶ **See** "Customizing the Hyphenation Prompt," **p. 152**
▶ **See** "Specifying the Macros Folder in Location of Files," **p. 410**
▶ **See** "Using QuickFinder To Search for Files," **p. 931**

## Documents/Backup Files

When you choose Files from the Preferences dialog box, the Files Preferences dialog box initially displays the Document dialog box options shown in figure 9.8, in which you can specify a default document folder and file extension, authorize the creation of timed backups as well as original document backups, and specify a default folder for backup files.

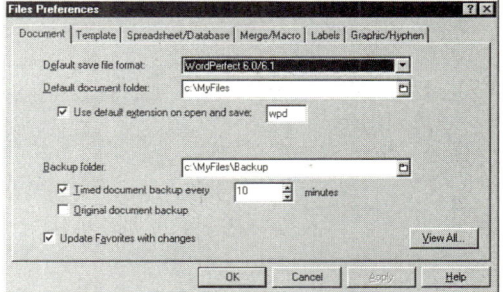

**FIG. 9.8**
The Files Preferences dialog box opens to display the Document file options.

**Document Folder and Extension**   At installation, WordPerfect creates a MYFILES folder at the root level (not in the WordPerfect path) and uses it as the default folder for saving documents, although you may use the Custom installation option to specify a different folder. To change the default document folder later, at the bottom of the Files Preferences dialog box, choose Default Document Folder and enter the path for the folder in the text box.

WordPerfect 7 uses WPD as the default file extension. Deselect Use Default Extension On Open And Save to turn off this feature. To save documents using a different default extension, enter the extension you prefer in the adjacent text box. If you change extensions, bear in mind that WordPerfect and Windows are set up to use the WPD extension with the Object Linking and Embedding (OLE) and Dynamic Data Exchange (DDE) features of Windows. OLE and DDE are used when you create links between a WordPerfect document and an object, such as a spreadsheet or a graphics image, in a document created using a different application. Consider the material in Chapter 18, "Importing Data and Working with Other Programs," before deciding to change the WPD extension.

The FAVORITES folder is automatically updated to incorporate any changes you make in the default file folder and extension. Choose Update Favorites With Changes to remove the check from the check box if you do not want the Favorites updated.

**Backup Options** WordPerfect offers two types of backup features to help you protect your files: Timed Document Backup and Original Document Backup. Use Timed Document Backup to guard against losing work because of power or equipment failure. WordPerfect is set up at installation to make a backup copy of the current document every 10 minutes, but you can specify another time interval or choose Timed Document Backup to turn off this feature. To change the interval, enter the number of minutes in the adjacent text box using the keyboard or click the up or down arrow button to change the default interval of 10.

Backup features are not a substitute for regularly saving your work and making backup copies of document files on separate disks.

Choose Original Document Backup to guard against accidentally overwriting work that you did not intend to replace. For example, if you save a document, then edit it and save it again, the edited version (on-screen) normally replaces the original version (on disk). Original Document Backup saves the edited version of the document with the original file name and the original version with a BK! extension.

## Templates

When you choose File, New to open a new file, you can use existing or create new document templates, or form files, for newsletters, monthly reports, financial statements, or other standard document formats. The templates you create and use are saved in the folder you specify for templates in the Template tab shown in figure 9.9. At installation, WordPerfect created a default folder for template files, a default template file named WP7US.WPT.

To change the information in Template tab, follow these steps:

1. Choose Default Template folder and enter the path for the folder where templates are to be stored, or click the list button at the right of the Default Template folder text box to use the Select Default Template Folder dialog box to find the folder you want.

**FIG. 9.9**
Choose the Template tab in the Files Preferences dialog box to provide a default and additional templates folder, a default template file name, and an additional objects template file name.

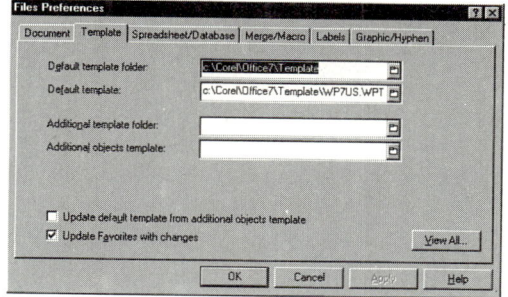

 **T I P**  To select the list button with the keyboard, select the desired option, and press Alt+↓.

2. Choose De̱fault Template, and enter the file name for the default template file, or click the list button at the right of the text box to use the Select Default Template dialog box to locate the file you want. The Select Default Template dialog box is identical to the Open Files dialog box. Refer to Chapter 3, "Retrieving and Editing Documents," for instructions on using the Open Files dialog box.

   If you enter a template name that does not exist, WordPerfect creates a template based on the template WP7US.WPT, or on the template specified as the additional objects template, if you have provided one.

3. To specify an additional folder for storing templates, choose Additional Template folder, and enter the path for the folder, or click the list button at the right of the text box to use the Select Default Template Folder dialog box (refer to fig. 9.7) to find the folder you want.

4. Choose Additional Objects Template, and enter the file name for an additional template file that contains additional objects such as keyboards, menus, template macros, toolbars, and styles. Or click the list button at the right of the text box to use the Select Additional Objects Template dialog box to find the file you want to use as the additional objects template.

5. To cause the standard template to be continually overwritten by the additional objects template, select Update Defau̱lt Template From Additional Objects Template.

6. Choose Update Favorites With Changes if you do not want to update the FAVORITES folder.

## Labels

The Files Preferences options for labels files offer some additional customizing preferences. At installation, WordPerfect places labels files in the COREL\OFFICE7\WPWIN7\SYSTEM folder. The folder can be changed by choosing the Labels tab to open the dialog box shown in figure 9.10.

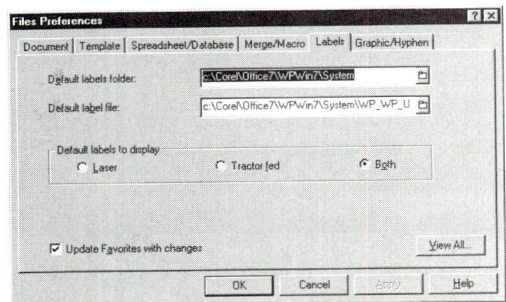

**FIG. 9.10**
Choose Labels in the Files Preferences dialog box to specify a default labels file, default labels folder, and to choose the type of labels you want displayed in the Labels dialog box.

When you choose Format, Labels, the Labels dialog box displays a list of approximately 190 custom label definitions for both laser and dot-matrix printers. Although you can limit the label list to only one printer type from within the Labels dialog box, if you have only one type of printer you can change the default for which type to display.

To customize the preferences for labels files, follow these steps:

1. Choose Default Labels folder and enter the folder name where you want WordPerfect to look for printer and label files, or click the list button at the right of the text box to choose the folder from the Select Default Labels Folder dialog box.

 **TIP** To select the list button with the keyboard, select the desired option, and press Alt+↓.

2. If you create a label file of custom labels and want it used as the default, change the default label file name by choosing Default Label File, and enter the file name in the text box. To browse your drive for the file, click the list button at the right of the text box or press Alt+down arrow.

3. To limit the list of labels displayed in the Labels dialog box, choose Laser, Tractor Fed, or leave Both selected.

4. If you do not want Favorites updated with your changes, choose Update Favorites With Changes to remove the check from the adjacent check box.

# Customizing Document Summaries

Document summaries are used to create a database of information about your documents without the necessity of retrieving each document. Instructions for creating document summaries are in Chapter 5, "Formatting Pages and Documents," including more detailed information about the Document Summary features that you can customize here. A review of that discussion will help you make appropriate configuration decisions.

▶ **See** "Using Document Summaries," **p. 201**

 To configure the document summary preferences, choose <u>S</u>ummary from the Preferences dialog box to open the Document Summary Preferences dialog box shown in figure 9.11.

**FIG. 9.11**
The Document Summary Preferences dialog box enables you to specify how you identify the subject of a document, provide a descriptive type, and also use descriptive names.

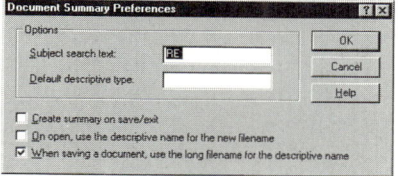

## Subject Search Text

One category of information is the subject of the document. The Document Summary feature automatically retrieves, or extracts, into the Subject field the text (until a hard return is encountered) that follows RE: in the document. If you routinely use **Subject:**, **Reference:**, or other text in your documents, enter the text you prefer to use in the <u>S</u>ubject Search Text text box.

## Default Descriptive Type

WordPerfect can provide you with a default descriptive type such as "letter" or "proposal." If one type of document is predominant in your work, specify your most frequent descriptive type as the default. To do this, enter the document type in the <u>D</u>efault Descriptive Type text box.

 Specifying a default descriptive type for document summaries can save you time, even if you create your most frequent document type only 30 or 40 percent of the time.

You can override this default entry by typing a different descriptive type in the <u>D</u>efault Descriptive Type text box in the Document Summary Preferences dialog box.

## Create Summary on Save/Exit

You can choose to have WordPerfect open the document summary dialog box when you save or exit your document. The summary dialog box appears again each time you save or exit until you fill it in. Choose Create Summary On Save/Exit to turn on the option. Choose it again to turn off the option.

▶ See "Creating a Summary on Save/Exit," **p. 204**

## Use Descriptive Names

Windows 95 moves you past the familiar eight-character filename format of DOS, making it possible for you to use long file names that include multiple words. To use a long file name, simply type the long name in the Name text box when you save the file.

▶ See "Saving a Document to Disk," **p. 70**

If you create a document summary and provide a multi-word description in the Descriptive Name field, WordPerfect can use the description as the actual file name. Choose On Open, Use Descriptive Name For New Filename; thereafter, the descriptive name you provide in the document summary is proposed as the file name when you save the file.

You may prefer to provide a file name when you save the file and complete a document summary later. Choose When Saving A Document, Use The Long Filename For The Descriptive Name, and the file name is placed in the document summary Descriptive Name text box when you create the summary.

# Customizing Convert Options

You can merge a WordPerfect merge form file with data files created in other programs and saved as DOS text. To do so, you must tell WordPerfect about the codes and characters used to divide *fields* (individual pieces of information, such as phone numbers) and *records* (a group of fields containing information about one subject) in the DOS text file. All records contain the same group of fields arranged in the same order.

▶ See "Setting File Preferences for Imported Files," **p. 561**

Database and spreadsheet programs usually provide options for saving data as DOS text files, enabling you to specify characters or codes to insert at the end of fields (or columns) and records (or rows). Choose the Options button to customize margins, paper size, fonts, and other standards to use when converting files. Choose Convert from the Preferences dialog box to display the Convert Preferences dialog box.

# Customizing Window Features

A major attraction of the graphical user interface is that so many features are available at the click of a mouse or a shortcut keystroke. The Power Bar, Toolbars, and status bar are designed to place as many features as possible only a click away. However, as WordPerfect continues to grow in power and size, you may find that your most frequently used features are being buried at the end of submenus or at the bottom of several layers of dialog boxes. To help you with this dilemma, WordPerfect enables you to add and remove buttons from the Power Bar and Toolbars, and to create your own Toolbars for special projects.

If your preference is to move that feature up to one of the main pull-down menus, you can do that, too. You can add features, scripts, and macros to the main pull-down menus and submenus, and even launch other programs directly from the WordPerfect menus. For users who are more comfortable with the keyboard, features, scripts, macros, and other programs can also be assigned to keystroke combinations.

Whether you are customizing a Toolbar, the Power Bar, the keyboard, or menus, you can add commands from pull-down menus and submenus, text scripts, a command to launch another program, or macros.

**NOTE** You can open the Preferences dialog box for each of these features by using the QuickMenu that appears when you right-click directly on the desired screen feature.

## Toolbars

 WordPerfect 7 comes with 15 specialized Toolbars. You can copy and edit any of them, or make your own creations from scratch. You can choose to display text only, pictures only, or both, and change the location of the Toolbar or convert it to a palette you can move around the screen as necessary. Choose Toolbar from the Preferences dialog box to open the Toolbar Preferences dialog box shown in figure 9.12.

▶ See "The Toolbar," **p. 22**
▶ See "Customizing a Toolbar," **p. 420**

Using the Toolbar Editor to edit existing Toolbars and create your own designs is the subject of Chapter 13, "Working with Toolbars." There you can find instructions for using the Toolbar Editor to create your own Toolbars, and editing existing Toolbars to better suit your needs.

**FIG. 9.12**
In the Toolbar Preferences dialog box, you can choose from the 15 Toolbars available with WordPerfect or create your own.

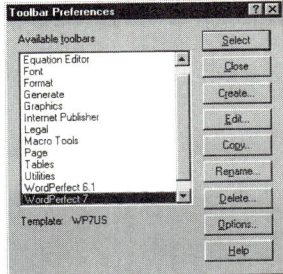

## The Power Bar

By choosing P<u>o</u>wer Bar from the Preferences dialog box, you can choose from about 100 features to add to the Power Bar. You can choose features to add buttons, move buttons by dragging them to new locations on the Power Bar, and delete buttons by dragging them off the Bar.

▶ **See** "The Power Bar," **p. 23**
▶ **See** "Customizing the Power Bar," **p. 426**

## The Status Bar

At the bottom of the WordPerfect screen is a sculptured status bar. By default, the status bar displays the Insert mode indication on the far left; next is the name of the active printer, the Select mode indicator (dimmed) at left center, the date and the time in the center, and the position of the cursor in the document on the right. When you use the mouse to select text or choose <u>E</u>dit, Se<u>l</u>ect, Select appears in black letters to show that WordPerfect is in Select mode. The Insert button changes to display information about the status of features such as columns, macros, merges, paragraph style, and tables when appropriate. Refer to Chapter 1, "Getting Started," for more information on the status bar.

▶ **See** "The Status Bar," **p. 24**

You can easily customize the status bar to notify you about other WordPerfect operating modes. Choose St<u>a</u>tus Bar from the Preferences dialog box, or right-click the status bar and choose <u>P</u>references to open the Status Bar Preferences dialog box (see fig. 9.13).

Scroll the highlight bar through the features in the S<u>t</u>atus Bar Items list to see a description of each feature at the bottom of the dialog box.

Customizing Window Features | 323

**FIG. 9.13**
The Status Bar Preferences dialog box lists the features you can include on the status bar.

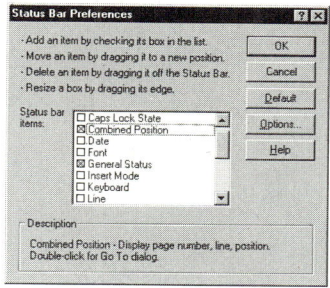

To change the features or the appearance of the status bar, follow these steps:

1. In the Status Bar Items list box is a check list of features that can be included in the status bar. Choose as many of the features as you want to add or remove from the status bar by selecting each to add or remove the check in the adjacent check box.

2. WordPerfect may display a message box stating `Status Bar cannot be redisplayed. Please resize or delete an item`. To make room for more items, use the mouse to do one or more of the following:

   - Drag the left or right side of each box on the status bar to change the size of existing items.
   - Drag an item off the status bar.
   - Drag an item to a new position to change its order.

3. Choose Options to display the Status Bar Options dialog box (see fig. 9.14).

**FIG. 9.14**
Use the Status Bar Options dialog box to change fonts for the status bar text and to customize the appearance of the status bar.

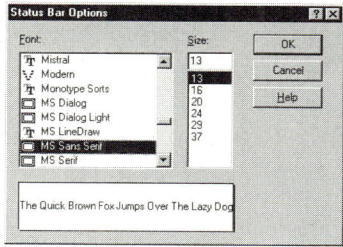

4. Choose Font, scroll through the list of fonts, and choose the font for the status bar text.

5. To change the font size, choose Size and enter a size in the text box or choose a size by scrolling through the list of available sizes.

6. Choose OK twice to return to the Preferences dialog box.

When choosing what to display, you may find that you are dissatisfied and want to start over. Rather than trying to remember what features to remove, choose Default to return to the original items.

## The Pull-Down Menus

 By using the Menu Editor, you can add commands to the Menu Bar or to any level of the pull-down menus. Choose Menu Bar from the Preferences dialog box to open the Menu Bar Preferences dialog box shown in figure 9.15.

**FIG. 9.15**
Use the Menu Bar Preferences dialog box to select a different menu, copy or edit an existing menu, or create new menus for specific applications.

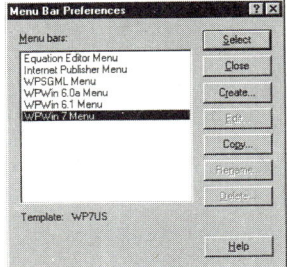

Menus are stored as part of a template. WordPerfect includes six menus in the Standard template: the default WPWin 7 menu, WPWin 6.1 menu, WPWin 6.0a menu, the WPSGML menu, the Internet Publisher menu, and the Equation Editor menu which is displayed automatically when you open the Equation Editor.

You can open the Menu Editor to create and edit menus from the Menu Preferences dialog box or by using the Create Object command in the Template Editor. Instructions for creating and editing menus are found in Chapter 11, "Using Templates."

# Creating and Customizing Keyboards

WordPerfect comes with three keyboard layouts:

- The *WPWin 7 keyboard* (the default) contains the commands described in this book.
- The *Equation Editor keyboard* features a selection of Greek characters, symbols, and commonly used equation commands such as SQRT. You can use the Equation keyboard during document creation and while working in the Equation Editor.

- The *WPDOS 6.1 Keyboard* uses the WordPerfect for DOS function keys and cursor movements such as F4 to Indent, and Home, Home, Up arrow and Home, Home, Down arrow to move to the top and bottom, respectively, of a document.
  - ▶ **See** "The Pull-Down Menus," **p. 20**
  - ▶ **See** "Using Objects in Templates," **p. 378**
  - ▶ **See** "Associating Features and Events," **p. 381**

## Selecting Another Keyboard

During installation, WordPerfect selects the default WPWin 7 keyboard for your use. You can change keyboards at any time by following these steps:

1. From the Preferences dialog box, choose **K**eyboard. The Keyboard Preferences dialog box appears (see fig. 9.16).

**FIG. 9.16**
When you open the Keyboard Preferences dialog box, the highlight bar indicates the name of the active keyboard.

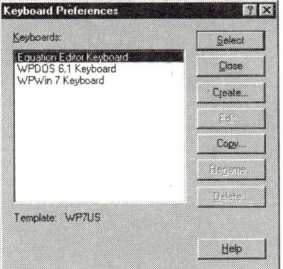

2. Choose the name of the keyboard layout you want to use. To quickly move the highlight bar to a keyboard name, or if you created so many keyboards that not all are visible in the list box, type the first letters of the name of the keyboard in the text box that opens at the top of the list.

3. Choose **S**elect or press Enter to begin using the keyboard.

The newly chosen keyboard remains active every time you start WordPerfect until you choose another keyboard layout.

## Creating, Copying, and Editing Keyboards

The Keyboard Preferences dialog box also includes command buttons that open the Keyboard Editor, which you can use to redefine the function of every key on the keyboard. You can also copy existing keyboards or create a keyboard that begins with the WPWin 7 default keyboard layout, and then customize these new keyboards to suit your needs. So, as you become comfortable with adding buttons to Toolbars and the Power Bar and using other keyboards, you might decide you are ready to add a few shortcuts of your own to the keyboard.

You cannot edit the keyboards that are installed by WordPerfect. To begin working with keyboards, you must create a new keyboard based on one of the WordPerfect keyboard definitions. To create a new keyboard definition that you can customize, follow these steps:

1. In the Keyboard Preferences dialog box, move the highlight bar to the keyboard definition you want to use as the basis for a new keyboard, then choose Create. The Create Keyboard dialog box appears.

2. In the New Keyboard Name text box, enter a name for your proposed keyboard. (In this example, the name is "Newsletter.")

3. By default, the keyboard you create is stored with the current template. If you prefer to store the keyboard with the default template, choose Template, Default Template. Choose OK or press Enter to return to the Create Keyboard dialog box.

4. Choose OK or press Enter. The Keyboard Editor appears, in which you can customize the new keyboard (see fig. 9.17).

**FIG. 9.17**
The Keyboard Editor displays the key assignments on the left for the Newsletter WPWin 7 keyboard definition that is being created.

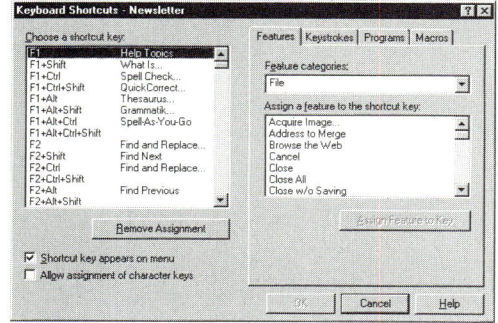

You can edit any of your personal keyboard creations. In the Keyboard Preferences dialog box, highlight the keyboard you want to edit and choose Edit to open the Keyboard Editor.

If you are pleased with a customized keyboard, you might want to use it as the pattern for another keyboard rather than continue to edit it further. To use another keyboard definition as a pattern for a customized keyboard, highlight the keyboard name in the Keyboard Preferences dialog box and choose Copy. In the Copy Keyboard(s) dialog box, highlight a keyboard name in the Select Keyboards To Copy list and then choose Copy. In the Overwrite/New Name dialog box, type a name for the copied keyboard in the Object text box and then choose OK or press Enter to return to the Keyboard Preferences dialog box. Edit the copied keyboard using the Keyboard Editor.

## Making Keyboard Assignments

In the Keyboard Editor, you can create new key assignments, edit key assignments that already exist, and delete an assignment. The keys available to use as shortcut combinations include the Alt or Ctrl key pressed with letters, numbers, keypad keys, punctuation marks, or other keys such as End, Page Up, and arrows.

By using the Keyboard Editor, you can assign any of the following functions to a keyboard:

- *Features*. WordPerfect provides a comprehensive list of the commands on the pull-down menus and submenus so you can assign a keyboard shortcut keystrokes to open dialog boxes or insert codes. For example, when you use chapter numbers, seven steps are needed to increment the chapter number and return to the document. Assigning the Chapter Number Increase feature to the keyboard causes WordPerfect to insert the [Chap Num Inc] code at the cursor location when you press the key assignment.

**NOTE** While you are editing and testing a keyboard, assign the Keyboard Preferences feature to the keyboard, perhaps to Alt+K, to enable you to move from your document back to the dialog box quickly.

- *Keystrokes*. WordPerfect provides a text box in which you enter text to assign to a keystroke. You can reassign Alt+C, for example, so that it types your company name. Then when you need to type your company name, press Alt+C instead. Or try assigning a standard closing paragraph to the keyboard. You can assign a sizable paragraph of text to a key, and the text can include hard returns such as for a signature block, but otherwise must be unformatted.

- *Programs*. You can start another program from within WordPerfect. For example, if you use an address book program to store the addresses for correspondents, you might assign the program to Alt+A. You can, of course, use the Windows Shortcut Key feature found in File Preferences and the Program Information Files, but the shortcut combinations allowed by Windows require three keys, whereas WordPerfect allows two-key shortcuts.

- *Macros*. You can assign macros to any key on the keyboard, which enables you to use more than just the Alt+letter combinations for two-key macros. You can also make keys "smart," allowing a macro to figure out what the key should type. You can reassign the asterisk, for example, so that WordPerfect types a bullet at the left margin when you press the * key.

**TIP** If you use only a few letters from the Greek alphabet, assign these characters to keys on your standard keyboard rather than switching to the Equation keyboard when you need a character or two.

To make a keystroke assignment, follow these steps:

1. In the Keyboard Preferences dialog box, use the Create, Copy, or Edit command described earlier to display the Keyboard Editor shown in figure 9.17.
2. Choose the combination of keys to which you want to make an assignment by scrolling through the keys in the Choose A Shortcut Key list box, or type the first letters of the keys to open a text box at the top of the list and move the highlight bar to the first key beginning with those letters.
3. Choose the tab, such as Features, for the type of assignment you want to make:

**TIP** If you don't use the numeric keypad, you can reassign these number keys without losing other features. In the Choose A Shortcut Key list box, keypad keys begin with Num. Remember that Num Lock must be active to use these assignments.

4. Choose Assign Feature To Key.
5. Choose Shortcut Key Appears On Menu at the bottom of the Keyboard Editor to display the shortcut key to the right of the menu command.
6. If a key assignment is not correct, highlight the key in the Choose A Shortcut Key list box and choose Remove Assignment.
7. Repeat steps 2–5 until you have made all the key assignments you want.
8. Choose OK or press Enter to return to the Keyboard Preferences dialog box.
9. Click Select to use the keyboard immediately, or choose Close to return to the Preferences dialog box.

The procedure used to make a key assignment varies somewhat based on the type of assignment. The following sections examine each type individually.

**Assigning Features** When you want a key assignment to perform a feature, select the keystroke combination you want to use, then follow these steps from the Keyboard Editor:

1. Choose the Features tab.
2. In the Feature Categories drop-down list, choose the name of the main menu in which the feature you want can be found.
3. Choose Assign A Feature To The Shortcut Key, then move the highlight bar to the feature you want to assign.
4. Choose Assign Feature To Key.

In addition to commands available on the various pull-down menus, you can also make any of these assignments:

- If you want to assign a feature that is on a submenu to a key, choose Submenus from the end of the Feature Categories drop-down list and then choose the submenu you want displayed.
- To have a key assigned to select a specific amount of text, choose Selection from the list of Feature Categories; from the list displayed next, choose the desired select action, such as Select Paragraph Next.
- To have a key assigned to move the cursor to a different location in the document, choose Navigation; then choose the desired movement, such as Move Table Row End.

**Assigning Keystrokes**   *Keystrokes* are a keyboard script consisting of a small amount of text that is typed into the current document when you press the keys to which the script is assigned. Choose the Keystrokes tab to open a typing text box; then choose Type The Text To Be Inserted In Your Document When The Shortcut Key Is Pressed. Enter the text you want assigned to the keyboard.

When you type the script, the text wraps unless you press the Enter key to insert a hard return. Wrapped text conforms to the margins of your document when you play the script. Choose the Assign Keystrokes To Key command button when you have entered all the text.

You can assign special characters to a keystroke combination or include special characters in text, such as accented letters in a French or Spanish company name or city. Use either of the following methods to include special characters in a script:

- To include characters from the WordPerfect character set, place the cursor where you want the character and press Ctrl+W.
- To insert characters from the IBM character set, hold down the Alt key while you type the character number, using the numeric keypad. If you use the section symbol (Alt+21) frequently, for example, assign it to a key.
    - ▶ **See** "Accessing Special Characters," **p. 640**
- You can include command keystrokes such as Ctrl+S or F6 as well as characters in a script. To do so, you use the SendKeys Markup Language. To learn how to use this feature, select the Macros, Macros Programming topic in Help then find the SendKeys topic using Index. If the Macro Help module has not been installed from the CD-ROM, WordPerfect displays a Help topic that lists the steps for installing WordPerfect Macro Help.

> **CAUTION**
> Scripts are not interchangeable with macros. You may find that shortcut key you want to use does not work when you play the script. If this happens, create a macro to perform the task, then assign the macro to the keyboard.

**Assigning Programs**    First, choose the key to which you want to assign a program and choose the Programs tab. Next, choose Assign Program To Key; the Open dialog box appears with Executable Files selected in the For Type text box.

Use the Folders list box to scroll through folders to find the application file. Choose the application EXE or COM file in the list box; the file name appears in the Name text box. Choose Open to assign the program to the key.

  You can assign a DOS "old favorite" to a shortcut key.

**Assigning Macros**    When you assign macros to the keyboard, you first create the macro. The macro can be stored in a template or saved on a disk. Follow these steps to assign a macro:

1. Choose the key to which you want to assign a macro.
2. Choose the Macros tab; then choose the Assign Macro To Key button to open the Select Macro dialog box.
3. Choose the application EXE or COM file in the list box; the file name appears in the Name text box. Use the Folders list box to scroll through directories to help you find the application file.

  You can use the QuickFinder in the Select Macro dialog box to help you locate a file.

▶ **See** "Using QuickFinder To Search for Files," **p. 931**

4. Click the Select button or press Enter to assign the program to the key.

After you select the Macros tab, you can see instead a list of macros that have been stored in the current template by following these steps:

1. Choose Assign Template Macro To Key to display the Select Template Macro dialog box. If the macro you want is not displayed, click Location, then choose one of these locations for the macro you want:
   - Current Template (TEMPLATE.WPT)
   - Default Template (TEMPLATE.WPT)

**TIP** The default template choice is available if the current template is also the default template.

To use your choice as the default location for macros, choose <u>U</u>se As Default. Choose OK.

2. Enter the name of the macro you want to assign in the <u>N</u>ame text box or choose it from the M<u>a</u>cros In Template (template.wpt) list box.
3. Choose Select to assign the macro to the keystroke combination.

   ▶ **See** "Creating a Macro," **p. 388**
   ▶ **See** "Understanding Where Macros Are Recorded," **p. 394**
   ▶ **See** "Understanding Macro Storage," **p. 950**

**TIP** If you use a named macro frequently, consider assigning it to a keyboard where you can provide a shortcut combination—using the Ctrl or Alt key, for example.

> **CAUTION**
> Be careful when you delete macros or change the default folders if the folder contains macros. If the affected macros are assigned to a keyboard, the keyboard no longer functions properly when you try to execute those macros.

## Deleting and Renaming Keyboards

To delete a keyboard definition you no longer use, highlight the keyboard name in the Keyboard Preferences dialog box and choose <u>D</u>elete. WordPerfect asks whether you want to `Delete keyboard from list?`. Choose <u>Y</u>es. ●

Chapter 10

# Using Styles

*by Rick Winter and Judy Petersen*

Styles are the best-kept secret of WordPerfect for Windows. Simple to apply, yet challenging to master, styles are an extraordinarily powerful way to format similar types of text, and yet are woefully underused. If you hope to master word processing, you have to master styles; it's that simple. Because styles can incorporate nearly any WordPerfect formatting feature—as well as text, graphics, and even other styles—you need a good foundation in WordPerfect to define your own styles.

If you are new to WordPerfect for Windows, or if you have never bothered with styles, you can save a great deal of time and trouble by learning to use styles now, before you create many documents with manual formatting.

After providing an overview of styles and style classifications, this chapter teaches you how to create, edit, and use styles. While reading this chapter, keep in mind the Templates feature of WordPerfect for Windows. A template can include styles, as well as macros, text, menu items, feature bars, and abbreviations. The next chapter introduces templates.

▶ See "Understanding Templates," **p. 364** ■

**Using document, paragraph, and character styles**
Learn about the different types of styles and when to use each.

**Creating styles**
Design styles that provide consistency when you use them to format documents.

**Working with documents and templates**
Use your style creations in your documents. Adding your best styles to templates you create helps standardize your work product.

**Editing styles with the Styles Editor**
It is easy to fine-tune styles as your needs change.

**Using styles from other files**
When you create a style that really does the job, you can retrieve it to use in other documents.

# Understanding Styles

*Styles* are primarily formatting tools. Think of a style as a named collection of formatting codes, graphics, text, and other elements. By defining styles for the formatting combinations that you use most often, you save time by reducing the number of steps necessary to format your documents. Because most of us produce the same types of documents repeatedly, a small investment of time in creating a library of custom styles pays off handsomely.

A style consists of various defined formatting elements that you apply collectively to all or part of a document. These elements might include type size, text enhancements (such as boldface or italics), text alignment, line spacing, and graphics.

Figure 10.1 shows a newsletter with five styles:

- *Letterhead*. Includes page margins, the Jeep graphic, and the address text with large caps in individual text boxes.
- *Dateline*. Includes the horizontal lines and enables you to type the volume, issue, and date information between the lines.
- *Head/Text*. Includes centering the text and 14-point bold.
- *Subheading*. Includes centering and bold.
- *Flyercolumns*. Accommodates a wide price box in the right column.

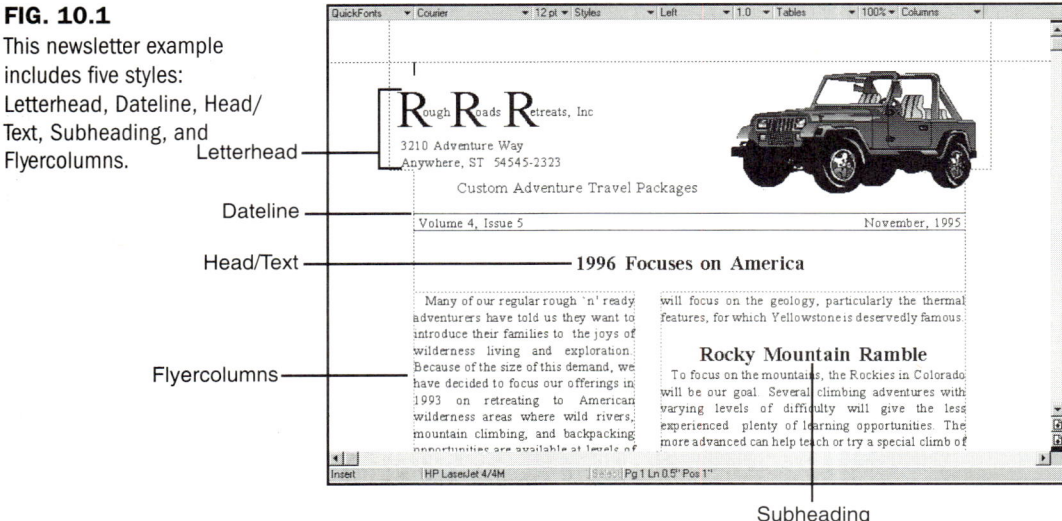

**FIG. 10.1**
This newsletter example includes five styles: Letterhead, Dateline, Head/Text, Subheading, and Flyercolumns.

## Benefits of Using Styles

One of the most important features of styles is that when you want to change formatting, you change the style instead of the individual formatting around the text. If you want to change bylines from italic to bold, for example, you edit the Byline style, and all text formatted with that style throughout the document changes from italic to bold.

If you work repeatedly with the same type of document, or if you work with long documents, styles offer many benefits including the following:

- Saving time and keystrokes.
- Creating a consistent look within a single document.
- Creating a consistent look within groups of documents of the same type, allowing your organization to present a more professional image.
- Enabling groups of writers who work together to standardize their formatting easily.
- Providing a familiar road map to regular readers, thus helping them find important information quickly.
- Making document revisions easier and less time-consuming.
- Enabling you to see how a revision affects an entire document, not just a portion.
- Enabling you to save a number of format codes, text, and graphics with memorizable names.

## Styles Versus Macros

You might be asking yourself, "What's the difference between styles and macros?" You may also ask, "If I already have macros for formatting my documents, why should I use styles instead?"

Although macros can automate some formatting tasks, save keystrokes, and help achieve consistency, macros are less useful than styles for formatting. Macros insert regular formatting codes, just as though you chose the formatting options one-by-one from the menus. After you run a macro, the document formatted by the macro is indistinguishable from a document formatted by hand, and you cannot easily reformat the document if you change your mind. When you use styles, on the other hand, you retain control over the formatting because you can redefine the styles as often as you please. Styles thus provide more flexibility and control than macros.

▶ **See** "Comparing Templates to Macros, Merges, and Styles," **p. 366**
▶ **See** "Using Macros for Common Formatting Tasks," **p. 404**
▶ **See** "Creating a Macro," **p. 388**

# Considering Types of Styles

WordPerfect for Windows styles can be classified in several ways. One way to classify styles is by the sections of documents that the styles affect. Paragraph styles, for example, apply only to complete paragraphs.

Another way to classify styles is by their location. Styles can be built into the current document including initial styles at the beginning of a document. Styles are also part of the entire program (system styles), and part of templates.

Yet another way to classify styles depends on where you create and edit them. For example, you create document, paragraph, and character styles through the Style List dialog box. You create outline styles using the Outline Bar. You create graphics box and line styles through the graphics dialog boxes and feature bars.

## Document, Paragraph, and Character Styles

WordPerfect for Windows offers three main types of styles:

- Document
- Paragraph
- Character

The style type determines how you apply the style and how it affects your document's formatting.

**Document Styles**   *Document styles* are most often used at the beginning of a document or a document section to control features such as paper size, margins, tabs, justification, line spacing, and page numbering. Document styles primarily contain formatting codes that stay in effect indefinitely, along with text, graphics, and other style codes. Prior to WordPerfect 6 for Windows, document styles were defined as *open styles*.

You cannot turn off document styles, but you can override their effect by using another style or by manually inserting formatting codes into the document after the document style code. If, for example, you use a document style to change to landscape paper size, the landscape paper size stays in effect until you use another document style that changes the paper size, or manually insert a different Paper Size code into the document.

**NOTE**   WordPerfect's formatting codes fall into two categories: *paired* and *document*. Paired codes consist of On and Off codes, and apply only to a portion of a document. Font attributes—including boldface, italics, and underlining—are paired codes. You cannot insert or remove one of the codes without inserting or removing the other. When you apply bold to a section of text, for example, WordPerfect inserts a bold code at the beginning of the section and another at the end of the section.

Document codes are single formatting codes that affect all following text until another code later in the document changes that formatting. `Margins`, `Page Numbering`, and `Tab Set` codes are examples of document codes.

**Paragraph Styles**  The paired styles of WordPerfect 5.x are divided into two categories beginning with WordPerfect 6.0: *paragraph* and *character*. Paragraph styles, as you would expect, affect entire paragraphs. You typically use paragraph styles for titles, subtitles, items in numbered or bulleted lists, and bibliographic entries.

When a paragraph style is turned off, the formatting options revert to the settings that were in place before the style was turned on. If you turn on the bold attribute as part of a paragraph or character style, for example, the bold attribute is turned off when the style is turned off. This also applies to open codes—such as margin changes, tab settings, and line spacing—when they are used in paragraph or character styles.

Because paragraph styles always apply to entire paragraphs, you do not need to select the current paragraph in order to apply a style to it; you can position the insertion point anywhere in the paragraph to apply the style. However, selecting text in one or more paragraphs before applying a paragraph style also works. If you select text to turn on a paragraph style, the style automatically turns on at the beginning of the first paragraph and off at the end of the last paragraph. If you already assigned a paragraph style to that paragraph, the new style replaces the old one.

When you apply a paragraph style before you type text rather than after the text is entered, WordPerfect applies the current style to the next paragraphs each time you press Enter to end the current paragraph. You can, if you prefer, create styles that invoke, or *chain*, to another style or choose to have WordPerfect revert to the previous settings.

A new type of style, the paragraph (paired-auto) style, was introduced in WordPerfect 6.1 for Windows. Previously, all styles could be edited only in the Style Editor. If you change the format of a paragraph that uses a paragraph (paired-auto) style, the style itself is immediately modified to incorporate the change(s) you made to the paragraph in the document. As with all other types of styles, once the style is edited, the change is reflected wherever the style is used in the document.

**Character Styles**  Character styles are primarily text attributes such as bold, italics, font size, and the font face. You use character styles to enhance a single character, phrase, or extended text passage.

You can apply a character style to text as you type by turning the style on, typing the text, and then turning the style off. When a character style is turned off, the formatting options revert to the settings that were in place before the style was turned on. To apply a character style to existing text, however, you must select the entire text and not just position the insertion point in a paragraph. For more detailed instructions, see "Using Styles Together" later in this chapter.

## Initial Style

At the beginning of each document is the [InitialStyle] code. This code enables you to group the starting codes for the document together in one place. You can edit the [InitialStyle] code the same way as other codes through the Style List dialog box (see "Editing Styles" later in this chapter) or by choosing Format, Document, Initial Codes Style. To make this [InitialStyle] apply to all new documents, select the Use As Default check box in the Styles Editor dialog box.

▶ **See** "Creating the Initial Codes Style," **p. 199**

## System Styles

WordPerfect 7 for Windows 95 controls the default settings for most document elements through a type of style called system styles. *System styles* represent the built-in settings for features such as headers, footers, endnotes, footnotes, and outline styles, as well as the settings for graphic boxes, text boxes, graphic captions, watermarks, equations, lines, borders, and graphic fills. System styles also control the format of generated features, including indexes, tables of contents, lists, and tables of authorities.

A common complaint about earlier releases of WordPerfect was that although the program provided exceptionally precise control over certain kinds of formatting, such as kerning and letter spacing, you could not change many of the program's default settings. A graphic box, for example, always was positioned on the right and was half as wide as the space between the left and right margins. You could not automatically include a Tab or Indent code in a footnote or endnote. There was no foolproof way to ensure the use of a particular font for document substructures such as headers, footers, footnotes, endnotes, and box captions. In WordPerfect 7 for Windows 95, however, you can change the settings for these elements by editing the system style, or you can modify the settings by copying a system style to a document or to a template and then editing the copy.

## Template Styles

All documents created using WordPerfect for Windows are based on a template. *Templates* are a collection of styles, macros, abbreviations, toolbars, keyboards, and menu choices, as well as boilerplate document text. In addition to being able to save styles in a style library, you can save styles, as well as all the other features, in a template. You create, edit, and apply styles in a template just as you would in a document (see "Creating

Styles," "Editing Styles," and "Using Styles" later in this chapter). You use styles within templates as you would with any document.

▶ See "Using Objects in Templates," **p. 378**

## Outline Styles

*Outline styles* are a special category of text styles. WordPerfect has improved the original design of outline styles by integrating them with collapsible outlining and the Outline Bar. The result is that outline styles in this version are far more powerful, yet easier to apply. Because the topics of outlining and outline styles are covered in-depth in Chapter 15, "Organizing Documents with Outlining," this chapter discusses outline styles only in relation to other types of styles.

▶ See "Introducing Outline Styles," **p. 486**

Outline styles are potentially confusing because you define and apply them differently from non-outline styles. You can edit and apply outline styles using one of two methods:

- Through the Style List dialog box. Choose Fo_r_mat, _S_tyles, and make sure that _O_ptions, _S_etup, S_y_stem Styles is selected.
- Through the Outline Define dialog box. Choose _T_ools, _O_utline, _O_ptions, _D_efine Outline, select the type of outline and choose _E_dit, _E_dit Style.

But you can define new outline styles and assign a hierarchical level to outline styles only through the Outline Define List dialog box.

## Graphics Styles

Although the casual user need not be aware of the fact, styles also control paragraph, column, and page borders, as well as tables, lines, boxes, and fills. (For detailed instructions on creating and editing graphics styles, see Chapter 21, "Using Advanced Graphics Techniques.") These styles control line attributes, such as thickness, color, line spacing, spacing between lines and text or graphics, shading, and pattern (such as solid, dashed, or dotted).

▶ See "Setting the Initial Font," **p. 197**
▶ See "Creating the Initial Codes Style," **p. 199**
▶ See "Understanding Graphics Box Styles," **p. 262**
▶ See "Understanding Templates," **p. 364**
▶ See "Editing a Template to Your Specifications," **p. 374**

# Creating Styles

WordPerfect provides several methods for creating new style definitions. You can base a style on a paragraph; enter formatting codes directly into a style; embed one style in another style; copy a style to a new name and modify the copy; or copy formatting codes, text, and graphics from your document into a style definition.

## Working with a Document or a Template

You create styles for a document or a template in the same way: through the Style List dialog box. The first step is to open the appropriate document or template.

**Opening a Document**   If you want to create or edit styles in an existing document, choose File, Open; or press Ctrl+O. Then choose the name of the file that you want to retrieve.

If you want to create or edit styles in a new document, press Ctrl+N.

**Accessing a Template**   To create or edit styles in a template, follow these steps:

1. Choose File, New; or press Ctrl+T. The Select New Document dialog box appears (see fig. 10.2).

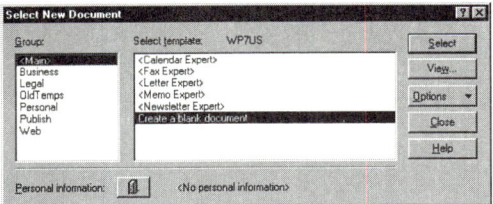

**FIG. 10.2**
The Select New Document dialog box lists several dozen templates that ship with WordPerfect 7 for Windows 95, as well as any templates that you add. Select Options for commands available to customize and create templates and manage template groups.

2. Highlight the appropriate template in the Select Template list box, selecting a more specific category of templates from the Group list box to show only templates of that type.
3. Choose Options, Edit Template (refer to fig. 10.2). The Template Feature Bar and any text and graphics within the template appear (see fig. 10.3).

**FIG. 10.3**
The Template Feature Bar appears below the Power Bar. The text and table features are associated with the Legal Fax Cover Sheet template file.

Template Feature Bar

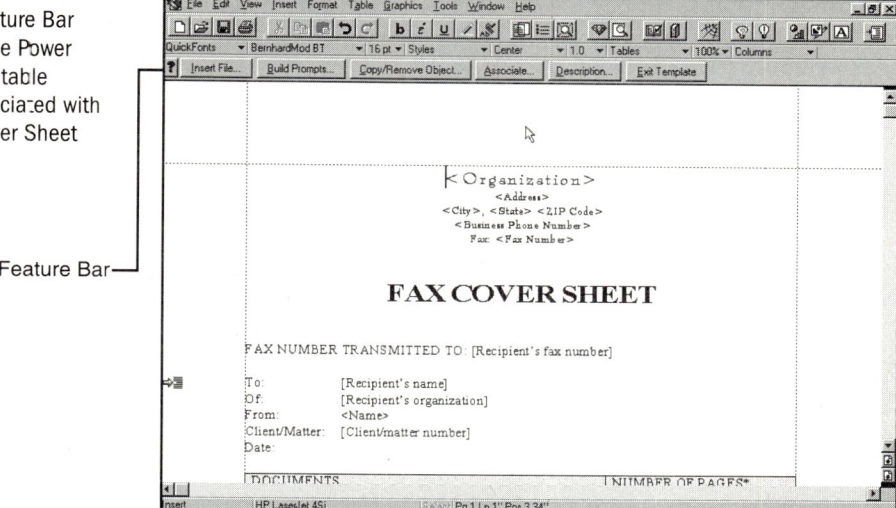

## Bringing Up the Style List Dialog Box

After you open a new document, an existing document, or a template, the next step is to bring up the Style List dialog box.

To get to the Style List dialog box, choose For̲mat, S̲tyles; or press Alt+F8 (see fig. 10.4). Many procedures in this chapter start from the Style List dialog box.

**FIG. 10.4**
The Style List dialog box shows the system style <None>, <InitialStyle>, <_Confident>, and heading styles that come with the Legal Fax Cover Sheet template.

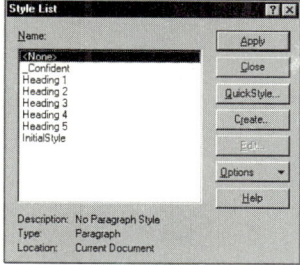

For instructions on listing existing styles, see "Displaying Style Names" later in this chapter.

## Creating a QuickStyle

One of the easiest ways to create a style is to first format some text as you want the style to look and then use the QuickStyles feature.

To use QuickStyle, follow these steps:

1. Format a text selection or a paragraph with the features that you want to include in the style, as shown in figure 10.5.

**FIG. 10.5**
In this example, the text is 18 points and made bold.

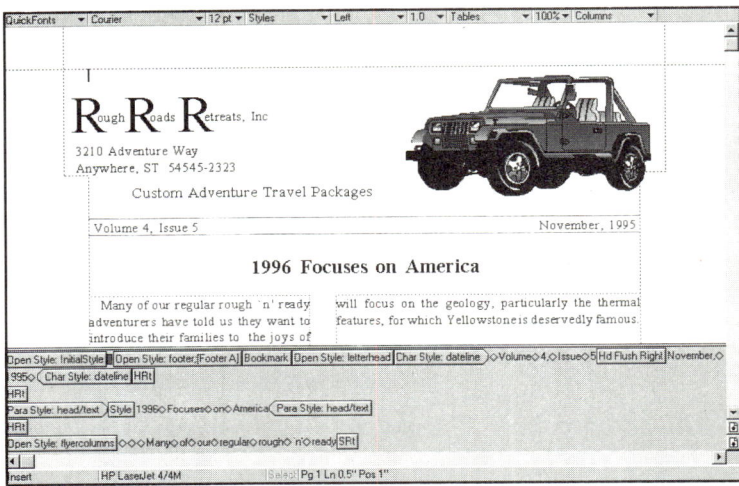

2. Position the cursor anywhere in the formatted text. You do not have to select the text, whether you are creating a character or paragraph style.
3. Bring up the Style List dialog box as described in the preceding section.

 You can also select the Styles button on the Power Bar and choose QuickStyles from the list that appears.

4. Click QuickStyle in the Style List dialog box. The QuickStyle dialog box appears.
5. In the Style Name text box, type the name of the style, using 20 or fewer characters.
6. If you want to include a description of what the style does, type it in the Description text box.
7. Click the appropriate radio button to indicate whether you want a Paragraph or Character style. Figure 10.6 shows how the QuickStyle dialog box might look at this point.
8. Choose OK to return to the Style List dialog box.

The newly created style appears in the Name list box. From here, you can Close the dialog box, Create another style, or Edit another style.

**FIG. 10.6**
A completed QuickStyle dialog box shows that this style will be a character style.

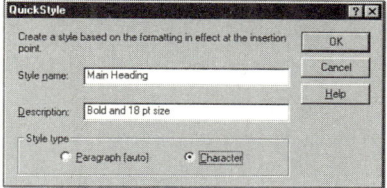

To see information about the style you just created, highlight its name in the Name list box. The information appears below the list box, as shown in figure 10.7.

**FIG. 10.7**
The description supplied in step 6 appears, and the Type appears as Character.

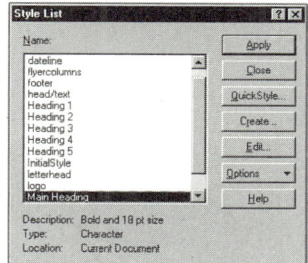

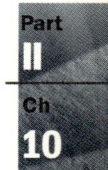

## Creating a Style Through the Style List Dialog Box

In addition to using QuickStyles to generate a style, you can enter your own codes directly with a new style.

From the Style List dialog box, follow these steps:

1. Click Create. The Styles Editor dialog box appears, as shown in figure 10.8.

**FIG. 10.8**
The Styles Editor dialog box includes a menu bar, a Contents box in which to insert codes, and check boxes to see the codes and to control the Enter key action.

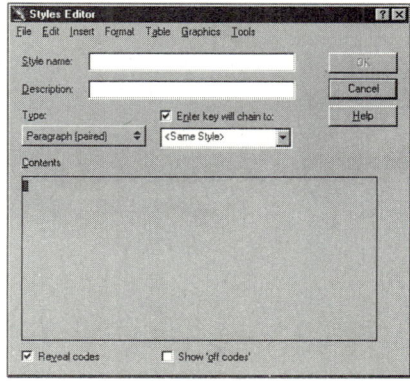

2. In the Style Name text box, type the name of the style, using 20 or fewer characters.

3. If you want to include a description of what the style does, type it in the Description text box.

4. Choose the type of style that you want to create from the Type pop-up list. WordPerfect's default style type is Paragraph (paired), but you can choose Paragraph (Paired-Auto), Document (Paired) or Character (Paired) instead.

5. Move to the Contents box, and type text or choose items from the pull-down menus (see fig. 10.9).

**FIG. 10.9**
The Contents box shows that graphics, formatting, and text are entered for the style Letterhead.

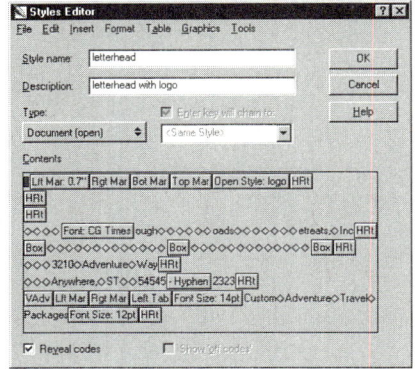

If you make a mistake, you can edit any choice in the Styles Editor dialog box. (This procedure is described in the following section, "Editing Styles.")

6. When you finish creating a style, choose OK to return to the Style List dialog box.

7. In the Style List dialog box, you can create another style, edit an exiting style, or apply a style. When you finish with the Style List dialog box, choose Close to return to the document window.

▶ See "Keeping Text Together," **p. 159**
▶ See "Using Headers and Footers," **p. 173**
▶ See "Numbering Pages," **p. 163**

## Editing Styles

In addition to creating styles, you can use the Style List and Styles Editor dialog boxes to edit a style. You can delete the entire style, or delete and insert codes within the style. In the Styles Editor dialog box, you can change the name, description, or style type. In the Style List dialog box, you can copy information into the style from the document, copy the entire style and make changes, use the style as a code within another style, or link the style to another style. Remember that you can reach the Style List dialog box by choosing For̲mat, S̲tyles; or by pressing Alt+F8.

## Displaying Style Names

When you edit styles, you need to keep in mind the three types of styles: current document, template, and system. When you edit a style for the current document, the style changes for only that document unless you copy the style to another document or template. Do not confuse current document as a location for styles with document as a type of style (as opposed to paragraph and character styles).

If you edit a template style, all text formatted with the style in any document created with that template changes. You can change a system style to affect all documents by editing the style in the default template.

You cannot permanently change a system style that would affect all documents. When you edit a system style, WordPerfect changes the style for the current document or current template.

To display different kinds of styles, follow these steps:

1. In the Style List dialog box, click O̲ptions.
2. Choose S̲etup from the pop-up list. The Style Setup dialog box appears, enabling you to choose which styles are displayed (and, therefore, accessible).
3. To display styles of different types, choose one or more of the following check boxes in the Display Styles From area, as shown in figure 10.10:
    - *C̲urrent Document.* Displays styles associated with the current document.
    - *D̲efault Template.* Displays styles associated with the template that you are editing or with the template that defines the current document.
    - *A̲dditional Objects Template.* Displays the styles associated with an additional template for the current document, if you have specified one using Preferences.
    - *Sy̲stem Styles.* Displays styles for the program such as graphic captions, headers and footers, outline styles, and much more.

**N O T E** To define the default and additional objects templates, choose E̲dit, P̲references, F̲ile; choose the Template tab; and then indicate the file names in the appropriate text boxes. For more information, see Chapter 9, "Customizing WordPerfect."

**FIG. 10.10**
To show styles for only the on-screen document and to save styles only to this document, choose Current Document in both locations in the Style Setup dialog box.

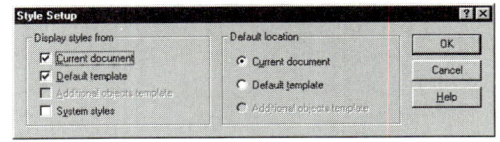

4. To save new styles to a specific file, choose one of the following options in the Default Location area:

   - *Current Document.* Saves the style only to the current document.
   - *Default Template.* Saves the style to the template that defines the current document.
   - *Additional Objects Template.* Saves the style to a supplemental template file if you have specified one.

5. When you finish with the Setup dialog box, choose OK.

**N O T E** To activate Additional Objects Template in the various Options features in the Style List dialog box, choose Edit, Preferences, File, Templates and designate an Additional Objects Template.

## Deleting a Style

When you no longer need a style, or if you make an irreparable mistake, delete the style from your style list as follows:

1. In the Name list box of the Style List dialog box, highlight the style to be deleted.

**N O T E** Pay attention to the information at the bottom of the dialog box. Make sure that you delete the style for the current document. If you want to delete the style for all documents based on the same template, make sure that the Location area indicates Template.

2. Choose Options, Delete. WordPerfect displays the Delete Styles dialog box, which contains two options (see fig. 10.11).

**N O T E** The System styles provide the default settings for the features—such as headers and footers, tables of contents, and graphic boxes—that are part of the WordPerfect program. You cannot, therefore, delete these styles.

**FIG. 10.11**
If you choose Include Codes in the Delete Styles dialog box, your style is gone and cannot be brought back with Edit, Undo.

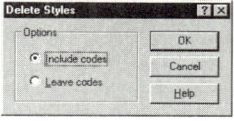

3. Choose one of the following options:

   - *Include Codes.* Deletes the style definition as well as all the style codes used in the document.
   - *Leave Codes.* Deletes the style definition but converts the style codes in the document to regular formatting codes.

4. Choose OK. WordPerfect returns to the Style List dialog box. The deleted style is removed from the Name list box.

## Copying and Modifying a Style Definition

Suppose that you want to create a style similar to another style already created for the existing document, or that you want to copy a style to your template or supplemental template file.

To copy a style, follow these steps:

1. In the Name list box of the Style List dialog box, highlight the name of the style. Choose Options, Copy. The Styles Copy dialog box appears, containing three options (see fig. 10.12).

**FIG. 10.12**
To avoid overwriting existing styles in your templates, choose Current Document in the Styles Copy dialog box.

2. Choose one of the following Copy To options:

   - *Current Document.* Copies the style to a new name. You are prompted for the name (see step 4 below).
   - *Template.* Copies the style name and contents to your template.
   - *Additional Objects Template.* Copies the style name and contents to your additional object template if you have specified one.

3. If you chose Template or Additional Objects Template in step 2 and the name already exists, a confirmation box appears asking whether you want to overwrite the

current styles. Choose Yes to change the template style or No to return to the Style List dialog box.

4. If you choose Current Document in step 2, the Styles Duplicate dialog box appears, as shown in figure 10.13. Type the name of the style in the Style Name text box, and then choose OK. Both styles—the old name and the duplicate name—appear in the Style List dialog box. If you want to, you can edit the copied style.

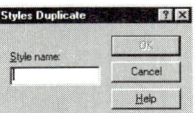

**FIG. 10.13**
In the Styles Duplicate dialog box, the style name can include up to 10 characters, just as when you create a style.

## Copying Text, Graphics, and Formatting onto the Clipboard

If you want to copy text, graphics, or formatting codes from the document to a style, first copy these elements to the Windows Clipboard by following these steps:

1. If you want to turn on Reveal Codes to assist your selection, choose View, Reveal Codes; or press Alt+F3.

2. Position the insertion point before the codes or text, and then use the keyboard or mouse to select the text and codes that you want to use.

3. Choose Edit, Copy; or press Ctrl+C to place a copy of the selected text and codes on the Clipboard.

Once the codes and text are on the Clipboard, they can be pasted into the Contents box in the Styles Editor. The procedure for doing so is described in the next sections.

▶ **See** "Working with Reveal Codes," **p. 93**
▶ **See** "Understanding WordPerfect's Hidden Codes," **p. 91**

## Bringing Up the Styles Editor

Whether you copy from the Clipboard or make direct changes to the style definition, you need to bring up the Styles Editor dialog box for any style you want to change.

1. Choose Format, Styles; or press Alt+F8 to bring up the Styles List dialog box.

2. In the Name list box, highlight the style that you want to change.

> **N O T E**  You need to have the appropriate style type (Current Document, Template, or System) selected from the Style Setup dialog box to display your style. See "Displaying Style Names" earlier in this chapter.

3. Click Edit. The Styles Editor dialog box appears, as shown in figure 10.14.

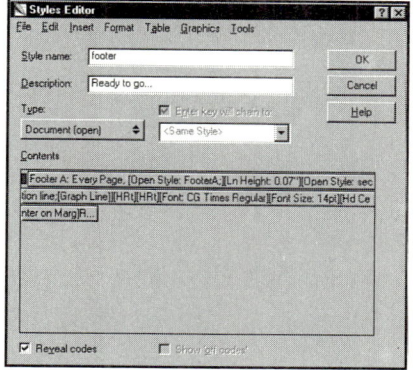

**FIG. 10.14**
To replace the description, press Tab until you reach the Description text box, or use the mouse to highlight the description. Typing the first letter of the new description removes the old description.

## Editing a Style Definition

You can edit a style in several ways, including inserting or deleting text and codes, or changing the style name, style description, or style type. If you edit the contents of the style, make sure that the Reveal Codes check box is selected on the Styles Editor dialog box.

 **TIP** To edit a system style so that the edited style will be available in future documents, be sure to choose Default Template in the Default Location section of the Style Setup dialog box.

To edit the style, perform one or more of the following steps:

- Choose Style Name, and then type a new style name.
- Choose Description, and then type a new style description.
- Choose Type, and then use the pop-up list to change the style type to Document, Paragraph, Paragraph (Paired-Auto) or Character.
- Edit the Contents box by following the procedure in the following section.
- Place another style into the current style definition by following the procedure in "Nesting Styles" later in this chapter.
- Have another style turn on automatically when you turn off this style by following the procedure in "Chaining Styles" later in this chapter.

When you finish editing the style, choose OK in the Styles Editor dialog box, and then choose Close in the Style List dialog box.

## Editing Styles Editor Contents

To edit the codes and text of the style, follow the same procedure that you would use to edit text and codes with the Reveal Codes feature. For more information, see Chapter 3, "Retrieving and Editing Documents."

▶ **See** "Working with Reveal Codes," **p. 93**

▶ **See** "Understanding WordPerfect's Hidden Codes," **p. 91**

Display the Styles Editor and place the insertion point in the Contents box. The insertion point becomes a blinking rectangle. Perform one or more of the following steps:

- Move the insertion point with the mouse or arrow keys.
- Press Backspace to delete the text or codes before the insertion point.
- Press Delete to delete the text or codes after the insertion point.
- Choose Edit, Paste or press Ctrl+V to bring information from the Clipboard into the Contents box.
- Choose other items from the Styles Editor menu bar to add codes and graphics.
- To place special text or formatting codes after a paired style (paragraph or character) is turned off, mark the Show "Off Codes" check box and position the insertion point after the [Codes to the left are ON - Codes to the right are OFF] code in the Contents box. This is useful to add spacing, formatting, or a graphic line below the text that is formatted with the paired style.

**NOTE** You can use keystroke combinations—such as Ctrl+Enter for Page Break and F9 to access the Font dialog box—to add codes to the Contents box. Other keystrokes, such as Tab, are ignored. When the Styles Editor is active, Page Break, Hard Return, and Tab are available at the bottom of the Insert menu.

# Using Styles Together

When you have successfully created a number of styles you use frequently, you can increase the power of styles in your work by using several styles together. A style that includes your address or logo can be included, or *nested*, in other styles that create documents such as your letterhead or the banner for the office newsletter. Similarly, styles that you usually follow with another specific style can be placed in sequence, or *chained*, so that pressing the Enter key applies the next style.

## Nesting Styles

Embedding one style in another is a very efficient way to control groups of related styles. For example, you might have a dozen styles based on a single style that contains your logo. If you ever change the logo style, all styles containing the logo style instantly reflect the change.

When you are in the Contents box of the Styles Editor dialog box, choose Format, Styles (or press Alt+F8) to bring up the Style List dialog box. Highlight the style you want, and then choose Apply. A copy of the highlighted style appears at the location of the insertion point in the Contents box of the Styles Editor dialog box.

**NOTE** A paragraph style cannot be nested in another paragraph style.

## Chaining Styles

In some cases, you might want to have one style turn on immediately after another turns off. For example, you might use a chained style for a newsletter in which each article title in one style always is followed by a byline in a different style.

**NOTE** You can link only from a paragraph or character style. When you edit a document style, the Enter Key Will Chain To option is dimmed.

To link two styles, follow these steps:

1. In the Style List dialog box, highlight the style you want to use first.
2. Click Edit to bring up the Styles Editor dialog box.
3. Make sure that the Enter Key Will Chain To check box is selected.

**TIP** A system style cannot be chained to another style.

4. Use the drop-down list below this check box to choose the style to link to (see fig. 10.15). Only styles that you have created specifically for this document show in this list; template and system styles do not appear.
5. If you have no further editing to do in the Styles Editor dialog box, choose OK to return to the Style List dialog box. Then choose Close to return to the document window.

**FIG. 10.15**
In this example, you might choose to have the Head/Text appear when you press Enter after typing the text in the Dateline style.

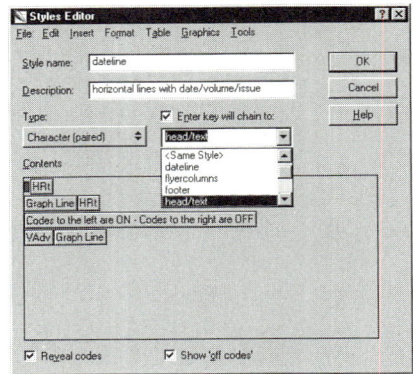

> **N O T E**  The default selection for the Enter Key Will Chain To pop-up list is <Same Style>. This is useful for body text where you can press Enter; the style continues for all paragraphs. To turn this style off, apply the <None> paragraph style.

▶ **See** "Formatting Lines and Paragraphs," **p. 130**
▶ **See** "Formatting Characters," **p. 126**
▶ **See** "Customizing File Preferences," **p. 312**
▶ **See** "Toolbars," **p. 321**

### TROUBLESHOOTING

**I have created a section heading style for the financial report I write every month. I am creating a new report and cannot find the new heading style.** When creating a style you want to be available in the future, be sure to choose Default Template in the Styles Setup dialog box. To make this choice in the Style List box, choose Options, Setup. Alternatively, you can create a template for the monthly report. Create the style while creating the template; the style will be available when you use the report template but not in any other documents.

**I've edited a system style and now I am unhappy with how it works.** You can quickly restore the original system style by selecting the style in the Style List dialog box, then choosing Reset from the Options drop-down list.

# Using Styles

As you create and edit styles, you will most likely apply the styles to your document to see the results and then make further editing changes in the styles. You generally can apply a style in either of two ways:

- Turn on the style code at a position in the document.
- Select text and then apply style codes.

To use chained styles and styles that chain to the same style, turn the style on and type your text. To apply text enhancements (bold, change in fonts), it may be easier to type the text first and then highlight the text to apply the style. When you press Enter at the end of the text, WordPerfect follows the instructions you provided to chain to the same style or to the style you specified.

## Inserting Styles

To turn on any type of style, follow these steps:

1. Choose Format, Styles; or press Alt+F8. The Style List dialog box appears.
2. Highlight the style name in the Name list box (see fig. 10.16).

**FIG. 10.16**
When you highlight the style, you can check information about the style in the bottom of the Style List dialog box.

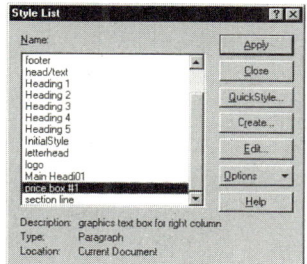

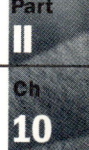

3. Click Apply.

The steps for turning on a style are simple. However, the following factors are affected when you turn off the style:

- Whether the style is a document, paragraph, or character style
- Whether the style is inserted amid text
- Whether the style is chained to another style

The following sections explain how these factors influence the way each type of style is turned off.

## Using Power Bar Buttons

The Power Bar includes buttons to help you work with styles. To use the Styles button to apply a style, click the pull-down arrow or the button face and scroll through the list of styles. After you choose your style, the button face displays the name of the current style.

The list of styles displayed using the Styles button includes only the current document styles, several WordPerfect heading styles, and any system styles you have used so far.

## Applying Document Styles

Because document styles do not have an Off code, there is no need to highlight text. The document style code appears in the document, and all text following the code takes that code's formatting.

▶ **See** "The Power Bar," **p. 322**
▶ **See** "Customizing the Power Bar," **p. 426**

## Applying Paragraph Styles

Unlike document styles, paragraph styles do have On and Off codes. The procedure for turning off the paragraph style depends on whether you first apply the style and then type text, or just select existing text. The procedure also depends on whether the paragraph style is linked to another style.

> **N O T E** A *paragraph* in WordPerfect for Windows is defined as any text followed by a hard return, so even a short line of text without any punctuation can be a paragraph.
>
> In a standard letter, for example, the date, each line of the address, and the closing, as well as full paragraphs within the letter, are all considered to be paragraphs for style-type purposes.

If you want to apply a paragraph style to an existing paragraph, position the insertion point anywhere in the paragraph, and then follow the procedure in the preceding section. If you want to apply the paragraph style to more than one paragraph, highlight the paragraphs first and then insert the style. As long as you highlight any portion of a paragraph, the style is applied to the entire paragraph. If you apply a paragraph style within existing text, the Enter Key Will Chain To check box (style linking) has no effect.

If you apply a paragraph style before you type the text, what occurs when you press Enter depends on the status of the Enter Key Will Chain To check box:

- If the text box indicates <None>, the style turns off.
- If the text box indicates that the style will chain to itself with <Same Style>, the style remains turned on.
- For paragraph styles that chain to the <Same Style>, if you have added text or codes after the [Codes to the left are ON - Codes to the right are OFF] code in the Contents part of the Styles Editor, these codes take effect after you press Enter, and the style turns on again at the beginning of the next paragraph.

■ If the check box is marked and indicates a different style, pressing Enter links to the chosen style by turning off the first style and turning on the next.

In either case, if you want to turn off the paragraph style or not use the chained style, be sure to choose the <None> style after you press Enter. The <None> style is a special style that turns off any paragraph style and prevents chaining. If you select E<u>n</u>ter Key Will Chain To so the check is removed from its adjacent box, the type of style changes to Character.

> **CAUTION**
> Be careful when you edit a paragraph formatted using a Paragraph (Paired-Auto) style. If you make a change that affects the entire paragraph—such as changing the font size or indenting the paragraph—the Paragraph (Paired-Auto) style is immediately edited to include the change.

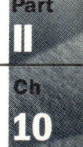

## Applying Character Styles

Character styles should apply only to a portion of text, not to specific paragraphs. Although it makes sense to chain paragraph styles, it is less appropriate to chain character styles (but the program allows you to do this). A better procedure is to choose E<u>n</u>ter Key Will Chain To <None> for character styles. This option allows you to turn on the character style, type text, and then press Enter to turn off the style. If you want to insert a hard return, you have to press Enter a second time.

To apply a character style to existing text, first select the text, and then follow the procedure in the preceding section.

▶ See "Finding and Replacing Formatting Codes," **p. 118**
▶ See "Formatting Characters," **p. 126**
▶ See "Formatting Lines and Paragraphs," **p. 130**

# Working with Styles from Other Files

As mentioned earlier in the chapter, styles come from one of four places: the document, template, supplementary template, or system. Templates allow you to create and save styles, macros, or menus, and to add generic text and graphics for each type of document you work with, such as letters, memos, and reports.

▶ See "Using Objects in Templates," **p. 378**
▶ See "Finding Files," **p. 928**

System styles are associated with WordPerfect features such as captions, line styles, and outline styles throughout the program. You can change a copy of the system styles for each template.

You can change a copy of the template and system styles only for the current document. You can make any changes you want to the styles for the current document, but the changes occur only in that document.

## Using System Styles

If you change a system style in a document, you change the style only for the current document. If you change a system style for a template, however, only the new files you create are affected. Files you created before the style change are not affected.

## Using Templates

 As mentioned in the preceding section, changing a template or a system style in a template affects all files that are based on the template. To edit a template (not a document based on the template), choose File, New; or press Ctrl+T. Then choose Options, Edit Template.

Now, when you follow the directions in this chapter for editing styles, the styles displayed are those in the current template.

## Saving Styles to Another File

If you want to use your styles for other documents, you can save the styles into a document, a style library, or a template.

To save a style to a document, follow these steps:

1. In the Style List dialog box, choose Options, Save As. The Save Styles To dialog box appears.

2. Type the name of the file in the Filename text box, or click the Lookup button (see fig. 10.17), and choose a file in the list of files.

**FIG. 10.17**
Enter a file name and choose the style type to save this style to the default template folder.

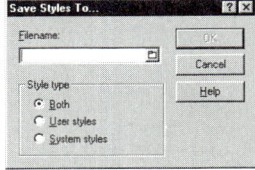

3. The Style Type area of the Save Styles To dialog box allows you to save some or all of your styles. Choose one of the following options:
    - *Both*. Saves all styles to the specified document.
    - *User Style*. Saves current document styles and template styles to the specified document.
    - *System Styles*. Saves only system styles to the specified document.

> **NOTE** You also can save the styles in a blank document by typing a new file name; previous versions of WordPerfect refer to such a file as a *style library*. One function of templates in version 7 is to offer more flexibility than style libraries do, but if you want to save only styles (and no other features associated with the template), simply type an unused file name in the Filename text box. Because the new file contains only styles, choose an extension such as STY. The new file is saved to the OFFICE7 folder.

4. After you finish making choices in the Save Styles To dialog box, choose OK to save the styles and return to the Style List dialog box.

To copy a style to the default or supplemental template, select the style, then choose Options, Copy in the Style List dialog box. The Styles Copy dialog box contains options for copying to the Template or Additional Objects Template (refer to fig. 10.12).

## Retrieving Styles from Another Document or Template

You can combine the styles in your current document with styles from another document or template.

To retrieve styles into the current document, follow these steps:

1. In the Style List dialog box, choose Options, Retrieve. The Retrieve Styles From dialog box appears.
2. Type the name of the file in the Filename text box, or click the file tool on the dialog box and choose a file in the list of files.

    You can choose a WordPerfect document (with a WPD extension) or a WordPerfect template file (with a WPT extension).

3. The Style Type area of the Retrieve Styles From dialog box allows you to retrieve some or all of the styles. Choose one of the following options:
    - *Both*. Retrieves all styles from the specified document.
    - *User Styles*. Retrieves document styles and template styles from the specified document.
    - *System Styles*. Retrieves only system styles from the specified document.

4. After you finish making choices in the Retrieve Styles From dialog box, choose OK to retrieve the styles and return to the Style List dialog box.

**CAUTION**
If you already have a style in the current document that has the same name as the style you are retrieving, an error dialog box appears, asking if you want to overwrite the current style.

**TROUBLESHOOTING**

**I have created a master document that contains several subdocuments. Several of the styles in the subdocuments are not working, and now when I try to edit one of the styles in a subdocument, the style has been changed.** You have probably repeated style names in the master document and the subdocuments. The master document style takes precedence over styles of the same name in the subdocuments. When the subdocument is condensed and saved, the master document style replaces the style in the subdocument. Be sure you use different names or use the same styles in master and subdocuments.

**I want to edit the format of a bulleted paragraph but cannot find these styles in the Styles List box.** Bulleted and numbered paragraphs are edited from within the Bullets and Numbers dialog box accessed via the Insert menu.

▶ **See** "Introducing Outline Styles," **p. 486**

# Examining Some Styles in Use

The four examples that follow illustrate how you can use some of WordPerfect's formatting capabilities in document, character, and paragraph styles.

## Letterhead Document Style

A letterhead is an excellent application for styles, especially if you take advantage of the formatting capabilities of WordPerfect for Windows. Creating a letterhead in WordPerfect is helpful if your printer does not have a paper bin or if you want to fax files without printing them.

The example Letterhead style is an open style that uses a `Delay` code to change the top margin beginning on page 2 and includes text and a graphics image (see fig. 10.18). The Letterhead style uses an advance code to force the letter to begin exactly 2 1/2 inches below the top of the page.

**FIG. 10.18**
The letterhead is produced by the codes and text shown in the Reveal Codes area. First, create the letterhead as a document, and then fine-tune it before replicating the codes in the Style Editor.

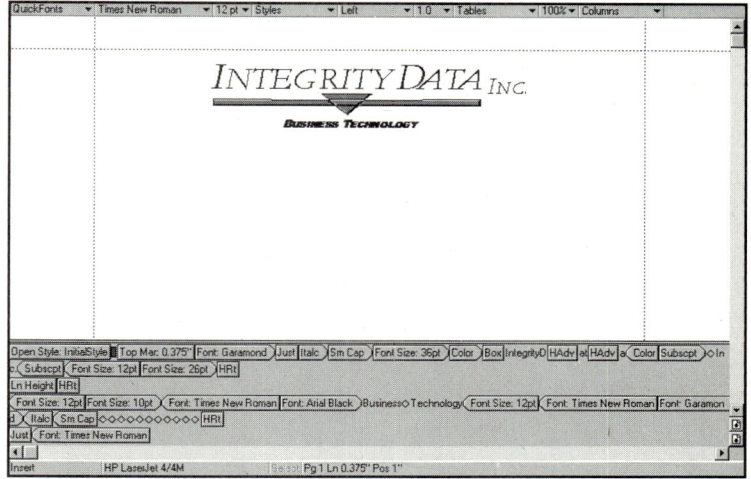

- See "Using Objects in Templates," **p. 378**
- See "Finding Files," **p. 928**

**NOTE** If you use text in a style definition, WordPerfect does not see that text during a search, spell check, or grammar check.

**TIP** Because Letterhead style is used so frequently, avoid wasting disk space by using WordPerfect's Image On Disk option described in Chapter 21, "Using Advanced Graphics Techniques," instead of including the actual image in each file.

## Quotation Character Style

The Quotation style shown in figure 10.19 controls the formatting for quoted text in a scholarly article. The Quotation style was created as a character style, but it could have been created as a paragraph style as well.

The Quotation style shown in figure 10.19 turns on italics, and chooses the small-font attribute. The Quotation style also takes advantage of WordPerfect's paragraph format feature to change the paragraph left and right offsets to 1/2 inch, the spacing between paragraphs to 1 1/2 lines, and the first-line indent to 1/2 inch. To override the first-line indent when using this style, press Shift+Tab.

- See "Formatting Lines and Paragraphs," **p. 130**
- See "Formatting Characters," **p. 126**

**FIG. 10.19**
The Quotation style makes it easy to format embedded quotations. If you want to change the style for all quotations, you can edit the style.

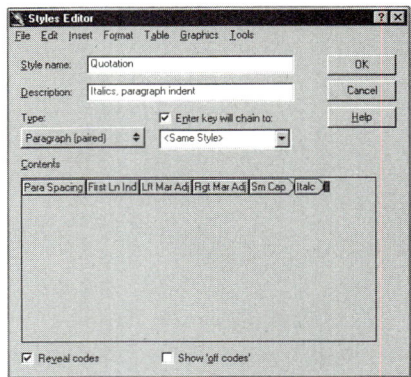

## Border Text Paragraph Style

The Border Text style (see fig. 10.20) is a paragraph style that uses a thick paragraph border and `Block Protect` to keep the paragraph together on a page. Because this style is designed for use with single paragraphs, Enter Key Will Chain To is set to `<None>` to turn the style off. Justification is set to `Full` because text within a border looks better with full justification than with left justification.

▶ **See** "Keeping Text Together," **p. 159**
▶ **See** "Using Graphics Borders," **p. 255**

**FIG. 10.20**
The Border Text style adds a thick border and `Block Protect` to a paragraph. The `Block Protect` code prevents the paragraph from splitting when a page break occurs.

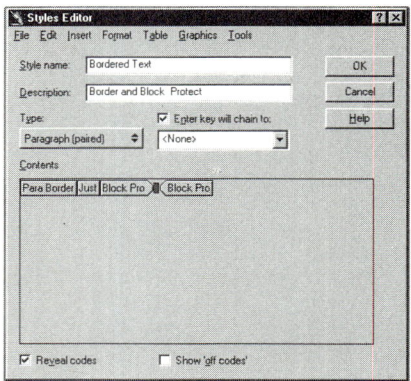

## Q&A Linked Paragraph Styles

The Q&A styles are paragraph styles—Q and A—that are designed to help you to format a series of questions and answers (see fig. 10.21). The Q and A styles illustrate style chaining, a powerful capability of WordPerfect for Windows.

**FIG. 10.21**
The Q and A styles create the format displayed in the document window.

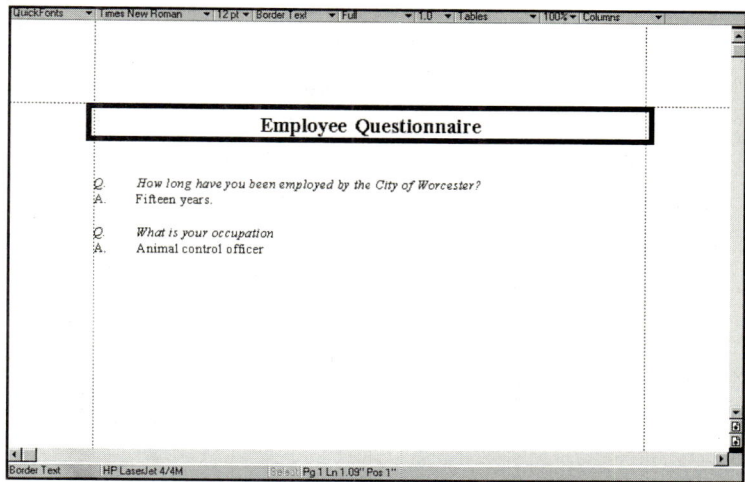

The Q style consists of an `Italic` code, the text `Q.`, and an `Indent` code. The A style consists of the text `A.` and an `Indent` code. The A style also contains a `Hard Return` code with the `Style Off` codes, to add space between the answer and the next question.

▶ **See** "Formatting Lines and Paragraphs," **p. 130**
▶ **See** "Formatting Characters," **p. 126**

The Q style is linked to the A style, which in turn is linked to the Q style (see fig. 10.22). To use these styles, turn on the Q style and type your question. When you press Enter, WordPerfect turns off the Q style and turns on the A style. Type the answer to the question, and then press Enter. WordPerfect turns off the A style and turns on the Q style again. When you finish typing the questions and answers, open the Style List dialog box and choose `<None>`.

**FIG. 10.22**
The Enter Key Will Chain To text box in the Styles Editor dialog box shows that these styles are linked. By using a link of this sort, you can alternate between two styles by pressing Enter.

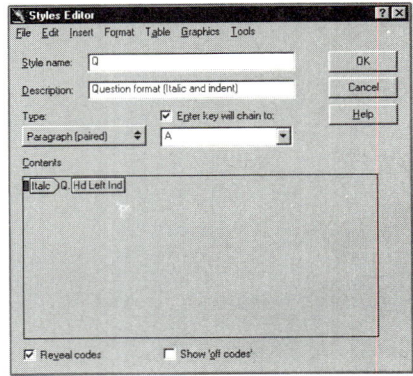

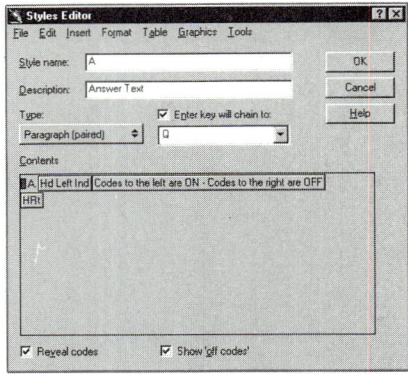

CHAPTER 11

# Using Templates

*by Gordon McComb*

**W**ordPerfect enables you to create documents based on previously designed templates—a sort of "write by the numbers," where the document gives you the basic framework. Fill in the missing text, and your document is complete.

You can create a memo template, for example, that contains the basic formatting and text for your company's interoffice memos. To write a new memo, just create a document that is based on your memo template. Fill in the blanks—who the memo is for, the subject of the memo, and so on—and the document is ready to be saved or printed.

WordPerfect comes with many templates that you can use immediately. You also can edit these templates to better suit your taste. You can provide your own name and phone number, for example, in several of the templates (such as the Meeting Agenda or the Greeting Card) so you don't need to retype this information each time you use the template. You also can create custom templates if you don't find what you want in the template assortment that accompanies WordPerfect. ■

**Understanding the rationale behind the use of templates**

What do they do? Why do I need them? Answers to these questions and more in this chapter.

**Applying templates to documents**

Learn how to use WordPerfect's existing templates and how they can assist you in your everyday document generation tasks.

**Editing templates to your specifications**

You see how to modify one of WordPerfect's existing templates to make it perform as you want.

**Creating new templates**

Create custom templates to suit your own requirements.

**Adding Toolbars, keyboards, and other tools to templates**

Templates can be customized to maximize user productivity and ease of use.

**Using WordPerfect's Letter Expert feature**

The Letter Expert guides you through the creation of a letter, in various formats. Learn how and why it is used.

# Understanding Templates

A *template* is a preformatted page or document layout, used as a model for other documents. Templates contain text that does not vary between documents of a certain type. Templates also can contain a number of WordPerfect for Windows tools, including styles, abbreviations, macros, keyboards, toolbars, or menus. These tools are customized specifically for use with that particular type of document. By using a template, you can keep all the tools you need for a particular type of document close at hand, while ensuring that the correct document formatting is consistently used.

The result of using templates is that all copies of a particular type of document look much the same. All memos, for example, have a similar form. Company standards are automatically followed, the possibility of style mistakes is almost eliminated, and standard text is entered without typographical errors (assuming, of course, that you designed the template properly).

Regarding the memo example from the introduction of this chapter, for instance, you can have a memo template that contains the company letterhead, as well as address and date information. When you use this template, the Memo toolbar and Style Library are activated to help you to format the body of the memo. These tools are specifically designed to assist your work with memos.

The template feature is complex, especially if you probe its more elaborate variations. Learning to make the feature work for you is easy, however, and well worth the effort, considering the time you can save and the consistency you can achieve with documents in future typing sessions. You don't need to master the advanced uses of templates just to be able to build a memo from a memo template.

The simplest definition of templates is *prefab forms*. WordPerfect 7 includes a wide array of templates for commonly used documents and forms. You can change these templates to your specifications. You can also create new templates for other types of documents that you use often. When the time comes to create a document, you retrieve the proper template and edit it to meet your needs.

A template can contain text only, formatting only, or both. A letter template, for example, might contain only your return address or company letterhead. A report template may contain a single embedded code to force double-spacing.

A template for bulletin board announcements might consist of the word Announcement, a graphic, and a text box that contains codes for a certain font.

A purchase order template might include a table complete with formulas to compute the extended cost, amount due, and other critical information. In fact, this template is one of the many that comes with WordPerfect for Windows (see fig. 11.1).

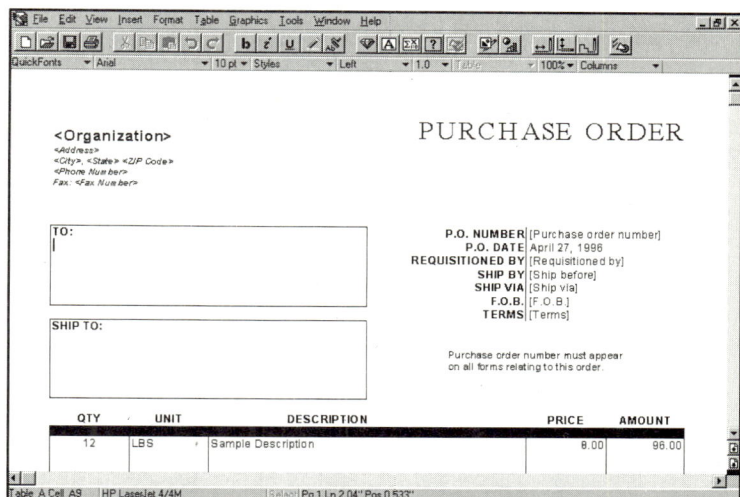

**FIG. 11.1**
This is the purchase order template, before the template prompts have been replaced with personal address user-specified information.

Templates are just WordPerfect files. By convention, template files are given a WPT file extension, and are stored in the TEMPLATE folder under the main \COREL\OFFICE7 folder (these folder names assume that you chose the Standard option when installing WordPerfect for Windows). Individual templates may also be stored in additional folders under the TEMPLATE folder. These additional folders, such as LEGAL and BUSINESS, group like templates together.

Because templates are WordPerfect files, you can open, edit, and print the files just like any other WordPerfect file.

 Whether or not you have explicitly used the template feature of WordPerfect, you have used templates to create new documents. Every new document you start with WordPerfect is based on the default template, which is usually WP7US.WPT (this is the file for the U.S. English version of WordPerfect; the two-letter country abbreviation differs for each international version). That is, choose File, New. WordPerfect displays the Select New Document dialog box, shown in figure 11.2. From the Select Template list, choose Create A Blank Document and click Select.

 You only need to type the personal information that WordPerfect asks for the first time you use a template.

**FIG. 11.2**
As you scroll through the list of templates, you see that each one is summarized in the Select Template box.

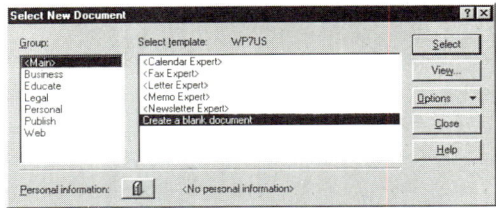

WordPerfect creates a new, blank document. The document is based on all formatting and text that may be in the WP7US.WPT file. If WP7US.WPT contains the text `This is WordPerfect for Windows`, all the new documents you create in WordPerfect automatically contain this text.

 **N O T E**  If you want to start a new, blank document quickly without the trouble of going through the Select New Document dialog box, press Ctrl+N or click the New Blank Document icon in the default WordPerfect 7 Toolbar. Either of these methods bypasses the Select New Document dialog box and immediately starts a new, blank document.

You can edit the WP7US.WPT default template to suit your individual taste, adding as many features as you like. You can change margins, tabs, or the base font, or add text to the template.

## Comparing Templates to Macros, Merges, and Styles

Templates are yet another link in WordPerfect's long list of document automation features, which includes macros, merges, and styles. It may be convenient to lump templates with macros, merges, and styles, but it is also important to note that each automation feature has its own special set of uses and limitations.

▶ See "Creating a Macro," **p. 388**
▶ See "Using Merge," **p. 588**
▶ See "Understanding the Merge Process," **p. 611**

Although templates can be used to solve a lot of problems and provide a great deal of flexibility, other automation features may be better suited for the task. It's also important to note that both macros and styles can be "embedded" in a template, so you can use all three together.

In fact, an ideal use of templates is to "package" all these elements into one file, to make it easier to distribute document-building tools. For example, you can distribute a memo template to all employees, ensuring that they all use the same form, styles, and macros for memos.

Templates are best suited for creating documents that contain specific text or formatting, or both. The legal fax cover sheet is an excellent example of a perfect template: the template includes the words FAX COVER SHEET at the top and has places to type the name of the person to receive the fax, the subject of the fax, and so on. When you use the template, WordPerfect inserts this text—along with all accompanying formatting, such as centered text, font changes, or font attributes—into a new document. You need only fill in the blank parts (who the fax is for and so on), and then print the document.

Templates are not as well suited when you need the user to enter information in a specific order, or when you must be sure that the user provides the correct information. Macros and merges are better suited for this task because you can include intelligence that ensures proper entry.

Conversely, one benefit of templates is that the template contains the overall text and formatting of an entire document. If the template is a form that the user fills in, the formatting—as an integral part of the document—is automatically applied. This process is unlike styles, which must be applied manually.

**N O T E** There's no rule that says you must use styles, macros, or templates. In fact, many document-building chores require that you combine all of WordPerfect's features for maximum benefit.

When deciding on whether to use templates, macros, merges, or styles, keep the following points in mind:

- Templates define the text and formatting for an entire document. If you need to insert only a line or two of text, use a macro.
- The same applies to styles. If you want to apply the formatting for only a portion of a document, use one or more styles rather than a complete template.
- By themselves, templates have no intelligence. A template cannot insert one graphic if a certain set of criteria is met and another graphic if another set of criteria is met. Macros and merges can be endowed with intelligence. If needed, you can embed a macro in a template if you want to combine the features of a template with the smarts of a macro.
- Templates cannot connect to a data file and therefore cannot be used as part of a merge. If you need to prepare a form letter to send to clients, use the merge feature instead. The form document becomes the "template," and the data document provides the information you want to insert into the template when the two documents are merged.

## Applying Templates to Documents

When the time comes to create a particular type of document—a sign, for example—perform these steps:

1. Choose File, New; or press Ctrl+Shift+N. The Select New Document dialog box appears, containing a list of available templates and template groups (refer to fig. 11.2).

2. Highlight the template you want; then choose Select. A new document, based on the template you selected, opens for you.

3. If you want to choose a template that is contained in a different group, such as a template in the Publish group, select the template group you want in the Group list. Templates within that group are shown in the Select Template list box.

You can use templates that contain only formatting and regular text. After WordPerfect opens the document, just write text as usual. However, templates that must be filled in require that you respond to one or more prompts to provide the information needed for the template.

**TIP** If the text in the Select Template list doesn't tell you enough about a template, highlight a template and click View. The View window appears, showing you the text and basic formatting of the template.

As you highlight the templates in the Select Template list, the template file name (minus the WPT extension) appears above the Select Template list. This information can help you identify the actual template file (should you want to copy it), move it to another folder, and so on.

Almost all the templates that come with WordPerfect for Windows are designed as forms to be filled in. For example, when you use the Meeting Agenda template (filename AGENDA.WPT), you are asked for the location, title, and time of the meeting, among other critical information.

**NOTE** The first time you use a template that requires you to fill in information, WordPerfect asks you to provide personalizing information such as your name, company name, address, and phone number. You enter this information once; thereafter, each time you use a template, WordPerfect inserts this information for you in the proper spots in the template.

Suppose that you want to create a balance sheet using the Balance Sheet template. To do so, choose File, New; or choose Ctrl+Shift+N. Choose Business in the Group list, then choose the Balance Sheet template. Click Select.

WordPerfect for Windows creates a new document based on the Balance Sheet template. An automatic macro (contained within the template) runs that displays an information box, telling you that you can enter personal information. Click OK. The Corel Address Book dialog box appears so you can enter information, such as your company name and address, if you want. Choose close when you are finished (or if you don't want to use the Address Book at this time). The Template Information dialog box prompts you to fill in the document (see fig. 11.3). You can fill in fields for the template and then save or print the document when you are finished.

**FIG. 11.3**
Fill in the template fields or click Personal Information to change your personalized information.

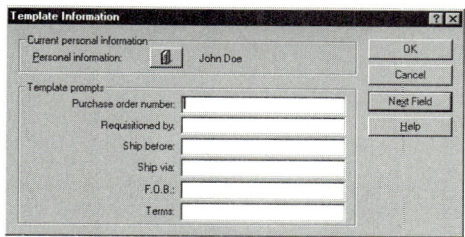

> **TIP** The Template Prompts section contains prompts specific to defined fields in the template that is being used for the new document.

## Using the Template Feature Bar

When editing or creating a template, WordPerfect displays the Template Feature Bar, which consists of seven option buttons (see fig. 11.4). The Feature Bar helps you access the special features of templates. Table 11.1 describes the Template Feature Bar options.

**FIG. 11.4**
Use the Template Feature Bar to access advanced template editing features.

Template Feature Bar

**Table 11.1  The Template Feature Bar Options**

| Button | Function |
|---|---|
| ? | Displays a menu list of Template Feature Bar functions. |
| Insert File | Enables you to insert text and graphics from another file at the current insertion point. |
| Build Prompts | Enables you to create your own Template Information dialog boxes for adding data to a template. |
| Copy/Remove Object | Copies an object (such as a style or macro) from another template, or deletes a selected object. |
| Associate | Associates a macro with any of more than a dozen events, such as saving a file, closing a file, or leaving WordPerfect. |
| Description | Describes the template; this descriptive text appears in the Description box in the Templates dialog box. |
| Exit Template | Saves any changes to the template and closes the template. |

Keep the following in mind when using the Template Feature Bar:

- If you use a mouse, you can access any option in the Template Feature Bar by clicking the appropriate button.
- If you use the keyboard, you can access an option button by pressing Alt+Shift, then the letter associated with the button (such as C for Copy/Remove Object, or A for Associate).

# Using the Templates Provided with WordPerfect for Windows

As you read in the earlier section, "Using Templates," WordPerfect for Windows comes with 48 ready-made templates. Table 11.2 lists these templates and what they do.

**Table 11.2  WordPerfect for Windows Predefined Templates**

| Template | Group | Description |
|---|---|---|
| ACHIEVE | Publish | Certificate of achievement |
| AGENDA | Business | Meeting agenda |

| Template | Group | Description |
|---|---|---|
| BALANCE | Business | Balance sheet |
| BROCHUR1 | Publish | Brochure—Traditional |
| BROCHUR2 | Publish | Brochure—Elegant |
| CALEXP | Main | Calendar Expert |
| EXAM | Education | Exam builder |
| EXPENSE | Business | Expense report |
| FAXEXP | Main | Fax Expert |
| GRADES | Education | Grade schedule |
| GRAPH | Education | Graph paper |
| GREETING | Publish | Greeting card |
| INCOME | Business | Income statement |
| INVOICE1 | Business | Invoice—Sales |
| INVOICE2 | Business | Invoice—Sales and service |
| INVOICE3 | Business | Invoice—Service |
| LAWFAX | Legal | Legal fax cover sheet |
| LAWTIME | Legal | Legal time sheet |
| LETTREXP | Main | Letter Expert |
| MEMOEXP | Main | Memo Expert |
| NEWSEXP | Main | Newsletter Expert |
| PHONEMSG | Business | Telephone message pad |
| PLEADING | Legal | Pleading paper |
| PRESS | Business | Press release |
| PURCHASE | Business | Purchase order |
| REPORT | Education | Report containing title page and table of contents |
| RESUME1 | Personal | Resume—Traditional |
| RESUME2 | Personal | Resume—Contemporary |
| RESUME3 | Personal | Resume—Cosmopolitan |
| SIGN1 | Publish | Sign—Landscape |
| SIGN2 | Publish | Sign—Southwest border |
| SIGN3 | Publish | Sign—Seminar announcement |

*continues*

### Table 11.2 Continued

| Template | Group | Description |
|---|---|---|
| TERM1 | Education | Term Paper—American Psychological Association (APA) |
| TERM2 | Education | Term Paper—Chicago Manual of Style (Turabian) |
| TERM3 | Education | Term Paper—Modern Language Association (MLA) |
| THANKYOU | Publish | Thank you card |
| THINKPAD | Personal | Numbered list |
| WBLANK | Web | Create a blank Web document |
| WEBEXP | Web | Web Page Expert |
| WP7US | Main | Create a blank document |

Most of the templates supplied with WordPerfect for Windows are stored in separate folders to create *template groups*. All these folders are contained under a *master template folder*, usually TEMPLATE. This folder is identified in the Template tab of the Files Preferences dialog box. If you don't see a list of template names when you choose File, New (or press Ctrl+Shift+N), one of two things might have happened:

- You performed a custom installation of WordPerfect and did not choose to include template files in the WordPerfect folder. To include these files, start the install program, choose Custom install, then select Corel WordPerfect from the Components list. If the Templates component WordPerfect Templates doesn't have a checked box beside it, check the box to activate it and continue installing the software.

- WordPerfect was not looking in the proper folder for the template files. Choose Edit, Preferences, Files, then select the Template tab.

  Enter the proper folder (for example, C:\COREL\OFFICE7\TEMPLATE) in the Default Template Folder text box.

**N O T E**  Saving the new document has no effect on the template. The original template is unchanged and remains blank so it's available for you to use for more documents.

### TROUBLESHOOTING

**When I choose File, New, no templates appear.** The template documents must be placed in specific folders. These directories are set up when you first install WordPerfect. The main template folder (usually \COREL\OFFICE7\TEMPLATE) is identified in the File Preferences dialog box. Make sure this folder is specified in the File Preferences dialog box, or else WordPerfect won't be able to locate your template files.

**When I choose File, New, all the templates appear at once, rather than in groups.**
WordPerfect uses subfolders under the main TEMPLATE folder to create groups for template files. As it comes "out-of-the-box," WordPerfect comes with more than a half-dozen group subfolders, including BUSINESS, PUBLISH, and WEB.

The individual templates are supposed to be placed within these subfolders. However, if for some reason the files are moved to the main TEMPLATE folder, they appear together in the Select New Document dialog box. If you want your templates in groups, you must create the group subfolders as specified in this chapter, and move the files to their associated groups.

**When I create a new document with a template, WordPerfect fills it with personal information for someone else, but not me.** WordPerfect stores one set of personal information. If someone else has used your copy of WordPerfect, that personal information may not be up-to-date for you. You can change the personal information at any time by clicking the Personal Info button whenever a Template Information dialog box appears. Make any necessary changes, and choose OK.

**I can't find one or more of the templates that are supposed to come with WordPerfect.**
Templates are files; therefore, they can be deleted. If a template you want to use is missing from the list of templates, you need to reinstall the template files from the original WordPerfect CD-ROM.

## Working with Templates

You are not limited to working with WordPerfect for Windows default templates. You can edit the predefined templates to suit your needs or create your own templates. The new template can be one that you create from scratch or one that you base on a predefined WordPerfect template. When you no longer need one or more templates, you can delete them.

## Editing a Template

Most of the templates that come with WordPerfect for Windows can be used straight "out of the box," without modification, as long as you have previously provided personalized information (refer to the earlier section, "Applying Templates to Documents"). For example, the Greeting Card sheet template (filename GREETING.WPT) is formatted so that when you use it, WordPerfect automatically inserts the name for the card.

Although WordPerfect's templates don't require modification before you can use them, you might still want to add or modify text or formatting to suit your tastes. For instance, you might want to use a different font, change the wording of the greeting, or perhaps add a different graphic than the one provided.

 To edit a template, choose File, New; or press Ctrl+Shift+N. Choose the template you want to edit (select a new group if the template you want is in another group) and choose Options, Edit Template. The selected template document opens, showing you the contents of the template, as well as the Template Feature Bar (see fig. 11.5).

**FIG. 11.5**
An opened template is ready for editing. Templates are like regular WordPerfect documents, so you can use any formatting features to make the template look the way you want. Feel free to experiment with template designs.

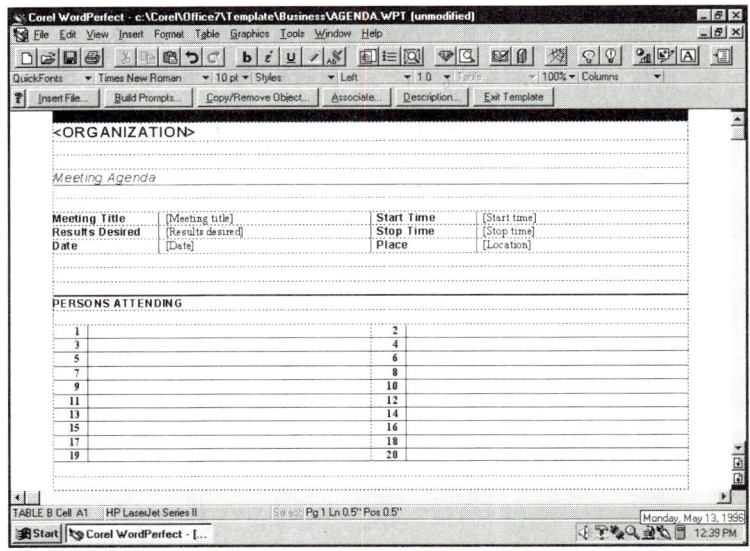

After the template document opens, you can edit it as you would any WordPerfect document. You may add or remove text, change the formatting, and so on.

**NOTE** The changes that you make in a template by following the steps in this section make permanent changes in the template, but not in any document you've previously created using the template. Be careful not to delete template elements that are hard to replace or add features that are not useful. You may want to create backups of your template files as a safety measure in case something goes horribly wrong.

When you finish editing the template, save it so that it is available for future use. Click Exit Template on the Template Feature Bar. WordPerfect asks whether you want to save the changes; choose Yes. The program saves and then closes the edited template.

## Creating a New Template

Just because WordPerfect for Windows comes with previously made templates doesn't mean you can't create your own. You'll want to create your own templates if the ones that come with WordPerfect are not suitable to your needs, or if you regularly produce specialized documents.

For example, you can create a template for quickly producing "standard operating procedure" documents for your company. You might use another custom template for making it easier to write the notes for the weekly meeting. In short, there is no limit to the number and type of templates you can create for use in WordPerfect.

**Creating a Template from Scratch**   To create a new template, in the Select New Document dialog box, choose Options, New Template. Once again, WordPerfect starts a new document for you, and displays the Template Feature Bar.

Select the formatting and text of the document as desired. After you finish with your changes, click Exit Template. Answer Yes to save the changes. The Save Template dialog box appears (see fig. 11.6).

**FIG. 11.6**
Provide a name and description for your new template, and specify the group in which you want to store the template.

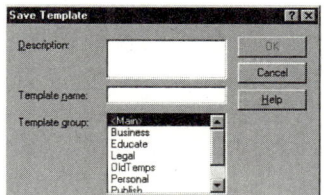

In the Save Template dialog box, provide a name for the template (don't use an extension; WordPerfect does that for you). Provide a brief description of the template and indicate in which existing template group to store your new template. Choose OK. The template is saved, and then closed.

> **NOTE** You can create a new template from any standard WordPerfect document. Just follow the previous steps, and then insert the document you want to use into the template document by clicking the Insert File button on the Template Feature Bar.

**Basing a New Template on an Existing Template**   When you create a new template, WordPerfect doesn't base it on another template—unless you specifically ask it to. This means that the new template doesn't carry forward any formatting or text of another template. In most cases, this method is how you want to create most new templates.

However, WordPerfect also enables you to create a new template based on an already existing template. The new template *inherits* all the traits of the *parent*, or original, template. You can keep the new template as-is (as a clone of the parent), or you can change formatting, text, and other features to customize the new template.

To base a new template on an existing one, follow these steps:

1. Choose File, New to display the Select New Document dialog box.
2. Locate the template you want to use as the basic template. Select the template with a *single* click of the mouse. You want to simply highlight, not activate, the template.
3. Choose Options, Edit Template. The template is opened for you.
4. Immediately choose File, Save As. The Save Template dialog box appears, where you provide a new name for the template. You can also provide a new description and new location.
5. Choose OK to save the template.

You can now alter the template as you want. Remember that the new template has all the features of the original template. You can delete these features, add to them, and so on. After you finish, click Exit Template on the Template Feature Bar. Answer Yes to save the changes you've made to the template. You can now use the new template as usual.

**Using the Prompt Builder**   When you create a custom template you might also want to design your template so that it uses the same automated field-entry syntax found in the templates that come with WordPerfect. WordPerfect has a special template feature that enables you to embed special data-entry fields into your document that prompt the user for information when a new document is created based on your template.

Fortunately, you don't need to understand the field-entry syntax, because WordPerfect comes with a feature to assist you in providing the field-entry prompts in templates you create or edit. To use the automatic field-entry feature, click the <u>B</u>uild Prompts button in the Template Feature Bar. In a moment, the Prompt Builder dialog box appears (see fig. 11.7). After using the Prompt Builder dialog box, choose OK to close the box. WordPerfect updates the prompt information in the template.

Keep the following in mind when using the Prompt Builder dialog box:

- Ask for user information in the Template Information dialog box (this is the dialog box that first appears after choosing a template from the Select New Document dialog box), and choose <u>B</u>uild Prompts from the Template Feature Bar. In the Prompt Builder dialog box, choose <u>A</u>dd. The Add Template Prompt dialog box appears. Type the text of the prompt, and choose OK.

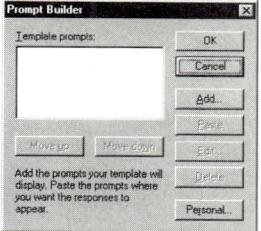

**FIG. 11.7**
Use the Prompt Builder dialog box to insert your own prompts and entry fields for automatic template fill-in.

- To reorder the prompts in the Template Information dialog box by selecting the prompt you want to reposition in the <u>T</u>emplate Prompts list, then click Move <u>U</u>p or Move Do<u>w</u>n.
- Specify where you want the user's data for a particular prompt inserted, and place the insertion point at the desired spot in the document. Choose <u>B</u>uild Prompts from the Template Feature Bar. In the Prompt Builder dialog box, select the prompt you want to insert in the <u>T</u>emplate Prompts list, then click <u>P</u>aste.
- Edit the text of a prompt, and choose <u>B</u>uild Prompts from the Template Feature Bar. In the Prompt Builder dialog box, choose the prompt to edit in the <u>T</u>emplate Prompts list, then click <u>E</u>dit. Edit the prompt text, then choose OK.
- Delete a prompt (it will no longer appear in the Template Information dialog box), and choose Build Prompts from the Template Feature Bar. In the Prompt Builder dialog box, choose the prompt to delete in the <u>T</u>emplate Prompts list, then choose <u>D</u>elete.

- Specify where the user's personal data will appear (such as the user's name, phone number, and so forth), and place the insertion point at the desired spot in the document. Choose Build Prompts from the Template Feature Bar. In the Prompt Builder dialog box, click Personal. The Personal Fields dialog box appears. Choose the field to use, and choose Paste.

**NOTE** The Add Template Prompt dialog box gives you the option of typing a prompt into the user's personal address book. If you want, you can associate a prompt with an address book entry, so that the template information is automatically provided if the user elects to use an address book entry when filling out the template. To tie an address book field to a template prompt, choose one of the field names in the Link to Address Book Field button.

When writing the prompt text be sure to keep it short—no more than 20 or 30 characters. In addition, keep the number of prompts to a minimum—no more than four or five is ideal (the maximum is 12).

## Deleting Templates You No Longer Need

You can delete templates you no longer need so they don't clutter the Templates dialog box. In the Select New Document dialog box, highlight the template you want to delete. Choose Options, Delete Template. Confirm that you want to delete the template by answering Yes.

## Creating New Template Groups

WordPerfect allows you to create new groups for storing templates. You might create a new group for templates you regularly use in your office, such as templates for filling out regular reports, or producing documentation for a client.

To create a new template group, in the Select New Document dialog box choose Options, New Group. Specify the name of the group (eight characters or fewer), and choose OK.

To rename an existing group, choose Options, Rename Group. You cannot rename the Main group. Choose Options, Delete Group to delete an existing group. You cannot delete the Main group.

# Using Objects in Templates

One of the greatest features of WordPerfect for Windows templates is that you can embed styles, macros, abbreviations, Toolbars, keyboards, and menus in the template. Whenever you use the template, these styles, macros, and other objects are available. If you have the default Toolbar displayed, for example, and the template contains its own embedded Toolbar, WordPerfect removes the default Toolbar and displays the Toolbar from the template in its place.

Conversely, if you aren't using the template, the objects are not available, so they don't get in the way. Objects embedded in templates enable you to create styles, macros, abbreviations, Toolbars, keyboards, and menus that are context-sensitive. These specific objects are available to you only in the context of the template.

Of course, you do not need to use objects to use templates. But it's nice to know this powerful feature is available should you want to use it.

**N O T E** If you do not specify an embedded object for a template, WordPerfect uses the object (if any) in the default template (usually WP7US.WPT). For example, if you do not specify a new keyboard layout for your template, WordPerfect merely uses the standard keyboard layout in the default template.

## Adding an Object to a Template

Objects are added when you create or edit a template. You can add any type of object; the object does not have to already exist to be able to add it to the template.

To add an object to a template, follow these steps:

1. Create or edit the template in the usual manner (see the previous sections "Editing a Template" and "Creating a New Template" for more information).
2. Create the object you want by defining it using WordPerfect's normal feature editing tools. For example, to create a new menu, choose Edit, Preferences, Menu Bar.
3. Define the object in the same way that you change WordPerfect's preferences, such as with Toolbars and macros.

   ▶ **See** "Templates," **p. 316**
   ▶ **See** "Creating a Macro," **p. 388**
   ▶ **See** "Working with the Toolbar," **p. 417**

Objects are defined in the same way you use the corresponding feature outside of templates. If you are creating a macro object, choose Tools, Template Macro, Record. Record the macro in the usual fashion. If you are creating a style, display the Style List dialog box (Alt+F8), where you create the style as you do for a regular WordPerfect for Windows document.

The following table shows how to create the individual objects using WordPerfect's commands.

| Object | Displays | Choose |
|---|---|---|
| Style | Style List | Fo<u>r</u>mat, <u>S</u>tyles |
| Template Macro | Record Template Macro | <u>T</u>ools, Tem<u>p</u>late Macro, <u>R</u>ecord |
| Abbreviation | Abbreviations | <u>I</u>nsert, <u>A</u>bbreviation |
| Toolbar | Toolbar Preferences | <u>E</u>dit, P<u>r</u>eferences, <u>T</u>oolbar |
| Keyboard | Keyboard Preferences | <u>E</u>dit, P<u>r</u>eferences, <u>K</u>eyboard |
| Menu Bar | Menu Preferences | <u>E</u>dit, P<u>r</u>eferences, <u>M</u>enu |

## Copying Existing Objects from Other Templates

WordPerfect for Windows enables you to borrow objects contained in other templates. This feature saves you the time of re-creating objects that you may want to use over again.

To copy an object from another template, follow these steps:

1. Create or edit the template in the usual manner (see the previous sections "Editing a Template" and "Creating a New Template" for more information).

2. Click <u>C</u>opy/Remove Object in the Template Feature Bar, or press Alt+Shift+C. The Copy/Remove Template Objects dialog box appears (see fig. 11.8).

**FIG. 11.8**
Use the Copy/Remove Template Objects dialog box to copy objects from existing templates and to remove objects you no longer need from the template you are currently editing.

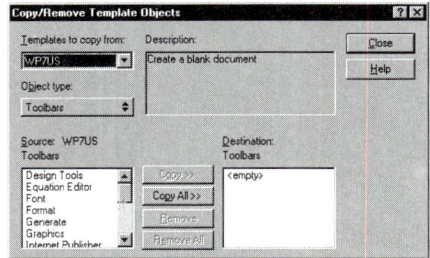

3. In the Templates To Copy From list, choose the template that contains the object you want to copy.

4. Click Object Type and specify the type of object you want to copy: Menu Bars, Macros, Macros on Disk, Toolbars, Abbreviations, Styles, or Keyboards.

5. Locate the object you want to copy in the Source box and highlight it. Click Copy to move the objects to the Destination box. Or, if you want to copy all of the objects in the Source box, click Copy All.

6. After you make your choices, click Close.

## Removing Objects from the Current Template

The Copy/Remove Template Objects dialog box, described in the preceding section, also is used to delete objects no longer needed in the template. The following series of steps assumes that you are already editing the template.

To delete an object, follow these steps:

1. In the Template Feature Bar, click Copy/Remove Object. The Copy/Remove Template Objects dialog box appears.

2. Click Object Type and specify the type of object you want to delete.

3. In the Destination box, select the object you want to delete and click Remove; if you want to delete all the objects listed in the Destination box, click Remove All.

4. After you finish, click Close.

# Associating Features and Events

In the previous section, you learned how to embed objects into templates. Embedded objects—such as styles, macros, Toolbars, and keyboard layouts—are context-sensitive to the template you are using. Only when using a given template are the embedded objects available to you. This restriction helps to avoid clutter and streamlines your use of WordPerfect.

Besides embedding objects in templates, you can associate macros, Toolbars, menus, and keyboards to specific WordPerfect for Windows editing modes (called *features*). You can associate a particular Toolbar, for example, so that it appears whenever you use the Equation Editor or the Tables Editor. As you change modes, the Toolbar also changes.

To give templates even more of a power boost, you can associate a macro with any of 15 different *events*, or triggers. When one of these triggers occurs, the specified macro is played.

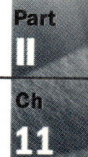

## Associating to a Feature

As far as templates are concerned, WordPerfect has numerous main editing modes:

| | |
|---|---|
| Main editing window (normal document editing) | Graphics |
| Comments | Headers |
| Endnotes | Main |
| Equation Editor | Outline |
| Footers | Tables |
| Footnote | Watermark |

By using templates, you can associate a different Toolbar, menu, and/or keyboard to each of these editing modes. As you change modes, the Toolbar, menu, or keyboard layout changes dynamically and automatically.

To set an editing mode association, follow these steps:

1. Create or edit the template in the usual manner (see the "Editing a Template" and "Creating a New Template" sections earlier in the chapter for more information).

2. Click Associate on the Template Feature Bar or press Alt+Shift+A. The Associate dialog box appears (see fig. 11.9).

3. If not already selected, click the Features option.

**FIG. 11.9**
The Associate dialog box permits you to associate certain WordPerfect for Windows features (editing modes) to Toolbars, menus, and keyboard layouts.

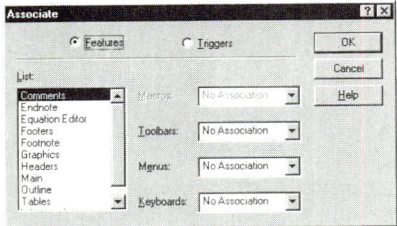

4. Choose the editing mode you want to associate, such as Comments, Equation Editor, or Watermark.

5. In the respective lists, click Toolbars, Menus, or Keyboards to specify the object you want to associate to. If no association is desired, choose No Association.

> **NOTE** The Toolbar, menu, or keyboard object already must be embedded in the template before an editing mode can be associated to the template. If you don't see the object you want to use, close the Association dialog box (choose Cancel), and create or copy the object to the template you are editing. See the previous section "Using Objects in Templates" for more information.

6. Repeat steps 4 and 5 for each additional association.
7. Choose OK when you finish.

## Associating Macros to Triggers

Macros are not associated in the same manner as Toolbars, menus, and keyboard layouts. Rather than associate a macro to a given editing mode, macros are associated to triggers. WordPerfect for Windows recognizes the following events as triggers to which you can associate a macro.

| Trigger | Macro Runs... |
|---|---|
| Post Close | After document is closed (choose File, Close). |
| Pre Close | Before document is closed. |
| Post New | After opening a new document (choose File, New). |
| Pre New | Before opening a new document. |
| Post Open | After opening a document. |
| Pre Open | Before opening a document. |
| Post Print | After printing begins (choose File, Print). |
| Pre Print | Before printing begins. |
| Post Startup | After WordPerfect starts (note there is no Pre Startup). |
| Post Switch Doc | After switching to a different document (choose Doc In Window). |
| Pre Switch Doc | Before switching to a different document. |
| Post Tables | After switching to table edit (choose Table). |
| Pre Tables | Before switching to table edit. |

To associate a macro to one of these triggers, follow these steps:

1. Create or edit the template in the usual manner (see the "Editing a Template" and "Creating a New Template" sections earlier in this chapter for more information).
2. Click Associate in the Template Feature Bar, or press Alt+Shift+A. The Associate dialog box appears.
3. Click the Triggers option.
4. In the Triggers List box, choose the trigger you want to use, such as Pre Open or Post Startup.
5. In the Macros list, choose the macro you want to associate with the selected trigger. If no association is desired, choose No Association.

**N O T E**  The macro object must already be embedded in the template before it can accept a trigger association. If you don't see the macro you want to use, close the Association dialog box (choose Cancel), and create or copy the macro to the template you are editing. See the previous section "Using Objects in Templates" for more information.

6. Repeat steps 4 and 5 for each additional macro trigger association.
7. Choose OK when you finish.

## Planning for Embedded Macros

While there are no serious side effects of using objects in templates, you should keep the following in mind:

- Avoid embedding more than a few macros (especially large ones) in a single template. Embedded macros can cause the template file to become larger (an increase of between 5K and 10K for even a relatively simple macro is not uncommon). The larger the template, the slower WordPerfect is in using it.

- If you must associate or embed more than a few macros in a template, consider using a "starter macro" in the template, and placing the full macro as a separate disk file. For the starter macro, use the macro CHAIN command and follow it with the name of the macro you want to use. Enclose the name in quotes, as in CHAIN ("mymacro.wcm"). This causes WordPerfect to immediately play a macro called MYMACRO.WCM (the macro is assumed to be in the default macros folder).

- To edit an embedded macro, edit the template as described earlier in "Editing a Template." Choose Tools, Template Macro, Edit. Highlight the macro you want to edit, and then choose Edit. The macro is opened for you. You may now edit the macro. Save the changes when you are done, and close the document window.

# Using the Letter Expert

The Letter Expert is something of a "hidden" feature of WordPerfect. With the Letter Expert, you can write and format entire business letters in a matter of minutes. WordPerfect comes with over a dozen pre-written business letters; you just insert the letter you want and fill in the blanks.

To use the Letter Expert, follow these steps:

1. Choose File, New; or press Ctrl+Shift+N. The Select New Document dialog box appears.

2. Choose <Letter Expert>, then choose Select.

3. In a few moments, WordPerfect displays the Letter Expert dialog box (see fig. 11.10). In this dialog box, type the name and address of the person to whom you're sending the letter.

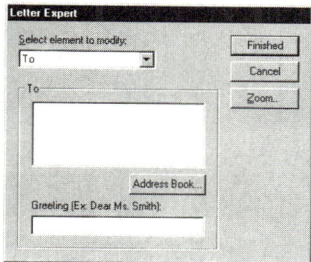

**FIG. 11.10**
Start the letter by filling in the Letter Expert dialog box, including the name and address of the recipient of the letter.

4. Choose Appearance from the Select Element To Modify list.

5. From the Text Format drop-down list, specify the format of the letter: Full Block, Modified Block, Semiblock, or Simplified.

6. Choose Closing from the Select Element To Modify list.

7. Specify the closing options you want.

8. Choose any of the other options from the Select Element To Modify list, and make changes in the letter accordingly.

9. When finished setting up the letter, choose Finished. WordPerfect starts the letter for you and inserts the opening of the letter.

10. You should now be able to locate the insertion point and begin entering the body of the letter.

You can now spell check the letter, save it, and print it, as desired.

## Using WordPerfect's Other Template Experts

In addition to the Letter Expert described in the preceding section, WordPerfect comes with several other template experts that can make your work faster and easier. The following experts work in about the same way and prompt you for the information needed to complete each step:

- *Calendar Expert*. Choose <Calendar Expert> in the Main template group. Use the Calendar Expert to create a customized calendar that suits your own personal style.

- *Memo Expert*. Choose <Memo Expert> in the Main template group. Use the Memo Expert to quickly prepare memos.

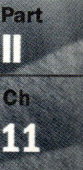

- *Newsletter Expert.* Choose <Newsletter Expert> in the Main template group. Use the Newsletter Expert to create any of several styles of newsletters.
- *Fax Expert.* Choose <Fax Expert> in the Maintemplate group. Use the Fax Expert to prepare a fax cover sheet.

## TROUBLESHOOTING

**I can't associate two macros to the same trigger.** This is working as designed. WordPerfect only lets you trigger an event (like opening a new template) to one macro at a time. If you want to use more than one macro, you need to use the CHAIN command to play the macros one after another. If you want to run a macro and use the built-in <dofiller> macro, edit your macro so that the last command is TemplateFill(). Use this macro as the trigger association, rather than <dofiller>. WordPerfect plays your macro, then runs the <dofiller> macro so the template can be filled in.

**When I try to insert a Letter Expert letter, no letter appears.** The Letter Expert documents must be placed in the TEMPLATES folder (usually \COREL\OFFICE7\TEMPLATE). Make sure this folder is specified in the File Preferences dialog box, or else WordPerfect won't be able to locate your Letter Expert files.

CHAPTER 12

# Creating Macros

*by Gordon McComb*

Don't let the word *macro* fool you. It's not some arcane feature that only WordPerfect wizards use. Macros are for everyone—beginner or expert—and they benefit all users the same way: macros are shortcuts that help speed up your work.

The simplest macro—the kind you'll use the most—is a recording of the keys you press and the commands you choose. When you *play back* your macro, your keystrokes and commands are repeated, and much faster than when you originally recorded them. With a macro, you can automate the time-consuming and dreary tasks you do every day with WordPerfect for Windows. You can, for example, set up letters, prepare fax cover sheets, or write memos.

The main purpose of macros is to make Corel WordPerfect 7 do the work for you. The more menial tasks you can get WordPerfect to perform, the more time you can spend improving the content and look of your documents. If sheer output is your goal, macros enable you to speed up the preparation of documents so that you can turn out more work in the same period of time. ∎

### Record and play back macros
Learn the basics of recording and playing macros of your own creation.

### Re-record macros that don't work correctly
When recorded macros don't work properly, it's often easier to just start over and record from scratch. You learn why and how here.

### Use macros for common writing, editing, and formatting tasks
Macros were created to accelerate your word processing. See how you can benefit by creating your own macros.

### Access macros
Macros can be activated in a variety of methods. This chapter covers the different methods and locations.

You already know that macros help save you time. Now take a brief look at the other benefits macros provide:

- *Increase your productivity.* Instead of spending several minutes writing and formatting a cover sheet for every fax you send, a macro can help you write and print the cover sheet in seconds.
- *Improve your accuracy.* Although WordPerfect's built-in spelling checker helps you find spelling and typographical errors, it will not locate wrong phone numbers, shipping addresses, or social security numbers. If you type this kind of information often, you can use a macro to ensure that it is accurate every time.
- *Enhance consistency.* Did you use a 14-point font or an 18-point font for the title of last month's meeting notes? With a macro, you never have to worry about forgetting the formats you used the last time. Your documents will be more consistent—and therefore, more professional. While the style and template features of WordPerfect can also be used to make sure your documents look the same, a macro is often easier to set up and use.
- *Reduce complex tasks.* WordPerfect isn't known for making all tasks especially easy. Take, for example, the steps required to retrieve a graphics file, position it on the page, and set a particular border and background color. A job like this requires several dozen steps and can take minutes to perform. A macro, however, enables you to accomplish the same job in seconds and with little more effort than pressing two keys.

If you used the macro feature of earlier versions of WordPerfect for Windows, you'll find only a few changes in the way you record and play back macros in WordPerfect 7. Version 7 also uses a similar approach to its macro language—the way your actions are recorded and stored. If you plan on writing your own macros, as opposed to just recording them, you'll find you don't have to relearn everything from scratch.

# Creating a Macro

WordPerfect requires very little preparation before you can record a macro. Usually, you don't have to do anything more than start the macro recorder. As a precaution, save any documents you're currently working on. Unless you specifically want to do so, don't record your macros using a document that already contains text you don't want to change. The macro you record may change the contents of your document in ways that you may not anticipate.

## Important Considerations

Although recording macros is simple and straightforward, don't use the Macro Record feature of WordPerfect in a haphazard fashion; if you do, you may accidentally change the document you are currently working on. Keep the following points in mind before recording your macros:

- *Save any documents you have open.* Although serious glitches during macro recording are rare, don't take chances. This step is particularly important if you are recording a macro that will modify existing text. If you save the document first and something goes wrong while you record the macro, you can retrieve the saved version and try again.

- *Unless your macros modify existing text, open a new document before starting macro recording.* This precaution helps ensure that the macro does not disturb another document you are working on.

- *If your macro modifies existing text, note the conditions that are present when you record the macro.* Be sure to reproduce those conditions before you play the macro. If you record a macro that changes wording in a form letter you send out to customers, for example, be sure to retrieve the form letter the next time you play the macro.

- *Be aware of where you are in WordPerfect before you start macro recording.* Consider WordPerfect's operating state so that you can remember to always play back your macro in the same way. If, for example, you record a macro in the header window, remember to only play the macro in a header, not at the main document screen.

- *Before recording a macro, make a dry run of the steps you want to record.* WordPerfect can't tell if you make a mistake or choose the wrong command. Although minor mistakes usually pose no harm and can remain in your macro, you want to record your macros with the fewest number of mistakes possible. If you are making a macro of some complex task, write down the steps as a script you can follow during recording.

- *WordPerfect records the keys you press and the commands you choose.* The program does not record the amount of time you take to perform the steps. Go slowly and take your time.

**NOTE** Recording macros using standard conditions is highly recommended. If your macro is supposed to add text to a header, for example, start recording at the main document screen, and then open the header window. Type the text you want, and close the header window. By following this procedure, your macro includes all the commands needed to reproduce the conditions required for successful playback.

## Steps To Record a Macro

You can use the keyboard or the mouse to record your macro. Either way, recording a macro requires the following five steps:

1. Choose <u>T</u>ools, <u>M</u>acro, <u>R</u>ecord; or press Ctrl+F10. The Record Macro dialog box appears (see fig. 12.1).

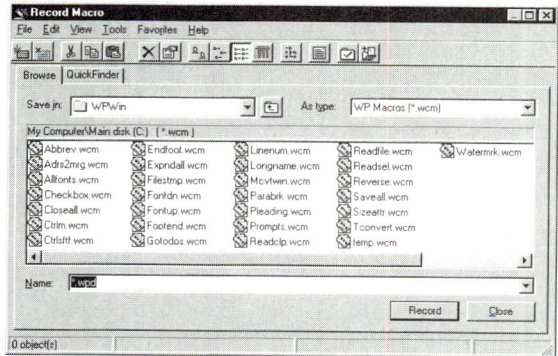

**FIG. 12.1**
The name you type in the <u>N</u>ame text box becomes the macro's file name.

2. In the <u>N</u>ame text box, type a name for your macro. This name is the macro's file name, which can include one to eight characters and any valid character for DOS file names. Macros are automatically given a WCM extension.

3. Choose Record or press Enter. After a few moments, WordPerfect activates the macro recorder. Look for the `Macro Record` indicator in the status bar; this lets you know that your actions are being recorded. (This prompt does not appear if your status line is not set to show the General Status group.)

4. Perform whatever action you want your macro to record. You can use the keyboard to enter text or choose commands from menus. You can also use the mouse to choose commands from menus.

**N O T E** When a macro is recording, WordPerfect does not allow you to use the mouse to move the insertion point or block text. You are restricted to keyboard access only for such commands.

5. After you have entered the keystrokes, stop the macro recorder by choosing <u>T</u>ools, <u>M</u>acro, <u>R</u>ecord; or press Ctrl+F10. The `Macro Record` prompt disappears and your macro is complete.

**N O T E** Immediately after you end a macro recording session, WordPerfect saves your macro and compiles the commands contained in the macro file. During this compiling phase, WordPerfect displays a `Compiling Macro` message, which usually appears for less than a second. On a very fast computer and a short macro, the message may just flash briefly on-screen.

## A Practical Application Using Macros

A simple and common writing job is typing your name and the closing on a letter, for example:

> **Milton Farnsworth III, Esq.**
>
> **Very truly yours,**

Typing this example takes about 10 seconds, not including typographical errors. Although 10 seconds doesn't seem like a long time, consider the number of times that you may need to type this block of text each day, week, or month. The 10 seconds can add up to many extra hours by the end of the year.

Because typing a closing is a common task in WordPerfect for Windows, recording a macro to type the close for you makes sense. Follow these steps to create a macro for this task, but feel free to use your own name (or your employer's name) instead of the name shown in the example:

1. As a safeguard, save any document you are currently working on.
2. Choose File, New to open a new document.
3. Start macro recording by choosing Tools, Macro, Record; or press Ctrl+F10. The Record Macro dialog box appears (refer to fig. 12.1).
4. For the name of the macro, type **vty**, for "very truly yours." You don't need to type a file extension.
5. Choose Record or press Enter. Wait a few moments for the `Macro Record` prompt to appear in the status bar.
6. Type **Very truly yours,**. If you make a mistake, press Backspace to clear the error, and retype the text.
7. To add space between the close and your name, press the Enter key three or four times.
8. Type **Milton Farnsworth III, Esq.** (or any other name).
9. Stop macro recording by choosing Tools, Macro, Record; or press Ctrl+F10. The `Macro Record` prompt disappears.

# Chapter 12 Creating Macros

**N O T E** During macro recording, what you type is entered into the current document. Because you don't need this text, you can close the document window without saving the document.

**T I P** If the document you're currently working on might be disrupted by the macro, be sure to save and close your document before you play the macro.

Now that you have recorded this macro, you can add a closing to any letter just by positioning the insertion point and executing the macro. The next section explains in detail how to play back a macro.

## Playing a Macro

Macros are even easier to play than they are to record. You just tell WordPerfect you want to play back a macro, specify the name of the macro you want, and press Enter.

To play back a macro, follow these steps:

1. Choose Tools, Macro, Play; or press Alt+F10. The Play Macro dialog box appears (see fig. 12.2).

**FIG. 12.2**
Type the name of the macro you want to play in the Play Macro dialog box.

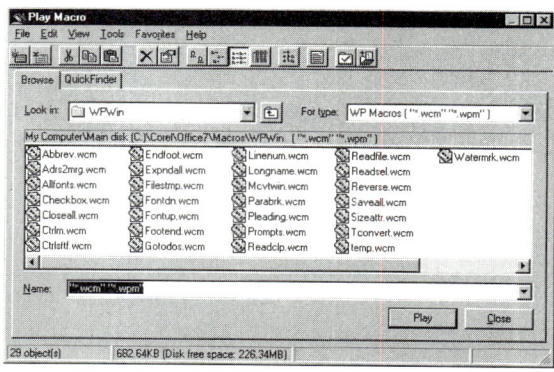

2. In the Name text box, type the name of the macro you want to use. For example, if you want to play the macro you recorded earlier, type **vty**.

   Because WordPerfect always adds the WCM extension to macros that you record, you don't need to type this extension when you specify the name of the macro you want to play.

3. Choose Play or press Enter. WordPerfect plays the macro.

As you use WordPerfect for Windows' Macro feature, you'll eventually forget the names you gave your macros. Fortunately, WordPerfect helps you locate the macro you want by letting you scan through the available macro files. To scan the list of available macros, follow these steps:

1. Choose Tools, Macro, Play; or press Alt+F10. The Play Macro dialog box appears (refer to fig. 12.2). This is the standard "open file" dialog box you see when you open a file, so you use it in the same way. Locate the file you want, or choose a different folder or disk drive to see the macro files there.

    In the Play Macro dialog box, you can use the scroll bar to scroll through the list of macros.

2. In the listing of files, highlight the macro you want to play, then choose OK or press Enter.

# Re-Recording a Macro

Suppose you are recording a macro and you make a mistake—you cut and paste instead of copy and paste, for instance. Don't worry. You can stop macro recording and try again. When you make a mistake while you record a macro, you can simply re-record over the mistake; no one is the wiser.

You may also want to re-record a macro that isn't current. If you get promoted from vice president to president, for example, you will want to re-record any macro that identifies you as a V.P.

Consider these points before you re-record a macro:

- If you're re-recording a macro because you made a mistake the last time, the mistake may not be bad enough to warrant a new macro. Suppose, for example, that you entered one too many hard returns and had to remove it. The extra hard return and the deletion are recorded, but they have no ill effect when the macro is played back.

- Some mistakes aren't recorded. Suppose you open the wrong dialog box. You immediately realize your mistake and choose the Cancel button. Under most circumstances, WordPerfect does *not* record this action. As a general rule, actions are recorded only when you make a change in a dialog box or type text in the document.

- WordPerfect does *not* record your fishing through various menus with the mouse or keyboard.

To re-record a macro, follow the steps in the earlier section "Steps to Record a Macro." When WordPerfect tells you that you already have a macro with the same name, answer Yes, that you want to replace it.

# Understanding Where Macros Are Recorded

WordPerfect can record macros in any of several places. So far, you've read how a macro is recorded and stored as its own separate file, with a WCM file extension. The file is stored in the folder specified for macros in Preferences. (If no folder is specified, the macro is stored in the current document folder.)

This is just one way to record a macro for future use. Macros can also be recorded in a template document. To record a macro in a template:

1. Choose Tools, Template Macro, Record. The Record Macro dialog box appears.
2. Click Location. The Macro Location dialog box appears (see fig. 12.3).

**FIG. 12.3**
In the Macro Location dialog box, specify where you want to store the macro when you record it.

3. Select either Current Template or Default Template (usually WP7US.WPT). If you're new to the subject of templates, see Chapter 11, "Using Templates."
4. If you want to choose a new default location, check the Use As Default option.
5. Choose OK or press Enter.
6. Type the name of the macro you want to record in the Name box. The macro name can be up to 31 characters and can contain spaces.
7. Choose Record or press Enter to start recording.

## The Current Template Location Option

Use the Current Template location option to record the macro in whatever template file is being used for the currently open document. For example, if the currently open document is based on the resume template (choose File, New; choose the Personal group; then choose one of the several resume template selections), the macro is recorded in the selected resume template file. The macro is only available when you use the resume template.

Even if you didn't use a template for the currently open document, by default all new documents are based on the WP7US template (the WP7US.WPT template file). If you didn't select a different template, the WP7US template is the current template; therefore, recording a macro to the current template stores it in the WP7US.WPT file.

Use the Current Template option when you want to store a macro that you plan to use only with that template. For example, if you use a resume template, you may want to record a macro that inserts your education history. Such a macro has little use outside a resume template, so storing it with the template consolidates files.

### The Default Template Location Option

Use the Default Template location option to record the macro in the template file used to create all new documents (normally WP7US.WPT). This option is dimmed (unavailable) if the current template and the default template are the same.

Use the Default Template option when you want to store a macro that you can access when using any template. Storing macros in the default template helps you consolidate files, while ensuring that the macros are always available to you.

▶ See "Understanding Templates," **p. 364**

## Understanding Macro File Names

When creating macros that do not reside inside a template, you must give a name to every macro you record. WordPerfect uses that name as the file name for the macro. Each macro you record is stored on your computer's hard disk drive as a separate file. Storing the macros separately makes copying, renaming, or deleting your macros easier, because they are treated like any other file on your computer.

> **NOTE** When using the Current Template and Default Template macro location options, you must still name the macro, but you are not limited to valid DOS file names. You can include spaces, punctuation, and other characters not allowed in file names (up to 31 characters).

The remainder of this section assumes that you are using file macros recorded and played with the Tools, Macro commands (as opposed to the Tools, Template Macro commands).

The following sections introduce points you should keep in mind when naming your macros.

## Unless Noted Otherwise, Macros Use the WCM Extension

WordPerfect uses a standard naming scheme for macros. The WCM extension is not mandatory; however, it is highly recommended. When you use the WCM extension, you don't need to provide a unique extension when specifying the macro you want to play. If you use a different extension, you must also explicitly type the extension.

For example, if your macro is named TEST.WCM, you need only type **TEST** in the Play Macro dialog box, and WordPerfect plays the TEST.WCM macro. However, if the macro is named TEST.MAC, you must type **TEST.MAC** to tell WordPerfect the exact file name you want to use.

Ordinarily, you never have to give much thought to the WCM file extension requirement, unless you write your macros from scratch or rename a macro file. In these cases, make sure that the file names you specify include the required WCM extension.

## All Macros Use Only Valid Windows 95 File Names

Because WordPerfect macros are individual files (except those macros that are stored in templates; see the previous section for more information), you must follow standard Windows 95 filenaming practices and give your macros names that Windows 95 can accept. Keep in mind the following as you name your macros:

- The macro name can contain up to 255 characters, but for simplicity, the name should be as short and descriptive as possible.

- Avoid the use of the following characters in Windows 95 file names, as these characters cannot be used in the DOS-compatible "alias" file name that is also created for the file:

    + , : = [ ]

- If you plan on using the macro with a version of WordPerfect for Windows running under Windows 3.1, save the macro using the DOS 8+3 filename standard. The macro name cannot contain any of the following characters:

    A space

    A period (WordPerfect for Windows uses the period between the file name and extension)

    The characters ^ + = \ / [ ] " ; : ? * < > |, which are either used in DOS or reserved for future use, and, therefore cannot be used in names of files under Windows 3.1

# Creating Instant Play Macros

If you have a macro that you use fairly often, you may find the routine of playing macros tedious (choosing Tools, Macro, Play, typing the macro name, and pressing Enter). WordPerfect 7 provides a shortcut to playing commonly used macros—the Ctrl+key method.

## Renaming a Previously Recorded Macro for Ctrl+Key Playback

You might not discover how often you'll use a certain macro until you have used it for a while. Although you gave the macro a regular name when you first recorded it, you can still play the macro by using the Ctrl+key method. All you need to do is rename the macro file.

To rename a previously recorded macro so that you can play it using the Ctrl key, follow these steps:

1. Choose File, Open; or press Ctrl+O. The Open dialog box appears.
2. Find and select the macro you want to rename. If the file is not listed, change folders and disks as needed.
3. Choose File, Rename; or press F2. A box is placed around the file name and the name is highlighted. This indicates that the name may be edited.
4. Type **ctrl*x*.wcm**. For the *x*, substitute the letter you want to use with the Ctrl key to play that macro (see fig. 12.4). If you want to play the macro by pressing Ctrl+Y, for example, rename the file **CTRLY.WCM**. Be sure to include the WCM file extension!
5. Press Enter.

**FIG. 12.4**
Rename a macro file as you would rename any file in Windows 95.

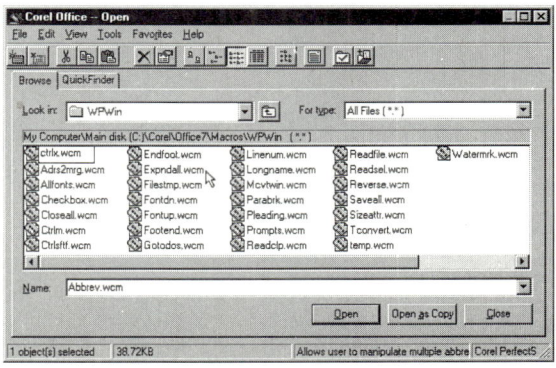

**N O T E**  Be careful not to use a Ctrl+letter combination already in use by WordPerfect 7 for accessing a feature. Ctrl+key macros are ignored if WordPerfect already has a shortcut feature assigned to the same keys. For example, if you name a macro *ctrlo.wcm*, pressing Ctrl+O displays the Open dialog box, rather than runs the CTRLO.WCM macro.

## Ctrl+Key and Shift+Ctrl+Key Combinations Already in Use

Table 12.1 lists the Ctrl+key and Shift+Ctrl+key combinations that WordPerfect already uses for shortcuts to features (when using the standard WordPerfect 7 keyboard layout, as defined in Edit, Preferences, Keyboard). Do not use these combinations for Ctrl+key and Shift+Ctrl+key macros; otherwise WordPerfect will ignore the macro and execute the shortcut instead, as described in the preceding note.

**Table 12.1  Ctrl+Key and Shift+Ctrl+Key Combinations Already in Use**

| Key | Pressing Ctrl+Key | Pressing Shift+Ctrl+Key |
|---|---|---|
| A | Select all | Expand abbreviation |
| B | Bold | Insert bullet |
| C | Copy text | Drop cap |
| D | Date text | Date code |
| E | Center justification | *<None>* |
| F | Find and replace | Find next |
| G | Go to | *<None>* |
| H | Outline body text | PrintHistoryDlg |
| I | Italic | *<None>* |
| J | Full justification | *<None>* |
| K | Case toggle | *<None>* |
| L | Left justification | Line break |
| M | PerfectScript command inserter | *<None>* |
| N | New blank document | New document |
| O | Open document | Outline define |
| P | Print dialog box | Print document |
| Q | Find QuickMark | Set QuickMark |
| R | Right justification | Redo |

| Key | Pressing Ctrl+Key | Pressing Shift+Ctrl+Key |
|---|---|---|
| S | Save document | Save all |
| T | Template | *<None>* |
| U | Underline | *<None>* |
| V | Paste | Paste simple |
| W | WP characters | *<None>* |
| X | Cut | *<None>* |
| Y | *<None>* | *<None>* |
| Z | Undo | Undelete |

## Playing Macros in Other Ways

WordPerfect provides three other methods with which you can play macros without using the Play Macro dialog box:

- *Assign a macro to a keyboard layout.* Keyboard layouts are special WordPerfect 7 files that enable you to change the meaning of the keys on your keyboard. You can assign a macro—that is, tell WordPerfect to play a macro whenever you press a certain key or key combination—to any of several hundred key combinations.

- *Add a macro button to a Toolbar.* When you click the button for the macro, the macro plays. The Toolbar, however, can only be used with the mouse. If you don't have or use a mouse, you can't take advantage of this option.

- *Choose any of up to the last four recently played macros by picking it from the Macro submenu.* Choose <u>T</u>ools, <u>M</u>acro. The menu that appears is the Macro submenu. At the bottom of this submenu, WordPerfect automatically places up to the last four macros you replayed, with the most recently played macro shown first.

For more information on the first two methods, see the section "Playing Macros Using Other Methods" later in this chapter.

# Stopping a Macro

Stopping a macro is sometimes necessary if something goes wrong during recording or playback. For example, you might discover that the macro is adding text to the wrong part of your document, so you want to stop it from doing any more damage. Or you might need to pause the macro so you can leave your desk to perform some other task.

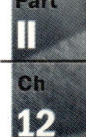

## Stopping a Macro During Recording

 If you need to stop recording, choose Tools, Macro, Record; or press Ctrl+F10. (If you're in a dialog box, you must exit the dialog box before you can stop macro recording.)

You can stop a macro at any time, even before WordPerfect 7 has a chance to record any of your actions. Although the macro may be *empty* (it has no commands to tell WordPerfect what to do), the macro file is created anyway. You can delete this file or record over it.

 If pressing Esc has no effect, press Ctrl+Break. Not all keyboards have a Break key. If yours does, it may be labeled Pause on the top and Break on the side.

## Stopping a Macro During Playback

To stop a macro during playback, press the Esc (Cancel) key. If you press the Esc key soon enough, you may be able to limit the damage. Keep in mind, however, that most macros play very quickly, and you probably will not have time to press the Esc key before the macro ends.

# Using the Macros that Come with WordPerfect

WordPerfect comes with a small selection of macros. Many of these macros are handy additions to what WordPerfect can already do for you. Included, for example, are macros that help you prepare a memo or convert spaces to tabs. The macros that come with WordPerfect also include more complex macros that you can use as examples of how to write more sophisticated macros. (To learn more about sophisticated macros, see Chapter 30, "Advanced Macro Techniques.") Table 12.2 lists some of the more useful macros that come with WordPerfect 7 and their functions.

**Table 12.2  Selected List of Macros Included with WordPerfect**

| Macro | Function |
|---|---|
| ALLFONTS.WCM | Creates a document listing the name and some sample text from every font available to the current printer. |
| CLOSEALL.WCM | Closes all documents currently open and prompts to save any that have been modified. |
| ENDFOOT.WCM | Converts endnotes to footnotes in a document or selected text. |
| FILESTMP.WCM | Places the file name and path of the current document in a header or footer. |

| Macro | Function |
|---|---|
| FONTDN.WCM | Decreases the font size of the selected text by 2 points. |
| FONTUP.WCM | Increases the font size of the selected text by 2 points. |
| LONGNAME.WCM | Converts a file from a short to a long file name by extracting the document description from the document summary. |
| PARABRK.WCM | Inserts graphical paragraph breaks between paragraphs. |
| PLEADING.WCM | Formats a standard legal "pleading paper." |
| REVERSE.WCM | Creates white text on black background (or other color options as set by the user) in document text or tables. |
| SAVEALL.WCM | Saves all documents currently open and prompts to save any that have been modified. |
| WATERMRK.WCM | Aids in creating a watermark using a WordPerfect WPG file. |

### TROUBLESHOOTING

**I can't find a macro that I just recorded.** WordPerfect stores macros either on the computer's hard disk drive or in the current template. If you record a macro in a template, you will not be able to find it if you later try to play a macro on disk, and vice versa. Be mindful where you are recording the macro, either on disk or in a template. Be sure to choose the appropriate macro play command, in the Tools menu, to play back your macro. For example, to play a disk file macro, choose Tools, Macro, Play. To play a template macro, choose Tools, Template Macro, Play.

**I can't find the macros that come with WordPerfect.** When WordPerfect is installed, the macro files are placed in a folder of their own, usually called MACROS. If you selected the Standard install option, this folder is located in the COREL\OFFICE\WPWIN subfolder. The files may be missing if they were not installed in the first place (meaning that the person who installed WordPerfect elected not to include them). You will need to install the macros from the original WordPerfect disks if you want to use them.

The files may also not be found if WordPerfect is looking in the wrong place for the macro files. Check the folder specified for macros in the Files Preferences dialog box (choose Edit, Preferences, Files).

# Using Macros for Writing and Editing Tasks

The most common macros are those that help you write and edit your documents. If you find yourself performing the same task repeatedly—you type the same list of names or addresses, or other information one or more times a day, for example—consider the job a good candidate for a macro. You can play the macro rather than retype the same information.

Listed in this section are several macros you can use to start your writing and editing macro collection. These macros perform common tasks, and you will probably use them quite often. For this reason, consider giving them Ctrl*x* names, as described in the section "Creating Instant Play Macros" earlier in this chapter.

> **CAUTION**
> The macro examples detailed in this chapter are given full names rather than Ctrlx names in the event that you already have a Ctrlx macro of the same name. If you do use Ctrlx names, be sure to use a name that's not currently in use; otherwise, you may accidentally erase a macro you want to keep.

## A Macro To Transpose Two Characters

The fingers of even the world's best touch typists sometimes get ahead of one another, and the result is transposed characters. Perhaps the most commonly transposed word is *teh* for *the*.

For all its other features, WordPerfect 7 lacks a built-in system to switch transposed characters. Most typists make the extra effort to delete and then type over the transposed characters. But you can record a simple macro that switches the positions of the characters and saves several keystrokes.

To record the transpose macro, first type two characters, such as **ab**. Make sure the cursor is to the immediate right of the *b*. After you record the macro, the characters are reversed to *ba*. To create the transpose macro, follow these steps:

1. Choose <u>T</u>ools, <u>M</u>acro, <u>R</u>ecord; or press Ctrl+F10. The Record Macro dialog box appears.
2. In the <u>N</u>ame text box, type **transp**, and choose Record or press Enter to start recording.
3. Press Backspace.
4. Press the left-arrow key (←).
5. Choose <u>E</u>dit, U<u>n</u>delete; or press Ctrl+Shift+Z. The Undelete dialog box appears.
6. Click <u>R</u>estore to undelete the previously deleted character.
7. Press the right-arrow key (→).
8. Choose <u>T</u>ools, <u>M</u>acro, <u>R</u>ecord; or press Ctrl+F10.

The letter transpose macro is complete.

To use the transpose macro, position the insertion point after the transposed characters. Then play the macro.

**N O T E** Rename the transpose macro so that you can run it by using the Ctrl+key shortcut, as explained in the earlier section "Creating Instant Play Macros." One possible name is CtrlSftT.WPM; you play the transpose macro by pressing Ctrl+Shift+T.

## A Macro To Write a Memo

Writing memos is such a common job that most people don't think twice about the mechanics involved in preparing a memo. But each memo you write contains a great deal of the same *boilerplate text*, or text that doesn't change from memo to memo. A macro makes the perfect memo-writing assistant, typing the boilerplate text for you. All you have to do is fill in the blanks.

In addition to the message, most memos contain four fields of information that you fill in:

- The date of the memo (Date:)
- Who the memo is from (From:)
- Who the memo is to (To:)
- The subject of the memo (Subject: or Re:)

To be most useful, you can make the memo-writing macro stop so that you can fill in each of the four fields of information. After you fill in the blanks, press the Enter key, and the macro continues.

You can tell WordPerfect to pause a macro during playback so that you can type the needed text. Whenever WordPerfect encounters a pause instruction, the macro stops temporarily and lets you type. When you press Enter, the macro starts again. For the memo-writing macro, you tell WordPerfect to pause two times so that you can enter the memo information. You will make the macro enter the fourth field of information— the date—by itself.

To record the memo macro, follow these steps:

1. Choose <u>T</u>ools, <u>M</u>acro, <u>R</u>ecord; or press Ctrl+F10. The Record Macro dialog box appears.
2. In the <u>N</u>ame text box, type **mymemo**, and choose Record or press Enter to start recording.
3. Type **Date:** and a space.

4. Choose Insert, Date, Date Text; or press Ctrl+D. This inserts the current date.
5. Press Enter twice to add a blank line between the Date field and the field that follows.
6. Type **From:** and your name. Press the Enter key twice.
7. Type **To:** and a space.
8. Choose Tools, Macro, Pause. Choose Tools, Macro, Pause again. This inserts a pausing command.
9. Press the Enter key.
10. Type **Subject:** and a space.
11. Repeat steps 8 and 9 to insert another pause instruction.
12. Choose Tools, Macro, Record; or press Ctrl+F10.

The memo macro is finished. Clear the document by choosing File, Close, No.

To play the memo macro, choose Macro, Tools, Play; or press Alt+F10. Type **mymemo** and press Enter. The macro inserts the date and the From: line (with your name). It then inserts the To: line, and pauses and waits for you to enter text.

Type the text and press Enter. The Enter key unpauses the macro, which continues to the next memo field, where you type the name of the memo's recipient.

Repeat this process until you have filled in all the memo fields. When the macro finishes, you can complete the rest of the memo.

# Using Macros for Common Formatting Tasks

As with writing and editing, you can simplify common formatting tasks—changing the margins, for example—by recording them as macros. To change the margins of a document from the regular 1-inch margins to 2-inch margins on all sides, you must perform at least 10 steps—more if you use the mouse. If you must change the margins of your documents often, you can save a great deal of work by recording the margin change as a macro and then playing the macro whenever you want the new margins.

**NOTE** Another time-saver is the Styles feature of WordPerfect 7, discussed in detail in Chapter 10, "Using Styles." You can use styles to change the formatting of your documents. A style can contain one or many formatting changes. In fact, if you need to make many formatting changes (set new margins or tab stops, add a header and footer, and so on), use styles instead of macros.

▶ See "Understanding Styles," **p. 334**
▶ See "Creating Styles," **p. 340**

Follow these steps to record a macro that changes the left and right margins to 1 1/2 inches.

1. Choose <u>T</u>ools, <u>M</u>acro, <u>R</u>ecord; or press Ctrl+F10. The Record Macro dialog box appears.
2. In the <u>N</u>ame text box, type **marg15**, and choose Play or press Enter to start recording.

3. Choose Fo<u>r</u>mat, <u>M</u>argins; or press Ctrl+F8. The Margin Format dialog box appears.
4. Change the <u>L</u>eft margin to **1.50**".
5. Change the <u>R</u>ight margin to **1.50**".
6. Press Enter until the program returns to the main WordPerfect editing screen.
7. Choose <u>T</u>ools, <u>M</u>acro, <u>R</u>ecord; or press Ctrl+F10 to complete the recording of the margin setting macro.

To use the macro, place the insertion point where you want to change margins, and play the macro.

# Playing Macros Using Other Methods

In this chapter, you have learned how to play macros by using the Play Macro dialog box, and by pressing the Ctrl key and a letter key. Two more ways exist to play macros: using a keyboard layout and using the Toolbar. Both methods enable you to play your favorite macros without using the Play Macro dialog box.

## Assigning a Macro to a Keyboard Layout

WordPerfect is a "do-it-your-way" kind of program; you can personalize it so that it behaves in the way *you* want, not the way some programmer thought it ought to be. One of the ways to personalize WordPerfect is to create a *keyboard layout*. With a keyboard layout you can change the meaning of almost any key on the keyboard. You can assign unused key combinations to favorite macros. Your keyboard layout is saved in a special file, to which WordPerfect refers each time it starts. You can change keyboard layouts whenever you want and turn off this feature when you no longer want to use it.

Chapter 9, "Customizing WordPerfect," details keyboard layouts—how they work and how to create them. In this chapter, you concentrate on creating a new keyboard layout and assigning a macro to a normally unused key combination. You use the TRANSP character-transposing macro detailed earlier in this chapter as the macro to assign to the keyboard layout; however, you can substitute any other macro.

**NOTE** Only the keys that you specifically change in a keyboard layout differ from the original layout that WordPerfect uses. The functions of all the other keys remain the same.

**NOTE** The following instructions assume that you are assigning a macro on disk, rather than a template macro, to a keyboard layout.

To create a keyboard layout and assign a macro to it, follow these steps:

1. Choose Edit, Preferences. The Preferences dialog box appears.
2. Double-click the Keyboard icon. The Keyboard Preferences dialog box appears (see fig. 12.5). At least one keyboard layout is listed: WPWin 7 Keyboard. This keyboard layout is the one built into WordPerfect 7 and cannot be deleted or edited.

**FIG. 12.5**
The Keyboard Preferences dialog box lets you select and create new keyboard layouts.

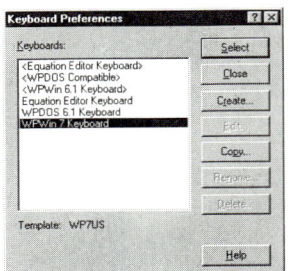

3. Click Create. The Create Keyboard dialog box appears.
4. Provide a name for your new keyboard layout. The name can be up to 32 characters, and can contain spaces.
5. Choose OK or press Enter. The Keyboard Shortcuts dialog box appears (see fig. 12.6).
6. In the Choose A Shortcut Key list (on the left side of the Keyboard Shortcuts dialog box), find and select the key or key combination you want to use.
7. Select the Macros tab.
8. Choose Assign Macro To Key. The Select Macro dialog box appears.
9. Type the name of the macro you want to play (in this case, **TRANSP.WCM**), and choose Select.

**FIG. 12.6**
The Keyboard Shortcuts dialog box enables you to change the functions of just about any key and key combination on the keyboard.

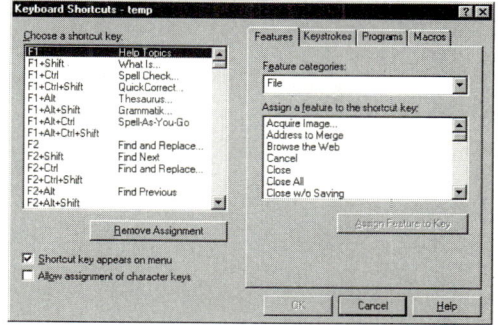

10. When WordPerfect asks if you want to save the macro name with the full path, answer Yes or No. Answering Yes records the macro with its path; answering No records just the name of the macro. As a general rule, choose Yes unless you are going to share your keyboard layouts and macros with other people.

11. Choose OK to close the Keyboard Editor.

12. Highlight the new keyboard and choose Select.

The selected macro is now accessible by pressing the key or key combination you chose.

To play the TRANSP macro, type some text (so that you have something to transpose), and press the keys you assigned in step 6. If you used Ctrl+F12, for example, press these keys to transpose two characters.

 **TIP** To turn off your custom keyboard layout, choose Edit, Preferences; then choose Keyboard. Highlight WPWin 7 Keyboard and choose Select.

You can assign additional macros to your custom keyboard layout by repeating steps 6–10.

### TROUBLESHOOTING

**I want to record a macro that exits WordPerfect, but when I try, the Exit command in the File menu is dimmed out (unavailable).** WordPerfect will not allow you to leave the program while a macro is recording. A macro that exits WordPerfect is not possible.

**I tried recording a macro where I switch to another Windows program. When the macro is played back, nothing happens.** WordPerfect only records actions inside the WordPerfect program and other selected Corel applications (such as Quattro Pro and Presentations). As long as you stay within WordPerfect or one of these other applications, your actions are recorded in the macro. Once you leave these programs, macro recording is suspended until you come back. If you need a macro that controls other Windows programs, use the Macro Recorder facility that comes with Windows.

**A macro that has worked before is now ending in an error message.** Macros must be played back under the same circumstances in which they were recorded. The most common reason for a macro to end in an error message is that the macro searches for text that it can't find in the current document. Other reasons a macro can end in an error message include:

- A macro that opens a document when nine documents are already open.
- A macro that creates a header when played in the Header window.
- A macro that selects a font that is not supported by your printer.
- A macro that opens a document that no longer exists on your computer's hard disk drive.

## Adding a Macro to a Toolbar

If you use a mouse with WordPerfect 7, you have another option to playing macros: you can click a button on a Toolbar. Unlike the keyboard, which requires that you remember the key combinations you used, the Toolbar has the advantage of showing you the available macros. The disadvantage to the Toolbar is that you are limited to the number of buttons you can display at one time. Although you can scroll the Toolbar to see more buttons, it's better to use the Toolbar when all your regular buttons are always in view.

▶ See "Customizing Keyboards," **p. 324**
▶ See "Customizing a Toolbar," **p. 420**

Associating a macro with a Toolbar is a little easier than assigning a macro to a keyboard layout. Chapter 13, "Working with Toolbars," discusses Toolbars in depth, but a few basic steps exist. The following exercise adds a button to the current default Toolbar. Unless you have switched to a different Toolbar, the default is WordPerfect, which comes with WordPerfect 7. You can use a different Toolbar, however, or create a Toolbar of your own. Chapter 13, "Working with Toolbars," provides more details on how to do this.

**NOTE** The following instructions assume you are assigning a macro on disk, rather than a template macro, to the Toolbar.

To add a macro button to the current Toolbar, follow these steps:

1. Choose Edit, Preferences; then choose Toolbar. The Toolbar Preferences dialog box appears (see fig. 12.7).
2. Choose Edit. The Toolbar Editor appears.

**FIG. 12.7**
Use the Toolbar Preferences dialog box to create and edit Toolbars.

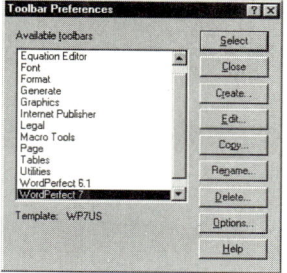

3. Choose the Macros tab.
4. Choose <u>A</u>dd Macro. Type the name of the macro you want to play (such as TRANSP.WCM), and choose <u>S</u>elect.
5. When WordPerfect asks if you want to save the macro name with the full path, answer <u>Y</u>es or <u>N</u>o. Answering <u>Y</u>es records the macro with its path; answering <u>N</u>o records just the name of the macro. As a general rule, choose <u>Y</u>es unless you are going to share your Toolbars and macros with other people.
6. Choose OK to close the Toolbar Editor.
7. Choose Close until you are back at the document window.

 To use the new button on the Toolbar, display the Toolbar if necessary by choosing <u>V</u>iew, <u>T</u>oolbars/Ruler. The Toolbar item must have the check box selected. Once the Toolbar is displayed, locate and then click the new button on the Toolbar to play your macro.

 To select the macro you want from the Macro menu, choose <u>T</u>ools, <u>M</u>acro, and the name of the macro; or press Alt+T, M, and the number of the macro.

**N O T E** WordPerfect also includes a handy feature bar you can use when writing and editing macros. When you edit a macro file (choose <u>T</u>ools, <u>M</u>acro, <u>E</u>dit), the Macro Feature Bar automatically appears. Or you can manually display the feature bar by choosing <u>T</u>ools, <u>M</u>acro, <u>M</u>acro Bar. For information about the Macro Feature Bar, see Chapter 30, "Advanced Macro Techniques."

# Managing Macro Files

After you begin to use the Macros feature of WordPerfect 7, you'll want to consider how you can best manage your macro files; otherwise, you may forget what macros you have and lose track of where they are on your computer's hard disk drive.

When you record a macro, WordPerfect puts it in one of two places:

- *The main WordPerfect folder.* This folder contains the bulk of WordPerfect's files, including WPWIN.EXE (the WordPerfect program itself).
- *A special folder just for macros.* This folder is specified in the Location of Files dialog box. To see this dialog box, choose Edit, Preferences; then choose Files. The File Preferences dialog box appears. Choose Merge/Macro to see the folder (or folders) used for macros.

The more macros you record, the more reason you have to create a folder just for them. A good place for your macro folder is \COREL\OFFICE7\MACROS\WPWIN\ (this folder contains the main WordPerfect files; the exact name of the folder may be different on your computer, depending on how WordPerfect 7 was installed). A MACROS folder under \COREL\OFFICE7\MACROS\WPWIN\ is automatically created for you if you use the Standard option when installing WordPerfect.

## Creating a Folder for Macros

You can use the Windows Explorer to create a new folder for your macros. Follow the instructions provided in the Windows User Guide. Alternatively, you can use WordPerfect's Open dialog box to create new folders by choosing File, Open, New, Folder. See Chapter 29, "Advanced File Management," for more information.

Check to see whether a folder for macros already exists. The folders are always listed first in the Windows Explorer list of files.

## Moving Files into the MACROS Folder

A MACROS folder is useless unless macro files are placed there. You must scan through the list of files using the Windows Explorer (or WordPerfect's Open dialog box) to pick out the macro files.

## Specifying the Macros Folder in Location of Files

You need to tell WordPerfect where to find the macro files by following these steps:

1. Choose Edit, Preferences; then choose Files. The File Preferences dialog box appears (see fig. 12.8).

**FIG. 12.8**
Use the Files Preferences dialog box to tell WordPerfect for Windows where to look for macro files.

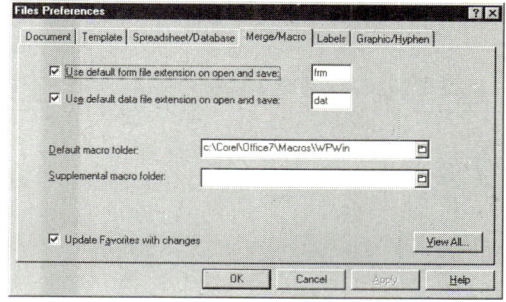

2. Choose the Merge/Macro tab.
3. Choose Default Macro Folder.
4. Type the full path of the folder that contains the macro files, such as **C:\WPWIN7\MACROS**.
5. Press Enter or choose OK.

**N O T E** If you are on a network, you can also specify an alternate folder for *shared macros*, which are macros stored on a network server that your entire office might use. To specify a path for shared macros, choose Supplemental Macro Folder. Type the full path of the folder that contains the shared macros, and press Enter.

6. Choose OK or Close until you return to the main WordPerfect editing screen.

## Giving Macros Descriptive File Names

Placing your macros in a central repository folder is the first step in managing your growing macro library. If you create many macros, however, after a period of time you may forget what certain macros do, and you may even forget that you recorded a macro to handle a particular task.

You can guard against macros falling into obscurity by always giving your macros descriptive file names, which is not quite as easy as it sounds because you are limited to a maximum of eight characters for each name. Whenever possible, give your macros abbreviated names that reflect the tasks they perform, such as DBLSPACE for a macro that sets line spacing to two, or SPELLWRD for a macro that performs a spell check on the current word.

Avoid generic terms like MYMACRO or TEST, and be specific in describing the macros function. A macro named FONTCHNG probably changes fonts, but to what font?

Because Windows 95 has the ability to use long file names, you may want to take advantage of this feature. Refer to the previous section "All Macros Use Only Valid Windows 95 File Names" for more information on using long file names with macros.

## Deleting Macros You No Longer Need

Recording a macro doesn't mean that you have to keep the macro around forever. Unnecessary macro files clutter up your computer's hard disk drive, and they take up valuable space that can be better used by the files you do want to keep. Delete macro files you no longer use.

To delete a macro you no longer want to keep, follow these steps:

1. Choose File, Open, or press Ctrl+O. The Open dialog box appears.
2. Find and highlight the file you want to delete (change the folder and drive, if necessary).
3. Choose File, Delete; or press Delete.
4. WordPerfect asks whether you want to send the file to the Recycle Bin; answer Yes.
5. Repeat steps 2–4 for each additional macro file you want to delete.
6. Choose Cancel.

**TIP** You may select multiple files to delete at the same time by pressing the Ctrl key while you select the files.

**NOTE** Macros that were recorded into either the default or current template are not deleted by removing a file on your computer's hard disk drive.

Rather, to delete a macro in a template, choose Tools, Template Macro, Play. A list of the macros contained in that template is displayed. Choose the macro you want to delete; then choose Delete.

CHAPTER 13

# Working with Toolbars

*by George Beinhorn and Judy Petersen*

This chapter discusses using and customizing WordPerfect's many Toolbars and the Power Bar.

*Toolbars* are an innovative way to carry out commands. Instead of searching through menus or issuing multiple keyboard commands, you simply click a button with the mouse to carry out the desired function. WordPerfect comes with a variety of preconfigured Toolbars for specialized tasks, such as editing equations, working with fonts, or editing graphics. You can configure your own customized Toolbars, and you can place any WordPerfect feature on the Toolbar. You can even assign macros to a button, and you can quickly switch between Toolbars. ■

- **Use Toolbar and Power Bar buttons**
  Toolbars and the Power Bar put many of WordPerfect's features a mouse-click away.

- **Switching between Toolbars**
  Whether you are working in a table or formatting pages, WordPerfect has special-purpose Toolbars that make your work easier.

- **Adding, deleting, and moving Toolbar and Power Bar buttons**
  You can customize the WordPerfect Toolbars and the Power Bar, or design one of your very own.

- **Moving the position of the Toolbar on-screen**
  When you configure WordPerfect to suit your work habits, you also can move the Toolbar to another position.

# Why Use the Toolbar and Power Bar?

WordPerfect 7 makes locating program commands easy. Using the mouse with pull-down menus soon becomes natural, and after you become familiar with the menu structure, you can quickly access commands with keystrokes.

So why use buttons? Toolbars are unique in that you can make them perform multiple commands, and you can customize them with your own most-used program functions and macros. You can create several Toolbars for specific tasks, and you can toggle the Toolbar display on and off with a single mouse click on the Power Bar. Figure 13.1 shows the default WordPerfect 7 Toolbar.

**FIG. 13.1**
The default Toolbar includes buttons for common WordPerfect commands. To display other supplied Toolbars, click the Toolbar with the right mouse button and choose a Toolbar from the pop-up QuickMenu.

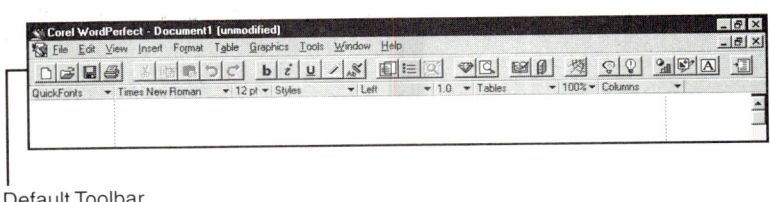

Default Toolbar

The Power Bar is equally convenient but serves the slightly different purpose of performing common, everyday chores that mostly have to do with creating and formatting text and turning on special features such as tables and columns. The Power Bar offers the added advantage of bypassing dialog boxes because selecting any of the Power Bar buttons displays a drop-down list of choices.

In practice, you will probably find that you prefer to perform some tasks with the keyboard and others with the Toolbars and the Power Bar. A unique advantage of the Toolbars and Power Bar is that you never forget a program command. In fact, moving the mouse cursor onto a button displays a description of its function in the title bar.

Above and beyond the Toolbars' everyday utility, clicking buttons to execute complicated program commands and macros is fun!

# Hiding and Viewing the Toolbar

You can turn the Toolbar on and off in four ways:

- Choose View, Toolbar.
- Click the right mouse button anywhere on the Toolbar to display the QuickMenu, and choose Hide Toolbar.
- Add the Toolbar button to the Toolbar or Power Bar, and then click the Toolbar button.
- Choose View, Hide Bars or press Alt+Shift+F5.

 To quickly toggle the Toolbar off, add a Toolbar button to the Power Bar.

When you choose View, Hide Bars or press Alt+Shift+F5, WordPerfect displays the Hide Bars Information dialog box. If you choose OK in this dialog box, the menu bar, Power Bar, Scroll Bars, Toolbar, Ruler Bar, and status bar are removed from the screen. To restore the bars to the screen, press Alt+V and choose Hide Bars, or just press Esc.

Hiding all bars is useful when you need to view a larger area of a document.

 To temporarily turn off all bars for a "clean screen," choose View, Hide Bars or press Alt+Shift+F5. Choose OK. To turn bars on again, press Alt+Shift+F5 (you don't have to choose OK).

# Switching Between Toolbars

WordPerfect provides 15 predefined Toolbars. There are two ways to switch to a different Toolbar:

- You can choose Edit, Preferences, Toolbar to display the Toolbar Preferences dialog box shown in figure 13.2; then highlight a Toolbar in the list and choose Select.
- You can right-click the current Toolbar to display the QuickMenu and switch to another Toolbar by clicking its name. Figure 13.3 shows the Toolbar QuickMenu.

**FIG. 13.2**
The Toolbars available with WordPerfect are listed in the Toolbar Preferences dialog box.

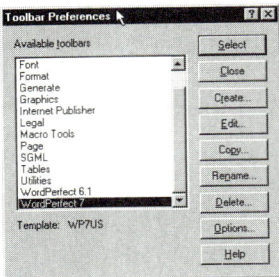

**FIG. 13.3**
To quickly switch to another Toolbar, right-click the Toolbar to access the Toolbar QuickMenu. The default is the WordPerfect 7 Toolbar.

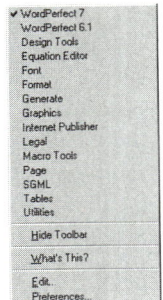

You can customize the Power Bar, but you cannot switch to another Power Bar, and you can display only one row of Power Bar buttons. To access a greater number of program operations with the mouse, customize the Toolbar.

# Examining the Toolbar and Power Bar Icons

If you look closely at the Toolbar icons, notice that their design identifies the type of task they perform. For example, the first button on the Toolbar is New Blank Document. The button displays an icon of a page, which represents a document in the world of Windows. Similarly, the Print button shows a printer, and the icon on the Cut button is a pair of scissors.

Just as WordPerfect grays out unavailable menu options, Toolbar buttons that are currently unavailable are grayed.

Some buttons serve as visual indicators; for example, the font attribute buttons such as Bold, Italic, and Underline. Whenever your insertion point is between a pair of attribute codes, the button for that attribute appears pressed in.

The default appearance for the buttons on the Power Bar is text only. The text describes the current status of each button, such as the name of the font face in use, the font size, the number of columns, if any, and the zoom percent. The down-arrow on the button indicates that a drop-down menu of choices appears when the button is selected.

## Working with the Toolbar

You may want to customize one of WordPerfect's supplied Toolbars, removing buttons that you seldom use and installing buttons that perform frequently used tasks. You can also rearrange the buttons to suit your personal preference.

 You can select common formatting functions by clicking the Ruler Bar, Power Bar, or Toolbar, or by using a QuickMenu.

### Positioning the Toolbar On-Screen

By default, the Toolbar appears horizontally at the top of the screen, under the main menu. You can move the Toolbar to the bottom edge of the screen, under the horizontal scroll bar, or vertically at the left or right edge of the document window. Additionally, you can display the Toolbar in a rectangular "palette" anywhere on-screen.

You can position the Toolbar with the mouse. Move the mouse pointer to a space between buttons on the Toolbar until it becomes a hand, and drag the Toolbar to a new location. You can position the Toolbar at the top, left, bottom, or right edge of the screen.

If you drag the Toolbar into the document window, the bar outline becomes a rectangle. When you release the mouse button, the Toolbar becomes a palette. To move the palette, point to its title bar and drag it to a new location. To resize the palette, move the mouse pointer onto an edge until it becomes a double-headed arrow, and drag the edge of the palette to the desired size. Figure 13.4 shows the Toolbar displayed in a palette.

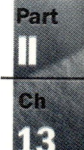 If the palette obscures options on the dialog box, use its title bar to drag it to a new location.

**FIG. 13.4**
Whether the Toolbar appears as a bar or a palette, you can drag it to a new location. As you drag, the Toolbar's shape is indicated by a gray-lined box.

To move the Toolbar using the keyboard, complete these steps:

1. Choose Edit, Preferences to display the Preferences dialog box.
2. Choose Toolbar, and then choose Options.
3. In the Toolbar Options dialog box (shown in fig. 13.5), choose Left, Top, Right, Bottom, or Palette; then choose OK.
4. Choose Close; then choose Close again to return to the editing screen.

**FIG. 13.5**
You can place the Toolbar at the left, top, right, or bottom edge of the screen. Placing the Toolbar in a palette enables you to drag it out of the way of on-screen text.

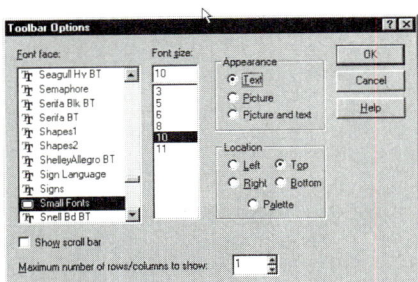

To restore the palette to a horizontal or vertical Toolbar, drag it to an edge of the screen until the outline becomes an elongated horizontal or vertical bar, and release the mouse button.

## Working with Large Toolbars

Many of the Toolbars supplied with WordPerfect, including the default Toolbar, contain more buttons than can fit in a single row or column on-screen. If a Toolbar extends past the edge of the screen, WordPerfect can display scroll arrows at the right end of the Toolbar (for a horizontal Toolbar) or at the bottom of the Toolbar (for a vertical Toolbar). To scroll the Toolbar, just click the arrows.

If you prefer to avoid scrolling the Toolbar, you can display up to three rows of buttons on-screen. Both options are set in the Preferences dialog box by following these steps:

1. Choose Edit, Preferences, Toolbar, Options. Or, right-click the Toolbar to display the QuickMenu, and choose Preferences, Options.

2. In Maximum Number Of Rows/Columns To Show, choose or enter **1**, **2**, or **3**.

   If you prefer, choose Show Scroll Bar.

3. Choose OK, Close, Close.

Toolbars with more than one row displayed leave little room on-screen for your document. To conserve editing space, you can change the style of Toolbar buttons, as described in the following section.

**NOTE** Try this alternative to coping with rows of Toolbar buttons. Add the Toolbar button on the Power Bar so that you can quickly hide (and later unhide) the Toolbar when you need to see more of your document. You may need to remove a button from the Toolbar to make room for the Toolbar button.

## Changing the Button Style

WordPerfect can display Toolbar buttons with text and pictures (the default), or with pictures or with text only. Switching to text-only or pictures-only saves screen space and displays more buttons on-screen without the need for scrolling.

**TIP** Buttons formatted with the Picture option take up the least space horizontally on Toolbars; the Text option takes the least vertical space on Toolbars.

To change the button style, follow these steps:

1. Choose Edit, Preferences, Toolbar, Options. Or, right-click the Toolbar to display the QuickMenu, and choose Preferences, Options.

2. In the Toolbar Options dialog box (refer to fig. 13.5), choose Text, Picture, or Picture And Text. Your changes are reflected on-screen behind the dialog box.

3. Choose OK, Close, Close to return to the editing screen.

Figure 13.6 shows the same Toolbar formatted as pictures only, text only, and pictures and text.

**FIG. 13.6**
Display the most buttons on a text only or pictures and text Toolbar by moving the Toolbar to the left or right edge of the screen.

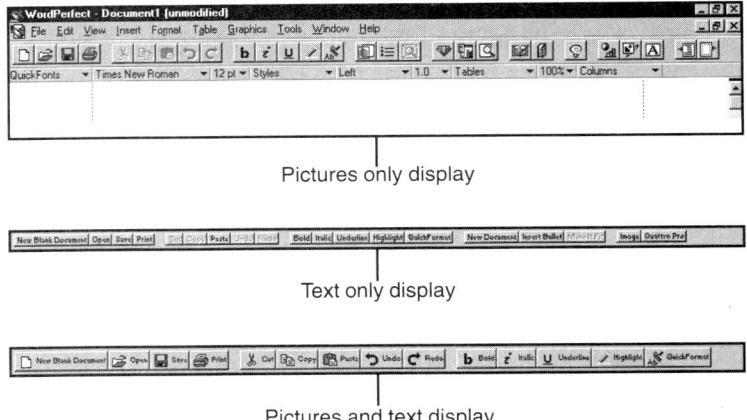

Pictures only display

Text only display

Pictures and text display

# Customizing a Toolbar

You can reposition buttons on a Toolbar, and you can assign program functions, keystrokes, or macros to buttons. Before you customize the Toolbar, however, remember that you can perform many common WordPerfect operations with the Power Bar and Ruler Bar.

WordPerfect allows you to restore the default Power Bar. The WordPerfect Toolbar cannot be edited permanently and you cannot restore another Toolbar to its default configuration. It's therefore a good idea to make a backup copy of a Toolbar before you edit it by following these steps:

1. Choose Edit, Preferences, Toolbar.
2. In the Toolbar Preferences dialog box, choose Copy.
3. In the Copy Toolbars dialog box, select a Toolbar from the Select Toolbars To Copy text box, and choose Copy.
4. In the Overwrite/New Name dialog box, type a new name for the copied Toolbar in the Object text box.
5. Choose OK.

WordPerfect lists the copy of the Toolbar in the Available Toolbars list box, where you can now select it (or the copied Toolbar) and choose Edit to customize. The new Toolbar is also included on the Toolbar QuickMenu.

## Moving Toolbar Buttons

You can move the buttons on the Toolbar. You might want to place the buttons you use most frequently at the left end of the bar, for example. You can group buttons by adding spacers between the groups.

To reposition buttons on the Toolbar, follow these steps:

1. Choose Edit, Preferences, Toolbar, Edit. Or, right-click the Toolbar to display the QuickMenu, and choose Edit.

   WordPerfect displays the Toolbar Editor dialog box (see fig. 13.7).

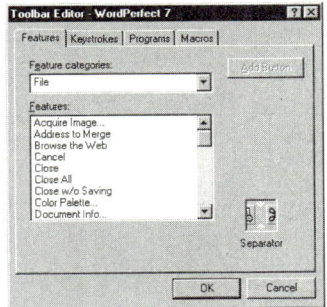

**FIG. 13.7**
You can use the Toolbar Editor dialog box to move buttons. You can also delete a button by simply dragging it off the Toolbar.

2. With the Toolbar Editor displayed, drag a button to a new location.
3. To insert a spacer between buttons, drag the spacer symbol at the bottom of the dialog box between two buttons on the Toolbar and release the mouse button.
4. To delete a button, drag it off the Toolbar; or right-click and choose Delete.
5. Choose OK, Close, Close to return to the editing screen. Or choose Cancel to return the Toolbar to the way it was before editing.

## Assigning Program Features to Buttons

You can assign any WordPerfect program feature to a Toolbar button. For example, you might decide to add a Save All button to the Layout Toolbar if you frequently perform page layout operations with several files open at once. To assign a program feature to a Toolbar button, follow these steps:

1. Choose Edit, Preferences, Toolbar, Edit. Or, right-click the Toolbar and choose Edit.
2. In the Toolbar Editor—Graphics dialog box (refer to fig. 13.7), choose the Features tab.

3. Choose F<u>e</u>ature Categories and select a category of commands from the list.

   The categories correspond to the WordPerfect menus. When you choose a category, WordPerfect displays the commands from the corresponding menu in the F<u>e</u>atures list.

4. In the F<u>e</u>atures list box, select the feature you want to add to the Toolbar.

   WordPerfect highlights the <u>A</u>dd Button and displays the button's graphic and title. The title explains the button's function and appears in the document window's title bar when you move the mouse cursor onto the button.

5. Choose <u>A</u>dd Button to add the button to the bar.

6. Move the buttons and add optional spacers as described in the preceding section, "Moving Toolbar Buttons."

7. Choose OK, <u>C</u>lose, <u>C</u>lose to return to the document window.

 **TIP** If you make a mistake while editing a Toolbar, press Esc to remove all newly added buttons from the Toolbar.

You can also add a new button by choosing a feature from a WordPerfect menu while the Toolbar Editor dialog box is displayed. To move the Toolbar Editor out of the way of the program menus, click the dialog box title bar and drag it. You can also click an empty area or spacer in the Toolbar and drag it to a new location.

## Assigning a Text Script to a Button

You can create buttons that play back text by following these steps:

1. Choose <u>E</u>dit, P<u>r</u>eferences, <u>T</u>oolbar, <u>E</u>dit. Or, right-click a button on the Toolbar and choose <u>E</u>dit.

2. Choose the Keystrokes tab.

3. In the <u>T</u>ype The Keystrokes This Button Will Play text box, type the script.

   WordPerfect word-wraps the text in the box. You cannot apply formatting. Text entered with a script button takes on the formatting currently in effect at the insertion point location in a document.

4. Choose <u>A</u>dd Keystrokes. WordPerfect creates a new button for the script.

5. Choose OK, <u>C</u>lose, <u>C</u>lose to return to the document window.

Move the mouse pointer to the new script button, and you see a box with the first word of the script. Refer to the later section "Customizing a Button's Text and Picture" for instructions on how to edit this button.

**N O T E**  You can include command keystrokes such as Ctrl+S or F6 as well as characters in a script. To do so, you use the SendKeys Markup Language. To learn how to use this feature, select the Macros, Macros Programming topic in Help, and then find the SendKeys topic using Index. If the Macro Help module has not been installed from the CD-ROM, WordPerfect displays a Help topic that lists the steps for installing WordPerfect Macro Help.

Scripts are not interchangeable with macros. You may find that the keystroke you want to use does not work when you play the script. If this happens, create a macro to perform the task, and then assign the macro to the keyboard.

## Assigning Macros to Buttons

You can create Toolbar buttons that insert text and carry out complex strings of program commands. For example, you can create a button that retrieves a memo template and moves the insertion point to the first text-entry area. Another button could open a new document and retrieve an invoice form. To learn more about macros, see Chapter 12, "Creating Macros," and Chapter 30, "Advanced Macro Techniques."

▶ **See** "Adding a Macro to a Toolbar," **p. 408**

To create a Toolbar button that runs a macro, follow these steps:

1. Choose Edit, Preferences, Toolbar, Edit. Or, right-click a button on the Toolbar and choose Edit. WordPerfect displays the Toolbar Editor—Graphics dialog box.

2. Choose Macros and then choose Add Macro. WordPerfect displays the Select Macro dialog box (see fig. 13.8).

3. To add a macro, type its name or select it from the Filename list box and choose Select.

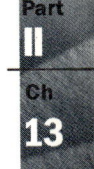

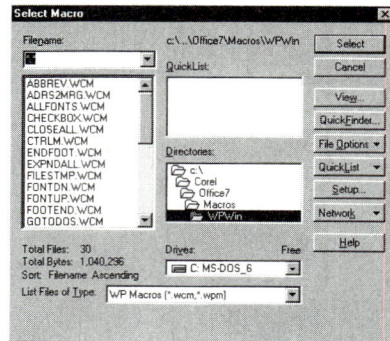

**FIG. 13.8**
In the Select Macro dialog box, choose the macro you want to add to the Toolbar.

You can also add a macro that is part of a template. Template macros are useful for performing document-specific tasks, such as moving from a Date: field to a Name: field on an employee health insurance records form. Follow these steps:

1. Choose Add Template Macro in the Toolbar Editor dialog box.
2. Enter the name of the macro in the Name text box or choose the macro from the Macros In Template list box, which includes all the macros in the template.

   If the macro you want is in the default template rather than the current template, choose Location and select Default Template. You can also choose to use the current template as the default by choosing Use As Default.

   Choose OK. The macros from the template you selected are now listed.
3. After selecting a macro, choose Select to return to the Toolbar Editor dialog box.

WordPerfect creates a new button and places it on the Toolbar. Because all the macro buttons look alike, try customizing the picture if you add more than one button.

## Customizing a Button's Text and Picture

Not only can you create a new Toolbar button as described in the preceding section, but you can customize its appearance with your own text graphic symbol.

To customize a button's appearance, follow these steps:

1. Choose Edit, Preferences, Toolbar, Edit. Or, right-click a button on the Toolbar and choose Edit. WordPerfect displays the Toolbar Editor dialog box.
2. Double-click the button you want to customize, or right-click the button and choose Customize from the QuickMenu. WordPerfect displays the Customize Button dialog box (see fig. 13.9).

**FIG. 13.9**
You can customize the text or graphic image of a button. To maintain a look consistent with other WordPerfect task-specific buttons, you may want to copy and customize existing buttons.

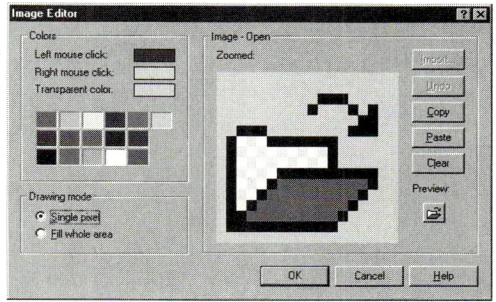

3. To change the button's text, choose Button Text and type the new text.

   You can type up to 25 characters, but WordPerfect uses only the amount of text that can fit on a button in one line on the current button display mode: text and picture, picture only, or text only.

4. To change the description that WordPerfect displays when you move the mouse cursor onto the button, choose QuickTip and type the new description. You can type up to 130 characters.

5. Choose OK, Close, Close to return to the document window.

You can edit a button's graphic icon or create a button with a graphic image of your own design by following these steps:

1. From the Customize Button dialog box (refer to fig. 13.9), choose Edit.

   WordPerfect displays the Image Editor dialog box (see fig. 13.10).

 **TIP** To create a button graphic from scratch, choose Clear to clear the Zoomed Image display.

**FIG. 13.10**
In the default configuration of the Image Editor dialog box, clicking in the image area draws, and clicking the right mouse button deletes.

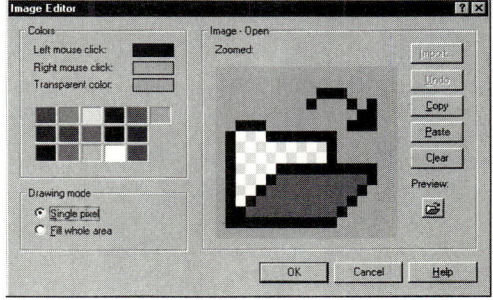

2. To draw, first click the left mouse button on a color in the Colors area. The Left Mouse Click sample display changes to the color you selected.

3. Move the cursor into the image area and click the left mouse button to insert a square of color.

4. To erase, make sure that the Right Mouse Click sample display shows the same background color as the image display, and click with the right mouse button on the area of color that you want to remove.

 You can drag to "paint" with the mouse, but clicking on one area (pixel) at a time is safer—you're less likely to run over and change an adjoining area's color unintentionally.

5. To fill a large area with color, choose Fill, point the mouse cursor to an enclosed area in the image display, and click. WordPerfect fills the enclosed area with the color that's currently assigned to the left mouse button.

Your changes are shown in the small sample display in the lower-left corner of the dialog box. You can paint in the sample display, but you cannot add colors outside the area covered in the Zoomed Image display. For example, you cannot fill a button with a color.

6. To undo your most recent changes, choose Undo.

7. After you finish drawing, choose OK until you return to the editing screen.

When you find a graphic image you like and want to use it on a button, you can retrieve the image from the Windows 95 Paint Accessory or another paint program and select the portion of the image you want to use. Choose Edit, Copy In Paint Program, switch to WordPerfect, and choose Paste in the Image Editor.

You can capture the current screen at any time in Windows 95 using the Print Screen key. Then choose Paste In Paint to insert the captured image. You can now select part of the image to copy to the Toolbar Image Editor. By using this method, you can easily capture icons for other programs that you want to add to a Toolbar.

# Customizing the Power Bar

The Power Bar is intended as a tool for invoking a handful of frequently used functions, such as choosing a font or style, creating and sizing a table, and justifying text. The Power Bar handles these common chores so that you can place more advanced commands on the Toolbar.

You can customize the Power Bar just as you can the Toolbar, but you can't move the Power Bar to a new location on-screen.

## Hiding and Viewing the Power Bar

You can toggle the Power Bar on and off in three ways:

- Choose View, Toolbars and choose Power Bar to remove the X from the check box.
- Right-click anywhere on the Power Bar and choose Hide Power Bar.
- Choose View, Hide Bars or press Alt+Shift+F5.

Choose this third option if you need to view a larger area of a document. Refer to the earlier section, "Hiding and Viewing the Toolbar," for more information about this technique.

## Customizing Power Bar Button Faces

As with the Toolbar, you can change the font face and size of the text on the Power Bar buttons to display text, pictures, or both. To customize these buttons, follow these steps:

1. Choose Edit, Preferences, Power Bar. Or, right-click anywhere on the Power Bar and choose Options. WordPerfect displays the Power Bar Options dialog box shown in figure 13.11.

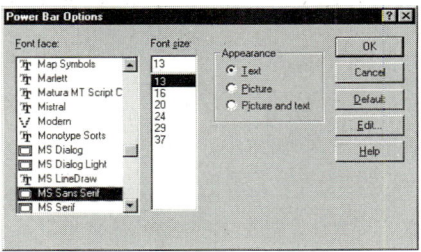

**FIG. 13.11**
Use the Power Bar Options dialog box to select a font face and size and to change the appearance of the button face.

2. Select a font to use for the button text from the Font Face list box.
3. From the Font Size list box, select a new size for the button text.
4. Select whether to display Text, Picture, or Picture And Text on the face of the button.
5. Choose OK to close the dialog box.

Using only pictures enables you to add many more buttons to the Power Bar. In fact, with all the shortcut keys now available in WordPerfect, you can easily include all your most frequently used features that require multiple keystrokes to access. Then dispense with the Toolbar altogether.

You can also edit the pictures on the button faces if you want. The instructions are the same as for customizing the Toolbar text and pictures.

## Adding, Moving, and Deleting Power Bar Buttons

To add, move, or delete a Power Bar button, follow these steps:

 **T I P**  To quickly edit the Power Bar, click it with the right mouse button and choose Edit from the QuickMenu.

1. Choose Edit, Preferences, Power Bar, Edit. Or click the Power Bar anywhere with the right mouse button and choose Edit. WordPerfect displays the Toolbar Editor— Power Bar dialog box shown in figure 13.12.

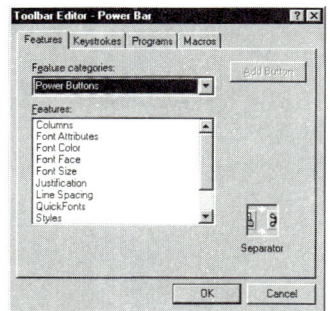

**FIG. 13.12**
By using the Toolbar Editor– Power Bar dialog box, you can add special Power Buttons, a variety of commands from the menus, macros, and scripts to the existing Power Bar.

2. To add a button to the Power Bar, choose whether you want to add Features, Keystrokes, Programs, or Macros. Follow the instructions earlier in this chapter for adding buttons to the Toolbar.

    **N O T E**  Choose Power Buttons in Feature Categories text to display a list of Power Bar buttons that drop down a menu when chosen.

▶ See "Using Power Bar Buttons," **p. 353**

3. To move a button, drag the button to the new location while the Toolbar Editor—Power Bar dialog box is displayed.

4. To delete a button, drag the button off the Power Bar while the Toolbar Editor—Power Bar dialog box is displayed.

5. To add a spacer between buttons, drag the Spacer symbol to the desired location on the Power Bar.

6. Choose OK to return to the document window.

To restore the default Power Bar buttons, choose Default from the Power Bar Options dialog box. Before you close the Toolbar Editor—Power Bar dialog box, move the box out of the way of the Power Bar and check the results of your editing. If you are not satisfied with your changes, choose Cancel and all the changes you made are removed.

### TROUBLESHOOTING

**When I add buttons to the Power Bar, they aren't on the Power Bar when I return to the document window.** Be sure you click Add Button each time you choose a feature to add. It's easy to just choose OK after choosing a feature when you want to add only one.

**I tried again, making sure to click Add Button, and the button is still not on the Power Bar.** If the Power Bar is full, additional buttons you add won't be visible. You'll need to return to the Editor and remove one or more buttons to make room for your additions to display. Study your word processing needs carefully. You may find that you rarely use standard newspaper columns, change justification, or zoom. To remove any of those or other buttons, just grab the button with the mouse and drag it off the Power Bar.

**But I don't want to give up any buttons. Is there another solution?** If you still can't make room for the button you want, display the Power Bar with pictures only. Alternatively, move buttons such as Zoom to the Toolbar you use most often. The Toolbar contains scroll arrows that enable you to display more of the Toolbar, or you can display the buttons in several rows.

PART

# Specialized Procedures

**14**   Working with Text Columns   433

**15**   Organizing Documents with Outlining   461

**16**   Working with Tables   495

**17**   Creating and Modifying Charts with WP Draw   535

**18**   Importing Data and Working with Other Programs   559

**19**   Assembling Documents with Merge and Sort   587

CHAPTER 14

# Working with Text Columns

*by Gordon Nelder-Adams and Gabrielle Nemes*

Columns can add visual impact to documents and make text easier to read. With WordPerfect's powerful Columns feature, you can format all or part of a document into columns. You can choose the number of columns, the width of each column, the manner in which text flows from column to column, and the width of the gutters (the empty spaces between columns). You can start and stop columns as often as you want within your document, or even on a single page. You can also print lines between your columns, put borders around them, and use background shading or patterns.

In this chapter, you learn about four types of columns in WordPerfect: balanced newspaper columns, newspaper columns, parallel columns, and parallel columns with block protect. ■

### Define newspaper columns
Newspaper columns are often used to create short, easy-to-read lines such as those found in newspapers. You'll learn how to effectively create and use newspaper columns.

### Define parallel columns
Parallel columns are a powerful formatting tool often used to organize text logically into rows and columns, similar to the table feature. You'll learn how to use parallel columns for documents such as itineraries or scripts.

### Type and edit in columns
Creating and editing text in columns requires an understanding of how columns are formatted. You'll learn the special codes that are created when working with columns and how to use them to your advantage.

### Change the column type and column widths
You can easily change the size, number, or type of columns used in your document even after you've created your document text.

### Use column Border and Fill styles
Add borders around columns to draw special attention to their contents. Further dress up the columns by adding fills, or shading, to the text. You'll learn how to add and customize these attributes.

# The Types of Columns

Suppose you're creating a newsletter, schedule, or script. Your document isn't like a memo or letter where all the paragraphs of text stack on top of one another. Your document requires columns of text neatly assembled on the page.

At first glance, it may seem that putting text into columns is a rather difficult chore. Fortunately, WordPerfect 7 is as equally comfortable formatting text in multiple columns as it is in single columns.

Each type of column has its own particular strengths and weaknesses, which makes it ideal for particular document layouts. This section helps you understand how each column type looks and acts so you can choose the best column type for your document.

Figures 14.1 and 14.2 show examples of WordPerfect's column types. Figure 14.1 illustrates two types of newspaper columns, while figure 14.2 shows parallel columns. These columns types are further described in the following paragraphs.

*Newspaper columns* wrap text from column to column, flowing the complete length of each column (usually the full length of the page) before wrapping to the top of the next column. Newspaper columns are most often used in newsletters where columnar text usually fills an entire page. You can easily type text in Newspaper Column mode.

*Balanced newspaper columns* typically contain continuous text that flows down one column, then wraps to the top of the next column so that text is evenly balanced between each column. This means that if the columnar text is only long enough to fill a portion of a page, the text is evenly divided between each column so that the columns are as close to the same length as possible. This column type is ideal for documents where you want as much text as possible to stay together in the same section, such as the top or bottom of the page. You might also use this column type when you know that the columnar text won't fill a complete page. Because text is constantly adjusting to balance the columns, creating text in Balanced Column mode is awkward. It's easiest to first create all your text, then turn on balanced columns.

*Parallel columns* contain short blocks of text side by side in rows, like a table. Unlike a table, however, text in a parallel column can easily flow across a page break without special formatting. You'll use parallel columns for text such as scripts. Because reformatting text in parallel columns can be awkward, you'll want to define the parallel column first, then create your text in the columns whenever possible.

*Parallel columns with block protect* are similar, except that if a column in one row extends beyond a page break, WordPerfect moves the entire row to the next page, exactly like a table.

## The Types of Columns

**FIG. 14.1**
The same newsletter is displayed using balanced newspaper and newspaper columns to show their difference.

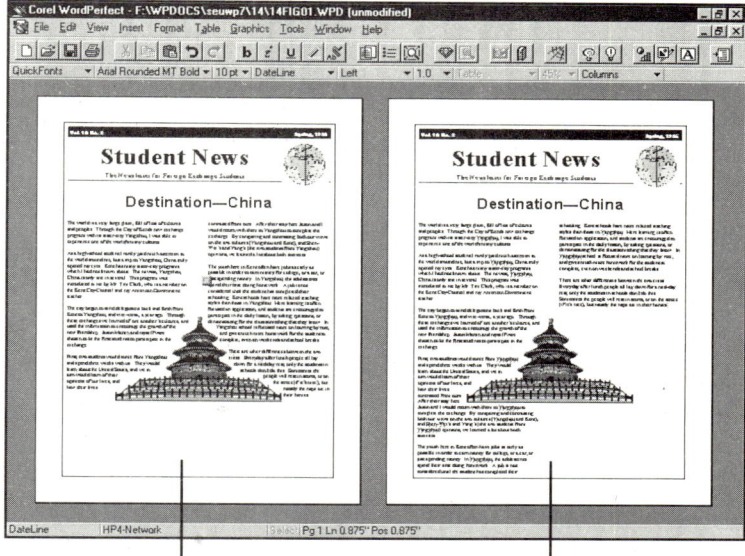

Balanced newspaper columns are the same length

Newspaper columns flow the entire length of a page

**FIG. 14.2**
Parallel block protected columns and parallel columns organize text into rows.

Parallel block protected columns stay together on a page

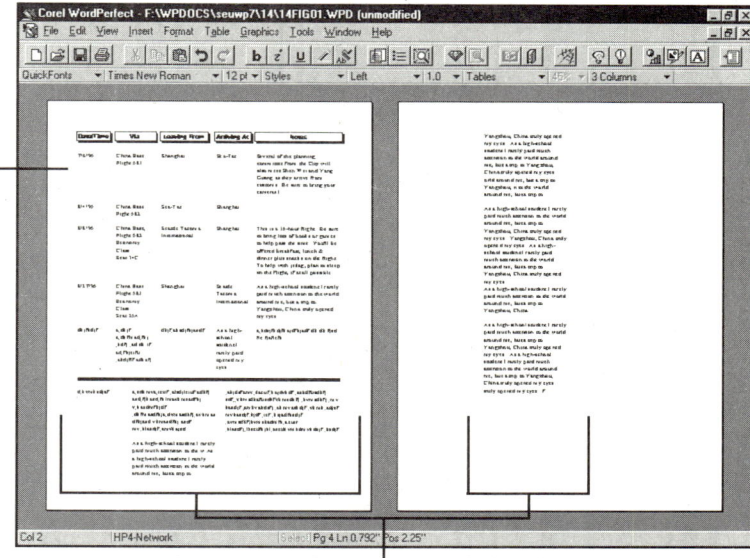

Parallel columns can cross a page break

In the sections that follow, you learn more about using WordPerfect's Column feature and controlling column formatting by using the Power Bar, Columns dialog box, Ruler Bar, and column guidelines.

## Newspaper Columns

With WordPerfect's Newspaper Columns feature, you can lay out an entire document—or sections within a document—in columns. Columnar format adds visual appeal and is often easier to read than text that spans the full width of the page, especially at smaller point sizes. When you read text printed on a normal page, your eye often has trouble scanning from the end of one line to the beginning of the next. For this reason, newspapers and most large-format magazines are printed in several columns.

In addition, with standard newspaper columns, if the document has two full-length columns and you turn columns off in the middle of the second column, WordPerfect leaves the first column as-is and forces any text that follows onto the next page, leaving the remainder of the second column empty.

### Defining Newspaper Columns Using the Power Bar

WordPerfect lets you control every aspect of column formatting, including the number and width of columns, width of the gutter (the space between columns), and Border and Fill styles. If you find WordPerfect's default values acceptable, with a single mouse action you can select two, three, four, or five evenly spaced columns by using the Columns button on the Power Bar (see fig. 14.3).

▶ **See** "The Power Bar," **p. 23**

To select newspaper columns using the Power Bar, follow these steps:

1. If the Power Bar is not displayed, choose <u>V</u>iew, <u>T</u>oolbars/Ruler. Then check the Power Bar check box.
2. Start with a new document, or place the insertion point in an existing document where you want columns to begin.
3. Using the mouse, click the Columns button. A drop-down list appears.
4. Select the number of columns you want to create.

If you select a block of text before you define columns, WordPerfect inserts the column definition code and starts the columns at the beginning of the selection. Columns are then automatically turned off at the end of the selection.

**FIG. 14.3**
Guidelines and the column definition code represent the current column definition.

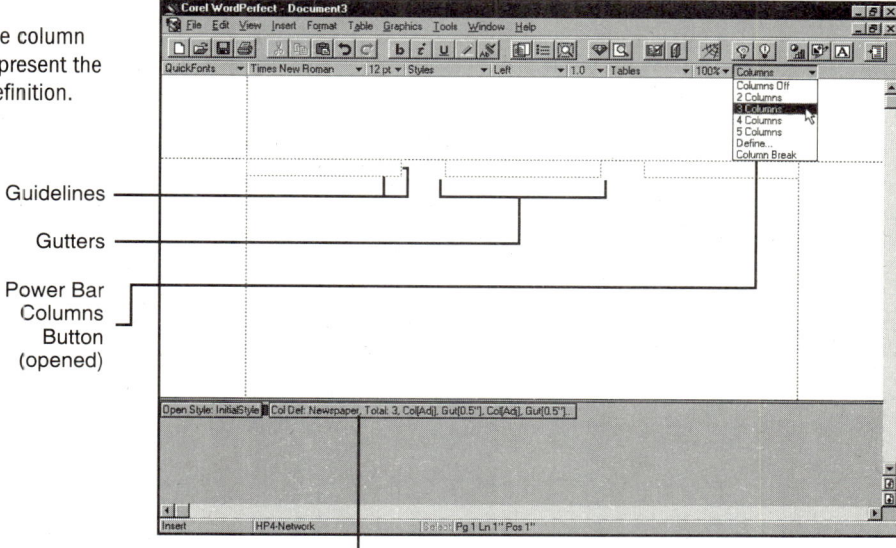

Guidelines
Gutters
Power Bar Columns Button (opened)

Expanded Column Definition code

WordPerfect inserts a column definition code into your document at the beginning of the current paragraph, and displays guidelines for your chosen column definition (refer to fig. 14.3). The column definition code specifies the type and number of columns. If you are editing an existing document, WordPerfect reformats all text below the code in columns with a half-inch gutter space between each pair of columns. If you are creating a new document, all subsequent text you type is formatted into columns. In Reveal Codes, the column definition code resembles the following:

```
Col Def: Newspaper, Total: 3, Col[Adj], Gut[0.5"], Col[Adj], Gut[0.5"]...
```

To turn columns off, choose Columns Off from the Power Bar's Columns button options, or choose Format, Columns, Off. If the insertion point isn't in the last column, WordPerfect inserts one or more [THCol] codes (temporary hard column) to preserve the column structure. The program then inserts the Column Off code, which in Reveal Codes appears as follows:

```
Col Def: Off
```

▶ **See** "Working with Reveal Codes," **p. 93**
▶ **See** "Creating the Initial Codes Style," **p. 199**

# Defining Newspaper Columns Using the Columns Dialog Box

You can use the pull-down menu from the Power Bar's Column button to choose two, three, four, or five evenly spaced newspaper columns. In each case, the gutter width remains fixed at 0.5 inch with the column widths evenly divided between the left and right page margins. If any of these default settings are not acceptable, you can specify the settings you prefer by using the Columns dialog box (see fig. 14.4).

To access the Columns dialog box, use one of these methods:

- Click the Columns button on the Power Bar, then select Define.
- Choose Format, Columns, Define.

WordPerfect then opens the Columns dialog box. If the insertion point was in columnar text before accessing the dialog box, the box displays the current settings. Otherwise, the settings displayed are WordPerfect's defaults.

**FIG. 14.4**
You can specify all column settings in the Columns dialog box.

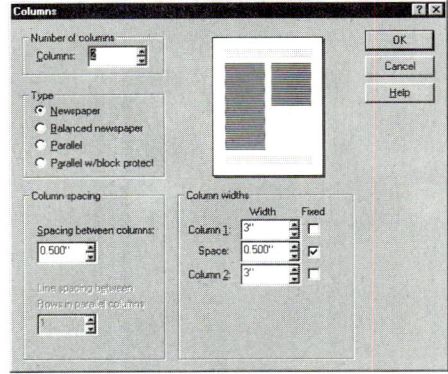

 You can also quickly access the Columns dialog box by double-clicking the Columns button on the Power Bar. As with all of the buttons on the Power Bar, you can quickly access the definition box for the button feature by double-clicking the button.

Before calling up the Columns dialog box, it's easiest if you decide how many columns you need, how much space you want between columns, and whether you want all columns to be the same width. Don't worry if you don't get your settings exactly right. You can easily change these column layout settings at any time using the Ruler Bar and guidelines.

**NOTE** If you want your entire document to be in columns, place the `Column Def` code in your document's Initial Codes style. This makes it harder to delete the code accidentally and is less distracting in Reveal Codes. To do so, choose Format, Document, Initial Codes Style. The Styles Editor dialog box then opens. Verify that your insertion point is in the Contents area of the dialog box, then in the dialog box menu choose Format, Columns, Define to access the Columns dialog box. Complete all the column settings you need for your document, then click OK twice to return to your document window.

To select more than five newspaper columns or to change the distance between columns, follow these steps:

1. Position the insertion point where you want the columns to begin.
2. Open the Columns dialog box using one of the methods described previously.
3. The Columns text box is selected when the Columns dialog box appears. The default is two columns. If you want three or more columns, type the desired number in the text box, or use the increment/decrement arrows to change the number. You can define up to 24 columns.
4. Newspaper is the default column type. If another column type is selected, choose Newspaper.
5. The default 0.5-inch gutter between your columns is often too wide. To change this value, choose Spacing Between Columns and type a new value, such as **0.2** or **0.25**. You can insert a decimal value or a fraction, such as **1/3** or **1/5**. You can also click the increment arrows to change the value by 0.1 inch at a time. Because some gutter space is necessary, avoid settings that approach zero. WordPerfect doesn't accept a value that, when multiplied by the number of gutters, is greater than the document's width.
6. Choose OK or press Enter when you are satisfied with your settings.

**NOTE** By default, WordPerfect assumes inches when you enter any measurement in any of its format settings. You can, however, use other measurement units for more precise settings. WordPerfect then automatically translates your entered units into the default measure unit, usually inches. For example, if you type **18p** (for *points*), WordPerfect automatically converts your entry to .250 inches. You can use **m** for millimeters, **c** for centimeters, or **w** for WordPerfect units (measured at 1,200 per inch).

WordPerfect inserts the column definition code. If you are not satisfied with your column margins when you see the formatted text, you can return to the Columns dialog box and change the settings. With the insertion point anywhere within the defined columns, repeat the preceding steps, and make the desired changes. You can also easily use the guidelines or ruler to visually adjust the column settings. See the section "Changing the

Appearance of Columns" later in this chapter for more information on using the guidelines and Ruler Bar.

To turn columns off, choose Columns Off from the Columns button options on the Power Bar, or choose Format, Columns, Off. WordPerfect inserts a Column Off code into your document.

## Defining Newspaper Columns with Custom Widths

When you define columns, WordPerfect automatically calculates the width and position of each column based on the number of columns, distance between columns, and current settings for left and right margins.

For example, if you select 2 columns, leaving the distance between columns at 0.5 inch and margins at one inch on each side, each column will be three inches wide. If you change the side margins to 0.5 inch, WordPerfect adjusts the column widths to 3.5 inches. If you adjust the width of one column, WordPerfect automatically adjusts the width of the other columns to keep them between the margins.

The *gutters*—the spaces between columns—are not available for text, and you always have one less gutter than the number of columns. With two columns, you have one gutter; with six columns, you have five gutters.

You can control the width of columns to some extent by changing the settings for left and right page margins and Spacing Between Columns. If either setting is changed, WordPerfect automatically recalculates the column widths and reformats the document accordingly. If you want more precise control, you can specify exact widths for each column and gutter in the Column Widths section of the Columns dialog box.

WordPerfect displays a thumbnail sample of the columns' appearance above the Column Widths settings in the dialog box. When you change the width of one or more columns or gutter spaces, WordPerfect changes the sample's appearance to reflect the current settings (see fig. 14.5).

You can also change the width of each column or gutter space and select whether that width should remain fixed (unchangeable). Before you set any custom widths, the Columns dialog box shows the WordPerfect-calculated widths of the columns, with the widths of the spaces between columns set to the current Spacing Between Columns value; the width of each gutter space is fixed. Whenever WordPerfect adjusts column widths, it does not adjust the width of any column or gutter marked as Fixed. You should, therefore, set any fixed column and gutter widths first so that WordPerfect does not automatically adjust a column setting you enter.

**FIG. 14.5**
When you change the column widths, WordPerfect changes the thumbnail sample in the Columns dialog box to show the effect of your changes.

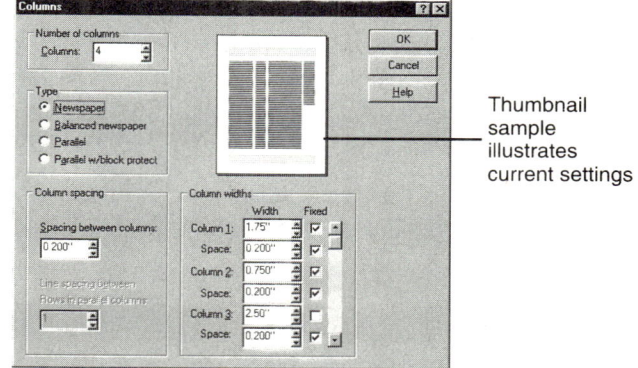

Thumbnail sample illustrates current settings

To set custom column widths, follow these steps:

1. Place the insertion point where you want the columns to begin and double-click the Columns Power Bar button. Leave the column Type set to Newspaper.
2. Type the number of columns you want in the Columns text box.
3. Choose Spacing Between Columns, and enter a value, such as **0.25**.
4. Set the widths of those columns which will be designated as fixed by first selecting the Width text box for the column number and typing the desired width. Then click the Fixed check box to the immediate right of that column's width to mark the column width as unchangeable. As you set each fixed column, WordPerfect adjusts the remaining columns to span the distance between the left and right page margins.
5. If you want to change the width of the space between columns, press Tab until WordPerfect selects the current value, or click the space text box immediately below the value for that column. Type a value or click the increment buttons to change the current value by 0.1-inch increments.
6. To change the width of other columns or gutter spaces, repeat steps 4 or 5. When you define more than three columns, a scroll bar appears that enables you to scroll to modify additional column width values. You can also press Tab or Shift+Tab to move forward or backward through the column width values.
7. Click OK or press Enter. WordPerfect inserts a column definition code and returns you to the document window.

If you later change your margins, WordPerfect adjusts your custom column widths for those columns not marked fixed, but maintains them in their relative proportions. For example, if you fix the width of one column and then change your margins, WordPerfect

adjusts the widths of the remaining columns and maintains them in their relative proportions. If you prefer to fix your column widths, but let the gutter space between them vary with margin changes, mark all columns as Fixed and remove the marks from the gutter spaces. If you don't want WordPerfect to adjust any column or gutter widths, mark all columns and gutter spaces as Fixed. In this case, WordPerfect begins the first column at your left margin setting, and ignores the right margin setting.

You can also adjust column and gutter widths using the Ruler Bar and guidelines. See the section "Changing Column Widths" later in this chapter.

## Working with Columnar Text

Entering text in newspaper columns is the same as entering text in a normal document. Text automatically wraps at the end of each line within the column and from the bottom of one column to the top of the next.

You can force text to start a new column by pressing Ctrl+Enter, thus inserting a hard column break. If you press Ctrl+Enter while typing in the last column in a column set, a new column set begins..

Because columnar text generally has a much narrower line width, you might need to adjust other formatting elements, such as the type size or typeface. If your type size is too large for the column width, left-justified text may have a ragged-right margin, and with justification set to Full, some lines may look abnormally spread out or compressed. Text set in a point size too small for the column width is difficult to read. In general, the more columns you define, the smaller your point size should be. Avoid using font sizes for general text which fall below 8 points, however, because tiny text can also be difficult to read. As a good rule of thumb, you should average 10 or 12 words per line. Proportionally spaced fonts also adjust better than fixed-width fonts, and some fonts at the same point size are narrower than others.

You might want to hyphenate some words manually; however, avoid placing hyphens on several successive lines. If WordPerfect is hyphenating for you, you may need to adjust the Hyphenation Zone settings in extreme cases for tighter hyphenation. Again, this problem is far less troublesome with proportionally spaced fonts than with fixed-width fonts.

If necessary, consider decreasing the number of columns to make each remaining column wider. Personal preference with regard to appearance should be your final guide, however.

▶ **See** "Using Hyphenation," **p. 148**

**Moving the Insertion Point** Insertion point movement within a column is the same as in a normal document, but moving between columns is not. You cannot move the insertion point to an empty column, just as you cannot move the insertion point to an empty position on a page.

The easiest way to move from one column to another is to select a new insertion point with your mouse. If you do not have a mouse, or if you prefer to use the keyboard, WordPerfect offers several commands for moving the insertion point between columns. If you create a macro to move between columns, you must use these commands, because macros don't record mouse movement.

Alt+right arrow moves the insertion point one column to the right, and Alt+left arrow moves the insertion point one column to the left. Alt+End moves the insertion point to the last line in a column, while Alt+Home moves the insertion point to the first line in a column.

More powerful but more complex is the Go To command (Ctrl+G). Typically, you use the Go To dialog box to go to a specified page number or to the top or the bottom of the current page. When the insertion point is located within a column, however, the following additional options become available:

| | |
|---|---|
| Top of Column | Next Column |
| Bottom of Column | First Column |
| Previous Column | Last Column |

To choose one of these Go To options from the keyboard, follow these steps:

1. Choose Edit, Go To or press Ctrl+G. The Go To dialog box appears.

> **TIP** You can also open the Go To dialog box by double-clicking the page number indicator in the status bar.

2. Choose Position, or press Shift+Tab.
3. Select the desired option.
4. Choose OK or press Enter. WordPerfect moves the insertion point to the desired location.

WordPerfect displays columns side-by-side on-screen, exactly as they will print. When you scroll down through text in a column and reach the bottom, WordPerfect automatically moves the insertion point to the top of the next column. If that column is only partially visible on-screen, however, WordPerfect does not move the text on-screen to make the entire column visible. This problem is particularly noticeable if you zoom the display to a setting higher than 100 percent. If you need to see the full column width, scroll to the right edge of the column using the horizontal scroll bar. You can, alternatively, move the insertion point to the right edge of the column by pressing the End key. WordPerfect adjusts the screen so that the insertion point is visible.

**Editing in Columns** Editing text within columns is not much different from editing standard text. WordPerfect has no special keys for selecting text within columns. You must be aware, however, of the codes that create the columns themselves. Deleting a [Col Def] code reformats the document as normal text to the end of the document or to the next [Col Def] code, if any, and can drastically alter the pagination of the document due to the additional space that is no longer taken up by the gutters. If Reveal Codes is not active, however, deleting [Col Def] codes by accident is less likely. (See Chapter 9, "Customizing WordPerfect," for more information on insertion point movement options.)

▶ **See** "Moving the Insertion Point with Go To," **p. 64**

In Reveal Codes, formatting codes can easily be deleted. This is useful if several parts of your document have different column structures and you want to change the format of one part to match that of the preceding section. To do so, delete the intervening [Col Def] code or codes.

If you delete a [Col Def] code accidentally, immediately select Undo (Ctrl+Z). Alternatively, you can select Undelete (Shift+Ctrl+Z), then Restore. Undo reverses your last action, while Undelete enables you to restore any of your last three deletions. If you don't Undo or Undelete immediately, you must re-create your column definition.

If the insertion point is in columnar text, WordPerfect treats page break commands as column breaks. To force a column break at some point, choose Column Break from the Power Bar's Columns button; choose Format, Columns; or press Ctrl+Enter. This code forces the following text to the top of the next column and ends the current column.

You can turn columns off by choosing Format, Columns, Off or by choosing Columns Off after clicking the Power Bar's Columns button. If you want to turn columns back on at some later point in the document, choose Format, Columns, Define, or choose Define after clicking the Power Bar's Columns Button. WordPerfect retains the previous column settings; you can accept or change them as you like. If you choose a specific number of columns from the Power Bar, you lose any custom column widths.

Justification and alignment codes also work in columns the same as in normal text. To center a heading, for example, you can use Center Align (Shift+F7) for a single-line heading or Center Justify (Ctrl+E or Format, Justification, Center) for a multiline heading. In either case, WordPerfect centers the text between the current margins, whether they are full-page or column margins. The other alignment and justification commands act in a similar manner. (See Chapter 4 for more information on aligning and justifying text.)

▶ **See** "Using Hyphenation," **p. 148**
▶ **See** "Centering and Flush Right," **p. 131**
▶ **See** "Using Justification," **p. 147**

### TROUBLESHOOTING

**When I change the widths spacing between columns in the Columns dialog box, the column widths change as well.** WordPerfect tries to automatically adjust the column widths to ensure that the columns will span the width of the page. As you change column widths and spacing, other column widths and spacing may be adjusted so that everything fits properly on the page. If you set a column width or spacing and don't want it to be changed, place a check mark in the Fixed check box next to the column width or spacing.

## Balanced Newspaper Columns

In WordPerfect 7, the default column type is newspaper columns, where text completely fills the first column, usually the full length of the page, before wrapping to the next column (see fig. 14.6). Balanced newspaper columns, however, keep all columns approximately the same length on the page as you type (see fig. 14.7).

**FIG. 14.6**
In newspaper columns, WordPerfect fills each column before beginning the next one.

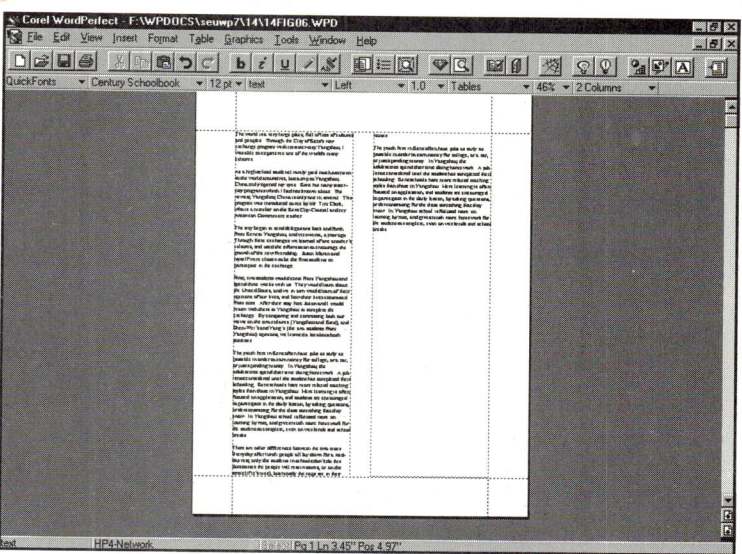

You can create balanced newspaper columns by using the Columns dialog box in the same way that you create newspaper columns, except that you choose the Balanced Newspaper type instead of Newspaper. (You cannot create balanced newspaper columns without accessing the Columns dialog box in some fashion.)

**FIG. 14.7**

In balanced newspaper columns, WordPerfect adjusts the length of each column as you type so that all columns are approximately the same length.

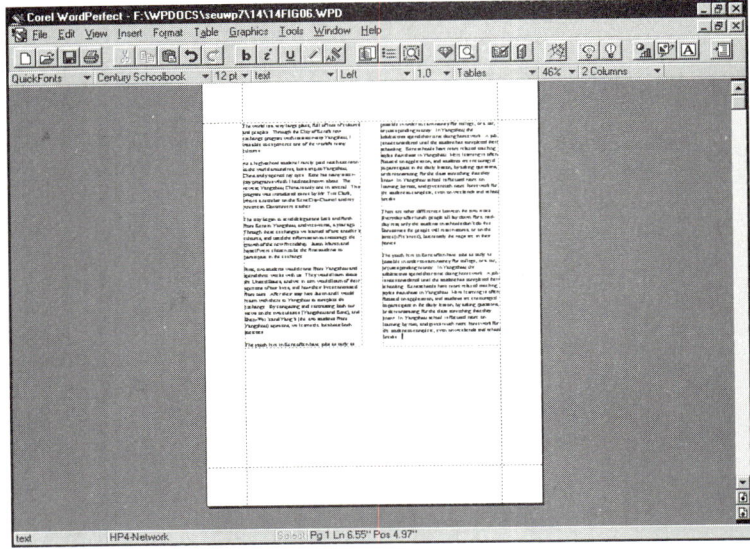

> **NOTE** Even when you are creating balanced newspaper columns, all your columns may not be exactly the same length. For example, fitting four lines of text evenly into three columns is impossible. Additionally, widows and orphans, paragraph spacing, larger type sizes for headings, or the addition of graphics can all cause your columns to have slightly uneven lengths. However, no column should be more than one or two lines shorter or longer than the average number of lines in all columns.

To turn off newspaper columns, choose Format, Columns, Off, or choose Columns Off from the Power Bar's Columns button. WordPerfect moves the cursor to the left margin, a double space below the end of the first column. You can now add additional text beneath the columnar text.

## Parallel Columns

Parallel columns, though closely related to newspaper columns, also have much in common with WordPerfect's Tables feature. Whereas newspaper columns typically feature large amounts of text flowing continuously from column to column, parallel columns contain shorter blocks of text that are read across the page from left to right in rows. These blocks of text can be any length, from individual words and short phrases to long paragraphs. You can use parallel columns for a wide variety of documents, from itineraries to screenplays.

Parallel columns come in two flavors: standard parallel columns and block protected parallel columns. *Standard parallel columns* typically hold large amounts of text, as displayed in figure 14.8. They are especially useful for screenplays or other document types where a single text block may be several paragraphs or even several pages long. Each column works together with the remaining columns to comprise an entire row or column set. Text within individual columns in the column set can extend across a page break. When you have finished entering text in the last column of the set, WordPerfect inserts a double space, then starts a new column set or row.

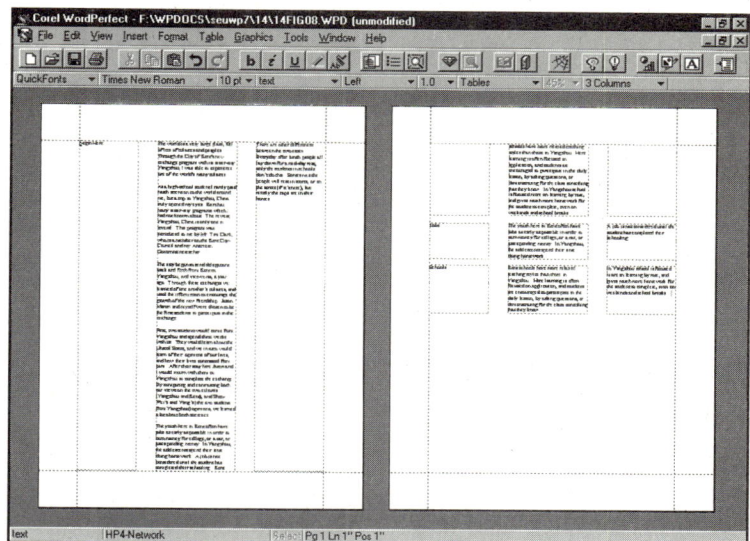

**FIG. 14.8**
Parallel columns can extend from page to page.

*Parallel block protected columns* also work in sets or rows, as displayed in figure 14.9. However, text in block protected parallel columns cannot cross a page break. Should text in any column of a block protected set be longer than the allowable space on the page, the entire row moves to the next page.

 **TIP** For most columnar features that need columns and rows, the Tables feature of WordPerfect is often easier to work with, provides more formatting features and more power than does working with parallel block protected columns.

▶ See "Incorporating Columns," **p. 731**
▶ See "Working with Tables," **p. 495**

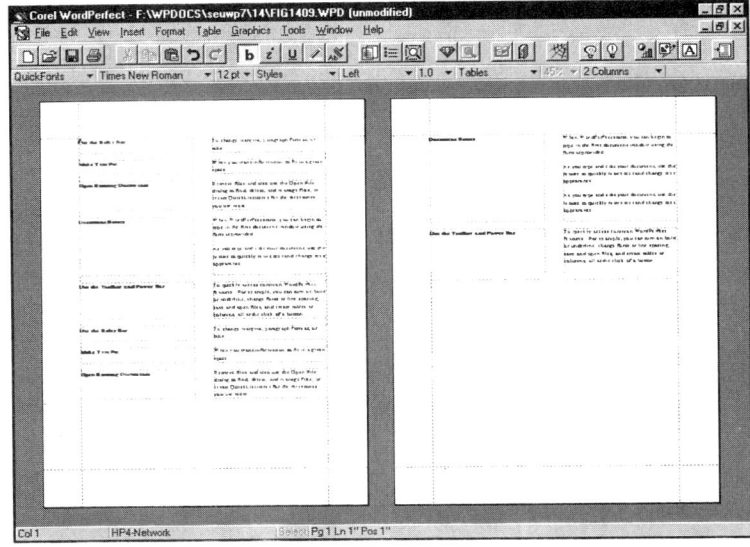

**FIG. 14.9**
Parallel block protected columns keep complete rows together on a page.

## Defining Parallel Columns

The steps for defining parallel columns are similar to those for creating newspaper columns. You can define parallel columns, however, only through the Columns dialog box. Unlike newspaper columns which are usually spaced evenly and need little (if any) adjustment after definition, parallel columns are usually of greatly differing widths. The best column width settings for parallel columns depend on the actual contents of each column. For the best results, you usually need to edit your parallel columns definition after you enter some text. Although you should plan in advance the number of columns you need and their approximate widths, don't spend a lot of time making complex calculations that you will probably change anyway. You can easily change the appearance of the column using the column guidelines or the Ruler Bar. See the section "Changing Column Widths" later in this chapter.

WordPerfect either inserts a [Col Def:Parallel...] code or a [Col Def:Parallel w/Blk Prot...] code, depending on which type of parallel columns you selected. Column guidelines illustrate one complete row, and the Ruler Bar, if visible, displays a left and right margin for each column between your page margins. You can change the widths of your columns, but before doing so, you might want to type several rows of text.

## Typing Text in Parallel Columns

When you type text in parallel columns, you must manually insert a column break at the end of each block of text, unlike newspaper columns where text automatically flows from column to column. This tells WordPerfect where to break text between columns. If you do not insert a column break, WordPerfect treats all text that follows as part of the same column.

Column breaks are created by pressing Ctrl+Enter. Although in normal text this keystroke inserts a [HPg] code, in columnar text, Ctrl+Enter inserts a [HCol] code instead. After you finish typing the block of text in the first column, insert a column break. WordPerfect then moves the insertion point to the second column. Do the same for each subsequent column. After you finish the text block in the last column, again insert a column break. WordPerfect moves the insertion point to the beginning of the first column, below any text you have entered.

Parallel columns with block protection look and act almost exactly the same as standard parallel. In Reveal Codes, the column definition code appears as [Col Def:Parallel w/Blk Prot], but WordPerfect provides no other indication that block protection is active. Each text block still ends in a [HCol] code. If a text block extends past the page break at the bottom of a page, however, WordPerfect moves the entire row of text blocks to the next page.

A simple itinerary using parallel block protected columns is illustrated in figure 14.10. To create the columns in a similar itinerary, follow these steps:

1. Define parallel columns as described in the preceding section. Choose 4 columns with 0.25-inch space between them. Set fixed column widths for columns 1 and 2 at 0.75 inches. The remaining columns automatically adjust to fit within the left and right margins. Click OK when you have finished defining your columns and to return to the document window.
2. Turn on Bold by pressing Ctrl+B or clicking the Bold button on the Toolbar, and then type **Date**.
3. Press Ctrl+Enter to go to the next column. In Reveal Codes, you can see a [HCol] code.
4. Type **Time**, and press Ctrl+Enter to go the third column.
5. Choose Format, Line, Center or press Shift+F7. Type **Place**, and press Ctrl+Enter to go to the final column.
6. Again, choose Format, Line, Center or press Shift+F7. Type **Comments**, and turn off Bold.
7. Press Ctrl+Enter to return to the first column.
8. Continue to enter text in column format, allowing text to wrap within each column as required. Remember to press Ctrl+Enter at the end of each column. You can use any text attributes, choose justification or alignment options, change line spacing, and so on.

9. When you finish typing in columns and want to resume typing normal text, turn columns off by choosing Fo_r_mat, _C_olumns, _O_ff.

**FIG. 14.10**
A simple itinerary can use parallel block protected columns.

| | | Cozumel Dive Trip Itinerary | | |
|---|---|---|---|---|
| Date | Time | Place | | Comments |
| 9/29 | 8:00 AM | Meet at SFO; check in for flight | | Don't forget your ticket and passport! |
| 9/29 | 9:44 AM | Departure, Mexicana Flight 823 | | It's an 8 hour flight; bring a book or a game to pass the time. |
| 9/29 | 2:16 PM | Arrive Cozumel; go through Customs; take bus to hotel; check in | | |
| 9/29 | 9:00 PM | Carlos & Charlie's downtown | | Don't come on an empty stomach |
| 9/30 | 10:00 AM | Meet at Chancanab State Park for check-out dive | | Dive shops are available to rent tanks and other gear. Wet suit not necessary! |
| 9/30 | 8:00 PM | Costa Brava | | The best seafood on the island! (And cheap) |
| 10/1 | 8:30 AM | Meet at Tropical Divers for boat trip to Palancar Reef | | Back at 5:00 |
| 10/1 | 7:30 PM | Meet back at Tropical Divers for night dive | | They will provide underwater flashlights |

 **TROUBLESHOOTING**

**I accidentally started a new row of columns rather than turning them off. How can I delete the row?** If you forgot to turn off columns and pressed Ctrl+Enter instead, turn on Reveal Codes. Then delete the final [HCol] code and turn off columns as described in the previous section or by using the Columns button on the Power Bar.

# Adding Space Between Rows in Parallel Columns

When you create parallel columns, WordPerfect essentially turns columns off at the end of each row and turns them back on immediately at the beginning of the next row. (WordPerfect 5.1 literally did just that, but WordPerfect 7 only displays its standard [HCol] column code between rows.) If you choose borders or a fill for parallel columns, however, these features affect only the rows of text and not the lines between rows.

By default, WordPerfect 7 leaves one blank line between rows of parallel columns. You can increase or decrease that value in the Columns dialog box. When either parallel column type is selected, you can choose Line Spacing B_e_tween Rows in Parallel Columns and type in any decimal value, or click the increment/decrement buttons to increase or decrease the value by half-line (.5) increments. You can type any standard line spacing value, such as **1.5** or **2.0**, or you can decrease the space by typing values such as **0.75** for three-quarter line or **0**, which removes the space between rows completely.

The actual amount of space WordPerfect leaves between rows is a multiple of the value you enter and the current type size. If you later select larger or smaller type, the distance between rows changes accordingly.

## Editing Parallel Columns

Editing in newspaper columns is essentially the same as editing in normal text. When you edit parallel columns, however, you must remain aware of the codes that give the columns their structure and work within that structure. You can then cut and paste text between columns, insert new groups of columns between existing ones, and move groups of columns to different locations.

You can cut and paste text from one location to another with few restrictions. You must pay attention, however, to your location within the columns. Because each column ends with a [HCol] code, if you block and copy text from more than one column at a time, your block includes a [HCol] code. When you paste that block into another column, WordPerfect pastes the [HCol] code as well. The code ends the column, moves any following text to the next column, and moves each subsequent text block in the column structure one column to the right. As a result, text that was in the last column is now in the first column. Fortunately, to restore your column structure, you can merely delete the extra [HCol] code so the following text reverts to its previous position. In the same manner, if you delete a [HCol] code by accident, you can press Ctrl+Enter to insert a new code.

If you need to add a new event to the middle of the itinerary, simply place the cursor at the beginning of the following event and begin typing. After you finish your new text in the first column, press Ctrl+Enter to move to the second column. WordPerfect pushes the following blocks of text ahead of you. Continue on in this manner, pressing Ctrl+Enter at the end of each column. At the last column, insert one last column break, which moves the following text block to the beginning of the next row.

## Moving Parallel Columns

Moving rows of parallel columns is not difficult, although you need to be sure that you preserve the column structure. When you move one or more rows of parallel columns, make sure that you include the [HCol] code at the end of the last column in any row. You can see exactly which codes are selected by using Reveal Codes.

To move a row of parallel columns, follow these steps:

1. Place the insertion point before the first character in the group of columns you want to move. Then press Shift+down arrow, or press Select (F8) and the down-arrow key.

2. Choose <u>E</u>dit, Cu<u>t</u>; or press Ctrl+X.

3. Move to the new location by clicking at the beginning of a new row or pressing the up-arrow or down-arrow key. Then choose <u>E</u>dit, <u>P</u>aste or press Ctrl+V. WordPerfect pastes the block at the new location.

 You cannot move a row of columns above a column definition without losing the column format.

You can also use WordPerfect's drag-and-drop feature to move a row to a new location. To do so, point just to the left of the first character in a row with the mouse pointer, and drag downward to select the row. Then point at the selected text and drag to the beginning of a different row. Pay special attention to the insertion point when using drag and drop to move rows. When you release the mouse, the block appears in the new location (see fig. 14.11).

# Changing the Appearance of Columns

After you have created your columns, and perhaps even typed several lines or rows of text, you can still easily change the appearance of columns. You might need to change the width of each column or the gutter space between the columns. Or, you might want to dress up the text by adding borders, lines, or shadows around or between the columns.

While you can always modify the widths of both the columns and gutters using the Columns dialog box, it is far easier and more intuitive to use either WordPerfect's Ruler Bar or the column guidelines. Using one of these methods allows you to view your column layout interactively as you make changes. You can use the Ruler Bar or column guideline methods of adjusting column layout for any of WordPerfect column types.

## Changing Column Widths Using the Ruler

Using the default column widths typically results in columns which are not appropriately sized for their content. After you enter some text into columns, you can see which columns are too wide and which are too narrow. Using the Ruler Bar to adjust column or gutter widths provides an easy method of resizing columns to better represent the data being presented. The Ruler Bar displays margin and column information along its top edge. By reviewing the Ruler Bar, you can quickly see the left and right column edges, paragraph margins for the column in which the insertion point resides, and distance (gutter space) between each column.

**FIG. 14.11**
The insertion point marks the location where the new row will drop.

Drag the insertion point to the very beginning of a row

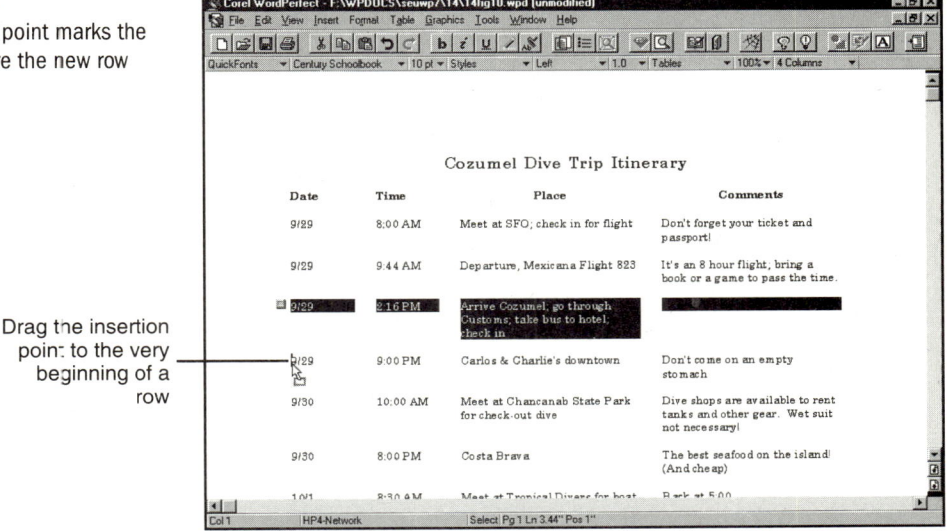

You can drag any of the icons, or the gutter spaces, in the Ruler Bar to adjust the widths of your columns and gutters, or to adjust the paragraph settings. Whenever you drag a margin or column guide in the Ruler Bar, a vertical line appears to aid in placing the setting with respect to the existing text. When you drag a gutter space, a double line appears (see fig. 14.12).

▶ **See** "Setting Margins," **p. 135**

When you drag a column edge to narrow a column, WordPerfect makes the adjacent gutter wider by the same amount. When you drag a gutter, WordPerfect makes the column on one side of the gutter wider and makes the column on the other side narrower by the same amount.

To adjust the columns in your sample itinerary, follow these steps:

1. Place the insertion point in the first row of text blocks. If your insertion point is not in the first row, changing column widths inserts a new column definition in the current row, affecting all rows which follow, instead of editing the first column definition.

2. If the Ruler is not displayed, choose Toolbars/Ruler, place an X in the Ruler Bar check box, then choose OK.

3. Using the mouse, drag the gutter space between the first two columns. Two vertical lines appear; drag to the left until the left vertical line approaches the text in the first column.

4. Release the gutter space. The text in column 2 moves to the left; columns 3 and 4 remain unchanged.

5. Drag the gutter between columns 2 and 3 to the left the same way that you dragged the first gutter.

6. Finally, drag the gutter between columns 3 and 4 so that the two columns are about the same width.

By adjusting the column widths, the entire document takes up far less space, and the text is reasonably well balanced between columns. You can make further adjustments at any time to fine-tune column widths, remembering first to place an insertion point in the first block of text.

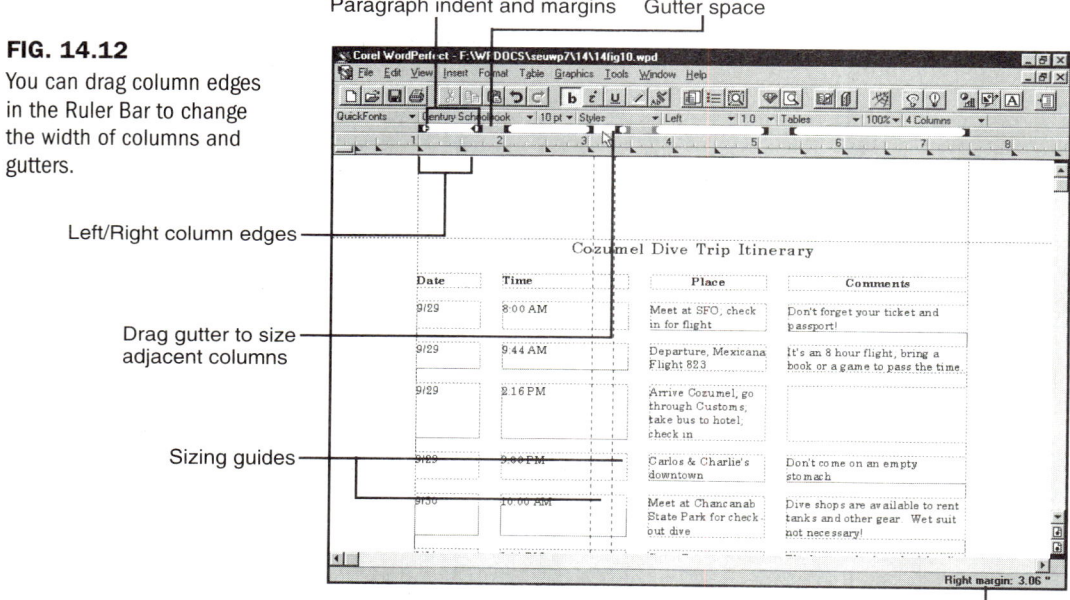

**FIG. 14.12**
You can drag column edges in the Ruler Bar to change the width of columns and gutters.

## Changing Column Widths Using the Column Guidelines

Similar to using the Ruler Bar, you can drag column guidelines to adjust the widths of your columns and the gutter spaces. While you'll probably want to adjust all of the rows in the columns, you can make adjustments at any location. Remember, however, that if you've not placed the insertion point in the first line or row, an additional column definition code is added to your document; the appearance of the columns is affected from that point forward.

▶ See "Guidelines" **p. 1095**

When you drag a single column guideline, you effectively change the width of the column's associated gutter space. For example, if you drag the right edge of a column, making the column area narrower, the gutter space immediately following that column becomes wider.

To change a column width using a column guideline, follow these steps:

1. In parallel columns, place the insertion point in the first row.

**NOTE** If column guidelines are not visible, you can turn them on by choosing View, Guidelines, and then choosing Columns in the Guidelines dialog box.

2. Position the mouse pointer over a column guideline until it turns into a single bar with arrows on both sides.

3. Drag the guideline to its new location, then release. As you drag a guideline, a vertical dashed guide appears to help you position the guideline accurately. The columnar text adjusts to accommodate the new column width.

Similar to adjusting a single column width by dragging a column guideline, you can adjust column widths on both sides of a gutter by dragging the gutter itself. To do so, position the mouse pointer between two columns. Drag the gutter left or right to adjust the columns on either side of the gutter. Vertical dashed guides appear on either side of the gutter as you drag the gutter space to assist you in placing the gutter exactly where you want it. When you are satisfied with the gutter location, release the mouse pointer.

## Adding Borders, Fills, or Shadows to Columns

You can "dress up" the appearance of a document by adding borders between or around columns. Background shading or a pattern can be added as well. You can choose any of WordPerfect's default Line or Fill styles, or customize them according to your own desires.

Column borders are similar to paragraph and page borders. Like paragraph borders, column borders do not surround headers, footers, or page numbers, but column borders let you put lines between columns, which the other border types do not. You may want to experiment to find which border types are appropriate for a particular document.

▶ See "Using Graphics Borders," **p. 255**
▶ See "Customizing Borders," **p. 666**
▶ See "Customizing Graphics Boxes," **p. 669**

You can select a Border style, Fill style, or both from the Column Border/Fill dialog box. As with the Columns dialog box, when you choose an option, WordPerfect displays an image of the current settings in Preview window of the dialog box.

To add column borders or fills, first choose Format, Border/Fill, Columns. WordPerfect displays the Column Border/Fill dialog box displayed in figure 14.13. As you make your selections, you can quickly view their effect on your columns by clicking the Apply button. (You may need to temporarily drag the Column Border/Fill dialog box out of the way to view the effect.) The choices available on each of the tabs in the Column Border/Fill dialog box are listed with a brief explanation in the following sections.

**FIG. 14.13**
The Column Border/Fill dialog box is used to add interest to your columns.

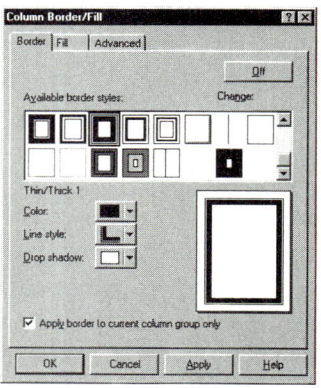

**The Border Tab**   The Border tab is visible when you open the Column Border/Fill dialog box. It is used to select the basic Border style and settings you want to use. Each of the choices in the remaining Fill and Advanced tabs modifies your selection from the Border tab. As you continue to define your border, you can view the changes in the dialog's preview window.

Borders surround either individual rows in parallel-style columns, or individual columns in newspaper-style columns. By default, WordPerfect adds your border to only the column group which is selected, or in which your insertion point resides. You can add the border to all of the column groups by removing the check from the Apply Border To Current Column Group Only box.

To add and customize a border, use these steps:

1. From the Available Border Styles palette, click the icon that represents the Border style you want to use (see fig. 14.13). As you select a Border style, a thumbnail view of your choice appears in the preview window.

2. To further define your border, you can customize its color, line style, and drop shadow.

   To make the selections using the mouse, click the drop-down arrow next to the Color, Line Style, or Drop Shadow icons. Then double-click from the resulting palette to make your selection.

   As you make your selections, the preview window updates to reflect your choices. Figure 14.14 displays the available palettes.

**FIG. 14.14**
Customize your border selection by assigning colors, line styles, and drop shadows.

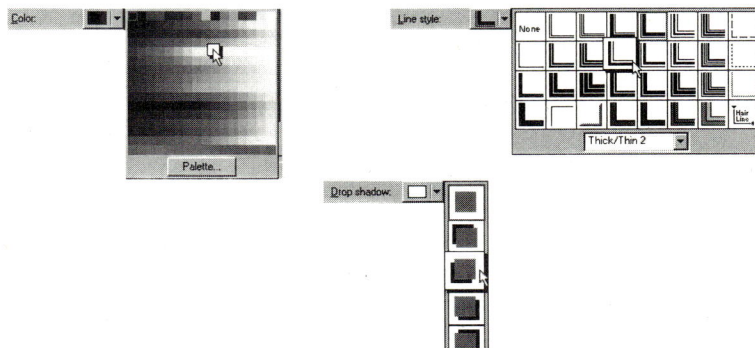

**The Fill Tab** The Fill tab adds shading or patterns to the inside of your column or column selection. You can choose the intensity of the fill-in percentages, or even assign a color or pattern.

To choose a Fill style, first open the Fill tab by clicking the Fill tab with your mouse, or pressing Ctrl+Tab until the Fill tab is visible. The Fill tab will move to the front of the dialog box selection tabs, as shown in figure 14.15. Next, select a fill style by clicking one of the fill icons in the Available Fill Styles palette. Or you can use the cursor arrows followed by the Enter key to make your selection. Similar to the Border options, you can further customize fill options, selecting custom foreground and background colors and fill patterns.

If your output device is a 300 dpi laser printer, the 10 percent Shaded Fill style provides a light gray background, which is quite noticeable without making your text harder to read. A 20 percent shaded fill is significantly darker, and a 30 percent shaded fill begins to make your text hard to read. In general, 30 percent and darker fills are useful only on higher-resolution printers and typesetters. If your printer is capable, however, you can choose the 100 percent shaded fill and set your text color to white to achieve white text on a black background. If you have a color printer, you can choose any two colors for the foreground and background, respectively, which is particularly effective with the gradient Fill styles.

**FIG. 14.15**
The Fill tab sets the fill options for your column.

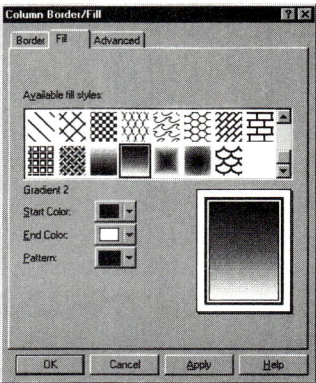

**The Advanced Tab**   You can further customize your fill and border selections using the Advanced tab. Click Advanced, or press Ctrl+Tab to bring the Advanced tab to the front (see fig. 14.16).

**FIG. 14.16**
The Advanced tab allows you to customize selections made on the Border and Fill tabs.

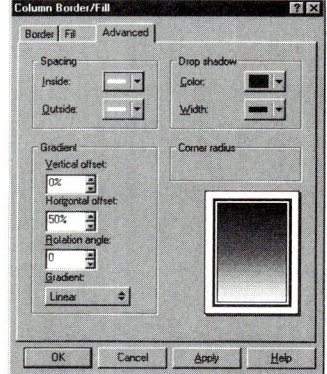

Using mouse or keyboard techniques similar to those noted in the Border Tab section, and make the custom settings you want to apply to your columns. The settings are used as follows:

- *Spacing.* Sets the amount of white space both inside the columns and outside each of the columns to which you are applying your border. The inside border spacing determines the distance the border appears from the text within the column. Therefore, by selecting a wide inside border space, you set the columnar text further away from the column border.

- *Drop shadow.* Determines the color and width of a drop shadow selection from the Border tab.

■ *Gradient.* Used when a gradient Fill style is selected from the Fill tab. You can modify both the vertical and horizontal offsets (the center, or darkest point of the gradient). You can also rotate the gradient and select the Gradient style.

### TROUBLESHOOTING

**How do I add lines between each of my columns?** To add vertical lines between each of your columns, scroll through the icons in the Available Border Styles palette until the Vertical Center Line style is visible. Then select the style by double-clicking the icon.

**Selecting the Vertical Center Line style from the Border styles palette places a line between all of the columns. How do I add a line only between some of the columns?** To insert a vertical line between any columns in a document, choose Graphics, Custom Line. The Create Graphics Line dialog box appears. Choose Vertical in the Line Type area, then choose Column Aligned from the Horizontal button options. In the After column box, specify which column you want the line to appear after. For example, if you want the line to appear between the second and third columns, select 2 in the After Column box. Choose OK to return to the document. A line appears between the columns.

**When I add lines between my columns using the Border Styles palette, the lines are broken between the rows. How do I add continuous lines between parallel columns?** WordPerfect breaks parallel-style columns between each row and essentially considers each row to be a separate column definition. To add non-breaking lines that extend completely between parallel columns, use the Graphics, Custom Line steps in the previous question.

# CHAPTER 15

# Organizing Documents with Outlining

*by Eric Baatz and Gabrielle Nemes*

An outline is an effective tool with which to present the main points and organization of a document. Additionally, the act of creating an outline enables you to determine what information you want your document to contain and in what order the topics should be presented.

Simple outlines can be used to automatically number paragraphs. You can use digits, such as 1., 2., or typical outline appearance such as I., A., 1., a., and so on. You can even use multiple level numbers such as 1.1, 1.2, or 1.1.1., 1.1.2., 1.2.1., and so on.

As described in this chapter, you'll want to use either WordPerfect's Outline or Bullets & Numbers features to add numbers to the beginning of each paragraph. Then while you edit your document, adding or rearranging paragraphs, the numbers in front of each paragraph will automatically update, keeping everything in precise order!

WordPerfect enhances both aspects of outlines by making your final document look good and by providing active, intelligent assistance that speeds up the mechanics of outline creation beyond anything you can do with a pen and paper. ■

### Make simple lists using WordPerfect's Bullets & Numbers feature
Simple lists start with bullet or number characters and are an effective method of drawing attention to important items in your document.

### Create a variety of outlines using WordPerfect's predefined outline types
WordPerfect 7 provides nine ready-to-use outline definitions that incorporate the most commonly used outline styles.

### Manipulate outlines
You can rearrange your outlined text in any order: moving, hiding, or displaying individual items or complete outline families. Each outline number automatically updates, keeping your thoughts organized and up-to-date.

### Create customized outlines
Custom outline definitions can easily be created allowing you to create an outline layout that exactly meets your requirements.

## Understanding What Outlines Can Do

A WordPerfect outline can consist of more than Roman numerals as outline characters. Figure 15.1 shows examples of some outlines that use WordPerfect's supplied outline definitions. In addition, you'll be able to customize the appearance of any of the outline elements, such as the type of character used for the outline number, and how the text relates to the number.

**FIG. 15.1**
In these four WordPerfect outlines, each uses a different outline definition.

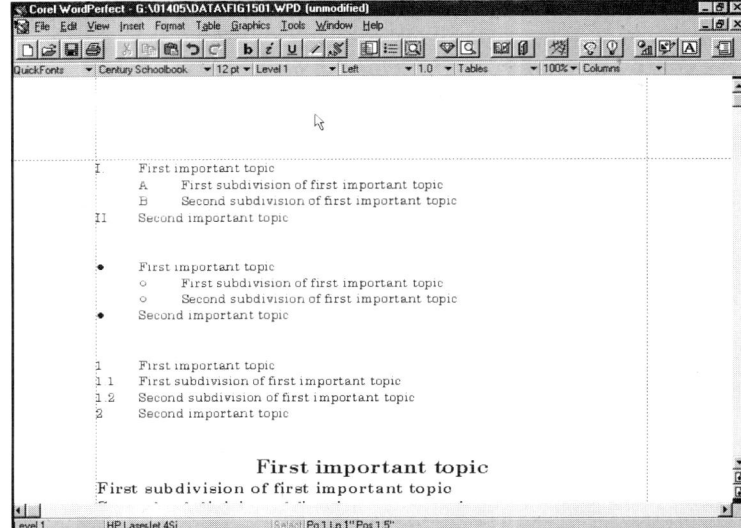

In addition to making the final appearance of an outline look sharp, WordPerfect makes outlines interactive. As you work with outlines, you can concentrate on writing particular points while hiding other parts of the outline. Then you can show the complete outline when you are finished or need to review the entire outline. This enables you to construct documents from outlines by adding text and ideas as you go. Of course, when you insert or delete material, WordPerfect automatically maintains whatever, if any, numbering you are using.

## Using Bullets & Numbers

Using outlines may be too complex if you only want a simple list or numbered paragraphs, such as the examples shown in figure 15.2. Those lists, and similar ones, can be produced by choosing Insert, Bullets & Numbers, selecting a bullet or number to insert, and choosing OK.

**FIG. 15.2**
Here are three simple lists and an example of numbered paragraphs that are easy and quick to make with Bullets & Numbers.

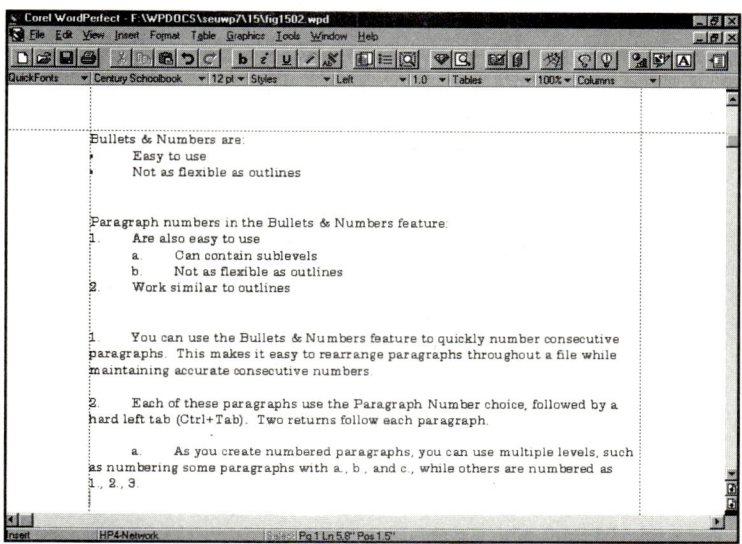

You'll want to use the Bullets & Numbers feature for most simple numbering requirements—especially when you only need to use one or two levels. When you know you will want to use several different levels, or when you'll want to hide parts of your document while you work on other sections, be sure to use the Outline feature. You can use the Outline feature to produce the same type of lists and paragraphs that appear in figure 15.2. See the section "Creating Simple Numbered and Bulleted Outlines" later in this chapter for more information.

## Creating a Simple List with Bullets & Numbers

A *simple list* is one or more paragraphs that begin with bullets or numbers. If numbers are used, they increase from paragraph to paragraph and sometimes also contain simple subnumbers or levels.

WordPerfect predefines five types of bullets (Small Circle, Large Circle, Diamond, Square, and Triangle) and six types of numbering styles (Numbers, Uppercase Roman, Uppercase Letters, Lowercase Roman, Lowercase Letters, and Paragraph Numbers), as shown in figure 15.3. All these bullet and number styles work similarly with the exception of the Paragraph Numbers style that handles returns and indents slightly differently than do the other styles. See the section titled "Understanding the Bullets & Numbers Styles" later in the chapter for more information.

**FIG. 15.3**
The Bullets & Numbers dialog box is used to select the number type and number options that you want to use.

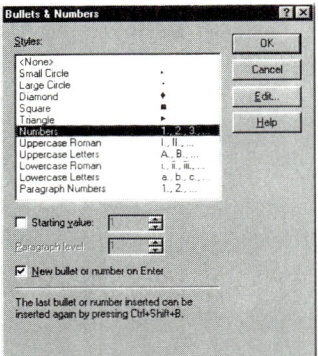

To create a simple list, follow these steps:

1. Move the insertion point to the left margin of the line in which you want to create the simple list.
2. Choose Insert, Bullets & Numbers. The Bullets & Numbers dialog box appears (refer to fig. 15.3).
3. Select the style you want. If it is a numbering style, look at the value in the Starting Value field. If it's not 1, check the Starting Value check box and enter **1** in the Starting Value field.
4. Review the New Bullet Or Number On Enter field. Click the check box to toggle the check mark so that a new number or bullet is automatically added to your document each time you press the Enter key.
5. Choose OK. WordPerfect returns to your document, adds the number style to your document, and places the insertion point after the style, ready for you to enter text.
6. Type your text and press Enter. If you want a blank line, press Enter again.
7. If you do not want to use an automatically entered bullet or number, press Backspace to quickly delete it. If, however, you want another bullet of the same type or the next number and you did not check the New Bullet Or Number On Enter check box, press Ctrl+Shift+B and then enter more text.

 Click the Insert Bullet button on the default toolbar to start a bulleted list or to insert the next number or bullet in sequence at the location of the cursor.

You also can create a simple list by first entering the text and then applying a Bullets & Numbers style. The general steps are as follows:

1. Move the insertion point to the left margin of the line in which you want to create the simple list.

2. Enter the text for each item, then press Enter. (Press Enter twice if you want a blank line between items.)
3. Select all the items.
4. Choose Insert, Bullets & Numbers. The Bullets & Numbers dialog box appears (refer to fig. 15.3).
5. Select the style you want. If it is a numbering style, look at the value in the Starting Value field. If it isn't 1, check the Starting Value check box and enter **1** in the Starting Value field. Choose OK.

> **NOTE** To change the level of the paragraph numbers you insert—for example, to change *1.* to *a)*—choose the Paragraph Numbers style in the Bullets & Numbers dialog box. You can define a starting paragraph level by changing the value in the Paragraph Level box.

## Making Fewer Keystrokes with Bullets & Numbers

You can create a series of bullets or numbers with fewer keystrokes than the previous steps by checking New Bullet Or Number On Enter in the Bullets & Numbers dialog box. Then, whenever you press Enter after typing your text, you immediately get a new bullet or number without having to press Ctrl+Shift+B.

To terminate the automatic numbering of paragraphs if you checked New Bullet Or Number On Enter, choose Insert, Bullets & Numbers. The Bullets & Numbers dialog box appears. Select <None> in the Styles list box, then choose OK. The previously generated bullet or number disappears.

> **TIP** Backspace or delete any number or bullet you don't want in your text. Numbers on Enter will not start again until you insert another number using Ctrl+Shift+B or add it from the Bullets & Numbers dialog box.

▶ See "Editing Styles," **p. 344**
▶ See "Accessing Special Characters," **p. 640**

## Understanding the Bullets & Numbers Styles

The term *style* refers to a set of formatting codes and text which are grouped together so that the codes can be used as a single unit. You very likely use manual styles in your everyday work already. These styles probably consist of simple typing habits. For example, typing a number, a period, then two spaces to begin each paragraph is a style of typing numbered paragraphs. WordPerfect allows you to group these elements (the number, period, and spaces) together under a single code—*the style code*.

The styles associated with Bullets & Numbers also follow a consistent typing convention: a bullet or number character is generally followed by an indent. To keep it simple for you, however, WordPerfect has grouped these formatting instructions together in paragraph styles which are associated with each Bullet & Number style. Therefore, when you select one of the Bullets & Number choices, your text is automatically formatted!

Styles can be created or modified by you. In this section, you learn how the Bullets & Numbers styles look and how to make changes to them. This enables you to fully customize your lists. You can learn more about defining and modifying styles in general by referring to Chapter 10, "Using Styles."

**The Bullets & Numbers Styles**   In both Outlines and Bullets & Numbers, styles are automatically used when you select the type of outline or bullet you want to include in your document. You can view the styles by turning on Reveal Codes—using Alt+F3, or by dragging the Reveal Codes Bar. After selecting one of the Bullets & Numbers styles, you see codes similar to those that appear in figure 15.4.

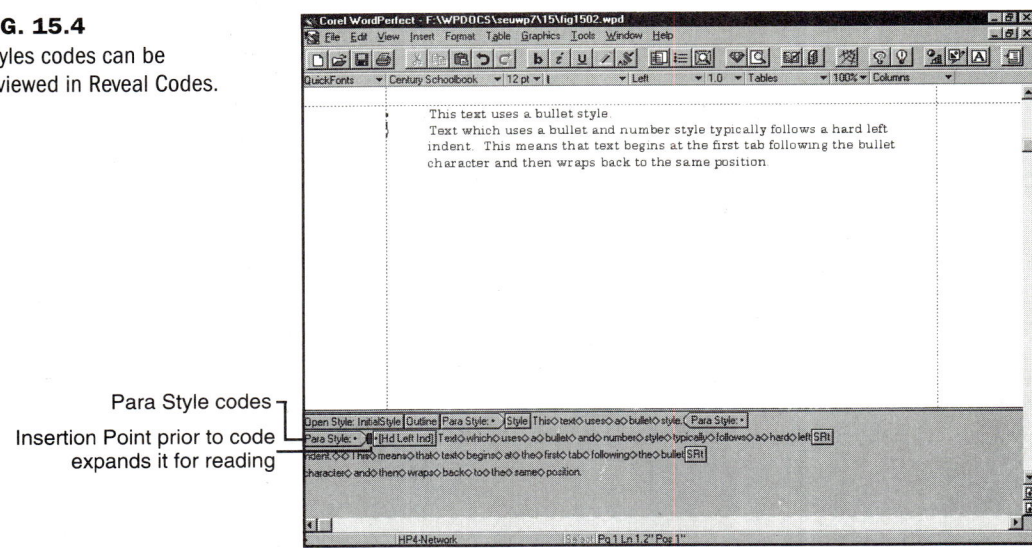

**FIG. 15.4**
Styles codes can be reviewed in Reveal Codes.

Para Style codes
Insertion Point prior to code expands it for reading

All the styles contain similar formatting codes, with the exception of the Paragraph Numbers style. These formatting codes affect the appearance of the bullet or number, and the method the text wraps around the number. With the exception of the Paragraph Number style, each of the other styles inserts a bullet or number at the left margin followed by a hard left indent. An indent positions text at the next tab, wrapping to the tab position at the end of each line, as shown in figure 15.4.

When you press Enter when using a Bullets & Numbers style, the next character or number in sequence is inserted into your document, assuming that you've checked the New Bullet Or Number On Enter check box. If you like, you can then press Enter again to add a blank line between the previous bulleted item and your new item.

**Paragraph Numbers**   The Paragraph Number style works differently than all other Bullets & Numbers styles in the way in which it formats text and behaves when you press Enter.

When you choose the Paragraph Number style, the number style is inserted into your document from the Bullets & Numbers dialog box, similar to the other styles. However, the Paragraph Number style does not include a hard left indent after the number. This enables you to include the type of formatting you want to use immediately after the number without modifying the existing style. For example, you can press the space bar twice to add two spaces after the number, or you can add a tab immediately after a paragraph number by pressing Ctrl+Tab. (The keystroke Ctrl+Tab creates a left tab code which you can view in Reveal Codes.)

Pressing the Tab key alone changes the existing paragraph number to the next number level. For example, if the current paragraph number is 1., pressing Tab inserts a tab prior to the paragraph number and changes it to a.. Conversely, if you want to change the current number to a previous level, position the insertion point immediately after a paragraph number and press Shift+Tab.

One other slight difference becomes apparent when you've checked the New Bullet Or Number On Enter check box in the Bullets & Numbers dialog box. When you press Enter with all other styles, a new number is added to the document. Immediately pressing Enter again adds a blank line and moves the number to the next line—effectively allowing you to double-space between paragraphs.

With the paragraph numbering style, however, pressing Enter twice adds two numbers. You then need to delete the number on the line which should be blank. All remaining paragraph numbers are updated correctly. Note that you can solve the problem by temporarily setting the spacing between paragraphs to 2 by choosing Format, Paragraph, Format and changing Spacing Between Paragraphs to 2.

**Modifying Bullets & Numbers Styles**   The great thing about Bullets & Numbers is that it has only a few options. However, you can make any number of changes to the appearance of Bullets & Numbers by using the following two general techniques:

- Because bulleted or numbered paragraphs are paragraphs, you can use any applicable WordPerfect layout technique to modify their look. For example, you can use paragraph formatting to change the spacing between bulleted or numbered paragraphs. You also can choose Format, Paragraph, Format and modify the Left Margin Adjustment to indent lists.

- You can edit the styles that Bullets & Numbers invoke. See the section "Editing and Creating Outline Styles" later in this chapter for the general techniques.

> **CAUTION**
>
> When you edit a Bullets & Numbers style, you are editing the style in your document's template, not in the document itself. Thus, you are affecting future documents, not just the current one. Therefore, if several users share the same template, they will also be affected by your modification.

As an example of editing a Bullets & Numbers style, you can add a blank line after a numbered paragraph by following these steps:

1. Move your insertion point to the left margin of the line in which you want to create the numbered list.
2. Choose Insert, Bullets & Numbers. The Bullets & Numbers dialog box appears.
3. Select Numbers from the Styles list box.
4. Click Edit. The Styles Editor dialog box appears.
5. Check the Show Off Codes' box. A new code (On/Off) is added to the end of the existing codes in the Contents box which reads `Codes to the left are ON—Codes to the right are OFF`. All formatting and text that precedes this On/Off code appears when you first turn on the Paragraph Number style. Any formatting codes or text that you add after the On/Off code appears when the Paragraph Number style is turned off. (A Paragraph Number style is usually turned off by pressing Enter at the end of the text which follows the number.)
6. Move the insertion point after the On/Off code in the Contents field.
7. Press Enter to insert a hard return code. A hard return code is automatically inserted each time you press Enter while typing text in your document.
8. Choose OK.
9. Look at the value in the Starting Value field. If it isn't 1, check the Starting Value check box and enter **1** in the field.
10. Choose OK. WordPerfect returns to your open document with the insertion point ready for you to begin typing.
11. Type your text and press Enter. A blank line appears automatically after your text.

**TROUBLESHOOTING**

**I chose a bullet or number in the Bullets & Numbers dialog box; now every time I press the Enter key, WordPerfect inserts another bullet or number.** The New Bullet Or Number On Enter option in the Bullets & Numbers dialog box has been selected. To insert just one bullet or number (pressing Enter starts a new line, without a number), choose Insert, Bullets & Numbers, then deselect New Bullet Or Number On Enter.

**I'm selecting a number style in the Bullets & Numbers dialog box, but WordPerfect won't let me specify a paragraph number level.** Only one of the number styles in the Bullets & Numbers dialog box supports paragraph number levels. In the Bullets & Numbers dialog box, choose the Paragraph Numbers style. You can set an initial paragraph level in the Paragraph Level box. Once the number has been inserted in the document, you can alter the paragraph level by pressing Tab to move to the next level, and Shift+Tab to change to a previous level.

# Introducing Outlines

There are two ideas at the heart of outlining:

- Information is presented hierarchically, meaning that a general idea is presented first, and then a related, more specific idea is indented under the first idea. Ideas on the same level, therefore, have the same amount of indentation from the left margin.
- Information at a given level of the outline looks similar to information at the same level elsewhere in the outline.

In WordPerfect, an *outline* is a series of paragraphs, called *outline items*. Each outline item starts with an optional *number* and is indented to the same level as the text's logical level in the hierarchy. Each outline item then contains text which relates to the outline level. You can think of the outline number as a counter, incrementing sequentially from the beginning of the outline to the end. You can format the number to look like an Arabic numeral, Roman numeral, uppercase or lowercase letter, bullet, or virtually any character you desire.

 **TIP** Where a tab or indent positions text depends on how you set up your tab settings (see Chapter 4, "Formatting Text").

For many styles of outline, the indentation level corresponds directly to the number of tabs or indents that separate the beginning of the indented text from the left margin. In the Paragraph outline style, for example, the Level 1 number is at the left margin, and the text is preceded by one indent. The Level 2 number is preceded by one indent and the text by two indents (see fig. 15.5).

> **NOTE** Although Tab and Indent both move the insertion point to the next tab stop, they are different. Indent causes second and subsequent lines to be aligned directly under the beginning of the first line. Tab does not, wrapping subsequent lines of text to the left margin. You must use the correct one immediately before entering text. In an outline style, however, if you want to use a tab action, you must press Ctrl+Tab.

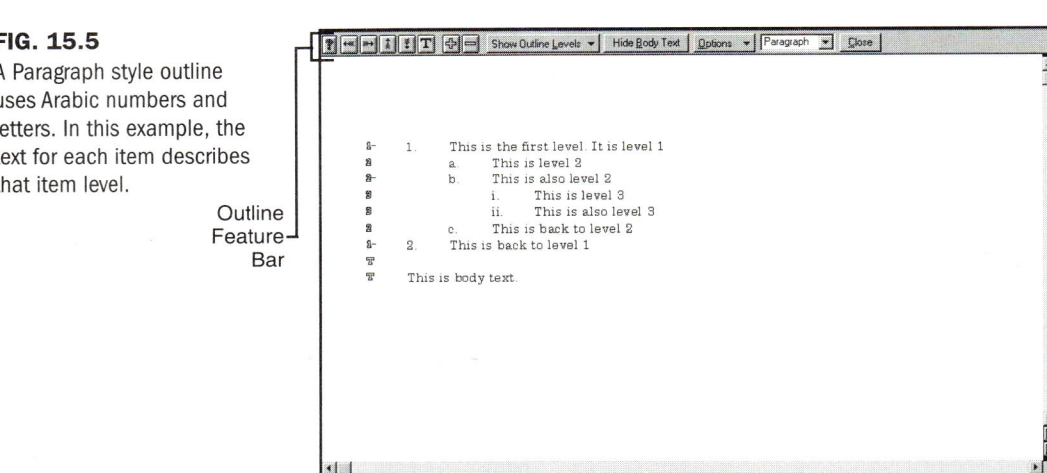

**FIG. 15.5**
A Paragraph style outline uses Arabic numbers and letters. In this example, the text for each item describes that item level.

Outline Feature Bar

▶ See "Setting and Using Tabs," **p. 138**

The following terms are related to WordPerfect's Outline feature:

- *Outline item.* A paragraph of an outline.
- *Body text.* A paragraph within an outline that does not have a number and may not have the same level of indentation as pieces of the outline that surround it. With WordPerfect, you can easily change body text into an outline item and back again.
- *Family.* A group of related material consisting of all the numbered paragraphs and body text that are indented directly underneath the first item of that group. With WordPerfect, you can easily renumber, show, move, and delete families.

- *Outline mode.* An editing state in which you have access to the Outline Feature Bar, visual indications of the level of each outline item and whether some outline items are hidden, and support for selecting and moving outline families. Outline mode is started by choosing Tools, Outline. Figure 15.5 shows Outline mode.
- *Outline Feature Bar.* A WordPerfect defined set of buttons that makes it easy to define an outline and to manipulate its structure. The Outline Feature Bar automatically appears near the top of your screen when you enter Outline mode. Unlike a toolbar, you cannot modify it. Figure 15.5 shows the Outline Feature Bar just above the text.
- *Outline definition.* A group of styles, each of which uniquely defines the appearance of the number and text for each level of the outline. WordPerfect provides several predefined outline definitions that you can use, modify, or refer to as examples of how to use many of Outlining's features; for example, Paragraph, Headings, and Outline.

# Introducing the Outline Feature Bar

The Outline Feature Bar provides keyboard and one-button access to many of outline's capabilities and is the gateway to all of outline's functionality. Choose Tools, Outline; click the Outline button; or double-click the Status Bar Outline On/Off item to display the Outline Feature Bar (see fig. 15.5). The Outline Feature Bar contains the tools you'll use when creating or editing an outline.

Table 15.1 describes the individual buttons on the Outline Feature Bar.

**Table 15.1 Summary of the Outline Feature Bar**

| Icon | Keystroke | Function |
|---|---|---|
| ? | Alt+Shift+F10 or Alt+Shift+space | Feature Bar help. Allows access to other feature bars, provides menu access to Outline Feature Bar functionality, lists the Outline Feature Bar keystrokes, and provides access to Help. |
| ← | Alt+Shift+P | Previous level. Decreases the outline item's level by one. This is the equivalent of pressing Shift+Tab. (Decreasing an item's level may cause its formatting to change; for example, the form of its number and indentation from the left margin.) |

*continues*

### Table 15.1 Continued

| Icon | Keystroke | Function |
|---|---|---|
| | Alt+Shift+N | Next level. Increases the outline item's level by one. This is the equivalent of pressing Tab. (Increasing an item's level may cause its formatting to change; for example, the form of its number and indentation from the left margin.) |
| | Alt+Shift+M | Moves family up. Moves the outline item or selection up one item without changing its level. |
| | Alt+Shift+W | Moves family down. Moves the outline item or selection down one item without changing its level. |
| | Alt+Shift+T | Toggles item as body text. Changes an outline item to body text that starts at the left margin or changes body text to an outline item. |
| | Alt+Shift+S | Shows all levels of the current outline family. Shows/redisplays the collapsed family under the current outline item. |
| | Alt+Shift+I | Hides all but the current level of the outline family. Hides/collapses the family under the current outline item. |
| Show Outline Levels | Alt+Shift+L | Chooses outline display level. Hides or shows selected levels 1–8. |
| Hide Body Text | Alt+Shift+B | Turns display of body text on or off. Hides or shows body text. |
| Options | Alt+Shift+O | Chooses outline options. Displays the Outline Options menu, which allows you to change or define the current outline type, end the outline, and change the outline level and current paragraph number. |
| Paragraph | Alt+Shift+D | Selects outline definition. Selects the outline definition you want to use for your outline. |
| Close | Alt+Shift+C | Closes feature bar. Removes the Outline Feature Bar from the window. |

**TIP** To add an Outline button to a Toolbar, use the secondary mouse button to choose Edit from the Toolbar QuickMenu. Choose Tools in the Feature Categories field, and select Outline in the Features field.

Rather than trying to define, in a rather abstract fashion, what each Outline Feature Bar button and pull-down menu does, you'll use the Outline Feature Bar buttons as you learn to create and edit outlines.

# Creating an Outline

WordPerfect 7 installs with nine predefined outline types. These outline types are based on formatting and attributes commonly used in outlines that you create by hand. The difference, of course, is that you'll no longer need to keep track of each number and outline level by hand. Each of the predefined outline types contains eight levels. Figure 15.6 illustrates four of the predefined outline types, showing all eight levels of each type.

**FIG. 15.6**
Four of the predefined outline types are illustrated here. Notice that each type uses a different method for each level.

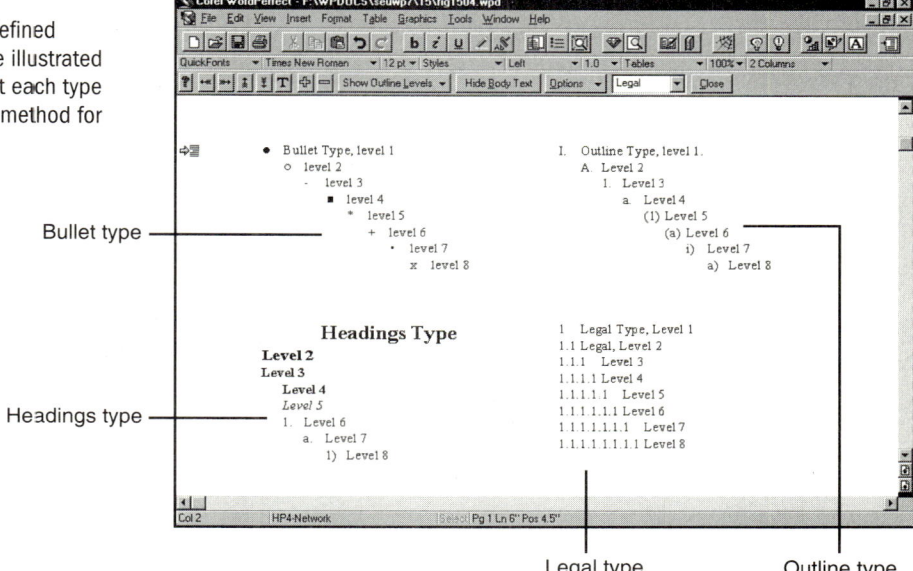

- Bullet type
- Headings type
- Legal type
- Outline type

Creating an outline using any of WordPerfect's predefined outline definitions is simple! The general steps for creating an outline are as follows:

1. Move your insertion point to the left margin of the line in which you want to create the outline.

2. If the Outline Feature Bar is not already visible, choose Tools, Outline. The Outline Feature Bar appears. A Level 1 outline item is created in your document (based on the default Paragraph outline definition), and the insertion point is placed so you can enter your text.

If the style of the inserted outline item is not the one you wanted, you can do one of three tasks.

Choose an alternate outline type by clicking the drop-down list for Outline Definitions on the Feature Bar and select the definition you want to use. Alternatively, you can use the keyboard by pressing Alt+Shift+D. Then press the down arrow to thumb through the defined outline definitions. Press Enter when the definition you want to use is displayed.

 Alternatively, Press Shift+Ctrl+O to open the Outline Define dialog box. Select the outline definition you want, check S̲tart New Outline, and choose OK or press Enter. An outline item is created and the insertion point is placed so you can enter your text.

3. Type the text; then press Enter. The insertion point is automatically positioned at the same level to enter the text for the next item.

 4. To enter text for the next level in sequence, before you enter any text, press Tab. Alternatively, click the Next Level button on the Feature Bar. Each tab increments the current level by one (and probably indents your text to the next tab stop, although whether that happens depends on the definition of outline you are using). If you increment the level too many times, you can decrease the level by pressing Shift+Tab, or by clicking the Previous Level button on the Outline Feature Bar.

> **TIP** If you want to insert a blank line between outline items, press Enter a second time immediately after entering an item's text.

 5. If you want body text in an outline, click the Outline Feature Bar's Body Text button, or press Ctrl+H anytime before pressing Enter to end your text.

If you want the body text to look like an unnumbered paragraph of an outline item, you should indent (press F7) or tab at the left margin of the body text to align it with the outline item. Use Indent if the outline item's text is indented with an indent, and use Tab if the text is indented with a tab.

 6. After entering the last item's text, choose O̲ptions, E̲nd Outline, or click the Close button on the Outline Feature Bar.

Table 15.2 summarizes the keystrokes that have special meaning within an outline.

## Table 15.2 Special Keystrokes for Creating and Editing Outlines

| Keystroke | Function |
| --- | --- |
| Enter | When pressed following text, ends the outline item. When pressed twice, inserts a blank line between outline items. |
| Tab | When the first character of an outline item, changes an item level to the next level in sequence (which frequently increases the item's indentation and changes the format of its number). |
| Shift+Tab | When the first character of an outline item, changes an item level to the previous level in sequence (which frequently decreases the item's indentation and changes the format of its number). |
| Ctrl+H | Changes an outline item to body text that starts at the left margin, or changes body text to an outline item. If the Outline Feature Bar is visible, you can also use Alt+Shift+T to toggle between outline text and body text. |

# Creating Simple Numbered and Bulleted Outlines

A *list* is really a simple outline with one level. You can easily create simple outlines by using WordPerfect's built-in outline definitions.

To create an unindented, numbered list, such as the one shown in figure 15.7, complete the following steps:

1. Move the insertion point to the left margin of the line in which you want to create the outline.

2. If the Outline Feature Bar is not already visible, choose Tools, Outline. The Outline Feature Bar appears, and an outline item for the default outline definition is inserted into your document.

3. Select the Paragraph outline definition from the Outline Definitions button on the Outline Feature Bar.

   Or press Ctrl+Shift+O. The Outline Define dialog box appears. Select Paragraph, and then choose OK or press Enter.

4. After entering each item's text, press Enter. The next number is automatically generated.

5. After entering the last item's text, click the Close button on the Outline Feature Bar, or choose Options, End Outline rather than pressing Enter.

**FIG. 15.7**
A simple unindented, numbered list can be created by using the predefined WordPerfect Paragraph outline definition.

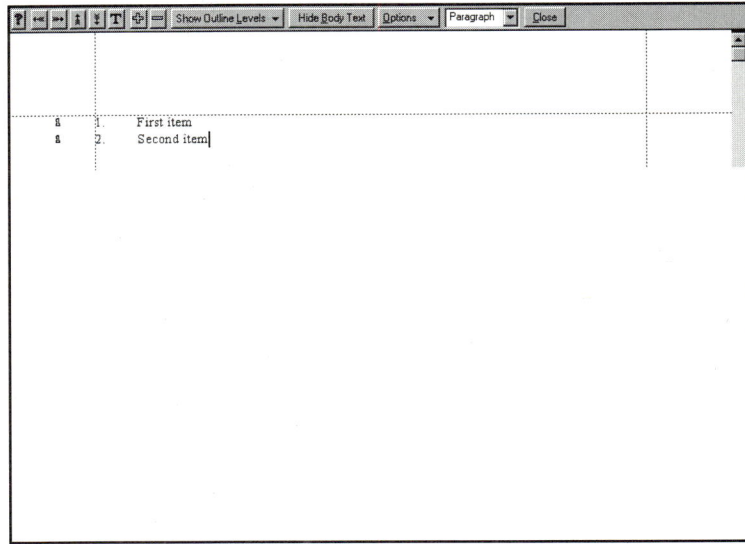

To create an unindented bulleted list, as shown in figure 15.8, follow the previous steps to create an unindented numbered list, except select Bullets as your outline definition rather than Paragraph in step 2.

**FIG. 15.8**
A simple unindented, bulleted list can be created by using the WordPerfect-supplied Bullets outline definition.

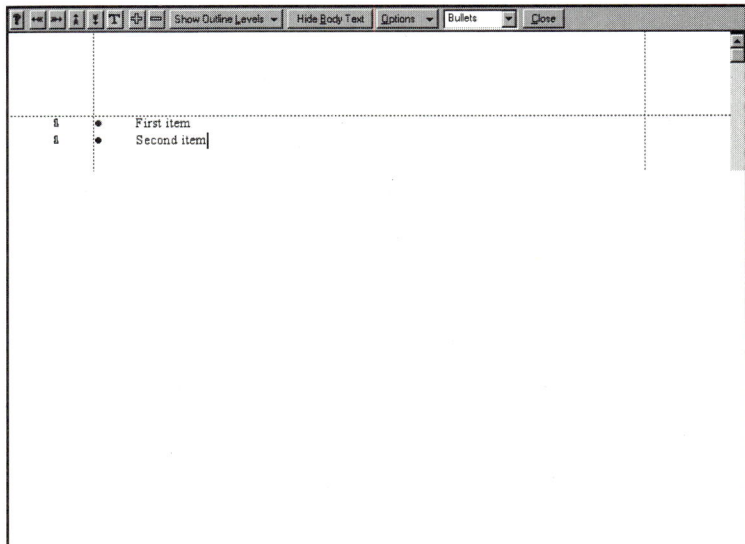

If you want to use a different bullet than the WordPerfect default, see the section "Creating Your Own Bulleted List Definition" later in this chapter.

## Creating Incrementing Numbers in Normal Text

To create incrementing numbers within a paragraph, complete the following steps:

1. Enter the text that comes before the first incremented number.
2. If the Outline Feature Bar is not already visible, choose Tools, Outline. The Outline Feature Bar appears.
3. From the Outline Definition button on the Feature bar, select Numbers, or choose Options, Define Outline. Alternatively, choose Numbers from the Outline Define (Ctrl+Shift+O) dialog box and choose OK.
4. Choose Options, Change Level, and enter the level you want to use into the Outline Level field. Choose OK or press Enter to return to the document window.
5. Enter the text that comes after the incremented number.
6. Repeat step 5 when you need an incremented number; however, you can only enter one incremented number within a paragraph.

You can change the style of the numbers—for example, from 1 to "(1)"—by editing the format of the numbers used by the Numbers outline definition or by creating your own outline definition (see the section "Editing and Creating Outline Definitions" later in this chapter).

# Displaying and Editing an Outline

Long and complicated outlines can be annoying to work with because their length or depth makes it difficult to see only the part in which you are currently interested. Several options available on the Outline Feature Bar control what portion of an outline is displayed. Using the Outline Feature Bar, you can:

- Hide/collapse individual families under their first outline item
- Hide all outline items of a specified level and their families
- Hide the entire outline excluding body text
- Hide only body text

You can mix these options. For example, you can hide all Level 3 outline items, and then collapse one or more individual Level 1 items. Figure 15.9 shows an example of a simple outline with several levels and body text.

**N O T E** You can easily distinguish the level of each outline item by reviewing the non-printing level icons that appear in the left margin next to the actual outline text. The level icons typically appear by default. If the icons do not appear or are distracting, turn them on or off by choosing Options, Show Level Icons.

**FIG. 15.9**
This complete outline is used in the hiding and showing examples.

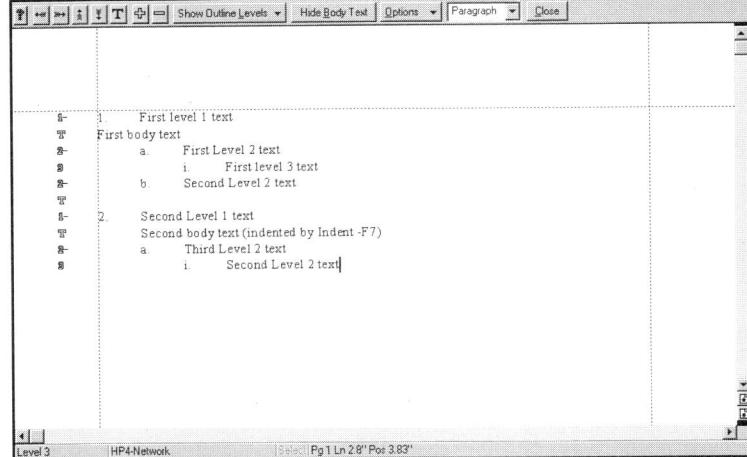

## Hiding and Showing Families and Levels

Sometimes it is advantageous to hide parts of an outline while working on other parts. This allows you to focus on just a specific point without being distracted by other, surrounding points. WordPerfect lets you hide entire outline families, body text, or the entire outline.

 **Hiding an Outline Family** To hide an outline family, that is, to collapse the family so only its first level item is visible, place the insertion point in the first level of the family and click the Outline Feature Bar's Hide Family button, or press Alt+Shift+I. You also can move the cursor to the left of the first level of the family, until the cursor changes to a vertical, double-headed arrow; then double-click the primary mouse button.

Figure 15.10 shows the result of collapsing the first Level 1 family and the vertical, double-headed arrow cursor.

**FIG. 15.10**
The plus sign to the left of the first level 1 indicates hidden members of that outline family.

Double-click to hide/show family

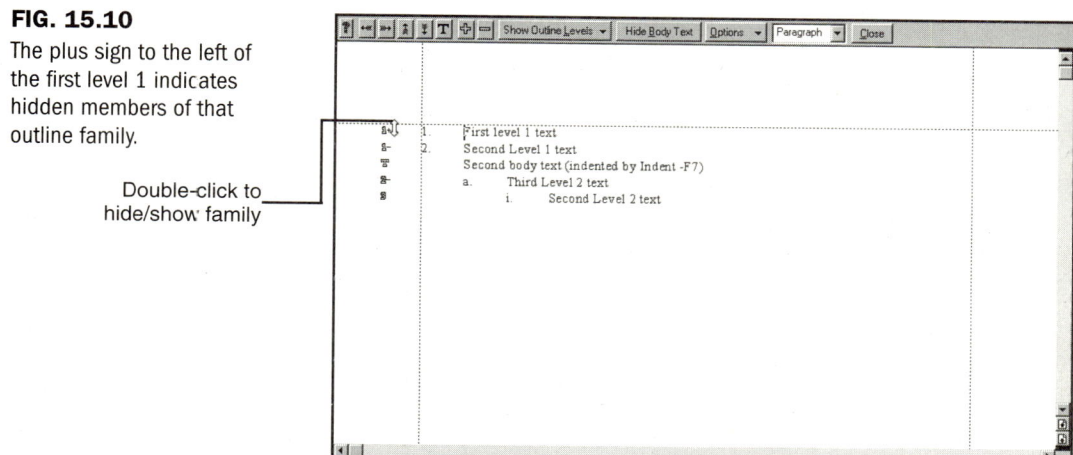

**Showing a Hidden Outline Family**   To show/redisplay a collapsed outline family, place the insertion point in the visible outline item and choose the Outline Feature Bar's Show Family button, or press Alt+Shift+S. You can also move the cursor to the left of the visible outline item until the cursor changes to a vertical, double-headed arrow; then double-click the primary mouse button.

**Hiding All Outline Families Under a Specified Level**   To hide all the outline families under a specified level for the entire outline, place the insertion point in the outline and click the Show Outline Levels button. Choose the lowest number that you still want shown. All levels underneath your specified level (that is, all the families of your specified level) are hidden. Figure 15.11 shows the result of showing only Level 1 for the outline in figure 15.9. Notice, however, that body text still shows.

**Showing All Hidden Outline Families**   To show/redisplay all the hidden levels of an outline, place the insertion point in a visible outline item and click the Feature Bar's Show Outline Levels button; then choose 8 (all levels).

**Hiding Body Text**   To hide an outline's body text, as in figure 15.12, place the insertion point in the outline and click the Outline Feature Bar's Hide Body Text button, or press Alt+Shift–B, then 8.

**FIG. 15.11**
Showing only Level 1 of the outline shown in figure 15.9 results in this display.

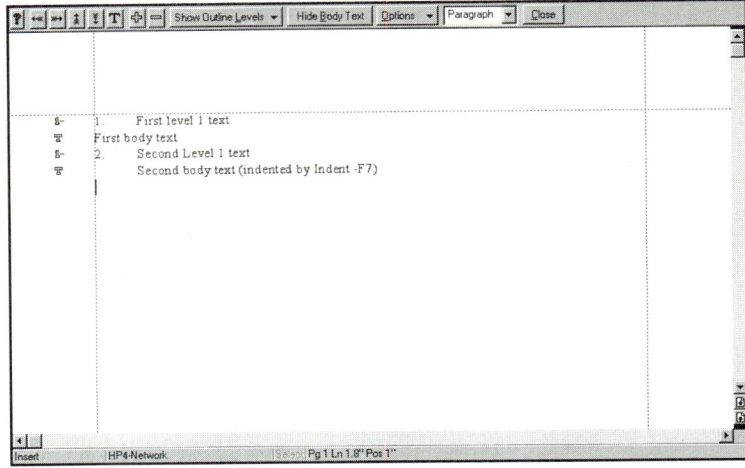

**FIG. 15.12**
Hiding the body text of the outline shown in figure 15.9 results in this display.

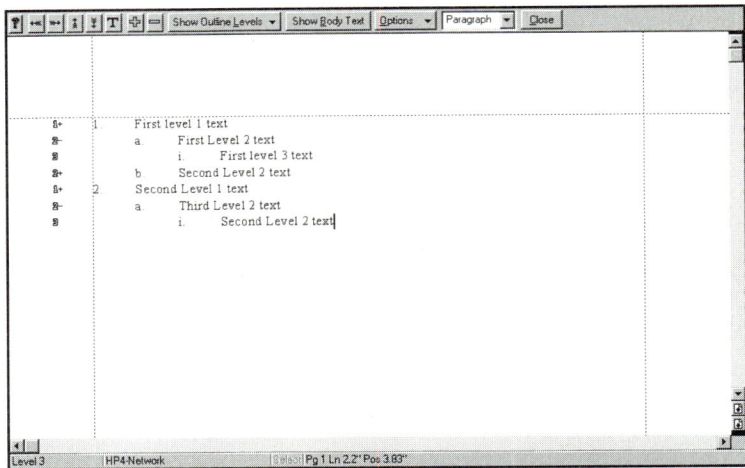

**Showing Hidden Body Text**  Body text is an integral part of an outline level. For body text to be displayed, the outline level that contains the body text must also be displayed. If all outline levels are currently showing, redisplay hidden body text by clicking the Outline Feature Bar's Show Body Text button. If, however, the outline level that contains the body text is not displayed, first display all outline levels by clicking the Show Outline Levels Feature Bar button, then choose 8. Then click the Show Body button.

## Editing Outline Text

*Outline items* are just normal text with an outline style applied to them. You edit text in outline items using the same techniques you would use with any other text. You can add or delete, cut or paste text or formatting just as you normally would. For example, as you continue to add levels to your outline you may find that it's helpful to adjust the tab settings. Adding more distance between the tabs can be especially important when working with one of the Legal outline types. For more information about adjusting tab settings, refer to Chapter 4, "Formatting Text."

## Modifying an Outline's Structure

By modifying an outline's structure, you renumber and rearrange an outline's individual items and its families, rather than change the text in an item. Although you can manipulate an outline by cutting and pasting the outline's text and hidden codes, doing so is very difficult because selection of normal text does not pick up the hidden codes that describe an outline's structure. Working around that by using the Reveal Codes display or the left margin's QuickMenu to select paragraphs is tedious, at best. However, when the Outline Feature Bar is visible, it's easy to select families for copying, deleting, and cutting, and it's especially easy to move a family without worrying about hidden codes. Of course, WordPerfect automatically adjusts the numbering of the outline to reflect each change made.

### Adjusting Levels

 To change the level of an outline item to the next level in sequence, position the insertion point anywhere in the item and click the Outline Feature Bar's Next Level button, or press Alt+Shift+N. If the insertion point is positioned just in front of an outline item's text, you also can press Tab.

 To change the level to the previous level, position the insertion point anywhere in the item and click the Outline Feature Bar's Previous Level button, or press Alt+Shift+P. If the insertion point is positioned just in front of an outline item's text, you also can press Shift+Tab (Back Tab).

To increase or decrease several levels at once, position the insertion point anywhere in the outline item and choose Options, Change Level. Enter the level to which you want to assign the outline item, then choose OK.

**TIP** You can change several outline items to the same level by first selecting them, then choosing <u>O</u>ptions, <u>C</u>hange Level.

## Changing To and From Body Text

 The Change To Body Text Outline Feature Bar button is a *toggle*, which means that it changes a current outline item or selected items both to body text and back to an outline level.

To change an outline item to body text, place the insertion point anywhere in the outline item you want to change and click the Outline Feature Bar's Change To Body Text button, or press Alt+Shift+T. The text is placed at the left margin. You may want to adjust its indentation using Tab or Indent (F7).

To change body text to an outline item, place the cursor anywhere in the body text you want to change and click the Outline Feature Bar's Change To Body Text button, or press Alt+Shift+T. The text is given the next number at the same level as the outline item that immediately precedes the text. You may want to adjust the level.

 **TIP** You can use Ctrl+H to change to or from Body Text if the Outline Feature Bar is not active.

## Copying, Cutting, and Pasting Families

To cut, copy, or delete an outline family, select the family and then use normal WordPerfect techniques to perform the cut, copy, or delete action. Selecting a family is easiest if the Outline Feature Bar is visible. To do so, move the cursor to the left of the top item of an outline family, until the cursor becomes a double-headed arrow; then click to select the entire family. Then use standard text methods of cutting, copying, or deleting text. For example, you can quickly access the cut, copy, and delete functions through a QuickMenu (see fig. 15.13). The QuickMenu is accessed by pointing to the selected text and clicking the right mouse button. Then click the function you want to use. Or you can use the shortcut keys for Cut (Ctrl+X) or Copy (Ctrl+C).

 **TIP** If you delete something accidentally, immediately choose <u>E</u>dit, <u>U</u>ndo, or press Ctrl+Z, to restore it.

## Modifying an Outline's Structure 483

**FIG. 15.13**
You can delete the selected outline family by using a QuickMenu.

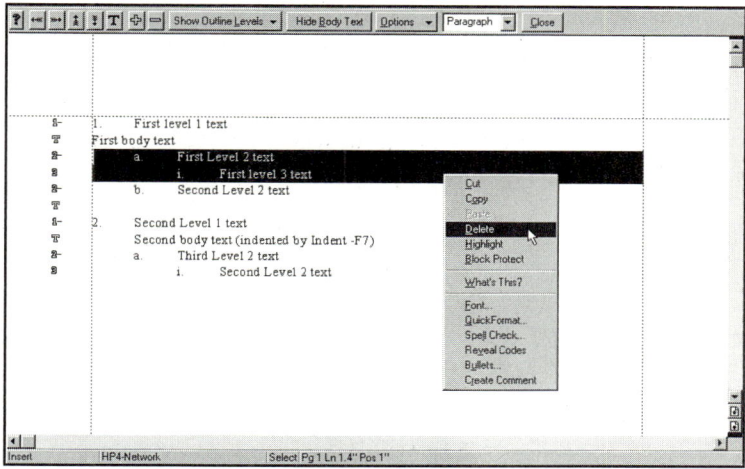

To move a family within an outline, complete the following steps:

1. If the Outline Feature Bar is not visible, choose Tools, Outline.
2. Move the mouse pointer near the outline level number in the left margin, across from the top item of the family that you want to move. It changes to a double-headed arrow. Press the primary mouse button to select the family.
3. While continuing to press the primary mouse button, move the cursor in the direction in which you want to move the family. A thin, horizontal line appears. Continue to hold down the primary mouse button and move the cursor until this line is where you want the family to appear (see fig. 15.14).
4. Release the primary mouse button. The family is inserted in the new location.

To move just the first item of a family, first select it as an entire paragraph by pointing to the item and clicking four times. You can then drag the selected paragraph to a new location within the outline. If you like, you can perform a normal cut and paste from the keyboard. Be sure to turn on Reveal Codes to be sure that all paragraph numbering codes are also included within your selection.

To move a family or an individual item between outlines, you must cut and paste. The Copy (Ctrl+C) and Cut (Ctrl+X) commands place the family into the Clipboard. To insert the contents of the clipboard into your document, place the insertion point where you want the text to be inserted, and choose Edit, Paste, or Paste from the QuickMenu. Alternatively, press Ctrl+V.

**FIG. 15.14**
As you drag the mouse, a thin horizontal line appears to the new position for the outline family.

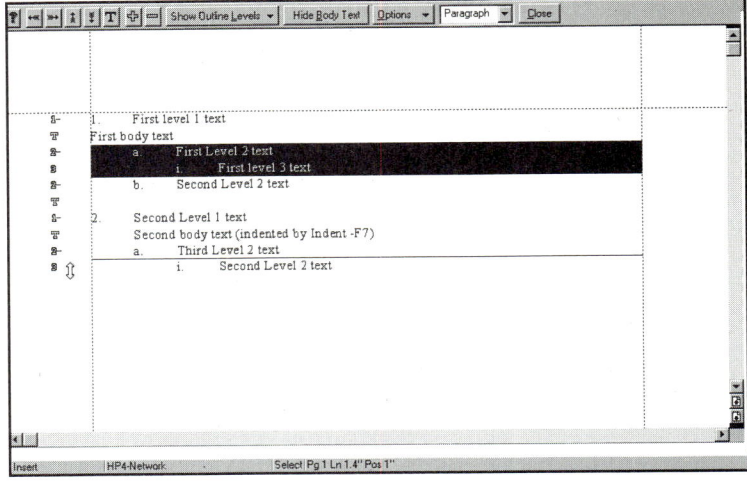

> **N O T E** The Clipboard is not cleared when you use it. This allows you to place multiple copies of an outline family into your document by copying the family to the Clipboard and pasting multiple times.

▶ See "Transferring Selected Text to Another Location," **p. 104**

## Renumbering an Outline

The values of outline numbers are normally maintained by WordPerfect automatically. You can, however, force an outline item to have a specific number or force succeeding outline numbers to start from a specific number by doing the following:

1. Place the insertion point anywhere in the outline item whose number you want to change.
2. If the Outline Feature Bar is not visible, choose Tools, Outline.
3. Choose Options, Set Number. The Set Paragraph Number dialog box appears.
4. Enter the desired number, and choose OK or press Enter.

The number you enter has a special format because it specifies values for all its sublevels, not just the one you want to change. Not only can you set a simple numbering scheme, but you can also specify complex numbering schemes by using a combination of Arabic numerals, spaces, commas, or periods. For example, entering the string **2,3.1** tells the outline that you want to set the number to the current second level number followed by a comma, then the current third level number followed by a period, and the current first level number.

You can also use question marks as placeholders which force the current values to remain unchanged, for example, entering the string **?,?.1**. Figure 15.15 shows an outline and how it changes after setting several paragraph numbers.

**FIG. 15.15**
You can control the value of an outline item's number by changing paragraph numbers for one or more levels.

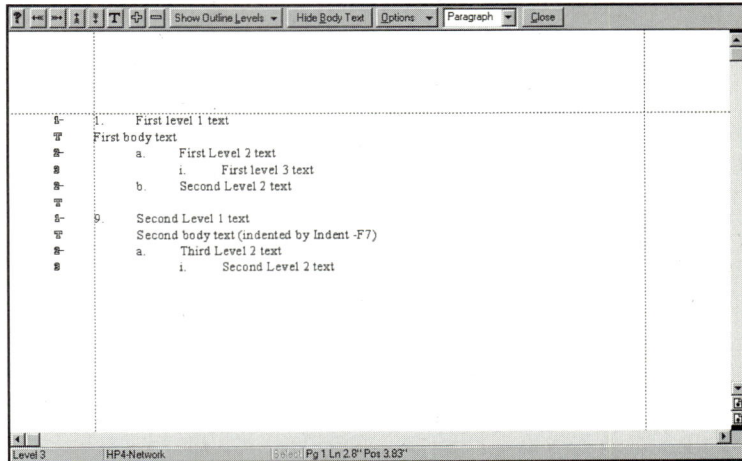

## Changing an Outline's Definition

To change to a different outline definition, perform the following steps:

1. Place the insertion point anywhere in the outline.
2. If the Outline Feature Bar is not visible, choose Tools, Outline.

3. Click the Outline Definitions button on the Feature Bar and select the new outline definition. Alternatively, you can press Shift+Ctrl+O, and then make your choice from the Outline Define dialog box.

**TROUBLESHOOTING**

**I don't see the outline numbers and symbols that are supposed to appear on the left side of the document window.** The outline numbers and symbols (icons) only appear when WordPerfect is in Outline mode. To change to Outline mode, choose Tools, Outline. You can turn on or off the level icons by choosing Options, then checking or unchecking Show Level Icons. When checked, the outline numbers and symbols appear along the left edge of the document window.

**I don't see all the levels in my outline.** One or more levels have been hidden. Levels can be hidden when WordPerfect is in regular editing mode or in Outline mode. If the Outline Feature Bar is not already visible, choose Tools, Outline to switch to Outline mode. Choose Show Outline Levels (or press Alt+Shift+L). Choose 8 to see all levels.

**I want to insert a bulleted item in my numbered outline, but when I change to the Bullet definition, my entire outline changes from numbered to bullet format.** WordPerfect is working as designed. The easiest way to insert a bulleted item in a numbered outline is to insert a new line where you want the bullet to appear. Change the format to body text. Then choose Insert, Bullets & Numbers. Find the bullet style you want to use, and choose OK.

# Introducing Outline Styles

The preceding sections have shown what can be done with WordPerfect's predefined outline definitions. Understanding outline styles reveals how predefined outlines accomplish what they do and allows you to create outlines to fit your needs. Ultimately, styles enable outlines to escape the rigid box of numbers and indentation levels to become simply a systematic way of controlling the look of your document.

Each of WordPerfect's outline definitions consists of a set of outline *styles*. The styles include both the appearance of the number and any appropriate formatting which appears immediately before and after the outline number.

The following sections assume that you already understand what styles are and how to use them in general (see Chapter 10, "Using Styles" for more information). They concentrate on how you access outline styles, how styles relate to the basic pieces of an outline, and how to create several popular types of outlines.

A fundamental idea of WordPerfect is that every paragraph has a style associated with it which determines the paragraph's formatting. When you begin an outline, you are simply saying that each succeeding paragraph is formatted according to an outline style.

Introducing Outline Styles 487

Depending on how the outline style is defined, it may or may not display a number, and it may or may not indent the paragraph or apply other formatting attributes.

Although most outlines have numbers and step-like indentation, you will not have discovered the full power of outlines until you realize that WordPerfect outlines are not required to use numbers or indentation. The WordPerfect Headers outline definition is a good example. (Review figure 15.1 to see an example of the Headers outline definition.)

The following examples generally assume that the system style definitions are visible and available for editing. To verify that they are, follow these steps:

1. Be sure that the Outline Feature bar is visible. If it isn't, choose Tools, Outline.
2. Choose Options, Define Outline from the Feature Bar. The Outline Define dialog box appears.
3. Choose Options, Setup to view the Style Setup dialog box. Be sure that the System Definitions box is checked.
4. Click OK to return to the Outline Define dialog box and OK again to return to your document window.

## Using the Define Outline Dialog Box

The Outline Define dialog box (see fig. 15.16) is the place from which to start manipulating outline styles.

**FIG. 15.16**
The Outline Define dialog box shows the system definitions. Use this dialog box to start an outline or to create, modify, or copy an existing outline style.

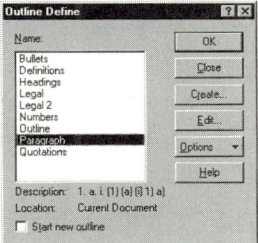

To access this dialog box, do one of the following:

- Press Alt+Shift+O.
- If the Outline Feature Bar is not visible, choose Tools, Outline. Then choose Options, Define Outline from the Feature Bar.

Table 15.3 summarizes the controls in the Outline Define dialog box, many of which are discussed more fully in other sections of this chapter.

### Table 15.3 Controls in the Outline Define Dialog Box

| Control | Function |
| --- | --- |
| OK | Starts the selected definition. This is the equivalent of double-clicking a listed definition. You are returned to the document window, and the first level of the outline definition appears. If you were working on an existing outline before accessing the Outline Definition box, all levels of the existing outline are rewritten to the selected outline definition. |
| Close | Closes the Outline Define dialog box without activating the selected outline definition. |
| Create | Allows you to create your own outline definition. You specify its name, and WordPerfect specifies its initial attributes. You edit the attributes to your needs. |
| Edit | Allows you to modify the selected style. |
| Options | Presents a pop-up list of Setup, Copy, Delete, Reset, Retrieve, and Save As choices. |
| | *Setup.* Allows you to specify the sources for outline styles (the current document, the default template, or the supplemental template) and the type of outlines you want displayed. |
| | *Copy.* Copies and renames the selected outline style to the current document, the template, or the supplemental template. You can then edit it to your specifications. |
| | *Delete.* Deletes the selected outline style. You cannot delete one of the WordPerfect-supplied system definitions. |
| | *Reset.* Restores an edited WordPerfect-supplied system definition to its unmodified state. You cannot reset an outline style you create. |
| | *Retrieve.* Retrieves user and/or system outline styles from a file. |
| | *Save As.* Copies all the user or system outline styles, or both, to a file which you name. |
| Start New Outline | If this is checked when OK is chosen, a new outline is started immediately following the paragraph in which the insertion point resides. The new outline uses the selected definition. |

## Editing and Creating Outline Definitions

An Outline definition can contain both numbers and styles that control the final appearance of each outline level. If an outline style is created for any levels, it typically contains a set of format codes, and sometimes text.

Creating an outline definition, therefore, allows you to define each level's numbering scheme, if any, and formatting style where desired. Editing an outline definition lets you modify every aspect of each level's appearance. Copying an existing definition that does almost what you want, and then editing the copy allows you to create a new outline definition without having to manually define every setting of each level.

▶ See "Outline Styles," **p. 339**

▶ See "Editing Styles," **p. 344**

To edit an outline definition, complete the following steps:

1. From the Outline Define dialog box, select the definition you want to edit.
2. Click Edit. The Edit Outline Definition dialog box appears (see fig. 15.17).

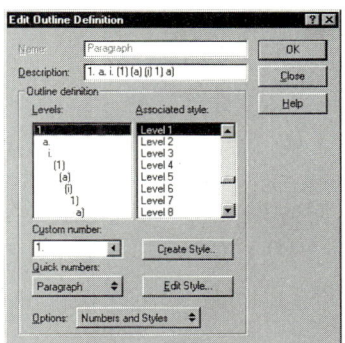

**FIG. 15.17**
The Edit Outline Definition dialog box shows the system Paragraph definition in this figure. From here, you can modify every aspect of the outline definition.

3. Work your way through the Edit Outline Definition dialog box, making the appropriate choices. (See table 15.4 for the editing operations of this dialog box.) Then choose OK.

    Modifications to an outline definition or style in the current document do not affect other documents, but they will affect other outline definitions which use the same outline styles in this document.

> **TIP** You can back out of any part of a dialog box without making a change by pressing Esc.

> **CAUTION**
>
> Styles edited through the Outline Definition Styles Editor will only be stored with the current document. However, WordPerfect allows you to access the System Styles Editor while editing an outline style. You can then open the level style again. Any changes you make through the System Styles Editor are saved to the current, often the default, template.
>
> Modifications to system styles should only be made through the System Styles Editor accessed by choosing Format, Styles where system styles are available. These modifications affect future documents. You can always reset system styles to their unmodified state, but you must be aware that any system style changes also affect other users who share the same templates.

**Table 15.4 Items in the Edit Outline Definition Dialog Box**

| Item | Function |
| --- | --- |
| Name | Identifies the outline definition. Editing this field renames the definition. If the selected definition is predefined by WordPerfect, this option is grayed so you cannot edit it. (However, you can rename an outline definition when you copy it.) |
| Description | Allows you to enter the text you want displayed in the Description field for the definition in the Outline Define dialog box. It's handy to list the level numbering appearance here. |
| Levels | Shows the number for each level. Clicking a number selects the associated level style in the Associated Style field. |
| Custom Number | Allows you to define, or customize, a number type to be used for the selected level. (Use the Quick Numbers pop-up list to select from WordPerfect's predefined number types.) In general, what you enter appears literally in your document. The pop-up list from which you select your number type allows you to choose from six number characters and four bullet characters. The number characters have the following meanings:<br><br>*1*—Numbers (for example, 1, 2, and 10)<br><br>*A*—Uppercase ASCII letters (for example, A, B, and Z)<br><br>*a*—Lowercase ASCII letters (for example, a, b, and z)<br><br>*I*—Uppercase Roman numerals (for example, I, II, and X)<br><br>*i*—Lowercase Roman numerals (for example, i, ii, and x)<br><br>*0*—Numbers with leading zeroes (for example, 01, 02, and so on)<br><br>The bullets are *Bullet* (WordPerfect character set 4, character 0), *Hollow Bullet* (4,1), *Square Bullet* (4,2), and *Small Bullet* (4,3) |

| Item | Function |
|---|---|
| | By pressing Ctrl+W, you can open the WordPerfect Characters dialog box so that you can insert any WordPerfect character into Custom number. You can also surround the number type with other characters. |
| | Note that a number is displayed only if its corresponding level style includes [Para Num] and [Para Num Displ] hidden codes. Not all outline definitions use level styles, however. |
| Quick Numbers | Allows you to choose Paragraph, Outline, Legal, or Bullets to set all eight entries of the Levels item to predefined values. Editing the Custom Number field sets the Quick Numbers choice to User Defined. |
| Associated Style | When a Level *N* outline item is created, the style specified by the *N*th entry of Associated Style is applied to the paragraph. To associate an Associated Style with a level, select the level in the Levels field, select the desired style in Associated style, and choose OK. |
| Create Style | Opens the Styles Editor dialog box in which you can define a new style for the selected level. The Styles Editor dialog box is explained in Chapter 10. |
| Edit Style | Opens the Styles Editor dialog box containing the definition for the currently selected level style. The Styles Editor dialog box is explained in Chapter 10. |
| | When you modify a style, you are affecting all the outline definitions in the current documents that use that style. |
| Options | Controls which of the preceding fields are active. |
| | Choosing Numbers Only deactivates Associated Style, Create Style, and Edit Style. Choose this when you do not want to add additional formatting to the appearance of the level number or to change the formatting of the paragraph when the level is used. This allows you to embed a series of numbers that WordPerfect manages into a paragraph. (For example: I want (a) some candy and (b) a toothbrush.) |
| | Choosing Styles Only deactivates Custom Number and Quick Numbers and clears Levels. WordPerfect's predefined Headings outline definition is a good example of a Styles only definition. |
| | Choosing Numbers and Styles activates all the fields. Most of the predefined outline definitions use both Numbers and Styles. |

 **TIP** To view your outline level styles while in the Style List dialog box (choose Format, Styles or press Alt+F8 from the document window), choose Options, Setup. Then check System Styles and choose OK.

**N O T E** Your printer may not be able to print all the characters you want to use as bullets, or you may not like how it prints them. Before using bullets, therefore, print a test document that uses all the bullet characters at all the point sizes you use.

To create your own outline definition, perform the following series of steps:

1. From the Outline Define dialog box, select the definition that is closest to what you want. Choose Options, Copy. The Outline Definition Copy dialog box appears.
2. Choose the destination of the copy (Current Document or Template) and choose OK. The Outline Definition Duplicate dialog box appears.

    Note that you can duplicate an outline definition to the current document and then edit the definition. Copying to a template is used to copy an outline definition you have created to the current template so that it will be available to other documents.
3. Enter a name for your copy and choose OK.
4. Select the newly named style in the Outline Define dialog box. Choose Edit, and edit the style following table 15.4. Choose OK.
5. If desired, repeat step 2 to copy the style to the current template.

Alternatively, perform the following steps:

1. From the Outline Define dialog box, choose Create. The Edit Outline Definition dialog box appears.
2. Type the name of the new definition. Now complete the settings you want to use for each of the levels of your definition, following table 15.4. Choose OK.
3. If desired, copy the style to the current template.

**Creating Your Own Bulleted List Definition**   You can either modify the predefined WordPerfect Bullets definition or create a new one. This section illustrates how to modify the WordPerfect definition. You can create a new definition using these steps:

1. From the Outline Definition dialog box, select the Bullets definition, and choose Edit.
2. In the Edit Outline Definition dialog box, choose Levels and then select the bullet that you want to change.
3. Choose Custom Number. Enter the new character by typing it or by using the WordPerfect Characters dialog box (Ctrl+W).

**Creating an Outline that Uses Tabs and Not Indents**   The predefined WordPerfect outline level styles use indents to produce outline text that aligns to the right of an outline number. For example, the first level item in the Bullets definition looks like the following:

- This line of text is long
- enough to wrap to two lines.

You may prefer a level style that produces text like:

- This line of text is long

    enough to wrap to two lines.

The following steps create a new definition that is a modification of the predefined WordPerfect Paragraph outline definition. The basic idea is to replace the Indents with Tabs for each level's style:

1. From the Outline Define dialog box, select the Paragraph definition; then choose Options, Copy.
2. In the Outline Definition Copy dialog box, choose Current Document, and then choose OK or press Enter.
3. In the Outline Definition Duplicate dialog box, name the copy *ParaTab*, and then choose OK or press Enter. You will be returned to the Outline Define dialog box. The new ParaTab definition will appear on the list of definition names.
4. In the Outline Define dialog box, select ParaTab. Then choose Edit.
5. Select the first level in the Levels list, then select Level 1 from the Associated Style list.
6. Choose Create Style. The Styles Editor dialog box opens, displaying a copy of the Level 1 style.

    Remember that editing a level style also affects all other outline definitions that use the same level style. Therefore, we've created a new level style which will be unique to this outline definition. Figure 15.18 displays the Styles Editor dialog box, with the completed level style.

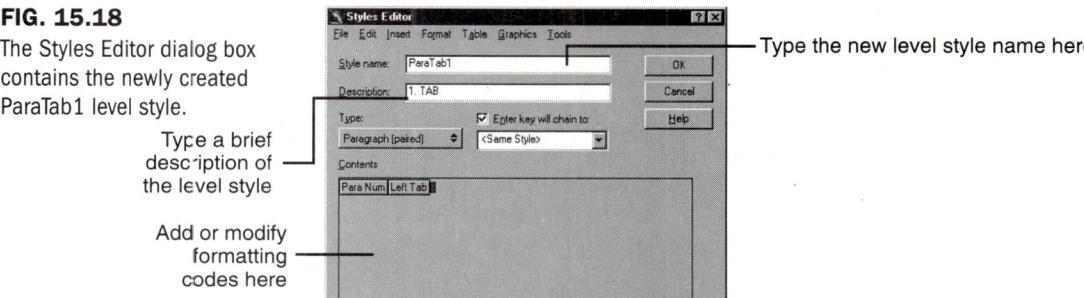

**FIG. 15.18**
The Styles Editor dialog box contains the newly created ParaTab1 level style.

Type a brief description of the level style

Add or modify formatting codes here

Type the new level style name here

7. Type the new level style name in the Style Name field. The example uses the name *ParaTab1*.
8. If desired, type a brief description in the Description field. This is a helpful method of reminding yourself what the style will do. The example uses the description *1. TAB*.
9. In the Contents field, place the insertion point after the last [Hd Left Ind]. Press Backspace to delete the [Hd Left Ind] code. Insert a left tab by pressing Ctrl+Tab. Choose OK to return to the Edit Outline Definition dialog box.
10. Repeat steps 5–8 for Levels 2–8, selecting both the number level and its associated style for each level. Be sure to create a new level style for each number level.
11. When all levels and styles are complete, from the Edit Outline Definition dialog box, choose OK or press Enter. You will be returned to the Outline Define dialog box.
12. Select your new definition and choose OK to begin using it. If you do not want to use your new definition, choose Close.

## Saving Your Definitions

If you create an outline definition that you find useful, you may want to save it so you can reuse it in another document. WordPerfect provides two methods for doing so.

From the Outline Define dialog box, you can choose Copy to copy an individual outline definition to the current template file, or the supplemental template file (if you have one assigned). This allows the outline definition to be automatically included in the list of outline types on all documents that are based on the current or supplemental template files.

You also can choose Options, Save As to copy all the outline definition, including its level styles, to a file. This allows you to retrieve the new definition into any document you may want. To retrieve a saved style file from the Outline Define dialog box, choose Options, Retrieve. Type the name of your style file, then choose OK. The retrieve definition then appears in your Outline Define Definitions list. ●

CHAPTER 16

# Working with Tables

*by Read Gilgen*

**O**f all WordPerfect's special features, the Tables feature offers more practical uses and enables you to enhance the effectiveness and attractiveness of your documents more than any other feature. That statement is a bold one, but as you learn in this chapter, it is easily substantiated. ■

### Create tables
Create tables for text or numbers, consisting of any number of rows and columns.

### Work with data in tables
Entering text and moving around in a table makes working with table data easy.

### Add and delete cells, rows, and columns
If you need more rows or columns, or if you have too many, you can modify your table quickly and easily.

### Modify the table structure
Create uneven and oddly shaped table cells by joining and splitting cells and changing column widths.

## Understanding Tables

Just what is a table? Although people use the term in many different contexts, in WordPerfect a table consists of rows and columns of data arranged and formatted to make the data easy to read or understand. For example, consider the following list:

| **Item** | **Part Number** | **Bin Number** |
|---|---|---|
| Widget | 34-222 | 24-A |
| Gadget | 33-245 | 26-B |
| Doodad | 33-249 | 13-F |

Typically, you might format this list only by separating the columns with tabs and by using underlining and different fonts to make the information easier to follow. Not only are such lists boring, but, you can easily lose your place, especially if the lists are wide and contain many details.

On the other hand, consider the same list as a printed WordPerfect 7 table (see fig. 16.1).

**FIG. 16.1**
An example of how simple data can be arranged in a WordPerfect table.

| **Item** | **Part#** | **Bin#** |
|---|---|---|
| Widget | 34-222 | 24-A |
| Gadget | 33-245 | 26-B |
| Doodad | 33-249 | 13-F |

Already you can see a difference—the program separates the items clearly, and the entire table is neat and attractive.

The structure of a table is very much like the structure of a spreadsheet, and in fact, you can even use WordPerfect tables for spreadsheet functions (see Chapter 31, "Advanced Tables"). In a table, WordPerfect labels the rows with numbers (1, 2, 3…) and the columns with letters (A, B, C…). The intersection of a column and a row is a *cell*. You identify each cell according to the row and column in which it resides (A1, B3, C14, and so on). In figure 16.1, for example, the word Widget is in the first column (A) and the second row (2); therefore, Widget is in cell A2.

All other table features are options. For example, you can change the appearance of the lines that WordPerfect uses to separate table cells, or you can omit them altogether. You can change text justification, and you can add text attributes. You can adjust the width and height of any column or row. You can even create formulas to calculate numeric information.

By using WordPerfect's table formatting options, you can create any kind of table—from simple lists to complex invoices, from schedules to calendars, from programs to scripts, and more.

In this chapter, you first learn how to create and modify a table by using a sample invoice as a model (see fig. 16.2). You learn how to enter text into tables, change the table structure, format table text, and convert existing data into a table format.

Designing, creating, and modifying a table is a visual and artistic venture. Although this chapter describes how to obtain certain results when creating a table, you have your own needs and opinions of what looks good. Don't be afraid to experiment, and don't be upset if the results are not quite what you expected. Simply try again.

**FIG. 16.2**
With WordPerfect's Table feature, you can even create complex forms, such as an invoice.

| Quantity | Description | Unit Cost | Amount |
|---|---|---|---|
| 2 ea | Deluxe Tour Packages | $834.00 | $1,668.00 |
| 2 ea | Tickets in End Zone | $63.50 | $127.00 |
| 1 ea | Game Football (autographed) | $75.00 | $75.00 |
| | | | $0.00 |
| **Comments:** Deposits must be received 14 days prior to departure. Thank you for your business. | | Subtotal | $1,870.00 |
| | | Tax (5.5%) | $102.85 |
| | | TOTAL | **$1,972.85** |

Badger Tours, Inc.
1234 Rose Bowl Avenue
Madison, WI 53700
(608) 555-4321

December 1, 1999

Before you actually create a table, you can save a great deal of time by doing some preliminary planning. First, ask yourself what you want to accomplish with your table. Do you merely want to present straightforward information more clearly, or do you want to design a more complex, heavily formatted form?

Next, determine the approximate number of rows and columns you want. You can have up to 64 columns and 32,767 rows (or 2,097,088 cells), although it's unlikely you'll ever use that many. You do not have to know the exact number of rows or columns you'll need, because you can add or insert them while you work with your table. Knowing this information in advance, however—especially the number of columns—can make creating, modifying, and using your table much easier.

You can also benefit from determining and selecting the font style and size you want to use before you begin. Again, this is not critical, because you can change fonts as you work with your table.

Finally, consider the number and placement of your tables. You may need to place two tables of dissimilar structure one after the other, rather than trying to create just one table. Also, you may need to place two tables beside each other, in which case you may want to use columns or graphics boxes (see Chapter 14, "Working with Text Columns" or Chapter 21, "Using Advanced Graphics Techniques," for information on table boxes).

Even in their simplest form, tables are easy to create and can be quite effective. Mastering the basic procedures described in this section is important. The more complex procedures, explained later in this chapter and in Chapter 31, "Advanced Tables," build on what you learn here.

▶ See "Using Basic Math and Formulas in Tables," **p. 995**
▶ See "Parallel Columns," **p. 446**
▶ See "Customizing Graphics Boxes," **p. 669**

## Creating a Table

At least two different methods of creating a table are available. You can use WordPerfect's menu system to specify the number of rows and columns you want in the table, or you can use the mouse to choose the table size you want from the Power Bar.

To use the menus to create a table, follow these steps:

1. Position the insertion point in your document where you want to insert the table.
2. Choose Table, Create or press F12. WordPerfect displays the Create Table dialog box, which prompts you to specify the number of columns and rows you want in your table (see fig. 16.3).

**FIG. 16.3**
The Create Table dialog box lets you specify the number of columns and rows you want in your table.

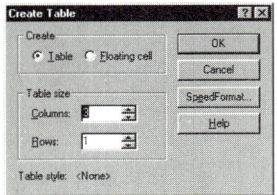

3. In the Columns text box, type the number of columns you want (for example, **4**).
4. In the Rows text box, type the number of rows you want (for example, **5**). Choose OK or press Enter to display the table you have defined.

If you specify four columns and five rows, WordPerfect displays the table shown in figure 16.4.

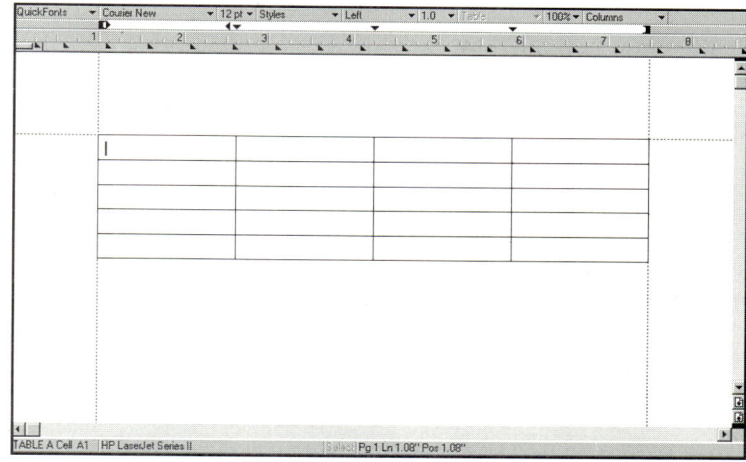

**FIG. 16.4**
In this simple table with four columns and five rows, notice that the columns are evenly spaced and extend from margin to margin, and the Toolbar now shows table-specific functions.

By default, all the cells in a WordPerfect table are surrounded by single lines, and the table has no border.

To use the Power Bar to create a table, follow these steps:

1. If the Power Bar isn't already displayed, select View, Toolbars/Ruler, and from the dialog box, select Power Bar, and then click OK.

    WordPerfect displays several buttons on the Power Bar. One of the default buttons is the Tables button, located between the Spacing (1.0) and Zoom buttons.

2. Position the insertion point in your document where you want to insert your table.

3. Click the Table QuickCreate button, and hold the mouse button down to display a large grid.

4. Drag the mouse down and to the right until the pop-up grid highlights the number of columns and rows you want (see fig. 16.5). If you need more columns or rows than is displayed on the grid, keep dragging the mouse; WordPerfect expands the grid up to 32 columns by 45 rows. At the top of the grid, WordPerfect specifies the number of columns and rows, in that order, that you have selected (4 × 5 in this example).

**FIG. 16.5**
In the Table button pop-up grid, click the button and drag the mouse to select the number of rows and columns you want in your table.

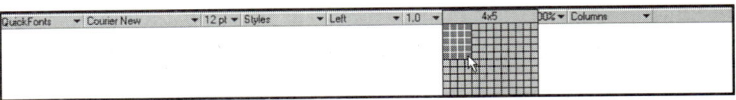

5. After you have displayed the number of columns and rows you want, release the mouse button. WordPerfect creates the table according to the size you indicated.

**TIP** If you decide you don't want to create a table, simply drag the mouse pointer to the top of the grid and when No Table appears, release the mouse button.

## Converting Tabular Columns to Tables

You may have existing text you want to place in a table, and you don't want to retype the text. Fortunately, WordPerfect provides a simple method for creating a table from text that is formatted in tabular columns. In fact, this capability may be the easiest yet most practical use for tables you will have.

Suppose that you have a list of company employees that includes their names, offices, and telephone numbers. The columns of data are separated by single tabs, as follows:

| | | |
|---|---|---|
| Engel, Peyton | VH287 | 3-2555 |
| Lindaas, Brad | VH390 | 3-5454 |
| Prochniak, Mary | VH271 | 3-2435 |

To convert data in tabular columns to a table, follow these steps:

1. Position the cursor at the beginning of the first line of data. Using the employee list as an example, place the cursor just before the letter E in `Engel`.

2. With the mouse or keyboard, select all the text to the end of the last line of data—for example, just after the 5 in `3-2435`. Don't include the final hard return, or you end up with an extra row in your table.

3. Choose Table, Create. WordPerfect displays the Convert Table dialog box (see fig. 16.6). Alternatively, you can click the Tables QuickCreate button on the Power Bar and choose Tabular Columns from the drop-down list.

4. Choose Tabular Column (the default), and choose OK. WordPerfect converts your tabular columns of data into a table (see fig. 16.7).

**FIG. 16.6**
The Convert Table dialog box is used for converting preexisting data to a table.

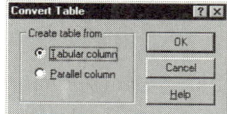

**FIG. 16.7**
After converting data from tabular columns into a table, you might need to use column width and other formatting to adjust the layout of the data.

| Engel, Peyton | VH287 | 3-2555 |
| Lindaas, Brad | VH390 | 3-5454 |
| Prochniak, Mary | VH271 | 3-2435 |

This procedure seems quite easy because it *is* easy; however, the key to successfully converting tabular columns to a table lies in the format of the original text. Make sure that each column is correctly aligned by a tab setting. Also, make sure that only one tab separates each column of data. If, for example, you use WordPerfect's default half-inch tab settings and use two tabs to separate the office numbers from the short employee names and only one tab to separate the office numbers from the long names, WordPerfect adds extra cells in the table for the blank tabs. Consequently, the result can be quite messy.

After you convert your data to a table, you can use the procedures you learn in this chapter to change column widths, modify column and cell attributes, and use line and fill options to format your table.

## Moving Within a Table

When you first create a table, WordPerfect positions the cursor at the upper-left corner of the table, in cell A1. Notice that the status bar, at the bottom of the screen, displays the name of the current table (Table A in this case) and the cell location of the cursor, Cell A1. When you move the cursor to a new cell, WordPerfect indicates on the status bar the location of the new cell.

To move the cursor one cell to the right, press the Tab key. The status bar now indicates that the cursor is in cell B1. To move the cursor one cell to the left, press Shift+Tab.

Note that if the cursor is in the last cell of a row, pressing Tab moves the cursor back to the first cell of the next row. Pressing Shift+Tab while the cursor is in the first cell of a row moves the cursor to the last cell of the previous row.

Sometimes using the mouse to position the cursor in the cell is a quicker and easier way to move from one cell to another. If you are typing, however, using the Tab key usually is easier. You can also use the arrow keys to move from one cell to another. If the cells are filled with text or numbers, however, using the Tab key or mouse is generally easier. Using the Tab key, the mouse, or the arrow keys to move within a table provides the same results. Choose the method which is easiest and helps you work in the most efficient manner (see table 16.1).

**Table 16.1 Moving the Insertion Point in a Table**

| Action | Result |
|---|---|
| Tab | Advances one cell to right |
| Shift+Tab | Moves one cell to the left |
| Arrow keys | Move any direction |
| Home, Home | Move to left column in row |
| End, End | Move to right column in row |
| Mouse click | Click directly in the target cell |

## Entering Text

When you enter text into your table, consider each cell a miniature document with its own margins and formatting. As you enter text, WordPerfect wraps the words within the cell, vertically expanding the row to accommodate what you type (see fig. 16.8). You can enter and edit text in a cell just as you do in any document.

**FIG. 16.8**
A table can contain more than one line of text in a cell. Notice that the row automatically expands to accommodate the text you enter.

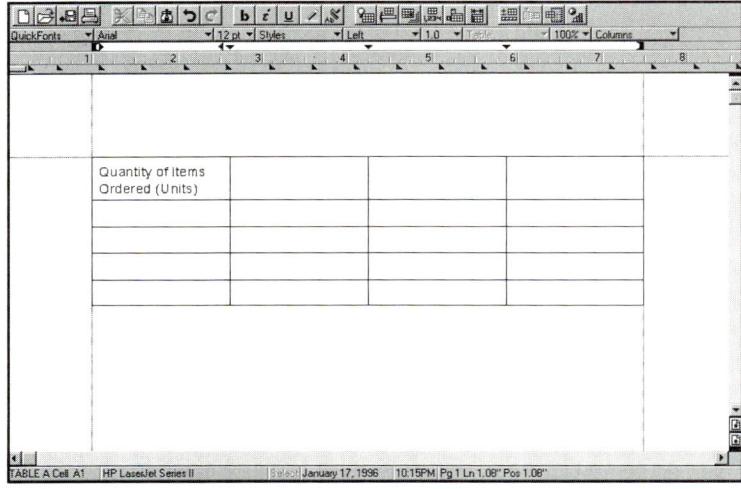

Suppose that you want to create a four-column invoice table in which you list the quantity, description, unit price, and extended cost of various products. You simply move the cursor from cell to cell and type the information you want in each cell.

> **NOTE** As you follow the development of the sample invoice table, you many not see explicit instructions to enter text. Nevertheless, when you see new text in these figures, enter that text into your own invoice table. Refer to figure 16.2 to see the completed invoice.

## Adding Rows to a Table

If you planned your table carefully, you probably have the right number of columns, but even the best planning often cannot predict the number of rows you will need. Fortunately, WordPerfect makes it easy to add extra rows in a table.

Suppose that you have filled your entire table and need an additional row at the end. With your cursor in the last cell of the last row (in cell D5, for example), simply press Tab. WordPerfect adds a row and advances the cursor to the first cell of the next row. You can now enter information in the empty cells of your new row. (See the later section "Editing the Table Structure" for more information on inserting and deleting rows and columns.)

## Selecting Text and Cells

Within a single cell, you select text the same way you do in a document. You can use the mouse to select text, hold down the Shift key and use the cursor keys, or press Select (F8) and use the cursor keys.

To select text from more than one cell, you must use the Select key (F8). This key allows you to precisely select the text you want. If you use the other methods of selecting, after you cross a cell boundary, WordPerfect begins selecting entire cells. For example, if you click the mouse in the middle of the text in cell A1 and begin dragging the mouse toward cell B1, WordPerfect highlights just the text until the mouse pointer crosses over into cell B1. At that point, the entire cells (A1 and B1) are highlighted and the mouse pointer changes to an arrow (see fig. 16.9). As you continue to drag the mouse to other cells, these cells also become part of a block.

You can use this method to select rows of cells, columns of cells, and entire tables of cells. However, to select a single cell, position the mouse pointer within the cell you want to select and move the pointer slowly toward the left line of the cell until the pointer changes to a horizontal arrow. This arrow indicates that you are about to select cells rather than just contents.

**FIG. 16.9**
You can select entire cells by dragging the mouse pointer across the edge of the cell until the pointer turns into an arrow. Continue dragging the pointer across cells to select multiple cells at once.

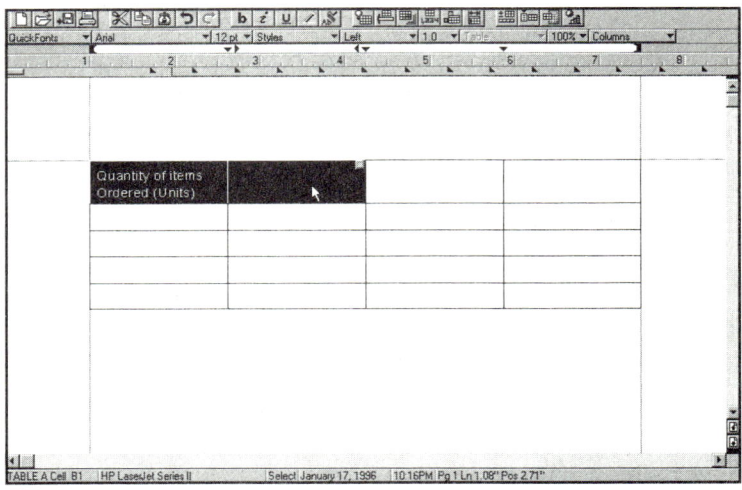

Click once to select the cell. Click twice to select the entire row of cells. Click three times to select the entire table.

To select a column, move the pointer toward the top line of any cell in the column until the pointer turns into a single upward-pointing arrow. Click once to select the cell, twice to select the column, and three times to select the entire table.

## Deleting Text from Cells

To delete text from a cell, you can position the cursor anywhere in the cell and use Backspace or Delete. You can also use Undelete (choose Edit, Undelete, Restore; or press Ctrl+Shift+Z) or Undo (choose Edit, Undo; or press Ctrl+Z) to restore deletions made in this manner.

A quicker and easier method for deleting the contents of entire cells is to select the entire cell using the method described in the preceding section. For example, if you want to remove all the text from cell A1 of the invoice table, move the mouse pointer to the left side of the cell. When the pointer turns into a horizontal arrow, click once and then press Backspace or Delete; WordPerfect removes the entire contents of the cell.

**N O T E** If you delete the entire contents of a cell, you cannot use Undelete to restore the deleted text. However, you can Undo the action.

You can use the same method for deleting the contents of an entire row, column, or table. However, because deleting the contents of rows or the entire table can be a bit more destructive, WordPerfect displays a dialog box asking exactly what you want to delete. For example, if you select all of row 1 and press Delete or Backspace, the Delete dialog box appears with the Rows radio button selected (see fig. 16.10). If you choose OK, you actually remove the entire row from the table. If you first choose the Cell Contents radio button, then choose OK, only the contents of that row is removed; the row itself remains.

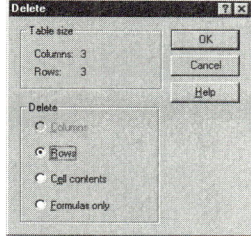

**FIG. 16.10**
The Delete dialog box enables you to delete the contents of cells or entire rows or columns.

If you select all the cells in the table, WordPerfect displays the Delete Table dialog box (see fig. 16.11), which offers several options:

- Entire Table
- Table Contents
- Formulas Only
- Table Structure (Leave Text)
- Convert To Merge Data File
- Convert To Merge Data File (First Row Becomes Field Names)

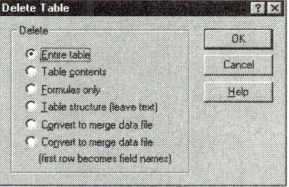

**FIG. 16.11**
The Delete Table dialog box enables you to delete the entire table, all the data in the table, or convert the table to a merge data file.

## Cutting, Copying, and Pasting Text

You can cut, copy, and paste text to and from table cells the same way you do in text documents. Within a single cell, select the text you want to cut or copy, and use any of the various methods for cutting or copying. Then position the cursor in the destination cell and paste the text. You can move text from a cell to the document, from one cell to another, or from the document to a single cell.

By selecting entire cells, you can quickly and easily cut or copy all the text along with its formatting to a new location. For example, suppose that you want to copy all of row 1 to row 2. Select the entire row by dragging the mouse pointer across all the cells (or you can move the mouse pointer toward the left edge of the cell and when the horizontal arrow appears, click twice). When you choose Cut or Copy (either from the Edit menu or by clicking the right mouse button), the Table Cut/Copy dialog box appears (see fig. 16.12).

**FIG. 16.12**
You can use the Table Cut/Copy dialog box to cut and paste entire rows, columns, or groups of cells.

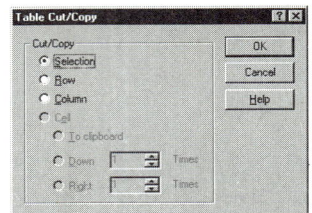

 Use Undo (choose Edit, Undo; or press Ctrl+Z) if you mistakenly cut or copy the wrong text.

In this dialog box, you can choose to move the current selection (single cell or block of selected cells), the entire row, or the entire column. To cut or copy the entire row, click the Row radio button, and then choose OK. Position the cursor where you want to paste the row, and paste the contents of the cells you just cut or copied.

 You can use the drag-and-drop method to move table cells from one location to another. After selecting the cells you want to move, simply use the mouse to drag the selection to the new table location and release the mouse button.

## Using the Tables QuickMenu

When the insertion point is positioned inside a table, you can access a QuickMenu that is specific to table operations. All you have to do is click the right mouse button. For example, to quickly perform a copy operation, you can select the cells you want to copy, access the QuickMenu by right-clicking (see fig. 16.13), and choose Copy from the QuickMenu.

**FIG. 16.13**
With the cursor in a table, right-click to access this time-saving menu.

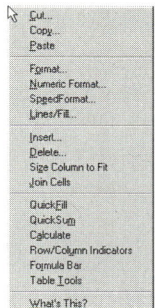

## Using the Table Edit QuickSpot

When you position the mouse pointer inside a table cell, an Edit Table QuickSpot appears in the upper-right corner of the cell. If you click this QuickSpot, the Tools dialog box appears (see fig. 16.14). You can use this dialog box to change a bit more directly many of the same things you can change with the Tables menu or the Tables QuickMenu.

**FIG. 16.14**
The Edit Table Tools dialog box offers quicker access to many table editing features.

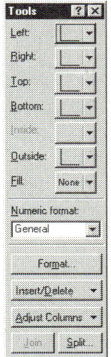

Although the Edit Table QuickSpot dialog box is more graphical and a bit more direct than the QuickMenu, it also tends to cover the area you are working on and, because it does not close automatically, it can get in the way. You can drag it out of the way, or unless you find something you really need in this dialog box, use the Tables QuickMenu instead.

## Deleting, Cutting, or Copying a Table

To delete, cut, or copy an entire table, including its structure, position the cursor before the table, press Select (F8), and move the cursor to extend the selection beyond the end of the table; then delete, cut, or copy the table.

To restore a deleted table, you can use Undo (Ctrl+Z). If you cut or copied the table, you can paste it in the new location. You can also Undelete the table if you deleted it.

 **TIP** If you select all the cells in a table and press Backspace or Delete, WordPerfect offers you the options of deleting the data, the entire table, or converting the data to another format.

## Saving and Printing a Table

A table is always part of a document, even when the table is the only element in the document. The procedure for saving tables, therefore, is exactly the same as the method for saving documents (see Chapter 2, "Creating and Saving a Document," for more information).

If you want to save just a part of your table, first select the cells you want to save, and then choose File, Save As (or press F3). WordPerfect asks if you want to save the Entire File or just the Selected Text. If you choose Selected Text and provide a file name, WordPerfect saves just the selected cells along with their format and contents. When you want to print a table, the process is the same as printing any other document. However, you should keep the following points in mind:

- WordPerfect normally does not split table rows with page breaks. The entire last row on a page prints with a line at the bottom of the row of cells, and the next entire row prints at the top of the next page with a line at the top of the row of cells.
- Table lines print properly, regardless of the font you use or the format of the text and graphics in the cells.
- Because WordPerfect prints table lines graphically, you can print tables on any dot-matrix or laser printer that is capable of printing graphics.
- Graphic printing takes longer than regular text printing without graphics. Depending on the printer you use, printing tables can dramatically increase the printing time of your document. On laser printers, tables do not slow printing significantly.
- You can decrease printing time on a slow printer by turning off table lines (see the next section, "Editing the Table Structure"). However, choosing dotted or dashed lines actually increases printing time over solid single or double lines.

 **TROUBLESHOOTING**

**I'm not too steady with the mouse. When I try to use the Table grid to create a table, I sometimes get the wrong number of rows or columns.** You can use the menu item Table, Create and fill out the dialog box to specify the number of rows and columns.

**Sometimes when I try to select cells in a table, the contents of those cells end up in some other part of the table.** You're probably inadvertently using WordPerfect's drag-and-drop feature. Be careful not to click again on the selected text after you've released the mouse button. If this happens, just click the Undo button on the Toolbar (or choose Edit, Undo) and try again.

# Editing the Table Structure

Up to this point, you learned about the default WordPerfect table settings, which include the following:

- Evenly spaced columns and rows that fit neatly between the margins of your document
- No special formatting of the contents of the cells
- Single lines that separate the cells of the table
- No special border around the table
- Left-justified tables (the tables themselves are justified at the left side of the document)

The real beauty of the Table feature, however, is that you can easily make all kinds of adjustments to these default settings. When you make changes to the shape and size of table cells, columns, and rows, you are editing the layout of the table, or the table structure.

## Tools for Editing a Table

WordPerfect offers several methods for changing the layout of your table: the menu system, QuickMenu, mouse, Table Toolbar, and Ruler Bar. Indeed, the only difficulty in editing your tables may be choosing which method to use.

Before you can access any of these tools, you must position the insertion point somewhere inside the table. You then can access the tools in these different ways:

- Select the Table menu by choosing Table from the main menu. WordPerfect then displays the Table menu (see fig. 16.15).
- Select the QuickMenu by clicking the secondary (right) mouse button (refer to fig. 16.13 for an example of what the QuickMenu looks like).
- Move the mouse pointer toward the edge of a cell until the pointer turns into a single or double arrow, enabling you to select cells and move column lines.

**FIG. 16.15**
The most complete collection of table options is found in the Table menu.

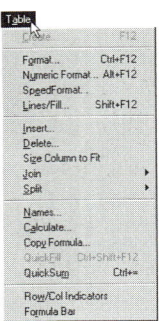

- When you create a new table using the default WordPerfect document template, WordPerfect automatically displays the special Tables Toolbar, which contains several buttons for editing table format and structure. If you use some other template or see another Toolbar, click anywhere in the table, then choose View, Toolbars/Ruler and the Table Toolbar will be listed. You could alternatively position the pointer anywhere on the Toolbar and click the secondary (right) mouse button for a QuickMenu of Toolbars and choose the Table Toolbar.

- Select the Ruler Bar by choosing View, Toolbars/Ruler and check the Ruler Bar option.

Although the Table menu is fairly accessible, learning to use these other tools can save you lots of time as you edit and format your tables.

## Changing Column Widths

Often, instead of evenly spaced columns, you need a table with columns of unequal width. To quickly change the width of a column, position the mouse pointer directly on the line separating two columns until the pointer changes into a double arrow (see fig. 16.16). When you click and hold down the mouse button, WordPerfect displays a dotted guide that helps you position the new column margin. Notice that a QuickTip box also appears, displaying the exact widths of the column to the left and the column to the right. Simply drag the column divider right or left until you have the desired width.

You can perform the same task by dragging the inverted triangles on the Ruler Bar (see fig. 16.17).

To change column widths proportionally, hold down the Shift key before you begin to move the column separators. In the invoice form, for example, hold down Shift and drag the line between columns B and C to the right until the last two columns are 1 inch wide (refer to the number on the right side of the QuickTip box). Now, without holding down Shift, move the line between columns A and B to the left until column A is 1 inch wide.

**FIG. 16.16**
You can change column widths by dragging the column divider with the mouse.

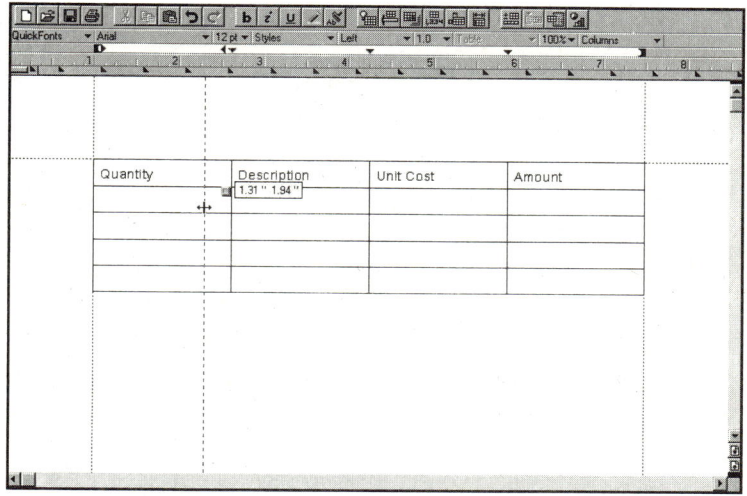

**FIG. 16.17**
Use the mouse to drag the inverted triangles on the Ruler Bar to size your table columns.

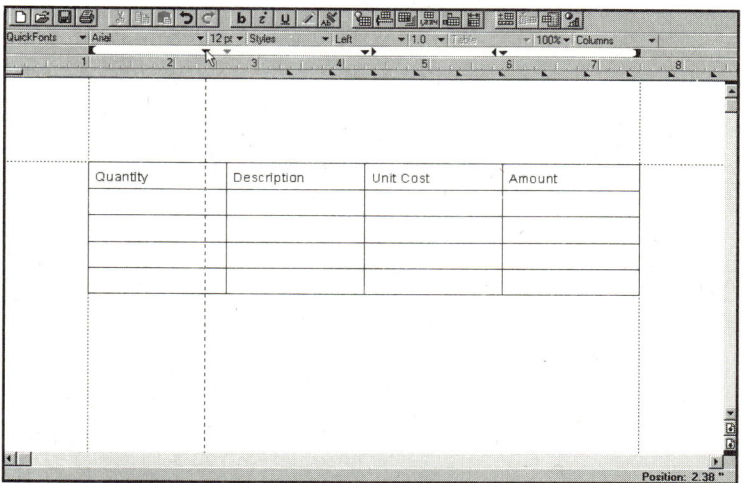

> **NOTE** If you prefer to use the keyboard to size your column widths, you can position the cursor in the column you want to change and press Ctrl+, (Ctrl and the comma key) to reduce the width of the column, or press Ctrl+. (Ctrl and the period key) to expand the width of the column.

Adjusting column width in this manner is not very precise. If you already have text in the columns and can see that the columns are wide enough, or if the measurements don't really matter, this method is adequate.

Sometimes you simply want to be sure that the columns are wide enough to display each cell's information on one line (for example, a list). To adjust a column's width to fit the text in its cells, position the cursor in the column you wish to adjust, click the secondary (right) mouse button, and from the QuickMenu choose Si_z_e Column To Fit. Columns adjusted in this manner expand to the right, thus reducing the width of columns to the right.

If, on the other hand, you want exact column measurements, position the cursor in any cell of the column you want to adjust and choose T_a_ble, F_o_rmat. WordPerfect displays the Properties for Table Format dialog box (from here on, I refer to this simply as the Table Format dialog box). This is a *tabbed dialog box*, which means that the bottom portion of the dialog box changes depending on which tab is selected at the top. Choose the Column tab, and WordPerfect displays the dialog box shown in figure 16.18.

**FIG. 16.18**
The Table Format dialog box is used in this case for formatting table columns.

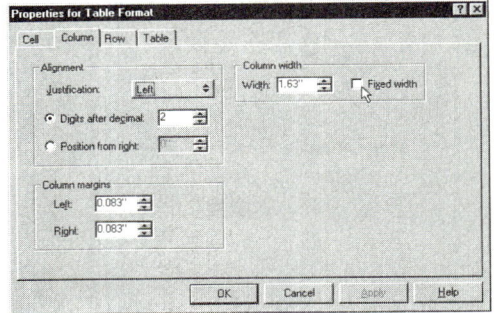

> **TIP** You can also choose the Table Format dialog box from the QuickMenu, or by clicking the Format Table button on the Toolbar.

To work with a specific column, click anywhere in the column and then bring up the Table Format dialog box and move to the Column tab. In the upper-right corner of the dialog box, choose Wid_t_h and type **1"**. Also, choose the Fi_x_ed Width check box to prevent proportional sizing of columns from affecting this particular column.

For example, in the sample invoice form, type **3.5"** in column B. You then can select both columns C and D, and set both columns to **1"** at the same time.

> **N O T E** You can specify the column width measurement in inches (the default unit of measurement) or in fractions of an inch, such as 1 5/16. Other units of measurement include centimeters (2.55c = 1 inch), points (72p = 1 inch), or WordPerfect units (1200w = 1 inch). WordPerfect automatically converts these measurements into the measurement type you are using as a default.

## Changing the Table Size

After you create a table, you often discover that it has too many or too few columns or rows. You learned earlier how to add rows at the end of a table by pressing Tab while in the last cell of the table. You can also insert or delete many rows or columns at one time. For example, suppose that you created an invoice table with five rows, and you discover that this table must have at least eight rows.

To add three rows to the end of the table, position the cursor in any cell of the last row and choose Table, Insert. WordPerfect displays the Insert Columns/Rows dialog box (see fig. 16.19).

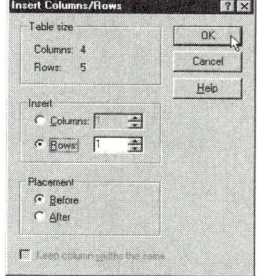

**FIG. 16.19**
The Insert Columns/Rows dialog box enables you to add rows or columns to your table.

By default, WordPerfect assumes you want to insert a single row preceding the current cursor position. In this case, you want to add three rows after the current cursor position; type **3** in the Rows text box, choose the After radio button, and choose OK.

Choosing Before inserts the specified number of rows or columns at the location of the cursor, pushing the rows down or columns to the right to make room for the new rows or columns. Suppose, for example, that you already typed the column heading information, but now want to add an extra row for your company name at the beginning of the table. Position the cursor anywhere in the first row and choose Insert from the QuickMenu (or from the Table menu). From the Insert Columns/Rows dialog box—which by default inserts one row before the cursor—choose OK. WordPerfect inserts a row at the top of the table, and the row that contains Quantity, Description, and so on, becomes the second row.

> **NOTE** Be aware that columns or rows you add or insert assume the special formatting attributes—such as lines and text formats—of the column or row that is selected when you choose Insert.

To decrease the size of the table, you can delete rows or columns. Position the cursor in the row or column you wish to delete, and from the Table or QuickMenu menu choose

Delete. Specify the number of columns or rows you want to delete and choose OK. The Delete dialog box also enables you to delete only the contents of specified rows or columns.

> **CAUTION**
> You cannot use Undelete to restore deleted rows or columns. Instead, if you accidentally remove a row or column, choose Edit, Undo (or press Ctrl+Z) to restore that column or row.

## Joining Cells

Suppose that you want the row at the top of your invoice to consist of one cell that extends all the way across the top of the table. You want one cell, rather than the four currently displayed, because you need more room to display your company name and logo. WordPerfect enables you to join two or more cells into one. To join the top four cells of the table, follow these steps:

1. Select all the cells in the first row from cell A1 to cell D1.
2. Access the Table menu and choose Join, Cell or right-click to bring up the QuickMenu, and choose Join Cells.

WordPerfect joins the cells, and the first row now consists of one large cell, A1. Cells B1, C1, and D1 no longer exist (see fig. 16.20).

**FIG. 16.20**
The invoice table contains several joined cells which become one large cell.

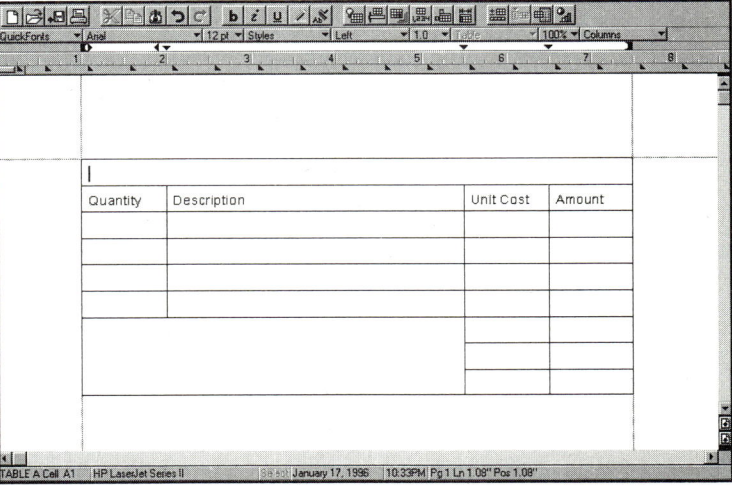

You can use this method to join any number of cells in rows, columns, or blocks. Joined cells become one cell, occupying the space formerly occupied by the individual cells. Suppose, for example, that in the lower-left corner of your invoice you want a box for comments. Select cells A7, A8, A9, B7, B8, and B9; then use Join Cells to create one large cell for your comments (refer to fig. 16.20). Any text you enter in this cell must fill it entirely before the cell expands.

 **TIP** If you've selected several cells and then decide you want to add the next cell to the group, you don't have to start all over. Just hold down the Shift key and press the appropriate arrow (the arrow headed in the right direction for your additional cell).

## Splitting Cells

WordPerfect also enables you to split a cell into two or more cells. Suppose that you now want to split the top cell into two cells: a small cell on the left for a graphic of your company's logo, and a longer cell on the right for your company's name and address. Position the cursor in cell A1, and from the Table menu choose Split, Cell, or from the QuickMenu menu choose Split Cell. WordPerfect displays the Split Cell dialog box (see fig. 16.21).

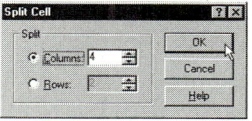

**FIG. 16.21**
The Split Cell dialog box enables you to split a cell into two or more rows or columns.

Because you want two columns, type **2** in the Columns text box and choose OK. WordPerfect evenly divides the cell into two cells, but the left cell is as wide as columns A and B, and the right cell extends across columns C and D. To get the results you really want—a small cell on the left corresponding to column A and a wide cell on the right extending across columns B, C, and D—follow these steps:

1. Split cell A1 into two cells. WordPerfect now displays three cells in the top row.

2. Join cells B1 and C1. You now have the cells you want in row 1 (see fig. 16.22).

You can also split a cell into two or more rows. Simply position the cursor in the cell, choose Split Cell from the QuickMenu, and in the Split Cell dialog box choose Row and specify the number of rows you want.

**FIG. 16.22**

Row 1 is split into a small and a large cell. You may have to split a cell into smaller units and then join cells to create the combination of small and large cells on the same row.

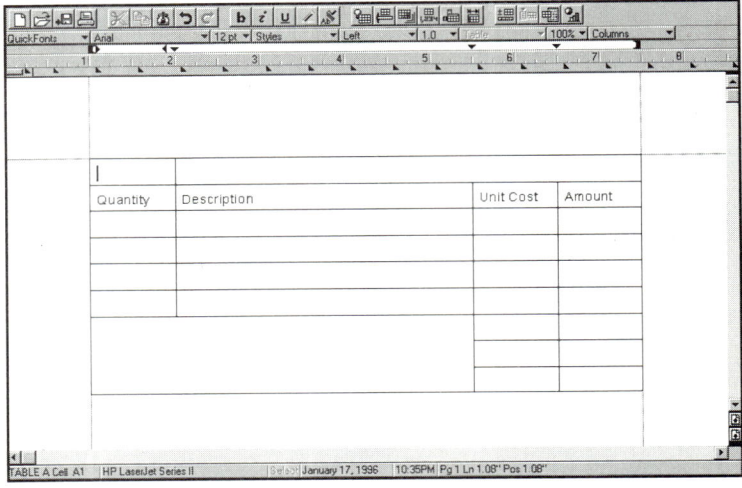

Joining and splitting cells may take some getting used to, but the procedure is easy and the effect can be quite attractive.

## Changing Row Height

WordPerfect automatically determines the amount of vertical space in a row, based on the amount of text in its cells. The cell requiring the most vertical space sets the height for the entire row.

Sometimes you need to set a specific row height, either to limit the amount of text you can enter into the row's cells or to make sure that a row contains a minimum amount of space, regardless of whether the cells contain data. A good example of the latter situation is a calendar in which you may want a fixed row height, regardless of the number of events on any given day.

For the invoice example, you want the top row of your invoice to occupy 2 inches of vertical space, even though the logo and address really need only 1 1/2 inches. To set a specific row height in row 1, follow these steps:

1. Position the cursor in row 1.

2. Choose Table, Format; or choose Format from the QuickMenu.
3. From the Table Format dialog box, choose the Row tab. WordPerfect displays the options for formatting a row (see fig. 16.23).

**FIG. 16.23**
To format an entire row of cells, choose the Row tab in the Table Format dialog box.

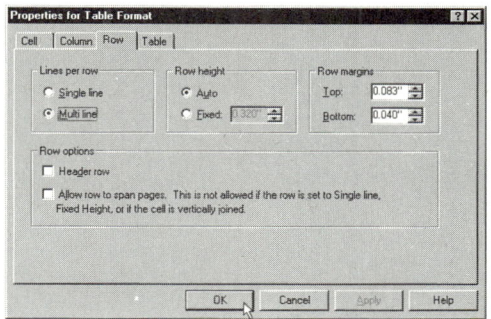

In this dialog box you can select the following combinations of options:

- *Auto Row Height* and *Multi Line Lines Per Row.* This combination, the default, automatically adjusts the row height to accommodate as many lines as necessary.

- *Fixed Row Height* and *Multi Line Lines Per Row.* This combination uses a fixed height and enables you to enter multiple lines, but only up to the specified height. You use this combination when you create a calendar, for example.

**CAUTION**
Make sure that any fixed height you select is high enough to accommodate at least one line of text. Otherwise, text which may appear on-screen will not print.

- *Auto Row Height* and *Single Line Lines Per Row.* This combination automatically adjusts the row height to accommodate a single line of text, regardless of the text's height (font size). If you choose these options and press Enter while entering text in your table, the cursor automatically advances to the next cell.

- *Fixed Row Height* and *Single Line Lines Per Row.* This combination maintains a fixed height but enables you to enter only one line of text. The font size for that line of text must be small enough to fit into the specified row height.

4. Because you want a fixed height of 2 inches, choose Fixed and type **2** in the text box. Leave Multi Line selected so that you can have as many lines as can fit in 2 inches.

5. Choose OK to set the row height for your first row.

## Creating Header Rows

Because a table can consist of up to 32,767 rows, it may span several pages. If you create a long table, you may want certain information (such as column headings) to repeat at the top of each page. If the table extends to multiple pages, suppose that you don't want the company logo to repeat, but you do want the column heading information to appear at the top of each page. To accomplish this, you specify this row as a *header row*. To create a header row, follow these steps:

1. Position the cursor in the row you want to designate as a header row (for example, row 2).

2. Choose Table, Format; or choose Format from the QuickMenu.
3. Choose the Row tab.
4. Select the Header Row to place a check mark in the checkbox.
5. Choose OK.

WordPerfect displays an asterisk (\*) next to the cell reference on the status bar (for example, Cell A2\*) to indicate that the row is a header row.

**NOTE** You don't have to begin with the first row, but if you want more than one header row, the rows you specify must be contiguous.

# Formatting Table Text

The preceding section focuses primarily on features that help you create the layout, or structure, of a table. You also want to make sure that the text itself contributes to the effectiveness of your presentation. Therefore, you need to understand how text attributes and text alignment apply to table cells.

## Understanding Formatting Precedence

Each time you choose a text formatting option, you have to consider whether that attribute should apply to the entire table, to a column, or to a cell or group of cells. Whether an attribute you assign to a table affects a given cell depends on the priority of what you assign. Changes you make to a specific cell or group of cells have precedence, or priority, over changes you make to columns. Changes made to cells or to columns have precedence over changes made to the entire table.

Suppose, for example, you specify that the data in a single cell should be centered (the heading of a column, for example) and then specify that the data for the entire column should be decimal-aligned. The change made to the column has no effect on the center alignment change you made to the individual cell.

Keep this in mind, especially as you format columns. Any changes to a cell you may have made (and forgotten about) are not changed when you specify something different with Columns or Tables formatting.

## Accessing the Table Format Dialog Box

 To format a cell, column, row, or entire table, you can access the Table Format dialog box by choosing Table, Format, by choosing Format from the QuickMenu, or by clicking the Table Format button on the Toolbar. WordPerfect displays the Table Format dialog box (see fig. 16.24).

The dialog box controls that are displayed at the bottom of this dialog box depend on which tab is selected at the top. Most of the procedures in the following sections take place in the Table Format dialog box. From there, simply choose the appropriate tab for the procedure being discussed (for example, Cell).

**FIG. 16.24**
The Table Format dialog box is a tabbed dialog box that changes depending on the tab you have selected.

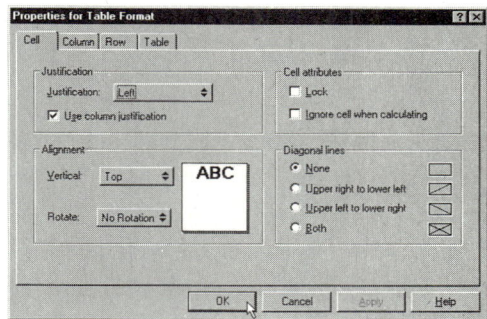

## Formatting Columns

To modify the text formatting of all the cells in a column, position the cursor in the column you want to format, access the Table Format dialog box, and choose the Column tab. WordPerfect displays the dialog box controls for formatting columns (see fig. 16.25).

To format several adjoining columns simultaneously, position the cursor in any cell in the leftmost column of the columns you want to format. Next, select that cell and the cells on the same row in columns to the right that you want to include. Then access the Table Format dialog box and choose the Column tab.

**FIG. 16.25**
To format columns, use the Column tab in the Table Format dialog box.

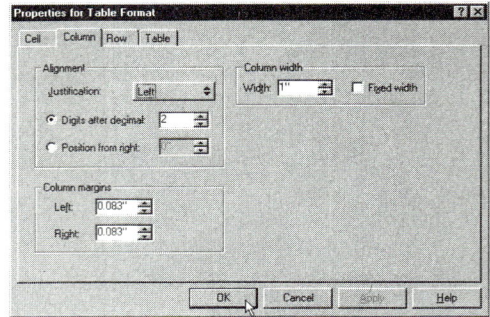

Perhaps one of the most commonly needed column formats is Justification, found in the Alignment section. Choose from the following options:

- *Left*. Used for most kinds of text.
- *Right*. Used for certain kinds of whole numbers and text headings for columns of right-aligned numbers.
- *Center*. Useful for columns containing data that you will probably scan vertically—columns listing Yes, No, and N/A, for example.
- *Full*. Used sparingly in tables, because text that extends to both margins in relatively wide columns often has large gaps of white space between words.
- *All*. Enables you to evenly space letters of a title or heading between both margins. Use this setting as sparingly as you use Full.
- *Decimal Align*. Enables you to align numbers at the decimal point, normally two digits from the right edge of the column. You can specify the actual distance in terms of digits (the default is 2) or by a specific measurement.
- *Mixed*. If you have selected two or more columns and the justification differs in either column, Mixed displays as the default.

Using your invoice as an example, align your columns so that the Quantity column is right-justified and the two Cost columns align at the decimal point. To right-justify the Quantity column, for example, follow these steps:

1. Position the cursor in any cell in column A.
2. Access the Table Format dialog box and choose the Column tab.
3. In the Alignment section of the dialog box, choose Justification, Right.
4. Choose OK to right-justify the column.

To align both the Cost columns at the decimal point, position the cursor in any cell in column C, and select that cell and the cell to the right in column D. From the Table

Format dialog box, choose the Column tab, Justification, Decimal Align to align the two columns at the decimal point.

The column headings now assume the new column alignments, as does the text or numbers you type into any cell in these columns. As you enter text, the program right-justifies the text on the left side of the decimal. As soon as you type a period, WordPerfect left-justifies the text on the right side of the decimal point.

By default, WordPerfect displays decimal-aligned text two digits from the right edge of the cell and places the characters on the right side of the cell. To change either of these settings, move to the Column tab of the Table Format dialog box. Choose Digits after Decimal, then specify the number of digits you need after the decimal. Choose Position from Right to specify a distance between the right edge of the cell and the last digit.

In addition to column width, explained earlier in this chapter in the section "Changing Column Widths," you can also specify the left and right text margins for your columns. The default is 0.083" (1/12 of an inch).

## Formatting Cells

After you format a column of cells, you may find that you need to change the justification or attributes of a single cell or group of cells within that column. For example, although the two price columns in your invoice now align text at the decimal point, the headings in those columns would look better if they were right-justified. To right-justify these headings, you need to change the formatting of the two cells containing these headings.

To change the format of a single cell, position the cursor in the cell you want to change, access the Table Format dialog box, and choose the Cell tab. WordPerfect displays the controls for formatting cells (refer to fig. 16.24).

To change the format of a group of cells, select the cells you want to change before you choose the Cell tab from the Table Format dialog box. The changes you choose apply to all the cells you selected.

> **NOTE** Although it might seem logical to choose the Row tab to format all the cells in a row, you must select all the cells first and then choose the Cell tab from the Table Format dialog box to format the row of cells.

To right-justify the column headings in columns C and D of your invoice, select the two cells, choose the Cell tab from the Table Format dialog box, and choose Justification, Right. Choose OK to apply the change to the two cells.

Many of the options for formatting cells are identical to those used for formatting columns, such as the Justification options. Other options used only for formatting cells include:

- *Use Column Justification.* By default, each cell assumes the attributes that are in effect for the column in which it resides. Thus, when you first choose the Table Format (Cell) dialog box, the Use Column Justification check box is selected. If you select a justification that differs from the column type, WordPerfect deselects this box. To reassign the column defaults, choose the Use Column Justification check box. WordPerfect automatically turns off any cell attributes that conflict with the default column formats.
- *Vertical Alignment.* By default, WordPerfect vertically aligns all text in a cell at the Top of the cell. Choose Bottom or Center to change the vertical alignment of the text in a cell. Rotate gives you the option to rotate the text within a cell by choosing 90 Degrees, 180 Degrees, or 270 Degrees. For more information on rotating text, see "Adding Other Enhancements to a Table" later in this chapter.
- *Lock.* This option protects a cell from being altered.
- *Ignore Cell When Calculating.* If the cell contains numbers that you don't want calculated during a math operation, you can specify that WordPerfect ignore the numbers. (For details on Lock or Ignore When Calculating, see Chapter 31, "Advanced Tables.")
- *Diagonal Lines.* You can add diagonal lines to cells by choosing one of the options, including Upper Right To Lower Left, Upper Left To Lower Right, or Both.

**NOTE** In previous versions of WordPerfect, you also applied text attributes such as Bold, Italics, and Relative Size through the Table Format dialog box. Now you apply attributes to table text the same way you manipulate regular text. See "Adding Text Attributes in Cells" later in this chapter for information on changing text attributes for entire cells or groups of cells.

## Formatting the Entire Table

Most of the changes you make to tables are to columns and cells. Sometimes, however, you may want to use a certain format as a default for your entire table. When you choose the Table tab in the Table Format dialog box, WordPerfect presents the same controls used for columns and cells (see fig. 16.26).

▶ **See** "Locking Table Cells," **p. 1005**

**FIG. 16.26**
The Table Format dialog box has the Table tab selected.

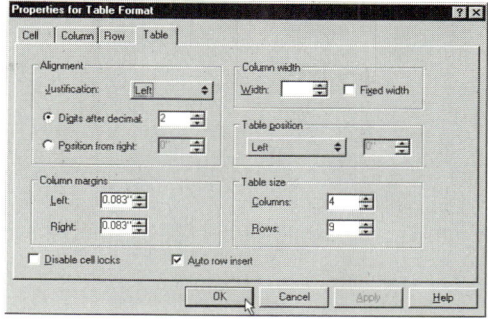

The options you select apply to the entire table, except, of course, in columns or cells you already modified.

Three options that apply only to tables are:

- *Disable Cell Locks.* This option lets you quickly disable any cell locks you may have set. After you finish modifying the locked cells, select this box again to reset the locks.

- *Table Position.* By default, tables are left-justified in your document. This option lets you change the justification of the table itself, not the text in the cells of the table.

- *Auto Row Insert.* Deselect this check box to prevent WordPerfect from adding a new row to the table when you press Tab in the last cell of the table.

### TROUBLESHOOTING

**I changed the format of my table column to decimal-aligned, but the text still appears left-aligned.** This is an easy mistake to make, and it's commonly caused by making a change to the table or to a column, but cell formatting is in place and it takes precedence. The easiest way to correct this is to select the cells, move to the Cell tab of the Table Format dialog box, and set the Justification correctly. This way, no other formatting scheme can have precedence over your cells.

**After making a justification change to a column, one of the cells doesn't seem to accept the new change.** This is usually because you formatted a single cell at some point. To make the cell match the rest of the column, position the cursor in that cell, choose Format from the QuickMenu, and with the Cell tab selected, make sure the Use Column Justification check box is selected.

# Changing Table Lines, Borders, and Fills

One part of a table's effectiveness is the lines that help the reader better understand the information. For tables in which a user needs to fill in information, lines also help the user know where to enter appropriate data. By default, WordPerfect surrounds each cell with a single line, giving the appearance that the table also is surrounded by a single line. In fact, there is no border at all around a WordPerfect table. In addition to lines, you can also fill the entire table or individual cells with varying patterns and colors of shading. WordPerfect's lines, borders, and fill options provide nearly limitless control over the appearance of your tables.

## Using SpeedFormat

While you can customize lines, fills, and borders, WordPerfect's Table SpeedFormat consisting of predefined "expert" table styles is perhaps an easier way to add lines, fills, and other formatting to existing tables. To access these expert designs, position the cursor in your table, and from the QuickMenu choose SpeedFormat. WordPerfect displays the Table SpeedFormat dialog box (see fig. 16.27).

**FIG. 16.27**
Use the Table SpeedFormat feature to select predefined table format styles or to create your own expert styles.

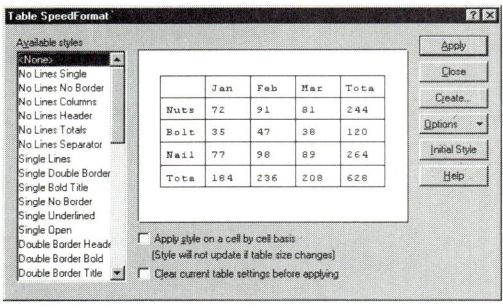

The Available Styles list box has many predefined table formats and you can scroll through the list to find one that looks interesting. When you click a style, WordPerfect displays a sample table in the preview box. For example, if you select the Fancy Totals style, WordPerfect formats your table with a colored title bar and no lines except to set off the totals (see fig. 16.28).

You can clear all formatting first and then apply the expert style you choose by selecting the Clear Current Table Settings Before Applying check box. You also can simply select the style and add it to any formatting changes you already have made to the table.

You can even create your own "experts" that you can use over and over again. For information on creating your own SpeedFormat styles, see Chapter 31, "Advanced Tables."

**FIG. 16.28**
When you select a Table SpeedFormat style such as Fancy Totals, you apply a predefined set of formats, lines, and fills to your table.

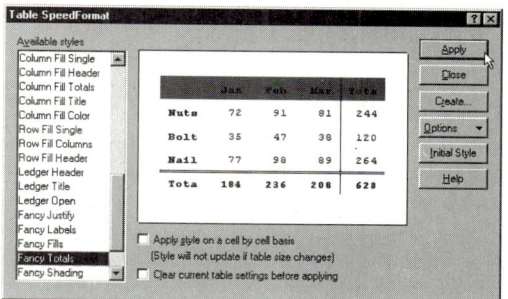

## Changing Lines

Changing the default single line between cells is simple. You can change to another line style or decide to use no line at all. Suppose, for example, that you want to use a thick line to separate the first row that contains your company address from the body of the invoice. To change the line style, follow these steps:

> **TIP** You can select multiple cells with the mouse by dragging the mouse pointer from one cell to another.

1. Position your cursor in the cell (or select the group of cells) you want to change. In your invoice table, for example, move to cell A1 and select the entire first row of cells.

2. Choose Table, Lines/Fill. Alternatively, you can press Shift+F12, or you can right-click and choose Lines/Fill from the QuickMenu. WordPerfect displays the Properties for Table Lines/Fill dialog box (see fig. 16.29).

   This dialog box defaults to controls for the Outside Of Current Selection and lists the current style for each of the line segments included in the selected cells. Unless you change them, each line uses the default (Single Line).

3. You can choose the line segment you want to change (for example, Bottom) from a palette of line styles by choosing that line's line style button. After clicking the line style button, you can also choose a line style from a drop-down list.

4. After choosing each line style you want, choose OK or press Enter. WordPerfect makes the change to your table.

> **NOTE** Depending on the resolution of your computer's monitor or the scale of your document display, single lines may not appear at all, or double lines may appear as a thicker single line. To be sure you have the correct line, you can increase the zoom percentage of your document.

**FIG. 16.29**
The Table Lines/Fill dialog box is used to change lines styles for cells, groups of cells, the entire table, or the table border.

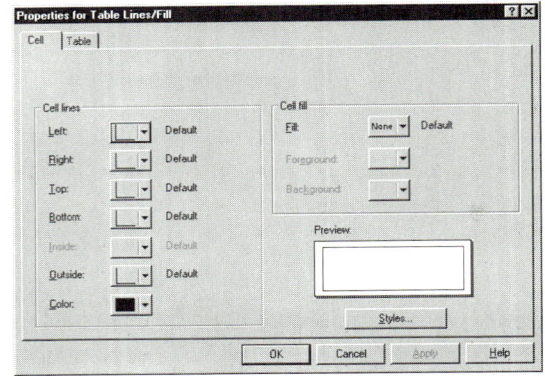

## Turning Off Cell Lines

You may find that as you work on a table it's useful to see the cell lines on the screen, but you don't want to print the lines. In your invoice, for example, you want to place your company's logo in cell A1, and use the left side of cell B1 as the left margin for your company's name and address. To turn off the line between the two cells, position the cursor in cell B1, choose Lines/Fill from the QuickMenu, and change the Left line segment to <None>.

To turn off printing all the cell lines in a table, select all the cells, select Lines/Fill from the QuickMenu, and change all the Inside and Outside lines to <None>. By using this method, none of your table lines print.

 **TIP** If you use parallel columns to format your text, consider using tables without lines instead. The effect is the same, but working with tables is much easier than working with parallel columns.

You can also change the default line style to <None> by choosing Lines/Fill from the QuickMenu, then choosing Table, Define Line Style, and choosing None. Note, however, that any changes you made to individual line segments still print.

## Using Table Cell Guides

If you still want to know where the cell lines are located, even though you don't want to print them, you can choose to display table cell guides. Choose View, Guidelines and then select the guidelines you want to see while you work on this document from the Guidelines dialog box. To make this the default, choose Edit, Preferences, Display. From the Display Preferences dialog box, choose the Document tab and select the Table Gridlines check box in the Show area. Choose OK, and then Close to return to your table. In the invoice table, for example, you now see a dashed line between cells A1 and B1. However, this line does not print.

## Understanding Default Line Styles

The default style for table lines is a single line. Although it may seem that a single line appears on all four sides of a cell, only two sides typically make up a cell: the left and the top. If you were to "explode" a typical table of three rows and three columns, the cells would resemble the cells shown in figure 16.30. (Notice that lines appear on the right and bottom sides of cells on the right and bottom of the table.)

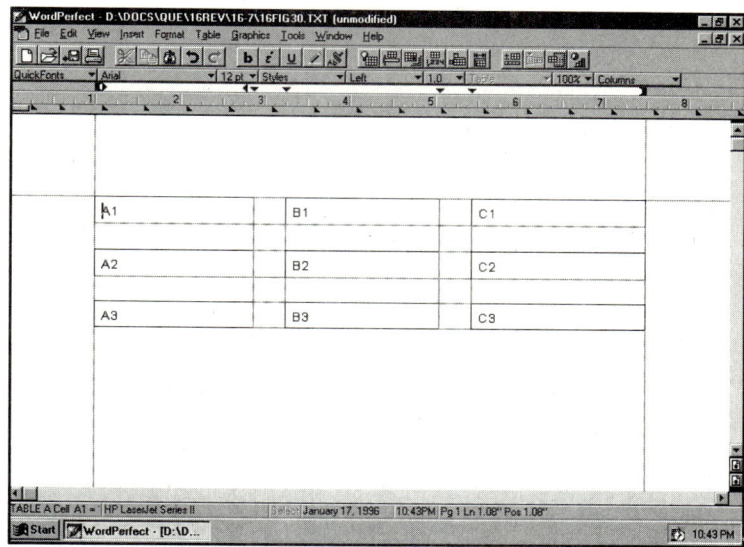

**FIG. 16.30**
An "exploded" WordPerfect table illustrates default line segments.

When you specify a line style other than the default, you force WordPerfect to display that style at the location you specify. But you must be careful: if you make changes to the right or bottom lines of a cell (perhaps you want to specify a single line for the right side of a cell) the cell line may not align with the other single lines in that column or row. In figure 16.31, for example, notice that the single line between cells A2 and B2 does not align with the other lines between columns A and B. To avoid this situation, make changes only to the top and left sides of cells whenever possible.

If you change both adjoining cell sides, you can create interesting effects because both lines print. Suppose, for example, that in your invoice table you select the Double Line style for the bottom of row 2, and the Single Line style (not Default) for the top of row 3. You force WordPerfect to print both styles of lines—a single line beneath a double line.

**FIG. 16.31**

If you change lines other than the default left and top lines, your table lines may not align properly.

| | | |
|---|---|---|
| This cell's default right line (none) has been replaced by a single right line. | | |
| | | |

## Changing Borders

The border around a WordPerfect table is separate from the lines that surround each of the cells in the table. By default, a WordPerfect table border has no border style. Suppose you want a double line around the outside edges of your table. To change a border style, follow these steps:

1. From the Table menu or from the QuickMenu, choose Lines/Fill.

2. From the resulting Table Lines/Fill dialog box, choose the Table tab to display table-related lines and fill options.

3. In the Table Border area, choose the Double style from the Borders palette. Note the resulting effect in the preview box.

4. Choose OK or press Enter to return to your table.

WordPerfect's Tables Border feature is both powerful and flexible. In addition to the standard list of styles, you can customize your border to include special combinations of lines, shading, and even drop shadow border effects (see Chapter 31, "Advanced Tables," for details).

## Changing Fills

WordPerfect enables you to fill individual cells, groups of cells, or the entire table with black, colors, or shades (percentages of black, which are shades of gray). Unless you have a color printer, however, the most practical use for this feature is to shade cells you want to set apart from the rest of the table. Suppose, for example, that you want to set off the column headings (Quantity, Description, and so on). To shade a cell or group of cells, follow these steps:

**TIP** If you plan to print text in the cell you are filling, choose 20% fill or less. Higher percentages of shading usually make reading text contained in that cell difficult.

1. Position your cursor in a cell on the row you want to change (or select the group of cells). In your Invoice table, move to a cell in the second row and select the entire second row of cells.

2. From the Table menu or the QuickMenu, choose Lines/Fill. WordPerfect displays the Table Lines/Fill dialog box (refer to fig. 16.29).

3. From the Cell Fill area, choose the Fill palette button and from the palette of shading styles, choose 20% Fill. Choose OK to return to your table.

You can select different shading or fill styles for any number of cells in your table. You can even create your own custom fills, including gradient shading and special patterns. WordPerfect also provides expert help so you can choose special formats for entire tables from a list of predefined or customized table format styles (see Chapter 31, "Advanced Tables," for details).

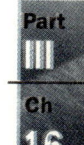

# Adding Other Enhancements to a Table

You can add graphics, set the text attributes for entire cells, format only portions of cell text, and add rotated text to your tables. The only remaining task before you can use your invoice table is to add the graphic image for your company logo and enter the company name and address.

## Adding Graphics to a Table

Each cell of a table is a self-contained miniature document, and you can place both graphics and text within a cell, just as you do in a document. To add *pizzazz* to the invoice table by adding a graphic to the upper-left corner of the invoice (see fig. 16.32), follow these steps:

▶ **See** "Customizing Table Lines and Borders," **p. 990**
▶ **See** "Customizing Cell and Table Shading," **p. 993**

1. Position the cursor in cell A1, the cell in which you want to place the image. Although you easily can move the graphics to another cell, beginning in the cell where you want to place the graphic is best.

2. Choose Graphics, Image. WordPerfect displays the Insert Image dialog box.

3. Choose the graphics file you want (ROSE.WPG, for example, is a graphics figure that comes with WordPerfect for Windows) and double-click it to bring it into your table.

4. Make any changes to the graphic as you desire, using tools you see on the Graphics menu or on the feature bar. (See Chapter 7, "Integrating Text and Graphics," for more information on adding graphics to your document.)

To get the exact results you want, you may have to experiment further, adjusting the size of the graphic and its position.

**FIG. 16.32**
The invoice table contains graphics and special text effects.

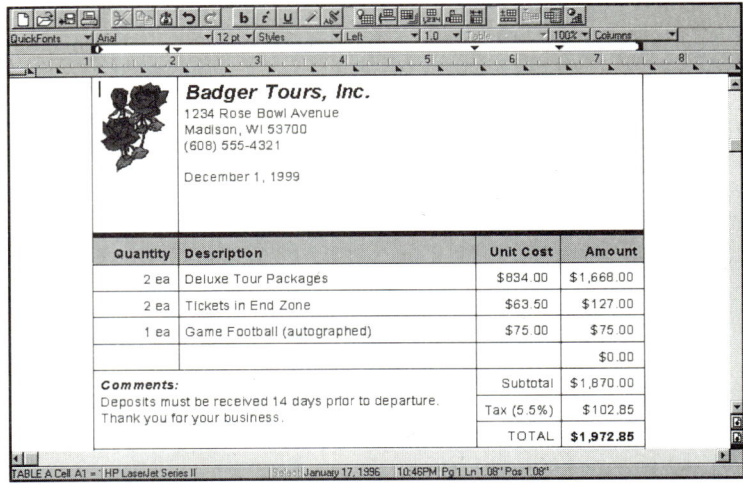

## Adding Rotated Text

As mentioned earlier, adding rotated text to table cells is as easy as accessing the Table Format dialog box and choosing a Rotated Text option. Other table formatting options are useful when using rotated text. Suppose you want to create a checklist such as the one in figure 16.33. Follow these steps:

**FIG. 16.33**
You can quickly and easily rotate text in cells at 90, 180, or 270 degrees.

| | Apples | Bananas | Cherries | Grapefruits | Kiwis | Navel Oranges | Tangerines |
|---|---|---|---|---|---|---|---|
| July | | | | | | | |
| August | | | | | | | |

1. Create the table you want (for example, eight columns by three rows).
2. Type the text in the cells you want to rotate. Don't worry at this point that the text doesn't fit properly. If you don't type the text first, you can't format the cell for rotated text.
3. Select the cells you want to rotate.
4. Access the Table Format dialog box and choose the Cell tab.
5. Choose Rotate, and the degree you want (for example, 90 degrees).
6. Choose Vertical, Bottom to align the text at the bottom of the cell.
7. Choose Justification, Center to align the text in the center horizontally.
8. Choose OK to rotate your text.

The columns with rotated text now are much wider than they need to be. Select all of those columns, and choose T<u>a</u>bles, Si<u>z</u>e Column To Fit. That's it!

**N O T E** WordPerfect actually takes text you type and places it in graphics text boxes. To edit the information in your rotated cells, you must double-click the cell, and in the Text edit screen, make your changes and choose <u>C</u>lose from the Feature Bar. See Chapter 7, "Integrating Text and Graphics," for more information on working with text graphics boxes.

## Adding Text Attributes in Cells

In earlier versions of WordPerfect, entire cells could be formatted for text attributes such as Bold, Italic, or Relative Size directly from the Table Format dialog box. The advantage to formatting an entire cell in this way is that any text or numbers that you type in that cell automatically format with the attributes you selected. Even if someone else fills in the data, you can be assured that the proper text attributes will be applied.

Fortunately, you can still format entire cells with text attributes, even if the process is not so evident. Follow these steps:

1. Select the cell or cells you want to format. Even if you wish to format just a single cell, you must select that cell first.

2. Choose the text attribute you want to apply, such as Bold or Italic. You can choose such attributes from the Toolbar by pressing a shortcut key (Ctrl+B for Bold, for example), or by accessing the Font menu (choose F<u>o</u>rmat, <u>F</u>ont; or press F9).

Now, whatever you type in the formatted cells automatically appears with the appropriate format attributes.

## Adding Text with Different Attributes

Normally when you add text to a cell, it takes on the attributes assigned to that cell. Sometimes, however, you must enter text with different attributes. For example, you may want to use a large boldface italic font for the company name, but normal text for the rest of the text in the cell (refer to fig. 16.32).

▶ **See** "Using Graphics Borders," **p. 255**

In this case, you enter the text into the cell just as you would enter text in any document. Then select the company name and choose Fo<u>r</u>mat, <u>F</u>ont; or press F9. In the Font dialog box, click the Relative Si<u>z</u>e pop-up menu and choose <u>L</u>arge. In the <u>A</u>ppearance section of the dialog box choose <u>B</u>old, and <u>I</u>talic. You could also choose a different <u>F</u>ont Face. Choose OK, leaving the remainder of the address in the normal font and size.

**TROUBLESHOOTING**

**I turned off all my table lines, but now I can't tell where the different cells are.** Just choose View, Guidelines, then select Tables in the Guidelines dialog box. This changes the document window so that the cell grid is displayed. These lines won't print, but they'll let you see what you're doing.

**I can't seem to position my graphics image properly in a table cell.** Graphics images require enough room to display properly. You may have to reduce the size of the graphics image or increase the width or height of the table cell. There is no exact rule for accomplishing this task, so keep trying (and using Undo) until you get it the way you want it.

# Exploring Other Uses for Tables

In the preceding sections, you learned the basics of creating and modifying tables by using a sample invoice. So many potential uses for tables exist that an entire book could be written describing samples and exploring tables options. This section gives you a taste of some specific and common practical applications for tables. In Chapter 31, "Advanced Tables," you learn how to build on these basics. Also, as you work with WordPerfect templates, note some of the creative ways tables are used to format documents.

## Creating Phone Message Forms

The Tables feature is an excellent tool for creating preprinted forms. If, for example, standard phone message forms don't meet your needs, you can create your own (see fig. 16.34).

▶ **See** "Using Data Fill to Simplify Data Entry," **p. xx** (31)

You want your forms (and tables) to be both functional and attractive. The advantage to creating your own forms with WordPerfect is that before you print a large quantity of the forms, you can test several versions of the form on the people who will actually use them.

## Creating Forms for Electronic Fill-In

The invoice form you created in this chapter can be printed and filled in manually, but you also can fill in such forms on the computer and print the result.

WordPerfect offers special math and spreadsheet functions that you can add to a form to provide greater functionality. Figure 16.35 is an invoice form that contains formulas. You only have to enter the quantity and the unit cost; then the form calculates the extended price, sums the charges, adds the sales tax, and gives the total for the invoice. Another example is a Grade Book form for tracking student grades as described in Chapter 31.

▶ See "Using Basic Math and Formulas in Tables," **p. 995**

▶ See "Designing More Complex Tables: The Grade-Tracking Table," **p. 1006**

**FIG. 16.34**
A sample preprinted phone message form can be created with the Tables feature.

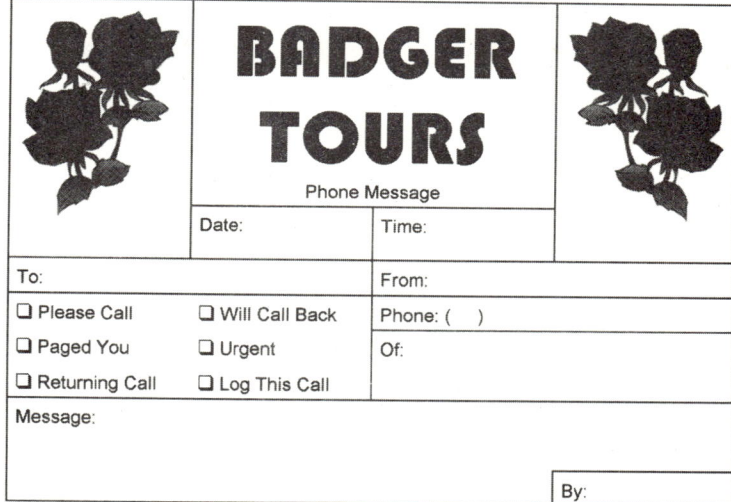

**FIG. 16.35**
The complete invoice table uses math functions to calculate the total amount of the invoice.

**Badger Tours, Inc.**
1234 Rose Bowl Avenue
Madison, WI 53700
(608) 555-4321

December 1, 1999

| Quantity | Description | Unit Cost | Amount |
|---|---|---|---|
| 2 ea | Deluxe Tour Packages | $834.00 | $1,668.00 |
| 2 ea | Tickets in End Zone | $63.50 | $127.00 |
| 1 ea | Game Football (autographed) | $75.00 | $75.00 |
| | | | $0.00 |
| **Comments:** Deposits must be received 14 days prior to departure. Thank you for your business. | | Subtotal | $1,870.00 |
| | | Tax (5.5%) | $102.85 |
| | | TOTAL | **$1,972.85** |

CHAPTER 17

# Creating and Modifying Charts with WP Draw

*by Pat Freeland, Alan Westenbroek, and Gary Pickavet*

Profits are up sharply! The Denver office is leading the company in sales! Jones is the best salesperson by far!

These statements may be wonderful news, but you need to add more information to help your reader understand their meanings. One way is to add several paragraphs of text to make your points.

You can illustrate your points more quickly, however, with charts. A chart can replace mountains of words and make the point more clearly. WP Draw, which enables you to create charts and drawings, has been included with version 7 of WordPerfect. Now, it is possible to create a chart in WordPerfect based on data you supply from a table, a spreadsheet, or right in WP Draw. ∎

### Identify the parts of a chart
You learn what a chart is, as well as the various parts of a chart and their uses.

### Identify the types of charts available and their uses
What type of chart should you use to present your data to your readers to have the greatest impact? In this chapter, you learn about the best choices.

### Create a chart
Once you've decided on the type of chart, learn how to create a chart and, if necessary, change the underlying data in the chart.

### Change the appearance of the chart
WordPerfect offers features that enable you to extensively change the way your chart looks. You learn how in this chapter.

# Understanding Chart Basics

A *chart,* sometimes called a *graph,* is a picture of numeric data. In version 7 of WordPerfect, the data can be in a table, spreadsheet, or a chart datasheet.

You can create a table in WordPerfect, as you learned in Chapter 16, "Working with Tables." You can also import into WordPerfect a spreadsheet you created in programs such as Excel or Quattro Pro, or a database created in a database program such as Paradox.

It's up to you whether the table appears in the document itself; in some cases it isn't necessary to display both the chart and the data. You may be interested in illustrating the growth of profits, for example. A chart with a line gracefully sweeping upward may do the job perfectly without a table of figures close by.

> **NOTE** A table or spreadsheet is a series of rows and columns. The rows are designated with numbers, the columns with letters. The intersection of a row and column is a *cell.* Labels, values, and formulas are entered into these cells.

Figure 17.1 shows a simple bar chart with the important parts labeled. Each bar in the chart refers to a single number in a table. The top of a bar is called a *data point.* Naturally, each type of chart represents data points differently. A line chart, for example, shows data points as marks on a line, sometimes at a place where the direction of the line changes.

Along the left side of the chart is the *vertical y-axis.* Numbers appear next to this axis, generally starting with zero and ending slightly higher than the largest number in the table. Each data point is compared in height to the numbers on the y-axis.

The bottom of the chart is the *x-axis.* In most charts, the names of the items being compared appear along this axis. In figure 17.1, the performance of several offices is being compared for the four quarters of the year. The names of the quarters are along the x-axis.

**FIG. 17.1**
This simple three-dimensional bar chart shows quantities by both quarter and region.

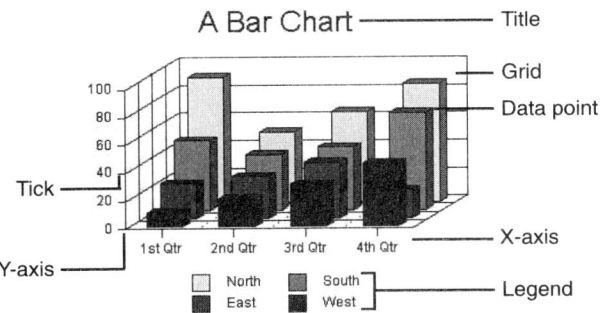

The little boxes and descriptions at the bottom of the chart is the *legend*, which matches the pattern or color of each data point with one of the series in the table. In figure 17.1, the legend tells which color or pattern is associated with which office.

The horizontal lines running across the chart is the *grid*, which is used to help compare data points with the y-axis and each other.

▶ See "Creating a Table," **p. 498**
▶ See "Importing and Working with Spreadsheet/Database Data," **p. 573**

# Understanding How Data Affects a Chart

The way you arrange data in a table determines how WordPerfect displays the data in the chart. Table 17.1 shows the data used for the chart in figure 17.1. The names of the items being compared—the quarters—are in the top row of the table. They are the labels that appear on the x-axis.

**Table 17.1  Data Used To Create the Graph in Figure 17.1**

|       | 1st Qtr | 2nd Qtr | 3rd Qtr | 4th Qtr |
|-------|---------|---------|---------|---------|
| North | 90      | 50      | 65      | 85      |
| South | 50      | 40      | 45      | 70      |
| East  | 25      | 30      | 40      | 20      |
| West  | 10      | 20      | 30      | 45      |

The series are the numbers entered in the rows. One number is in each series for each quarter. The name of the series is in the left column. In table 17.1, there are four series: North, South, East, and West. When you create the chart, each number in the series is converted into a data point. One data point from each series is grouped with data points from the other series. In figure 17.1, the data points for each series of each quarter are displayed in a group of four bars.

Table 17.2 contains the same data as table 17.1, but it has been rearranged so that the series are now the offices, not the quarters. The chart in figure 17.2 is based on the data in table 17.2 and allows the reader to see the data represented differently. Office names, not quarters, are on the x-axis.

**Table 17.2 Data with Quarters, Instead of Offices, Represented in Rows**

|         | North | South | East | West |
|---------|-------|-------|------|------|
| 1st Qtr | 90    | 50    | 25   | 10   |
| 2nd Qtr | 50    | 40    | 30   | 20   |
| 3rd Qtr | 65    | 45    | 40   | 30   |
| 4th Qtr | 85    | 70    | 20   | 45   |

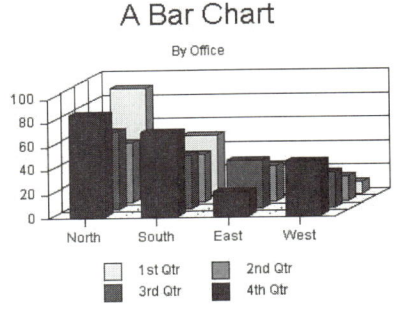

**FIG. 17.2**
A new bar chart based on rearranged data makes a different point. The bars are grouped by quarter in figure 17.1, and by regional office in this figure.

# Understanding the Chart Types

WordPerfect enables you to choose seven basic chart types: bar charts, line charts, radar charts, high/low charts, area charts, scatter charts, and pie charts. The following list describes the seven types of charts and explains why you might choose each. (Don't worry if the one you choose doesn't work out right; you can always change it.)

- *Bar chart.* Each data point is represented by a bar that starts at the x-axis and rises parallel to the y-axis to a height corresponding to the value it represents (refer to fig. 17.2).

    Bar charts are used for a quick comparison of related information or for showing trends in groups of related information. Generally, this type of chart should be used only when small amounts of data are involved; otherwise, a bewildering collection of tiny bars appears, looking like a cluster of match sticks.

    *Stacked bar charts* are a variation of bar charts. Stacked bar charts stack all bars in one bar to enable the user to see the contribution of each to the whole.

- *Line chart.* Figure 17.3 shows a line chart based on the data in table 17.1. Each data point is a marker on a line; one line for each series connects the data points for that series. Line charts are commonly used to display trends.

**FIG. 17.3**
Line charts are often used to show the relationship between two factors. They can help your reader quickly understand relationships and trends even with large quantities of data. Each data point is a marker on a line, and the lines show the progression of the data points.

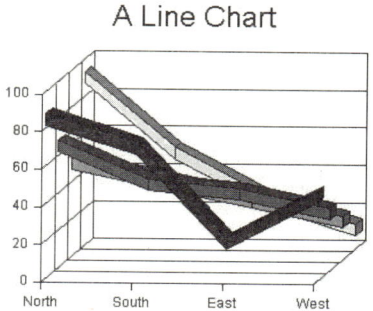

- *Radar chart.* Each data point is represented by a mark that can be placed anywhere within the x-axis and y-axis. Radar charts are used to show data over a period of time. They can be used to show variations and are ideal for plotting trends.
- *High/Low chart.* Figure 17.4 shows a high/low chart. Each figure displays four separate numbers in a series. The vertical bar represents the spread between the highest and lowest value of an item. The left "wing" of the bar represents the value of the item at the beginning of a specified time period, and the right "wing" represents its value at the close of the time period.

**FIG. 17.4**
A high/low chart is commonly used to show the performance of individual stocks for a given period of time.

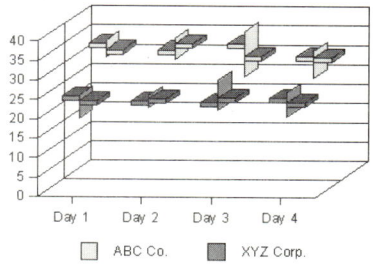

- *Area chart.* Figure 17.5 shows an area chart. It is really a line chart with the space between the line and the x-axis filled with a color or pattern. Area charts are used to display broad trends. The contrast between the areas below and above the line call attention to the trend illustrated by the slope of the line.
- *Scatter chart.* This type of chart is unique in that the top row of the table on which the chart is based contains values, not labels. The data points in the chart represent the relationship between the data in the series and the data in the top row of the table that appears on the x-axis.

**FIG. 17.5**
An area chart is a variation of a line chart. The space between the line for each of the series and the x-axis is filled with a color or pattern.

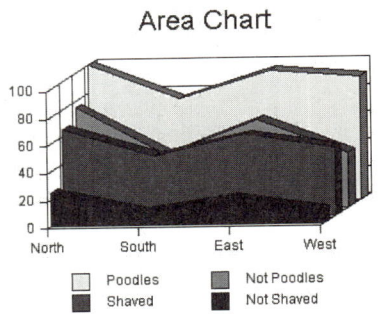

For example, you might want to show the relationship between temperature (entered in the top row) and sales of gloves, hats, mittens, and suntan cream (each item entered in the left column).

- *Pie chart.* Figure 17.6 shows a pie chart. Pie charts are used to show the contribution of each part to the whole. Only one set of values can be displayed in a pie chart. Pieces of the pie correspond to values entered in a column below the label at the top of the column. Negative numbers cannot be displayed by a pie chart, because you cannot have a negative piece of pie.

  Generally, it is best to use no more than six numbers for a pie chart—too many pieces can cause confusion. If more than six numbers are involved, it's better to create several separate pie charts or use one label for several of the smaller pieces.

**FIG. 17.6**
A pie chart can show the relationship of only one set of values. The pieces of the pie show what portion each item is of the whole.

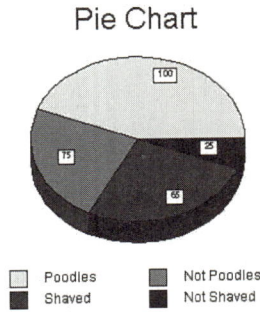

> **TIP** Negative numbers may be used in bar, line, area, and scatter charts, but they won't be displayed correctly in high/low and pie charts.

> **NOTE** Sometimes one series may deserve special attention. The sales of one product, for example, may need to be displayed in a different way to set it apart. To differentiate one piece of data in a pie chart, the piece can be *exploded,* or separated from the rest of the pie.

Another way to set one series apart from the other series is to represent its data with a chart type different from the type used for the others. In a bar chart, the sales figures for the company's flagship product could be displayed as a line rather than as a bar. (See the section "Making Changes to a Series" later in this chapter for details on how to change the chart type for one series.)

> **TIP** Pie charts can be compared by using stacked bar charts because they both depict data as it relates to the whole. Each stacked bar represents a pie. The chart type you use depends on the message you want to deliver. The saying "A picture is worth a thousand words" is only true if you use the right picture.

## Creating the Chart

Before you create a chart, you need to create a table of data for the chart to represent. This table can be a spreadsheet created in a dedicated spreadsheet program such as Quattro Pro; it can be entered in a table created in WordPerfect, or it can be data you enter directly into the datasheet when you're using the Chart Editor. See Chapter 16, "Working with Tables," for information on how to create a table and enter data. Be sure you also read and understand the section "Understanding How Data Affects a Chart" earlier in this chapter.

 Choose Graphics, Chart. WordPerfect changes the menus and toolbars to show that you're editing a chart object. The datasheet and a chart with the default type appear in the document with a heavy border around it (see fig. 17.7). By default, WordPerfect generates a bar chart.

If you created a spreadsheet in another program, choose Data, Import or press Ctrl+O. In the Filename field of the dialog box that appears, type the path and file name of the spreadsheet you want to import, or click the folder icon to display the Select File dialog box to help you locate the file.

The Import Data dialog box also displays any named ranges contained in the selected spreadsheet. It has a Range field where you can type a specified spreadsheet range. This enables you to bring only a portion of an entire spreadsheet file into the datasheet without having to delete any unwanted data.

The data from the file you import appears in the datasheet and replaces the data currently visible.

**FIG. 17.7**
In WordPerfect in WP Draw Chart mode, the datasheet is a separate window that you can close or move around.

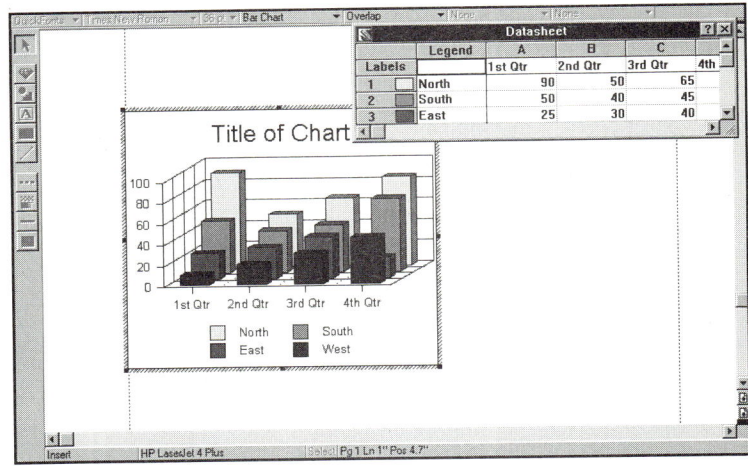

 **TIP** To get data from a program saved in a format not supported by the importer, copy it to the Clipboard and paste it into the datasheet by choosing Edit, Paste.

It is also possible to start entering data in the table section of the editing window. Place the cursor in a cell and type the data you want to place in that cell. You move from cell to cell by pressing the appropriate arrow key or by clicking the desired cell. For long-distance moves, click the Go To Cell button and choose Edit, Go To Cell or Ctrl+G from the Chart Edit Menu Bar. Type the cell address of the cell you want to change and press Enter.

The Tables feature in WordPerfect enables you to create a table with more features, such as formulas, than is possible in the table section of the chart edit window. Therefore, you may prefer to create a table in the document, generate a chart, and then later delete the table from the document if you don't want it to be visible.

> **NOTE** After the chart has been created, it does not look at the data in the document to place its data points. Therefore, the chart isn't affected by data deletions. However, unlike the WP Draw datasheet which can be closed and opened, if you delete the table from your document, you'll no longer be able to edit the chart data values.

 After you place the table in the document, put the cursor anywhere in the table and choose Graphics, Chart. WordPerfect changes its menus and toolbars to reflect the fact that you're creating and editing an embedded chart object. The chart appears with the data from your table already loaded. By default, WordPerfect generates a bar chart.

## Touring the WP Draw Interface

The major features of the WP Draw interface are explained in the following list:

- *Menu.* Across the top of the window is the pull-down menu bar, which WordPerfect alters to provide the commands you need while editing a WP Draw object. Items in this menu enable you to make changes to the chart, the data, and the display of the editing window. You access and use this menu the same way you use any of WordPerfect's other pull-down menus.

- *Main Toolbar.* WP Draw replaces WordPerfect's default Toolbar with its own. This Toolbar is similar to the one used in WordPerfect, but it uses functions relating to WP Draw. Many of these buttons provide quicker ways to accomplish the tasks included in the menu. If the Toolbar is hidden, you can make it visible by choosing View, Toolbar.

- *Drawing Toolbar.* On the left side of the chart editing window is a palette of tools. These buttons enable you to make changes to the style, format, and appearance of objects in your drawing.

**NOTE** You can move the Tool palette, which by default is to the left of the window. Notice that the mouse cursor changes to a hand as you move the mouse cursor across a blank area of the Tool palette. You can place the mouse pointer in that area and click and drag the entire Tool palette to another area of the screen. If the WP Draw window is not maximized, you can place the palette outside of the WP Draw window.

**NOTE** You can customize WP Draw's Toolbar just like any other. Choose Edit, Preferences, Toolbar to access the Toolbar Preferences dialog box. You can add, delete, or move buttons and change the bar's position. You can also hide or display the Toolbar by choosing View, Toolbar.

### TROUBLESHOOTING

**I can't find the Toolbar.** WordPerfect provides the flexibility to show or hide different elements of the screen, including toolbars. If you are missing one, choose View, Toolbars/Ruler.

**WP Draw either takes forever to start or it won't start at all.** The good part about Object Linking and Embedding (OLE) is how easy and seamless it makes integrating data from different places. The bad part involves the amount of memory and system resources it requires. The performance of machines with less than 8M of memory usually suffers when using OLE. If WP Draw starts slowly or fails to start, you may need more memory in your computer. Sometimes you can get around this by closing other applications you don't need at the moment. Exiting Windows and restarting can also free up system resources and get you going.

**My chart looks great on-screen, but I can't read it once it's printed.** Many black-and-white printers don't do a very good job of translating colors to differing shades of gray. To do it yourself, select the chart object in your document, right-click to display the QuickMenu, and choose Image Tools. Select the Black & White tool and adjust the threshold settings until you see a clear difference in the different elements of your chart.

## Moving Between the Chart and the Rest of the Document

When you want to return to the document, choose Close from the Toolbar. You can also click anywhere outside the chart's borders, and WordPerfect will return to editing the document.

Click anywhere in the chart and selection handles appear around the chart's frame. Any commands used affect the selected chart.

To leave the document and reenter Chart Edit mode, select the chart you want to edit. With the chart selected, choose Edit, Chart Object, Edit. Double-clicking the selected chart also switches to Chart Edit mode.

# Changing the Underlying Data

After you create a table and generate a chart, you may need to change some of the data. It is possible that you either made a mistake in data entry or some of the numbers changed since you created the chart.

If your chart was created based on data in a datasheet, you must make the change in the datasheet for any data change to be reflected in the chart. If your chart was created from data in a table in the document, you must make changes in the table for any data change to be reflected in the chart.

> **CAUTION**
>
> If you delete the table in the document that your chart was created from, you will no longer be able to make changes to the data values in your chart. Consider moving the table to a different page or area of your document if you don't want it to print with the chart.

To change data in the datasheet, move the cursor to the cell in which you want to enter new data and type the correction. You can also double-click the cell; choose Edit, Cell; or press F11 to display the Edit Current Cell dialog box. The advantage to using the Edit Current Cell feature is that the contents of the current cell appear separated from the rest of the table, making it easier to concentrate on the contents of one cell at a time. A small cell edit window appears on-screen with the contents of the current cell in an edit box in the middle. When you complete the correction, click OK or press Enter.

To navigate around the datasheet, use the arrow keys, the Go To feature (Ctrl+G), or the scroll bars. Be careful when using the scroll bars; they move the focus of the screen but do not move the cell highlighter, so be sure to click a cell in the visible window before pressing an arrow key or entering data. If you don't click a cell, use an arrow key to return to the area of the screen previously visible. Otherwise, the data you type is entered in a cell off-screen.

You can choose Cut, Copy, and Paste from the Edit menu to move and copy data from cell to cell. You can also access these features from the Toolbar. By clicking and dragging across several cells and then using the Edit menu, you can copy and move the contents of several cells at once. To move the data in column A to column E, for example, click and drag across all the cells in column A that have data. Selected cells appear black with white text. Choose Edit, Cut (Ctrl+X). Then move the cell highlighter to the top cell in column E and choose Edit, Paste (Ctrl+V).

 To select an entire column or row, click the row number or column letter.

> **CAUTION**
>
> Choosing Edit, Clear removes the contents, formatting, or both from selected cells, but does not place them in the Clipboard. They are erased permanently and cannot be pasted elsewhere. In addition, Undo is not an option on the WP Draw Edit menu. Choosing Edit, Clear All can be even more disastrous because it completely removes all data from the entire datasheet. Notice that a prompt appears when you choose Clear All, asking if you really want to clear all data. Make sure you really want to empty the table before answering the prompt.

To update the chart with changes to the datasheet, choose View, Redraw or press Ctrl+F3. Alternatively, you can choose View, Auto Redraw and changes made to the datasheet will be made to the chart immediately. The chart will also be updated when you exit WP Draw and return to your document.

To update a chart that is based on data from a table in your document, move the mouse pointer over the chart, then right-click the chart. From the QuickMenu that appears, choose Update Chart From Table. The chart is updated with the data from the table.

## Formatting Data

When numbers are entered in cells, they may appear without any formatting (dollar signs, commas, or extra decimal places) or with the wrong formatting. You apply formatting to the current cell—or to a selected group of cells—by choosing Data, Format or pressing Ctrl+F12; or by right-clicking the datasheet item you want to format to display the QuickMenu and choose Format. Standard formats available include comma separators, currency symbols, and percent signs. Choosing one of the main formats enables you to determine the number of decimal places the data has in the cells and how negative numbers are displayed.

To change the number of decimal places, choose Precision and type the number of decimal places you want for the highlighted numbers. Choose Floating to allow WordPerfect to determine the number of decimal places in a number.

 Typing a format symbol such as a dollar sign automatically applies the currency format to a cell. The format remains the same, even if the number is changed.

You display negative numbers with a minus sign or parentheses by clicking the appropriate box in the Negative Numbers section of the Format dialog box.

If you have Auto Redraw on, applied formats become visible in the chart after you click OK. Otherwise, applied formats can be seen by choosing View, Redraw or pressing Ctrl+F3.

## Widening and Narrowing Columns

Some columns may have data that is too long for the cell's width. If you need to see the whole cell entry, widen the columns. This has no effect on the chart; it affects only the datasheet. The easiest way to widen or narrow a column is to click and drag a *column divider* (the vertical line between the column letters). Drag it to the right to widen the column and to the left to narrow the column. Widening or narrowing one column narrows or widens all columns.

Another method for changing column width involves choosing Data, Column Width and typing the width in number of characters. Clicking and holding down the increment/decrement arrows next to the Width number box increases or decreases the number in the box. This new width is applied after you press Enter or click OK.

## Removing or Adding Columns and Rows

After entering data and creating a chart, you may discover you forgot to enter a set of numbers. If this set goes in the middle of the table, you need to insert a row or column.

To insert a row or a column, select a cell in the row or column in which the insertion will be made. If you want to insert a blank column before column C, for example, select a cell anywhere within column C and choose Edit, Insert, Column (to insert a row, choose Row instead of Column). An empty column appears and existing data is moved to the right. To insert multiple columns or rows, type in the number box the number of rows or columns you want to insert.

 The quickest way to insert or delete a column or row is to right-click its label and choose Insert or Delete.

Selecting a cell and choosing Edit, Delete, Row or Column removes the row or column and its data from the table. Data that is either in rows below the deleted information or in columns to the right of the deleted information moves up or to the left to fill the vacancy created by the deletion.

### CAUTION
Use the Delete command carefully—you can easily remove data that you did not intend to delete.

As an alternative to deleting columns or rows, consider using the Exclude Row/Column feature in the datasheet. This is especially useful if you want to prepare a chart without a piece of information (for example, one of the regions in an annual report), but that you may want to include later.

To exclude a column or row in a datasheet from appearing in the chart, click a cell that is in the row or column you want to exclude or drag to include multiple rows or columns. Choose Data, Exclude Row/Col. The Exclude dialog box appears, enabling you to choose Rows or Columns. Make your choice, and the row or column will appear grayed out in the datasheet and will no longer appear in the chart. To bring back a column or row, follow this procedure again, only choose Data, Include Row/Col.

 To quickly include or exclude a row or column, right-click the row number or column letter, then choose the Include or Exclude choice for row or column from the QuickMenu.

> **N O T E** It is not necessary to add a column or row if you plan to add data at the edge of the datasheet. If, for example, you have data in the first three rows and want to add data to row four, simply go to the correct cell and enter the data. Insert rows and columns only when data must be added between existing rows or columns.

# Changing the Appearance of the Chart

After the chart is created, it's time to stand back, look at the chart with a critical eye, and determine what needs to be done to make its message clear and its appearance pleasing.

In the sections that follow, you learn how to make changes to the entire chart and how to change one series to make it stand out. Because of the number of available changes, it's tempting to pile modification after modification on the chart. Be careful—your point could be lost in a bewildering flurry of enhancements.

## Adding Titles

Adding some descriptive titles to your chart is a good idea. You will at least want to change the title of the chart, which reads "Title of Chart." Keep the titles simple and be sure they emphasize no more than one point, such as "Sales Are Up!" or "Regional Sales Performance."

Add titles to the chart by choosing Chart, Title or by right-clicking the default title and choosing Title Properties. To add a subtitle to the chart, choose Chart, Subtitle. In the property sheet that appears, type the text for the title or subtitle.

In addition to entering the title or subtitle text, in the property sheet you can change many other appearance options for the title and subtitle:

- Choose the Title Font tab to change the font face, style, size, color, and appearance.
- Choose the Text Fill tab to change the fill style, patterns, and colors for the text characters.
- Choose the Text Outline tab to change the character outline line width, style, and color.
- Choose the Box Type tab to choose the type and color of the border to place around the title.
- Choose the Box Fill tab to select fill styles and colors for the title box.
- To change the location of the title in the chart, choose Position. You can place the title at the left, right, or center of the top of the chart.

To add a title for the x-axis and either or both y-axes, choose Chart, Axis, and choose the axis you want to add a title for. (See the section "Making Changes to a Series" later in this chapter for more information about adding a second y-axis.) In the property sheet that appears, choose the Title Font tab and type the title name in the text box next to the Display Title check box. As with the chart title, you can change many other appearance options for the axis title.

You can make the axis titles vertical or horizontal. Choosing horizontal for a long y-axis title or vertical for a long x-axis title squeezes the chart to make way for the title.

The property sheet and alignment options for the chart titles and axis are also available directly using a QuickMenu. Right-click the title area or axis area and choose the desired alignment or properties item from the QuickMenu.

As you make your choice of fonts, attributes, and appearance items, click Preview to see how the changes affect your chart.

The chart looks better if you use one font for all text. If you use several fonts in a small area, the chart looks confusing and cluttered.

## Including a Legend

By now you've got an attractive chart with lots of colors and a meaningful title, but the effectiveness of the chart is lost if you don't know what the data points represent.

The legend removes any doubt about which data point goes with which element in the series. Each series has its own color or pattern. The legend shows which color or pattern goes with which series. If, for example, all the bars in a chart corresponding to your salesperson, Jessica, are red, the legend shows the word Jessica next to a red box.

Choose Chart, Legend; or right-click the legend and choose Legend Properties. The Legend property sheet that appears enables you to make changes to the legend. First, of course, you need to choose Display Legend to activate the other items in the dialog box.

Legend Type enables you to place each color or pattern in a vertical or horizontal arrangement. If, for example, you choose Horizontal, the legends are displayed next to each other rather than above or below each other, giving you a rather wide legend box.

Position enables you to place the legend inside or outside the actual chart and to choose what side of the chart to place the legend. Unchecking Place Legend Inside Chart places the legend outside the chart. This makes sense if the chart is already cluttered or if the legend hides some data points. Placing the legend outside is not a good idea if the legend forces the chart to squeeze too much in any direction to accommodate the legend.

The default name of the legend box is Legend. To display the legend title or change it, choose the Title Font tab in the Legend property sheet. Then choose Display Legend and type in some other text if you prefer to give the box a different title.

The Title Font tab includes choices that enable you to change the font face, style, size, and appearance of the legend box title. The Text Font tab enables you to make the same choices for the legend text.

The Box Fill tab enables you to change the fill style and fill options for the legend box.

## Using Labels

*Labels* are numbers placed near parts of the chart that tell the exact number associated with that part. Labels can be displayed or suppressed for the x-axis and y-axis and for data points. When placed near data points, they are called *data labels*. Figure 17.8 shows a bar chart with data labels at the top of each bar. Notice that the display of the labels normally displayed with the y-axis is suppressed, partially to show that such suppression is possible, but also to show that having numbers at data points and at the y-axis is superfluous. Notice also that the display of the x-axis labels is staggered.

**FIG. 17.8**
This graph has data labels added to data points and removed from the y-axis. Labels on the x-axis are staggered.

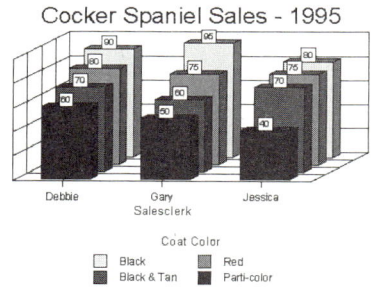

To make choices about data labels, choose Chart, Data Labels. A check in the Display Data Labels box means that the label will be visible.

The Position tab enables you to determine where the label will appear relative to the data points. The Font tab includes choices that enable you to change the font face, style, size, and appearance of the data labels. The Box Fill tab enables you to change the fill style and fill options for the data point display box.

To display labels for the x-axis and either or both y-axes, choose Chart, Axis and choose the axis you want to work with. In the dialog box that appears, choose Labels and make sure Display Labels is checked. As with the data labels, you can change many other appearance options for the axis labels.

The Labels tab on the x-axis allows several choices. Choosing to show ticks on labels only is useful if there are many labels showing. Choosing Stagger is useful when each label is long enough to interfere with the display of adjacent labels. If staggered, labels are placed at varying distances from the chart so that they have more space to be displayed.

Choosing Skip Labels determines whether every label in the top row of the table is displayed. When the labels are very long or when the display of every label becomes monotonous, you can choose to display only some of those labels. Choosing a value of 1 means that you display every other label, 2 skips two labels and displays every third label, and so on.

## Changing Chart Types

WP Draw enables you to quickly change your chart type by choosing Layout/Type from the Chart menu. You can also take advantage of several predefined chart types and styles in the Chart Gallery. For example, figure 17.9 shows a horizontal bar chart.

**T I P** Although WordPerfect enables you to easily change chart types, a certain chart type may not be appropriate for certain types of information. Refer to the section "Understanding the Chart Types" earlier in this chapter to learn more about selecting the right kind of chart for each type of information.

To change a chart from one type to another, Choose Chart, Layout/Type, and select the chart type you want. Keep in mind that not all chart types are appropriate for all data. If, for example, your datasheet contains two or more series, you wouldn't want to use a pie chart.

The Chart Gallery has a range of chart types already defined for you. To access it, choose Chart, Gallery. You can select from different types on the left of the dialog box and apply specific style and formatting options by choosing the button with the sample chart you want. Check the 3D box to make a 3D chart or clear it for a two-dimensional chart.

**N O T E** After choosing a chart from the Chart Gallery, you can fine-tune the preset options by choosing Chart, Layout/Type. ■

> **CAUTION**
> One reason for choosing a two-dimensional display is that some smaller values may be hidden behind larger ones. A forest of high bars in the front can completely conceal a short bar in the back.

**FIG. 17.9**
The bar chart from figure 17.8 is displayed horizontally with the same clarity as when displayed vertically. Others charts, such as line charts, may appear confusing when rotated to the horizontal position.

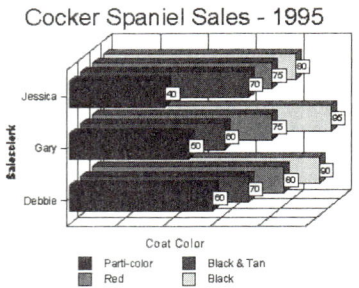

The four styles available in the Layout dialog box include:

- *Cluster.* This style spreads the bars out so that they don't overlap and no bars are hidden by the others.
- *Overlap.* This style is opposite of cluster. The bars are permitted to overlap and some may be hidden.
- *Stacked.* This style takes all the bars for one range and stacks them so that the reader can see how each bar contributes to the whole. Each stacked bar is a true representation of the total value for the stack.
- *Stacked 100%.* This style stacks the bars and makes all composite bars the same height. The contribution of each component to the whole is shown as a percentage rather than as an actual amount.

## Making Other Changes

The WP Draw Chart menu contains four other items that change the entire chart: Axis, Grids, Frame, and Perspective.

**Modifying the Axes**   Choose Chart, Axis and select the axis you want to change. You can make the following types of changes (some of the options are only available for either the x- or y-axis, not both):

- *Scaling Method.* You can choose Linear, which is the default, or Logarithmic. Logarithmic displays each tick on the axis as a power of the one below. For example, the numbers might be 10, 100, 1000, 10000, and so on. All numbers are the same distance apart.
- *Automatic Maximum Value.* An x in the box means the program automatically sets the highest axis value a bit higher than the highest value in the data. You may type in a number higher (but not lower) than the highest value in the data. The higher the number you type, the smaller the data points.

- *Automatic Minimum Value.* This is generally set at zero, but you can set it to a negative value or to a value just below the lowest value in the data so that the differences between data points are more noticeable.

 **TIP** Create a y-axis title to remind the reader that the numbers on the y-axis are in the millions, if you use the label scale factor to divide each by one million.

- *Automatic Major Grid Value.* A gridline crosses the chart for each major value. An x in the box means the program automatically sets the increment. If the maximum value in a chart is 100 and you set the major grid value at **2**, a line appears every two numbers.
- *Label Scale Factor.* This is a number divided into each number on the axis to make it appear smaller. If the numbers along the y-axis range from 1 million to 10 million, dividing each by 1 million displays them as 1 through 10, which is easier to read.

Click the Preview button to see the results of the changes.

**Changing the Grid and Tick**   The *grid* is the set of lines that appears across the chart (refer to fig. 17.1). The *tick* is the little extension of the grid along the axis that points away from the axis. You can change the tick so that it points inward, outward, or both (or does not appear at all). To change the tick, choose Chart, Axis and select the axis you want to change. From the displayed property sheet, choose the Tick Options tab and make the desired changes.

You can choose Chart, Grids to add or remove the grid. You can change the grid color, line style, and, for the x-axis, the major and minor gridline ratio.

**Modifying the Frame**   The *frame* is the box in which the chart appears. When the chart is two-dimensional, there is only one frame. Change the chart to three-dimensional and a left side of the frame appears. Choose Chart, Frame to display the Frame property sheet. The Display Options tab enables you to add or remove parts of the frame, and change the border width and color. The base height command raises the floor of the chart.

The Fill Attributes tab enables you to change the fill style and fill options for the frame.

**Adjusting the Perspective**   After choosing Chart, Perspective, you can rotate the display of the chart. Choosing the Right Angles Axes box toggles between displaying the chart so that the x-axis and y-axis are displayed as though they are at right angles. To rotate the display of the chart horizontally or vertically, change the number of degrees in the Horizontal or Vertical box. A quicker way to rotate the chart is to use the sliders next to the chart in the center of the dialog box.

## Making Changes to a Series

A table often contains not only the data for each series and item, but also the totals. At times you may want to include the totals in your chart, but the data points for the totals will be much higher than the data points for the other series.

To keep totals from looking like just another series—and to keep the data points from looking disproportionately large—consider changing the graphic display of the total.

Figure 17.10 shows WP Draw's Chart Edit mode with a table that includes totals. The chart in the edit window contains a bar for the totals row, which is considerably higher than the bars for the other series.

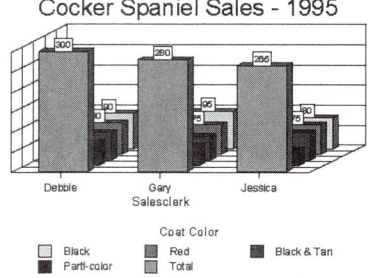

**FIG. 17.10**
A bar chart showing data and totals. The totals line is a series with its own set of bars, but they are disproportionately large. In this chart, the large bar for totals does not look correct next to the bars for the other series.

> **N O T E**  Changing the display of one series is a good idea if that series deserves special attention. For example, you may want to alert readers to the performance of one product, the data concerning one corporate location, or the contribution of foreign sales.

Depending on the point you're trying to make and the nature of the data displayed in the chart, there are several ways to change the appearance of the data points for one series.

To change the display of one series, choose Chart, Series or double-click one of the bars of the series you want to change. To use the QuickMenu, point the mouse at the series you want to change, click the right mouse button, then choose Series Properties. The Series property sheet appears.

The series number and name appears at the top of the property sheet. Any changes you make affect the series whose name appears, so be sure that the name of the series you want to change appears there. Click the left arrow to move to a lower series number, or the right arrow to move to a higher series number, until the proper name appears. The Series property sheet has the following functions:

- *Type/Axis*. Under this tab you can select the chart type for an individual series.

  Choose Bar Shape (only available when a bar chart is selected) to change the shape of the bar in a bar chart.

- *Fill Attributes*. Under this tab, you can choose from four different fill styles to get the look you want in your chart.

  When you choose the pattern or gradient fill styles, you can choose two colors—a pattern or gradient color (depending on the fill style selected), and a background color. You can choose from 256 colors—some solid, or some with a muted pattern.

  Choose the Pattern fill style to choose from 32 designs, each of which displays the foreground and background colors you choose in the pattern you select.

  Choose the Gradient fill style to display 32 gradient fill patterns. By using one of the gradient fill options, you can choose to blend the gradient background colors in a variety of ways.

  To fine-tune the gradient fill, choose More Options. The Gradient Settings dialog box appears, enabling you to customize the gradient fill to be used.

  By using one of the Gradient Type options, you can choose to blend the gradient and background colors in a linear fashion (from one side to the other of the chart element), in circular fashion (the two colors form a circular pattern blending from the center outward), or in rectangular fashion (similar to circular, except that the two colors form a rectangle).

  **N O T E** Choosing Horizontal Offset in the Gradient Settings dialog box (visible when Circular is selected) moves the center color left or right as you change the percentage. Setting Offset higher than 50 percent moves the center color right; setting Offset lower than 50 percent moves the color left. Changing the Vertical Offset moves the center color down if you set it higher than 50 percent and moves it up if you set it lower than 50 percent.

  Further fine-tuning is possible with the Angle and Blending commands. Angle, an active choice with Linear and Rectangular patterns, enables you to rotate the two colors around each other. Blending is usually Auto-Step blending, in which the two colors gradually blend together. When you choose Fixed, you set a number into the window that determines how many stripes will appear in the chart element. Rather than gradually blending the colors, each stripe is a distinct step in the blending of the two colors.

  Choose the Texture fill style to choose one of 32 textures. The 32 textures are grouped into four categories. Choose Category to choose from the four categories.

  To fine-tune the texture fills, choose More Options. The Texture Settings dialog box appears, enabling you to customize the way texture fills are displayed.

Choose the Picture fill style to choose a picture fill from a variety of choices. The picture fill choices are grouped into six categories. Select Categor*y* to choose from the six categories.

To fine-tune the picture fills, choose *M*ore Options. The Picture Settings dialog box appears, enabling you to customize the way picture fills are displayed.

- *Line Width/Style.* This tab enables you to select options for the lines used in the series. What you change is determined by the series type. If you are changing one series in a bar chart, for instance, *line* refers to the lines at the corners of the bars. The Line Width/Style tab enables you to select the color, style, and thickness of the line.

To see the results of the changes, click the Pre*v*iew button.

> **CAUTION**
> The appearance of a chart on a color monitor is quite different from its appearance when printed in black and white. Be sure that your changes do not make the printed copy more difficult to interpret.

The Series property sheet is where you select the type of chart for the one series. Figure 17.11 shows the results of choosing *L*ine as the type of chart for the totals series.

In figure 17.11, the line is floating above the bars because all numbers for all data points correspond to the numbers on the y-axis to the left. You may want to display the line for totals in front of the bars, which makes the bars appear higher. To display the line in front of the bars, select Y2 as the axis for the totals series. A second y-axis appears at the right side of the chart and is used only for the totals series.

**FIG. 17.11**
The totals series has been changed so that it is now represented by a line chart.

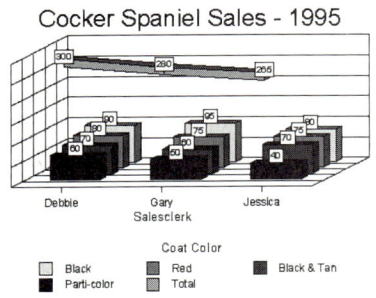

> **N O T E** When you use two y-axes, be sure to give each a title so that the reader knows what data series goes with which axis. Select *C*hart, *A*xis, *S*econdary Y; or right-click the Y2 axis and choose Secondary Y Axis Properties. Choose the Title Font tab, make sure Display *T*itle is checked, and type the Y2 title.

## Making Changes to Individual Chart Types

The changes listed in the preceding section are possible with all the chart types, but each type has unique qualities that can be changed by choosing Chart, Layout/Type or Chart, Series. Some changes are possible with several types of charts. Degree of overlap, for example, is part of the Chart, Layout/Type property sheet for only bar charts.

**Pie Chart Changes**   Choose Chart, Layout/Type to make the pie chart three-dimensional, tilt the pie, link two pies together, or explode pieces.

**TIP**  Clicking 3D toggles the pie between three- and two-dimensional.

The Layout/Type property sheet gives you the following choices:

- *Depth*. Thickness of the pie. The maximum is 100.
- *Size*. Overall diameter of the pie. The maximum is 100.
- *Angle*. When the pie is rotated about its center. The number is in degrees; therefore, the maximum is 360.
- *Tilt*. Determines the degree to which the back of the pie appears higher than the front. Values range from 10 to 90 degrees.
- *Sort Slice*. Arranges the pie chart slices by size. This option is not available with linked pies.
- *Explode Slice*. Enables you to pull out one or more of the pie pieces to provide emphasis to the series.

**NOTE**  To explode a pie piece, choose Explode Slice from the Layout/Type property sheet. The Explode Slice dialog box appears. Type the number of the piece (trial and error will determine which piece is which number) and type the distance between the piece and the pie. An easier way to explode one or more pieces of the pie is to click the piece and drag it to the desired position.

**Scatter Chart Changes**   The only unique change possible in a scatter chart involves choosing Chart, Series; picking one series; and changing the appearance of the individual data points. Eleven styles of points are available, including an X, box, triangle, and several types of stars. Use the Marker Size box to change the size of the data points.

**High/Low Changes**   The normal display of the high/low data points is a vertical bar with two wings. Choose Chart, Layout/Type to change this default and choose Bar/Error Bar, Error, or Area. Change the size of the resulting data points with the size options.

# Placing the Chart in the Document

Once you're satisfied with how the chart looks, you need to decide how it should be placed in the document. Chapter 7, "Integrating Text and Graphics," and Chapter 23, "Desktop Publishing with WordPerfect," investigate the options and considerations important to the placement of any graphic within a document.

After you place the chart in the document, you can still make changes. Double-click the chart to switch back to WP Draw's Chart Edit mode. Click the chart with the right mouse button to open the QuickMenu, which allows changes to the chart.

Items in the lower part of the QuickMenu are used to affect the appearance of the chart in the document. For example, you can add a caption outside of the chart box.

Although size is one of the choices in the menu, you may prefer to click and drag one of the selection handles to resize the chart box.

Choose Image Tools from the QuickMenu. A dialog box appears that enables you to make several changes to the chart.

▶ **See** "Using Graphics Boxes," **p. 262**
▶ **See** "Printing Graphics," **p. 286**

# CHAPTER 18

# Importing Data and Working with Other Programs

*by Robert Raleigh*

In many offices, several types of programs are used—word processing, spreadsheets, graphics programs, and databases, for example. Exchanging data between programs, therefore, becomes more and more important.

Most programs create data files in unique formats. Each program understands its own format but usually requires an interpreter to exchange its information with other programs, especially if the data contains complex formatting instructions. The process of interpreting a data file into the style used by other programs is called *document conversion*. Most word processing programs, including WordPerfect, include built-in document conversion from—and to—many other word processing formats.

One reason for the success of Windows is that it establishes standards for the sharing of data. Besides the Clipboard, Windows also offers DDE and OLE, different but equally useful approaches to intelligent data

- **Import files created by other programs**
  WordPerfect can automatically convert files from many other applications.

- **Export documents to other programs**
  Learn how to export documents for when you need to send your files out into the world.

- **Import and link documents with DDE**
  You can import files (or parts of documents) and retain a link to the original material.

- **Embed, link, and edit objects with OLE**
  Windows' OLE is a powerful way to mix and match data from all your favorite applications. Learn how to use OLE in WordPerfect.

- **Import and link data from spreadsheet and database programs**
  WordPerfect provides some custom tools for interpreting spreadsheet and database data.

sharing. WordPerfect supports all these methods of smart data sharing.

In addition to supporting the Windows Clipboard and both DDE and OLE, WordPerfect for Windows has its own tools for importing data and working with other programs.

Even with the powerful data exchange methods provided by WordPerfect and Windows, the results of a conversion are not always perfect; complex formatting can complicate the conversion process. So don't expect perfect results. ■

# Understanding the Conversion Process

WordPerfect makes document conversion as seamless as possible. You can open or insert a file into a WordPerfect editing window, and if the file is not in WordPerfect 7 format, the conversion process begins automatically.

> **NOTE** If you select a file after choosing File, Open, the selected file opens in an empty document window. If you select a file after choosing Insert, File, the file is inserted into the current document at the cursor position. ■

To convert a file from—or to—another format, WordPerfect must store information about that format. WordPerfect stores information about many different text, spreadsheet, database, and graphic file formats.

By using the information that is stored for the selected file format, WordPerfect automatically brings the document into the main editing window with the original text and most, if not all, of the formatting intact. You may have to answer prompts regarding the conversion while it takes place. The time required to perform the conversion can range from a few seconds to several minutes, depending on the size of the file and the hardware configuration of the system on which you are operating WordPerfect (see fig. 18.1).

**FIG. 18.1**
The Conversion dialog box displays the Conversion in progress message.

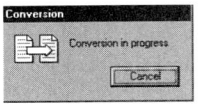

The amount of original formatting retained in the converted document depends on the complexity of the formatting in the original document.

Another way to convert a document from one format to another is to copy and paste data from the first document to the second by using the Windows Clipboard. To use this method, both the program using the original format and the program using the new format must be installed on the system on which the conversion takes place. The Clipboard conversion process is totally seamless. After data is selected and copied from the originating document—for example, from Word Pro—it is stored on the Clipboard both in its native format and in standardized Windows format. If the data is pasted into another program—for example, WordPerfect—it is automatically converted to the format used by that program.

> **CAUTION**
> You might lose formatting when copying text across the Clipboard.

In addition to recognizing many document formats, WordPerfect recognizes many graphics formats and automatically converts files in those formats into WordPerfect format when the contents of a graphics file are placed in a WordPerfect graphics box. For general information on opening and retrieving documents, see Chapter 3, "Retrieving and Editing Documents." For information on integrating text and graphics, see Chapter 7, "Integrating Text and Graphics."

# Setting File Preferences for Imported Files

This section discusses setting defaults for imported files. The types of files that are affected by these defaults are ASCII delimited text files, Windows metafiles, and any file that is imported with an ASCII code page (character set) that is different from the expected character set.

Import preferences are customized in the Convert Preferences dialog box (see fig. 18.2). To display the Convert Preferences dialog box, choose Edit, Preferences; then choose Convert.

> **TIP** One option, Code Pages, can be customized either by clicking the Options button in the Convert Preferences dialog box, or by choosing Edit, Preferences, Environment, Code Page. (See "Setting Preferences for Code Pages and Other Options" later in this chapter for more information.)

When you import an ASCII delimited text file, you must accept or adjust the values of options that define the format of the file. When you import graphics data through the Clipboard, you accept options regarding the retention of metafile data. When you import any data file, you accept the option setting for code pages. You can customize the defaults for these types of options in the Convert Preferences dialog box by choosing the drop-down list control and selecting a code from the list of common codes (refer to fig. 18.2) or by typing the information in the text boxes.

**FIG. 18.2**
In the Convert Preferences dialog box, you can customize import preferences.

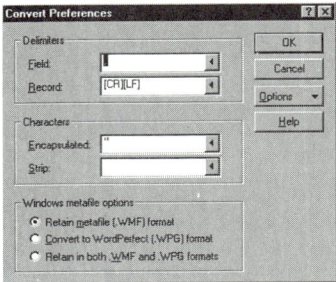

## Setting Preferences for ASCII Delimited Text Files

The delimiters in an ASCII delimited text file separate the data into fields and records. The data also may contain extra characters (typically quotation marks) that encapsulate field values. Not all ASCII delimited text files have the same field and record separators or the same, if any, encapsulation. When you import an ASCII delimited text file, WordPerfect prompts you to accept or change the format settings. You can avoid customizing these settings every time you import an ASCII delimited text file if you adjust the default settings to match the settings for your incoming data.

 Many database and spreadsheet programs have a built-in export option that creates an ASCII delimited text file from a database or spreadsheet file.

If the database or spreadsheet file that you want to import is not formatted in one of WordPerfect's supported file formats, you still can import it by converting the database or spreadsheet from its native format to an ASCII delimited text file format.

## Setting Preferences for Metafiles

When graphic data is copied (or cut) to the Clipboard, that data is automatically formatted in Metafile format, a standardized Windows format. When you paste the graphic data into a WordPerfect document, the data is retained according to your Metafile option settings. You can adjust the default Metafile options by choosing Edit, Preferences, Convert. You can ask WordPerfect to retain Windows Metafiles in both Metafile format (WMF) and WordPerfect Format (WPG)—the default—or in just one of these two formats.

The default setting for the Windows Metafile option, Retain Metafile WMF Format, keeps the original format. An image retained in WPG format can be displayed in WordPerfect on other platforms, and when it is edited with WordPerfect's Image Editor, more editing options are available than when the image is retained in WMF format. The appearance of an image usually is close to identical in either format. Some images look slightly better in one format; others look better in the other format.

**TIP** To use images in WordPerfect for DOS, you must be in WPG format.

## Setting Preferences for Code Pages and Other Options

You can set four different types of convert options by clicking the Options button in the Convert Preferences dialog box. These option types include Code Pages, Document, WP 4.2 Fonts, and DCA/DisplayWrite Fonts. To see or change the settings for any of these options, click Options in the Convert Preferences dialog box, and then choose an option type.

*Code pages* are DOS-defined lists that define the character sets used in different languages. Every file contains a code page definition in its prefix. If a document was saved with a code page for a language other than the one built into your hardware, the data may contain characters that WordPerfect does not recognize. Regardless of the file's format, when WordPerfect opens a document containing an unrecognized character, it usually replaces the character with a space.

As a partial solution to this problem, you can set WordPerfect's Convert feature to recognize different code-page definitions. You can set the Input code page to Hebrew, for example, before you import a file with a Hebrew code page. A file with a code-page format that is not in the list of input-supported code pages is automatically imported with the DOS code page—unless the file is in ANSI format, in which case it is imported in the Windows code-page format. You can customize the input and output files' code pages.

▶ **See** "Using Merge," **p. 588**
▶ **See** "Understanding Data Files," **p. 596**
▶ **See** "Understanding the Merge Process," **p. 611**

Other types of options in the Options list are applied when a conversion is performed to or from a specific file format. Changing any of these options to match imported or exported files results in a more accurate conversion.

After you change any of the options in the Options list, choose OK or Save to save changes and return to the Convert Preferences dialog box.

After you finish setting preferences in the Convert Preferences dialog box, choose OK; then, in the Preferences dialog box, choose Close.

For information on importing spreadsheet and database files, see the section "Importing and Working with Spreadsheet/Database Data" later in this chapter.

# Importing and Working with Word Processing Data

In this section, you learn to import and work with word processing data. The section covers the following topics:

- Importing documents with WordPerfect's Convert
- Saving converted documents
- Converting documents to an intermediate format
- Importing documents with the Clipboard
- Importing documents with Dynamic Data Exchange (DDE)
- Embedding document objects with OLE

## Importing Documents with WordPerfect's Convert Feature

This section discusses the use of WordPerfect's Convert feature to import document files that are saved on disk. WordPerfect 7 for Windows converts files from and to more than 50 other word processing formats. The following formats are supported by the WordPerfect 7 Convert feature:

| | |
|---|---|
| ANSI, text/delimited text/generic | Office Writer 6.0–6.2 |
| ASCII, text/delimited text/generic | Professional Write 1.0, 2.2 |
| Borland Sprint (import only) | Quattro Pro 1.0, 5.0, 6.0 |
| DisplayWrite 4.0–5.0 | QuickFinder Log (import only) |
| EDGAR | Rich Text Format (RTF) |
| Excel Spreadsheet, 3.0, 4.0 | RTF Japanese |
| HTML | RTF Help File |
| IA5 (import only) | Spreadsheet DIF |
| IBM DCA FFT | Volkswriter 4 |
| IBM DCA RFT | Windows Write |
| Kermit (7-Bit Transfer) | WordPerfect for Macintosh 2.0–3.1 (import only) |
| Lotus 1-2-3 Spreadsheet, 1.0–4.0 for Windows, 3.0 and 3.1 for DOS | WordPerfect 4.2–7 |
| Microsoft Word 4.0-5.5 | Word Pro 1.2–3.0 |
| Microsoft Word for Windows 1.0–7.0 | WordStar 2000, 1.0–3.0, 3.–7.0 |

MultiMate 3.3–4.0, Advantage II 1.0
Navy DIF Standard

WPWorks Word Processor 2.0 (import only)

XYWrite III Plus 3.55–4.0

**NOTE** If you need to convert a large number of documents to or from the WordPerfect 7 format, consider using ConvertPerfect 2.0 or a third-party conversion program that supports the WordPerfect 7 format and converts documents in a batch process. ConvertPerfect is a standalone utility program available from Corel.

**Starting the Conversion Process** The conversion process begins as soon as you choose a document for editing and WordPerfect determines that the file is not in WordPerfect format. To convert a document file from another format to WordPerfect format, follow these steps:

1. Choose File, Open; or press Ctrl+O.

   Alternatively, choose the name of the document you want to open from the bottom of the File menu; or choose Insert, File to display the Insert File dialog box.

2. In the Open File dialog box, change the folder, if necessary, to the folder that contains the document to be converted. For example, in the Name text box, type **c:\wordpro\docs** and press Enter. Alternatively, you can browse folders or choose a folder using the Favorites or Folder list.

3. Scroll through the list of files until the file that you want to convert is highlighted (for example, AMINEWS.SAM).

   If the file you are searching for doesn't appear, you may need to choose a different option from the For Type drop-down list. Choose All Files (*.*) to see every file in a folder.

4. Double-click the file name or press Enter. Depending on the actual format, one of several actions can occur as soon as you choose a file.

   If the file uses a WordPerfect 7 format, it opens immediately. If the file uses a WordPerfect 5 or 6 format, the file is converted immediately, then opened.

   When the file uses any other format WordPerfect recognizes, the Convert File Format dialog box appears (see fig. 18.3), which displays a suggested format. In almost every case, the suggested format is correct; all you must do is double-click its name or choose OK. If it's not the format you are looking for, select an alternate file format from the Convert File Format From drop-down list.

**FIG. 18.3**
If WordPerfect needs to convert a file's format, it suggests a format that seems to match the format of the incoming file.

If the file uses a supported spreadsheet or database format, WordPerfect automatically displays the Import Data dialog box. For more information on importing spreadsheet and database files, see "Importing and Working with Spreadsheet/Database Data" later in this chapter.

If the file seems to use an unsupported format, an Unknown format message appears in the Convert File Format From message box. In this case, you need to determine the original file format and select it from the drop-down list (or determine whether or not you can bring its information into WordPerfect). For detailed information, see "Converting Documents to an Intermediate Format" and "Importing Documents with the Clipboard" later in this chapter.

5. As soon as you see that Convert has correctly identified the format of the document, choose OK. The conversion begins.

 **TIP** If the document is password-protected, the Password dialog box appears. Type the password and press Enter to continue with the conversion process.

**NOTE** In the rare case that WordPerfect incorrectly detects the file's format, the conversion is unsatisfactory. To use a conversion format other than the one suggested by WordPerfect, scroll down the list of formats and select another one. If you don't know for sure what the actual format is, and if the document is in the data folder of another program, try converting from the format for that program.

During the conversion, you might need to answer questions about the conversion process. The Position Hyphen dialog box, for example, may prompt you to make a decision about hyphenating a particular word. You can temporarily disable the Hyphenation feature by clicking Suspend Hyphenation. If, after the conversion is complete, the result is unsatisfactory, you may want to try the conversion again, this time supplying different answers to these conversion questions.

After the conversion process is complete, the document appears on-screen.

**Editing a Converted Document** Before you edit a converted document, examine the new document carefully to determine whether the conversion result is acceptable. If important formatting or other details have been lost or incorrectly converted, consider trying another conversion approach.

Document conversion works best on documents with simple formatting and a minimum of graphics. The success of the conversion depends on the formatting complexity of the original document.

The document shown in figure 18.4 contains many elements found in complex documents. The newsletter-style page has a masthead, graphics image, and columnar layout. The types of problems that occur when you convert a document with formatting as complex as this are the same whether the document originates in Word for Windows, Word Pro, or another word processing program for which WordPerfect has a conversion format.

**FIG. 18.4**
This Word for Windows document contains complex formatting.

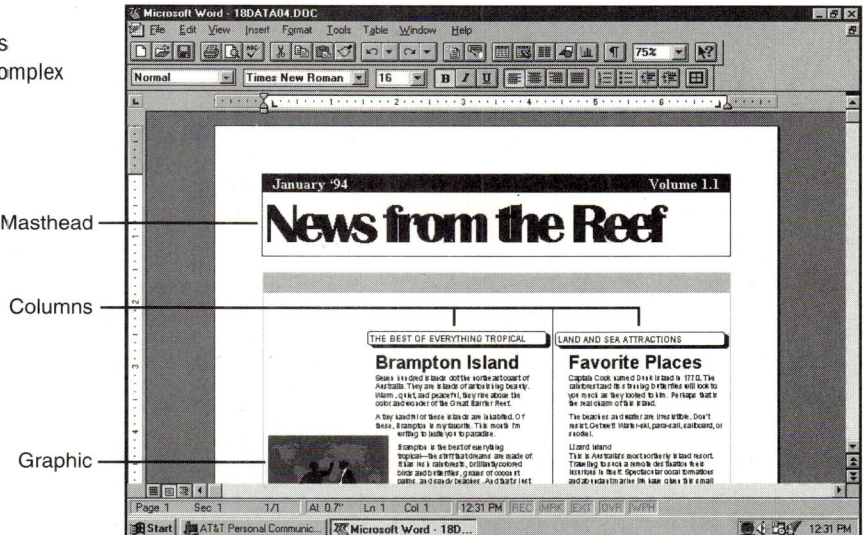

After this newsletter (a Word for Windows document) is converted by WordPerfect's Convert function, the resulting document appears as shown in figure 18.5. All the body text in the editing screen is retained, as is the masthead and graphic. Some repositioning and other formatting is required to "clean up" this document after the conversion, however.

With documents as complex as this newsletter, the best method may be to simply copy and paste text and graphics separately via the Clipboard. Converting the document text by copying and pasting sometimes results in a better conversion than the one performed by WordPerfect's Convert function.

**FIG. 18.5**

The Word document shown in figure 18.4 has been converted by WordPerfect for Windows. All elements are retained, but some cleanup is definitely required.

For detailed information on combining text with graphics, refer to Chapter 7, "Integrating Text and Graphics."

 **Saving a Converted Document** When you use the Save feature (choose File, Save or press Ctrl+S) to save a file that is converted from another format, WordPerfect displays a message box stating the original format of the file and asking whether you want to overwrite it in WordPerfect 7 format. If you choose OK to the overwrite question, WordPerfect replaces the original file with the converted file. If you want to save the file back in its original file format, choose that format and then choose OK.

 It's usually a good idea to assign a new name to a converted file, leaving the original intact. That way, if the conversion is unsatisfactory, you can always return to the original.

## Exporting Documents with WordPerfect's Convert Feature

You convert a WordPerfect document to another supported format by bringing the document to an editing window and using the Save As feature to save it in another format. To convert the document in the current WordPerfect editing window, follow these steps:

1. Choose File, Save As; or press F3. The Save As dialog box appears.
2. In the Save As dialog box, change the folder, if desired.
3. If necessary, select the Name option and then type a new file name.
4. The As Type drop-down list suggests a WordPerfect 6.0/6.1 format. Use the Format list to choose the appropriate export format.

> **TIP** You can change the default file save format by choosing Edit, Preferences, Files, Documents.

   5. Choose OK or press Enter. A `Conversion in progress` message appears while the convert and save operations take place.

When you save a document in the WordPerfect 7 format, all its formatting feature and function codes remain intact. The next time the document is opened or inserted into a WordPerfect 7 editing window, its appearance on-screen is the same as when it was saved, unless one of the following problems occurs:

- The program cannot locate the printer definition that was active when the document was saved.
- The program is set for automatic document formatting and for using an active printer driver other than the driver that was active when the document was saved.
- The document was created using fonts not installed in the current system.

In these situations, WordPerfect attempts to format the document in a manner that duplicates its original appearance.

When a document is edited in WordPerfect and saved in any other format, however, the save operation automatically and permanently removes all WordPerfect formatting or feature and function codes not recognized by the file format in which it is saved. If the document contains a table and is saved in WordPerfect 4.2 format, for example, the program automatically replaces the table structure with protected parallel columns that simulate the structure, if not the appearance, of the original table. Even if you immediately retrieve the document and resave it in WordPerfect 7 format, the original table structure is lost unless you manually re-create it.

## Converting Documents to an Intermediate Format

If WordPerfect cannot convert its documents to another word processing program's format, and if the other word processing program cannot convert its own documents to WordPerfect format, a possible solution lies in using an intermediate format that is supported by both programs. The extent of formatting that is preserved depends on several factors, including how well the first program handles the conversion to the intermediate format.

**Using RTF as an Intermediate Format**   *Rich Text Format (RTF)* is a standard document format used by Windows programs. RTF is designed to let programs use the same codes to represent document formatting details such as margins, indents, columns, justification, typeface, font size, boldface, italics, and underlining. In theory, word processing programs that use this common format can exchange documents with virtually all formatting elements transferring intact. RTF is not perfect, but it does a good job of translating documents between word processing programs.

You can convert documents to RTF format via WordPerfect's File, Open or Insert, File commands, or with the Clipboard.

 If WordPerfect can't read a document created in another program and no intermediate shared format exists, use the Clipboard to convert the document.

The major limitation of the RTF format is that it does not support conversion of graphics images or graphic text boxes. When RTF proves to be the best conversion alternative for the text in a document, use RTF for text conversion and import the graphics separately, using a format supported by WordPerfect.

**Using ASCII Text or ANSI Text as an Intermediate Format**   When all else fails, save the document to be converted in ASCII text or in ANSI text format. These categories produce lowest-common-denominator results. Very little, if any, of the original formatting is preserved, but the ASCII/ANSI formats retain most (if not all) of the original document's text. It can be easier to convert a very long document to ASCII text or ANSI text and then convert it again to the second word processing program than to retype the document. Use ANSI text format as an intermediate format between two Windows programs; use ASCII text as an intermediate format.

 For the best results, when importing an ANSI or ASCII text file, choose the ANSI Text or ASCII Text CR/LF To Srt option. This removes the hard line break at the end of every line. ANSI and ASCII files always end each line with a [HRt] code rather than word wrap. Hard line breaks cause lots of trouble if you ever want to edit the imported document.

## Importing Documents with the Clipboard

The Windows Clipboard provides a quick and easy way to transfer data from one program to another. You can transfer both formatted text and graphics from one word processing program to another via the Clipboard. Because Windows programs are required to use certain standardized data formats when transferring information to the Clipboard, the Clipboard can also be an important conversion tool.

In many cases, the Clipboard preserves formatting features such as margins, indents, columns, typeface, and font size, as well as boldface, italics, underlining, and other complex elements. The Clipboard can also transfer tables and graphics from one document to another. Text on the Clipboard is retained in RTF as well as in the originating program's format.

When you copy a document to the Clipboard and then paste the document into another word processing program, you may preserve all the text and graphics simultaneously. When the document is too complex to be translated successfully all at once, you can try breaking the translation down into more than one operation—that is, you could translate the text first and then the graphics.

The Clipboard has different capabilities, depending on whether you are transferring data between two Windows programs or from a DOS program to another program. When you are copying a document from a DOS program, the Clipboard can transfer only unformatted text.

The following sections explain how to copy with the Clipboard. Notice that you must follow different procedures for copying data to the Clipboard from Windows programs or DOS programs. You must use the correct procedures, or the Clipboard does not work correctly.

**Placing Text on the Clipboard**  To copy data to the Clipboard from a Windows or DOS program, follow these steps:

1. Start the program from which you want to copy data, and open the file containing the data that you want to copy.
2. If you are running a Windows program, maximize it to full screen.

    If you are running a DOS program, the program should be running in a window; if the program has started full screen, press Alt+Enter to reduce the program to a window.

3. Select the data that you want to copy.
4. Copy the selected data to the Clipboard.

    If you are copying data from a Windows program, choose Edit, Copy or press Ctrl+C. The data is copied to the Clipboard.

    To copy from a DOS program, choose Edit, Mark from the Control menu, select the text you want to copy, and then choose Edit, Copy from the Control menu.

**Pasting Data from the Clipboard**  After data is copied to the Clipboard, the next step is to paste the data into the destination program. Notice that you must follow different procedures for pasting data from the Clipboard into Windows programs and DOS programs running in Windows.

To paste data, follow these steps:

1. Start the program into which you want to paste data from the Clipboard. If you are copying into a DOS program, make sure that the DOS program is running in a window.

2. Open the document into which you want to paste the data.
3. Place the insertion point in the document where you want to insert the data.
4. Paste the data into the program.

    If you are pasting into a Windows program, choose Edit, Paste or press Ctrl+V.

    If you are pasting into a DOS program, use the Control menu and choose Edit, Paste. Data from the Clipboard is pasted into the destination document.

To copy data from one DOS program to the Clipboard and paste it into another DOS program from the Clipboard, follow the preceding directions for copying data from a DOS program, and then follow the preceding directions for pasting data into a DOS program.

## Importing Documents with DDE

Windows Dynamic Data Exchange (DDE) is useful for importing document information into WordPerfect when the important consideration is current information rather than appearance. After you import data with a DDE link, the imported data can be updated (that is, replaced) from the source data. You can make any changes you want to the linked data in WordPerfect without affecting the source data (for example, you could reformat it).

> **CAUTION**
> Keep in mind that any changes made to linked data are lost whenever the linked data is updated from the source data.

WordPerfect is DDE-capable as a client; it can be linked to any Windows program that is DDE-capable as a server. Many Windows applications, including Word Pro and Word for Windows, can be linked to WordPerfect with a DDE link.

For detailed instructions on creating a DDE link, see "Creating a DDE Link to Data in Another Program" later in this chapter.

For more information on opening and retrieving documents, refer to Chapter 3, "Retrieving and Editing Documents." For more information on integrating text and graphics, see Chapter 7, "Integrating Text and Graphics." For more information on saving documents, refer to Chapter 2, "Creating and Saving a Document."

# Importing and Working with Spreadsheet/Database Data

WordPerfect's built-in Spreadsheet/Database Import feature provides an easy-to-use, powerful tool for importing spreadsheet and database data. The imported data can be copied, or copied and linked at the same time. The Clipboard is another tool for importing spreadsheet and database data. In addition, because WordPerfect is DDE- and OLE-capable as a client, both DDE and OLE are available as tools for importing spreadsheet data from programs that are DDE- or OLE-capable as servers.

Figure 18.6 shows a WordPerfect document containing data that has been copied and pasted (via the Clipboard) from a Quattro Pro spreadsheet.

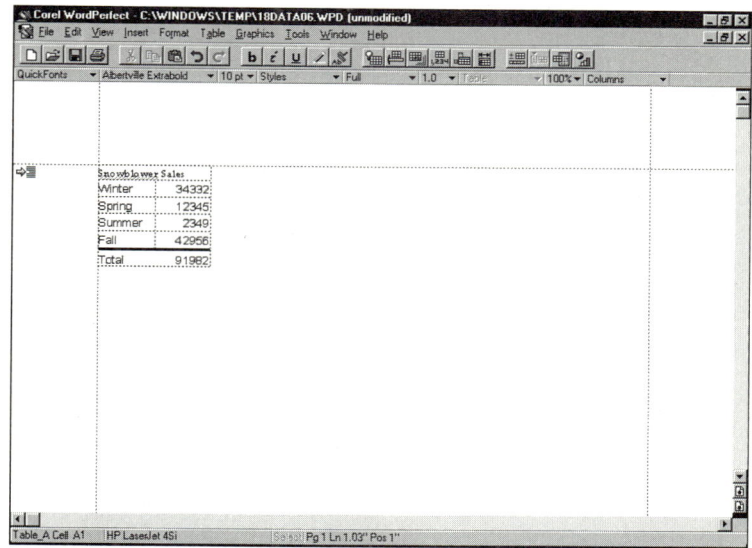

**FIG. 18.6**
This WordPerfect document contains data pasted from the Clipboard after being copied from a Quattro Pro spreadsheet. Calculations are retained as answers rather than as calculations.

## Copying Spreadsheet/Database Data

You can use WordPerfect's Spreadsheet/Database Import to copy data from a spreadsheet or a database, or you can use the Clipboard. When you copy data, the data in WordPerfect is independent of the data in the source file. You can change the data in WordPerfect without affecting the source data, or you can change the data in the spreadsheet/database file without affecting the document in WordPerfect.

### Copying Spreadsheet/Database Data with the Import Feature
The Spreadsheet/Database Import feature has several advantages over the Clipboard in copying spreadsheet/

database data. One advantage is that calculations in the source data are retained in the copied data. You also have the choice of copying the data into a table format, merge data file format, or text format; when you paste from the Clipboard, the data is formatted as a table. Another advantage of a WordPerfect Import is that you can copy from a file on disk; the source file does not have to be open when you perform the copy operation.

**TIP** Before defining the WordPerfect Import, start the program that was used to create the source data, and load the file containing the source data. If the file is a spreadsheet file, find the range of cells you want in the link, and record the range's address so that the information is available for reference during the link-definition process. If the file is a database file, decide which fields and records you want to import.

To copy spreadsheet/database data with WordPerfect's Import feature, follow these steps:

1. Place the insertion point where you want to place the imported data.
2. Choose Insert, Spreadsheet/Database, Import. The Import Data dialog box appears.
3. If the suggested Data Type doesn't match the format of the file that you want to import, choose the Data Type option to select another type. Figure 18.7 shows the list of available data types.

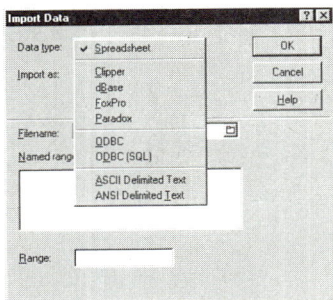

**FIG. 18.7**
The list of data types appears in the WordPerfect Import Data dialog box. The same Data Type options (and Import As options) are available when you choose Import or Create Link.

4. Table is the default setting for Import As. Accept this setting if you want to preserve calculations in the imported data. If you would rather import the spreadsheet as a Merge Data File or as Text, make that choice from the Import As list.
5. Choose the Filename option, if necessary, and type the path and name of the file that you want to import, or click the button to the right of the Filename text box to open the Select Data Filename dialog box.
6. Select a file name and choose OK. WordPerfect examines the selected file.
7. If the detected file format belongs to a spreadsheet, the Named Ranges list box displays the entire <Spreadsheet> range and any named ranges.

In the Range text box, type the range of cells that you are importing from the spreadsheet file, or choose a range from the Named Ranges list. The default range is the entire spreadsheet. (If the range is very wide, follow the instructions in the section "Working with Wide Spreadsheets and Database Records," later in this chapter.)

The completed information for copying spreadsheet data appears in figure 18.8.

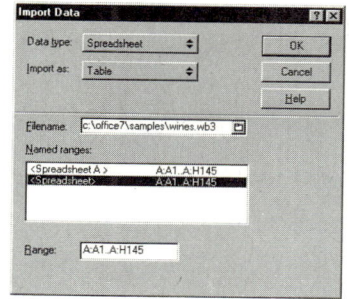

**FIG. 18.8**
The Import Data dialog box contains complete information for importing the cell range A1:H145 from a Quattro Pro spreadsheet.

8. If the detected file format belongs to a database, the Fields list box appears in the lower portion of the dialog box. All fields are listed and selected for import. (You can deselect fields you don't want to import.) Beneath the Fields list box is an option for using field names as headings. When this option is selected, field names are used as headings in a table or as field names in a merge data file.

Figure 18.9 shows the Import Data dialog box with completed options.

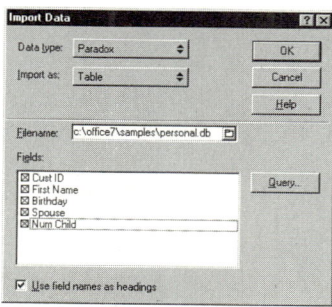

**FIG. 18.9**
The Import Data dialog box contains complete information for importing data from a Paradox file.

9. Choose OK to complete the import operation.

The specified data is copied from the source file on disk. A conversion message appears on-screen while the data is being converted to WordPerfect format. When the conversion is complete, the imported data is inserted into the WordPerfect document.

▶ **See** "Examining Advanced Merge Topics," **p. 618**

**N O T E** Depending on your particular import task, one or more of the following points may be helpful:

- To convert mathematical functions as calculations rather than answers, import data as a Table. Always check mathematical operations for accuracy. Place the insertion point in a cell containing a calculation to see the calculation (on the Table Feature Bar).
- You can customize option settings for imported ASCII delimited text files. See the section "Setting File Preferences for Imported Files," earlier in this chapter.
- When you import data from DataPerfect, in addition to choosing the file name, you must choose a Panel. The Panel list box is displayed beneath the Filename text box.
- To access any of the SQL databases, you must log onto the database. After you select the SQL database from the list of data types, choose Logon, and type the Server Name or File Path and Dictionary Path for Netware SQL. Then type the User ID and Password, and choose Logon.

**Copying Spreadsheet/Database Data with the Clipboard** Copying and pasting spreadsheet data with the Clipboard is quick and easy, especially when both programs are Windows products. You simply select and copy the source data, and then paste it into your WordPerfect document.

**N O T E** When you copy and paste data that includes embedded graphics, the results are not perfect. If it's not satisfactory, try copying the data without the graphics. An embedded graph can also be copied separately with the Clipboard, but the pasted graph is likely to be distorted no matter how it is copied.

Keep in mind that when you copy and paste with the Clipboard, formulas are not copied as formulas, as they are if you use WordPerfect's Import/Link feature and import the data as a table.

Most database programs make selecting an entire data record difficult, if not impossible. This places a severe limitation on the practicality of using the Clipboard for importing database data. Access is a notable exception to this selection problem. Access enables you to choose record selectors to select a single record, contiguous records, or an entire table. (A database in Access consists of tables.) You can even hide columns (fields) that you don't want to import. After you complete the selection procedure, you can copy the selected data to the Clipboard and then paste it into a WordPerfect document.

For more information on using the Clipboard to copy data, refer to the section "Importing Documents with the Clipboard" earlier in this chapter.

## Copying and Linking Spreadsheet/Database Data

If maintaining current spreadsheet and database information in a WordPerfect document is important, use WordPerfect's built-in Spreadsheet Import/Link feature to link data at the same time that it is copied. You can update the data in your document at any time to make sure that the data is current. Additionally, you can set the default link options so that WordPerfect automatically updates the linked data each time it opens or inserts the document.

> **CAUTION**
> When you create a link that is updated whenever the document is open, all data is updated, including any formatting changes that you made for cosmetic reasons.

**Creating a WordPerfect Spreadsheet/Database Link** To create a WordPerfect link, follow these steps:

1. Place the insertion point in your WordPerfect document where you want to copy and link the imported data.
2. Choose Insert, Spreadsheet/Database, Create Link. The Create Data Link dialog box appears. Except for its name, this dialog box looks exactly like the Import Data dialog box.
3. In the Create Data Link dialog box, take the same steps that you would take in the Import Data dialog box. (Refer to the section "Copying Spreadsheet/Database Data with the Import Feature" earlier in this chapter.)

   The specified data is copied from the file on disk. A conversion message appears on-screen while the data is being converted to WordPerfect format. When the conversion is complete, the data is inserted between a pair of codes in the WordPerfect document. If Link Options are set to display link icons, the link icons are visible in the editing screen, just above and below the data. (See the section "Setting Options for WordPerfect Links" later in this chapter.)

**Editing a WordPerfect Link** You can edit an existing WordPerfect link to change any of the link information that you specified in the Create Data Link dialog box. To edit an existing WordPerfect link, follow these steps:

1. Move the WordPerfect insertion point inside the link that you want to edit.
2. Choose Insert, Spreadsheet/Database, Edit Link. The Edit Data Link dialog box appears.
3. Change any of the specifications that you defined in the Create Data Link dialog box. For example, you could reduce the linked spreadsheet range to remove blank rows.

> **CAUTION**
> Deleting either of the pair of codes (the codes can be viewed in Reveal Codes, but can be deleted whether Reveal Codes is open or not) removes both codes and destroys the link. The spreadsheet data continues functioning as an imported spreadsheet. The only way to restore the link is to delete the spreadsheet data and define a new link, as described in the preceding section, "Creating a WordPerfect Spreadsheet/Database Link."

**Updating Data that Is Linked with a WordPerfect Link**   To ensure that data is current in all WordPerfect spreadsheet/database links, ask WordPerfect to update all links. Follow these steps to update WordPerfect links:

1. Choose Insert, Spreadsheet/Database, Update. You are prompted with `Update all data links?`.
2. To update links, choose Yes.

**Setting Options for WordPerfect Links**   You can adjust the default settings for WordPerfect spreadsheet/database link options in the Link Options dialog box. To adjust the settings of link options, follow these steps:

1. Choose Insert, Spreadsheet/Database, Options. The Link Options dialog box appears.
2. The Link Options dialog box contains two options: Update On Retrieve (the default) and Show Link Icons. You can change either or both options.
3. Choose OK to exit the dialog box and save your settings.

## Handling Special Spreadsheet/Database Conditions

This section discusses special situations that can occur when you import spreadsheet/database data. For example, some spreadsheets and database files contain data that is in a very wide format. Unsupported formats can be imported as ASCII-delimited text files, but this also requires special consideration. This section explains these issues.

**Working with Password-Protected Files**   Password protection is part of a document's formatting that WordPerfect checks before allowing you to import a file. You must remove the password from a file created by a spreadsheet or database program before you can import or link to it.

**Working with Wide Spreadsheets and Database Records** WordPerfect tries to make imported spreadsheet/database data fit between the left and right margins of the document. When WordPerfect imports data that is wider than the document margins, formatting problems arise. One or more columns are compressed (table format) or data is wrapped to the next line (text format). If the data string is too wide to fit between the margins, you can accommodate the data in any of the following ways:

- Reduce the column (field) widths in the source file.
- Reduce the font size or font type that is active at the location where WordPerfect inserts the imported data.
- Reduce the width of the left and right margins at the location where WordPerfect inserts the imported data.
- Choose a landscape-sheet definition for the page where WordPerfect inserts the imported data if the printer supports this mode, or choose a larger paper size, if possible.
- Use the methods described in Chapter 16, "Working with Tables," and Chapter 31, "Advanced Tables," to resize the table so that it doesn't exceed the space between the margins.
- Use more than one import operation, and import the data in sections. Import one cell range or one set of columns at one place in the WordPerfect document, and import another set at another place.

**TIP** Use the horizontal scroll bar and adjust the Zoom factor when you're working with a wide table in WordPerfect.

▶ See "Changing the Table Size," **p. 513**
▶ See "Creating a Table," **p. 498**

**Working with Unsupported Formats** To use a spreadsheet other than one created by Lotus 1-2-3, Excel 4.0 or before, Quattro/Quattro Pro, Quattro Pro for Windows, or PlanPerfect, you must convert the spreadsheet to one of the formats recognized by WordPerfect.

Most spreadsheet programs enable you to convert a spreadsheet to Lotus 1-2-3 format. For more information on converting a spreadsheet, see the documentation for the spreadsheet program.

If WordPerfect cannot convert data from the spreadsheet and the spreadsheet program cannot convert the file to a format supported by WordPerfect, converting the spreadsheet to an ASCII format first is a possible solution. Use the spreadsheet program to make an ASCII copy of the spreadsheet file. If the spreadsheet program can create an ASCII delimited text file, you can import the ASCII file into WordPerfect as a table or merge data file. If the ASCII file does not have delimiters, your only option is to open (or insert) the ASCII file as a text file.

When your database is not in one of WordPerfect's supported file formats, you can convert the file to an ASCII delimited text file and then import the ASCII file into WordPerfect. Many database programs have a built-in export option for converting their own database files to ASCII delimited text format. After the database file is in ASCII delimited format, you can import it as a table or merge data file, or you can merge the ASCII file without converting it first. See Chapter 19, "Assembling Documents with Merge and Sort," for information on merging.

**N O T E** For information on setting defaults for imported ASCII delimited text files in WordPerfect, see "Setting File Preferences for Imported Files" earlier in this chapter.

## Importing Spreadsheet Data with DDE

A Windows DDE link is an alternative to the WordPerfect spreadsheet link. (See "Copying and Linking Spreadsheet/Database Data" earlier in this chapter, for information on creating a WordPerfect spreadsheet link.) A DDE link gives you automatic updates when both programs are in memory at the same time and when the source (server) file is opened before the WordPerfect document is opened. This is the only advantage that a DDE link has over a WordPerfect spreadsheet link; with either type of link, you can update linked data simply by asking for an update. When the ability to have automatic updates under these circumstances is an overriding consideration, use a DDE link.

To create a DDE link in WordPerfect to data in any Windows spreadsheet program that is DDE-capable as a server (including Excel, Quattro Pro for Windows, and Lotus for Windows), follow the steps for creating a DDE link to data in another program later in this chapter. While you are creating the link, the Paste Special dialog box appears. In the Paste Special dialog box, select the spreadsheet data and choose Paste Link. The data is imported and linked.

## Importing Spreadsheet Data with OLE

When you want the convenience of being able to update linked spreadsheet data while you are editing the WordPerfect document that contains the link, you can have that convenience by creating an OLE link to the data. An OLE link creates an embedded object in your document; you can move and size the object with the mouse. Because the object is a copy of the data from the original file rather than of text, its appearance may not be perfect. With a small and simple spreadsheet, the result may be acceptable. Further, if an OLE package object is linked, you see an icon that represents the link rather than a copy of the data itself.

For more information on creating an OLE link to a spreadsheet, see "Creating an OLE Link to Data in Another Program" later in this chapter.

## Exporting Spreadsheet/Database Data

With WordPerfect's powerful built-in Tables feature, the need to export data to a spreadsheet or database may never occur. One method for exporting data to a spreadsheet is to format the data in WordPerfect tabular columns (this works best if you use a monospace font), save the document in ASCII text format, and import the file into the spreadsheet. You then can parse the data into cells. See the documentation for your spreadsheet program for information on converting, translating, and importing data and on parsing data.

- See "Understanding Tables," **p. 496**
- See "Creating a Table," **p. 498**
- See "Understanding the Merge Process," **p. 611**

If a WordPerfect merge data file becomes too large and cumbersome to maintain in WordPerfect, you may want to export the merge data file to a database program. You can export data from WordPerfect to dBASE, for example, by converting the merge data file to ASCII delimited format with WordPerfect's internal convert process and then appending that file to a file with an appropriate structure. See your database program's reference manual for instructions on importing data from other programs.

# Importing and Working with Graphics Data and Other Types of Data

The list of data types that can be imported into WordPerfect includes graphics images, text, charts, spreadsheets, database data, sound clips, and video clips. Guidelines for importing data from other word processing programs and from spreadsheet/database programs are presented earlier in this chapter. This section discusses the importation of data types—for example, graphics, sound, and video.

 To see which applications on your hardware installation support DDE/OLE, choose Insert, Object and look at the Object Type list in the dialog box.

WordPerfect supports graphics formats from many of the most popular Windows and non-Windows graphics programs. You can import into a WordPerfect document a file saved in any compatible graphics format simply by placing that file in a graphics box. For more information about working with graphics images, see Chapter 7, "Integrating Text and Graphics."

The quickest and easiest method of importing data into WordPerfect is to select the data in the source program, copy it to the Clipboard, and paste it into a WordPerfect document. If the data is clip art—that is, a graphics file on disk—you can create a graphics box and insert the image into the WordPerfect graphics box.

 **T I P** You can export data from WordPerfect 7 to another program by copying and pasting or by using DDE or OLE.

If you want to keep imported data current, and if the source program has DDE capability as a server, you can choose to import the data with a DDE link. If you want the convenience of editing the imported data while you are editing your WordPerfect document, and if the source program has OLE capability as a server, you can choose to import the data with an OLE link. Either of these techniques is appropriate, for example, for keeping data from an imported chart current in WordPerfect.

**N O T E**  The instructions in this section for creating Windows DDE and OLE links can be applied to the importation of data from any source that is DDE- or OLE-capable as a server. (If a program is DDE-capable as a server, it isn't necessarily OLE-capable as a server.)

## Creating a DDE Link to Data in Another Program

To create a DDE link in a WordPerfect document to data in another program, follow the instructions in this section. The other program must be DDE-capable as a server, and the file containing the data to be linked must have a name (that is, it must have been saved). Creating the link is easiest if you have already started the server application and the data file containing the data to be linked is already open (the server application could, of course, also be WordPerfect). After these conditions are met, follow these steps to create a DDE link:

1. Select the data that you want to link.

2. Copy the selected data to the Clipboard by choosing Edit, Copy or by pressing Ctrl+C.

3. Start WordPerfect. (Don't close the other program; just minimize it.)

4. Open the document into which you want to import the data, and place the insertion point where you want to create the link.
5. Choose Edit, Paste Special. The Paste Special dialog box appears.
6. Choose Paste Link, then choose OK, to place a copy of the source data in the WordPerfect document. The beginning of the linked data is identified in Reveal Codes with a code, and the end of the linked data is identified with a code. The code contains an identifying link number.

If Paste Link is unavailable, you haven't saved the original document. Choose Cancel, save the original document (in its parent application), then repeat these steps.

A DDE link is updated automatically when the server file and the client file are open at the same time and the source file has been opened first. You can update the client file at any time, however, after saving any changes in the source data. To do so, follow these steps:

1. Deselect any graphics (including OLE objects).
2. Choose Edit, Links to display the Links dialog box.
3. Highlight the name of the link that you want to update.
4. Choose Update Now.
5. Choose Close to exit the Links dialog box.

## Creating an OLE Link to Data in Another Program

OLE enables you to place an object from one application within a document created by another application. When you place a file by choosing Insert, Object, you can choose to either link or embed the object. A *linked object* is automatically changed in the client application when it's changed in the server/parent application. An *embedded object* doesn't retain that close association, although when you edit an embedded object, the parent application automatically opens to perform the edit. You can edit an embedded object without changing the original object. Linked objects retain their connection with the server/parent application.

For example, you could embed a Corel Photo-Paint object in a WordPerfect document. When double-clicked, Photo-Paint opens, enabling you to edit the object. When you are finished editing the object, you are returned to the WordPerfect document that contains the now-modified object. This ability is called *in-place editing*.

To create an OLE embedded object in a WordPerfect document from data in another program that is OLE-capable as a server, follow these steps:

1. Choose Insert, Object. The Insert Object dialog box appears (see fig. 18.10).

**FIG. 18.10**
The Insert Object dialog box displays a list of objects that can be inserted from the current hardware installation.

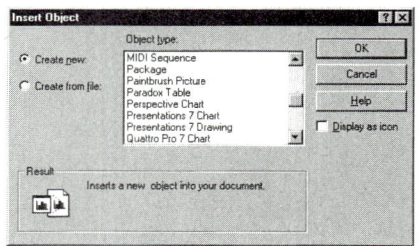

2. Select the Object Type from the list of available object types on your hardware installation. The name of the type includes the name of its server application. Then choose OK.

3. The server application starts, taking control of WordPerfect's menus and Toolbar. Create the item (document, image, or sound clip, for example) that you want to embed in WordPerfect.

    If the item you want to use has already been created and saved in a document, you can embed or link an object from a file by choosing Create From File in the Insert Object dialog box.

 **TIP** Another way to embed an object is to choose Edit, Paste Special (in WordPerfect) and select Object after placing the object in the Clipboard.

4. Exit the server application by clicking in the document to deselect the object. WordPerfect's menus and Toolbar return.

> **NOTE** These steps work only if the OLE server application supports in-place editing. If it does not, the OLE object is edited in a separate window. To return to WordPerfect in this case, you must exit the OLE server application the way you normally would (by choosing File, Exit, or a similar method).

An even simpler way to create embedded objects is to drag text or objects from one application Window into another. You can also drag text or objects from an application window to the desktop, thus creating a *scrap*, which can then be dragged into applications any time to create embedded OLE objects. (Not all applications support this method, however.)

Pressing Ctrl+Shift while dragging an object into WordPerfect will link the information rather than embed it. You can also right-click the information or file, drag it to WordPerfect, then click Link in the pop-up menu.

You can select the embedded object with the mouse and then move or resize it.

To edit the embedded object at its source, double-click the embedded object. The source application starts, taking control of WordPerfect's menus and Toolbar and displaying the embedded object in the WordPerfect document window. After you make your editing changes, exit the source application by clicking in the document to deselect the object. (This description applies only to applications that support in-place editing.) If the embedded object is a sound or movie clip, a double-click plays the clip.

For more information on combining text and graphics, see Chapter 7, "Integrating Text and Graphics." ●

CHAPTER 19

# Assembling Documents with Merge and Sort

*by C. Brian Scott and Judy Petersen*

Consider the following situation.

You have just been named the coordinator for the upcoming Office Automation conference, and your first task is to send a letter announcing the first meeting to the other employees assigned to help with the conference. How do you produce the letter and prepare it for mailing to everyone who should receive it?

You must design a new form for use in your office. How do you design the form to make sure that users get the right information in the right place, formatted the right way?

The WordPerfect 7 Merge feature provides an answer in both situations. Merge enables you to combine fixed information (the form, its text, and merge codes) with variable information. The variable information can come from a data file, or it can be entered by the user.

This chapter explains the merge feature, tells you how to construct simple merges, and introduces advanced features that can be used in complex merges.

### Create data files and form files for merging
Use data files to name the fields in the file and use the field names in your form. Use form files for preparing a generic letter you need to send out to several people.

### Use Merge to prepare a form letter mailing
The Merge feature enables you to also create envelopes and labels from a mailing list.

### Use keyboard input in a merge
WordPerfect 7 makes data entry nearly foolproof. Learn how to effectively use the keyboard to input information you want to merge.

### Merge data into a table
Although you maintain a data file in table format, at times you might need to merge data from a data text file into a table.

### Sort data files and select records
By using the Sort feature, you can sort the data file itself as well as other kinds of files.

This chapter also explains the Sort feature. You can use Sort to order the information in files, whether or not the file is to be used as a data file for a merge operation. ■

# Using Merge

*Merge* is the process of combining variable information with a file containing fixed information to produce one or more new files. The file with the fixed information is referred to as a *form file*. The variable information can come from user input at the keyboard or from another file referred to as a *data file*.

Many people use a *mail merge* to create customized form letters together with envelopes or labels. In this type of merge, the form file is the letter and the data file is the mailing list. You can also use merge to create "fill-in-the-blank" forms. You can design the forms to be filled in by users at the keyboard or with variable information from a data file.

# Performing a Simple Merge

This section demonstrates a typical simple merge. The basic features shown here apply to any merge operation for a mass mailing. Later sections of this chapter provide detailed explanations of the various features used in the demonstration.

Refer to the conference-letter example presented earlier in the chapter. To prepare the mailing, you need to create a letter (the form file), a mailing list (the data file), and envelopes for the letters.

## Creating the Data File

Although you can create the data and form files in any order, creating the data file first is the easiest approach; you can name the fields in the file and use the field names in your form. For this example, you need the following information for each person who is to receive the letter: first name, last name, address, city, state, and ZIP code.

> **NOTE** A *field* is a single item of information (for example, a first name) that you use in your form. (See "Understanding Data Files" later in this chapter for more details.) You can combine the first and last names in a single field, but if you do, you cannot use just the first name in the salutation of the letter.

To create the data file with the listed fields, follow these steps:

1. Choose <u>T</u>ools, M<u>e</u>rge, or press Shift+F9. The Merge dialog box appears (see fig. 19.1).

**FIG. 19.1**
In the Merge dialog box, select the type of merge file to be created, and begin the merge.

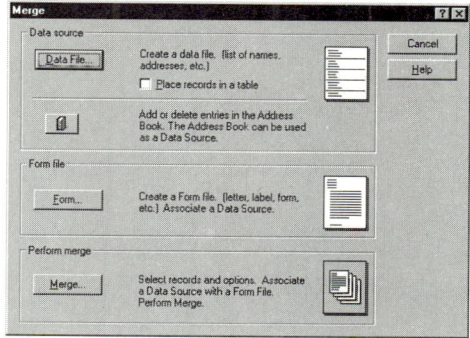

2. Choose Data File. The Create Merge File dialog box appears.

   If the active document is new, the Create Data File dialog box will appear instead of the Create Merge File dialog box. In this case, skip to step 4.

3. Choose whether to Use File In Active Window or to Create The File In A New Document Window, then choose OK. The Create Data File dialog box appears (see fig. 19.2).

**FIG. 19.2**
Enter the names of the fields in the Field Name List box. You can add, delete, edit, and rearrange the order of the fields by using the controls in this box.

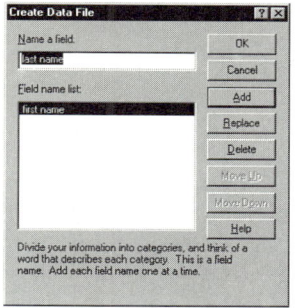

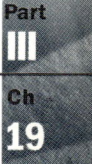

4. Type **first name** in the Name A Field text box, and then press Enter.
5. Continue to enter the remaining field names: **last name**, **address**, **city**, **state**, and **zip code**.
6. Choose OK. The Quick Data Entry dialog box appears (see fig. 19.3).

   You are ready to type in the mailing list information. For this example, you need to mail the letter to three employees:

   Peter Wilson, 3740 NE Alameda, Portland, OR 97212

   John Reed, 3416 SE 117th Avenue, Portland, OR 97266

   Terry Macnamara, 2216 SE 57th Street, Portland, OR 97215

**FIG. 19.3**
Use the Quick Data Entry dialog box to enter information in your data file. You can enter, edit, and delete records, or choose Field Na̲mes to open the Edit Field Names dialog box.

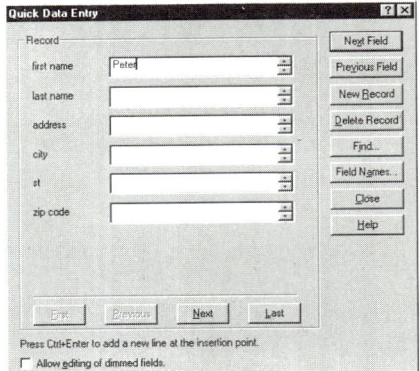

7. Be sure the insertion point is in the text box next to the First Name prompt. Click the text box, use the Ne̲xt Field or Pre̲vious Field controls, or press Tab or Shift+Tab to position the insertion point.

8. Type **Peter**, then press Enter. Because Ne̲xt Field is the default control when you begin data entry, pressing Enter moves the insertion point to the next field.

9. Continue entering the field information for Peter Wilson as shown previously. When you finish typing the ZIP code, press Enter to insert the completed record in the file. The insertion point returns to the first field prompt, and you can enter another record.

**N O T E** When you enter text in fields, do not include punctuation, such as the comma that usually follows a city name, or spaces at the end of words when the entry is only one word. Punctuation, spacing, fonts, and other formatting is entered in the form file we will create later.

10. After you enter the data for all three records, choose C̲lose. A dialog box appears, asking if you want to save changes to disk.

11. Choose Y̲es. The Save Data File As dialog box appears.

12. Type a suitable file name, such as **conference.dat**, and then choose S̲ave or press Enter to save the file.

 **TIP** If you want to keep your merge data files in a folder other than the current default folder, be sure to include the path to the folder.

**N O T E** Use a DAT file extension for your merge data files; then you can easily select only data files by choosing the WP Merge Data (*.dat) file type. WordPerfect recognizes files with a DAT extension as merge data files, and files with an FRM extension as form files.

The completed data file resembles figure 19.4.

**FIG. 19.4**
A hard page break separates the records in the data file. Notice the field names in the first record at the beginning of the file.

Hard page break

Current field name

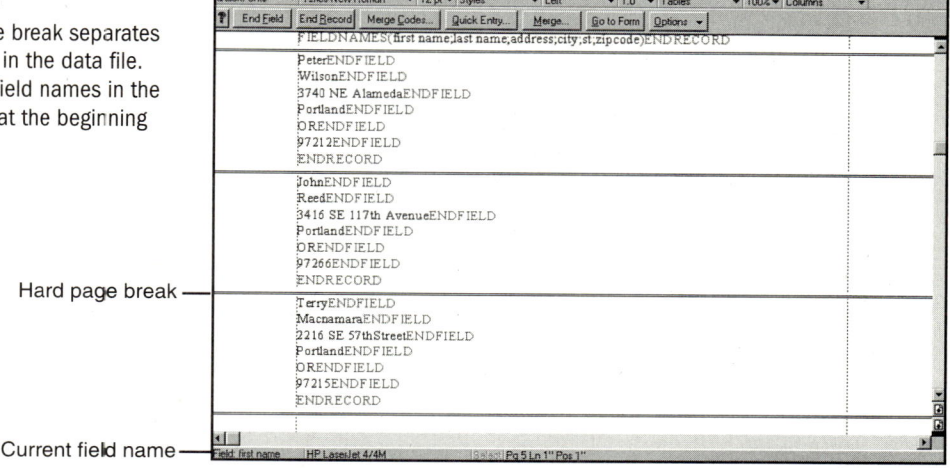

> **NOTE** A WordPerfect 7 merge file is always displayed with a Merge Feature Bar. The Merge Feature Bar gives you quick access to the merge features you use most often with that file. See the section "Understanding the Merge Feature Bar" later in this chapter for more details. Use Alt+Shift+*underlined letter* to choose items on the Merge Feature Bar via the keyboard.

## Creating the Form File

You have completed the mailing list. Now, you need to prepare the letter about the date and time of the next meeting to send to the people on the list. You can draft a generic notice and use mailing labels to send it out, but personalized letters generally receive a more favorable response. To prepare a personalized letter that contains the meeting information, follow these steps:

1. Choose Go to Form from the Merge Feature Bar.
2. The Associate dialog box appears with a message explaining that there is no associated file. Choose Create.
3. Type the inside address as follows:

    **Metro West Soccer Club**
    **Coach Development Committee**
    **P.O. Box 80317**
    **Portland, OR 97280**

4. Press Enter four times to make three blank lines after the inside address.

5. To date the letter to the time of the mail merge (regardless of the date you type the form), use the DATE merge code. To insert the DATE code, click <u>D</u>ate from the Merge Feature Bar.

6. Press Enter four times to create three blank lines after the date.

7. Click <u>I</u>nsert Field from the Merge Bar. The Insert Field Name or Number dialog box appears (see fig. 19.5).

**FIG. 19.5**
The Insert Field Name or Number dialog box lists the fields in the order in which they appear in the associated data file.

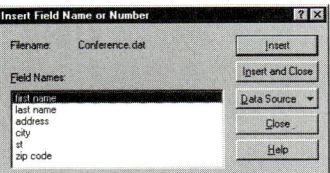

8. Move the highlight bar to `first name`, and click <u>I</u>nsert or press Enter; you can also double-click the item in the <u>F</u>ield Names list box. The line `FIELD(first name)` appears in your document at the insertion point.

 **T I P** You also can double-click the item in the <u>F</u>ield Names list box to insert the field in the document.

9. Press the space bar once to place a space between the first and last name, and then choose and insert `last name` from the Insert Field Name Or Number dialog box.

10. Follow the same procedure to insert the field codes for the rest of the address. Press Enter to move down a line, then insert address. Press Enter to move down one more line, and insert the city field code, type a comma, then press the space bar. Next insert state, press the space bar once or twice, and finally insert the ZIP code.

11. Press Enter twice to create a blank line before the salutation. Type **Dear**, press the space bar, and then insert the first name field code and type a colon. <u>C</u>lose the Insert Field Name or Number dialog box.

12. Press Enter two times to position the insertion point for typing the body of the letter. The remainder of the letter is plain text, without merge codes. Type the following text, using your own name as the author:

> **This will confirm our recent phone conference about the first meeting. We will hold an organizational meeting of the Office Automation Conference committee at 1:00 p.m. on Tuesday, April 16, 1996, in the board room at the main office, 4832 SW Belmont.**

Please bring your suggestions, and those of your staff, for workshop and panel topics. I look forward to seeing you there!

Sincerely,

*your name*

Chairman

Figure 19.6 shows the finished document.

**FIG. 19.6**
The completed sample letter includes text and merge codes where variable data will appear.

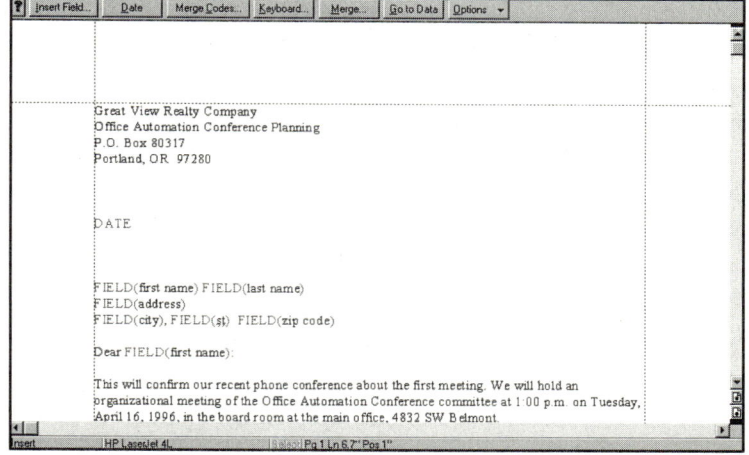

13. Choose File, Save As, or press F3 to save the file. Use an appropriate name, such as **orgmeet.frm**.

> **NOTE** Use an FRM file extension for your merge form files; then you can easily select only data files from the Open dialog by choosing the WP Merge Forms (*.frm) file type when you use any of WordPerfect's features for selecting a file. WordPerfect recognizes files with a DAT extension as merge data files, and files with an FRM extension as form files.

## Creating Envelopes

Although you can create envelopes and letters separately, a form letter mailing is easiest to prepare when you create the envelopes as you perform the merge. To create envelopes for the sample merge, proceed as follows:

1. Click Merge. The Perform Merge dialog box appears (see fig. 19.7). WordPerfect 7 displays the name of the data file associated with the form file you just created.

**FIG. 19.7**
The Perform Merge dialog box shows the data file associated with the current form file. Use this box to choose the files to be merged, direct the merge output, and to create envelopes.

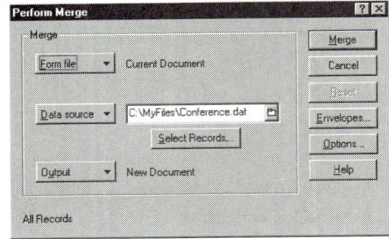

2. Click Envelopes. The Envelope dialog box appears (see fig. 19.8).

**FIG. 19.8**
The Envelope dialog box, which includes a Field button, enables you to insert the return address and the mailing address into the form, save mailing addresses, choose saved addresses, and define envelopes.

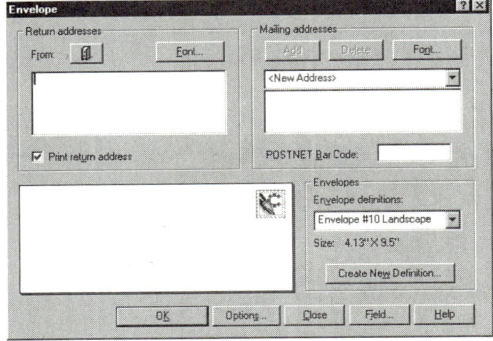

3. Click the From box, and then type the return address as shown in the sample letter.
4. Click the Mailing Addresses text box, and then click the Field button. The Insert Field Name Or Number dialog box appears.
5. Choose first name from the Insert Field Name or Number dialog box, and then click Insert and Close. The field first name is inserted into the Mailing Addresses text box (see fig. 19.9).

**FIG. 19.9**
By using the Insert Field Name or Number dialog box, you can quickly and accurately insert merge codes for the mailing address.

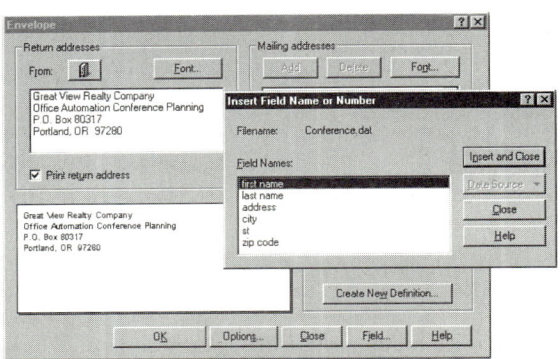

6. Continue to insert the fields for the remainder of the mailing address. Format the address using the same techniques used the first time (such as inserting spaces, commas, and hard returns, where appropriate). Choose Close after you finish to return to the Envelope dialog box.

7. To use the POSTNET bar code on the envelopes, click Options, and choose whether to Include and position above address or Include and position below address, then choose OK. Choose the POSTNET Bar Code text box that now appears in the Envelope dialog box, then click Field. Choose zip code in the Field Names list of the Insert Field Name or Number dialog box, and click Insert and Close.

The envelopes are now defined for the merge, and your screen resembles figure 19.10.

8. Choose OK or press Enter. The program returns to the Perform Merge dialog box.

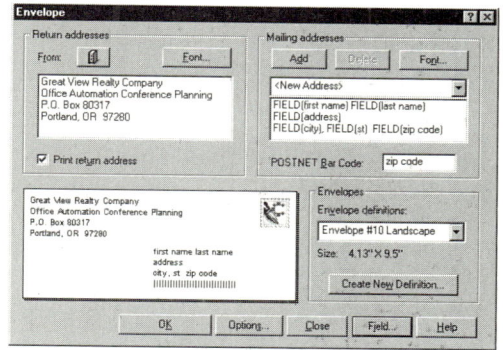

**FIG. 19.10**
The completed Envelope dialog box contains the return address and merge codes for the mailing address.

## Performing the Merge

You are now ready to perform the merge. To merge the files you have just created, follow these steps:

1. Make sure that New Document appears in the Output pop-up button.

2. Choose Merge or press Enter to complete the merge operation. The merge creates a file that contains a letter, immediately followed by an envelope, for each record. Each letter and envelope is separated from the others by hard page breaks.

 If your printer doesn't have an envelope feeder, you may find it more efficient to create envelopes separately from the letters for larger printing jobs. Because the envelopes are all clumped together at the end of the file (after the letters), it would be easier to select the envelope pages and save them to a separate file.

After the merge is completed, you can print the resulting file to generate the letters for mailing. You can also save the file, although in most situations saving only the form files and data files is more efficient than saving the merged file.

# Understanding Data Files

Data files hold the variable information used in a merge. That variable information can be of any type. The data may be personal information such as names, addresses, and phone numbers, or more varied data such as contract clauses, airline schedules, or recipes. For WordPerfect to use the information, you must organize the data into fields and records.

## Understanding Records and Fields

Each *record* in a data file contains information that is related in some way. Each record in a mailing list, for example, contains information about one person or company. Records are subdivided into fields. A *field* contains the smallest item of information that you intend to use in a form file associated with the data file. Each field of a record in a mailing list contains a single item of information, such as a name, street address, or phone number.

You decide the organizational structure for your data when you create the data file. As a result, when you create the data file, you must give careful consideration to what level of detail your fields must provide. You may choose to divide personal information, for example, into just three fields: name, address (including the city, state, and ZIP code), and phone number. You have much greater flexibility in using the data, however, if you divide the same information into more fields, for example: first name, last name, street address, P.O. box, city, state, ZIP code, and phone number. As a rule, the more fields you use, the more flexibility you have in using the data.

WordPerfect identifies fields by name or number (relative position in the record). Use the same number of fields and the same field order in every record in your data files, even if some records have blank fields. WordPerfect identifies numbered fields only by their relative position in the record. If you have records with different numbers of fields in different orders, you may get unintended results when you perform a merge that calls for fields by number.

> **CAUTION**
> Avoid assigning the same name to more than one field. WordPerfect accepts the duplicate names, but when you later merge using the data file, you will not be able to retrieve the data you want.

## Understanding the Types of Data Files

WordPerfect uses two types of data files: *data text files* and *data table files*. In a data text file, fields are separated from each other by an ENDFIELD code, and records are terminated by an ENDRECORD code. In a data table file, each row of the table is a record and each cell is a field. You saw an example of a data text file in figure 19.4. Figure 19.11 shows the same data in a data table file format.

▶ See "Understanding Tables," **p. 496**

You use the same process to create a data table file that you use to create a data text file. If you want to use a data table file, choose Place Records in a Table in the Merge dialog box that appears in the first step of creating a data file in the previous section "Creating the Data File" before choosing Data File in the second step. WordPerfect then creates the table for you as you enter the field names.

**FIG. 19.11**
This data table file holds the same data as the file shown in figure 19.4. The field names are the column headings in the first row of the table.

| first name | last name | address | city | st | zip code |
|---|---|---|---|---|---|
| Peter | Wilson | 3740 NE Alameda | Portland | OR | 97212 |
| John | Reed | 3416 SE 117th Ave. | Portland | OR | 97266 |
| Terry | Macnamara | 2216 SE 57th | Portland | OR | 97215 |

The two data file types have these relative features:

| Feature | Data Text | Data Table |
|---|---|---|
| Field Delimiter | ENDFIELD code | table cell |
| Record Delimiter | ENDRECORD code | table row |
| Maximum Number of Fields | Unlimited | 64 |
| Maximum Number of Named Fields | 255 | 64 |
| Maximum Number of Records | 32,767 | 32,767 |
| Maximum Size of Fields | Unlimited | Must fit in cell (less than one page) |

Your choice of data file type depends on the data you plan to use in the file. Data table files work best with a relatively small number of short fields. Although data table files can hold up to 64 fields, the font and paper you select (for the document window in which you create the table) limit the practical size of a table. If you create 64 cells in a data table row, you may not be able to read any of the data. The data table shown in figure 19.11 is close to the practical size limit for standard letter-size paper in portrait orientation with 1-inch margins and a 12-point font.

## Understanding Field Names

WordPerfect can recognize fields by number or by name. When you first create a data file, WordPerfect gives you the opportunity to enter field names before you move to the main document window. Entering field names is illustrated in the earlier section, "Creating the Data File." If you do not use field names, WordPerfect automatically numbers the fields. The program numbers the fields in a data text file sequentially, from the beginning of the record to the end; fields in a data table file are numbered sequentially by cell, from left to right.

Working with a form file is easier when you have created the file with named fields whose names correspond to the information in the fields. When you want to locate information or enter data into a specific field, the field name helps you find the right field quickly. When the main document window for a data file is active, the WordPerfect status bar identifies the field in which the insertion point is located. Further, the Quick Data Entry dialog box displays the fields' identification next to the data entry text boxes. If you haven't used field names, only field numbers appear in these displays.

> **NOTE** Field names can be all upper- or lowercase characters, or a mix of both. You can also use spaces and punctuation marks.

WordPerfect's 255 named-field limit enables you to use named fields in virtually any project that uses Merge.

## Using the Quick Data Entry Dialog Box

WordPerfect 7 makes data entry simple and nearly foolproof. After you have entered field names in a new data file, WordPerfect displays the Quick Data Entry dialog box (see fig. 19.12). You can also access the Quick Data Entry dialog box by clicking Quick Entry from the Merge Feature Bar that is present when you edit a merge data file.

To enter data through the Quick Data Entry dialog box, position the insertion point in the text box for the first field, type the information for the field, and then press Enter. The insertion point advances to the text box for the next field. Repeat this process to enter data for each field. If you have no data for a field, press Enter to leave the field blank. When you complete the last field, press Enter to save the record in the data file. The insertion point moves to the text box for the first field to enable you to enter another record. This process is identical for both data text files and data table files.

**FIG. 19.12**
The Quick Data Entry dialog box enables you to enter, delete, and edit records quickly in merge data files.

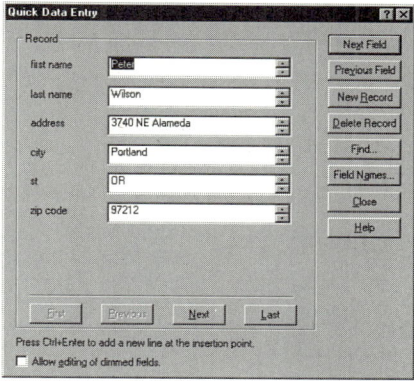

The Quick Data Entry dialog box displays the record in which the insertion point is located when you choose Quick Entry from an existing merge data file. You can position the insertion point in the displayed record by clicking the text box for the field you want to edit, or by choosing the Next Field or Previous Field controls. The controls along the bottom of the dialog box enable you to quickly select the record you want to edit.

Table 19.1 lists and describes the Quick Data Entry dialog box options.

**Table 19.1  Controls in the Quick Data Entry Dialog Box**

| Control | Action |
| --- | --- |
| Next Field | Moves the insertion point to the next field in the displayed record. |
| Previous Field | Moves the insertion point to the previous field in the displayed record. |
| New Record | Clears the text boxes for entry of new record data (the new data is placed in the data file where the insertion point was located when you chose Quick Entry). |
| Delete Record | Deletes the displayed record from the data file. |
| Find | Opens the Find Text dialog box to enable you to search for text in the data file; displays the record in which the matching text is located. |
| Field Names | Opens the Edit Field Names dialog box in which you can add, delete, or edit field names; any changes you make in this dialog box apply to all records in the data file. |
| Close | Closes the Quick Data Entry dialog box, writes the data entries to the data file, and makes the data file the active window. |
| Help | Opens WordPerfect Help and displays the topic About Quick Data Entry. |

*continues*

**Table 19.1 Continued**

| Control | Action |
|---|---|
| First | Displays the first record in the data file. |
| Previous | Displays the record that immediately precedes the currently displayed record. |
| Next | Displays the record that immediately follows the currently displayed record. |
| Last | Displays the last record in the data file. |
| Allow Editing Of Dimmed | By default, fields containing Fields Merge functions are protected from changes when the data file is edited. Choosing this option enables you to edit any field with a function. The function is lost if the field is edited. |

## Entering Data Directly in an Existing Data File

Adding or editing records in an existing data table file is similar to editing any table. Adding a row adds a new record; entering data in a cell edits the field defined by the column heading. Choose Row from the Merge Feature Bar, then choose Insert. From here, you can add a row above the current row; add a row below the current row; or add a row to the end of the table.

▶ **See** "Editing the Table Structure," **p. 509**

**TIP** Use Alt+Shift+*underlined letter* via the keyboard to choose Feature Bar buttons.

To enter a new record directly in an existing data text file, follow these steps:

1. Position the insertion point where you want to begin the record (begin either at the end of the data file or immediately after the record you want your new record to follow).

   **NOTE** Changing your mode from View to Draft before editing a data text file enables you to see more than one record at a time. Records are separated by both an ENDRECORD code and a [HPg] (Hard Page Break) code. In Page mode, the [HPg] codes cause only one page (therefore, one record) to appear on-screen at any one time. In Draft mode, the [HPg] breaks appear on-screen as double horizontal lines.

2. Type the data for the field. Notice that the status bar shows the name of the field in which the insertion point is located.

3. After you finish typing the data for the field, click End Field from the Merge Feature Bar or press Alt+Shift+F. WordPerfect inserts an ENDFIELD code followed by a [HRt] code. The insertion point moves to the next line for the beginning of the next field.
4. Repeat steps 2 and 3 to enter data in each field.
5. After all the fields are complete, click End Record from the Merge Feature Bar. WordPerfect inserts an ENDRECORD code followed by a [HPg] code, and moves the insertion point to the beginning of the next record.

## Editing the Data File Structure

As records are added to a data file, it may become obvious that fields should be added or removed from the data file. For example, the Office Automation Conference Planning data file could contain data about the speakers and panelists as well as the committee members. This would result in fewer data files to track and would increase the power of the form files.

To include all participants in a single file, add a field for position of each participant. To add a field to the CONFERENCE.DAT data text file:

1. Click Quick Entry from the Merge Feature Bar. The Quick Data Entry dialog box appears.
2. Choose Field Names to display the Edit Field Names dialog box (see fig. 19.13), and select address from the Field Names list.

**FIG. 19.13**
In the Edit Field Names dialog box, select the field name that will follow the new field.

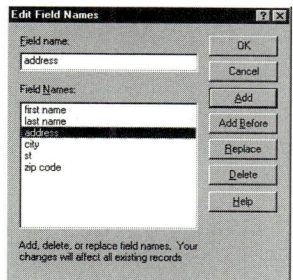

3. Type **position** in the Field Name text box, then choose Add Before.
4. Choose OK to return to the Quick Data Entry dialog box.
5. Type **committee** in the position text box for each record, clicking the Next button to move from record to record after each record is updated.

6. Choose Close, then Yes; then click Save, Yes in the Save Data File As dialog box to save the changes to disk.

The process of inserting a new field in a data table file is a bit easier:

1. Select the column that will be to the right of the new field, in this case, the Address column.
2. Choose Table, Insert to display the Insert Columns/Rows dialog box.
3. Choose Columns, then OK to return to the table.
4. Type **position** in the first cell in the new column and **committee** in the remaining three cells in the column.

## Understanding the Merge Feature Bar

When you use the Merge feature to create a file, WordPerfect identifies the file as a merge file and always displays it with the appropriate Merge Feature Bar. Figure 19.14 shows the Merge Feature Bars for data text files and data table files.

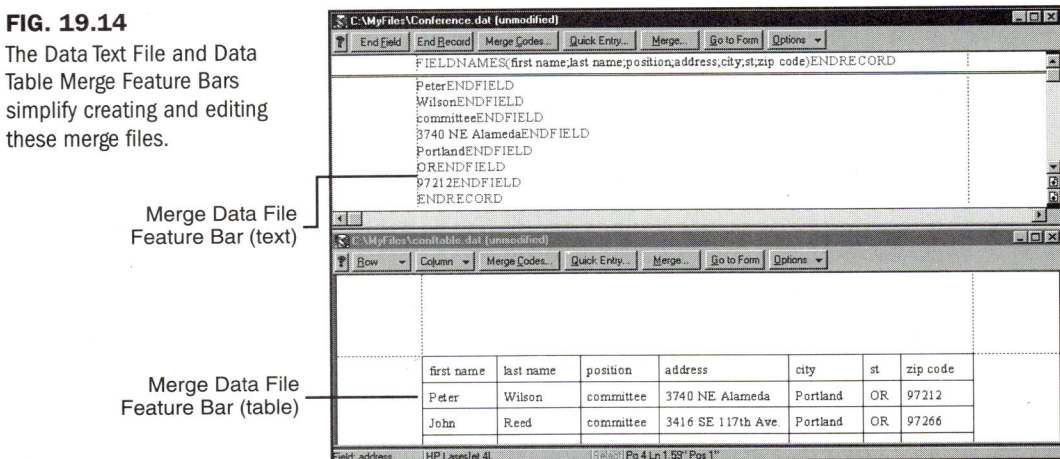

**FIG. 19.14**
The Data Text File and Data Table Merge Feature Bars simplify creating and editing these merge files.

The Merge Data File Feature Bar provides instant access to the most common merge actions. Table 19.2 lists and describes the controls on the Merge Feature Bar for data files.

### Table 19.2 Controls on the Merge Data File Feature Bar

| Control | Action |
|---|---|
| Insert Field... | Enables you to insert or delete a table row (data table files only). |
| Column ▼ | Enables you to insert or delete a table column (data table files only). |
| Merge Codes... | Displays the Insert Merge Codes dialog box to provide access to all merge codes. |
| Quick Entry... | Displays the Quick Data Entry dialog box to enable you to enter and edit records. |
| Merge... | Displays the Perform Merge dialog box to enable you to create new merge files or begin a merge. |
| Go to Form | Displays the associated form file; if no form is associated, enables you to select or create an associated form file. |
| Options ▼ | Displays a menu of these additional file manipulation options:<br>• Sort. Displays the Sort dialog box that enables you to sort the records in the data file (see the "Using Sort" section for more details).<br>• Display Codes. Displays full merge codes in the file. Has no effect on a merge data file.<br>• Display As Markers. Displays merge codes as a diamond icon. Has no effect on a merge data file.<br>• Hide Codes. Suppresses all display of merge codes (codes are visible only in Reveal Codes). Has no effect on a merge data file.<br>• Remove Merge Bar. Removes Merge Bar to prevent WordPerfect from treating file as a merge file. |
| ? | Displays menu of choices for other feature bars. |

**NOTE** Adding a row adds a record, and adding a column adds a field. You can insert a new row above or below the current row or at the end of the file. You can place a new column to the left or right of the current column, or at the end of the data file.

# Understanding Form Files

*Form files* are WordPerfect 7 files that contain text, merge codes, or both. A form file serves two functions in a merge operation:

- It supplies the instructions for the merge process.
- It holds the constant information that is combined with the data file to produce the final document.

Most form files contain both text and codes, but you can use a form file that contains only merge and formatting codes.

Every merge requires a form file. The merge instructions come from merge codes placed in the form file. Merge instructions can be simple or complex; they can range from causing a pause for user input to controlling a complex application. WordPerfect 7's merge codes comprise a programming language with which you can create sophisticated applications. At the same time, the default merge setups make basic mail merges easy.

## Using the Merge Feature Bar for Form Files

The Merge Form File Feature Bar, shown in figure 19.15, provides quick access to merge codes and other program functions you use to create form files.

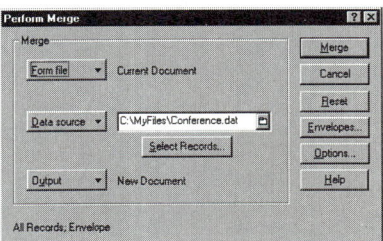

**FIG. 19.15**
The Merge Form Files Feature Bar gives you instant access to the merge codes and program functions you use most often in creating and editing form files.

You can choose the Insert Field, Keyboard, and Date codes directly from the Merge Feature Bar; all other merge codes are readily accessible. Table 19.3 shows each of the choices available on the Merge Feature Bar for form files.

**Table 19.3  Controls on the Merge Form File Feature Bar**

| Choice | Action |
|---|---|
| ? | Displays menu of choices for other feature bars. |

| Choice | Action |
|---|---|
| **Insert Field...** | Places a FIELD(`field name`) code at the insertion point. |
| **Date** | Places a DATE code at the insertion point. |
| **Merge Codes...** | Displays the Insert Merge Codes dialog box from which you can choose any of WordPerfect's 82 merge codes. |
| **Keyboard...** | Inserts a KEYBOARD(`[prompt]`) code at the insertion point (see "Understanding the Keyboard Code" later in this chapter for more details). |
| **Merge...** | Displays the Perform Merge dialog box that enables you to create a data file or another form file, or begin a merge. |
| **Go to Data** | Makes the associated data file the active window; opens the associated data file if it has not been opened; if no associated data file exists, prompts you to select or create one. |
| **Options ▼** | Displays a list of options, as follows:<br>• **D**isplay Codes. Displays full merge codes in the file.<br>• Display As **M**arkers. Displays merge codes as a diamond icon.<br>• **H**ide Codes. Suppresses all display of merge codes; codes are visible only in Reveal Codes.<br>• **R**emove Merge Bar. Removes Merge Bar to prevent WordPerfect from treating a file as a merge file. |

## Associating Form and Data Files

When you create a form file, WordPerfect enables you to designate a particular data file as the source of the field information. The data file you designate is *associated* with the form file. In the form file, WordPerfect stores an internal reference that points to the associated data file. When a data file is associated with a form file, the following features become available:

- *Insert Field*. Causes the Insert Field Name Or Number dialog box to display the list of named fields from the associated data file.

- *Go To Data*. Takes you to the associated data file. If you have not yet opened that data file in your current session, the file opens in an unused document window.

**NOTE** The Go To Data feature works only if you saved the form file after you made the data file association.

- *Go To Form*. After a data file is associated with the form, this takes you to the associated form file. The link from the data file to the form file is not durable; the association lasts only until the data file is closed.

When you first choose to create a form file, WordPerfect prompts you to designate an associated data file (see fig. 19.16). The program also prompts you to associate a data file when you click <u>G</u>o To Data from the Merge Bar in a form file that does not already have an associated data file (see fig. 19.17). If you click <u>I</u>nsert Field from the Merge Feature Bar and you have no associated data file, you see the prompt shown in figure 19.18.

**FIG. 19.16**

When you first create a form file, WordPerfect prompts you to designate an associated data file.

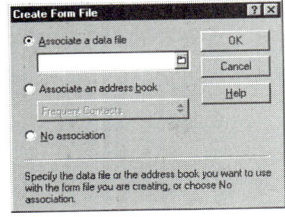

**FIG. 19.17**

Selecting Go to Data when no data file has been associated causes WordPerfect to prompt you to select or create an associated data file.

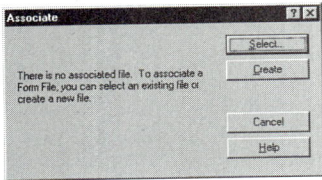

**FIG. 19.18**

A warning message appears in the Insert Field Name or Number dialog box if you click <u>I</u>nsert Field when no data file is associated with your form file. Choose <u>D</u>ata Source, then choose Data File to specify a data file.

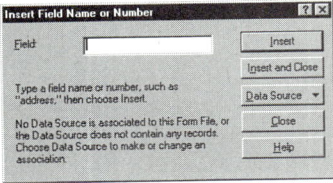

You need not associate a data file with every form file. The association is useful only when the form file uses FIELD( ) codes. Form files that use direct keyboard entry only do not need an associated data file.

## Understanding Merge Codes

*Merge codes* are codes that direct the operation of WordPerfect's merge function. You cannot type merge codes directly into a WordPerfect 7 document; only the program can insert these codes.

Most merge codes require additional parameters, called *arguments*, to operate correctly. Arguments are enclosed in parentheses at the end of code names. The FIELD(*field*) code, for example, includes the argument (*field*). In this example, the code requires an argument—either a name or number—that identifies the particular field in the data file from which information is to be extracted during the merge. Some merge codes accommodate optional arguments, but do not require them. *Optional arguments* are displayed in square brackets in the Insert Merge Codes dialog box. The KEYBOARD([*prompt*]) code, for example, enables you to include a prompt, but does not require it. Other merge codes, such as ENDFIELD, do not accept any arguments.

Merge codes that take arguments appear in Reveal Codes as paired codes, similar to WordPerfect's paired formatting codes. For example, the code to insert the contents of the last name field in your document appears as FIELD(last name) on the editing screen. When viewed in Reveal Codes, however, you see a paired code surrounding the name of the field, as shown in figure 19.19.

**FIG. 19.19**
The FIELD(last name) merge code in the document text appears as the redline attribute to distinguish merge codes from regular text.

The FIELD(last name) merge code in Reveal Codes

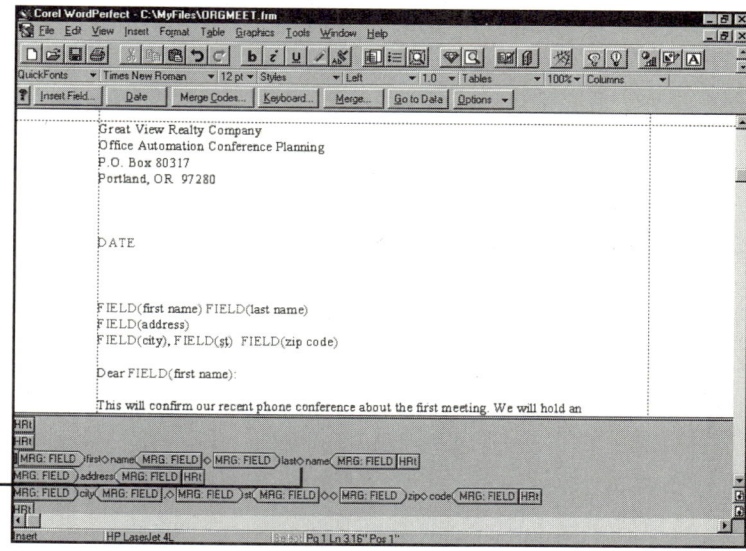

You need not insert the parentheses for merge codes. The parentheses are not actually characters, but are part of the codes. If no parentheses appear next to a merge code, that code does not require arguments.

You can insert the ENDFIELD, ENDRECORD, DATE, FIELD( ), and KEYBOARD( ) codes by choosing them from the Merge Feature Bar. You can insert any of the 82 other merge codes available in WordPerfect by choosing the desired code from the Insert Merge Codes dialog box, shown in figure 19.20. To do so, follow these steps:

1. Place the insertion point where you want to insert the code and click Merge Codes from the Merge Feature Bar. WordPerfect displays the Insert Merge Codes dialog box (see fig. 19.20).

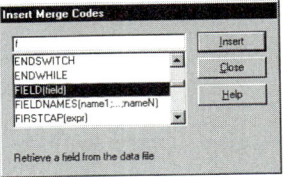

**FIG. 19.20**

Pressing the first letter of a code name takes you to the first code that begins with that letter. Continue entering letters or use the arrow keys or scroll bar to move to the code you want.

2. Type the first few characters of the code's name to jump to the code you want to use. Highlight the code, and then click Insert or press Enter to insert the code in your document.

3. If the code accepts or requires parameters, a message prompts you to enter those. After you enter the parameter, choose OK or press Enter, and WordPerfect inserts the code in your document.

4. To continue entering codes, move the insertion point to the desired location and choose the next code.

5. When you are finished entering codes, choose Close to return to your document.

**NOTE** The Insert Merge Codes dialog box stays on-screen, but is inactive so that you can insert additional merge codes into your document as needed. You can also move the insertion point to other positions in the document or even type more document text. You can move or close the dialog box if it gets in your way.

You can read about using additional merge codes in the upcoming sections "Understanding the Keyboard Code" and "Working with User Input."

## Controlling Merge Codes Display

WordPerfect 7 enables you to control the display of merge codes in a file. The default setting is to show full merge codes. After you have fine-tuned the form file so that merges consistently work the way you expect, the full display of the merge codes may be distracting. If you prefer to not see the merge codes in a file, you can change the way the codes are displayed.

To change the way merge codes are displayed in your files, click Options from the Merge Feature Bar. Among the options listed in the drop-down list are three that control the merge codes display. The default setting is Display Codes. Choosing Display as Markers places a diamond-shaped marker in your file where each merge code is located. The marker hides the code, including any parameters or nested merge expressions. Hide Codes completely eliminates any display of the codes on the regular editing screen. To see codes you have hidden or displayed as markers, use Reveal Codes.

**NOTE** If merge codes are displayed in full, you can edit parameters for the codes on the main editing screen. You cannot edit hidden codes or codes displayed as markers.

## Understanding the Keyboard Code

The purpose of the KEYBOARD([prompt]) code is to pause the merge to allow input from the keyboard, making it possible to insert unique information not available in the merge data file into each merged document. In addition, the KEYBOARD code is particularly useful for jobs that many users do not think of as merge projects because the form file is not merged with a data file. Imagine being able to create fill-in-the-blank documents that, when merged, pause at each blank and prompt you for the required information.

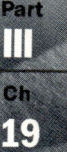

The optional prompt parameter can be used to tell the operator what to type at the location of the pause. Prompt text appears in a Merge Message dialog box that remains visible until the operator closes it or continues the merge. By default, the window is located at the bottom-center of the screen. You can drag the message dialog box to another location, resize it, or close it if it gets in your way.

When the merge pauses for keyboard entry, WordPerfect displays choices on the Merge Feature Bar that enable you to Continue from the pause, Skip Record, Quit or Stop the merge. Even if you close the Merge Message dialog box, the Merge Feature Bar remains visible, indicating that you are in the middle of a merge operation. While the merge is paused, you can use nearly all of the program's functions, including opening and editing other files. When you have completed your actions during the pause, choose Continue to proceed with the merge.

If you click Quit while the merge is paused, the remainder of the form file is placed in your document, but the program processes no more merge codes. Any remaining merge codes are now in your new document, so you can complete the merge later using the new file as the form. If you click Stop while the merge is paused, the merge immediately terminates at the location of the insertion point, and the program inserts no further text or codes from the form file.

In the Office Automation Conference example, once the speakers and panelists are selected and entered into the data file, you need to send each a letter notifying them of the time their workshop or panel will meet. By using the address and salutation containing merge codes from the letter written in the section "Creating the Form File" earlier in this chapter, the new body of the letter can include the following sentence:

> The meeting in which you will participate is scheduled for KEYBOARD(*Type the time, followed by a.m. or p.m., of the workshop or panel*) on August 21, 1996.

To enter the KEYBOARD( ) code, click Keyboard from the Merge Form File Feature Bar and type the text for the prompt message. When finished typing, choose OK or press Enter.

During the merge process, the prompt text appears in the Merge Message dialog box, and whatever you type in response is inserted in the document at the location of the KEYBOARD( ) code (see fig. 19.21). After you complete the response to the prompt, choose Continue to proceed with the merge.

**FIG. 19.21**
The sample letter is paused for keyboard entry of the time of the workshop on panel.

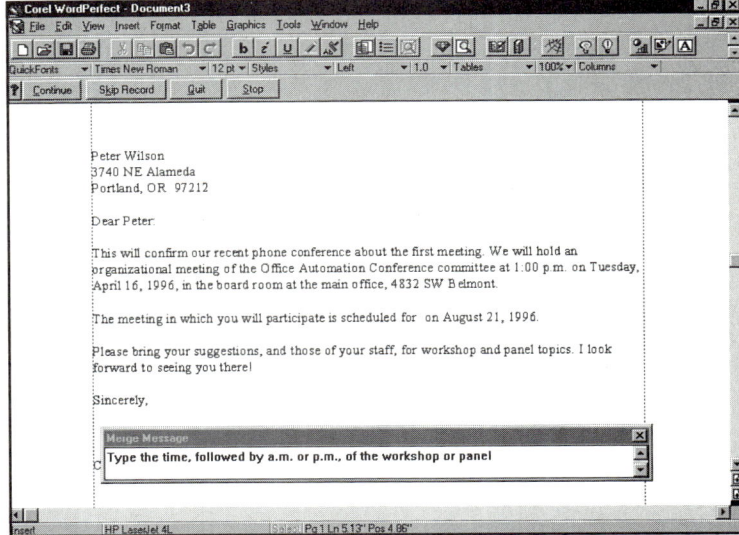

If you often send the same letter many times to different people, you can set up a form letter that prompts for the name, address, and salutation. WordPerfect inserts the prompt messages inside the parentheses of the KEYBOARD( ) code. You can modify the letter for interactive use, written in the section "Creating the Form File" earlier in this chapter, by changing the inside address and salutation prompts as follows:

> KEYBOARD(*Type the Addressee's name, address, city, state, and ZIP code.*)
>
> Dear KEYBOARD(*Type the salutation.*)

# Understanding the Merge Process

After you prepare your form file and data file, you can perform a merge. To begin a merge from a screen that does not contain a merge file, choose Tools, Merge, Merge; or press Shift+F9 and choose Merge. If you have a merge file in the active window, click Merge from the Merge Feature Bar. The Perform Merge dialog box appears (refer to fig. 19.7). Use this dialog box to select the form file and data file and begin the merge process.

## Understanding the Perform Merge Dialog Box

When you perform a merge from a window that does not contain a merge file, the Perform Merge dialog box appears (see fig. 19.22). The insertion point is in the Form File text box, awaiting your entry. You can select general merge options, but before you can perform the merge, you must select a form file.

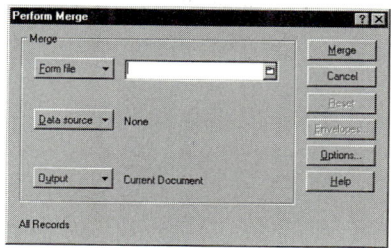

**FIG. 19.22**
The Perform Merge dialog box appears before a form file is selected. You must select a form file before you can perform a merge.

**Selecting the Merge Files**  Type the name (and path, if needed) of the form file you want to use. If you are uncertain of the name or location of the form file, click the Browse button at the right end of the Form File text box and use the Select Form File dialog box to locate the file. Alternatively, click the Form File button; a drop-down list appears, offering the following alternatives:

 Press Alt+down arrow to use the keyboard to open the Form File drop-down list button.

- *File On Disk*. Produces the Select Form File dialog box, which enables you to search anywhere on your system to locate the form file you want to use. If you have used WordPerfect's suggested file extension of FRM for your form files, the dialog box displays only the form files in a folder, because WP Merge Forms (*.frm) is the default selection in the For Type text box.
- *Current Document*. Enables you to use the document in the active window as the form file.
- *Clipboard*. Enables you to use a form that has been previously copied to the Windows Clipboard. If you select a form that has an associated data file, the file name for the associated data file appears in the Data Source text box when you move the insertion point to that box.

If you have previously performed a merge during your current session, the name of the form file you most recently used is displayed in the Form File text box, and the data source you used with that form appears as the default source. If you reached the Perform Merge dialog box by clicking Merge from the Merge Feature Bar of a merge form file, Current Document is the default for the Form File text box, and the name of the form file's associated data file is in the Data Source text box.

After you choose a form file, you can choose a data file (if you need a data file and have not yet chosen one). Choose the data file by using the same methods you use to choose a form file.

In most situations, you need not change the setting for Output. The default location is New Document if the active window is being used when Merge is chosen. If the active window is unused, the default location for merge output is Current Document. If you have many records to merge with the form file, you may want to change the destination to the Printer. With this destination, each completed record goes immediately to the printer as a separate print job. You can also direct output to a File On Disk—a good arrangement if your computer has limited amounts of memory.

Last, you can immediately distribute the merged documents by e-mail. When you choose E-mail, a Merge to E-mail dialog box appears in which you use the drop-down list to Select Fieldname of E-mail address. A text box is also provided where you can specify a Subject line.

> **CAUTION**
> If you have not tested the merge files you plan to use, do not merge the documents to the printer. To avoid wasting time, toner, and paper, either merge a few selected records or merge to the Current Document so you can review the output to see if the results are satisfactory.

To change the default location, click the Output button and select the desired destination from the drop-down list. If you choose to send the output to a disk file, you can enter the name of the file or use the Select Output File dialog box to choose an existing file.

**Setting Merge Options**   Choose the Options button at the bottom of the dialog box to set options for the merge. The Perform Merge Options dialog box appears (see fig. 19.23). The options you set in this dialog box remain in effect during your current session (unless you change them).

**FIG. 19.23**
The Perform Merge Options dialog box provides options with which you can determine how the merge operates.

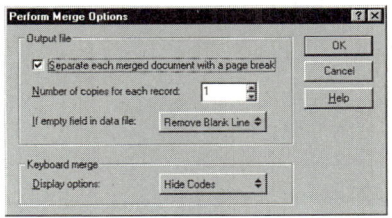

The Number Of Copies For Each Record option enables you to set the number of times each record in a data file is merged with the form.

By default, WordPerfect places a hard page break between each merged record. However, when creating output such as a membership roster or phone list, you will want the data to print continuously or in columns down the page without page breaks. Choose Separate Each Merged Document With A Page Break to deselect this option.

> **NOTE**  A PAGEOFF code can be added at the end of the form file to suppress the page break between merged records, but a PAGEOFF code permanently affects the form file in which you place it. A PAGEOFF code is not affected by the setting of this option.

Empty fields (such as when there is no street address) in a merge file leave blank lines in the merged document. You can choose how WordPerfect handles a blank field using the If Empty Field In Data File option. The default is to remove a blank line in the merged record. This option is particularly useful when you are merging letters with an address list that may contain some blank fields, such as a list in which only some business owners use a separate company name in their address. You can choose to have the blank line left in the document, however, by choosing Leave Blank Line from the drop-down list.

Choose <u>D</u>isplay Options and then choose an option from the pop-up button to control how merge codes are displayed when a merge is paused for data entry from the keyboard. This choice affects the code display only during the merge process; it does not affect the display of codes in the form file or data file after the merge is completed. The default setting is <u>H</u>ide Codes. <u>S</u>how Codes enables you to see unprocessed merge codes in full while the merge is paused. Show as <u>M</u>arkers displays a diamond-shaped marker for each unprocessed code.

If you have changed the options, when you choose OK to return to the Perform Merge dialog box, you see the words Options Modified to the right of the phrase All Records in the lower-left corner of the Perform Merge dialog box; the <u>R</u>eset control is now activated. Choosing <u>R</u>eset returns all options to their default settings.

**Selecting Records** If you only want to use some of the records from the data file in the merge, choose <u>S</u>elect Records. The Select Records dialog box appears with the Selection Method option <u>S</u>pecify Conditions selected (see fig. 19.24). You can specify a range of records, select records by setting conditions, or select records by specifying both a range and setting conditions.

**FIG. 19.24**
Select <u>S</u>pecify Conditions in the Select Records dialog box to choose a record set that matches conditions you define. This condition specifies records for persons with a speaker or panelist position.

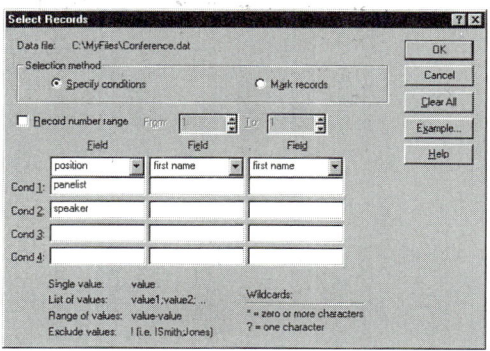

Once the position field is added to the Office Automation Conference data file, you can select only committee members, only speakers, or only panelists to receive a mailing.

**Specifying a Range** To specify a range of records, choose <u>R</u>ecord Number Range, then enter the record number in the Fr<u>o</u>m and <u>T</u>o boxes. WordPerfect sequentially numbers records in a data file from beginning to end. If you have an exceptionally large data file, you can specify a range to limit the number of records used during the selection and merge process.

**Defining Conditions**   Conditions are based on fields present in the data file. To set a condition, do the following:

1. In the first column, choose Field.
2. Use the drop-down list on the Field text box to choose the field you want to use as a condition (for example, last name).
3. Position the insertion point in the Cond 1 text box below the Field column, and type the condition in the box.
4. Use the same procedure to set any other conditions you want to use.

Each condition line defines a set of records that are to be selected (or excluded) from the data file. You can define more than one condition for a single row; only records that meet all conditions in the row are selected. Specifying more than one row of conditions selects records that meet any row of conditions.

WordPerfect provides excellent help for defining conditions. The Help dialog box shown in figure 19.25, for example, provides examples of the records selected for various example conditions. You can access this Help dialog box by clicking Example in the Select Records dialog box. For additional guidance on selection statement syntax, you can click More from the Example Select Records dialog box to produce the screen shown in figure 19.26.

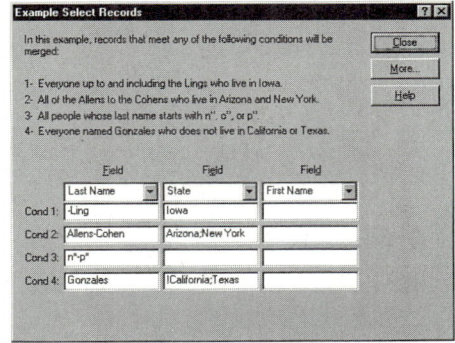

**FIG. 19.25**
When the Specify Conditions option is selected, choose Example from the Select Records dialog box, and WordPerfect 7 displays these examples of conditions for selecting records.

**FIG. 19.26**
Select More from the Example Select Records dialog box to see these examples of valid entries to use in defining the conditions for selecting records.

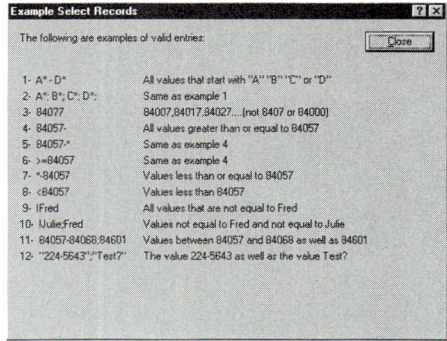

**Marking Records**  You can also select records from the data file by marking them manually. This procedure is useful for selecting a relatively small number of records that share no consistent pattern for selection.

To mark records, follow these steps:

1. Choose Mark Records from the Select Records dialog box; the dialog box changes to offer manual marking options (see fig. 19.27).

**FIG. 19.27**
If you choose the Mark Records option, the Select Records dialog box enables you to manually mark the records in the data file.

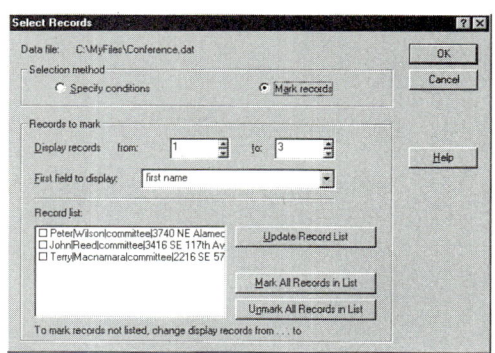

2. Set the range of records to be displayed.

   You can work with a range of records by setting the starting and ending numbers in the From and To boxes for Display Records. The default is to display all records.

   WordPerfect displays 32–35 characters of the selected range of records in the Record List text box. By default, the display begins with the first field defined in the data file. You can change the display to begin with any field in the data file.

3. Choose First Field to Display.

4. Use the drop-down list of the First Field to Display text box to choose the field you want to display first—for example, the last name field.

5. Choose Update Record List. The selected range of records appears in the Record List list box, beginning with the field you selected.

6. Select the records you want to use. Choose Mark All Records in List to include all records in the Record list in the merge.

   To change an individual mark, click the record. Choose Unmark All Records in List to remove all record markings.

7. After you finish marking records, choose OK to return to the Perform Merge dialog box.

## Creating Envelopes and Labels

Creating envelopes as part of a form letter merge is covered in detail in the section "Creating Envelopes" earlier in this chapter. The following sections describe how to create envelopes or mailing labels from a mailing list.

**Merging Envelopes Only**   To create an envelope form to merge with a mailing list, follow these steps:

1. Starting in an unused document window, choose Tools, Merge; or press Shift+F9. The Merge dialog box appears.

2. Choose Form, and then specify the data file containing the mailing list to associate with the form.

3. Choose OK. You now have a form file containing no text.

4. Choose Format, Envelope. The Envelope dialog box appears.

5. Complete the Return Addresses and Mailing Addresses areas of the Envelope dialog box, as described in the section "Creating Envelopes" earlier in this chapter.

6. To include the POSTNET bar code, choose Options to specify whether WordPerfect places the bar code above or below the mailing address.

7. Choose Append To Doc. The Envelope dialog box closes, and you see the envelope in the active document window. The form is ready to be merged with your mailing list.

> **TIP**   If you saved a mailing address that contains field codes for the address you want to use, you can choose this mailing address from the drop-down list of addresses.

**Creating Mailing Labels**   Creating mailing labels is essentially the same as creating any form file. When you create mailing labels, however, you work with a label-sized page.

To create a merge form file for labels, choose Tools, Merge, or press Shift+F9. Choose Form and designate the associated data file. Then choose Format, Labels, and choose a label definition.

After you select the label definition, create a regular form file on the small page that displays. Proceed as described in the section "Creating the Form File" earlier in this chapter, to insert field codes to define the address.

> **NOTE**  Consider centering the text from top to bottom, so it doesn't print off the edge of the label. You can also add left and right margins.

▶ See "Choosing a Label Definition," **p. 191**

### TROUBLESHOOTING

**I want to use a mailing label format to print a roster of members in alphabetical order. Neither the spacing nor the order of the addresses is correct.** Because there are several changes that must be made to a form that prints mailing labels to get what you want, try creating a new file. Select just the field codes and text, and paste them into a new file. Begin the roster form file by setting up parallel columns. Then add an extra hard return at the end of the form so a blank line is inserted between addresses, and end the form with a PAGEOFF code. Save the new form file. Now all you have to do is remember to sort the data file by last name when you perform the merge.

**When certain fields in my data file are blank, I want the merge to insert specific information rather than just remove or leave a blank line.** You can set up options based on the presence or absence of data in a field. Choose Merge Codes from the feature bar to select IFBLANK or IFNOTBLANK, as appropriate, to test for the presence or absence of data. At the end of the text where you want to insert or other instructions for the option, insert an ENDIF code.

▶ See "Working with Labels," **p. 191**

# Examining Advanced Merge Topics

WordPerfect's merge codes comprise a true programming language that enables you to create sophisticated applications. Exploring the extent of that language is beyond the scope of this chapter. The information in the following sections provides a sampling of some advanced merge topics.

## Working with User Input

Merge is an excellent tool for creating forms that are to be filled in individually. Rather than taking variable information from a data file, you supply the variable information for these forms from the keyboard. Typing information from the keyboard in response to prompts can be inefficient, however, if the form repeatedly asks for the same information. You can easily make keyboard merges more efficient by capturing variable information the first time it is typed, and then reusing that information wherever necessary without additional user input.

**Understanding Variables**   WordPerfect uses *variables* to hold data that can be manipulated by merge programming codes or macros. Just as an algebraic variable can have many values, so too can a merge variable have different values. For example, the variable name can be assigned the value John Doe, or Richard Roe, or some other name.

You assign a value to a variable by using ASSIGN(*var;expr*), ASSIGNLOCAL(*var;expr*), or any of the merge codes that work with user input, or a macro. For example, the merge code ASSIGN(name;John Doe) places the value of the expression "John Doe" in the variable "name." After a variable has a value, you use a merge code, such as VARIABLE(*var*), to insert the *value* of the variable identified by the *var* parameter in your text at any place you would otherwise type that information.

**Capturing User Input**   Suppose that you have an office form that uses KEYBOARD( ) codes to prompt the user through interactive completion of the form. The form uses the author's name several times in the document. You could use the KEYBOARD code to prompt for the author's name each time, but with minor effort you can capture the author's name to a variable when the name is first typed. The program then inserts the name wherever the variable appears in the document.

To capture the author's name the first time it is typed, position the insertion point where the author's name is first used, and then follow these steps:

1. Choose the Merge Codes button on the Merge Feature Bar to access the Insert Merge Codes dialog box and select the GETSTRING(*var[;prompt][;title]*) code. Then click Insert to display the Insert Merge Code dialog box, as shown in figure 19.28.

**FIG. 19.28**
The Insert Merge Code dialog box for the GETSTRING code assists you in entering parameters for the code.

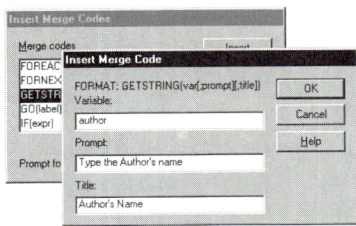

2. In the Insert Merge Code dialog box, choose Variable, type **author** for the variable name, and then press Tab.
3. Choose Prompt, type **Type the Author's Name**, and then press Tab.
4. Choose Title, type **Author's Name**, and then press Enter to insert the code in your form. After the file is merged, whatever the user types in response to the prompt is assigned to the variable named *author*.
5. Insert a VARIABLE(*author*) code. This code is required to place the value assigned to the variable into the document. After the file is merged, the contents of the variable *author* are placed at the location of the VARIABLE(*author*) code.

To include the author's name at other locations in the document, position the insertion point where you need the author's name, and insert another VARIABLE(*author*) code. When you perform a merge with a form file containing the GETSTRING code, WordPerfect prompts you for the author's name (see fig. 19.29). After the merge is complete, the text you typed in response to the Author's Name prompt is inserted at the location of each VARIABLE(*author*) code.

Figure 19.30 shows an example of a memorandum form that uses the GETSTRING code to capture and use the author's name in both the heading and signature line.

**FIG. 19.29**
When you are prompted for keyboard input, the dialog box title and prompt message are the entries you included in the GETSTRING code.

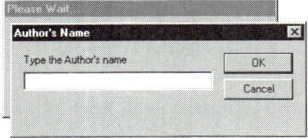

**FIG. 19.30**
A sample memorandum shows how the GETSTRING code can be used to capture keyboard input and display the result at the location of VARIABLE codes.

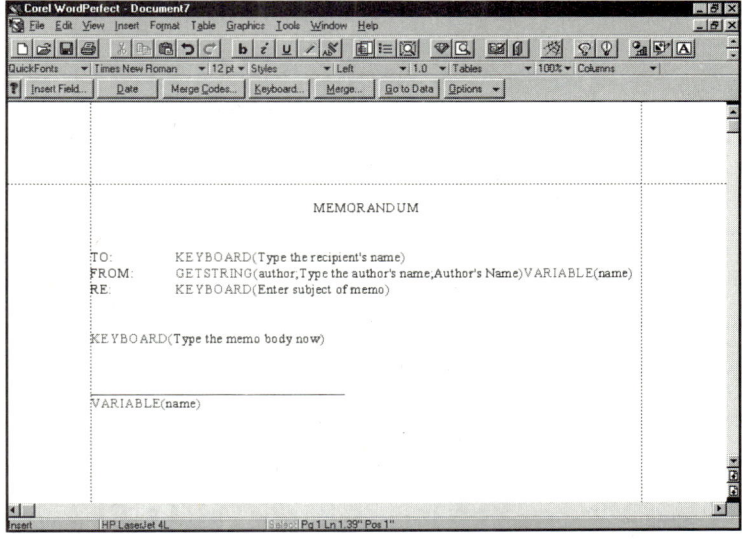

**Controlling User Input**   The previous section shows how you can capture user input to a variable and then use that variable information in your document. The codes, however, do not control the appearance of text the user puts in the document. Whatever the user types in response to the prompt is assigned to the variable and is used throughout the document. You don't have to rely on the user, however, to enter text correctly. WordPerfect 7 has additional merge codes that enable you to control the appearance of text entered by a user.

The codes CAPS(*expr*), FIRSTCAP(*expr*), TOLOWER(*expr*), and TOUPPER(*expr*) enable you to force text input from a user to be inserted into the merged document in the way you want the text to appear. The word *expr* in these codes refers to data (an expression) that is to be acted upon by the code. Usually these codes operate on text contained in a variable:

- CAPS. Capitalizes the first letter of each word in the expression.
- FIRSTCAP. Capitalizes the first letter of the first word in the expression.
- TOLOWER, TOUPPER. Changes all characters in the expression to lowercase and uppercase, respectively.
- CAPS, FIRSTCAP. Works only on text that is all lowercase; the user cannot change the case of text in positions other than the first characters of words.

Suppose the corporate standard for the memorandum shown in the preceding section required that the names of the author and recipient be in small caps. You can put formatting codes in the form to apply the small caps attribute to text entered by the user. The small caps attribute, however, correctly formats text only if it has initial caps. WordPerfect makes it possible for you to get the result you want, regardless of how the user types the text. Figure 19.31 shows the merge codes in the memorandum that accomplish the desired result.

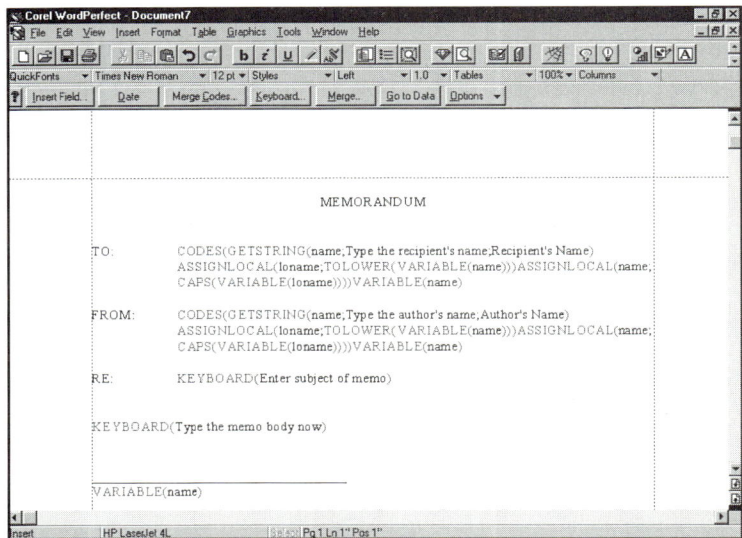

**FIG. 19.31**
A memorandum form with merge codes force user input to appear in the document as small caps.

## Using Data Files from Other Sources

With WordPerfect 7, you can use data files produced by supported programs in merge operations, and you need not convert them prior to the merge. WordPerfect 7 converts supported files on-the-fly. You can use WordPerfect *secondary merge format files* (now known as *data text files*) from prior versions of WordPerfect and from WordPerfect Office Notebook as data text files. Data files created by most major word processing programs can also be used.

In addition to files from word processing programs, WordPerfect supports the import and use of data files created by spreadsheets and database programs. Field names used in the source application are recognized and used by WordPerfect as field names. To use a data file from another application, simply select the file as the data file either while performing a merge or associating a data file. WordPerfect performs any conversions necessary to make the file usable.

WordPerfect has an important feature that enables data files to be linked to your document. After you establish a link to a data file, the linked data in your WordPerfect file is updated whenever the source data file changes. To import or link to a spreadsheet or database file, choose Insert, Spreadsheet/Database, and then choose either Import or Create Link. Figure 19.32 shows a list of the database formats that WordPerfect supports for import and linking.

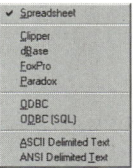

**FIG. 19.32**
WordPerfect enables you to create links to data files created by any of the supported programs listed.

In addition to direct use of files from other applications, WordPerfect can use ASCII delimited text as a data text file without prior manipulation. ASCII delimited text typically surrounds each field with quotation marks (" ") and separates fields with commas. Records are a single line of text terminated by a carriage return and a line feed. ASCII delimited text appears as follows:

```
"Peter","Wilson","3740 NE Alameda","Portland","OR",97212
"John","Reed","3416 SE 117th Avenue","Portland","OR",97266
"Terry","Macnamara","2216 SE 57th    Street","Portland","OR",97215
```

WordPerfect automatically recognizes DOS text and prompts you for the characters to be stripped during the merge.

## Merging into Tables

Although you can maintain a data file in table format, at times you may need to merge data from a data text file into a table. When you merge text file data into a table in WordPerfect, a new row is automatically added to the table for each record.

Suppose you have a data text file with named fields in the following order: First Name, Middle, Salutation, Last Name, Spouse, Office, Address, City, State, ZIP Code, Work Phone, Home Phone, Fax Number, and Notes. You want to prepare a table from the data file that contains only the full name, address, and position. Follow these steps to prepare the table:

1. Starting in a new document window, choose Tools, Merge; or press Shift+F9.
2. Choose Form, select the data file to associate with the form, and then choose OK.
3. Create a table of three columns and two rows. Make the first row a header row and enter column headings of **Name**, **Address**, and **Position** in the first row. (See Chapter 16, "Working with Tables," if you are unsure how to create the table.)

4. Position the insertion point in the last cell of the first row. Click Merge Codes from the Merge Feature Bar and choose the LABEL(*label*) code; then click Insert.

5. In the Insert Merge Code dialog box, type a name for the label, such as **loop**, then choose OK or press Enter.

6. Position the insertion point in the first cell of the second row.

7. Click Insert Field from the Merge Feature Bar, then choose and insert the first name field.

8. Press the space bar, then repeat step 7 to choose and insert the last name field.

9. Continue in the same way to insert the address, city, state, and ZIP code fields in the second cell, and the position field in the third cell. Also add appropriate spacing, commas, and hard returns as needed. Then click Close to close this dialog box.

10. With the insertion point positioned in the third cell following the Position field code, insert the NEXTRECORD code.

11. Insert the GO(*label*) code. At the prompt, type the same label name (**loop**, in this example) that you used in step 5; the screen now resembles figure 19.33.

**FIG. 19.33**
This table form file displays merge codes to merge data into the table. The table automatically expands to accommodate the records from the data file.

| Name | Address | PositionLABEL(loop) |
|---|---|---|
| FIELD(first name) FIELD(last name) | FIELD(address) FIELD(city), FIELD(st) FIELD(zip code) | FIELD(position) NEXTRECORD GO(loop) |

12. Save the form with an appropriate name, such as **table.frm**.

13. Perform the merge in any of the ways described in the section "Performing the Merge" earlier in this chapter.

# Using Sort

In addition to the WordPerfect 7 merge functions, which can be used for sorting data files and selecting individual records when merging, you can sort the data file itself as well as other kinds of files. The Sort feature enables you to manipulate any file that is formatted in a way that WordPerfect can recognize. You can use Sort to arrange records, lines, columns, or other text alphabetically or numerically, based on the value of sort keys, and you can use sort to extract text that meets conditions you define.

## Understanding Sort Record Types

Sort recognizes five types of data files, as described in table 19.4.

**Table 19.4  How Sort Handles Data Files**

| Record Type | Record Termination | Record Subdivisions |
|---|---|---|
| Line | Each line is a record, terminated by an HRt. | Fields<br>Words |
| Paragraph | Records are terminated by two hard returns. | Lines<br>Fields<br>Words |
| Merge text data file | Records end with an ENDRECORD code. | Fields<br>Lines<br>Words |
| Parallel columns | Records are a parallel row of columns. | Columns<br>Lines<br>Words |
| Table | Each row is a record. | Cells<br>Lines<br>Words |

The terms used in the right column of table 19.4 are descriptive terms for the recognized subdivisions of a record of the type shown in the left column. The list of recognized subdivisions for a particular record type is set out in order from largest to smallest. In a table, for example, a record (a single row) is divided into cells, which are subdivided into lines, which are themselves subdivided into words. Notice the difference between paragraph records and merge data records.

Fields and lines in ordinary text are usually the same. Tabs or indents on a line, however, separate the line into fields. ENDFIELD codes separate fields in merge data files. Words are separated by spaces, forward slashes (/), and hyphen characters; for example, the date 7/19/96 is actually three words.

> **NOTE**  The regular hyphen is not treated as a word separator. To separate sort "words" with a hyphen, use the hyphen character (choose Format, Lines, Other Codes, Hyphen Character, Insert) instead. When you want to lock words together, such as "John Smith III" or "Van Nuys," replace the regular space between the words with a hard space (choose Format, Lines, Other Codes, Hard Space, Insert). Words joined by a hard space are treated as a single word during a sort.

## Understanding Sort Keys

*Sort keys* are the definitions for the record subdivisions that you use to arrange a data file. Figure 19.34 shows a list of participants in the Office Automation Conference presently listed alphabetically by first name.

**FIG. 19.34**
In the text file list of conference participants, tabs separate the columns and hyphen characters are included in the phone numbers.

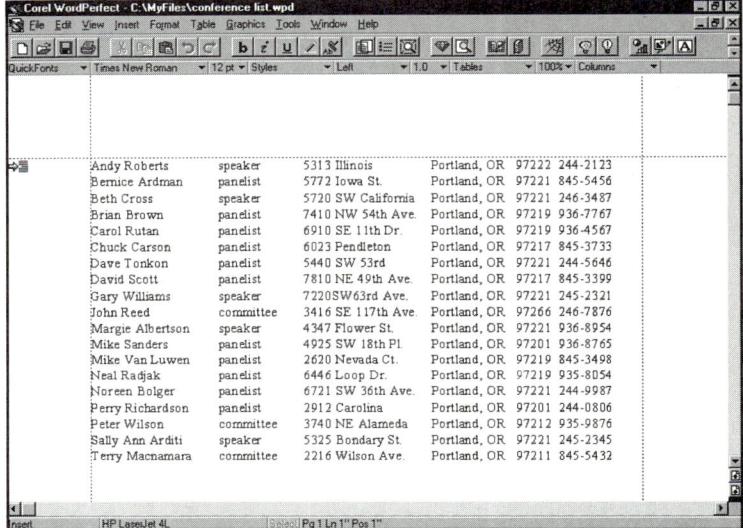

You can sort this list to reorder it alphabetically by the participants' last names. To accomplish this task, begin with the file open on-screen, and follow these steps:

1. Choose Tools, Sort, or press Alt+F9. The Sort dialog box appears, as shown in figure 19.35.

    The default is set to order the records by the first word in the first cell in a table. In this case, the last names of the participants are not the first word of the first field. To use the last name as a key, you must create a new key statement.

**FIG. 19.35**
The Sort dialog box enables you to select a predefined table, line, merge file, paragraph, column sort, or one of your previous sorts. You can also create new sorts or edit an existing sort.

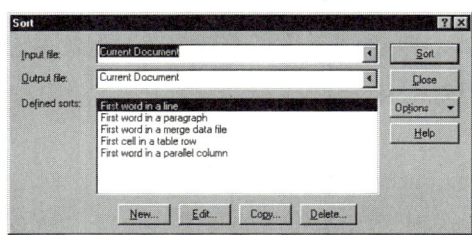

2. Click <u>N</u>ew to open the New Sort dialog box shown in figure 19.36.
3. Enter **Last Name Sort** in the <u>S</u>ort Name text box. This descriptive name is added to the list in the Sort box and will be easy to recognize in the future.
4. Type **1** in the Field text box.
5. Type **–1** in the Word text box. Use –1 rather than 2 to sort by the last word (last name) in the field. When there are multi-word first names or titles such as Dr. in the name field, the minus sign causes WordPerfect to count from the right rather than from the left.

**FIG. 19.36**
The New Sort dialog box enables you to establish keys to sort and select records from data files.

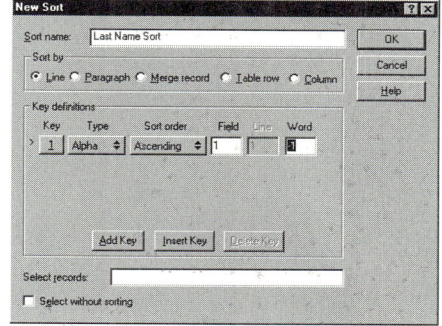

6. Choose OK or press Enter, then Sort to perform the sort. Figure 19.37 shows the sorted list.

**FIG. 19.37**
The list of participants from figure 19.34 is sorted by the last name of the participant. In this Reveal Codes view, notice the [HSpace] code between Van and Luwen that keeps this name together during the sort.

HSpace code keeps the name together

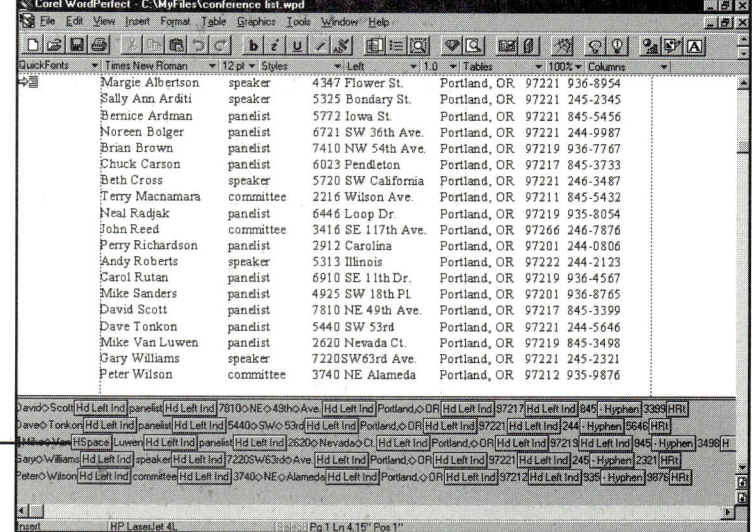

Sorting merge data files is exactly the same process as the previously illustrated sort. In fact, you can use the same menu choices to begin either sort. You can also begin a sort of a merge data file by choosing Options, Sort from the Merge Feature Bar of the data file.

# Using Multiple Keys to Sort and Select Records

Suppose that you have a mailing list containing more than 1,000 business names and addresses spread across five ZIP codes. The data is organized in the same way as the data file in the previous example, but the type of business is in the column used for the position in the conference example. You want to send a marketing letter to those business owners in a single ZIP code whose businesses are of a certain type. You also want the list in alphabetical order by the owner's last name.

Using the conference data file as an example, you can define the sort keys as follows:

1. Choose Tools, Sort, or press Alt+F9.
2. Select Last Name sort and click Edit. Make sure that Sort By is set to Line and that the first sort key is still set for Field 1 and Word –1.
3. Choose Insert Key.
4. Type **5** in the Field text box (change the contents of the Word text box from –1 to **1**). This sets the primary key to the ZIP code field (refer to fig. 19.38).
5. Choose Key 2, and then choose Insert Key.
6. Type **2** in the Field text box and then enter 1 in the Word text box. This entry sets the second key to the position field.

> **CAUTION**
> Although the phone number and ZIP code fields in this example contain numeric data, the key type has been left as alphanumeric. These keys sort properly because the numbers are all the same length. When unequal length numbers are sorted as alphanumeric data, the numbers are ordered by the value of the leftmost digit, then the second digit, and so on. For example, the numbers 9, 124, 28, and 3,029 would be sorted alphanumerically as 124, 29, 3,028, 9.

Now that the keys are set, you can enter select statements to extract the records you want from the data file. A *select statement* assigns a value to a sort key you defined and chooses from the file being sorted only those records in which the key data values match the select value.

Using the previous data file as an example, select all records for speakers with a 97221 ZIP code. To assign select values to extract the records that meet these conditions, follow these steps:

1. Position the insertion point in the Select Records text box.
2. Type **Key1=97221 & Key2=Speaker** (see fig. 19.38).

**FIG. 19.38**
The logical selection operators ¦ (OR) & (AND) = <> > < >= <= are displayed in the status bar while you create or edit selection statements in the New Sort dialog box.

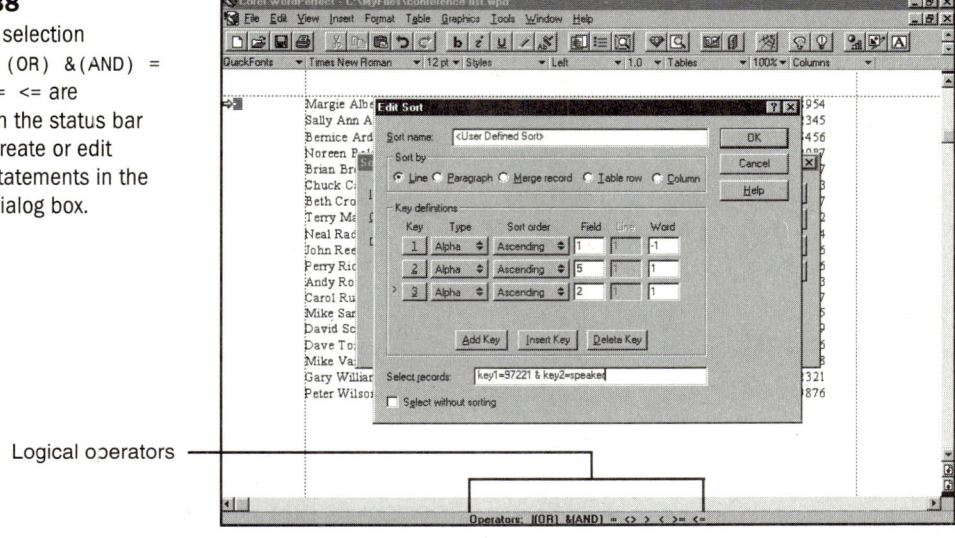

Logical operators

3. Choose OK or press Enter, then choose Sort. The results of the sort and select operation are shown in figure 19.39.

**FIG. 19.39**
The records for four participants appear as the result of performing the selection. Notice that the selected records have been sorted in alphabetical order by the person's last name.

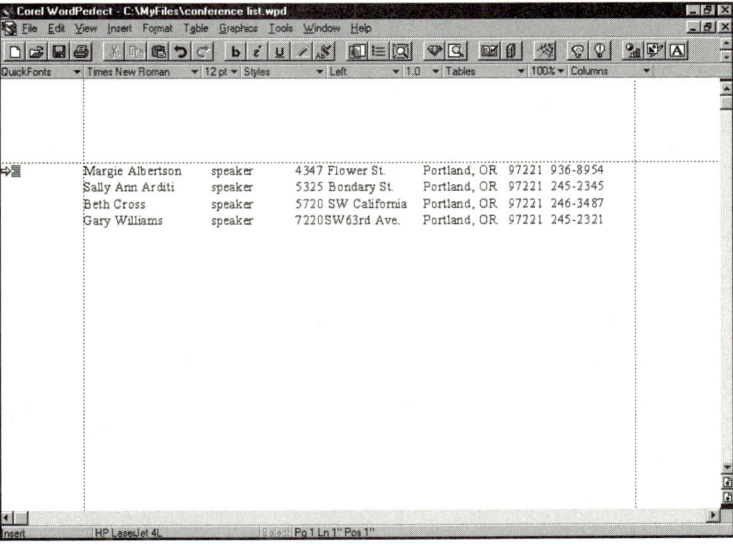

## TROUBLESHOOTING

**I have a file of employee names with the job title and social security number in tabular columns on the same line. I can't successfully sort the file by job title or social security number, only by first or last name.** Check in Reveal Codes to see if there is more than one tab code between columns. If you have not set tabs for the document, you often must press Tab more than once to line up the data. However, tabs are recognized as separating each line into fields. Set tab stops for the three columns of data and remove any extra tab codes to assure that only three fields of data are on each line.

**I have multi-word names, including some that are followed with M.D. or Ph.D. How can I sort the list of names by last name?** It's simple. Use a hard space between each word in the last name and between the last name and the initials. Insert hard spaces from the Other Codes dialog box found by choosing Format, Line.

PART IV

# Professional Output

**20** Using Fonts and Special Characters   633

**21** Using Advanced Graphics Techniques   657

**22** Using WordPerfect Draw and TextArt   683

**23** Desktop Publishing with WordPerfect   723

**24** Using the Equation Editor   759

CHAPTER 20

# Using Fonts and Special Characters

*by Gordon Nelder-Adams and Laura Acklen*

**W**ant a quick way to make your documents more effective? It's easy when you use fonts. A document can communicate its purpose more effectively if it looks interesting and is easy to read. Carefully choosen fonts for the body text, headings, or other elements such as headers, footers, and captions draw attention to points of interest and creates a more pleasing appearance.

WordPerfect for Windows provides a great deal of flexibility and control over fonts and their appearance, both on-screen and in printed text. You can use fonts that are built into your printer, installed with Windows, or provided by WordPerfect itself. You can also purchase additional fonts and install them for use in your Windows programs. WordPerfect also includes special font files, called *character sets*, that contain thousands of characters, symbols, and foreign language alphabets you can use in your documents. Figure 20.1 shows some of the TrueType fonts that come included with the WordPerfect program. ■

**Understanding Windows font management**

There are many different types of fonts that can be used with Windows 95 applications.

**Installing TrueType fonts**

The Control Panel provides a shortcut to the FONTS folder, where you can add and remove TrueType fonts from the FONTS folder.

**Inserting special characters**

WordPerfect's character sets contain more than 2,400 special characters and symbols that you can use in your documents.

**Creating and editing overstrike characters**

Two characters can be combined into one overstrike character to create special characters and symbols.

**Adjusting automatic font changes**

Fine-tune the fonts WordPerfect chooses for size and appearance attributes. Find matches for printer, display, and document fonts so they are all consistent.

**FIG. 20.1**
WordPerfect includes these and other TrueType fonts that you can use with all your Windows 95 programs.

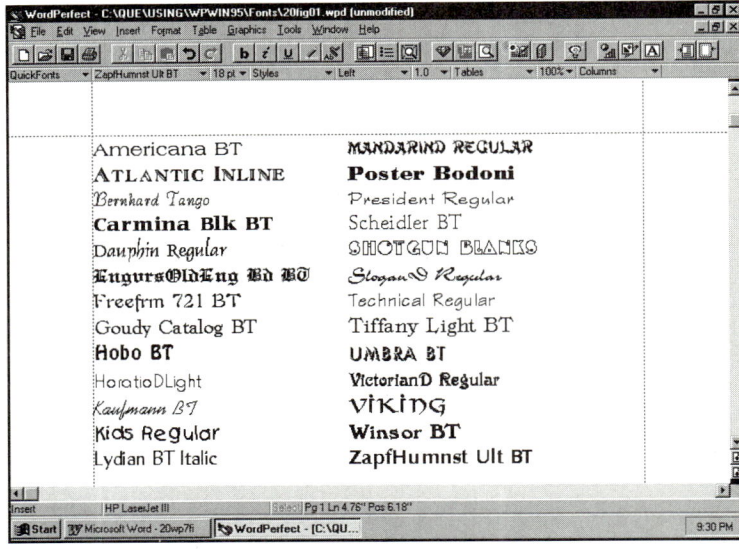

# Understanding Windows Font Management

Computer programs use fonts in two ways: to create printed output and to display text on-screen. All programs that run under Windows 95, including WordPerfect 7, can use the installed TrueType fonts to do both: display text on-screen and print the characters on paper. WordPerfect uses the printer drivers that you installed with Windows 95 to generate printed output. (This is different from previous versions of WordPerfect, which included WordPerfect printer drivers.) See Chapter 8, "Basic Output: Printing, Faxing, and E-Mail," for more information on selecting printer drivers.

**N O T E** If you create a document with a Windows printer driver selected and give a copy of the document to a WordPerfect 6.x for DOS user using WordPerfect printer drivers, the document content will be correct, but the user might need to reselect the fonts.

For font management purposes, you can divide fonts into two broad categories:

- *Printer fonts.* Found in your printer's native font format. Printer fonts can be *internal fonts*, *cartridge fonts*, or *soft fonts*.
- *Graphic fonts.* Created "on-the-fly" (as needed) by Windows. These fonts are called graphic fonts because they are often printed as graphics, and Windows uses them to display text on-screen.

*Internal fonts* are built into your printer. All printers have one or more internal fonts, which almost always include a Courier font. Some printers have many internal fonts, and some have only one or two.

*Cartridge fonts* are similar to internal fonts, but are built into cartridges that can be inserted into a printer. Not all printers accept font cartridges. The most common cartridges are designed for use in Hewlett-Packard LaserJet (and compatible) printers.

You must purchase your printer and font cartridges separately. Although you can purchase many font cartridges, your printer probably has no more than one or two font cartridge slots, which limits the number of cartridge fonts you can use at one time. After you insert a font cartridge into the printer, the fonts are in effect "built in," and you can use them in exactly the same way you use internal fonts.

*Soft fonts* are fonts stored in files on your hard drive. Before your printer can use these fonts, they must be downloaded (copied) to your printer from your hard drive. Windows does this for you automatically.

There are advantages and disadvantages to each type of font. Because internal fonts and cartridge fonts are "built in," printing with these fonts is extremely fast. Unfortunately, most printers can hold relatively few internal and cartridge fonts at one time. If you want to use other fonts, you often have to turn off your printer, remove a cartridge, and install a new cartridge.

Because soft fonts must be downloaded to your printer before they can be used, printing with soft fonts takes longer than printing with internal or cartridge fonts. You can save some time by downloading fonts to your printer's memory, which makes the fonts resident before printing. However, most printers can hold only a limited number of resident fonts in memory.

Although printing with soft fonts is usually slower than printing with internal or cartridge fonts, soft fonts are far more flexible because you can use any soft font stored on your hard drive at any time. If you have room on your hard drive, you can easily acquire and store thousands of soft fonts.

In the past, soft fonts were stored in many files—one file for each size. The larger the type size, the larger the font file. A 48-point font file could take more than 200K of space on a hard drive. These files took up so much disk space that you were often limited to three or four typefaces, with a limited selection of sizes.

*Scalable fonts*, the latest in soft font technology, have only one file per typeface because the file contains a set of instructions to "scale" each character for the desired size, rather than containing every character in a specific size. Scalable fonts reduce the amount of required storage space and makes it possible to use a wider variety of typefaces and sizes in your documents.

Microsoft incorporates TrueType font technology into the Windows 95 operating system. Although Windows comes with a limited selection of fonts, you can easily add more fonts to your system. In fact, many popular applications include collections of TrueType fonts. Every TrueType font that you install in Windows is immediately available to your Windows application.

 **TIP** TrueType fonts are differentiated from other types of fonts by a TT icon next to the font name.

TrueType fonts have several advantages over downloadable or printer-resident fonts:

- TrueType fonts include matching screen and printer fonts so the appearance on-screen always matches the printed copy.
- TrueType fonts are used with practically every Windows program. If two computers have TrueType fonts installed, you can create a document on the first computer and print it on the second computer without losing the original appearance.
- TrueType fonts print on all types of printers, although the appearance varies with the quality of the printer. Also, depending on your printer's resources, you can choose to have TrueType fonts downloaded to the printer, or printed graphically.

  ▶ See "Adding Fonts for Your Printer," **p. 292**

## Installing TrueType Fonts

When you install WordPerfect, the Setup program automatically copies a number of TrueType fonts into Windows, which makes the fonts available not only to WordPerfect, but also to all your other Windows programs. These fonts are specialized fonts that contain the WordPerfect character sets.

▶ See "Installing Fonts," **p. 1087**

**NOTE** Other third-party font packages (Adobe Type Manager, for example) can be used in Windows 95, and subsequently, WordPerfect 7. Refer to the installation guide that comes with the font package for information on installing the fonts into Windows.

The TrueType font format was jointly developed by Microsoft and Apple, and TrueType font support is built directly into Windows 95 and Apple System 7.x. TrueType fonts contain the instructions necessary to size the font, so you can select virtually any point size. TrueType takes care of sizing, or scaling, the characters so they are the right size. Should you decide to purchase additional TrueType fonts, you can install them directly into Windows.

TrueType font files are identified by a TTF filename extension. To install TrueType fonts, you only have to tell Windows where the files are, and then mark which fonts you want to install. Windows then copies the fonts to the FONTS folder. Some font packages compress the fonts on the distribution disks, and typically have an Install program that decompresses the fonts and copies them directly to your FONTS folder. If the fonts are not compressed, you can copy them to the FONTS folder directly from the floppy disks.

> **NOTE** The steps for installing and removing fonts may differ, depending on the type of printer you have. Refer to the documentation that came with your printer for the specific steps to install and remove fonts.

To install TrueType fonts in Windows 95, follow these steps:

1. Click the Start button to open the Start menu.
2. Choose Settings, Control Panel.
3. Double-click the Fonts icon in the Control Panel. The Fonts folder window appears (see fig. 20.2).
4. Choose File, Install New Font. The Add Fonts dialog box appears, as shown in figure 20.3. When you first access this dialog box, you might see `Temp Installer Font (TrueType)` in the List Of Fonts list box.

**FIG. 20.2**
The Fonts folder window displays a list of installed TrueType fonts. From here you can add or remove TrueType fonts.

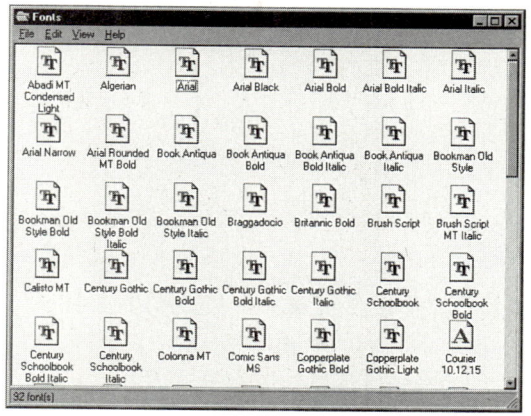

> **NOTE** Even when selecting the correct FONTS folder, the list does not always immediately update. If you highlight the FONTS folder in Windows 95, those fonts have already been copied and exist within the folder. These are not the fonts to be installed, but are the fonts that have already been installed.

**FIG. 20.3**
You can highlight a range of fonts to install, or click Select All to install all the fonts.

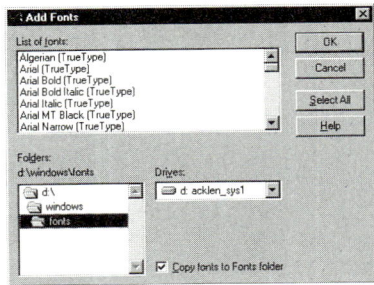

**N O T E** When you first access the Add Fonts dialog box, the user may see `Temp Installer Font (TrueType)` in the List of Fonts list box. Further, even when selecting the correct fonts folder, the list does not always immediately update. If you highlight the FONTS folder in Windows 95, those fonts have already been copied and exist within the folder. These are not the fonts *to be* installed, but instead are the fonts which have already been installed.

5. From the Drives drop-down list, select the drive that contains the fonts you want to install namely, \COREL\OFFICE7\APPMAN\WKSFILES\FONTS on the installation CD. If necessary, select the folder that contains the font files.

   Windows builds a list of the available fonts. If the drive or folder contains many TrueType files, Windows may take a few seconds to build the list.

6. Select the fonts you want to add. You can click a single font to highlight it, then Ctrl+click to highlight a second font, or click the first file, then Shift+click the last file to highlight a range of fonts. Or, click Select All to highlight the entire list.

7. Make sure that the Copy Fonts To Fonts Folder check box is marked, then choose OK. Windows copies the font files to the FONTS folder and adds the font names to the list of available fonts.

**CAUTION**
If you want to install fonts from a network drive without using space on your computer, make sure the Copy Fonts To Fonts Folder check box isn't checked.

8. Close the FONTS folder. Then, if still open, close the Control Panel.

   You can use the newly installed fonts immediately; you do not need to restart Windows before the fonts are available.

If you decide that you don't like a particular font, or that your list of available fonts is getting too long, you can remove one or more fonts. When you delete the font from the FONTS folder, Windows removes the font file itself from your hard disk, freeing up the disk space.

To remove TrueType fonts from Windows 95, follow these steps:

1. Click the Start button to open the Start menu.
2. Choose Settings, Control Panel.
3. Double-click the Fonts icon in the Control Panel. The Fonts folder window appears.
4. Select the fonts you want to remove. You can click a single font to highlight it, then Ctrl+click to highlight a second font, or click, then Shift+click to highlight a range of fonts.
5. Choose File, Delete or press Delete. Windows displays a dialog box prompting you to confirm removal of the font(s).
6. Choose Yes to remove all selected fonts.

 If you accidentally delete the wrong font(s) from the FONTS folder, which deletes the file(s) from your hard disk, you can restore the font file(s) from the Windows Recycle Bin—unless, of course, you have emptied the Recycle Bin since deleting the font(s). Open the Recycle Bin window, select the file(s), then choose File, Restore to restore the fonts to the FONTS folder.

7. When all selected fonts have been removed, close the Fonts folder window, and then close the Control Panel.

# Installing WordPerfect's TrueType Fonts

There is a wide variety of attractive TrueType fonts included with the WordPerfect program. However, to avoid wasting disk space, these fonts are not installed automatically. Many people already have an adequate selection of fonts on their system, and adding more fonts only creates confusion. For this reason, you have to install the WordPerfect TrueType fonts separately. You can do this by choosing a Custom installation in the Corel WordPerfect Suite 7 Setup program.

**NOTE** Before you start the Setup program, you need to shut down any Corel applications. If you forget this step, the Setup program prompts you to shut down the applications and then continue running the Setup program.

To install the TrueType fonts that come with WordPerfect, follow these steps:

1. Start AUTORUN.EXE on the installation.
2. Select Bonus Applications.
3. Choose Next, then Yes to move past the License Agreement.

4. Choose <u>N</u>ext to move past the registration information.
5. Choose C<u>u</u>stom to select a custom installation, then choose <u>N</u>ext.
6. Verify the destination (for example, C) for your files, then choose <u>N</u>ext.
7. Double-click CorelFLOW3, deselect all check boxes except for the TrueType Fonts check box, then make sure the TrueType Fonts check box is selected.
8. Choose OK to close the CorelFLOW 3 dialog box.
9. Deselect the Corel Screen Saver Option, and the Optional Shared Components option.
10. Choose Next, then <u>I</u>nstall. The Setup program copies the TrueType fonts from the CD directly to the FONTS folder, so they are ready to use immediately. Remember, you can use these fonts with *any* Windows 95 program, not just WordPerfect.
11. When finished, Corel displays the Setup Complete dialog box. Choose OK to close Setup.

# Accessing Special Characters

Although a computer keyboard has only a few dozen keys, WordPerfect can access several thousand special characters, such as typographic or scientific symbols and letters in foreign alphabets. The program makes accessing non-keyboard characters simple. Most applications require that you know where and in which font each *glyph* (character, symbol, or anything else contained in a font) is located. WordPerfect simplifies this problem. Unlike almost any other program, WordPerfect does not make you remember in which font the character is located. If you need to insert a plus or minus sign (+ or −) in your document, the keystrokes needed are the same regardless of the printer and font you are using.

You can access all these characters through the WordPerfect Characters feature. WordPerfect groups the characters into 15 character sets. Each character set contains dozens or hundreds of related letters or symbols. Table 20.1 lists the character sets available in WordPerfect 7.

### Table 20.1  WordPerfect Character Sets

| Character Set Number | Name of Character Set | Examples | Number of Glyphs |
|---|---|---|---|
| 0 | ASCII | Characters available from the keyboard | 127 |
| 1 | Multinational | Accented characters | 242 |

| Character Set Number | Name of Character Set | Examples | Number of Glyphs |
|---|---|---|---|
| 2 | Phonetic | International Phonetic Alphabet | 145 |
| 3 | Box Drawing | Single and double lines | 88 |
| 4 | Typographic Symbols | Quotation marks, em dash | 102 |
| 5 | Iconic Symbols | Dingbats, happy face | 255 |
| 6 | Math/Scientific | Less than, empty set | 238 |
| 7 | Math/Scientific Extensions | Large math symbols | 229 |
| 8 | Greek | Alpha, omega; includes breathing marks | 219 |
| 9 | Hebrew | Aleph, gimel; includes vowel points | 123 |
| 10 | Cyrillic | Characters for printing various Slavic languages | 250 |
| 11 | Japanese | Phonetic Japanese | 63 |
| 12 | User Defined | Usually empty | 255 |
| 13 | Arabic | Block printing version of Arabic | 196 |
| 14 | Arabic Script | Script version of Arabic | 220 |

In all, WordPerfect's character sets contain 2,478 characters. Except for character set 12 (User Defined), all the characters are available to any WordPerfect user who has access to a printer capable of printing graphics. The following list describes each character set:

- *ASCII (Set 0)*. Normal typewriter characters available directly from the keyboard.
- *Multinational (Set 1)*. Modified from previous versions of WordPerfect, two Multinational character sets have been combined into one larger set. In this set, you find all the characters you need for writing in Western European languages and Central European languages that use the Roman alphabet. In addition to complete characters, the various accents and marks (diacriticals) are provided independently. See the "Overstrike" section later in this chapter for an explanation of how to create additional characters you may need.
- *Phonetic (Set 2)*. Found in WordPerfect 6.x for Windows, consists of the characters in the International Phonetic Alphabet (IPA). Most users have no need for any of

these characters, but if you do need to use the IPA, the characters are available to you. As with the Multinational set, the various diacriticals are provided both as independent characters and combined with the basic letter form.

- *Box Drawing (Set 3)*. Used for the Line Draw feature in earlier versions of WordPerfect and remain for compatibility with older documents. You seldom need to directly choose any of these characters.

- *Typographic Symbols (Set 4)*. Contains common symbols such as bullets, daggers, currency symbols, and ligatures. Some of these characters are very useful. Perhaps the most often used are the true open and close quotation marks ("curly quotes"). Compare the use of straight quotation marks:

    He said, "See Spot run."

With typographic quotation marks:

    He said, "See Spot run."

Other commonly used typographic symbols are the em dash (—) used to set off an aside or change of subject, and the en dash (–) used for dates such as 2–01–95. Several fractions and other useful symbols are also found in this character set.

**N O T E** WordPerfect 7 includes a special SmartQuotes utility. This utility automatically substitutes typographical quotation marks for the straight keyboard quotation marks as you type. If you use typographical quotes often, you might consider activating the SmartQuotes utility. To do so, choose Tools, QuickCorrect, Options. Then place check marks in the Turn on Single Quotes and Turn On Double Quotes options. Choose OK then Close to get back to the document.

- *Iconic Symbols (Set 5)*. Includes less commonly used symbols defined in your PC's ROM such as the male ( ) and female ( ) signs and the happy face ( ), as well as the ITC Zapf Dingbats character set. Dingbats is a major addition from previous versions of WordPerfect, which did not include these symbols.

 **T I P** To see what the WordPerfect character number and set are for any special character, turn on Reveal Codes (choose View, Reveal Codes or press Alt+F3) and position the insertion point to the left of the special character. The code expands to show you the character number and set number. Now, press Ctrl+W, then type the two numbers, separated by a comma, to insert the character.

**N O T E** In WordPerfect 5.x for DOS, dingbats were mapped to the User Defined character set (Set 12). If you edit a document created in WordPerfect 5.x for DOS that contains dingbats, you may need to edit the file to correct these characters. The character number is likely to be the same, but the character set is now 5 instead of 12. For example, if the character was 12,200, it is likely to be the character now found at position 5,200 in WordPerfect 7. If there are several such characters in the document, you can use the Replace feature to quickly correct the situation.

- *Math/Scientific (Set 6).* Most often used to create equations. However, you can use these characters at any place in a document. This character set includes a wide variety of symbols, including the plus or minus sign, degree symbol, and various symbols used in Set Theory.

  ▶ **See** "Using WordPerfect Characters," **p. 776**

- *Math/Scientific Extensions (Set 7).* Contains symbols almost never used outside of an equation. These characters are pieces of large mathematical symbols (such as the top, middle, and bottom of a summation sign), and are used by WordPerfect's Equation Editor. Certain large complete symbols are also defined in this set.

- *Greek (Set 8).* Consists of normal capital and minuscule Greek letters used in mathematical expressions and also the accented letters (including breathing marks) used for writing Greek (classic and modern).

- *Hebrew (Set 9).* Consists of Hebrew. The vowel points are included.

- *Cyrillic (Set 10).* Consists of the characters necessary for Russian, Serbian, and other languages written in the Cyrillic alphabet.

- *Japanese (Set 11).* Includes the Hiragana and Katakana characters necessary for writing phonetic Japanese. This set does not include Kanji characters.

- *User Defined (Set 12).* Provided so that you can make use of fonts containing characters not included in WordPerfect's other character sets. If you install an "expert" font or a font containing typographical ornaments, the characters appear in Set 12. Foreign language fonts containing characters not defined elsewhere (such as Thai) could also make use of this character set. Unless you install such a font, the characters in this set print as blanks.

- *Arabic (Set 13) and Arabic Script (Set 14).* Found in WordPerfect 6.1 for Windows, these characters are used for writing in Arabic.

WordPerfect makes using special characters in your documents easy. You can select characters from a menu, enter a specific character set and character number, or use mnemonic shortcuts for common characters. Each method is discussed in subsequent sections.

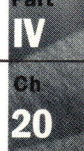

## WordPerfect Characters

If you are unsure of exactly where the character you need is located, you can use the WordPerfect Character feature. To access WordPerfect Characters, choose Insert, Character or press Ctrl+W. The WordPerfect Characters dialog box appears (see fig. 20.4).

**FIG. 20.4**
You can select any available character from the WordPerfect Characters dialog box.

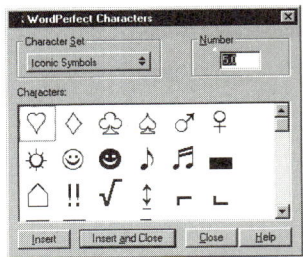

**TIP** If you know the set and number of the character you want, you can type the set and number in the Number text box and press Enter. To insert a playing card club symbol, for example, type **5,2** and press Enter.

If you click a special character, the character's set and number appear in the Number text box. To switch to another character set, choose character set and select another character set from the pop-up list. Double-click a special character in the Characters list box to have WordPerfect insert the character into your document.

The WordPerfect Characters dialog box is *modeless*, which means that you can work in your document while the dialog box remains on-screen. If you simply double-click a character, WordPerfect inserts the character and does not close the dialog box. If you don't intend to insert another character immediately, you can choose Close to close the dialog box. You can also click once on a character to select it, and then choose Insert And Close to insert the character into your document and close the dialog box.

## Compose

With more than 2,400 characters available, remembering the character set and number of frequently-used characters can be difficult. Although you can always select a character directly from the Characters list box, WordPerfect also provides some keyboard shortcuts for some of the most common characters. The Compose feature lets you use mnemonics to "assemble" characters from pairs of more common characters.

A *mnemonic* is a memory device. For example, the name Roy G. Biv is a common mnemonic to remind you of the colors of the rainbow: Red, Orange, Yellow, Green, Blue, Indigo, and Violet. Many of the Multinational Characters and Typographic Symbols can be accessed with mnemonics. For example, to insert a u umlaut (ü), open the WordPerfect Characters dialog box by pressing Ctrl+W, type **u"**, and press Enter. The following table provides additional examples of mnemonics.

| Keystrokes | Character | Keystrokes | Character |
|---|---|---|---|
| a" | ä | a' | á |
| a' | à | a^ | â |
| n~ | ñ | f- | ƒ |
| c, | ç | ss | ß |
| ao | å | a= | ª |
| co | © | ro | ® |
| rx | R$_x$ | tm | ™ |
| m- | — | n- | – |
| !! | ¡ | ?? | ¿ |
| /2 | ½ | /4 | ¼ |
| >> | » | << | « |
| >= | · | <= | < |
| +- | ± | ~~ | ~ |
| ** | ● | · | ■ |
| *O | ○ | *o | o |
| Y= | ¥ | L- | £ |
| c/ | ¢ | P\| | ¶ |
| AE | Æ | ae | æ |

Notice that many of these mnemonics are case-sensitive. For example, e' creates é, but É creates E. Also, in most, but not all cases, the order in which you type the characters is not important.

 **TIP** If you frequently need to use certain special characters, add the characters in the preceding table to a keyboard layout.

▶ See "Customizing Keyboards," **p. 324**

# Overstrike

WordPerfect offers a way to create characters that aren't otherwise available: by combining two existing characters. When you create an overstrike, WordPerfect literally prints one character on top of another. This feature is seldom necessary because of the huge range of characters and symbols provided in the various character sets, but it can be useful in certain special situations.

**Creating Overstrikes**   To create an overstrike character, follow these steps:

1. From the Format menu, choose Typesetting, and then select Overstrike. The Overstrike dialog box appears (see fig. 20.5).

**FIG. 20.5**
You can combine two characters using the Overstrike dialog box.

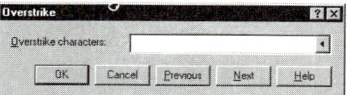

2. Enter the characters you want to combine. You can enter the characters in any way you want. You can use WordPerfect Characters (Ctrl+W), the Alt+number pad method, or type standard keyboard characters. You can enter as many characters as you like, although more than two or three characters printing on top of each other becomes illegible.

**N O T E**   When using the Alt+number pad method, press and hold the Alt key while entering the number in the numeric keypad (on the right side of the keyboard). Release the Alt key when you are done entering the number. Press 0*xxx* (such as **0128**) to insert a character using the ANSI character set, and *xxx* (such as **128**) to insert a character using the ASCII character set. Note that WordPerfect does not support the IBM character set, such as the IBM box drawing characters.

Num Lock must be turned on in this example. If not, you can press Alt+Shift+*number*.

3. Choose OK to insert the overstrike character into your document.

4. After inserting the desired characters in your document, you can apply font attributes just as you would to an ordinary character. By combining glyphs of different sizes, appearance, and positions (superscript and subscript), you can create exactly what you need.

**N O T E**   If you want to apply a font attribute to an overstrike character, open the Attributes list by clicking the arrow at the right side of the Overstrike Characters text box, then select the attribute you want to use. Type the characters between the attribute on/off codes.

 If you use an overstrike character frequently, create a macro that inserts the character into your document. (See Chapter 12, "Creating Macros.")

**Editing Overstrikes**   After an overstrike character is created, you may need to edit it. To do so, follow these steps:

1. Choose Format, Typesetting, Overstrike. The Overstrike dialog box appears.
2. Choose Previous or Next until the desired overstrike character appears in the Overstrike Characters text box.
3. Add, delete, or change any of the characters or attribute codes in the overstrike sequence.
4. After you finish, choose OK. Alternatively, choose Reset to abandon your changes.
    - ▶ See "Using Find and Replace," **p. 111**
    - ▶ See "Customizing Keyboards," **p. 324**
    - ▶ See "Creating a Macro," **p. 388**
    - ▶ See "Using the Equation Editor," **p. 759**

### TROUBLESHOOTING

**I have collected a number of fonts, but I don't remember what they all look like.** WordPerfect comes with a macro that lets you create a "catalog" of available fonts. The macro is named ALLFONTS.WCM, and is contained in the MACROS folder. To use the macro, open a new, blank document. Play the macro by choosing Tools, Macro, Play. If necessary, change to the \COREL\OFFICE7\MACROS\WPWIN7 folder (or its equivalent if the macros were installed to a different folder). Double-click the ALLFONTS macro in the list. The macro takes a moment to make the catalog of fonts. Once the macro is finished with the font catalog, you can print it for future reference. You should, however, avoid using the ALLFONTS macro if you have more than 255 fonts installed in your system.

**I don't get typographical (curly) smart quotes when I press the " key.** There are three reasons typographical open and close smart quotes may not appear when you press the " (quote) key. One obvious reason is that the SmartQuote feature has been turned off. To turn it on, choose Tools, QuickCorrect. In the QuickCorrect dialog box that appears, choose Options. Place a check mark in the Turn On Single Quotes check box and the Turn On Double Quotes check box to turn smart quotes on.

Another reason is that when you are editing a macro (the Macros Feature Bar appears), WordPerfect automatically turns smart quotes off.

And finally the smart quotes may seem not appear if the font you are using—such as Courier—lacks curly quotes.

# Font Mapping

When you use a font attribute such as bold or italic, WordPerfect actually selects a different font to print those characters. The program maintains a font mapping table of *Automatic Font Changes* (*AFCs*) for each font, which tells WordPerfect which font to choose for changes in Appearance, Relative Size, Orientation, and WordPerfect character sets. (See Chapter 4, "Formatting Text," for information on Appearance and Relative Size font attributes.)

If you don't like the way the AFCs are working, you can change them. Not only that, but you can change the way display and document fonts are selected. For example, when you use fonts that are built into your printer, WordPerfect also has to choose which graphics font to display on-screen to represent the printer font. Also, when a document calls for a font that isn't installed on your system, WordPerfect has to choose which installed font to use to represent the document font.

## Understanding AFC Attributes

Although you use completely different commands in WordPerfect to select font attributes, insert special characters, or print landscape fonts, the program uses Automatic Font Changes in each case. When you edit Automatic Font Changes, WordPerfect lists every type of AFC under one heading, but they can be grouped into four general categories—Appearance, Relative Size, Character Sets, and Orientation.

 **TIP** If you need to use combinations of attributes that WordPerfect isn't selecting the way you want, you can create a character style that specifically selects the desired font.

**Appearance** An *appearance attribute* is font style, such as bold, italic, or underline. These attributes are frequently used to emphasize a section of text, setting it off from the rest of the text. Combinations of appearance attributes are handled in a series. For example, if you apply the bold attribute and then the italic attribute, WordPerfect first finds the bold AFC font and then finds the italic AFC font for the bold font. For font families that don't contain a complete set of Regular, Bold, Italic, and Bold Italic font styles, this process can cause some unexpected results, because WordPerfect will choose a font outside of the immediate font family. As a result, you may obtain different results if you switch the order in which you apply the attributes.

WordPerfect tries to find an appropriate font when you choose an appearance attribute. For example, if your base font is Times New Roman and you apply the bold appearance attribute to some text, WordPerfect chooses Times New Roman Bold when printing (and displaying) that text. If an appropriate font does not exist, WordPerfect attempts to approximate it. If you choose the bold attribute, for example, and no appropriate font exists, WordPerfect prints the text twice, using the base font, to make the printed text darker.

**Relative Size**   When you use the relative size attributes with non-scalable fonts, WordPerfect uses AFCs to choose a font size that is a percentage of the size of your base font. The Large font attribute is 120 percent of normal, for example, so if your base font is 10 point, large text will be 12 point. As for the other sizes: Fine is 60, Small is 80, Extra Large is 200, and Very Large is 150 percent of the base font. If WordPerfect can't find a font that matches the new size, it may choose a font outside of the font family, and you may get unexpected results. If you use scalable fonts, however, you can be sure the same font will be used, because WordPerfect can generate virtually any size font from a scalable font.

**T I P**   Relative size attributes are stored in the Windows 95 Registry. You can change the relative size percentages by running the supplied macro SIZEATTR.WCM.

**WordPerfect Character Sets**   If a special character isn't available in the current font, WordPerfect uses an AFC to select a font that contains most or all of the character set in which that character can be found. If WordPerfect finds the desired character in any of the available fonts—not just the selected font—it prints the character. Nearly every WordPerfect character is available in the TrueType fonts that WordPerfect installs automatically, but other installed fonts may contain different versions of the same character; one of these versions may provide a closer match to the current body text font. As a result, you may want to change the AFC to select a more pleasing font to print special characters.

If the character isn't available, WordPerfect creates and prints a graphical representation of the character. The only exceptions to this process are characters in the User Defined character set. WordPerfect doesn't create graphical representations of these characters because it has no way of knowing what characters are defined in that set. WordPerfect also doesn't graphically create characters from character set 0 (ASCII).

**Orientation**   *Orientation* refers to the direction the text is printed on the page. Portrait orientation prints from left to right across the short end of the page (like this page). Landscape orientation prints from left to right across the long end of the page. WordPerfect offers four orientations—Portrait, Landscape, Reverse Portrait, and Reverse Landscape. WordPerfect can print TrueType fonts in any orientation; however, dot-matrix internal printer fonts usually can only be used in Portrait mode.

The only time you might need to adjust the Orientation Automatic Font Changes is for laser and inkjet printer fonts. Some lasers (such as PostScript and the Hewlett-Packard

III and IV series) can rotate fonts while others (such as the LaserJet II and earlier Hewlett-Packards) cannot. Inkjet printers (such as the Hewlett-Packard DeskJet series) usually cannot rotate fonts.

## Editing Automatic Font Changes

If you aren't happy with WordPerfect's choice of Automatic Font Change for a particular font, you can edit WordPerfect's Font Mapping table. Notice that these changes are made through the Font dialog box, not through the Print dialog box as you might expect.

**TIP** One of the biggest reasons users edit the font changes is to change redline to a completely different typeface. This allows reliable faxing of edited and/or compared documents.

To edit AFCs, follow these steps:

1. Choose Format, Font or press F9. The Font dialog box appears.

2. Choose Font Map. The Edit Printer/Document Font Mapping dialog box appears (see fig. 20.6). The Face drop-down list box displays the currently selected font. The Automatic Font Change list box at the bottom of the dialog box lists the available attributes and other Automatic Font Change categories. The Face drop-down list box displays the Automatic Font Change for the selected printer font and highlighted AFC option.

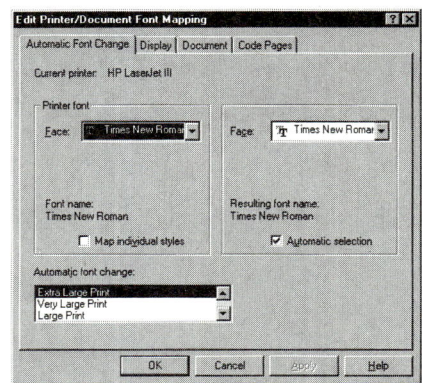

**FIG. 20.6**
The Edit Printer/Document Font Mapping dialog box lets you select different AFCs for any font.

3. From the Face drop-down list, select the font whose Automatic Font Changes you want to review or change.

   **NOTE** Most fonts are part of a font family made up of several font styles—usually Regular, Bold, Italic, and Bold Italic. By default, WordPerfect creates AFCs for font families as a group. If you want to review or change AFCs for the individual styles within a given family, select the Map Indi_v_idual Styles check box. WordPerfect then adds Style and Size drop-down list boxes under the Face list boxes.

4. Select the category you want to review or change from the Automa_t_ic Font Change list box at the bottom of the dialog box. WordPerfect displays the currently mapped font in the Fa_c_e list box. If no font is listed, there is no font change for that particular AFC.

5. If you want to change the displayed AFC, select a different font from the list of available fonts from the Fa_c_e drop-down list. The name of the new font appears under the Resulting Font Name and WordPerfect removes the check from the A_u_tomatic Selection check box immediately beneath this list box.

6. Repeat steps 4 and 5 to review or change the AFC for another AFC category for the same font; repeat steps 3–5 to review or change the AFCs for another font.

7. Choose OK to return to the Font dialog box and have WordPerfect save the changes in the printer driver and supporting files; or choose Cancel to abandon your changes. Then choose OK to return to the document window.

If you aren't happy with a new AFC that you've chosen, you can repeat the preceding steps to map a different font for that particular AFC, or you can mark the A_u_tomatic Selection check box to return to WordPerfect's default AFC for that font.

## Editing Display Font Mapping

When you use a font built into your printer, WordPerfect selects a similar graphic font to represent the printer font on-screen. If you disagree with a choice WordPerfect has made, you can change the display font mapping to choose another graphic font for the on-screen representation of a printer font.

To change the display font mapping, follow these steps:

1. Choose Fo_r_mat, _F_ont or press F9. The Font dialog box appears.

2. Choose Font _M_ap. The Edit Printer/Document Font Mapping dialog box appears.

3. Click the Display tab. WordPerfect switches to the Display page of the Edit Printer/Document Font Mapping dialog box (see fig. 20.7).

4. Select from the Printer Font _F_ace drop-down list the printer font whose display font you want to review or change. WordPerfect displays the currently mapped font in the Fa_c_e list box.

5. To change the display font mapping for the printer font, select a different font from the Display Font Fa_c_e drop-down list. The name of the new font appears under the Resulting Font Name and WordPerfect removes the check from the A_u_tomatic Selection check box.

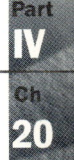

**FIG. 20.7**
You can choose which display font WordPerfect uses on-screen to represent fonts built into your printer.

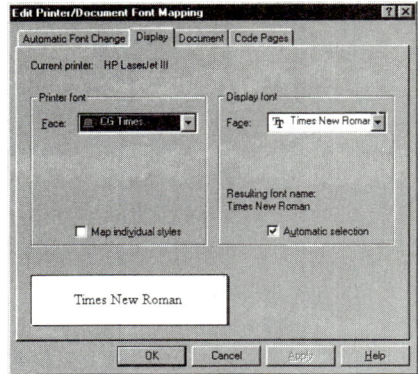

6. Repeat steps 4 and 5 to review or change the display font mapping for another printer font.
7. Choose OK to return to the Font dialog box and have WordPerfect save the changes in the printer driver and supporting files; or choose Cancel to abandon your changes. Choose OK to return to the document window.

To undo the changes, repeat steps 1–4; then mark the A̲utomatic Selection check box for the selected font, which returns the display font mapping for the selected printer font to WordPerfect's original choice.

▶ **See** "Formatting Characters," **p. 126**

### TROUBLESHOOTING

**When I print my document, the text looks all jagged, and printing is very slow.** Under normal circumstances, WordPerfect uses the fonts built into the printer or available through Windows (such as TrueType and ATM) to print the document. However, both WordPerfect and Windows can print text graphically—that is, by sending the dots that make up each character to the printer, rather than the characters themselves. Usually this is not advisable, because the text can look jagged, and it can take much longer to print a document. If you are using a Windows and TrueType fonts printer, turn off graphical text printing. From the Print dialog box, click the Printer tab to switch to the Printer page. Choose P̲roperties, click the Fonts tab, then deselect the Print TrueType As G̲raphics check box.

There is another setting you may need to change. From the Printer page of the Print dialog box, deselect the Prin̲t Graphically check box, then choose C̲lose.

**WordPerfect uses the wrong fonts when I open a document created by someone else on another computer.** Not every computer has the same collection of fonts. If someone creates a document with a given font, but you don't have that font, WordPerfect attempts to match the missing font as best as it can with one you do have. Sometimes, this matching is not accurate.

If you consistently get the wrong font, use the font mapping procedures outlined earlier in this chapter to force WordPerfect into substituting a different font. Or, install the missing font so it's on your computer as well.

# Working with Multiple Languages

WordPerfect has released more than 30 foreign language versions of WordPerfect, including not only Western European languages such as French, Spanish, and German, but also versions such as Russian, Greek, and Japanese. No matter which version of WordPerfect you own, if you need to create or edit documents in more than one language, WordPerfect provides several kinds of support:

**NOTE** WordPerfect has traditionally been available in more than 30 foreign languages. Contact Corel Corporation to find out more about the foreign language version of the Corel WordPerfect Suite 7 you require.

- You can enter, display, and print any of more than 2,400 foreign language characters and other symbols using the WordPerfect Characters dialog box. You can also use the Compose feature to insert common accented characters such as é (see the earlier sections "WordPerfect Characters" and "Compose").

- If you carry on correspondence in a foreign language, you need to be able to use dates, times, and currency in the correct formats. You can insert a language code into a document, and WordPerfect will use the appropriate conventions for that language.

- If you use a foreign language frequently, you also want to check the spelling of the non-English portions of your documents. You can purchase a WordPerfect foreign language module that contains dictionary files for use with the Speller, Grammatik, and Thesaurus. Language modules also contain alternate keyboard layouts that let you type the characters used in that language far more quickly than using WordPerfect Characters or Compose.

- You can purchase a foreign language version of WordPerfect itself, in which all the menus, prompts, and dialog boxes appear in the foreign language as well.

## Entering a WordPerfect Language Code

When you buy WordPerfect, you receive a version for a specific language and country. You can buy an English version of WordPerfect for the United States, for example, or an English version for Australia, or one for the United Kingdom. Likewise, you can purchase a French version or a Canadian French version. WordPerfect refers to the combination of language and country as the package language and abbreviates the language with a two-letter language code. The package language for the United States, for example, is English-U.S., and the corresponding language code is US. The Australian package language is English-Australian, and its language code is OZ; the British versions are English-U.K. and UK.

WordPerfect uses the language code in several ways. With any version of the program, you can insert a language code to tell WordPerfect to use foreign dates and times. For example, in U.S. English the standard date text is "February 1, 1996;" but in UK English the proper format is "1 February 1996." In French it's "1 février 1996" and in Spanish it's "1 de febrero de 1996." In tables, WordPerfect uses the language code to insert the appropriate number formats and currency symbols, such as pounds (£) or yen (¥). This information is contained within the Language Database File, PFDTLR.DAT.

> **NOTE** PFDTLR.DAT cannot be retrieved into WordPerfect to be edited. You must edit the settings for the language by choosing Tools, Language, then clicking the Edit LRS button.

If you have purchased a foreign language module, inserting a foreign language code also tells WordPerfect to use the appropriate dictionary for the Speller, Thesaurus, and other language features. If you have passages of a foreign language within an English-language document, you can insert multiple language codes to tell WordPerfect to switch back and forth between languages when spell-checking. See Chapter 6, "Using Writing Tools," for more information on using writing tools in a foreign language.

To insert a language code in a document, follow these steps:

1. Move the insertion point to where you want the change to take effect, or select a block of text.
2. Choose Tools, Language. WordPerfect displays the Language dialog box (see fig. 20.9). The current language code is highlighted.
3. Select a language.
4. Choose OK or press Enter.

WordPerfect inserts a [Lang:XX] code in your document, where *XX* is the two-letter language code. If you select French-National, for instance, the code is [Lang:FR]. The new language stays in effect until WordPerfect encounters a different language code. If you select a block of text, WordPerfect places the language code for the new language before the text and, at the end of the block, reverts the language to the original language.

**FIG. 20.9**
Choose a different language code for WordPerfect to be able to insert dates, times, and currency correctly for that language.

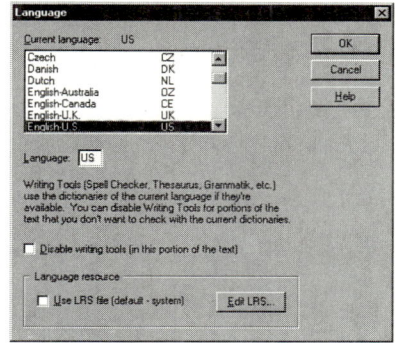

If you now insert a date or time in the document, WordPerfect uses the format of the new language.

**N O T E**  If you use footnotes that span more than one page and want WordPerfect to include "(continued. . .)" messages in a different language, you must insert a language code into the Initial Codes style.

## Using Foreign Language Keyboards

When you type in a foreign language, you frequently use characters and symbols that aren't used in American English. You can certainly insert these characters using WordPerfect Characters or Compose. If you have to insert more than a few characters, however, this procedure quickly becomes tedious. If you are typing in a foreign alphabet such as Cyrillic or Greek, you would have to leave the WordPerfect Characters dialog box open to the correct alphabet, then double-click to insert each character—clearly not a practical solution.

Instead, you can use an alternate keyboard file. If you only need to insert an occasional foreign character, you may want to create your own keyboard file, adding the character(s) you need to use. If you do extensive work in a foreign language, however, you should purchase the appropriate language module from Corel Corporation. The language modules include not only files to be used with the writing tools such as Speller, Thesaurus, and Grammatik, but also keyboard files customized for the language.

When you purchase a language module, you can use its keyboard file in several ways. If you will be creating entire documents in the foreign language, create a template designed for working in that language, and assign the foreign keyboard file to that template. You can then select that template whenever you want to create a foreign language document, and WordPerfect automatically selects the foreign keyboard. See Chapter 11, "Using Templates," for more information.

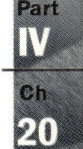

If you need to switch back and forth between languages and keyboards within a document, you must choose Edit, Preferences, Keyboard, and then select the desired keyboard to change to a different file. To make this procedure easy to use in practice, you should record a macro that selects the foreign keyboard and assigns it to your normal keyboard file; then record a macro that selects the normal keyboard and assign it to your foreign keyboard file.

▶ **See** "Creating and Customizing Keyboards," **p. 324**

▶ **See** "Using Templates," **p. 363**

▶ **See** "Creating Macros," **p. 387**

## Working with Character Maps

Languages such as English, French, Spanish, and German all use the Roman alphabet. Although you can insert characters from other alphabets, such as Greek, WordPerfect assumes that most of the letters in your documents will use the standard Roman alphabet. If you use a foreign language module such as Greek, Hebrew, or Russian (which uses the Cyrillic alphabet), most of the characters in your foreign language documents will not be in the Roman alphabet.

WordPerfect language modules for such languages contain a different character map for the foreign alphabet. Each character map contains a subset of more than 2,400 WordPerfect characters most likely to be used in languages that use that alphabet.

When you use the standard character map for English, each Greek letter that you insert into a document takes up more room on disk than a character in the English alphabet. If you only insert an occasional Greek character, this extra room is a small fraction of the document's total size, but if you create an entire document in Greek, the document takes up much more room on disk than an equivalent document in English.

If you purchase the Greek language module, however, you can select the Greek character map, which tells WordPerfect to assume that most of the characters in the document will be Greek. In this case, the Greek letters take up less room on disk, and inserting an English character takes more. If you purchase a Russian or Hebrew language module, the same principal applies for the Cyrillic and Hebrew character maps.

You can only choose a different character map if you have purchased a language module for a language in a different alphabet. If you do have a different character map available, however, you should choose that character map whenever a document has more characters in that language than in English. To choose a different character map, choose Format, Document. Then choose Character Mapping and select a character map from the list. (Without a foreign language module, this list will be empty.)

▶ **See** "Working with Other Languages," **p. 235**

# CHAPTER 21

# Using Advanced Graphics Techniques

*by Susan Plumley and Alan Westenbroek*

By using WordPerfect, you can add a variety of graphics to your documents: horizontal and vertical lines, paragraph and page borders, and graphics boxes that hold text, images, tables, equations, and spreadsheets. In Chapter 7, "Integrating Text and Graphics," you learned how to add basic graphics to a document to create interest, separate text, and emphasize your message. This chapter shows you how to customize the graphics elements to get the most out of WordPerfect's capabilities.

Customizing graphics elements includes changing the thickness and color of lines and borders, adding shadows and fill to graphics boxes, setting margin spacing within a border, adding captions to graphics boxes, and much more. WordPerfect enables you to modify the graphics elements in your documents in many ways.

Even though you can create many varied lines, borders, and boxes in WordPerfect, keep some basic guidelines in mind when using graphics elements. First and foremost, you want to provide a consistent design with the graphics so as not to overwhelm the message. ■

### Insert a drop cap
Draw attention to a sentence or paragraph by leading off with a large capital letter.

### Customize graphics lines
You learn how to customize horizontal and vertical lines as well as how to create your own graphic lines.

### Customize borders
Page and paragraph borders come in hundreds of shapes and sizes. You learn how to use all of the options to create the perfect border for your document.

### Customize graphics boxes
Graphic boxes are created with a default set of options, which makes it fast and easy to add graphics to your document. In this chapter, you learn how to adjust the settings for just the right presentation.

### Retrieve and edit images
Graphic images in many popular formats can be retrieved and edited using the Image Tools. You learn how to adjust brightness or contrast, change color or fill, rotate, move, and scale the image.

### Create graphics with Drag To Create
Using the mouse, you can click and drag anywhere in a document to create a graphics box.

Graphics lines, borders, and boxes should support the text, not confuse the reader or overwhelm the message. Be consistent with your use of graphics; that is, if you use single line styles and 10 percent fill on the first page, use that same formula throughout the document with little or no variation. Second, be careful not to crowd text and graphics on the page; a crowded page is difficult to read. Use plenty of *white space*—areas without text or graphics that provide a rest for the reader's eyes.

This chapter shows you how to customize the graphics elements—lines, borders, and graphics boxes—in your documents. In addition, this chapter gives you helpful tips on how to provide the most comfortable reading environment while adding interest and emphasis with graphics. ■

## Inserting a Drop Cap

A *drop cap* is the large initial letter that sometimes begins a page or chapter. This is an easy way to add that extra "finished" look to a formal or fancy document.

 If you prefer, you can use the keyboard shortcut, Ctrl+Shift+C, rather than choosing from the pull-down menus.

To add a drop cap in WordPerfect, place your insertion point anywhere in the paragraph you want to begin with a drop cap and choose Format, Drop Cap. WordPerfect selects the first letter of the paragraph, makes it larger, and wraps the other text around it. WordPerfect also displays a feature bar with options for changing the font, size, alignment, position, and border style of the drop cap. The default drop cap style, which is approximately five times larger than the text in the paragraph, is perfect for many occasions, but you can experiment with the options to get the look that's just right for your specific application. Click Close on the Drop Cap Feature Bar to close the bar.

## Customizing Lines

WordPerfect enables you to customize the horizontal and vertical lines you add to your documents. In Chapter 7, "Integrating Text and Graphics," you learned how to create lines and alter them by using the mouse. You also can alter, or edit, lines by using the Edit Graphics Line dialog box, which gives you more control over the changes you make.

▶ **See** "Customizing Lines Using the Mouse," **p. 252**

Suppose that you want to add lines to separate stories in a newsletter. You want to make them shorter than the column width. Use the Edit Graphics Line dialog box to make the changes to the lines. Figure 21.1 illustrates this effect. Notice, too, the use of thick lines to emphasize the masthead, or title area of the newsletter.

## Customizing Lines

**FIG. 21.1**
All lines in the newsletter are thick, thus creating consistency; however, the lines separating stories are shorter than the column to add emphasis to the text.

In WordPerfect, you can change the style, position, color, and spacing of any horizontal or vertical line. The *style* of the line refers to whether the line is single, double, thick, extra thick, and so on. *Position* describes the placement of the line on the page—for example, whether the line starts on the left, right, or center of the page or column. If you have a color monitor—or better yet, a color printer—you also can assign a color to the lines in your documents. Finally, *spacing* refers to any margin area you set above or below the line to separate it from text. This section shows you how to customize these options for horizontal and vertical lines.

## Changing Line Style

*Line style* refers to the type of line you choose: single, thick, thick double, triple, thick triple, and so on. In Chapter 7, "Integrating Text and Graphics," you created the default horizontal and vertical lines—single lines. You can create a default line and then change the line style, or you can choose a line style as you create a line.

**NOTE** The following instructions can be used for either horizontal or vertical lines.

To create a line using a style other than the default single, follow these steps:

1. Choose Graphics, Custom Line. The Create Graphics Line dialog box appears (see fig. 21.2).

**TIP** To create a line, choose Graphics, Horizontal Line, Vertical Line, or Custom Line.

**FIG. 21.2**
The Create Graphics Line dialog box offers you a number of ways of controlling line appearance and position.

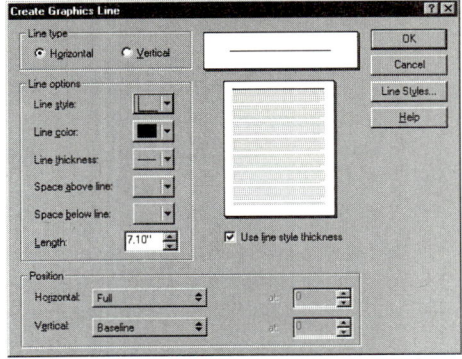

2. Choose a style from the Line Style pop-up palette.
3. In Line Type, choose Horizontal or Vertical.
4. Choose OK to close the dialog box and return to the document.

To change the line style of a line after the line is created, follow these steps:

 In the Create Graphics Line dialog box, you can also set other options for the line, all of which are described in the following sections.

1. Point to the line you want to edit and click the left mouse button. When a graphics line is selected, selection handles appear around the line. You can use these selection handles to move and resize a line.

 You can also point to a graphics line and right-click the mouse button to open a QuickMenu. If you right-click a vertical line, choose Edit Vertical Line from the QuickMenu; if you right-click a horizontal line, choose Edit Horizontal Line from the QuickMenu.

2. Choose Graphics, Edit Line. The Edit Graphics Line dialog box appears.
3. Choose a style from the Line Style pop-up palette.
4. Choose OK to close the dialog box and return to the document.

## Changing Line Thickness

You can further customize a line by changing its thickness. You can control the thickness of any line by using the Edit Graphics Line dialog box.

 The Edit Graphics Line dialog box and the Create Graphics Line dialog box are identical.

Customizing Lines  661

To change line thickness, follow these steps:

1. Open the Line Thickness pop-up palette and either choose a line thickness visually or type a value in the text box (see fig. 21.3).

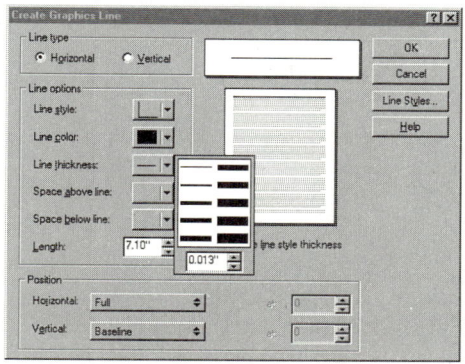

**FIG. 21.3**
Choose one of the sample lines or use an exact measurement by typing a value. As you change the thickness value, the sample in the thickness button changes so that you can view the change.

 To change back to the default line style thickness, choose Use Line Style Thickness.

2. Choose OK to close the dialog box and return to the document.

 Alternatively, point at the graphic line and right-click to open a QuickMenu; choose Edit Horizontal Line (if it's a horizontal line), and the Edit Graphics Line dialog box appears.

**NOTE** All instructions from this point on refer to the Edit Graphics Line dialog box; however, the same options are available in the Create Graphics Line dialog box.

## Setting Line Color

You can also change the color of lines you add to your document. Unless you have a color printer, the colored lines print a shade of black or gray.

To change a line's color, follow these steps:

1. In the Edit Graphics Line dialog box, click the Line Color button. The Line Color palette appears (see fig. 21.4).
2. Select a color from the palette.
3. Choose OK to close the dialog box and return to the document.

**FIG. 21.4**
Use the Line Color palette to change the color of lines in your document. Choose the Use Line Style Color check box to revert back to the default color—black.

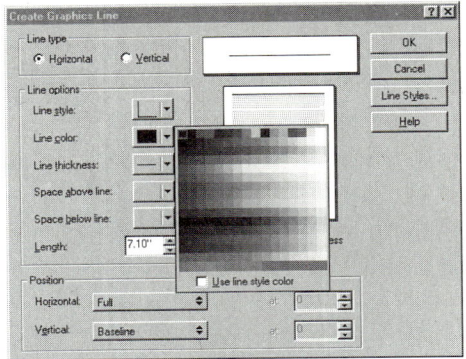

 **TIP** Don't use more than two different shades of black or two different colors for lines within a document. Remember to be consistent with your design so that the reader can concentrate on your message.

## Customizing Horizontal Lines

WordPerfect includes some specific options you can customize for horizontal lines, including position, spacing, and line length. By using these options, you can place a horizontal line exactly where you want it, create short or long lines, and change the space above or below the line.

The default horizontal line you create extends from the left to the right margin and is located on the baseline; the line length is dependent on the area between the margins. In addition, the default line uses no spacing above or below the line. The following sections describe how to change the horizontal line defaults.

**Horizontal Position**  The horizontal position sets where the left end of the line begins. To customize the horizontal position of a line, follow these steps:

1. Choose Graphics, Edit Line. The Edit Graphics Line dialog box appears (refer to fig. 21.3).
2. In the Position group, choose Horizontal. A pop-up list of choices appears (see fig. 21.5).

**FIG. 21.5**
When altering the horizontal position of a line, you might also need to change the line length to better fit the page.

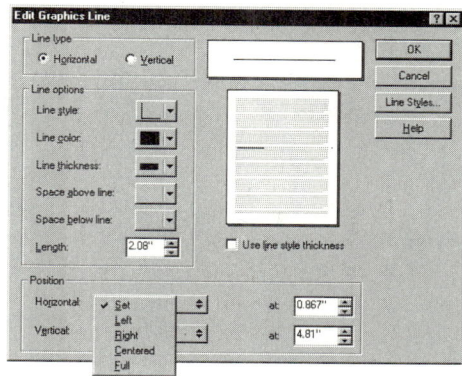

The following table describes each of your horizontal position choices:

| Option | Result |
| --- | --- |
| Set | Sets a value in the At box to indicate where the left side of the horizontal line begins; when you choose Set, the At box becomes available. |
| Left | Sets the line to begin at the left margin. |
| Right | Sets the line to begin at the right margin. |
| Centered | Centers the line in the column or on the page. |
| Full | Sets the line to extend from the left to the right margin (default). |

3. Choose the Horizontal Position option you want and choose OK to close the dialog box and return to the document.

**NOTE** The preceding steps also apply to the Create Graphics Line dialog box.

**Vertical Position** The vertical position sets the line position between the top and bottom margins. To alter the vertical position of a horizontal line, follow these steps:

1. Select the line you want to edit, then choose Graphics, Edit Line.
2. In the Edit Graphic Line dialog box, choose Vertical in the Position section. The following table describes your choices.

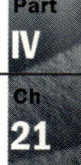

| Option | Result |
|---|---|
| Set | Appoints a specific value in the At box to define the vertical position of the line from the top edge of the page. Editing the text in front of a line set to a specific value does not alter the line's position. |
| Baseline | Places the line on the baseline on which the insertion point is positioned (default). Adding or deleting text before a graphic line set to a vertical position of Baseline alters the position of the line. |

3. Choose an option and choose OK to close the dialog box.

**Line Length**  You can adjust the length of a horizontal line to any length between the left and right margins. To change the line length, follow these steps:

1. In the Edit Graphics Line dialog box, type a value in the Length text box.
2. Choose OK to close the dialog box.

## Customizing Vertical Lines

Just as you can change the position and length of a horizontal line, you can change the position and length of a vertical line. The vertical line options, however, are slightly different. This section explains how to change the horizontal and vertical position of a vertical line and how to change the line length.

**Horizontal Position**  You can change the horizontal position of a vertical line, but you must be careful how the line affects your text. Experiment with changing the position of a vertical line to get the hang of it.

To change the horizontal position of a vertical line, follow these steps:

1. In the Edit Graphics Line dialog box, choose Horizontal in the Position group. The following table describes the options.

 **TIP**  To insert a vertical line between columns, choose Column Aligned from the Horizontal pop-up list in the Edit Graphics Line dialog box.

| Option | Result |
|---|---|
| Set | Sets a specific value, in the At box, from the left edge of the paper. |
| Left | Sets the line along the left margin of the page (default). |

## Customizing Lines

Right  Sets the line on the right margin of the page.

Centered  Centers the line on the page. If you have text in one column—stretching from the left margin to the right—the Centered line runs directly through your text.

Column Aligned  Sets the line to position after any column; sets the column in the After Column text box. This is a handy option for placing lines between columns in a newsletter, report, and so on.

2. Choose an option and choose OK to close the dialog box.

**Vertical Position**  The vertical position of a line describes where the top of the line begins. To change the vertical position, follow these steps:

1. In the Edit Graphics Line dialog box, choose Vertical in Position/Length. The following table describes available options:

| Option | Result |
| --- | --- |
| Set | Sets a specific value, in the At text box, from the top edge of the paper to describe where the vertical line begins. |
| Top | Sets the line to begin at the top margin, not the top edge of the paper. |
| Bottom | Sets the line to begin at the bottom margin of the page. |
| Centered | Centers the line between the top and bottom margins. |
| Full | Sets the line to extend between the top and bottom margins (default). |

2. Choose an option and choose OK to close the dialog box.

▶ **See** "Using Graphics Lines," **p. 250**

**Line Length**  Setting the line length of a vertical line gives you more control over its vertical position. For example, set a line's vertical position to begin at the bottom; if the line length extends from the top to the bottom margins, you can't tell any difference. However, if you set the line length to three inches, the vertical positioning is more noticeable.

To set the line length of a vertical line, in the Edit Graphics Line dialog box, type a value in the Length text box and choose OK to close the dialog box.

# Customizing Borders

In Chapter 7, "Integrating Text and Graphics," you learned how to create a paragraph and a page border, and even to customize the border somewhat. This section takes you a step further.

WordPerfect enables you to customize more than just the line style of a border; you can add spacing to the inside and outside of a border, change the color of the lines, and add a drop shadow. In addition, you can customize the type of fill and the color of the fill in a border.

As explained in Chapter 7, to create a paragraph border, choose Format, Border/Fill, Paragraph. To create a page border, choose Format, Border/Fill, Page.

▶ **See** "Using Paragraph Borders," **p. 256**
▶ **See** "Using Adding a Page Border," **p. 258**

## Setting Spacing

WordPerfect enables you to set the space between a border and outside text, and the border and inside text. In addition, you can view the spacing in the preview box as you change it. You can set the spacing as a numerical value or by sight.

> **CAUTION**
> Be careful to leave space around a paragraph or page border to keep from crowding text and making it hard to read.

To change the spacing assigned to a border, follow these steps:

1. In the Paragraph Border/Fill or Page Border/Fill dialog box, click the Advanced tab (see fig. 21.6).

> **CAUTION**
> You must have a border style selected in the Available Border Styles list box, or the options in the Advanced page will be grayed out (unavailable).

2. Click the Inside or Outside pop-up palettes and choose a spacing amount visually, or type a spacing value in the text box.
3. Choose OK to change the spacing and close the dialog box.

**FIG. 21.6**
Whether you set the spacing by sight or by numerical value, you can view the spacing in the example box.

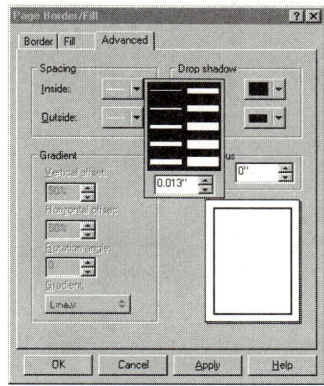

## Changing Color

You can apply one of a variety of colors to a paragraph or page border. To change the color of a border, follow these steps:

1. In the Page Border/Fill or Paragraph Border/Fill dialog box, click the Color button in the Border tab. An array of available colors appears (see fig. 21.7).

> **CAUTION**
> You must have a border style selected in the Available Border Styles list box, or the Color button will be grayed out (unavailable).

**FIG. 21.7**
If you're printing to a laser printer, it's probably best to stick to black. But if you have a color printer or a high-end output device, put that palette to work for you!

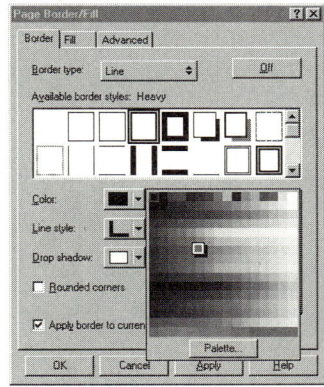

2. Select the desired color, and choose OK.

 **TIP** Limit colors of borders to no more than two within each document to create consistency and unity.

3. Choose OK to change the border's color and close the dialog box.

## Changing Corners

Round-cornered borders create an interesting effect in a document. You can change the border corners for page borders to anything from slightly rounded to almost circular. To change the corners of a page border, follow these steps:

1. In the Page Border/Fill dialog box, choose Rounded Corners.
2. To change the corner radius (the amount of "roundness"), click the Advanced tab and type a value in the Amount text box. Larger values make for rounder corners.

 **TIP** As you change the curvature of the corners, watch the example box to get an idea of how much curve you want.

3. Choose OK to change the corners and close the dialog box.

## Adding a Drop Shadow

A *drop shadow* gives your document a professional look by adding depth to the page. For example, you can add a drop shadow to a paragraph border for special announcements, advertisements, or special areas of a form. A drop shadow also looks good when applied to a page border for a letterhead, title page, or flyer. To create a drop shadow, follow these steps:

1. In the Paragraph Border/Fill or Page Border/Fill dialog box, click the Border tab, then choose a drop shadow direction from the Drop Shadow palette.
2. Click the Advanced tab and choose an option from the Width pop-up palette in the Drop Shadow group (see fig. 21.8).

**FIG. 21.8**
You can select a width visually or type a value in the text box.

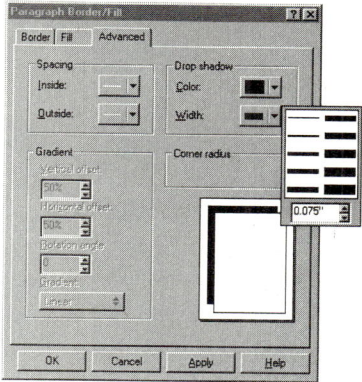

3. Choose the color of the shadow from the Color pop-up palette.
4. Choose OK to create the drop shadow and close the dialog box.

## Adding Fill

As described in Chapter 7, "Integrating Text and Graphics," you can also add fill to a paragraph or page border. In addition to a variety of fills—including lines, checkerboard, fish scale, waves, mesh, and more—you can add a variety of colors to your fill. To add fill to a border, follow these steps:

1. Choose Format, Border/Fill, Page or Paragraph. The Page Border/Fill or Paragraph Border/Fill dialog box appears.
2. If necessary, choose Line from the Border Type pop-up list.
3. Click the Fill tab and choose a fill style from the Available Fill Styles area.
4. Choose the colors you want from the Foreground and Background color palettes.
5. Choose a pattern from the Pattern pop-up palette (some patterns and fill styles are mutually exclusive).
6. Choose OK to add fill to the border and close the dialog box.

## Customizing Graphics Boxes

WordPerfect enables you to add graphics images—such as clip art, WP Presentations images, scanned images, and so on—to your documents to add interest and diversity. In addition, you can add text boxes for callouts, quotes, announcements, and so on. You can also add graphics boxes to hold equations, tables, or inline figures. WordPerfect offers

many ways to spice up your documents. Chapter 7, "Integrating Text and Graphics," shows you how to create a variety of graphics boxes.

▶ **See** "Using Graphics Borders," **p. 255**

WordPerfect offers 11 graphics box styles you can use; however, you may want to change line style, color, spacing, captions, and so on. WordPerfect enables you to do all this and more. You can adjust the text flow around the graphics box, for example, or rotate the contents within a box. This section shows you how to customize graphics boxes to suit your documents and purposes. Figure 21.1 illustrates a graphic with a custom wrap that lets the text contour around the graphic image.

The Edit Box dialog box, shown in figure 21.9, allows you to control many attributes of a graphics box. To open the Edit Box dialog box, click a graphic's QuickSpot.

**FIG. 21.9**
The Edit Box dialog box enables you to change the border, fill, style, size, position, text wrap, and content of the graphics box. You can add a caption or choose other graphics boxes to edit while in this editing mode.

## Choosing a Box Style

You can choose the style of box you want by using the Graphics menu or the Toolbar. The Graphics menu offers four box options: Image, Text Box, Equation, and Custom Box. If you do not want to use a Image, Text, or Equation box, choose Custom Box and select the style of box you want to create.

 You can add a box style you use often to the Graphics menu by choosing Graphics, Graphics Styles, Menu. Select the box style in the Items list and choose OK, then Close.

You can choose a new graphics box style at any time by using the Edit Box dialog box. To change a box style, follow these steps:

# Customizing Graphics Boxes

**T I P** You can point the mouse at the graphics box and right-click; a QuickMenu appears from which you can choose some of the editing options.

1. Select an image, then click the QuickSpot button in the upper-left corner. The Edit Box dialog box appears (refer to fig. 21.9).
2. Choose an option from the Box Styles drop-down list.
3. To close the Edit Box dialog box, click the Close button in the upper-right corner.

## Choosing Contents

You can choose the contents of a graphics box to be an image, text, or equation, or the box can remain empty (something you might do to hold a space for an image until the image is available). In addition, you can position the contents within the box horizontally and vertically. You can choose to center the contents horizontally, for example, or position the contents to the left or right of the graphics box. You can also center the contents vertically, or position the contents to the top or bottom of the box.

**N O T E** If the contents of the box consist of text, you can additionally rotate the contents 90, 180, or 270 degrees if you want, as well as adjust the position of the text within the box. To do so, click Content in the Edit Box dialog box and choose a Vertical Position option or one of the options in the Rotate Text Counterclockwise section.

To choose the contents of the graphics box, follow these steps:

1. In the Edit Box dialog box, click the Content button. The Box Content dialog box appears (see fig. 21.10).

**FIG. 21.10**
Choose the Content category first, and then either choose a file to import to the graphics box, or create your own text, image, or equation.

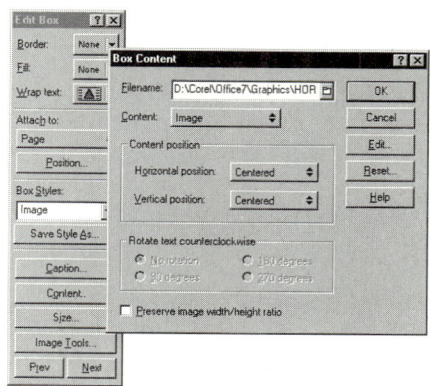

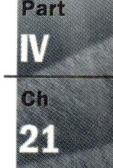

2. Choose <u>C</u>ontent; a pop-up list appears. Your choices are listed in the following table:

| Option | Result |
|---|---|
| <u>E</u>mpty | The box remains empty. |
| <u>I</u>mage | Choose an image file from the hard disk drive; the image can be clipart, WP Draw, scanned art, or any variety of other graphics. |
| <u>T</u>ext | Choose a file name or create the text in the box. |
| E<u>q</u>uation | Create an equation for the box. |
| Image On <u>D</u>isk | Choose an image file from a floppy disk. The image will be linked to the document, meaning that you must insert the disk containing the image each time you open the document. |

3. Choose any other options such as positioning or rotation.
4. Choose <u>F</u>ilename if you want to import a file and select a file. If you choose <u>T</u>ext from the <u>C</u>ontent pop-up list, click the <u>E</u>dit button to create your own text.
5. Choose OK to close the Box Content dialog box and save your changes.

**TIP** For most graphic images, choose <u>P</u>reserve Image Width/Height Ratio to maintain the image's proportion when changing the proportion of the graphics box.

If the <u>C</u>ontent you select is <u>T</u>ext, WordPerfect returns to the editing window with the insertion point in the graphics box. Type and format the text.

**N O T E** If you have a great amount of text to enter in a text box, consider typing the text in a WordPerfect document, formatting, and then saving it. Then use the <u>F</u>ilename option in the Box Content dialog box to import the text.

If you choose to edit the equation contents of a box, the Equation Editor appears.

If you choose to edit the image contents of a graphics box, WP Presentations appears.

## Creating a Caption

WordPerfect enables you to add captions to the graphics boxes you create. You can position the caption on the left, right, top, or bottom of the graphics box. You can also place the caption inside, outside, or on the border of the box. In addition, you can left-, right-, or center-align the text in the caption, offset the text, rotate the text, and number the captions. To add a caption to the graphics box, follow these steps:

1. Click Caption in the Edit Box dialog box. The Box Caption dialog box appears (see fig. 21.11).

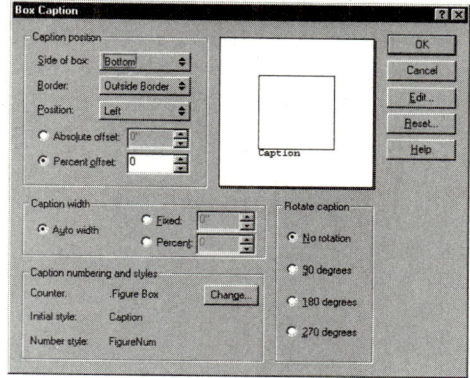

**FIG. 21.11**
When you create a caption, WordPerfect automatically numbers the caption according to the number of like box styles you have created. For example, if this is the third figure box, the caption number is 3.

2. Choose options for the placement, position, rotation, and so on of the caption.
3. Choose Edit. The dialog box closes and returns you to the graphics box editing screen. The insertion point is in position for the caption; type the text.
4. If you are finished editing the box, close the Edit Box dialog box. If, however, you want to further edit the graphic box, leave the Edit Box dialog box open.

 If you change your mind and want to delete a caption after you've created it, choose Reset in the Box Caption dialog box.

## Choosing Position Options

As you learned in Chapter 7, "Integrating Text and Graphics," you can easily position a graphics box by selecting it with the mouse and moving it to a new position. You can also reposition a graphics box by using the Box Position dialog box. To position a graphics box, follow these steps:

 To reposition a graphic with the mouse, drag it to a new position.

1. Click Position in the Edit Box dialog box. The Box Position dialog box appears (see fig. 21.12).

**FIG. 21.12**
You can position the graphics box horizontally and vertically by entering a value in inches, centimeters, points, or WP units.

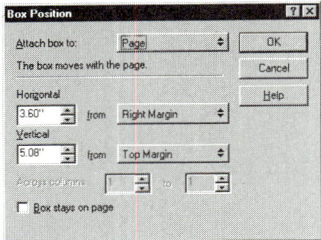

**N O T E** Horizontal placement can be measured from the right or left margin, center of paragraph, or left of the page. Vertical placement is measured from the top of the paragraph.

2. Choose the type of box placement from the Attach Box To drop-down list:

| Option | Result |
| --- | --- |
| Page | The box is anchored to the page no matter what text editing is performed. |
| Paragraph | The box remains with the paragraph the insertion point is in when you create the box—a paragraph anchor. |
| Character | The box moves with surrounding text as if it were one of the characters on the line. |

3. Type a value in the Horizontal text box, then choose where the measurement should start by selecting an option in the From pop-up menu.
4. Type a value for Vertical placement, then choose where the measurement should start by selecting an option in the From pop-up menu.
5. Choose OK.

   ▶ **See** "Using Graphics Boxes," **p. 262**

## Choosing Size Options

Perhaps the easiest way to size a graphics box is with the mouse. However, you may want an exact size for fitting within a column, matching the exact width-height ratio, and so on. To set an exact size for the graphics box, follow these steps:

 **T I P** To size a graphics box with the mouse, select the box. Click and drag one of the box's handles to resize.

1. Click Size in the Edit Box dialog box. The Box Size dialog box appears (see fig. 21.13).

**FIG. 21.13**
Set the width and height of the graphics box by typing values in the text boxes. Choose Full to fill the page with the image, or choose Maintain Proportions to create a proportioned image.

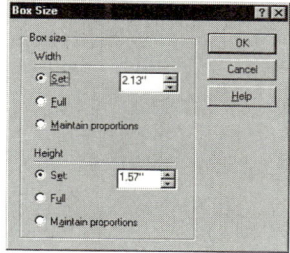

2. Choose the Width and the Height of the graphics box.
3. Choose OK.

**NOTE** You can mix and match sizing options. For example, choose Width to be Full, and Height to be Maintain Proportions, which makes the image the full width between the margins and proportionally adjusts the height of the image.

## Editing Border and Fill

Editing the border and fill of a graphics box is the same as editing the border and fill of a graphics border. For more information, see the earlier section "Customizing Borders." To edit the border and fill of a graphics box, choose options from the Border and Fill pop-up palettes in the Edit Box dialog box.

## Adjusting Text Wrap

Graphics boxes you use in your documents normally are accompanied by text. When placing a graphics box in a page or column of text, you must decide how that text flows—or wraps around—the graphics box. WordPerfect gives you several choices for text wrap. To adjust text wrap for a graphics box, choose an option from the Wrap Text pop-up menu (see fig. 21.14). You can refer back to figure 21.1 to see an illustration of Contour text wrap.

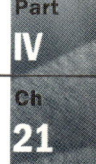

**FIG. 21.14**

Choose how the text wraps around the graphics box by choosing an option from the menu. The icons next to each option show the type of wrapping.

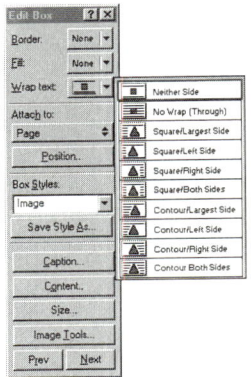

# Retrieving a Graphics Image

WordPerfect enables you to import many types of graphics files; you can import vector graphics (draw images) and bitmapped graphics (paint images). *Vector graphics* are images created using mathematical formulas to create lines and curves. They can be sized and distorted without losing any resolution. *Bitmapped graphics* are images created using a series of dots (called *pixels*). When resized, they often lose some of their clarity. Figure 21.15 illustrates examples of vector and bitmapped graphics.

**FIG. 21.15**

The image on the left (the beautiful rare marsh crane) is a vector graphic. The image on the right (the flower) is a bitmapped image.

WordPerfect enables you to use a variety of files, including WP Graphics (WPG), Encapsulated Postscript (EPS), PC Paintbrush (PCX), Tagged Image Format (TIF), and more. Images from most drawing, painting, and scanning programs can be imported to WordPerfect for Windows.

If you want to quickly import a graphics image, you can create a default figure box and retrieve an image without editing the graphics box. The box appears in the document, and you can resize and reposition it by using the mouse. Of course, you also can edit the graphics box by using the graphics box editing screen, if you find it necessary.

To retrieve an image into a figure box, follow these steps:

1. Choose Graphics, Image. The Insert Image dialog box appears (see fig. 21.16).

**FIG. 21.16**
If you don't have image files of your own, choose from the clip art provided with WordPerfect; the path to the WordPerfect clip art files is C:\COREL\OFFICE7\GRAPHICS. All WordPerfect graphics use a WPG extension.

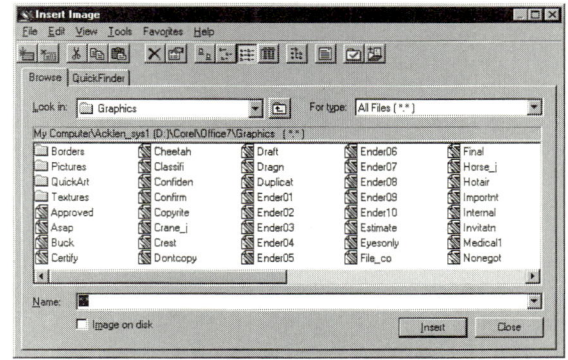

2. In the Name text box, type the name of the file to be retrieved, or select the filename from the list.
3. Choose Insert.

 **TIP** You can use images created in Presentations as an image file. See Chapter 22, "Using WordPerfect Draw and TextArt," for more information.

## Editing a Graphics Image

When you retrieve a graphics image, you might need to adjust the image to make it more suitable to your document. Editing an image includes adjusting brightness or contrast, changing color or fill, and even rotating, moving, and scaling the image.

**N O T E** Editing also includes adding lines and shapes to the image with WP Draw, which you can learn more about in Chapter 22, "Using WordPerfect Draw and TextArt."

You can edit graphics images so that they complement and emphasize the text in your document. For instance, if you have an image of a ship that's facing the wrong way for its placement in your document, you can alter the position of the image by mirroring it. This section shows you how to edit graphics images.

WordPerfect's graphics box editing screen includes a toolbox—Image Tools—to enable you to customize and edit images. To display the Image Tools palette, click Image Tools in the Edit Box dialog box, or right-click the graphic and choose Image Tools from the QuickMenu. Figure 21.17 illustrates the Image Tools toolbox.

**FIG. 21.17**
Icons represent each tool in the Image Tools toolbox.

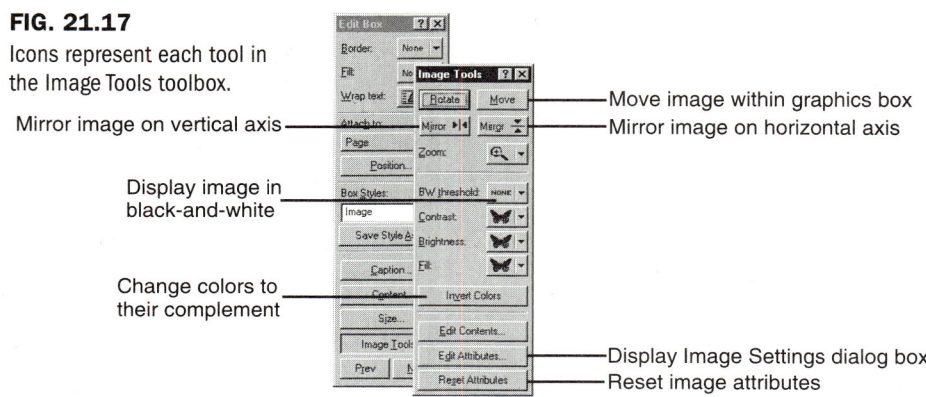

- Move image within graphics box
- Mirror image on horizontal axis
- Mirror image on vertical axis
- Display image in black-and-white
- Change colors to their complement
- Display Image Settings dialog box
- Reset image attributes

You can reverse all editing effects at any time by choosing Reset Attributes in the Image Tools toolbox.

 **T I P** To close the Image Tools toolbox, click the Close button in the upper-right corner.

## Rotating Images

You can rotate an image within the graphics box by using the Rotation tool. Figure 21.18 illustrates an image being rotated.

**FIG. 21.18**
Drag any of the rotation handles to rotate the image. All handles enable the image to rotate on a center vertical axis.

To rotate an image, follow these steps:

1. Click Image Tools in the Edit Box dialog box to display the Image Tools toolbox.

 **T I P** You can point the mouse at the graphics box and right-click to display a QuickMenu. Choose Image Tools.

 2. Click the Rotate button. Small double handles appear in the corners of the image.

3. Move the mouse over one of the new handles appearing inside the graphics box until the double-headed arrow appears.
4. Click and drag the handle until the image is rotated the way you want.

## Moving an Image

You can crop—or move the image within the graphics box—by using the Move tool in the toolbox. This tool is handy for repositioning the image to move unwanted areas out of view. To crop an image, follow these steps:

1. In the Image Tools Toolbox, click the <u>M</u>ove tool.
2. Click and drag the image to a new position within the graphics box.

## Scaling an Image

The Scaling tool is exceptionally handy for enlarging an area of an image to cover the entire graphics box. Suppose that an image contains one small section you want to enlarge; you want that small section to be all that shows. Use the Scaling tool by following these steps:

**TIP** To better see the image, especially when using the scroll bars to scale, move the Image Tools toolbox by clicking the window's title bar and dragging it to another location.

1. In the Image Tools toolbox, choose the <u>Z</u>oom tool. A palette menu appears.
2. Choose the method of scaling. You have three choices of scaling the image:

   *Magnifying Glass*. Enables you to draw a box around the area you want to enlarge (see fig. 21.19).

**FIG. 21.19**
Use the Magnifying Glass scale control tool for quick and easy image editing.

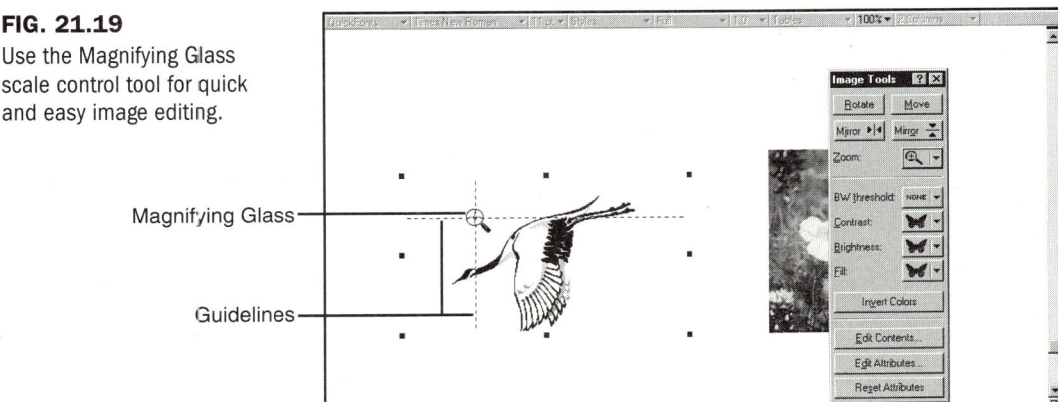

*Up/down arrows*. Add a scroll bar to the figure box. Click the up arrow and the image becomes smaller; click the down arrow and the image becomes larger. Figure 21.20 illustrates the scroll bars.

*1:1 ratio button*. Changes the image back to its original size.

**FIG 21.20**
You can resize the image by using the scroll bar.

## Changing Colors

By using the Image Tools, you can change the colors of an image to its complementary colors, or you can change an image to black and white. *Complementary colors* are those that are opposites on the color wheel: red and green, yellow and purple, and blue and orange, for example. Thus, an image that is red and blue changes to green and orange if you change to complementary colors. For more control over the color of an image, use WP Presentations.

To change colors of the image to its complementary colors, follow these steps:

1. Choose Invert Colors on the Image Tools toolbox.
2. To change the colors back, choose the tool again.

 **T I P** If the image is in black and white, choosing to change to complementary colors switches black to white and white to black in the image.

To change a color image to black and white, follow these steps:

1. Choose a threshold value from the BW Threshold pop-up palette on the Image Tools toolbox.
2. To change the image back, choose Reset Attributes.

## Changing Contrast

Changing the contrast of an image changes the difference between the colors. For example, if you're using a black-and-white image, you can adjust the contrast so that everything is black or white. You can also adjust the contrast so that grays appear and the contrast is not so strong. Figure 21.21 illustrates the contrast tool and a black-and-white figure using a lesser degree of contrast.

**FIG. 21.21**
When changing contrast, make changes in small increments—one step at a time—to see how the changes affect the image. Experimentation is the best guide because each image is different.

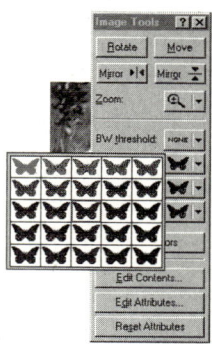

 To change the contrast of an image, choose an option from the Contrast pop-up palette on the Image Tools toolbox.

## Changing Brightness

Changing the brightness is similar to changing contrast, except that *brightness* refers to the intensity of the colors. Experiment with the brightness of the image as you would with the contrast before deciding which setting is best.

 To change the brightness of the image, click the Brightness button in the Image Tools toolbox. A palette appears; choose the preferred brightness.

## Setting Fill

The Fill attributes button controls the lines and fill of the image. You can display the image with fill, as just lines, or as a transparent object. To set the fill for an image, follow these steps:

1. Choose the Fill tool. A palette appears.
2. Choose an option from the Fill pop-up menu on the Image Tools toolbox. The first box represents color or black fill; the second box represents a transparent fill with only lines; the third box represents opaque white fill with lines.

## Mirroring Images

You can choose to mirror an image on its vertical (up-and-down) or horizontal (left to right) axis. Use the mirror tools when you need to flip an image to better suit your document.

  To flip an image, choose either the horizontal or vertical mirror tool in the Image Tools toolbox.

## Using the Image Settings Dialog Box

 You can accomplish all the image editing techniques covered in this section through the use of the Image Settings dialog box. Choose Edit Attributes in the Image Tools toolbox to display the dialog box shown in figure 21.22. The main difference between editing the image with the tools and editing with the Image Settings dialog box is the difference between using the mouse and entering a value for the options. For example, to rotate an image with the Image Settings dialog box, you enter a value between -360 and +360 degrees.

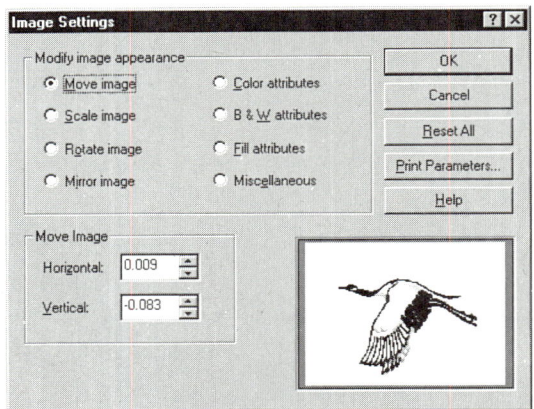

**FIG. 21.22**
As you choose an option in the Modify Image Appearance area, the options in the lower-left corner of the dialog box change. In addition, the image changes in the example box so that you can see the results of the editing.

# Creating Graphics with Drag To Create

The Drag To Create feature enables you to quickly and easily size and position any type of box. By using Drag To Create, you simply click and drag anywhere in your document to create a graphics, text, or custom box.

To use Drag To Create, choose Graphics, Drag To Create. A check mark appears next to the menu item when it is activated. Now choose the type of box you want from the Graphics menu as you normally would. Click the mouse in the document and drag to create an outline of the box you are creating. When you release the mouse button, the box appears.

CHAPTER 22

# Using WordPerfect Draw and TextArt

*by Rick Winter, Sue Plumley, and Alan Westenbroek*

You have seen that working with graphics is fun and helps stimulate ideas, and that graphics add interest to your documents. In addition to the advanced graphics capabilities mentioned in Chapter 21, "Using Advanced Graphics Techniques," WordPerfect 7 comes with WP Draw and TextArt. These modules cost nothing extra and add most of the capabilities that come with separate stand-alone programs such as Corel Presentations and Harvard Graphics. ■

- **Access WP Draw**

  WP Draw is the default WordPerfect 7 drawing module and a complete drawing program that fully supports OLE 2.0 standards.

- **Create and edit shapes such as lines, rectangles, and circles**

  Modifying or adding simple graphic shapes to an existing clip art image can result in effective and attractive documents.

- **Include clip art images within your own drawing**

  WordPerfect 7 includes more than 100 clip art and QuickArt images. You learn effective methods of accessing and including them in your own drawings.

- **Add text to your graphic**

  Explanatory or decorative text can be an important addition to a graphic. Learn how to add text elements to a graphic.

- **Scan images into WP Draw**

  Scanned images such as logos can identify and personalize a drawing.

- **Use TextArt to create text with a variety of shapes and special effects**

  Molding text into an effective shape can add interest to an otherwise dull headline. TextArt enables you to dress up your text for interest!

**NOTE** When you installed WordPerfect 7, you probably used the Setup program from the Corel WordPerfect Suite 7. You may have used Setup's Typical installation selection for the complete Suite, or included Presentations when performing a Custom installation. By doing so, Corel Presentations was also installed.

Presentations is a full-featured graphics program that allows you to create and edit sophisticated graphics along with powerful slide presentations. When installed, Presentations automatically becomes your draw module within WordPerfect rather than WP Draw.

Because WP Draw is a scaled-down version of Presentations, you can use the instructions in this chapter. Presentations has additional features that are not included with WP Draw. For more information about Presentations, refer to the section in Chapter 28, "Using Presentations with WordPerfect."

# Starting WP Draw

How you start WP Draw depends on whether you are creating a new drawing or editing an existing one.

## Creating a New Drawing

To start WP Draw to create a new drawing, follow these steps:

1. Position the insertion point in your WordPerfect document where you want to insert your graphic.

2. Choose <u>G</u>raphics, <u>D</u>raw. WP Draw opens a drawing area within the current document, substituting the WordPerfect menu and Toolbar with its own. The drawing area is surrounded by a border that includes eight sizing handles.

**TIP** Sizing handles look like small black squares, and appear at each corner and at the middle of each side. You can drag any of the sizing handles to make the drawing area within your document larger or smaller.

With WP Draw open, you can now create graphics using any of the WP Draw tools, as you learn in this chapter.

3. To exit WP Draw and switch back to WordPerfect, just click outside the thick border around the drawing area.

> **NOTE** Because WP Draw is an OLE-based application, you can create a WP Draw object in any application that supports OLE. From that other application, use its Insert Object command (the location varies from application to application) to create a WP Draw 7 Drawing.

## Editing an Existing Graphic

To start WP Draw to edit an existing graphic, double-click an embedded WordPerfect graphic (see fig. 22.1).

**FIG. 22.1**
WP Draw is launched, enabling you to modify the image.

## Updating Your Document

Using WP Draw to create a drawing doesn't actually add the image to your document until WP Draw is instructed to do so. Likewise, when you edit a WordPerfect graphic in a document using WP Draw, you must update your document to save those changes to the document. When ready, you can add the graphic to your document, spreadsheet, or presentation using one of the following methods:

- From the WP Draw Toolbar, click the OLE Update button to add the new or edited graphic to the document and continue working in WP Draw.

- Click the OLE Close button to add the new or edited graphic to the document and exit WP Draw.

- Click anywhere else in the document to deselect the graphic. WordPerfect regains control of its Toolbar and menus and updates the drawing.

Remember, you have embedded the graphic in your document. If you do not save the document in WordPerfect (or another program), the graphic and any other changes since the last save are lost.

**N O T E** If you do not see your graphic in the document, you may be in Draft view or have graphics turned off. In WordPerfect, for example, you must choose View, Graphics to see your graphics.

▶ See "Using Help," **p. 45**

# Exploring WP Draw

Whether you enter WP Draw from WordPerfect for Windows or another program, you see the same WP Draw controls (refer to fig. 22.1). WP Draw works in much the same way as do other graphics products. The WP Draw controls are intuitive, and you can quickly become familiar with them, even if you are accustomed to using other graphics products.

## Glancing at the Pull-Down Menus

WP Draw's menu bar is almost identical to WordPerfect's. In fact, notice that the only difference between the two menus are that the WordPerfect menu includes a Table option while WP Draw does not. The choices listed under the main menu headings differ, however. Table 22.1 provides a general description for each of the items on the WP Draw menu bar.

▶ See "Understanding the Editing Screen," **p. 16**

▶ See "Working with Multiple Documents," **p. 43**

▶ See "Customizing a Toolbar," **p. 420**

**Table 22.1  Functions Accessible Through the WP Draw Menus**

| Item | Function |
|---|---|
| File | Remains unchanged from WordPerfect's default File menu. |
| Edit | Undoes last command; cuts, copies, pastes, selects, and controls links; and rotates selected items. |
| View | Shows or does not show tools such as Toolbar, ruler, grid, and Reveal Codes; and changes view size of picture. |

| Item | Function |
|---|---|
| <u>I</u>nsert | Inserts drawing elements, other objects, date, and time. |
| Fo<u>r</u>mat | Adds or changes text or graphic layout options. |
| <u>G</u>raphics | Changes the order and orientation of graphic elements and controls Contour Text. |
| <u>T</u>ools | Starts any of the writing tool modules (such as Spell Checker and Thesaurus) and Macro tools. |
| <u>W</u>indow | Displays more than one document window or moves to a different document window. |
| <u>H</u>elp | Finds more information about WP Draw. |

## Using WP Drawing Tools

The WP Draw screen also includes its own Toolbar. The buttons provide you with shortcuts to the most frequently used procedures within WP Draw. Although the default for the program is having the Toolbar on, if the Toolbar does not display choose <u>V</u>iew, <u>T</u>oolbar.

Table 22.2 lists and describes the functions of the buttons on the Toolbar.

**Table 22.2  Functions of the WP Draw Toolbar**

| Button | Function |
|---|---|
|  | Updates the OLE object in the document. |
|  | Updates the OLE object in the document and closes WP Draw. |
|  | Saves the current drawing. |
|  | Cuts the selected item(s) to the Clipboard. |
|  | Copies the selected item(s) to the Clipboard. |
|  | Pastes the contents of the Clipboard. |
|  | Undoes the last action. |

*continues*

## Table 22.2 Continued

| Button | Function |
|---|---|
| | Redoes the last undo. |
| | Makes the selected text bold. |
| | Makes the selected text italic. |
| | Makes the selected text underlined. |
| | Flips the selected item vertically. |
| | Flips the selected item horizontally. |
| | Views or hides the ruler. |
| | Views or hides the grid. |
| | Snaps drawing objects and tools to the grid points. |
| | Copies the attributes of the selected object. |
| | Applies copied attributes to the selected object(s). |
| | Opens the Font Properties dialog box. |
| | Lets you change the properties of lines. |
| | Lets you change the fill attributes of objects. |
| | Launches Ask the PerfectExpert. |
| | Launches your Web browser. |

## Viewing the Tool Palette

The Tool palette on the left side of the screen enables you to select, view, create, and modify graphic items (see fig. 22.2). The tools are divided into three sections: Selection, Drawing, and Attribute.

**FIG. 22.2**
The Tool palette enables you to create and edit graphics quickly.

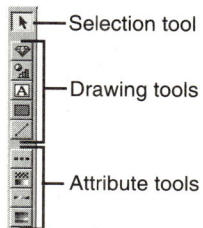

## Viewing the Ruler and Grid

The View menu offers two features that can help make your work more precise. These features are the WP Draw ruler and grid (see fig. 22.3). The ruler displays at the top and left side of the drawing window. The grid marks the drawing window's background display with evenly spaced vertical and horizontal lines. The grid helps you position graphics more accurately on the page.

**FIG. 22.3**
The View menu enables you to display the ruler and grid. Use View, Grid/Snap, Grid/Snap Options to change the spacing for the grid.

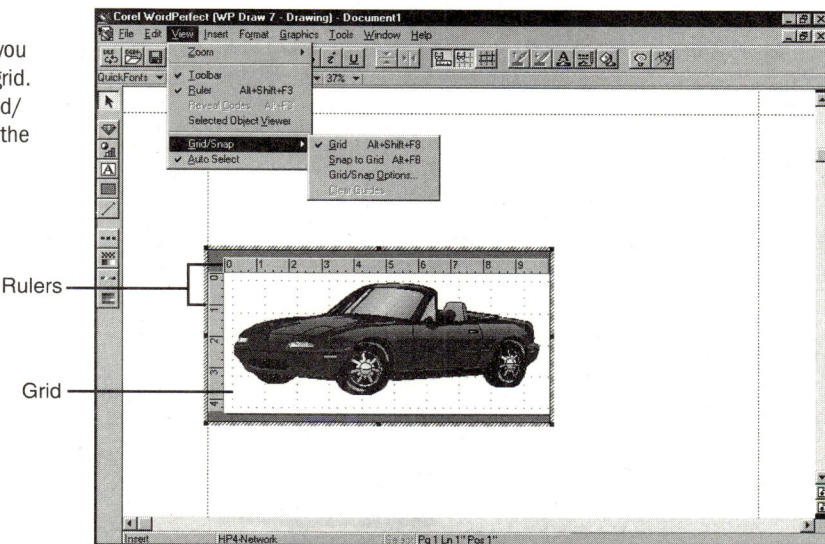

To turn the ruler on or off, choose View, Ruler. To turn the grid on or off, choose View, Grid/Snap, Grid. If you want the lines and boxes you are creating to align with the grid, choose View, Grid/Snap, Snap To Grid.

## Creating Shapes

To draw a shape, you need to select the shape tool from the Drawing Tools palette. When you move the mouse pointer into the drawing area, the cursor changes to a crosshair. Depending on the shape you choose to draw, click to start the object, click to add points, and double-click to end the object; or you click and drag the mouse to draw the object. The different kinds of shapes you can create are shown in figure 22.4.

**FIG. 22.4**
You can create a variety of shapes by using the WP Draw drawing tools.

In WP Draw, you can choose attributes (such as line width, fill pattern, or font) before you begin drawing shapes or entering text, or you can apply the attributes after you finish creating the shape or text. If you choose attributes before you begin drawing, those attributes apply to all shapes you create (until you change the attributes). If you apply attributes after drawing, you select the shapes or text (objects) to which you want to assign the attributes. The attributes, then, only apply to the selected objects.

You can select attributes by using the various attribute tools or through the options in the Format menu in the WP Draw menu bar. The Attribute tools provide basic choices; the Format menu options provide more specific choices.

For more information on changing attributes, see "Changing the Shape Attributes" later in this chapter.

## Using the Drawing Tools

The Drawing tools are located in the Tool palette on the left side of the WP Draw window. Each Drawing tool has a specific use, but some tools have more than one function. You can draw a rectangle or a perfect square with the Rectangle tool, for example, and you can draw an oval or a perfect circle with the Ellipse tool. To use a tool, you must first click it with the mouse.

The drawing tools are grouped into five categories. To select a specific tool from each group, click and hold down the mouse over the group tool you want. A palette of choices appears from which you can select the object type you want to draw. Now drag the pointer over the specific tool you want to use. For example, when you click and hold the Closed Shapes group tool, you can then choose between the shapes of rectangles and circles, among others. To draw a rectangle, continue to press the mouse while you drag the pointer to the rectangle shape. Release the mouse pointer to complete your selection. Table 22.3 lists the object types available for each drawing tool.

> **NOTE** In Presentations, the drawing tools are grouped into four categories; QuickArt and Charts are now located on the same tool button.

**Table 22.3  Object Types Available for Drawing Tools**

| Tool Name | Function |
| --- | --- |
| QuickArt | Inserts a QuickArt graphic. |
| Charts | Displays the Charts palette from which you can choose to create either a data chart or an organization chart. |
| Text | Displays a Text palette from which you can choose to create a text area (which you can then size) or a single text line. |
| Closed Shapes | Enables you to create a rectangle, rounded rectangle, circle, ellipse, polygon, and closed curve, arrow, or regular polygon. |
| Line | Enables you to create a line, curve, ellipse section, multi-part line, free-hand, and circle section tools. |

As you select a tool, the mouse pointer appears as an arrow. When you move to the drawing area, the mouse pointer changes to a crosshair or a hand with a box. A crosshair indicates that you are ready to begin creating your chosen object. The hand and box pointer indicate that you must press and drag the mouse within the drawing window to identify the space to be used for your object. For example, when you want to create a text area, the hand and box pointer appears. Click and drag the mouse pointer (the hand and box) from one corner to the opposite corner, then release. The text area border appears, surrounding the area you indicated.

## Using the Mouse and Keyboard To Draw

The following information describes the general procedures for drawing with the mouse and the keyboard. The descriptions of these procedures assume that you use the left mouse button as the primary button. If you've reassigned your mouse buttons so that the right button is primary, be sure to adjust these procedures. You need a mouse to draw an object, but you can control drawing by using the mouse and the keyboard together.

**Drawing with the Left Mouse Button**  Depending on which shape on the Drawing Tools palette you have selected to draw, you can use one of three general procedures to create the shape with the mouse:

- To create rectangles, rounded rectangles, ellipses, and elliptical arcs, and to define the area for a chart, figure, and text, press and hold the mouse and drag the mouse pointer from one corner to the opposite corner of the drawing or drawing area.

- To create lines, polygons, closed curves, and curves, click the left mouse button for each corner or change in direction. Then double-click the left button to end. If you want to completely start over before you double-click, press Esc. To remove a corner or change in direction, press Backspace.

- For freehand drawing, press and hold the mouse and drag the mouse pointer across the drawing area. When you release the mouse button, the drawing is completed.

**Moving the Shape with the Right Mouse Button**  If you are in the middle of drawing a shape and want to reposition the location of the shape, press and hold the right mouse button and drag the shape to the new location.

**Deleting with Esc and Backspace**  When you draw lines, polygons, closed curves, and curves, you can completely start over before you finish the shape by pressing Esc. Similarly, you can back up one step in a jointed drawing by pressing Backspace. For example, assume that you are drawing a jointed line. You've drawn three of the four sides and realize that the third joint is incorrectly placed. Press Backspace to delete the last joint, then continue drawing.

To remove a shape immediately after you create it, choose Edit, Undo; or press Ctrl+Z. This technique works only if you have not pressed any other keys or performed any other function since you created the shape. You can continue to Undo changes to your drawing, which reverses each of your drawing steps. Suppose you are drawing a polygon and have anchored the first three corners, and then change your mind about the position of the last-placed corner. Press Backspace, and the last-placed corner is removed.

**Constraining the Shape with Shift**   To draw a straight vertical, horizontal, or 45-degree line or polygon edge, hold down Shift before you click or drag the mouse. To create a square, rounded square, circle, or radius of a circle, hold down Shift when using the Rectangle, Rounded Rectangle, Ellipse, or Elliptical Arc tools or options.

▶ **See** "Using the Mouse," **p. 14**

### TROUBLESHOOTING

**WP Draw takes forever to start, or won't start at all.** WordPerfect uses OLE 2.0 to accomplish switching transparently between its different modules. OLE is a powerful tool, but has steep RAM requirements. Machines with less than 8M of memory usually exhibit poor performance when using OLE 2.0. If WP Draw is slow starting or fails to start, you may need more memory in your computer.

**When I double-click an image for editing, the WP Draw window that opens is too small to work with. How can I make it bigger?** The WP Draw window just large enough to fit around the image you are editing. Sometimes, especially if the image is small, the WP Draw window is too small to allow for precise editing. A simple solution is to increase the Zoom size of the actual display. Open the drop-down Zoom button on the Power Bar to change to a larger display (zooming in closer to the actual image makes it larger on-screen). To get even closer, select Zoom To Area from the Zoom button, then drag to select the area that you really need to get close to.

**I can't get all of my images to line up neatly.** Precisely placing images by hand can sometimes be nearly impossible. A simple method to line up images is to first select all the images to be aligned. Then right-click to access the WP Draw QuickMenu. Select Align, then choose one of the alignment options. You can align elements to their left, right, top, or bottom edges, or you can align them to their left/right, top/bottom, or both center points.

# Drawing a Shape

After you start WP Draw, you can draw lines, rectangles, ellipses, and curves, and add figures. You can even use the mouse as a pencil and draw freehand. If you don't have the time to create your own drawings, you can choose from the QuickArt clip art drawings that install with WordPerfect, figures that come with WordPerfect, or from thousands of clip art figures available on the market.

A *figure* or *image* is a drawing you have created and saved from a graphic program or a from figure that was created by someone else (also called *clip art*). You can save a graphic in WP Draw as a figure by itself; click the Save button on the Toolbar.

## Drawing a Line

The Line tool allows you to draw a straight line. If you want to change the line into an arrow, choose Fo_r_mat, Li_n_e Attributes and select _B_eginning, _E_nding, or B_o_th Ends under _A_rrowhead in the Line Options area to draw the arrowhead at the first point, the last point, or both ends, respectively.

> **N O T E** The steps here are different for Presentations. Instead, you can choose Fo_r_mat, Object Properties; click the Line Joints/Ends tab in the dialog box; and choose Beginning, End, or Both Ends.

To draw a line or polygon, follow these steps:

1. Select the Line tool from the Drawing tools.
2. Move the crosshair mouse pointer to the beginning of the line.
3. Hold down the left mouse button to begin the line or border.
4. Drag to where you want the line to end, and release the mouse button.

To create straight vertical or horizontal lines or to create a line with a 45-degree angle, hold down Shift while you drag the pointer in step 4.

## Drawing Lines, Polygons, Curves, and Closed Curves

In addition to drawing straight lines, you can draw a line with multiple changes in direction. You can draw other shapes that have multiple sides as well. These shapes include polygons, closed curves, and curves.

A *polygon* is a multi-sided enclosed shape such as a triangle, pentagon, or hexagon. You can fill the polygon or leave it empty with only the border showing. Squares and rectangles are polygons, but WP Draw provides the Rectangle and Rounded Rectangle tools to help you draw those shapes. A *regular polygon* is one in which all sides have an equal length.

The current line color and line pattern applies to curves as well as lines and becomes the border of polygons, closed curves, and other shapes. You can change the fill pattern, fill color, and turn the Fill attribute on or off. For more information on this technique, see the section "Filling Solids" later in this chapter.

To draw a multiple-sided line, curve, polygon, or closed curve, follow these steps:

1. Select one of the following tools: Multi-Part Line, Curve, Polygon, or Closed Curve.
2. Position the crosshair pointer where you want to begin drawing the line or shape, and click the left mouse button.
3. Move the crosshair pointer to the position where you want to place the second point of the shape.
4. Click the left mouse button to begin the next side of the shape or a change in direction for the line (see fig. 22.5).
5. Repeat steps 3 and 4 for each change in direction of the line or side of the polygon.
6. Double-click the mouse for the last point of the line or polygon.

When you are drawing lines and polygons, to create straight vertical or horizontal lines or to create a line with a 45-degree angle, hold down Shift before you draw the line in step 3.

**FIG. 22.5**
Click the left mouse button to indicate a change in direction when you draw lines, curves, closed curves, and polygons.

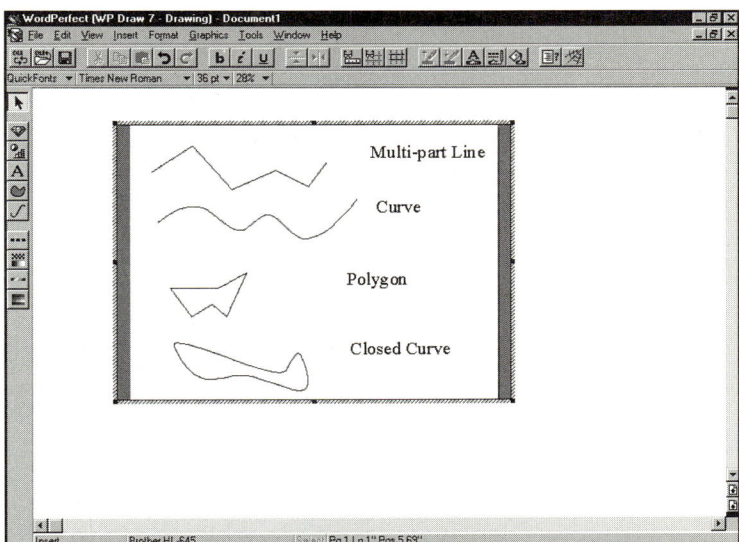

## Drawing Rectangles, Arcs, and Ellipses

A *rectangle* is a four-sided polygon. An *ellipse* is a shape with no corners. Ovals and circles are examples of ellipses. An *arc* is a portion of an ellipse's border. In WP Draw, you use the same technique to draw rectangles, ellipses, regular polygons, arrows, and arcs.

▶ See "Using Graphics Lines," **p. 250**
▶ See "Using Graphics Borders," **p. 255**

▶ **See** "Changing Table Lines, Borders, and Fills," **p. 524**
▶ **See** "Creating the Chart," **p. 541**

**N O T E**  You can use the Polygon tool to create a rectangle, but you have only your eye to vertically and horizontally align such a rectangle. When you print the rectangle, it may not be perfectly parallel to the sides of the paper. To help you draw rectangles that are parallel to the sides of the paper, use the WP Draw Rectangle tool or the Rounded Rectangle tool.

To draw a rectangle, arc, regular polygon, or ellipse (as shown in fig. 22.6), follow these steps:

1. Select one of the following tools:

   | Rectangle | Rounded Rectangle |
   | Circle | Ellipse |
   | Elliptical Arc | Regular Polygon |

2. Position the crosshair pointer where you want to begin the shape (in the case of a regular polygon, you must also specify the number of polygon sides).

3. Press and hold the left mouse button, and drag the crosshair pointer toward the position where you want to create the opposite corner of the shape. An outline of the shape appears as you drag the mouse.

4. When the crosshair pointer reaches the position where you want the opposite corner of the shape, release the mouse button. The screen displays the completed shape.

**FIG. 22.6**
Hold down Shift when you draw an ellipse to turn it into a circle. Choosing the Circle tool will draw a circle from the center out. Likewise, with a square, hold down Shift while you draw the rectangle to turn it into a square.

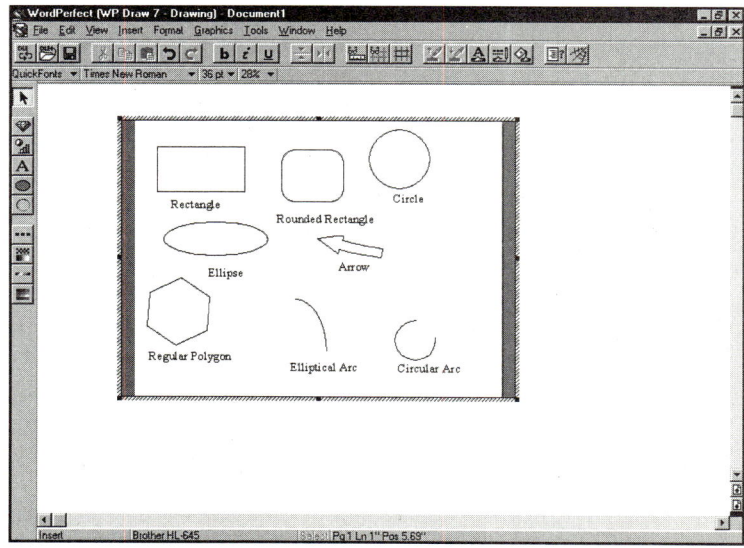

**NOTE** For Arrows, click once when you start the arrow, then click again when to end the arrow. You can also "twist" either end of an arrow by clicking and dragging rather than just clicking. For Circular Arcs, you can click and drag to anchor the beginning and ending points of the arc, then stretch the curve of the arc by moving the mouse, and double-click to finish.

**NOTE** By default, WP Draw shapes as you draw them—usually with solid blue. You can easily change the color, turn off the color, or even use fill patterns by using the attribute tools on the Tools palette. Likewise, you can easily change the color, width, and pattern for the shape's lines or borders.

For example, to change the fill color of an object, open the fill color palette by clicking the Fill Color tool. Now click the color you want to use. Your selected color is applied either to the currently selected object or, if no objects were selected, to all new objects as you draw them. More information about the Fill Color tool, as well as the other attribute tools, can be found later in this chapter.

## Drawing Squares and Circles

A *square* is a rectangle that is of equal length on all sides. In WP Draw, a *circle* is an ellipse in which all points of the border are an equal distance from the center point.

**TIP** Although you can draw rectangles with the Polygon tool, use the Rectangle or Rounded Rectangle tool if you want the rectangle's sides to be exactly horizontal and vertical.

You use the same tools and techniques to draw a square or circle that you use to draw a rectangle or ellipse, except you hold down the Shift key as you draw.

## Drawing Freehand

Using the Freehand tool is similar to drawing with a colored pencil. If you are a good artist and skilled at using the mouse, you can draw fairly sophisticated shapes in WP Draw.

To draw a freehand shape, follow these steps:

1. Select the Freehand tool.
2. Hold the mouse button down as you drag the crosshair across the drawing area to draw the shape.
3. Release the mouse button when you finish drawing the shape.

## Drawing Arrows

Two types of arrows can easily be drawn using WP Draw:

- A line with an arrowhead positioned at the beginning, end, or both ends of the line. Arrows of this type are often used in documentation, placed over the top of text or screen shots.
- Best described as a large, sweeping, arrow. This arrow type is used more as a graphic element rather than a "pointing" tool.

Both of these arrows types can be seen in figure 22.7.

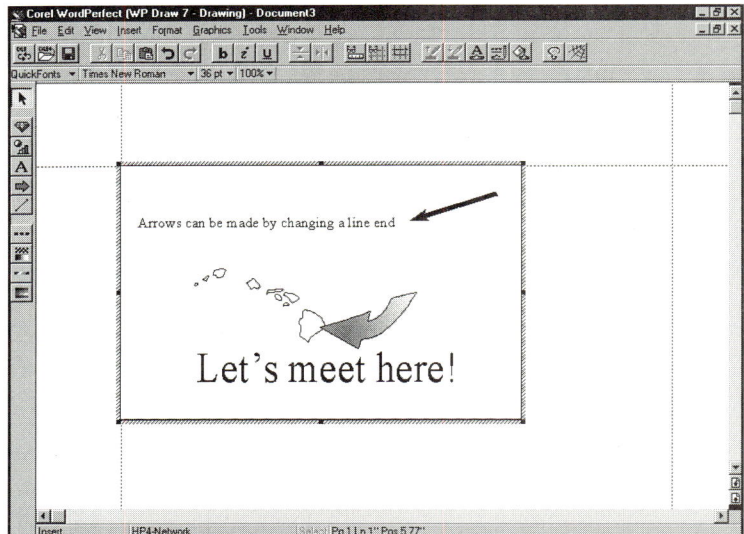

**FIG. 22.7**
Arrows can be used to call attention to another element in a drawing.

**Creating Line End Arrows** The simplest arrows can be created by adding arrowheads to the ends of a line. Like changing another attribute, you can add an arrowhead either before or after you actually draw your line. As previously discussed, if you make attribute changes (in this case, adding the arrowheads) before drawing a line, the arrowhead automatically appears on each new line as you draw it. If, however, you first select a previously created line, the arrowhead is only added to the selected line.

To add or change arrowhead attributes, use these steps:

1. From within the WP Draw window, choose Format, Object Properties. The Object Properties dialog box opens.

2. Choose the Line Joints/End tab (see fig. 22.8).
3. Choose the Arrowheads location you want to use.

**FIG. 22.8**
The Object Properties dialog box enables you to customize fills, line widths and styles, and line ends and line joints for each object in your drawing.

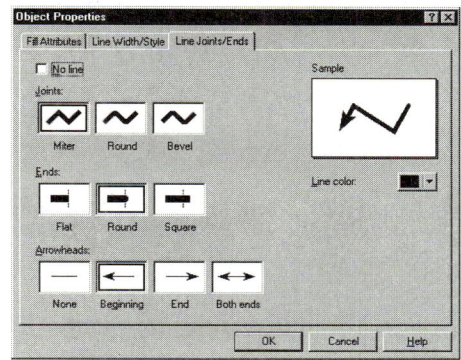

**Creating Sweeping Arrows**   Sweeping arrows are typically used as graphic elements in a figure. WP Draw enables you to actually draw and manipulate the arrow by twisting the arrowhead, its tail, and so on. To create a sweeping arrow, from the WP Draw window, select the Arrow tool from the Closed Shapes Tool palette. The mouse pointer now appears as a crosshair when placed over the drawing window. Then, do one of the following:

- To draw a simple arrow, click the drawing to indicate the starting position for the arrow point. As you move your mouse, you can see the arrow shape and size. When the arrow is at the right length, click to lock in its shape.

- To draw a curved sweeping arrow, click and hold the mouse pointer to define the total approximate length for the arrowhead and its tail, then release the mouse. Now move the mouse pointer. As you do, you see the arrow take shape. When the shape is correct, click the mouse button.

- To draw an arrow with double curves, follow the steps in the previous bullet. However, rather than just clicking the mouse button, click and hold the mouse button again to add a second curve length. When the length is about right, release the mouse button. Now move the mouse pointer and watch the second curve appear. When the shape is correct, click the mouse button.

 As with any object, you can easily size your arrow after it has been created by selecting it and dragging one of its sizing handles.

# Retrieving and Positioning Clip Art

Most of us are not artists and are too unskilled with the mouse to create anything except crude drawings with the Freehand tool. Luckily for us, great libraries of clip art (or pre-drawn art) are available, including a number of figures that come with WordPerfect.

If you installed WordPerfect to the default folders, your clip art is located in the \COREL\OFFICE7\GRAPHICS folder. This folder contains many figures that you can place in your document directly through the Graphics Figure features. If you want to modify the clip art, you can bring the figure into WP Draw and change it.

**FIG. 22.9**
These figures are available from the C:\OFFICE\WPWIN\GRAPHICS\PICTURES\FOODPROD folder.

To add clip art to your drawing within WP Draw, as shown in figure 22.9, follow these steps:

1. Select the QuickArt tool.
2. Move the mouse pointer into the drawing area; the pointer becomes a hand with a rectangle.
3. Drag the pointer from one corner of the area where you want to place the graphic to the opposite corner.
4. Release the mouse button; the QuickArt Browser dialog box appears (see fig. 22.10).

5. If necessary, change the Look In drop-down list to display WordPerfect's GRAPHICS folder. If you installed WordPerfect 7 in the default location, the graphics are in the \COREL\OFFICE7\GRAPHICS folder. You can quickly move to the default graphics directly by choosing it from the Go To/From Favorites list.

**FIG. 22.10**
More than 100 clip art files come with WordPerfect. Open folders or scroll to the file you want in the File list box.

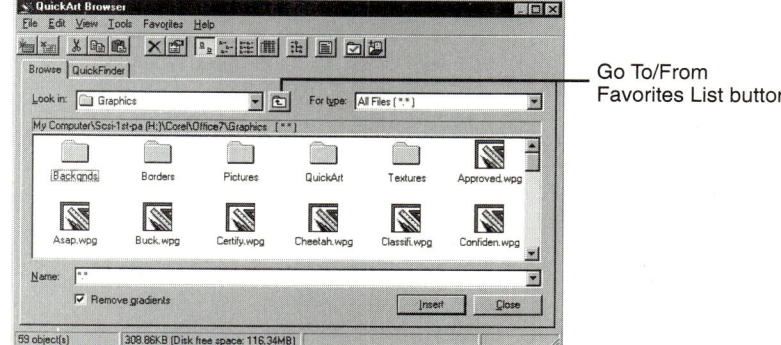

Go To/From Favorites List button

6. If you have other clip art or different programs, you can change the file type in the For Type drop-down list.

7. Select the name of the file by typing the file name in the Name text box or by choosing from the scroll list box.

8. When you have selected the file for the graphic that you want to use, choose Insert or double-click the file.

▶ See "Retrieving a Graphics Image," **p. 676**
▶ See "Finding Files," **p. 928**

 **T I P** You are not limited to the WPG files found in the GRAPHICS folder. In the \COREL\OFFICE7\GRAPHICS\QUICKART folder is a file called STANDARD.QAD. By using WordPerfect or Presentations, users can access this file which contains many QuickArt images.

To remove QuickArt from the STANDARD.QAD file, follow steps 1-5, then double-click STANDARD.QAD. You are presented with a hierarchical structure of QuickArt images that are stored in different categories. Double-click any category to find the QuickArt you want, then choose Insert.

**N O T E** An alternative way to bring a figure into the drawing area is to choose Insert, File, and then choose the figure's name from the Insert File dialog box. When you bring in a figure this way, you can edit individual pieces of the figure.

*continues*

*continued*

When you use the Figure tool to retrieve a figure, the entire figure is grouped together. Notice that when you drag on the figure, the entire figure moves. To edit portions of such a figure, double-click the figure. A blue-hashed bounding box appears around the figure. During this mode you can edit portions of the figure.

**NOTE** WordPerfect can directly use graphic files from a large number of different vendor formats. The following is a list of available file types:

| | |
|---|---|
| WP Graphics (WPG) | Adobe Photoshop bitmap (PSD) |
| AutoCAD (DXF) | Bitmaps (BMP) |
| CALS Bitmap (CAL) | Computer Graphics Metafile (CGM) |
| Corel PHOTO-PAINT (CPT) | Adobe Illustrator/Encapsulated Postscript (EPS) |
| Freelance Graphics (PRE) | Graphics Interchange Format (GIF) |
| GEM Paint Image (IMG) | Harvard Graphics (PRS, SH3, CH3) |
| HP Graphics Language (HPG) | Joint Photgraphic Experts Group (JPG) |
| Kodak Photo CD (PCD) | Lotus PIC (PIC) |
| Macintosh PICT (PCT) | MacPaint (MAC) |
| Micrografx Draw/Designer (DRW) | PC Paintbrush (PCX) |
| Picture Publisher 4 bitmap (PP4) | Powerpoint (PPT) |
| Scitex CT bitmap (SCT) | TIFF bitmap (TIF) |
| Truevision Targa bitmap (TGA) | Wavelet bitmap (WVL) |
| Windows Metafiles (WMF) | WordPerfect Masters (MST) |
| WordPerfect Presentations (SHW) | |

Be certain that any clip art you purchase has one of these file type formats available, or can export to one of these file types (most graphic packages will). Although you can retrieve and work with these file types in WP Draw, the best graphics type for editing is WordPerfect's own graphic file type, WPG.

# Inserting a Chart into Your Drawing

As a rule, the easiest way to enter Chart Edit mode from WordPerfect document is via the Chart button on the Toolbar or by choosing <u>G</u>raphics, Cha<u>r</u>t. If you are working in a WP Draw window, however, you also can insert a chart into a WP Draw drawing, by choosing

Insert, Data Chart. This can be a handy method of combining the chart with drawing shapes or figures.

To insert a chart into the drawing, follow these steps:

1. Double-click the drawing to display the drawing in WP Draw.
2. Choose the Chart tool.
3. Move the mouse pointer into the drawing area; the pointer becomes a hand with a rectangle.
4. Press and hold the left mouse button and drag the pointer from one corner of the graphic area to the opposite corner; release the mouse button. The Data Chart Gallery dialog box appears.
5. Choose a chart type from the Chart Type list, select a visual example of the chart formatting you want, then choose OK. The Datasheet appears along with a chart.

▶ **See** "Creating the Chart," **p. 541**
▶ **See** "Changing the Appearance of the Chart," **p. 548**
▶ **See** "Changing the Underlying Data," **p. 544**

# Editing a Figure

After you retrieve a figure or draw any of the shapes available with WP Draw, you may want to edit or delete all or parts of the drawing. If you want to change the attributes, see the section "Changing the Shape Attributes" later in this chapter.

## Selecting an Item

Before you can change an item such as a drawn shape or an imported figure, you first must select the shape or figure.

To select an item, follow these steps:

1. Choose the Select tool.
2. Click the item to select it (see figs. 22.11 and 22.12).
3. If you want to select more than one item, hold down Ctrl or Shift and click another item.

You can select all items by choosing Edit, Select, All, or by choosing the Select tool and then dragging around the objects you want to select.

**FIG. 22.11**
When you select an item in the drawing window, small black handles surround the item.

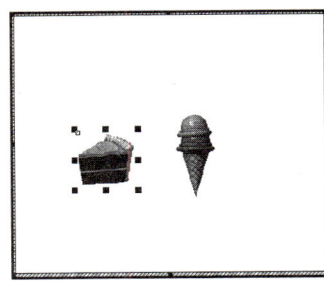

**FIG. 22.12**
When you select more than one item, the black handles surround all objects, and a small white handle appears next to each individual item within the selection group.

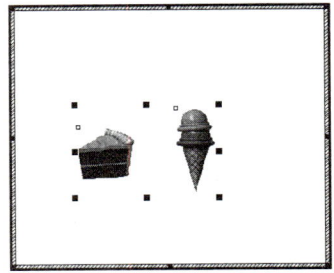

## Deleting an Item

After you have selected an item(s), you can delete them by pressing Delete. If you accidentally delete the wrong item, immediately choose Edit, Undo; or press Ctrl+Z.

If you want to delete everything in the drawing area, choose Edit, Clear, press Ctrl+Shift+F4, or simply press Delete. At the Clear dialog box prompt, choose Yes.

## Moving an Item

If you have one or more items selected, you can move the selection.

To move items, follow these steps:

1. Select the item or items to move.
2. Press and hold the left mouse button and drag the mouse pointer from the center of one of the items. As you drag, a gray outline of the shape moves with the mouse pointer.
3. Release the mouse when the item(s) are in the proper position.

Editing a Figure 705

**N O T E**  If you are moving a single item, you can select and move the item in one step by dragging the item. If you try to move multiple items and they become deselected, you did not drag from the inside of one of the selected items. If the item you are clicking has no fill pattern, you must click its border to select it.

## Copying an Item

You can repeat an item on the same drawing, copy it to another drawing, copy it to a document within WordPerfect, or even copy the item to another program. The following sections explain the techniques for accomplishing these tasks in WP Draw.

**Copying Within the Drawing Area**   To create a copy of an item within the same drawing, follow these steps:

1. Choose the Select tool.
2. Position the mouse pointer on the item you want to copy.
3. While pressing both the Ctrl key and the mouse button, drag to the location you want your copy to appear.
4. Release both the mouse button and the Ctrl key. The copied item appears in the new location while the original item is unchanged.

**T I P**  To duplicate an item within a drawing window and keep it on the same vertical or horizontal axis, or at a 45-degree angle to the original item, press and hold both the Shift key while you drag the item.

**Copying to Another Document or Program**   To copy an item directly to a document, follow these steps:

1. Select an item on your drawing.
2. Choose Edit, Copy; or press Ctrl+C. Windows copies the item to the Clipboard.
3. Move to another open document by changing to that document's window, or to another program by using Alt+Tab or the taskbar.
4. Position the insertion point where you want to place the copy of the item.

5. Choose Edit, Paste or press Ctrl+V.

**N O T E**  If the application you are pasting the WP Draw object into supports OLE, you can choose Edit, Paste Special, WP Draw 7 Drawing Object. This action pastes the graphic as a WP Draw OLE object which can then be edited using WP Draw. Activate WP Draw from within that application by double-clicking the object.

## Changing the Size and Shape

You can make an object larger or smaller by dragging one of the handles surrounding the object.

If you change only the width or height of a graphic image, you can significantly alter the proportions of the figure or shape (see fig. 22.13).

**FIG. 22.13**
You can create special effects by changing the width or height of an item. This example uses a widened figure.

You also can alter the size, shape, and orientation of a selected figure by the following methods:

- To flip the selected figure top to bottom, use the Flip Top/Bottom tool.
- To flip the selected figure to a mirror image, use the Flip Left/Right tool.
- To rotate the selected figure, choose Edit, Rotate and drag one of the corner selection markers. If you drag one of the side selection markers, and you will skew the object instead of rotating it.
- If two items are stacked on top of each other, select one and choose Graphics, Order, Front to bring the selected item in front of the other item. Or, choose Graphics, Order, Back to move the selected item behind the other item.
  - ▶ See "Transferring Selected Text to Another Location," **p. 104**
  - ▶ See "Editing a Graphics Image," **p. 677**

# Changing the Shape Attributes

You can apply attributes such as colors and patterns to shapes before or after you create the shapes. If you select attributes before drawing the shapes, the attributes apply to all shapes you subsequently draw. To modify existing shapes, select the shape(s), and then change attributes. These changes affect only the shapes you selected; they do not affect non-selected shapes or shapes you draw later.

You can change an attribute with an attribute tool, or for more choices, you can change an attribute through the Fo_r_mat menu.

## Applying Color

You can use a number of methods to apply color to a shape. WP Draw offers two color palettes in addition to the _C_olor Palettes menu choice on the Fo_r_mat menu. You also can define colors from options on dialog boxes for line, fill, text, and shadow.

The easiest way to change colors is through the Line Color palette and the Fill Color palette. In WP Draw, *line color* refers to the color for lines, curves, elliptical arcs, and freehand drawing; the term also refers to the border surrounding closed curves, polygons, ellipses, and rounded rectangles. You can fill the area inside the border with a different color or colored pattern, referred to as *fill color*.

▶ **See** "Printing Documents with Graphics or Color," **p. 206**
▶ **See** "Using Color," **p. 750**
▶ **See** "Creating a Color Document," **p. 756**

## Using the Color Palettes

To change the line color, follow these steps:

1. Click the Line Color palette; the current color palette appears.
2. Click the color you want to use for the line or border.

To change the fill color, follow these steps:

1. Click the Fill Color palette; the current color palette appears, offering choices for the Pattern or Gradient color and for the Background color. (Refer to the next section for more information about how these two color options are used.) For most single-color images, choose from the Pattern/Gradient Color palette.
2. Click the color or colored pattern you want to use to fill your shapes.

## Using More Options To Change Colors

If you select a pattern other than a solid for your shapes, the pattern can have two colors. One portion of the pattern (for example, the lines) is the foreground color, and the other portion of the pattern (for example, the space between the lines) is the background color.

When you select the Fill Color palette, you can change the foreground color with the left mouse button and the background color with the right mouse button.

To choose or define a new color palette, follow these steps:

1. Choose Format, Color Palettes; the Color Palettes dialog box appears (see fig. 22.14).

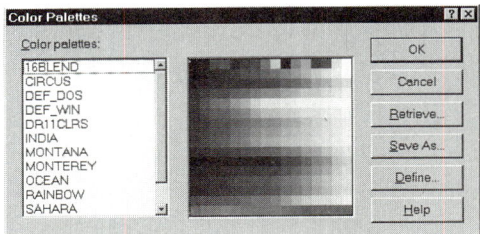

**FIG. 22.14**
Use the Color Palettes dialog box to create custom color palettes.

2. If you saved a different color palette earlier (through the Save As command button), select it from the Color Palettes list or click the Retrieve button and select the appropriate color palette file name. Choose OK to return to the Color Attributes dialog box.

   If you do not see the color you want on the current palette, click the Define button to display the Define Color Palette dialog box (see fig. 22.15).

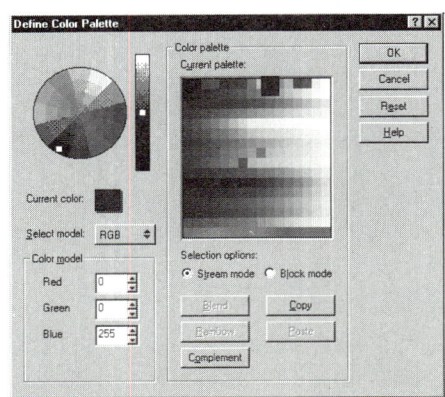

**FIG. 22.15**
In the Define Color Palette dialog box, a color wheel appears and the current color is displayed in a box under the color wheel.

3. Click the color in the Current Palette area that you want to change.
4. Change the current color by changing to one of the Select Model types (RGB, Red Green Blue; HLS, Hue Lightness Saturation; CMYK, Cyan Magenta Yellow Black) and by changing the values for each of the portions of the color models. You also can change the current palette by changing the Selection Options section below the palette. If you want more description on these options on the Define Color Palette dialog box, click the Help button.
5. Repeat steps 3 and 4 for every color you want to change in the Current Palette.
6. When you finish making your selections, choose one of the following:
    - OK to save the changes.
    - Cancel to ignore the changes.
    - Reset to return the current palette to the default palette.
7. After you return to the Color Palettes dialog box, you can save your change to a palette name. Click the Save As button and select a file name and folder for your palette. You don't need to add the extension; WP Draw automatically adds a PRC extension to your file name.
8. Choose OK to return to the drawing.

## Filling Solids

As mentioned in the previous section, you can create a patterned fill for a solid, have an empty fill for the solid, or turn off the border for the solid.

To change the pattern for solids, follow these steps:

1. Click the Fill Attributes tool. The expanded Pattern palette appears.
2. Click one of the displayed patterns (see fig. 22.16). If you have a color monitor, the current pattern is surrounded by a heavier box.

When your shape is a closed curve, circle, arrow, polygon, ellipse, rectangle, circle, arrow, or rounded rectangle, you have the choice of turning the border on or off around the shape, or you can turn the fill on or off. If the fill is off, your image shows only the border for the shape.

Click the Line Attributes tool and select None to turn the border on or off.

Click the Fill Attributes tool and select None to turn the fill on or off.

**FIG. 22.16**
In addition to the None choice, the pattern palette shows 64 different patterns.

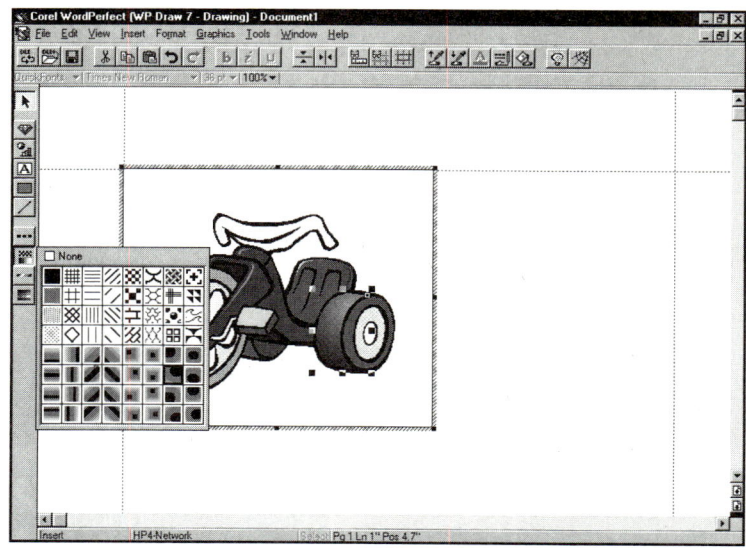

## Changing the Line or Border Pattern

Similar to changing line colors, changing line patterns also affects the borders surrounding objects.

To change the line pattern, follow these steps:

1. Click the Line Attributes palette. The expanded Line Style palette appears.
2. Click one or more of the options on the Line Attributes palette (see fig. 22.17).

   Choose the <u>N</u>one check box to have no line show around solid shapes.

   ▶ **See** "Customizing Lines," **p. 658**
   ▶ **See** "Customizing Borders," **p. 666**

**FIG. 22.17**
The Line Attribute palette gives you three choices: None, 10 values of line thickness, and 16 values of line patterns.

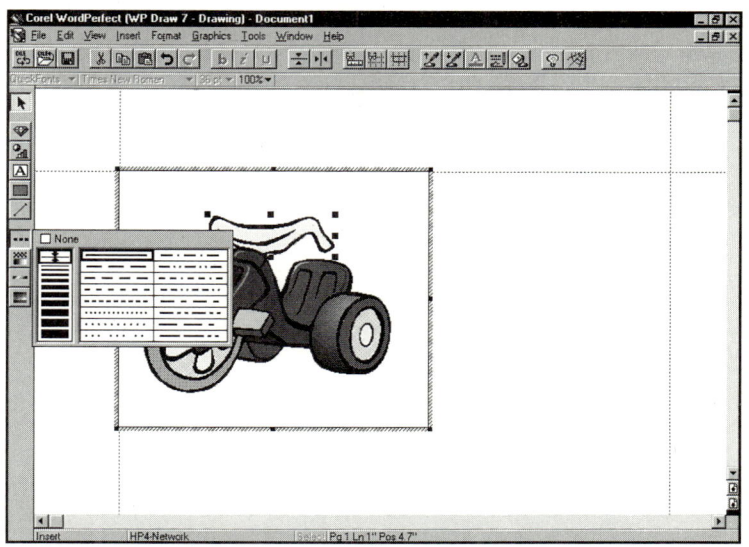

 **TROUBLESHOOTING**

**How can I change the curve of a sweeping arrow?** WP Draw creates sweeping arrows using Bezier curves. You can easily change the curved segments by double-clicking the arrow, then dragging the resulting handles. When you click some handles, you see a light dashed line which also contains handles at each end. Drag the control handles for the curve to modify the actual curve's steepness, or angle.

It's helpful to experiment with the Bezier Curve tool which appears in the Line Tool palette. You can also find additional information about Bezier curves in WP Draw's Help text.

**I can't find a gradient that exactly meets my needs. How can I customize a gradient?** A wide selection of predefined gradient styles appears on the Fill Attributes palette. You might need to create a customized gradient from scratch, or perhaps you can select a gradient fill from the palette and then edit it slightly. The easiest method is to choose the gradient that is closest to your requirements, then edit the Object Properties for the element to which you want to apply the gradient. To do so, select the object, then choose Format, Object Properties. From the Fill Attributes tab, verify that Gradient is selected in the Fill Style field, then click the More Options button. The Gradient Settings dialog box opens, from which you can customize your gradient settings.

**Are there any other fill options I can use besides those that appear on the Fill palette?**
Similar to gradients in the previous question, you can select from one of many textures or backgrounds for your object. Select your object, then from the Object Properties dialog box (choose Format, Object Properties), open the drop-down menu from the Fill Style button. Depending on your selection, you can add textures or even background pictures to your object.

Note that if the textures or background pictures were not installed during Setup, they may not be available. You need to run Setup for WordPerfect 7 again, specifically selecting the textures and background files from the WP Draw Components list.

# Using Text in WP Draw

WordPerfect not only lets you add text, but gives you a great amount of control over how that text appears.

## Adding Text to the Drawing

After you select the location for your text within a drawing, adding text to a graphic is just like adding text to a document.

To add text to your drawing, follow these steps:

1. Click the Text tool and choose either the Text Area option or Text Line tool.
2. To create a text area, position the mouse crosshair pointer in the upper-left corner of where you want the text to start.
3. Hold down the left mouse button and drag the mouse pointer from the upper-left corner to the lower-right corner of where you want text to appear. A text box appears on-screen.
4. To create a text line, simply click where you want the text to appear.
5. Type text and place formatting characters within the text box.
6. When you finish typing the text, click outside the text box or click another drawing tool.

 You can use a Hard Return in a Text Area, but not in a Text Line.

> **CAUTION**
> Be sure you select Text Area if think you later might want to size the height of the text box, or if you want to type multiple lines. The size of the text area for a Text Line is dependent on the font size and length of the actual text entered. If you've chosen Text Line and then want to break your text into several lines (by inserting hard returns within the text), you have to delete the Text Line, then recreate the text using the Text Area tool.

## Using Common Text Features

Many of the text features available in WordPerfect 7 also are available in WP Draw. These features are covered throughout "Part I: Basic Tasks." For example, to delete or change the format of existing text, first select the text box, highlight the text with the mouse, and type the new text or add a format, such as Ctrl+B for bold. The procedures are essentially the same for text within a WP Draw drawing (see table 22.4). Any of the text formatting commands available from the Toolbar affect your text in WP Draw.

**Table 22.4 Text Features Available in WP Draw**

| Feature | Shortcut Keys | Description |
|---|---|---|
| Font Properties | F9 | Change font face, style, size, appearance, and attributes (color, pattern). |
| Normal | Ctrl+N | Change back to no changes in appearance. |
| Bold | Ctrl+B | Bold selected text or type bold text. |
| Italic | Ctrl+I | Italicize selected text or enter italicized text. |
| Date | Ctrl+D or Ctrl+Shift+D | Place current date as text or a code. |
| Find and Replace | F2 or Ctrl+F | Find and/or replace existing text. |
| Format | Center: Shift+F7<br>Flush Right: Alt+F7<br>Indent: F7<br>Back Tab: Shift+Tab | Change line position of text. |
| Justification | | Change document justification to Left, Right, or Center. |

*continues*

| Feature | Shortcut Keys | Description |
| --- | --- | --- |
| Speller | Ctrl+F1 | Spell check the text. |
| Thesaurus | Alt+F1 | Look for a word. |
| Characters | Ctrl+W | Add a special character such as a bullet, copyright symbol, or foreign letter. |

▶ See "Revising and Editing Text," **p. 86**
▶ See "Formatting Characters," **p. 126**
▶ See "Accessing Special Characters," **p. 640**
▶ See "Understanding Windows Font Management," **p. 634**
▶ See "Choosing Fonts," **p. 740**

## Wrapping Text Around an Object

If you want to mold your text into a non-linear shape, you can use WP Draw's new contour text capability. To change the shape of your text line, follow these steps:

1. Enter the text you want to contour.
2. Using one of the drawing tools—such as line or circle—draw the shape to which you want your text to conform.
3. Select your text.
4. Select the graphics object you drew. Figure 22.18 shows a line and text after both items have been selected.

**FIG. 22.18**
To contour text, select both the text and the graphics object that will control the contour.

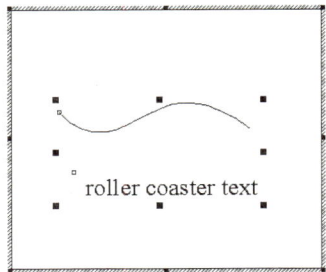

5. Choose Graphics, Contour Text. The Contour Text dialog box appears (see fig. 22.19).

WP Draw allows you to specify where the text will be positioned in relation to the selected graphics object. Choose Position to select one of the following options: Top Left, Top Center, Top Right, Bottom Left, Bottom Center, or Bottom Right. These selections enable you to place your text on the top or bottom of the selected graphics object and also place your text left, right, or center justified on the graphics object. The default Position is Top Left.

The option Display Text Only determines whether you will be able to see the graphics object used to contour the text. The default option is On, which means the graphics object will not be visible after you have performed the contour operation. If Display Text Only is not selected, you see both the contoured text and the graphics object.

**FIG. 22.19**
The Contour Text dialog box enables you to specify how the text is contoured to the selected graphics object.

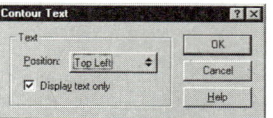

6. Accept the default options from the Contour Text dialog box. Your text appears as shown in figure 22.20.

**FIG. 22.20**
After using the default options of Position Top Left and Display Text Only from the Contour Text dialog box, the sample text follows the shape of the original line.

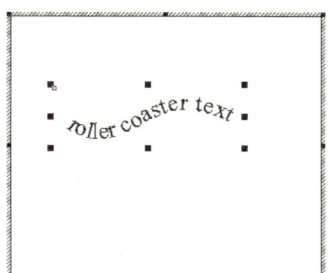

 **TIP** To undo the contour, select the contoured text and choose Graphics, Separate or Edit, Undo (Ctrl+Z).

# Scanning or Capturing an Image into WP Draw

If you have a scanner and scanner program or video capture board, you can bring a copy of a photograph, typeset image, or still frame from video into your documents.

## Selecting the Image Source

You must tell WP Draw what kind of scanner or video capture hardware you have. You need to select it only once; it will remain defined for all your WordPerfect sessions. To select the image source, choose Insert, Select Image Source. The Select Source dialog box appears, as shown in figure 22.21. Choose the device in the Sources box, and click the Select button.

**FIG. 22.21**
The Select Source dialog box shows the name(s) of your TWAIN software in the Sources section.

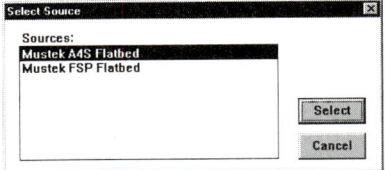

## Acquiring the Image

After you select the source, you can capture an image by following these steps:

1. Place the photograph or object on the scanner, or cue up the videotape or laser disc if you are capturing from video.

2. Choose Insert, Acquire Image. WP Draw brings up the TWAIN capture interface for the device you selected.

3. Complete the procedure for capturing the image according to the software instructions. The dialog box that appears depends on your software.

**N O T E** WordPerfect uses the TWAIN interface for image capture. This means you see the same window and controls no matter which program you're using to acquire the image. If you can capture in CorelDRAW! or Photoshop, you can capture in WordPerfect.

# Adding the Drawing to Your WordPerfect Document

After you finish creating and editing your drawing, you need to switch back from WP Draw and place the drawing in your WordPerfect document.

To place the drawing in your document, simply click outside of the WP Draw window to deselect the drawing.

▶ See "Customizing Graphics Boxes," **p. 669**
▶ See "Editing a Graphics Image," **p. 677**
▶ See "Planning the Page," **p. 729**

# Using TextArt

You can use TextArt to create company logos and display heads for your documents quickly and easily. TextArt enables you to change fonts, type styles, and alignment of the text on-screen; but more importantly, TextArt enables you to distort and modify the text so it conforms to various shapes. You also can add a shadow, use different outlines and fills, and resize the text in TextArt.

After creating the text, you can save the text in a file for use later, place it in a WordPerfect document in a movable frame, or insert it in a graphics box for a different effect such as a Watermark box.

## Understanding the Tools

Figures 22.22 and 22.23 show the TextArt interface. The General tab lets you control the text to be shaped, font, style, text shape, justification, and text color. The Options tab gives you control over finer details, such as the text pattern, shadow, outline, rotation, and smoothness.

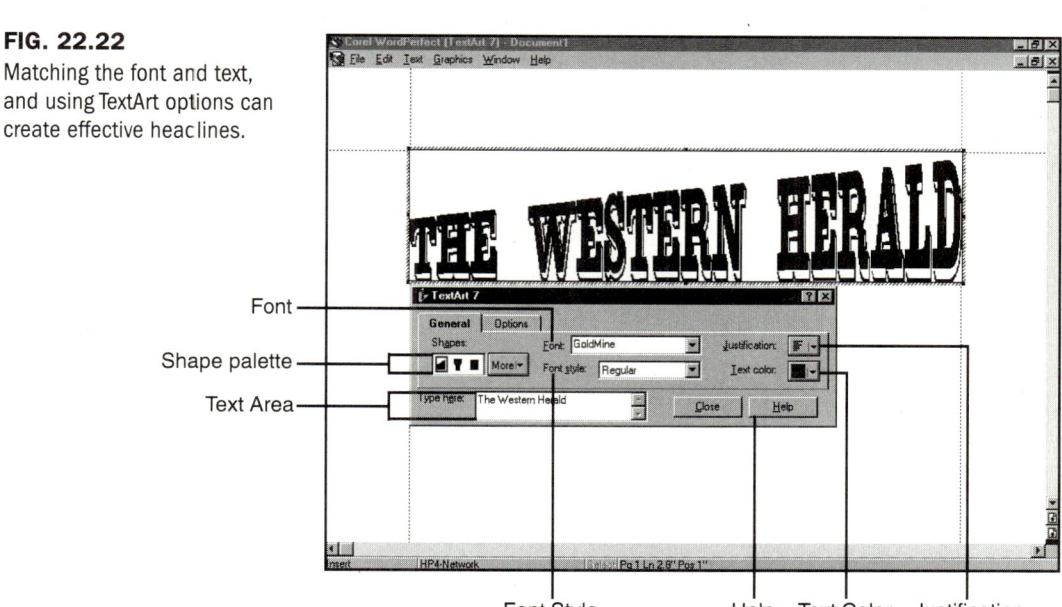

**FIG. 22.22**
Matching the font and text, and using TextArt options can create effective headlines.

To enter text for formatting, click the mouse in text box and type your text. The sample box illustrates the text you enter and the formatting. You don't have to select the text to apply formatting to it; TextArt applies any formatting you choose to all text in the text box.

**FIG. 22.23**
The Options tab gives you finer control over text appearance.

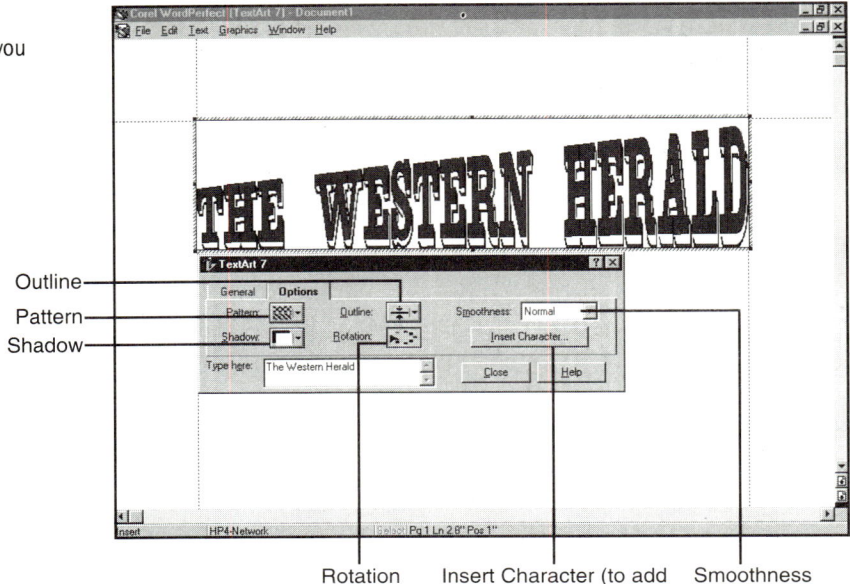

- TIP: The more text you enter on one line, the more distorted the text becomes. Use short lines of text when possible.

After you enter the text, you can use the TextArt tools to change the shape, color, size, and so on. You also can change the font, style, and alignment at any time. TextArt automatically redraws each time you make a change.

Following are brief descriptions of each tool in the TextArt 7 dialog box. These tools appear on the General tab:

- *Font*. Displays a list of selectable typefaces for the text.
- *Font Style*. Displays a list of font styles (such as bold or italics) available for the currently selected typeface.
- *Justification*. Aligns text to the left or right edges of the displayed text box or centers the text between the edges.
- *Text Color*. Opens a color palette from which you can choose the color for the text.
- *Shapes Palette*. Choose the More button to open a palette from which you can select additional shapes for the text. Choose a shape in which to mold the text; some fonts look better with certain shapes, so try several fonts when you find a shape you like. Figure 22.21 illustrates text molded in one of the shapes.

You can further define the appearance of your text by selecting theOptions tab on the TextArt 7 dialog box by using these tools:

- *Pattern*. Open the Pattern palette to select an alternate pattern and color for your text.
- *Shadow*. You can modify the shadow location, text color, and shadow color from the Shadow palette.
- *Outline*. Selecting an alternate outline color and size affects the border (outline) of each letter within your text.

 **TIP** Use a white outline if the letters seem too close or crowded.

- *Rotation*. Rotates the text within the text area from 0 to 360 degrees. Figure 22.24 illustrates rotated text. As you rotate the text, the angle of rotation appears in the TextArt 7 dialog box title bar.
- *Smoothness*. Determines the amount of resolution used to define curves. Setting Smoothness to Very High removes jagged edges from the molded text. It can, however, adversely affect print time and the required printer memory.
- *Insert Character*. Displays the character set in the Character dialog box. Use this to access characters not readily available from the keyboard, such as the copyright symbol.

**FIG. 22.24**
When you rotate text, experiment until you get the effect you want.

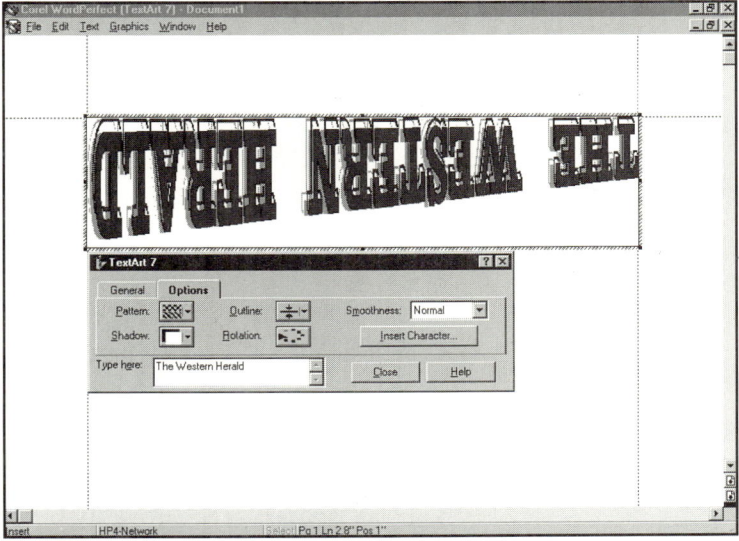

## Saving TextArt

After completing your design in TextArt, you can save your text as a file to use again in TextArt or as a graphic file to use in WordPerfect and other programs.

To save a copy of the text, choose File, Save As. Select the Selected Image option and choose OK. Then save the file using the regular Save As dialog box.

## Using TextArt

Using TextArt is 90 percent experimentation. The more you explore and test the program, the more you learn how to use it. No one can tell you exactly how to judge the height of text in any certain shape. You have to explore the possibilities.

To use TextArt, follow these steps:

1. Choose Graphics, TextArt or click the TextArt tool.
2. Type the text in the Type Here text box.

    If you need a special character, click Insert Character and select the character to insert it in the text box. Click Insert, and then choose Close.

3. Select a font, style, and alignment for the text.
4. Experiment with the shapes, color, shadow, size, and so on.
5. To optionally save the text to a file, choose File, Save As, select Selected Image, and choose OK. The Save As dialog box appears. Choose the file type options and name the file; then choose OK to return to TextArt.
6. When you have finished with your TextArt creation, select Close from the TextArt 7 dialog box, then click your document to deselect the TextArt object.

### TROUBLESHOOTING

**TextArt creates my text OK, but won't display a shadow behind it.** Make sure you have a shadow selected with the Shadow tool, and make sure it has a color other than white. In addition, it can be difficult to see a shadow behind some typefaces. Experiment with the Shadow position until you can see the shadow behind your text.

**I get an Out of memory error on my laser printer when printing documents that include TextArt images.** Out of Memory errors at print time can be frustrating. TextArt images in particular can be incredibly complex and can take a lot of printer memory, especially when the image is large or complex. There are several things you can try:

- Edit your TextArt image, reducing the setting for Smoothness to Normal.
- Print at a lower resolution. Select a lower resolution at print time from the Resolution field in the Print dialog box.
- Modify your printer's properties so that graphics are printed as raster graphics rather than vector graphics. Printer Properties can be set from the Printer choice of your Windows 95 Start menu, or through WordPerfect 7's Print dialog box, Printer tab. With the Printer Properties dialog box displayed, select the Graphics tab, then choose Use Raster Graphics. Note that if you work on a network, you might not have sufficient network rights to allow modifying the printer's properties.

CHAPTER 23

# Desktop Publishing with WordPerfect

*by Susan Plumley and Gabrielle Nemes*

With desktop publishing, you can use a personal computer to create attractive, visually interesting, typeset-quality documents. Desktop publishing involves integrating text and graphics on the same page and printing to a high-resolution laser printer or image typesetter. Word processors enable you to enter and edit text; some word processors allow you to format the text and the page for a more professional look than a document created with a typewriter.

A word processor that enables you to accomplish true page layout—design a professional-looking document using various typefaces and type styles, columns, graphic lines, borders, images, and so on—is also a desktop publishing program. WordPerfect 7 for Windows 95 is just such a program.

Desktop publishing and the principles of layout and design are really nothing more than personal preference. This chapter offers guidelines for designing professional-looking documents and shows you how WordPerfect's features can help. You must keep in mind, however, that your own eye is the final judge of the appearance of your document. ■

### Plan margins and columns in a document

One of the most important principles of desktop publishing involves laying out a page using design elements such as white space, emphasis, and balance. This chapter offers some suggestions on how to use WordPerfect's Margin and Columns features to effectively plan document appearance.

### Align the text and use line spacing

As you continue to design your desktop-published document, you'll want to use WordPerfect's Justification, Line Spacing, and Leading features to make your document attractive and easy to read.

### Choose typefaces and type sizes

Typefaces and type sizes can be used to add emphasis to important sections of text or to encourage the reader to read further. You'll learn how and when to use particular typefaces and type sizes in your document.

### Add color to your documents

Color is an important element in desktop publishing. WordPerfect enables you to add color to your document on-screen and to print in color if you have a color printer. This chapter shows you how to use color effectively in your documents.

# A Word About Using WordPerfect for Desktop Publishing

WordPerfect has many features you can use to perform desktop publishing tasks. Among the most important of these features is WYSIWYG (*What-You-See-Is-What-You-Get*), which enables you to view on-screen exactly what will be printed interactively as you create your document. When you're laying out a page, you have a specific design to follow, and you must be able to see the layout develop as you work. In addition, WordPerfect includes many other features that enable you to create a professional-looking document: styles, templates, columns and tables, fonts, various typographic controls, graphics, and advanced printing capabilities. Other chapters introduce many of these features.

While WordPerfect can be very successfully used for desktop publishing, it truly is a word processing package with a lot of fun and powerful tools that allow you to create outstanding, professional advertising pieces. A few quick tips to help you create your desktop-published document are listed below:

- Use the various options for Zoom and View so that you can quickly enlarge portions of your document. For example, use Zoom To 200% to precisely place two lines that must meet exactly. On the other hand, when laying out your page, you want to work with Zoom set at Full Page view so that you can see how your placement of each object relates to the others.

- As much as possible, leave the guidelines visible. You can quickly drag guidelines to change margins, column widths, and table columns to line things up exactly where you need them.

- Similar to the guidelines, display the Ruler Bar. You can find it as another useful method of dragging around tabs and margins.

- Use a watermark as a background against which you can lay various elements. (A *watermark* is usually text or graphics which appear *behind* the text on every page, similar to a header or footer.) This can be an especially helpful method when you want to place elements that span columns. Change the watermark page as often as you need, adjusting the columns, tables, or whatever. Remember that the watermark page shows through the actual document text. It can, therefore, effectively become a grid which is especially useful when you need to be precise. When your layout is complete, delete the Watermark code. Magic! Refer to the section in this chapter "Custom Column Widths" for more help in using watermarks.

- Place your small text items, including tables, inside graphic boxes. This action allows you to move them around with the mouse, dropping them in several places until the page looks just right. This is far easier than trying to align or place text using tabs or indents. (But don't do this for the text that comprises the main body of your newsletter. It needs to logically flow from column to column, page to page.)

- Print your document, or at least the page on which you are working, often. You can often spot mistakes or areas that need additional refining once you see your design on paper.
- Work with odd numbers—1, 3, and 5. You can find that for many publications, three columns or three graphic images look better on a page than do two or four columns or images.
- An asymmetric layout can be dynamic! Try setting images or quotes out in a wide margin. You'll be surprised at the visual power the object gains just by setting it out on its own.
- Don't be afraid to break a few rules—just be careful not to make your publication too junky. Refer to the sections later in this chapter for tips on the numbers and compatibility of fonts.
- Lastly, use lots of white space. You can often say more effectively by writing very little and surrounding your little bit of text and graphics by lots of nothing. White space gives your eye a breather.

  ▶ See "The Ruler Bar," **p. 25**
  ▶ See "Using Graphic Boxes," **p. 262**
  ▶ See "Using Zoom and View To See the Printed Output," **p. 279**
  ▶ See "Using Graphics Boxes," **p. 262**

# Designing Successful Publications

A successful publication or presentation grabs the reader's attention and holds it. You can attract the reader's attention in a variety of ways: use very large text as an eye-catching headline, display a graphic image that entices the reader, or use color for emphasis.

After attracting the reader, the design of your document can also help sustain attention—although ultimately, it's your message that must maintain the reader's interest.

The first step in designing a professional-looking document is to plan the overall look of the document:

- How will the text appear—typefaces, type size, columns, text alignment?
- What graphics elements and images will appear—lines, borders, clip art, scanned art, art created in WordPerfect Draw or Presentations?

- How do the graphics relate to the text—illustrate, separate, guide the eye, emphasize?
- Will you use colors in your document—one, two, or more?
- If you are using color in your document, what division of color will you use—graphic borders one color, text another?

The next step is to plan each page of the document. Is there a logical sequence to the text and graphics? How does each page relate logically to the whole? Design each page of a document so that it can stand alone but also correspond with the whole. Guide the reader through the document page by page. Add graphics to enhance and reinforce the text. Balance text and graphics elements on the page to entice the reader.

Designing a professional-looking document takes time, experimentation, and the willingness to change what doesn't work. Consider the following points when planning your document:

- *Amount of copy.* Ascertain the amount of text and number of graphics to help you decide the type of document, number of pages, and so on.
- *Type of document.* Decide whether your message is best suited for a newsletter, brochure, flyer, on-screen presentation, or other type of document.
- *Page orientation.* Determine whether the type of document suggests a landscape or portrait orientation. Consider the copy as well as the graphics. If the graphics are taller than they are wide, use a portrait orientation; if the text consists of long paragraphs, it may be more readable using a multicolumn format in a landscape orientation.
- *Size of the document.* Determine document size based on the type of document (flyers are usually 8 1/2 × 11 inches, for example), method of reproduction (laser printers limit paper size), and method of distribution (mailings, for example, have size and weight limits).
- *Number and type of column.* Choose the number and type of columns that best fit the copy and type of document.
- *Type.* Determine typefaces, type size, and type attributes according to design guidelines.
- *Color.* If you can print in color and want to use color in your document, choose the number of colors for the final document and how the colors will be distributed within the document.
- *Who will produce your document.* If you print your document in-house using your own equipment, you can freely use all elements and capabilities of WordPerfect that can be produced by your own printers. Printing in color is a good example.

However, if you plan to produce your document using a commercial print house, you should contact them first to determine exactly what the file you provide must look like. Should it contain all of the layout elements on one page? If you plan to produce a document which uses several colors, must the colors be separated by you? Can your printer read a WordPerfect 7 file? If not, what file format does it require?

▶ **See** "Selecting Page Size and Type," **p. 179**

▶ **See** "Working with Text Columns," **p. 433**

In addition to the physical characteristics of the document, further aesthetic considerations (design guidelines) play a part in the page layout. These guidelines, which apply design principles to page layout, help you make your documents more effective. Consider the following topics when planning your desktop-published documents:

Look at other publications to get ideas for designs. Keep a folder of designs you like and don't like, and refer to them as you plan your documents.

- *Consistency.* Whether your document consists of one page or many, you should establish a consistent format. Consistency creates unity in your documents and helps the reader maintain interest in your message. Design elements such as margins, columns, typeface, type size, spacing, and alignment should remain the same throughout your document to create consistency.

- *Emphasis.* You can emphasize certain elements of your document to create an area of interest. Emphasis keeps the document from being monotonous for the reader; too much emphasis can create chaos, however. Emphasize only *one* object—text or graphics—per page.

- *Balance.* Balance the text and graphics in the document to create an even, pleasing, and simple appearance. A balanced document leads the reader logically from topic to topic without distracting jumps in column number, text blocks, or graphic images. Especially when working with graphics, print the page, then turn the paper 180 degrees. Does your layout appear equally as balanced when rotated as it is when right-side up? It should.

- *Proportion.* Just as balance helps keep a page uniform, so too does proportion. A graphics image or headline that is too large can overpower the other elements on the page. Keep all elements proportionally equal so that they work together instead of fight each other for the reader's attention.

- *White space.* White space—the area of the document that contains no text or graphics—is an important addition to any design. White space provides contrast, emphasis, and a rest for the reader's eyes. Text and graphics that are surrounded by white space have more impact. Margins and *gutters* (the space between columns and the space between inside margins where pages come together) are the most effective ways of implementing white space; however, other methods include using left- or right-aligned text, spacing between paragraphs, and adding space above and below a headline.

- *Color.* Adding color to a publication can enhance your message, improve readability, and attract attention—or it can create confusion in your document. Use no more than three or four colors per publication. Make sure the colors you use are not too bright or harsh—or too light or dark—to be read comfortably.

Figure 23.1 shows a desktop publication—a newsletter—that employs the design guidelines previously listed. Use the design guidelines listed in this section as you plan your publications and presentations. The remainder of this chapter explores desktop publishing with WordPerfect in more detail.

**FIG. 23.1**
When designing a document, use guidelines such as consistency, emphasis, white space, and balance, as in this example.

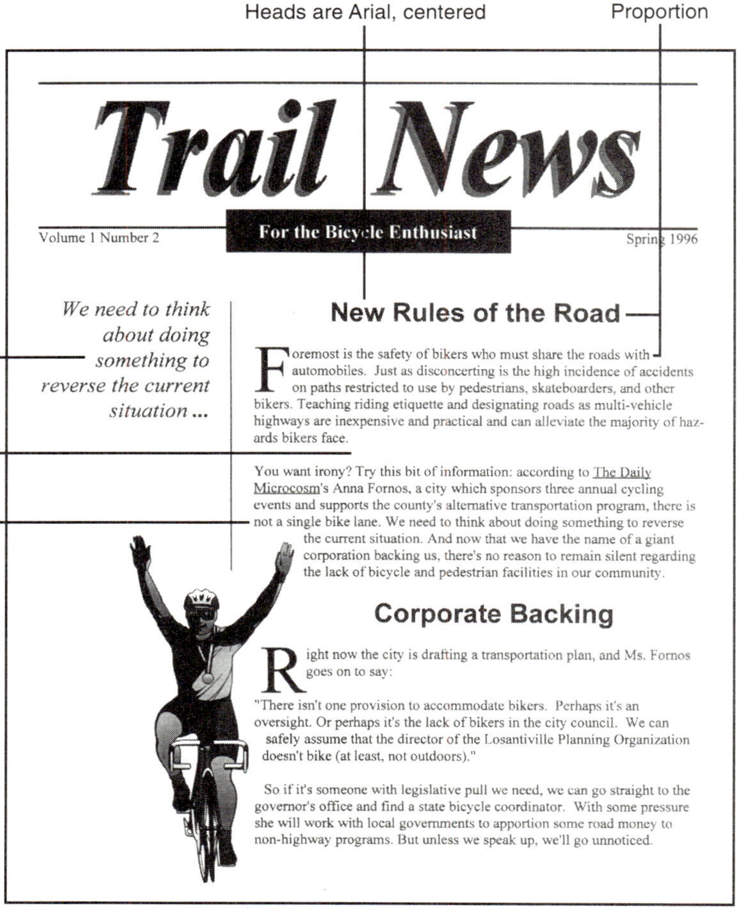


Trail News

For the Bicycle Enthusiast

Volume 1 Number 2

Spring 1996

*We need to think about doing something to reverse the current situation ...*

## New Rules of the Road

Foremost is the safety of bikers who must share the roads with automobiles. Just as disconcerting is the high incidence of accidents on paths restricted to use by pedestrians, skateboarders, and other bikers. Teaching riding etiquette and designating roads as multi-vehicle highways are inexpensive and practical and can alleviate the majority of hazards bikers face.

You want irony? Try this bit of information: according to The Daily Microcosm's Anna Fornos, a city which sponsors three annual cycling events and supports the county's alternative transportation program, there is not a single bike lane. We need to think about doing something to reverse the current situation. And now that we have the name of a giant corporation backing us, there's no reason to remain silent regarding the lack of bicycle and pedestrian facilities in our community.

## Corporate Backing

Right now the city is drafting a transportation plan, and Ms. Fornos goes on to say:

"There isn't one provision to accommodate bikers. Perhaps it's an oversight. Or perhaps it's the lack of bikers in the city council. We can safely assume that the director of the Losantiville Planning Organization doesn't bike (at least, not outdoors)."

So if it's someone with legislative pull we need, we can go straight to the governor's office and find a state bicycle coordinator. With some pressure she will work with local governments to apportion some road money to non-highway programs. But unless we speak up, we'll go unnoticed.

# Planning the Page

To create an effective publication or presentation, you must lay some groundwork. First, decide what you want to communicate:

- What is the purpose of your document?
- Do you want to sell, inform, announce, or explain?
- Who is your audience? Customers, potential customers, employees?
- Consider the type of document—is the final output a brochure for a few people, or a flyer mailed to thousands? You'll use different techniques and different preference rules for single page announcements than you will for lengthy publications.

The next step is to write the text and select or create graphics—images, tables, spreadsheets, and so on—that support the text. If you've determined that you want to include graphics with your document, be very sure that the graphic supports the impression you're trying to make. A graphic that's been included just to "break up the text" detracts from the value of your message. When you are satisfied with the content of the document, you are ready to begin planning the page.

You must consider many factors when planning the page. Physical factors include the amount of copy, size of the document, and number of pages. In addition, keep in mind the design guidelines as you plan. This section gives you some guidelines and ideas for planning your page, as well as tips on how to use WordPerfect features to make your job easier.

## Determining Page Margins

*Margins*—the areas surrounding text blocks and graphics—serve as a buffer zone to contrast the text and graphics. Margins provide white space on the page to improve readability and emphasize the message. Plan the margins of the page as a first step to page layout.

> **NOTE** Use margins to help maintain consistency throughout your document. When you determine the margins, stay with that formula; don't change the margins for the sake of design, and don't change the margins to squeeze in an extra bit of text.

The size of the margins depend on the amount of copy and type of document. If you have a lot of copy and few pages to work with, for example, you might use smaller margins, or perhaps a smaller type size. Be careful, however, not to cram too much text onto too few pages. You'll be better off to cut your text or increase the number of pages.

If you're producing a brochure with two folds, the outer margins must reflect the margins between the panels. However, try to plan as much margin space as possible with all documents. Where possible, always leave at least a 3/8-inch margin on all sides of a page. More is better; margins of 1/2 inch or 1 inch are not only acceptable, but preferable. The margin can be a very effective method of adding white space to your pages.

You can vary the margins on a page for interesting white space, so long as you stay consistent throughout your document. Suppose you design a one-page advertising piece. The minimal amount of copy gives you room to adjust the margins for a more interesting page layout. Figure 23.2 shows an advertising flyer that has wide left and top margins. The advertisement has an openness to it because of the wide margins, added white space around the figure, and right-aligned text.

 **TIP** If you vary the margin on one page of a multipage document, repeat the same margin on every page to ensure consistency.

> **NOTE** You can change the margins of your document using the guidelines, or from the Margin dialog box. (Choose Format, Margins.) For more information on setting margins, see Chapter 4, "Formatting Text."

**FIG. 23.2**
Wide left and top margins create interest and attract attention in this advertisement; in addition, right-aligned text emphasizes the white space.

## Incorporating Columns

As you learned in Chapter 14, "Working with Text Columns," WordPerfect enables you to use several types of columns in your documents. Columns add visual appeal, and columnar text can be easier to read than a full page of text. A full page of 10- or 12-point body text can be difficult to read because when you reach the end of the line, your eye must jump a long way to get to the beginning of the next line. Placing your text in columns alleviates this problem. One simple rule is keep your lines to an average of eight to 10 words.

Choose the type of column that best suits your document's needs. Because the main purpose of any document is to present information to the reader in a format that is easy to understand and follow, text should flow in a logical order. Don't be so creative with your columns that you confuse the reader.

 To format columns in WordPerfect, double-click the Columns button on the Power Bar, or choose Format, Columns, Define.

Too many columns clutter the page and confuse the reader. When using portrait orientation, generally use no more than three columns per page. In landscape orientation, which offers more flexibility, you can use four or five columns. This section gives examples of some types of columns you can use in your documents and when to use them.

**NOTE** If the text is suited for more columns—such as lists consisting of short line lengths—you can fit four or five columns to a page.

▶ See "Setting Margins," **p. 135**
▶ See "Working with Text Columns," **p. 433**

**Newspaper Columns**   The text in a newspaper column flows the entire length of the first column and then wraps to the top of the next column. Use newspaper columns for a large amount of text, such as a newsletter, book, or report. Figures 23.3 and 23.4 show a newsletter that incorporate newspaper columns.

Figure 23.3 displays balanced columns; the text in each column is approximately the same length. While WordPerfect automatically keeps the text in balanced columns to approximately the same length, you may find that placing a graphic in or between columns interrupts WordPerfect's capability to properly balance them. Therefore, where possible, play with the location of your graphic image so that the column lengths remain the same.

Figure 23.4, on the other hand, uses a standard newspaper column definition. Text is placed all the way to the bottom of each column, contouring around the graphic image.

**FIG. 23.3**
Balanced newspaper columns in a newsletter promote the smooth flow of text and guide the reader's eye.

**FIG. 23.4**
Newspaper columns extend the full length of each column. Continuing a story from the third column to the next page may encourage the reader to open the newsletter.

 Any extra hard returns at the end of your text can throw the balance off. Remove extra blank lines before choosing the Balanced Newspaper option. Refer to Chapter 14, "Working with Text Columns," for more information on working with balanced newspaper columns.

**Custom Column Widths**   With WordPerfect, you can create custom column widths. Using custom column widths breaks up the page so that it isn't monotonous to the reader. If you use custom column widths, however, plan them carefully so that you don't present a chaotic layout of text and graphics. Keep the layout simple. Just because WordPerfect lets you create up to 24 columns of varying widths doesn't mean the layout will look good.

Two asymmetric column layout techniques are often used in layout of published materials. The first is based on three column widths. Then, either columns 1 and 2 or columns 2 and 3 are "joined" to present text in two columns as shown in figure 23.1. For example, visualize a page divided into three vertical columns—perhaps each column is 2 inches wide with about a one-half inch space between each column. Now imagine the same page with only two columns—the first column is still two inches wide, but the second column is now a combination of columns 2 and 3, or four and a half inches wide.

The second method uses five columns widths to create an asymmetric two-column layout. Two-fifths are used for one of the columns, while three-fifths are used for the other column, as shown in figure 23.5. For more information on creating custom column widths, as well as adding borders or shading in columns, see Chapter 14, "Working with Text Columns."

**FIG. 23.5**
Custom columns in a newsletter are based on five-column widths. The left column uses three-fifths, and the right column uses two-fifths.

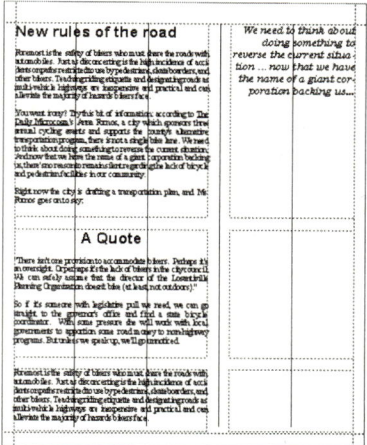

 **TIP** Use the same custom widths throughout the document to avoid inconsistency. Use no more than two or three columns per page.

An easy method to work with asymmetric columns is the watermark method. The general steps for the one-third, two-thirds layout follow:

1. From the document window, choose Format, Watermark. Then choose either Watermark A or Watermark B and choose Create.

2. Create three newspaper columns by double-clicking the Columns button the Power Bar to quickly open the Columns Define dialog box. Enter 3 in the columns text box, select Newspaper. Click OK to return to the watermark page.

3. Add border lines between each column by selecting Format, Border/Fill. Then select Columns.

4. Click the Column Between icon from the Available Border Styles palette, then click OK.

5. With the insertion point in column 1, press the Enter key until the column guidelines and column border lines extend the full length of the watermark page, as shown in figure 23.6. Click <u>C</u>lose on the Watermark Feature Bar (or press Ctrl+F4) to return to the document window. The lines from the watermark are now visible in your document window.

**FIG. 23.6**

Create three columns with lines between them in a watermark.

6. In the document window, create two columns, either newspaper or balanced newspaper, depending on your layout.

7. With your column guidelines visible, drag the gutter between the two columns until it is centered over one of the watermark-visible column border lines, as shown in figure 23.7.

8. With your columns positioned, open Reveal Codes and delete the Watermark code. You can now place your text and other elements based on an asymmetric two-column layout.

   ▶ **See** "Using Watermarks," **p. 272**

If the newsletter consists of more than one page, you can switch the position of the two columns on the second page—and the fourth page, sixth page, and so on. By doing this, the wide column appears to the inside, or the outside, of both odd and even pages. This *mirroring* adds interest to the layout while maintaining consistency. You must manually do this in WordPerfect, however, because WordPerfect does not support mirrored columns. A sample of mirrored columns can be seen in figure 23.8.

Planning the Page 735

**FIG. 23.7**
Two columns are created based on the width of the columns visible in the watermark.

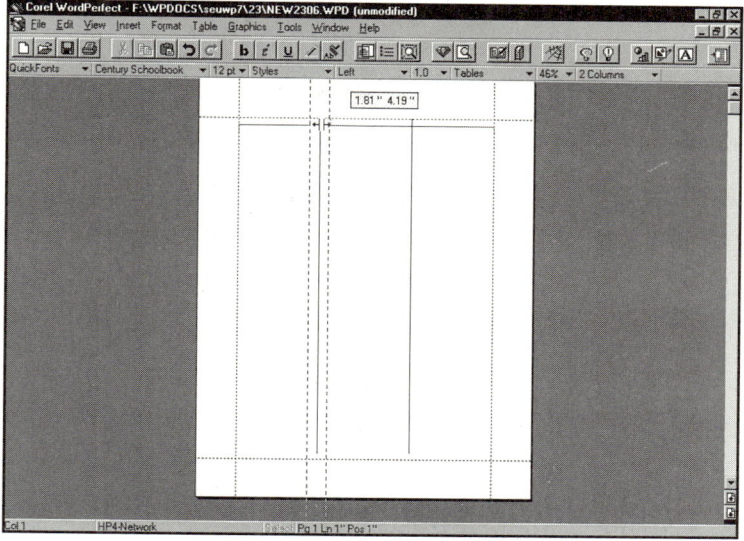

**FIG. 23.8**
Although difficult to create, mirrored columns can be an effective, easy-to-read, format, especially when lots of headings are used.

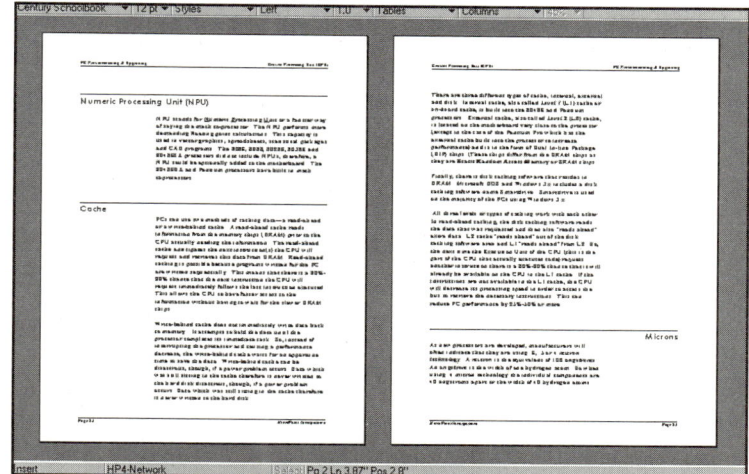

**Gutter Space and Columns**   Consider the gutter, the space between columns, as additional margin space. Documents need gutters to separate the text, but gutter space also provides valuable white space that acts as a resting point for the reader's eye. Narrow gutters make text hard to read and may force the reader's eyes to jump to the next column. On the other hand, very wide gutters may separate columns too much, thus separating related text.

**NOTE**  Don't substitute a graphics line for gutter space. If you use lines between columns, add extra gutter space to compensate. Also, be sure to use plenty of gutter space when you use justified text.

### TROUBLESHOOTING

**When I format text in two or more newspaper columns, the column(s) to the right are higher than the left column.** When you tell WordPerfect to create columns, a Column Definition `[Col Def]` code is automatically placed at the beginning of the paragraph in which the insertion point resides. The column text, therefore, starts at the top of the current paragraph. If your insertion point is on a blank line when you create columns, the Column Definition code starts that blank line.

It's a common mistake, however, to press Enter after creating columns, which then forces the text to begin one line lower—one line after the `[Col Def]` code— in the first column than in the remaining columns. If there are extra blank lines after the insertion point, the text won't be even across the tops of the columns. To start all columns lower on the page, add any extra blank lines you want by pressing Enter before the Column Definition code (`[Col Def]` in Reveal Codes; turn on Reveal Codes to see it). As you add blank lines to the page, the tops of all the columns are pushed down and remain even.

**The text in my document looks scrawny when the document is formatted at more than two columns wide.** For most layouts, the maximum practical number of columns per page is four (maybe five) when working with a landscape paper size. With a two-column treatment, WordPerfect's default gutter spacing of 1/2 inch is acceptable; but with three and four columns, the 1/2 spacing makes the columns too narrow. When formatting the text to more than two columns, be sure to change the gutter space. Try a spacing of 1/4 inch between columns, and make adjustments until the text looks right. Use the Ruler Bar to see the effects of your spacing changes as you make them.

# Refining the Page

Now that you have planned the page using margins and columns, refine the page layout by formatting the text. This section describes working with text in blocks—as page elements rather than individual characters. Decide on the alignment and line spacing—the appearance of the paragraphs—before you decide on fonts. For information about choosing fonts, see the section "Choosing Fonts" later in this chapter.

The methods for organizing text elements depend on the amount of copy, type of document, and message you want to present. While justified text organized in columns, for example, lets you fit the most copy on a page, you'll see uncomfortable "rivers of white" running through your text copy, especially if the columns are narrow. One-and-a-half or double-line spacing, for instance, makes the text more readable in an advertisement, but makes entire blocks of text in a newsletter harder to read. Short phrases in an advertisement may be better received if the text is center-aligned. Consider the design guidelines—white space, consistency, emphasis, and so on—when you organize text on the page.

This section contains tips on how to refine the page layout for a professional-looking document. WordPerfect features enable you to perform page-refinement tasks and experiment with options before deciding on the one that best suits your document. This section discusses text alignment and line spacing.

## Aligning Text

*Text alignment* is a method of organizing words in a document. You can also use text alignment to create consistency and emphasis in your documents. All text—body text, headlines, tabs—requires an alignment (left or right aligned, centered, fully justified, or all lines justified). As always, make sure that the alignment remains consistent throughout the entire document; too many alignment changes can distract the reader. To change alignment, use the Justification button on the Power Bar, or choose Format, Justification. Figure 23.9 illustrates the appearance of a newsletter using different text justification settings.

**FIG. 23.9**
Text justification can control the readability and effectiveness of your message.

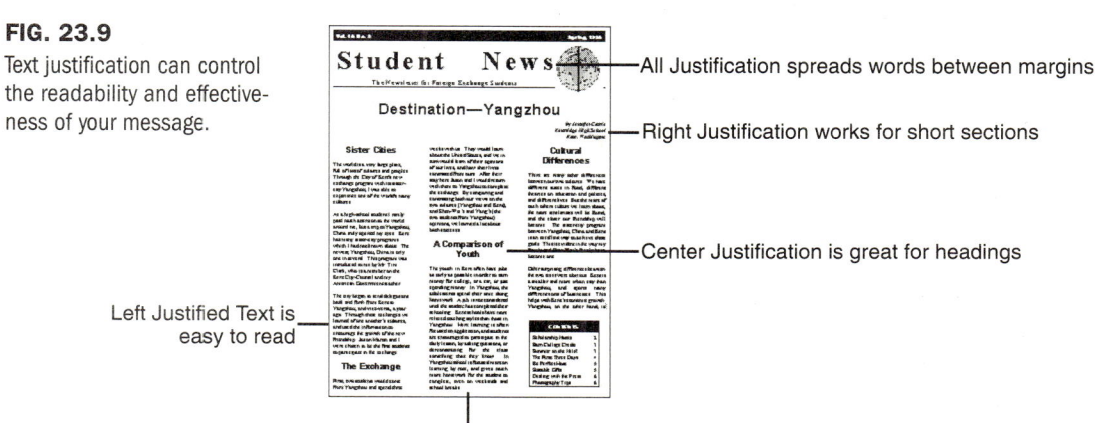

- All Justification spreads words between margins
- Right Justification works for short sections
- Center Justification is great for headings

Left Justified Text is easy to read

Full Justification is more formal

**Left Justification**  *Left-aligned text*—flush-left and ragged-right text—is perfect for body text and headlines. The ragged-right edge adds valuable white space, and the flush-left edge helps the reader find the next sentence. Left-aligned text, which provides a more open informal feeling to your documents, is more readable. Use left-aligned text in newsletters, reports, advertisements, forms, or any other document.

Left-aligned text offers the following advantages:

- Word spacing is even, unlike word spacing with justified text, in which the spacing between words varies.
- With narrow columns, the reader's eye is directed quickly and easily to the beginning of the next sentence.
- Left-aligned heads and subheads enable the reader to find the next topic easily.

**NOTE** Be sure that the ragged right text is not too ragged. Hyphenating left-aligned text helps keep the right margin somewhat uniform. Try not to hyphenate the ends of more than two lines in a row, however, because too many hyphens can make reading difficult.

**Right Justification**   *Right-aligned text*—flush-right and ragged-left text—gives you eye-catching headlines when used with justified body text. You can use right-aligned text in documents with short phrases, such as an advertising piece (refer to fig. 23.2). Reserve right-aligned text for heads and subheads, single words, and occasionally short phrases; typically you'll not want to use right alignment for body text, because the reader must be able to find the beginning of each line easily—a task that is extremely difficult with right-aligned body text. Right-aligned text can be effective, however, when listing short subjects in a column. When designing a document using right-aligned text, make sure the overall page design reflects the alignment. Notice in figure 23.2 that all elements—including the margins—reinforce the right alignment.

The advantage of using right-aligned text is that it's unique—because it's difficult to use successfully—and attracts attention.

**Center Justification**   *Centered text*—ragged-left and right text—is used primarily for headlines, subheads, and captions. Center alignment adds visual interest and an air of dignity to a document. You can use centered text for short lists, names and addresses, dates, and even invitations or announcements. Because your eye does not easily travel from line to line when text is center-aligned, it's best not to use center alignment for body text.

Centered text for a headline complements either justified or left-aligned body text (refer to fig. 23.1). When using centered headlines, make sure the text is large enough—24- or 36-point for headings, 14- to 18-point for subheads, for example—to differentiate it from the body text. Centered text offers the advantages of even word spacing and visual interest.

**Full Justification**  *Full justification*—flush-left and flush-right text—is often used for long articles, reports, newsletters (refer to fig. 23.9), and books. A page of justified text appears organized, but can be difficult to read. Justified text is also more formal than left-aligned text and allows you to fit the most amount of copy on a page. When you use full justification, consider using hyphenation so that large gaps between the words in unhyphenated justified text don't form "rivers" of white space. This can be distracting to a reader.

The advantages of using fully justified text are that you can fit more copy on a page and create an even, organized, formal page.

**All Justified**  Text that uses the All Justification formatting should only be used for special effects. All Justification spreads text evenly between the left and right margins on lines that end both with soft [SRt] or hard returns [HRt] codes. The newsletter in figure 23.9 uses All Justification in its masthead. ([HRt] codes appear when you press Enter; [SRt] codes appear at the end of line where text wraps automatically to the next line.) Full Justification, on the other hand, only spreads text on those lines which end with a soft return (refer to fig. 23.9).

## Using Line Spacing

Line spacing sets the amount of space that occurs between lines of text. In typographic terms, line spacing is referred to as *leading* (pronounced *LED-ing*). Because WordPerfect has origins as a word processing package, leading is typically adjusted using line spacing settings. By using line spacing settings, you can adjust the line spacing within a paragraph and between paragraphs. The default line and paragraph spacing in WordPerfect is 1.0. To change line spacing, use the Line Spacing button on the Power Bar, or choose Format, Line, Spacing to access the Line Spacing dialog box.

 You can open any related dialog box (except the justification button) by double-clicking the Power Bar button.

The tallest character in a particular typeface and size is the guideline for measuring line spacing. Uppercase letters, *ascenders* (b, k, and d, for example), and *descenders* (g, j, and p, for example) must have enough space to prevent them from overlapping letters on lines below or above them. Typical line spacing is 20 to 30 percent of the size of the font, which allows a little extra space above and below a line.

In WordPerfect, 1.0 (the default) is equal to the type size plus 30 percent. Professional typesetters typically use no more than 20 percent of the size of the font as their leading spaces between lines, although WordPerfect by default uses 30 percent. A 30 percent leading amount is easy to read for documents with long lines of text and relatively small type sizes, such as 10 or 12 point. In columns or for larger type sizes, try setting your line spacing to 0.9 or 0.8. The commonly used line spacing values are 1, 1 1/2, and 2; these are the values with which you're probably most familiar. WordPerfect, however, enables you to set line spacing to any measurement from 0.01 to 160. You seldom need to set line spacing at either extreme; however, you may want to adjust line spacing at some point in your documents.

The majority of line spacing uses the default, 1.0. You can increase line spacing to make crowded text more readable. Decreasing line spacing may make the text unreadable.

▶ **See** "Formatting Lines and Paragraphs," **p. 130**

▶ **See** "Using Hyphenation," **p. 148**

Double spacing between paragraphs is the most common paragraph spacing. Most people, therefore, usually press Enter twice at the end of a paragraph, before starting the next. A better method of adjusting spacing between lines and paragraphs, especially if you plan to use your WordPerfect text with other desktop publishing programs, is to use paragraph format options. In this manner, you can, for example, leave the default line spacing to 1.0 for text within a paragraph and then use 1.5 or 2.0 as the spacing to occur between paragraphs. To set paragraph spacing, use these steps:

1. Position your insertion point where you want the new paragraph spacing to begin, then choose Fo*r*mat, P*a*ragraph, *F*ormat.

2. In the *S*pacing Between Paragraphs text box, type the number of lines you want to insert at the end of a paragraph. You can alternatively enter the lines using the spin control.

3. Click OK to return to your document window.

   ▶ **See** "Customizing Formatting Options," **p. 145**

## Choosing Fonts

A *font* (family) includes all sizes and styles of a particular typeface. A *typeface* is a specific style or design of letters; Arial and Times New Roman are two different typefaces, both of which install with Windows 95. Type styles and weights include normal, italic, bold, or bold italic. A *type size* indicates the font's size, usually expressed in points (72 points equals approximately 1 inch). WordPerfect refers to these portions of a type family as its *attributes*.

**N O T E** The terms *font* and *typeface* are often used interchangeably, although they are different. A *typeface* is the complete set of all characters, punctuation, numbers, or other characters. A *font* on the other hand, refers to the combination of typeface, type size, weight, and style. Figure 23.10 illustrates four examples of fonts. WordPerfect refers to the combination of typefaces and attributes as *fonts*.

**FIG. 23.10**
Fonts refer to the combination of typeface, type size, weight, and style.

Two different typefaces

Arial
Times New Roman

Two different fonts

*Century Schoolbook, 20 point, bold, italic*
**Century Schoolbook, 14 point, bold**

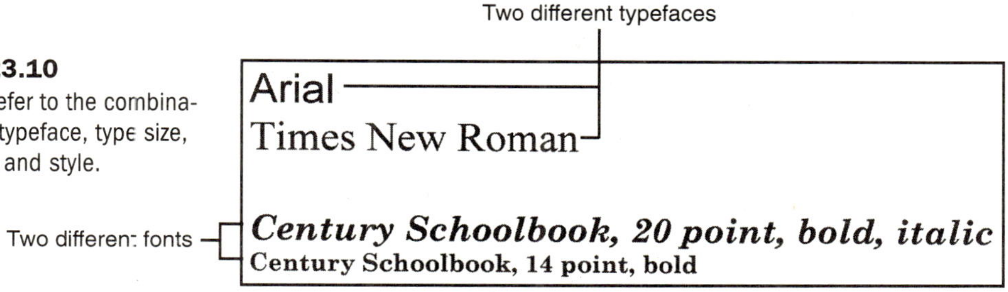

The combination of WordPerfect and Windows provides you with many different fonts for your documents. In addition to your printer fonts, WordPerfect installs several TrueType fonts. TrueType fonts are commonly used by most Windows 95 applications. They can be easily sized and printed with almost all printers. As with all elements of page design, following certain guidelines ensures that the chosen fonts complement—rather than confuse—your message. This section contains tips on how to use fonts to create a successful document.

▶ See "Installing TrueType Fonts," **p. 633**

## Using Typefaces and Attributes

You're probably familiar with the typefaces available in WordPerfect. Depending on your Windows setup and printer, as few as five typefaces or as many as 500 may be available. No matter which typefaces you have, you need to follow basic guidelines when designing your documents.

In using typefaces and attributes, one important rule is to avoid using more than three typefaces in one document. Too many typefaces not only distract the reader, but also interfere with the message. Remember that the consistency guideline applies to typefaces, as well.

 **T I P** Avoid using Courier, which has an unprofessional dated appearance in a typeset document. Wherever possible, use a serif font, such as Times Roman, Century Schoolbook, instead.

Generally, you use only two typefaces per document; a sans serif and a serif typeface work nicely together. A *serif*—the decorative component of some typefaces—is the fine stroke across the end of the main strokes of characters. Times Roman is a serif typeface. An example of a *sans serif* typeface—no serifs—is Arial.

Most desktop publishers use a sans serif typeface for headlines, subheads, captions, callouts, and headers and footers. A serif typeface is often used for body text. Serif type is easier to read because the serif adds a horizontal flow to the text, making the letters easily recognizable. While you can use serif type for headlines, you may want to avoid using sans serif for body text because it's often difficult to read in small type sizes. Figure 23.11 illustrates several popular serif and sans serif typefaces.

**FIG. 23.11**
Sans serif fonts are often used for headlines, while easier-to-read serif fonts are typically used for body text.

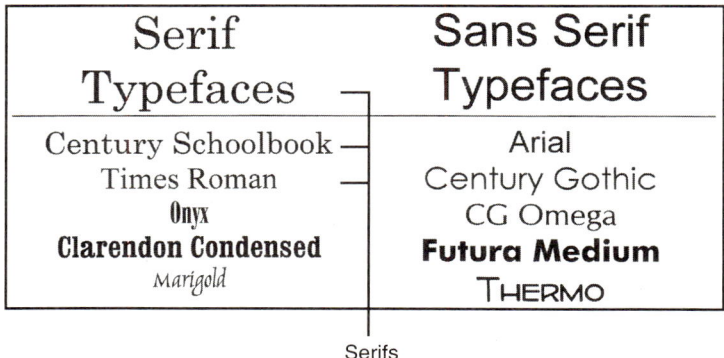

As you choose typefaces for documents, you also choose type styles, or *attributes*. Common attributes include underline, bold, italic, and bold italic. Other attributes include condensed type, superscript, and subscript. Attributes emphasize a word or group of words; applying an attribute to a small amount of text is more emphatic than applying it to large blocks of text. Also, a large block of text that is bold or italic can be very difficult to read. Avoid using many different attributes in a document. Also avoid overusing any attribute; using one too often diminishes its importance.

> **NOTE** Although underlining is a common attribute, limit its use in documents. Professional typesetters use underlining *only* at the bottom of a column of numbers. Use italic or bold rather than underlining for a more professional-looking document.

## Using Type Sizes

*Type size* is the size of a font measured in points from the top of the tallest capital letter to the bottom of the lowest descender. 10-point type in one typeface may not be exactly the same height as 10-point type in another typeface. Figure 23.12 shows some common type sizes and uses. All the type examples in the figure are Times Roman. Generally, however, you use attributes such as bold or italic with subheads, headings, and display type (either large—60-point and larger—or especially decorative typefaces that are used to attract the reader to the document).

**FIG. 23.12**
Use the sizes represented in the figure as a guideline for sizing text in your documents. You can also use bold and italic to emphasize text.

**Body Text**
9-point
10-point
11point
12-point

**Subheads**
12-point
14-point
16-point

**Headings**
18-point
24-point
36-point
48-point

**Display Type**
60-point
72-point

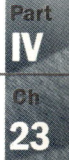

The following table describes common type sizes.

| Type Style | Size | Uses |
|---|---|---|
| Body text | 9, 10, 11, 12 | The bulk of text in a document. |
| Subheads | 12, 14, 16 | Categorize main topics or act as headlines. Use bold or italic type. |
| Headings | 18, 36, 48 | Represent main topics with headings. Headings can be bold, italic, or all uppercase. |
| Display heads | 60, 72, 96, 126 | Use display type—for large and sometimes ornamental text—sparingly in a document. |

 Create display type by entering the size in the Font Size text box (found in the Font dialog box). Only enter a number larger than 72 points if your printer can support it.

**FIG. 23.13**
Just two typefaces, two type styles, and three type sizes, combined with a simple border, create an eye-catching, professional-looking advertisement.

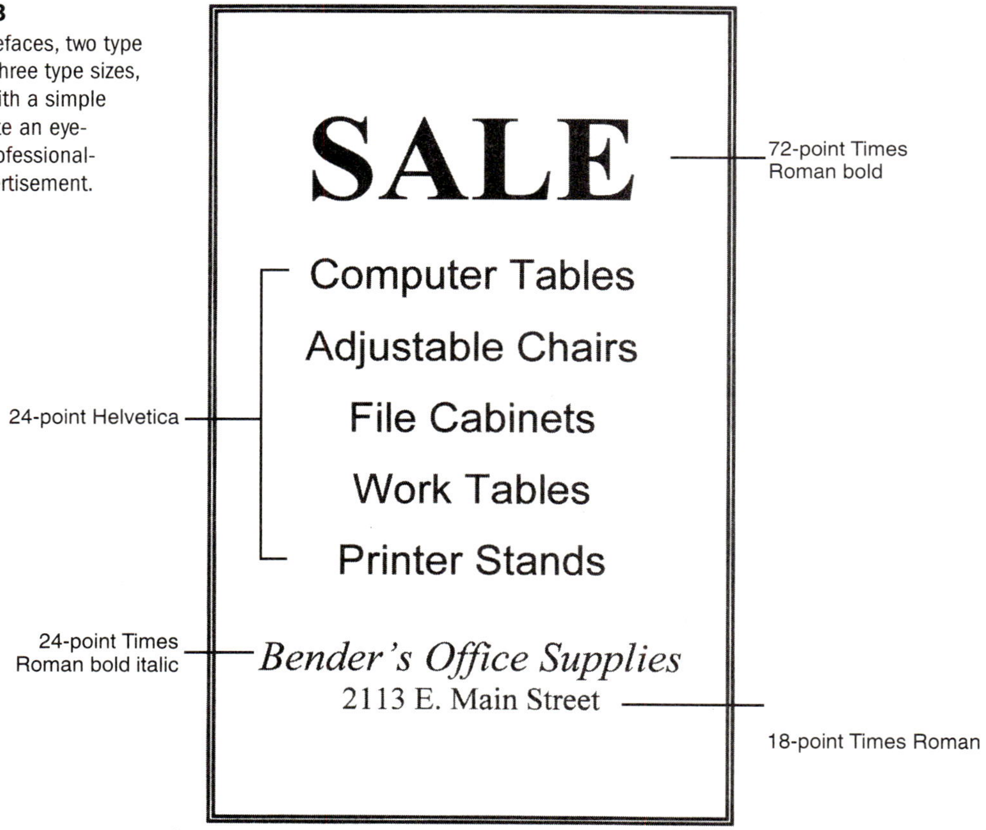

**SALE** — 72-point Times Roman bold

Computer Tables
Adjustable Chairs
File Cabinets — 24-point Helvetica
Work Tables
Printer Stands

24-point Times Roman bold italic — *Bender's Office Supplies*
2113 E. Main Street — 18-point Times Roman

As with typefaces, limit the number of type sizes you use in any one document. Use no more than three type sizes if possible: one size each for body text, headings, and subheads, for example. Figure 23.13 illustrates a flyer that uses the appropriate number of typefaces, type sizes, and attributes.

# Using Typographical Controls

*Typography* refers not only to typeface, type style, and type size, but to aesthetics and readability. When creating type for documents, your goal is to produce attractive and easy-to-read material that invites the reader to continue further. To accomplish this task, you can use WordPerfect's typographical controls to adjust the type on the page.

WordPerfect's typographical controls include leading, kerning, letterspacing, and word spacing. Each of these options regulates the way the type appears in documents and the way the type prints. You won't use all three options at one time, and you won't use any of the options all the time. You will, however, need to control leading, kerning, letterspacing, and word spacing at some point in your desktop publishing projects. The following sections explain each of WordPerfect's typographical controls and when to use them.

**Leading**  *Leading* is the same thing as line spacing, or the amount of space between two lines of text within the same paragraph. You're probably familiar with single-, one-and-a-half, and double-line spacing; these are common leading settings. WordPerfect, however, enables you to adjust the leading in smaller increments in the Word/Letter Spacing dialog box.

As you change type sizes, WordPerfect continues to set line spacing as 30 percent of the current type size. This results in lines being too far apart, or too close together, as shown in figure 23.14. You can adjust leading heights by using the Typesetting options or the Line Spacing options available in WordPerfect. Setting leading heights affects an entire paragraph and, therefore, does not stabilize lines within a paragraph that may use different type sizes. To set leading heights using Typesetting options, use these steps:

1. Choose Format, Typesetting, Word/Letter Spacing. The Word and Letter Spacing dialog box appears.
2. Click the Adjust Leading check box, then type the adjustment you need in the Between Lines text box.
3. Click OK to return to your document window.

**FIG. 23.14**
Leading adjustments add or decrease the spacing between lines.

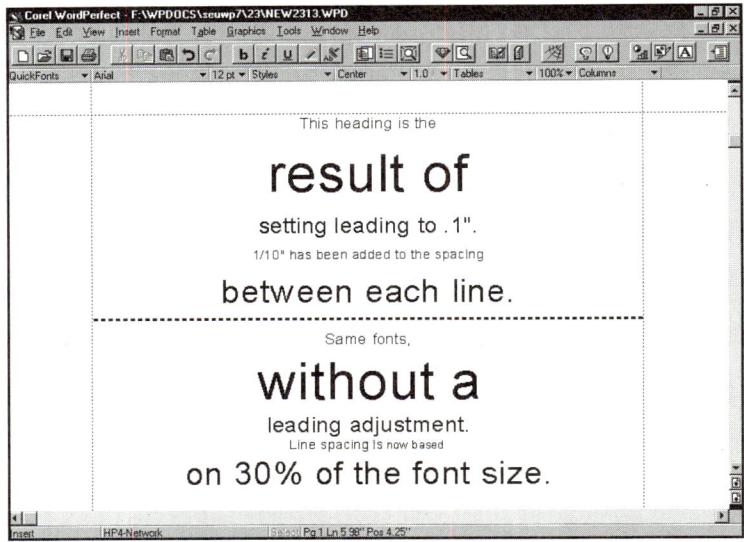

**Kerning** *Kerning* is the reduction of space between certain letter pairs so that the characters appear more pleasing to the eye. Some letters take up more space than others, which is not a problem when the text is small—for example, 14 points and smaller; however, kerning is sometimes necessary with larger text. Kerning is often useful with certain pairs of letters, for example:

| | | |
|---|---|---|
| Yo | At | Av |
| AV | LT | OA |
| Ta | Te | We |

Figure 23.15 illustrates 24-point Times Roman letter pairs as well as a headline before and after kerning.

> **NOTE** You can't kern monospaced fonts, such as Courier, because they allow the same amount of space for all letters.

The easiest way to kern two letters in a heading or in display type is to follow these steps:

1. Position the cursor between the two letters to be kerned.
2. Choose Format, Typesetting. From the cascading menu that appears, choose Manual Kerning. The Manual Kerning dialog box appears as shown in figure 23.16.

**FIG. 23.15**
Kerning is most effective when used on large type—headings and display type.

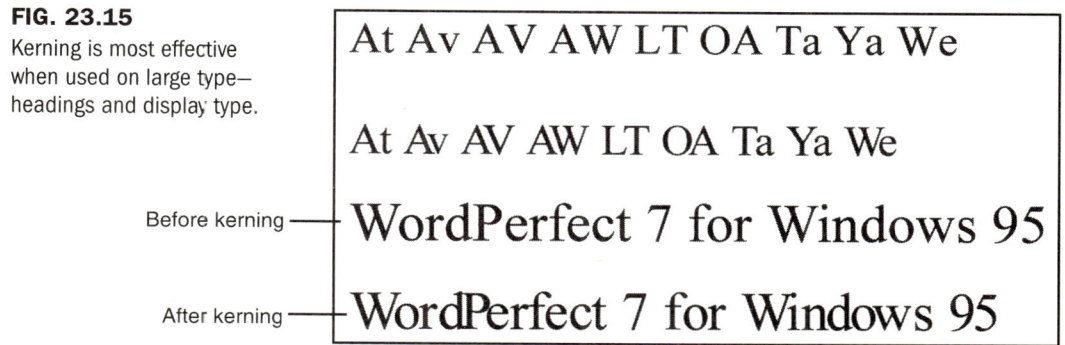

Before kerning

After kerning

**FIG. 23.16**
The Manual Kerning dialog box is used to tighten spacing between pairs of letters.

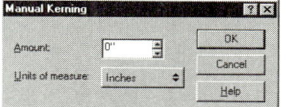

3. Click the up/down buttons in the Amount spin control. As you change the Amount value, you'll see that the space between the letters changes. (If necessary, drag the Manual Kerning dialog box to a location on the screen which allows you to view the text as you make your adjustments.)

4. When your kerning adjustment is complete, click OK to return to your document window. A horizontal advance Code appears in Reveal Codes that sets the kerning adjustment.

**N O T E** Rather than using the mouse in step 2, you can also type exact kerning adjustments. In Units of Measure, choose the type of measurement you want to use: Inches, Centimeters, Millimeters, Points, or 1200ths. Then, in the Amount text box, type a value—either positive or negative—to adjust the spacing between the two letters.

 You can turn on automatic kerning in the Word/Letter Spacing dialog box. See the next section for more information about this dialog box.

**Letterspacing** Using WordPerfect's letterspacing controls is a way of minimizing the large gaps of space that occur when you use full justification. Justification—aligning text both flush left and flush right—applies extra space between words to force the text to be flush with both margins. Figure 23.17 illustrates justified text before and after using letterspacing.

**FIG. 23.17**
Letterspacing can be used to add a fraction of space between characters and reduce the space between words.

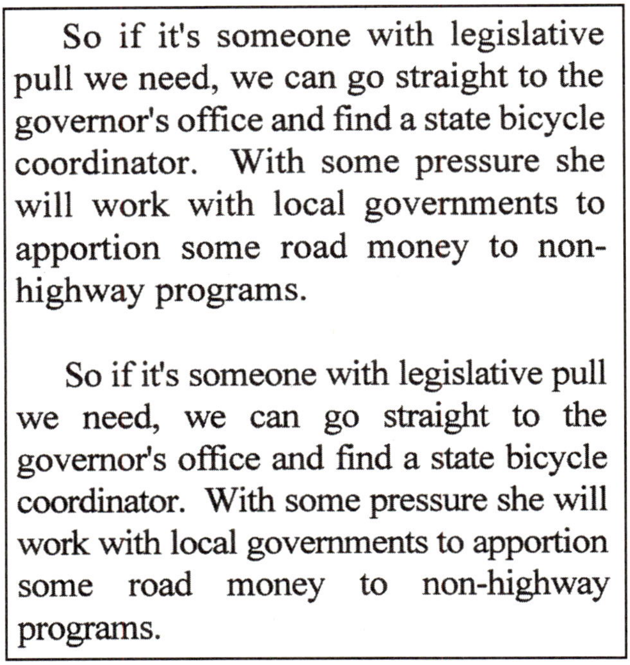

> So if it's someone with legislative pull we need, we can go straight to the governor's office and find a state bicycle coordinator. With some pressure she will work with local governments to apportion some road money to non-highway programs.
>
> So if it's someone with legislative pull we need, we can go straight to the governor's office and find a state bicycle coordinator. With some pressure she will work with local governments to apportion some road money to non-highway programs.

To apply letterspacing to your text, perform the following steps:

1. Either select the text to be adjusted, or position the cursor at the beginning of the text to be adjusted, in which case your action affects all text after the cursor.

2. Choose Format, Typesetting. From the cascading menu that appears, choose Word/Letterspacing. The Word/Letter Spacing dialog box appears (see fig. 23.18).

3. In the Letterspacing area, choose Percent of Optimal. Optimal letter spacing is the width of the capital letter I. Enter a value in the text box, or use the arrows to increase or decrease the value.

4. Choose OK to close the dialog box and view the results on the document screen.

WordPerfect Optimal letterspacing is the default setting and is adequate in most instances. However, you can experiment with the settings. Start by changing the percentage in small increments—5 or 10 percent at a time. Then view the changes and adjust the letterspacing if necessary.

**FIG. 23.18**
Adjust typographical controls for your text in this dialog box.

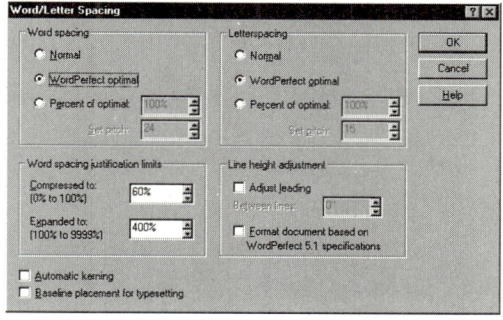

**Word Spacing**  Word spacing, like letterspacing, can be adjusted in justified text to create a more pleasing and readable block of text. You can adjust the word spacing in the same way you adjust letterspacing. Figure 23.19 shows text before and after word spacing is applied.

**FIG. 23.19**
Word spacing tightens or loosens the distance between words.

> So if it's someone with legislative pull we need, we can go straight to the governor's office and find a state bicycle coordinator. With some pressure she will work with local governments to apportion some road money to non-highway programs.
>
> So if it's someone with legislative pull we need, we can go straight to the governor's office and find a state bicycle coordinator. With some pressure she will work with local governments to apportion some road money to non-highway programs.

To change the word spacing in WordPerfect, perform the following steps:

1. Select the text or position the cursor in the text to be adjusted.
2. Choose Fo_r_mat, _T_ypesetting. From the cascading menu that appears, choose _W_ord/Letterspacing. The Word/Letter Spacing dialog box appears (refer to fig. 23.18).

3. In the Word Spacing area, choose Pe_r_cent of Optimal and enter a value.
4. Choose OK to close the dialog box and return to the document.

Optimal word spacing is the default setting in WordPerfect; however, you can experiment with the settings by choosing Pe_r_cent of Optimal. Increase or decrease the percentage in small increments until you are happy with the word spacing.

The Word Spacing Justification Limits section of the dialog box enables you to set default word spacing limits for your document. The compression limits refer to how much space can be reduced between words when the text is justified. You can set the limit from 0 percent, which is much too close to read easily, to 100 percent, which may be a bit too far apart. WordPerfect sets a default value of 60 percent, which provides comfortable reading.

Expansion limits refer to how much space can be added between words when the text is justified. The expansion limits range from 100 to 9999 percent, with WordPerfect's default set at 400 percent, or middle range. When set lower than 400, the words begin to close up space; when set to higher than 400, more space separates the words.

In general, use the expansion and compression limits WordPerfect sets, and use word and letterspacing to adjust the text. If you decide to try changing the compression and expansion limits, do so in small increments—such as 100 percent at a time—until you see the effects you want.

### TROUBLESHOOTING

**I looked for the fonts Helvetica and Times Roman, but WordPerfect doesn't offer these.** The names *Helvetica* and *Times Roman* are registered trademarks for popular typefaces. WordPerfect (and Windows in general) offers substitute typefaces (fonts) that are very nearly identical in appearance to the real Helvetica and Times Roman. Use Times New Roman as the equivalent of the Times Roman font; use Arial as the equivalent of the Helvetica font.

# Using Color

WordPerfect enables you to use color in your documents, both on-screen and in printed materials. You can display text, lines, borders, fills, and graphic images in color on-screen. If you have a color printer, WordPerfect can print these same elements in color. Using color with documents is as easy as formatting text or adding graphics. You can use WordPerfect's palette of colors or create your own custom colors.

Naturally, as with other design elements—type, graphics, columns, and so on—be careful to present the color in your documents within the design guidelines, and be sure not to overwhelm or distract the reader. Consider the following guidelines when using color in your documents:

- Limit the number of colors to two or three; consider the paper color as one of the colors if you use a paper color other than white.
- Be consistent with the use of color; if you choose dark blue for headings, use dark blue for headings throughout the document.
- Use contrasting colors such as red and blue.
- Don't use light colors such as yellow or white for text, because these colors make text difficult to read. Instead, use light colors for screens, lines, or graphic elements.
- Use a splash of color for emphasis; for example, use dark blue for text, and then use a splash of yellow for one element, such as a screen or thick graphic border.
- Don't forget white space in your designs. If you fill every area with color, the colors compete for the reader's attention; use white space to give the reader's eye a break.

This section shows how to apply color to type and graphics and how to create attractive, professional color documents. This section is a prerequisite to the "Printing in Color" section later in this chapter. Many of the techniques you learn here will be helpful when you are ready to print your document.

When applying color to a document, first apply the color on-screen. When you are satisfied with the way the text and graphics look, you can print your finished document. You can apply color to selected sections of text only, or you can apply color to all the text. You can use color with graphic elements—such as lines, borders, and fills (screens)—or you can use color with graphic images, such as clip art or art from WordPerfect Draw.

## Using Color with Text

When using color with text, make sure the color enhances the text. The text must be easy to read. Use color sparingly: for example, red headings with black body text, green display type in an advertisement, or blue body text with red headings on white paper. If you must use three colors, use two colors consistently throughout the document and the third as an emphasis point.

 You can apply colors to styles for faster and easier formatting.

The easiest way to apply color to text is after you have entered and formatted the text. When the document is complete, add color. To apply color to text, follow these steps:

> **N O T E**  If you select the text before you change the color of the font, only the selected text is changed. If, however, you position the cursor within the text, all text following the cursor is changed until you change the font color again.

1. Choose Format, Font, or double-click either the Quick Font, Font, or Size buttons on the Power Bar. The Font dialog box appears.
2. In the Color Options area, click the Text Color pop-up button. The default color palette appears (see fig. 23.20).

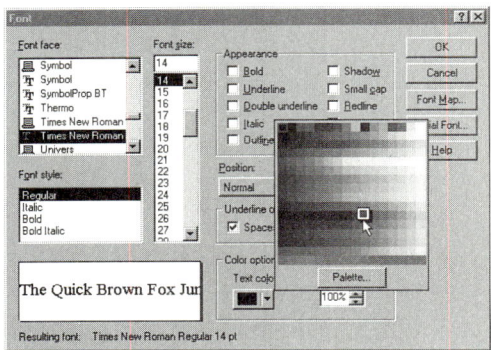

**FIG. 23.20**
The color printing palette offers various shades of colors you can apply to a font. You can also choose a shade of black, creating a gray screened effect for interesting headings or display type.

3. As you move the mouse pointer or use the cursor arrows to move through the color palette, the current color "jumps" forward. Click or press Enter to select the current color.
4. Choose OK to close the dialog box.

In addition to changing the color of a font, you can also change the shading of the selected font. In the Color Options area, change the value in the Shading text box; note the change in the Resulting Font preview box as you change the shading.

Furthermore, you can create your own custom colors and shades by choosing Palette in the Color pop-up palette. Figure 23.21 illustrates the Define Color Printing Palette dialog box. You can choose various colors in the palette and change its composition, or blend, copy, and invert colors. After you've created a color you plan to use often, save it by typing a name in the Name text box. You can save a group of colors as a custom palette to use over and over in your documents by clicking Save As from the Define Color Palette dialog box.

**FIG. 23.21**
The default palette is one created using 256 colors; choose colors from the color wheel, or create the color by entering values in the Color Model area.

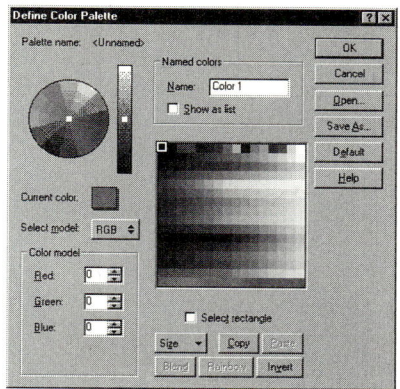

> **NOTE** When you create a palette in the Define Color Printing Palette dialog box, that palette replaces the original in the Color Options area of the Font dialog box, that is, until you change it again.

> **NOTE** Size defines the number of colors in the palette. You can drag the mouse over several colors in the palette, then click Blend to create shades of one color or to blend two colors together; you can click Rainbow to create colors which stand adjacent to one another on the color wheel. You can further choose to create or edit your color mix using one of three color models RGB (red, green, blue), HLS (hue luminosity saturation), and CYMK (cyan, yellow, magenta, back) using the Model button. You can also choose to Invert your color choice. Inverting selects the color directly opposite the chosen color on a color wheel. For example, black is the invert of white, yellow the invert of blue, and so on.

## Using Color with Graphics

You can also apply colors to graphic lines, borders, fills, and images using a color palette like the one used for fonts. Choosing Format, Border/Fill allows you to choose colors for page, paragraph, and column borders. In addition, you can define custom colors and fills for graphic lines while defining lines by choosing Graphics, Custom Line. You can change the color of images using WordPerfect Draw or Presentations; for more information about WordPerfect Draw, see Chapter 22, "Using WordPerfect Draw and TextArt."

**Lines** To change the color of a graphic line, create a line, or choose one to edit, follow these steps:

1. Access the Create/Edit Graphic Line dialog box by choosing Graphics, and then either Custom Line to create a line or Edit Line to customize a line.

2. In Line options, choose Line Color. The palette appears; choose the color for the line and choose OK to close the dialog box.

  **TIP**  If you want to revert to the original line color, access the Edit Graphic Line dialog box. In the color palette for Line Color, check the Use Line Style Color check box.

**Border**   To change the color of a page, paragraph, or column border, follow these steps:

1. Access the Border/Fill dialog box by choosing Format, Border/Fill. Then choose Paragraph, Page, or Column. The Border/Fill dialog box associated with your selection opens (see fig. 23.22).

2. For Page borders only, choose Line as the Border Type. Note that you can only change the colors of Fancy borders by first adding the border to your document, then editing the border using WordPerfect Draw or Presentations.

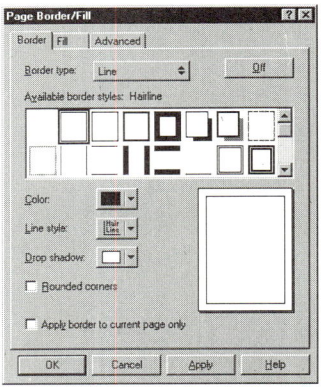

**FIG. 23.22**
The Page Border/Fill dialog box is the route to using borders and fills and customizing their appearance.

3. Open the Color palette, then select the color you want to use. To further define available colors, click the Palette button.

4. Choose OK to return to your document window.

**Fill**   To change the fill for a paragraph, page, or column, follow these steps:

1. Access the Border/Fill dialog box by choosing Format, Border/Fill. Then choose Paragraph, Page, or Column. The Page Border/Fill dialog box opens (refer to fig. 20.22).

2. For Page Fill only, you must first select a Line border type before you can change the fill for the paragraph. The Line border type can be no border. To select a Line border type, select Line from the Border Type field.

3. Click the Fill tab or press Ctrl+Tab until the Fill tab appears.
4. Select the fill you want to use from the Available Fill Styles palette. As you select a fill, notice that the preview window updates to reflect your changes.
5. You can further define your fill style by selecting a Start Color (foreground) and an End Color (background). Start and End Color options only appear when you choose a gradient fill, as shown in figure 23.23. All other fill styles allow you to select foreground and background colors.

**FIG. 23.23**
Choose a fill style and color that complements the contents of the border. Don't choose a dark blue gradient or honey-comb fill for a border with text to be read.

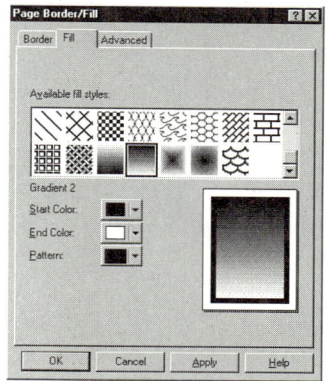

6. You can also select a pattern for your fill by choosing Pattern. If you've chosen a shaded fill such as 10 percent, your pattern selection will use your fill shade.
7. Click the Apply button to apply your choices to your document without closing the Page Border/Fill dialog box. When your choices are complete, click OK.

 Do not use a heavy fill—50 percent or more—when you use dark colors; you want the reader to be able to see the text through the fill.

**Using the Advanced Border/Fill Options** The Advanced tab of the Border/Fill dialog box allows you to further customize your Border and Fill options. The Advanced tab applies its fields as discussed in this section. Figure 23.24 displays the Advanced tab.

Setting Inside and Outside spacing controls the distance your border appears from its associated text. For example, setting a larger inside spacing forces the border further away from the text which the border surrounds. Setting an outside spacing, on the other hand, sets the distance from which other text sits away from the "bordered" text.

If you've chosen a border style that includes a drop shadow, you can further customize both the color and width of the shadow in the Drop Shadow area.

**FIG. 23.24**
The Advanced tab of the Border/Fill dialog box customizes settings for both the Border and Fill tabs.

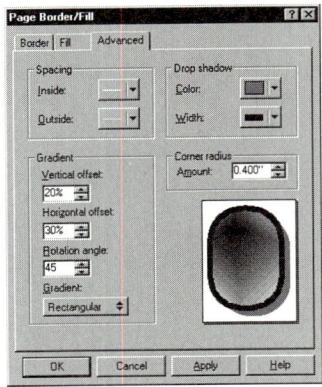

The Gradient fields apply only to gradient fill choices. For example, using the offsets and rotation angle fields allow you to customize where the Start color appears in the fill, and the angle in which the Start and End colors meet.

The Corner Radius Amount field sets the exact curve to be used when you've chosen Rounded Corners on the Border tab.

## Creating a Color Document

If you have a color printer, you can print your documents in a full range of colors. Although printing thousands of newsletters is not feasible using your own color printer, printing 10 special reports to show the board members may be. You must consider the number of documents to print and the cost to print them before you decide to print in color.

 Look at as many color publications—magazines, brochures, rack cards, newsletters, and so on—as you can. Use samples to give you ideas for your documents.

In addition, make sure you follow all design guidelines and suggestions to ensure that your document looks professional and attractive. Following is a list of considerations when applying color to a document:

- Bear in mind the number of printed copies and the number of pages per copy; judge the feasibility of color printing by calculating the cost per copy.
- Lay out the page and format all text before adding color. Use the design guidelines as you format the document.
- Choose only two or three colors for the entire document.
- Remember that the design guidelines—consistency, emphasis, balance, proportion, and white space—apply to color as well as to text and page formatting.

**TROUBLESHOOTING**

**When I tried to change the kerning of a pair of letters, nothing happened.** WordPerfect offers a means to adjust the spacing between two letters. This is more often used in desktop publishing to adjust the kerning of the letter pair—for example, when kerned closer together, the letters VA look more visually appealing, because the left side of the A tucks in neatly to the right side of the V. The kerning adjustment—accessible by choosing Fo_r_mat, _T_ypesetting, _M_anual Kerning—works only with proportionally spaced fonts. These are fonts where characters take up only as much space on the line as they need to; i's take up less space than W's. Kerning does not work with monospaced fonts, such as Courier, because with these fonts, all the characters are meant to take up the same amount of space on the line.

**When I try to print a document with graphics, the text appears on the printed page, but not the graphics.** WordPerfect allows you to turn off graphic printing and print just the text. Among other things, this feature lets you quickly create a "proof" of the text of a document, without spending the time to print the graphics that are in place. To enable graphic printing, choose _F_ile, _P_rint, and check the Print Graph_i_cs option.

CHAPTER 24

# Using the Equation Editor

*by Gordon Nelder-Adams and Gordon McComb*

**E**veryone knows Einstein's famous equation, $E=MC^2$. Einstein had no trouble writing an equation like this on his chalkboard. But even a man of Einstein's genius may have had trouble figuring out how to show such equations in his favorite word processor (which undoubtedly would have been WordPerfect for Windows!).

Fortunately for the Einsteins of the world, WordPerfect 7 comes with an extremely powerful Equation Editor—a special tool designed just for creating equations of all shapes and sizes.

Mathematical equations have their own grammar and syntax, which are analogous to the grammar and syntax of written and spoken English. Just as you use a text editor to create and edit sentences, you can use WordPerfect's Equation Editor to create and edit equations. Although WordPerfect's text-editing tools are ideal for creating words, sentences, and paragraphs, mathematical equations require more specialized tools to create multiple type sizes, special characters, varying line spacing, and complex alignment. ▪

**Type entries in the Editing Pane**

You learn how to create equations by entering English-like commands in an Editing Pane.

**View equations in the Display Pane**

See the results of the commands you entered in the Editing Pane displayed as an equation in the Display Pane.

**Insert commands, functions, and symbols from the equation palettes**

The Equation Editor supports many mathematical functions that can be used to create your own equations.

**Create superscripts and subscripts, fractions, sums and integrals, roots, and matrices**

You don't have to be a rocket scientist to create complex equations. This chapter guides you through the more complex and intricate equations.

**Embed equations in text**

After creating an equation you learn how to embed it into your document.

# Understanding the Equation Editor

You can use WordPerfect's Equation Editor to create complex, multilevel equations that would look perfectly at home in a calculus textbook, scientific paper, or engineering diagram. You can also use the Equation Editor to create simple fractions, square roots, and other common algebraic functions more likely to be helpful to the average user.

The Equation Editor uses a specialized syntax similar to the language you use to read equations out loud. For example, the syntax for creating a fraction is simply "a over b." After you enter a description of an equation, the Equation Editor performs all of the formatting for you, automatically placing each element in the correct position, using the appropriate type sizes, and scaling mathematical symbols such as sums, integrals, roots, and parentheses to fit. The Equation Editor automatically positions, sizes, and aligns the elements in mathematical expressions such as complex ratios, built-up fractions, and multilevel subscripts and superscripts. The Equation Editor does not solve equations for you, nor does it check the mathematical validity of any equation you create.

When you create an equation, WordPerfect places it in a graphics box. You can then adjust the equation's size, shape, and position as you do any other graphics box. WordPerfect also provides all the symbol fonts necessary to display equations in your document exactly as they will print, so you can see an equation as you create or edit the surrounding text. The program can print equations on any printer, from a nine-pin impact printer to a PCL laser printer or a PostScript typesetter.

# Starting the Equation Editor

The Equation Editor is a specialized graphics editor; therefore, the mechanics of creating, saving, and positioning equations are similar to those used for figures and other graphics boxes.

▶ **See** "Using Graphics Boxes," **p. 262**
▶ **See** "Customizing Graphics Boxes," **p. 669**

Because you can choose which types of graphics boxes to include in the Graphics menu, before you can create an equation you must verify that Equation is listed as an option. To do so, choose the Graphics menu. If Equation is not listed, follow these steps to add the option:

1. With the Graphics menu still displayed, choose Graphics Styles.
2. Choose Box to display options for Graphics Box styles.
3. Choose Menu. The Edit Graphics Menu dialog box appears, which lists the available Graphics Box styles. Check boxes to the left of the styles indicate which styles appear in the menu (see fig. 24.1).

**FIG. 24.1**
The Edit Graphics Menu dialog box lets you choose which Graphics Box styles to display in the Graphics menu.

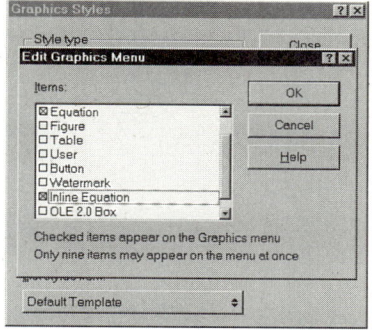

4. Select the Equation check box.
5. If you want to create inline equations, which can be embedded within a paragraph, select the Inline Equation check box.
6. Choose OK and then <u>C</u>lose to return to the document window.

To start the Equation Editor and create a new equation, choose <u>G</u>raphics, Equation. The Equation Editor appears on-screen, temporarily replacing the normal document editing screen (see fig. 24.2).

**FIG. 24.2**
The Equation Editor has its own menus and Toolbars, equation palettes for inserting commands and special characters, an Editing Pane for typing equation text, and a Display Pane for displaying equations as they will print.

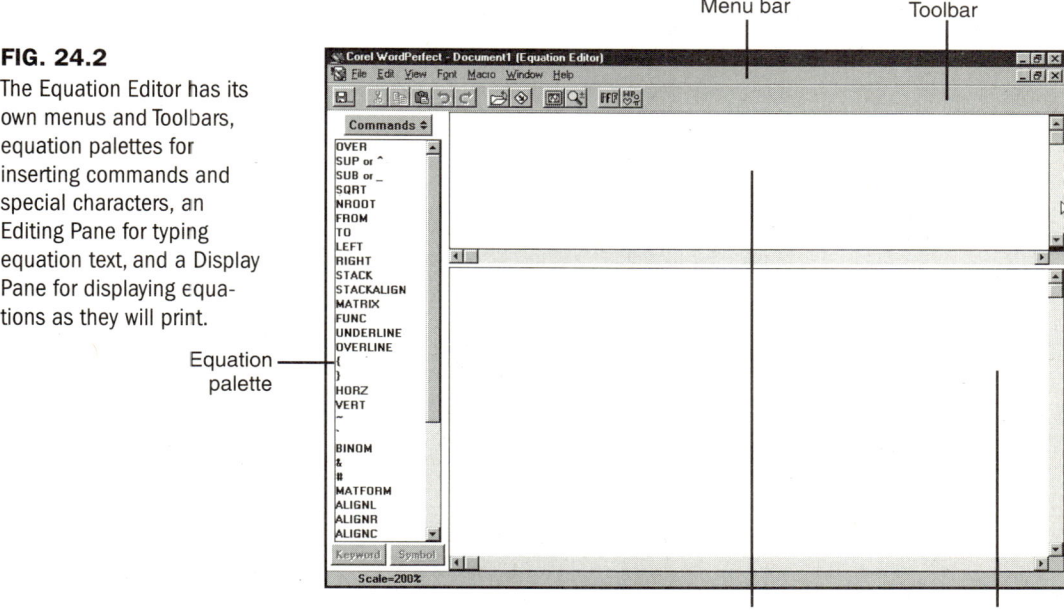

# Examining the Equation Editor

The Equation Editor consists of five main elements:

- The Editing Pane
- The Display Pane
- The Equation palette
- An abbreviated menu bar
- The Equation Editor Toolbar

▶ **See** "Using Graphics Boxes," **p. 262**
▶ **See** "Customizing Graphics Boxes," **p. 669**

Making full use of the Equation Editor requires using all five of its elements, as well as other available features, including the WordPerfect Characters dialog box and specialized equation keyboards.

When you call up the Equation Editor to create a new equation, the Editing Pane and Display Pane are empty (refer to fig. 24.2). You can switch between the Editing Pane, Display Pane, and equation palettes with the Next Pane and Previous Pane commands (F6, Shift+F6).

The Editing Pane, located at the top of the Equation Editor, is a simple text-editing window in which you type the text of an equation. The Editing Pane lets you use all the basic text-editing commands and techniques, but provides none of the normal formatting options. You can move by character, word, line, or to the top and bottom of an equation with the normal directional keys. You can select text by using Shift either with the directional keys or with the mouse. You can delete selected text, or cut or copy it to the Clipboard, and paste it back once or many times. You can use Edit, Find and Replace (F2) to search for a word or number in a large equation or to replace it with an alternative throughout an equation. (You can also move information between the normal document screen and the Editing Pane by cutting or copying to the Clipboard.)

You cannot, however, use any of WordPerfect's normal formatting commands, such as font attributes or justification, in the Editing Pane. Instead, you type a text description of the equation you want to create, using special commands and symbols to format the equation. Each description can consist of text, variables, symbols, numbers, functions, and commands. You can insert these elements by typing directly from the keyboard, by selecting them from an equation palette, or through the WordPerfect Characters dialog box.

You can also perform basic file operations in the Equation Editor. You can save the contents of the Editing Pane as a separate file, and retrieve other equation descriptions into the Editing Pane to modify or build on.

To see the current appearance of your equation, choose View, Redisplay, or press Ctrl+F3, or double-click the Display Pane. WordPerfect displays the equation in the Display Pane (the lower half of the Equation Editor). If your equation is not syntactically correct, the program displays an error message instead of the equation.

As its name implies, the Display Pane displays an image of your equation as it will print. WordPerfect usually magnifies this image for ease of viewing, although you can zoom in or out to enlarge or reduce the view of a particular segment or the entire equation, and you can scroll in the window to display different parts of your equation. You cannot, however, make any changes in the Display Pane. If some part of your equation is incorrect, you must make changes in the Editing Pane.

**NOTE** WordPerfect doesn't automatically display your equation in the Display Pane, nor does the program automatically update the display when you make changes in the Editing Pane. The Equation Editor cannot display an equation if its syntax is not correct, which is often the case while you are in the process of building an equation. After you create or change an equation, therefore, you should redisplay the equation to see the results.

When you need to insert a character, symbol, command, or function into an equation, you can type it from the keyboard or insert it from an equation palette. The Equation Editor has eight palettes, similar in concept to the 15 character sets available in the WordPerfect Characters dialog box. Each palette provides quick access to a group of WordPerfect characters, formatting commands, or mathematical functions used frequently in the Equation Editor. You can browse through the palettes to find the symbol, command, or function you need, and then insert it into the Editing Pane.

The Equation Editor has a menu bar of its own, similar to WordPerfect's menu bar, but with fewer entries. The Equation Editor menu bar contains the following menus:

- *File menu*. Lets you save equations and return to the document, cancel changes, and save and retrieve equations as separate files. WordPerfect refers to "retrieving" equations as "Insert File."
- *Edit menu*. Lets you perform the standard editing undo, redo, undelete, cut, copy, paste, find, and replace operations. You can also Redo, display Undo/Redo History, or set Equation Preferences via the Edit menu.

- *View menu.* Lets you redisplay equations in the View Pane, zoom the display of the View Pane, or turn the palettes and Toolbar off or on.
- *Font menu.* Lets you choose a font to be used in the Equation Editor, and call up the WordPerfect Characters dialog box.
- *Macro menu.* Lets you record or play macros to automate Equation Editor tasks.
- *Window menu.* Lets you switch between the Equation Editor and an open document, and tile or cascade all open windows.
- *Help menu.* Lets you call up the WordPerfect Help system.

Finally, the Equation Editor has its own Toolbar and keyboard, which are automatically activated whenever you call up the Equation Editor. Each contains features and functions useful in the Equation Editor.

# Creating a Simple Equation

Before examining the Equation Editor's syntax and command structure in detail, create a few simple equations and observe how WordPerfect interprets them.

## Creating Proper Spacing in an Equation

The Equation Editor doesn't interpret normal spaces between words in the same manner that WordPerfect does. Instead, you have to instruct the Equation Editor where to add spaces and how much space to add. To see how the Equation Editor uses spacing, follow these steps:

1. Choose Graphics, Equation. The Equation Editor appears. The insertion point is in the Editing Pane, and the equation palette is displayed.

2. Type the following equation, using the space bar to create the spaces before and after the plus (+) and equal (=) signs:

   **2x + 3y = 24**

3. Choose View, Redisplay, or press Ctrl+F3. Your equation appears in the Display Pane, but it doesn't look quite the way you typed it. Instead, it appears as follows:

   2x+3y=24

   The Equation Editor doesn't interpret spaces that you type in the Editing Pane as spaces in the printed equation. In many cases, equations require spacing far narrower than standard spacing, so the Equation Editor demands that you explicitly enter spacing instructions by using a tilde (˜) to create a normal space and a grave accent mark (`) to create a thin space, which is one-quarter the width of a normal space.

4. Edit your original equation so that it reads as follows in the Editing Pane:

    2x˜+˜3y˜=˜24

5. Choose <u>V</u>iew, <u>R</u>edisplay, or press Ctrl+F3. In the Display Pane, your equation now appears like this:

    2x + 3y = 24

6. Choose <u>F</u>ile, <u>C</u>lose, or press Ctrl+F4. Your equation appears horizontally centered in your document.

The tilde (˜) and grave accent mark (`) can be called *formatting spaces,* because they are the codes that control the spacing format of printed equations. If you don't use formatting spaces in your equations, WordPerfect runs the clauses in your equation together. As you work in the Editing Pane, however, the Equation Editor treats the formatting space codes as it does any other character for the purposes of cursor movement and text editing.

Normal spaces, created by pressing the space bar, don't affect the appearance of the printed equation, but make working in the Editing Pane much easier. Normal spaces separate items and improve the readability of the text in the Editing Pane. They also break an equation up into "words," which you can move through quickly using the Ctrl+left-arrow and Ctrl–right-arrow keys, as in a normal document.

Just as pressing the space bar inserts a nonprinting space, pressing the Enter key in the Editing Pane inserts a nonprinting hard return. The hard return moves the cursor to the next line in the Editing Pane without affecting the appearance of the printed equation. Like normal spaces, hard returns improve the readability of equations in the Editing Pane by letting you put individual clauses on lines by themselves. If you want a printed equation to contain two or more lines, you must use the STACK or STACKALIGN commands. See the later section "Creating Multiline Expressions with STACK and STACKALIGN" for more information.

In practice you should use a combination of normal spaces and formatting spaces when you create and edit equations, to make the equation easier to work with in the Editing Pane, and to ensure the proper formatting of the printed equations.

## Creating a Simple Fraction

You also use regular spaces in the Editing Pane to separate commands and variables. OVER, for example, is the Equation Editor command that creates a fraction. You type **a OVER b** to create the following equation:

$$\frac{a}{b}$$

Because the printed equation contains no spaces, you don't need to use tildes. You might assume, therefore, that you can omit regular spaces from the typed equation as well. Typing **aOVERb**, however, produces the following equation:

*aoverb*

Without the spaces around OVER, the Equation Editor cannot recognize it as a command, and instead treats the entire phrase as a single, six-letter variable.

Create the following sample equation using the OVER command:

$$\frac{2x}{3y} = 24$$

To create the equation, follow these steps:

1. Choose <u>G</u>raphics, <u>E</u>quation.
2. In the Editing Pane, type the following equation:

   **2x over 3y ~=~ 24**

   **N O T E**  You don't need to capitalize or lowercase the OVER command; Equation Editor commands are not case-sensitive.

3. Choose <u>V</u>iew, <u>R</u>edisplay, or press Ctrl+F3. Your equation now looks like this:

$$2\frac{x}{3}y = 24$$

Again, this is not quite what you want. The Equation Editor recognized the OVER command, but it did not recognize "2x" and "3y" as belonging together. The Equation Editor makes very few assumptions about which letters, characters, and symbols should be grouped together and which should not. Just as you must indicate formatting spaces by inserting tildes and grave accent marks, you must use braces ({ }) around groups of characters on which you want the Equation Editor to perform some action.

4. In the Editing Pane, change the text again to read as follows:

   {2x} over {3y} ~=~ 24

5. Choose <u>V</u>iew, <u>R</u>edisplay; or press Ctrl+F3. Now the equation appears as desired.

## Creating Superscripts and Subscripts

Superscripts and subscripts are as common as fractions in many equations. WordPerfect's normal text attributes do not work in the Equation Editor, so you must use commands to create superscripts and subscripts in equations. These commands are SUP and SUB, respectively. Because these two commands are used so frequently, WordPerfect provides abbreviated forms of the commands. In place of SUP you can use a caret (^) to create a superscript, and in place of SUB you can use an underline (_) to create a subscript.

Therefore, to produce the simple expression $x^2$, you can type **x SUP 2**, or simply **x^2**. To produce $x_1$, you can type **x SUB 1**, or simply **x_1**. As with OVER, you must use regular spaces around SUP and SUB. You don't need to use spaces around the caret and underline characters because their meanings are always unambiguous, and the Equation Editor reserves their use for these commands.

You can nest multiple levels of super- and subscripts, using braces if necessary. Examine the following typed equations and their printed appearances:

| (a) | (b) | (c) | (d) |
|---|---|---|---|
| x^e^n | x^e^n-1 | x^e^{n-1} | x^e^n_1 |
| $x^{e^n}$ | $x^{e^n}-1$ | $x^{e^{n-1}}$ | $x^{e^{n_1}}$ |

As you can see, WordPerfect chooses a smaller point size for each successive level. Also, note the difference that adding braces makes between equations (b) and (c).

Finally, you can add both a superscript and a subscript to the same character. For example, to create the following expression:

$$x_1^2$$

you type the following:

   **x_1^2**

To make the superscript appear immediately over the subscript, you must type the subscript first, then the superscript.

## Editing Equations

If you discover a mistake in an equation after you have closed the Equation Editor and returned to your main document, or you need to edit the equation for some other reason, you can return to the Equation Editor to make further changes in an equation.

To edit an existing equation, follow these steps:

1. Choose Graphics, Edit Box, or press Shift+F11. If you only have one graphics box in your document, WordPerfect immediately selects the box and displays the Edit Box dialog box.

   If you have more than one graphics box, WordPerfect displays the Select Edit Box to Edit dialog box. Choose Equation Box, and then enter the number of the equation you want to edit in the Document Box Number box. WordPerfect selects the box and displays the Edit Box box.

2. Choose Content, or press Alt+O. WordPerfect displays the Box Content dialog box.

3. Choose Edit. The Equation Editor appears, displaying the selected equation.

 **TIP** To edit an equation quickly, double-click the equation with your mouse. The Equation Editor opens and automatically retrieves the equation.

## Reviewing Key Concepts

Now that you've created a few equations and have some feel for how the Equation Editor works, you are ready to examine some concepts and terminology in more depth. Although learning the syntax of individual commands is important, understanding the concepts on which those commands are based is equally important.

At first glance, many commands can appear to be confusing and arbitrary collections of symbols. With a little background knowledge, the command syntax becomes logical and necessary. In the following sections, you learn some definitions and general rules of syntax. Then you examine the parts of the Equation Editor in more detail, before returning to more specific examples of Equation Editor formatting commands.

## Defining Terms

A *command* is a reserved word or character that tells the Equation Editor to perform a formatting action on the text that follows. OVER, SUP, and SUB (or ^ and _) are examples of commands. Table 24.1 contains a full list of Equation Editor commands and their meanings.

A *function* is a word recognized by the Equation Editor as a standard mathematical function such as *log* or *sin*. A full list of functions can be found in table 24.3, located in the later section "Using Functions and Commands To Create Equations."

A *symbol* is any character that is not a standard letter or number. Symbols frequently used in the Equation Editor can be found in the Greek, Symbols, Arrows, Large, Sets, and Other equation palettes. The complete set of WordPerfect characters is available by choosing Font, Character, or by pressing Ctrl+W.

A *key word* is an alphabetic description of a command, function, or symbol. Commands and functions are key words by definition. However, just as SUP and SUB can be represented by ^ and _, each symbol can be inserted as a key word or an individual character. Thus, BETA is the key word for the symbol B. You can use either the key word or the equivalent character in the equation text to make the symbol appear in the printed equation.

A *variable* is any sequence of letters and numbers that the Equation Editor doesn't recognize as a command, function, or other key word. Variables can be one or more characters and must start with a letter of the alphabet, but can contain numbers also. Any word not having a special meaning is treated as a variable. A variable must be followed by a nonalphabetic character, such as a symbol, normal space, or hard return. Examples of variables include *x*, *B1*, and *velocity;* by default, the Equation Editor prints variables in italic type.

A *number* is any non-negative integer (such as 0, 1, or 387) that is followed by a space, alphabetic character, symbol, or period. Thus, although B2 is a variable, 2B is the number 2 followed by the variable B. The Equation Editor doesn't recognize real numbers (negative numbers and decimals, such as −2 or 3.1) as units, and treats minus signs and decimal points as separate characters. To make the Equation Editor treat real numbers as units, you must use braces around real numbers to group them, such as {−2} or {3.1}.

### Table 24.1 Equation Editor Commands

| Command Key Word | Description |
| --- | --- |
| OVER | Fraction |
| SUP or ^ | Superscript |
| SUB or _ | Subscript |
| SQRT | Square root |
| NROOT | Nth root |
| FROM | Limits |
| TO | Limits |
| LEFT | Left delimiter |
| RIGHT | Right delimiter |
| STACK | Vertical stack |
| STACKALIGN | Vertical stack with character alignment |
| MATRIX | Matrix |
| FUNC | User-defined function |
| UNDERLINE | Underline |
| OVERLINE | Overline |
| { | Start group |
| } | End group |
| HORZ | Horizontal move |
| VERT | Vertical move |
| ~ | Normal space |
| ` | Thin space (1/4 of normal space) |
| BINOM | Binomial |
| & | Column separator |
| # | Row separator |
| MATFORM | Matrix column format |
| ALIGNL | Align left |
| ALIGNR | Align right |
| ALIGNC | Align center |

| Command Key Word | Description |
| --- | --- |
| PHANTOM | Placeholder |
| . | No delimiter |
| \ | Literal |
| BOLD | Bold attribute |
| ITAL | Italic attribute |
| OVERSM | Fraction small |
| BINOMSM | Binomial small |
| LINESPACE | Vertical (line) spacing |
| LONGDIV | Long division |
| LONGDIVS | Long division (square symbol) |
| SCALESYM | Scale symbol |

# Understanding Syntax

Text in an equation resembles a sentence. Commands act the part of verbs, numbers act the part of variables, and other symbols take the place of nouns. Just as each language has its own rules of grammar and syntax, the Equation Editor has specific rules that govern how you combine the various elements of an equation. The Equation Editor doesn't check to see whether your equation makes sense, only that it is syntactically correct. In the Equation Editor, as in English, you can construct a sentence that is syntactically correct but means something other than what you intended, or one that is missing an essential part of speech and is meaningless. It's up to you to ensure that the equation makes sense.

Your equation text must provide the necessary commands for what actions are to be taken, and what groups of characters those commands should act upon. The Equation Editor then performs the mechanics of positioning the various elements of an equation, selecting the proper type sizes, and creating graphic symbols where necessary. As long as your equation's syntax is correct, the Equation Editor shows it in the Display Pane, although the displayed equation may not be exactly what you intended. If your syntax is faulty, however, when you choose View, Redisplay, the Editor displays an `ERROR: Incorrect Syntax` message in the status bar and moves the insertion point to a part of your equation text that it recognizes as faulty. If your equation has more than one error, you may have to edit and attempt to redisplay several times.

The following syntax rules apply to all equations. Some commands have additional syntax rules, as described in the "Using Functions and Commands to Create Equations" section later in this chapter.

- Commands are not case-sensitive. You can type a command in all uppercase, all lowercase, or in mixed case. **OVER**, **over**, and **Over** are all acceptable commands.

- All commands must be separated from variables that come immediately before and after them. You can use the space bar, press Enter, or insert a symbol to separate a command from a following variable or number.

    You can place a number immediately before a command, but if you place a number immediately after a command, the Equation Editor interprets the two elements as a single variable. For example, typing **3OVER 5** creates the fraction 3/5, but typing **3OVER5** creates the expression 3OVER5. The best practice, therefore, is to use spaces around commands at all times. When you choose a command from the equation palette, the Editor automatically puts a space before and after the command and displays the command in uppercase letters.

- Commands act only on individual elements of an equation, whether those elements are numbers, variables, or characters. If you want a command to act on several elements as a group, you must put braces ({ }) around the elements you want to combine. The Equation Editor then formats everything between the pair of braces as a single group.

 **TIP** Putting spaces around commands is a good way to avoid syntax errors.

- You can create groups within groups by using additional pairs of braces.
- Braces must appear in pairs. Mismatched braces are the most common cause of syntax errors.
- When formatting equations, the Equation Editor groups elements in the following order of precedence:
    1. Groups formed by braces ({ })
    2. Diacritical marks (such as overbars, vectors, and tildes)
    3. Primes, SUB, SUP, FROM, and TO
    4. Roots
    5. OVER, BINOM
    6. Other elements from left to right

- Groups formed by braces ({ }) take precedence in all cases. When the Equation Editor doesn't format a clause as you desired, you can always override its defaults by establishing a group.

# Working with the Equation Editor Features

As you saw in the examples earlier in this chapter, you can create and edit many equations in the Editing Pane using only the keyboard, without employing the other resources the Equation Editor provides. Making full use of the Equation Editor, however, requires making full use of its features: the keyboard, specialized equation keyboards, the equation palettes, the WordPerfect Characters dialog box, and the Equation Editor Toolbar.

## Using the Editing Pane

The Editing Pane provides a full text-editing environment with most of the editing features available in a normal document. You can use the normal directional keys to move by character, word, line, or to the top or bottom of an equation, or you can select any insertion point with the mouse. You can select text by using Shift with the directional keys or by using the mouse. You can delete selected text, or you can cut or copy it to the Clipboard and paste it back once or many times. You can also move information between the normal document screen and the Editing Pane by cutting or copying to the Clipboard.

You can enter letters, numbers, and other keyboard characters by typing directly in the Editing Pane. You can also insert many mathematical symbols and characters using the equation palette, but if you need to include the following common characters in an equation, you must enter them from the keyboard:

$+ - * / = < > ! ? . | @ , ; :$

Several other common characters must also be entered from the keyboard, but have special meaning to the Equation Editor. These are:

$\sim \ ` \ " \ \backslash \ \# \ \& \ \{ \ \} \ ( \ ) \ [ \ ]$

You have already seen how the tilde (~) and grave accent mark (`) are used. The meanings of the other characters are described in the later section "Using Functions and Commands To Create Equations."

## Using an Equation Keyboard

Just as WordPerfect supplies a Toolbar customized for use in the Equation Editor, the program also supplies an equation keyboard with keys mapped to Equation Editor functions. Although you cannot edit this keyboard, you can copy it and then edit the copy as you would any other keyboard, moving commands from one function key to another or assigning macros or special characters to Ctrl+key combinations.

While in the Equation Editor, you can select which keyboard it uses. To do so, follow these steps:

1. Choose Edit, Preferences. The Preferences dialog box appears, with most options grayed.
2. Choose Keyboard. The Keyboard Preferences dialog box appears.
3. Highlight the Equation Editor Keyboard, and choose Select.
4. Choose Close to close the Preferences dialog box.

The new equation keyboard will now be selected whenever the Editing Pane is active. See the WordPerfect manual for a complete list of shortcut keys contained in the equation keyboard. You can add any command or other key word you use frequently to this keyboard, and assign that text to a keystroke combination.

▶ **See** "Creating, Copying, and Editing Keyboards," **p. 325**

## Using the Equation Palettes

The equation keyboard lets you insert common characters and symbols with a single keystroke combination, but you are limited by the number of keys available on a keyboard. Unless you use the equation keyboard frequently, you may have trouble remembering which characters are assigned to which keys. Although not as quick to use, the equation palettes provide access to many more symbols and mathematical functions, as well as to the main Equation Editor formatting commands.

The Equation Editor displays one palette at a time, at the left of the screen. At the top of the currently displayed palette is the equation palette pop-up list, a large button that displays the name of the current palette. You can browse through the palette to find the symbol, command, or function you need; then you can insert the item you choose into the Editing Pane. Table 24.2 lists the names of the palettes and their contents.

### Table 24.2 The Equation Palettes

| Palette | Contents |
|---|---|
| Commands | The main Equation Editor formatting commands. |
| Large | Large and small versions of common mathematical and scientific terms including brackets, braces, sums, and integrals. |
| Symbols | Common mathematical symbols. |
| Greek | The entire Greek alphabet, in upper- and lowercase letters. |
| Arrows | Single and double arrows pointing in various directions, as well as circles, squares, and triangles. |
| Sets | Mathematical set symbols. |
| Other | Diacritical marks and ellipses. |
| Function | Trigonometric and other mathematical functions. |

You can insert commands and functions only as key words. You can insert items from the other groups as key words or as the symbols their key words represent. Symbols such as Greek letters and other characters always print as symbols, regardless of whether you enter them in the Editing Pane as key words or symbols. Key words are usually quicker to type than to select through an equation palette, but they take up more room in the Editing Pane. If you use symbols, your equation text will more closely resemble the printed equation, but selecting symbols through the palettes takes longer than typing key words (although you can insert some symbols quickly from the equation keyboard).

When you insert a command, function, or symbol into the Editing Pane from an equation palette, the Equation Editor puts a space before and after the item, whether it is inserted as a key word or as a symbol.

To use an equation palette, move the insertion point in the Editing Pane to where you want to insert a command or symbol; then perform the following steps:

1. Choose the desired palette by pressing the equation palette pop-up list button with your mouse. When the list of palettes appears, drag up or down and release to select the desired palette.

   Alternatively, choose Next Pane (F6) to activate the equation palette. Then press Alt+Page Up or Alt+Page Down to cycle through the palettes until you reach the desired palette.

2. Highlight a symbol or command in the selected palette using your mouse or the directional keys. As each item is highlighted, its key word appears in the status bar. If the entire menu will not fit in the space available on-screen, a vertical scroll bar appears that you can click with your mouse. You can also continue to scroll using the up- and down-arrow keys, or use Page Down and Page Up to move to the bottom or top of the palette.

3. At the bottom of the palette are two buttons labeled Keyword and Symbol. Click either button with your mouse to insert the item in the form indicated. (Because commands and functions can only be entered as key words, the Symbol button is grayed when either of those menus is displayed.)

Alternatively, press Enter to insert the item as a key word.

**N O T E** You can double-click an item to insert it as a key word, or hold down the Ctrl key and double-click to insert the item as a symbol.

If you need more room on-screen, you can turn off the equation palette by choosing View, Palette. Use the same actions to turn the palette back on.

## Using WordPerfect Characters

Although the equation palettes provide access to a wide variety of characters commonly used in equations, they do not contain every available WordPerfect character. If you need to enter some other character into an equation, you have access to the full set of nearly 2,000 characters that WordPerfect recognizes. To access these characters, choose Font, Character; or press Ctrl+W. The WordPerfect Characters dialog box appears in the lower-right corner of the Equation Editor, partially obscuring the Display Pane.

You can choose from the 15 different character sets (0–14), select a character, and insert it into the Editing Pane in a manner nearly identical to using the equation palettes. If you only need one special character, you can close the dialog box after you insert the character. To insert additional characters, you can leave the dialog box open and switch between it and the Editing Pane. You can redisplay equations while the WordPerfect Characters dialog box is open, but they will be partially hidden until you close the dialog box. See Chapter 20, "Using Fonts and Special Characters," for more information on WordPerfect characters.

## Altering the Equation Display

By default, the Equation Editor displays equations in the Display Pane at 200 percent magnification, or twice actual size. If you create large equations, however, your equations may not fit entirely in the Display Pane. You can change the degree that the Equation Editor magnifies equations, from a low of 10 percent (one-tenth actual size) to a high of 1,000 percent (10 times actual size). The status bar at the bottom of the screen displays the current degree of magnification.

 To change the degree of magnification, choose View, Zoom Display. WordPerfect displays the Zoom Equation Display dialog box (see fig. 24.3). Choosing any percentage option from 50 to 200 percent changes the display to that magnification. You can choose one of several standard magnifications—50%, 75%, 100%, 150%, or 200%—or choose Other, and enter any percentage from 10 to 1,000 percent. You can type in a value, or click the scroll buttons to change the percentage in 5 percent increments. The Equation Height option increases or decreases the magnification so that the equation fills the entire height of the Display Pane. The Equation Width option changes the magnification so that the equation fills the entire width of the Display Pane. The Full Equation option changes the display height or width as necessary to display both the entire width and height of the equation in the Display Pane. At some magnifications, the entire equation may not fit in the Display Pane.

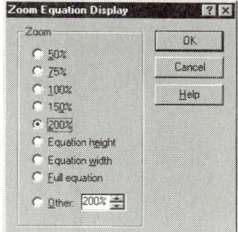

**FIG. 24.3**
You can change the view of the Display Pane to show an equation at several degrees of magnification, or the equation's full height or width.

The Equation Editor always displays scroll bars in the Editing Pane and View Pane. You can use these scroll bars to move the equation in the Display Pane without changing its magnification.

Moving or resizing an equation in the Display Pane does not affect the printed appearance of the equation. To change the printed size, see the "Changing Equation Box Options" section later in this chapter.

## Using the Equation Toolbar

The Equation Editor has its own Toolbar, to which WordPerfect has already added buttons for the most useful Equation Editor options. Whenever you call up the Equation Editor, WordPerfect displays this Toolbar by default. You can switch to a different Toolbar once you are in the Equation Editor, although all buttons for features not available in the Equation Editor will be grayed.

- See "Customizing Keyboards," **p. 324**
- See "Working with the Toolbar," **p. 417**
- See "WordPerfect Characters," **p. 644**

As with any other Toolbar, you can edit the Equation Editor Toolbar to assign various menu commands, keyboard scripts, or macros to individual buttons. You can change its position on-screen, and choose to display button text, pictures, or both. If you need more room on-screen, you can turn off the Toolbar by choosing View, Toolbar.

### TROUBLESHOOTING

**When I insert a space in an equation, WordPerfect ignores it when it displays the equation in my document.** Spaces and other "white space"—such as tabs and hard returns—are ignored in the Equation Editor. To insert a space in the equation, use the tilde (~) character for a full space, and the grave accent (`) character for a one-quarter space.

**When I use the ` key, it doesn't create a half space like it's supposed to.** The character for creating a one-quarter space in an equation is the ` character, or grave accent. It's not the apostrophe character. Using the apostrophe character instead of the grave accent character inserts the apostrophe. On most computer keyboards, the grave accent character is in the upper-left corner, on the same key as the tilde (~). You can also insert the grave accent by choosing it in the Commands list on the left side of the Equation Editor window.

**I don't see an Inline Equations command in the Graphics menu.** As it comes "out of the box," WordPerfect doesn't display the Inline Equation command in the Graphics menu. If you want to create inline equations, you should add the command to the menu. See the section "Starting the Equation Editor" earlier in this chapter for details on adding the Inline Equation command to the Graphics menu.

# Using Functions and Commands To Create Equations

Although the Equation Editor automatically performs certain formatting tasks, such as printing variables in italic and functions in standard type, you must provide most formatting instructions yourself. You have seen several commands used, including OVER, SUP, and SUB (^ and _). The following sections explore other useful commands, from basic to complex, that you can use to format equations to your exact needs.

# Using Functions in the Equation Editor

The Equation Editor follows accepted mathematical rules in formatting equations. In particular, this requires setting recognized mathematical functions in regular type and setting variables in italic type. As a result, any word that the Editor doesn't recognize as a function, command, or other key word is treated as a variable and is automatically set in italic. The words recognized by the Equation Editor as functions are standard terms for trigonometric, logarithmic, and other mathematical functions. Table 24.3 lists the functions and their descriptions.

**Table 24.3  Equation Editor Functions**

| Key Word | Description |
| --- | --- |
| cos | Cosine |
| sin | Sine |
| tan | Tangent |
| arccos | Arc cosine |
| arcsin | Arc sine |
| arctan | Arc tangent |
| cosh | Hyberbolic cosine |
| sinh | Hyperbolic sine |
| tanh | Hyperbolic tangent |
| cot | Cotangent |
| coth | Hyperbolic cotangent |
| sec | Secant |
| cosec | Cosecant |
| exp | Exponent |
| log | Logarithm |
| ln | Natural logarithm |
| lim | Limit |

*continues*

**Table 24.3 Continued**

| Key Word | Description |
|---|---|
| liminf | Limit inferior |
| limsup | Limit superior |
| min | Minimum |
| max | Maximum |
| gcd | Greatest common denominator |
| arc | Arc function |
| det | Determinant |
| mod | Modulo |

You can type functions directly or insert them from the Function equation palette. The palette always uses lowercase letters when inserting functions into the Editing Pane, and automatically puts a space before and after each function. As with commands, functions require either a space, hard return, or symbol on either side to be recognized by the Equation Editor.

Although you can enter functions in either upper- or lowercase, the lowercase used by the Function equation palette is the normal mathematical practice. In mathematical typesetting, functions are often separated from variables by a thin space (`), which is 1/4 the width of a normal space.

For example, you type

    B`cos`theta ~+~ A

to produce the equation shown in figure 24.4.

The Equation Editor recognizes the letters *A* and *B* as variables and therefore italicizes them. It recognizes *cos* as a function and formats it in normal type. It recognizes *theta* as the key word for a Greek letter. Thin spaces separate *cos* from the letter *B* and *theta*, but full spaces separate the plus sign from the whole first clause and from the letter *A* that follows.

**FIG. 24.4**
The Equation Editor's Function equation palette lets you insert trigonometric functions, which are commonly followed by a thin space.

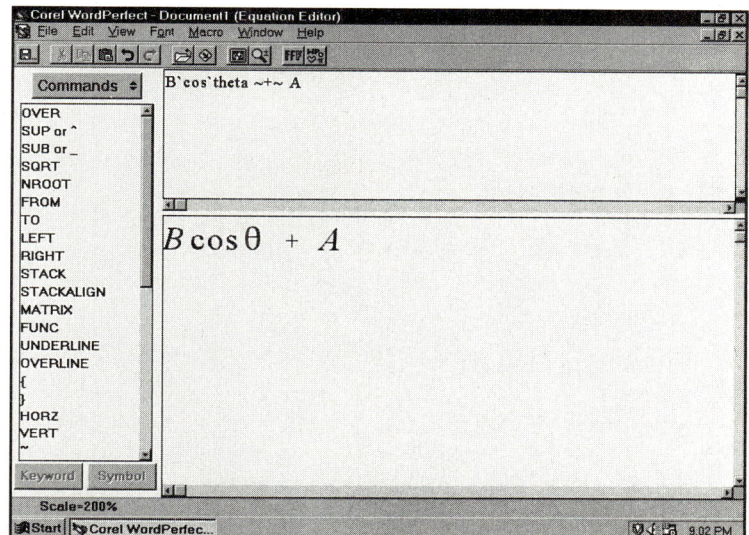

## Using FUNC, BOLD, and ITAL to Format Equations

The Equation Editor does nothing with functions but display them as typed, in normal (non-italic) font. If the Equation Editor does not recognize a character or word you entered as a function, command, symbol, or other key word, it treats your entry as a variable and italicizes it. Suppose that you want to create the following equation for Present Value:

$$\text{Present Value} = \text{Payment} \left( \frac{1 - (1 + \text{interest rate})^{-\text{number of payments}}}{\text{interest rate}} \right)$$

You may be tempted to type the following:

**Present~ Value ~=~ Payment~ ({1 ~-~ (1 ~+~ interest~ rate)^ {-number~ of~ payments}} over {interest~ rate})**

The Equation Editor does not recognize any word except over as a key word, and therefore treats the rest as variables, with the following result:

$$\textit{Present Value} = \textit{Payment} \left( \frac{1 - (1 + \textit{interest rate})^{-\textit{number of payments}}}{\textit{interest rate}} \right)$$

To format this equation without italic type, you must use the command FUNC, which instructs the Equation Editor to treat the item that follows it as a function. The item can be a single variable, a grouped word or phrase, or an entire equation. The Editor then formats the indicated text normally instead of italicizing it. To correct the preceding equation text, insert the command FUNC at the beginning and surround the rest of the equation with braces, as follows:

FUNC {Present~Value~=~Payment[t]l ({1 ~-~ (1 ~+~ interest~ rate)^{-number~ of~ payments}} over {interest~ rate})}

The equation now appears as desired. Whenever you use FUNC, make sure that you properly group the desired text with braces ({ }).

Because the Equation Editor always formats functions in normal type by default, it also provides the command ITAL to italicize functions. You use ITAL in exactly the same manner as FUNC, and you can use both simultaneously. You can use FUNC on an entire equation, for example, and use ITAL to italicize a smaller group within the equation.

You can use a third command, BOLD, in a similar manner to set part (or all) of an equation in bold type. UNDERLINE and OVERLINE are similar to BOLD and ITAL, in syntax and usage.

**NOTE** WordPerfect's normal Bold (Ctrl+B), Italic (Ctrl+I), and Underline (Ctrl+U) commands have no effect in the Equation Editor.

## Using a Backslash (\) To Format Literals

When you include a common word in your equation text that also happens to be a key word for a mathematical symbol, such as *and, or, in,* or *not,* the Equation Editor formats the word as a symbol instead of as a word. You can correct this situation by placing a backslash (\) immediately before the misinterpreted word, in the following manner:

\and

The backslash is a command that instructs the Equation Editor to treat the following symbol or command as a literal, that is, to render it exactly as typed. If you use braces ({ }) in an equation, for instance, the Equation Editor assumes that you are trying to group the text in between, and does not print the braces. To cause them to print, place a backslash before each brace, as in the following example:

\{ equation \}

You must also use a backslash if you want to print characters such as a tilde (~), ampersand (&), pound sign (#), the backslash itself (\), or other key words such as BOLD or UNDERLINE.

## Forming Fractions with the OVER, LEFT, and RIGHT Commands

You have already seen the OVER command used to create a fraction in the form

x over y

where x and y can be individual characters or groups. As with multiple levels of superscripts and subscripts, the Equation Editor can create fractions within fractions, as long as each successive level of fractions is properly grouped with braces so that it can be treated as a single item. For instance, the equation text

{{x^2 ~+~ 5} over y} over 2

creates the following result:

$$\frac{\frac{x^2 + 5}{y}}{2}$$

where $x^2 + 5$ is placed over y, and the entire fraction is then grouped and placed over 2.

You can also use a variant of the OVER command, OVERSM, to set the numerator and denominator in the next smaller size of type than the rest of an equation. In all other respects, OVERSM works in exactly the same manner as OVER.

More complex equations frequently use parentheses, brackets ([ ]), and braces ({ }) as delimiters to enclose individual clauses. When surrounding a single line of text, these symbols can be used as they are (although each brace must be preceded by a backslash to print). Used by themselves, however, these characters are not tall enough to properly enclose multiple-line fractions.

You can use the commands LEFT and RIGHT with delimiters to create dynamic delimiters that automatically expand to the height of the equation they surround. Table 24.4 lists the available delimiters.

## Table 24.4 Dynamic Delimiters

| Delimiter | Description |
| --- | --- |
| ( | Left parenthesis |
| ) | Right parenthesis |
| [ | Left bracket |
| ] | Right bracket |
| < or LANGLE | Left angle bracket |
| > or RANGLE | Right angle bracket |
| \{ or LBRACE | Left brace |
| \} or RBRACE | Right brace |
| \| or LINE | Single vertical line |
| DLINE | Double vertical line |

You can rewrite the Present Value equation in an abbreviated form, as follows:

**PV ~=~ PMT~ LEFT [ {1 ~-~ (1~+~ i)^{–n}} OVER i RIGHT ]**

with the following result:

$$PV = PMT \left[ \frac{1 - (1 + i)^{-n}}{i} \right]$$

In this example, the parentheses are used normally, the brackets are used with LEFT and RIGHT to create dynamic delimiters, and the braces are used to group the numerator, and therefore do not print. The Equation Editor automatically expands the height of the brackets to match the enclosed text.

If you enclosed multiple levels of an equation with delimiters, the Equation Editor adjusts the height of each pair of delimiters to the appropriate height. For example, typing the following:

**a ~+~ LEFT \{` b OVER {c ~+~ LEFT \{` d ~+~ e OVER {f ~+~
LEFT\{` g OVER {h ~+~ DOTSAXIS} ` RIGHT \} }
` RIGHT \} } ` RIGHT \}**

creates the following equation:

$$a + \left\{ \dfrac{b}{c + \left[ d + \dfrac{e}{f + \left\{ \dfrac{g}{h + \cdots} \right\}} \right]} \right\}$$

The Equation Editor automatically positions and sizes the braces correctly. The DOTSAXIS keyword, located in the Other equation palette, creates the centered ellipsis (…).

You must always use the LEFT and RIGHT commands as a pair, although you do not need to use the same left and right delimiters. If you want to use a single delimiter, you can substitute a period (.) for the delimiter that you don't want to print. For example, typing the following:

**LEFT . {7x} OVER {x¯+¯3} RIGHT LINE_0^5**

creates the following equation:

$$\left. \dfrac{7x}{x + 3} \right|_0^5$$

## Creating Sums and Integrals

Although you can create most of the equations you have seen thus far outside of the Equation Editor, specialized constructs such as sums and integrals are nearly impossible to create any other way. Using the Equation Editor, these constructs are no more difficult to produce than a simple fraction.

You use the SUM and INT operators with the FROM and TO commands to create a sum or an integral using the following syntax:

    operator FROM x TO y

where `operator` is SUM or INT, and $x$ and $y$ are variables for the beginning and ending limits. For example, typing the following

**INT FROM 0 TO inf ¯ x^2 ¯+¯ 2**

creates the following equation:

$$\int_0^\infty x^2 + 2$$

And typing the following

>   SUM FROM {i=1} TO N F_i ` DELTA t_i

creates the following equation:

$$\sum_{i=1}^{N} F_i \Delta t_i$$

The use of FROM and TO is optional. You can use none, one, or both, but you cannot use TO without FROM. You can trick the editor, however, by using a space (`) after FROM.

FROM and TO always place the limits below and above the symbols, respectively. If you want the limits to appear to the side, use SUP and SUB instead. Notice that you must use braces around limits, such as {i=1}, for them to be treated as a single item.

Also, notice the use of keywords for symbols. INF is the key word for infinity, and is not case-sensitive. Keywords for Greek letters, however, *are* case-sensitive, because the Greek alphabet contains both upper- and lowercase characters. Therefore, DELTA is typed in all capitals to create a capital Delta symbol.

If you want to enlarge a sum or integral symbol, you can use the command SCALESYM following the syntax:

```
SCALESYM (% of normal) operator
```

Therefore, the equation text

>   SCALESYM 200 INT

creates an integral sign twice the normal size. Although SCALESYM is most useful with SUM and INT, it can be used with any character.

You can use the FROM command to position items below other functions and symbols. For example, typing the following:

>   **lim FROM {t–> inf} ` x(t)**

creates the equation:

$$\lim_{t \to \infty} x(t)$$

Notice that the combination of a minus sign and a greater than sign (–>) creates a right arrow in the equation. No keyword exists for this symbol, or for any other symbol in the Arrows equation palette.

## Creating Roots

Another mathematical construct difficult to create without the Equation Editor is the root. The command for creating a square root is SQRT, and the command for nth root is NROOT. The syntax for SQRT is shown in the following:

```
SQRT { expression }
```

Both SQRT and NROOT are dynamic operators and automatically expand in height and width to enclose any expression enclosed by braces ({ }). You should always use braces to group root expressions, unless you are creating the root of a single number. For example, the statement

```
SQRT {x^3+1}
```

creates the following equation:

$$\sqrt{x^3+1}$$

As with other constructs, the information within the braces can be simple or complex, and can include additional roots, fractions, or any other command or symbol the Equation Editor can use.

The syntax for NROOT is as follows:

```
NROOT n { expression }
```

where *n* denotes the root number. The root commands can also be nested. For example, typing the following:

```
NROOT 4 { a `+` SQRT { b `+` SQRT c }}
```

creates the equation

$$\sqrt[4]{a+\sqrt{b+\sqrt{c}}}$$

## Using the Matrix Commands

Matrices and determinants contain elements that must be properly aligned in rows and columns. When you create a matrix, you must indicate the beginning of each new row with a pound sign (#), and within each row, you must separate each column with an ampersand (&). You can specify further the way in which each row is formatted by including the MATFORM command in conjunction with ALIGNC, ALIGNL, or ALIGNR. Table 24.5 describes the matrix commands and their functions.

### Table 24.5  Matrix Commands

| Command | Function |
|---|---|
| MATRIX | Creates a matrix structure in the Equation Editor by specifying the row and column location of every subgroup. |
| MATFORM | Specifies the horizontal alignment format to be applied to each subgroup (left, right, or centered within the column) in combination with the commands ALIGNC, ALIGNL, and ALIGNR. |
| ALIGNC | Aligns its accompanying variable in the center of the current subgroup or matrix column. |
| ALIGNL | Aligns its accompanying variable on the left margin of the current subgroup or matrix column. |
| ALIGNR | Aligns its accompanying variable on the right margin of the current subgroup or matrix column. |
| & | Column separator. |
| # | Row separator. |

To create a matrix with three columns and three rows, type the following:

**MATRIX {a1 & b1 & c1 # a2 & b2 & c2 # a3 & b3 & c3}**

which creates the following equation:

$$\begin{matrix} a1 & b1 & c1 \\ a2 & b2 & c2 \\ a3 & b3 & c3 \end{matrix}$$

You must surround the entire matrix with braces ({ }), type an ampersand (&) between each column, and type a pound sign (#) between each row. Each row must have the same number of columns, and you can create a maximum of 47 columns.

Matrices are usually bounded by square brackets or vertical lines. In most cases, therefore, you will use the LEFT and RIGHT commands, in conjunction with the appropriate delimiters, to surround the matrix. Thus, the following text:

**LEFT LINE ` MATRIX {aaa & bbb & ccc # 11 & 22 & 33 # x & y & z} ` RIGHT LINE**

creates the following equation:

$$\begin{vmatrix} aaa & bbb & ccc \\ 11 & 22 & 33 \\ x & y & z \end{vmatrix}$$

If all the elements in a column are not the same width, the Equation Editor centers them around a common midpoint. If you prefer to have one or more columns aligned to the left or right, you can include a MATFORM command, which specifies the alignment of each column with the ALIGNL, ALIGNC, and ALIGNR commands. The syntax is as follows:

```
MATFORM { align1 & align2 & align3 ...}
```

where `align1` is either ALIGNL, ALIGNR, or ALIGNC to specify whether the column is aligned to the left, right, or center. The syntax of MATFORM used with MATRIX is as follows:

```
MATRIX { MATFORM { align1 & align2 & ... } a1 & a2 ... # b1 & b2 ... # ... }
```

Place the command after the MATRIX key word, immediately inside the left brace and before the contents of the matrix. If you use MATFORM to specify the alignment for one column in the matrix, you must specify the alignment for every other column in the matrix. To realign the first and last columns of the previous equation, you can change the equation text as follows:

**LEFT LINE ` MATRIX {MATFORM {ALIGNL & ALIGNC & ALIGNR} aaa & bbb & ccc # 11 & 22 & 33 # x & y & z} ` RIGHT LINE**

which creates the following equation:

$$\begin{vmatrix} aaa & bbb & ccc \\ 11 & 22 & 33 \\ x & y & z \end{vmatrix}$$

As with any other Equation Editor construct, each element in a matrix can be quite complex, as long as the entire expression that makes up the element is surrounded by braces to create a group.

## Creating Multiline Expressions with STACK and STACKALIGN

The Equation Editor assumes that each equation text, no matter how complex, is a single equation centered on a common baseline. Spaces and hard returns in the Editing Pane can make your equation text easier to read but don't change the printed appearance of the final equation.

Often, however, you want to stack several shorter equations on top of one another within the boundaries of a single equation box. The Equation Editor provides two commands that perform this task in slightly different ways: STACK and STACKALIGN. STACK simply creates a vertical stack of expressions; STACKALIGN also creates a vertical stack of expressions, but requires that you identify on which character each expression should be aligned. The syntax for STACK is as follows:

```
STACK {line1 # line2 ...}
```

As with MATRIX, STACK uses the pound sign (#) as a row separator. To stack two equations, such as:

```
2x + 3y = 3200
x - 2y = 8
```

you type the following:

**STACK {2x ~+~ 3y ~=~ 9 # x ~-~ 2y ~=~ 8}**

$$2x + 3y = 9$$
$$x - 2y = 8$$

Notice that these two equations are centered around a common midpoint. This alignment is the default alignment, which you can change by using some of the same commands you use to align matrices: ALIGNL and ALIGNR. For example, to align the two equations along their left edges, you could edit the equation text as follows:

**STACK {2x ~+~ 3y ~=~ 9 # ALIGNL x ~-~ 2y ~=~ 8}**

to create the following result:

$$2x + 3y = 9$$
$$x - 2y = 8$$

Usually, however, you want to align two or more equations along a specific point such as an equal sign, which you can accomplish with the STACKALIGN command. The syntax for STACKALIGN is nearly identical to that for STACK, except that each line of the equation must also contain an ampersand (&) following the character upon which the equations should be aligned. The previous equation text could again be edited as follows:

STACKALIGN {2x ~+~ 3y ~=&~ 9 # x ~Å~ 2y ~=&~ 8}

to align the equations on their equal signs, as follows:

$$\begin{aligned} 2x + 3y &= 9 \\ x - 2y &= 8 \end{aligned}$$

The equations now line up in a pleasing manner. Another example:

STACKALIGN {DELTA f ~=&~ f(a ~+~ DELTA x) ~-~ f(a)
#=&~ SQRT {9 ~+~ 0.3} ~-~ SQRT 9
#=&~ SQRT {9.3} ~-~ SQRT 9 }

creates the following equation:

$$\begin{aligned} \Delta f &= f(a + \Delta x) - f(a) \\ &= \sqrt{9 + 0.3} - \sqrt{9} \\ &= \sqrt{9.3} - \sqrt{9} \end{aligned}$$

Notice that the equation text could have been written in a continuous string without affecting the printed output of the equation(s). Pressing Enter to place each part of the equation on a different line, however, makes the entire equation easier to read and work with. This technique is helpful when you work on large or complex equations.

You can also use the PHANTOM command to help align equations. PHANTOM tells WordPerfect to leave space in an equation for a character or group of characters, but not to actually print them. Thus

```
PHANTOM {x+1}
```

tells WordPerfect to leave a space in the equation the exact width of the clause x+1. This command is particularly useful in stacked equations for matching the same clause in the line above or below. PHANTOM can also be used to create placeholders in matrices.

## Using Other Commands and Symbols

Although you will probably find the Commands, Functions, and Greek equation palettes to be the most useful, don't overlook several other palettes.

The diacritical marks found in the Other palette can be considered either commands or symbols; each prints a characteristic mark, but prints that mark over another character. Common diacritical marks include vector (VEC), overbar (BAR), tilde (TILDE), hat (HAT), and left and right accent marks (ACUTE and GRAVE). The Other palette also contains key words that create several kinds of ellipses, including horizontal, vertical, and diagonal. To add a diacritical mark to a character, press the space bar to add a space after the character; then type or insert the key word for the mark. Typing the following:

**x BAR DOTSLOW y VEC**

creates the equation

$$\bar{x} ... \vec{y}$$

Notice that a diacritical mark must be typed before a subscript or superscript. Typing a diacritical key word after a subscript puts the diacritical mark on the sub- or superscript.

The Large palette contains symbols that are commonly used in a larger size (as well as smaller equivalents of each). Some examples are SUM and SMALLSUM for large and small sums, and INT and SMALLINT for large and small integrals.

The Arrows palette contains a wealth of single and double arrows pointing in all directions. For example, the left and right harpoons are useful in chemical equations, such as

$$HCO_3^- \rightleftharpoons H^+ + CO_3^{2-}$$

The Symbols palette contains many other common symbols, from primes, mathematical operators such as the partial derivative, and multiplication and division symbols, to logical symbols such as therefore, and abstract symbols such as infinity.

The examples in this chapter provide only a small sample of the many characters and symbols available in the equation palettes. Virtually any mathematical character or symbol is available, and you can access still more through the WordPerfect Characters dialog box.

# Changing Equation Box Options

Although created by the Equation Editor, WordPerfect's equations are contained in graphics boxes that are functionally identical to a figure box or other graphics box. Each type of graphics box has its own graphics box style, which contains settings for default anchor type, position, size, border and fill styles, caption, and text wrap. The default equation box style anchors an equation to the current paragraph, and sets the box width to the full width of the page, even if the equation is only an inch or two wide. The height of the equation determines the height of the equation box. By default, the equation box has no border, fill, or caption.

As with any other graphics box, you can change an equation box's position, size, anchor type, border, or fill style individually, or even choose a different graphics box style. To change one of these options, click the equation using the right mouse button. WordPerfect displays a QuickMenu from which you can choose the desired option. If you want to change several options, or change the options for more than one equation box, choose Edit Box from the Quick Menu. WordPerfect displays the Graphics Box Edit Box palette (see fig. 24.5).

The procedures for changing graphics box settings in general are described in detail in Chapter 21, "Using Advanced Graphics Techniques," and need not be repeated here. Several specific settings, however, are particularly useful for equations.

**FIG. 24.5**
The Edit Box dialog box lets you change an equation's position, size, border, fill, and caption, among other options.

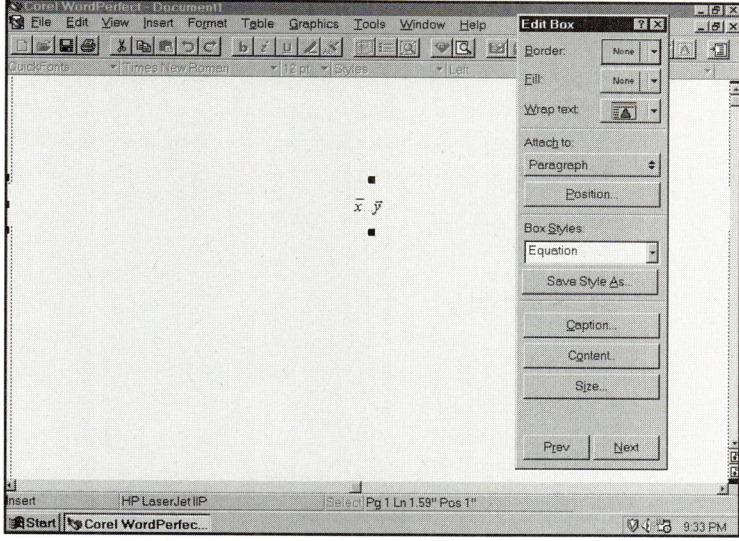

## Numbering Equations

Although an equation doesn't have a caption when it's first created, you can add a caption after you return to the document screen. Why would you want to caption an equation? Because the default caption style for equation boxes is simply a number in parentheses, aligned flush right adjacent to the equation. This is the standard format for numbering equations in journals and texts. Furthermore, equation boxes are automatically numbered in sequence just as are figure or table boxes.

You cannot create or edit an equation caption from within the Equation Editor; you must first close the Editor and return to the normal document window. To add an equation number caption, click the equation using the right mouse button, and choose Create Caption from the QuickMenu. WordPerfect adds the caption in the form of an equation number.

WordPerfect automatically numbers equations in sequence. If you add or delete equations, the program automatically renumbers all equations. To change the equation numbering sequence, change the Equation Box counter. Choose Insert, Other, Counter. Then highlight Equation Box, and choose Increase, Decrease, or Value. The first two options insert a code that increases or decreases the value of the following equation by 1, and automatically adjusts if you add or decrease equations. If you choose Value, you must enter a specific number, and WordPerfect permanently sets the value of the following equation to that number. When finished, choose Close to return to the document window.

## Embedding Equations in Text

You may want a simple expression (such as the square root of a number) to appear in the text of your document, but even a simple equation created by the Equation Editor by default takes up the full width of the screen and is half an inch tall. By changing the graphics box settings, you can reduce the size of the equation box to the size of the equation, and include the equation in the text of your document. WordPerfect calls such an equation an *inline* equation, and includes a special box style for this type of equation.

You create an inline equation just as you would create a normal equation, except that you choose a different option from the Graphics menu. To create an inline equation, follow these steps:

1. From the editing screen, choose Graphics.
2. Choose Inline Equation. (If the Inline Equation option is not listed, follow the steps in the earlier section "Starting the Equation Editor" to add Inline Equation to the Graphics menu.) WordPerfect displays the Equation Editor.
3. Create the inline equation as you would create a normal equation.
4. Choose File, Close, or press Ctrl+F4. WordPerfect displays the inline equation embedded in your text at the position of the insertion point.

If you have already created a normal equation, you can change it to an inline equation by changing its box style. To change a normal equation to an inline equation, follow these steps:

1. Right-click the equation to access the Graphics QuickMenu; then choose Edit B*o*x.
2. Choose Inline Equation from the Box Styles drop-down list box.
3. When finished, close the Edit Box dialog box by clicking the document. WordPerfect shrinks the dimensions of the box to the size of the equation.

## Changing the Equation Font

When you install WordPerfect, the program automatically installs TrueType fonts for all the WordPerfect character sets, which include the special characters and symbols necessary to print equations. As a result, unless the printer cannot accept either downloadable fonts or graphics, it can print WordPerfect equations.

By default, WordPerfect formats and prints equations in the same font and point size as a document's initial font. You can change the font or point size for an individual equation, or for all equations in a document.

 To change the font for an equation, in the Equation Editor choose F*o*nt, Equation *F*ont. WordPerfect displays the Equation Font dialog box, a variant of the normal Font dialog box. You can choose a different font or size, or both. You can also choose a font Co*l*or and, where appropriate for the font, an alternate F*o*nt Style.

To change the font for all equations in a document, you change the font settings in the Equation Box style. Follow these steps:

1. Choose *G*raphics, *G*raphics Styles. The Graphics Styles dialog box appears.
2. Highlight Equation; then choose *E*dit. WordPerfect displays the Edit Box Style dialog box.
3. Choose *S*ettings. The Equation Font Settings dialog box appears.
4. Choose a different font face, font size, or both.
5. Choose OK or Close to close all open dialog boxes.

All equations in the document now print with the new font settings, unless you change the font for one or more individual equations.

▶ **See** "Customizing Graphics Boxes," **p. 669**

# Saving and Retrieving Equation Files

If you create equations infrequently, or if the equations you create are significantly different from one another, you must create all your equations from scratch. If, however, you repeatedly use the same commands or frequently create equations that are slight variations of one another, you can make your task easier by reusing your work. From the Equation Editor, you can save part or all of an equation text to a file on disk. You can also retrieve previously saved equations—or even WordPerfect documents—into the Equation Editor.

To save an equation as a separate file, in the Equation Editor choose File, Save As (F3). The Save Equation As dialog box appears. WordPerfect automatically suggests WordPerfect Graphics 2 *.WPG as the file name extension. You can use any file name or extension you want. When you later insert a saved equation into the Equation Editor, the program lists all files within the displayed folder. You do not need to type the WPG extension; WordPerfect adds it for you automatically. You can save the equation in the current folder, or change the folder before saving.

By default, the program saves equations in WordPerfect Graphics 2 (WPG) format. This allows you to retrieve the file into a drawing program, such as WordPerfect Presentations. You can then create technical illustrations containing equations. You can also save an equation as a standard WordPerfect 7 document, as WordPerfect 5.1/5.2 documents, or in a WordPerfect Graphic 1 format. To save an equation in a different file format, in the Save As dialog box choose As Type, then choose a file type.

To insert a previously saved equation into the Equation Editor's Editing Pane, place the insertion point where you want the inserted equation text to appear; then choose File, Insert File. The Retrieve Equation Text dialog box appears, listing all files in the current folder. If you don't see the equation you want, you can select a different folder. When you find the correct file, double-click the file name, or highlight the name and choose Retrieve. The contents of the file appear at the insertion point in the Editing Pane.

You can follow the preceding steps to insert a standard WordPerfect document into the Editing Pane also. The Equation Editor strips the inserted document of all codes and formatting, leaving only text, WordPerfect characters, and hard returns. Any soft returns are changed to hard returns, and the Equation Editor treats the result according to its usual rules.

If you save many equations as separate files, you may want to create one or more separate folders for those files and add the location(s) to your QuickList for easy access.

**TROUBLESHOOTING**

**When I use an equation function, like "theta," WordPerfect displays the text of the function, rather than the symbol for the function.** When using functions and commands, WordPerfect requires you to insert spaces so that it can understand the equation syntax you've provided. For example, typing **Btheta** displays the text "Btheta," rather than B and the theta symbol. To properly display the equation, insert either a space or a space character (~ or `) before and after all equation functions and commands, such as B theta or B~theta.

**Nothing happens when I press Ctrl+B to make text bold in the Equation Editor.** Character formatting for bold and italic is ignored in the Equation Editor. Instead, use the BOLD and ITALIC commands to format characters in an equation as bold or italic, respectively. Only the next character or symbol after a BOLD or ITALIC command is bolded or italicized. You need to repeat the BOLD and ITALIC commands to format additional characters and symbols in your equation as bold and italic.

**The font that I use for equations doesn't match the font I use for the rest of the document.** The Equation Editor uses its own default font, and is separate from the font used in the body of the document. You can change the Equation Editor font to match the rest of the document by changing the style for equation graphics boxes. See the section "Changing the Equation Font" in this chapter for details on selecting a different equation font.

# PART V

# Large Documents

**25**  Using Footnotes and Endnotes   801

**26**  Assembling Document References   823

**27**   Working with Large and Multi-Part Documents   869

**28**  Using WordPerfect with the Corel WordPerfect Suite   899

CHAPTER 25

# Using Footnotes and Endnotes

*by Laura Acklen*

Mention the word *footnotes*, and most people picture volumes of scholarly works laden with obscure references. Many people also remember—painfully, no doubt!—the difficult chore of typing footnotes for research papers. But with WordPerfect, footnotes (and endnotes) are easy to create, and they aren't just for academics anymore.

Footnotes and endnotes provide additional information about what is being said in the body of the text without interrupting the flow of that text. They may contain reference details, such as the name of the author and the title of the work; the page number on which the reference is found; and so on. They may also provide parenthetical or interpretive explanations of technical material. Footnotes and endnotes should not contain essential information, however, because by their very location, the author is telling you that they are not required reading.

**Create and edit footnotes**

WordPerfect's Footnote feature makes it easy to include reference information in a document without interrupting the flow of the text.

**Move, copy, and delete notes from a document**

WordPerfect automatically adjusts the placement and numbering of footnotes as you move, copy, and delete them in a document.

**Change the style of the footnote information**

The Styles Editor can be used to alter the style of the footnote reference number and the footnote text to meet specific requirements.

**Create a page for endnotes**

Endnotes are placed on a page by themselves at the end of the document, or wherever an Endnote Placement code is found.

Typing footnotes and endnotes on a typewriter can be a tedious and frustrating process, especially if the references move around during editing. Fortunately, WordPerfect makes creating, editing, moving, and renumbering footnotes and endnotes easy.

Typically, footnotes are placed at the bottom of the page on which the footnote reference number appears. This arrangement makes it easier for the reader to find the additional information. Endnotes, on the other hand, are listed together on a page. They are usually at the end of the document, or, in the case of long documents, at the end of every section. This arrangement is easier for typists because they don't have to remember to allow room at the bottom of each page for the notes. In WordPerfect, the methods for working with footnotes and endnotes are virtually the same. Because footnotes are more widely used, this chapter focuses first on footnotes and then explains how endnotes differ. ■

## Using Footnotes

A footnote consists of two parts: the footnote reference number and the footnote text. The footnote reference number appears in the text. The footnote text, with a corresponding footnote number, is at the bottom of the page. If the footnote text is lengthy, WordPerfect splits the footnote and carries it over to the next page. Figure 25.1 shows a sample document with footnotes.

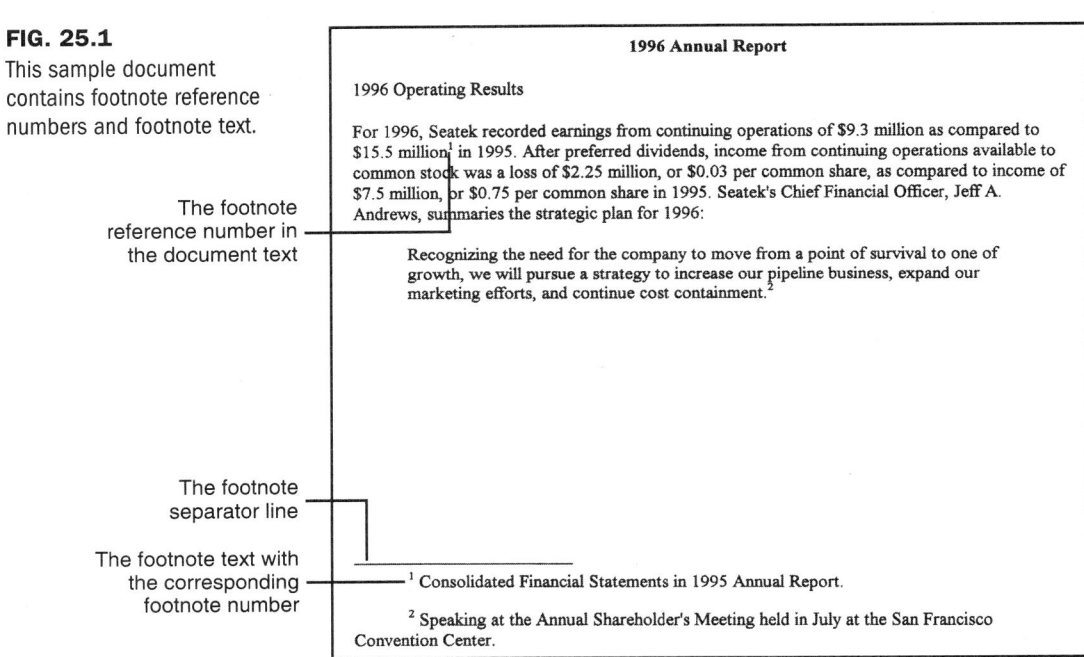

**FIG. 25.1**
This sample document contains footnote reference numbers and footnote text.

The footnote reference number in the document text

The footnote separator line

The footnote text with the corresponding footnote number

**N O T E**  You can use the Cross Reference feature to reference a footnote number anywhere in the text—for example, `See footnote number 13 on page 27`. After you modify the document, you can update the page number and footnote number by choosing Tools, Ge<u>n</u>erate.

▶ See "Marking References to Footnotes and Endnotes," **p. 868**

## Inserting Footnotes

You may choose to create footnotes as you type the text of the document, or you may create the notes later when you have the necessary information. A footnote should be inserted where you want the footnote reference number to appear in the text.

> **CAUTION**
> You can create footnotes in tables, but not in a header row. If you create a footnote in a table header row, WordPerfect converts it to an endnote.

If you want to experiment with footnotes but don't have text of your own to work with, type the text that appears in figure 25.1, without the footnote reference numbers or the footnote text at the bottom of the page. This chapter walks you through creating and modifying the footnotes in this sample section of text.

**N O T E**  Choose F<u>o</u>rmat, <u>P</u>aragraph, <u>D</u>ouble Indent or press Ctrl+Shift+F7 to indent the quotation from both the left and right margins. If you use indented quotations often in your writing, create a Quotation style that indents, single spaces, and, if necessary, selects a smaller font. See Chapter 10, "Using Styles," for more information on creating and using styles.

To create a footnote, complete the following steps:

1. Position the insertion point where you want the footnote reference number to appear in the text. For the sample document, position the insertion point at the end of the indented quote.

2. Choose <u>I</u>nsert, <u>F</u>ootnote, <u>C</u>reate.

   WordPerfect moves the insertion point down to the footnote area of the document editing window. However, if you are using Draft View mode, the insertion point is moved into a separate Footnote window. In either case, the text `Footnote` appears in the title bar, and the Footnote/Endnote Feature Bar is added at the top of the window.

**N O T E**  If you are using Draft View mode, footnotes (or endnotes) don't appear in the document editing window. Therefore, creating and editing footnotes is accomplished through a separate Footnote window. You must change to Page View mode or print the document to see the footnotes (and endnotes).

Notice that WordPerfect has automatically inserted the correct footnote number underneath a separator line.

3. Type the text of your footnote. For the sample document, type the footnote text shown in figure 25.1.

When you are finished typing the footnote text, your screen should look like the one shown in figure 25.2.

**N O T E**  If you accidentally delete the footnote number in the footnote text, and it is too late to restore it by using the Undo or Undelete features, use the Note Number button on the Footnote/Endnote Feature Bar to reinsert the footnote number. Don't retype the number yourself; you need to insert the correct code so that WordPerfect can update the note number automatically if you later change the order of the notes. Position the insertion point at the beginning of the footnote text, and click Note Number.

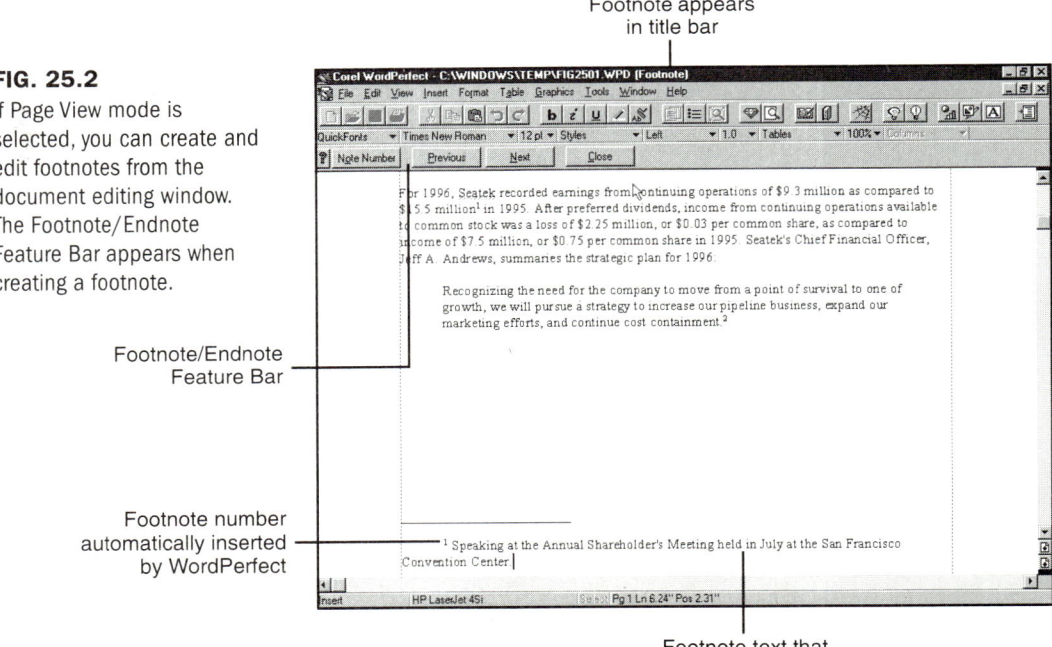

**FIG. 25.2**
If Page View mode is selected, you can create and edit footnotes from the document editing window. The Footnote/Endnote Feature Bar appears when creating a footnote.

4. After you finish typing the footnote text, click <u>C</u>lose from the feature bar.

   WordPerfect moves the insertion point back to the document text area and inserts a superscript footnote reference number (see fig. 25.3).

**FIG. 25.3**
The sample text with the first footnote reference number appears at the end of the quotation.

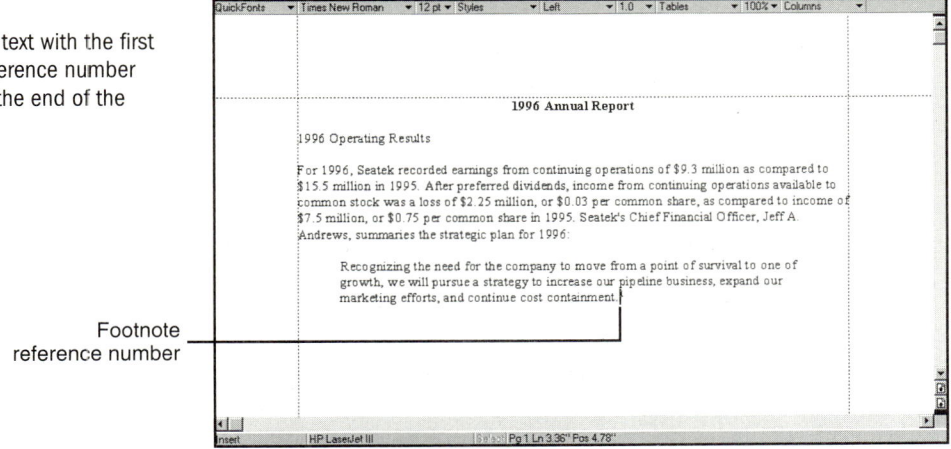

**NOTE** If the text that you want to appear in a note already exists in a document (this one or any other), you can use several WordPerfect features to insert the text into a note without having to retype it. The Copy and Paste or Delete and Undelete features can duplicate text so that you can insert it into a note. You can even use the Insert File feature to insert an entire document into a note.

**TIP** If you double-click a footnote (or endnote) code in Reveal Codes, the Edit Footnote (or Endnote) dialog box appears. Here you can type the number of the note you want to edit.

The footnote reference number in the text represents a footnote code that contains both the footnote reference number and the footnote text. Because a code is used instead of typing in a number, WordPerfect can update the footnote numbers as you insert or delete footnotes. To look at a footnote code, position the insertion point directly before or after the footnote number in the text and turn on Reveal Codes (choose <u>V</u>iew, Reveal <u>C</u>odes). Figure 25.4 shows the footnote code in Reveal Codes.

To insert a footnote before another existing footnote, follow the same steps that you used to create a new footnote. In the sample document, create a new note at the end of the phrase `...$15.5 million...` in the first sentence of the first paragraph. Type the following text for the note contents:

**Consolidated Financial Statements in 1995 Annual Report**

**FIG. 25.4**
The Reveal Codes window at the bottom of the screen shows the footnote code at the end of the paragraph.

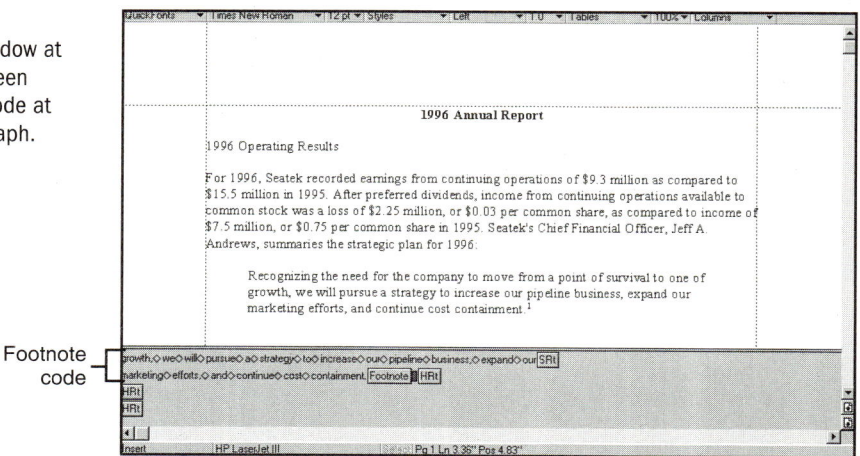

Notice in figure 25.5 that WordPerfect has automatically numbered the new footnote as footnote number 1 and renumbered the existing footnote (underneath it) to footnote number 2.

WordPerfect places the footnote text at the bottom of the page with a corresponding footnote number. The program automatically inserts a separator line and a blank line between each footnote. Use the scroll bar to move down to the bottom of the page to view your footnotes, as shown in figure 25.6.

> **NOTE** If there is too much space between the footnotes, edit the notes and look for an extra blank line after the footnote text. You probably pressed Enter after typing the footnote text. Look through the footnotes and delete the extra blank lines. Because WordPerfect automatically inserts one blank line between notes, extra lines are not usually necessary.

WordPerfect prints footnotes (and endnotes) in the Document Initial Font, which may be different from the font you have chosen for the body text. The Document Initial Font is shown on the Power Bar when the insertion point is in the footnote (or endnote) area of the document editing window. If you want to change the font in the document and have the footnote (and endnote) text match it, you can change the font by choosing For̲mat, D̲ocument, Initial F̲ont, which affects both the document and the note text. The insertion point must be positioned in the body of the document (not in the footnote) to choose Initial F̲ont.

Using Footnotes

**FIG. 25.5**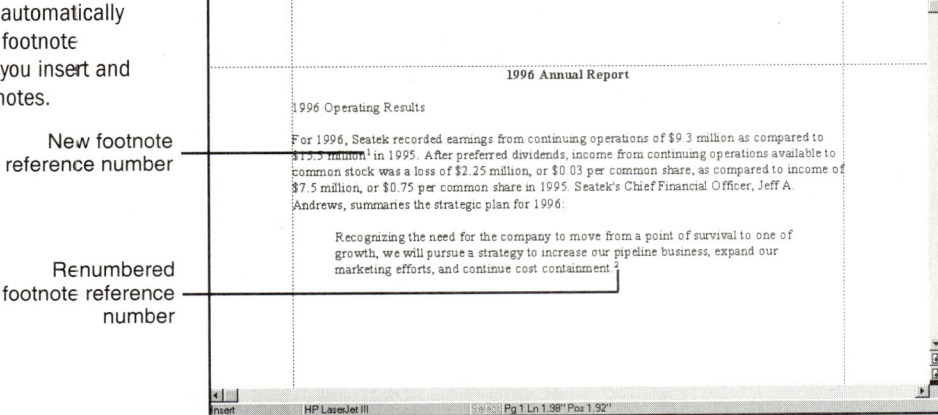
WordPerfect automatically updates the footnote numbers as you insert and remove footnotes.

New footnote reference number

Renumbered footnote reference number

**N O T E** Use the mouse to move from editing one footnote to editing another footnote on the same page. Simply click to place the insertion point and then edit. You cannot use the keyboard to navigate between footnotes. However, if the Footnote/Endnote Feature Bar is displayed, you can click Previous or Next.

**FIG. 25.6**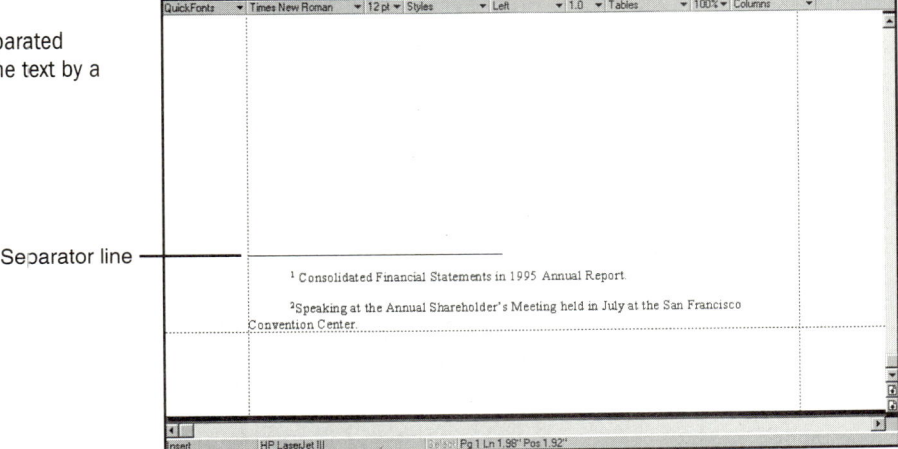
Footnotes are separated from the rest of the text by a separator line.

Separator line

A second method is to insert a font code before the note text in the note area of the document editing window. Keep in mind that you have to do this for each note. Likewise, if you change the margins in the document and you want the note text to use those margins, you can either make the margin change by choosing Format, Document, Initial Code Style, or set the margins in the note area of the document editing window for each note.

## Editing Footnotes

The steps for editing footnotes differ depending on the type of view mode you work in. Page View mode is best if you work with a lot of footnotes, because you can edit the footnotes right inside the document editing window. If you use Draft View mode, you have to switch to a separate footnote window before you can edit the footnote.

If you use Page View mode, you can edit a footnote by scrolling down to the bottom of the page and clicking in the footnote text. Insert or delete text as necessary to make the changes, then click in the text area of the document editing window to move back into the body of the document.

If you use Draft View mode, you have to use the Edit Footnote dialog box to switch to the Footnote window where you can edit a particular footnote. You can edit any footnote in the document, from any position in the document, by specifying the footnote number in the Edit Footnote dialog box. WordPerfect searches for that footnote and displays the footnote text in a Footnote window for editing. This footnote window has a Footnote/Endnote Feature Bar in it to make it easier for you to move to the previous or next footnote.

To edit a footnote, complete the following steps:

1. From anywhere in the document (except within a footnote), choose Insert, Footnote, Edit. Figure 25.7 shows the Edit Footnote dialog box.

**FIG. 25.7**
Type the number of the footnote you want to edit in the Edit Footnote dialog box and let WordPerfect locate the footnote for you.

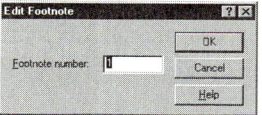

WordPerfect automatically displays the number of the previous footnote in the document. For example, if the insertion point is between footnotes 2 and 3, WordPerfect inserts the number 2 in the Edit Footnote dialog box.

> **CAUTION**
> If you type the number of a footnote number that doesn't exist in the document, WordPerfect displays a Not found message. Choose OK, and try again.

2. If the number of the footnote shown is the one you want to edit, choose OK or press Enter. Otherwise, type the appropriate number, and then choose OK or press Enter.

   WordPerfect moves the insertion point to the requested footnote text and displays the Footnote/Endnote Feature Bar across the top of the window.

 If you work in Page View mode but prefer to use the Footnote/Endnote Feature Bar, you can use these same steps to edit the footnotes.

3. Make the necessary changes.

   At this point, you have the option of returning to the document text or editing other footnotes.

4. If you want to edit or view other footnotes, click Next or Previous from the feature bar to browse through the notes.

5. Click Close from the feature bar when you are ready to return to the document text.

 If you use footnotes often, use WordPerfect's Toolbar feature to create a toolbar with the Create Footnote and Edit Footnote buttons already on it.

## Copying Footnotes

If two or more footnotes have the same footnote text, you can create the first footnote and then copy that footnote to another location in the document. In the sample document, for example, use the text from the first footnote as the text for a new second footnote. Rather than typing that text a second time, copy the first footnote and insert it as the second footnote.

▶ See "View Modes," **p. 28**
▶ See "Selecting Text," **p. 29**
▶ See "Understanding WordPerfect's Hidden Codes," **p. 91**
▶ See "Customizing a Toolbar," **p. 420**

The Copy function is really a two-step process. First, select and copy the text. Then paste the text into a new location. Follow these steps to copy and paste the footnote:

1. Save the document (so that you can go back to your original if you make a mistake later).
2. Select the footnote reference number in the text. For this example, select the first footnote reference number in the sample document, making sure that only the 1 is highlighted.

3. To copy the footnote, choose Edit, Copy; or press Ctrl+C.
4. Move the insertion point to the location where you want to insert the copied footnote. In the sample document, position the insertion point after 1995 in the second sentence of the first paragraph.

> **TIP** Because the footnote number is very small, you may find it difficult to select using the mouse. Use the Shift+arrow keys method of selecting text instead. Hold down the Shift key then press the left (or right) arrow key to select the footnote number.

5. To paste the footnote, choose Edit, Paste or press Ctrl+V.

You now have two footnotes with identical text. Notice that WordPerfect has automatically renumbered the footnote at the end of the quotation (formerly footnote number 2) to footnote number 3.

> **TIP** Once text is selected, you can also click the right mouse button and choose Cut, Copy, and Paste from the QuickMenu.

## Moving Footnotes

As you edit your document, you may have to move sections of text from one place to another. If the text contains footnotes, WordPerfect moves the footnotes along with the text and renumbers them according to their new locations.

> **CAUTION**
> If the footnote reference number is the last character in the selected text, be sure to extend the selection to include it, or the footnote will be left behind.

▶ **See** "Selecting Text," **p. 99**

Sometimes, however, you need to move only the footnote and not the text around it. For example, you might insert a footnote in the wrong place. Moving is a two-step process: cutting and pasting. First, select and cut the text (in this case, a footnote); then paste the text at the new location. The steps for moving a footnote follow:

## Using Footnotes    811

> **TIP** You can also use the drag-and-drop method to move footnotes.

1. Save the document (in case you later make a mistake).
2. Select the footnote reference number in the text. In the sample document, select the second footnote reference number at the end of the second sentence in the first paragraph.

3. To cut the footnote, choose Edit, Cut or press Ctrl+X.
4. Move the insertion point to the new location for the footnote reference number. In the sample document, position the insertion point after the phrase `...7.5 million...` in the second sentence of the first paragraph.

5. To paste the footnote, choose Edit, Paste or press Ctrl+V.

## Deleting Footnotes

If you decide that footnote information is unnecessary, or if you have created a footnote in error, you may need to remove a footnote. The footnote reference number and footnote text are both contained in a footnote code. If you delete the code, WordPerfect removes the footnote reference number, and the footnote text no longer appears at the bottom of the page.

To delete a footnote, position the insertion point to the right of the footnote reference number and press Backspace. Alternatively, position the insertion point to the left of the footnote reference number and press Delete.

## Setting a New Footnote Number

If you have a large number of footnotes in your document, you may decide to restart the numbering at the beginning of each section. Or you may opt to split a large document into several files using the Master Document feature (because WordPerfect runs faster with smaller files). If this is the case, you need to specify a new footnote number to use. When you specify a new number, WordPerfect renumbers all the subsequent footnotes beginning with that new number.

To specify a new number, position the insertion point before the first footnote (in the body of the document) that will have a new number assigned. Choose Insert, Footnote, New Number. WordPerfect displays the Footnote Number dialog box, as shown in figure 25.8.

▶ **See** "Adding Footnotes and Endnotes," **p. 893**

**FIG. 25.8**
Type a new footnote number to restart the numbering for all subsequent footnotes.

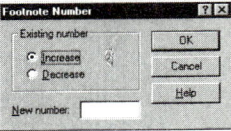

## Using Footnote Options

You can change many aspects of your footnotes' appearance if WordPerfect's style doesn't suit your needs. For example, you may want to use a different numbering style or separator line.

To access the footnote options, choose Insert, Footnote, Options. WordPerfect displays the Footnote Options dialog box (see fig. 25.9).

**FIG. 25.9**
The Footnote Options dialog box always displays the settings that are in effect for that particular area of the document.

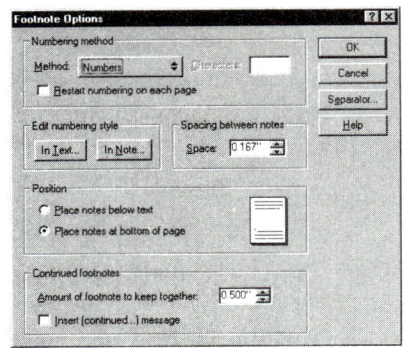

Changes that you make in the Footnote Options dialog box affect either the entire document or only the footnotes on that page through the end of the document. For example, if you click the In Note button, any changes you make here affect the whole document (because you are editing a style). However, if you select a different option from the Method pop-up list, the new numbering method only affects footnotes which occur after the insertion point. In general, if you want the changes to affect all the footnotes, position the insertion point at the top of the document (or before any footnotes) before accessing the Footnote Options dialog box.

**Changing the Numbering Style** WordPerfect offers several numbering styles for footnotes, the default being Arabic numerals (1, 2, 3). If you want to change to a different numbering style, choose Method in the Numbering Method area of the Footnote Options dialog box. A pop-up list of numbering styles appears. Choose the numbering or lettering scheme you want to use.

**NOTE** If your document contains a mixture of footnotes and endnotes, you may want to use characters for footnotes and numbers for endnotes. Because characters can quickly become long and cumbersome, use a series containing a number of different characters (a, b, c, #, *, ~) or restart numbering on each page.

To use symbols other than numbers or letters, choose the Characters option on the Method pop-up list. Next, in the Characters text box of the Footnote Options dialog box, type the characters you want to use. If you specify a series of characters like *#~, WordPerfect numbers footnotes *, #, ~, **, ##, ~~, ***, and so on.

**Restarting Numbering on Each Page** If your document contains a large number of footnotes, you might want to restart the footnote numbering with 1, or with the first character in your character series, at the top of every page. Click the Restart Numbering On Each Page option in the Footnote Options dialog box (refer to fig. 25.9). This feature is especially useful if you are using asterisks or other characters (instead of numbers or letters) to number your footnotes.

**Editing the Numbering Style in Text** The appearance of the footnote reference number in the text is controlled by a style that you can modify to suit your specific needs. By default, the footnote reference number appears in superscript in the text. If your printer doesn't support superscript, or you want to use another type of formatting, you can edit the style with the Styles Editor. The Styles Editor has its own pull-down menu for features that you can use in styles.

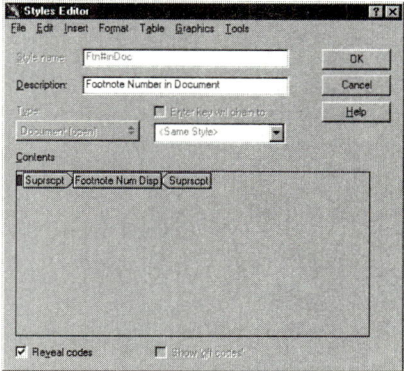

**FIG. 25.10**
As with other styles in WordPerfect, the Footnote Number in Document style can be edited with the Styles Editor.

To edit the style for the footnote reference number in the text, click In Text under Edit Numbering Style in the Footnote Options dialog box. The Styles Editor appears with the contents of the style displayed, as shown in figure 25.10. If necessary, choose Reveal

Codes to display the codes in the style. Insert or delete codes as necessary to make the desired changes. Choose OK when you're finished.

WordPerfect does not insert a code in the document when you make changes to the footnote styles. Instead, the program makes changes to the document's Ftn#inDoc System Style, which affects all footnotes in the document. See Chapter 10, "Using Styles," for more information on editing styles.

**Editing the Numbering Style in Notes**   The format of the footnote text (including the footnote number) is controlled by a style which you can modify to suit your specific needs. You may want to change the style to match a change you made to the style for the footnote reference number in the document, or you may have to follow specific guidelines for formatting footnotes. The format assigned by default is a left tab followed by a superscripted footnote number, followed by the note text.

To edit the style for the footnote text, click In Note under Edit Numbering Style in the Footnote Options dialog box. The Styles Editor appears with the contents of the style displayed, as shown in figure 25.11. If necessary, choose Reveal Codes to display the codes in the style. Insert or delete codes as appropriate to make the format changes.

WordPerfect does not insert a code in the document when you make changes to the footnote styles. Instead, the program makes changes to the document's Footnote System Style, which affects all the footnotes in the document.

▶ **See** "Editing Styles," **p. 344**

**FIG. 25.11**
The Styles Editor dialog box shows the codes in the Footnote style.

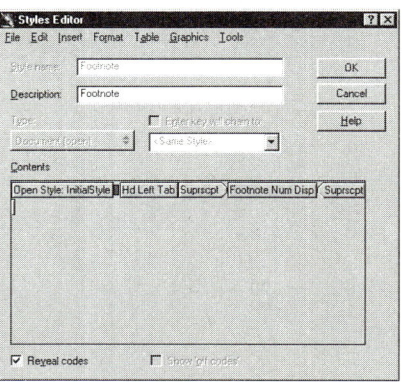

**Changing the Spacing Between Notes**   WordPerfect automatically inserts a blank line between footnotes. If you want to increase or decrease the size of this space, click Space under Spacing Between Notes in the Footnote Options dialog box. Change the number by typing a specific measurement or by using the arrows to increase or decrease the size.

**Specifying the Position for Footnotes**   In most cases, footnotes should be at the bottom of the page; this is the default in WordPerfect. However, if you want your footnotes to print immediately below the last line of text, you can click Place Notes Below Text in the Position section of the Footnote Options dialog box.

**Splitting Long Footnotes**   Normally, WordPerfect reserves enough space at the bottom of a document page for all the footnotes on that page. However, if a page has several footnotes that are particularly long, WordPerfect may split a footnote between the current page and the following page. You can specify how much of the footnote to keep together on the current page in the Amount Of Footnote To Keep Together text box in the Continued Footnotes section. By default, if there isn't enough room for at least a half inch of text, WordPerfect moves the text and footnote to the next page.

If a footnote is split between two pages, you can have WordPerfect automatically insert a (Continued...) message on the last line of footnote text on the current page and a (...continued) message on the first line of footnote text on the following page. To activate this option, click the Insert (Continued...) Message option in the Footnote Options dialog box.

> **N O T E**   WordPerfect can print the footnote "continued" messages in a different language if necessary. Specify the appropriate language in the Document Initial Style with the Styles Editor dialog box by choosing Format, Document, Initial Codes Style, then choosing Tools, Language. Select the language from the list.

**Choosing a Separator Line**   WordPerfect automatically places a line between the document text and the footnotes. This line helps the reader to distinguish between the two parts of the page. By default, the separator line is a single line that's two inches long. There are a number of line styles and other options available for the separator line. Click Separator from the Footnote Options dialog box to open the Line Separator dialog box (see fig. 25.12).

**FIG. 25.12**
The Line Separator dialog box is used to modify the separator line between the footnotes and the document text.

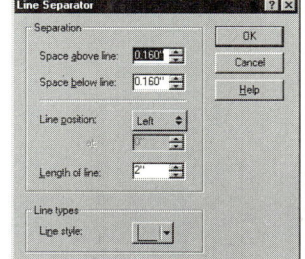

In the Line Separator dialog box, you can increase or decrease the amount of space above and below the separator from the standard one blank line. You can change the Line Position from Left (flush with the left margin) to Center (center of the line), Right (flush with the right margin), or Full (extend from the left to the right margin), or you can Set a specific position. You can also change the length of the line from the default of 2 inches. Finally, if you want to use something other than a single line, you can select from a long list of line styles.

If you make any changes in the Line Separator dialog box, WordPerfect inserts a code in the document at the top of the current page. Only the footnotes on the current page and subsequent pages will have the new separator line.

To change the separator line for the sample document, follow these steps:

1. From the Line Separator dialog box, choose Line Position and set it to Center.
2. Double-click the Length Of Line text box, then type **3** to set the length to 3" (three inches).
3. Choose Line Style, then the Thick/Thin 1 button (top line, fourth from the left) in the palette.
4. Choose OK to close the Line Separator dialog box. To return to the document, choose OK again (or choose Cancel if you did not make any changes in the Footnote Options dialog box).

Figure 25.13 shows the modified separator line in the sample document.

**FIG. 25.13**
The new separator line gives a more informal appearance to the sample document.

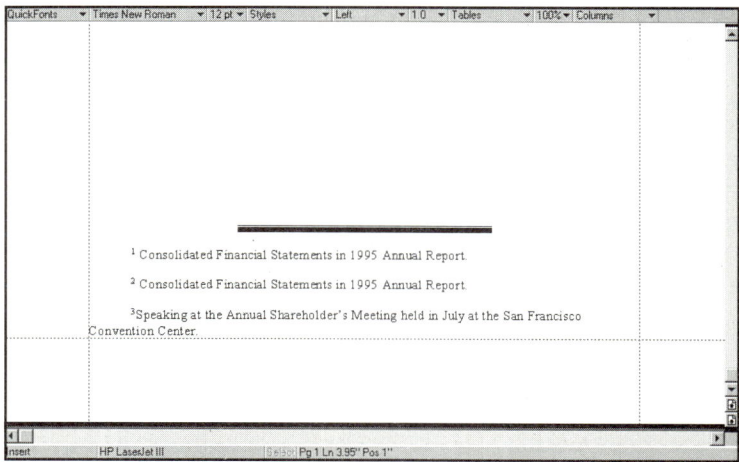

**Changing Footnote Options for the Entire Document** If you want to change the options for all the footnotes in a document, there are a couple of ways to do it:

- You can position the insertion point at the top of the document before making any changes in the Footnote Options dialog box.
- You can place the Footnote Options codes in the Document Initial Codes style (choose Fo_r_mat, _D_ocument, Initial Codes St_y_le). The advantage of placing the codes in the Document Initial Codes Style is that the codes won't be accidentally deleted or moved during editing.

### TROUBLESHOOTING

**When I insert a footnote number on a new page, the numbering starts again at 1.** The _R_estart Numbering On Each Page option is selected in the Footnote Options dialog box. To use continuously numbered footnotes for the entire document, choose _I_nsert, _F_ootnote, _O_ptions. In the Footnote Options dialog box, remove the check beside the _R_estart Numbering On Each Page option.

**I can't edit the separator line between the text and footnote area by clicking the line.** The footnote separator line is not a standard WordPerfect graphic line. It is not edited by selecting it and then choosing a command from the Graphics menu. Rather, to change the separator line, choose _I_nsert, _F_ootnote, _O_ptions. In the Footnote Options dialog box, click _S_eparator to change the appearance of the separator line. If desired, you can remove the line by choosing None in the Li_n_e Style palette.

**I deleted a footnote, but the footnote reference number remains in the text.** The footnote number in the footnote itself and the footnote number in the document are two separate entities. Deleting the text of the footnote and the number in the footnote area does not automatically remove the footnote reference number in the text of the document. You must remove the reference number manually. Or, if you want to remove a footnote entry entirely—both its reference number in the text and the footnote itself—simply delete the reference number in the text of the document. The text of the footnote is automatically deleted.

# Using Endnotes

The methods for creating and editing endnotes are much the same as those for footnotes. The main difference between the two types of notes is that you can list endnotes together on a page by themselves. Usually found at the end of the document, endnotes can be listed anywhere in a document. For example, in long documents, it is common to print a page of endnotes at the end of each section.

Endnotes have several advantages over footnotes. If your footnotes are lengthy, they can be split between two pages, which makes them more difficult to read. In addition, multiple footnotes can reduce the amount of text available on a page. Because endnotes are grouped together on a page, lengthy notes are easier to read, and they do not take up valuable space in the body of the document.

## Inserting Endnotes

As with footnotes, you may choose to create endnotes as you type the text of the document, or you may create the endnotes later when you have the necessary information. You insert an endnote where you want the endnote reference number to appear in the text.

To create an endnote, do the following:

1. Position the insertion point where you want the endnote reference number to appear in the document text.
2. Choose Insert, Endnote, Create.

WordPerfect moves the insertion point to the endnote area of the document editing window, which, by default, is one line below the last line of text on the current page. If you are using Draft View mode, the insertion point is moved into a separate Endnote window. A Footnote/Endnote Feature Bar is available in the Endnote window.

WordPerfect inserts the correct endnote number in the endnote area. While the footnote number is a superscript number followed by a tab, the endnote number is normal size and followed by a period to separate it from the text of the endnote.

## Editing and Manipulating Endnotes

When editing, the only difference between footnotes and endnotes is that in Page mode, endnotes are placed after the text instead of at the bottom of the page, and in Draft mode, WordPerfect displays the Endnote window instead of the Footnote window. Deleting, moving, and copying endnotes works exactly the same way as for footnotes.

## Using Endnote Options

The Endnote Options dialog box has most of the same options as the Footnote Options dialog box, with a couple of exceptions. Because endnotes are grouped together on a page, the Position options are not necessary. Also, there is not an option to print a continued message if a footnote is split between pages.

**NOTE** Endnote text is frequently indented next to the endnote number. To indent the endnote text from the Endnote Options dialog box, click In Note, and insert an Indent (F7) after the period in the Endnote style in the Styles Editor dialog box.

## Placing Endnotes

In long documents, it is often preferable to compile a list of endnotes at the end of each section, rather than at the end of the document. You can specify where to insert the endnotes with the Placement option on the Endnote menu. The Endnote Placement dialog box has two options: Insert Endnotes At Insertion Point and Insert Endnotes At Insertion Point And Restart Numbering. To insert endnotes within the document, rather than at the end of the document, follow these steps:

1. Position the insertion point where you want the endnotes listed. If you want the endnotes on a new page, press Ctrl+Enter to create a new page. If necessary, create a heading for the page (for example, type **Notes** and format it centered, underlined, and bold).
2. Choose Insert, Endnote, Placement to display the Endnote Placement dialog box.
3. Choose either option: Insert Endnotes At Insertion Point or Insert Endnotes At Insertion Point And Restart Numbering.
4. Choose OK.

WordPerfect inserts an [Endnote Placement] code at the insertion point. Figure 25.14 shows the endnotes page for the sample document.

### TROUBLESHOOTING

**I deleted an endnote, but the endnote reference number remains in the text.** The endnote number in the endnote itself, and the endnote number in the document, are two separate entities. Deleting the text of the endnote and the number in the endnote area does not automatically remove the endnote reference number in the text of the document. You must remove the reference number manually. Or, if you want to remove an endnote entry entirely—both its reference number in the text and the endnote itself—simply delete the reference number. The text of the endnote is automatically deleted.

*continues*

*continued*

> **When I insert an endnote, the endnote appears immediately below the insertion point.**
> Before inserting the first endnote of the document, place the insertion point where you want the endnotes to appear (usually at the very end of the document). Choose Insert, Endnote, Placement, and choose one of the two placement options in the Endnote Placement dialog box. When finished, move the insertion point back to where you want the endnote reference to appear, and then create the endnote.

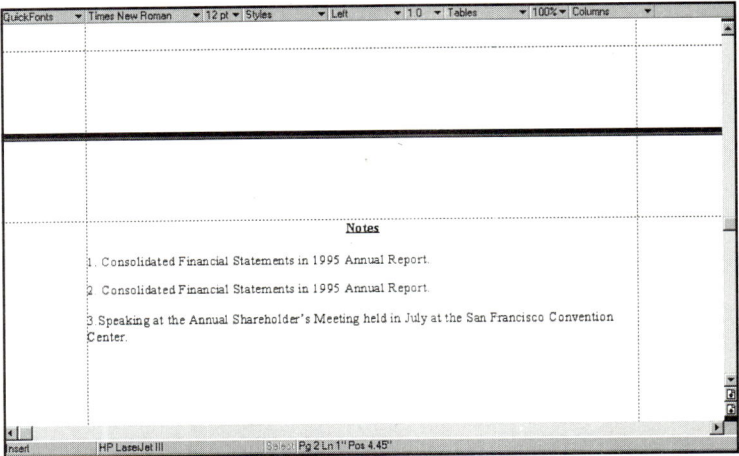

**FIG. 25.14**
The endnotes for the sample document are compiled on a titled page.

# Converting Footnotes to Endnotes and Endnotes to Footnotes

Sometimes requirements for a document can change, and you may find yourself needing endnotes instead of footnotes, or vice versa. If this is the case, you can use one of the macros that comes with WordPerfect (called *shipping macros*) to convert footnotes to endnotes and endnotes to footnotes. The two macros are called FOOTEND and ENDFOOT, respectively.

To convert footnotes to endnotes, follow these steps:

1. Choose Tools, Macro, Play.

> **CAUTION**
> In most cases, the WPWIN subfolder of the MACROS folder is open in the Play Macro dialog box. If you don't see the FOOTEND and ENDFOOT macro files, you need to switch to this subfolder before continuing.

2. Type **footend** in the Name text box.

3. Choose Play.

   As the macro runs, WordPerfect displays a message box indicating that the footnotes are being converted to endnotes. A counter is also displayed so you can watch the progress.

 If, for some reason, you don't have access to the shipping macros, you can convert your footnotes to endnotes manually. Simply cut the text out of the footnote, create an endnote, then paste the text into the endnote. Likewise, if you need to convert your endnotes, cut the text out of the endnote, create a footnote, then paste the text into the footnote. After you move the footnote text to the endnote, be sure to delete the appropriate reference numbers.

To convert endnotes to footnotes, follow these steps:

1. Choose Tools, Macro, Play.

2. Type **endfoot** in the Name text box.

3. Choose Play.

   As the macro runs, WordPerfect displays a message box indicating that the endnotes are being converted to footnotes. A counter is also displayed so you can watch the progress.

These two macros make it easy to switch back and forth between footnotes and endnotes; you can quickly decide which one works best for you. ●

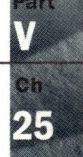

CHAPTER 26

# Assembling Document References

*by Gary Pickavet and Gabrielle Nemes*

WordPerfect 7 is a truly powerful word processor, yet its power doesn't stop with composing a document. WordPerfect also provides tools that enable you to perform complex document processing tasks, such as generating different kinds of references automatically, allowing you to track revisions, compare versions of a document, and mark the changes.

WordPerfect provides a variety of document reference types: lists, tables of contents, tables of authorities, indexes, and cross-references. These references enable you to mark document text and have WordPerfect automatically create tables listing the items and their page numbers. WordPerfect can even mark graphics box captions automatically to be included in a list. When you revise a document, the power of the document reference feature is most apparent—you can add or delete information anywhere in the document without worrying about the page numbers assigned to the marked items. After you revise the document, you simply use the Generate feature when you want WordPerfect to update the tables.

### Use highlighting to add comments or call attention to portions of a document

Marking text makes it easy for you to quickly locate sections when you view or print a document.

### Add revisions or annotations made to a document

Several persons can easily add revisions to a document, each in a separate color, while you retain final editing control. You'll learn how to add your editing touch to a document.

### Compare two documents to locate their differences

It can be difficult to find changes to a document that has been modified by other people and then returned to you. You learn how to compare the text between the changed document and the original document.

### Create and customize tables of content, indexes, tables of authorities, and lists

You learn how to automate these important reference functions.

### Add cross-references

The capability to maintain accurate cross-references is a powerful feature of WordPerfect. Learn how to add and generate references to pages, figure numbers, chapter numbers, and so on.

Before computerized word processors, a significant amount of time was required at the end of a project for designing, creating, modifying, and proofreading tables of exhibits, tables of contents, indexes, and other reference materials. With automatic generation of references, WordPerfect makes creating references almost effortless and saves countless hours.

Lawyers preparing legal briefs once had to spend much time poring over a document, noting all the legal citations. After finding all the legal citations and noting their page numbers, the writer had to create a table of authorities listing each citation and the page number. WordPerfect's Table of Authorities feature was designed specifically to solve this problem and allow these tables to be created with minimum effort.

Showing the differences between old and new versions of a document by using strikeout and redlining is another time-consuming task often performed manually. WordPerfect allows you to track revisions made by every person who edits a document. You can also use the Compare Document feature to mark all changes made between a new version and a previous version of a document. Deleted material is marked with the Strikeout font attribute, and new material with the Redline font attribute.

# Keeping Track of Document Revisions

In today's world of easy e-mail, routing documents electronically means that more people have active access to an actual document file rather than merely a printed copy. And, of course, the more people who can work with a file, the more changes, or *revisions,* are typically made. Adding revisions and managing those revisions is an important part of managing document workflow.

Consider the implication of asking five people to review a complex document. Now imagine the chaos that might occur if each person added, deleted, or rearranged even a small portion of the text. Without the capability to electronically track those changes, it might quickly become impossible to even determine where—or *if*—revisions were made.

WordPerfect 7, therefore, allows two simple methods of adding revision marks to a document, and one method of highlighting a portion of a document for emphasis. It then becomes a simple matter to review a document for changes.

## Highlighting for Emphasis

You can add highlighting to existing text in a document, similar to using a marker highlighter on a written document. Highlighting, while drawing attention to areas of a document, is not considered a revision. Highlighted portions look nice, are easy to spot, can appear in any color your monitor supports, and can be printed. But highlighted portions cannot be tracked as revisions, annotations, or changes.

Adding highlighting to a document adds a pair of on/off highlighting codes, such as [Highlight:Yellow]. The code reflects the color you've chosen as your highlight color. To add highlighting to your document, use one of the following methods:

1. If you plan to highlight several areas of text, click the Highlight tool in the Toolbar. The mouse pointer changes to a pen highlighter (see fig. 26.1).
2. Drag the pen highlighter over the text you want to highlight, then release the mouse. The selected text appears highlighted.

**FIG. 26.1**
Dragging the Highlight pointer selects the text to be marked.

The Highlight tool

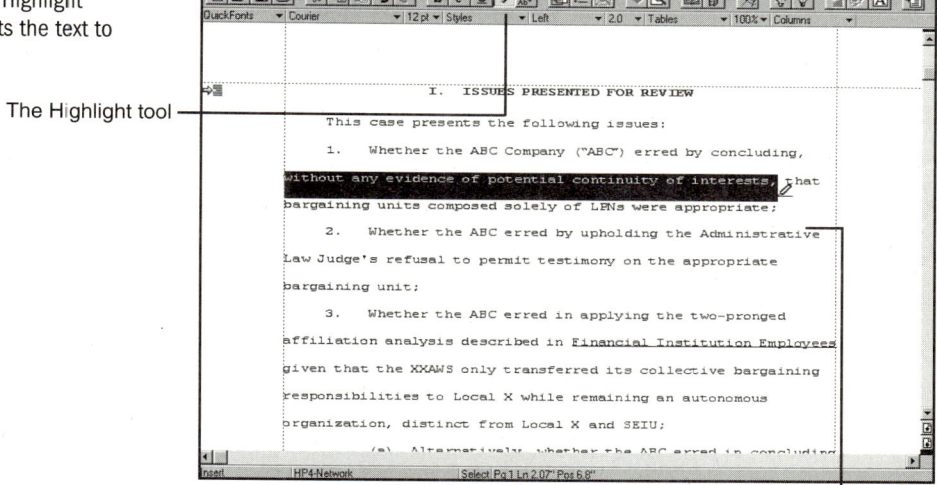

The Highlight pointer

3. When you're finished marking all text to be highlighted, click the Highlight tool in the Toolbar. The Toolbar button is no longer active, and the mouse pointer returns to normal.

You can also use the other method of highlighting:

1. Select the text to be highlighted.
2. Click the Highlight tool or choose Tools, Highlight, Highlight On. The selected text is then highlighted.
   ▶ **See** "Selecting Text," **p. 99**

You might want to ask different people to use different highlight colors, or perhaps you want to use different colors to draw attention to alternate points. To quickly change highlight colors, follow these steps:

1. Choose Tools, Highlight, Change Color.
2. Select the color you want to use from the Color drop-down palette. Be sure to select a color light enough, and perhaps bright enough, to allow the text to show through your highlight marking.
3. Choose a lighter shade of the color you have chosen by entering (or using the spin controls to select) a percentage in the Shading text box.
4. Choose OK. Text you highlight after changing the highlight color now uses the new color.

By default, the highlighting color is yellow and prints with a shaded background. You can, however, hide the highlighted text marks from both the screen and the printer. This allows you to use the Highlighting feature for adding personal annotations to the document, perhaps to draw your attention to particular sections, then printing the document with or without the background shading.

To hide or show highlighting in your document, choose Tools, Highlight, Print/Show Highlighting. Highlighted text and its associated codes still exist in the document when hidden. Showing and printing highlighted text works together. If you've checked the Print/Show Highlighting option, your marked text appears with its highlighting both on-screen and in the document when printed. If unchecked, the highlight shading do not appear in either place.

You can remove highlighting marks individually from each highlighted text portion. To do so, select the highlighted text, then choose Tools, Highlight, Remove Highlighting.

## Revising Routed Documents

WordPerfect 7 allows you to efficiently and easily route a document to other persons for review. Inviting other people to review and edit a document, however, can be confusing when each person makes changes to the document. The Document Review feature of WordPerfect enables you to determine exactly what changes were made, and by whom.

▶ **See** "Using Novell GroupWise or Other E-Mail Programs," **p. 295**

**Marking Revisions as You Edit**   When you receive a document for revision from someone else, you are considered a *reviewer*. You can then use Document Review feature to edit the document. As a reviewer, you can choose a personal color so that your additions or deletions are automatically marked in your color in the document as you edit the file.

Revisions to document text appear in two ways:

- Additions to a document appear in the reviewer's color.
- Deletions also appear in the reviewer's color, but are marked with strikeout, as shown in figure 26.2.

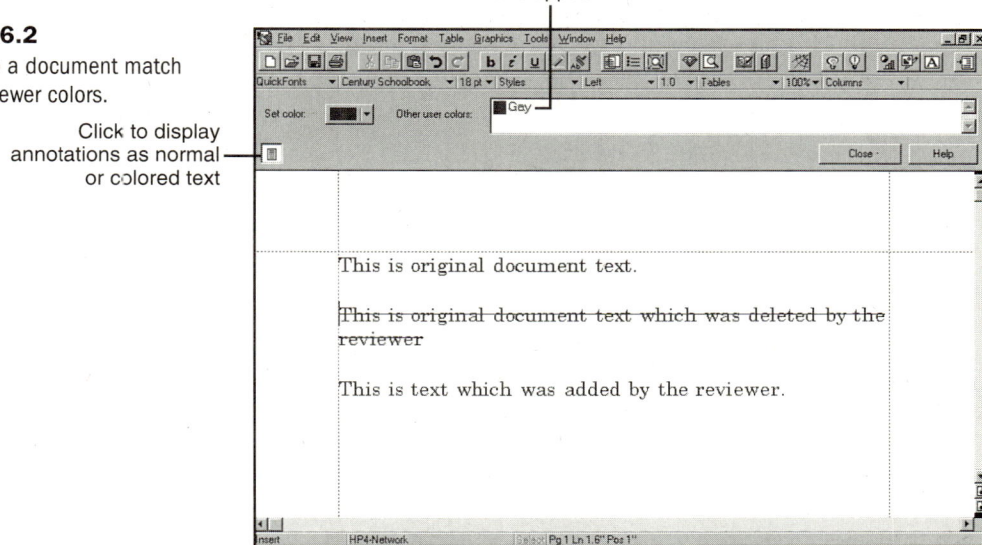

**FIG. 26.2**
Edits to a document match the reviewer colors.

Use these steps when reviewing a document:

1. Open the document as you normally would using File, Open. Now choose File, Document, Review, Reviewer.

   The document opens, with any changes made by other reviewers included in their chosen colors. The Reviewer Bar appears at the top of the document.

2. Choose the color you want to use for your revisions by choosing Set Color, then selecting a color from the color palette. (Be sure to select a color that no one else has used. You can see their colors in the Other Used Colors list box.)

3. Edit the document. You can make changes to additions made by other reviewers, but you cannot change text that has been deleted.

4. When you're finished, save the document as you normally would. WordPerfect saves your changes with your user color as set in step 2. If you've not changed your user color, WordPerfect looks at Environment Preferences for your name and saves your changes to the Document Review User list with your chosen color.

At times it can be confusing to edit the document with all the different colors and strikeout text on-screen. Temporarily hide the revision marks by clicking the display all annotations as normal/colored text button (refer to fig. 26.2).

**Reviewing Revisions Made by Others**   When you create a document, you become that document's *author*. After sending a document to others for revision, you can easily review it for modifications, noting all of the changes made. You can tell who made the change by comparing the color of the modification to a displayed list of user colors. You can also reject or accept the changes, and then save a final copy of the document.

To review all changes made to a document, follow these steps:

1. Open the document to be reviewed by choosing File, Open. Then choose File, Document, Review, Author.

   Your document opens with all revision marks visible, displayed in each reviewer's color. The Document Review Bar also opens at the top of the document, and the insertion point automatically moves to, and selects, the first revision (see fig. 26.3).

2. Step through the document, inserting or deleting each annotation using the buttons on the Document Review, as listed in the following table.

| Button | Description |
| --- | --- |
| | Displays all annotations (changes or revisions) to the text in color, or as normal text. |
| | Moves to the next annotation and selects it. |
| | Moves to the previous annotation and selects it. |
| | Accepts and inserts the currently selected annotation into the document. |
| | Inserts all annotations into the document. |
| | Deletes the currently selected annotation from the document. |
| | Deletes all annotations from the document. |

3. At any time during processing, you can save the document changes using File, Save on File, Save As to save the document with a new name on format.

4. When you have completed accepting or declining all revisions, choose Continue, or save the document normally.

# Keeping Track of Document Revisions 829

**FIG. 26.3**
Author review buttons enable you to insert or delete selected revisions.

Revision buttons

First revision is selected

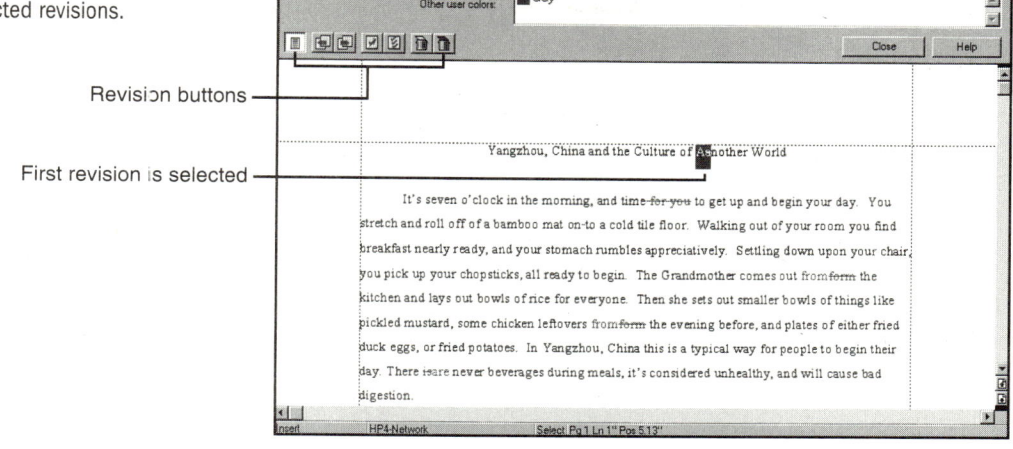

# Automatically Marking Revisions Using Compare Document

**NOTE** WordPerfect comes with several ready-made Toolbars that can be displayed on any side of your screen. One of these Toolbars, Generate, enables you to quickly choose each of the WordPerfect document reference features. When you plan to do a great deal of document reference work, consider displaying the Generate Toolbar (see fig. 26.4).

▶ See "Switching Between Toolbars," **p. 415**

Another method of comparing changes between document versions is to use the Compare Document feature. Manually identifying every change between document versions takes a great deal of time. WordPerfect's Compare Document feature completely automates the task, comparing an old version of a document on disk to the current on-screen document. WordPerfect indicates which text has been added, deleted, changed, and moved in the on-screen document.

Deleted material is shown with the strikeout text enhancement. New text is marked with the redline text enhancement. If you have a color monitor, the new text appears in red on-screen.

On laser printers, *strikeout* is typically printed as text with a line through it. *Redlined* text is printed with a shade behind the text. The actual enhancements printed depend on your printer and the enhancements it supports. Consult your printer manual for more information.

Part V
Ch
26

**FIG. 26.4**
Use the Generate Toolbar to choose document reference features.

The Generate Toolbar

> **CAUTION**
> Using this feature requires foresight. Many people perform revisions to a document by retrieving the current document, making the changes, and then replacing the old version of the document with the revised version. After you replace the old version of the document with the on-screen version, you cannot use the Compare Document feature because you have no old version to compare to the on-screen document.

If you plan to use the Compare Document feature after you revise an original document, save the revisions with a new name, rename the original document, or make a copy of the original document. By taking any one of these steps, you maintain the original version for use with the Compare Document feature.

**Comparing a New Version to an Old Version**  To compare the revised version of the document to the old version saved on disk, follow these steps:

1. Choose File, Document, Add Compare Markings. The Add Compare Markings dialog box appears, with the path and file name selected for the current document on-screen (see fig. 26.5).

2. If necessary, change the file name to match the name of your original document.

   To search for another file, click the filelist icon at the right of the text box. The Select File dialog box appears to help you select another folder or file name. Select the desired file and choose OK.

**FIG. 26.5**
Use the Add Compare Markings dialog box to specify the file to wh ch you want to compare the current document, and the method used by WordPerfect to compare the documents.

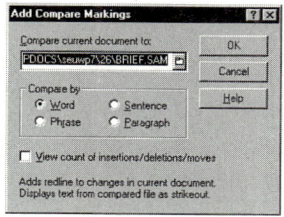

3. In the Compare By section of the Add Compare Markings dialog box, choose how you want WordPerfect to compare the documents. The Compare By options are described in the following table.

| Option | Description |
| --- | --- |
| Word | Any text that ends with a space, period, comma, colon, semicolon, question mark, exclamation point, hard return, hard page break, footnote or endnote number, or the end of a document. |
| Phrase | Text that ends with a period, comma, colon, semicolon, question mark, exclamation point, hard return, hard page break, or the end of the document. Note that a phrase does not end with a space as does a word. |
| Sentence | Text that ends with a period, question mark, exclamation point, hard return, hard page break, or the end of the document. |
| Paragraph | Ends with a hard return, a hard page break, or the end of the document. |

4. If desired, check the View Count Of Insertions/Deletions/Moves option to see a summary count of the changes found between the documents. When the option is checked, WordPerfect responds with a Document Compare Status dialog box when comparison is complete (see fig. 26.6).

**FIG. 26.6**
If requested, the Document Compare Status dialog box appears after Compare Document has finished adding markings.

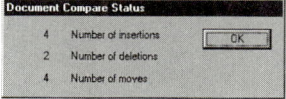

5. Choose OK. WordPerfect compares the documents, and a progress bar appears, displaying the percentage of completion as the documents are processed. When the comparison is finished, WordPerfect returns to your document.

**N O T E**  The Compare Document feature marks changes in footnotes, endnotes, and tables, but it doesn't mark changes in graphics boxes, watermarks, comments, headers, and footers.

WordPerfect modifies the on-screen version of the document and notes the differences. Removed text is marked with the strikeout enhancement. New text is displayed with the redline enhancement. Text that was moved is surrounded by two messages—the message THE FOLLOWING TEXT WAS MOVED precedes the moved text; the message THE PRECEDING TEXT WAS MOVED follows the moved text. Figure 26.7 shows a document that has been marked using the Compare Document feature.

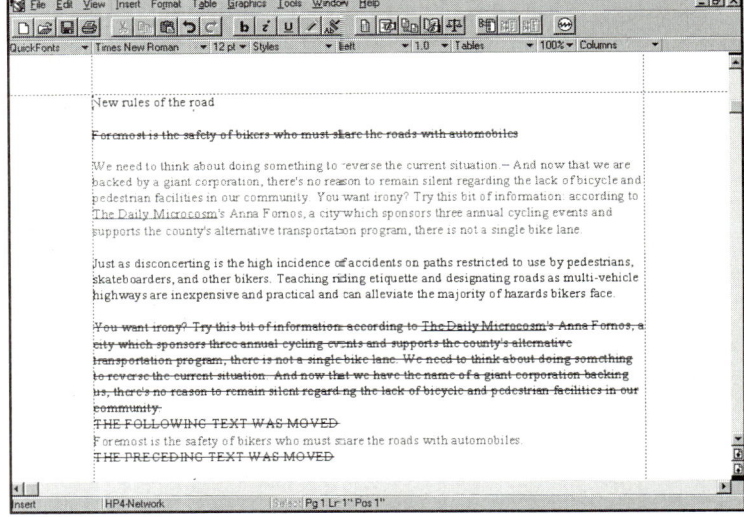

**FIG. 26.7**
A revised document shows changed sentences marked in strikeout and redline and may display messages about moved text.

WordPerfect also enables you to change the method of redlining to one other than the default WordPerfect printer driver method.

To change the way WordPerfect displays the redlining when your document is printed or displayed, follow these steps:

1. Choose F<u>o</u>rmat, <u>D</u>ocument, <u>R</u>edline Method. The Redline dialog box appears (see fig. 26.8).

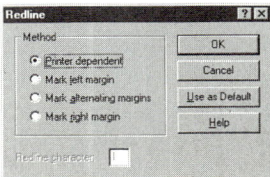

**FIG. 26.8**
The Redline dialog box shows a list of redlining display choices.

2. Choose one of the following options:
    - *Printer Dependent.* Uses the WordPerfect printer driver redlining method. Redlined text (which has been added) is printed on most laser printers with a gray shading behind the text.
    - *Mark Left Margin.* Places the selected redline character in the left margin of lines with added text.
    - *Mark Alternating Margin.* Places the selected redline character in the left margin of lines on even-numbered pages, and the right margin of lines on odd-numbered pages.
    - *Mark Right Margin.* Places the selected redline character in the right margin of lines.

3. To change the redline character from the default vertical bar, choose Redline Character and type the desired character in the box. This option is available only if you choose to use a redline method other than Printer Dependent. You can press Ctrl+W to open the WordPerfect Characters dialog box and insert a special character.
4. Choose OK. WordPerfect applies the changes and returns to your document.

> **TIP** Choose Use As Default to have WordPerfect use the selected redline method for future editing sessions as well as the current one.

In addition to changing how redlined text is displayed, you can modify the typeface your printer uses for redlined text. For example, suppose you are using Times New Roman as the font in your document. When you add new text, you want that redlined text displayed in Arial. This can be especially useful when you must fax a redlined document.

You can make this automatic font change using these steps:

1. Choose Format, Font, Font Map. The Font Map dialog box opens. Times New Roman should be listed as the current printer typeface in the Face list on the left. If it does not automatically appear in the Face list, select it from the drop-down list. (You need to change the Redline font for each font you use in the document.)
2. Select Redline from the Automatic Font Change list and select an alternate typeface from the Face list in the group box on the right. This typeface is now automatically used each time you use redlining in any document that uses the original printer font.
3. When your font changes are complete, choose OK to return to the Font dialog box, then OK again to return to your document window. When redline is used, it will now appear in your substituted typeface.

▶ **See** "Font Mapping," **p. 648**

## Purging Marked Changes from a Saved Document

If you saved your revised file immediately before using the Compare Document function, you have no reason to remove the redlining and strikeout from your document. After you print the document with the noted changes, simply close the document without saving it and open the latest version of the revised document. If you haven't saved the on-screen document, or if you accidentally save the on-screen document after you have marked it and replaced the latest revision, you can remove the strikeout and the redline text enhancement from the document.

To remove Compare Document markings, follow these steps:

1. Choose File, Document, Remove Compare Markings. The Remove Compare Markings dialog box appears.

2. To remove both the redlining enhancement and text with strikeout enhancements, choose Remove Redline Markings and Strikeout Text. Added text remains in the document without redline markings, while deleted text is removed from the document.

3. To remove only the text marked with the strikeout enhancements and leave the text marked with the redline enhancement, choose Remove Strikeout Text Only.

4. Choose OK to remove the Compare Document markings.

 You can also remove the Compare Document text and redline enhancements by choosing Edit, Undo; by pressing Ctrl+Z; or by choosing the Undo Toolbar button. If you choose any of these methods, you must choose Undo immediately after you use the Compare Document function.

# Creating Lists

*Lists* are used to display a roster of items that are referenced throughout a document. For example, you might want to include a list of graphics, figures, exhibits, or even appendixes. WordPerfect's List feature is its most basic automatic reference feature. By marking items you want to include on a list, WordPerfect searches the document and generates a list of the marked items, with or without their page numbers. Your generated list can appear anywhere in the document you specify.

Three basic steps are required to create lists:

- *Mark*. Mark the text to be included in the list and specify the list in which it is to appear. (You can skip this task if you only want lists generated from captions of the various graphics boxes provided by WordPerfect. WordPerfect finds the captions automatically.)

■ *Define.* Indicate where you want WordPerfect to create the list and how you want the list to look.

■ *Generate.* Run Generate to create and revise the list of marked items and, optionally, page numbers.

Each of these steps is discussed in the sections that follow. When WordPerfect generates a list, the items appear in the order in which they appear in the document.

## Marking Text for Lists

To create a list, you must mark the text you want included in the list. (Note, however, that graphic boxes that do not contain captions will not be included in the list.) WordPerfect includes the marked text as the item description in the list.

It's a good idea to open the Reveal Codes window while you select text to be marked for inclusion in your list so that you can precisely place the insertion point. If you include the enhancement code while selecting and marking text, the enhancement is also included in the generated list. If, for example, you mark `Exhibit 1,` which is italicized, the text is italicized in the list if the `[Italic]` codes are included in the marked text. Review figures 26.9 and 26.10 to see how to include or omit enhancement codes when your list is generated.

▶ See "Reveal Codes," **p. 41**

**FIG. 26.9**
Codes between `[Mrk Txt List]` codes are included in the generated list.

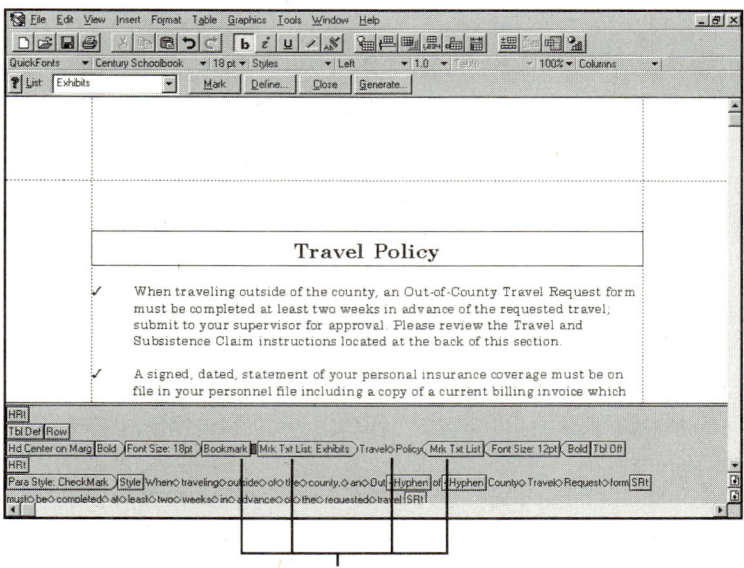

These enhancement codes are between the `[Mrk Txt List]` codes

**FIG. 26.10**
Enhancement codes outside the [Mrk Txt List] codes are not included in the generated list.

These enhancement codes are outside the [Mrk Txt List] codes

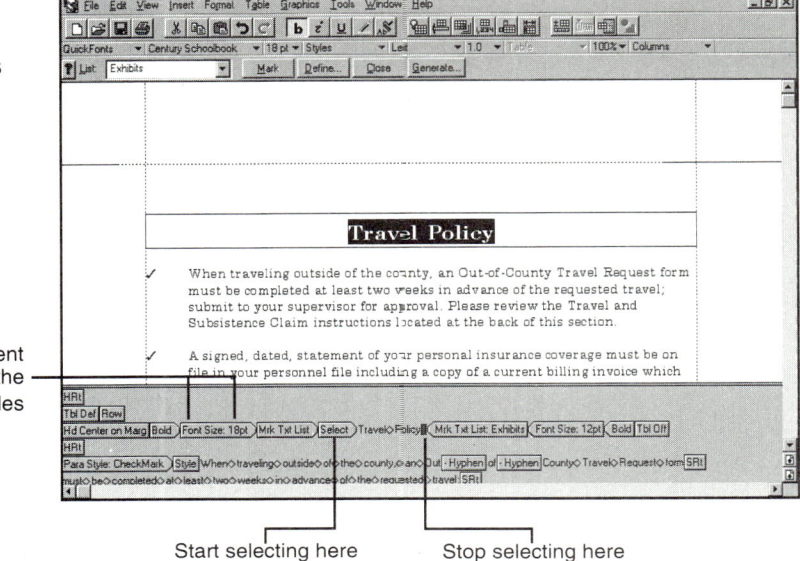

To mark text that you want to appear in a list, follow these steps:

1. Choose Tools, Generate, List. The List Feature Bar appears (see fig. 26.11).

**FIG. 26.11**
The List Feature Bar enables you to enter and select list names, mark list entries, define a list, or run Generate to create and update lists you've defined.

2. Select the text.

3. Click List to move the insertion point to the List text box. For a new list, type a descriptive name in the List text box.

   If this is the first list defined in your document, the List text box is empty. If you are marking subsequent occurrences of text for existing lists, the list name that you last used appears in the List text box. If the desired name of a previously entered list name is not displayed, open the pop-up list button by clicking or pressing the up or down cursor arrows to show the current list names. Select the desired list name.

4. Click Mark on the List Feature Bar. The text is marked for inclusion in the selected list, and WordPerfect returns to your document.

> **TIP** To access the mnemonics in the feature bars, press Alt+Shift+*letter*.

When you mark text to be placed in a list, WordPerfect inserts the code [Mrk Txt List] at the beginning and end of the selected text. These codes do not print; however, you can see them by opening the Reveal Codes window (choose View, Reveal Codes; or press Alt+F3). To see which list the marked text belongs to, move the insertion point so that it immediately precedes the code before or after the marked text. The code expands and displays the name of the list to which the selected text belongs. Figure 26.9, for example, displays the code for a list named "Exhibits."

Alternatively, click the code in the Reveal Codes window to quickly place the insertion point before the code and expand it.

> **NOTE** You can change the Reveal Codes Display Preferences so that WordPerfect always shows codes in detail and so the list name always appears in the code. Because this causes all codes to appear expanded with their values, you might prefer to expand the codes when you need to know the list name rather than having WordPerfect display all codes as expanded.
>
> To turn on display of full code detail, from a document window choose Edit, Preferences. The Preferences dialog box will appear. Next choose Display, then click the Reveal Codes tab. Finally, turn on detailed display by checking Show Codes in Detail in the Options group. Choose OK, then Close to return to the document window.

If you change your mind about what you want the text in your list to say, edit the text between the Mark Text codes. If you decide you do not want an item included in the list, delete the code marking the list item. The next time you generate the list, WordPerfect modifies or removes the list text, as appropriate.

## Defining a List

 You can define the appearance and placement of a list either before or after you mark list items. As you define your list, you can specify the numbering format you want to use for the list, the format of the page number, what type of graphics box captions you want included in the list, and the default settings for the style that determines how your list is formatted.

It's probably easiest to define where you want the list placed and to set any list formatting options at the same time. Follow these steps to insert a list definition into your document which uses the default list format settings:

1. Place the insertion point at the location in your document where you want the list to appear.

To place the list on its own page, insert a hard page break (press Ctrl+Enter). If you want, you can type a title for the list.

2. If the List Feature Bar is not displayed, choose Tools, Generate, List.

3. From the Feature Bar, click Define. The Define List dialog box appears. Any lists which you have already defined, or for which you have marked entries, appear in the list box (see fig. 26.12).

**FIG. 26.12**
The Define List dialog box shows the names of lists for which entries have been marked or which have already been defined, the style applied to the list, and the numbering format for the list.

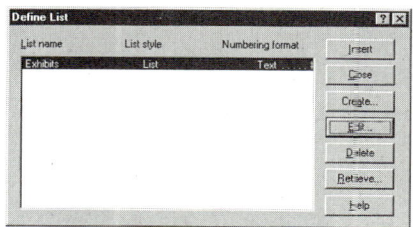

4. To use an existing list name, select the list name.

5. To create a new list, click Create. The Create List dialog box appears. Type a name for the list in the List text box, then choose OK. The new list appears as selected in the Define List dialog box.

6. Click Insert. The Define List dialog box closes and the List Definition code is added to your document.

When you define a list, WordPerfect inserts a [Def Mark] code in your document. If you want to see which type of document reference is being defined and its name, click the [Def Mark] code. The code expands, similar to the following:

    [Def Mark: List, Exhibits: None]

The text << List will generate here >> is inserted into your document between two [Gen Txt] codes. This text is replaced by the list when you run Generate.

 **TIP** To see these codes, open the Reveal Codes window by choosing View, Reveal Codes, or by pressing Alt+F3.

**Editing an Existing List Definition**   If you want to change the appearance of your lists, you need to edit its definition. You are then able to specify the numbering format you want to use for the list, format of the page number, and default settings for the style that determines how your list is formatted.

You can set the appearance of your list when you first define your list definition, or you can later change the appearance of a list. Follow these steps to edit an existing list definition:

1. If the List Feature Bar isn't visible, choose Tools, Generate, List.
2. From the Feature Bar, click Define. The Define List dialog box appears.
3. Choose the list whose appearance you want to modify. Scroll the selection highlight bar to the desired list.
4. Click Edit. The Edit List dialog box appears (see fig. 26.13).

**FIG. 26.13**
The Edit List dialog box enables you to change the appearance of your list and select graphics box captions to be automatically selected for the list.

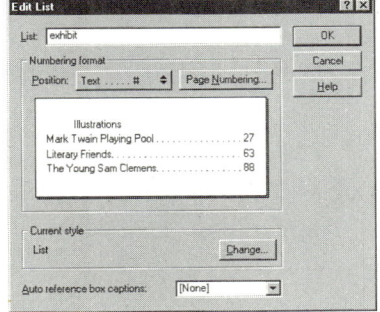

The following sections describe the various options for changing the appearance of your list. These options can be set when you first define or create a list, or later when you edit the list definition. Follow the steps in the appropriate section.

**Choosing the Numbering Position for a List**   Five numbering positions for lists are available and are illustrated in the table in step 4, in the following list of steps. The default numbering position is a right-justified page number with dot leaders.

To change the position of the page number, follow these steps:

1. If you've previously defined this list, delete the [Def Mark] code for the list using Reveal Codes.
2. Choose Define from the List Feature Bar, then choose Edit. The Edit List dialog box appears.
3. From the Edit List dialog box, choose Position.
4. Choose the desired page number option from the resulting pop-up list. You can see the appearance of your selection in the preview window. The options are listed in the following table.

| Numbering Format | Text Result |
| --- | --- |
| No Numbering | Map of the US |
| Text # | Map of the US 38 |
| Text (#) | Map of the US (38) |
| Text    # | Map of the US 38 |
| Text    # | Map of the US.38 |

5. If you are through making changes to the definition, choose OK. You are returned to the Define List dialog box.

6. Choose Insert to add the list definition to your document, or Close to discard your changes.

**Changing the Page Number Format for a List**   You can change the appearance of the page numbers for the items in a list. The page number format can be the same as the page number formatting in your document, or you may want the page number printed with your list items to use a different format.

To change the page number format for a list, follow these steps:

1. From the Edit List dialog box, click Page Numbering. The Page Number Format dialog box appears, showing two choices: Document Page Number Format and User-Defined Page Number Format (see fig. 26.14).

**FIG. 26.14**
The Page Number Format dialog box enables you to design custom page number formats for your lists.

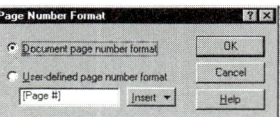

2. Choose Document Page Number Format to format the page numbers in your list the same way page numbers are formatted in your document.

   Alternatively, choose User-Defined Page Number Format to set the page number format differently for this list. By using the Insert drop-down list, you can also include a Secondary Number, Chapter Number, Volume Number, or even Total Pages in the document (such as School Problems-Chapter 4 Page 12 of 15). For detailed information about working with page number formats, see Chapter 5, "Formatting Pages and Documents."

   The code [Page #] in the User-Defined Page Number Format text box represents the page number. If you want text to appear before or after the page number, type the text, then click Insert and select the page number option. Finally, type any text to follow the number. To have the page number appear as - 1 -, for example,

type a dash and space before and after the page number code in the text entry box
(- **[Page #]** -).
3. Choose OK to return to the Edit List dialog box.
4. Choose OK to return to the Define List dialog box, then <u>I</u>nsert to add your definition to your document, or <u>C</u>lose to discard your changes.

▶ **See** "Customizing the Page Number Appearance," **p. 165**

**Changing a List's Default Style**   WordPerfect provides a default style for each of its document references. The style name used for lists is appropriately called List. You can modify the List style, and WordPerfect applies your modifications to all lists that use this default style; or you can create a new style that you apply only to certain lists.

To modify the default style of a list, follow these steps:

1. From either the Edit List or Create List dialog boxes, click <u>C</u>hange. The List Style dialog box appears showing the various document reference styles as well as styles you have created. The style called List is highlighted.
2. Choose <u>E</u>dit. The Styles Editor dialog box appears.

    The default style for lists contains the codes to create a hanging indent (`[Hd Left Ind][Hd Back Tab]`). WordPerfect enables you to customize this List style as you would any style. For detailed information about styles, see Chapter 10, "Using Styles."
3. Make any desired changes and choose OK. WordPerfect returns to the List Style dialog box.
4. Choose <u>C</u>lose, OK, and <u>C</u>lose to return to your document.

In addition to editing the existing List style, from the List Style dialog box you can also highlight another style and click <u>S</u>elect to change from the default style list to another existing style. Or you can click C<u>r</u>eate to design a new style to be applied to a list. When you create a style, WordPerfect inserts the style in the Styles box in the List Style dialog box.

▶ **See** "Editing Styles," **p. 344**

**Making a List of Graphics Box Captions**   For most lists, you mark in your document text what you want to include in the list. Then when you generate the list, WordPerfect copies the marked text to the selected location and formats the list. If you use graphics boxes in your document, you can have WordPerfect automatically place the captions from each type of graphics box into a separate list.

> **N O T E**  You can mix marked text in a list with graphics box captions. It's usually less confusing, however, to keep separate the lists for which *you* mark text from WordPerfect's automatically selected lists.

To make a list of graphics box captions, follow these steps:

1. Place the insertion point at the location in your document where you want the list to appear, adding a page break and list title if you want, as necessary.

2. If the List Feature Bar isn't visible, choose Tools, Generate, List.
3. From the Feature Bar, click Define. The Define List dialog box appears. The lists you have already defined appear in the list box.
4. Click Create. The Create List dialog box appears.
5. Type a list name in the List text box.
6. Click Auto Reference Box Captions at the bottom of the dialog box.
7. Use the drop-down list button at the right of the Auto Reference Box Captions text box to display the list of WordPerfect graphics boxes.
8. Select the type of graphics box for which you want to have WordPerfect automatically select the box captions, and place in the List.
9. Choose OK. The Define List dialog box reappears.
10. Click Insert. The Define List dialog box closes and inserts a [Def Mark] code in your document. The captions from the type of graphics box you selected are included in the selected list the next time you run Generate.

You are now ready to generate your list, as explained in the next section.

## Using Generate To Create and Update Document References

After you mark text, determine on which list to place the text, and define the appearance and location of the lists, you are ready to create the lists. Generating document references can take a long time. As with any function that automatically modifies your document, it's a good idea to save your document before running Generate. If you have any system problems, or if you must abort the Generate process for some reason, you can then easily start over.

All references in a document—lists, tables of contents, tables of authorities, cross-references, indexes, and endnotes—are generated and updated each time you perform the Generate function. To ensure that all page numbers and cross-references are correct, you usually want to generate references immediately before you print. If you modified your document since the last time you generated references, be sure to regenerate your document before printing to ensure accuracy of your lists.

When you run Generate, WordPerfect creates new lists where you've indicated. WordPerfect deletes any lists previously generated and rebuilds new lists based on the text currently marked in your document. Tables of contents, tables of authorities, cross-references, and indexes are all deleted and rebuilt when you use Generate.

 To create and update your document references, it's easiest to click the Generate button on the Toolbar; choose Tools, Generate, Generate; or press Ctrl+F9. Alternatively, you can follow these steps:

> **TIP** It's a good idea to save your document before running Generate.

1. If the List Feature Bar is not displayed, choose Tools, Generate, List.
2. From the Feature Bar, click Generate. The Generate dialog box appears. The Generate dialog box enables you to have WordPerfect perform the job of locating, gathering, sorting, and listing all of a document's (and optionally its subdocuments') references. Doing this manually is very tedious and time-consuming.
3. Choose OK to create or update lists and any other references in the document.

By default, Generate updates all document references in subdocuments. This task can be very time-consuming because WordPerfect must open each subdocument, generate any document references in the subdocument, and then save the subdocument. If you are using subdocuments and do not want WordPerfect to generate and save them, uncheck the Save Subdocuments option. For more information about working with subdocuments, see Chapter 27, "Working with Large and Multi-Part Documents."

# Creating a Table of Contents

WordPerfect enables you to form a comprehensive table of contents (ToC) for documents you create. Tables of content can include as many as five levels of headings and subheadings. Each level is automatically indented to indicate the subordinate levels. As with a list, each marked item included in the table of contents can include the item's page number. When you perform the Generate function, WordPerfect creates, and subsequently updates, the table of contents entries and their page numbers.

## Marking Text for a Table of Contents

Selecting items for a table of contents is as easy as highlighting text and any desired enhancement codes, and then selecting the desired ToC level.

WordPerfect provides five levels of headings and places a blank line before each Level 1 ToC entry. Subordinate items with levels below 1 are not separated by blank lines (see fig. 26.15).

To mark text for a ToC entry, follow these steps:

1. Choose Tools, Generate, Table of Contents. The Table of Contents Feature Bar appears (see fig. 26.16).
2. Select the text. Include any enhancement codes to be applied to the text (for example bold or italic) that you also want included with the Table of Contents.

 **TIP** Include any automatic paragraph numbering codes within the selected text to also include them in the table of contents.

**FIG. 26.15**
A sample table of contents shows two levels and the default formatting, which places a blank line before each level 1 ToC entry.

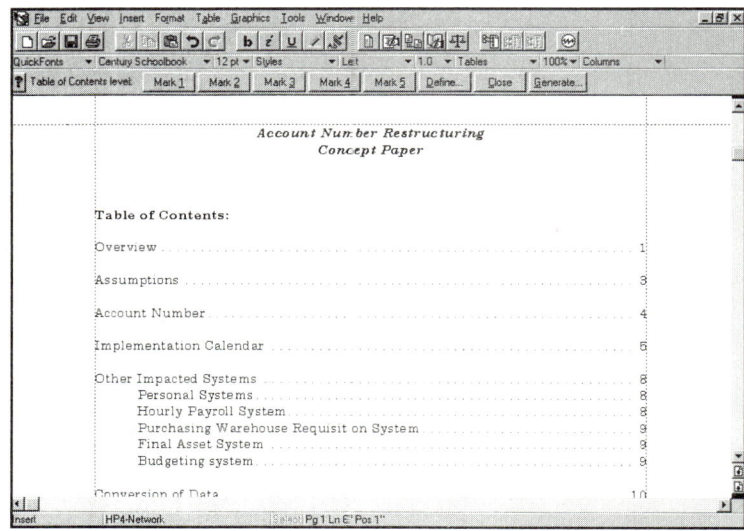

**FIG. 26.16**
Use the Table of Contents Feature Bar to mark entries, define a table of contents, or run Generate to create and update the table of contents.

 **NOTE** By using Reveal Codes (choose View, Reveal Codes; or press Alt+F3), you can easily include or exclude text enhancement codes that occur at the beginning of selected text. When you mark a ToC entry with codes within the text, WordPerfect applies the code to the text in the ToC. If the code starts before the marked text, the enhancement is not applied to the text that appears in the generated ToC.

If you capture an item with a text enhancement code that you don't want to print in the ToC, you can edit the table of contents after it has been generated. However, any changes you make in the generated table of contents are replaced the next time you generate the document references because WordPerfect deletes the old ToC and creates a new one.

3. Choose the ToC level number (Mark 1 through Mark 5) for this item; or press Alt+Shift+(1-5). The selected text is marked with the appropriate ToC code and level number.

To see the text and enhancement codes that are or will be included in the table, open the Reveal Codes window. The text and enhancement codes are surrounded by a [Mrk Txt ToC] code. To see the level number, click the code in the Reveal Codes window. The insertion point moves to just before the code; the code expands; and the level number (1 through 5) appears at the end of the code. To change the ToC entry, edit the text between the codes (which also changes the text in the document). The next time you generate the document references, WordPerfect inserts the revised text in the table of contents.

If you decide that you no longer want the item included in the table of contents, delete either of the [Mrk Txt ToC] codes surrounding the text. WordPerfect deletes both codes in the pair and removes the item from the table of contents the next time you generate document references.

 **TIP** WordPerfect's predefined heading styles (available through the Styles Power Bar Button) include table of content marks. To avoid having to manually mark headings for styles, use these predefined styles in your document, or add table of content marks to your own custom heading styles.

## Defining a Table of Contents

Either before or after you mark the text to be included in the table of contents, you can select the location of the table of contents and define its appearance.

To define where you want the table of contents to appear, follow these steps:

1. Place the insertion point at the location where you want to place the table of contents. If desired, add a page break (Ctrl+Enter) so that the resulting table of contents is on a page by itself. As shown in figure 26.15, you might want to also add a title to your table of contents page.

 2. If the Table of Contents Feature Bar is not displayed, choose Tools, Generate, Table of Contents.

**846** Chapter 26  Assembling Document References

3. Click <u>D</u>efine. The Define Table of Contents dialog box appears (see fig. 26.17).

4. Choose <u>N</u>umber of Levels (1-5) and enter a number, 1 through 5, to indicate how many ToC levels you want included in your document's ToC. Alternatively, you can use the up and down arrows to change the value.

 **TIP** Choosing all five levels for your ToC is usually easiest. Only those entries for which levels have been assigned are actually included in the ToC.

5. To change the default numbering position for any of the levels, select the level (1-5) you want to change and choose one of the five available numbering positions. (Level numbers are available only to the number of levels you indicate in step 4.) For a detailed description of the available formats, see the earlier section "Choosing the Numbering Position for a List." Repeat this step for each level that you want to change.

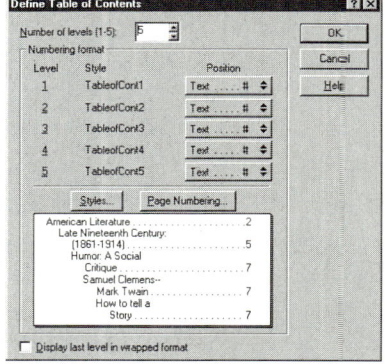

**FIG. 26.17**
The Define Table of Contents dialog box enables you to choose how many levels to include in your table of contents and to change the look of the ToC. A preview window shows you how the table of contents is formatted.

6. To change the default style for any of the levels, click <u>S</u>tyles. Selecting, creating, and editing styles for each table of contents level is similar to editing styles for lists. For information on changing the default style or creating a custom style, see the earlier section "Changing a List's Default Style."

7. You can change the look of the page numbers for the items in a table of contents by following the same procedure used for changing page number format for lists. For information on changing the page number format, see the earlier section "Changing the Page Number Format for a List."

8. Click <u>D</u>isplay Last Level in Wrapped Format if you want the ToC entries for the last level to wrap to the next line without indenting. If you choose this option, all last level headings—and optionally their page numbers—follow one another as though they are one paragraph of information. If the entries are longer than one line, the text wraps.

**NOTE** If you select the Display Last Level in Wrapped Format option, only the first three numbering formats in the Numbering Mode section are available for the last level.

9. Choose OK. The Define Table of Contents dialog box closes, and WordPerfect returns to your document. The text

    `<< Table of Contents will generate here >>`

    appears between two `[Gen Txt]` codes. The text is replaced by the table of contents when you run Generate. WordPerfect also inserts a `[Def Mark]` code into your document.

**NOTE** If you want to see which type of document reference is being defined and its name, click the [Def Mark] code. The table of contents code expands similar to the following:

`[Def Mark: TOC, 2: Dot Ldr #]`

10. If necessary, press Ctrl+Enter to insert a hard page break at the end of the table of contents page to separate the table of contents from the rest of your document.

11. If you place the table of contents before your document text, make sure that you set the page number to **1** at the top of the first page of document text to ensure that your document is properly numbered and has correct page numbers in the table of contents.

> **CAUTION**
> Table of contents pages also count as document pages. Therefore, if you don't reset the page number to 1, the document is misnumbered—the numbers in the ToC will not be correct. To set the first ToC page as page 1, from a document window choose Format, Page Numbering, Value/Adjust. The Value/Adjust Number dialog box opens. In the Set Page Number box, bype or use the spin box to set the number 1. Choose OK to return to your document.

After you define the location and appearance of the table of contents and have marked the table of contents entries in your document, you are ready to generate the table of contents.

 You can run Generate several ways. Click the Generate button in the Generate toolbar; from the menus, choose Tools, Generate, Generate; or press Ctrl+F9. Alternatively, from the Feature Bar, click Generate. WordPerfect generates all document references—including the table of contents. For complete instructions on generating document references, refer to the earlier section "Using Generate to Create and Update Document References."

**TROUBLESHOOTING**

**When I generate a table of contents, only the first word in each heading in the table of contents appears.** When you defined the headings for the table of contents, you didn't select the entire heading first. If you merely put the insertion point at the beginning of the heading, WordPerfect assumes that's the extent of the text you want included in the table of contents. If you want the entire line, select it, and then choose the table of contents heading level you want (1 through 5).

**All the headings in my table of contents are the same level, instead of level 1, level 2, and so forth.** You must be careful to specify the heading level you want for the table of contents. After selecting the text you want included in the table of contents, choose the button in the Table of Contents Feature Bar for the level you want: Mark 1 for level 1, Mark 2 for level 2, and so forth. In addition, when defining the table of contents (click Define in the Table of Contents Feature Bar) make sure that you specify the number of headings you plan to use for the table of contents.

# Creating a Table of Authorities

A *table of authorities* is a list of all references to other materials and the page locations on which the reference occurs throughout a document. While used heavily by the legal profession, you can also use the Table Of Authorities feature to easily create and maintain a bibliography for any heavily referenced text. When you edit your document—perhaps moving text between pages—you'll want to regenerate your table of authorities to keep all page references current.

**NOTE** Few professions probably have to handle more paperwork than the legal profession. Court cases require enormous amounts of correspondence, transcripts, and other written materials, such as legal briefs. *Table of authorities* is the term used by the legal profession to create a bibliography for a legal brief.

The WordPerfect Table of Authorities (ToA) feature makes creating a table of authorities easier. The time savings realized while allowing WordPerfect to generate an automatic reference list for just one document makes spending the time required to learn how to use the feature worthwhile.

Creating a ToA is not difficult, but it does require you to carefully mark your document. Because the Table of Authorities feature is so heavily used by lawyers, the following steps refer to each reference as a *legal citation*. Remember, though, that you can use this feature to list any reference material you use in your document, such as books, magazines, or quotations. Although you must perform several steps, they are straightforward:

1. Decide what groupings or categories of legal citations or references you have in your document.
2. Mark the first occurrence of each citation. Define precisely how the citation reference should read and how it should be formatted when printed in the ToA. You can add hard returns, underlining, and so on so that the reference is complete. This task is called *marking the full form*.
3. Assign a unique keyword or phrase to be associated with that particular reference. This is the *short form*.
4. Mark all subsequent occurrences of a citation with the associated keyword or phrase to tie these occurrences to the full form. This task is called *marking the short form*.
5. Define where you want to place the ToA and what formatting options you want to apply.
6. Generate the document references (which creates the ToA).
7. Print the document.

WordPerfect sorts the authorities within each section alphabetically. Figure 26.18 shows a sample table of authorities for a legal brief.

**FIG. 26.18**
A Table of Authorities for a legal brief might look like this example.

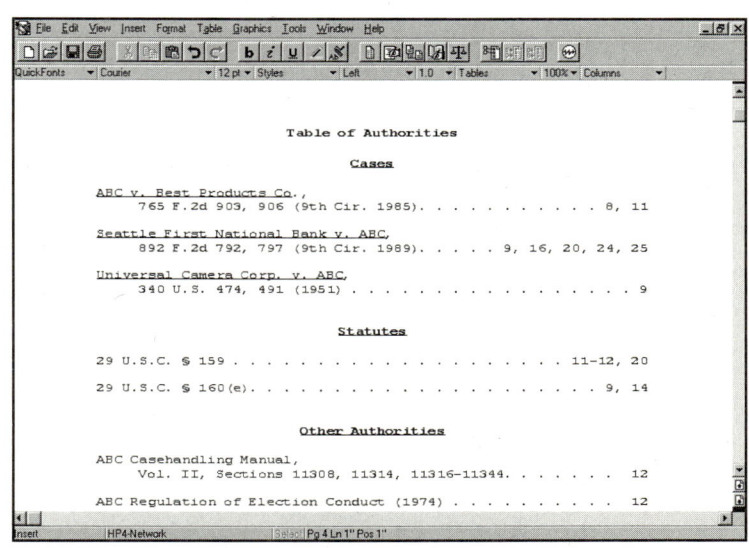

## Marking Text for a Table of Authorities

Before you begin marking citations for the table of authorities (ToA), decide how many sections you plan to have and how you will refer to these sections. As you mark each citation the first time, you assign it to a section. Suppose, for example, that you decide to have three sections: one for Cases, one for Statutes, and one for Other Authorities (refer to fig. 26.18). Sections for non-legal documents might refer to Books, Magazines, or Other Authorities.

Before you begin marking text, you should understand how WordPerfect uses the ToA full form and ToA short form. The *ToA full form*, which you enter only once, contains the text of the complete citation as it appears in the generated table of authorities and the section in which the authority is to appear.

As part of the ToA full form code, you also assign a ToA short form. The *ToA short form* is a unique identifier you assign to tie citations together when the table of authorities is generated.

It sometimes helps to think of a ToA full form as you would your own name and address. The combination of both is the full listing of who you are and where you live—the full form. Now, think of the ToA short form as your nickname. Each time you refer to yourself in your document, except for the very first time, you use only your nickname—the short form. In a legal brief, a full form might read

```
Human Rights Commission v. Association of School Districts,
97 Wn.2d 118, 121 (1982)
```

while the associated short form might read

```
Human Rights Commission
```

> **CAUTION**
> Using the same ToA short form for more than one ToA full form causes the error message `A Full Form has already been defined with this Short Form.`

After you create the ToA full form for a citation, you mark the location of subsequent occurrences of the same citation with the unique short form name assigned to the citation. By doing this, you enable WordPerfect to build the table of authorities with page numbers showing every place where the citation occurs.

**Marking Full Form Entries** The first time reference text occurs in a document, it should include the full citation. All subsequent references to the same reference are then marked as short forms. When you mark a citation for the first time, therefore, you need to mark it as the ToA full form. This means that you define the actual text to be placed in the table of authorities.

To mark a citation as a ToA full form, follow these steps:

1. Choose Tools, Generate, Table of Authorities. The Table of Authorities Feature Bar appears (see fig. 26.19).

**FIG. 26.19**
Use the Table of Authorities Feature Bar to mark short form entries, create and edit full form entries, define a table of authorities, or run Generate to create and update the table of contents.

2. Select all the text for the citation that you want included in the ToA.
3. Click Create Full Form. The Create Full Form dialog box appears (see fig. 26.20).

   The first time you mark a full form, the Section Name entry box is blank unless you have already defined your ToA. You can use numbers to identify the sections where the full forms are to be included, although it's usually easiest to keep track of the sections if you title them with more descriptive names such as Cases, Statutes, and Rules.

**FIG. 26.20**
The ToA Create Full Form dialog box enables you to enter the section name and short form name for the ToA full form.

4. To enter the section name, choose Section Name. For a new section, type the name.

   For an existing section name, you can select a section name from the list of existing section names. Click the Section Name drop-down list button, then select a section name from the resulting list. The selected name appears in the Section Name field.

 Open the Reveal Codes window to make sure that you mark the exact text—including any text attributes such as underlining or bold—you want to include as the full form.

5. A portion of the selected citation appears in the Short Form text box. If desired, edit the short form to more appropriately represent the method used for reference later in your document. You might want to delete all but the descriptive text for the citation from the short form name.
6. Choose OK to edit the full form. The ToA Full Form Editing window appears. The text you selected in your document appears in the text editing area (see fig. 26.21).

**852** Chapter 26 Assembling Document References

7. Edit the citation so that it appears exactly as you want it to appear in the table of authorities. You can format the text by adding or removing text attributes such as underlining or bold. You might want to add hard returns and tabs to force the citation to appear on more than one line, or perhaps indented on the second line. When you are finished, choose Close. WordPerfect returns to your document.

 You can apply text enhancement codes (such as bold, italic, or small caps) or formatting codes (such as indent) to the full form citation.

▶ See "Formatting Text," **p. 121**

**FIG. 26.21**
The Table Of Authorities Full Form editing window lets you view the full form text you've selected. In the Full Form Editing window, edit the text until it looks exactly as you want it to appear in the generated table of authorities.

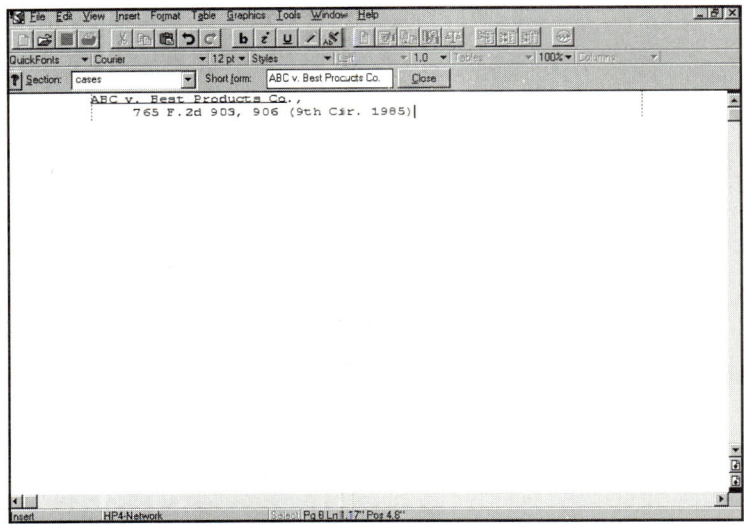

When you mark text for a full form entry to be included in a table of authorities, WordPerfect inserts the code [ToA] at the beginning of the citation. If you want to see more information about the Table of Authorities code, click the [ToA] code. The code expands, similar to the following:

    [ToA:section name;short form text;Full Form]

 These codes do not print. To see these codes, open the Reveal Codes window by choosing View, Reveal Codes; or by pressing Alt+F3.

**CAUTION**
If you edit the legal citation in your brief, the text in the full form is *not* modified. You must edit the full form to change the appearance of the citation in your table of authorities.

**Editing Full Form Entries**  After you mark a full form citation, you can edit its short form identifier, the section name it belongs to, or its full form text.

To edit a full form entry, follow these steps:

1. From the Table of Authorities Feature Bar, choose <u>E</u>dit Full Form. The Edit Full Form dialog box appears (see fig. 26.22).

**FIG. 26.22**
The Edit Full Form dialog box lists the unique short form identifier and assigned section for each of the full forms you have marked.

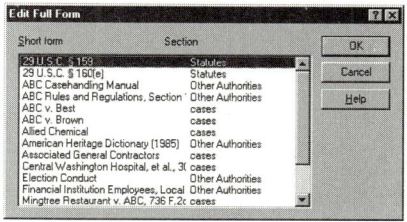

2. Select the citation you want to edit. Scroll the highlight bar to the desired citation.
3. Choose OK. The Full Form Text editing window appears with the full form text. In addition to changing the actual text or appearance of the long form, you can choose from the following options:
    - *Short <u>F</u>orm.* Changes the short form identifier. Edit the short form as desired.
    - *Section.* Changes the section in which you want this full form entry to appear. Either type a section name or click the Section drop-down list button to select from a list of available sections.
4. Choose <u>C</u>lose to save the changes.

The edited full form text and section changes do not appear in the table of authorities until you generate the document references.

**Marking Short Form Entries**  After you enter the ToA full form, you mark subsequent occurrences of the citation by using the ToA short form name that you associated with the ToA full form.

> **N O T E**  Because WordPerfect displays the last short form used in the <u>S</u>hort Form text box on the Table of Authorities Feature Bar, you may find it more efficient to mark all related short forms for one citation before moving to the next. You can find each occurrence of the citation quickly by using Find (F2, or Ctrl+F). It's helpful, when using the Find method of marking short forms, to first set a QuickMark (Ctrl+Shift+Q) at the location of the full form. After finding and marking all remaining short forms, you can quickly return to the original long form by finding the QuickMark (Ctrl+Q). You can then locate to the next new long form citation and begin again.

To mark a citation by using the ToA short form identifier, follow these steps:

1. Move the insertion point so that it immediately precedes the citation.
2. From the Table of Authorities Feature Bar, make sure that the short form displayed is the one you want to use. If not, select the short form from the drop-down list, or type the short form you want to use in the Short Form field.
3. Click Mark. WordPerfect inserts a hidden code into your document for that short form.
4. Repeat steps 1 through 3 until all citations are marked.

 Marking ToA entries can take a great deal of effort. Be sure to save your file periodically to protect your work!

**N O T E** The short form name must be unique for each full form, but it also should be descriptive so that you can easily associate the short form with the citation full form.

When you mark a citation with a short form code, WordPerfect inserts the code [ToA]. If you want to see the short form name for the code, click the code. The code expands and displays the name of the short form such as [ToA:,short form text;]. If you decide to delete the reference, simply delete the code. If you want a different short form name for a citation, delete the code and repeat the preceding steps.

 To see these codes, open the Reveal Codes window by choosing View, Reveal Codes; or by pressing Alt+F3.

## Defining a Table of Authorities

Before WordPerfect can generate the table of authorities, you must define where you want the table placed. You may want to title the page and place headings before each section. The following steps show how to define the location and options for a table of authorities. You can define your table of authorities page either before or after you mark your citations. The table of authorities shown in figure 26.23 is used as an example.

**Creating the ToA Page**   To define the location for a table of authorities, perform the following steps:

1. Move the insertion point to the location in your document where you want the table of authorities to appear.
2. As required, press Ctrl+Enter to place a hard page break and start the table of authorities on a new page. (The table of authorities should be a separately numbered part of the document.)

3. Pages used for a table of authorities usually carry their own set of page numbers. You should, therefore, set a page numbering scheme and value by choosing Format, Page Numbering. If you are defining the table of authorities to appear before your document text, be sure to also reset the page number values on the first page of that text, similar to defining a Table of Contents page.

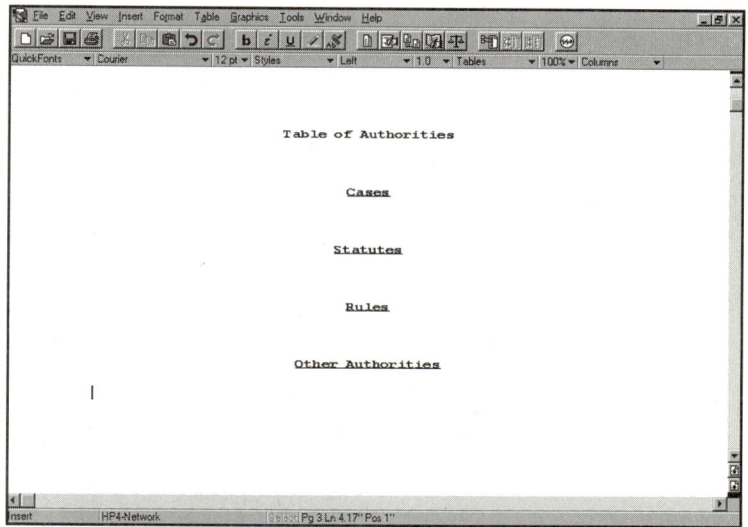

**FIG. 26.23**
The sections of a sample table of authorities. When you run Generate, WordPerfect builds the table of authorities and places the full form entries in the appropriate section.

4. If desired, type a title for your table of authorities page. Include any formatting you want to appear in the final table of authorities. You might also want to mark the table of authorities title as a table of contents entry so that it also appears in the table of contents.

5. Now create headings for each section which will be generated for the table of authorities. Include any text formatting you want to use. Be sure to turn off any text attributes individually for each heading. You should also follow each heading with two or three hard returns to separate it from the next heading.

**Placing the ToA Section Definitions** You can now place the definition mark for the sections you've listed in your table of authorities page. To define the location and options for a table of authorities section, do the following:

1. Position the insertion point on the table of authorities page under the heading for the section to be defined.

2. From the Table of Authorities Feature Bar, click Define. The Define Table of Authorities dialog box appears (see fig. 26.24).

3. Select the section name you want to place on your ToA page.
4. Click Insert. The Define Table of Authorities dialog box closes, and WordPerfect returns to your document. The text

    << Table of Authorities will generate here >>

    and a [Def Mark] code are inserted into your document. The text is replaced by the Table of Authorities when you run Generate.
5. Repeat steps 1 through 4 to define the location for each remaining section of the ToA.

**FIG. 26.24**

The Define Table of Authorities dialog box lists the names of the sections you used when you marked the ToA full form entries.

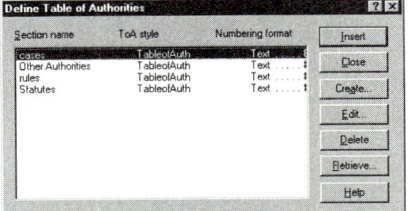

6. If required, press Ctrl+Enter to insert a hard page break at the end of the ToA page.
7. If the next page is your document text, restart the page number at 1 to ensure that your citations are referenced to the correct page numbers of the document text.

When you define a table of authorities, table of contents, list, or index, WordPerfect inserts a [Def Mark] code in your document. If you want to see which type of document reference is being defined by the code, click the code so it expands. For a table of authorities, the code resembles the following example:

    [Def Mark: ToA, <section name><numbering format>]

These codes do not print, but you can see these codes by opening the Reveal Codes window (choose View, Reveal Codes; or press Alt+F3).

**Formatting the ToA Entries**   You can also change how the entries generated by the table of authorities appears. To change table of authorities options, follow these steps:

1. From the Table of Authorities Feature Bar, click Define. The Define Table of Authorities dialog box appears (refer to fig. 26.24).
2. Choose the section name for which you want to change options.
3. Click Edit. The Edit Table of Authorities dialog box appears (see fig. 26.25).

**FIG. 26.25**
The Edit Table of Authorities dialog box enables you to change the appearance of the table of authorities, including the numbering format and style used to format the text.

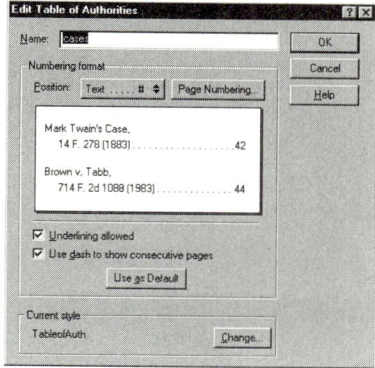

4. Set the formatting options for the section. You can change these settings:

   - *Position of the page number.* The default numbering position for each ToA entry is a flush-right page number preceded by dot leaders. To change the numbering position, or to turn off dot leaders, click Position in the Edit Table of Authorities dialog box. Choose from the five available numbering positions. For a detailed description of the available formats, see the earlier section "Choosing the Numbering Position for a List."

   - *Appearance of the page number.* Changing the page number format for a ToA is similar to setting the page number format for lists. For information on changing the page number format, see the section "Changing the Page Number Format for a List," earlier in this chapter.

   - *Underlining.* In the text of a legal brief, the court case references are normally underlined. You can choose to display or omit the underlining in the ToA. By default, underlining appears in the ToA because Underlining Allowed is checked. To turn off underlining in the generated ToA, remove the check from Underlining Allowed.

   - *Consecutive pages.* By default, a ToA definition connects sequential pages using a dash (for example, 7–10). To force generation of sequential pages to be separated by commas (7, 8, 9, 10), remove the check from Use Dash to show consecutive pages.

   - *Saving your settings as default.* Click the Use As Default button to use the current settings for underlining and dashes for sequential pages for all new table of authorities sections.

- *Changing the ToA style.* To change the style definition used for a table of authorities, click Change in the Current Style group. Selecting, creating, and editing styles for a table of authorities is similar to editing styles for lists. For detailed information on changing the default style, see the section "Changing a List's Default Style," earlier in this chapter.

5. When your settings are complete, choose OK and then Close to return to your document.

**Generating the Table of Authorities**   When all citations have been marked and the table of authorities page has been defined, you are ready to generate the table.

You can run Generate several ways:

- Click the Generate button on the Generate Toolbar.
- From WordPerfect's menus, choose Tools, Generate, Generate.
- Press Ctrl+F9.
- From the Feature Bar, click Generate.

WordPerfect generates the Table of Authorities along with all other document references—any lists, the table of contents, the index, and cross-references. For complete instructions on generating document references, refer to the earlier section "Using Generate to Create and Update Document References."

**N O T E**   If you incorrectly type a ToA short form or have no ToA full form corresponding to the short form, when you generate the table of authorities, WordPerfect displays the message Generate TOA - Full form not found. WordPerfect places the ToA short form name, preceded by an asterisk (*), at the beginning of the first section of the table of authorities when you generate it. If this situation occurs, simply locate the incorrect short form, delete the code, and enter the correct short form. If the full form is missing, find the first occurrence of the citation, delete the short form, and create a full form.

# Creating an Index

Manually generating a good index is a time-consuming task. Sifting through a long document looking for each reference to a word or phrase can also be subject to error. WordPerfect makes this task much quicker and easier.

WordPerfect's Index feature creates an alphabetized list of index headings and subheadings for a document. You can manually mark the words to be included in the index, use a file with the words you want to use as index words for the document, or use a combination of both methods.

▶ **See** "Finding Words and Phrases," **p. 111**

As an alternative to marking each occurrence of a word or phrase in a document for inclusion in the index, WordPerfect offers another way to build an index: the concordance file. A *concordance file* is a normal WordPerfect file into which you place words or phrases that you want to include in the index. WordPerfect reads the list of words in the concordance file, determines on what pages the words appear in your document, and places the entry in the index.

Creating an index uses a similar procedure as creating a list or a table of contents. You mark the words or phrases to include as major or subheadings—optionally, create a concordance file—define the location and formatting for the index, and then generate the index.

## Marking Text for an Index

You can mark text for an index in two ways: you can manually mark each occurrence of the index word in the on-screen document, or you can list the words and phrases in a concordance file. Each method has advantages and disadvantages. You may want to use the methods together.

Three obvious advantages to marking index entries manually are:

- You can quickly spot misspelled or mistyped words or phrases. When WordPerfect generates the index, only exact matches appear together with the page numbers for each occurrence. Misspelled index entries do not match and appear on separate lines.

    Suppose that in your document you marked the text Instructional Expenses Accounting as an index entry, and elsewhere in your document you marked the text Instructional Expense Accounting. When you generate the index, the entries are listed separately because the text is not identical (Expense and Expenses).

    If you placed the text Instructional Expense Accounting into a concordance file, Instructional Expenses Accounting would not appear at all in the index because it is not an *exact* match.

- You can mark text with both a heading and a subhead listing. Subheadings are listed alphabetically and normally indented under a heading. Suppose that you are indexing a document with a section describing computer training for Macintosh and

IBM computers. You may want to mark Training Opportunities as the heading and Macintosh and IBM each as subheadings. The resulting index is shown as follows:

Index:

Training Opportunities .............. 13

   IBM ......................................... 13

   Macintosh .............................. 14

- You can cross-index entries. In addition to marking the phrase Training Opportunities as listed in the previous paragraph, you might mark IBM *and* Macintosh each as major headings with Training Opportunities as subheads under each:

Index:

IBM ............................................... 13

   Training Opportunities .......... 13

Macintosh ................................... 14

   Training Opportunities ......... 14

**Marking Text Manually**   Marking each occurrence of an index word provides the greatest flexibility, but is the most time-consuming. This method requires you to find and mark every occurrence of the index word in the document. Items not marked are not included in the index.

To mark text manually as an index word, follow these steps:

1. Choose Tools, Generate, Index. The Index Feature Bar appears (see fig. 26.26).
2. Select the index text.

**FIG. 26.26**
Use the Index Feature Bar to mark index entries as headings and subheadings, define an index, or run Generate to create and update the index.

**N O T E**  Any enhancements—bold or underline, for example—are not applied to the index text in the index.

3. Choose Heading. The selected text is placed into the Heading text box.

4. Click <u>M</u>ark to insert an index code containing the selected text into your document.

   To place this reference as a subheading under another heading, type the text of the heading into the Heading entry box. Press Tab or click <u>S</u>ubheading. The insertion point moves to the Subheading entry box, and the text you selected in your document appears as the subheading. Click <u>M</u>ark to insert an index code containing the selected text into your document.

**NOTE** The heading and subheading don't have to be the same as the marked text. You can highlight the text you want indexed, and then type the text you want to appear in the document index in the Heading or Subheading text boxes. When the index is generated, the text in your index mark is used with the page number where the mark appears.

After you have created a heading or subheading, you can reuse the phrases for additional entries by clicking the Heading or Subheading drop-down list buttons to display and select the previously entered index items.

When you mark an entry as an Index heading, WordPerfect inserts the code [Index] at the location of the insertion point. If you want to see the text of the index, click the code so it expands and displays the heading such as [Index: *heading text*]. If you mark an entry as a subheading after typing a heading in the Heading text box, the expanded WordPerfect code shows [Index: *heading text;subheading text*]. These codes do not print, but you can see these codes by opening the Reveal Codes window (choose <u>V</u>iew, Reveal <u>C</u>odes; or press Alt+F3).

**CAUTION**
When you mark text as an index entry, the heading and subheading text you type is inserted in the index code. If you subsequently modify the originally selected index text, the text in the index code does not automatically change. You must delete the original index code in your document and re-mark the text to be included. If you no longer want the item included after you mark text for inclusion in the index, delete the [Index] code using the Delete or Backspace keys or by dragging it out of the Reveal Codes window. WordPerfect removes the item from the index the next time you generate document references.

**Marking Text by Using a Concordance File** You can create an index without manually marking text by using the Concordance feature. A *concordance file* contains the words and phrases that you want to use as major headings in a document. When you define the index for your document, as explained in the section "Defining an Index" later in this chapter, WordPerfect allows you to reference a concordance file to be used when the index is generated. The words and phrases you place in the concordance file become your index items, and the referenced page numbers reflect all occurrences of the words in the document.

WordPerfect includes and shows the page numbers of only items that are an exact match with a concordance entry. An entry of Print in the concordance file, for example, does not match Printing in your document; consequently, WordPerfect doesn't create an index reference for Printing.

On the other hand, the match is not case-sensitive. An entry in the document of print matches Print in the concordance file, causing that page number to be included in the index.

To create a concordance file, follow these steps:

1. Click the New Blank Document button on the default Toolbar. Alternately, choose File, New; or press Ctrl+Shift+N. In the Select New Document dialog box, choose Create a Blank, and then click Select. A blank file appears.

2. Type the entries that are your index items. Type one entry to a line, pressing Enter at the end of each line.

3. Choose File, Save; or press Ctrl+S. Name your concordance file, then choose Save.

 **TIP** Keep your concordance file and your primary document window open at the same time. Each time you use a word in your primary document that is appropriate as an index entry, click the concordance file window, add the word to the list, then click your primary document, and continue composing.

WordPerfect makes each entry in the concordance file a heading. Normally, you just enter the words in the concordance file; marking the words isn't necessary. However, if you want a concordance file entry to be listed in your document's index as a subheading, mark the concordance file entry as a subheading and type the heading under which the subheading is to be listed.

## Defining an Index

Similar to defining other document reference pages, you define the index's placement and formatting. To define an index, follow these steps:

1. Place the insertion point at the location where you want the index to be generated (normally at the end of your document).

    If you want to place the index on a page by itself, insert a hard page break (press Ctrl+Enter). You may want to type a page heading (such as **INDEX**).

2. From the Index Feature Bar, click <u>D</u>efine (if the Index Feature Bar isn't visible, choose <u>T</u>ools, Ge<u>n</u>erate, <u>I</u>ndex). The Define Index dialog box appears (see fig. 26.27).

3. If you want to use the default formatting options for your index without a concordance file, choose OK. (See the text that follows for help in customizing the format of your index.)

The Define Index dialog box closes, and you are returned to your document. The text

        << Index will generate here >>

is inserted into your document between two [Gen Txt] codes. This text is replaced by the index when you run Generate.

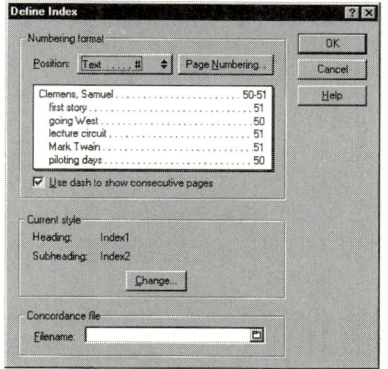

**FIG. 26.27**
The Define Index dialog box enables you to change the appearance of your index and specify a concordance file. A preview window shows you how the index will look.

When you define an index, table of authorities, table of contents, or list, WordPerfect inserts a [Def Mark] code in your document at the location of the insertion point. If you want to see which type of document reference is being defined by the code, click the code. The code expands. For an index, the code resembles the following example:

    [Def Mark: Index, Dot Ldr #]

You can also change how an index is formatted. To define an index with a different appearance, follow step 1, then customize the index using the following options. When you're finished, choose OK to return to your document. Customize your index using these options:

- *Numbering Position*. The default numbering position is a flush-right page number with dot leaders. To change the numbering position, from the Define Index dialog box, click <u>P</u>osition. Choose from the five available numbering positions. For a detailed description of the available formats, see the earlier section "Choosing the Numbering Position for a List."

- *Page Number Appearance.* You can change how the page numbers for the items in an index look. Changing the page number format is the same for indexes and lists. For information on changing the page number format, see the earlier section "Changing the Page Number Format for a List."
- *Consecutive Pages.* If you want groups of sequential pages printed out separately (for example 7, 8, 9, 10) instead of combined (for example, 7–10), uncheck the default Use Dash to Show Consecutive Pages option.
- *Index Style.* To change the default style for the index Heading or Subheading levels, click Change. Selecting, creating, and editing styles for an index is similar to editing styles for lists. For detailed information on changing the default style, see the earlier section "Changing a List's Default Style."
- *Concordance File.* To generate the index using a concordance file, choose Filename and type the file name in the text box.

  Alternatively, choose the list button at the right of the Filename text box. The Select Concordance File dialog box opens to help you find the desired file.

If, after you define the index, you want to change its location or numbering format, you must delete the current [Def Mark:Index] code, and then define the index and desired format information at the new location. The next time you generate, WordPerfect deletes the generated index at the old location and places the newly generated index information at the new location.

Now that you have marked the index entries and optionally selected a concordance file of index entries, you are ready to generate the index. For complete instructions on generating document references, refer to the earlier section "Using Generate to Create and Update Document References."

### TROUBLESHOOTING

**I want to use a concordance entry as both a heading and subheading in the index. How can I do so?** If you mark a concordance file entry as a subheading, it will not automatically create a heading in your document's index. If you want a word or phrase in the concordance file to be listed as a subheading and also want it listed as a heading, mark the concordance file entry again—this time as a heading. Two [Index] codes precede the word in the concordance file.

# Using Automatic Cross-Referencing

Using automatic cross-referencing makes a complex document much easier for a reader to understand. With automatic cross-referencing, you can let the reader know where a figure is located or provide a detailed explanation of a concept (for example, `See fig. 3 on page 22` or `See the detailed description of the widget that begins on page 114`). You can cross-reference any item. You control the definition of the referenced items (the targets) and the references to them.

In the past, writers often avoided using cross-references because the task was time-consuming and prone to errors. Each time the document was revised, the writers had to manually find, review, and correct the cross-references. Now, WordPerfect makes cross-referencing a snap. References are automatically and reliably updated each time you run Generate.

When WordPerfect generates the document references, it matches *targets* (the location where you are telling the reader to look) and references (the location where you talk about the target). The name of your target is a unique identifier that links the target with its reference.

The target name must be an exact match. During document reference generation, a reference to the name `account` does not match and cross-reference if you entered the target name as `accounts`. Matching is not case-sensitive, however. This means that a reference linked to the target name `Accounts` is matched with a target defined as `accounts`.

WordPerfect uses the target name to link references with their targets only when it generates document references. The target name is not printed with the document.

You can use cross-referencing in different ways. You can use simple cross-referencing in which there is one reference to one target:

    See the detailed description of helium on page 234

You can also have a reference to multiple occurrences of a unique target name:

    See the graphics check boxes on pages 2, 12, 20

Or you can reference a single target in different ways:

    See fig. 1 on page 4

To use cross-references, follow this basic procedure:

1. Define one or more references to each target.
2. Mark the referenced item(s) (the targets).
3. Generate the document references to update the page numbers to all targets.

Depending on what works best for you, you can mark a target when you create it and mark the references to it later, or you can mark the references as you write them and mark the target later. Generally, if you are composing a new document and want to handle the references and targets as you write, mark the reference before the target. Then when you come to the place where you want the reader to look, mark the target.

## Marking References and Targets

To mark a reference, follow these steps:

1. Type any desired introductory text such as **See description on page** at the desired location.
2. Place the insertion point where you want to insert the reference code.
3.  Choose Tools, Generate, Cross-Reference. The Cross-Reference Feature Bar appears (see fig. 26.28).

**FIG. 26.28**
Use the Cross Reference Feature Bar to choose and work with types of references.

4. Choose a reference type from the Reference drop-down list (see fig. 26.29). For example, if you want the reference to show the page number of the target, choose Page. As you can see in figure 26.29, you can refer the reader to other than page numbers.

**FIG. 26.29**
WordPerfect provides several reference types to which you can refer readers.

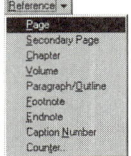

5. Type the target name you want to use into the Target box. You can refer to the same target as many times as you need to in your document. After you've defined a target the first time, the target name continues to be available in the Target box. The last target name you used may already be in the Target box. If you previously entered a reference to the target you want to reference and it is not displayed, choose a target from the drop-down list.

6. Click Mark Reference. WordPerfect inserts a reference code such as

   [Ref Pg: target name;?]

   in your document. The question mark in the code will be replaced with the correct cross-reference number when the document is generated. Also, unless the target is placed at the same time you mark its reference, you see a question mark in your document text as a place holder—See description on page ?. WordPerfect replaces the question mark with the page number of the target when you generate the document references. If more than one target exists with the entered target name, WordPerfect lists multiple page numbers separated by commas. If you make a mistake while you type the target name, delete the code and mark the reference again.

   After you mark references to a target, you must mark the target before you generate the document references. If you don't, the question mark shown at the reference is not replaced with the document reference.

To mark a target, follow these steps:

1. Position the insertion point within the first word in the target text. If you are marking an item other than text (for example, a graphics box), position the insertion point to the immediate right of the graphics box code.

2. If the Cross-Reference Feature Bar is not displayed, choose Tools, Generate, Cross-Reference.

3. The last target name you typed appears in the Target box. If the name is correct, click Mark Target.

   For a new target, type the name in the Target box. Or if you have already created the target, choose it from the drop-down list. Then choose Mark Target.

When you define a target, WordPerfect inserts a [Target(*target name*)] code in your document. If you made a mistake typing the target name, delete the code and mark the target again.

## Marking References to Footnotes and Endnotes

Sometimes you want to reference a footnote in the main text of your document (See discussion in footnote 4 on page 12, for example). To mark a footnote as a target, you must be in the Footnote editing window.

You mark endnotes the same way you mark footnotes. Be sure to place the target codes for endnote references in the endnotes themselves.

If you mark a target in the footnote editing window, the target moves to other pages with the footnote if you add or delete text in the document.

As with other document references, run Generate when all cross-references are complete. Because marking text takes a lot of effort, be sure to save your document before running Generate.

You can wait to run Generate until after you've completed all marks for all document reference types.

▶ See "Using Footnotes and Endnotes," **p. 801**

### TROUBLESHOOTING

**When I generate an index (or any document reference), WordPerfect says** `No def codes found.` In addition to marking entries for the index, you must make sure that you define the index somewhere in the document. The index is usually defined at the very end of the document, but it can be placed anywhere. To define the index, place the insertion point where you want the index to go. Click Define in the Index Feature Bar. If desired, choose the index options you want to use, and choose OK. After it is defined once, you do not need to define the index again unless you want to modify the index options.

**When I generate a document with cross-referencing, WordPerfect displays a ? (question mark) where the reference is supposed to go.** The ? (question mark) denotes an unresolved cross-reference. The question mark is normal when you are defining the cross-references before the document has been generated. If a question mark remains after generating the document, it means that a reference was made to an undefined target. Check the target name of the unresolved cross-reference to make sure that it is spelled correctly. And make sure that the target exists someplace in the document. Click the arrow beside the Target box to see a list of the targets in the document.

CHAPTER 27

# Working with Large and Multi-Part Documents

*by Gordon Nelder-Adams and Laura Acklen*

You can create documents of any length—from a short letter to a manuscript hundreds of pages long—by using WordPerfect. WordPerfect imposes no specific limits on document size; the only real limit is the amount of available disk space.

Large documents can be awkward to work with. Moving the cursor in a large document from one point to another can take several minutes, particularly on older computers or those that have less memory. If you break a large document into smaller, more manageable files, editing becomes much easier. However, you must keep the page numbers consistent in each file, and you cannot easily generate a table of contents, list, or index of your entire document.

WordPerfect's Master Document feature provides the solution to this problem. This feature lets you work with smaller documents for ease of use and then, when you need to work with the document as a whole, combine the small documents into one large file. ■

**Creating a master document**

Insert a series of subdocuments into a document to create a master document that can be expanded and condensed as needed.

**Generating document references in master documents**

Define a table of contents, list, index, or table of authorities in the master document.

**Using styles to ensure consistent formatting**

The Styles feature allows you to combine multiple formatting commands into a single unit that can be applied to the text in subdocuments to ensure a uniform appearance in the master document.

**Insert page numbering codes**

Use the Page Numbering feature to keep track of the correct chapter/section numbers and page numbers in both the master document and subdocuments.

**Editing a master document**

Add footnotes, cross references, headers, and footers to a master document. Also use the Find, Replace, and Spell Checker features to edit the text.

# Creating Master Documents and Subdocuments

The Master Document feature is ideally suited for any large project—college dissertation, user manual, or complex legal contract, for example. Writers often collaborate on a large project and then combine their work into one document. Without WordPerfect's Master Document feature, combining separate efforts is a time-consuming task that presents many challenges in numbering pages, creating a table of contents, and indexing the final document. These challenges take time away from the actual research and writing effort of the authors.

You use two types of files with this feature: a master document and one or more subdocuments. A *subdocument* is a normal WordPerfect file that is one of the smaller pieces of your large document. The *master document* is essentially an outline of the final document and contains codes that identify each of the subdocuments. You can include text in a master document. A master document also typically contains definitions for document reference features such as a table of contents, lists of tables or figures, or an index.

Using the Master Document feature involves the following basic steps:

1. Create the individual subdocuments.
2. Create a master document with codes that identify the subdocuments and, if desired, definitions for document reference features.
3. Expand the master document. Expanding combines all the individual subdocuments into a single long document.
4. If necessary, edit the expanded document to create a consistent format throughout or add document references.
5. Print the master document.
6. Condense the master document. Condensing removes the subdocuments from the master document, optionally saving any changes you have made to subdocuments while they were within the expanded master document.

You can use the Master Document feature with any document that can be divided into sections. Most books, for example, are divided into individual chapters. A class syllabus or training manual can be divided into individual lectures. For illustration purposes, this chapter creates an office procedures manual—a document used by most businesses.

An office manual may contain many types of information—from personnel policy to accounting, organization charts, floor plans, phone lists, and more. Several people or departments usually create or compile this information. Some parts of the manual, such as the personnel policy section, might be revised infrequently; whereas other parts, such as the phone list, might be updated monthly. These separate files are combined to produce a complete manual.

▶ See "Creating Lists," **p. 834**

Using the Master Document feature for this project is desirable for the following reasons:

- Sections can be created by a number of people in different departments, and then easily combined.
- The individual subdocuments can be created in any order, regardless of the order in which they will appear in the master document.
- The author or authors of each section can revise their documents at any time, and use them as separate files unrelated to the office manual.
- You can ensure consistent pagination throughout the manual and create a comprehensive table of contents and index that can be updated quickly each time a subdocument is revised.

## Creating Subdocuments

A subdocument is a WordPerfect document of any length and containing any text or formatting codes. Unlike WordPerfect's Merge feature, which requires certain types of merge codes in data files, a subdocument requires no Master Document feature codes to make it act as a subdocument (although certain codes are required in master document files).

WordPerfect places no limits on the number of subdocuments you can combine into a master document. When you use a master document for a large project, divide the job into as many logical or manageable sections as you want and create a subdocument for each. In addition, a subdocument can contain links to other subdocuments, making a subdocument in one master document a master document in its own right. This concept is covered in the later section, "Creating Subdocuments Within Subdocuments."

When you expand a master document, WordPerfect retrieves a copy of the entire contents of each designated subdocument—each with its own set of format codes—into one large document. In any WordPerfect document, format codes you insert—margins, tab sets, and fonts, for example—affect the format of all text that follows until another code of the same type appears. As a result, the format codes in each subdocument can affect the formatting of every following subdocument in the expanded master document.

When a subdocument takes its place in a master document, the subdocument's formatting can change substantially, depending on the format codes from preceding subdocuments. Therefore, when you create a subdocument, use only formatting codes essential to your subdocument's appearance, and reset any formatting changes to the defaults whenever possible. For example, if you need to insert a nonstandard tab set for a particular group of paragraphs, remember to reset your tabs back to every half inch at the end of that group.

You can prevent many formatting errors by using styles. *Paragraph styles* can ensure consistency of headings and body text throughout a master document. You can create a Begin Subdocument style that sets defaults for all formatting that might change from subdocument to subdocument, and then use this style at the beginning of each subdocument. You might also create separate style libraries—with identical style names but different style contents—for master documents and subdocuments. When the subdocuments are expanded into the master document, the master document's styles take precedence over subdocument styles of the same name. These techniques are covered in the later section, "Using Styles with Master Documents."

#### CAUTION
When it expands a master document, WordPerfect ignores the Initial Codes style in each subdocument. Therefore, place any codes essential for your subdocument's format in the body of the document, not in its Initial Codes style.

▶ **See** "Considering Types of Styles," **p. 336**

## Building a Master Document

To build a master document, insert one or more subdocument codes into any normal document. The subdocument code identifies the file name of a subdocument and creates a link between the master document and subdocument. In practice, most master documents contain many subdocument links. Building a master document requires the following three basic steps:

1. Decide what files you want to use as subdocuments with the master document.
2. Create a new WordPerfect file or open an existing file to which you want to add subdocument codes.
3. Insert subdocument codes into the master document.

You can insert the subdocument codes in any order. When you expand the master document, individual subdocuments are retrieved in the order in which their codes appear in the master document. Table 27.1 lists the files to be included in the office procedures manual.

 **TIP** Establish naming conventions for your master document and subdocument filename extensions, such as MD for master documents, and SUB for subdocuments, to indicate the type of file.

### Table 27.1  Subdocuments Included in the Office Procedures Manual

| File Name | Description |
| --- | --- |
| TITLE.PG | The title page |
| COMPANY.HIS | The company's history and mission statement |
| OFFICE.PRO | The heart of the manual—a detailed description of office procedures |
| PERSONNL.POL | The company's personnel policies |
| EMERGNCY.PRO | Emergency procedures |
| NETWORK.GDL | Guidelines for logging on to and using the company's local area network |
| ORG.CHT | The company's organization chart |
| PERSONNL.LST | A list of room numbers and phone numbers for all employees |
| FLOORMAP | A floor map of the building |
| CALENDAR | A list of office holidays and other scheduled events |

**N O T E**  WordPerfect 7 also accepts file names of up to 255 characters, including spaces. (These file names appear with a WPD extension in your subdocuments.) However, if you share files with users of previous versions of WordPerfect, you should use the standard DOS filenaming rules of eight characters, followed by an *optional* three character extension. If you inadvertently give a file with a long file name (for example, Lindsey Letter) to someone who uses a previous version of WordPerfect, a DOS version of the file name for the file is shown (for example, _INDSE~1.WPD).

To create a PROCEDUR.MD master document, begin with an empty document. If the active window is not empty, click the New Blank Document button on the Toolbar, or choose File, New, Select. WordPerfect displays a blank document. You are now ready to insert subdocument codes in the document.

To insert a subdocument code, follow these steps:

1. Move the insertion point to where you want to place the subdocument. (If you are starting from a new document, the insertion point is already at the top of the document, so you can skip this step.)

**T I P**  If you prefer, you can right-click in the left margin area (next to the flashing insertion point) and select Subdocument from the QuickMenu to open the Include Subdocument dialog box.

2. Choose File, Document, Subdocument. WordPerfect displays the Include Subdocument dialog box, a variant of the Open dialog box (see fig. 27.1), which lists the files in the current folder.

**FIG. 27.1**
Select a file name in the Include Subdocument dialog box to create a link between a master document and the selected file.

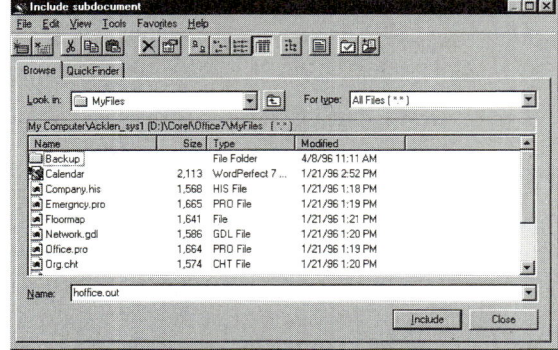

3. Type the subdocument's file name or select the file from the file list, then choose Include. For the first subdocument in the office procedures manual, for example, you would type in the filename **title.pg**.

**N O T E**  A subdocument doesn't need to be present when you type its name in the Include Subdocument dialog box. When you expand the master document, however, the subdocument must be in the specified location.

WordPerfect inserts a subdocument code into the master document. In Page mode or Two Page mode, the code appears as an icon in the left margin (see fig. 27.2). In Draft mode, the code can be seen in the document, resembling a document comment with the text Subdoc:*FILENAME*, where *FILENAME* is the name of the subdocument file (see fig. 27.3). In any mode, you can see a similar code in the Reveal Codes window.

Because the subdocument link uses the complete path to a subdocument, the subdocument need not be in the same subfolder as the master document. In fact, your subdocuments can be stored in different subfolders. However, if you move the subdocument from the folder designated in the code, WordPerfect cannot locate the subdocument when you expand the master document. You need to move the file back to its original location, or delete and recreate the subdocument link.

Repeat the preceding steps for each subdocument link you want to include in a master document.

**FIG. 27.2**
In Page mode, a sub-document link appears as an icon in the margin, as well as a code visible in Reveal Codes.

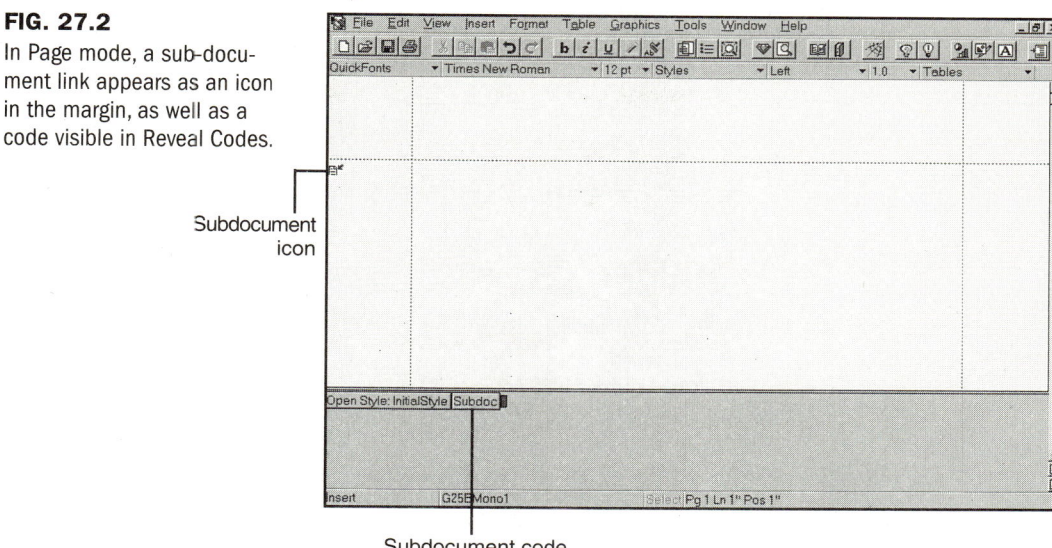

Subdocument icon

Subdocument code

**FIG. 27.3**
A master document with subdocument links is separated by page breaks. In Draft mode, the subdocument codes resemble document comments.

Subdocument code

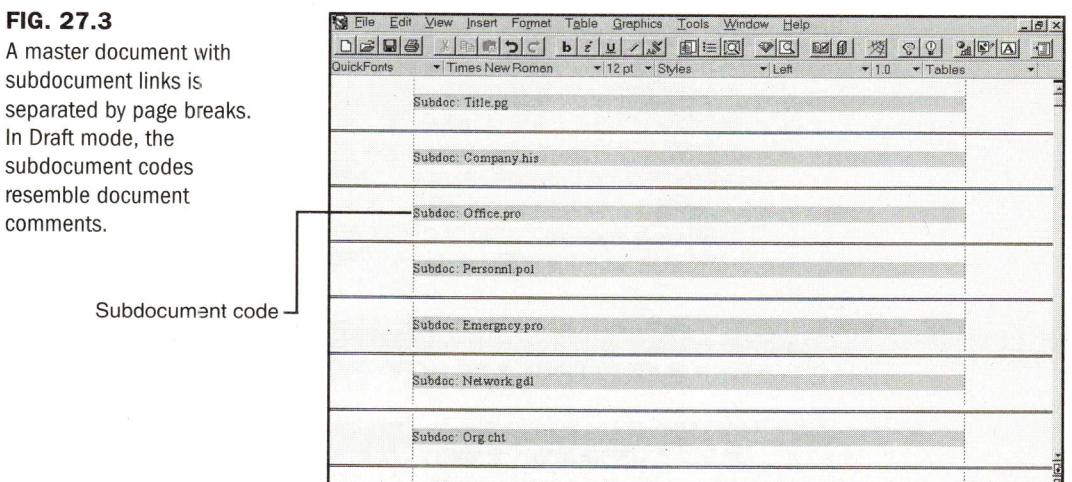

You may want each subdocument to begin on a new page. In some books, for instance, each chapter begins at the top of a page. In other books, each chapter begins immediately after the preceding chapter, wherever on the page the division may fall. To force page breaks in your master document, simply press Ctrl+Enter to insert a Hard Page code before you insert each subdocument link.

You also can use WordPerfect's Force Page command, which lets you specify that a chapter start on a new page, an odd-numbered page (the right-hand page in a double-sided publication), or an even-numbered page (the left-hand page). To force page breaks in your master document, choose Format, Page, Force Page, and then choose Current Page Odd, Current Page Even, or New Page. If you specify Odd, and the page following the code falls on an even-numbered page, WordPerfect inserts a Temporary Hand Page break before the page to force the text to the following odd-numbered page.

After you have inserted all the subdocument links, save the master document. For this example, the file is saved with the name PROCEDUR.MD. For more information on saving master documents, see the section "Saving a Master Document" later in this chapter.

Figure 27.3 shows the first series of subdocument codes in the PROCEDUR.MD master document, displayed in Draft mode. In this example, page breaks are used to separate the subdocuments, forcing each to begin on a new page.

## Adding, Deleting, and Moving Subdocuments

You can change the structure of your master document at any time, regardless of whether your master document is expanded. You may need to add a new subdocument code, delete an existing code, or move a code to a different location in the master document.

To add a subdocument, move the insertion point to where you want to insert the code. Turning on Reveal Codes (choose View, Reveal Codes; or press Alt+F3) may help you position the insertion point precisely, particularly if your master document contains formatting codes for page numbering or headers and footers. Then follow the steps in the preceding section to insert the subdocument code. The next time you expand the master document, WordPerfect adds the new subdocument.

Deleting a subdocument is easier when the master document is condensed because you need to delete only one code. When the master document is expanded, each subdocument begins with a [Subdoc Begin] code and ends with a [Subdoc End] code, and deleting a subdocument requires deleting these two codes as well as all text and formatting between them.

To delete a subdocument from a condensed master document, turn on Reveal Codes (choose View, Reveal Codes; or press Alt+F3), and then move the insertion point immediately to the left of the [Subdoc] code. Press Del, and WordPerfect removes the code from your document. If you placed a [HPg] code (indicating a Hard Page break) after the subdocument code to separate it from the following subdocument, you also may want to delete this code to prevent a blank page from appearing in the middle of your document. Alternatively, you may want to insert a different subdocument code at the same position.

Deleting a subdocument from an expanded master document is more complicated. You can either block and delete everything from the [Subdoc Begin] code through the [Subdoc End] code, or you can follow the steps for condensing a single subdocument in the later section, "Condensing a Master Document," and then delete the single [Subdoc] code.

There are several ways to move a subdocument from one location to another within your master document. First, you can delete any existing codes for the particular subdocument, and then insert a new code at the desired location. WordPerfect always retains the last three blocks of text or codes you delete, so you can undelete the old code(s) instead of inserting a new subdocument code. Second, you can block (and move) everything from the [Subdoc Begin] code through the [Subdoc End] code. See Chapter 3, "Retrieving and Editing Documents," for more information on blocking, moving, and deleting text and codes.

> **CAUTION**
>
> If you move a subdocument in an expanded master document, make sure that you move both the [Subdoc Begin] code and the [Subdoc End] code. If these codes are mismatched, WordPerfect cannot properly condense the master document.

After you delete a subdocument from a condensed master document, the next time you expand the master document, that subdocument will not be included. Remember, if you add, delete, or move a subdocument in an expanded master document, you need to regenerate document references such as table of contents, lists, or index to update the page numbers for the current subdocuments.

# Creating Subdocuments Within Subdocuments

Any subdocument can be a master document. If, for example, the personnel policy section of the office procedures manual, PERSONNL.POL, becomes very large, you can break it into individual sections covering sick leave, vacation, holidays, overtime, and so on. Then you can treat the personnel files both as a separate document and as part of the larger office manual.

When you expand PROCEDUR.MD (the office procedures manual master document), if WordPerfect finds subdocument links within the PERSONNL.POL file, the program expands those subdocuments into PERSONNL.POL. When you condense PROCEDUR.MD, WordPerfect also condenses the subdocument files in PERSONNL.POL.

# Expanding a Master Document

After you insert all the subdocument codes in the master document, creating links between the master document and each of the subdocuments, you can expand the master document. When you expand the master document, WordPerfect retrieves a copy of each subdocument into the master document, in effect combining many smaller documents into one large document. You can then use several of WordPerfect's features and functions on the expanded document much more efficiently than on the individual subdocuments. You can use Find and Replace to change a particular phrase throughout the entire document in one operation, instead of repeating the operation for each subdocument. Likewise, spell checking an expanded master document is more efficient than spell checking each subdocument individually.

Most important, though, is that after you expand a master document, you can add page numbers, headers and footers, and other page formatting for a consistent appearance throughout the entire document. You can also easily generate document references across the entire master document. Both tasks are difficult, if not impossible, when working with subdocuments alone.

> **NOTE** As mentioned earlier, WordPerfect doesn't impose restrictions on the number of subdocuments you can include in a master document. However, the amount of free disk space on your computer does impose a practical limit on the combined size of the master document and all its subdocuments. As a rule of thumb, the free disk space should be at least three times the size of the combined size of your subdocuments. When you expand your master document, this document occupies as much disk space as the subdocuments, and WordPerfect requires an equal amount of space to hold temporary files while you work with the expanded document. If you run out of disk space while working in an expanded master document, you might be unable to save any changes you make.

WordPerfect provides the option of expanding all or only selected subdocuments in a master document. The procedure you follow to accomplish either task is much the same. To expand one or more of the subdocuments within a master document, follow these steps:

1. Open the master document.

2. Choose File, Document, Expand Master.

   WordPerfect displays the Expand Master Document dialog box (see fig. 27.4). The Subdocuments list box displays the names of all the subdocuments for which you have inserted a [Subdoc] code. The X in the check box before each file name indicates that the file will be included when you expand the document. By default, all subdocuments are checked.

**FIG. 27.4**

The Expand Master Document dialog box lists all the subdocuments in the master document.

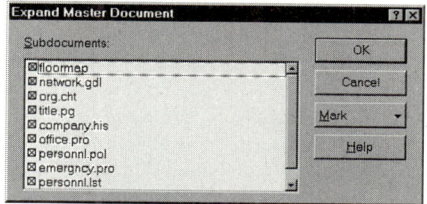

3. If you do not want to expand all the subdocuments, you can choose which ones to expand.

   To unmark all selected subdocuments, choose Mark, Clear All. (To re-mark all subdocuments, choose Mark, Mark All.)

   To mark an individual subdocument, unmark all subdocuments, and then click the desired subdocument's name so that the box to its left is checked.

   To unmark an individual subdocument, click the desired subdocument's name so that the box to its left is unchecked.

   Figure 27.5 shows the Expand Master Document dialog box with six subdocuments marked.

4. Choose OK or press Enter.

**FIG. 27.5**

You can expand selected subdocuments by marking them in the Expand Master Document dialog box.

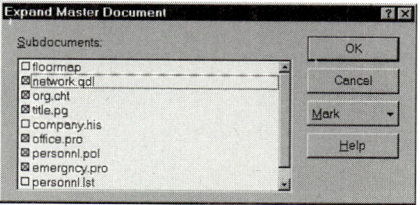

WordPerfect retrieves a copy of each subdocument you marked. If the program cannot find a file, a Subdocument Error dialog box is displayed (see fig. 27.6). You can enter a new file name and/or location, or click the file folder button to browse for the file. You can also choose Skip to tell WordPerfect to ignore the missing file and move on to the next subdocument, or Cancel to abandon the expansion process entirely.

When WordPerfect expands a master document, the program removes the original [Subdoc] code and places a [Subdoc Begin] code at the beginning of the subdocument and a [Subdoc End] code at the end of the subdocument (see fig. 27.7).

**FIG. 27.6**
If WordPerfect can't find a file while expanding a master document, this dialog box enables you to enter a new name and/or location.

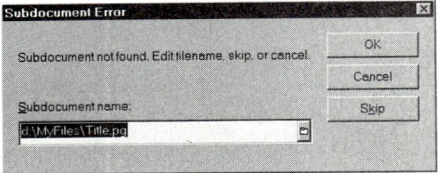

### CAUTION

Never delete an individual [Subdoc Begin] or [Subdoc End] code in an expanded master document, unless, of course, you want that portion of the document to remain expanded. WordPerfect requires that these codes be in pairs to manage your subdocuments. When you condense a master document, the program removes subdocuments according to these paired codes, and if it can't find half of a pair, WordPerfect displays an error message and halts the procedure. If you delete a code by mistake, immediately choose Undo (choose Edit, Undo; or press Ctrl+Shift+Z) to restore the code. If you discover the deletion only while condensing, you must delete the remaining code before you continue condensing, and you must delete the contents of the subdocument, or block and save the contents as a separate file. To delete a subdocument from your master document, see the earlier section, "Adding, Deleting, and Moving Subdocuments."

**FIG. 27.7**
When you expand a master document, WordPerfect places [Subdoc Begin] and [Subdoc End] codes at the beginning and end of each subdocument.

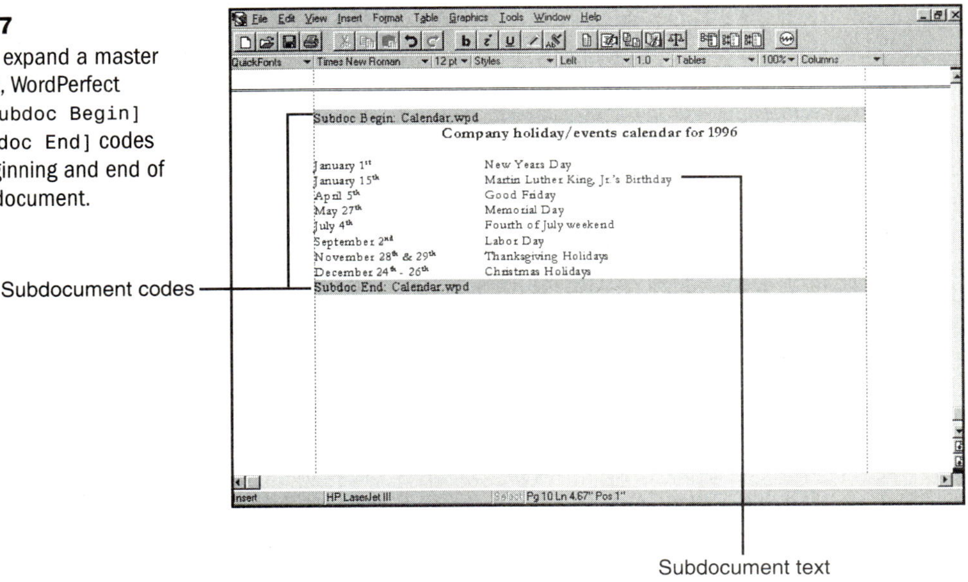

Subdocument codes

Subdocument text

### TROUBLESHOOTING

**WordPerfect can't find a file when expanding a document, but the file is still on the computer's hard disk drive.** WordPerfect stores the complete path and name to a subdocument in the subdocument code. If you move the file to a different directory, WordPerfect won't be able to find it. There are three solutions to this problem. First, you can move the file back into its original directory. Second, you can remove the subdocument code in the master document file, then insert a new Subdocument code with the new directory. Third, when the "Subdocument not found" message box appears, you can type the correct path and file name (or you can browse for it), expand the master, and then when you condense the master document, make sure you save the subdocument to the new location.

**In Draft Display mode, some files are shown with a complete path in the gray Subdocument comment box, and some are not.** WordPerfect is working as designed. The files shown with a full path—such as C:\LINDSEY\MYSTERY\OUTLINE.BEN—are not stored in the default folder. The default folder in WordPerfect is the folder that comes up whenever you first open the Open File dialog box. This folder is specified in the Files Preferences dialog box (choose Edit, Preferences, Files). Files not shown with a full path (name only) are stored in the default folder, so WordPerfect knows where to look for them. Note that if you change the default folder, WordPerfect won't be able to find those files, and you will get an error message when you expand the master document. Should this happen, you need to condense the master document, delete the codes without a path, and reinsert them.

## Saving a Master Document

After you expand a master document, you can save it in its expanded or condensed form. If you only need to update page numbering and document references and then print—and you don't need to edit the expanded document—then no good reason exists to save an expanded master document. Saving an expanded document is like saving a second set of subdocument files.

An expanded master document takes up about as much space on disk as all its subdocuments combined.

If you do need to edit the expanded master document, however, you may find that saving the full document in its expanded form is practical. Expanding and saving a large master document can waste time if you're not finished with the expanded document. If you plan to use the expanded document again soon, save the document in expanded form.

You save a master document just as you would save any other document. (See Chapter 2, "Creating and Saving a Document," for more information on file saving options.) If your master document is expanded, WordPerfect saves it in its expanded form. If you don't want to save the expanded document, either close the document without saving, or condense the master document before saving. The following section covers this process in detail.

## Condensing a Master Document

When you finish working with an expanded master document, you can condense it. When you condense a master document, WordPerfect reverses the operations it performed when expanding. The program removes the subdocuments from the master document, and replaces each pair of [Subdoc Begin] and [Subdoc End] codes with a single [Subdoc] code.

If you edited the subdocuments while they were part of the expanded master document, you can save the versions of the subdocuments contained in the master document over the earlier versions of the subdocuments on disk. When you save subdocuments while condensing, WordPerfect overwrites any earlier versions of the subdocuments without prompting for confirmation.

> **CAUTION**
> If you save subdocuments while condensing but don't want to overwrite the original versions of the subdocuments, you must move the subdocuments before condensing, or WordPerfect replaces them with the newer versions of the subdocuments in the master document.

> **CAUTION**
> By default, WordPerfect saves subdocuments when you condense a master document. If you made changes to the master document that you don't want saved in the subdocuments, unmark the subdocuments before you start the condense process. Otherwise, your changes will be saved over the original file.

Whenever you make changes to an expanded master document, save subdocuments while condensing, unless the changes are only temporary. If you make extensive changes to a colleague's document, however, he or she may not appreciate your replacing the original version. In this case, make sure that you move or copy the original version before condensing.

Just as you can choose to expand only selected subdocuments, you can also choose to condense and/or save only selected subdocuments. To condense an expanded master document, follow these steps:

1. Choose File, Document, Condense Master.

   WordPerfect displays the Condense/Save Subdocuments dialog box, which closely resembles the Expand Master Document dialog box. In the Condense/Save Subdocuments dialog box, however, each subdocument is listed twice: one entry to be marked for saving the subdocument, and one entry to be marked for condensing the subdocument (see fig. 27.8).

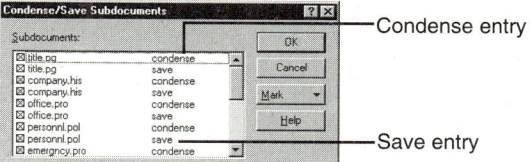

**FIG. 27.8**
By default, WordPerfect marks all subdocuments for condensing and saving.

2. Mark which subdocuments you want to save and which subdocuments you want to condense. You can perform any of the following actions:

   To deselect a marked subdocument, click the subdocument's name. WordPerfect unchecks its box.

   To select an unmarked subdocument, click the subdocument's name. WordPerfect checks its box.

   To mark all items to be condensed, choose Mark, Condense All. WordPerfect checks all subdocuments with an accompanying "condense" entry.

   To mark all items to be saved, choose Mark, Save All. WordPerfect checks all subdocuments with an accompanying "save" entry.

   To unmark all items to be condensed, choose Mark, Clear Condense. WordPerfect unchecks all subdocuments with an accompanying "condense" entry.

   To unmark all items to be saved, choose Mark, Clear Save. WordPerfect unchecks all subdocuments with an accompanying "save" entry.

3. Choose OK or press Enter. WordPerfect removes from the master document all subdocuments marked to be condensed, and saves all subdocuments marked to be saved. Any changes to an unmarked subdocument are discarded.

# Creating a Table of Contents, List, Index, or Table of Authorities

In Chapter 26, "Assembling Document References," you learn about features you can use to assemble document references. When you combine those features with the Master Document feature, you can assemble document references that span all the subdocuments in an expanded master document. You can create a table of contents, table of authorities, lists of tables, figures, or other repeating items, an index, or cross-references for the entire master document.

This section describes the steps required to generate a table of contents for a master document. The steps to generate a table of authorities are nearly identical, and the steps to generate lists or an index are similar.

▶ See "Creating a Table of Contents," **p. 843**
▶ See "Creating a Table of Authorities," **p. 848**

Creating a table of contents in a master document requires the following basic steps:

1. Mark the text to be included in the table of contents.
2. Select a location for the table of contents and insert a table definition code.
3. Generate the table (and any other document references).

**NOTE** Create a Mark Text Toolbar to save time when you are marking many entries for table of contents or other document references. Add buttons for marking and defining the table of contents, lists, index, cross-references, and table of authorities (if needed), and a Generate button.

▶ See "Customizing a Toolbar," **p. 420**

When you generate a document, WordPerfect scans the entire document for document reference marks, including table of contents marks. The program copies the text between each pair of codes and its table of contents level, assembles the marked text at the table of contents definition mark, and formats the table according to the definition.

## Marking Text for the Table of Contents

Marking the text to be included is the first step in creating a table of contents. You can mark any text in any document to be included in a table of contents. That text can be in an individual subdocument, a condensed master document, or an expanded master document.

**TIP** Instead of opening each subdocument and marking text for table of contents and other document references, expand the master document and mark the expanded document. Then compress and save the master document and modified subdocuments.

Block the text and any format codes for each heading that you want to include in the table of contents. As you mark text for inclusion in the table of contents, note the highest level number you use so that you can define the table of contents properly.

## Defining the Tables of Contents

After you mark the headings or other text for inclusion in the table of contents, you can define the table of contents and its options. The table of contents definition specifies the location of the table, the number of levels to include when the table is generated, and how WordPerfect should format each level.

To define the table of contents in a master document, follow these steps:

1. Open the master document, select a location for the table of contents, and move the insertion point to that location.

2. To place the table of contents on its own page, insert a [HPg] code (hard page) by pressing Ctrl+Enter. Type any desired heading, and press Enter several times.

3. Create the table of contents definition.

   ▶ **See** "Defining a Table of Contents," **p. 845**

4. If necessary, press Ctrl+Enter to insert a hard page break at the end of the table of contents. If you want to add lists of tables, figures, or other items, define them on the following pages. When you generate the table and other document references, WordPerfect adds pages as needed to hold the entire table.

   **NOTE** Instead of marking each heading individually for inclusion in the table of contents, put the table of contents marks into styles, and use those styles to format your headings. See the later section "Using Styles with Master Documents" for more information.

5. Insert a new page number code where the body of your master document begins, so that your body text always starts with page 1. Generally, this position immediately precedes the subdocument code linking the first subdocument containing body text, and follows any definitions for table of contents or lists. (The title page may be a subdocument, but comes before the table of contents, and is usually not considered body text.) For information on inserting a new page number code, see the later section, "Inserting a New Page Number."

> **CAUTION**
> If you don't insert a page number code at the beginning of your body text, your table of contents and body text are part of the same numbering sequence. When you generate document references, any tables or lists that grow longer than one page change the body text page numbers, and the generated references are no longer correct.

6. Save the master document with the defined table of contents.

After you define the table of contents and any other formatting options, you are ready to generate the table.

## Generating Tables, Lists, and Indexes

After you mark your master document and subdocuments for table of contents entries or other document references and define the location and formatting options for the table of contents and other lists and indexes, you can use the Generate command to create or update the actual table of contents, list, or index.

The first time you generate a table of contents, WordPerfect scans the entire document for table of contents marks. The program copies any text and codes between each pair of [Mrk Txt ToC] codes, noting the table of contents level for each mark. WordPerfect then assembles the marked text at the location of the table of contents definition mark and formats each item according to the style, numbering mode, and page number format you defined.

> **NOTE** If you defined a list or index in addition to the table of contents, you cannot generate just one type of document reference. Whenever you use the Generate command, WordPerfect generates all references in a document, deletes the contents of any previously generated tables, lists, or indexes, and creates brand-new ones.

When you generate document references for a condensed master document, WordPerfect automatically expands the master document, generates the document references, and then condenses the master document again. If this procedure modifies any subdocuments, by default WordPerfect saves any modified subdocuments over the originals. If you don't want subdocuments modified by a Generate command to be saved over their original versions, you can tell WordPerfect not to save modified subdocuments when you generate.

▶ See "Creating an Index," **p. 858**
▶ See "Creating a Table of Contents," **p. 843**

To generate or update the table of contents for your master document, follow these steps:

1. Choose Tools, Generate, Generate, or press Ctrl+F9. WordPerfect displays the Generate dialog box (see fig. 27.9).

2. Deselect the Save Subdocuments option, and then choose OK.

**FIG. 27.9**
Deselect the Save Subdocuments option if you don't want modified subdocuments to replace the original subdocuments during a generate operation.

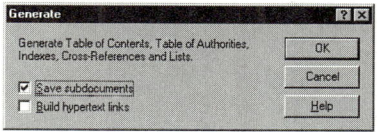

  After you generate the table of contents, you may discover typographical or formatting errors in the generated table. Because each entry in the table of contents is copied from the body of the expanded master document, an error in the table of contents indicates an error in the text. Instead of correcting the table of contents entry, fix the error in the body text and regenerate the table of contents.

**CAUTION**
If you edit any text in a generated table of contents, list, or index, your changes will be lost the next time you generate.

## Using Styles with Master Documents

WordPerfect 7 makes extensive use of styles. A *style* is a named collection of format codes that you can apply to a section of text or graphics. WordPerfect formats all text marked with a particular style identically. If you edit the style definition, WordPerfect automatically reformats any text marked with that style.

Styles are useful for ensuring consistent formatting throughout a document or between several documents—an important capability when you work with master documents. This section covers several uses of styles particularly applicable to master documents. For more information about styles, refer to Chapter 10, "Using Styles."

You can use four types of styles with text: Paragraph, Paragraph-Auto, Character, and Document. Paragraph styles format the contents of an entire paragraph. Paragraph-Auto styles automatically update all paragraphs when the style is changed for one paragraph.

Character styles format any text that appears between paired [Char Style] codes, and essentially act like paired font attribute codes. Document styles contain all their formatting codes in a single [Open Style] code.

> **NOTE** In previous versions of WordPerfect, styles were referred to as *Paired* styles and *Open* styles. Also, WordPerfect 6.0 for Windows offered only the standard Paragraph style, not Paragraph-Auto.

Whenever you combine many documents prepared by many people, you can expect the formatting of those documents to be different. If you have a collection of subdocuments in various formats, you can easily apply styles to those documents to reformat them according to the needs of your project. A more efficient method, however, is to create a template containing the styles for your project. You can then share that template with your colleagues so that they can use the styles when they create their subdocuments.

When a master document contains styles, those styles take precedence over any other styles of the same name in any of the subdocuments. Styles with unique names in subdocuments are added to the master document's styles. If several subdocuments use a style name not used by the master document, WordPerfect uses the first style definition it encounters as it expands the subdocuments.

If all the subdocuments contain different style names, a master document's style list can become huge and unmanageable. When you edit the subdocuments, rename styles to ensure consistency or delete unnecessary styles. If the master document and all subdocuments use the same style names—even if the contents of those styles are different—WordPerfect reformats all the subdocuments according to the style definitions in the master document when a master document is created.

Although you can use styles in the master document, styles are more useful in the individual subdocuments—particularly the codes at the beginning of each subdocument and the headings within each subdocument.

## Using Open Styles To Begin Subdocuments

When you expand a master document, each subdocument effectively becomes part of one large document, and WordPerfect ignores each subdocument's Initial Codes style and Initial Font Document. As a result, each subdocument assumes whatever formatting is in effect at the end of the previous subdocument, including font, justification, margins, line spacing, tab sets, and more. Likewise, any format changes made in the subdocument have a similar effect on all subdocuments that follow.

To ensure consistency of format throughout the master document, you should create a standard format for the entire document and insert all the codes that specify that format at the beginning of each subdocument. Each subdocument automatically begins with the preferred format options. Each author can then make necessary deviations from that format within his or her subdocument without affecting other subdocuments. By combining all these formatting codes into one Open style, you can apply all the formatting codes into a single style. If necessary, at a later date you can edit the style and thereby reformat all the subdocuments in the master document.

You should create an Open style for the beginning of each subdocument with a name, such as SubdocInit. In the style, include all the formatting that defines your preferred master document's appearance and that may be changed within a subdocument. The following items are a suggested minimum:

- Margins (top, bottom, left, and right)
- Tab set
- Line spacing
- Paragraph spacing
- Font
- Font size
- Paper size/type
- Page numbering

Other useful items include the following:

- Force page
- Increment chapter or volume number
- Header or footer discontinue
- Footnote numbering

You can place the style at the beginning of each subdocument or in a master document immediately before each subdocument code.

## Using Paragraph and Character Styles To Format Headings

You can put nearly any WordPerfect formatting code into a Paragraph or Character style. These codes can determine font, font size, text alignment or indentation, chapter or outline number, and table of contents marks. For example, WordPerfect's default Heading 1 style—a Paragraph style designed to be used on main titles—contains the following codes:

    [Bold][Very Large][Hd Center on Mar][Mrk Txt ToC: 1]

The first three codes make the paragraph bold, very large (relative to the body text size), and centered. The [Mrk Txt ToC] code marks the paragraph as a first-level table of contents entry. As a result, whenever you apply the Heading 1 style to a paragraph, you automatically mark that paragraph for inclusion in the table of contents. Because the other formatting codes appear before the mark text codes, the table of contents entry includes only text, not the formatting codes.

Most main headings and high-level subheadings appear on a line by themselves and are followed by hard return codes ([HRt]), which, by definition, make them paragraphs. Use Paragraph styles to format such headings. For lower-level headings that are not paragraphs in their own right, use Character styles. Character styles can contain the same types of codes as Paragraph styles.

You can use WordPerfect's default styles, edit these styles to your liking, or create entirely new styles. In any case, by applying styles to your headings, you can quickly and consistently format the headings of any document. In addition, applying a style to a heading automatically marks the heading for inclusion in the table of contents if the style contains table of contents codes.

You can use styles most effectively with a master document project if you distribute a Style Library to everyone working on a subdocument. If this is not possible, you can still save time by using styles to format the subdocuments after you receive them.

▶ **See** "Considering Types of Styles," **p. 336**

# Inserting Page Numbering Codes

Without the Master Document feature, sequentially numbering a master document is a monumental task: you need to count the number of pages in the first document, insert a page number code with the next sequential page number at the beginning of the second document, and repeat the process for each successive document. If you add pages to or delete pages from any document, you must renumber the pages in all subsequent files. With the Master Document feature, however, if you insert a new page number code into the master document, WordPerfect automatically renumbers all pages from that point forward.

Alternatively, if you frequently change the number of pages in a master document, you may not want to repeatedly print and duplicate the majority of the document simply to correct the page numbers. WordPerfect lets you insert codes that identify individual subdocuments as chapters or volumes and include the chapter or volume number with the printed page numbers, such as "II-1." You can then begin the numbering of each subdocument with page 1, and if you edit that document, you don't need to reprint the remainder of the master document.

## Inserting a New Page Number

If you want your master document numbered sequentially, you must insert a new page number code in the document after any table of contents or list definitions and before the beginning of the body of the document. In the sample office procedures manual, for example, the first page after the table of contents is the company history and mission statement. If you place a new page number code with a value of 1 in the master document immediately before the COMPANY.HIS subdocument code, the company history now begins on page 1. WordPerfect numbers all subsequent pages sequentially from that point.

▶ See "Numbering Pages," **p. 163**

**NOTE** WordPerfect prints page numbers where the top or bottom line of your document would otherwise print, shortening each page of your document by two lines. If you decrease the size of your top or bottom margin to approximately 2/3 inch (depending on the location of your page numbers), you can regain the lost space, and your page numbers will appear to print in the margin.

## Inserting Chapter Codes

Just as you can have WordPerfect print the current page number, you can place a chapter code at the beginning of each subdocument and have WordPerfect insert the current chapter number into page numbers, headers and footers, or text. Chapter numbers are particularly useful if you don't need to sequentially number all pages in a master document. You can start numbering each chapter at page 1 and include the chapter number with the printed page number so that, for example, Chapter II, page 3 prints as II-3.

▶ See "Numbering Pages," **p. 163**

Unlike page numbers, which WordPerfect automatically increments at each page break, chapter numbers do not change until you instruct the program. If you use chapter codes at the beginning of each subdocument, you must insert a Chapter Number Increment code. If you want to start numbering each chapter at page 1, also insert a Page Number Set code. In the master document, at the beginning of the body text, insert a Page Number Position code. Also insert a Chapter Number Method code to format chapter numbers using letters, numbers, or Roman numerals.

**NOTE** Include a Chapter Number Increment code in your Subdocument Initial Code style so that each subdocument automatically starts a new chapter. If you include a Chapter Increment code for your subdocuments at the beginning of your master document, you must decrement the chapter number to 0. Choose Fo_r_mat, Page _N_umbering, Value/Adjust, then click the Chapter tab. Click the _S_et Chapter Number text box, then type **0**.

You also can have WordPerfect insert the current chapter number anywhere in body text, a header or footer, or a style by choosing Format, Page Numbering, Insert in Text. Choose Chapter from the Number list box, then click Insert. WordPerfect inserts a code that displays and prints as the current chapter number.

▶ See "Numbering Pages," **p. 163**

# Using Headers and Footers with Master Documents

Headers and footers can make a large document easier to read. You can include almost any information in a header or footer, including chapter title or number, volume numbers, document headings, topics, author name, and page numbers. When you include this type of information in headers and footers, your readers can find relevant information more readily. Chapter 5, "Formatting Pages and Documents," covers the process of creating and editing headers and footers in detail. This section discusses using headers and footers with master documents.

WordPerfect lets you use two headers and two footers simultaneously (Header A, Header B, Footer A, and Footer B), in addition to automatic page numbers. If you use two headers, you can print one header on odd-numbered pages and one header on even-numbered pages, or you can print both headers on all pages; footers work the same way. Although you can only have one Header A and one Header B on a given page, you can have a different Header A or B for each chapter or section of your document. These options give you great flexibility.

In the office procedures manual, for example, Header A may read `Office Procedures Manual` and appear on even-numbered pages for the entire document. For the odd-numbered pages, you may want to create a different Header B for each subdocument containing a chapter number and title. The header for the first chapter might read

`Part I—Company History and Mission Statement.`

The document title would thus appear on all even-numbered (left-hand) pages, and the section number and title would appear on all odd-numbered (right-hand) pages. You can include page numbering codes within a header or footer, or you can use automatic page numbers, as described earlier in this chapter.

▶ See "Using Headers and Footers," **p. 173**

# Adding Footnotes and Endnotes

Footnotes and endnotes are also useful with a master document. If you plan to use footnotes or endnotes, however, exercise caution with the codes you use to control their format. Footnote and endnote format is controlled in two ways:

- *System style*. A default system style for each element controls such details as default font, margins, indentation, and appearance of the footnote or endnote number. You can have only one footnote or endnote system style per document.

- *Note options*. Footnote (or endnote) option codes control other options, such as spacing between footnotes, separator line, and whether numbers should restart on each page. You can have many option codes in a document.

Use footnote or endnote option codes only in the master document, not the subdocuments. Like many WordPerfect codes, an option code placed in the middle of a document changes the format of that feature for the remainder of the document. If you place a footnote or endnote option code in a subdocument, all notes before the code have one appearance, and all notes after the note have another.

For detailed information on creating and editing footnotes and endnotes, see Chapter 25, "Using Footnotes and Endnotes."

## Numbering Footnotes

WordPerfect gives you the option of numbering footnotes sequentially throughout a master document or of numbering each chapter or section separately. Like page numbers, by default WordPerfect numbers footnotes sequentially throughout an entire document. If you print a subdocument by itself, its page numbering and footnote numbering both start at 1. If you print that same subdocument in its place in an expanded master document, its page and footnote numbers depend on how many of each appear in previous subdocuments.

Just as you can insert a new page number code, you can insert a new footnote number code to restart numbering at any given value. Choose Insert, Footnote, New Number, then type **1** in the New Number text box. If you want all subdocuments to start numbering at 1, place this code in your SubdocInit style.

## Placing Endnotes

By default, WordPerfect places endnotes at the end of a document. If instead you want endnotes to appear at a particular location within a document—such as the end of a subdocument—you can insert an endnote placement code. Any endnotes you create before the code are printed at the location of the code, and any endnotes you create later in the document are printed at the end, or at a subsequent endnote placement code. You can insert an endnote placement code at the end of each subdocument, or you can insert a single code near the end of your master document—immediately before an index definition, for example.

▶ See "Using Footnotes," **p. 802**
▶ See "Using Endnotes," **p. 817**

The Endnote Placement dialog box contains two options: Insert Endnotes At Insertion Point, and Insert Endnotes At Insertion Point And Restart Numbering. If you are placing endnotes at the end of each subdocument and want to restart numbering for each, choose the latter. If you are placing all endnotes near the end of your master document, choose the former.

## Using Cross-References

When you combine individual documents in a master document, you can cross-reference items in other subdocuments—a process that is impossible without the Master Document feature. You can reference chapter titles or section headings in other subdocuments, for example.

To cross-reference items between subdocuments, insert a reference code with a particular target name into one subdocument, and then use that same target name for a target code in a different subdocument. If you are creating many cross-references, expand the master document so that the reference and target are in the same large document.

▶ See "Using Automatic Cross-Referencing," **p. 865**

## Using Search, Replace, and Spell Check in a Master Document

You can use many WordPerfect features with the Master Document feature. You can perform functions—a spell check or find and replace, for example—more efficiently on one expanded document than on many separate subdocuments.

The sample office procedures manual has many sections contained in separate subdocuments. Using find and replace, or spell check functions without the Master Document feature requires that you open each subdocument, perform the desired operation, and save the revised file—a tedious and time-consuming task. Also, with so many separate files, you may forget to check some of the files. With the Master Document feature, however, you can expand the master document and perform operations knowing that all files will be checked.

▶ See "Spell Checking the Document," **p. 210**
▶ See "Using Find and Replace," **p. 111**

To search and replace, or run a spell check across all the subdocument files linked to your master document, you simply open and expand the master document, and then perform the necessary operation.

# Printing a Master Document

Expanding your master document produces one large document containing all the text and codes of the master document and each of the linked subdocuments. After you insert the appropriate page numbering codes and generate the document references, you have created a complete version of the document. Printing the expanded document produces a comprehensive final document.

## Printing the Entire Document

You print an entire expanded master document just as you print any other document. First choose File, Print or press Ctrl+P. Then press Enter to select the default value of Full Document and begin printing.

## Printing Selected Pages or Chapters

As with any document, you can print selected pages of an expanded master document. If you have inserted a new page numbering code for your body text, however, you may have to specify the page range in a different fashion.

Every new page number code inserted in a document creates a new *logical section* for page numbering purposes. For example, if your title page, table of contents, and other preface material take up eight pages, and you insert a new page number code to start numbering the body text at page 1, your document now has two page 1s (one in the body and one in the front matter). If you simply tell WordPerfect to print pages 1–4, the program prints the title page and subsequent pages. If you specify pages 20–50, WordPerfect prints that page range from the body text, because the first section of the document doesn't contain pages numbered greater than 8. To print pages 1–8 of the body text, however, you must tell WordPerfect that you want pages 1–8 of the second section of the document.

If you inserted chapter codes, you can print one or more chapters instead of printing a page range. If necessary, you can also specify a page range within a specific chapter. To print selected pages or chapters, do the following:

To print pages:

1. Choose File, Print. WordPerfect displays the Print dialog box.
2. Choose Multiple Pages from the Print drop-down list. WordPerfect activates the Page Range section below the Print list box.
3. Type the beginning page in the From text box, then type the ending page in the To text box.
4. Choose Print.

To print chapters:

1. Choose File, Print. WordPerfect displays the Print dialog box.
2. Choose Advanced Multiple Pages from the Print drop-down list. A small indicator section appears with an Edit option button. These indicators show which chapters, volumes, secondary pages, or pages you select for printing.
3. Choose Edit. The Advanced Multiple Pages dialog box appears.
4. If necessary, delete the current selections in each text box.
5. Choose Chapter(s), then type the chapter number or range of chapters in the text box. In the range, use a dash to separate the beginning and ending chapter numbers. If you want to print non-contiguous chapters (for example, chapters 3 and 7 rather than chapters 3 through 7), use a space to separate the chapter numbers.
6. If necessary, indicate the range of pages within the selected chapter in the Page(s)/Label(s) text box.
7. Choose OK, then choose Print.

Normally, you won't want to print a condensed master document. However, because a master document can contain text of its own as well as the generated table of contents, lists, and index, you may want to print the condensed master document to see those items. To print the condensed master document, print the document before expanding it. If the master document is already expanded, condense it and then print. Remember, the subdocument links are formatted as comments and do not print.

▶ **See** "Using Basic Printing Skills," **p. 278**

## TROUBLESHOOTING

**I've expanded a master document, and the formatting I used in the original subdocuments is lost.** If you use styles for formatting, WordPerfect gives precedence to the style definitions in the master document. If you have a StyleA defined in a subdocument, and a StyleA defined in the master document, WordPerfect ignores the definition for StyleA in the subdocument and goes with the definition in the master document. Because of this precedence, you should give styles unique names if you want their definitions to remain when they are expanded into a master document. Avoid using the InitialStyle style to define styles unique to the individual files.

**I'm trying to print only certain sections of my document with the Multiple Pages and Advanced Multiple Pages options and I can't get it to work.** Make sure you are typing the page numbers in order. If you type **27**, **13**, **9**, for example, only page 27 will print. When you use the Advanced Multiple Pages options, pay attention to the order of precedence: Volume, Chapter, Secondary Page, Page. For example, if you type **3** in the Volume text box, only the chapters within volume 3 will print, even if you specify pages and chapters that are in another part of the document.

**WordPerfect takes an inordinate amount of time to generate a very large expanded master document.** The larger the expanded master document, the more time it takes to generate it. Long documents of several hundred pages are not uncommon, and these can take several minutes—depending on the speed of your computer—to generate. Because large documents can take so long to generate, it is advisable to do it just once—when you are putting the finishing touches on your document and preparing it for printing. If you must generate large documents often, consider ways to speed up the process by using a faster computer. A PC with no less than 16M of RAM improves the speed of the generating process.

CHAPTER 28

# Using WordPerfect with the Corel WordPerfect Suite

*by Diane Koers*

The Windows operating environment offers a unique opportunity to share information easily with other Windows programs. Although WordPerfect can do many things by itself—including creating charts or drawings—you may want to use projects that have already been created using other programs.

The import or linking feature of WordPerfect can save you from having to repeat your work. With WordPerfect, you have the capability to import and or link files created in other Corel WordPerfect Suite applications such as Quattro Pro, Presentations, or Paradox. Before looking at methods of using the major Corel Wordperfect Suite applications together, this chapter explores the use of the Address Book, which is a useful tool for the entire suite. ■

**Share information between multiple applications**

You learn how to use drag-and-drop to share information from one WordPerfect application to another.

**Use the Address Book feature**

You learn how to add, edit, delete, and use information in the Address Book.

**Link WordPerfect with Quattro Pro or Presentations**

Learn how to link a Quattro Pro spreadsheet or a Presentations chart or drawing into a WordPerfect document.

**CorelFLOW and WordPerfect**

Learn how to incorporate a flow chart created from CorelFLOW into a WordPerfect document.

**Envoy and WordPerfect**

Learn how to publish your WordPerfect document to Envoy so that others can view the information electronically.

**QuickTasks**

Learn how the many Corel Office QuickTasks can save you time when you need to complete a project quickly.

# Using the Address Book

The Corel WordPerfect Suite comes with an Address Book accessible from within WordPerfect and other Corel Office programs, allowing you to store names, addresses, phone numbers, e-mail addresses, and other pieces of information. This information can then be inserted into a WordPerfect document. You can also dial the phone from the Address Book.

**NOTE** When the Address Book is installed (and it typically is), Corel searches for any other available messaging systems and then adds a Profile to Windows 95, which links those messaging systems to the Corel WordPerfect 7 settings. This means that if you have an Address Book identified with your existing messaging system (such as Exchange, which is installed with Windows 95), that address book and its entries become the address book used within WordPerfect and the other suite applications.

This also means that as you add additional names into the address book through WordPerfect, the new info will be available to all other applications that recognize the messaging system (such as Word, Schedule+, and Exchange Server).

**TIP** If you want a separate address book, you must edit your Corel Settings profile to link to an alternate address book, or create an alternate profile altogether. This can be done through the Control Panel's Mail and Fax utility.

## Creating an Address Book

Multiple address books can be created to separate your family's or friends' information from business information. Any number of address books can be added.

To create an Address Book:

1. Choose Tools, Address Book, or click the Address Book icon. The Address Book opens.
2. Choose Book, New. The Create New Address Book dialog box appears.
3. In the dialog box, type a name for the new Address Book such as **My Friends** or **Vendor List** (see fig. 28.1).
4. Click OK. A new tab is inserted into your Address Book.

**FIG. 28.1**
The Address Book helps you organize your contacts.

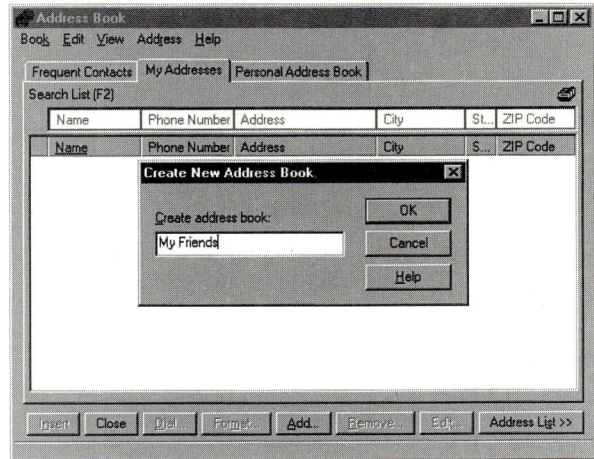

## Renaming an Address Book

OK, so you changed your mind. You don't want to call the Address Book "My Acquaintances." You want to call it "My Friends." No problem—WordPerfect enables you to rename any Address Book you created.

To rename an Address Book:

1. Choose Tools, Address Book, or click the Address Book icon. The Address Book opens.
2. Click the Address Book tab you want to rename.
3. Choose Book, Rename. The Rename Address Book dialog box opens.
4. In the dialog box, type the new name for this Address Book.
5. Click OK. The Address Book tab is renamed.

## Deleting an Address Book

Occasionally you will want to delete an Address Book. Again, no problem—WordPerfect enables you to delete any Address Book you created.

To delete an Address Book:

1. Choose Tools, Address Book, or click the Address Book icon. The Address Book opens.
2. Select the Address Book tab you want to delete.

3. Choose Boo<u>k</u>, De<u>l</u>ete. The Delete Address Book dialog box appears with a list of the books eligible to be deleted.

4. Highlight the Address Book to remove, then click OK.

   You are informed that any information in that particular Address Book will be deleted and cannot be restored.

5. Click <u>Y</u>es. The Address Book is deleted.

**TROUBLESHOOTING**

**I'm trying to delete the Frequent Contacts or My Addresses but I don't get those choices available to delete. Why not?** Frequent Contacts and My addresses tabs are default tabs in the Address Book, and WordPerfect does not allow you to delete those two. Any Address Book tabs that have been added by you can be deleted by you.

## Adding an Address to the Address Book

You can now add information to the newly created Address Book. You can add personal names or organizations. WordPerfect does not limit the number of names or organizations you can add to your Address Books.

**Adding an Organization**   When you create an organization, the information you enter is available for each person who works for that organization. For example, suppose you create an organization named ABS Production Products. You enter the business address, phone number, and other information. Then you create personal entries for John Smith, Mary Jones, and Susan Williams who all work for ABS Production Products. All you need to do is specify that they work for ABS, and their information is updated automatically. You do not have to retype their company information each time.

To add a new organization to an Address Book:

1. Choose <u>T</u>ools, Address <u>B</u>ook, or click the Address Book icon. The Address Book opens.

2. Click the appropriate tab such as My Friends.

3. Click <u>A</u>dd at the bottom of the Address Book dialog box. The New Entry dialog box appears, as in figure 28.2.

4. In the <u>S</u>elect Entry Type list box, choose Organization and click OK. The New Organization Properties dialog box appears.

5. Enter the organization's name, address, and other desired information.
6. Choose OK. The address entry is added to the Address Book.

**FIG. 28.2**
Add as many entries to each Address Book as you like.

In the Address Book, the entries are listed in alphabetical order. Organizations are designated with a small icon representing a building next to them. This allows you to quickly distinguish between the two types of entries.

> **TIP** To save time, enter an **Organization** before you enter a **Person**. That way, if you have several people working at the same organization, you save yourself some typing time.

**Adding an Individual**   To add an individual to your Address Book:

1. With the appropriate tab of the Address Book selected, click Add at the bottom of the Address Book dialog box. The New Entry dialog box appears.
2. From the Select Entry Type list box, choose Person, then click OK. The Properties for New Entry dialog box appears (see fig. 28.3).
3. Enter the individual's First Name, Last Name, Address, and other desired information.

**N O T E**   Notice as you enter information into the Organization text box, if the organization has already been added, as you type a few characters of the organization name, it appears in the dialog box. You do not have to finish typing this entry.

If, however, the organization did not previously exist, it is created as you type in the name in the Organization text box. You can optionally click Edit to add the organization address or other information.

4. Choose OK. The address entry is added to the Address Book.

**FIG. 28.3**
While typing the information in the Properties for New Entry dialog box, you can click the Custo<u>m</u> button to add your own customized fields into the Address Book.

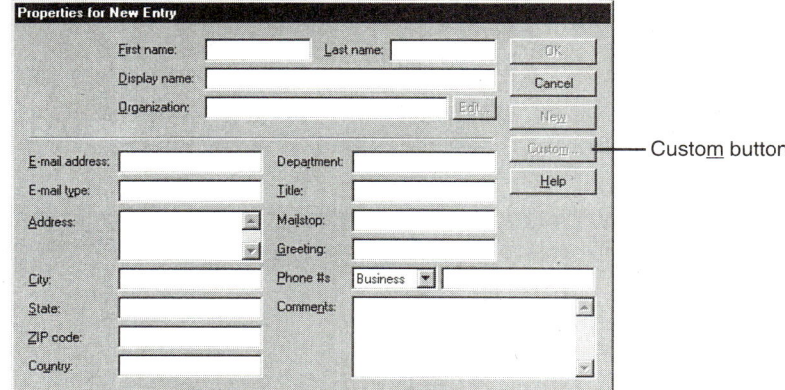

Custo<u>m</u> button

### TROUBLESHOOTING

**The Exchange address book opens in WordPerfect, even though I specified the Corel Settings profile for WordPerfect and the Corel Suite** The default Windows 95 profile uses Exchange settings, and the Exchange/Windows 95 client (without Exchange Server) address book will not allow you to add new addres books. Export the current MS Exchange address book, then change the default profile to the Corel Settings profile (both through Mail and Fax Services and through the Corel Suite Address Book), reload and configure any necessary services, and then import the saved address book into the Corel Address Book.

## Editing an Address Book Entry

Occasionally you need to edit existing names in the Address Book. If you make a change to an Organization, all Persons from that Organization will be modified as well. Suppose you entered an organization of ABS Products, and created Persons of John Smith and Susan Jones who work for ABS Products. ABS Products has now changed their name to ABS Production Products. You only need to change the name of the Organization. The other two names will have their organization changed to ABS Production Products at the same time.

To edit an Address Book entry:

1. With the appropriate tab of the Address Book selected, select the organization or person to be modified.

2. Click the Edit button from the bottom of the Address Book dialog box. The Properties dialog box appears.

3. Make any desired changes and click OK. The modifications are now in place in the Address Book.

**NOTE**  If you enter the Properties dialog box but do not make any changes, the OK button will not be available. Click Cancel to close the dialog box.

## Deleting an Address Book Entry

To remove a name or organization from the Address Book:

1. With the appropriate tab of the Address Book selected, highlight the organization or person to be deleted.
2. Click Remove. You are prompted to verify you want to delete this entry.
3. Click Yes. The entry is deleted.

**CAUTION**
Use caution with deleting entries. There is no chance to undo a deleted entry.

## Inserting an Address into a WordPerfect Document

To insert an address in a WordPerfect document, follow these steps:

1. Position the insertion point at the desired location for the address.
2. Choose Tools, Address Book, or click the Address Book icon. The Address Book opens.
3. Choose the desired tab, then select the name you want to insert in the document.
4. Choose Insert. The person's name and address are inserted into the WordPerfect document.

 You can also just double-click an Address Book entry to add it to the document.

## Choosing To Paste, Link, or Embed

When bringing in data from other programs, you must choose whether to paste the information, to link it with a feature called Dynamic Data Exchange (DDE), or to link and embed it into your document with a feature called Object Linking and Embedding (OLE).

When you choose to paste information via the Windows Clipboard from one Corel Office application to another, the data is copied one time only—meaning that if the source information is changed, the information in the WordPerfect document is not updated.

If you choose to link the information using DDE, when the source information in modified, your WordPerfect document can then be updated, either manually or automatically. You cannot change the original information from inside of WordPerfect when the data is linked. You must launch the originating program (such as Quattro Pro), edit the document, save it, then return to WordPerfect to have the WordPerfect document updated.

The third choice —to link the information using OLE—takes linking a step further. Not only is the information tied to the original source, but you also have the capability to modify the source document from within WordPerfect. Choosing to edit the original launches the program that created that data, so you can edit it without leaving your WordPerfect document. Therefore, the data is always current in both programs. (You can also embed an object in WordPerfect, which brings a mere copy of the information into WordPerfect. You can launch the original application within WordPerfect in order to edit the object, but the original file is not updated.)

**NOTE** When an object is embedded into WordPerfect document, the overall file size of the document is increased.

## Using Quattro Pro with WordPerfect

If you have a spreadsheet already created in Quattro Pro and need the information to be included in a report created in WordPerfect, you can bring in the Quattro Pro information. The information can be imported and, if desired, linked. Linking the documents enables you to update the WordPerfect document if the original Quattro Pro spreadsheet changes, and also enables you to update the spreadsheet itself from within WordPerfect. Depending on the type of link, you can also update the spreadsheet from within WordPerfect. Depending on the type of link, you can also update the spreadsheet from within WordPerfect.

## Importing a Spreadsheet from Quattro Pro

You must decide how you want the imported data to appear in your WordPerfect document. The Import As choices are Table, Text, or Merge Data File. If the data is brought in as a Table, the table will have gridlines, and most of the original formatting will be displayed as well. If the data is imported as Text, the cell information will be separated by the WordPerfect document tabs.

If you bring the data in as a Merge Data File, each row of your spreadsheet will be a record, with the beginning row classified as the data fields. Each column is designated as a field. The appropriate ENDFIELD and ENDRECORD commands will appear in the WordPerfect document, along with the Merge Feature Bar.

▶ **See** "Understanding Records and Fields," **p. 596**

To insert a Quattro Pro spreadsheet:

1. Choose Insert, Spreadsheet/Database. A submenu appears.
2. Click Import. The Import Data dialog box appears.
3. Specify the file name of the desired Quattro Pro spreadsheet.

   When you select the name of the file to be imported, if that spreadsheet has any range names, those choices will also be available in the Named Ranges list box. The default choice for WordPerfect is to select the entire worksheet; however, you can specify the specific area to be imported. Figure 28.4 illustrates a spreadsheet with range names specified. See your *Quattro Pro User's Guide* for instruction on naming ranges.

4. Specify the Range of the spreadsheet to be imported.
5. Choose OK. The spreadsheet is imported into your WordPerfect document.

**FIG. 28.4**
If you do not specify a specific range, WordPerfect assumes the entire spreadsheet is to be imported.

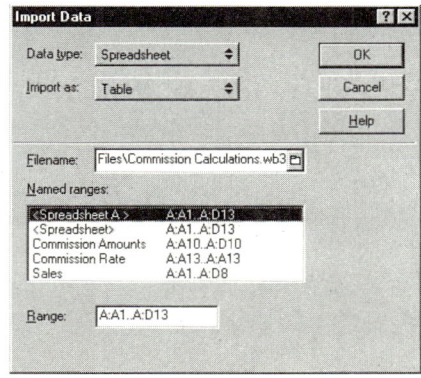

## Converting Spreadsheet Formulas

As the file is imported as a table, the formulas created in the original Quattro Pro spreadsheet will import as long as the cells being referenced are being imported as well. For example, in the Quattro Pro spreadsheet shown in figure 28.5, the amounts in row 10 are being calculated from cell A13. If you were to import the spreadsheet and not include cell A13 in the import, then the commission amounts will not reference formulas, but will include the current value in the cells of row 10.

**FIG. 28.5**
Importing a Quattro Pro spreadsheet into a WordPerfect table will also import any formatting.

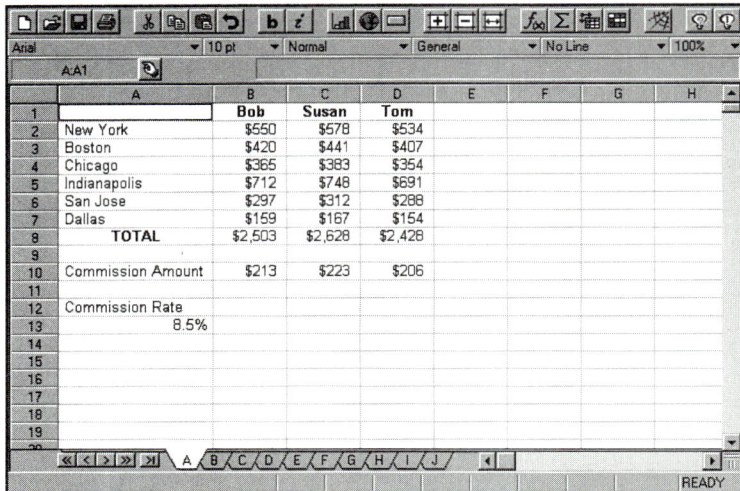

# Using Presentations with WordPerfect

The WordPerfect program has a drawing feature that uses the basics of the Presentations program. Not all Presentations features are available through the WordPerfect drawing portion.

If you've loaded the Corel Suite, however, the WP Draw module is replaced with Presentations automatically. Presentations then becomes your drawing program within WordPerfect. For more information on WP Draw, see Chapter 22, "Using WP Draw and TextArt."

> **NOTE** If you have installed the Corel WordPerfect Suite, the WP Draw module is replaced with Presentations automatically. Presentations then becomes your drawing program within WordPerfect.

## Linking a Presentations Chart

Although you can create charts in WordPerfect's Charting feature, you may have already created the chart in Presentations. Just like spreadsheet data, the chart can be inserted into WordPerfect as one-time data or as a link that can be updated.

To link a Presentations chart:

1. Position the insertion point at the location you want the chart to be inserted.
2. Choose Insert, Object. The Insert Object dialog box appears.
3. Choose Create From File if the chart has already been created and saved in Presentations (see fig. 28.6).

**FIG. 28.6**
Clicking Display As Icon hides the object for faster screen refreshing.

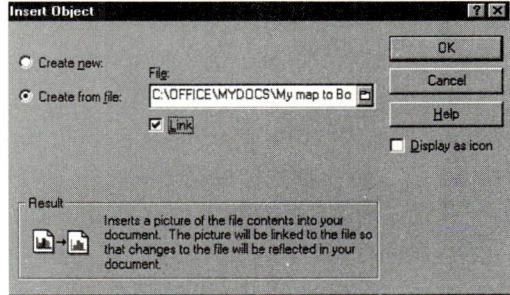

4. Specify the File Name.
5. Click Link.
6. Click OK. The chart is inserted in the WordPerfect document.

Because you chose to link the chart, WordPerfect inserts a picture of the chart so the WordPerfect document is updated in case the original chart changes.

You also can edit the original chart through WordPerfect by double-clicking the chart. This opens Presentations (within the WordPerfect window) so that the chart can be edited. When you exit Presentations, you are prompted to save your changes back to the original chart file. This option updates both the original file and the object within WordPerfect.

But, you can also edit the original chart through WordPerfect by double-clicking. This opens Presentations (within the WordPerfect window) so that the chart can be edited.

When you then exit Presentations, you are given the chance to save your changes back to the original chart file. This updates both the original file and the picture within WordPerfect.

> **CAUTION**
>
> When saving a Presentations chart or graphic, you should save it as a WPG 2.0 type if you intend to also use the file with older software versions (not just of WordPerfect, but also other drawing programs and spreadsheets—those other programs that import a WPG image). Those software applications probably do not recognize WPG 3.0 format yet.

## Inserting a Presentations Drawing

WordPerfect recognizes many types of graphics file formats, including WPG (WordPerfect Graphic). When a drawing is saved in Presentations, the file is formatted as a WPG file. Inserting a Presentations drawing is the same as inserting any standard graphic into WordPerfect. The drawing is inserted into the WordPerfect document where it can be manipulated for size.

To insert a Presentations drawing:

1. Position the cursor at the desired location for the drawing.

2. Choose Graphics, Image, or click the Image icon. The Insert Image dialog box appears.
3. Locate the folder where the Presentations drawing is located and select the drawing.
4. Click Insert. The drawing is inserted into the WordPerfect document.

   ▶ See "Resizing a Graphics Box," **p. 270**

**N O T E** To edit the drawing, double-click it. The Presentations program is launched, and the embedded drawing can be modified. Also, once you've edited the image in Presentations, the box contents change to an OLE object.

## Exporting a WordPerfect Outline for a Presentations Slide Show

Not only can you bring information created in other Corel Office programs into WordPerfect, but you can also take information from a WordPerfect document into other Corel Office programs. An example of this is to create an outline in WordPerfect to be used in a Presentations slide show.

If you have already created the outline for an upcoming project, why should you have to recreate it again in Presentations?

▶ **See** "Creating an Outline", **p. 473**

To export a WordPerfect outline to Presentations:

1. Save the WordPerfect outline by choosing File, Save, or by clicking the Save icon.
2. Begin the Presentations program.
3. At the Presentations opening screen, choose Create a New Slide Show.
4. Click OK. The New Slide Show dialog box appears.
5. From the Select A Template Group, choose Bullet Chart.
6. Click OK. A new slide show window opens, ready for your edits.
7. Choose View, Outliner. You are now switched to the Outline view.
8. Choose Insert, File, and specify the name of the WordPerfect outline to use.
9. Click Insert. The WordPerfect outline is now in Outliner view.

You are now ready to make any further changes in Presentations. See your *Presentations User's Guide* for further information about Corel WordPerfect Suite's Presentation program.

# Using CorelFLOW

Included with the WordPerfect Suite product is a program called CorelFLOW. This product is used to create diagrams and flow charts and enables you to embed or link a CorelFLOW diagram to a WordPerfect document. CorelFLOW does not automatically install when you set up the Corel Suite. It is available through Bonus Applications on the installation CD.

To insert a CorelFLOW diagram:

1. Position the cursor where you want the drawing to be located.
2. Choose Insert, Object. The Insert Object dialog box appears.
3. Choose Create From File if the diagram has already been created and saved to the disk.
4. Specify the folder and file name of the desired CorelFLOW diagram. Look for files with a CFL extension.

5. If you want to link the file instead of embedding it, click the box marked L̲ink. (See the section "Paste, Link, or Embed?" at the beginning of this chapter.)

6. Choose OK. The diagram is inserted into your WordPerfect document. You may want to resize the graphic image after it comes into the WordPerfect document.

**N O T E** Instead of inserting the CorelFLOW diagram from a file on disk, you can choose Create N̲ew and then select CorelFLOW 3.0 Diagram from the Object T̲ype list box. Draw new diagram inside the CorelFLOW window.

▶ **See** "Resizing a Graphics Box," **p. 270**

# Publishing a WordPerfect Document to Envoy

Envoy is a publishing medium that enables you to exchange and distribute WordPerfect and other documents electronically across various computers and operating systems such as between Windows and Macintosh. The Envoy program enables your readers to view the document including all fonts, colors, graphics, and page layouts as designated in the originating WordPerfect document without having to have the WordPerfect program located on their system.

By distributing a document via Envoy across a network, the reader can instantly access the document without having to change the original. The reader can also add annotations such as highlighting and QuickNotes.

You can create an Envoy file from any Windows 95 application that prints. The file is converted to the Envoy file format with the EVY extension. The Envoy Viewer program can view any file created in this format.

To publish a WordPerfect document to Envoy:

1. Choose F̲ile, Pub̲lish to Envoy.

   The Envoy Viewer starts. If the window is not visible, you may need to minimize WordPerfect to see it. If Publish to Envoy is not available on your File menu, then Envoy is not installed. Run Setup again to install it.

2. From Envoy, choose F̲ile, S̲ave (or press Ctrl+S).

**TIP** If the Envoy Viewer starts but isn't visible, minimize WordPerfect so that you can see the Envoy Viewer with your published document.

3. Give the Envoy document a file name.
4. Click Save. The file is saved in the Envoy EVY format.
5. Choose File, Exit. You exit the Envoy program and return to WordPerfect with your document still intact.

**TIP** You can also print to the Envoy 7 driver through the Print dialog box.

**TIP** To make each page fit into a single Envoy Viewer screen, select a half-page size in Landscape orientation when you create the file in WordPerfect.

# Using QuickTasks

Corel Office includes a series of common tasks, many of which are performed in WordPerfect, such as creating a certificate, a fax cover sheet, an income statement, or agenda. These tasks are called *QuickTasks*. The QuickTasks are organized into categories such as Publishing or Financial. There is even a QuickTask to aid you in browsing your favorite daily Internet Web pages.

It is not necessary to be in the WordPerfect program to use the QuickTasks. If you select a task to be created in WordPerfect, the program automatically launches for you.

Some of the QuickTasks use a WordPerfect template to assist you. You may be prompted for information important to the creation of the particular document task. For example, if you are using QuickTask to create a certificate, you are prompted for the name of the person receiving the award and the reason for the award. If you are using QuickTask to create a grading sheet, you are asked for the class name and the date. This information is then used in the newly created document and filled in at the appropriate location.

To use QuickTasks:

1. From the Windows 95 Start menu, choose Corel WordPerfect Suite 7, Accessories, Corel QuickTasks.
2. Select the desired task, such as Create Certificate.

You also can access QuickTasks by choosing Help, Help Topics, Show Me, and then selecting the Do It For Me option button in PerfectExpert.

3. Click Run. The QuickTask begins.
4. Follow any prompts in the dialog boxes. (The prompts will vary depending upon the task you selected.)

    The QuickTasks feature creates a new document and may ask you for information to put in it. Depending on which QuickTask you chose, the QuickTask may then pause until you finish editing the document.

5. If applicable, click Continue to complete the project.

    The Finish Document dialog box appears and prompts you for any additional features you would like QuickTasks to do for you including Spell Check, Save, or Print.

6. Select any desired features for QuickTasks (or whatever application you are using) to complete for you, then click Finish.

 If you do not want QuickTasks to complete any of these tasks, click Cancel or press the Esc key, and the dialog box disappears.

## One for All and All for One

Just as one person does not make up a group, one software product doesn't do everything. Although products like WordPerfect can do *almost* everything, we still need the sister products that come with the Corel WordPerfect Suite such as Quattro Pro or Presentations to finish the jobs we all have to do. Hopefully, this chapter has given you some insight on how these products will integrate together to make your computing world a little easier. ●

PART VI

# Techniques from the Pros

**29** Advanced File Management   917

**30** Advanced Macro Techniques   949

**31** Advanced Tables   981

**32** Interactive Documents   1021

**33** Publishing Documents on the World Wide Web   1041

CHAPTER 29

# Advanced File Management

*by Laura Acklen*

In earlier chapters of this book, you learned how to perform basic file-related tasks such as retrieving, saving, and closing documents. You will soon have quite a collection of files, however, and will discover that you need to organize your work. Learning how to manage files is one of the most important skills you can acquire.

WordPerfect's file management tools are powerful and easy to use. To understand how these tools can help you, suppose that you go to a library that has no card catalog and whose books are randomly placed on the shelves. Finding what you need requires a very special librarian who has read *and* remembers everything in the collection and who knows exactly where to find each book.

Fortunately, librarians have shelving systems, catalogs, and references to find and retrieve information efficiently. Likewise, effective use of your collection of documents depends on your ability to find and retrieve the information you need. WordPerfect's file management tools actually surpass the skills of most librarians. To ignore these important skills is akin to searching for a book in a library by browsing the shelves. ■

### Manage system files
The file management features in WordPerfect can be used to move, rename, copy, and delete files.

### Organize files into folders and subfolders
Create an electronic filing system with folders and subfolders to organize your files so you can locate them quickly.

### Customize file and folder lists
The file and folder lists can be altered to display additional information to help you locate the file or folder that you need.

### Locate files with QuickFinder
The QuickFinder feature is a powerful search engine that can be used to locate files based on a wide variety of criteria.

### Set up and use shortcuts in the FAVORITES folder
Add shortcuts to the Windows 95 FAVORITES folder to quickly access frequently-used files and folders.

### Use the QuickFinder Manager to create fast searches that locate files quickly
The QuickFinder Manager, an extension of the QuickFinder feature, gives you the ability to create indexes of your files so you can locate information in the files more efficiently.

# Using the File Management Tools

In WordPerfect 7, file management tools are incorporated into dialog boxes that appear when you need to choose a file. These dialog boxes, called *file management dialog boxes*, appear when you use Open, Save As, Insert File, Insert Image, Select File, Retrieve Equation Text, or any other feature that requires you to specify a file. You can use the file management tools to move, copy, rename, delete, print, and change the properties for a file.

It's important to understand that you can work with virtually any file on your system, not just WordPerfect files. When you need to work with more than one file, you can mark a series of files and then work with them as a group. You also can create new folders to organize related files into groups.

 Although the file management tools are available in every file management dialog box, this section uses the Open dialog box as an example. To access the Open dialog box, click the Open button on the WordPerfect 7 Toolbar, or choose File, Open. Figure 29.1 shows the Open dialog box.

 **T I P** You can also press Ctrl+O to display the Open dialog box.

**FIG. 29.1**
The Open dialog box is the most frequently used file management dialog box.

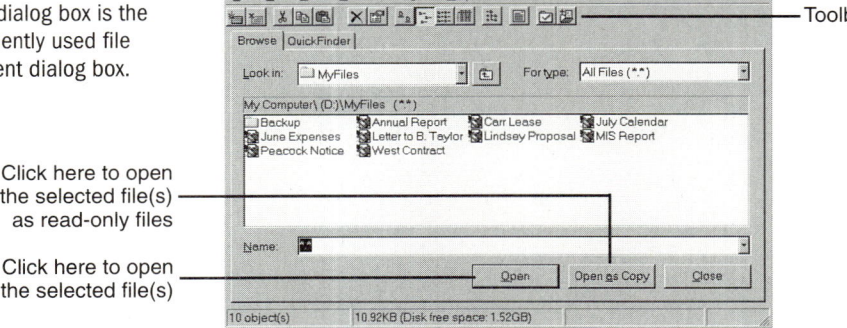

Click here to open the selected file(s) as read-only files

Click here to open the selected file(s)

 **T I P** You can also right-click a file to display a file management QuickMenu, which contains the file management commands.

## Copying and Moving Files

In this latest release of WordPerfect, the technique for moving and copying a file is identical to moving and copying sections of text. You first select the file (or group of files). Then, if you want to copy the file, choose Copy; if you want to move the file, choose Cut.

Both these commands are available on the Edit menu and the QuickMenu (see fig. 29.2). You then switch to the folder (called a *directory* in previous versions of Windows) where you want to place the file(s), then choose Paste from the Edit menu or QuickMenu.

To display the QuickMenu for a file, right-click the file. You can also click the Cut, Copy, and Paste icons on the toolbar to copy and move files.

**FIG. 29.2**
The QuickMenu contains a list of file management commands.

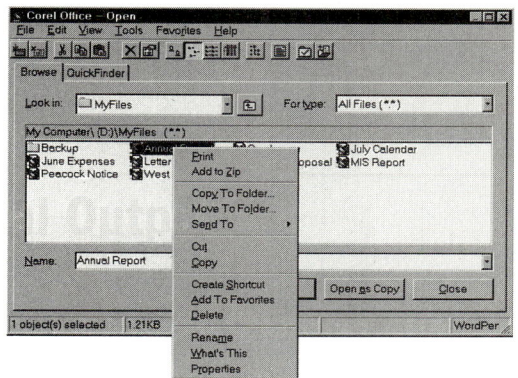

Copy a file before making heavy revisions. Then if anything happens to the document during revision, you can always return to the original copy.

When you choose Copy (or Cut), the name and location of the file (or files) is saved to the Windows Clipboard until you paste the file(s). Then, after you choose Paste, WordPerfect locates the file(s) and copies (or moves) it to the new folder. The interval between copying (or moving) and pasting the file can be as long as you like, as long as you don't copy or cut anything else to the Clipboard.

> **CAUTION**
> If you select another file or group of files and choose Copy (or Cut), you lose the information for the file that you forgot to paste. You have to go back to the folder where the file is located and cut or copy the file(s) again.

If an identical file exists in the destination folder, WordPerfect displays the Confirm File Replace dialog box asking if you want to replace the existing file (see fig. 29.3).

**FIG. 29.3**
WordPerfect prompts you before replacing an existing file with the same name.

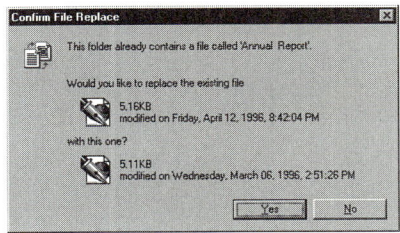

## Renaming Files

When you save your files, you probably try to give them as descriptive a name as possible. Months later, however, the file name might not seem appropriate. You can easily rename a file by clicking the file name once, waiting a second, then clicking again. If you prefer to use the keyboard, select the file and press F2. Either way, a box appears around the file name, and the current name is selected (see fig. 29.4). Type a new name in the box and press Enter to rename the file.

> **CAUTION**
> Make sure you click the file name, not the file icon. Clicking the file icon selects the *file*, not the file *name*. You have to select the file name to rename the file.

**FIG. 29.4**
To rename a file, select the file name, then type a new name.

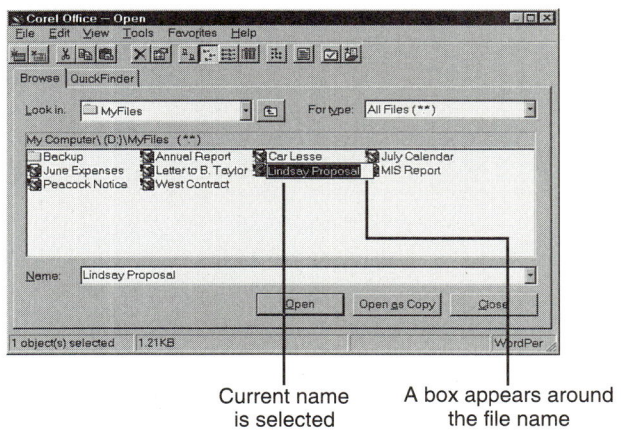

Current name is selected     A box appears around the file name

## Deleting Files

If you no longer need a file, you can delete it from the system. You can delete almost any file; the only exceptions are some program files and files that are marked specifically so they cannot be deleted. To delete a file or group of files, select the file(s), then choose

Delete from the File menu or QuickMenu. You can also click the Delete icon on the Toolbar.

 **T I P** Selecting a file (or group of files) and pressing the Delete key also displays the Confirm File Delete message box.

A Confirm File Delete message box appears, as shown in figure 29.5. Make sure you read the name of the file in the Confirm File Delete message box carefully before responding. Choose Yes to delete the file, or No to cancel the delete operation.

> **CAUTION**
> If you have deselected the Display Delete Confirmation Dialog option in the Properties dialog box of the Recycle Bin, you won't get a Confirm File Delete message box.

**FIG. 29.5**
So you don't delete a file accidentally, you must confirm the deletion of every file.

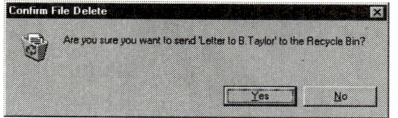

When you delete a file, Windows 95 moves it to the Recycle Bin. If you change your mind, you may be able to recover the file from the Recycle Bin, but only if you haven't emptied it. (When you empty the Recycle Bin, you physically delete the files from the system.) If the Maximum Size of the Recycle Bin (in the Recycle Bin Properties dialog box) has been reached, and you have deleted other additional files, it's possible your file may have been deleted by Windows. Instead, consider using the Cut and Paste commands on the Edit menu to move a file (or group of files) to a floppy disk, which you can then store in a safe location. This technique is known as *archiving*.

## Changing File Attributes

Every file is assigned certain attributes that tell Windows and WordPerfect how to handle the file. In WordPerfect 7, you can set and clear four file attributes:

- Archive
- Read-Only
- Hidden
- System

Select a file, then choose File, Properties. Place a check mark next to the appropriate check box in the property sheet for the file (see fig. 29.6).

>  **TIP** You can also click the Properties icon on the Toolbar to open the property sheet for a selected file.

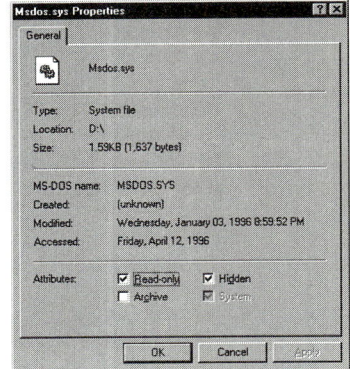

**FIG. 29.6**
You can use the Properties dialog box for the file to set four attributes.

The Archive attribute acts as a reminder to backup programs—such as Microsoft's Backup or Fastback Plus—that this file needs to be backed up. If you deselect the Archive option, the file is excluded from the backup—even if it was modified.

The Hidden attribute designates a file as being hidden, so it does not appear in folder listings. You must know the name of the file to work with it. This attribute is helpful if you are working on confidential files. Although the Hidden attribute may be more secure, you won't have to worry about forgetting the file name if you simply save the file to a disk and keep the disk in a locked drawer.

The Read-Only attribute prevents a file from being modified or deleted. These files can be retrieved and edited in WordPerfect, but they must be saved under a new name. They can also be copied to a new file name. Either way, the original file remains unchanged.

The System attribute designates a file as a system file.

## Opening a File as a Copy

As an alternative to setting a read-only attribute on a file, you can use the Open As Copy option to open a file as a copy, so that the original cannot be modified accidentally. When a file is opened as a copy, it cannot be saved to the original file name. This prevents accidental modification of important files, such as form files or contracts. To open a file as a copy, select the file(s), then choose Open As Copy in any file management dialog box (refer to fig. 29.1).

When you open a file by choosing Open As Copy, the title bar for the document window contains the name of the file and the text (Read-Only) so you know the file has been opened as a read-only file. When you save the file, the Save As dialog box opens automatically, and you have to type a new name for the file. If you accidentally type the original file name, WordPerfect displays a message box indicating that the file already exists and asks if you want to replace it. If you answer Yes here, another message box appears stating that the file was opened as a read-only file and cannot be saved to the original file name.

## Printing a File

You can print a file without retrieving it into a document window by selecting the file (or group of files) and choosing Print from the File menu or the QuickMenu. WordPerfect sends the file directly to the printer.

## Working with More Than One File

If you need to perform a file management function (copy, move, delete, or print) on more than one file, you can select, and then work with, the files as a group. To select a file, click the file name, or use Tab to move to the file list box and then use the arrow keys to move the selection bar to the correct file.

To select a series of contiguous files (files that are next to each other in the list), click the first file name, hold down the Shift key, then click the last file name, or use the arrow keys to highlight the first file, and hold down the Shift key and use the arrow keys to highlight additional files.

To select noncontiguous files, click the first file name, then hold down the Ctrl key and click the other file names. If you want to select all the files and folders in the list, choose Edit, Select All or press Ctrl+A. You can click a blank spot in the window to deselect everything.

## Creating, Renaming, and Removing Folders

Setting up an electronic filing system is just like setting up a filing system for your printed documents. Just as you would take out and label a manila file folder, you can create a folder on the disk and give it a name. Organizing files into folders by account, subject, or project helps you locate the files you need quickly and easily.

To create a folder, choose File (from the file management dialog box), New Folder (or open the QuickMenu and choose New, Folder). The new folder is inserted in the list box with a default name of New Folder. Give the folder a more meaningful name by renaming it. See the earlier section "Renaming Files" if you need a quick review.

While a folder name might seem appropriate when you create the folder, over time the contents of that folder can change. It makes sense to update the name of the folder to match the contents. As you saw earlier in the "Renaming Files" section, you can rename a folder by clicking the folder name, waiting a second, and then clicking the folder name again (or pressing F2). Type a new name, then press Enter.

If you decide that you no longer need a folder, you can remove it from the hard drive. When you archive files that are no longer current, for example, you can choose to remove the folder, also.

To remove a folder, select the folder name in the Look In list box, then choose File, Delete; use the QuickMenu, or click the Delete icon on the Toolbar. WordPerfect displays a Confirm Folder Delete message box similar to the Confirm File Delete message box you saw in the "Deleting Files" section. If you confirm to move the folder, all the files and/or subfolders are moved to the Recycle Bin as well.

### TROUBLESHOOTING

**I moved (or copied) a file to another folder, but now I can't find it.** There is a chance that you might be looking for the wrong file name. Or, you could be looking in the wrong folder. Either way, the fastest way to find the file is to use QuickFinder to search for it. You can either search for the file name, or if you are unsure about the file name, you can search for it based on the text in the file. See the section "Finding Files" later in the chapter for more information on QuickFinder.

**I accidentally deleted an important file—can I get it back?** First of all, make sure you don't empty the Windows 95 Recycle Bin. If the file is still in the Recycle Bin, you can restore it by selecting the file and choosing Restore from the File menu. However, if you have emptied the Recycle Bin, don't do anything else on your computer. Don't save a file, open another file, print a file—don't do anything until you have tried to undelete the file with an Undelete utility. If the utility isn't successful at bringing your file back, you can restore the file from your latest backup. If you don't have a backup with that file on it, as a last resort you can retype the document from a printed copy.

**I can't seem to select more than one file in my file list. When I try to select the second file, it deselects the first one.** Selecting multiple files can be tricky. You have to remember to hold down the Ctrl key when you select the second and subsequent files. If the files are all in a row, you can click the first one, then hold down the Shift key while you click the last one.

▶ See "Saving a Document to Disk," **p. 70**
▶ See "Saving a Document with a Different Name or File Format," **p. 75**
▶ See "Opening a File," **p. 82**
▶ See "Using Insert File To Combine Files," **p. 85**

# Customizing the File/Folder List Display

The View menu contains options that enable you to specify how you want files and folders listed in the file management dialog boxes. The same four options you are accustomed to seeing in Windows Explorer and My Computer (and other Windows 95 applications) are available here, as shown in figure 29.7:

- *Large icons*. Displays the folders and files with large icons, which makes it easier to read the file names. Icons are arranged alphabetically, from left to right.

- *Small icons*. Displays the folders and files with small icons, which makes it possible for more folder and file icons to fit in the window. Icons are arranged alphabetically, from left to right.

- *List*. Displays the folders and files with small icons, arranged alphabetically, from top to bottom.

- *Details*. Displays the folders and files with small icons, along with the size, type, and creation/modification date and time. Icons are arranged alphabetically, from top to bottom.

In addition, a Tree View option divides the list box into two sections. A tree diagram of the drives and folders on your system (and network, if applicable) appears on the left side; a list of folders and files in the selected folder appears on the right side.

**FIG. 29.7**
You use the options on the View menu to customize the list box in file management dialog boxes.

These four options are consistent throughout Windows 95 applications

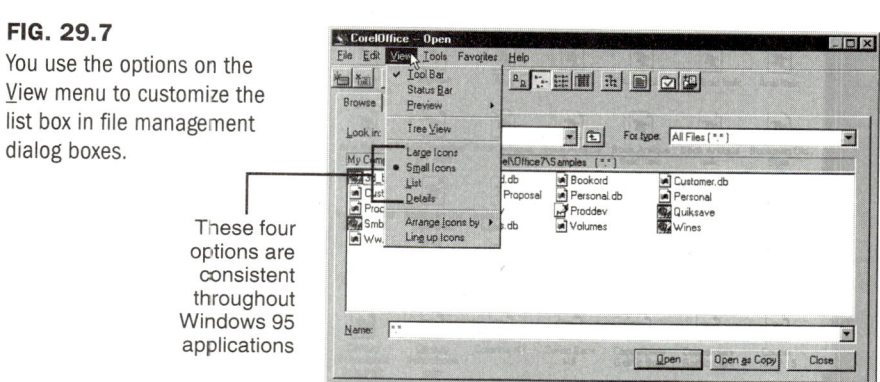

> **N O T E** You can tell WordPerfect to change the default folder each time you change to a different folder in a file management dialog box. The default folder is the one WordPerfect uses to save a file if only a file name is given (instead of the full path name), and also is the one that is selected when you open a file management dialog box.

Choose Edit from a file management dialog box, and select Change Default Folder (so it is checked). If you don't want to change the default folder each time you change folders in a file management dialog box, deselect this option, thus removing the check mark.

## Arranging Files and Folders in the List Box

Making changes to the way files and folders are arranged in the list box can make the difference between finding a file and not finding a file. Larger file icons make it easier to spot a particular file type; smaller icons make it easier to display more files in the window. The Details option arranges the files and folders so you can see all the details (size, date modified, and type of file).

Sorting, or reordering, the files and folders in the list box enables you to group related files together. For example, arranging files by date in descending order shows you the files you modified on a given date. When you are displaying the file list using the Details option, four buttons (Name, Size, Type, and Modified) stretch across the top of the list box. Click any of the buttons one time, and the file list is then sorted by that column. Click the button again, and the file list is sorted in reverse order.

Finally, switching to the Tree View gives you a broader view of your system. When you work from many folders spread across several drives, Tree View can make it easier to navigate through all the drives and folders. This type of view is similar to the arrangement of the Open File dialog box in previous versions of WordPerfect for Windows.

**Displaying File and Folder Information** In figure 29.4, the icons in the list box are shown in small size by default. While this view allows you to see more files at one time, larger icons make it easier to read file names and identify file types. To switch to larger icons, choose View, Large Icons or click the Large Icons button on the Toolbar. Figure 29.8 shows the list box with the larger icons displayed.

**FIG. 29.8**
The Large Icons setting makes it easier to identify the different types of files.

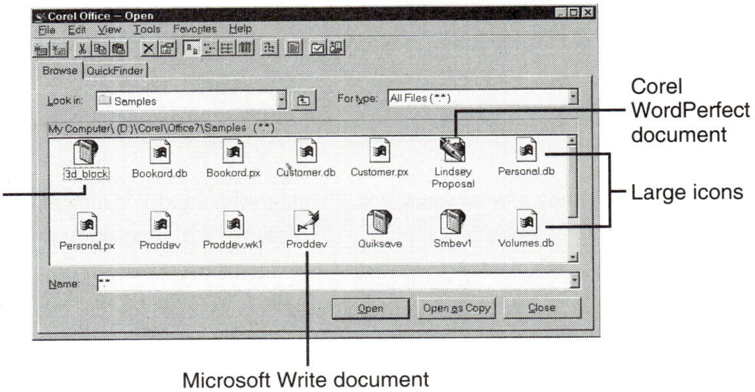

The Large Icons and Small Icons settings arrange the icons alphabetically with folders first, then files. The icons are arranged across columns, from left to right. The List option arranges the icons alphabetically, from top to bottom. This way, you can read *down* the list of files, in alphabetical order, rather than trying to read *across* the columns. To switch to List view, choose View, List or click the List icon on the Toolbar.

 The Large Icons, Small Icons, and List options only display the folder or file name with the icon. When you need to know more about the folder or file, use the Details option. This view adds the size of the folder or file, the type of file, and the date and time created or modified. To switch to the Details view, choose View, Details or click the Details icon on the Toolbar.

In Details view, a set of column headings is added to the top of the list box, as shown in figure 29.9. The information for some files in the Type column has an ellipsis (...) at the end. This means there is more information than fits in the column. You can resize any column to see more of the information by clicking and dragging the column border. When you move the mouse pointer over the border between columns, the mouse pointer changes to a resizing mouse pointer. Click and drag this pointer to resize the columns.

**FIG. 29.9**
Click and drag the column borders to resize the columns.

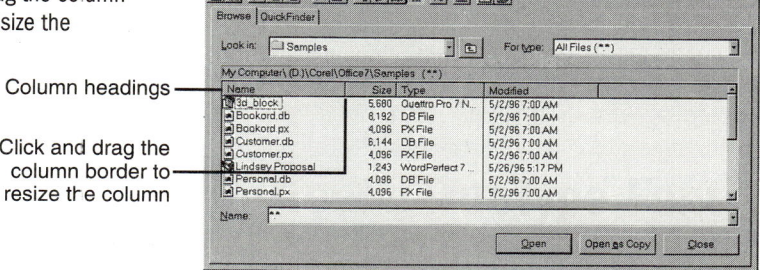

Column headings

Click and drag the column border to resize the column

**Sorting the File List** By using the Arrange Icons By options, you can specify the method for sorting files in the list. You can sort folders and files by file name, size, type, and revision date/time. This is an easy way to group related files together. For example, if you sort the files by date, you can see all the files that you worked on in a given time period. Or, you might choose to sort the files by type so you can group all your WordPerfect document files together. To sort the folders and files, choose View, Arrange Icons By, then choose Name, Size, Type, or Date.

 If you switch to Details view, you can click the column headings to sort folders and files. For example, if you want to sort by the modification date, click the Modified column heading. If you want to sort by the name, click the Name column heading. Clicking the same column heading switches between an ascending or descending sort.

## Switching to Tree View

 If you've used earlier versions of WordPerfect, you are accustomed to several list boxes in the Open dialog box. One list box contains the list of drives, one contains the list of folders, and one contains the list of files. The list of folders has always been shown in a "tree diagram" format where the folders and subfolders are shown as branches of the trunk which represents the current drive. This format is also available in this newest version of WordPerfect. To switch to a tree diagram format, choose View, Tree View, or click the Tree View icon on the Toolbar.

When you turn on Tree View view, the list box that formerly listed all folders and files in the current folder is divided into two sections (see fig. 29.10). The left side is a tree diagram of the drives and folders available on your system. The right side is the list of folders and files in the currently selected folder.

**FIG. 29.10**
Tree View view makes it easier to navigate through the drives and folders on your system.

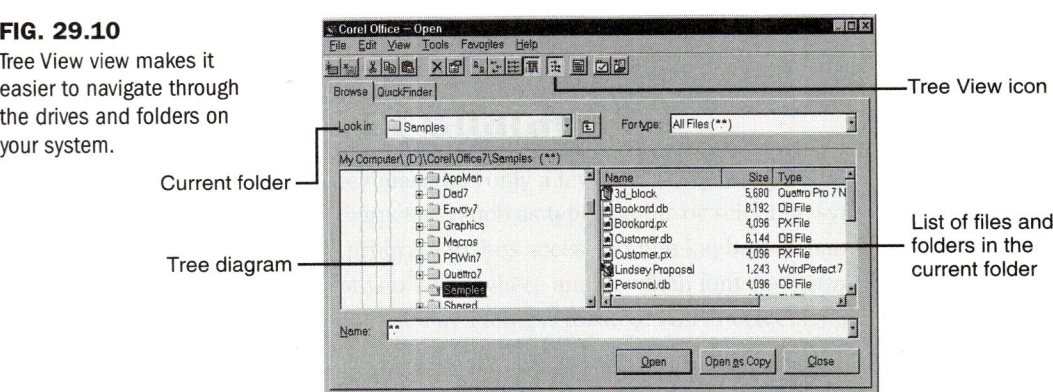

# Finding Files

With today's large hard drives, you can store literally thousands of files on one disk, which makes the task of locating files a daunting one. Learning the methods that you can use to search for files is one of the most important skills you can master. In previous chapters, you learned how to browse through file lists in the file management dialog boxes. You scrolled through the current list of files and changed folders to look at lists of files in other folders. This approach has several major disadvantages:

- Disk drives may contain so many folders that looking through each folder is tedious and time-consuming.

- Folders may contain so many files that scanning the file names to find the file you want is impractical.

- You may have assigned a file name that, at the time, seemed to adequately describe the file contents. Days later, however, the file name may not seem meaningful.
- You may not remember the name of the file.

Although organizing files into folders and subfolders can help reduce the time you take to find a particular file, this method isn't always foolproof. WordPerfect provides a number of methods that you can use to locate files in a folder, subfolder, or disk. From displaying a specific file list to using the search options in the QuickFinder page of the file management dialog boxes, you are sure to find the file(s) you are looking for. In addition, WordPerfect also includes a file search utility, called QuickFinder, and the ability to add shortcuts to the Windows 95 FAVORITES folder described in later sections in this chapter.

## Listing Files by Type

The For Type option appears in most file management dialog boxes. A drop-down list of file types (such as text, macros, and documents) is available (see fig. 29.11). This list references certain file name extensions that are assigned to files to indicate the file type (for example, WPD for WordPerfect documents). In most Windows 95 applications, file extensions are hidden from view because they are used primarily by the applications to identify special types of files (such as macros or templates). To view a file's extension, right-click the file and choose Properties from the QuickMenu. The extension is shown in the MS-DOS file name.

**FIG. 29.11**
The For Type drop-down list has options that help you group WordPerfect files with a certain extension together.

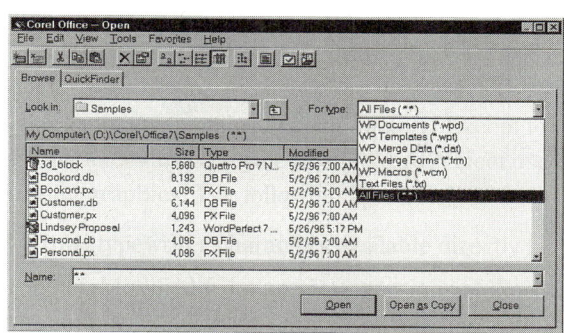

> **NOTE** WordPerfect 7 can maintain two file names for each file:
> - Long file name
> - MS-DOS file name
>
> In previous releases of WordPerfect, you could assign the standard MS-DOS file name of eight characters and a three-letter extensions, separated by a period. For example, LINDSEY.LTR is a

*continues*

*continued*

MS-DOS file name. You also had the option of creating a descriptive file name in the document summary, which could then be displayed in the file list to make it easier to identify a file.

In WordPerfect 7, descriptive file names have been replaced by the longer file name made possible by Windows 95. File names can be as long as 255 characters and can now include spaces. For example, LINDSEY LETTER is a long file name. When you give a file a long file name, WordPerfect automatically assigns a MS-DOS file name with the first six characters of the long file name, followed by a tilde and a number, depending on how many file names began with those same six characters. An extension of WPD is automatically added to identify the file as a WordPerfect document. For example, the file LINDSEY LETTER would be assigned the name LINDSE~1.WPD. The two file names make it possible for you to share documents with people who use earlier versions of WordPerfect that only recognize MS-DOS file names.

 If you can't see the WPD extension on your WordPerfect documents, you need to launch Explorer and change the Windows filename viewing option. Click the Start button on the taskbar, and select Programs, then Windows Explorer. Choose View, Options, and remove the check from the Hide MS-DOS File Extensions For File Types That Are Registered check box. Choose OK, and close Explorer. The next time you open a file management dialog box in WordPerfect, you can see the WPD extensions on your file names.

When you select one of the file types from the For Type drop-down list, WordPerfect displays a new file list with only the files that have the selected extension. This feature comes in handy when you are trying to locate a merge file, for example, in the midst of other types of files.

## Creating a Partial Listing Using DOS Wildcard Characters

Occasionally, you might need to be able to work from a specific list of files rather than from the list of every file in a folder. You can create a custom list of files by using DOS wildcard characters to represent a portion of the file name. By listing only files that match the pattern, you can narrow down the list to a manageable size.

Two DOS wildcard characters—* and ?—are available. The asterisk (*) stands for *any number* of characters, and the question mark (?) stands for *any one character*. The following examples in table 29.1 use these wild cards.

**Table 29.1  Using MS-DOS Wildcard Characters**

| Wild Card | Locates |
| --- | --- |
| *.* | All file names. |
| *.LTR | All files names with an LTR extension. |

| | |
|---|---|
| REPORT*.* | All files names that begin with REPORT, such as REPORT95.LST, REPORT.TBL, and REPORTS.FIN. |
| M*.FRM | All files that begin with an M and have an FRM extension, such as M.FRM, MEMO.FRM, MINUTES.FRM, MISSING.FRM, and MBTA.FRM. |
| L?ST | The files that are named LIST, LAST, and LOST, but not LEAST. |

You can create a custom list of files from any folder dialog box. Type the file pattern you want to display in the Name text box, and then choose Open or press Enter.

## Using QuickFinder To Search for Files

Although the previously mentioned features are helpful and easy to use, the QuickFinder feature provides the real muscle for locating files. QuickFinder goes beyond searching for patterns in file names to searching for patterns of words in documents. If you fill in the document summaries, you can search any item in these summaries. You can expand the search for files from the current folder to a subfolder of the drive, or even the entire drive. You can use the QuickFinder File Indexer to create indexes of files that can be searched much more quickly. (The QuickFinder File Indexer is covered later in the section "Using the QuickFinder File Indexer.")

To access the QuickFinder page in a file management dialog box, click the QuickFinder tab. If this is the first time you have clicked the QuickFinder tab, you see a QuickFinder Fast Search Setup Expert dialog box. Choose the Don't Pre-Search button. The QuickFinder dialog box appears (see fig. 29.12).

**FIG. 29.12**
Use the QuickFinder page of a file management dialog box to specify the criteria for a file search.

Search for patterns in file names

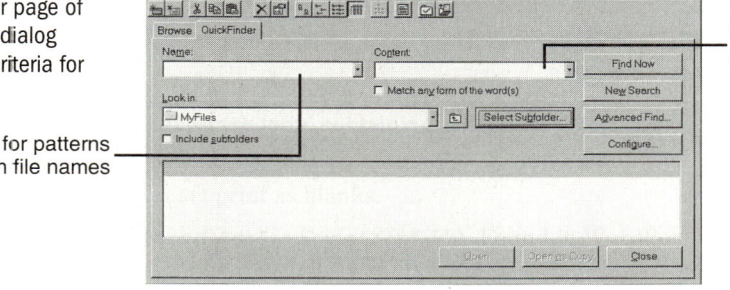

Search for word patterns in files

**Searching for Files by Name**   For those times when you know the name of the file but not where it is stored, type the file name in the Name text box. Next, choose where you want to search for the file. You can search through a folder, subfolder, or entire drive. Click the Look In drop-down list arrow to choose from the list of drives and folders on your system. Once you have chosen a drive or folder, you can select a particular subfolder by clicking Select Subfolder. This option opens the QuickFinder Select Subfolder dialog box where you can browse through the selected drive or folder and choose a specific subfolder. Click a folder and choose Select to return to the Open dialog box.

The name of the drive, folder, or subfolder you have chosen appears in the Look In list box. If you want to include subfolders in the search, place a check mark in the Include Subfolders check box.

**Searching for Word Patterns in Documents** To search for a particular word or word pattern, click the Content text box and type the word (or word pattern). If you type **Taylor**, for example, WordPerfect searches for files that contain the word Taylor anywhere in the file.

Place a check mark in the Match Any Form Of The Word(s) check box to search for different forms of the word(s) you typed in the Content text box. For example, if you search for the word **evict**, QuickFinder looks for other forms of the word, such as *evicting*, *evicted*, or *eviction*.

You can build more complex searches by using the advanced search options. Click Advanced Find to open the Advanced Find dialog box, as shown in figure 29.13. The top section of the dialog box has the same Look In section as the QuickFinder page, with one exception. If you have created custom searches with the QuickFinder Manager, choose Custom Search, then choose a custom search from the Look In drop-down list. (The QuickFinder Manager is covered in more detail in the "Using QuickFinder Manager" section later in this chapter.)

> **NOTE** If you have not yet created a fast search file, the Custom Search option is dimmed in the Advanced Find dialog box.

**FIG. 29.13**
You can build more complex searches with the options in the Advanced Find dialog box.

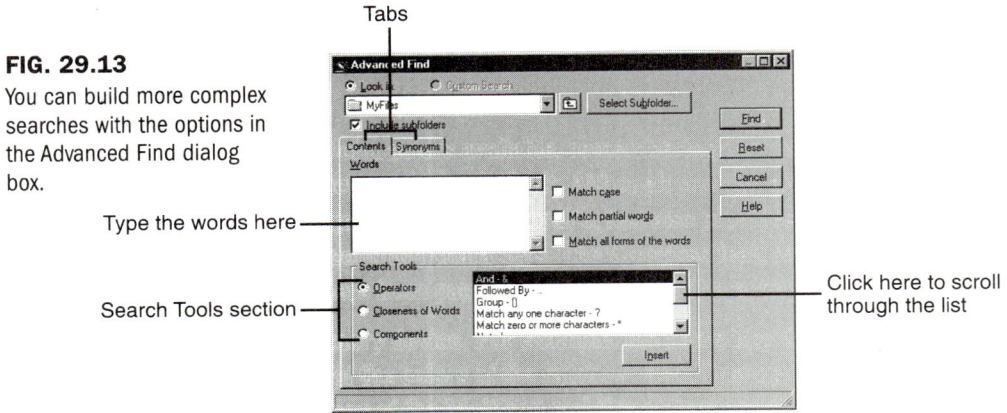

There are two tabs underneath the Look In section: Contents and Synonyms. By default, the Contents tab is selected, so the Contents page is displayed. The Contents page is an expansion of the Content text box in the QuickFinder page. Click the Words text box and type the word or word pattern you want to search for.

You can significantly narrow the scope of the search by conducting a case-sensitive search or a partial word search in addition to the different word form search. You can also use the Search Tools section to specify how the words are found in the documents.

**Specifying Case-Sensitive Searches** The Match Case option enables you to specify whether or not you want a case-sensitive search. The default search is not case-sensitive. If you place a check mark in the Match Case check box, WordPerfect compares the case of the words (not just the word itself) for a correct match.

**Searching for Partial Words** When you need to search for a partial word, so you can catch similar words in the search, you use the Match Partial Words option. For example, when searching through technical papers, you might want to find all the documents with the words *psychoanalyst*, *psychologist*, and *psychedelic*; you can search for the word *psych* with the Match Partial Words option selected and WordPerfect would locate documents that contain words beginning with *psych*.

**Finding Different Forms of a Word** The Match Any Form Of The Word(s) check box is the same as the option on the QuickFinder page of the Open dialog box. This option searches for different forms of the word(s) you typed in the Words text box. For example, if you search for the word **evict**, QuickFinder looks for other forms of the word, such as *evicting*, *evicted*, or *eviction*.

**Using Operators** A series of search operators appears in the list box in the Search Tools section. First, position the insertion point after the word. Select the operator, then click Insert. When you select an operator from the list, a symbol that represents the operator is inserted in the Words text box.

**TIP** If you prefer, you can type the operator symbols with the keys on the keyboard, rather than selecting them from the Search Operators dialog box.

The following table provides a list of the operator symbols and their descriptions.

| Search Operator | Description |
| --- | --- |
| & | And |
| \| | Or |
| ! | Not |

*continues*

*continued*

| Search Operator | Description |
|---|---|
| .. | Followed by |
| ( ) | Group |

The following examples in table 29.2 show valid search patterns that use operators.

**Table 29.2 Using Operators in Searches**

| Pattern | Files Selected Contain... |
|---|---|
| `Benjamin&Taylor` | *Benjamin* and *Taylor*. |
| `Benjamin|Taylor` | *Benjamin* or *Taylor*. |
| `Benjamin&Taylor|Andrews` | *Benjamin* and also *Taylor* or *Andrews*. |
| `Benjamin&"recycling efforts"` | *Benjamin* and the exact phrase *recycling efforts*. |
| `!Taylor` | Does not contain *Taylor*. |
| `Taylor!Andrews` | *Taylor* but not *Andrews*. |
| `Benjamin..Taylor` | *Benjamin* followed by *Taylor*. |
| `(recycling plastic paper)` | All three words, in any order. |
| `"aquifer"` | Only the exact phrase: *aquifer*. |

**Using Wildcard Characters**  The ? and * are called *wildcard characters* and can also be used to limit a list of files (see the section "Creating a Partial Listing Using DOS Wildcard Characters" earlier in this chapter). Use these wildcard characters to search for partial words, which will further limit your search.

The following examples show valid search patterns that use wildcard characters.

| Pattern | Files Selected Contain... |
|---|---|
| `ta?` | tan, tar, tab, tad and so on. |
| `expen*` | expense, expenditure, expend. |
| `"elect*"` | Finds the exact pattern as a portion of something longer: *elect, election, electoral, electing, electricity.* |

However, if you need to search for a word that actually contains an asterisk or a question mark, you'll need to turn off the wildcard search. Use the Treat "*" And "?" As Characters (Not Wildcards) and Treat "*" And "?" As Wildcards options in the drop-down list of search operators to turn the wildcard search capability on and off.

**Specifying the Closeness of Words**  You can limit the search to finding words and word patterns only if they are found within certain boundaries. Position the insertion point before the word pattern you want affected by the search limitation and choose Closeness of Words to display a list of options in the list box (see fig. 29.14).

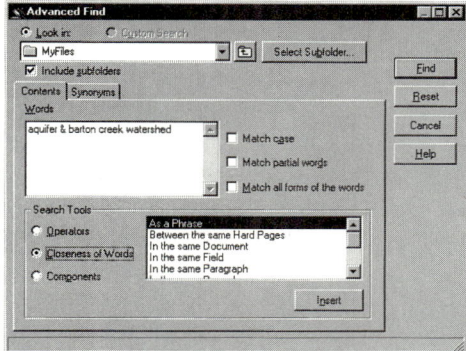

**FIG. 29.14**
The Closeness of Words option limits the search to certain boundaries within the document.

When chosen, each option inserts a forward slash (\), followed by the selection's name. The exception is the Within # Words option, which inserts a forward slash (/), followed by the number 5, which you can change to the desired number.

**Specifying Which Part of the Document To Search**  You can restrict the search to a certain part of a document, rather than searching the entire document, which can greatly reduce the time taken to perform the search. You might decide to limit the search, for example, to the first page only.

To specify what part of the document to search, position the insertion point before the word pattern you want affected by the search limitation and choose Components to display a list of options (see fig. 29.15). Select an option from the list and click Insert. When chosen, each option inserts a forward slash (\), followed by the selection's name.

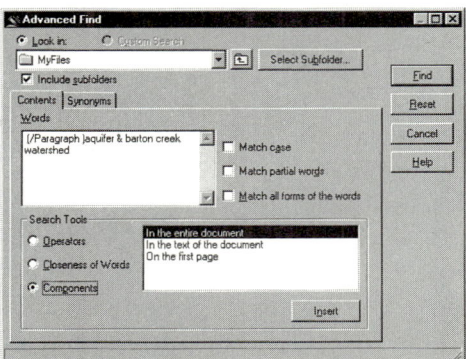

**FIG. 29.15**
You can use the Components options to limit the search to a certain part of the document.

**TIP** If you prefer (and you can remember them), you can type the slash and the document component name rather than choosing them from the menu.

The In The Entire Document option searches the document text and all substructures (headers, footers, and so on). The On The First Page option searches only the first page, and the In The Text Of The Document option limits the search to the document text (no substructures).

**Expanding Word Searches**   The Synonyms tab switches to the Synonyms page of the Advanced Find dialog box (see fig. 29.16), which is used to expand QuickFinder searches by including synonyms of words in the Words text box. This is helpful if you aren't exactly sure which word is used in the document. This should reduce the number of searches you perform because you can include search words and selected alternatives in a single search.

The Concept Net section enables you to choose from a list of synonyms so you can search for a word and related words in one step. Clicking the Look Up button produces a list of synonyms for the original search word. For example, if you type the word **distribute** in the Words text box and click Look Up, WordPerfect's Thesaurus provides a list of synonyms in the list box on the right. You can choose from synonyms such as *circulate*, *disburse*, and *publish*. WordPerfect searches for the word *distribute* and any of the synonyms you select from the Concept Net section.

**FIG. 29.16**
The Concept Net section is used to expand word searches by searching for synonyms of a word.

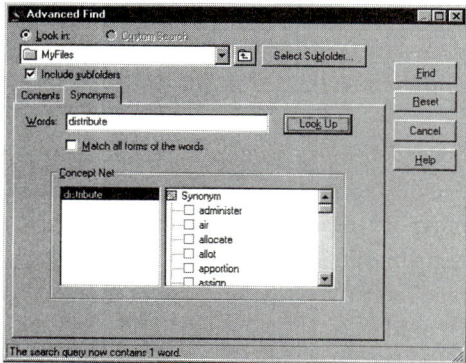

▶ **See** "Using Document Summaries," **p. 201**
▶ **See** "Customizing the Document Summary Fields," **p. 205**

**TROUBLESHOOTING**

**I'm trying to search for text in a file, and WordPerfect says it can't find the file. I know it's in the folder somewhere—what am I doing wrong?** Make sure the operators you are using are placed in front of the text you are searching for. Also, try using a partial word search using * or ? so you have a greater chance of finding what you are looking for. Try using the Match Any Form of the Word(s) option or the Concept Net section to search for alternate word forms. Remember, the phrase you type must be found in the document, or WordPerfect tells you the file is not found.

# Using the FAVORITES Folder

Although organizing files into folders and subfolders is a good management practice, remembering the exact location (and typing it correctly) can be difficult. You can save yourself the trouble by creating shortcuts to the files and folders you use most often. These shortcuts are stored in the FAVORITES folder, which is created when you install Windows 95. You can create as many shortcuts as you need to make it easier to navigate through your system. You can even assign descriptive names to help you remember the contents of a particular folder or file.

## Opening the FAVORITES Folder

 File management dialog boxes include two Favorites icons on the Toolbar: Go To/From Favorites and Add To Favorites. Clicking the Go To/From Favorites icon opens the FAVORITES folder and displays the contents in the list box (see fig. 29.17). You can also choose Favorites, Go To/From Favorites, if you prefer.

**FIG. 29.17**
You can have an unlimited number of shortcuts in the

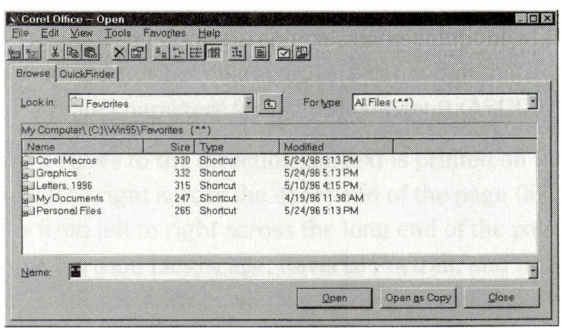

To choose a shortcut to a folder, click the shortcut icon, then choose Open, or double-click the shortcut icon. The new folder name appears at the top of the file management box, and the new list of files appears in the list box. To choose a shortcut to a file, click the file icon, then click Open. WordPerfect opens the file in a new document window.

## Adding Shortcuts to the FAVORITES Folder

You can add as many shortcuts to the FAVORITES folder as you need. Any folder or file on any drive can be referenced by a shortcut.

To add a shortcut to a folder, open the folder, then choose Favorites, Add, or click the Add To Favorites icon. A pop-up list with two options appears, as shown in figure 29.18. Choose Add Favorite Folder to create a shortcut for the currently selected folder, and add it to the FAVORITES folder.

**FIG. 29.18**
You use the Add To Favorites option to create shortcuts to folders and files.

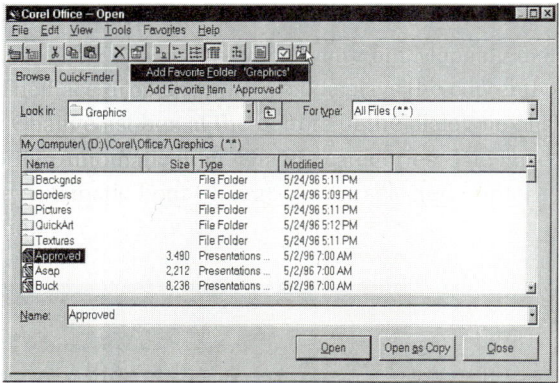

To add a shortcut to a file, select the file, then choose Favorites, Add, or click the Add To Favorites icon. Choose Add Favorite Item to create a shortcut for the currently selected file, and add it to the FAVORITES folder.

When you create a shortcut, the name of the folder or file is used as the shortcut name. You can, however, give a shortcut a more descriptive name to make it easier to remember the contents. Right-click the shortcut, then choose Rename. Type a new name for the shortcut, then press Enter.

## Deleting Shortcuts from the FAVORITES Folder

The shortcuts in the FAVORITES folder make it faster for you to access the folders and files you use the most. However, over time, the FAVORITES folder can become cluttered with outdated shortcuts. It's a good idea to periodically clean out the folder, deleting old shortcuts that you don't use anymore. To delete a shortcut, right-click the shortcut icon, then choose <u>D</u>elete, or press the <u>D</u>elete key. WordPerfect displays a message box asking if you are sure you want to send the shortcut to the Recycle Bin. Read the message carefully to make sure the correct shortcut is being deleted, then choose <u>Y</u>es to send the shortcut to the Recycle Bin.

### TROUBLESHOOTING

**I can't get one of my shortcuts to a file to work. I click the file, then choose Open and nothing happens.** If the file (or folder) has been deleted, moved or renamed, the shortcut won't be able to find it. Try to locate the file by browsing through other folders on your system, or try to find the file by searching for a piece of text in the file (using QuickFinder). When you find the file, delete the old shortcut, then create a new shortcut for the file.

## Using the QuickFinder Manager

In the "Finding Files" section earlier in the chapter, you learned how to use the QuickFinder feature to locate files with certain word patterns. As powerful as this feature is, the QuickFinder Manager takes the concept one step further by allowing you to create a Fast Search that speeds up the search process. A *Fast Search* is a compressed file that contains a list of all the words in all the files in a particular folder or group of folders. (This type of file is also called an *index file*.) It's much faster for QuickFinder to search through one file than to search through each individual file. The result is a dramatic increase in the speed of the search.

You should create a Fast Search for the folders (and groups of folders) that you search most often. For example, during a trial, you might search through a folder of depositions dozens of times. Create a Fast Search for that folder and search through the Fast Search file rather than searching through each deposition.

### Starting the QuickFinder Manager

You use the QuickFinder Manager to create and edit a Fast Search. You can create a standard Fast Search, which contains a single folder and its subfolders, or you can create a custom Fast Search, which contains one or more folders with or without their subfolders. You can create an unlimited number of Fast Searches, but you should try to keep them small—create a Fast Search for each element in a project rather than one Fast Search for the entire project.

To start the QuickFinder Manager, select File, Open, then click the QuickFinder tab in the Open dialog box. Click the Configure button, and the QuickFinder Manager dialog box appears, as shown in figure 29.19. Existing Fast Searches are shown in the list box. The tabs at the top of the dialog box switch back and forth between the Standard Fast Search Setup and the Custom Fast Search Setup, and QuickFinder visibility.

> **CAUTION**
> Unless your computer has large amounts of memory and drive space, you probably should not try to index your entire hard disk. Instead, create indexes for the different classes and types of documents you have.

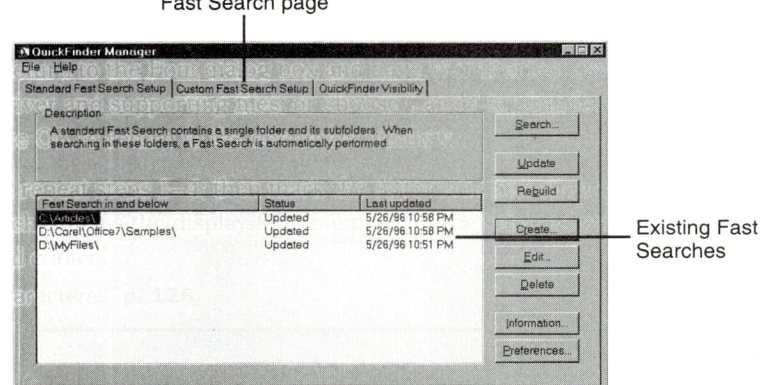

**FIG. 29.19**
The QuickFinder Manager dialog box contains a list of existing Fast Searches in the list box.

## Creating a Standard Fast Search

You can create two types of Fast Searches: Standard and Custom. A *Standard Fast Search* can only contain one folder with all its subfolders. A *Custom Fast Search* can contain multiple folders, with or without their subfolders. Both types of Fast Searches are easy to create and maintain.

If you organize your files into folders and subfolders, your files are already grouped together by subject and are quite easy to work with. If you recall, *archive files* are files you plan to move from your hard disk to floppy disks or a tape backup cassette. Follow these steps to create a Standard Fast Search for the archive folder:

> **NOTE** By default, QuickFinder creates a Fast Search information file in the folder you selected for the Standard Fast Search. The secondary location for the Standard Fast Search file is C:\COREL\OFFICE7\SHARED\QFINDER7.

1. From the QuickFinder Manager dialog box, click C<u>r</u>eate. The QuickFinder Standard Fast Search dialog box appears, as shown in figure 29.20.

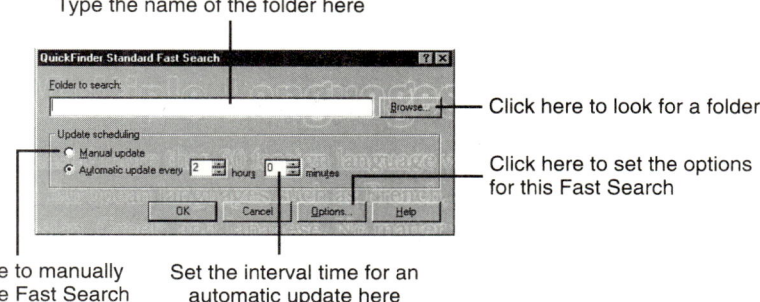

**FIG. 29.20**
Use the Create QuickFinder Standard Search dialog box to create a Fast Search for one folder and its subfolders.

2. You need to tell QuickFinder which folder to include in the Fast Search. (Remember, a Standard Fast Search can only have one folder with its subfolders.) In the <u>F</u>older To Search text box, type the full path name of the folder you want to include. For this example, type **c:\archive**.

> **N O T E** In a Standard Fast Search, the subfolders of the chosen folder are automatically included. If you don't want to include the subfolders, create a Custom Fast Search instead, which can be created without including the subfolders.

3. By default, an automatic update is selected in the Update Scheduling section. The default update interval is two hours. This means that while your system is running (in Windows 95), QuickFinder updates the Fast Search files every two hours. You can choose <u>M</u>anual Update, or use the spinner to set the number of hours and/or minutes.

4. If necessary, click <u>O</u>ptions to open the Options dialog box where you can change the settings for the Fast Search. These settings are discussed in the section "Setting Preferences in the QuickFinder Manager." The changes you make through the QuickFinder Fast Search Options dialog box only affect the current Fast Search. To change the settings for all Standard Fast Searches, click <u>P</u>references in the QuickFinder Manager dialog box.

5. Choose OK to create the Fast Search.

WordPerfect adds the new Fast Search to the list box in the QuickFinder Manager dialog box. The word Updating in the status column next to the new entry indicates the Fast Search is being updated. When the updating is completed, the word Updated appears in the Status column. The date and time the Fast Search was updated appears in the Last Updated column.

The next time you use QuickFinder to search for a file, by name or content, in this folder, a Fast Search is automatically performed. In other words, QuickFinder knows if you have created a Fast Search for a folder, and if you have, searches the Fast Search file instead of each file in the folder.

## Creating a Custom Fast Search

A Custom Fast Search is more flexible than a Standard Fast Search in that you can build a list of folders to search, rather than conducting a separate QuickFinder search for each folder. Also, you can choose to exclude certain subfolders. For example, if you want to include the files in the C:\LINDSEY folder but not the files in the C:\LINDSEY\DEPOSITIONS subfolder, you need to create a Custom Fast Search. Follow these steps to create a Custom Fast Search for some of the files included with the WordPerfect programs:

**NOTE** If you have a Custom Fast Search, the Fast Search information file is created in the C:\COREL\OFFICE7\SHARED\QFINDER7 on your drive.

1. From the QuickFinder Manager dialog box, click the Custom Fast Search Setup tab, then click Create. The QuickFinder Custom Fast Search dialog box appears, as shown in figure 29.21.

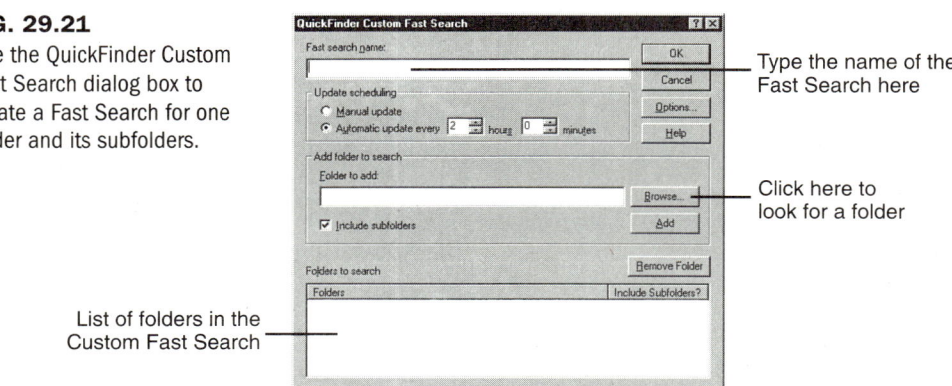

**FIG. 29.21**
Use the QuickFinder Custom Fast Search dialog box to create a Fast Search for one folder and its subfolders.

Type the name of the Fast Search here

Click here to look for a folder

List of folders in the Custom Fast Search

2. Type a descriptive name for the Custom Fast Search in the Fast Search Name text box. For this example, type **Corel Office Files**.

3. By default, an automatic update is selected in the Update Scheduling section. The default update interval is two hours. This means that while your system is running (in Windows 95), QuickFinder updates the Fast Search files every two hours. You

can choose <u>M</u>anual Update, or use the spinner to set the number of hours and/or minutes.

4. If necessary, click <u>O</u>ptions to change the settings for the Fast Search. These settings are discussed in the section "Setting Preferences in the QuickFinder Manager." The changes you make through the QuickFinder Fast Search Options dialog box only affect the current Fast Search. To change the settings for all Standard Fast Searches, click <u>P</u>references in the QuickFinder Manager dialog box.

5. You need to tell QuickFinder which folders to include in the Fast Search. In the <u>F</u>older To Add text box, type the full path name of the folder you want to include. For this example, type the path for your Corel Office sample files (**C:\Corel\Office7\Samples**).

6. If you don't want to include subfolders in the Fast Search, remove the check mark in the <u>I</u>nclude Subfolders check box.

7. Click <u>A</u>dd or press Enter to add the folder to the Fo<u>l</u>ders To Search list box.

8. In the <u>F</u>older To Add text box, type the full path name of the second folder you want to include. For this example, type the path for the Corel Office MYFILES folder (**C:\Corel\Office7\Myfiles**).

9. Click <u>A</u>dd or press Enter to add the folder to the Fo<u>l</u>ders To Search list box.

10. Continue adding folders to the list of Fo<u>l</u>ders To Search until you have added all the relevant folders to the list. If necessary, click the <u>B</u>rowse button to open the QuickFinder—Select Folder dialog box where you can look through the available drives for another folder.

11. Click OK to return to the QuickFinder Manager dialog box.

WordPerfect adds the new Fast Search to the list box in the QuickFinder Manager dialog box. The word Updating in the Status column next to the new entry indicates the Fast Search is being updated. When the updating is completed, the word Updated appears in the Status column. The date and time the Fast Search was updated appears in the Last Updated column.

The next time you use QuickFinder to search for a file, by name or content, in a folder used in a Custom Fast Search, a Fast Search will only be performed if you have the Custom Fast Search selected in the Advanced Find dialog box. Once you have selected C<u>u</u>stom Search, choose the search name from the drop-down list. In other words, QuickFinder won't use the Custom Fast Search file unless you tell it to.

## Editing a Fast Search

As you add new folders and subfolders to your system, you might want to edit your Fast Searches to add these new folders or to remove the folders that are no longer applicable.

> **NOTE** If you want to add a new Fast Search, follow the steps in the earlier sections "Creating a Standard Fast Search" and "Creating a Custom Fast Search."

To edit an existing Fast Search:

1. Choose File, Open, and click the QuickFinder tab.
2. Click the Configure button.
3. Select the Fast Search in the list box, and click Edit.

   In a Standard Fast Search, you can change the method of updating, and you can edit the options. In a Custom Fast Search, you can also add and delete the folders to search.

4. In a Custom Fast Search, add or remove folders in the Folders To Search list box. To remove a folder, select it in the list box, then click Remove Folder.

   To add a folder, type the full path of the folder in the Folder To Add text box, or click Browse to open the QuickFinder—Select Folder dialog box where you can look for a folder. Highlight a folder, then choose Select.

5. If necessary, change the method of updating or modify the options for the fast search.
6. Choose OK to save your changes and to update the Fast Search.

## Updating a Fast Search

Searching for files with a Fast Search is effective only if you maintain it well. A Fast Search can quickly become outdated as documents are added and deleted from folders. When you create a Fast Search, the default setting is to automatically update the Fast Searches every two hours (while the system is running). If you prefer, you can change the update interval to a specific number of hours or minutes. You can also choose to manually update a file, so you can update the file whenever you like.

To update a Fast Search, select a Fast Search in the list box, then click Update. The status column displays the message Waiting to update, then Updating, and then Updated when the update process is complete.

## Displaying Fast Search Information

Each Fast Search has an information sheet that you can view. To display the information sheet for a Fast Search (either Standard or Custom), select the Fast Search, then click Information. The QuickFinder Fast Search Information dialog box opens, as shown in figure 29.22.

**FIG. 29.22**
The QuickFinder Fast Search Information dialog box appears for the Corel Office Files Fast Search.

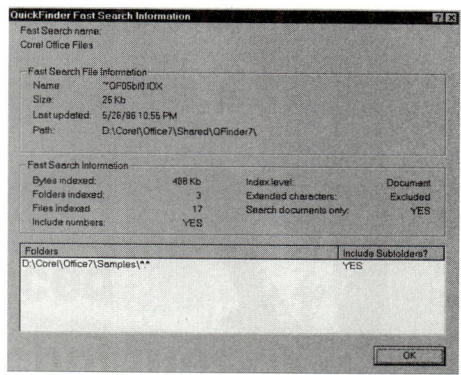

The name of the Fast Search is shown in the upper-left corner. The next section tells you the name of the Fast Search information file, which has an IDX extension. (The IDX extension is often used to indicate an index file.) The size of the file of the IDX file is shown—notice how much smaller this file is compared to the total number of bytes indexed (shown in the Fast Search Information section). The index file is much smaller, because it's compressed. The path of the IDX file is given so you know where the file is stored on your system.

In the Fast Search Information section, the total number of bytes indexed as well as the number of files and folders; this is shown to give you an idea of how much information is contained in the Fast Search. The other four options show you the settings you chose when you created the Fast Search. These settings are covered in detail in the next section.

> **CAUTION**
> Take care to not accidentally delete a Fast Search Information File (with the IDX extension). The name of the file is cryptic and can easily be mistaken for a misplaced temporary file.

## Setting Preferences in the QuickFinder Manager

When creating a Fast Search, you can specify what the index will contain, which files to exclude, what level of indexing will be done, and how to handle extended characters. To change these options for all new indexes, click Preferences in the QuickFinder Manager dialog box (see fig. 29.23).

To change the preferences for a new index, click Edit in the QuickFinder Manager dialog box, then Options; the dialog box shown in figure 29.24 appears.

**FIG. 29.23**
Changes made in the QuickFinder Preferences dialog box affect all new Fast Searches.

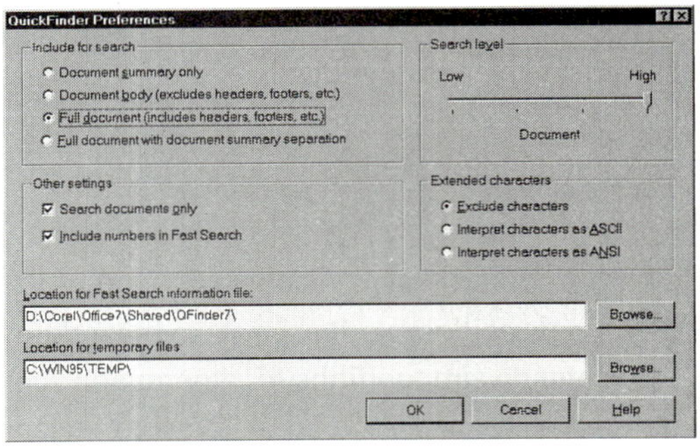

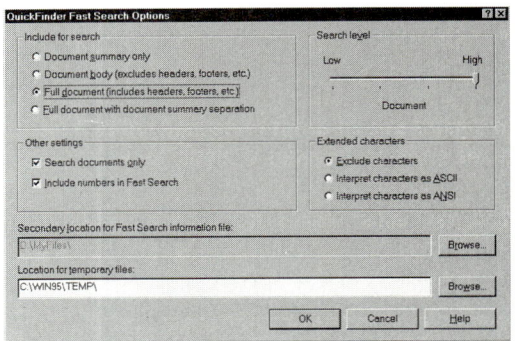

**FIG. 29.24**
Changes made in the QuickFinder Fast Search Options dialog box affect the current Fast Search only.

The options for an existing index file can also be changed. Click Edit in the QuickFinder Manager dialog box, then Options; the changes are reflected the next time the index is generated.

The QuickFinder Preferences and QuickFinder Fast Search Options dialog boxes contain the following components:

- *Include For Search.* This section controls what information in the file is indexed. You can choose Document Summary Only, Document Body (Excludes Headers, Footers, Etc.), Full Document (Includes Headers, Footers, Etc.), and Full Document With Document Summary Separation.

- *Search Level.* This slider controls the level of the search, which, in turn, defines the setting for the Closeness of Words option when a search for multiple words is performed. If, for example, you select an index level of Paragraph, WordPerfect flags only the files in which the words are found in the same paragraph.

- *Search Documents Only.* Check this box if you want to index documents only, and ignore program files such as DLL, EXE, and COM.
- *Include Numbers in Fast Search.* Check this box to include numbers in the fast search.
- *Extended Characters.* This is set to Exclude Characters by default. If necessary, you can change it to interpret the extended characters as ASCII (DOS standard) or ANSI (Windows standard).
- *Secondary Location For Fast Search Information File.* This text box lists the C:\COREL\OFFICE7\SHARED\QFINDER7 folder by default. If you want the index files created in another folder, type another folder name.
- *Location For Temporary Files.* This text box lists the name of the folder where your temporary files are created. ●

CHAPTER 30

# Advanced Macro Techniques

*by Gordon McComb*

WordPerfect 7 Macro feature goes far beyond recording the keys you press and the commands you choose. You can write macros from scratch, using a sophisticated and powerful macro language. This language is similar to other computer programming languages such as BASIC or Pascal, except that the macro programs you write are designed to be used solely in WordPerfect.

These and other macros are detailed in this chapter. Along with these macros, you learn the basics of WordPerfect's powerful macro programming language. You learn about several dozen of the most important programming commands and how to use them to construct your own sophisticated macros. You also learn how to open macros and how to print macros for future reference. ■

### Store macros for easier access
This chapter shows you how and where to store your macros for easy, convenient access.

### Use macros in templates
Learn about creating macros that function in association with WordPerfect's Template feature.

### Print and edit macros
Macros are a slightly modified WordPerfect document so you can use standard WordPerfect procedures for editing and printing.

### Use the Macro Feature Bar
Learn the uses of the Macro Feature Bar which contains special macro-related functions that assist you in your macro-writing efforts.

### Create advanced macros with the macro programming language
You learn the more advanced product and programming commands to create more sophisticated macros.

### Create a macro that automatically formats a fax cover sheet, prompting you for the information needed to fill out the sheet
Finally, you put your knowledge to use in creating a fax cover sheet macro.

# Understanding Macro Storage

In Chapter 12, "Creating Macros," you learned that macros can be stored either inside a template or as a separate file. When stored inside a template, the macro becomes part of the template file. The commands that make up the macro are placed in a special area of the template so that you can access the macro while you are using the template.

Macros that are separate files are really WordPerfect documents. Because of this, you can readily open and edit your macro files.

Whether your macros are embedded in a template or recorded as a stand-alone file, you do not need a separate "macro editor" facility. This is different from the macro feature in earlier versions of WordPerfect for DOS, in which macros are contained in their own special file format. In these earlier versions, you had to use a special editing window to write and edit macros.

## Opening a Macro Stored in a Template

To open a macro stored in a template document (to view, edit, or print it), follow these steps:

1. Choose Tools, Template Macro, Edit.
2. Choose Location.
3. Choose the location of the template, either Current or Default; then choose OK. (If the template that contains the macro is not listed, you need to create a new document based on the template before following these steps.)

**NOTE** If the Current template and the Default template use the same file, the Default Template choice is grayed.

4. WordPerfect displays the macros contained in the template. Select the macro you want, and click Edit. The macro is opened.

## Opening a Macro File

To open a stand-alone macro file (to view, edit, or print it), follow these steps:

1. Choose File, Open; or press Ctrl+O. The Corel Office —Open dialog box appears.
2. If necessary, select the folder containing the macro you want to view. Then, open the folder that contains your macro file, then select the macro file you want to open.
3. Choose Open or press Enter.

With either method, WordPerfect opens the macro file and displays it in the document window (see fig. 30.1). The strange words you see are part of WordPerfect's macro programming language.

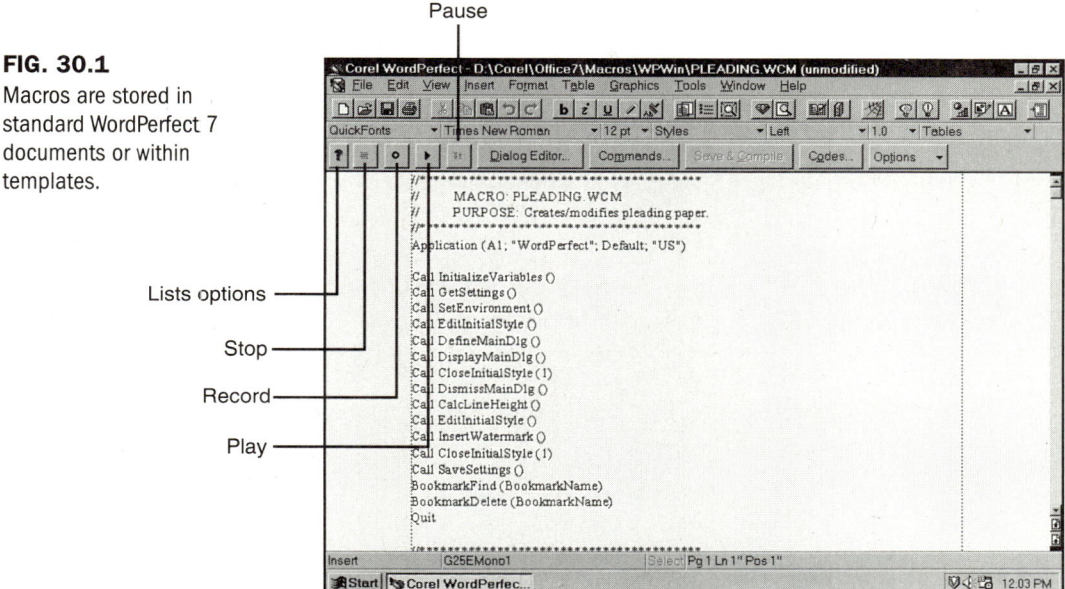

**FIG. 30.1**
Macros are stored in standard WordPerfect 7 documents or within templates.

Don't worry if the language looks complex or indecipherable. The language actually is straightforward and logical. In time, you will learn it and will be able to speak it fluently. The remainder of this chapter is devoted to helping you understand the language.

## Printing a Macro File

Macros can be printed as you would print any WordPerfect document. This lets you create a hard-copy version for future reference. Printing also is handy when you are working with longer macros. Putting the macro on paper enables you to trace more easily its operation and track down any problems that may be occurring.

> **NOTE** You can print a file macro directly from the Print dialog box. After displaying the Print dialog box, choose Document on Disk from the Print drop-down list, then click Edit. Enter a Document Name or click the folder button to select a file from the Document on Disk dialog box. Click OK to return to the Print dialog box. Finally, click Print to begin printing.

# Using the Macro Feature Bar

WordPerfect 7 includes a handy feature bar you can use when writing and editing macros. When you edit or record a macro file (choose Tools, Macro, Edit or Record), the Macro Feature Bar automatically appears (refer to fig. 30.1). Or, you can manually display the feature bar by choosing Tools, Macro, Macro Bar. The Macro Feature Bar also appears when recording a macro.

> **NOTE** If you are editing a template macro, choose Tools, Template Macro, Template Macro Bar. The Macro Feature Bars for file macros and template macros are actually the same.

The Macro Feature Bar offers the following 10 option buttons (the labeling on the first five buttons is icons; the labeling on the remaining buttons is text):

- *?*. Lists the available options in the Macro Feature Bar.
- *Stop*. When playing or recording a macro, click this button to stop the macro play or macro record.
- *Record*. Click this button to start recording a macro. WordPerfect switches to a new document window so you can perform the steps you want included in the macro. When you stop recording, the newly-opened window is closed (without saving what you've done). You are taken back to the document window that contains the macro you just recorded.

> **NOTE** When recording a macro into the current document, you can stop the macro only by clicking the Stop button in the Macro Feature Bar. Use this feature with care!

- *Play*. Click this button to play the macro currently shown on-screen. The macro must have already been saved and compiled first. (WordPerfect must first *compile* a macro before it can be played; this step is automatic and done entirely by WordPerfect.)
- *Pause*. When playing or recording a macro, click this button to temporarily pause the macro. This is the same as choosing Tools, Macro (or Template Macro), Pause.
- *Dialog Editor*. Click this button to create or edit a dialog box.
- *Commands*. Click this button to display the PerfectScript Commands dialog box, which makes it easier to insert macro commands.
- *Save & Compile*. Click this button to save the current macro file and compile it.
- *Codes*. Click this button to display the macro Codes dialog box, which allows you to insert special macro codes.

- *Options.* Click this button to choose one of four options: save as a file macro, save as a template macro, close the macro, remove the Macro Feature Bar.

### TROUBLESHOOTING

**I recorded a macro that opens a dialog box and makes some changes in the box. When I look at the macro, the command for opening the dialog box isn't there.** WordPerfect records complete actions, not the separate steps it takes to perform the action. So, if you record a macro that includes opening a dialog box, what WordPerfect records is what you actually do inside the dialog box. If you like, a WordPerfect macro can open a dialog box and pause there, waiting for you to manually choose options.

# Introducing the WordPerfect Macro Language

Macros are composed of commands that tell WordPerfect what to do. When you record a macro, WordPerfect inserts a command for every complete action you take, such as opening a file, entering text, or deleting a paragraph. Because each step is a complete and separate action, each action is recorded in the macro as a separate command.

## Recording a Sample Macro

To record a macro, follow these steps:

1. Choose Tools, Macro, Record; or press Ctrl+F10. The Record Macro dialog box appears.

2. Type **TESTMAC** and press Enter. After a few moments, the Macro Record prompt appears in the left corner of the status bar.

3. Type **This is a test** and press Enter.

4. Choose Format, Margins; or press Ctrl+F8. The Margins dialog box appears.

5. Set the Left and Right margins to 0.5" and choose OK.

6. Choose Format, Font, Bold, and then choose OK. Or press Ctrl+B.

7. Type **This is bolded text** and press Enter.

8. Choose Format, Font, Bold, then choose OK. Or press Ctrl+B.

9. Choose Tools, Macro, Record; or press Ctrl+F10. The macro recording stops.

Now look at the commands WordPerfect recorded in the macro file. Open the TESTMAC.WCM macro as detailed earlier in "Opening a Macro File." You should see the following text:

```
Application (WordPerfect; "WordPerfect"; Default; "US")
Type (Text:"This is a test")
HardReturn ()
MarginLeft (MarginWidth: 0.5")
MarginRight (MarginWidth: 0.5")
AttributeAppearanceOn (Attrib: Bold!)
Type (Text:"This is bolded text")
HardReturn ()
AttributeAppearanceToggle (Attrib: Bold!)
```

These nine lines make up the entire TESTMAC macro.

## Examining the TESTMAC Macro

The following list examines the commands WordPerfect recorded in the TESTMAC macro. Some commands are followed by a set of parentheses and text inside the parentheses. This is important, as you learn later in the chapter.

- `Application (WordPerfect; "WordPerfect"; Default; "US")`. The `Application` command is always inserted at the beginning of recorded macros. It provides specifics on how to translate the macro commands.

- `Type (Text: "This is a test")`. This command inserts the text `This is a test` at the current cursor position when the macro is played. You use the `Type` command whenever you want a macro to insert text.

- `HardReturn ()`. This command enters a hard return at the current cursor position. You use the `HardReturn ()` command (notice the open and close parentheses) whenever you want to start a new line.

- `MarginLeft (MarginWidth: 0.5")` and `MarginRight (MarginWidth: 0.5")`. These commands set the left and right margins to one-half inch. Notice that there are two margin commands: one for the left margin, and one for the right margin.

- `AttributeAppearanceOn (Attrib: Bold!)`. This command turns bold on.

- `Type (Text:"This is bolded text")`. Another `Type` command; this one inserts the text `This is bolded text`. A `HardReturn ()` command follows.

- `AttributeAppearanceToggle (Attrib: Bold!)`. This command turns bold on or off (in this case off, because bold was previously on).

**NOTE** Most commands are fairly self-explanatory, but they may appear more cryptic in some macros you record. As long as you remember what you did to record the action, you can readily decipher the meaning of most macro commands. Remember this when writing your own macrcs. If you are not sure what command to use, simply record the action you want your macro to take. When you are done, open the file and look at the macro command WordPerfect recorded for you.

## Using Two Kinds of Commands

On a broad scale, WordPerfect 7 uses two types of macro commands:

- *Product function* commands control specific features of WordPerfect—therefore, the name *product function*. When you type on the keyboard to enter text, WordPerfect inserts a Type command. When you change the margins of a document, WordPerfect inserts a Margin command. By convention, product function commands generally appear in mixed case (upper- and lowercase). The majority of WordPerfect's macro commands are the product function type.

- *Programming* commands work independently of any feature found in WordPerfect and are designed to add intelligence and control to your macros. By convention, programming commands generally appear in all uppercase.

From an operational standpoint, you don't have to concern yourself much with the difference between product function commands and programming commands. In fact, the remainder of this chapter refers to both as *commands*.

All macro commands are described in the Macros online help. Use these steps to open Macros help:

1. Choose Help, Help Topics.
2. Double-click the Macros book in the Contents tab.
3. Open the Macro Programming topic, then click the Index tab. The Index tab lists each macro command along with other commonly used search words.

**NOTE** If you did a Typical install of WordPerfect, then after you open the Macro Programming topic in step 3, you are taken to a help screen that tells you the Macro Help file (WPMH7US.HLP) is not installed. The Help screen contains steps that show you how to install the file. Follow the steps outlined in WordPerfect Help, then return to step 1.

4. Type a few letters of the macro command or word you want to look up. The index entry list is updated, highlighting the first entry that matches your typed letters.
5. Choose Display or press Enter to open the help text for the selected entry.

6. When finished reading the help text, close Macro Help by pressing Alt+F4, or clicking the Close button.

 **TIP** You can quickly add a Macro Help button to a Toolbar. To do so, point to the Toolbar with your mouse, then right-click. Choose Edit from the resulting QuickMenu. From the Features tab, select Help from the Feature Categories drop-down list. Double-click Macros from the Features list. The Macros Help button is added to the end of the currently displayed Toolbar. Choose OK to close the Toolbar Editor dialog box.

**N O T E** If you are not able to access full Macro Help, you need to install WordPerfect Macro Help from your installation CD. The complete Macro Help file is not automatically installed when you install WordPerfect using a Typical or Compact installation. If Macro Help is not available, reinstall WordPerfect using the Custom install choice. Be sure to manually check WordPerfect Macro Help for installation from the WordPerfect 7 Components list.

**N O T E** You can quickly add a Macro Help button to a Toolbar. To do so, point to the Toolbar with your mouse, then right-click. Choose Edit from the resulting QuickMenu. From the Features tab, select Help from the Feature Categories drop-down list. Double-click Macros from the Features list. The Macros Help button is added to the end of the currently displayed Toolbar. Choose OK to close the Toolbar Editor dialog box.

## Comparing Product Commands Versus the WordPerfect 5.1 Macro Model

As mentioned in the earlier section, "Understanding Macro Storage," macros in earlier versions of WordPerfect for DOS (such as versions 5.0 and 5.1) are recorded differently than in WordPerfect 7.

In WordPerfect 5.1 for DOS, for example, your actions are recorded as keystrokes. The combination of the keystrokes determines the overall action, whether entering text into the document, setting margins, and so on.

In WordPerfect 5.1 for DOS, the TESTMAC macro looks like the following:

```
{DISPLAY OFF}
This is a test{Enter}
{Format}170.5"{Enter}
0.5"{Enter}
{Enter}
{Enter}
{Bold}This is bolded text{Bold}
```

The problem with recording macros as a series of keystrokes is that they are tied to the keyboard. What if you are using a mouse or some other input device? Because you are not always clear what they do, keystroke macros are harder to maintain. You have to be very familiar with WordPerfect, for example, to know that {Format}170.5" means, "Change the left margin to half an inch." Compare the readability of the WordPerfect 7 macro with its clunky 5.1 counterpart.

Notice, too, that 5.1 commands are context-sensitive, making it harder to determine exactly what the macro is doing. For example, which {Enter} codes are used to navigate through menus, and which are used to insert hard returns in the document?

Finally, keystroke macros are highly dependent on WordPerfect's interface. During the lifetime of WordPerfect 5.1 for DOS, WordPerfect Corporation wanted to add a variety of features to the program. Doing so, however, would have "broken" a large number of macros—including many shipped with the product! This is no longer a problem in WordPerfect 7.

If you are familiar with WordPerfect 5.1 for DOS macros, you need a period of adjustment to become familiar with the way macros work in WordPerfect 7. If you approach the change in macro languages with an open mind, you will find that the new way has great potential.

However, if you have some experience in the macro language of WordPerfect 6.0/6.1 for DOS, you will find striking similarities between it and the language used in WordPerfect 7. The languages are similar, but not identical. If you are a user of WordPerfect 6.0/6.1 for Windows, you should notice very little change in the macro commands you currently use. After you learn one language, you should have no trouble mastering the other.

# Understanding the Syntax of Macro Commands

Macro commands follow a predictable format, called *syntax*. If you use the wrong syntax, WordPerfect refuses to play the macro because it doesn't understand what you are trying to do. This is similar to trying to speak in a foreign language and mixing up verbs, nouns, and other parts of speech.

The syntax of WordPerfect's macro commands is relatively simple and follows certain conventions:

- All commands are one word, with no spacing and no special characters. For example, AttributeAppearanceToggle is allowed, but Attribute Appearance Toggle is not.

- The capitalization of the command does not make a difference. The consistent capitalization is for your benefit. `Type` is the same as `type`, `TYPE`, `TyPe`, and all other variations.

- Proper spelling is an absolute must. WordPerfect 7 doesn't know what you mean if you use the command `HardRetrun` rather than `HardReturn`. Spelling mistakes such as this cause WordPerfect to display a `Syntax error` message when the macro is compiled (see fig. 30.2). This compiling stage is usually performed immediately before the macro is played the first time or when the macro was saved.

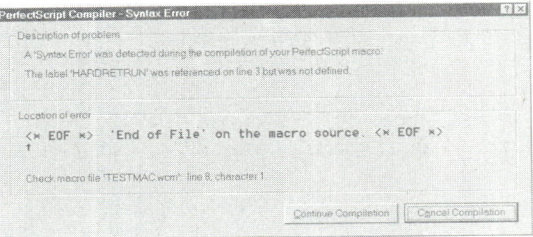

**FIG. 30.2**
WordPerfect 7 warns you when you make a mistake in your macro. You must fix the mistake before the macro will play or compile.

- Many commands consist of two parts: the command name and one or more parameters. The *parameters*, which tell WordPerfect exactly what you want to do with the command, always are enclosed in a pair of parentheses. The `Type` command, for example, uses one parameter—the text you want to type—such as:

    `Type (Text: "I am Text")`

    This text is enclosed in quotation marks.

- By default, WordPerfect adds the parameter name inside the parentheses. For example, the parameter name for the `Type` command is `Text`, and appears in a recorded macro as

    `Type (Text: "I am Text")`

    This parameter name is optional, and is not usually required by WordPerfect to properly play back macros.

- Some commands need two or more parameters. The parameters are separated from one another with a semicolon (;). The `GETSTRING` command, for example, uses four parameters, which look like this:

    `GETSTRING (Response;"This is the message";"Title";30)`

- WordPerfect 7 doesn't care about spaces between the command name, parentheses, and semicolon characters.

- Not all commands use parameters. With these, the parentheses are not absolutely required, but are highly recommended. `HardReturn()` and `HardReturn` do the same thing.

Don't worry about remembering all these syntactical rules. The more you work with WordPerfect advanced macros, the more the special grammar of the macros commands becomes second nature to you.

# Getting To Know the WordPerfect Macro Language

Although WordPerfect's macro language contains more than 2,000 commands, most macros consist of the same small handful. This section details this core group of macro commands and how they are used.

## Understanding Variables

Many macro commands use a variable. A *variable* is a special place that holds information in your computer's memory (see fig. 30.3). This information may change each time the macro is run. Some commands, such as GETSTRING and MENULIST, fill a variable so that its contents can be used elsewhere in the macro. Other commands, such as IF, CASE, Type, and several others mentioned in this chapter, peek inside the variable and use whatever information it contains.

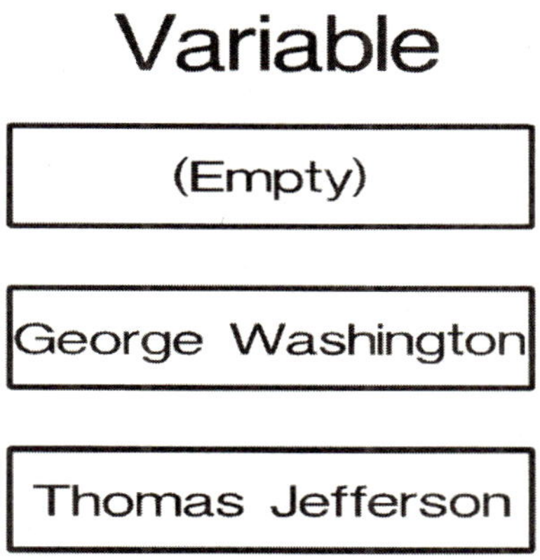

**FIG. 30.3**
Variables contain information that can vary each time the macro is played.

Variable

(Empty)

George Washington

Thomas Jefferson

Variables are useful because they enable you to store information once and then use it many times in a macro. You can ask the user to enter his or her name, for example, and store the response in a variable whose contents can be reused many times during the macro.

Keep the following points in mind when using WordPerfect macro variables:

- Variables are identified by name, and you get to choose the name. You may have as many variables in a macro as you want—until WordPerfect runs out of memory and cannot store any more.
- You can use almost any word for a variable name, up to the maximum length of 50 characters.
- Avoid variable names that conflict with existing macro commands. Don't use `HardReturn` as a variable name, for example, or WordPerfect could become confused.
- Variable names can contain numbers and letters but cannot start with a number. Few special characters are allowed in variable names, except the underscore. You can use the underscore to break up a long variable name made up of several words—for example, `This_Is_My_Variable`. For ease of use, choose short, descriptive words for variable names.
- The contents of variables are usually erased when the macro ends. However, variables assigned using the `PERSIST` or `PERSISTALL` commands are available as long as WordPerfect is running.

## System Variables

Asking for the user's name with a `GETSTRING` command is one way to give information to a macro. Another way is to use system variables. A *system variable* tells the macro something about WordPerfect, such as the number of the current page, the name of the current document, and the absolute location of the cursor on the page.

System variables are *read-only*; you can access the information contained within them, but you cannot store any information within them—that's WordPerfect's job.

WordPerfect 7 offers more than 250 system variables. These variables are listed in the PerfectScript Commands dialog box, detailed in the section, "The Macro Command Inserter," later in this chapter. All system variables start with a question mark (?), as in the following list:

- `?Page`. Provides the current page number.
- `?Name`. Provides the file name, if any, of the current document.
- `?BlockActive`. Indicates whether block is turned on or off. The value obtained from `?BlockActive` is True if block is on and False if block is off.

- `?InTable`. Indicates whether the insertion point is currently in a table. The value obtained from `?InTable` is True if the insertion point is in a table, and False if it is not.

- `?DocBlank`. Indicates whether the current document is blank. The value obtained from `?DocBlank` is False or True: False if the document is not blank; True if the document is blank. The following is an example of using a WordPerfect system variable:

```
If (?DocBlank = False)      // if document is not blank
    FileNew()               // open a new document window
EndIf
```

As you can see in the preceding example, two general types of information are provided by system variables: actual values (`?Page`, `?Name`) and the "logical" states of True and False.

**TIP** The large number of system variables makes it impossible to list all of them here. To learn more about WordPerfect's system variables and how they are used in macros, see the System Variables entry in the Macros online help. Choose Help, Help Topics, then double-click Macros from the Contents tab. Select Macros, Macro Programming; the WordPerfect Macros Help dialog box appears. In the Contents tab, select Lists of Commands, then choose System Variables.

## Commands That Ask for User Input

One common requirement of an advanced macro is that it interact with the user. This interaction is usually in the form of a dialog box or message prompt. WordPerfect provides several user input commands. The most common commands are GETSTRING and MENULIST.

Both commands display a message and save the user's response inside a variable. See the sections "Understanding Variables" and "System Variables" earlier in this chapter for more information on variables.

**The *GETSTRING* Command**   When the macro is run, the GETSTRING command displays a WPWin dialog box, which includes a prompt and an entry blank for text (see fig. 30.4). What the user types goes into the entry blank. The user's response is stored in a variable for later use. The following example displays a GETSTRING dialog box:

```
GETSTRING(Response;"Type your name";"WPWin";30)
```

This example prompts `Type your name`. The text `WPWin` is used for the title of the dialog box; the title appears at the top of the box. In response to this box, the user types his or her name, and chooses OK. This text is stored in a variable named *Response*, which can then be used as the parameter in a Type command like:

    Type (Response)

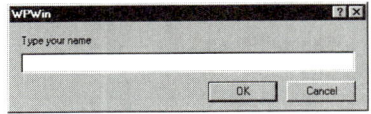

**FIG. 30.4**

The GETSTRING command displays a dialog box where you type text in response to a message that appears in the box.

The last parameter in the GETSTRING command limits the length of the response to 30 characters. This parameter is optional. If you leave it out, the WordPerfect limits the entry to 255 characters.

*Response* appears without quotation marks in the Type command. You are interested in the *contents* of the *Response* variable, so don't put the variable name *Response* in quotations.

**The *MENULIST* Command**  You use the MENULIST command to display a menu of choices. When you select an item from the menu, the number of that item is stored in a variable. Other commands in your macro—usually IF or CASE—determine the number in the variable and perform some specific action. See the later section, "Commands That Make Decisions," for more information on IF and CASE.

The syntax for MENULIST is somewhat complex because it has many parts. Some of its parameters are optional, meaning that you can leave them out if you don't want to use them. At a minimum, MENULIST needs you to fill in two items: the name of the variable that will hold the user's response, and the text for one or more menu items, as in the following example:

    MENULIST (Response; {"First Item";"Second Item";"Third Item"})

*Response* is the name of the variable that contains the number of the user's choice. The text for the three menu items is enclosed in quotation marks and is separated by semicolons. All three items are placed inside a pair of curly braces. Figure 30.5 shows how WordPerfect displays the MENULIST dialog box.

You can add more items inside the braces, up to a maximum of 26 items. If you use less than nine items, the items are automatically numbered 1–9, which you may use to select the option with the keyboard. If you use more than nine items, then the items are preceded with a letter of the alphabet (A–Z) rather than numbers (1–9). When the MENULIST dialog box appears, select any item, and the number of the item is stored in the *Response* variable. Pick the fourth item, for example, and the *Response* variable contains the number 4. Picking the "M" item stores the number 13 in the *Response* variable.

**FIG. 30.5**
The MENULIST command displays one or more options from which you can choose.

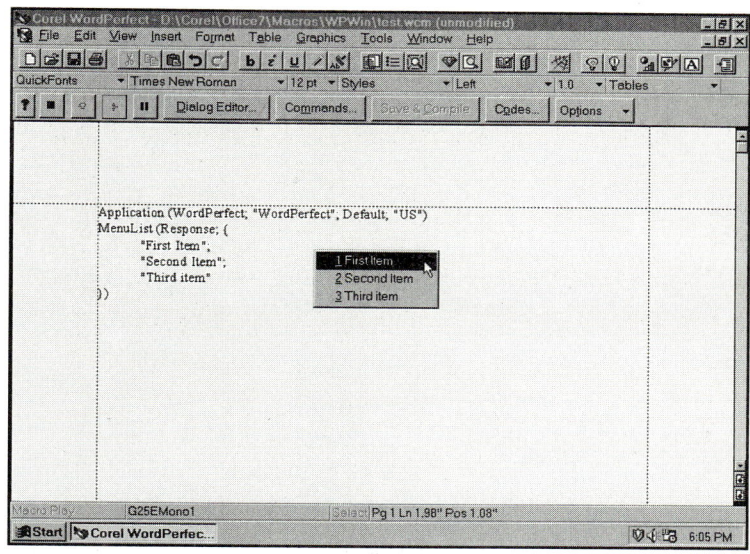

 The MENULIST dialog box lets the user skip making a choice by choosing Esc. In this case, *Response* contains the value 0.

## Commands That Make Decisions

You can make your macros "intelligent" by using commands that make decisions. Decision-making commands typically are used with user input commands, such as GETSTRING and MENULIST. Depending on the response from the user, the macro does either one thing or another. WordPerfect offers two powerful decision-making commands: IF and SWITCH/CASE.

**The *IF* Command**   The IF command is familiar if you have any experience with a programming language; it is found in all modern computer languages. The IF command determines whether a statement is true or false, which in turn enables your macros to make decisions. A typical IF statement tests whether one value is equal to another value, as in the following example:

    IF (1=1)

The result of this statement is true: 1 equals 1. In a real-life macro, the IF statement contains one or more variables. Your macro may compare one variable against another, or it may compare a variable against a known value, as follows:

    IF (Response=1)

*Response* is the name of a variable previously created and filled with the MENULIST command (see the earlier section "The MENULIST Command" for more information). This variable contains a number, and the IF statement tests whether that number is 1. If the number in *Response* is 1, then the IF statement is True. If the number in *Response* is something else, then the IF statement is False.

The IF command is never used by itself; it is always used with a matching ENDIF command. Commands between the IF and ENDIF commands are part of the IF structure—tasks for the macro to do if the IF statement is True. See the following example:

```
IF (Response=1)
     Type ("True")
ENDIF
```

If *Response* is equal to 1, the macro returns True; otherwise, the macro skips to the ENDIF command and performs any commands following it.

**N O T E** Try to get into the habit of formatting the various parts of the IF structure. The indentation of the steps between the IF and ENDIF helps you visually see the relationships of all the commands and makes the macro easier to read.

The ELSE command also is used with IF and is optional. ELSE tells WordPerfect what you want the macro to do when the IF statement is False. Consider the following example:

```
IF (Response=1)
     Type ("True")
ELSE
     Type ("False")
ENDIF
```

Your macro returns True or False depending on the outcome of the IF statement:

- If *Response* equals 1, the IF statement is True, and the macro returns True.
- If *Response* does not equal 1, the IF statement is False, and the macro returns False.

The equal sign (=) is an *operator*, which tells WordPerfect how you want the values in the IF statement evaluated. The = sign is the most common operator, but WordPerfect supports several other types. The most useful operators are shown in table 30.1.

**Table 30.1  *IF* Statement Operators**

| Operator | Use | Example |
| --- | --- | --- |
| = | Equals | *Response*=1 |
| <> | Not equal to | *Response*<>1 |
| <= | Less than or equal to | *Response*<=1 |
| >= | Greater than or equal to | *Response*>=1 |

**N O T E**  Complex IF tests can use additional logical operators such as AND or OR. For more information about other operators, refer to the Macros online help.

**N O T E**  You are not limited to just one command for the True and False parts of an IF structure; you can include as many commands as you need. The following macro, for example, beeps and types a line of text if the IF expression is False. When the IF expression is True, the macro types two lines of text, with each line separated by a hard return:

```
IF (Response=1)
    Type ("This IF statement")
    HardReturn()
    Type ("Turned out to be true")
ELSE
    BEEP
    Type ("This IF statement turned out to be false")
ENDIF
```

**The *SWITCH* Command**   As you read in the preceding section, the IF command is used to determine whether a statement is True or False. If the statement is True, the macro does one thing; if the statement is False, the macro does another. The IF statement is limited to "either/or" tests. This is fine for most types of decision-making, but not all.

The SWITCH command does a job similar to the IF command, but it lets you compare a value against any number of possibilities. SWITCH also enables you to define an action if the value doesn't match any of the possibilities. You are not limited to just two outcomes. With SWITCH, you can specify a different outcome for each possible value. Because of its flexibility in determining how the macro should respond depending on the test value, SWITCH is ideal for use with the MENULIST command, described in the earlier section "The MENULIST Command."

Like IF, the SWITCH command is never used by itself. SWITCH is always used with an ENDSWITCH command to mark the end of the SWITCH structure, and it's always used with at least one CASEOF command. You use a separate CASEOF command for every possible value you want to check for. The value that follows the CASEOF command is the value you are checking for. The following example uses the SWITCH and CASEOF commands:

```
SWITCH (Response)
    CASEOF 1:    Type ("Response is 1")
    CASEOF 2:    Type ("Response is 2")
    CASEOF 3:    Type ("Response is 3")
ENDSWITCH
```

In this example, WordPerfect types "Response is x" (*x* is a number from 1 to 3), depending on the number in the *Response* variable.

To use SWITCH, follow these rules:

- Place the reference value (usually a variable) in parentheses after the SWITCH command. In the example, the reference value is a variable named *Response*.
- Place each test value after the CASEOF command, and follow it with a colon. The example has three test values: 1, 2, and 3.
- Following the CASEOF command, include the command(s) you want executed if the test value matches the reference value.
- You are not limited to just one command after each CASEOF, as shown in the preceding example. You can add any number of additional commands as needed. To make reading the macro easier, place each command on a line of its own.
- Place the ENDSWITCH command after the last CASEOF.

A handy but optional command you can use with SWITCH is the DEFAULT command. DEFAULT tells WordPerfect what command(s) you want executed if no test values match the reference value. Include the DEFAULT command after the last CASEOF and before the ENDCASE, as follows:

```
SWITCH (Response)
     CASEOF 1:     Type ("Response is 1")
     CASEOF 2:     Type ("Response is 2")
     CASEOF 3:     Type ("Response is 3")
     DEFAULT:      Type ("Response not 1, 2, or 3")
ENDSWITCH
```

**N O T E**  WordPerfect also supports the CASE command, which performs a similar job as SWITCH. The CASE command isn't as versatile and is mainly provided for compatibility with macros created with earlier versions of WordPerfect for Windows. See the Macros online help for more information on the CASE command.

## Commands That Control the Flow of a Macro

The simplest macros start at the beginning and proceed to the end. All recorded macros work this way. In more advanced macros that you write yourself—particularly those that use the IF and CASE decision-making commands—you may want to redirect the flow of your macro so that WordPerfect executes different parts of it at different times.

WordPerfect provides several useful commands to control the flow of the macro. You can start at point A, then jump to a different part of the macro, depending on what you want the macro to do. The flow control commands can also be used to streamline the design of your macro. You can, for example, use the CALL command, detailed in a later section "The CALL Command," to repeat a set of commands two or more times.

**CAUTION**

When using the flow control commands, you must be careful that you don't create *spaghetti code*—macros that jump all over the place. Careless use of the flow control commands can make your macros harder to write and harder to fix if something goes wrong.

**The *LABEL* Command**  The LABEL command is used with the CALL and GO commands. The LABEL command specifies a certain spot in the macro—sort of like a street address—where you want the macro to divert control. The LABEL command uses one parameter, the label name, which optionally ends with an @ symbol. You can choose your own name, which can be up to 30 characters long (don't use spaces). The following example uses the LABEL command:

    LABEL (MyLabel@)

The label name is MyLabel@. You now can use the CALL or GO commands to change the flow of the macro to this label.

**TIP** Label names can be used only once in your macro. If you try to create two labels with the same name, WordPerfect displays an error message.

**The *CALL* Command**  The CALL command is used to branch temporarily to a different part of the macro, usually to perform some set of commands. Programmers refer to this as *branching to a subroutine*. A *subroutine* is any self-contained group of commands. The start of the subroutine is identified with a LABEL command. The LABEL command tells WordPerfect exactly where in the macro you want to jump.

The CALL command uses one parameter, the name of the label you want to jump to, as follows:

    CALL (MyLabel@)

Elsewhere in your macro, you write the following:

    LABEL (MyLabel@)

**TIP** The LABEL (MyLabel@) can be anywhere in the macro. It can be before or after the CALL command, but by convention, subroutines are placed most often toward the end of a macro.

**The *RETURN* Command**  WordPerfect needs to be told when a subroutine ends. For this you use the RETURN command. You place the RETURN command after the last command in the subroutine. When WordPerfect encounters the RETURN command, it returns execution to the spot immediately after the CALL command (see fig. 30.6).

**FIG. 30.6**

The CALL, LABEL, and RETURN commands work together to control precisely the flow of macro execution.

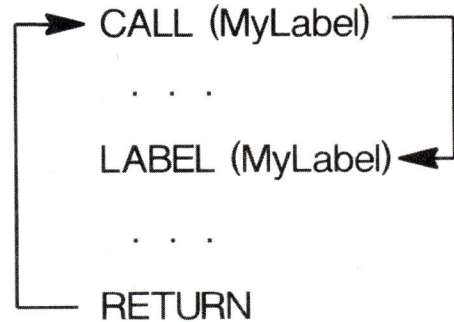

Consider the following example:

```
CALL (MyLabel@)
Type ("I'm back from the subroutine")
HardReturn()

LABEL (MyLabel@)
Type ("This is the MyLabel subroutine")
HardReturn()
RETURN
```

In this example, WordPerfect calls the MyLabel@ subroutine. This subroutine types a line of text:

```
This is the MyLabel subroutine
```

The RETURN command that follows tells WordPerfect to go back to the point immediately after the CALL command. The macro then types another line of text:

```
I'm back from the subroutine
```

**The *QUIT* Command**  If you try the preceding example, you find that WordPerfect types This is the MyLabel subroutine twice:

```
This is the MyLabel subroutine
I'm back from the subroutine
This is the MyLabel subroutine
```

After calling the MyLabel@ subroutine and printing the first two lines of text, WordPerfect continues the macro to the end. It encounters the LABEL(MyLabel@) command, which it ignores, and types This is the MyLabel subroutine again. When it reaches the RETURN command, WordPerfect stops the macro because there is no CALL to return to.

Although some macros are written so that a called subroutine is repeated before the macro ends, the usual requirement is that the macro stops before reaching any subroutines. Your macro may contain several subroutines, for example, but only one should be executed when commanded by the macro, not all remaining labels in sequence. If you don't stop the macro before it reaches the subroutines, WordPerfect may erroneously execute the commands in the wrong subroutine.

Use the QUIT command whenever you want to stop the macro before it reaches the last command in the macro. The following applies the QUIT command, using the preceding example:

```
CALL (MyLabel@)
   Type ("I'm back from the subroutine")
   HardReturn()
   QUIT
LABEL (MyLabel@)
   Type ("This is the MyLabel subroutine")
   HardReturn()
RETURN
```

This time, the macro types each line only once. The QUIT command ends the macro before it has a chance to continue through the LABEL command.

**The GO Command**  The GO command is similar to the CALL command in that you use it to redirect WordPerfect to a LABEL elsewhere in the macro. The difference between GO and CALL is that WordPerfect doesn't automatically return to the GO command after finishing the subroutine. With GO, you have to tell WordPerfect where you want to go next. The following example uses two GO commands and two LABEL commands:

```
GO (MyLabel@)
LABEL (ReturnToThisSpot@)
   Type ("I'm back from the subroutine")
   HardReturn()
   QUIT
LABEL (MyLabel@)
   Type ("This is the MyLabel subroutine")
   HardReturn()
   GO (ReturnToThisSpot@)
```

The first GO command tells WordPerfect to branch to the MyLabel@ subroutine. At the end of the subroutine is yet another GO command, which redirects the macro back to a label called ReturnToThisSpot@.

Although the GO command has its use, you can see how it can lead to confusing and poorly written macros, as controls jump from one spot to the other. Whenever possible, use the CALL command because it includes a mechanism for automatically returning control of the macro when the subroutine is over.

## Commands That Run Other Macros

Most of the time you run macros by telling WordPerfect which macro to play. To select a macro, you first choose Tools, Macros, Play; or press Alt+F10. Then you type or select the name of the macro and choose Play. In addition to this manual method of playing macros, one WordPerfect macro can also play another.

This is handy if you have two separate macros and each macro does a specific task. One macro might start a letter, and the other might type some standard paragraph of text. By linking the two macros together, you can have WordPerfect run them both, even though you play just one macro. WordPerfect 7 supports two commands that run other macros: CHAIN and RUN.

**The *CHAIN* Command**   The CHAIN command runs a second macro when the first macro is finished. The CHAIN command should be the last command in the first macro. Include the name of the macro as the parameter for the CHAIN command, as in the following example:

```
CHAIN ("mymacro.wcm")
```

This plays the macro MYMACRO.WCM, which WordPerfect assumes to be in the default MACROS\WPWIN folder, as specified in the File Preferences dialog box. (If you are not sure where the default MACROS folder is located, choose Edit, Preferences, Files. Then choose the Merge/Macro tab. The default macros folder is listed in the Default Macro Folder edit box.) Note the quotation marks that enclose the "mymacro.wcm" macro name.

**N O T E**   If you want to CHAIN to a macro in another folder, include the full path and the macro name, as in

```
CHAIN ("c:\newmacs\ mymacro")
```

This plays the MYMACRO.WCM macro, which is in the C:\NEWMACS folder.

**T I P**   You may use the WordPerfect system variables ?PathMacros and ?PathMacrosSupplemental to access your macros without hard coding a folder name with your macro name. For example,

```
Chain(?PathMacros + "mymacro.wcm")
```

will look in the folder you specified in your Default Macro folder by choosing Edit, Preferences, Files, Merge/Macro.

**The *RUN* Command**   Like CHAIN, the RUN command plays a second macro, but the first macro doesn't have to finish first. When WordPerfect encounters the RUN command, it pauses the first macro and plays the second macro. When the second macro is finished, WordPerfect picks up where it left off with the first macro and continues executing it.

As with the CHAIN command, you indicate the macro you want to play as the parameter of the RUN command, as follows:

```
RUN ("mymacro.wcm")
```

> **CAUTION**
>
> When nesting macros, be sure the second macro (the one you nest to) does not end with a QUIT command. If it does, WordPerfect stops all macro execution and control does not return to the first macro. If you have a nested macro that includes a QUIT command, replace it with a RETURN command.

 **TIP** WordPerfect 7 also supports the NEST command, which does the same job as RUN. The NEST command is provided for greater compatibility with WordPerfect 6 for DOS macros.

> **CAUTION**
>
> The macros being chained or run must be compiled before the current macro is played.

## Other Useful Commands

Several other commands commonly used in macros defy easy categorization. These commands add "comments" to your macros, control the display, pause the macro at various points, display a short message at the bottom of the screen, and sound a beep on the computer's built-in speaker.

**The // (Comment) Command**   The macros you write today may look like hieroglyphics tomorrow. Two months from now, you may not remember what a particular command or subroutine does in your macro. Instead, add comments to your macros. *Comments* are annotations that you provide to help you remember how your macro works. Comments also are helpful for users who are not familiar with your macro.

To add a comment to a macro, type a double slash (//); then write the text for the comment. The comment ends when you press Enter.

You can write comments of any length, from one word to complete paragraphs. You can insert comments on a separate line in your macro or after a macro command. Several examples follow:

```
// The following is the "MyLabel@" routine
LABEL (MyLabel@)
    Type ("This is the MyLabel@ subroutine")
    HardReturn()
RETURN  // This returns to the command that CALLed MyLabel@
```

**N O T E**   While comments can span two or more lines (as long as you don't press Enter), limiting comments to a single line is a good idea. If you must write longer comments, add the double slash at the beginning of each line, as follows:

```
// This is the first line of the comment
// and this is the second line.
```

**The *DISPLAY* Command**   Use the DISPLAY command to control how and when WordPerfect updates the screen when a macro plays. With DISPLAY turned off, WordPerfect does not update the screen while the macro plays. Text, graphics, tables, and other elements inserted by the macro aren't shown until the macro ends.

With DISPLAY turned on, WordPerfect updates the screen while the macro plays. If the macro types some text, for example, each character is shown as it is inserted into the document.

Macros run faster when DISPLAY is turned off. But you may prefer to leave DISPLAY on so that you can see the progress of your macro.

> **CAUTION**
>
> Don't confuse the DISPLAY command with the CLS (CLear Screen) command found in some other programming languages, such as BASIC. Unlike the CLS command, WordPerfect's DISPLAY command does not blank the screen. DISPLAY (Off!) merely turns off screen updating so that typing and editing changes aren't seen while the macro runs.

The DISPLAY command is used with one argument, either On! or Off!, as follows:

```
DISPLAY (On!)    // Turns display on
DISPLAY (Off!)   // Turns display off
```

Notice the exclamation point after the words On and Off. The exclamation point tells WordPerfect you are using a built-in parameter value rather than a variable. The parameter values On! and Off! have a significant meaning to WordPerfect and are equivalent to the numbers 1 and 0, respectively. If you prefer, you can use the numbers instead of the parameter values:

```
DISPLAY (1)    // Turns display on
DISPLAY (0)    // Turns display off
```

All macros recorded by WordPerfect start with a DISPLAY(Off!) command. If you want the screen to be updated as the macro runs, either remove this command or change it to DISPLAY(On!).

> **N O T E**   Recorded macros don't contain the command Display(Off!), but the action is implied. You must add the DISPLAY(On!) command to the beginning of a macro to display the entire macro (until Display is turned off) as it runs.

You can use the DISPLAY command any number of times in a macro to control precisely when you want the screen updated and when you don't. For example, you might start with DISPLAY turned Off! as the macro creates a table. Then, midway through the macro you can turn it On! to display several lines of text that the macro inserts into the table. You can turn DISPLAY Off! again for the remainder of the macro, as it completes other formatting tasks.

Keep the following points in mind when using the DISPLAY command:

- Use the DISPLAY (On!) command before that part of the macro that contains the commands you want to show. If you want to show text being entered in the document, for example, place the DISPLAY (On!) command before the Type command, as follows:

    ```
    DISPLAY (On!)
    Type ("This text shown as it is entered")
    ```

- Similarly, use the DISPLAY (Off!) command before that part of the macro containing the commands you do not want to show, as in the following example:

    ```
    DISPLAY (Off!)
    Type ("This text is NOT shown as it is entered")
    ```

- When you use the DISPLAY (On!) command, WordPerfect displays any typing and editing the macro may have done so far.

- Use DISPLAY (On!) DISPLAY (Off!)—both commands immediately following each other—if you want to update the screen with any typing and editing the macro has done so far and then turn DISPLAY back off.

**The *PauseKey* Command**  You were introduced to the PauseKey command in Chapter 12, "Creating Macros," where you learned how to insert a PauseKey command when recording a macro. You can use the PauseKey command in any macro you write. When WordPerfect encounters the PauseKey command, it temporarily stops the macro. Macro playback doesn't resume until you press Enter. Following is an example of the PauseKey command:

```
Type ("This is the first line of text")
HardReturn()
PauseKey(Enter!)
Type ("This is the second line of text")
```

See the FAXCOVER macro later in this chapter for a practical example of how to use the PauseKey command.

**The *MacroStatusPrompt* Command**  The PauseKey command commonly is used with another handy command: MacroStatusPrompt. The MacroStatusPrompt command displays a short, one-line message in the status bar, located at the bottom of the screen. (Of course, you can use one command without the other.)

To use the `MacroStatusPrompt` command, indicate the text you want to show. Make sure that the text is 80 characters or less. Enclose the message in double quotation marks, as follows:

```
MacroStatusPrompt (On!; "Type your name, then press Enter.")
PauseKey(Enter!)
```

WordPerfect 7 automatically removes the message as the macro continues or when the macro ends.

For best results, limit the `MacroStatusPrompt` message to no more than 40 characters. Longer messages are harder to read.

**The *BEEP* Command**  Use the BEEP command to sound a tone on the computer's speaker. A common use of the BEEP command is to call attention to the message provided in a `MacroStatusPrompt` command. In the following example, WordPerfect sounds the beep, displays the prompt message, then pauses the macro:

```
BEEP
MacroStatusPrompt (On!; "Type your name, then press Enter.")
PauseKey (Enter!)
```

## Dialog Box Commands

WordPerfect 7 lets you create your own macro dialog boxes that look exactly like the program's own dialog boxes. There are two ways to create dialog boxes:

- To create a dialog box with commands, use the `DialogDefine` command, followed by one or more commands to insert "controls" into the dialog box. The dialog box displays with the `DialogDisplay` command.

- To create a dialog box with the Dialog Editor, you must create the basic macro first, then save and compile it. Using the Macro Feature Bar (choose Tools, Macro, Macro Bar), access the Dialog Editor by clicking the Dialog Editor button. You then create a new dialog box and add "controls" to it.

Because there are more than a dozen dialog box commands, requirements for their use—as well as using the Dialog Editor—are too lengthy to discuss here. For more information on creating dialog boxes for your macros, click the Dialog Editor button on the Macro Feature Bar, then choose Help, Help Topics. Next, click the Help Topics button, then open the How Do I book on the Contents page. Open the Use the Dialog Editor book for a list of topics that discuss this powerful feature in detail.

## The Macro Command Inserter

WordPerfect offers a convenient way to insert programming commands as you write your macros. Choose Tools, Macro, Macro Bar. The Macro Feature Bar appears. Choose Commands. The PerfectScript Commands dialog box appears (see fig. 30.7). Highlight a command; its syntax is shown to the right of the Commands list.

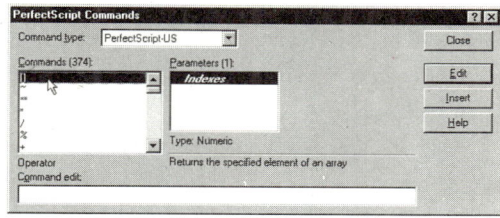

**FIG. 30.7**
Use the PerfectScript Commands dialog box to insert programming commands, system variables, and product function commands.

To insert a command, follow these steps:

1. Choose the command you want. You can use the keyboard or the mouse.
2. Press Enter.
3. If the command requires parameters, WordPerfect places the command name in the Command Edit text field, where you can fill in the parameters (see fig. 30.8). Type the parameters and click Insert. The command is inserted into the WordPerfect document window.

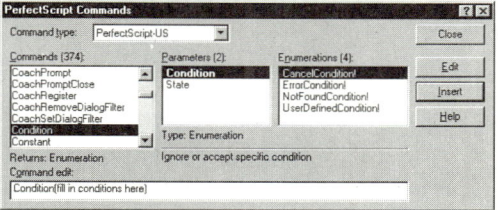

**FIG. 30.8**
The PerfectScript Commands dialog box helps you enter the correct parameters for each command that requires them.

## Useful Product Function Commands

As you read earlier in this chapter, WordPerfect has two kinds of macro commands: programming commands and product function commands. So far, discussion has been limited almost entirely to the most commonly used programming commands (exceptions include PauseKey and MacroStatusPrompt). Although more than 1,800 product function commands exist, only a small handful are used regularly. A brief description of these commands follows:

**NOTE** In addition to programming commands, the PerfectScript Commands dialog box also lists system variables and product commands. To display the system variables and product commands, choose the Command Type drop-down list and then choose WordPerfect. The commands in the Commands list change. System variables are listed first, followed by the product commands.

- `Close`. Closes the current document window.
- `DeleteCharNext` and `DeleteCharPrevious`. Delete the character (or code) to the right and left of the cursor, respectively.
- `FileNew`. Opens a new document window.
- `FileOpenDlg`. Displays the Open Document dialog box. When WordPerfect displays this dialog box during macro playback, it pauses the macro and waits for you to type the file name of a document to open.
- `FileSaveAsDlg`. Displays the Save Document dialog box. When WordPerfect displays this dialog box during macro playback, it pauses the macro and waits for you to type the file name of the document to save.
- `HardReturn`. Inserts a hard return in the document. It simulates pressing Enter.
- `PosCharNext` and `PosCharPrevious`. Position the cursor to the right or left of the cursor, respectively. If `SelectMode` is on (using the `SelectMode` command detailed below), these two commands are used to extend the block selection character-by-character.
- `SelectMode(On!)`. Turns block mode on and is the same as choosing Edit, Select; or pressing F8.
- `Tab`. Inserts a tab in the document. It simulates pressing the Tab key.
- `Type(Text)`. Inserts text into the document. The `Text` parameter indicates the text you want typed. The text can be the actual characters, or it can be the name of a variable, as in these examples:

        Type ("This is text") // Types the actual characters This is a test
        Type (Response) // Types the contents of the Response variable.

### TROUBLESHOOTING

**WordPerfect displays an error message when I try to play a macro I created with WordPerfect 6.0 for Windows.** While the macro language in WordPerfect 6.0/6.1 for Windows is almost identical to that in version 7, there are some changes and differences. Most macros created for version 6.0/6.1 of WordPerfect 7 will run without a hitch. If you encounter an error message, first try to recompile the macro. This can be done by opening the macro in WordPerfect 7 for Windows and resaving it. If that doesn't work, open the macro file and run the MCVTWIN.WCM macro conversion macro, which comes with WordPerfect 7 for Windows. It will go through the macro and correct for the changes between the two versions.

For best results, when prompted by the MCVTWIN.WCM macro, save the converted macro under a new name. This keeps the original intact in case you need to edit the macro manually to make any necessary changes.

**WordPerfect tells me a label was defined but not referenced.** When you use the LABEL command, WordPerfect expects you to reference it elsewhere in the macro. This is usually done with either a GO or a CALL command. Suppose, for example, you create a label called Start, with LABEL (Start). Elsewhere in the macro, WordPerfect expects to see a CALL (Start) or GO (Start) command—a reference to the Start label. If you get the error message that a label was defined but not referenced, you can ignore it and the macro will compile properly anyway. The message is a warning, not a "fatal" error. Just click the Continue Compilation button to continue.

**I can't see the text my macro types into the document.** WordPerfect normally does not display the text it types with the Type command until the macro is completely finished. This helps speed up macro execution. If you want to see the text before the macro has finished, insert a Display (On!) command prior to the Type command that you want to display.

# Extending Your Macro Programming Skills

The best way to learn about WordPerfect macros is to practice writing them. Following is a sample that will help you understand how to create sophisticated WordPerfect macros. The macro is commented at key points so that you can better follow the techniques used.

> **NOTE** If you forget how to use a command listed in the PerfectScript Commands dialog box, you have two alternatives. You can click Help in the PerfectScript Commands dialog box (which gives you online help for PerfectScript commands). You can also choose Help, Help Topics; double-click Macros from the Contents tab; then double-click Macro Programming (for help with WordPerfect commands). When you close the Help window, WordPerfect takes you back to the PerfectScript Commands dialog box.

> **NOTE** Some of the examples use commands not specifically discussed in this chapter. This is unavoidable because of the number of commands. If you encounter a command that is new to you, look it up in the online Macros Help that accompanies WordPerfect.

The FAXCOVER.WCM macro automates most of the steps in creating a fax cover sheet. The macro automatically inserts the current time and date, and asks the following pertinent questions:

- Who the fax is from?
- Who the fax is for?
- What is the fax number of the recipient?
- What is the subject of the fax?
- How many pages are in the fax transmission?

▶ **See** "Stopping a Macro During Recording," **p. 400**

FAXCOVER.WCM uses the `PauseKey` command to temporarily stop the macro for each piece of information it needs. You know exactly what and when to type, thanks to the `MacroStatusPrompt` command, as in the following example:

```
Application (A1; "WordPerfect"; Default; "US")
    // Center and bold the text "FAX COVER SHEET"
Center ()
AttributeAppearanceToggle (Bold!)
Type ("FAX COVER SHEET")
AttributeAppearanceToggle (Bold!)
HardReturn ()
HardReturn ()
DateFormat (DateFormatString: "Month Day#, Year(4)#")
DateText ()
HardReturn ()
HardReturn ()
    // Ask for and insert the sender's name
Type ("Sender's Name: ")            // Type descriptive text
MacroStatusPrompt (On!;"Sender's Name")  // Display prompt
PauseKey(Enter!)         // Pause and wait for Enter key
HardReturn ()     // Insert two hard returns
HardReturn ()
    // Ask for and insert the receiver's name
Type ("Receiver's Name: ")
MacroStatusPrompt (On!;"Receiver's Name")
PauseKey(Enter!)
HardReturn ()
HardReturn ()
    // Ask for and insert the receiver's fax number
Type ("Receiver's Fax Number: ")
MacroStatusPrompt (On!;"Receiver's Fax Number")
PauseKey(Enter!)
HardReturn ()
HardReturn ()
    // Ask for and insert the subject
Type ("Subject: ")
MacroStatusPrompt (On!;"Subject")
PauseKey(Enter!)
```

```
HardReturn ()
HardReturn ()
    // Ask for and insert the total pages
Type ("Total Pages: ")
MacroStatusPrompt (On!;"Total Pages")
PauseKey(Enter!)
HardReturn ()
HardReturn ()
```

# CHAPTER 31

# Advanced Tables

*by Read Gilgen*

In Chapter 16, "Working with Tables," you learned something about the power and versatility of WordPerfect's Tables feature. You also learned the basics of designing, building, formatting, saving, and printing tables. In this chapter, you take the next step toward your mastery of WordPerfect tables. You also learn how to create functional forms using WordPerfect's powerful spreadsheet and calculation capabilities.

### Position, join, split, and sort tables
Here's the rest of the story about customizing the layout of your tables.

### Import spreadsheets to a table
Automatically convert spreadsheets into WordPerfect tables, complete with data and formulas.

### Add graphics and customize table lines
Lines, fills, and borders are based on styles, which you can customize and save for use at any time.

### Add spreadsheet functionality to tables
WordPerfect tables enable you to use formulas and other spreadsheet-like procedures for simple to complex calculations.

### Work with floating cells
Give normal non-table text the capability to perform calculations using these unique floating table cells.

# Creating and Using Tables: The Next Step

Working with tables is somewhat like an artistic experience. The procedures included in this section are the tools you need to turn your tables into works of art: documents that meet your needs both functionally and aesthetically.

## Using the Tables Toolbar, QuickMenu, and Table Edit Tools

When working with tables, you can speed up your work considerably by using three special tools:

- Tables Toolbar (comes with WordPerfect)
- Tables QuickMenu
- Tools dialog box (accessed by clicking a Tables QuickSpot)

By default, when you first create a table, WordPerfect displays the Tables Toolbar. You can display the Tables Toolbar again by moving the insertion point inside the table.

To access the Tables QuickMenu, right-click anywhere inside the table (see fig. 31.1). Using the QuickMenu rather than first accessing the Table menu or even the Toolbar can save considerable time because you don't have to move the mouse to look for the menu.

**FIG. 31.1**
Right-click the table to access this handy menu of table-related features.

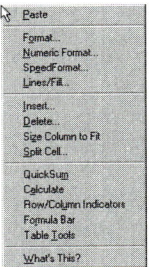

When you position the mouse pointer in a cell, WordPerfect displays an Edit Table QuickSpot in the upper-right corner of the cell. Click the QuickSpot; WordPerfect displays a Tools dialog box that contains some of the more commonly used Tables features such as Lines, Format, and Insert/Delete (see fig. 31.2). A drawback to this dialog box is that it remains on-screen until you close it, which means that sometimes it gets in the way of your work. You can, of course, just drag the Tools dialog box off to the side so it remains handy when you need it.

**FIG. 31.2**
The Tools dialog box for editing tables appears when you click a QuickSpot in a table cell.

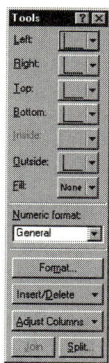

Become familiar with these tools, and use the one that works best for you to save time and effort.

> **N O T E** Unless specified otherwise, procedures described in the following sections assume you are using the QuickMenu. For example, "Choose Format" means to first access the QuickMenu as described previously, and then to choose Format from the QuickMenu. You can also access the Table menu that contains all of the QuickMenu items.

## Positioning Tables

By default, WordPerfect positions; tables at the left margin. When you create a table, WordPerfect allocates all the available space between the margins you specify; if you change column widths, however, your table may not extend from margin to margin.

You can change the horizontal position of a table in your document by choosing Format, and then selecting the Table tab. Then from the Table Position pop-up menu, specify whether you want to align your table at the left margin, right margin, or center, or whether you want the table to extend from margin to margin (Full). If you choose From Left Edge, you can specify the exact position of the table from the left edge of the paper. For example, 2" places the table 2 inches from the left edge of the paper, or 1 inch from the left margin.

If your table already extends from margin to margin, choosing Right or Center has no effect. If you choose Full and then change your margins or move the table to a location that has different margins, WordPerfect adjusts the table so that it fits within the new margins.

> **CAUTION**
> Avoid designating a table as "full" before all column width formatting is complete. Even if you set columns as fixed width, they readjust their width to force the table to "stretch" between the left and right margins. It's easiest to leave a table left aligned while sizing columns. Then change to full when formatting is complete.

## Placing Tables Side by Side

In normal body text, you cannot place two tables side by side. You could place your tables in graphics boxes, but creating and positioning such boxes can be a bit complicated. Instead, you can simply turn columns on, create your tables, and then turn columns off.

To create side-by-side tables using newspaper-style columns, follow these steps:

1. Define your columns as Newspaper type and turn them on. For example, for two columns, choose Format, Columns, Define, then in the Columns dialog box, choose Newspaper and choose OK.
2. Create the first of your tables.
3. Position the cursor just below the table you create, and press Ctrl+Enter to advance to the next column.
4. Create the second of your tables.
5. Turn off your columns. (See Chapter 14, "Working with Text Columns," for more information on creating and working with columns.)

As you expand or edit your tables, the columns also expand so the two tables are always parallel. Be aware, however, that such tables cannot extend across page boundaries. To prevent page breaks from rearranging side-by-side tables, first select all the rows of both tables, then choose Format, Page, Keep Text Together.

▶ See "Parallel Columns," **p. 446**

## Splitting Tables

Sometimes you need to position part of a table by itself in a different location. You can copy the whole table to the new location and then delete the rows or columns you don't need. An easier method, however, is to split the table into two separate tables and then move the part you want to its new location.

To split a table, position the cursor in the row of the table that you want as the first row of the second table. Choose Table, Split, Table. WordPerfect splits the table into two tables and adds the current border around each (see fig. 31.3). Notice, however, that because of the way table lines appear, the break between the tables may be barely noticeable.

Position the insertion point in cell A1 of the second table, press the left arrow key, then press Enter. The second table should move down a line.

**FIG. 31.3**
You can split a WordPerfect table into two separate tables.

| Cell A1 | | | |
| --- | --- | --- | --- |
| Cell A2 | | | |
| This used to be cell A3, but now is A1 of the second table. | | | |
| | | | |

## Joining Tables

If you decide you don't want split tables, or if you create two separate tables and later decide to join them, follow these steps:

1. Position the two tables one immediately after the other. There can be no text (not even blank lines or other hidden codes) between the two tables.
2. Make sure the two tables have an equal number of columns. Tables with different numbers of columns cannot be joined.
3. Position the cursor anywhere in the first table.
4. Choose T<u>a</u>ble, <u>J</u>oin, <u>T</u>able. WordPerfect joins the two tables.

If the tables cannot be joined, WordPerfect displays an error message to tell you why. For example, if you get the error message `Table to be joined must immediately follow this table`, make sure your cursor is in the first table and that no text or codes separate the tables.

**N O T E**  The joined tables take on the format characteristics, including column widths, of the first two tables.

## Creating Forms with Irregular Columns

You sometimes want to use tables to create forms that have somewhat irregular columns. You can split and join cells to accomplish the task, but you must remember that WordPerfect splits and joins cells along existing column lines. An easier method for creating a form with irregular columns is to create two separate tables, one immediately following the other; the result looks like a single table.

For example, to create a form that begins with three columns and then changes to four, create the first table with three columns; then position the cursor immediately below that table and create a second table with four columns. Change the bottom line style in the first table to `<None>` to complete the illusion of only one table. When printed, the two tables look like a single table (see fig. 31.4).

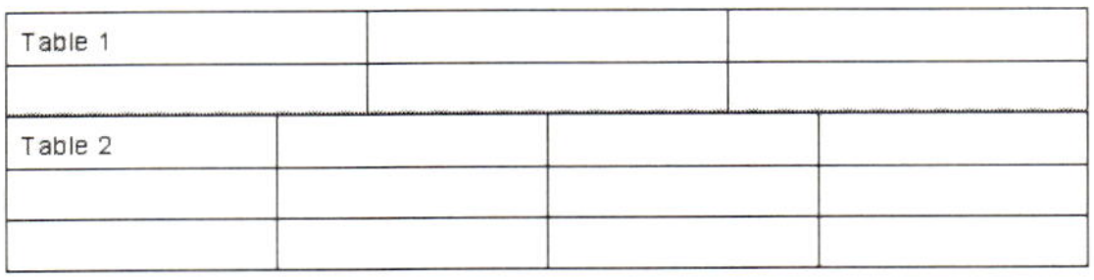

**FIG. 31.4**
Two tables of dissimilar column structure can be made to appear as one table by creating one table immediately following the other.

| Table 1 | | | |
|---|---|---|---|
| Table 2 | | | |
| | | | |

## Merging and Sorting Data in Tables

WordPerfect tables are perfect for rosters or lists of inventory parts, addresses, and so on. You can create table forms to which you can merge the information from your data files to create such lists. You can also easily sort lists of data in tables.

▶ **See** "Merging into Tables," **p. 623**

▶ **See** "Using Sort," **p. 624**

You can also use other merge codes in a table, just as you do in any form file. Suppose that you want to automate the Invoice table form you created in Chapter 16 (refer to fig. 16.2). You can place a DATE code in the form, along with a KEYBOARD( ) command to prompt for the invoice number, or another to prompt for the person who is being billed. You also can create a macro to start the merge automatically, and even assign that macro to a button on your Toolbar so that one click of a button brings up your invoice. This is just one of the many creative ways you can use tables to make your work easier and to produce quality documents.

## Importing a Spreadsheet to a Table

Spreadsheets have the same kind of layout as tables. To convert a spreadsheet to a table, open or insert the spreadsheet just as you open or retrieve any other document.

You can open any spreadsheet that is in a format recognized by WordPerfect. As of this printing, allowable formats include:

- PlanPerfect (versions 3.0–5.1)
- Lotus 1-2-3 (versions 1A–3.1) and Lotus 1-2-3 for Windows (versions 1.0–4.0)
- Excel (versions 2.1–7.0)
- Quattro Pro (versions 3.0–5.5)
- Quattro Pro for Windows (versions 1.0–7.0)
- Spreadsheet DIF

Most other spreadsheets are compatible with one of these formats, or can be saved in a compatible format.

When you attempt to open a file that WordPerfect recognizes as a spreadsheet, WordPerfect first displays the Import Data dialog box (see fig. 31.5). Here, WordPerfect enables you to specify how much of the file you want to import, and even lists any named ranges found in the spreadsheet. By default, spreadsheets are imported in table format.

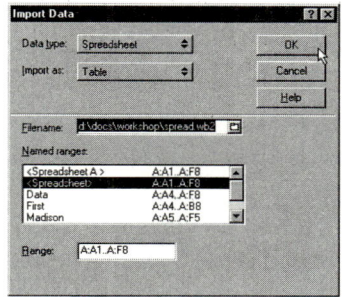

**FIG. 31.5**
The Import Data dialog box enables you to specify the file or named ranges you want to import into your document.

When you convert a spreadsheet to a table, the spreadsheet's blank rows convert to blank cells, as shown in figure 31.6.

**FIG. 31.6**
A table can be imported from a spreadsheet. Some editing of cell and column formats may be required before the data appears correctly.

| WORDPERFECT COSTS | | | | | |
|---|---|---|---|---|---|
| | License | Manual | Workbook | Complete | %Discount |
| List Price | N/A | N/A | N/A | $495.00 | 0.0% |
| Mail Order | N/A | N/A | N/A | $235.00 | 52.5% |
| Site License | $50.00 | $25.00 | $25.00 | $100.00 | 79.8% |

In addition, if the spreadsheet is too wide to fit within the margins, WordPerfect imports the whole spreadsheet, but does not print whatever extends beyond the right margin. Some useful strategies for importing spreadsheet data into tables include the following:

- Consider changing the paper orientation. More data can fit horizontally on a landscape page (11 × 8 1/2 inches) than can fit on a portrait page.
- Reduce the margins to allow more room for data. Remember, however, that most laser printers have minimum margin requirements, usually about 0.3 inches.
- Change to a smaller sans serif font. Helvetica, for example, requires less horizontal room than does Times Roman. An 8-point font usually is adequate for spreadsheet information.
- Have the person who created the original spreadsheet assign names to blocks or ranges of cells. Then as you import the spreadsheet, you can simply choose from the list of named ranges and import just the range of cells you need.

▶ **See** "Importing and Working with Spreadsheet/Database Data," **p. 573**
▶ **See** "Merging into Tables," **p. 623**

**TROUBLESHOOTING**

**I tried to open a spreadsheet, but I got an error message saying the file is not a supported format.** Although WordPerfect supports many different spreadsheet formats, you must be sure that the necessary conversion files are installed when you install WordPerfect. Run the WordPerfect 7 Setup, choose a Custom install, highlight PerfectFit Conversions, and click the Components button. In the PerfectFit Conversions dialog box, highlight Spreadsheet Conversions and click the Components button. Select the file conversion types you need, placing a check mark in each check box. Click OK twice and continue the installation.

# Using Custom Table Styles

In Chapter 16, you learned how to use basic line and fill styles to modify the appearance of your tables. WordPerfect also enables you to select a variety of predefined table designs.

## Creating Your Own Table SpeedFormat Styles

If you create a certain table format that you particularly like, you can save that style as a SpeedFormat style and use it again as often as you like. To create your own SpeedFormat style, follow these steps:

1. Make any format changes you want, including justification, text size, lines, and fills.
2. With the cursor in your table, choose SpeedFormat.
3. In the Table SpeedFormat dialog box, click Create. WordPerfect displays the Create Table Style dialog box.
4. In the Name text box, type a name for your table style.
5. Choose OK to save the new table style.

You can make this or any other table style the default by clicking Initial Style and choosing OK.

## Using Alternating Fills for Rows or Columns

One of the more popular styles for tables is an alternating pattern of filled rows or columns. Computer programming printouts, for example, used to use a "green bar" pattern to help readers follow the data. WordPerfect enables you to establish an alternating pattern of your choice, and as you expand your table WordPerfect automatically continues alternating that pattern.

To create alternating rows of dark green and light green, for example, follow these steps:

1. With the cursor in your table, choose Lines/Fill from the QuickMenu.
2. In the Properties for Table Lines/Fill dialog box, choose the Table tab.

**NOTE** The more technically correct name of many dialog boxes includes the phrase 'Properties for...", as in the Properties for Table Lines/Fill dialog box. From this point, however, the short name will be used, as in the Table Lines/Fill dialog box.

3. In the Alternating Fill area, choose Rows from the Type pop-up menu. WordPerfect then displays a modified Table Lines/Fill dialog box (see fig. 31.7).

**FIG. 31.7**
Choose the Table tab in the Table Lines/Fill dialog box to access the alternating fills feature. Your table then continues to alternate fills as it expands.

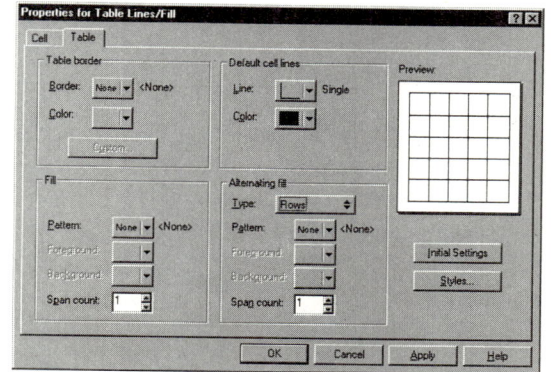

4. From the the Fill area, select 100% from the Pattern palette, then select green (or any other color) from the Foreground palette. This applies 100 percent shading to the entire table.
5. To set alternating rows to a lighter shade, from the Alternating Fill group, turn on alternating rows by selecting Rows from the Type pop-up list. Select 10% from the Pattern palette and green from the Foreground palette. The preview box displays the alternating dark/light row shading.
6. Change the Span Count for either the Fill or the Alternating Fill to determine the number of consecutive rows for each pattern and color, and note the results in the Preview box.

7. If you want to make this your default table style (for this and all subsequent tables you create), choose Initial Settings, and choose Yes.

8. If you want to make additional settings while in the Table Lines/Fill dialog box, you can apply those settings you've chosen so far by choosing the Apply button. When all of your settings are complete and you are ready to return to your document window, choose OK.

> **CAUTION**
> Any time you use a colored fill where you also intend to display text, be sure to select a color that isn't too dark (for example, dark green, or more than about 30% black shading) or too busy (for example, the wave pattern).

Now, as you enter data in your table and expand the rows in your table, every other row is solid green, and alternating rows are light green.

## Customizing Table Lines and Borders

You also can significantly enhance the appeal of tables by modifying the lines that separate their cells and customizing their borders.

### Customizing Lines

In addition to the predefined line styles described in Chapter 16, "Working with Tables," WordPerfect enables you to create your own custom line styles and effects. Furthermore, you can save your custom lines in style templates or in SpeedFormat table styles and use them over and over again.

Suppose that you want to separate the top row of your invoice (the column header row) from the rest of the table with something fancier than a simple thick line. You can create a style that includes, for example, two thick black lines separated by a thicker gray line, with no white space in-between (see fig. 31.8).

To create a custom line, follow these steps:

1. Position the cursor in the cell, or select the group of cells where you intend to use the new style. (This is not terribly important, however, because you can create the style first and then use it later.)

2. From the QuickMenu choose Lines/Fill, and from the Lines/Fill dialog box choose Styles. WordPerfect displays the Graphics Styles dialog box.

3. Click Create; WordPerfect presents the Create Line Style dialog box (see fig. 31.9).

**FIG. 31.8**
A customized table line consists of two thick black lines separated by a thicker gray line.

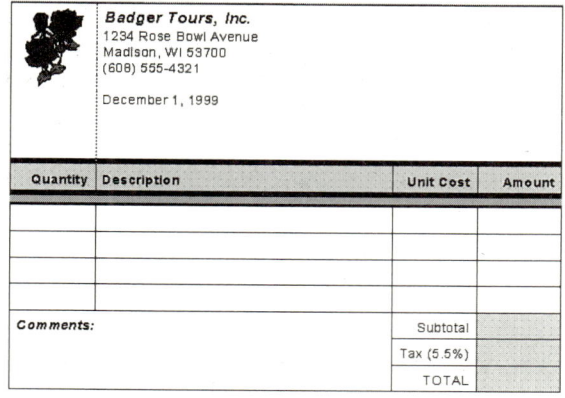

**FIG. 31.9**
The Create Line Style dialog box, the way it appears after following the steps to create a custom line, is used to customize your line styles.

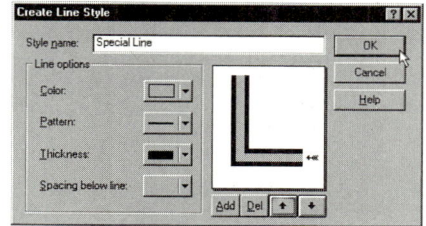

4. In the Style Name text box, type a unique name (for example, **Special Line**).
5. Click the Thickness palette button and in the text box enter **.05"**, then press Enter. Also, click the Spacing Below Line button and in the text box enter **0"**.
6. Click Add twice. This adds two more lines to the style, each 0.05 inches wide with no spacing between them. Notice that in the preview box, an arrow points to the bottom line. Move this arrow by clicking the up- and down-arrow buttons until it points to the middle of the three lines.
7. Choose Color and change the color to gray. Also, change the Thickness of this line to **0.1"**.
8. When you are finished, choose OK to close the Create Line Style dialog box.

If you want to keep your new line style with just the current document, simply use the line style wherever you want and save the document. However, if you think you want to use this line style over again, you can save it in your personal line styles library. (See Chapter 10, "Using Styles," for details on working with customized styles.)

To apply the newly created line style to an existing table, choose Styles in the Table Lines/Fill dialog box, and then choose the style from the bottom of the Styles list in the Graphics Styles dialog box.

## Customizing Table Borders

Table borders are separate from the lines of the table, and you change them separately from table lines. By default, WordPerfect displays no border at all around tables. The border you see is actually the default outside single lines of the table cells themselves. The advantage of this approach is that if you add or delete rows or columns or sort your table, any border you have selected remains a border and does not affect—nor is it affected—by table cell lines.

▶ See "Changing Table Lines, Borders, and Fills," **p. 524**
▶ See "Working with Styles from Other Files," **p. 355**

Unless you actually change the outside cell lines to something specific, their default single lines yield to any border style you select and do not appear. For example, to change the appearance of the table to look like tables in WordPerfect 5.1 or 5.2, you change the border style to double lines.

Suppose you want to surround your table with a three-line border and create a shadow effect. Perform the following series of steps to create a customized table border:

1. Choose T<u>a</u>ble, <u>L</u>ines/Fill, or from the QuickMenu, choose <u>L</u>ines/Fill.
2. Choose the Table tab so the dialog box displays the table-related options (see fig. 31.10).

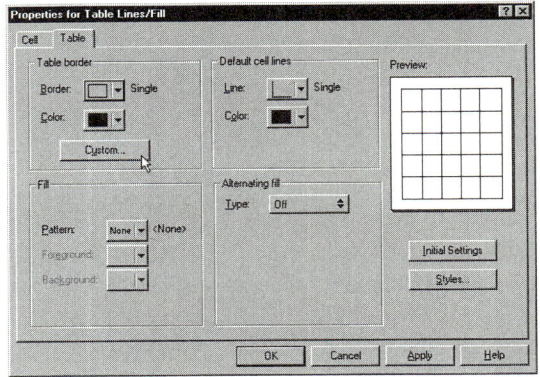

**FIG. 31.10**
Customize a Table Border style from the Table tab of the Table Lines/Fill dialog box.

From the Table Border area, normally you just select a <u>B</u>order line style from the palette or drop-down list beneath the palette. However, the style you want isn't there (for example, Triple is actually a thin-thick-thin triple with no shadow).

3. Click the <u>S</u>tyles button. WordPerfect displays the Graphic Styles dialog box.

> **NOTE** If you don't intend to create and save a custom border as a style, you can simply choose C<u>u</u>stom in the Table/Lines Fill dialog box and skip to steps 6-8.

4. In the Graphic Styles dialog box, click Create to display the Create Border Style dialog box.

5. In the Style Name text box, type the name of your special style—for example, **Triple-Shadow**.

6. Choose Line Styles and using either the button or the drop-down list, choose Triple (three regular thin lines).

7. You also can specify the type of drop shadow you want. Click the Drop Shadow Type palette button, and choose a drop shadow style—for example, with the shadow to the left and bottom.

8. Note how your newly defined border looks in the preview window (see fig. 31.11). If no further changes are needed, choose OK.

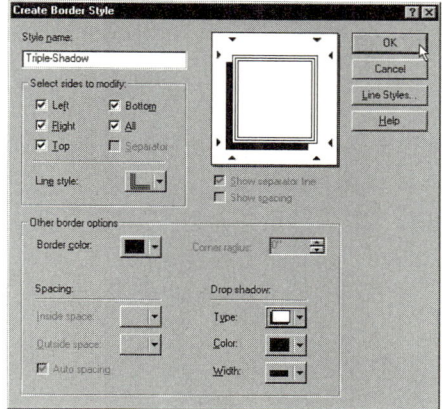

**FIG. 31.11**
Customize or create a new border style in the Create Border Style dialog box.

9. If you want this style just for this document, choose Close. However, if you want to save this border style for future use, in the Graphic Styles dialog box choose Options, Save As, and save the style in your personal styles library. (See Chapter 10, "Using Styles," for details on working with customized styles.)

10. In the Table Lines/Fill dialog box, click the Border palette button, and from the drop-down list choose the style you just created—for example, Triple-Shadow. Choose OK to return to your document. Note that custom styles always appear at the end of the list rather than alphabetically.

## Customizing Cell and Table Shading

WordPerfect uses the term *fill* to refer to shading cells, tables, and graphics boxes. By default, WordPerfect tables are not shaded or filled. But WordPerfect offers a wide variety of shading options, including percentages of shading, colors, and even gradient shading.

Suppose that you want to change the shading on the column heading row of your Invoice table. Follow these steps for changing cell shading, which are similar for changing table and graphics box shading:

1. Select all the cells in the row you want to shade—for example, the column headings row.
2. From the QuickMenu, choose Lines/Fill.
3. Choose the Styles button. WordPerfect displays the Graphic Styles dialog box.
4. Choose the Fill radio button.
5. Click Create to display the Create Fill Style dialog box.
6. Choose Gradient to display the gradient options of the dynamic dialog box.
7. In the Style Name text box, type the name of your special style—for example, **Special Shading**.
8. Under Pattern Options, from the Foreground Color palette choose gray, and leave the Background color at white.
9. Leave the Gradient at Linear, but change the Vertical Offset to **0**.
10. Notice what your style looks like in the preview box (see fig. 31.12); when everything is the way you want it, choose OK.

**FIG. 31.12**
Preview custom cell and table shading in the preview box of the Create Fill Style dialog box.

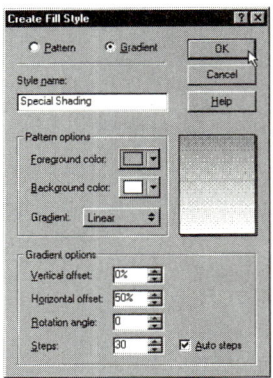

11. In the Graphic Styles dialog box, you can choose Options, Save As to save this fill style for future use. If, however, you want this style just for this document, choose Close.
12. Finally, in the Table Lines/Fill dialog box, click the Fill style palette button, and then from the drop-down list that appears beneath the palette of predefined styles choose

the style you just created—for example, Special Shading. Choose OK to return to your document.

Note that your cells are still selected, and your new shading may look strange. Simply click anywhere on your document to deselect the cell, and you then can see what the effect of your shading really is.

Remember that you are not limited to just one fill style (shading) in a table. For example, if you have a color printer, you could shade certain rows light green, others slightly darker green, and even others solid green. Even if you have a black and white printer, WordPerfect interprets colors with corresponding shades of gray. Appropriate uses of shading can have a dramatic impact on the readability of a table.

**NOTE** Don't forget that you can save your custom table format as an expert SpeedFormat style. See "Using Table SpeedFormat Styles" in Chapter 16.

### TROUBLESHOOTING

**When I create a custom line, it overlaps the text of the cell.** Thick lines, in particular, will overlap text in a cell because the cell doesn't automatically expand to accommodate the new line. You need to increase the cell margins (from the Table Format dialog box, choose the Column tab and change the Left or Right column margins, or choose the Row tab and change the Top or Bottom margins). You may also need to increase the column width or the row height or center the text vertically in the cell in order to have enough room for both the line and the text.

**After I change the fill for a row of cells, I can't read the text in those cells.** If you choose a shading that is too dark (30 percent or more, or a color such as blue), black text will be hard to read. Instead, choose a lighter shade (10 percent, for example) or color (yellow is quite light). If you really want a dark background, select the cells you want to fill, and then play the Reverse macro. This macro enables you to choose, for example, a black background with white printing. If that macro is not available (for example, on your network), you can change the shading and text colors yourself.

# Using Basic Math and Formulas in Tables

WordPerfect does such a great job with formatting text that it's easy to forget the many features that can take advantage of your computer's native capability to work with numbers. In this section, you learn not only how to add and subtract numbers in a table, but also how to use the table as a simple spreadsheet. This section also prepares you for the next section, in which you explore more complex formulas.

## Understanding Spreadsheets

If you use spreadsheet programs, you probably have noticed the similarity between WordPerfect's tables and a typical spreadsheet layout. Both arrange data in rows and columns, and the intersection of a row and a column is a cell.

Up to this point, you have learned about tables which allow you to arrange and format information. To use a table as a spreadsheet requires you to rethink the function of the table. In other words, you must switch from thinking about a table as a text formatter to thinking of it as a number processor. For example, you must consider whether cells are text only, or whether they have numeric values.

In the case of numeric cells, you specify number type and then let WordPerfect add formatting such as dollar signs, commas, or percent signs. If you use formulas, you must decide what you are trying to calculate. You also must be ready to analyze your table to make sure the numbers you see make sense, and be prepared to modify formulas that aren't functioning properly or that don't produce correct results.

## Designing a Spreadsheet

For simple tasks, jumping right in and building the layout and formulas in a table is okay. But often you find that the table's complexity increases as you begin to add functionality. In such cases, consider planning your table before you start to create it. A bit of planning during the early stages makes creating a functional table much easier.

On a separate sheet of paper, sketch the layout of your table. Pencil in the locations of calculations and the bits of information used to make those calculations. For example, when planning the formulas for your Invoice table, you might say to yourself, "I want to multiply the quantity times the unit cost to get the extended amount. I then want to add all the extended amounts, 5 1/2 percent sales tax, and shipping fees, and then produce a total amount due."

Don't be afraid to think in the broadest terms. WordPerfect's Tables functions are very flexible and powerful. Whether you need to perform complex interest payment schedules or simply add prices, WordPerfect's Tables functions are up to the task. Browse through the WordPerfect's online reference to see just what functions are available and what they can do.

> **NOTE** While WordPerfect's tables can handle powerful and complex spreadsheet functions, they are not intended to replace spreadsheet programs such as Quattro Pro or Excel. Instead, they afford you the ability to create and calculate spreadsheet data within a WordPerfect document. If what you are doing includes only spreadsheet data, you may want to use a spreadsheet program instead. In fact, because the basic WordPerfect suite comes with Quattro Pro, you might consider learning to use that program for your more complex spreadsheet needs.

Determine the number of columns you need and, if possible, the number of rows. Given the number of columns, try to determine how wide those columns must be and whether you need to change your paper size or orientation (for example, landscape) or reduce the size of your font (for example, 8-point Helvetica). Other format considerations, such as text attributes, lines, borders, and fills can be determined later. At this point, focus on the functionality of the table.

## Adding Spreadsheet Capabilities to a Table

By default, WordPerfect considers as text all information typed into a table cell, even numbers. When you begin to add formulas to tables, WordPerfect recognizes the values of any numbers you have entered and can use these numbers in formulas and calculations.

In WordPerfect, you really don't convert a table into a spreadsheet, as much as you begin to use the tool that adds spreadsheet functionality to your table: the Formula Bar.

To explore how WordPerfect handles numbers in tables—with and without the Formula Bar—begin by creating a simple 3-column × 4-row table. Also, before you continue, access the Tables QuickMenu and choose Row/Column Indicators (see fig. 31.13). These indicators help you know what cell you are looking at. Now try the following steps:

**FIG. 31.13**
Use Row/Column indicators when working with tables to better see your exact column and row location.

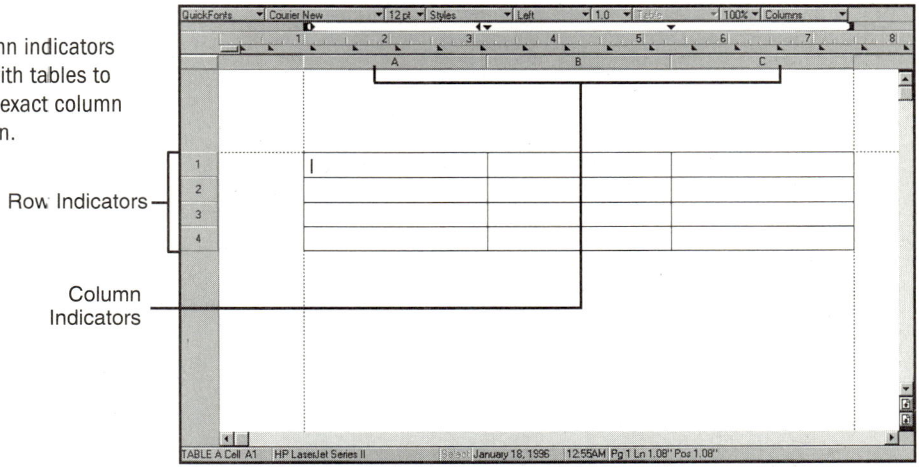

1. Type **2** in cell A1, and **3** in cell B1. Notice that the numbers appear just as you would expect them to. Later they can be used as reference values for formulas.
2. Type **7 South Park St** in cell A2, and **555-1234** in cell B2. Notice that although the phone number could be interpreted as numbers (for example, 555 minus 1234), WordPerfect displays the phone number as text.

3. Type **7/1/96** in cell A3 and **2** in cell B3. Again, WordPerfect displays the date rather than calculating 7 divided by 1 divided by 96.

4. Type **a1*b1** in cell C1. Again, WordPerfect sees the formula as text, displaying a1*b1 in the cell.

5. Now access the Formula Bar by choosing Formula Bar from the QuickMenu or from the Table menu. WordPerfect's Formula Bar (see fig. 31.14) treats as a formula that information that looks like a formula.

**FIG. 31.14**
Use WordPerfect's Formula Bar to help you enter and edit table cell formulas.

6. Now position your cursor in cell A4, select the Formula Bar edit box and type **7/1/96**. Press Enter or click the green check mark to enter the formula in cell A4. Note that the result this time is 0.0729166667.

7. Position your cursor in cell B4, click the Formula Bar edit box and type **555-1234**. Press Enter or click the green check mark and note the result in cell B4: -679.

8. Position the insertion point in C1 and note that in the Formula Bar edit box, WordPerfect displays the number 1. This is because WordPerfect considers the first number it encounters in a cell as the value of that cell. Now enter **a1*b1** in the Formula Bar edit box. When you press Enter, WordPerfect views what you typed as a formula and displays the result of multiplying those two cells (for example, 6).

9. Position the cursor in cell C2. Remember that the values in cells A2 and B2 were entered as text. Click the Formula Bar edit box, type **a2*b2**, and press Enter. The result, 3885, comes from multiplying the first separate number in each of the two cells (7 × 555).

**TIP**
For quick formula entry without using the Formula Bar, simply position the insertion point in the cell where you want the formula, and type the formula beginning with = or +. For example, in step 8 you could type **=a2*b2** directly in cell C2, and when you move the insertion point to another cell, WordPerfect automatically interprets it as a formula and displays the result in the cell.

**N O T E**  Fortunately, formulas do recognize numbers in cells that also contain text. You can enter, for example, **2 ea**. in a Quantity column, and a formula would recognize the 2 but ignore the text. However, you have to be careful because you may not expect such numbers to calculate. For example, if you add a list of numbers in a 2nd Quarter column, you may inadvertently add an extra 2 to your total.

10. Position the insertion point in cell A3 and note the value listed in the Formula Bar edit box (35246). WordPerfect has interpreted the date as a date value (more on this later) and is an exception to text being interpreted strictly as text.

In summary, to enter formulas in a cell, use the Formula Bar to enter formulas by way of the Formula Bar edit box.

> **TIP** For easiest formula entry, turn on and leave on the Formula Bar while working with tables that contain formulas.

## Formatting Numeric Data

You can use standard table formatting, such as alignment, for all table cells—both text and numeric—by choosing F_ormat from the QuickMenu. You also can add additional formatting to numeric cells by choosing _Numeric Format from the QuickMenu.

Consider the Invoice table you created in Chapter 16, "Working with Tables" (see fig. 31.15). The information in the Quantity column contains both numbers and text and needs no special formatting beyond right alignment. The Description column is all text. The Unit Cost and Amount columns, however, are best formatted as currency, whether for numbers or for formulas. To format either of these columns, position the cursor in the column you want to change and choose _Numeric Format from the QuickMenu (or press Alt+F12). When WordPerfect displays the Table Numeric Format dialog box, choose the Column tab (see fig. 31.16).

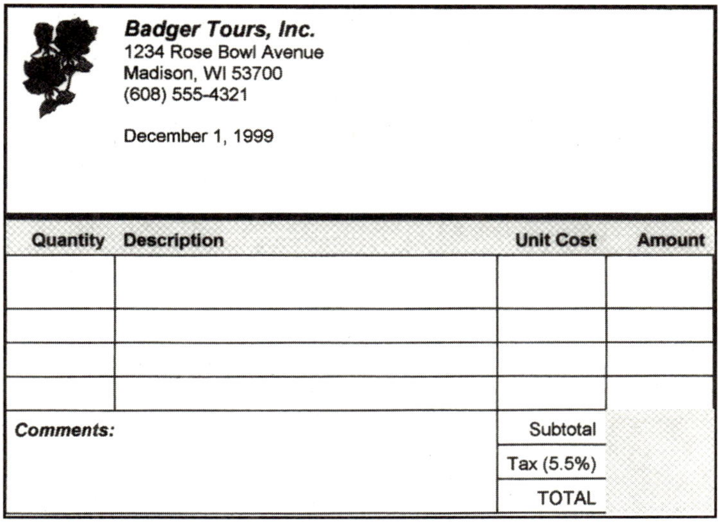

**FIG. 31.15**
In a table used as an invoice, cells have been formatted for currency by choosing T_ables, _Numeric Format.

**Badger Tours, Inc.**
1234 Rose Bowl Avenue
Madison, WI 53700
(608) 555-4321

December 1, 1999

| Quantity | Description | | Unit Cost | Amount |
|---|---|---|---|---|
|  |  |  |  |  |
|  |  |  |  |  |
|  |  |  |  |  |
|  |  |  |  |  |
| Comments: |  |  | Subtotal |  |
|  |  |  | Tax (5.5%) |  |
|  |  |  | TOTAL |  |

**FIG. 31.16**

The Table Numeric Format dialog box enables you to choose the numeric format for table cells.

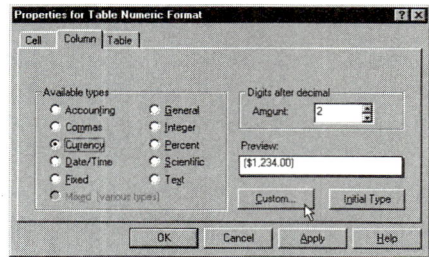

Because you are displaying currency values, choose Currency from the list of Available Types. In the Preview box, you can see what the format is for the number type you choose (for example, ($1,234.00)). In this dialog box, you also can choose how many digits to display after the decimal.

In the Table Numeric Format dialog box, you can set how many digits to display and whether to round to this digit for calculation purposes (be careful, you can lose money if you do this!). You can choose additional numeric formatting options by clicking Custom. WordPerfect displays the Customize Number Type dialog box (see fig. 31.17). Here you can specify how you want to display negative numbers (Minus Sign, Parenthesis, or CR/DR Symbol); whether to use the currency symbol and how it is to be aligned in the cell; and whether to use commas to separate thousands. You even can choose from a list of 48 international currency symbols.

**FIG. 31.17**

The Customize Number Type dialog box can be used for additional numeric formatting of table cells.

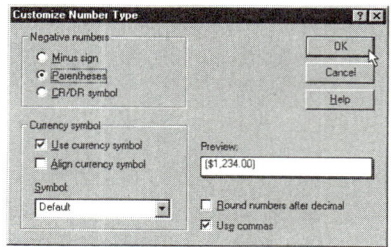

When you have chosen the format and options, choose OK to close the Customize Number Type dialog box, and then choose OK again to return to your document.

Unfortunately, WordPerfect does not automatically align numbers according to the number type you select. Therefore, to complete the formatting of the Unit Cost and Amount columns, choose Format from the QuickMenu, select the Column tab, and then choose Justification, Decimal Align. Choosing the Digits After Decimal option to specify how many characters appear to the right of the decimal point. Here, using the Position From Right option, you also can specify how far from the right margin of the cell you want to align your decimal point. By default, WordPerfect allows room for two digits. If you change this (for example, to 4), you aren't specifying how many digits to display, but instead how many digits away from the right margin you want your decimal point (for example, room for four digits, even if you only display two digits). If you use the Position From Right method, you specify the exact location of the decimal point. This method may be more difficult because how the digits actually display depends on the font style and size you are using.

Finally, the Unit Cost and Amount column headings may not look correct if you change the alignment of the columns. To correct this, select the two column heading cells, choose Format from the QuickMenu, and choose Justification, Right.

## Forcing Text Mode for Cells that Contain Numbers

Normally, WordPerfect considers combinations of text and numbers to be text, but does recognize the first separate numbers in such cells and uses them in calculations if you reference that cell in a formula. For example, if your column heading is Bin 1 and you add the column's values, the total equals one more than you expect, because the value 1 in Bin 1 is added to the total. You can avoid this problem in one of two ways:

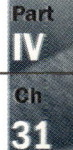

- Using the Formula Bar, enter the text in the Formula Bar text box, enclosed in quotes (for example, **"Bin 1"**). WordPerfect then inserts Bin 1 (without quotes) in the cell and treats it completely as text.

- If you have many such cells, this process could be quite tedious. Instead, select all the cells you want to force into Text mode, and from the QuickMenu choose Numeric Format. From the Cell tab of the Table Numeric Format dialog box that appears, choose Text Type from the Available Types list. The result of this is that any number entered in text-type cells is entered as text and ignored in all calculations.

If you want to enter numbers as values but ignore the value during calculations, you can enter the number as a regular value, then choose Format from the QuickMenu, and choose Ignore Cell When Calculating from the Cell tab of the dialog box. The advantage to this method is that when you deselect the Ignore Cell When Calculating check box, the value then can be calculated in a formula. Changing the Numeric format to Text, as described previously, does not permit this.

## Creating Formulas

You are now ready to create formulas that range in complexity from simple adding or multiplying of cells, to the use of functions such as PMT(), which is used to calculate loan payments. Begin with something basic. For example, use the Invoice table again and calculate the extended amount (Quantity × Unit Cost). Then add the Amounts column, and calculate and add the tax.

The first step in creating formulas (after creating the basic table, of course) is to turn on the Formula Bar (choose Formula Bar from the QuickMenu if it isn't already selected).

In your Invoice table, position the cursor in cell D3. Here you want the results of multiplying cells A3 and C3, so in the Formula Bar edit box type **A3*C3** and press Enter. WordPerfect displays the result of the formula in cell D3. In the General Status box of the status bar, WordPerfect displays the Table and Cell location along with the actual formula contained in the cell at that location.

**NOTE** The General Status box of the status bar may not be wide enough to display the entire formula contained in a cell. You can edit the status bar and widen the General Status box by choosing Edit, Preferences, Status Bar, and then by dragging the edge of the box to the right before choosing OK.

Because you knew that you wanted to multiply cell A3 times cell C3, you entered the formula directly into the Formula Bar edit box. However, what do you do if you forget the cell locations (for example, a large table in which you can't see all the different cells that you want to include in the formula)? Fortunately, WordPerfect allows you to "point" at the cells you want as you "compose" your formula.

To compose a formula by pointing, follow these steps:

1. Position the cursor in the cell where you want your formula—for example, in cell D3.

    If you already entered a formula in the cell, WordPerfect displays the formula in the Formula Bar edit box (to the right of the green check mark on the Formula Bar). Otherwise, the edit box is empty.

2. Click the mouse pointer in the Formula Bar edit box. Delete any formula you see there. Notice that in the Formula Bar, WordPerfect displays the message Formula Edit Mode is On.

3. Begin composing the formula by clicking the cells you want to include, and by typing any required math or function symbols in the Formula Bar edit box.

    For example, click the mouse pointer in cell A3. WordPerfect displays a highlighted A3 in the Formula Bar edit box. Type the asterisk (*). Finally, click the mouse pointer in cell C3. WordPerfect now displays A3*C3 in the Formula Bar edit box.

4. When you have the formula you want, enter the formula in the target cell (for example, **D3**) by clicking the green check mark just to the left of the Formula Bar edit box, or by pressing Enter.

If you decide to cancel the formula, click the red X on the Formula Bar, or press Esc.

> **CAUTION**
> When you first enter a formula, WordPerfect automatically calculates the formula and displays the result. Subsequent changes to cells referenced by this formula do not change the calculated result. Before you depend on the results you see, always choose Calculate from the QuickMenu or the Calculate button from the Formula Bar to update your table formulas. If you want to make calculation take place automatically, choose Table, Calculate and choose the Calculate Table option button in the Calculate dialog box.

## Copying Formulas

You now want to repeat this formula in the three remaining Amount rows. Fortunately, WordPerfect does not require that you enter this formula three more times. Instead, you can copy the formula by following these steps:

1. Position the cursor in the cell that contains the formula you want to copy (for example, in cell D3).
2. Choose Copy Formula from the Formula Bar or choose Table, Copy Formula. WordPerfect displays the Copy Formula dialog box (see fig. 31.18).

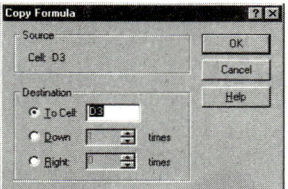

**FIG. 31.18**
The Copy Formula dialog box enables you to copy a formula from one cell to another. WordPerfect automatically adjusts the cell references in the formula to reflect its new location.

3. Note the location of the cell in the Source area (for example, D3) to make sure you are copying the correct formula.

   You can copy the formula to a cell Down *n* Times in the same column, or to the Right *n* Times in the same row.

   Choose Down and specify how many cells you want to copy the formula to (**3**, for example).

4. Choose OK. WordPerfect copies the formula to all three cells immediately below the current cell.

**TIP** The displayed results of your copied formulas may not be correct because they have not yet been calculated. Click the Calculate button from the Formula Bar or Calculate from the QuickMenu to update the results.

WordPerfect automatically adjusts the cell references in formulas to reflect the new location of the formula. This is called *relative referencing*. For example, move the cursor to cell D4 and notice that the formula reads A4*C4. In cell D5, it reads A5*C5, and so on.

> **CAUTION**
> Any inserted rows do not automatically include the formula. Relative referencing should remain correct on remaining rows, but, depending on where the row is inserted, summation formulas may not update correctly.

## Using Functions in Formulas

Already you can see the power of formulas in WordPerfect tables. But WordPerfect goes even further by providing nearly 100 special functions that you can use in your formulas to manipulate and calculate your data in exactly the same way you do in a full-featured spreadsheet. In this section, you learn the basics of working with functions.

To total the Amounts column in your Invoice table, follow these steps:

1. Position the cursor in the cell in which you want the subtotal (for example, in cell D7). Always start a formula in the exact cell in which you want to display the result.
2. If the Formula Bar is not displayed, choose Formula from the QuickMenu or from the Table menu.
3. In the Formula Bar edit box on the Formula Bar, type **sum(** and then type the range of cells to include—for example **d3:d6**. Type the closing **)** and press Enter, or click the green check mark on the Formula Bar.

A different but perhaps easier method is to use the mouse to select the functions and the cell range to include. Rather than performing step 3, simply click the Formula Bar edit box, and then click Functions on the Formula Bar to open the Table Functions dialog box; from the list, select SUM(List) and choose Insert. WordPerfect places the function in the Formula Bar edit box, with List highlighted. Using the mouse, select the cells you want to include (for example, cells D3–D6). WordPerfect automatically displays D3:D6 in place of the word List in the Formula Bar edit box. Press Enter or click the green check mark to enter the formula, SUM(D3:D6), in the table.

The results may be correct, but don't forget to click Calculate to make sure.

 **TIP** To add numbers directly above the formula cell, click QuickSum from the Formula Bar, or simply enter + as the formula for the cell. WordPerfect adds any numbers in the same column above the + sign.

The remaining formulas in the Invoice table are quite easy compared to using functions. In cell D8, you want to calculate the tax using the formula C7*.055 (5 1/2 percent tax). In cell D9, you want the total of the amounts plus the tax, so you use the formula C7+C8.

## Modifying, Deleting, and Calculating Cells and Formulas

When you finish building your table and its formulas, recalculate one more time. Choose Table, Calculate or click Calculate from the Formula Bar. Then examine the table to make sure the results make sense.

 **TIP** Most mistakes in formulas produce obviously wrong results. The best time to find and correct any mistakes is while the table and what you are trying to do are fresh in your mind.

To correct or change a formula, position the cursor in the cell that contains the formula. In the Formula Bar edit box on the Formula Bar, make any necessary corrections, or even start over. When you are through, click the green check mark or press Enter to insert the updated formula in your table. If you attempt to change the result of a formula directly in the table cell, WordPerfect prompts you that you are about to replace a formula. Choose Yes to replace the formula with the value you typed, or choose No to keep the formula in the cell.

To correct or change values in a referenced cell, move to that cell and make the changes. For example, if your unit costs just rose from $12.36 to $13.24, change the amount in the appropriate cell.

After making any changes to formulas or cell values, recalculate your table so that the information you see is the latest and most up-to-date version.

## Locking Table Cells

After you finish setting the formulas and attributes for a cell, you can lock the cell to protect it from further changes. Suppose that in the Invoice table, you don't want the user to be able to change the formulas in the Amount column cells. To lock a cell, follow these steps:

1. Position the cursor in the cell you want to lock.

2. From the QuickMenu, choose F<u>o</u>rmat.
3. In the Table Format dialog box, choose the Cell tab, and select the <u>L</u>ock check box.
4. Choose OK to return to your document. At this point, you cannot modify the contents of the cell without disabling cell lock. In the Table Format dialog box, click the Table tab, and choose <u>D</u>isable Cell Locks. You now can modify the contents of the cell or deselect the <u>L</u>ock check box.

**NOTE** You can use the Lock feature to speed data entry. After designing the entire form—for example, an Invoice form—lock the header cells and all the formula cells. When you fill in the form, pressing Tab moves you past any locked cells to the next unlocked cell.

# Designing More Complex Tables: The Grade-Tracking Table

The power and versatility of WordPerfect's Formula functions could fill an entire book. Therefore, this limited space focuses more on some of the procedures used to build a more complex table, and also introduces some of the powerful functions available in WordPerfect tables.

Suppose that you have to keep grades for your Spanish class. You don't have a grade-tracking program, nor do you have a spreadsheet (or you don't have time to learn the one you have). WordPerfect comes to your rescue by helping you build a table that can keep track of grades, provide totals and averages, and even create and print a report card that includes the student's letter grade.

Consider the grade-tracking table in figure 31.19. The purpose of this section is to explore the formula and other spreadsheet functions of tables, rather than review table-creating and formatting procedures. If you aren't sure of something, refer to Chapter 16, "Working with Tables," or preceding sections in this chapter.

**FIG. 31.19**
A grade-tracking table uses special functions to calculate totals, averages, percentages, and even letter grades.

| STUDENT NAME January 18, 1996 | Quizzes | | | Quiz Points | Exam 1 | Exam 2 | Paper | Total Points | Average % | Letter Grade |
|---|---|---|---|---|---|---|---|---|---|---|
| Possible Points | 85 | 70 | 100 | 100 | 150 | 150 | 200 | 600 | 100.0% | |
| Berndobler, Jerry | 83 | 65 | 92 | 94 | 136 | 130 | 175 | 535 | 89.2% | B |
| Bresser, Debra | 76 | 55 | 76 | 81 | 125 | 110 | 165 | 481 | 80.2% | C |
| Farmer, Mike | 85 | 69 | 96 | 98 | 144 | 143 | 190 | 575 | 95.8% | A |
| Larson, Jerry | 66 | 50 | 60 | 69 | 120 | 110 | 155 | 454 | 75.7% | D |
| Prochniak, Mary | 83 | 68 | 90 | 95 | 140 | 138 | 190 | 563 | 93.8% | A |
| Rinzell, Dennis | 50 | | 70 | 47 | 130 | 110 | 150 | 437 | 72.8% | D |
| AVERAGES | 73.8 | 61.4 | 80.7 | 80.7 | 132.5 | 123.5 | 170.8 | 507.5 | 84.6% | C |

The following summarizes how you can create the layout and format of the grade-tracking table:

- Accommodate in 11 columns the student names; each of the quizzes, tests, and papers; averages; and letter grades.
- Create enough rows to accommodate each member of the class, plus three rows for column headings, possible points, and averages.
- Measure and then specify a fixed width for each of the columns.
- Right-justify all the columns except the first (left-justified) and the last (centered).
- Join three cells for the Quizzes heading, and center the joined cell.
- Add line and fill changes after the entire table is built.

# Understanding Functions

Functions are both versatile and powerful, and can be divided into six basic groups or types:

- Arithmetic (AVE, SUM, QUOTIENT, and so on)
- Calendar (DATE and TIME, for example)
- Financial (NPV, PMT, and so forth)
- Logical (such as AND and FALSE)
- Special (BLOCK and LOOKUP, for example)
- Text (CHAR, LENGTH, and so on)

Most functions also require one or more arguments to complete the function. Multiple arguments must be separated by commas. For example, the SUM( ) function requires one argument: the list or range of cells to total. The PMT( ) function, on the other hand, requires five arguments: rate, present value, periods, future value, and type. All functions require a pair of parentheses following the function name, even when no argument is required—for example DATE( ). When you omit or mistype any part of the function, its arguments, or its punctuation, WordPerfect displays an error message suggesting how to correct it.

Thorough coverage of all WordPerfect table functions is beyond the scope of this book. See the *WordPerfect Reference* or the Help menu for information on functions. As you learn in the next section, a listing and mini-Help feature is available when you create formulas. Because the spreadsheet functions in WordPerfect are identical to those found in PlanPerfect—WordPerfect Corporation's old DOS-based spreadsheet program—you also can refer to the *PlanPerfect Reference* if you have it.

## Using a Function

Perhaps not the first, but one of the easier formulas in your grade-tracking table is the one that gives a class average for each quiz, test, and paper.

To create a formula to report an average, follow these steps:

1. If you haven't done so already, choose Formula Bar from the QuickMenu to display the Formula Bar. All the following procedures assume use of the Formula Bar.
2. Position the cursor in the last row of the first column of grades—B9 for example.
3. Click the mouse in the Formula Bar edit box, or press Alt+Shift+E.
4. Click the Functions button, or press Alt+Shift+F. In the Functions dialog box that appears, WordPerfect displays a list of nearly 100 functions. As you scroll through the list, WordPerfect displays a brief description of each function's purpose or use at the bottom of the dialog box. When you find the function you want—for example, AVE(List) (for averaging a list of numbers)—click Insert.
5. Specify the list, or range of cells, that are included in the average. You can type the range (for example, **B3:B8**), but it is much easier to use the mouse to select the cells in that range, because WordPerfect then automatically inserts B3:B8 in place of the word List in the formula.
6. Click the green check mark or press Enter to insert the formula in the table. If you haven't entered any student grades, the formula calculates to 0.

Your next task is to copy the AVE( ) formula eight times to the right. (You use another formula in the Letter Grade column.) After you copy the formula, notice that it changes automatically to reflect its new location. For example, in C9 the formula reads AVE(C3:C8). As explained earlier in the section "Copying Formulas," relative referencing enables you to copy formulas without having to edit them to match their new location.

## Using Formulas with Absolute References

Before you proceed, you should understand something about the difference between relative and absolute references so that your formulas work the way you expect them to when you copy them to other cells.

Each time you copy a formula, WordPerfect uses relative referencing, thus automatically changing the formula to reflect the formula's new location. Sometimes, however, you don't want one or more references in a formula to change. If you place brackets ([ ]) around a cell reference, it remains constant even when copied to a new location. This is called *absolute referencing*. You also can specify only the row or the column as absolute. For example, [A]2 means that row 2 changes relative to the new row as you copy down; however, as you copy the formula to the right, column A remains absolute in the copied formulas.

In the grade-tracking table, each instructor assigns different values to different testing activities. Assume that you grade the three quizzes using varying point values, but plan to give only 100 points total for all the quizzes. The formula for each student in column E, therefore, must divide that student's total quiz points by the total possible quiz points (the sum of all the points in cells B2–D2), and multiply by 100. Because each formula in the column references the same cells (B2:D2), you use absolute referencing.

To create a Quiz Points average formula using an absolute reference, follow these steps:

1. Position the cursor in cell E3 (the first student row) and then click the Formula Bar edit box.
2. Click Functions, find SUM(List), and click Insert. You can also simply type **sum(** (opening parenthesis) in the Formula Bar edit box.
3. Use the mouse to select the range of cells you want to include (for example, B3:D3). If you type the range, be sure to type a **)** (closed parenthesis) after D3—for example, **sum(B3:D3)**.
4. With the insertion point positioned after the closing parenthesis, type the division symbol (/).
5. Click Functions, choose SUM(List) from the list, and click Insert.
6. Use the mouse to select the range of cells by which you divide the student's scores; for example, **sum(B2:D2)**.
7. With the insertion point positioned after the closing parenthesis, type **\*100**. The formula now reads

    sum(B3:D3)/sum(B2:D2)*100

8. Finally, to make the sum of the cells in the range B2:D2 an absolute reference, type brackets on each side. The formula now reads

    sum(B3:D3)/sum([B2:D2])*100

With the sum of possible scores now established as an absolute reference, you can choose OK and safely copy the formula down to the other cells in column E. You even can copy the formula from E3 to E2 (the column heading row) to show the total possible points (100).

## Using the *SUM()* Function To Create a Total Points Formula

The formula for total points is relatively simple. You can use the SUM( ) function to add the range of cells from Quiz Points through the Paper (columns E–H). For example, the formula can read SUM(E2:H2).

That formula, however, works best for a final summary grade. To create a formula that reflects only the points possible to this point in the term, you can use a formula that lists only the cells of completed items—for example, SUM(E2, F2, H2). With this formula, the percentage averages and letter grades reflect a student's current standing in a more meaningful way.

The formula used on the student rows of column I should follow the pattern SUM(E3:H3). Although they may not have all the assignments completed or grades recorded, this formula gives a sum of what they have completed compared with the total number of points possible so far (at the top of the column).

## Creating the Percent Formula and a Percent Format

You calculate a student's final percentage average by dividing his or her total points by the total possible points in cell I2. Once again, you use absolute referencing to make sure each formula in the column divides by I2. For example, the formula in row three reads I3/[I2]. Copy the formula to the other student rows.

A perfect score results in 1, whereas most scores result in a decimal number less than 1. You can multiply the result by 100 to display a number that looks more like a percentage. But you also can format the entire column so that any number in the column appears as a percentage. To format a column for percentage, change the number type as follows:

1. Position the cursor in the column you want to format, for example, column J in the example.
2. From the QuickMenu, choose Numeric Format. Choose the Column tab, and from the list of number types choose Percent.

   Remember that number types enable you to predetermine the format of numbers you enter in a column.
3. You also can specify the decimal precision you want to display. For this example, choose Amount in the Digits After Decimal group on the Numeric Format dialog box. None of the other options apply here, but note them for future reference.
4. Choose OK to return to your document.

The value, 0.892, now appears as a properly formatted percentage: 89.2%. Remember, however, that if you reference a percentage cell in another formula, you must refer to the decimal value, not the displayed percentage (for example, 0.892, not 89.2).

## Using the *IF()* Function To Calculate the Letter Grade

One of the more powerful functions is the IF( ) statement, which you use to determine a result based on certain conditions. The syntax for this function is

        IF(CaseAisTrue, ThenResultB, OtherwiseResultC)

In column K of the grade-tracking table, for example, you want to indicate that the person receives a letter grade of "A" if his or her average is 92 percent or higher. In cell K3, you enter **IF(J3>=.93,"A","F")**. In plain English, this formula reads, "If the value of J3 is greater than or equal to 0.93, print an A in this cell, otherwise print an F." The percentage is entered as the decimal value to match properly the actual values in column J. Also, text strings can be part of a formula, but they must be surrounded by quotation marks.

This formula is a good start, but obviously you have a wider range of grades than just A's and F's. You need to use another IF statement in place of the F. In English, you say, "Otherwise, if J3 is greater than or equal to 0.85, print a B; otherwise, if J3 is greater than or equal to 0.76, print a C," and so on. The final formula looks like this:

        IF(J3>=.93,"A",IF(J3>=.85,"B",IF(J3>=.76,"C",IF(J3>=.7,"D","F"))))

Notice that the formula ends with four parentheses. For each opening parenthesis, you must add a closing parenthesis. If you enter the formula incorrectly, WordPerfect prompts you to modify it so all its functions, arguments, and punctuation are correct.

Copy this formula to all the student rows, as well as to the Averages row at the bottom. Functionally, the grade sheet is completed. Add lines and other cell formatting, lock formula cells, and save the grade sheet. You are ready to begin entering student names and grade scores.

# Using Names To Create a Report Card Table

As useful as the grade-tracking table is for monitoring student progress and how well the class is doing on your exams and quizzes, you can extend its power even further by using it to generate simple report cards. One method for doing this is to use floating cells (see "Using Floating Cells" later in this chapter). But another effective way is to use the Names feature to help transfer data from the master grades table to a report card table on a separate page in the same document.

## Creating the Form

Use the grade-tracking table as a model to create the report card table; make sure that the master grade-tracking table is completed and formatted just the way you want it. Then follow these steps:

1. Move to the bottom of your document and press Ctrl+Enter to create a new page.
2. Copy the entire grade-tracking table to this newly created page.
3. Position your cursor in row 4 of the copied table.

4. From the QuickMenu, click Delete and specify the number of rows you want to delete. Remove all but the first three rows. (Alternatively, split the table and delete the second of the two resulting tables.)

5. Be sure to save your work. Figure 31.20 shows the completed table.

**FIG. 31.20**
The student report card table is created by copying the grade-tracking table and deleting unneeded rows.

| STUDENT NAME January 18, 1996 | Quizzes | | | Quiz Points | Exam 1 | Exam 2 | Paper | Total Points | Average % | Letter Grade |
|---|---|---|---|---|---|---|---|---|---|---|
| Possible Points | 85 | 70 | 100 | 100 | 150 | 150 | 200 | 600 | 100.0% | |
| Berndobler, Gary | 83 | 65 | 92 | 94 | 136 | 130 | 175 | 535 | 89.2% | B |

## Creating Names in Tables

Every table has a name, and you can reference or go to a table in your document by using the name of the table. Unless you specify otherwise, WordPerfect names your tables `Table A`, `Table B`, and so on. When you copied your table in the preceding section, however, you ended up with two tables named `Table A`. (WordPerfect also copied the table name.)

You can easily assign descriptive names to your tables that make it easier to reference them in macros, formulas, and so on. To change the names of your tables, follow these steps:

1. Position the cursor in either table.
2. Choose Table, Names. WordPerfect displays the Table Names in Current Document dialog box (see fig. 31.21).

**FIG. 31.21**
The Table Names in Current Document dialog box lets you change the names of tables and cells, and then use those names as reference points for formulas, macros, and so on.

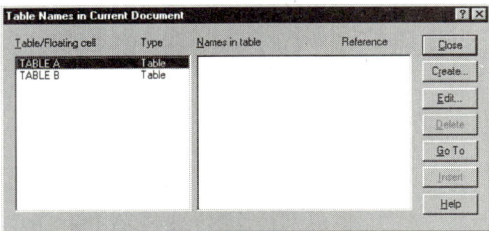

**NOTE** You cannot create or edit table names from the QuickMenu. However, you can do so by clicking the Names button on the Formula Bar.

3. Select the first Table A entry from the Table/Floating Cell list, and click Edit.
4. From the Edit Name/Reference dialog box that appears, type **Grade Sheet** in the Name text box and choose OK.

5. Select the second (remaining) Table A entry and choose Edit. Enter **Report Card** and choose OK.

6. Choose Close to return to your document.

You also need to name the first cell in the third row of the Report Card table as a reference point to which you can copy student data. To name a cell, follow these steps:

1. Position the cursor in the cell you want to name—for example cell A3 of the Report Card table.

2. Choose Table, Names. WordPerfect displays the Table Names in Current Document dialog box (refer to fig. 31.21).

3. Select the Report Card table from the Table/Floating Cell list and click Create. WordPerfect displays the Create Name dialog box (see fig. 31.22). In this dialog box, you can name a cell, range of cells, or entire row or column. You also can use the text in the cell to be named as the name for that cell.

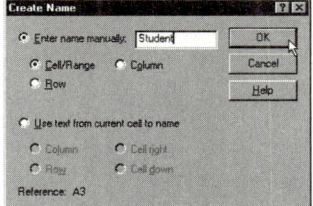

**FIG. 31.22**
The Create Name dialog box is used for naming cells, rows, and columns in a WordPerfect table.

4. In the Enter Name Manually text box, type **Student** and choose OK.

Now when you select the Report Card table in the Table Names in Current Document dialog box, STUDENT followed by A3 should appear in the Names in Table list.

5. Click Close to return to your document.

## Using Names in Tables

Table and cell names make it much easier to move from one location to another. For example, you can use the Go To command (Ctrl+G) to move from one table to another.

If you are in the Report Card table, press Ctrl+G and from the Table drop-down list, choose Grade Sheet and choose OK. If you want to go to a specific cell in another table, press Ctrl+G and choose both the table and the cell and choose OK (see fig. 31.23).

You also can use table/cell names as reference points in formulas. For example, if in your Invoice table you have a value in a cell named TOTAL and another named TAX, you can calculate the sales tax in your table by entering the formula with **INVOICE.TOTAL*TAX**. The table and cell are separated with a period.

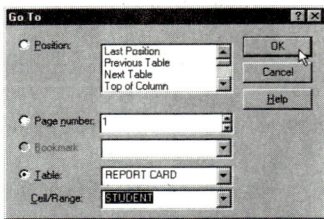

**FIG. 31.23**
Use the Go To dialog box to select a destination table and cell location.

Finally, you can use table and cell names as reference points in macros for copying data from one location to another. For example, you want to create a report card for each student by copying the data from his or her row on the master grade sheet table to the Student row on the Report Card table. After you position the cursor at the beginning of any row of grade information in the Grade Sheet table, include these basic steps in your macro (you also can perform these steps without using a macro):

1. Press Ctrl+Shift+Q to set a QuickMark bookmark.
2. Select the entire row of data by pressing Shift+F8 and then pressing Ctrl+right-arrow key. You also can hold down the Shift key and press End twice.
3. Choose Copy (Ctrl+C; or Ctrl+Insert), and from the Table Cut/Copy dialog box, choose OK (to copy selection).
4. Press Ctrl+G, and choose the Report Card table and the Student cell. Choose OK.
5. In the Student cell, choose Paste (Ctrl+V; or Shift+Insert).
6. Press Ctrl+Q to return to the original QuickMark bookmark location.

As you can see, table names and named cells give you tremendous power and flexibility as you work with table math and functions.

# Using Floating Cells To Create a Mortgage Loan Approval Letter

One of WordPerfect's unique new features, floating cells, provides the capability to use table functions and formulas in the body of your text. For example, you can use these cells to reference other floating cells or cells in any table such as in a mortgage loan letter that calculates payments based on current interest rates.

## Understanding and Creating Floating Cells

A *floating cell* is nothing more than a pair of codes that surround the same kind of information that you put in any table cell. Floating cells also can be formatted for number type, the same as in table cells.

To create a floating cell, position the cursor in your document text where you want to create the cell outside of an existing table. Then follow these steps:

1. Choose Table, Create. From the Create Table dialog box, choose Floating Cell. When you choose OK, the Formula Bar appears so you can enter a formula in the floating cell.
2. If you know the format you want for the floating cell, choose Table, Numeric Format and choose the number format you want to use.
3. WordPerfect automatically names floating cells—for example, FLOATING CELL A. If you plan to use the cell in a formula, you may want to use the Names feature to give it a more descriptive and shorter name—for example, **Amount**.
4. You can now enter the actual data for the floating cell in the Formula Bar edit box of the Formula Bar.

**NOTE** If the check mark next to the Formula Bar edit box is not green, then your cursor is positioned outside the pair of floating cell codes. Turn on Reveal Codes, move the cursor between the pair of codes, and the check mark turns green.

5. After you create the floating cell, assign the number type, and enter the data you want into the cell, you must move your cursor to the right, outside of the pair of floating cell codes. Press End or click the mouse to the right of the floating cell and continue with the text of your document.

## Using Calendar Math in a Floating Cell

Suppose you want to include in your letter a sentence stating that the loan offer is good for two weeks from today's date. You need to create two floating cells: one for today's date and one for the offer expiration date. The first cell contains the function MDY( ), using the Date/Time numeric format to display the current day. The second cell, also using the Date/Time numeric format, simply adds the contents of the first cell plus 14.

To create the closing paragraph of the loan letter (see fig. 31.24), follow these steps:

1. Type the paragraph until you reach the location of today's date (...beginning today, July 1, 1997,).
2. Choose Table, Create, Floating Cell, and choose OK.
3. Choose Table, Numeric Format, select Date/Time, and choose OK.
4. Choose Table, Names, and select FLOATING CELL from the Table/Floating Cell list, and click Edit.
5. In the Edit Name/Reference dialog box, type the name of the floating cell **Today**, choose OK, and then Close to return to the document window.

6. Click the Formula Bar edit box on the Formula Bar and enter **mdy( )**. Press Enter or click the green check mark to enter the formula into your document. The document should display today's date (for example, `July 1, 1997`).

7. Continue typing the paragraph until you reach the location of the expiration date (`…of this loan by`).

8. Repeat steps 2–4 to create a floating cell, formatted for Date/Time, and named **Expires**.

9. Click the Formula Bar edit box on the Formula Bar and enter **today+14**. Press Enter or click the green check mark to enter the formula into your document. The document should display today's date plus 14 days (for example, `July 15, 1997`).

10. Finish typing the paragraph and save the document.

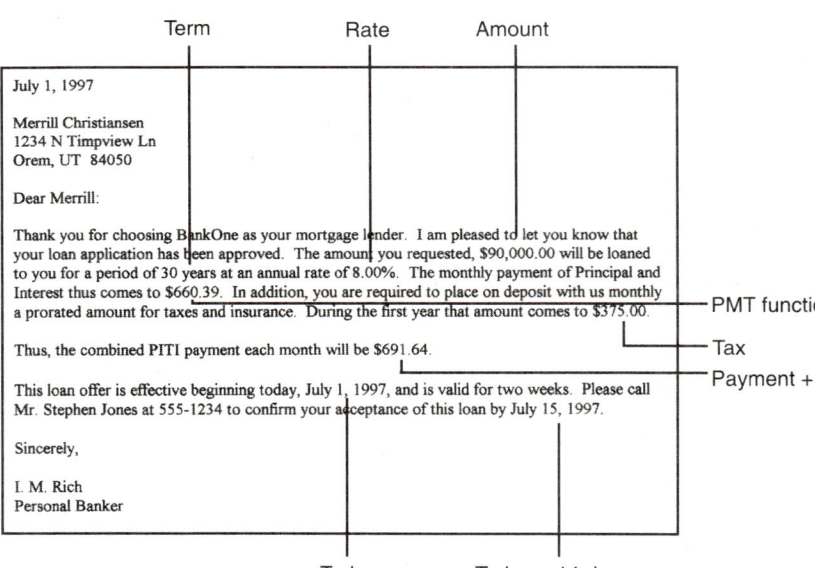

**FIG. 31.24**
By using floating cells, you can create a loan letter that uses functions in named cells to calculate a mortgage payment and the offer expiration date.

## Using the *PMT()* Function To Calculate a Loan Payment

The same principles you used to create the expiration date apply when using more complex formulas:

- Determine what arguments are required for the function.
- Create the floating cells (or table cells) that supply the information needed for the arguments.
- Name those cells so you can reference them easily.

- Create the floating cell that contains the function, assign a numeric format, and use named cells to create the formula.

The `PMT()` function is a good example of a powerful, yet relatively simple function. This function requires the following syntax and arguments:

`PMT(Rate,Present Value, Periods, Future Value, Type)`

- `Rate`. The annual interest rate. If you use periods other than years, the rate must be prorated. For example, 8 percent annual interest over 12 monthly periods must be expressed as `8%/12` (or `.08/12`).
- `Present Value`. The current or initial value of the loan expressed as a negative value because to the borrower, it is a negative amount (for example, `-90000`).
- `Periods`. The number of periods to be used in the calculation. A loan paid monthly for 30 years is for 360 periods (or `30*12`).
- `Future Value`. The amount of the loan when it is paid off—usually zero (0).
- `Type`. This indicates whether the payment is made at the end of a loan period (the default, 0) or at the beginning of the loan period (any non-zero value). This argument can be omitted altogether.

Thus, for a loan of $90,000, at 8 percent interest over 30 years, you use the following formula:

**pmt(.08/12, -90000, 360, 0, 0)**

Using the loan letter as a sample, enter the text you see until you reach each of the locations that contains a part of the `PMT( )` arguments. At that location, create a floating cell that contains the following:

- *Amount*. Name this **Amount**, choose Currency as the number type, and enter **90000** as the formula.
- *Period*. Name this **Years**, enter **30** as the formula (leaving the number type General).
- *Interest*. Name this **Interest**, choose Percent as the number type, and enter **8%** as the formula. Because the cell is formatted for percent, WordPerfect displays `8.00%` and also establishes the value of the floating cell as `.08`.

When you arrive at the payment amount, create the Payment floating cell, formatted for Currency, and enter the following formula:

**pmt(interest/12, amount, years*12, 0, 0)**

If you entered everything as indicated, the result should read `$660.39`.

## Simplifying Data Entry in a Floating Cell Letter

The amount of work required to enter each of the preceding entries is almost more work than it is worth. For example, to change the loan amount to $90,000, you must position the cursor between the Flt Cell codes. Then you delete the text that already is there and replace it with the new amount. You must do this in Reveal Codes to ensure that the new amount appears between the two floating cell codes.

A much easier method is to create a merge form using KEYBOARD( ) merge codes placed between the floating cell codes. Then when you merge the form, WordPerfect prompts you for the needed data and automatically inserts it in the proper floating cell location.

▶ See "Creating the Form File," **p. 591**
▶ See "Understanding the Keyboard Code," **p. 609**

You also can create a custom template document that prompts you for the necessary data and then fills it in at the proper locations.

▶ See "Creating a New Template," **p. 375**

> **CAUTION**
> Make sure your floating cell formulas and formats are the way you want them before you add the KEYBOARD( ) merge codes. If you change the formula, name, or number type in a floating cell, WordPerfect deletes any other data such as the merge code that may be in the cell.

Don't forget, after filling in the data, to update all the floating cells by choosing Table, Calculate, Calculate Document.

▶ See "Understanding Form Files," **p. 604**

### TROUBLESHOOTING

**After I create my table and formulas, the results don't appear to be correct.** There are no easy rules for making sure a table calculates correctly. However, try calculating the document first. Then examine each formula to make sure cell references and logic are correct. Finally, make sure you aren't inadvertently including a text cell that contains numbers in your formula (for example, adding a column that includes "2nd Quarter" so that the "2" is added to the total.) Proofreading formulas is as important as proofreading text, because incorrect formulas could cost you a lot of money.

**When I enter a dollar amount in a column, the cents sometimes wrap to the next line even though the original 0.00 displays properly.** Make sure the column is wide enough for the new number. The easiest method is to choose Size Column To Fit from the QuickMenu. If the numbers are in the last column, you probably have to change the width of the column. You also may need to change the amount of space reserved for numbers following the decimal point by choosing Format, and in the Column tab, specify the number of digits after the decimal.

# Using QuickFill To Simplify Data Entry

With WordPerfect you can create a calendar form using tables with fixed row height (see fig. 31.25). Although you could type in the days and dates by hand, WordPerfect's spreadsheet functions once again offer a simpler solution, as you learn in this section.

## Understanding QuickFill

The idea behind the QuickFill procedure is that WordPerfect can examine the first few entries in a series and automatically determine the pattern that is being used. The program then fills in the remaining blank cells in the series based on that pattern.

For example, if you want to enter a series of numbers in 15 cells, and the first three of those cells are 1, 3, and 5, WordPerfect would fill the remaining cells with 7, 9, 11, and so on.

**FIG. 31.25**
Use WordPerfect's QuickFill feature to automatically fill in days of the week and the calendar dates.

| | | | JUNE 1995 | | | |
|---|---|---|---|---|---|---|
| Sunday | Monday | Tuesday | Wednesday | Thursday | Friday | Saturday |
|  |  |  |  | 1 | 2 | 3 |
| 4 | 5 | 6 | 7 | 8 | 9 | 10 |
| 11 | 12 Summer Session Begins | 13 | 14 | 15 | 16 | 17 |
| 18 | 19 | 20 | 21 | 22 | 23 | 24 |
| 25 | 26 | 27 | 28 | 29 | 30 | |

## Using QuickFill To Enter the Days of the Week

In your calendar, the first row of seven cells should contain the days of the week. To automatically fill in these days, follow these steps:

1. Position the cursor in cell A1.
2. Type **Sunday** and tab to cell B1.
3. Type **Monday**.
4. Select all of the cells on the first row.
5. Choose Table, QuickFill, or press Ctrl+Shift+F12.

WordPerfect automatically fills in Wednesday, Thursday, and so on.

## Filling In the Dates of the Month

You can automatically fill in the dates of the month, although not quite so cleanly as you fill in the days of the week. To fill in the dates of the month, follow these steps:

1. Position the cursor in the cell that corresponds to the first day of the month and type **1**.
2. If this day falls on any day other than Sunday, you must then type in the remainder of the week by hand, then select the first row and choose Table, QuickFill. If the first day falls on Sunday, skip this step (or choose QuickFill from the Table Formula Bar).
3. Fill in the first two days of the first full week of the month (for example, **4** and **5**).
4. Select all the cells in the first full week through the end of the month and choose Table, QuickFill.
5. Delete the "extra" days at the end of the month.

## Other Uses for QuickFill

Anywhere you need a series of values and want to avoid typing them by hand, you can use the QuickFill feature. In addition to number sequences, you can also enter Days and Months:

> **Monday, Tuesday, Wednesday, ... (or Mon, Tue, Wed, ...)**
>
> **January, February, March, ... (or Jan, Feb, Mar, ...)**

For example, you could create a mortgage payment schedule, weight reduction schedule, jogging progress schedule, and more. In short, let WordPerfect do the work for you.

CHAPTER 32

# Interactive Documents

*by Mitch Milam*

**P**aper is fast becoming passé.

Document technology—the art of presenting textual information—has evolved greatly in the past few years. No longer must users read volumes of paper documents to find something that interests them. They can now view the documents on their computer screens in a format that is a very close, if not exact, representation of the printed output.

Even more importantly, references to related topics can be embedded directly into the document, enabling readers to move around the document much the way they would flip through a book using the table of contents, index, and other references to find related topics. The term used for interactive documents is *hypertext*.

Computer-based documentation not only saves our forests, but also provides companies and individuals a medium for presenting information that is easily distributed and updated. ■

**Use WordPerfect's Hypertext feature**

Create links to different parts of the same document and to parts of other documents. Also link to documents on the World Wide Web on the Internet.

**Run a WordPerfect macro using the Hypertext feature**

Create special hypertext links to run a macro when activated.

**Embed sound in your documents**

Use embedded sounds to emphasize a topic within a document.

Most modern computer applications show a trend toward large and complex online help systems and a reduction in the amount of printed material shipped with the product. After all, why print the manual when it is already at the user's fingertips under the Help option? ■

# Understanding Hypertext

*Hypertext* is a generic computer term that refers to a document's capability to immediately and automatically display nonsequential text when requested. WordPerfect takes this generic term and applies it to the creation of WordPerfect documents. Using WordPerfect's Hypertext feature, you can *link*, or connect, one section of a document to other sections of the same document or to sections of a different document; you can also run a macro. Figure 32.1 shows a flow chart of hypertext's text-switching and macro-running capabilities.

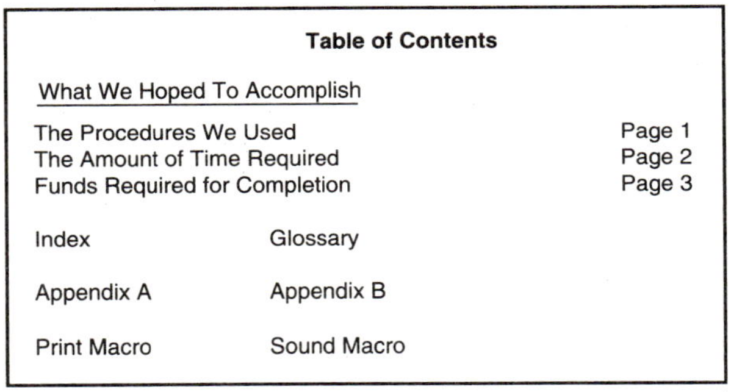

**FIG. 32.1**
This flow chart demonstrates Hypertext's capability to link a document to other sections of the same document or to sections of different documents.

|  | Table of Contents |  |
|---|---|---|
| What We Hoped To Accomplish | | |
| The Procedures We Used | | Page 1 |
| The Amount of Time Required | | Page 2 |
| Funds Required for Completion | | Page 3 |
| Index | Glossary | |
| Appendix A | Appendix B | |
| Print Macro | Sound Macro | |

WordPerfect uses the Bookmark feature to mark the locations that are referenced by the Hypertext engine. A *bookmark* is a hidden code that marks a location in the document. In Reveal Codes, you see the [Bookmark:<name>] code that marks the location of the bookmark. Bookmarks enable you to immediately jump from any position in the document to the bookmark. You can place bookmarks anywhere in a document.

WordPerfect uses a *button* to mark a hypertext link. A button can appear as either emphasized text or as an actual graphical button, like those found in Windows dialog boxes.

As you read this discussion on the Hypertext feature, keep in mind the following terms:

- A *link* is the connection between a button, word, or group of words marked in the document (WordPerfect, Envoy, or HTML document on the Web) with emphasized text, or the connection between a graphic image and its target.

- A *jump* is the switching operation that displays the target. You can invoke a jump by moving the cursor to the hypertext button and pressing Enter, or by clicking the hypertext button.
- A *return* is the switching operation that redisplays the original text passage.
- A *run* is a special type of jump that starts a WordPerfect macro.

# Working with WordPerfect's Hypertext Feature

WordPerfect provides an additional tool called a Feature Bar that appears below the ruler. The purpose of the Feature Bar is to provide additional buttons for quick access to features specific to the tool you have chosen. The Feature Bar changes depending on the tool you have selected. Figure 32.2 shows a WordPerfect document containing hypertext links with the Hypertext Feature Bar active.

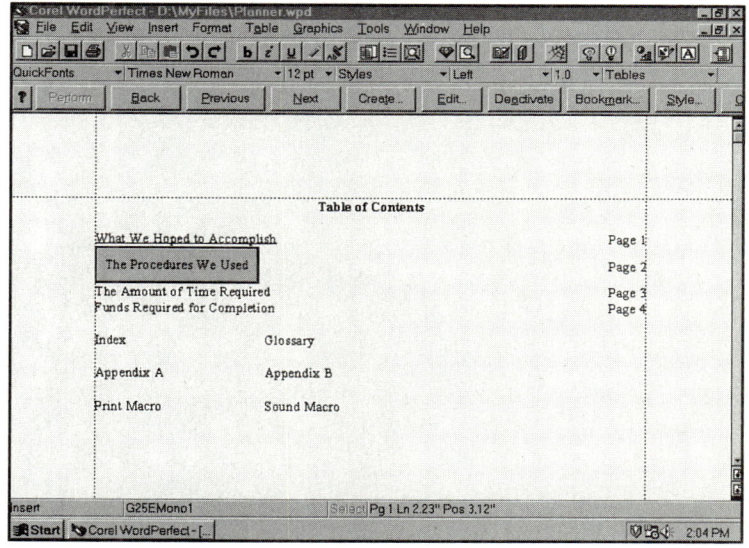

**FIG. 32.2**
The WordPerfect Hypertext Feature Bar supplies buttons for the different hypertext functions. You can select the button with the mouse, or press an Alt+Shift+letter combination.

The Hypertext Feature Bar buttons perform the following actions, as shown in table 32.1.

**Table 32.1 Description of the Hypertext Feature Bar**

| Button | Action |
|---|---|
| ? | Enables you to select the same functions contained in the Feature Bar's buttons and also to select other WordPerfect feature bars. |

*continues*

**Table 32.1  Continued**

| Button | Action |
| --- | --- |
| Perform | Activates the hypertext action of the current hypertext button. |
| Back | Returns to the point where the cursor was located before you performed a hypertext jump. |
| Previous | Jumps to the preceding hypertext button in your document. |
| Next | Jumps to the next hypertext button in your document. |
| Create/Delete | Enables you to create or delete a new hypertext button. If the insertion point is on a hypertext link, this button changes to Delete. |
| Edit | Enables you to modify an existing hypertext button. |
| Activate/Deactivate | Switches the current hypertext mode of the document. |
| Bookmark | Enables you to insert a bookmark in your document. |
| Style | Enables you to change the appearance of the text version of a hypertext button. |
| Close | Removes the Hypertext Feature Bar. |

You can select these buttons by clicking them or by pressing the Alt+Shift+letter combination.

When you first load a hypertext document, it is *activated*. This means that when you click a hypertext button or press Enter with the cursor on a hypertext button, the link is performed. Clicking Deactivate on the Hypertext Feature Bar switches the document from Hypertext mode to Edit mode and changes the Deactivate button to Activate. In Edit mode, you can edit the document, including the hypertext buttons, as you would any other WordPerfect document.

> **NOTE** Clicking the Close button removes the Hypertext Feature Bar but, because there are no menu equivalents to the Feature Bar, you lose most of the hypertext functionality. If Hypertext was active when you closed the bar, it remains active, but the only feature available to you is selecting a hypertext button in your document.

# Creating an Interactive Report

The best way to learn about Hypertext is by using it, so let's take an everyday report and make it interactive. Reports of any length have a table of contents at the beginning that enables the user to determine the contents of the report and on what page each topic starts. Figure 32.3 shows a report in WordPerfect before any hypertext features have been added.

The table of contents is the main jumping-off point in your document.

**FIG. 32.3**
A report in WordPerfect before adding Hypertext features.

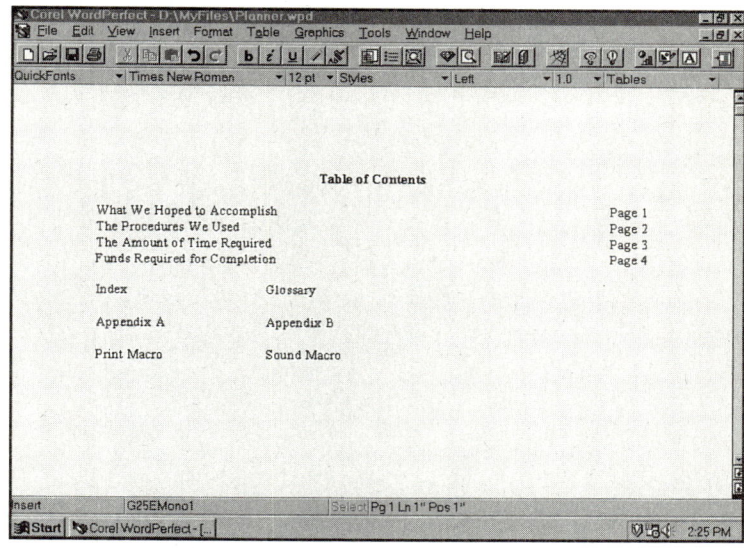

## Designing Your Hypertext Document

The first step in creating a hypertext document is creating the document itself. Follow whatever formatting and layout conventions you would use when creating a normal WordPerfect document. After you complete this step, print the document so that you have a working hard copy. The example used in this chapter is a project report. The report has four sections: an index, a glossary, and two appendixes. Each has an entry in the table of contents. The table of contents is located at the top of the document and will be used by the reader as the starting point for the document. From the table of contents, the user can jump to any section of the document.

The next step is creating a jump map. Like a road map that enables you to visually see the best way to navigate the roadways, a *jump map* allows you to define points of interest that are referenced with the hypertext links. A jump map consists of a table of entries defining the following information:

- Topic name
- Page number
- Bookmark name
- Locations where the topic can be referenced

**TIP** You can create a jump map at any time during the document's assembly. Waiting until the document is completed keeps you from wasting time modifying the jump map due to document editing changes.

**NOTE** If you are creating a multiple-document hypertext system, add the name of the document to the list of jump-map entries.

To create a jump map, perform the following steps:

1. Find a topic of interest. This topic could be the beginning of a chapter or section, graphics image, or relevant paragraph.
2. Create a named bookmark for the location. Remember that bookmark names must be unique. The actual bookmark is created in the next section of this chapter, "Marking a Hypertext Target with a Bookmark."
3. Review the document, and create a list of locations that could benefit from a reference to the current topic.
4. Repeat steps 1–3 until all topics of interest have been covered.

Table 32.2 shows an example of a jump map.

**Table 32.2  An Example of a Jump Map Used To Guide the Creation of Hypertext Links**

| Topic | Page | Bookmark | References |
|---|---|---|---|
| Hopes | 1 | Wishes | Table of Contents, page 1 |
| Procedures | 2 | Procedures | Table of Contents, page 2 |
| Time | 3 | Time | Table of Contents, page 3 |
| Funds | 4 | Funds | Table of Contents, page 4 |
| Index | 99 | Index | Table of Contents, page 30 |
| Glossary | 97 | Glossary | Table of Contents, page 31 |
| Appendix A | 90 | Appendix A | Table of Contents, page 32 |

Now that you have created a jump map, you are ready to create the bookmarks that will be used as targets for hypertext links.

**NOTE** Always work on a copy of the document(s). This procedure allows you to be creative without the worry of damaging the original work. You'll also have a backup in case you make a major editing mistake.

## Marking a Hypertext Target with a Bookmark

By using the jump map that you created in the preceding section, you can insert the bookmark targets that are referenced by your hypertext buttons. For example, to insert a bookmark at the section "What We Hoped To Accomplish"— one of the specified jump map locations—you can perform the following steps:

1. The first topic in your jump map is located on page 1 of the report. Move the cursor to the top of page 1.
2. Choose Insert, Bookmark, and select Create. Then enter the name of the bookmark **Hopes** and choose OK. WordPerfect inserts the hidden bookmark code at the current cursor location. This bookmark will be used by the Hypertext feature as a jump target.

   If you have text selected when you create the bookmark, WordPerfect uses the selected text as the bookmark name. If you don't have text selected, WordPerfect selects text for you and supplies it as the name. You can edit the name once the Create Bookmark dialog box is displayed.
3. Repeat steps 1 and 2 for each of the bookmark names in the jump map.

**NOTE** If you select text before accessing the Bookmark feature, the text within the selection is offered as the default bookmark name. If you create a bookmark by selecting existing text, WordPerfect marks the selected text in the document with beginning and ending bookmark codes instead of the default single code. The Hypertext feature works with both types of bookmark codes.

## Linking Text Within a Document

After you create all your reference bookmarks, you are ready to insert the hypertext links that provide the links to the bookmarks. To create a hypertext button using the default settings, perform the following steps:

1. Choose Tools, Hypertext/Web Links. The Hypertext Feature Bar appears.
2. Select the text What We Hoped To Accomplish to be used as the hypertext button. In some cases, you probably want to type text specifically for a button; at other times, you want to use existing text in the document. In this case, the existing text is used for the button.

   If you are using the text style of the hypertext button, you can simply select the text, and then create the hypertext button. The only change to the original text of your document will be in its appearance (font, color, bold, and underline). The button form of the hypertext button makes it stand out from the surrounding text but is also practically limited to a single word or two. You can create larger buttons, but in most cases, a large button distracts from the presentation of the text.
3. Click Create from the Hypertext Feature Bar. WordPerfect displays the Create Hypertext Link dialog box (see fig. 32.4).

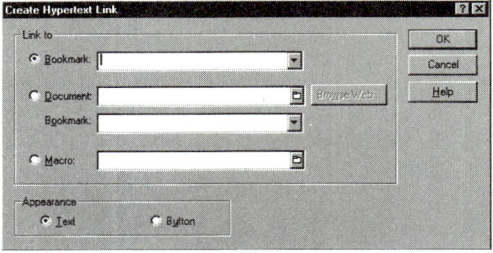

**FIG. 32.4**
Use the Create Hypertext Link dialog box to define or change the hypertext links in your document.

4. The dialog box contains three options that create different actions. For this example, choose Bookmark.
5. Enter the name of a bookmark and press Enter, or choose OK. For a list of bookmarks, use the Bookmark drop-down list.

Notice that the selected text has a changed appearance. On a color monitor, the text is green, boldfaced, and underlined. Figure 32.5 shows the effect of this operation. Notice the Hypertext On and Hypertext Off codes in the Reveal Codes window.

**FIG. 32.5**
The sample report shows a hypertext button created using the default style and appearance (text).

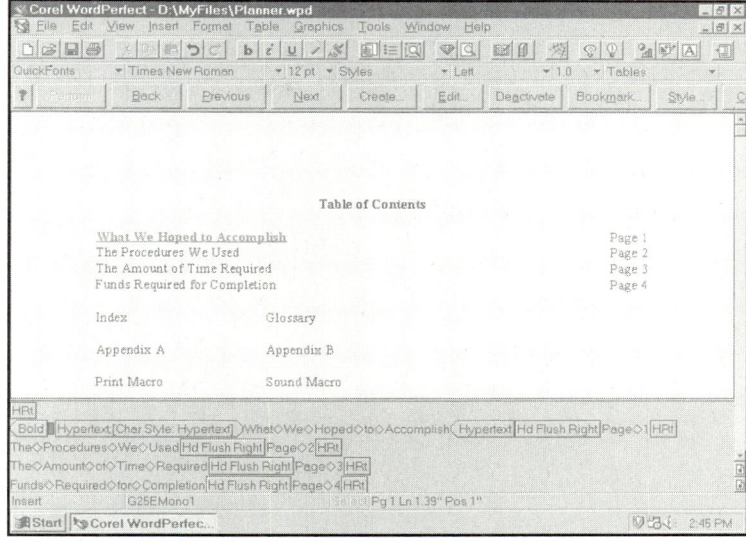

**N O T E**  The appearance of the hypertext button can be changed by modifying the hypertext style. Refer to the section later in this chapter, "Changing the Style of Hypertext Buttons," and Chapter 10, "Using Styles," for more information.

The default appearance WordPerfect has chosen for hypertext buttons is as text. You also can create a hypertext button that is displayed graphically. To create the button, select Button in the Create Hypertext Link dialog box instead of Text.

Graphical hypertext buttons can be blank or can contain text that you blocked before creating the button. Refer to figure 32.2 for examples of text and graphical hypertext buttons.

Functionally, the graphical hypertext buttons are different from text hypertext buttons in two ways:

- A character text box is created for the appearance of the button. If you blocked text that appears on the button, you find that text inside the text box.
- When Hypertext is active, clicking anywhere on the box activates the link.

The graphical hypertext buttons are actually graphics boxes used by the Hypertext feature. You can edit these buttons the same way you would edit a normal graphics box.

## Editing Hypertext Links

To edit an existing hypertext button, perform the following steps:

1. Look at the Hypertext Feature Bar to make sure that Hypertext is not active. If the Activate button appears in the bar, Hypertext is inactive, and you can continue with step 2. Otherwise, click Deactivate to return to Edit mode.

2. Place the cursor on the hypertext button that you want to edit.

 **TIP** You can also double-click the hypertext codes in Reveal Codes to edit the link, whether or not Edit mode is active.

3. Click Edit from the Hypertext Feature Bar. The Edit Hypertext Link dialog box appears (see fig. 32.6). In this dialog box, you can make any changes necessary.

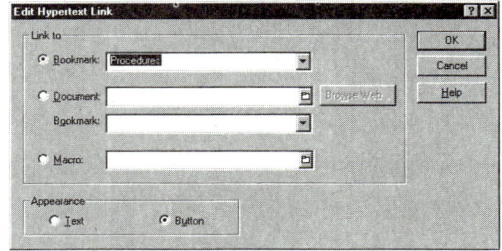

**FIG. 32.6**
The Edit Hypertext Link dialog box enables you to change the jump location and the appearance of the hypertext button.

To remove the hypertext button and restore the text of the button to normal, perform the following steps:

1. Place the cursor on the hypertext button that you want to edit.
2. Click Delete from the Hypertext Feature Bar. The hypertext button is removed, restoring the text to its original form.

## Linking Documents with Hypertext

The Hypertext feature can link the main document with one or more other documents. If the other document is a WordPerfect document, you can define a link to specific text, using bookmarks, within the second document. If you want to link to a non-WordPerfect document, the most you can do is display the entire document for the user to browse through.

You would create a multiple-document hypertext system if you had a variety of information stored in separate files that you wanted the user to view, or if the system was extremely large and you had broken the documents into smaller pieces for easier management.

To create a hypertext link to another document, perform the following steps:

1. Create bookmarks in the destination document. Refer to the earlier section in this chapter, "Marking a Hypertext Target with a Bookmark."
2. With the Hypertext Feature Bar active, click Create.
3. Choose Document.
4. Enter the name of the document. You can select the document name from a file list by selecting the folder icon located to the right of the edit box.
5. Choose Document, Bookmark.
6. Enter the name of the bookmark to which you want to jump. If you entered the name of a WordPerfect document, a list of available bookmarks appears. If you entered a document that is not in WordPerfect 6.x or 7 format, no bookmarks are listed. If you do not select a bookmark when the hypertext button is selected, the new document is loaded and your cursor placed at the top of the document.
7. Choose OK to return to the document.

**NOTE** If you distribute the hypertext document to other users through a network, try to put the linked secondary documents in a subdirectory common to all users. If a common subdirectory is not available to all users, do not add path names to the secondary document's file names, but be sure to distribute all other documents with the hypertext document.

## Linking Hypertext to Macros

WordPerfect's Hypertext feature also can run a WordPerfect macro. This capability can be useful if you want to display information that is not part of the document or to perform certain commands you feel would enhance the function of the document. To create a hypertext run link, perform the following steps:

1. Click Create from the Hypertext Feature Bar. The Create Hypertext Link dialog box appears.
2. Choose Macro.
3. Enter the name of the macro. Alternatively, select the macro from a file list by selecting the folder icon located to the right of the edit box.
4. Choose OK.

**NOTE** In multiple-document hypertext systems, you must be careful to distribute the macros along with the hypertext documents. On a network, all users must have access to the macros as well as the documents for the hypertext system to function correctly.

## Changing the Style of Hypertext Buttons

WordPerfect associates a style with the hypertext button. The default style is green, bold-faced, and underlined. In certain situations (if you are using a monochrome or LCD display, for example), you might find this style unacceptable. To change the hypertext style, perform the following steps:

1. With the Hypertext Feature Bar active, click the Style button. WordPerfect displays the Styles Editor dialog box (see fig. 32.7).

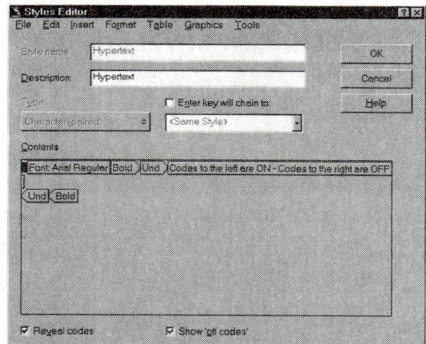

**FIG. 32.7**
The Styles Editor dialog box enables you to change the hypertext style. This figure shows the style after [Color:Green] was changed to an Arial font.

2. Modify the hypertext style in any way you want. Figure 32.7 shows the style after [Color:Green] was changed to an Arial font.

3. When you finish editing, choose OK to close the dialog box and return to the document screen.

**NOTE** When you modify the hypertext appearance style, it is modified for all hypertext buttons. You cannot modify the style of a single hypertext button. The hypertext style is a WordPerfect system style and can be edited like any other style. Refer to Chapter 10, "Using Styles," for more information.

▶ See "Editing Styles," **p. 344**

## Activating a Document with Hypertext

The final step in creating a document with the Hypertext feature is activating the document's automatic links. To activate the link, follow these steps:

1. Choose Tools, Hypertext/Web links. WordPerfect displays the Hypertext Feature Bar.
2. If the Activate button is displayed, click Activate. Hypertext is now active.

   ▶ See "Activate Hypertext," p. 310

# Creating a Link to a Web Page

WordPerfect makes it easy to create a link to a Web page. The page can be accessible on the global Web (available to the public) or limited to a private *intranet* that's available only within your company. With a Web link, clicking a hypertext element in a WordPerfect document automatically starts an Internet browser, if one is installed on the computer, and connects to the specified document on the World Wide Web.

WordPerfect 7 comes with Netscape Navigator, a popular browser for navigating the Web. If you have not installed Netscape, you need to do so before you can use WordPerfect's Web Hyperlink feature. To install Netscape, you must launch E:\BROWSER\DISK1\SETUP.EXE, and follow the prompts. The version of Netscape which is installed is called AT&T WorldNet Service.

To link to a Web page, follow the same basic steps outlined in the earlier section, "Linking Documents with Hypertext," except enter the URL of the Web page you want to link to. For example, if you want to link to Netscape's home page, type

   **http://home.netscape.com/**

into the Document box inside the Create Hypertext Link dialog box.

To link to a page on the Web:

1. With the Hypertext Feature Bar active, click Create. The Create Hypertext Link dialog box appears.
2. Choose Document.
3. Enter the name of the Web document you want to use. It must be a fully qualified URL, starting with the text **http://**.

If you don't know the URL of the document, click the Browse Web button. Netscape or another browser is launched for you. Use it to navigate the Web to find the page you want. When you locate the page, return to WordPerfect. The URL of the current document displayed in the browser is automatically inserted into the Document text box.

4. Choose OK to return to the document.

**NOTE** You are not limited to linking to pages on the World Wide Web. You can link to any resource on the Internet as long as you provide its full URL. This includes files on FTP and gopher sites. Netscape or another browser interprets the kind of Internet access you want by the protocol you use at the start of the URL (**http://**, **ftp://**, **gopher://**, and so on).

For example, to link to a file on an FTP site on the Internet (perhaps to download the file), use the format

**ftp://server.com**

where **server.com** is the name of the domain you want to connect to on the Internet.

You use the Web link as you would any other hypertext link. To *actuate* the link—connect to the desired page on the Web—merely activate it by clicking it within WordPerfect. See the next section for more information.

 **TIP** You can also link to Envoy documents merely by specifying the name of the document in the Document text box inside the Create Hypertext Link dialog box.

# Navigating a Hypertext Document

A WordPerfect document containing hypertext buttons offers two methods of navigating the hypertext links: manual and automatic. The manual navigation method allows you to perform a hypertext link when the Hypertext feature is inactive. When Hypertext is active, you can automatically navigate the document by using the mouse or the Tab key, as well as the Hypertext Feature Bar buttons.

## Jumping and Returning in an Active Hypertext Document

When Hypertext is active (and when the Hypertext Feature Bar is displayed), you can switch between different locations of the document with a single keystroke or mouse click, as described in the following list:

- To use the mouse to jump to the link's target location, click the hypertext button.

- To return to the position of the hypertext button that you last selected, click <u>B</u>ack from the Hypertext Feature Bar.
- To move to the next hypertext button, click <u>N</u>ext in the Hypertext Feature Bar, or press Tab. Then press Enter or use the mouse to activate the jump link for that button.
- To move to the preceding hypertext button, click <u>P</u>revious or press Shift+Tab. Press Enter or use the mouse to activate the jump link for that button.

The <u>N</u>ext and <u>P</u>revious feature buttons find the next available hypertext button located either above or below the current cursor position, even if the cursor is not located at a link code.

**N O T E** Tab and the Shift+Tab key combination perform their normal functions when the cursor is located at any position in the document other than when your cursor is inside the text hypertext button.

## Jumping and Returning in an Inactive Hypertext Document

Even when Hypertext is inactive, the links still are functional. To jump to a target in an inactive hypertext document, perform the following steps:

1. If the Hypertext Feature Bar is not active, display it by choosing <u>T</u>ools, H<u>y</u>pertext/Web Links.
2. Move the cursor to the left edge of a graphic hypertext button or within the text hypertext button.
3. Click Pe<u>r</u>form from the Hypertext Feature Bar.

To move from the target back to the hypertext button, click <u>B</u>ack from the Hypertext Feature Bar.

The feature buttons <u>N</u>ext and <u>P</u>revious function in the same manner as when the hypertext document is active.

## Jumping and Returning Between Documents

Jumping between documents is simply an extension of jumping around a single document. The major difference occurs when the document has been modified by any of the actions of either the hypertext system or the user. If the current document has been modified and the user selects a jump to another document, a dialog box appears, offering the following options:

- <u>Y</u>es saves the changes in the document and continues the jump.

- No abandons the changes in the document and continues the jump.
- Cancel abandons the changes and cancels the jump.

## Jumping to Web Pages

If the link is to a page on the Web, WordPerfect first starts Netscape or another browser in order to gain access to the Internet. After the connection is made, the browser automatically links to the desired page. You must manually switch back to WordPerfect to display its window. The Windows 95 taskbar makes this fairly easy: just locate the WordPerfect button in the taskbar, and click it. WordPerfect appears.

If there are many Web links in the document, keep the browser program open. This helps speed up navigation so the browser doesn't need to restart for each link.

## Running Macros with Hypertext

Running a macro from a hypertext document is just like using any of the other hypertext link options. If the macro modifies the current cursor position, just click Back to return to the preceding hypertext location.

### TROUBLESHOOTING

**Nothing happens when I click a hypertext link.** WordPerfect lets you enable or disable the Hypertext feature. With the feature disabled, clicking a hypertext link does nothing. To enable the Hypertext feature so that you can click a hypertext link, choose Tools, Hypertext/Web Links. Click Activate in the Hypertext Feature Bar. Choose Close to close the Hypertext Feature Bar. Hypertext is now active.

**WordPerfect displays a Macro XXX Not Found error when I click a hypertext link.** The macro you specified for the hypertext link cannot be found. Either the macro is missing completely, or it's not in your regular MACROS folder (usually \COREL\OFFICE7\MACROS\WPWIN). If your macro is on your hard disk drive, locate it and copy it to the MACROS folder.

**When I click on a hypertext link, WordPerfect displays a Bookmark not found error.** The bookmark you specified for the hypertext link could not be found. If you linked to a bookmark in the current document, be sure the bookmark is in the document. If it's not, place the insertion point at the proper spot in the document and create a bookmark there. If you linked to a bookmark in another document, open it, and check that the bookmark is there.

# Embedding Sound in a Document

Just as the Hypertext feature allows you to create interactive documents, WordPerfect's Sound feature enables you to enhance a document by embedding sounds that the user can play. You can use sounds to emphasize a point or to provide additional information that is understandable only in an audio presentation.

You should remember that sound clips occupy a large amount of space. How the sound clip was recorded and its length determine its file size. The higher the sound quality and the longer the clip runs, the larger the file size.

WordPerfect relies on the Windows Sound Recorder to record sounds. In most cases, however, the software shipped with the sound board provides superior recording and editing functions. This means that you must use another program to record and edit sound clips before you insert the clip into a document.

## Using WordPerfect with a Sound Board

Microsoft Windows provides a link between the Windows environment and the various sound boards available today. Because Windows controls the hardware, any application that can speak to the Windows sound drivers can use sound. WordPerfect is such an application. The program provides the interface between the user and the software that drives the sound hardware so that you can embed, record, and play sound clips as part of a WordPerfect document.

The configuration and setup of a sound card in a PC depends on the type of card being used and on its feature set. Follow the installation instructions to configure the sound card for your PC and Windows. Due to the number of sound cards on the market, this chapter cannot use the installation procedure for a specific card as a blanket example. You can, however, refer to Que's *Windows 95 Installation and Configuration Handbook* for additional information.

## Linking Sound Files to a Document

To insert a sound clip into your document, perform the following steps:

1. Choose Insert, Sound. WordPerfect displays the Sound Clips dialog box (see fig. 32.8).
2. Choose Insert. WordPerfect displays the Insert Sound Clip Into Document dialog box (see fig. 32.9).

**FIG. 32.8**
The Sound Clips dialog box enables you to insert, record, and play back sound clips.

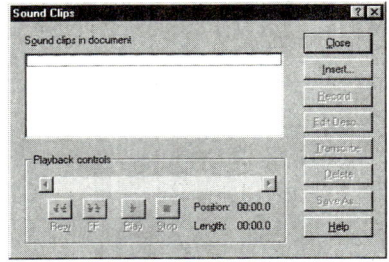

**FIG. 32.9**
Select a sound clip to be inserted into a WordPerfect document.

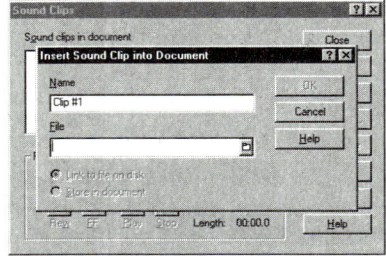

3. Type the file name of the sound clip in the File edit box, or select the folder icon to display the Select Sound File dialog box. In the Select Sound File dialog box, choose your sound file and click Select.

4. The Name edit box contains the name that WordPerfect uses when referring to the sound clip. The default naming scheme is Clip #X, with X being the next sequence number of the sound clips. You can change the name to allow you to identify the sound clip. In most cases, you can just enter the name of the sound clip file.

5. Choose either of the two clip-insertion options. The first option—Link To File On Disk—merely establishes a connection to the disk file that contains the sound clip. The second option—Store In Document—actually retrieves and stores the sound clip inside your WordPerfect document.

**N O T E** Storing a sound clip in a document makes the document larger and could make managing the document cumbersome. Also, if the original sound clip is modified for any reason, you must reinsert the re-recorded sound clip to incorporate the latest changes. However, using Link To File On Disk means that you must ensure that the clip doesn't change locations on disk, and is distributed with the document.

6. Choose OK to return to the document screen.

When you insert a sound clip into a document, WordPerfect places a small speaker icon in the document to inform you that a sound clip resides there (in Page view). Also, Reveal Codes shows a Sound code at the location of the inserted sound clip.

## Exploring the Sound Clips Feature

When you choose Insert, Sound, the Sound Clips dialog box appears (see fig. 32.10). Take a moment to review the features of this dialog box.

The Sound Clips In Document list contains the names of all sound clips in the current document, and also the description and storage method for each sound clip.

The Playback Controls buttons—Rewind (Rew), Fast Forward (FF), Play, and Stop—perform the same functions as their counterparts on a tape recorder. The horizontal scroll bar represents the current location in the sound clip when you click Play. The Position indicator displays the current position, in minutes and seconds, as you play the sound clip. The Length indicator shows the duration of the sound clip.

The dialog box also contains the following buttons, as shown in table 32.3.

**Table 32.3  Sound Clips Dialog Buttons**

| Button | Action |
| --- | --- |
| Close | Returns to the document screen. |
| Insert | Adds a new sound clip to the document. |
| Record | Launches the Windows Sound Recorder, which enables you to play, record, and edit sound clips. (Your sound board might include its own software for recording sounds). |
| Edit Desc | Enables you to edit the sound clip's description. |
| Transcribe | Removes the Sound Clips dialog box and activates the Sound Feature Bar, which enables you to access the Playback Controls from the document editing screen. |
| Delete | Removes a sound clip from the document. |
| Save As | Creates a file on disk containing a sound clip that is currently stored inside a document. |
| Help | Displays help information on the Sound feature. |

**FIG. 32.10**
The Sound Clips dialog box provides a central location from which you can insert, record, edit the description of, transcribe, delete, and play back sound clips within a WordPerfect document.

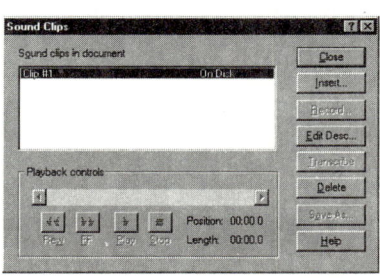

## Playing a Sound Clip

To play a sound clip from the document edit screen, click the speaker icon that represents the clip. Figure 32.11 shows a WordPerfect document with an embedded sound clip.

To play a sound clip from the Sound Clips dialog box, highlight the sound clip in the Sound Clips in Document list, and then click the Play button.

**FIG. 32.11**
When a sound clip is embedded in a WordPerfect document and the display view is set to Page, a speaker icon appears in the left margin. In Draft mode, the sound clip is a gray comment box, as shown here.

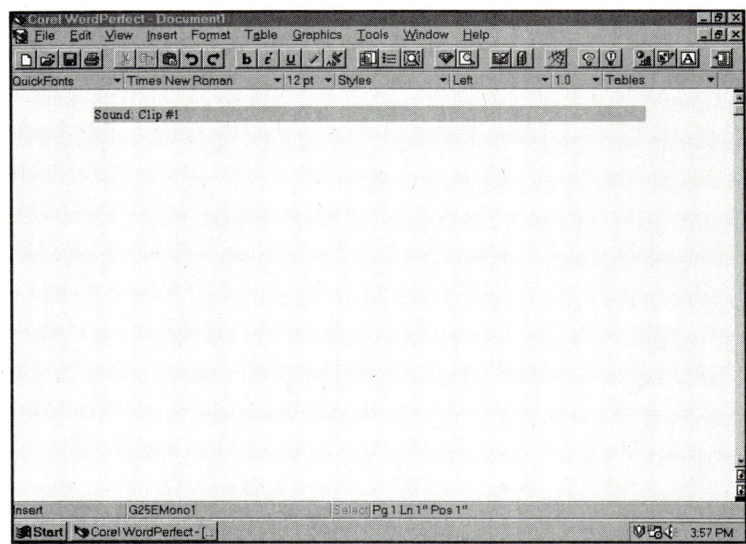

### TROUBLESHOOTING

**When I click on a sound to play it, WordPerfect displays a `WAVE sound output not available` error message.** WordPerfect uses the sound capabilities of Windows to play sounds. You must have a suitable sound card properly installed in your computer before you can play sounds.

**After inserting sound clips, my files get very large and take up a lot of space on my hard disk drive.** You specified the Store In Document option in the Insert Sound Clip Into Document dialog box. This places the entire sound file in your document. Sound files can be quite large; the longer the sound, the larger the file. To prevent your documents from growing in size when you insert a sound file, be sure to choose the Link To File On Disk option in the Insert Sound Clip Into Document dialog box.

CHAPTER 33

# Publishing Documents on the World Wide Web

*by Diane Koers*

Millions of people are learning to "surf the Net." Some are learning out of necessity—their job requires the research available on the Internet—and many are learning just for the fun of it. They want to see what all the excitement is about. The bottom line is that every day these millions of people can have access to the information you are providing them about your company. It is one of the least expensive forms of advertising available on the market today, and the number of people using the Internet is going to continue to grow for many years to come.

With the use of a product you are already familiar with—WordPerfect—and it's newest feature—the Internet Publisher—you can now create a document yourself to publish on the World Wide Web. Your customers will be able to download catalogs, view video about your company, or just become acquainted with your staff through information available on the Internet. Your readers can have the ability to create electronic forms, fill out information surveys, order your products, or send you e-mail. ■

- **Create a basic HTML document**
  Learn to use WordPerfect's Internet Publisher feature to design a Web page.

- **Format the HTML document**
  Learn how effective use of styles, colors, and other attributes can call attention to your document.

- **View the HTML document in the Netscape browser**
  What you see is not necessarily what you get. View the document in your Web browser to get the final results.

- **Publish the HTML document to the WWW**
  You created it, now what do you do with it? Learn some of the tricks of getting your Web page out on the Internet.

# What Is the World Wide Web?

There are many descriptions available of the World Wide Web, commonly referred to as the *Web*; one is that of an electronic encyclopedia—a very eclectic encyclopedia. When referring to a topic in an encyclopedia—say widgets for example—often some of the terms referred to in that reference (for example, polystyrene used in the manufacture of widgets) may lead you to look for more information somewhere else. So, you go to that reference, read through it, perhaps see something about where polystyrene is made, and go to that reference. Then you decide that you are ready to go back to the original reference on widgets.

The Web is similar to that encyclopedia. When you look up a reference on a page of the Web, there are references to similar articles. You can click that reference, and—zap—you are there reading about that reference. This can go on and on. You may have started looking up widgets, but ended up reading about Russian history. This is because the Web is interactive, using a feature called *hypertext links* to connect to other computers across the world.

The difference is the Web is made up of millions of articles called *Web pages*. Each one is created by a different author. This information is stored on computers all across the world. You can search for articles on any topic you can think of!

All that is needed to access the Web is a computer, a modem, a piece of software called a *browser*, and someplace to begin accessing the Web. It generally doesn't matter what kind of computer you are using—Mac, PC, Windows, DOS, or UNIX. Several browsers are available today; some popular ones are Netscape, Mosaic, and Lynx. Other places to access the Web are the online services such as CompuServe, America Online, Prodigy, and The Microsoft Network. If you plan on accessing the Web frequently, you might consider a direct Internet Service Provider (ISP) in your area. See the section "Finding a Service Provider" later in this chapter.

## What Is a Web Page?

When you enter the Internet, you go to a *Web site* (address) and you see a Web page. The first page of a site is called a *home page*. The home page is like an entry hall in your home. You've got to get in the front door and into the entry hall before you can go anywhere else in the house. It's the same way with a Web document. The home page will usually direct you to other locations.

A *Web page* is a simple document that can be created in any word processing program with text in a universal language called *ASCII* (pronounced "ask-ee"). There are specific commands to be included that dictate how the page looks; these are called *tags*. Tags can be added manually or by Internet Publishing software such as WordPerfect. The format of a document created to be used on the Internet is called *HTML* (an acronym for HyperText Markup Language). In this chapter, I refer to the document in WordPerfect as the *HTML document*. The document as it is displayed in a Web browser is referred to as the *Web document* or *Web page*.

The Web page can include pictures, graphic lines, sound, video, and other elements. These graphics or portions of the text can also tie into other Web pages. This is accomplished by creating *links*. Links are discussed later in this chapter in the section "Creating Links."

Figure 33.1 illustrates an example of a Web page as seen through Netscape. With WordPerfect's Internet Publisher feature, you can create the Web page using the skills you already have learned in WordPerfect, and not have to rely on learning how to be a programmer.

**FIG. 33.1**
A Web page can be seen by thousands of people each day.

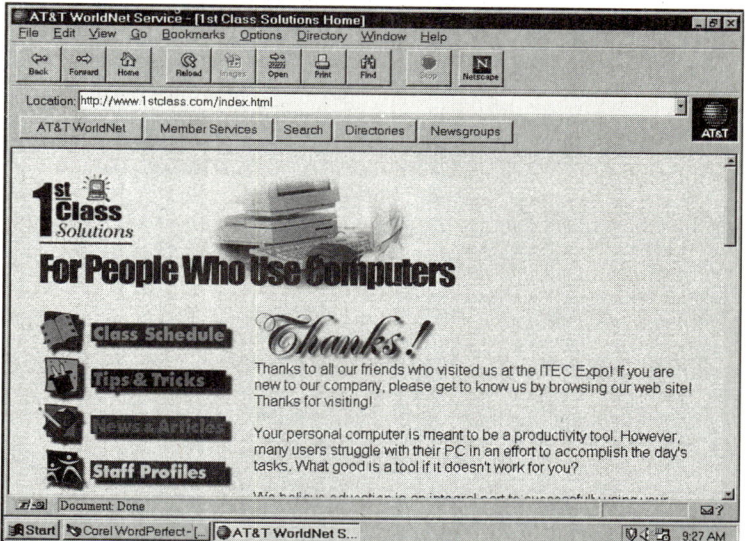

## Learning Web Terminology

Before you venture too far into the world of Web publishing, you should become more familiar with some of the terms used in this chapter. Table 33.1 defines some of these popular terms.

### Table 33.1 Web Terminology

| Term | Description |
| --- | --- |
| Home page | The initial screen seen by people who visit your Web address or Web site. |
| Web browser | Can be one of several programs available that allow you to see the finished Web page document on the Internet. |
| Netscape | A popular Web Browser; also known as Netscape Navigator. |
| HTML | HyperText Markup Language; the language used to create the page layouts of a document to be displayed in a Web browser. |
| URL | Uniform Resource Locator. A standardized address or way to locate a Web document on the Internet. Usually a URL consists of the service, host name, and path to the Web page. A URL example might be **http://yahoo.com** or **http://www.whitehouse.gov**. |
| Tags | HTML codes used in creating documents. A tag is enclosed in brackets such as `<H2>` or `</H2>`. With WordPerfect's Internet Publishing feature, you normally do not have to type these tags. WordPerfect assigns them for you. |
| Hypertext links | A point on the Web page where the user can click to go to other locations of that page, other Web pages, or other Web sites. A hypertext link can be a few words of text or could be a graphic picture. |
| Styles | A WordPerfect tool. WordPerfect uses styles to create Web pages with the Internet Publisher feature. |

▶ See "Understanding Styles," **p. 334**

# WordPerfect's Internet Publisher

WordPerfect includes a built-in feature called the Internet Publisher. It is a very easy to use tool that assists you in creating HTML documents for publishing on the World Wide Web.

As you apply styles to the WordPerfect document, the Internet Publisher assign tags to the text. A *tag* is the actual language coding for an HTML document to be seen in a Web browser such as Netscape or Mosaic.

Tags can be used to apply attributes, such as bolding, to text. You would see the text as bold in the browser; however, Internet Publisher assigns beginning and ending tags which appear as `<bold>`*text*`</bold>`. The advantage of using Internet Publisher is that you don't have to learn the exact HTML tag language. All you have to do is tell WordPerfect how you want certain text to look. Internet Publisher assigns the tags for you.

# The Basics of Creating an HTML Document

An HTML document normally has several components to it: a title, one or more headings, paragraphs of information, graphics, and the name and Internet address of the author. It also could contain lists or tables of information.

To create an HTML document, follow these steps:

1. Choose File, Internet Publisher. The Internet Publisher dialog box appears, as shown in figure 33.2.
2. Click New Web Document.

    As seen in figure 33.3, you are prompted to Select a New Web Document template. There is only one Web template that ships with WordPerfect 7, but you can create others, just like any other template.

**FIG. 33.2**
WordPerfect's Internet Publisher feature enables you to start with a new document or convert an existing document.

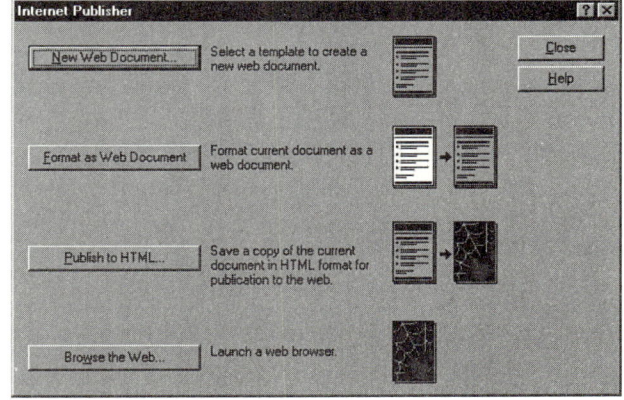

**NOTE** The Internet Publisher, like other WordPerfect features, has an "expert" to assist you. The Web Page Expert will begin a Web page for you, giving you basic elements to work with. I suggest that you start with the blank template and build from there. This gives you more flexibility in the design of the page and a great learning experience as to the concepts behind Web page publishing.

▶ **See** "Understanding Templates," **p. 364**

3. Choose Create A Blank Web Document, then click Select.

    The new document appears on-screen, and the WordPerfect Internet Publisher feature is now in effect. The dialog box as seen in figure 33.4 appears.

**FIG. 33.3**
You can create your Web page from a blank template or use the Web Page Expert template.

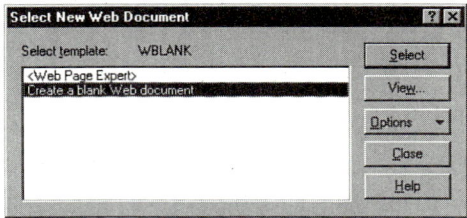

4. Click OK to acknowledge the announcement.

   Although the dialog box announced that only Web-compatible features are available, you will encounter a few choices on the menu that are not Web-compatible.

**FIG. 33.4**
Many features normally available in WordPerfect are unavailable to the Internet Publisher.

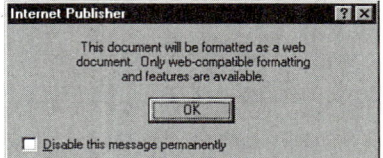

Several things are going to look different, most noticeably the background of your screen; it is no longer white like a normal WordPerfect document. The other item to notice is your Toolbar and Power Bar. Figure 33.5 shows the choices on both have changed to reveal only Web document features. Also many choices under the menu bar are grayed out and unavailable. Some menu selections even change. For example, take a look at the Format menu. The choices under this menu are totally different than in a regular WordPerfect document. These menu changes can save you lots of frustration from trying to use a feature that is not going to be accessible on a Web document.

**FIG. 33.5**
A special Toolbar and Power Bar with Web publishing features appears.

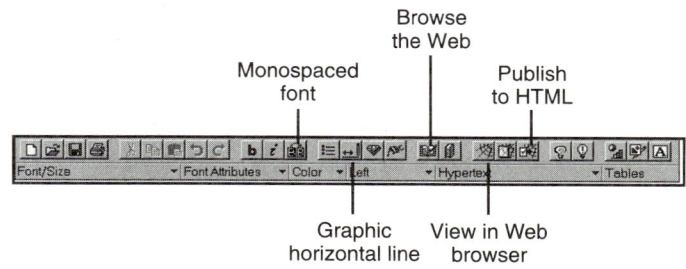

# Converting Standard WordPerfect Documents into HTML Documents

Although you may find it easier to create a document from the beginning using the Internet Publisher, a WordPerfect document can often be converted to HTML format.

> **CAUTION**
>
> If the document is complex and contains merge commands, columns, footnotes, or other WordPerfect features, it will not convert cleanly. Even something with a manual page break may give the Internet Publisher problems in converting.

Only a document with plain text and some formatting can be converted. The only formatting codes that are acceptable are bold or italics. Underlining, fonts, sizes, text color, and other choices cannot be used. If the document contains margin settings, line spacing, and other such settings, they are ignored during the conversion.

### TROUBLESHOOTING

**My original WordPerfect document had several graphic images in it. However, when I converted it, they were not there. What happened?** The only graphics that are recognized during the conversion are horizontal graphic lines. Graphic images should be added after the conversion has taken place.

**I converted a document to the Internet Publisher, but my formulas are not showing up in my tables.** Although the Internet Publisher converter recognizes tables, the actual formulas are not converted; only the results of the formula calculation will appear. WordPerfect Internet Publisher also puts lines around each cell of the table and in your Internet browser, and these lines appear as raised borders.

Figures 33.6, 33.7, and 33.8 illustrate how a document looks during the conversion from a WordPerfect standard document, to a WordPerfect HTML document, to viewing it in Netscape.

To convert an existing WordPerfect document to HTML:

1. Choose File, Internet Publisher.
2. Choose Format As Web Document.
3. Choose OK.

The existing WordPerfect file is converted using the Internet Publisher template to an HTML format. You can then continue to work on the document using HTML features.

**FIG. 33.6**
This is a WordPerfect document in its original format before conversion, including fonts and attributes.

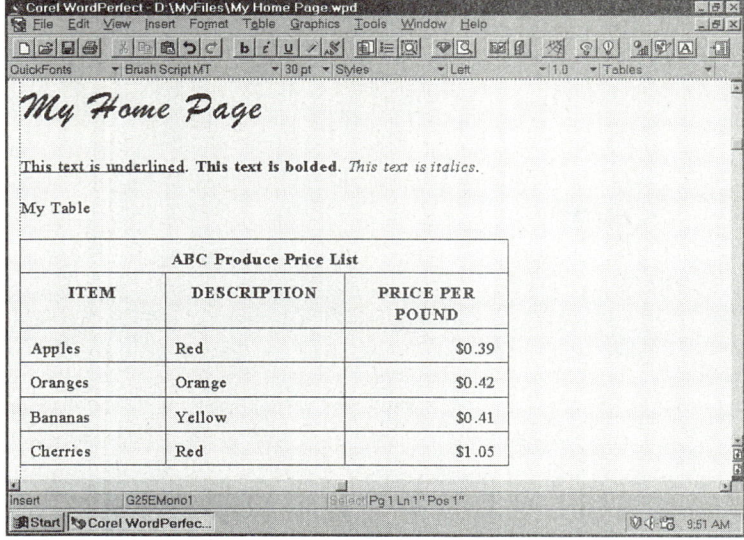

**FIG. 33.7**
This is the WordPerfect document after conversion, as displayed with the Internet Publisher feature. Notice that the original font choices are no longer displayed.

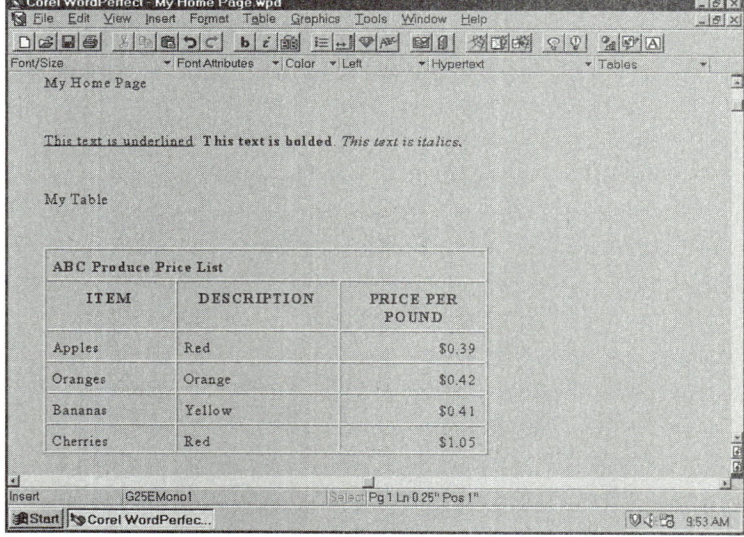

**FIG. 33.8**
This is the converted WordPerfect document as seen in a Netscape browser. Notice that the underlining attribute is no longer displayed.

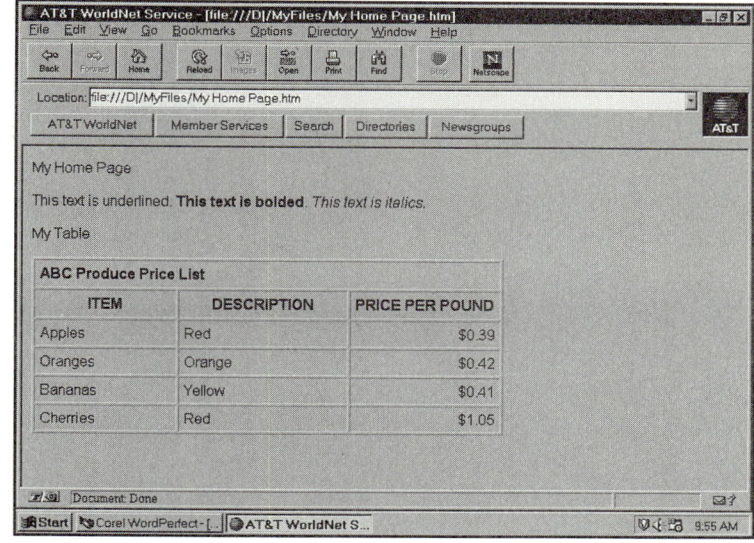

## HTML Document Title

HTML documents must have a title. The *title* is the text that appears in the title bar of your Web browser when your Web page appears. The title can be the first line of your Web page text, or it can be a totally different line of text that does not appear directly on the body of the Web page. An example of when you would use a custom title is if you want your reader to see a graphic image first, instead of text.

To give the HTML document a title:

1. Choose Format, Title.
2. Be sure the Title tab is displayed (see fig. 33.9).

**FIG. 33.9**
Unless you specify a custom title, WordPerfect uses the first heading as the title.

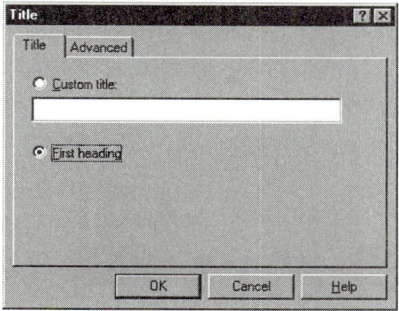

3. Click the Custom Title button, and then type the desired text in the box below it.

   Or, select First Heading to have WordPerfect enter the first line of text in your document as the title, also.

4. Click OK.

If you opted to use the Custom Title, you do not see this title in the HTML document. It appears in the title bar when you are viewing the document in your Web browser.

## Creating Body Text

The next step is to type the contents or the body of the page. This is when you type paragraphs of information that you want your reader to look at. You could also create a table here. When typing the text, follow standard word processing rules of letting the text wrap to the next line until you have completed the paragraph. Then press Enter to complete the paragraph.

> **NOTE** I am a firm believer in a word processing practice called *type first, edit later*. Over the years, I have found this to be a tremendous time-saver for me. It basically means to concentrate on what you want your document to say rather than how it looks. You do not have to stop and lose your train of thought while creating your document. After the text is typed, then you can select various portions of it and apply formatting as needed. In this chapter, I am using this concept.

There is no need to press Enter the second time for the standard blank line as you would in a normal word processing document. WordPerfect's Internet Publisher automatically places additional spacing in between paragraphs. The Internet Publisher is actually placing a paragraph tag every time you press Enter. That paragraph tag is what is telling the Web browser program to separate the paragraphs by a small amount of extra spacing. It also ignores any extra Enter commands it encounters in the HTML document.

If, however, you do want to press Enter, and you don't want the extra spacing between these paragraphs, you can insert a *line break*, which produces separate lines of text, but without extra spacing. Figure 33.10 illustrates the difference between a paragraph break and a line break. To create a line break, choose Insert, Line Break.

## Adding Headings

HTML documents need headings to separate the topics of your Web page. Just as this book has several types of headings, so should your HTML page. Headings are similar to an outline in that a Level 1 heading is larger than a Level 2 heading. You cannot choose the actual font for the heading because this is not determined by the HTML document; it's determined by the Web browser program. Netscape may show a Level 2 heading in a totally different font or size from a Level 2 heading in Mosaic. You have no control over which Web browser your readers are using.

**FIG. 33.10**
The shortcut key for a line break is Ctrl+Shift+L.

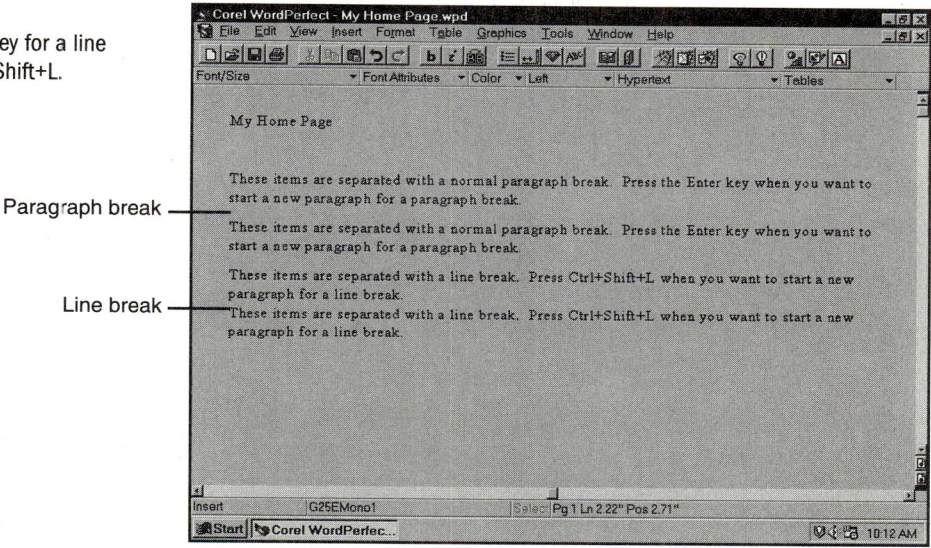

Paragraph break

Line break

An HTML document is capable of supporting up to six different heading types. You should note that some Web browsers only support up to five different heading styles. If you have used all six styles in your HTML document, the browser ignores the sixth style and makes it look like the fifth style. Most Web documents have two to three levels of headings.

 **TIP** It's a good idea to use the heading levels in a sequential manner; that is, don't skip from Heading 1 to Heading 3. Go from Heading 1 to Heading 2, or from Heading 2 to Heading 3, and so on.

Although you cannot apply fonts or point sizes to the headings, you can select extra appearance enhancements. These enhancements include Bold, Italic, Monospaced, or Blink. You can also change the size proportionally, such as Fine, Small, Large, Very Large, or Extra Large. The actual size of this font is going to vary with different Web browsers.

You are probably familiar with bold and italics. *Monospaced text* changes the text from a proportional typeface to a non-proportional typeface similar to the typewriter style Courier. Each character takes the same amount of space if you choose Monospaced. Monospaced is a good attribute to use to create the appearance of tabbed columns of text.

*Blink* text flashes on and off when displayed on the Web browser. On the HTML document, it looks similar to a shadow effect. Figure 33.11 illustrates these attributes and sizes.

**FIG. 33.11**
Blink text does not flash in the HTML document, only in the Web browser.

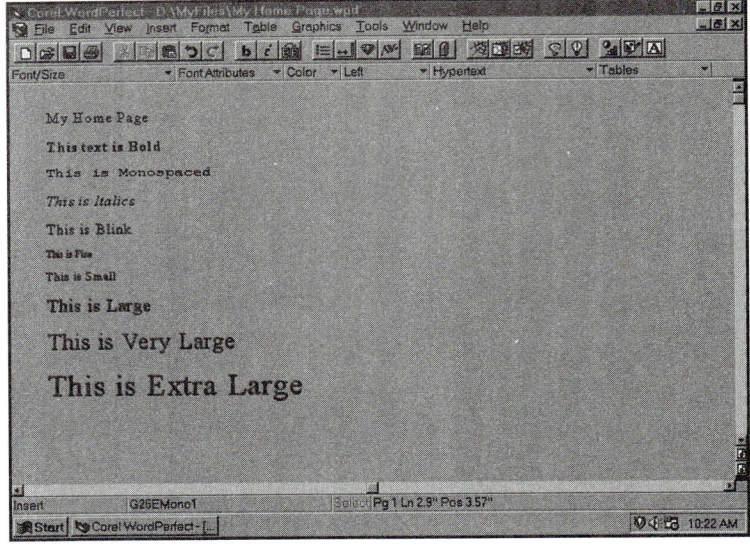

> **CAUTION**
> Use blink sparingly. It can be very distracting to the reader.

**N O T E**  Some Web browsers cannot display these appearance enhancements. For example, a character-based browser sometimes cannot display italics or underlining. Some browsers are incapable of displaying the Blink attribute.

To add a heading:

1. In the document, type the text for the heading.
2. Select the line of text for the heading.
3. Choose Format, Font. The Font dialog box appears (see fig. 33.12).

**FIG. 33.12**
The Internet Publisher Font dialog box does not display actual fonts by name; it displays styles.

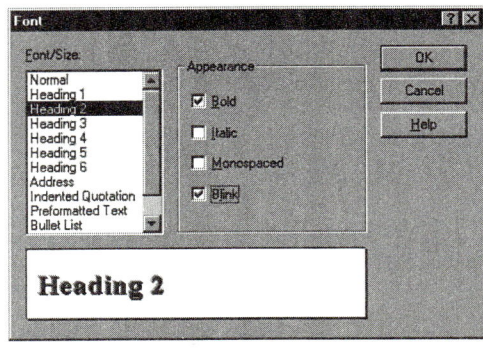

4. In the Font/Size box, select from the list of available headings, such as Heading 2.
5. In the Appearance box, select an appearance attribute (Bold, Italic, Monospaced, or Blink).
6. Choose OK.

## Adding Formatting

Character styles are used to change the appearance of a few words or characters in your HTML document. Character styles are the attributes discussed in the previous section: Bold, Italics, Monospaced, and Blink. The same information applies, in that many browsers might not be capable of displaying all attributes.

To apply character formatting:

1. Select the text to be formatted.
2. Choose Format, Font. The Font dialog box appears (refer to fig. 33.12).
3. Select the desired appearance attribute: Bold, Italics, Monospaced, or Blink.
4. Click OK. The text is now formatted.

Another type of formatting is applied to paragraphs of text. The text could be an indented quotation. Figure 33.13 shows an example of indented quotation text. With indented quotation, the left margin of the paragraph is moved in approximately 1/2 inch. Indented quotation is commonly used when you are quoting someone's words, or creating a subparagraph of a paragraph above it.

**FIG. 33.13**
Indented text is set apart from other body paragraphs for special attention.

Notice the indented paragraph

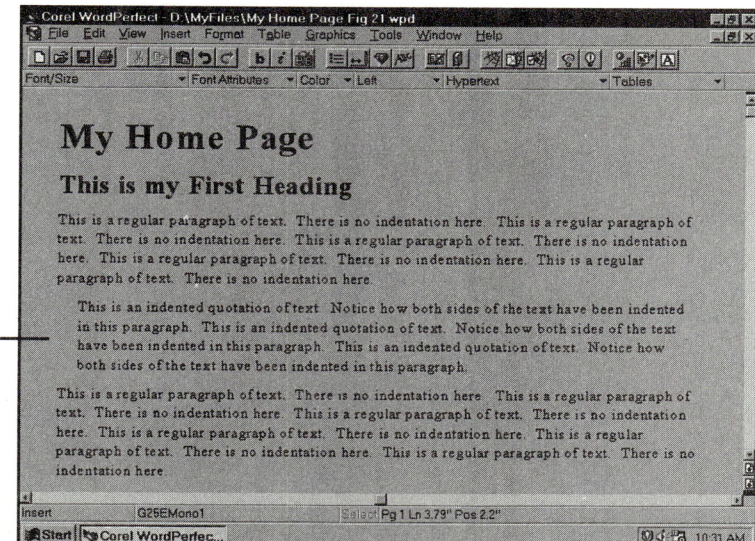

To create indented quotation text:

1. Place the cursor insertion point in the first line of the paragraph to be indented.
2. Choose Format, Font.
3. Select Indented Quotation from the Font/Size box.
4. Click OK. The specified paragraph is indented.

## Address Blocks

Occasionally you want to allow your readers to contact you or someone else, whether it is via e-mail or by a regular mailing address. To call attention to an address, WordPerfect's Internet Publisher provides a special appearance for this: an *address block*. In most Web browsers it appears as italicized text.

**TIP** Address block is a good style to use at the end of your document, where you should place the Web page author's name and Internet address.

The typed address block can contain multiple lines of text; however, in most Web browsers, the text runs together in a single line.

To change text into an address block:

1. Place the cursor insertion point in the text to be formatted as an address block.
2. Choose Format, Font.
3. Choose Address from the Font/Size selections.
4. Click OK. The text is then formatted as an address block.

## Creating Bullets and Lists

Three types of lists are supported by WordPerfect's Internet Publisher:

- Bullet list
- Numbered list
- Definition list

Lists can be created in several levels. The Tab key is normally ignored in an HTML document, but if you have defined a list, the Tab key creates the indentation for multi-levels.

Bullet list items are usually not in any particular order and are preceded with a bullet point. The style of the bullet varies according to the Net browser you are using. It could appear as a round circle ●, a hollow square ❑, or several other styles.

This is an example of a multi-level bullet list:

- ❏ Fruit
  - Apples
  - Oranges
  - Bananas
- ❏ Vegetables
  - Lettuce
  - Celery
  - Cabbage

A numbered list could be used to show a sequence of steps to follow. If you are displaying a procedure, a numbered list would be very appropriate. A numbered list can also be multiple levels.

This is an example of a numbered list:

1. Peel potatoes.
2. Cut into small pieces.
3. Place in pan.
4. Cover with water.
5. Cook 30 minutes or until tender.

A definition list allows you to display items similar to a glossary. The heading item is left-aligned, and the item under it is indented. You must press the Tab key at the second level to tell WordPerfect to indent it. This does not work like a Tab in a normal WordPerfect document. It works like an indent.

**NOTE** The Tab key indents text to the right, and Shift+Tab unindents, or moves text back to the left.

This is an example of a definition list:

Item One

> This is the descriptive information for item one. Notice that as the text wraps to the next line that it is indented also.

Item Two

> This is the descriptive information for item two. Notice that as the text wraps to the next line that it is indented also.

Item Three

> This is the descriptive information for item three. Notice that as the text wraps to the next line that it is indented also.

To indent text in a list, place the cursor at the beginning of any paragraph to be indented and press the Tab key.

To create a list:

1. Highlight the text to be modified into a list.
2. Choose Format, Font.
3. From the Font/Size selections, choose the type of list—Bullet, Numbered, or Definition.
4. Click OK. The items appear with your selected choice.

**TROUBLESHOOTING**

**I selected a numbered list and then typed my text. Now, every time I press Enter, the numbers are continuing. How can I turn it off?** At the line where you want to discontinue the numbering, press the Backspace key. This deletes the numbering style and returns the text to normal. The same is true if you have selected bullet points.

## Using Color

Even though you have no control over which font is being used or what size the text is to be, you do have the choice as to the color of the text. You can also pick a background color and even a wallpaper for the background. The default background color for an HTML document is gray. The color of hypertext links (discussed later in this chapter) also can be selected.

When a Text color is selected, it is consistent throughout the entire HTML document. WordPerfect does not allow you to make only a certain portion—say for example, a heading with your company name on it—to be red while the rest of the text is blue. If you choose to make the text red, it is red throughout your HTML document.

To assign a color:

1. Choose Format, Text/Background Colors. The Text/Background dialog box appears (see fig. 33.14).
2. Make your selections from the drop-down boxes available.

From this dialog box, you can choose the color for the regular text in your document as well as the hypertext links. The background color and background wallpaper is available, also.

3. Click OK.

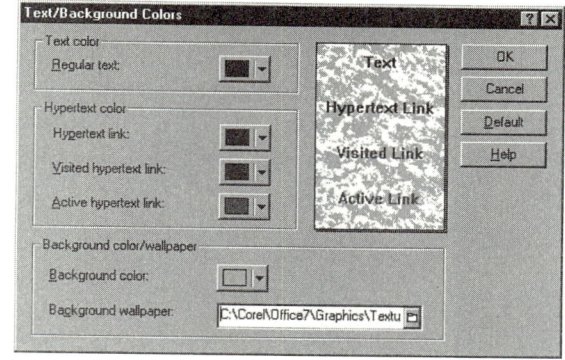

**FIG. 33.14**
You can specify a bitmap graphic file name to be used as wallpaper for your Web page.

 **TIP** Corel has included some wonderful graphics that can be used as wallpapers. Look in the TEXTURES folders for the subfolders called FABRICS, PAPER, STONE, or WOOD.

**CAUTION**
Make it easy on your readers. You want to grab their attention, but you don't want to blind them with color choices that are too bright or text that is too hard to read.

## Setting Alignment

Alignment in an HTML document works very much like in a standard WordPerfect document. If you want only a portion of the text to be centered, you must first select the text to be centered. Not selecting the text first results in the entire document (from the location of the insertion point down) to be centered or realigned. The shortcut keys are the same as in a standard WordPerfect document:

- Ctrl+L to left justify
- Ctrl+R to right justify
- Ctrl+E to center justify

A selection is also available on the Power Bar. There is no full justification option available in an HTML document.

To change alignment of text:

1. Select the text to be aligned.
2. Choose Fo*r*mat, *J*ustification.
3. Select *L*eft, *R*ight, or C*e*nter.

# Adding Graphics

"A picture is worth a thousand words." We've all heard that before, and it is absolutely true. It's one thing to write about your new invention, but what an advantage it is to have a picture to illustrate its usage as well. Graphics could be used to display your logo, a photograph, an illustration, or even be used as a link to another Web site.

**NOTE** Graphics should be in addition to your text, not in place of it. Some Web browsers are character-based only, which means they cannot display any type of graphic. If you tell your story in pictures only, these readers don't know what you were trying to say.

## Understanding Graphic Formats

A document created for the Web is actually only plain text. A graphic that you see on a Web page is really coming from a different document or file. The HTML document contains a tag that points to the graphic and its location. As an example, to insert a graphic called MYLOGO.GIF (located in the CLIPART folder) into your document, WordPerfect's Internet Publisher inserts the following tag:

```
<IMG SRC= "c:\clipart\mylogo.gif">
```

Dozens of types of graphic formats exist today, but there are only a few that can be used on a Web page. The two most widely used formats are *GIF* (*Graphics Interchange Format*) and *JPEG* (*Joint Photographic Expert Group*).

JPEG formats are the better quality of the two, especially for photographs because of color depth, but have a tendency to be larger in size and therefore slower for your viewer to load. GIF formats are usually much smaller than JPEG and therefore much faster to download; however, sometimes the quality is not as good.

Adding Graphics 1059

**TROUBLESHOOTING**

**The picture I want to use is not in a GIF or JPEG format. What can I do?** You can convert it using most image processing programs such as Adobe Photoshop or HiJaakPro. Corel's Presentations program can convert graphic files to either JPEG or GIF format. The Microsoft Paint accessory program that comes with Windows 95 cannot convert these files at all. There are also many shareware programs available on the Internet that can convert these files for you.

Although the WordPerfect menu enables you to insert several types of graphics, including text boxes and equations, these graphics are not acknowledged in the browser programs. Only graphics inserted with the GIF or JPEG format can be displayed.

To insert a graphic image:

1. Choose Graphics, Image.
2. Select the name of the desired graphic image.
3. Click Insert. The graphic comes into the HTML document.

The graphic might be quite large in size, but you can resize it like a normal WordPerfect graphic. To resize a graphic image, click once on the graphic to select it. Eight small handles appear. Place the mouse pointer over one of these handles and notice how the mouse pointer changes into a double-headed arrow. Drag these handles to resize the graphic image. Click your mouse anywhere else in your document to deselect the graphic.

▶ **See** "Resizing a Graphics Box," **p. 270**

If you change your mind and decide you do not want this graphic image on your Web page, click the graphic to select it and press the Delete key.

## Using Graphic Lines

An HTML document does not allow for page breaks in the way you would use them in a normal WordPerfect document. You need something to allow for a break in your topics. Using headings is one way. Creating a horizontal line or *rule* is another. See figure 33.15 for an example of a Web page with a horizontal line. Effective use of a horizontal line enables users to see a jump in the topics of your page and gives them a "breather" from their reading.

**TIP** Don't overuse horizontal lines in your document. Too many lines makes a document look "choppy" and can confuse the reader.

**FIG. 33.15**
Rules allow for a separation of topics.

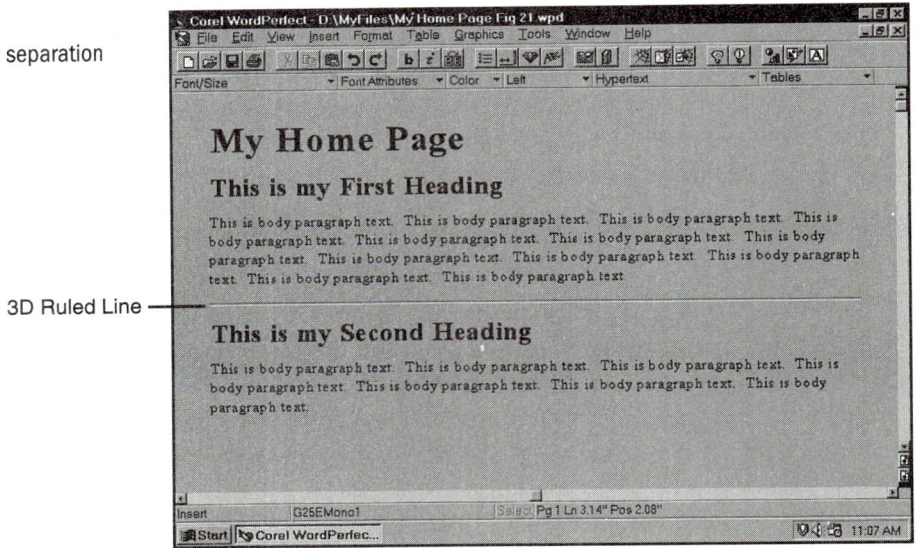

To create a horizontal line:

1. Place the cursor insertion point at the location for the line to appear.
2. Choose <u>G</u>raphics, <u>H</u>orizontal Line, press Ctrl + F11, or click the icon on the Toolbar. A line appears at the insertion point.

**TIP** Make sure you are on a blank line before creating a line. If you have text on the line, the paragraph breaks at the point where the line is inserted.

In an HTML document, using a horizontal line also places extra spacing between the text and the horizontal line.

**NOTE** Different browsers may display the horizontal rule differently. Some, such as Netscape, display it as a thin three-dimensional gray line. Others may display it as a flat black line. You have little control over the appearance of the horizontal line.

## Adding Special Characters

Occasionally you need a special character that is not on your keyboard in your HTML document. Perhaps you want to display the registered trademark ™ or the copyright symbol ©. These characters and several multinational characters can be added to an HTML document (see fig. 33.16).

**FIG. 33.16**
In the Typographic Character set, only characters 4,22 (Registered Trademark) and 4,23 (Copyright Symbol) are currently supported. In the Multinational Character set, numbers 23 to 89 are supported, excluding characters 2,24; 2,25; 2,74; 2,78; and 2,79.

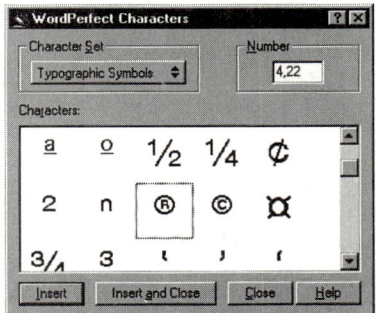

To insert special characters and symbols:

1. Place the cursor insertion point where you want the character to appear.
2. Choose Insert, Character; or press Ctrl+W. The WordPerfect Characters dialog box appears.
3. From the Character Set pop-up list, choose Multinational or Typographic Symbols.
4. Click the desired character.
5. Click Insert And Close to close the dialog box. The character is inserted into your document.

**NOTE** Certain characters and symbols might not be seen by all Web browsing programs. If possible, display your Web page with several different browsers to see the effects of using these commands.

# Creating Links

At this point, you have created a basic Web page that could be placed out on the Internet. Instructions for putting your page out on the Net are later in this chapter in the section "Getting Your Page Published."

The page, however, is still a relatively simple one. It provides the reader with something to read, and that's it. Many Web pages include hypertext links to allow the reader to quickly "jump" to another topic. That topic could be farther down in your page, on a different HTML document, or even to another Web site.

When should you use a link? It's really your choice, but if your document is relatively small—say, one or two screens full—you might not need a link. If your document is lengthy or it is only the beginning of several other documents, linking becomes necessary.

**TIP** If your document is long, you should put a link at the bottom that links back to the top of the document. Sometimes this is referred to as *Go Home* or *Return to Top*.

## Creating Bookmarks

In order to link to another location, you must first create a bookmark at the location to jump to. *A bookmark* in a WordPerfect document is similar to a bookmark in a real book. It's a placeholder, and marks specific locations in your document with an English-sounding name. It is much easier to tell WordPerfect to Go To *Managing Your Finances* than it is to Go To *Section 2, Page 14, Paragraph 5*.

▶ See "Marking a Hypertext Target with a Bookmark," **p. 1027**

To create a bookmark:

1. Place the cursor at beginning of the location, or highlight the area to be specified as a bookmark.
2. Choose Insert, Bookmark. The Bookmark dialog box appears.
3. Click the Create button. The Create Bookmark dialog box appears (see fig. 33.17).
4. Enter a name for the bookmark in the Bookmark Name box—for example, **Chapter Six** or **New Methods**.
5. Click OK. The bookmark is created.

**FIG. 33.17**
Bookmarks help you find a desired location in the document quickly.

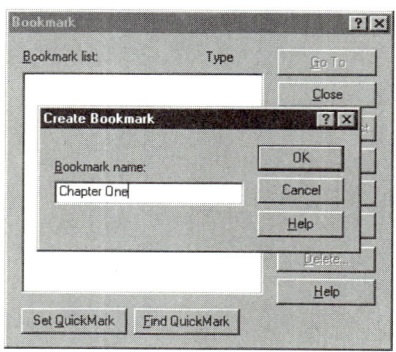

To quickly get to a specified bookmark, you can use several methods:

- Choose Edit, Go To.
- Press Ctrl+G.
- Double-click the page number at the bottom of the screen on the status line.

The Go To dialog box appears, as shown in figure 33.18. You can then choose to go to a specified page, or in this example, to go to a named bookmark. The last bookmark created appears in the bookmark section of this dialog box. Choose the bookmark name, click the Bookmark radio button, and click OK.

**FIG. 33.18**
The Go To box enables you to move quickly to the Last Position your cursor was located.

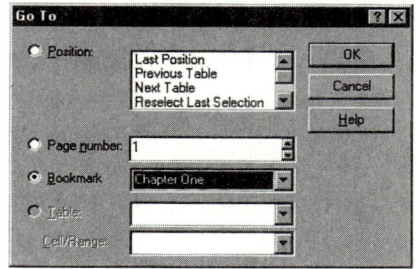

 Save yourself a little frustration—don't forget to click the Bookmark button in the Go To dialog box. It's an easy mistake to not actually click this button because a bookmark name appears, but by default, the button is not selected.

## Creating Hypertext Links

Bookmarks can get you around in a standard WordPerfect document, but when you are working with a Web page, you might also want the reader to quickly move from one place in your page to another. This process makes the Web page interactive for your reader. To do this you need a hypertext link.

▶ See "Understanding Hypertext," **p. 1022**

HTML hypertext links can create a link from one place in your document to another place in the same document. They can also create a link from one place in your document to another HTML document, whether it is another of your HTML documents or a Web page belonging to someone else. If you are planning to link to someone else's Web page, be sure to contact that person first for permission.

To create a hypertext link:

1. Highlight the text to be designated as the Jump Text. This is the location in the document where the reader may desire to "jump" to another location.
2. Choose Tools, Hypertext/Web Links. The Hypertext Feature Bar appears beneath the Toolbar and Power Bar (see fig. 33.19).

**FIG. 33.19**
Bookmarks can also be created or edited from the Hypertext Feature Bar.

Click here to create a hypertext link

Click here to create a bookmark

3. Click Create from the feature bar. The Create Hypertext Link dialog box appears (see fig. 33.20).

**FIG. 33.20**
If you are connected online, you can click the Browse Web button in this dialog box to access the Internet.

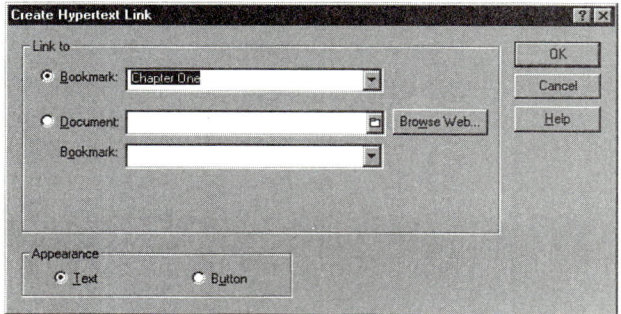

4. Enter the name of the Bookmark to jump to. Or select a different HTML Document and its Bookmark to jump to.
5. Select the appearance choice of either Text or Button.
6. Choose OK. The text selected as the hypertext link turns to a different color and is underlined, or it turns into a button.

> **NOTE** You should always create a link as text, and then optionally create a second link at the same location that appears as a button. Some Web browsers are character-based only and will not be able to display a graphic button.

>  **TIP** Many Web pages include a hypertext link to other Web sites. Often they refer to Other Fun Pages to Check Out, Related Web Sites, or Really Cool Web Pages.

## Editing A Hyperlink

After you have created your hypertext link, you might find you need to change it. Perhaps you want it to jump to a different bookmark or document than originally chosen.

To edit a hypertext link:

1. By using the keyboard, move the cursor to any part of the "jump" text. Be sure to use the cursor keys on the keyboard, and not the mouse.
2. Choose Tools, Hypertext/Web Links. The Hypertext Feature Bar appears.
3. Click the Edit button. The Edit Hypertext Link dialog box appears.
4. Make any desired editing changes, such as changing the bookmark or URL.
5. Choose OK. The Edit Hypertext Link dialog box closes, and the change you made is now in effect.

  **T I P**  To make editing easier, if your Hypertext Link Feature Bar is on-screen, you can temporarily deactivate hypertext by clicking the Deactivate button on the Hypertext Feature Bar. After editing, reactivate hypertext by clicking the Activate button on the feature bar.

## Editing the Appearance of a Button

A hypertext button, by default, contains no text. It appears as a gray box with no text to designate what it will do. It might be necessary to edit the appearance of the button. This button is really a graphic box and can be edited as any other graphic box by double-clicking the box. At that time, the Text Box Editor opens and enables you to type and format the text to appear in the button. Be aware that some browser programs cannot display a button.

To edit the appearance of a button:

1. Be sure hypertext is deactivated by clicking Deactivate on the Feature Bar.
2. Double-click the graphic button image. You are taken into the Text Box Editor.
3. Type and format the desired text for the button.
4. Click outside the graphic box to deselect it.

**N O T E**  If you are in Draft view instead of Page view, click Close on the feature bar to exit the Text Box Editor.

## Linking Graphic Images

Most of the time you create a hypertext link by selecting a block of text such as `Click here for more information`. Linking is not limited to text, however. In the earlier section "Creating a Hypertext Link," I discussed how to use a button instead of text, but also you can create a link with a graphic image.

Usually, graphics just lay on the page—looking quite nice, but doing nothing. You can make your Web page graphics interactive with hypertext links. With a graphic being interactive, your reader can click the image and jump to a different location.

To link a graphic image:

1. Insert the graphic image into the HTML document, as discussed earlier in the section "Adding Graphics."
2. Click the graphic image once to select it. Do not double-click it, or you are taken into the drawing program to actually edit the graphic. When it is selected, you see eight small "handles" around it. These are also the sizing handles discussed in the section "Adding Graphics."
3. With the graphic selected, choose Tools, Hypertext/Web Links. The Hypertext Feature Bar appears.
4. Click the Create button.
5. Specify the name of the Bookmark to jump to, or select a different HTML Document and (if desired) its Bookmark to jump to. Notice that because you have preselected a graphic image in the Appearance portion of this dialog box, the Text option is not available.
6. Choose OK.
7. Deselect the graphic image by clicking anywhere else in your document.
8. If the Hypertext feature has been deactivated, click the Activate button on the feature bar to reactivate hypertext.

Notice now as you move your mouse pointer over the picture of the graphic how it turns into a small hand with a pointing finger. Click anywhere on your graphic, and it jumps to the bookmark or location you specified.

# Finishing Your Document

The document is almost complete. There are a few tasks left to do, however. One is to spell check the document and check the grammar. Make sure the text is correct, and make sure the page is in a logical format with headings and subheadings. Also, very importantly, make sure the page is interesting. If what you are saying or displaying is not attractive, your readers may not stay at your Web page long enough to hear what you are trying to say or buy what you are trying to sell. Isn't that the reason why you are doing this? You want to bring readers onto your page to buy products or read your opinions.

Ask a friend to review your page. Sometimes it helps to have an outside source look at it for structural errors you might have overlooked. It is better to have a friend point out an error than one of your readers. Readers can notice any mistake in the document and, unfortunately, they don't usually forget it.

## Publishing to HTML

As you are working on the HTML document, you can view it with your Netscape browser. This gives you a different perspective of the document from the way WordPerfect is presenting it to you. You might notice some features that appear in WordPerfect which do not appear in the browser, for example, underlining. Note that the browser is the bottom line—how it appears in the browser is how the reader sees it.

The first step to seeing the document in the browser is to save it in an HTML format. This is the step that actually converts the document from WordPerfect format to HTML. Here is when WordPerfect converts all styles to HTML tags. You should save the document first as a WordPerfect document, then as an HTML document.

To publish to HTML:

1. Choose File, Save to save the WordPerfect document.

2. Choose File, Internet Publisher, Publish to HTML. The dialog box shown in figure 33.21 appears, prompting you for a file name. The default choice is to keep the same file name as given in WordPerfect, but assign it an extension of HTM.

**FIG. 33.21**
WordPerfect creates a separate folder to store the HTML graphics files.

3. Choose OK to accept the default choice.

If you have graphics or hypertext link buttons in your HTML document, they are saved in a separate folder that WordPerfect creates for you. The default choice is to create a folder called <*filename*>.HTG.

To illustrate this, say the name of your WordPerfect document is MYHOME.WPD and is stored in the C:\OFFICE\MYFILES folder. The HTML document is called MYHOME.HTM and is also stored in the C:\OFFICE\MYFILES folder. Any graphics or buttons, however, are stored by WordPerfect in the C:\OFFICE\MYFILES\MYHOME.HTG\ folder. If you inserted graphics into your document, WordPerfect converts them to GIF files before storing them in the newly created folder. This is controlled exclusively by WordPerfect's Internet Publisher.

> **CAUTION**
>
> Let WordPerfect do its job. Changing the file names or folders may cause the Internet Publisher to not function properly.

 To view the document in your Netscape Web browser, click the View in Web Browser icon or choose <u>V</u>iew, View in Web <u>B</u>rowser.

The Netscape browser appears with your document already loaded. You can now view the document in the same way your readers will view it. When viewed in the Netscape browser, the document shows a path on the top line of something like this:

```
C:\WINDOWS\TEMP\WP}00001.TMP
```

This path generally points to your temporary file directory as specified in your computer's AUTOEXEC.BAT file. The file is named WP}*NNNNN*.TMP where *NNNNN* is a file number specified by WordPerfect. When your document is actually published and out on a server, the path points to the server's name and address. An example might be:

```
http://www.1stclass.com/index.html
```

After viewing your document in the browser, you should exit the browser program as you normally would before returning to WordPerfect to make any editing changes.

## Getting Your Page Published

Now that your HTML documents are completed, you must decide how to get them out on the World Wide Web. The documents must be placed on a server. There are two options available:

- Set up your own server, which involves owning your own equipment and HTTP software. This is generally an expensive option, because of the cost of the hardware, software, and telephone line expenses involved and the cost of technicians to maintain all of it.

- Acquire space on an outside Web server. This option involves a monthly space rental fee.

## Finding a Service Provider

You can choose from one of many places available nationwide that are willing to rent space on their servers for your Web pages. If you are currently a member of an online service such as Prodigy, CompuServe, or America Online, you will also have access to store your pages—for a fee, of course.

In many cities, there are local Internet Service Providers (ISPs) who provide Internet access lines, enabling you to directly link up to the Internet via a local phone call. Check your telephone book for a listing of these providers. These ISPs often rent space on their servers for their subscribers. The price of the space rental varies depending on whether you are a business or an individual. You should thoroughly investigate the ISP you are thinking about, and consider not only their monthly space charges, but also the following:

- Do they charge you for each hit you get as well?
- What other "hidden" costs might be incurred?
- Do they have a good technical support system to assist you?

Ask to talk to other clients currently using their services.

**NOTE** When you have decided on a ISP, send them your HTML documents as well as any graphics or sound files to be included. These files are usually uploaded using FTP—File Transfer Protocol—or other software.

## Registering Your URL

Once you have decided where to publish your page, the next step is to set up your URL. Most ISPs assist you in deciding a URL address. Make sure you own the rights to your URL. That way, if you decide later to move your Web page to a different ISP or location, you can keep the same name.

A few general practices are involved in the naming of URLs. Most places use their company name, if it is available, such as **nbc.com** or **disney.com**.

**NOTE** The com extension after the company name designates a commercial business. A few other commonly used extensions are gov for government (as in **whitehouse.gov**) or edu (as in **purdue.edu**) for educational facilities.

Once you have been assigned your URL, you are responsible for registering your page with the various search engines, discussed in the next section.

## Marketing Your Page

The next step is to advertise your Web page. Put your URL on your business cards, any advertising brochures you send out, and on your letterhead and faxes. Anywhere your name goes, so should your URL. Many Web pages include a hypertext link to other Web sites. Because these authors are allowing their readers to jump to other pages, contact them about adding your page to their list. You may have even included some of these related sites when you designed your Web page.

### Webcrawler, Yahoo, and Other Search Programs

Other places to advertise your Web site include some of the Internet sites that search the Internet. These are sometimes called *search engines*. Many users log onto these search pages looking for a specific topic. A few of the more popular search sites are:

http://webcrawler.com  
http://www.yahoo.com  
http://www.submit-it.com  
http://www.lycos.com  
http://altavista.digital.com  
http://www2.infoseek.com

**NOTE** Although many search engines do not charge to register your site with them, some do have a registration fee. I have seen charges advertised in the range of $20 to $1,000. It is, however, an excellent place to market your page. Hundreds of thousands of users visit these pages daily to check out new sites. E-mail or contact the various search engines to check out their policies before you register your site with them.

### Locating Newsgroups

Contact a newsgroup affiliated with your subject matter. For example, if you are marketing genealogy-related products, locate a newsgroup that deals with genealogy. Don't try to market your page to unrelated newsgroups. This is not proper Internet netiquette.

If you don't know how to contact a newsgroup, try using a newsgroup search site such as http://www.dejanews.com.

## Final Notes

I would like to add a few final notes here, mainly to discuss a few miscellaneous aspects of Web publishing.

The first one is copyright. Be careful not to infringe on someone's copyrighted materials or drawings. If you are not sure if you are violating a copyright, contact an attorney who is familiar with copyright law, or scope out some of the do-it-yourself books available on copyright laws. It is definitely to your advantage to be sure before you publish.

 You can also contact the U.S. Copyright Office at their Web site: **http://lcweb.loc.gov/copyright**.

The other topic I want to briefly touch upon is called Net *etiquette or netiquette*. This is generally accepted practices of being on the Net. It also pertains to your published pages. Do not make untrue statements in your Web page, particularly about another person, company, or product. Do be considerate of your readers in the context and language of your page. Remember that children access the Internet and may come across your page. Also, when typing your page of text in WordPerfect, be sure to use a combination of upper and lowercase letters. Do not use all capital letters. This is determined to be *shouting* on the Internet, and you are likely to get nasty letters condemning this. (This is also called being *flamed*.)

Following a few considerate steps will make your Web page a more pleasant place to visit for your readers, and they most likely will come back from time to time. Keep the information on the page up-to-date, and add a little variety now and then.

# The Next Step—Forms

This chapter showed you how to create a page on the World Wide Web using WordPerfect. I introduced you to the features provided in WordPerfect Internet Publisher. However, there are many more things you can do with a Web page, such as creating interactive forms for your readers to fill out and return to you, or being able to download your complete catalog directly from your Web page.

To accomplish these tasks, you need a clear understanding of the HTML language. You can learn about these custom HTML tags from several books available on the market today. Among these books are Que's *Special Edition Using HTML*. I encourage you to look at these books. You will find a wealth of information in them regarding the additional codes you could use in creating your Web page.

Good luck, and have fun with it! ●

PART VII

# Appendixes

**A** Installing and Setting Up WordPerfect 7   1075

**B** Making the Transition to WordPerfect 7   1091

# APPENDIX A

# Installing and Setting Up WordPerfect 7

*by Tony Rairden, Cathy Kenny, and Read Gilgen*

**W**hether you are a novice computer user, a power user with an intense dislike for "automatic" install programs, or someone in between, WordPerfect's Install options can accommodate your needs and preferences. This appendix helps you with the initial installation of WordPerfect and with setting up WordPerfect 7. This chapter also shows you how to use the Uninstall program, which enables you to remove all or specific components of WordPerfect for Windows. ■

## Choosing What To Install

Since WordPerfect's acquisition by Corel Corporation, several marketing decisions make WordPerfect a better buy than ever. The basic WordPerfect is no longer sold by itself, but now comes bundled with other software programs. Corel calls this the *Corel WordPerfect Suite*, and it corresponds roughly to earlier versions of the PerfectOffice Suite for Windows 3.x. In order to receive all this functionality, you have to purchase the CD-ROM version. If all you have are floppy drives, you get a disk version with only WordPerfect.

If you do purchase the Corel WordPerfect Suite, these are some of the programs you receive:

- WordPerfect 7
- Presentations 7 (a complete graphics and presentations program)
- Quattro Pro 7 (a powerful spreadsheet program)
- Envoy 7 (a document electronic publishing program)

Bundled with this suite, you also can choose to install the following Bonus Applications:

- CorelFLOW 3 (a flow chart and diagramming program)
- Sidekick (a personal information manager)
- Dashboard (a program launching utility)
- QuickView Plus (a viewer for all popular document and graphics types)
- Clip art images, fonts, and a screen saver
- AT&T WorldNet Service (found in the BROWSER folder). You need to launch SETUP.EXE found in E:\BROWSER\DISK1 to install this application.
- Software Development Kit (SDK) (found on E:\SDK)

At current prices, purchasing a CD-ROM drive for your computer may cost you less than purchasing these programs separately on disk.

However, if all you need is WordPerfect, or if your company doesn't allow you to install "non-standard" software, you might have to choose which, if any, of these programs you will install along with WordPerfect.

## Installing WordPerfect for Windows

The Corel WordPerfect Suite ships on a single CD-ROM in an uncompressed format. WordPerfect, when purchased on floppy disk, ships compressed on 3 1/2-inch high-density (1.44M) disks. The following discussion assumes you are using the CD-ROM to install WordPerfect. See "Installing WordPerfect from Disks" later in this appendix for information on installing the stand-alone version of WordPerfect.

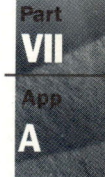

> **CAUTION**
>
> You must use WordPerfect's Setup program to install WordPerfect on your system. You can't decompress and install the individual files without the program. To access WordPerfect easily, you also need the changes that Setup makes to your Windows Registration file, icons, and Start menu items that Setup creates.

The WordPerfect Setup program does the following:

- Installs the programs you choose by decompressing and/or copying the required files into the appropriate folders.
- Installs icons on the Windows 95 Start menu, and modifies Windows to recognize and support WordPerfect and any other programs you install.

Don't be concerned about overwriting earlier versions of WordPerfect (Windows or DOS). WordPerfect 7 generates a totally separate installation, with its own discrete folder structures and access icons. You may continue to use the earlier version(s) without difficulty. However, you can't install WordPerfect 7 in the same folders as previous versions of WordPerfect.

## Preparing for Your Installation

Any time you install a major software program, you owe it to yourself to make backup copies of important files, and to clean up unneeded files to make room for the new program.

For example, if you are using versions of WordPerfect designed for Windows 3.x, you might want to make copies of your WPCSET.BIF and STANDARD.WPT files. While these files may not be affected by the installation of WordPerfect 7, there is always that possibility. In addition, although not required, now might be a good time to do a complete backup of your computer's hard disk(s).

Also, you need to make sure you have enough disk space to install WordPerfect. Depending on what you install, you will need about 260M of hard disk space in addition to any programs and documents you already have on your computer. You also need about 20M additional space for temporary installation files. If you're not sure how much disk space you have, the installation program will check for the required amount and give you the option to abort the installation if you don't have enough.

You can use the Custom installation procedure to eliminate portions of the program (such as the Spell Checker), but more likely than not you'll need or want the full complement of programs and features.

> **NOTE** You should defragment your hard drive before installing WordPerfect and then periodically (weekly works well for many people) with a utility such as the Disk Defragmenter in the MS Plus! Pack, MS-DOS 6's Defrag, Norton's SpeedDisk, or Central Point's Optimize.

Perhaps it goes without saying, but WordPerfect 7 is a Windows 95 application and requires that Microsoft Windows 95 first be installed on your system. (See *Windows 95 Installation and Configuration Handbook* by Que for information on setting up Windows 95.)

Finally, to avoid any potential problems during installation, close any applications you have running, especially WordPerfect products.

## Installing WordPerfect 7

After you make sure that your system has the necessary hardware (see Chapter 1, "Getting Started" in this book and "Installing WordPerfect" in the *Introduction to the WordPerfect for Windows Reference Manual*), software, and disk space for WordPerfect, follow these steps:

1. Insert the CD-ROM into your CD-ROM drive.
2. If Windows 95 is set up to automatically start CD-ROMs, the installation begins automatically.

   If nothing happens after you insert the CD-ROM, choose Run from the Start menu, and enter **[*d:*]autorun.exe** (where *d:* is the drive letter of your CD-ROM drive). The Autorun program appears (see fig. A.1) which launches Setup along with a musical introduction (if you have a sound board and speakers). You now have some choices and tasks before installation actually begins. Fortunately, you can back out at any time along the way by choosing Back or Exit from the Setup program.

On the first screen you can choose:

- *WordPerfect Suite Setup*. This is the choice you make to install the basic complement of programs (WordPerfect, Quattro Pro, Presentations, and Envoy) as an integrated suite. The typical suite installation requires about 135M disk space.
- *WordPerfect Setup*. If you don't have the disk space, or don't want to install other programs, this choice gives you WordPerfect by itself. The typical WordPerfect stand-alone installation requires 77M disk space.

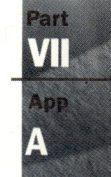

- *Bonus Applications.* Other programs that are not integrated with the WordPerfect Suite, but that come bundled with it, include CorelFLOW, SideKick, Dashboard 95, QuickView Plus, and the Corel Screen Saver. A typical installation of these programs requires about 61M disk space.
- *AT&T WorldNet Service.* This option is used to set up an Internet service provider and to install the Netscape browser. To install this service, open the Autorun program, go through E:\BROWSER\DISK1 and run SETUP.EXE.
- *Reference Center.* This is the new electronic version of the WordPerfect documentation, in Envoy format. You use this just like a printed reference manual.
- *Demos.* Corel has prepared several attractive, informative, and brief demonstrations of selected WordPerfect features.

**NOTE** The procedures for installing the first three options—WordPerfect Suite, WordPerfect, and Bonus Applications—are very similar. This section describes the WordPerfect Suite Setup (see "Installing Other Suite Programs" and "Installing WordPerfect Only" in this appendix for variations for installing the other two options).

**FIG. A.1**
After you insert your Corel WordPerfect Suite CD-ROM, the opening WordPerfect installation screen appears.

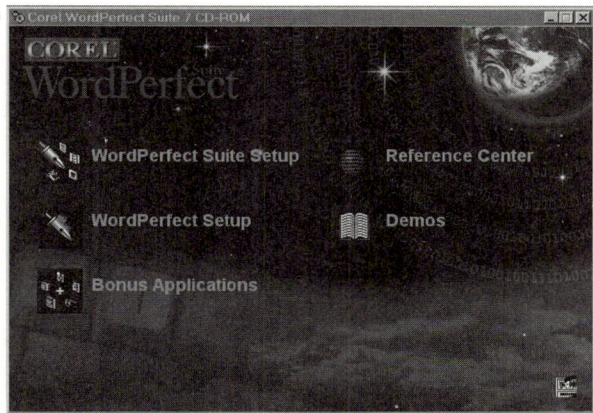

Choose WordPerfect Suite Setup, and the Setup welcome screen appears (see fig. A.2). Here you can click the Release Notes button to see any recent, late-breaking news about the program(s) you are about to install. Choose Next to continue with the installation.

If this is the first time you are installing the suite, you now see the License Agreement screen. If you choose Yes, you agree to abide by the licensing agreement. You can choose Back, Yes, No, or Help to stop at this point. To continue, choose Yes.

**FIG. A.2**
In the Setup welcome screen, you can see important late-breaking information about WordPerfect by choosing Release Notes.

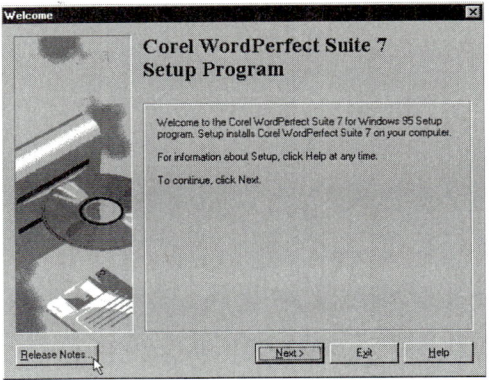

After briefly preparing for Setup, the Registration Information screen appears (see fig. A.3). Type in your name, then press Tab or Enter, type in your company name, then press Tab or Enter, and then type in the Serial Number of your copy of the software. Choose Next.

**NOTE** Your serial number can be found on the Proof of Purchase form that came with WordPerfect if this is your initial WordPerfect purchase. If you're upgrading from an earlier version of WordPerfect, use the serial number from that earlier version. If you can't find your serial number, enter your name and bypass the Serial Number box. The program runs without a serial number.

**FIG. A.3**
The Registration Information screen appears each time you use Install. The Serial Number you enter here appears in the Help, About WordPerfect dialog box, and is used when calling Corel Corporation for product support.

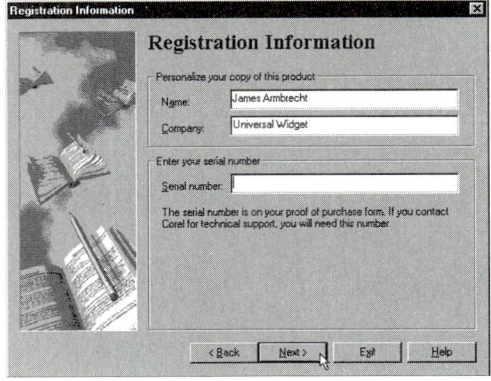

The Installation Type screen appears (see fig. A.4). You perform your initial installation from this screen. Use this screen for both stand-alone and network installations. (This appendix deals with stand-alone installations only. If you are installing to a network, refer users to the file NETWORK.TXT which is found on the CD in the COREL\OFFICE7\APPMAN\SETUP folder. This README file contains all the instructions necessary to install WP on a network.

**FIG. A.4**
Choose the type of installation you want to perform from the Installation Type screen.

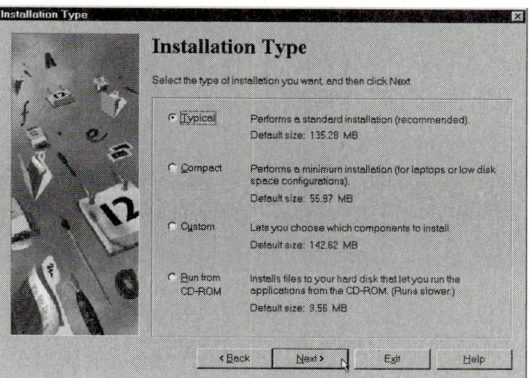

The following installation options are available:

- *Typical*. A Typical installation installs a basic set of all suite programs to the drive of your choice, in a predefined directory structure. This option requires approximately 135M disk space. Unless you have special requirements or need additional software elements, this is the recommended choice.

- *Compact*. If your disk space is limited (for example, on a laptop computer), choose the Compact option. This installs the minimum required files, and takes only 56M. However, although this installs minimal versions of WordPerfect, Quattro Pro, and Presentations, you are severely limited in what features you can actually use.

- *Network*. This option appears only if you are attached to a network, and enables network administrators to customize installation onto a network server. It also allows installation of files from a network server to a workstation.

- *Custom*. The Custom installation gives you considerable control over which files are installed and where they are placed. This option also enables you to save space by not installing WordPerfect features you know you won't use, or to install special features that most people don't need. The default Custom installation requires 141M.

- *Run From CD-ROM*. If you really want to conserve disk space, use this option which installs less than 10M of essential files and runs the rest from your CD-ROM drive. This requires, of course, that the WordPerfect CD-ROM be present in your CD-ROM drive whenever you use the program. The speed at which WordPerfect performs also is affected.

These options and those for most screens in Setup also are described in the Setup Help system, accessed from the screens by choosing Help.

**N O T E** Help must be accessed in WordPerfect's Setup by choosing the Help buttons offered in most screens. Install doesn't have a menu bar, and the F1 keystroke does nothing in Setup. If the screen doesn't have a Help button, Help is not available from that point in the installation.

For your initial installation of WordPerfect for Windows, use either the Typical or the Custom option if you have the necessary disk space. If you don't have enough disk space for a full installation, use Custom and deselect file groups under the Files option, or use Compact. (For information about the Custom Files option, see the section "Choosing Custom Installation" later in this appendix.)

## Choosing Standard Installation

If you choose Typical installation, Setup presents the Choose Destination screen (see fig. A.5), which also displays the available space on each drive. Select the drive on which you want to install; if you prefer a different location on one of the listed drives, choose Change Path, and in the Change Path dialog box indicate the different location where you want to install the program(s). Press Enter or choose Next.

**FIG. A.5**
In the Choose Destination screen, you can select any hard disk on your system for your WordPerfect installation.

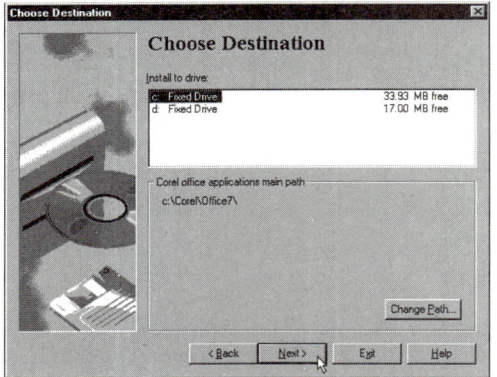

Setup next displays the Select Components screen (see fig. A.6). Here you have the option of not installing any of the suite components, in their entirety. Choose Next when you are ready to continue.

If you don't have enough space for the installation type you prefer, an Error dialog box appears. If you are overwriting an existing version of WordPerfect 7, click Yes to begin the install. If you aren't, click No. You either have to remove enough files from your drive to make room or change your installation plans.

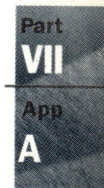

**Proceeding with the Actual Installation**  After making your drive selection and choosing the desired components of the suite, the Ready To Install dialog box appears, giving you one last chance to make changes before proceeding. Choose Install to begin, and Setup begins to transfer files from the CD-ROM to your hard disk. As the installation proceeds, you see a series of billboard-type screens containing helpful and informative messages about WordPerfect 7 for Windows 95. Also, an Installation Progress dialog box indicates what file is being installed to what folder, and what percentage of the installation has taken place (see fig. A.7).

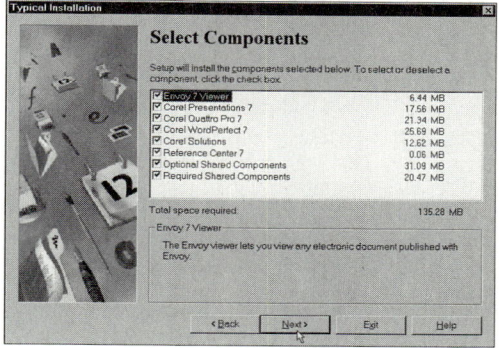

**FIG. A.6**
In the Select Components screen, you may choose entire programs that you want to install.

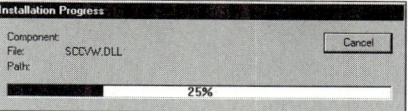

**FIG. A.7**
During the installation, a bar indicates how the installation is progressing.

From time to time you see the message `Committing data to the profile`, and when the transfer of files is complete, you see briefly `Updating the installation profile`. The Installation Profile keeps a detailed record of the Setup so that if you choose to remove the programs, Corel Uninstall knows exactly what to remove (see "Uninstalling WordPerfect" later in this appendix).

The Installation Progress dialog box also contains a Cancel button, which enables you to abort the installation at any point. If you do abort, you end up with a partial installation of WordPerfect that is unlikely to run. If you really want to remove the files installed during an aborted installation, your best course of action is to use a file management utility to delete all the WordPerfect files and their folders, then start over. If you intend to install all over again, there is no need to delete files, because you can install right over the aborted files.

**TIP** You might need to abort the installation (perhaps to do something else for a while). Later when you run the Setup program, you are asked if you want to resume the previous (incomplete) installation, or if you want to start all over again. If you choose to resume, the Setup program just picks up where it left off. This is also useful if the power goes out during the installation.

Finally, after all files are copied and the Profile has been updated, Setup displays the Configuring Your System screen. Because WordPerfect and its various components and other components of the Corel WordPerfect Suite are so tightly integrated, this step is necessary to coordinate the many files that have just been installed.

**Opening WordPerfect**  Once Setup is complete, you can open WordPerfect 7 from the Start button. If you installed the Corel WordPerfect Suite, a new category appears above the Programs icon: Corel WordPerfect 7. Choose this icon to get a list of any suite components you installed, including WordPerfect. Click WordPerfect to start up the program.

Having loaded Windows and WordPerfect, you might want to refer to Chapter 1, "Getting Started," before you proceed in this appendix.

WordPerfect can be extensively fine-tuned to suit your personal tastes and needs. Chapter 9, "Customizing WordPerfect," discusses customizing in depth.

**NOTE**  Your first temptation after installing a new version of WordPerfect is to try to customize it so that it works like your previous version of WordPerfect. Try to resist this temptation, and instead try things out using WordPerfect's defaults. Often you'll find you like the new ways better. If not, you can always customize later.

## Choosing Other Installation Types

With the exception of the Custom installation, all other installation types (for example, Compact and Run from CD-ROM) follow the sequence described in the preceding section. You first choose the destination drive, select the components you want to include or exclude, and follow the installation process.

## Choosing Custom Installation

If you choose the Custom installation from the Installation Type screen, the Custom Installation screen appears (see fig. A.8). Use Custom installation when you want to control directly the extent and locations of the installation. The default Custom installation installs approximately 7–8M more material than does the Typical installation.

Installing WordPerfect for Windows 1085

> **CAUTION**
> You should use the Custom installation only if you are reasonably sure of what you want to do. If not, you may include files you don't need, or exclude files that you do need.

The Custom Installation screen provides a list of all components that can possibly be installed. Those that are installed by default are already checked. Shaded check boxes indicate that only part of that component will be installed. To see what is missing, click the item, then choose Components. If you need a component that is not checked, simply check it to add the item to the installation process.

The Custom Installation screen also displays the intended destination (drive and path) of each component. If you want to install that component elsewhere, choose Change Path and indicate the new location. For example, you might want to install the bulk of the program on drive C, but in order to conserve space on that drive, you might install part of the program on drive D.

**FIG. A.8**
From the Custom Installation screen, you can control the selection and the locations for various elements of the WordPerfect program and the Corel WordPerfect Suite.

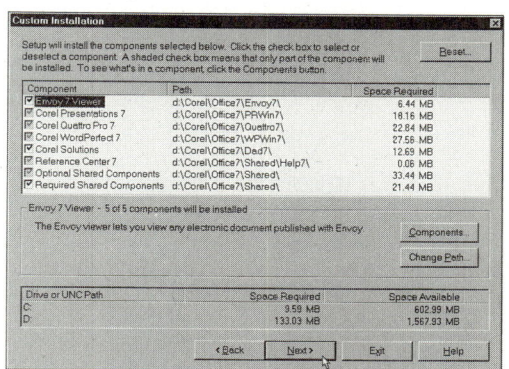

Examples of Typical components that require a Custom installation are the Corel True Type Fonts (8M), WordPerfect SGML options (6M), and the IBM Voice Type Control program (25M). To install the Corel True Type fonts, you must choose to install the Bonus Applications (do this from Autorun), then go into a custom install of CorelFLOW 3.

> **NOTE** To install a single component, go to the Custom Installation screen, unmark all the components except the one you need, and choose Next and OK.

If you begin to make changes, but then change your mind and can't remember what was originally selected, click Reset to access the Reset Custom Installation dialog box (see fig. A.9). If you click the Default Custom Installation option button, the default components (141M) are checked once again. Note that you can choose other install options, such as Typical, and then customize components and locations for just those files used in that installation. If you want to install one or a few options or files, choose Deselect All which clears all the selections so you can start from scratch. Click the Reset Paths To Default Locations check box to reset file locations as well as components to be included.

After you select the components and indicate the locations of your custom installation, choose Next and follow the installation procedures described in the preceding section.

**FIG. A.9**
If you want to reset the default installation options, or even deselect all options so you can choose just those you want, use the Reset Custom Installation dialog box.

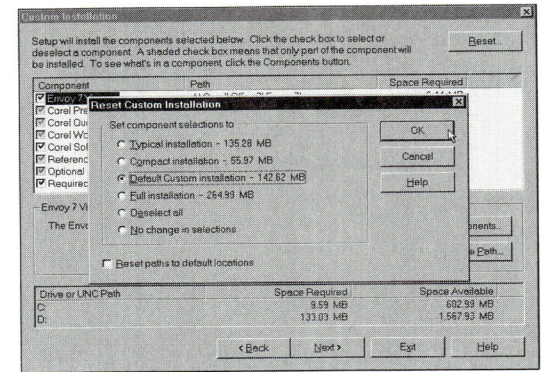

## Installing Other Suite Programs

Other installations, such as WordPerfect and Bonus Applications, follow the same pattern described earlier in this appendix. To install AT&T WorldNet Service, you need to run its own setup program.

## Installing WordPerfect Only from CD-ROM or from Disks

If you want to install only WordPerfect, you choose the options from Corel WordPerfect Suite 7 CD-ROM opening screen (refer to fig. A.1). If you must install WordPerfect from disks, that is the only program you are able to install; therefore, the procedure is the same for the CD-ROM WordPerfect Only option.

After choosing the WordPerfect option, and responding to the same welcome and licensing screens, you then also have the option of choosing which type of installation you desire (see fig. A.10).

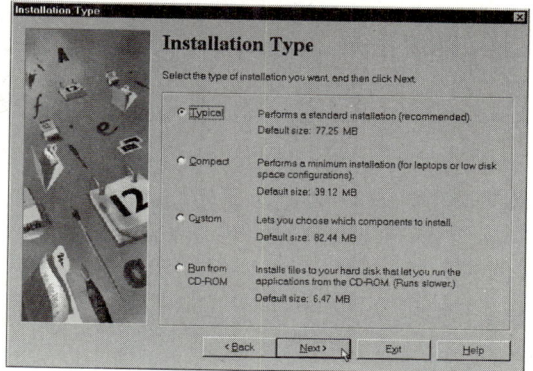

**FIG. A.10**
The Installation Type screen for the WordPerfect only installation still allows you to choose Typical, Custom, Compact, and CD-ROM installations.

The installation types include:

- Typical (77M required)
- Compact (43M)
- Custom (default is 86M)
- CD-ROM (6M, not available with the disk installation)

The components installed in the WordPerfect Only version include the Spell Checker, TextArt, graphics, and so on. Optional components include WordPerfect SGML options. You can access Corel Fonts through the Bonus Applications options (from Autorun).

## Installing Printer Drivers

In previous versions of WordPerfect, you had a choice of installing WordPerfect printer drivers or Windows printer drivers. WordPerfect no longer provides its own printer drivers, but instead relies entirely on those installed in Windows 95. If you need a particular printer driver, you must contact the printer manufacturer or Microsoft Corporation.

## Installing Fonts

As in previous versions of WordPerfect, the program ships with several True Type fonts, but only if you install from the CD-ROM version; the disk version does not come with additional fonts.

To install additional fonts from the Corel WordPerfect Suite CD-ROM, access the Bonus Applications install from Autorun, then choose the Custom install on CorelFLOW 3 when installing either the WordPerfect Suite or WordPerfect by itself. Then choose the Corel Fonts option. The Setup program automatically installs and registers 206 fonts, such as Bernhard, Broadway, Cooper, Oz Handicraft, Stencil, and others.

**NOTE** Of these 206 available fonts, 198 are found in the \COREL\OFFICE7\APPMAN\WKSFILES\FONTS folder, and eight are in the \SYMBOLS subfolder.

If you want more control over exactly which fonts you install, follow these steps:

1. Click the Windows 95 Start button; choose Settings, Control Panel; and double-click the Fonts icon to open the Fonts dialog box.
2. In the Fonts dialog box, choose File, Install New Font.
3. In the Add Fonts dialog box, go to the CD-ROM drive at D:\COREL\OFFICE7\APPMAN\WKSFILES\FONTS (where D is the drive letter of your CD-ROM drive). Windows 95 reads the fonts in that folder, and then displays a list of available fonts by name.
4. Select the fonts you want to install.
5. Check the Copy Fonts To Fonts Folder box, and choose OK.

To install fonts from other font packages, follow the directions provided by the vendor. All fonts are installed as part of Windows 95 and can be shared by any Windows 95 application.

# Updating and Adding onto WordPerfect

WordPerfect (Corel Corporation) is constantly working on new versions of its products. Major additions to the capabilities of the program are indicated by new "major version" numbers, which precede the decimal point in the version number: 5.0, 6.0. Lesser, but still significant enhancements are indicated by minor version numbers, which follow the decimal point. This version of WordPerfect is 7 for Windows 95; it surpasses the capabilities and features of WordPerfect 6.1 and 5.2 for Windows and 5.1 for DOS, and has a broader feature set than 6 for DOS.

In addition to major and minor version releases, WordPerfect sometimes adds enhancements and fixes minor problems with all its software products. These fixes are released as a "patch" to the software, and often can be downloaded via FTP or the World Wide Web directly from Corel.

# Using WordPerfect Startup Switches

WordPerfect has several startup options you can use by adding the appropriate switch to the command line you type to load the program (see table A.1). More than one switch may be used at a time—just make sure to put spaces between them. To use one or more of the switches when launching WordPerfect, follow these steps:

1. Access the Windows 95 Start button and choose <u>R</u>un.
2. Enter the entire path and file name for WordPerfect (for example, **C:\COREL\ OFFICE7\WPWIN7\WPWIN.EXE**).
3. Add the switch and its parameters (**/m=START**, for example) to the end of the command line, and then choose OK or press Enter. (The command line may extend beyond the initially visible space in the box.)

You can edit the properties for WordPerfect on the Windows Start menu. If you have a WordPerfect icon on the desktop, right-click the icon, click Properties Shortcut, then specify the startup options on the command line.

**Table A.1 Startup Options for WordPerfect 7**

| Option | Description |
| --- | --- |
| : | Starts WordPerfect, bypassing the "billboard" opening display screen. |
| *filename* | Starts WordPerfect with a specific file already open. Include the full path if the file isn't in your document default folder. |
| filename /bk-bookmark | Opens the specified file and goes directly to the bookmark name (for example, `/bk-conclusion`). |
| /m=*macroname* | Executes a specific macro when WordPerfect starts. |
| /d=*drive\directory* | Specifies the drive or folder where you want WordPerfect to store the temporary buffers, print queue, and overflow files it creates. |
| /x | Overrides Preferences settings with WordPerfect "out-of-the-box" default settings (for the current session only). |
| /l-language code | Instructs WordPerfect to use the Language Resource File (WP.LRS) and appropriate DLL files for the language code specified. |
| /nb | Turns off Original Backup (to save disk space). |
| /sa | Turns on Stand-alone mode; disregards network environment and settings. This option may provide greater speed of operation when the network facilities are not required. |
| /nt | Tells WordPerfect to operate in Network mode; also accesses network-oriented features for a stand-alone system. |

*continues*

**Table A.1 Continued**

| Option | Description |
| --- | --- |
| /sp | Instructs WordPerfect to use the personal setup file rather than a public one on a network. |
| /u=*username* | Identifies specific network user and machine. |
| /recover | Forces WordPerfect to rebuild table information in a document prefix when opened. |

# Uninstalling WordPerfect

If you decide you need to remove WordPerfect (or any other programs in the Corel WordPerfect Suite), choose Start, Settings, Control Panel, and double click the Add/Remove Programs icon. Select the program you want to remove and choose Add/Remove. This starts up the Corel Remove Program for Windows 95.

Choose Next to display the Select Applications To Remove screen (see fig. A.11). Check the application you want to remove (for example, Corel WordPerfect 7), and choose Next. The Uninstall program gives you one last chance to quit before you choose Remove. Corel Remove then deletes all files for that application, and cleans up all references to it in the Windows Registration file.

**FIG. A.11**
Use Corel's Remove program to uninstall WordPerfect or other components of the Corel WordPerfect Suite.

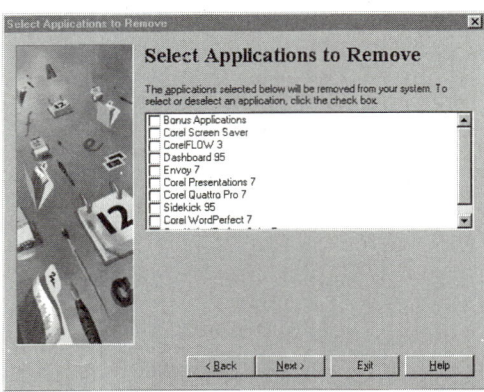

**N O T E**  Corel Remove does not allow you to remove only portions of a program. It's either all or nothing, so be careful when choosing to remove a program. If you accidentally remove the program, use the Setup program as described in this appendix to reinstall the program.

APPENDIX B

# Making the Transition to WordPerfect 7

*by Read Gilgen*

If you are currently a WordPerfect 6.1 for Windows user, making the switch to Corel WordPerfect 7 will be relatively easy. If you've been holding out and now are finally making the switch from a DOS version of WordPerfect, plenty of challenges lie ahead. Even if you are upgrading from earlier versions of WordPerfect for Windows, plenty of new features will not only challenge you, but enable you to take your word processing skills to new heights. This appendix can help you determine just what to look for. ∎

# Why Make the Switch?

You've spent lots of time learning and using your current version of WordPerfect. Is changing to WordPerfect 7 really worth the effort? Is it worth the cost? What do you lose in the process?

## Do You Have a Choice?

You might begin by asking yourself if you even have a choice. If you've held onto the DOS version of WordPerfect this long, most likely it's because you've had an older, less powerful computer. Perhaps you've just purchased a new computer and it came with Windows 95 already installed. Or maybe your company is making everyone switch to the new operating system.

One thing is certain: if you don't have Windows 95, you cannot use WordPerfect 7. Even if you do have Windows 95, you still can use earlier versions of WordPerfect. But if you want to take full advantage of the power of your new computer and operating system, and if you expect to reap the benefits of today's exciting developments in information processing, you really owe it to yourself to explore what WordPerfect 7 has to offer.

## Advantages

Perhaps the two biggest reasons for moving to WordPerfect are the graphical interface, which helps take the guesswork out of creating attractive documents, and the addition of a huge number of new and improved features. This appendix lists some of the more interesting and significant ones.

"But," you protest, "I've switched to WordPerfect 6.0/6.1 for DOS. What else could there be?"

The answer is "Plenty!" Although WordPerfect 6.0/6.1 for DOS made giant strides forward, much of what it contains already was present in WordPerfect 5.2 for Windows. WordPerfect 7 has added many features and improved the interface in ways that WordPerfect for DOS has not.

## Costs

The two major costs involved in moving to WordPerfect 7 are training and hardware. Consider the following:

- If you currently use an earlier version of WordPerfect for Windows (5.1, 5.2, 6.0, or 6.1), upgrading to WordPerfect 7 should be quite easy. Perhaps the more difficult part will be getting used to Windows 95, but feature for feature, WordPerfect 7 is very similar to WordPerfect 6.1 for Windows. WordPerfect has worked hard to become easier to use. Indeed, probably the most difficult thing you have to learn is how to stop doing things the hard way.

- If you currently use a DOS version of WordPerfect, you have to get familiar not only with WordPerfect 7, but also with an entirely new operating system. And unless you switched to WordPerfect 6.x for DOS with its graphical user interface, you also have a whole new way of looking at the way you do word processing. However, experience shows that if you already know any version of WordPerfect, making the switch to the latest Windows 95 version is relatively painless.

- If you currently use a PC, XT, or AT (286) computer, don't even consider using WordPerfect 7, because neither it nor Windows 95 even works on such computers.

- If you own a fast 386 computer with at least 8M of RAM, you *might* be able to use Windows 95 and WordPerfect 7. However, you will probably be quite frustrated by the slowness of the programs on your computer.

- The real minimum requirements for successfully using Windows 95 and WordPerfect 7 are a fast 486 computer (a speedy Pentium is better) and at least 16M RAM.

Ultimately, you must weigh these costs with those you incur by not upgrading or staying current. Eventually, support for older software versions will end, and increasingly what you create will not be compatible with the work done by others. In addition, you miss out on many new and exciting features that can make you more productive and make your work more enjoyable.

You can hardly purchase a new computer these days that does not meet these minimum requirements. So, if you have the hardware, you need to take the plunge and put it to the best use possible.

# New (and Improved or Relocated) Features in WordPerfect 7

Whether you're switching from WordPerfect for DOS, or upgrading from WordPerfect 5.x or 6.x for Windows, you want to know what's new in WordPerfect 7. Although a complete listing of all new features is impossible in this section, you find here a brief description, in alphabetical order, of some of the more important and intriguing new features. Features that are completely new are listed here, along with previously available features that saw significant enhancements. Features you may have missed by not upgrading to WordPerfect for Windows 6.x or 5.x are listed in separate sections later in this appendix.

## Address Book

WordPerfect's Address Book feature enables you to maintain one or more lists of names or organizations, and information about them. The Address Book data then can be inserted into documents, envelopes, or labels, using predefined and custom formats. You can create groups for multiple addresses, and can even use the entries to dial phone numbers.

Address books also serve as a handy central repository of information about customers, clients, members of organizations, or friends. (See Chapter 11, "Using Templates," for more information on the Address Book feature.)

## Ask the PerfectExpert

You now can ask WordPerfect, in plain English, about features you are interested in, and WordPerfect finds you the help you need. For example, you ask it, "How do I customize my address book?" and the PerfectExpert displays help topics on using the Address Book feature. The expert doesn't always guess perfectly what you want to know, but it's usually able to help you find what you want. (See the Introduction to this book for more information on where to find Help.)

## Corel

During the development of WordPerfect 7, WordPerfect and its family of business applications was purchased by Corel Corporation. Early indications are that graphics and Internet integration will be more prominent in this and future versions of WordPerfect.

Significantly, WordPerfect now is being sold as a suite of applications on CD-ROM. Among the announced programs bundled with WordPerfect are:

- Presentations 7 (a complete graphics and presentations program)
- Quattro Pro 7 (a powerful spreadsheet program)
- Envoy 7 (a document electronic publishing program)
- CorelFLOW 3 (a flowchart graphics program)
- Netscape Navigator (a powerful Internet browser)
- AT&T WorldNet Service (an Internet service provider)
- Sidekick (a personal information manager)
- Dashboard (a program launching utility)
- Clip art images, fonts, and a screen saver

If you don't have a CD-ROM drive, you may find that at current prices, purchasing a CD-ROM drive for your computer may cost you less than purchasing these programs separately on disk.

## Document Review

This feature (to open, choose File, Document, Review) is used for collaborative editing of documents. Those suggesting changes are called *Reviewers*, and the changes they make are highlighted, each with a different marking color. The originator of the document, the *Author*, can then examine each reviewer's changes and accept or reject them. If you use the Workflow feature (opened by choosing File, Workflow), Document Review is activated automatically.

## Flush Right with Dot Leaders

Most WordPerfect users do not know that flush right text with dot leaders has been a feature since early versions of WordPerfect for DOS (press the keystrokes for Flush Right twice; for example, Alt+F7 twice). Finally, you now have a menu listing by choosing Format, Line, Flush Right w/Dot Leaders.

## Guidelines

To make it easier to see your text margins, WordPerfect 7 now has guidelines that show the actual boundaries of your margins (top, bottom, left, and right), columns, and headers and footers. You also can drag the guidelines with the mouse to change any of these margin boundaries. (See Chapter 5, "Formatting Pages and Documents," for more information on using guidelines.)

## Help Online

Recognizing that many computers can now connect to the Internet, WordPerfect can provide online help via an Internet browser such as Netscape Navigator, which is included in the WordPerfect 7 Suite, or via CompuServe.

## Highlight

Highlight (to open, choose Tools, Highlight) acts like a colored marker to highlight text as you drag the mouse over it. You can print your text with the highlighting (in color if you have a color printer or shaded gray if you don't). This is particularly useful in a collaborative effort (see "Workflow" in this section, and also Chapter 26, "Assembling Document References," for more information on this feature).

## Internet Publisher

One of the more significant new features in WordPerfect 7 is the built-in Internet publishing features. You can create World Wide Web (HTML, or Hypertext Markup Language) documents from scratch or from existing documents, and you can see how they look right in WordPerfect. WordPerfect supports HTML 2.0 standards, plus several extensions found in Netscape Navigator and other browsers. Finished documents are published in HTML format for placement on your Web server. WordPerfect also ships with a copy of the latest version of Netscape Navigator. (See Chapter 33, "Publishing Documents on the World Wide Web," for more information on WordPerfect's Internet Publisher.)

## Print

Printing is now tied much more closely to the Windows 95 printing processes, thus eliminating WordPerfect 6.1's intermediate WordPerfect Print Process, as well as separate WordPerfect printer drivers. New features include a print history that lists (or hides) all completed print jobs, and where you cancel active print jobs. Also, you can now save your standard print settings for letters, legal documents, and so on by using the Named Print Settings feature with plain English names so you don't have to select the settings every time.

Multiple copy printing terminology has changed—*collate* is equivalent to having WordPerfect generate the copies, while *group* is equivalent to having the printer generate them. (See Chapter 8, "Basic Output: Printing, Faxing, and E-Mail," for more information on the new printing procedures.)

## QuickCorrect

This handy feature, which in its basic form was added to version 6.0a, quickly corrects common mistakes as you type them. For example, *teh* becomes *the*. It also corrects initial capitalization problems (for example, *TErry*). You can add words to the QuickCorrect list, and even use this feature as a shortcut for simple abbreviations.

The QuickCorrect feature also includes:

- *SmartQuotes*. Gives you typographically correct quote marks as you type.
- *QuickIndent*. Press Tab at the beginning of any line in a paragraph except the first line, and WordPerfect automatically gives you a hanging indent paragraph (all lines indented except the first line).

- *QuickBullets*. Automatically numbers or adds bullets to paragraphs if you type a number or a dash followed by an indent.
- *QuickLines*. Creates a single or double horizontal line if you type three - or = and press Enter.
- *QuickOrdinals*. Automatically adds a superscripted abbreviation after 1st, 2nd, and so on.

For information on QuickCorrect, see Chapter 6, "Using Writing Tools."

## QuickFonts

New on the Power Bar is the QuickFonts button, a list of recently used fonts displayed in their actual size and font.

## OLE Server

WordPerfect can now act as an OLE (Object Linking and Embedding) Automation server, which means other OLE programs such as Visual Basic, Delphi, Quattro Pro, or Excel can embed WordPerfect objects in their programs and jump back automatically to WordPerfect to edit those objects.

## QuickOpen

At the bottom of the File menu, WordPerfect now lists the last nine documents you worked with. Click a file's name to open it, or point at it with the mouse to display the file's location.

## QuickSpots

Many people simply forget to click the right mouse button to display the handy QuickMenus that were introduced in version 6. QuickSpots are small square buttons that appear in the upper-left corner of paragraphs, and in the upper-right corner of table cells and graphics objects when you point the mouse at them. Clicking the QuickSpot gives you a palette of formatting choices, and in the case of graphics, replaces the Graphics Feature Bar. (See Chapter 5, "Formatting Pages and Documents," for more information on QuickSpots.)

## Relocated Features

Several features have found new homes in WordPerfect 7 (see the table at the end of this appendix, "Where Do I Find It in WordPerfect for Windows?" for a more complete listing).

These include:

- *Page Numbers*. Formerly found by choosing Format, Page, page numbering now has its own menu entry under the Format menu (choose Format, Page Numbering).
- *Border/Fill*. The capability to add borders or fills to pages, paragraphs, or columns now has its own menu entry under the Format menu. See "Borders" later in this appendix for a more complete description of this feature.
- *Document Summary/Info*. These two items are now found by choosing File, Document, Properties.
- *Display Ruler Bar*. In previous versions you had to choose Edit, Preferences, Display to display the Ruler Bar. Now you simply choose View, Toolbars/Ruler, and check the Ruler Bar box. The Ruler then appears until you uncheck the box.
- *Preferences*. Environmental preferences were previously selected from the File menu. In WordPerfect 7, you choose Edit, Preferences to open a dialog box of icons representing Environment preferences and several other catgories of settings.

## Shadow Pointer

If you move your mouse over the text area of the document, a gray version of the insertion point appears where the insertion point would appear if you were to click the mouse button. This helps you determine precise mouse position before clicking. After a few seconds of no mouse movement, the shadow pointer disappears.

## Show Me

The Show Me tab in the Help Topics dialog box continues WordPerfect's quest to make learning how to use the program as painless as possible. Formerly limited to Coaches, this feature now includes Play a Demo, Guide Me Through It (Coaches), Do It For Me (QuickTasks), and a button for asking the PerfectExpert anything you can't find in the Show Me topics. (See the Introduction for more information on finding Help.)

## Spell As You Go

If you want to catch your mistakes as you make them, the Spell As You Go feature highlights (with a red dashed underline) words not found in the Spell Check dictionary. You can turn this feature off if you get annoyed that the computer seems to be smarter than you are. (See Chapter 6, "Using Writing Tools," for more information on Spell As You Go.)

## Tab Icons

When you change your tab settings, WordPerfect places a tab icon in the left margin which you can see if you work in Page mode.

## Tables

Many small enhancements have been made to tables, including the ability to have rows span page breaks, to rotate text in cells, to place diagonal lines in cells, and to see actual column measurements while dragging columns left or right. Also, the Table Expert is now called SpeedFormat. (See Chapter 16, "Working with Tables," and Chapter 31, "Advanced Tables," for more information on these new tables features.)

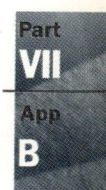

## Workflow

In an effort to help people like yourself work collaboratively with others, WordPerfect's Workflow feature (choose File, Workflow) enables you to create a document, then route it for editing or comments to others on your network. When the document is returned to you, you can examine the changes others have made (each person's changes are marked in a different color). You can move from change to change and accept or reject each one, or all the changes.

## Writing Tools

The Spell Checker, Thesaurus, and Grammatik (grammar checker) now appear in the same dialog box as tabbed options whenever you choose any of the three.

# What Did I Miss in WordPerfect 6.1 for Windows?

Several new features appeared in WordPerfect for Windows 6.1, most of which surpassed the feature set of WordPerfect 6.0 for Windows and even 6.1 for DOS. If you haven't used WordPerfect for Windows before, or if you didn't upgrade from versions 6.0 or 5.1/5.2, here are some of the features you've been missing.

## Drop Cap

You can quickly create a *drop cap* (a large letter that drops down one or more lines) for either the first letter of a word or for the entire first word. You can choose from 12 predefined drop cap styles, or you can customize your own. (For information on drop caps, see Chapter 21, " Using Advanced Graphics Techniques.")

## Find/Replace

Find and Replace are combined in the same dialog box. More significantly, however, WordPerfect integrates its PerfectSense technology to let you match word forms as well as exact word patterns. For example, you can replace *fly* with *drive*, and Replace also replaces *flew* with *drove*. (See Chapter 3, "Retrieving and Editing Documents," for information on Find and Replace.)

## Grammatik

One of the leading grammar checking programs, Grammatik, was purchased by WordPerfect Corporation and became fully integrated into WordPerfect beginning with version 6.0. This feature complements the Speller and Thesaurus tools that have made WordPerfect so valuable to writers. No longer do you need to be embarrassed by dangling participles or mismatched subjects and verbs. The version that shipped with WordPerfect for Windows 6.1 was significantly enhanced to provide more complete and accurate grammar checking, and to even suggest complete replacement sentences. Refer to Chapter 6, "Using Writing Tools," for more information about Grammatik.

## Graphics

In addition to full visual manipulation of graphic images (see "Graphics" in the next section), you can choose Drag To Create and then specify the exact location where you want your graphic image by dragging with the mouse. In the latest version of WordPerfect, graphic figures are now called *images*.

## Integration with Other Programs

WordPerfect for Windows integrates more completely with other Corel Office applications (such as Presentations and Quattro Pro). It also provides support for the following:

- Network Universal Naming Conventions (UNC)
- Mail (MAPI and VIM as well as WP/Novell products)
- OLE 2.0 objects
- OBEX (for Quattro Pro and Paradox, for example)
- ODBC database technology

- TWAIN (for scanning images directly into your document)
- ODMA support for document management software

For more information about integrating WordPerfect 7, see Chapter 18, "Importing Data and Working with Other Programs."

## Macro Dialog Editor

Along with its powerful macro commands, including those that enable you to create custom dialog boxes, WordPerfect sports a handy Macro Dialog Editor that enables you to create custom dialog boxes by design and example, rather than by programming commands. (For information on the Macro Dialog Editor, see Chapter 30, "Advanced Macro Techniques.")

## Make It Fit

This handy feature enables you to squeeze your document into a specified number of pages by reformatting automatically such things as font size, line spacing, and margins. For example, if you have two pages plus three lines on the third page, you can Make It Fit into two pages with just one command.

## Outline

While the Outline feature was enhanced significantly with version 6.0, you also can collapse outlines and still leave text such as hard returns, titles, and so on.

## Performance

In response to many concerns expressed by early users of WordPerfect 6.0 for Windows, WordPerfect Corporation focused on speed and reliability enhancements for version 6.0a. Similar improvements in performance appear in version 6.1. The program shows noticeable speed increases in basic formatting, scrolling, tables, graphics, outlines, printing, and opening large documents.

Reliability issues that were addressed include more accurate conversion of fonts in documents created by earlier versions of WordPerfect, and stability of the program when using certain video drivers.

The jury is still out as to whether these improvements also characterize WordPerfect 7, although stability of the operating system (Windows 95) does seem to be much better.

## QuickCorrect

(See "QuickCorrect" in the preceding section.)

## QuickFormat

A significant addition to the QuickFormat feature (see "QuickFormat" in the next section) is that you can specify that formats are being applied to headings. QuickFormat thus links all such formatted sections so a change to one heading also changes all other headings. (For information on QuickFormat, refer to Chapter 4, "Formatting Text.")

## Spell Check

The Spell Checker just continues to get better. Now words from your supplementary dictionary appear in the Suggested Replacements list. You also can link your QuickCorrect list (see "QuickCorrect" in the preceding section). Not only is the Spell Checker faster in this version, but when you check a document for the second time it checks only words that have changed.

## Tables

Many significant enhancements have been made to the Tables feature, in addition to the spreadsheet functions discussed in the next section.

The most important is the addition of the Table Expert feature (now called *SpeedFormat*) which lets you choose from predefined table layouts (formats, line, and fills) or create your own. (For more information on SpeedFormat, see Chapter 16, "Working with Tables.")

Another welcome feature is the command Size Column To Fit, where WordPerfect automatically adjusts column widths to match the longest line of text in that column.

Several other nifty additions include the ability to specify alternating shading in rows or columns. You also can display table row and column indicators just as in a spreadsheet program. You can save selected cells to a file in table format. Calculate has been added to the QuickMenu, and you can turn off Auto Row Insert (where pressing Tab automatically adds a row at the end of your table).

## TextArt

The TextArt program (see "TextArt" in the next section) has been significantly enhanced with many additional shapes and several new options, including *smoothing* to remove image jaggies. TextArt also is an OLE 2.0 server. Images created with TextArt in WordPerfect for Windows 6.1 cannot be used with earlier TextArt versions. (See Chapter 22, "Using WordPerfect Draw and TextArt," for more information.)

## Thesaurus

When you select a replacement word from the Thesaurus, it replaces the existing word with a grammatically correct equivalent. For example, if you choose *thrill* to replace *exciting*, you get *thrilling*.

## Templates

Templates were a significant addition to version 6.0 (see "Templates" in the next section). In version 6.1, you have many new templates as well as more ease-of-use features. For example, templates are now listed in groups rather than in one huge list.

Also, creating your own templates has been made easier with a Prompt Builder feature, and with the ability to record macros directly into a template. (For additional information on Template documents, see Chapter 11, "Using Templates.")

## Toolbar

The Button Bar is now called the Toolbar. Its look has changed dramatically in that the buttons are smaller, and placing the mouse pointer over a button pops up a QuickTip description of the button. Toolbars are now also shared among Corel WordPerfect Suite applications. (See Chapter 13, "Working with Toolbars," for more information.)

## Undo

The Undo feature has been changed to allow, by default, 10 levels of Undo. If that's not enough, you can change that to 300 levels. If you accidentally undo too many changes, you can use the new Redo feature to rebuild what you have undone. (For details on the Undo feature, see Chapter 3, "Retrieving and Editing Documents.")

## Upgrade Help

This handy Help feature enables you to learn how your previous word processor compares with WordPerfect. Pick a feature and the expert shows you where to find it, how to do it, or even does it for you. Earlier versions of WordPerfect are supported, as well as Ami Pro and Word.

## Uninstall

Most people never need to remove WordPerfect from their computer; but if you do, Uninstall does so quickly and easily. (For more information, see Appendix A, "Installing and Setting Up WordPerfect 7 for Windows 95.")

## Window Tile

You can now display tiled documents either horizontally (one above the other) or vertically (side by side). In addition, you now can "drag and drop" text from one window to another.

## WP Draw

You can now save images you create in WP Draw as separate WPG files in WPG 2.0 format. (See "WP Draw" in the next section.) In the Corel WordPerfect Suite, the more powerful and complete Presentations 7 program is used instead of WP Draw.

# If I Didn't Upgrade to WordPerfect 6.0 for Windows, What Did I Miss?

Several new features appeared in WordPerfect for Windows 6.0, most of which surpassed the feature set of WordPerfect 6.0 for DOS. If you haven't used WordPerfect for Windows before, or if you didn't upgrade from version 5.1/5.2, these are some of the features you've been missing.

## Abbreviations

You can define abbreviations for nearly any text, even text that includes attributes or other formatting. For example, you can tell WordPerfect that *asap* means "as soon as possible." When you later type **asap** and press Ctrl+Shift+A, WordPerfect expands the abbreviation.

## Bookmarks

You can insert bookmarks into your text, which you then can use as reference points. Either search for the bookmarks directly, or run macros that use these bookmarks as reference points. A variation on the named bookmark is the QuickMark bookmark, which is set easily by pressing Ctrl+Shift+Q, and found easily by pressing Ctrl+Q. A QuickMark bookmark also is inserted at the point of the cursor any time you save your document.

## Borders

In addition to borders that surround graphics boxes, you can add borders to paragraphs, whole pages, columns, and tables. You can create custom borders with special styles that include drop shadows and rounded corners (see Chapter 21, "Using Advanced Graphics Techniques," for more information on graphic borders).

## Coaches

WordPerfect's Help system always has been good. But coaches (now called *Guide Me Through It* in the Show Me tab of the Help Topics dialog box) give the term "help" a whole new meaning. Custom coaches not only provide information about a feature, but also "coach" you as you learn to use the feature. For example, a coach may tell you how to perform a certain procedure, then ask you to try it; but, if you prefer, the coach actually shows you step-by-step how it's done.

## Comments

The Comments feature has a completely new look. First, by choosing Preferences, Environment, you can specify your full name, your initials, and a color identification code. Then, when you create a comment, instead of displaying the comment, WordPerfect displays your initials with a small, color-coded tab in the margin. When you click the Comment tab, the full comment appears. When you create the comments, a feature bar assists you to insert your name, date, or time, along with your comments. (For information on comments, see Chapter 6, "Using Writing Tools.")

## Delay Codes

WordPerfect enables you to insert codes on the first page of your document, but to delay their implementation *n* number of pages. For example, if you don't want page numbering to start until the fourth page of your document, you can specify that the page numbering code you enter on page one is delayed four pages. The advantage of this, of course, is that all such codes are located in one easily found location, making editing much easier. Choose Format, Page, Delay Codes to use this feature.

## Document Summary

The Document Summary feature enables you to customize the fields of information required in the summary. You can choose from 51 different fields—more than enough for even the most demanding corporate situations. (For information on document summaries, see Chapter 5, "Formatting Pages and Documents.")

## Envelope

WordPerfect for Windows used to rely on a separate macro for addressing and printing envelopes. Now, this is a regular WordPerfect for Windows feature. Using the Envelope feature, you can capture an address from your document, add a return address, and print these on an envelope in the font of your choice, with or without a postal bar code. In addition, you can store commonly used addresses in the Address Book for later use.

## File Management

In versions 5.1/5.2, WordPerfect Corporation developed a separate File Manager program. In versions 6.0/6.1, it included the majority of File Manager features in the Open dialog box, including Copy, Delete, Move, or even Open or Print multiple files. In WordPerfect 7, the look has changed again to match other Windows 95 programs, although much of the earlier WordPerfect functionality has been retained as well. You also can display a folder tree (using visually attractive folder icons) along with your Favorite entries. You can sort files by size, date, or time. Finally, you can display just the file name, or choose which bits of file information (date, time, size, and so on) you want to display. (For more information on file management, refer to Chapter 29, "Advanced File Management.")

## Floating Cells

You can create separate spreadsheet-capable cells right in the text of your document. For example, a mortgage loan approval letter could tell the customer that her loan for $x$ amount is now approved at $y$ percentage for $z$ years. It could then use a fourth floating cell to calculate the mortgage payment with a spreadsheet function, using the values of $x$, $y$, and $z$. See Chapter 31, "Advanced Tables," for details on this exciting new feature.

## Fonts

Since the earliest WordPerfect for Windows versions, the program has come bundled with several useful fonts. Likewise, Corel's WordPerfect 7 also comes with many new TrueType fonts that can be used by WordPerfect and any other Windows program.

## Graphics

In addition to being able to create edit graphics and charts with a full-featured Graphics Editor (originally WP Draw, and now the complete Presentations 7 program), you also can wrap text on both sides of a graphic figure, and even contour text to the figure's shape. For information on graphics procedures, see Chapter 7, "Integrating Text and Graphics," and Chapter 21, "Using Advanced Graphics Techniques."

## Hidden Text

You can hide text that you don't want to display or print by adding a Hidden attribute from the Font dialog box. Then from the View menu, choose to display or hide everything found between the Hidden codes. (For information on hidden codes, see Chapter 3, "Retrieving and Editing Documents.")

## Hypertext

*Hypertext* refers to text that is "linked" to bookmarks in your document, to macros, or to other documents. When you click a hypertext link, WordPerfect automatically jumps to a linked location within your document or in another document. This feature is particularly useful for training or reference materials. You can also use hypertext to create buttons in your text to run macros.

## Interface Bars

Although WordPerfect introduced the Button Bar in WordPerfect for Windows 5.1, the program now has several specialty bars that aid you in creating and editing your document:

- *The Button Bar is now called the Toolbar.* Each shipping Toolbar includes basic editing tools (File Open, Cut, Paste, Print, Undo, and so on). You can drag the Toolbar to the left, right, top, or bottom with the mouse. You also can drag the Toolbar to the center of the screen, where it becomes a floating palette of buttons. In addition to being able to add or remove buttons from any Toolbar, you can modify existing Toolbar buttons (both the names and the bitmapped graphic icons).

- *The Power Bar.* Many basic format functions (for example, Font, Justification, Tables, or Zoom) now are found on the Power Bar. This means that you don't lose these basic functions when you change from the basic Toolbar to a specialty Toolbar.

- *Feature bars.* Feature bars appear on demand, or sometimes automatically when you select a certain feature. For example, if you choose Outline or Merge, feature bars related to these features appear, or when creating formulas in a table, you can display a formula bar to help you enter and edit the formulas.

- *Ruler Bar.* The feature buttons are gone from the Ruler Bar, making it less cluttered. Adding tabs to the Ruler Bar is easier, because to place a new tab you simply click the desired location. The QuickMenu lets you change the tab type, or access other Ruler Bar features.

- *Status bar.* Long a hallmark of the WordPerfect interface, the status bar now can be customized to meet your needs. Double-clicking with the mouse on status bar indicators takes you directly to an appropriate dialog box (Fonts, Go To, and so on).

## Keyboard

Changing key definitions in earlier versions of WordPerfect was nothing short of torture. Now, changing key assignments could hardly be easier. All you do, essentially, is match features from a list with keys on a simulated keyboard. The only two keys you can't reassign are Tab and Enter. For information on customized keyboards, see Chapter 9, "Customizing WordPerfect."

## Labels

This feature used to be a special macro that helped to create the Paper/Size definitions you needed. When you want to create labels now, simply choose a label definition from a WordPerfect list of commercially available label sizes and types. Furthermore, when you are in Page mode, you see the exact size and layout of the labels you create. (For information on labels, see Chapter 5, "Formatting Pages and Documents.")

## Merge

The Merge feature has a completely revamped interface. First, primary files now are called *forms*, and secondary files are called *data files*. Each must be identified by its type. You associate data files with form files, and save the associations, which makes merging a breeze—once you specify a form file, the data file name appears automatically.

Data entry is simplified by using the Quick Data Entry dialog box, which acts like a database input screen, using field names to prompt for the correct information. You can create data files in table format also.

The merging process is also changed dramatically. Now you can selectively merge, without having to Sort/Select separately. You can merge to a letter and to the envelope for that letter in the same merge. See Chapter 19, "Assembling Documents with Merge and Sort," for details on these improvements.

## Mouse

WordPerfect takes even more complete advantage of the mouse than earlier versions did. For example, you can move column margins in tables by dragging the column separators directly. You can point and click cells to add them to formulas. You can click Comments, Sound Clips, or Hypertext buttons to activate these features. And last, but certainly not least, you can right-click to access QuickMenus (see "QuickMenus" in this section).

## Outlines

WordPerfect's Outline feature has been made more powerful, yet easier to use. By using the Outline Feature Bar, you can change text to outline entries, and vice versa. You also can *collapse* your outlines. For example, if you want your students to have only the first and second levels of your outline of class notes, you can collapse the outline to two levels, print it for the students, then print an expanded version for yourself. The default outline style is a numbered list. See Chapter 15, "Organizing Documents with Outlining," for more information on outlining.

## Page Mode

True WYSIWYG editing is now possible when you use the Page mode in WordPerfect. In this mode, you can directly enter and edit headers, footers, footnotes, and page numbers. Because you can see these objects on-screen, simply click any of them (for example, a footnote), and begin editing. When you finish, click your text to continue editing your document. There is, of course, a Draft mode for doing things "the old way." (For information on Page mode, see Chapter 1, "Getting Started.")

## Printing

Because you see everything in Page mode, WordPerfect no longer needs a Print Preview mode. In fact, Page mode *is* a preview mode.

Finally, you can print documents in reverse order, as well as in booklet format (sequenced for back-to-back, camera-ready copy).

Refer to Chapter 8, "Basic Output: Printing, Faxing, and E-mail," for details on printing improvements.

## QuickFinder/Kickoff

Although QuickFinder was added to WordPerfect 5.2, it now is an integral part of WordPerfect, and can be accessed like any other feature. The QuickFinder enables you to search for a document based on words contained in the document file or file name.

Refer to Chapter 29, "Advanced File Management," for information on this powerful file-finding utility.

## QuickFormat

This new feature enables you to turn the mouse pointer into a style "paintbrush." For example, if you turn on QuickFormat while the cursor is inside Large, Bold text, then selecting other text with the mouse automatically applies the Large and Bold attributes to the selected text. You can continue applying attributes to selected text until you turn off QuickFormat. If you change the style, all locations where the style was used also change. See Chapter 4, "Formatting Text," for more details.

## QuickMenus

Perhaps the most significant addition to WordPerfect is the use of the right mouse button to open context-sensitive QuickMenus:

- Right-click the Toolbar to get a list of available toolbars and Toolbar options.
- Click a table to get a QuickMenu of table-related choices.
- Click the Ruler Bar to change tab stop types, format a paragraph, and so on.
- Click a comment to edit or delete it.
- Click the scroll bars for Go To, Bookmark, and Preferences features.

In short, you can get a QuickMenu for nearly anything just by right-clicking. At first, you'll have to force yourself to remember to use QuickMenus, but soon you'll probably wonder how you ever survived without them. (For information on QuickMenus, see Chapter 1, "Getting Started.")

## Repeat

WordPerfect for Windows users lost the ability to repeat a macro or keystroke in versions 5.1 and 5.2. Now you can repeat macros or keystrokes by choosing Edit, Repeat. (For information on repeating macros, see Chapter 12, "Creating Macros.")

## Reveal Codes

Most WordPerfect users appreciate the ability to locate and manipulate format codes and other control codes. While Reveal Codes has a slightly new look, its best new features relate to the mouse. For example, you delete codes simply by dragging them out of the Reveal Codes window. Also, you can go directly to the dialog box for a feature by double-clicking its code. (For information on Reveal Codes, see Chapter 3, "Retrieving and Editing Documents.")

## Revertible Codes

In earlier versions of WordPerfect for Windows, you could select text and choose a different font for that selection. WordPerfect would place the correct font code at the beginning of the selection, and place another code at the end of the selection to return to the earlier font. Now, however, when you select text and apply nearly any attribute or format setting, WordPerfect surrounds the selection with revertible codes.

Suppose that your text is in Courier font, and you select some text to change to Times Roman font. Text before and after the selected text remains in Courier. Later, if you change the document font to Helvetica, the text before and after the Times Roman selection automatically changes to Helvetica. Revertible codes also work for format changes, such as margin and tab settings. (For information on revertible codes, see Chapter 3, "Retrieving and Editing Documents.")

## Show Codes

In addition to the capability to display a character to show the location of hard returns in your document window, you can choose to display codes for spaces, tabs, and other items that otherwise would not be visible. (For information on displaying codes, see Chapter 3, "Retrieving and Editing Documents.")

## Sound

WordPerfect enables you to record and attach sound clips, or to place digitized music in your documents. Imagine clicking a sound bubble in your document and hearing your boss say, "I need this report by this afternoon!"

## Speller

If you thought that there was no way to improve the Speller, you are wrong. Now you can check words, sentences, paragraphs, or pages without first selecting them. You also can define your own custom dictionaries, and even include your own replacement words; for example, *post-nuptial fission* rather than *divorce*. For more details, refer to Chapter 6, "Using Writing Tools."

## Spreadsheet Features

WordPerfect tables now have the same kind of power formerly reserved for spreadsheet programs. With nearly 100 spreadsheet functions, you can create mini-spreadsheets within your WordPerfect documents.

For most WordPerfect users, this feature more than suffices, easily handling tasks such as reports, time sheets, and loan calculations. You even can import many spreadsheets directly into WordPerfect tables with their formulas intact.

For information on spreadsheet features in tables, see Chapter 31, "Advanced Tables." For details on importing spreadsheet information into WordPerfect, refer to Chapter 18, "Importing Data and Working with Other Programs."

## Subdivide Pages

Rather than using the Labels feature to create partial page brochures, you now use the Subdivide Page feature. Most importantly, you can print such pages in booklet format, in the proper order for camera-ready copy (for example, pages 4 and 1 on one side, and pages 2 and 3 on the other) without having to manually cut and paste to rearrange the pages. (For information on the Subdivide Page feature, see Chapter 5, "Formatting Pages and Documents.")

## Templates

Templates, a new concept in WordPerfect for Windows 6.0, help you to create documents that have a consistent look. More than styles, these templates serve as "boilerplates" to give you a great head start on document creation. You can embed macros or toolbars in your templates, and add "triggers" that set off actions. For example, a document can prompt for input, then fill in the document based on that input. WordPerfect supplies many standard templates for fax covers, reports, expense sheets, memos, and more, but you can create custom templates as well.

Refer to Chapter 11, "Using Templates," for more information on this powerful new feature.

## TextArt

An exciting addition to WordPerfect is the TextArt program that enables you to fit text of your choosing into predefined graphic shapes, such as banners or circles. You then use the resulting images in your document just as you do any graphic image. To learn more about creating TextArt images, see Chapter 22, "Using WordPerfect Draw and TextArt."

## Watermarks

You can use graphics or text as *watermarks*, which are lightly shaded backgrounds for your documents. For example, you might use a beach scene graphic as the watermark for your July calendar. (For information on watermarks, see Chapter 7, "Integrating Text and Graphics.")

## WP Characters

Although WordPerfect's special characters have been easily viewable and accessible since the 5.1 Windows version, the number of characters and special character sets has been increased to include phonetic symbols, two types of Arabic characters, and many new iconic symbols.

## WP Draw

No longer do you need a separate graphics program to create or edit WordPerfect graphics images. WP Draw, a scaled-back version of WordPerfect Presentations, shipped with earlier versions of WordPerfect. Now, with the Corel WordPerfect Suite, you get the complete Presentations program, including powerful drawing, editing, and charting tools. When you select a graphic image to edit, you now can do much more than rotate or size it; you can actually modify the graphic image.

For information on creating charts, refer to Chapter 17, "Creating and Modifying Charts with WP Draw." To learn more about editing graphic images, see Chapter 22, "Using WordPerfect Draw and TextArt."

# If I Didn't Upgrade to WordPerfect 5.2 for Windows, What Did I Miss?

Several new features appeared in WordPerfect for Windows, versions 5.1 and 5.2, and found their way to WordPerfect 6.0 for DOS. If you haven't used WordPerfect for Windows before, these are some of the features, in addition to those described in the preceding sections, that you've been missing.

## Auto Code Placement (and Replacement)

Under normal circumstances, you want certain format codes to take effect at the beginning of a page or a paragraph. For example, if you change a tab setting, or the left and right margins, you usually don't want that change to take place in the middle of a paragraph. WordPerfect for Windows automatically places such codes at the beginning of the current paragraph, or, if the codes are page-related, at the beginning of the current page.

Also, when you change a format setting, rather than placing multiple codes for the same format feature in your document, WordPerfect for Windows automatically updates the existing code.

## Document Conversion

Converting files from other word processing formats is automatic when you open such files in WordPerfect. As of this writing, WordPerfect recognizes and converts some 50 file formats, making it one of the most "compatible" word processing applications on the market.

## Dynamic Data Exchange (DDE) Links

With WordPerfect for Windows, you can use Dynamic Data Exchange (DDE) links not only to transfer data from one file to another, but to update the data automatically whenever the source file is changed. For example, you can link a fiscal year report to data in a spreadsheet—as the spreadsheet changes, the data in the report also changes. The feature only works, however, in Windows applications that support DDE.

## Fonts

WordPerfect 5.2 shipped with several Adobe Type 1 fonts that could be added to those you already use with Windows. Many of these fonts—such as Broadway, Hobo, or Murray Hill—had been in WordPerfect products such as DrawPerfect for several years. WordPerfect now comes with TrueType, rather than Adobe fonts. Refer to Chapter 20, "Using Fonts and Special Characters," for information on fonts used in WordPerfect 7.

## Grammatik

See "Grammatik" in the preceding sections.

## Graphics

Being able to see and easily manipulate graphic images is one of the major reasons for switching to WordPerfect 7. No longer do you have to guess where graphics and lines are located, or what they will look like when they print.

## Macro Language

WordPerfect for Windows macro language changed completely from that of WordPerfect 5.1 for DOS. Macro commands (in both the DOS and Windows versions of WordPerfect 6.x) now are based on the results of your actions (for example, "Set the margins to 1.5 inches at such-and-such location") rather than the specific keystrokes to accomplish the task. This makes it possible to include any action in a macro, regardless of whether you use function keys, menus, or mouse actions to accomplish that action.

In addition, WordPerfect has powerful macro dialog commands that enable you to create custom dialog boxes. To make macros as easy as possible to run, you can add them to your menus or toolbars.

## Multiple Documents

You can open up to nine documents simultaneously in WordPerfect 7. This gives you the flexibility of working with several different documents, without having to close one in order to use another.

## Object Linking and Embedding (OLE)

OLE is a sophisticated method of sharing data with other OLE-capable Windows programs. In addition to transferring data, as you do using DDE, you can embed actual objects (spreadsheet, Paintbrush picture, and so on) in your document. When you edit an embedded object, you are taken directly to the program that was used originally to create the object.

## QuickList

The QuickList feature enables you to create descriptions of file locations in plain English (for example, *Pretty Pictures* could refer to C:\COREL\OFFICE7\GRAPHICS). This feature has been replaced by Favorites, whereby in any Open File dialog box, you can quickly find an actual file location by clicking the appropriate Favorites entry.

## Undo

In addition to being able to undelete text, WordPerfect enables you to reverse an action (such as changing a margin setting) by choosing Edit, Undo; or pressing Ctrl+Z.

## WP Characters

Character sets in WordPerfect for Windows are easily viewable and accessible. Ctrl+W displays any of the 14 character sets and enables you to choose a character directly from the set to be inserted into your text.

## Zoom

One problem with document handling in WordPerfect for DOS is that wide documents cannot fit on-screen, forcing you to scroll horizontally to see the entire document. With the Zoom feature, you can increase or decrease the size of the text display from 50–200

percent (or to a specific percentage you choose), or you can force WordPerfect to fit the text between the margins of your display.

# Where Do I Find It in WordPerfect for Windows?

Even for veteran WordPerfect for Windows users, finding features in WordPerfect 7 may present some challenges. Not only do certain features have new names, but also the keystrokes used to access many features have changed. The following table is a brief, but certainly not comprehensive, comparison of features and locations that have changed.

| WordPerfect for Windows 6.x/5.x (Old Feature Name) | WordPerfect for Windows 7 (New Feature Name) | New Menu or Key Location (If Changed) |
|---|---|---|
| Search | Find/Replace | Ctrl+F |
| Print Preview | Page mode | Alt+F5 (Print Preview no longer needed) |
| | Repeat | Edit, Repeat |
| | Abbreviation Expand | Ctrl+Shift+A |
| Date Text | Date Text | Ctrl+D |
| Date Code | Date Code | Ctrl+Shift+D |
| | Paragraph Numbering | Ctrl+H |
| | Case Toggle | Ctrl+K |
| | QuickMark Find | Ctrl+Q |
| | QuickPrint | Ctrl+Shift+P |
| | QuickMark Set | Ctrl+Shift+Q |
| | Template | Ctrl+T |
| | Internet Publisher | File menu |
| | Document Review | File menu |
| | Send (E-mail) | File menu |
| | Workflow | File menu |
| QuickFinder | QuickFinder | Open dialog box |
| Printer Select | Printer Tab | Print dialog box |
| Preferences | Preferences | Edit menu |
| Retrieve File | Insert File | Insert menu |

| WordPerfect for Windows 6.x/5.x (Old Feature Name) | WordPerfect for Windows 7 (New Feature Name) | New Menu or Key Location (If Changed) |
|---|---|---|
| Footnote/Endnote | Footnote/Endnote | Insert menu |
| Spreadsheet Import | Spreadsheet/Database | Insert menu |
| Layout | Format | Format menu |
| Font | Font | Format menu |
| | Flush Right with Dot Leaders | Format menu |
| | QuickCorrect | Tools menu |
| | Spell As You Go | Tools menu |
| | Address Book | Tools menu |
| Macro | Macro | Tools menu |
| | Highlight | Tools menu |
| Figure | Image | Graphics menu |
| Figure Editor | Draw | Graphics menu |
| | Chart | Graphics menu |
| | Text Art | Graphics menu |
| Tables | Table | Table menu |
| | Table Formulas | Table menu |
| | Ask the Perfect Expert | Help menu |
| | Upgrade Help | Help menu |

# Summary

Whether you come to WordPerfect 7 from another word processing program, WordPerfect for DOS, or an earlier version of WordPerfect for Windows, many new and powerful features await you. Take time early to familiarize yourself with these features. As you do, your skill level will increase and you will find that WordPerfect makes your work much easier. ●

PART VIII

# Indexes

Action Index  1121

Index of Common Problems  1125

Index  1135

# Action Index

| When You Need To... | You'll Find Help Here... |
|---|---|
| **Editing** | |
| Use the mouse to drag and drop text. | See "Drag-and-Drop Editing" in Chapter 3 |
| Set tabs on the Ruler Bar. | See "Setting Tabs on the Ruler Bar" in Chapter 4 |
| Dress up a paragraph or page with a border. | See "Using Graphics Borders" in Chapter 7 |
| Format text with QuickFormat. | See "Formatting Text with QuickFormat" in Chapter 4 |
| Change character attributes with the Power Bar. | See "Changing Character Attributes" in Chapter 4 |
| Switch fonts and adjust letter spacing. | See "Choosing Fonts" in Chapter 3 |
| Insert special characters. | See "Accessing Special Characters" in Chapter 20 |
| Create a bulleted or numbered list. | See "Creating Simple Numbered and Bulleted Outlines" in Chapter 15 |
| Find hidden codes. | See "Understanding WordPerfect's Hidden Codes" in Chapter 3 |
| Attach comments to your document. | See "Using Document Comments" in Chapter 6 |
| Check your spelling and grammar. | See "Using Spell Checker" in Chapter 6 |

| When You Need To... | You'll Find Help Here... |
|---|---|
| **Special Formats** | |
| Include page numbers in headers and footers. | See "Using Page Numbers in Headers & Footers" in Chapter 5 |
| Create an outline with the Outline Feature Bar. | See "Introducing the Outline Feature Bar" in Chapter 15 |
| Insert and edit footnotes. | See "Using Footnotes" in Chapter 25 |
| Create a table of contents. | See "Creating a Table of Contents" in Chapter 26 |
| Use a macro to write a memo. | See "A Macro To Write a Memo" in Chapter 12 |
| Create a letterhead style. | See "Letterhead Document Style" in Chapter 10 |
| Use or modify a template. | See Chapter 11, "Using Templates" |
| Form fractions. | See "Forming Fractions with the Equation Editor" in Chapter 24 |
| Format an HTML document for the World Wide Web. | See "Adding Formatting" in Chapter 33 |
| **Graphics** | |
| Balance your newspaper columns. | See "Balanced Newspaper Columns" in Chapter 14 |
| Rotate a graphic image. | See "Rotating Images" in Chapter 21 |
| Wrap text around a graphic image. | See "Wrapping Text Around an Object" in Chapter 22 |
| Add a watermark. | See "Using Watermarks" in Chapter 26 |
| Make a list of figure captions. | See "Defining a List" and "Making a List of Graphics Box Captions" in Chapter 26 |
| Include a chart or drawing in your document. | See "Placing the Chart in the Document" in Chapter 17 and "Adding the Drawing to Your Document" in Chapter 22 |
| Add text, numbers, and graphics to a table. | See "Cutting, Copying, and Pasting Text" and "Adding Graphics to a Table" in Chapter 16 |
| Create a drop cap. | See "Inserting a Drop Cap" in Chapter 21 |
| Add graphics to a Web page. | See "Adding Graphics" in Chapter 33 |

| When You Need To... | You'll Find Help Here... |
|---|---|
| **Printing** | |
| Choose a different page size. | See "Customizing Page Size" in Chapter 5 |
| Create mailing labels. | See "Working with Labels" in Chapter 5 |
| Address envelopes. | See "Addressing an Envelope" in Chapter 5 |
| Control your print jobs. | See "Controlling the Printer and Print Jobs" in Chapter 8 |
| Fax a document from WordPerfect. | See "Faxing from WordPerfect 7" in Chapter 8 |
| **File Management** | |
| Use QuickFinder to find a file quickly. | See "Using QuickFinder to Search for Files" in Chapter 29 |
| Save with a different document name. | See "Saving a Document with a Different Name or File Format" in Chapter 2 |
| Import spreadsheet data. | See "Importing and Working with Spreadsheet Data" in Chapter 18 |
| Work with multiple documents. | See "Working with Multiple Documents" in Chapter 1 |
| Customize your display. | See "Customizing the Display" in Chapter 9 |
| Switch Toolbars using the QuickMenu. | See "Switching Between Toolbars" in Chapter 13 |
| Create a Web Page using WordPerfect's Internet Publisher. | See "The Basics of Creating an HTML Document" in Chapter 33 |

# Index of Common Problems

| Writing and Editing | |
|---|---|
| **If you have this problem...** | **You'll find help here...** |
| Address Book choices differ on some tabs. | p. 904 |
| Address Book tabs won't delete. | p. 902 |
| Alt key does not activate button on the Feature Bar. | p. 31 |
| Bullet is automatically added every time the Enter key is pressed. | p. 462 |
| Buttons cannot be added to the Power Bar. | p. 428 |
| Help window disappears when writing in WordPerfect. | p. 54 |
| Insertion point returns to the original spot when scrolling. | p. 26 |
| Mouse buttons difficult for left-handed users. | p. 103 |
| Sorting does not always work on tabular list. | p. 624 |
| Sorting order is incorrect with multi-word names. | p. 630 |
| Text box contents need to be deleted before entering new contents. | p. 41 |
| Text jumps around during typing. | p. 148 |
| Toolbar is not displayed. | p. 125 |
| Typographical ("curly") smart quotes do not appear when the quote key is pressed. | p. 147 |

## Formatting and Fonts

| If you have this problem… | You'll find help here… |
|---|---|
| Bullet styles are not listed in the Styles List dialog box. | p. 358 |
| Column widths change unexpectedly when altering the spacing between columns. | p. 445 |
| Custom heading style not found in the Style List dialog box. | p. 352 |
| Equation font doesn't match font used for the rest of the document. | p. 797 |
| Error message `WAVE sound output not available` appears when clicking a sound icon. | p. 1040 |
| Fonts shown incorrectly when editing a document created on another computer. | p. 652 |
| Helvetica and Times fonts are not listed in the Fonts dialog box. | p. 750 |
| Hidden Text option in the Font dialog box is shown dimmed and is not available. | p. 248 |
| Kerning two characters has no apparent affect. | p. 757 |
| Lines border style breaks lines between rows. | p. 459 |
| Lines border style places lines between all columns. | p. 459 |
| New row of columns is created when trying to turn columns off. | p. 450 |
| No name appears after inserting the file name in the document. | p. 248 |
| Page number changes affect only a part of the document. | p. 172-173 |
| Page numbering format is lost when defining a new chapter numbering format. | p. 173 |
| Page size definition that was previously defined cannot be found. | p. 184 |

| If you have this problem... | You'll find help here... |
|---|---|
| Styles in subdocuments are ignored when the master document is expanded. | p. 358 |
| Text looks too cramped when formatted with more than two columns. | p. 736 |
| Text is not aligned at the top of all newspaper columns. | p. 736 |

**Footnotes and Endnotes**

| If you have this problem... | You'll find help here... |
|---|---|
| Endnote appears at insertion point instead of at the end of document. | p. 820 |
| Endnote reference number remains in text after deleting the endnote. | p. 819 |
| Footnote numbering restarts at *1* on new page. | p. 817 |
| Footnote reference number remains in text after deleting footnote. | p. 817 |
| Separator line between text and footnote cannot be edited by clicking it. | p. 817 |

**Tables**

| If you have this problem... | You'll find help here... |
|---|---|
| Cell format is not updated after changing the cell format. | p. 523 |
| Contents of cells move to other cells when selecting text inside a table. | p. 509 |
| Custom line overlaps the text of a cell. | p. 995 |

*continues*

### Tables Continued

| If you have this problem... | You'll find help here... |
|---|---|
| Decimal portion of dollar amount wraps to next line in cell. | p. 1018 |
| Error opening spreadsheet file. | p. 988 |
| Graphic image is not positioned properly in the table cell. | p. 532 |
| Lines do not appear for the table. | p. 532 |
| Results of calculation are not correct. | p. 1018 |
| Table column appears left-aligned after changing to decimal-aligned. | p. 523 |
| Table too large/too small when defining a table with the Power Bar. | p. 508 |
| Text not legible after changing the fill for a row of cells. | p. 995 |

### Outlines

| If you have this problem... | You'll find help here... |
|---|---|
| Changing bullet styles in an outline changes all outline levels. | p. 486-494 |
| One or more levels in the outline do not appear. | p. 486 |
| Outline numbers and symbols don't appear on the left side of the document window. | p. 486-494 |
| Paragraph number level cannot be specified in the Bullets & Numbers dialog box. | p. 469-486 |

## Graphics and Equations

| If you have this problem... | You'll find help here... |
| --- | --- |
| Bold attribute does not appear when pressing Ctrl+B in the Equation Editor. | p. 797 |
| Chart appearance is different when printed than it appears on-screen. | p. 544 |
| Equation font doesn't match document font. | p. 797 |
| Graphic image is not positioned properly in table cell. | p. 532 |
| Graphics do not appear when the document is printed. | p. 757 |
| Graphics line is not deleted by pressing Delete or Backspace. | p. 261 |
| Half space does not appear when pressing the ` key in Equation Editor. | p. 778 |
| Inline Equations command is not shown in the Graphics menu. | p. 778 |
| Out of memory or application error occurs when running WP Draw. | p. 721 |
| Paragraph border does not appear when the paragraph border format is turned off. | p. 261 |
| Paragraph fill pattern covers printed text. | p. 261 |
| Shadow does not appear behind TextArt graphic. | p. 720 |
| Spaces in equation definition do not appear in the document. | p. 778 |
| Text of function name appears rather than the function symbol in Equation Editor. | p. 797 |
| TextArt won't display a shadow. | p. 720 |
| WP Draw does not start, or takes a long time to start. | p. 693 |

## Templates

| If you have this problem... | You'll find help here... |
|---|---|
| One or more templates that come with WordPerfect can't be found. | p. 373 |
| Templates appear together in the Select New Document dialog box instead of in groups. | p. 373 |
| Templates don't appear when choosing File, New. | p. 373 |
| Text does not appear when inserting a Letter Expert letter. | p. 386 |
| Two macros cannot be associated with the same template trigger. | p. 386 |
| WordPerfect inserts someone else's personal information when automatically filling out a template. | p. 373 |

## Document References and Master Documents

| If you have this problem... | You'll find help here... |
|---|---|
| ? appears when generating a document with cross-references. | p. 868 |
| All headings in table of contents are the same level. | p. 848 |
| Error message `No def codes` appears when generating index. | p. 868 |
| File not found when expanding a document. | p. 881 |
| Formatting in subdocuments is lost when expanding the master document. | p. 897 |
| Long delay occurs when expanding a large master document. | p. 897 |
| Only first word of headings appears in table of contents. | p. 848 |
| Some sections don't print when using multiple pages and advanced multiple pages options. | p. 897 |

| If you have this problem... | You'll find help here... |
| --- | --- |
| Subdocuments are shown with either complete path or no path in Draft mode comment. | p. 881 |

## Writing Tools

| If you have this problem... | You'll find help here... |
| --- | --- |
| Changes in the Grammatik writing style have no effect. | p. 232 |
| Grammatik always flags long sentences. | p. 232 |
| Grammatik flags correctly spelled words. | p. 232 |
| Spell Checker misses incorrectly spelled words. | p. 224 |
| Wrong word added to the QuickCorrect word replacement list. | p. 224 |
| Wrong word added to the Speller supplemental dictionary. | p. 224 |

## Macros, Merge, and Hypertext

| If you have this problem... | You'll find help here... |
| --- | --- |
| Command for recording the opening of a dialog box is not recorded. | p. 953 |
| Empty fields in a data file leave blanks in the resulting merge. | p. 618 |
| Error message `Label was defined but not referenced` appears. | p. 977-979 |
| Error occurs when playing macros created with WordPerfect 6.0 for Windows. | p. 976-977 |
| Error message `Bookmark not found` appears when clicking a hypertext link. | p. 1036 |

*continues*

## Macros, Merge, and Hypertext Continued

| If you have this problem... | You'll find help here... |
|---|---|
| Error message `Macro not found` appears when clicking a hypertext link. | p. 1036 |
| Macro doesn't record exiting WordPerfect. | p. 407 |
| Macro doesn't record switching to another Windows program. | p. 407 |
| Nothing happens when clicking a hypertext link. | p. 1036 |
| One or more macros that come with WordPerfect cannot be found. | p. 401 |
| Previously working macro now ends with an error message. | p. 408 |
| Recorded macro cannot be found on disk. | p. 401 |
| Saving macro file is stopped by syntax errors. | p. 976 |
| Spacing and order of addresses is not correct in merged mailing label. | p. 618 |
| Text doesn't appear in document as the macro types it. | p. 977-979 |

## File Management

| If you have this problem... | You'll find help here... |
|---|---|
| File is accidentally deleted. | p. 924 |
| File is accidentally saved under the wrong name. | p. 76 |
| File cannot be found after moving or renaming it. | p. 924 |
| File viewer shows the message `No viewer available`. | p. 85 |
| Files increase in size after inserting sound clips. | p. 1040 |

| If you have this problem... | You'll find help here... |
|---|---|
| Only one file at a time can be selected in file list. | p. 924 |
| QuickFinder search fails to locate files. | p. 937 |
| Shortcut to a file doesn't work. | p. 939 |

## Printing

| If you have this problem... | You'll find help here... |
|---|---|
| Choosing the Print command has no effect. | p. 282 |
| Document prints with the wrong letters and fonts. | p. 282 |
| Graphics do not appear when the document is printed. | p. 757 |
| Graphics look inferior when printing document. | p. 288 |
| Printer displays an error message when printing envelopes. | p. 289 |
| Printed text looks jagged and prints very slow. | p. 652 |
| Some sections don't print when using multiple pages and advanced multiple pages options. | p. 897 |

## Internet Publishing

| If you have this problem... | You'll find help here... |
|---|---|
| Formulas in tables are not converted to HTML. | p. 1047 |
| Graphic images disappear when the WordPerfect document is converted to HTML. | p. 1047 |
| Numbered list continues when Enter is pressed. | p. 1056 |
| Picture is not in a GIF or JPEG format. | p. 1059 |

# Index

## Symbols

` (accent mark) symbol, 765, 773
& (And) operator, 933
* (asterisk) wildcard character, 21
\ (backslash), 782
? button, 952-953
& (column separator), 770, 788
// (Comment) command, 971
... (ellipsis), 31
– (en dash), 642
} (End Group command), 770
— (em dash), 642
.. (Followed by) operator, 934
\ (forward slash), 935
( ) Group operator, 934
< (left angle bracket), 784
\{ (left brace), 784
[ (left bracket), 784
( (left parenthesis), 784
\ (literal), 771
*.LTR (wildcard), 930
. (No delimiter), 771
~ (normal space), 770
! (Not) operator, 933
| (Or) operator, 933
? (question mark) wildcard character, 216
> (right angle bracket), 784
\} (right brace), 784
] (right bracket), 784
) (right parenthesis), 784
# (row separator), 770, 788
| (single vertical line), 784
{ (Start Group command), 770
? (template feature bar), 370
` (thin space), 770
~ (tilde) symbol, 765, 773
* (wildcard), 934
*.* (wildcard), 930
? (wildcard), 934
1:1 ratio button (scaling option), 680
3D charts, 551

## A

abbreviations, 208, 245-247
Abbreviations dialog box, 246
aborting, *see* canceling
About WordPerfect command (Help menu), 48
absolute references, formulas, 1008-1009
accent mark (`) symbol, 765, 773
accessing
    Character feature, 644
    databases, 576
    dialog boxes, 33
    help
        Macro Help, 956
        WordPerfect, 1082
    macro files, 950-951
    menus, Application Control, 18
    special characters, 640
Acquire Image command (Insert menu), 716
Activate/Deactivate button (Hypertext Feature Bar), 1023-1024

**activating**
- documents, 44
- Hypertext in documents, 310
- links, 1033
- PerfectExpert, 51
- pull-down menus, 20
- SmartQuotes utility, 642
- styles, documents, 353
- *see also* starting

**actual values, 961**

**Add command**
- Favorites menu, 938
- Tools menu, 902-903

**Add Compare Markings dialog box, 830**

**Add Fonts dialog box, 638, 1088**

**Add Printer button (Print dialog box), 292**

**Add Template Prompt dialog box, 377-378**

**adding**
- fonts to printers, 292-293
- footers to master documents, 892
- graphics
  - to footers, 178-179
  - to headers, 178-179
- headers to master documents, 892
- network printers to printer list, 293
- startup options WordPerfect, 1088-1090
- subdocuments to master documents, 876-884
- *see also* inserting

**address blocks, converting text into, 1054**

**Address Book**
- addresses, inserting into document, 905
- creating, 900
- deleting, 901-902
- entries
  - deleting, 905
  - editing, 904-905
- messaging systems, 900
- organization, 903
- renaming, 901
- WordPerfect, improved features, 1094

**Address Book command (Tool menu), 900**

**Address Book dialog box, 902-903**

**addresses**
- editing envelopes, 189
- font size, envelopes, 189
- inserting into documents, 905
- labels spacing, troubleshooting, 618
- positioning, envelopes, 190

**addressing envelopes, 188-189**

**Advance command (Format menu), 196-197**

**Advance dialog box, 196-197**

**Advanced Find dialog box, 932, 936**

**Advanced Multiple Pages dialog box, 896**
- specifying page ranges, 284-285

**Advanced tab (Border/Fill dialog box), 755**

**AFCs (Automatic Font Changes), 648**
- attributes, 648-650
- editing, 650-651

**ALIGNC command, 770, 788**

**aligning**
- columns
  - tables, 520
  - text, 444
- graphics, 693
- text, 132, 737-739
  - all-justification, 739
  - center-justification, 738
- full-justification, 739
- HTML documents, 1057-1058
- left-justification, 737-738
- line spacing, 739-740
- right-justification, 738

**ALIGNL command, 770, 788**

**ALIGNR command, 770, 788**

**All option (Alignment section of Table Format dialog box), 520**

**all-justification, 739**

**ALLFONTS.WCM macro, playing, 647**

**Allow Editing option (Quick Data Entry dialog box), 600**

**Alt+number pad method, 646**

**And (&) operator, 933**

**Angle option (Layout/Type dialog box), 557**

**Annotate command (Options menu), 53**

**ANSI Text format**
- documents, converting to intermediate format, 570
- limitations, 570

**appearance attributes, fonts, 648-649**

**Appearance options (Font dialog box), 128**

**Application Control button, 18**

**Application Control menu, accessing, 18**
- commands
  - Move, 19
  - Size, 19

**applications**
- closing, 12
- macros, commands, 954

applying
  bullets and numbers in style lists, 464-465
  character styles to headings, 890
  graphics to labels, 192
  Paragraph Number style outlines, 467
  paragraph styles to headings, 889-890
  styles
    character, 355-356
    paragraph, 354-355

**Arabic character set (Set 13), 643**

**arc function, 780**

**Archive attribute (files), 922**

**arcos function, 779**

**arcs, drawing, 695-697**

**arcsin function, 779**

**arctan function, 779**

**area charts, 539**

**Arrange Icons By command (View menu), 927**

**arranging,** *see* **sorting**

**arrows**
  drawing, 698-699
    double curves, 699
    line end, 698-699
    sweeping, 699
    sweeping, troubleshooting, 711
    twisting ends of, 697

**Arrows palette, 792**

**Arrows palette (Equation Editor), 775**

**art,** *see* **clip art**

**ASCII character set (Set 0), 641**

**ASCII Delimited Text Files, setting conversion preferences, 562**

**ASCII Text format**
  converting spreadsheets, 579-580
  documents, converting to intermediate format, 570
  limitations, 570

**Ask The PerfectExpert, 1094**

**Ask the PerfectExpert command (Help menu), 47**

**assigning**
  features to keyboards, 328-329
  keystrokes to keyboards, 327-329
  macros
    to keyboards, 330
    to toolbar buttons, 423-424
  menus to keyboards, 327
  merge codes, 619
  program features to toolbar buttons, 421-422
  programs to keyboards, 327, 330
  special characters to keyboards, 329
  text script to toolbar buttons, 422-423
  values to variables, 619

**Associate dialog box, 382, 591**

**Associate option (template feature bar), 370**

**associating**
  data files with form files, 605-606
  editing features to templates, 382-383
  macros to triggers, 383-384
  troubleshooting, 386

**asterisk (*) wildcard character, 216**

**asymmetric columns, watermarks, 733-734**

**AT&T WorldNet Service**
  integrated applications, 1094
  WordPerfect setup options, 1079
  WordPerfect version of Netscape, 1033-1034

**attributes**
  Automatic Font Changes (AFCs), 648-650
  drawing shapes, 690
  files, 921-922
  fonts, 741-742
    applying to overstrikes, 646
    underlining, 742
  shapes, 707-712
    color, 707-709
    fills, 709
    line patterns, 710-712
  text, tables, 531

**Auto Code Placement feature, 126**

**Auto Redraw command (View menu), 545**

**Auto Row Insert option (tables), 523**

**Auto Start command (Customize menu), 228**

**Auto Start option (Spell Checker), 219**

**automatic backups, default settings, 56**

**automatic cross-referencing, 865-868**
  marking, 866-867

**Automatic Font Changes (AFCs), 648**
  attributes, 648-650
  editing, 650-651

**automatic formatting, 466**

**automatic hyphenation, 150**

**Automatic Major Grid Value option, editing axes (charts), 553**

Automatic Maximum Value option, editing axes (charts), 552
Automatic Minimum Value option, editing axes (charts), 553
automatic starts, Spell Checker, 219
automatically marking revisions, 829-831
Automatically Select Words option, 310
Autorun program, installation, 1078
axes (charts), 536-537
 adding titles, 549
 displaying labels, 550
 editing, 552
Axis command (Chart menu), 550-552

# B

Back button (Hypertext Feature Bar), 53, 1023-1024
Back tab, 138
backslash (\), in equations, 782
Backspace key, 87
 deleting shapes, 692
backups
 automatic, default settings, 56
 installing WordPerfect, 1077-1078
 toolbars, 420
balance, designing documents for desktop publishing, 727
balanced newspaper columns
 column type, 434-436
 customizing widths of columns, 440-442
 default, 439

bar charts, 536-538
bars, 536
Basic Counts dialog box, 231
BEEP command, 974
Beep On Misspelled option (Spell Checker), 219
beep options, 308
Bezier Curve tool, 711
BINOM command, 770
BINOMSM command, 771
blank documents, starting, 366
blank lines, inserting, 59
blending colors, 753
blink text, 1051
[Block Pro], indicates block protect, 160
Block Protect guidelines, 159-160
block protected parallel columns, 447
body text, 744
 HTML documents, 1050
BOLD command, 713, 771
 formatting equations, 782
bonus applications, WordPerfect setup options, 1079
booklets, printing, 286
Bookmark button (Hypertext Feature Bar), 1023-1024
Bookmark command (Insert menu), 1027, 1062
Bookmark dialog box, 1062
Bookmark option (Go To dialog box), 65

bookmarks
 creating, 1062-1063
 defined, 1022-1023
 navigating documents, 1022-1023
Border Fill command (Format menu), 256-257
Border Text Paragraph Style, 360
Border/Fill command (Format menu), 259, 733, 1098
Border/Fill dialog box, 754
borders, 255-261
 color, 754
 columns, 259-260
  adding, 456-457
 customizing, 666-669
  color, 667-668
  corners, 668
 documents, 258-259
  deleting, 261
  turning off, 260-261
 drop shadows, 668-669
 fills, 669
 spacing, 666
 graphics boxes, 675
 paragraphs, 256
  adding fills, 257
  deleting, 261
  troubleshooting, 261
 rounded, creating, 668
 tables, 528
  customizing, 992-993
Bottom command (Vertical menu), 530
Bottom option (Edit Graphics Line dialog box), 665
Box Caption dialog box, 673
Box Content dialog box, 671
Box Drawing character set (Set 3), 642

Box Fill tab, 548, 550
Box Position dialog box, 673
Box Size dialog box, 674
Box Style dialog box, 275
Box Type tab, 548
brightness, images, 681
browsers
   defined, 1044
   Netscape, 1044
      viewing HTML documents, 1068
Build Prompt option (Template Feature Bar), 370
Build Prompts button (Template Feature Bar), 377
bullets
   creating with Internet Publisher, 1054-1056
   diamond, 463
   large circle, 463
   small circle, 463
   square, 463
   triangle, 463
bullets and numbers
   automatic formatting, paragraph style, 466
   creating with fewer keystrokes, 465
   outlines
      creating, 463-464
      documents, 462-463
      modifying appearance, 467-468
   styles
      applying to lists, 464-465
      outlines, editing, 468
Bullets & Numbers dialog box, 465
button boxes, 266
buttons
   1:1 ratio (scaling option), 680

Add Printer (Print dialog box), 292
Application Control, 18
Back, 53
Build Prompts (Template Feature Bar), 377
Change To Body Text button (Outline Feature Bar), 482
Close, 17
Columns, 436-437
dialog boxes, 33-34
   lookup, 35-36
   QuickSpots, 39-41
   radio, 35
   selecting, 34
Document Control, 19
Document Review Bar, 828
Esc, 68
Font Face (Power Bar), 130
Font Size (Power Bar), 130
Help Topics, 53
Initial Font (Print dialog box), 292
Insert, 234
Insert Bullet, 464
Maximize, 18
Minimize, 18
Minimize (Spell Checker dialog box), 210
modifying styles, Hypertext, 1032-1033
Next Page, 27, 62
Note Number Footnote/Endnote, 804
OLE Close (WP Draw toolbar), 685
OLE Update (WP Draw toolbar), 685
Options, 53
Outline Definitions (Outline Feature Bar), 485
Paper Feed (Print dialog box), 292
Port option, 294
Power Bar
   adding, 428-429
   customizing, 427-428
   deleting, 428-429
   moving, 428-429
Previous Page, 27, 62
Properties (Print dialog box), 292
QuickFont (Power Bar), 130
QuickFormat, 122
selecting, Feature Bar, 31
Styles (Power Bar), 130
System Printers (Print dialog box), 292
toolbars, 416-417
   adding program features to, 421-422
   assigning macros to, 423-424
   assigning text script to, 422-423
   customizing appearance, 424-427
   displaying rows of, 419
   moving, 421
   rows, 419
   styles, changing, 419-420
WP Draw toolbar, 687-688
Zoom, 693

# C

Calculate command
   QuickMenu, 1003
   Table menu, 1003-1005
calculating
   formulas, 1005
   loan payments, 1016-1017
Calendar Expert, 385
calendar math, floating cells, 1015-1016
CALL command, 967
Cancel hyphenation of word code, 149
Cancel Printing command (Document menu), 282, 290

**canceling**
- Esc button, 68
- print jobs, 281-282, 290

**capitalization, checking with Spell Checker,** 212

**CAPS (merge code),** 621-622

**CAPS, FIRSTCAP (merge codes),** 621-622

**captions, graphics boxes,** 672-673

**capturing graphics with WP Draw,** 715-716
- selecting image source, 715-716
- TWAIN interface, 716

**cartridge fonts,** 635

**Cascade command (Window menu),** 44

**cascading documents,** 44

**CASE command,** 966

**CASEOF command,** 965-966

**CD-ROM, installation procedures,** 1078-1082

**Cell/Range option (Go To dialog box),** 66

**cells**
- charts
  - adding columns, 547-548
  - adding rows, 547-548
  - narrowing columns, 546
  - removing columns, 547-548
  - removing rows, 547-548
  - widening columns, 546
- floating
  - calendar math, 1015-1016
  - creating, 1014-1015
  - data entry, 1018
- tables
  - adding text attributes, 531
  - copying text, 505-506
  - customizing, 993-995
  - deleting text from, 504-505
  - entering text in, 502-503
  - formatting, 521-522
  - guidelines, 526
  - joining, 514-515
  - lines, 526
  - locking, 1005-1006
  - moving between, 501-502
  - pasting text, 505-506
  - selecting, 503-504
  - selecting all, 505
  - splitting, 515-516
  - troubleshooting selection of, 509

**Center command**
- Justification menu, 530
- Quick menu, 176

**Center option (Alignment section of Table Format dialog box),** 520

**Center Page(s) dialog box,** 158

**Center tab,** 139

**center-justification,** 738

**Centered option (Edit Graphics Line dialog box),** 663-665

**centering**
- lines, 131-132
- pages, 159
- text, 158

**CHAIN command,** 386, 970
- running macros, 970

**chaining styles,** 351-352

**Change Path dialog box,** 1082-1083

**Change To Body Text button (Outline Feature Bar), modifying outlines,** 482

**changing,** *see* **editing; modifying**

**Changing Footnote options (Footnote Options dialog box),** 817

**Changing the Spacing Between Notes option (Footnote Options dialog box),** 814

**chapter codes, inserting in subdocuments,** 891-892

**Chapter commands (Edit menu),** 896

**chapter numbers**
- inserting into documents, 892
- *see also* numbering

**Character command**
- Font menu, 769, 776
- Insert menu, 644, 1061

**Character dialog box,** 719

**Character feature,** 644

**character maps, foreign,** 656

**characters**
- appearance, 126-129
- attributes, changing with Power Bar, 130
- decimal align, changing, 144
- equations, 776
  - troubleshooting formatting, 797
- formatting, 126-130
- HTML documents, 1053-1054
- inserting into equations, 773
- size, 126-129
- special
  - accessing, 640
  - as font attributes, 649
  - Compose feature, 644-645
  - HTML documents, 1060-1061
  - mnemonics, 645
  - overstrikes, 645-647

types, 641-643
viewing character sets, 642
styles
  applying, 355-356
  documents, paired codes, 337-338
  font applications, 337-338
  headings, applying, 890
  paired style, 337
  text, 887-888
  types, 336-338
**Chart command (Graphics menu), 541, 702**
**Chart Gallery, 551**
  command (Chart menu), 551
  opening, 551
**Chart menu commands**
  Axis, 550, 552
  Chart Gallery, 551
  Data Labels, 550
  Frame, 553
  Grids, 553
  Layout/Type, 551
  Legend, 549
  Perspective, 553
  Series, 554
  Subtitle, 548
  Title, 548
**Chart Object command (Edit menu), 544**
**charts, 536-537**
  3D, 551
  area, 539
  bar, 536, 538
  clustered, 552
  columns
    adding, 547-548
    narrowing, 546
    removing, 547-548
    widening, 546
  creating, 541-544
  data, 537-538
    changing, 544-548
    formatting, 546
    pasting, 542

editing, 909-910
  series changes, 554-556
fill styles, 555-556
frames, editing, 553
grids, 537
  editing, 553
High/Low, 539
inserting, 909-910
  into drawings, 702-703
  subtitles into, 548
labels, 550-551
legends, 549-550
lines, 538
linking, 909-910
moving between documents and chart, 544
overlapping, 552
pie, 540
  editing, 557
placing in documents, 558
radar, 539
rotating display, 553
rows
  adding, 547-548
  removing, 547-548
scatter, 539
  editing, 557
stacked, 552
stacked 100%, 552
tick, editing, 553
titles, 548-549
troubleshooting, 544
types, 538-541
  changing, 551-552
updating, 545
vertical y-axis, 536
viewing on monitors, 556
x-axis, 536
  adding titles, 549
  displaying labels, 550
  editing, 552
y-axis
  adding titles, 549
  displaying labels, 550
  editing, 552
  titles, 556
**Charts palette, 691**
**check boxes, 34-35**

Print As Booklet, 286
Print Graphics, 287
Print in Color, disabling, 287
**Check Duplicate Words option (Spell Checker), 219**
**Check Footers command (Customize menu), 229**
**Check Footnotes command (Customize menu), 229**
**Check Headers command (Customize menu), 229**
**Check Irregular Capitalization command**
  Customize menu, 213
  Spell Checker, 219
**Check Words with Numbers command**
  Customize menu, 213
  Spell Checker, 219
**Checking Styles command (Customize menu), 228-229**
**Checking Styles dialog box, 229**
**Choose Bar Shape option (Series dialog box), 555**
**choosing,** *see* **selecting**
**Choosing a Separator Line option (Footnote Options dialog box), 815-816**
**circles, drawing, 697**
**Clear All command (Edit menu), 545**
**Clear command (Edit menu), 545, 704**
**Clear Condense command (Mark menu), 883**
**Clear Save command (Mark menu), 883**
**clearing tabs from Ruler Bar, 143**

**clicking (mouse operation), 15**

**clip art, 693**
    adding to drawings, 700-701
    copying figures, 705
        to Clipboard, 582
        to documents, 705
        positions, 705
    deleting figures, 704
    importing graphics, 582
    moving figures, 704-705
        to back, 706
        to front, 706
    pasting figures, 705
    positioning, 700-702
    retrieving, 700-702
    rotating figures, 706
    selecting figures, 703
    sizing figures, 706

**Clipboard**
    conversion capabilities, 570-572
    copying
        clip art, 582
        lines to, 85
        spreadsheets, 576
    data, pasting, 571-572
    formulas, pasting, 576
    importing documents, 570-572
    text, placing, 571

**Clipboard option (Perform Merge dialog box), 612**

**Close All Documents dialog box, 77**

**Close All feature, 77**

**Close button, 17**
    Hypertext Feature Bar, 1023-1024

**Close command (File menu), 71, 77**

**Close option (Quick Data Entry dialog box), 599**

**closed curves**
    creating, 692
    drawing, 694-695

**closed shapes (WP Draw), 691**

**closing**
    applications, 12
    dialog boxes
        keyboard, 41
        Print, 278
    documents, 71, 77
    help, 54
    Image Tools toolbox, 678
    Spell Checker, 215
    User Word List Editor dialog box, 222
    windows, 17
    WordPerfect 7, 12
    WordPerfect window, 18

**clustered charts, 552**

**[Cntr Cur Pg: On], indicates centering page on, 158-159**

**[Cntr Pgs: On], indicates current and subsequent pages on, 158-159**

**Coach feature, 54**

**Code Page option, 312**

**code pages**
    editing, 312
    Input File Code Page, 312
    Output File Code Page, 312
    setting conversion preferences, 563

**codes**
    auto placement, 126
    [Block Pro], 160
    [Cntr Cur Pg: On], 158-159
    [Cntr Pgs: On], 158-159
    [Condl EOP: #], 161
    deleting, 880
    displaying, 837
    ENDFIELD, 597
    ENDRECORD, 597
    [Force: Even], 158
    [Force: New], 157
    [Force: Odd], 158
    foreign language, inserting, 653-655
    [HPg], 157
    [HRt-SPg], 156
    initial, creating, 123
    keyboard, displaying, 609-611
    merge, 607-608
        displaying, 609
        inserting, 608
    [Open Style: InitialStyle], 199-200
    PAGEOFF, 613
    [SPg], 156
    [THPg] (Temporary Hard Page Break), 158
    turning on/off, 122
    viewing, 41
    [Wid/Orph: On], 161

**Codes button (Macro Feature Bar), 952-953**

**Codes command (Match menu), 152**

**Codes dialog box, 152**

**Codes Page Preferences dialog box, 312**

**codes, reveal, 41**

**Collate option, 281**

**Color Options (Font dialog box), 129**

**Color Palettes command (Format menu), 707-708**

**Color Palettes dialog box, 708**

**colors**
    blending, 753
    borders, 667-668
    creating with Internet Publisher, 1056-1057
    custom, creating, 752
    designing documents for desktop publishing, 728
    documents, 750
        creating, 756
        highlighting, 826
        printing, 286-287
    fonts, 129
    graphics, 753-756
    images, 680

inverting, 753
lines, customizing, 661-662
shapes, 707-709
    changing, 697
table fills, 990
text, 751-753

**Column Aligned option (Edit Graphics Line dialog box), 665**

**Column Border dialog box, enhancing column appearance, 456**

**Column Border/Fill dialog box, 38, 260, 456**

**column separator (&), 770, 788**

**columns**
    appearance, altering, 452
    asymmetric, watermarks, 733-734
    balanced newspaper
        column type, 434-436
            customizing widths of columns, 440-442
            default, 439
    borders, 259-260
        adding, 456-457
        color, 754
    charts
        adding, 547-548
        narrowing, 546
        removing, 547-548
        widening, 546
    codes, formatting, 444
    custom settings, applying to borders, 458-459
    defaults
        Balanced Newspaper, 439
        spacing, 439
    documents, 731-737
        ease of readability, 436
        enhancing appearance, 455-456
        types, 434-436
    fills, color, 754-757
    formatting, 731
    guidelines, 454
    gutter space, 735-736
    hyphenation of text, 442
    insertion point
        keyboard commands, 443
        moving to other column, 442-443
    matrices, *see* matrices
    measurements, default settings, 439-440
    newspaper columns, 733
        creating (Columns Dialog box), 438-440
        creating (Power Bar), 436-437
        turning off, 446
    Number of Columns text box (Columns Dialog box), 439-440
    parallel
        breaks, 449-450
        creating, 448
        defined, 446-447
        editing, 451
        moving, 451-452
        spacing, 450-451
        typing text, 448-450
        using column breaks, 449-450
    parallel block protected columns, creating, 449-450
    patterns, adding, 457
    scroll bar, viewing text, 443
    subdividing documents, 184-185
    tables
        aligning, 520
        alternating fills, 988-990
        creating forms, 985
        deleting, 513
        formatting, 519-521
        width, changing, 510-512
    tabular, converting to tables, 500
    text
        aligning, 444
        cutting and pasting, 451
        editing, 444-445
        formatting, 442
        inserting, 442
        troubleshooting, 736
    types, 434-436
    widths
        altering, 452-454
        custom, 732

**Columns button (Power Bar), creating columns, 436-437**

**Columns command (Format menu), 731, 984**

**Columns Define dialog box, 733**

**Columns Definition dialog box, 439-440**

**Columns dialog box, 34-35, 438-440, 445-446**

**commands**
    // (Comment), 971
    ALIGNC, 788
    ALIGNL, 788
    ALIGNR, 788
    Application Control menu
        Move, 19
        Size, 19
    applications (macros), 954
    AttributeAppearanceToggle (macros), 954
    BEEP, 974
    Block Protect, 159-160
    BOLD, 782
    CALL, 967
    CASE, 966
    CASEOF, 965-966
    Center, 158
    CHAIN, 386, 970
    Chart menu
        Axis, 550, 552
        Chart Gallery, 551
        Data Labels, 550
        Frame, 553
        Grids, 553
        Layout/Type, 551
        Legend, 549

Perspective, 553
Series, 554
Subtitle, 548
Title, 548
Conditional End Of Page,
  160-161
CorelOffice 7 menu,
  WordPerfect 7, 12
Create (Create Labels
  dialog box), 192-193
Customize menu
  Auto Start, 228
  Check Footers, 229
  Check Footnotes, 229
  Check Headers, 229
  Check Irregular
    Capitalization, 213
  Check Words with
    Numbers, 213
  Checking Styles,
    228-229
  Language, 228
  Main Word Lists, 220
  Prompt Before Auto
    Replacement, 228
  Save Rules, 228
  Suggest Spelling
    Replacements, 229
  Turn On Rules, 228
  User Word Lists,
    222, 228
Data menu
  Exclude Row/Col., 547
  Format, 546
  Import, 541
  Include Row/Col., 547
decision making
  IF, 963
  macros, 963-966
  SWITCH/CASE, 963
DEFAULT, 966
defined, 769
DialogCreate, 974
DialogDisplay, 974
DISPLAY, 972-973
Display menu, Hide
  Completed Jobs, 290
Document menu
  Cancel Printing,
    282, 290

Pause Printing, 290
Remove, 290
Edit menu
  Chapter, 896
  Chart Object, 544
  Clear, 545, 704
  Clear All, 545
  Convert, 561
  Copy, 506, 810, 918
  Cut, 506, 811, 918
  Delete, 547
  Find and Replace,
    152, 762
  Go To, 64
  Go To Cell, 542
  Insert, 547
  Paste, 542, 572, 810, 919
  Paste Link, 583
  Paste Special, 584, 705
  Preferences, 22, 74, 299,
    372, 415, 774
  Redo, 90
  Rotate, 706
  Select, 923
  Select All, 703
  Summary, 204
  Undelete, 88
  Undo, 89-90, 254, 692,
    704, 880
  Undo/Redo History, 90
ELSE, 964-965
ENDFIELD, 907
ENDIF, 964-965
ENDRECORD, 907
ENDSWITCH command,
  965-966
Equation Editor, 770-772
F1 (Help), 46
Favorites menu
  Add, 938
  Go To, 937
File menu
  Close, 71, 77
  Condense Master, 883
  Delete, 639, 920, 924
  Exit, 12, 79
  Expand Master, 878-881
  Insert File, 796
  Install New Font, 637
  Internet Publisher, 1045

New, 78, 368
New Folder, 923
Open, 14, 82, 918,
  950-951
Page Range, 896
Print, 69, 278, 280,
  895, 923
Properties, 203, 921
Publish to Envoy,
  912-913
Restore, 924
Save, 74, 796
Save As, 72, 376, 720
Send, 296
Subdocument, 874-876
Font menu
  Character, 769, 776
  Equation, 795
Footnote menu,
  Options, 817
Force Page (Format
  menu), 157
Format menu
  Advance, 196-197
  Border/Fill, 256-259,
    733
  Color Palettes, 707-708
  Columns, 731, 984
  Count Pages, 172
  Delay Codes, 186
  Document, 656, 806
  Documents, 123
  Drop'Cap, 658
  Envelope, 188-189, 617
  Font, 127, 262, 650, 752,
    953-954
  Force Page, 876
  Headers/Footers,
    174-176
  Initial Font, 198
  Initial Style, 199-200
  Justification, 147
  Justification All, 148
  Labels, 191, 318, 618
  Line, 131, 630, 739
  Line Attributes, 694
  Make It Fit Expert, 187
  Margins, 135, 258, 730,
    953-954

Object Properties, 694, 698, 711
Options, 190
Page Numbering, 170-171, 847, 892
Page Size, 180
Paragraph, 137, 740, 803
QuickFormat, 144
Redline Method, 200-201
Select, 163-164
Subdivide page, 184-185
Suppress, 172-173
Text/Background Colors, 1056
Title, 1049
Typesetting, 135, 646, 745
Watermark, 733
FROM, 785
FUNC, formatting equations, 782
GETSTRING, 960–962
GO, 969
Graphics menu
  Chart, 541, 702
  Contour Text, 714
  Custom Box, 275
  Custom Line, 659, 753
  Drag to Create, 682
  Draw, 684
  Edit Box, 768
  Edit Line, 660, 662, 753
  Equation, 761, 764
  Front, 706
  Graphics Styles, 670, 795
  Horizontal Line, 251, 1060
  Image, 268
  Inline Equation, 778, 794
  Insert, 677
  TextArt, 720
  Vertical Line, 252
HardReturn (macros), 954
Help menu
  About WordPerfect, 48
  Ask the Perfect-Expert, 47
  Help Online, 47
  Help Topics, 47-48, 955-956
  Upgrade Expert, 48
IF, 963-965
Image menu, Text Box, 670
Insert menu
  Acquire Image, 716
  Bookmark, 1027, 1062
  Character, 644, 1061
  Create Link, 577-578
  Date, 66
  Edit Links, 577-578
  Endnote, 818
  File, 82, 85-86, 701
  Find QuickMark, 310
  Footnote, 803, 811, 817, 893
  Import, 574-576, 907
  Link, 912
  Object, 911-912
  Other, 794
  Pages, 175-176
  Select Image Source, 716
  Sound, 1037-1038
  Spreadsheet/Database, 623
  Update, 578
inserting
  into equation palettes, 775-776
  macros, 975
ITAL, 782
Justification menu
  Center, 530
  Decimal Align, 521, 1000
  Right, 520, 1001
LABEL, 967
LEFT
  creating fractions, 783-785
  delimiters, 784
macro conventions, 957
MacroStatusPrompt, 973-974
MarginLeft (macros), 954
Mark menu
  Clear Condense, 883
  Clear Save, 883
  Condense All, 883
  Save All, 883
Match menu, Codes, 152
MATFORM, 788
MATRIX, 788
matrix, creating matrices, 787-789
MENULIST, 962-963
NEST, 971
New Page Size dialog box, New, 181-182
Options menu
  Annotate, 53
  Copy, 53
  Define a Bookmark, 54
  Delete Group, 378
  Delete Template, 378
  Display a Bookmark, 54
  Edit Template, 374
  Exit, 54
  Font, 54
  Keep Help on Top, 54
  New Group, 378
  New Template, 375
  Open a File, 54
  Print Summary, 287
  Print Topic, 54
  Rename Group, 378
  Save As, 993
  Use System Colors, 54
  Version, 54
OVER, 766-767, 783-785
PauseKey, 973
Product function commands, macros, 955-956
programming commands, macros, 955-956
Programs menu, Windows Explorer, 930
QuickMenu
  Calculate, 1003
  Center, 176
  Flush Right, 176
  Font, 176
  Format, 516

commands

  Image Tools, 677
  Indent, 176
  Lines/Fill, 526
  Numeric Format,
    999, 1010
  Paste, 176
  SpeedFormat, 524
  SpellCheck, 176
  Split Cell, 515
  Style, 275
  Update Chart From
    Table, 546
QUIT, 968
RETURN, 967-968
RIGHT
  creating fractions,
    783-785
  delimiters, 784
RUN, 970-971
Settings menu
  Control Panel, 63, 637
  Printer, 290
SQRT, 787
STACK, 790-791
STACKALIGN, 790-791
Start menu, Settings, 66
SUB, 767-768
SUP, 767-768
SWITCH, 965-966
Table menu
  Calculate, 1003-1005
  Copy Formula, 1003
  Create, 498
  Format, 512, 516
  Insert, 513
  Join, 985
  Join Cells, 514
  Lines/Fill, 525, 992
  Names, 1012
  QuickFill, 1020
  Split, 984
  Split Cell, 515
TO, 785
Toolbar menu, Options, 22
Tools menu
  Add, 902-903
  Address Book, 900
  Delete, 902
  Edit, 950
  Generate, 803, 887
  Generate Lists, 836
  Grammatik, 225
  Highlight, 825
  Hypertext/Web Links,
    1028-1029, 1064
  Language, 654, 815
  Macro, 647, 820
  Merge, 588, 611
  QuickCorrect, 224, 642
  Record, 953-954
  Rename, 901
  Sort, 626-628
  Spell Check, 209
  Spell-As-You-Go, 217
  Template Macro, 379
Type (macros), 954
user input
  GETSTRING, 961
  MENULIST, 961
  using, 961-963
Vertical menu, Bottom,
  530
View menu
  Auto Redraw, 545
  Details, 925, 927
  Graphics, 302
  Grid/Snap, 690
  Guidelines, 26, 57, 526
  Hidden Text, 128, 302
  Hide Bars, 30-31, 415
  Large Icons, 925-926
  List, 925, 927
  Options, 930
  Outliner, 911
  Page, 279
  Preview, 73
  Preview: Content, 84
  Preview: No Preview, 85
  Preview: Page View, 84
  Preview: Use separate
    window, 84
  Redisplay, 763
  Redraw, 545
  Reveal Codes, 41,
    122, 261
  Ruler, 690
  Show, 59, 146, 304
  Small Icons, 925
  Toolbar, 57, 415, 687
  Toolbars/Ruler, 23
  Tree View, 928
  View in Web browser,
    1068
  Zoom, 30, 279
  Zoom Display, 777
  Widow/Orphan
    protection, 161-162
  Window menu
    Cascade, 44
    Tile Side By Side, 44
    Tile Top To Bottom, 44

**Commands button (Macro Feature Bar), 952-953**

**Commands palette (Equation Editor), 775**

**comments, 208**

**Comments feature, 301-302**

**compact installation, 956**

**Compare Document feature**
  changing redline display, 832-833
  marking revisions automatically, 829-833
  removing redline display, 834

**Compose feature, special characters, 644-645**

**Concept Net section, 936**

**Concordance File option, 864**

**concordance files**
  creating, 862
  marking text to create indexes, 861-862

**Condense All command (Mark menu), 883**

**Condense Master command (File menu), 883**

**Condense/Save Subdocuments dialog box, 883**

condensing master documents, 882-884
**Conditional End of Page**
guidelines, 160-161
overriding command, 161
**[Condl EOP: #], indicates conditional end of page, 161**
configuring
printers, 291-292
user information in documents, 307
**Confirm File Delete dialog box, 921**
**Confirm File Replace dialog box, 919**
**Confirm Folder Delete dialog box, 924**
**Confirmation Deletion options, 309**
connecting
parts of documents with Hypertext, 1022-1023
WordPerfect document to web pages, 1036
**Consecutive Pages option, 864**
consistency, designing documents for desktop publishing, 727
constraining shapes, 693
contents, graphics boxes, 671-672
**Contents tab (Help dialog box), 48-49**
**Contour Text command (Graphics menu), 714**
**Contour Text dialog box, 714**
contouring text, 714-715
contrast images, 681
**Control Panel command (Settings menu), 63, 637**

controls
editing screen, 17-20
Application Control menu, 18-19
buttons, 17
document controls, 19-20
Merge Feature Bar, 603
Merge Form File Feature Bar, 604-605
typographical, 745
kerning, 746-747
leading, 745
letterspacing, 747-748
word spacing, 749-750
**conversion format, 566-569**
**Convert command (Edit menu), 561**
**Convert feature**
documents
importing, 564-565
word processing formats, 564
exporting documents, 568-569
**Convert File Format dialog box, 565-568**
**Convert Preferences dialog box, 320, 561**
**Convert Table dialog box, 500**
converting
code pages, 563
data file records, merge feature, 622-623
Document Comments, 244
documents
to ANSI Text format, 570
to ASCII Text format, 570
to HTML documents, 1047
to intermediate format, 569-570
to Rich Text Format (RTF), 569-570

to WordPerfect format, 565-566
unknown format, 566
endnotes to footnotes, 821
footnotes to endnotes, 820-821
measurements in documents, 303
Quattro Pro spreadsheet formulas, 908
spreadsheets
from unknown formats, 579-580
to ASCII file format, 579-580
tabular columns to tables, 500
text into address blocks, 1054
WordPerfect documents into HTML, 1047
**Copy Abbreviation dialog box, 247**
**Copy command**
Edit menu, 506, 810, 918
Options menu, 53
**Copy Formula command (Table menu), 1003**
**Copy Toolbars dialog box, 420**
**Copy/Remove Object option (template feature bar), 370**
**Copy/Remove Template Objects dialog box, 380-381**
copying
clip art figures, 705
to Clipboard, 582
to documents, 705
positions, 705
documents from disks to screens, 82
files, 918-919
footnotes, 809-810
keyboard definitions to other keyboards, 326

lines to Clipboard, 85
objects from other
  templates, 380-381
rows in tables, 506
spreadsheets
  with Clipboard, 576
  with Spreadsheet/
    Database Import
    feature, 573-576
styles
  documents, 347-348
  formatting codes, 348
  graphics, 348
tables, 507-508
text from table cells,
  505-506

**copyright law, publishing on the Web, 1071**

**Corel TrueType Fonts,** *see* **TrueType fonts**

**Corel WordPerfect Suite**
Address Book, 900
AT&T WorldNet Service, 1076
CD-ROM, 1087-1088
CorelFLOW3, 1076
Dashboard, 1076
Envoy 7, 1076
integrated applications
  AT&T WorldNet Service, 1094
  CorelFLOW 3, 1094
  Dashboard, 1094
  Envoy 7, 1094
  Netscape Navigator, 1033-1034, 1068, 1094
  Presentations 7, 1076, 1094
  Quattro Pro 7, 1076, 1094
  Sidekick, 1076, 1094
QuickView Plus, 1076
WordPerfect, 1076
*see also* WordPerfect 7

**CorelFLOW**
diagrams, inserting, 911-912
flow charts, inserting, 911-912

**CorelFLOW 3, 1094**

**CorelFLOW 3 dialog box, 640**

**CorelOffice 7 menu commands, WordPerfect 7, 12**

corners, borders, 668

**cos function, 779**

**cosec function, 779**

**cosh function, 779**

**cot function, 779**

**coth function, 779**

**Count Pages command (Format menu commands), 172**

**counting page numbers in documents, 172**

**Create a Mark Text Toolbar, 884**

**Create Bookmark dialog box, 1027**

**Create command**
Create Labels dialog box, 192-193
Table menu, 498

**Create Data File dialog box, 589**

**Create Data Link dialog box, 577-578**

**Create Full Form dialog box, 851**

**Create Graphics Line dialog box, 659**

**Create Hypertext Link dialog box, 1028-1034, 1064**

**Create Keyboard dialog box, 326, 406-407**

**Create Labels dialog box, 192-193**

**Create Link command (Insert menu), 577-578**

**Create Merge File dialog box, 589**

**Create New Address Book dialog box, 900**

**Create Table dialog box, 498**

**Create Table Style dialog box, 988**

**Create/Delete button (Hypertext Feature Bar), 1023-1024**

**Create/Edit Graphic Line dialog box, 753**

**Cross Reference feature, referencing footnote numbers, 803, 866**

**cross-referencing, 865-868**
items in subdocuments
  through master
  documents, 894
marking, 866-867
  footnotes/endnotes, 868
troubleshooting, 868

**Ctrl+Enter (inserting page breaks), 157**

**Ctrl+key shortcuts, 398-399**

**Ctrl+Shift+key shortcuts, 398-399**

**current documents, editing, 345-350**

**Current Document dialog box, 1012**

**Current Document option (Perform Merge dialog box), 612**

**Current Page Even option (Force Page dialog box), 157**

**Current Page Odd option (Force Page dialog box), 157**

**current pages, printing, 283**

**current templates (Macro location dialog box), storing macros, 394-395**
**curved sweeping arrows, drawing, 699**
**curves**
  creating, 692
  drawing, 694-695
**Custom Box command (Graphics menu), 275**
**Custom Box dialog box, 275**
**custom installation of WordPerfect, 1084-1086**
**Custom Line command (Graphics menu), 659, 753**
**Custom Page Numbering dialog box, 168, 171-172**
**Custom Search option (Advanced Find dialog box), 932**
**custom settings**
  columns
    borders, 458-459
    drop shadowing, 458-459
    gradients, 458-459
    spacing, 458-459
    print options, 287-289
**Customize Button dialog box, 424**
**Customize menu commands**
  Auto Start, 228
  Check Footers, 229
  Check Footnotes, 229
  Check Headers, 229
  Check Irregular Capitalization, 213
  Check Words with Numbers, 213
  Checking Styles, 228-229
  Language, 228
  Main Word Lists, 220

Prompt Before Auto Replacement, 228
Save Rules, 228
Suggest Spelling Replacements, 229
Turn On Rules, 228
User Word Lists, 222, 228
**Customize Number Type dialog box, 1000**
**customizing**
  Automatically Select Words option, 310
  borders, 666-669
    color, 667-668
    corners, 668
    drop shadows, 668-669
    fills, 669
    spacing, 666
    tables, 992-993
  cells of tables, 993-995
  columns
    borders, 455-456
    patterns, 455-456
    shadows, 455-456
    widths, 440-442
  confirmation deletion options in documents, 309
  document summaries, 205-206, 319-320
  environment options in documents, 306
  file conversion options, 320
  files preferences, 312-315
  format options, 145-146
  gradients, 711
  Grammatik, 228-229
  graphics boxes, 669
    borders, 675
    captions, 672-673
    contents, 671-672
    fills, 675
    positioning, 673-674
    size, 674-675
    styles, 670-671
    text wrap, 675
  hyphenation formatting in documents, 309

indexes, 863-864
keyboard
  definitions, 326
  layout, 324-325
labels
  description, 194
  file preferences, 318
  margins, 194-195
  per page, 194
  size, 194
lines, 658
  color, 661-662
  horizontal, 662-664
  with mouse, 252
  styles, 659-660
  tables, 990-991
  thickness, 660-661
  vertical, 664-666
menu display feature for documents, 308-309
page numbers, 165-168
Power Bar buttons, 24, 426-429
  adding, 428-429
  deleting, 428-429
  moving, 428-429
printers, 180
shading, tables, 993-995
Spell Checker, 217
toolbars, 420
  assigning macros to, 423-424
  assigning program features to buttons, 421-422
  assigning text script to buttons, 422-423
  editing screen, 23
  graphics, 424-427
  moving buttons, 421
  text, 424-427
  WP Draw, 543
windows appearance, 321
WordPerfect 7
  displays, 300
  Document display, 300-303

**Cut command (Edit menu), 506, 811, 918**

**cutting**
  footnotes, 811
  outline families, 482-484
  rows, tables, 506
  tables, 507-508
  text
    outlines, 482-484
    table cells, 505-506

**Cyrillic character set (Set 10), 643**

# D

**Dashboard, Corel WordPerfect Suite integrated applications, 1094**

**DAT file extension, merging data files, 590**

**data**
  charts, 537-538
    changing, 544-548
    formatting, 546
    pasting, 542
  clearing from datasheets, 545
  DDE Link, creating to other programs, 582-583
  embedding, 906
  entering in floating cells, 1018
  entering into data files
    in existing files, 600-601
    Quick Data Entry dialog box, 598-600
  entering with QuickFill, 1019-1020
    dates of months, 1020
    days of week, 1020
  graphics, importing, 581-582
  linking, Spreadsheet Import/Link feature, 577-578
  links
    editing, 577-578
    setting options, 578
    updating, 578
  OLE Link, creating to other programs, 583-585
  pasting, 571-572
  spreadsheets
    exporting, 581
    importing with DDE link, 580
    importing with OLE link, 580-581
  tables
    merging, 986
    sorting, 986

**data fields, troubleshooting, 618**

**data files**
  associating with form files, 605-606
  creating, 588-591
  data entry
    in existing files, 600-601
    Quick Data Entry dialog box, 598-600
  editing structure, 601-602
  fields, 596
    names, 596, 598
  merge feature
    converting, 622-623
    creating tables, 623-624
    defining conditions, 615
    marking records, 616-617
  records, 596
  Sort feature, 624
  types, 597-598
  user input information
    capturing, 619-620
    controlling, 621-622
    creating, 619-622

**Data Labels command (Chart menu), 550**

**Data menu commands**
  Exclude Row/Col., 547
  Format, 546
  Import, 541
  Include Row/Col., 547

**data points (charts)**
  changing in series, 554-556
  defined, 536
  editing high/low, 557

**databases**
  choosing records to be imported, 576
  finding, 50-51

**datasheets**
  ASCII file format, converting, 579-580
  copying
    Clipboard feature, 576
    Spreadsheet/Database Import feature, 573-576
  data entry
    changing, 545
    clearing, 545
    QuickFill, 1019-1020
    QuickFill, entering dates of months, 1020
    QuickFill, entering days of week, 1020
    troubleshooting, 1018
  designing, 996-997
  exporting data, 581
  forcing text mode, 1001
  formatting numeric data, 999-1001
  formulas
    absolute references, 1008-1009
    calculating, 1005
    converting, 908
    copying, 1003-1004
    creating, 1001-1003
    creating, letter grade formulas, 1010-1011
    creating, percent formulas, 1010
    creating, Quiz Points averages, 1009
    creating, reporting averages, 1008

creating, total points
  formulas, 1009-1010
deleting, 1005
functions in, 1004-1005
modifying, 1005
troubleshooting, 1018
importing
data, 580-581, 907
large, importing, 579
linking to WordPerfect, 906
navigating, 545
range of data
  imported, 907
to tables, 986-988
unknown formats,
  converting, 579-580

Date feature, 66, 713

dates, inserting into
  letters, 66

DDE (Dynamic Data
  Exchange) Link,
  582-583

Decimal Align command
  (Justification menu),
  521, 1000

Decimal Align option
  (Alignment section of
  Table Format dialog box),
  139, 520

decimal aligning
  character, changing, 144
  table columns, 520-521

Decimal tabs, 144

decision making
  commands
  IF, 963
  macros, 963-966
  SWITCH/CASE, 963

decrement arrows, 34

DEFAULT command, 966

Default Descriptive
  Type, 319

Default Labels Folder
  dialog box, 318

defaults
  folders, 315-316, 925
  graphic boxes, 262
  letter spacing, 748
  line spacing, 739
  lines in tables, 527
  lists, 841
  margins, subdividing, 185
  restoring tab settings, 140
  selecting folders as, 74
  settings, 56
  storing macros, 394-395
  table settings, 509
  templates, 316-317
  text formatting, 122-123
  user word lists, 209

Define a Bookmark
  command (Options
  menu), 54

Define Color Palette dialog
  box, 129, 708

Define Color Printing
  Palette dialog box, 752

Define Index dialog
  box, 863

Define List dialog box,
  838, 842

Define Table of Authorities
  dialog box, 855

Define Table of Contents
  dialog box, 846

defining
  data files, merge
    feature, 615
  indexes, 862-864
    troubleshooting, 868
  lists to create, 837
    default styles,
      changing, 841
    editing definition, 838
    graphics box options,
      841-842
    numbering position, 839
    page number
      format, 840
  Table of Authorities,
    854-858

  Table of Contents,
    845-849, 885

definition lists,
  1055-1056

delay codes, 162
  inserting into documents,
    185-188
  physical pages versus page
    numbers, 186

Delay Codes command
  (Format menu), 186

Delay Codes dialog
  box, 186

[Delay: #], 185-186

Delete Address Book
  dialog box, 902

Delete command
  Edit menu, 547
  File menu, 639, 920, 924
  Tools menu, 902

Delete dialog box, 505

Delete Group command
  (Options menu), 378

Delete key, 87

Delete Record option
  (Quick Data Entry
  dialog box), 599

Delete Styles dialog box,
  346-347

Delete Table dialog
  box, 505

Delete Template command
  (Options menu), 378

DeleteCharNext, 976-977

DeleteCharPrevious,
  976-977

deleting
  Address Book, 901-902
  Address Book entries, 905
  clip art figures, 704
  codes in master
    documents, 880
  columns of tables, 513

## deleting

document summaries, 204-205
files, 920-921
  troubleshooting, 924
footnotes, 811
  troubleshooting, 817
formulas, 1005
graphics boxes, 271
graphics lines, 261
keyboard definitions, 331
label definitions, 193
lines, 253-254
macros, 412
new key asssignments for keyboards, 327-331
objects in templates, 381
page borders, 261
page definitions for printers, 182
paragraph borders, 261
Power Bar buttons, 428-429
printer drivers, 292
rows of tables, 513
shapes, 692-693
shortcuts from Favorites folder, 938-939
styles, 346-347
subdocuments from master documents, 876-884
tables, 507-508
templates, 378
text, 87-88
  lines, 88
  restoring, 88-89
  single characters, 87
  tables, 504-505
  words, 88

**delimiters, 784**

**demos, 1079**

**Depth option (Layout/Type property sheet), 557**

**Description option (Template Feature Bar), 370**

**Description text box, 342**

**designing**
advanced tables, 1006
documents for desktop publishing, 725-728
documents for Hypertext, 1025-1026
spreadsheets, 996-997

**Desired Number Of Filled Pages text box, 187-188**

**desktop publishing, 723**
colors, 750-757
  graphics, 753-756
  text, 751-753
design, 725-728
guidelines, 724-725
planning page presentation, 729
  columns, 731
  columns, custom widths, 732
  columns, gutter space, 735-736
  margins, 729-730
refining page presentation, 736-740
  text alignment, 737-739
selecting fonts, 740
  attributes, 741-742
  type sizes, 742-745
  typefaces, 741-742
  typographical controls, 745

**det function, 780**

**Details command (View menu), 925-927**

**Details view, 927**

**diacritical marks (other palette), 791**

**Diagonal Lines option, 522**

**diagrams**
inserting
  CorelFLOW, 911-912

**dialog boxes, 31-41**
Abbreviations, 246
accessing, 33
Add Compare Markings, 830
Add Fonts, 638, 1088
Add Template Prompt, 377-378
Address Book, 902-903
Advance, 196-197
Advanced Find, 932, 936
Advanced Multiple Pages, 896
  specifying page ranges, 284-285
Associate, 382, 591
Basic Counts, 231
Bookmark, 1062
Border/Fill, 754
Box Caption, 673
Box Content, 671
Box Position, 673
Box Size, 674
Box Style, 275
Bullets & Numbers, 465
buttons, 33
  lookup, 35-36
  QuickSpots, 39-41
  radio, 35
  selecting, 34
Center Page(s) dialog box, 158
Change Path, 1082-1083
Character, 719
check boxes, 34-35
Checking Styles, 229
Close All Documents, 77
closing keyboard, 41
Codes, 152
Codes Page Preferences, 312
Color Palettes, 708
Column Border, 456
Column Border/Fill, 38, 260, 456
Columns, 34-35, 438-440
Columns Define, 733
Columns Definition, 439-440
Columns dialog box, 445-446

dialog boxes 1153

Condense/Save Subdocuments, 883
Confirm File Delete, 921
Confirm File Replace, 919
Confirm Folder Delete, 924
Contour Text, 714
Convert File Format, 565-568
Convert Preferences, 320, 561
Convert Table, 500
Copy Abbreviation, 247
Copy Toolbars, 420
Copy/Remove Template Objects, 380-381
CorelFLOW 3, 640
Create Bookmark, 1027
Create Data File, 589
Create Data Link, 577-578
Create Full Form, 851
Create Graphics Line, 659
Create Hypertext Link, 1028, 1064
Create Keyboard, 326, 406-407
Create Labels, 192-193
Create Merge File, 589
Create New Address Book, 900
Create Table, 498
Create Table Style, 988
Create/Edit Graphic Line, 753
creating macros, 974
Current Document, 1012
Custom Box, 275
Custom Page Numbering, 168, 171-172
Customize Button, 424
Customize Number Type, 1000
Default Labels Folder, 318
Define Color Palette, 129, 708
Define Color Printing Palette, 752
Define Index, 863
Define List, 838, 842
Define Table of Authorities, 855

Define Table of Contents, 846
Delay Codes, 186
Delete, 505
Delete Address Book, 902
Delete Styles, 346-347
Delete Table, 505
disabling, 57
Display, 141
Display Preferences, 141, 145, 300, 303-304
Document, 315
Document Initial Font, 33, 198
Document Summary Configuration, 205-206
Document Summary Preferences, 204, 319
e-mail, 612-613
Edit Box, 671, 677, 768
Edit Checking Styles, 229
Edit Current Cell, 545
Edit Data Link, 577-578
Edit Footnote, 805, 808
Edit Full Form, 853
Edit Graphics Line, 658, 660, 662
Edit Graphics Menu, 760
Edit Hypertext Link, 1030
Edit Label File, 196
Edit Labels, 194
Edit List, 839
Edit Named Settings, 288
Edit Outline Definition, 489
Edit Page Size, 181-182
Edit Printer/Document Font Mapping, 650
Edit Table of Authorities, 856
Edit Table QuickSpot, 507
Endnote, 805
Endnote Options, 818-819
Endnote Placement, 819, 894
Envelope, 188-189, 594, 617
Envelope Options, 190
Environment Preferences, 306

Equation Font, 795
Equation Font Settings, 795
Error, 1082
Exclude, 547
Expand Master Document, 878-881
Explode Slice, 557
File Open, 950-951
Files Preferences, 32-35, 312-315, 401
Find and Replace Text, 152
Finish Document, 914
Font, 32, 33, 127, 198, 650, 752, 795, 1052
Font Map, 833
Footnote Number, 811
Footnote Options, 812
Force Page dialog box, 157
Generate, 843, 887
GETSTRING, 961-962
Go To, 24, 64-66, 443, 1063
Gradient Settings, 555, 711
Grammatik, 225
Graphics Styles, 795, 990
Guidelines, 26, 57, 526
Help, 47, 48-52
Hide Bars Information, 415
Image Editor, 425
Image Settings, 682
Import Data, 541, 566-568, 574-576, 907, 987
Insert Columns/Rows, 513
Insert Field Name or Number, 592
Insert File, 86, 701
Insert Image, 268, 677, 910
Insert Merge Code, 619-620
Insert Merge Codes, 608
Insert Number in Text, 170-172
Insert Object, 584, 909-910
Insert Sound Clip Into Document, 1040
Installation Progress, 1083
Keep Text Together, 160-161
Keyboard Preferences, 325, 406-407, 774

## dialog boxes

Keyboard Shortcuts, 406-407
Label File, 195-196
Labels, 318
Language, 228, 237, 654
Language Resource Database Properties, 237
Layout, 552
Letter Expert, 385
Line Height, 134
Line Hyphenation, 150
Line Separator, 815
Line Spacing, 133, 739
Link Options, 578
Links, 583
list boxes, 36-37
Location of Files, 410
Macro Location, 394
Macros Help, 961
Mail To, 296
Main Word List Editor, 219
Make It Fit Expert, 187
Manual Kerning, 746
Margin, 730
Margins, 34, 135, 953-954
Menu Bar Preferences, 324
MENULIST, 963
Merge, 588
Merge Message, 609-611
Multiple Pages, 284
navigating, 32-33
New Organization Properties, 902-903
New Page Size, 181
New Slide Show, 911
Object Properties, 698, 712
Open, 14, 82, 220, 918
Open File, 86, 294, 397
opening, 739
Other Codes, 149, 630
Outline Define, 339, 474, 487, 493-494
Outline Definition Copy, 493-494
Outline Definition Duplicate, 493-494
Overstrike, 646-647
Overwrite/New Name, 326, 420
Page Border/Fill, 259
Page Number Format, 840
Page Numbering, 167-168
Page Numbering Font, 165-168
Page Size, 180-181
Pages, 175
Paragraph, 39
Paragraph Border/Fill, 256-257
Paragraph Properties, 125
Password, 566
PerfectFit Conversions, 988
PerfectScript Commands, 960-961, 975
Perform Merge, 593, 611
Picture Settings, 556
Play Macro, 820
Play Macro dialog box, 392-393
pop-up lists, 37-38
Position Hyphen, 150, 566
Power Bar, 24
Power Bar Options, 427
Preferences, 74, 300, 774
Print, 69, 652, 896, 951
    closing, 278
    displaying, 278, 281
Print To Printer name, 179-180
Printer Initial Font, 292
Printer Name, 197-198
Printers, 290
Prompt Builder, 377
Properties, 201, 240
Properties for New Entry, 903
Quick Data Entry, 598-600
QuickCorrect, 224, 238-239, 647
QuickCorrect Options, 239
QuickFinder, 931
QuickFinder Custom Fast Search, 942
QuickFinder Fast Search Information, 944
QuickFinder Fast Search Setup Expert, 931
QuickFinder Manager, 940
QuickFinder Preferences, 946-947
QuickFinder Select Subfolder, 932
QuickFinder Standard Fast Search, 941
QuickFormat, 144
QuickSpot Paragraph Properties, 137
QuickStyle, 342-343
Ready To Install, 1083
Record Macro, 390-391, 953-954
Recycle Bin Properties, 921
Redline, 201, 832
Rename Address Book, 901
Reset Custom Installation, 1085-1086
Retrieve Equation Text, 796
Retrieve Styles From, 357
Save As, 37, 72, 568-569
Save Data File As, 590
Save Document Summary, 205
Save Equation As, 796
Save Styles To, 357
Save Template, 376
Search Operators, 933
Select Box to Edit, 768
Select Default Template Folder, 316-317
Select Directory, 35
Select File, 541
Select Labels Location, 195-196
Select Macro, 330, 406-407, 423
Select New Document, 78, 368, 378, 862
Select Output File, 613
Select Page Numbering Format, 163-164
Select Printer, 24
Select Records, 614
Select Sound File, 1038
Select Source, 716
Set Paragraph Number, 484-485

Sort, 626-628
Sound Clips, 1037-1038
Spell Checker, 209, 213, 238
Split Cell, 515
Status Bar Options, 323-324
Status Bar Preferences, 25, 322-324
Style List, 340
Style Setup, 345-346
Styles Copy, 347-348
Styles Editor, 338, 344, 348-349, 468-469, 1032-1033
Subdocument, 874-876
Subdocument Error, 879-881
Suppress, 177
Tab Set, 142-143
Table Cut/Copy, 506
Table Format, 512, 516, 521
Table Lines/Fill, 525, 528, 989
Table Names in Current Document, 1013
Table Numeric Format, 999
Table SpeedFormat, 524, 988
Template Information, 377
text boxes, 34
Text/Background, 1056
Texture Settings, 555
Toolbar Editor, 421, 956
Toolbar Editor—Graphics, 421
Toolbar Editor—Power Bar, 428
Toolbar Options, 419
Toolbar Preferences, 321, 408-409, 415
Toolbars, 57, 125
Tools, 507, 982
Undo/Redo History, 90
Undo/Redo Options, 89-91

User Word List Editor, 219, 223, 228
Value/Adjust Number, 171-172
Values, 168-169
View File Location Preferences, 314-315
Word and Letter Spacing, 745, 748-749
WordPerfect Characters, 201, 644, 762, 776, 1061
WPWin, 961-962
Zoom, 279
Zoom Equation Display, 777

**Dialog Editor button (Macro Feature Bar), 952-953**

**DialogCreate command, 974**

**DialogDisplay command, 974**

**dictionaries, 209**
default user word list, 209
document user word lists, 209
adding words to, 215
main word lists, 209, 220-224
inserting into, 220-221
QuickCorrect
adding words to user word lists, 215
troubleshooting, 224
Spell Checker, 211
TEMPLATE, 372
user word lists, 209, 220-224
adding words to, 214-215, 223
creating, 221-222
editing, 223

**dingbats, 643**

**Disable Cell Locks option (tables), 523**

**disabling**
check boxes, 287
dialog boxes, 57
grammar rules in Grammatik, 227
scroll bars, 26
*see also* turning on/off

**Discontinue option (QuickFormat dialog box), 145**

**discontinuing**
footers in documents, 178
headers in documents, 178

**disks**
copying documents from, 82
saving documents to, 70-74

**Display a Bookmark command (Options menu), 54**

**Display As Markers option**
Merge Feature Bar, 603
Merge Form File Feature Bar, 605

**Display Codes option**
Merge Feature Bar, 603
Merge Form File Feature Bar, 605

**DISPLAY command**
DISPLAY (Off!), 972-973
DISPLAY (On!), 972-973
points to keep in mind when using, 973

**Display dialog box, 141**

**display heads, 744**

**Display Last Open Filenames menu displays, 308-309**

**Display menu commands, Hide Completed Jobs, 290**

**Display Options tab, 553**

**Display Pane (Equation Editor), 763, 776-777**

**Display Preferences dialog box, 141, 145, 300, 303-304**
**Display Ruler Bar (WordPerfect), 1098**
**Display Shortcut Keys menu displays, 309**
**displaying**
  bars, 125
  bookmarks, 54
  charts, 553
  codes in documents, 41
  dialog boxes, 64, 279
  documents, multiple, 43
  equations, 776-777
    troubleshooting, 763
  files, 925
  folders, 925
  font mapping, editing, 651-653
  formatting symbols in documents, 303-304
  hard returns in documents, 42
  hidden bars, 31
  highlighting, 826
  Image Tools palette, 677
  labels
    x-axis, 550
    y-axes, 550
  languages in documents, 307
  large icons, 926
  legend title, 550
  measurements in documents, 303
  merge codes in documents, 306
  page numbers, 62
  Parse Tree, 230-231
  Parts of Speech diagrams, 230-231
  print jobs, 290
  QuickMenu, 123
  reveal codes, 837
  rows of toolbar buttons, 419

Ruler Bar, 25, 140-141, 306
  spaces in documents, 42
  status bar, 25
  styles, 345-346
  Tables toolbar, 982
  tabs in documents, 42
  text
    columns (scroll bar), 443
    hidden, 128
  toolbars, 23
    Generate, 829
    troubleshooting, 125
  user information in documents, 307
  *see also* viewing

**displays, customizing, 300-306**
**DLINE (double vertical line), 784**
**Document command (Format menu), 656, 806**
**Document Control button, 19**
**Document Control menu, 19-20**
**Document dialog box, 315**
**Document Initial Font dialog box, 33, 198**
**Document menu commands**
  Cancel Printing, 282, 290
  Pause Printing, 290
  Remove, 290
**Document option (Spell Checker), 218**
**Document Review Bar buttons, 828, 1095**
**Document Summary, 1098**
**Document Summary Configuration dialog box, 205-206**

**Document Summary Preferences dialog box, 204, 319**
**document user word lists, 209**
  adding words to, 215
**documents**
  activating, 44
  Advance command, placing text on pre-printed forms, 196-197
  automatic cross-referencing, 865-868
    marking references, 866-868
  blank, starting, 366
  borders, 257, 259-260
    deleting, 261
    turning off, 260-261
  charts, 536-537, 541-544
    data, 537-538, 544-548
    formatting data, 546
    labels, 550-551
    legends, 549-550
    moving between documents and charts, 544
    placement, 558
    titles, 548-549
    types, 538-541
    updating, 545
    *see also* charts
  closing, 71, 77
  codes, 41, 337-338
    editing, 312
    viewing, 41
  colors
    creating, 756
    highlighting, 826
  columns
    ease of readability, 436
    enhancing appearance, 455-456
    subdividing, 184-185
    types, 434-436

comments, 241-244
    converting, 244
    creating, 241-242
    editing, 243-244
controls, 19-20
Convert feature, exporting, 568-569
converting
    editing, 566-568
    formatting complexity, 560-561
    into HTML documents, 1047
    to HTML documents, 1047
    to intermediate format, 570
    Rich Text Format (RTF), 569-570
    saving, 568
    specifying format, 566-569
    from unknown format, 566
    to WordPerfect format, 565-566
copying
    from disks to screens, 82
    formatting codes, 348
    graphics, 348
    styles, 347-348
creating
    graphic styles, 339-340
    Outline styles, 339
    QuickStyle, 342-343
    styles, 340, 343-345
    troubleshooting fonts, 652
defaults
    folders, 315-316
    margins, subdividing, 185
delay codes
    inserting, 185-188
    physical pages versus page numbers basis, 186

desktop publishing
    colors, 750
    columns, 731
    columns, custom widths, 732
    columns, gutter space, 735-736
    design, 725-728
    planning page presentation, 729
    refining page presentation, 736-740
    selecting fonts, 740
    text alignment, 737-739
displays
    customizing, 300-303
    Full Page, 305
    Margin Width, 305
    Page Width, 305
    Ruler Bar, 306
    Two-page mode, 304-305
    zooming, 305
drop caps, adding, 658
editing
    initial style, 338
    Redline font tool, 200-201
    Strikeout font tool, 200-201
    styles, 344-345
    system styles, 338
    template style, 338-339
endnotes, placing, 893-894
envelopes, addressing, 188-189
environment options
    Automatically Select Words, 310
    beep, 308
    confirmation deletion, 309
    customizing, 306
    hyphenation formatting, 309
    languages, 307
    menu display, 308-309
    Save Workspace feature, 308
    user information, 307

facing pages, setting, 162
faxing, 294-295
file extensions, modifying, 315-316
footers, 173
    adding graphics, 178-179
    creating, 173-176
    discontinuing, 178
    editing, 176
    replacing, 179
    searching, 179
    spellchecking, 178-179
    suppressing, 177
    working with page numbers, 176-177
formatting, 156
    displaying, 303-304
gopher sites, creating links, 1034
graphics, color, 753-756
graphics boxes, 262
    adding to letters, 271-272
    creating, 268-269
    deleting, 271
    moving, 269
    selecting, 269
    sizing, 270
    styles, 262
    troubleshooting, 275
    watermarks, 272-275
hard returns, displaying, 42
headers
    adding graphics, 178-179
    creating, 173-176
    discontinuing, 178
    editing, 176
    replacing, 179
    searching, 179
    spellchecking, 178-179
    suppressing, 177
    utilizing, 173
    working with page numbers, 176-177

HTML (HyperText
  Markup Language)
  address blocks,
    1054-1058
  alignment, 1057-1058
  body text, 1050
  bookmarks, 1062-1063
  character formatting,
    1053-1054
  color, 1056-1057
  converting WordPerfect
    documents into, 1047
  creating, 1045
  creating bullets/lists,
    1054-1056
  creating links, 1061
  graphics, 1058-1061
  graphics, formats,
    1058-1059
  graphics, lines,
    1059-1060
  headings, 1050-1053
  hypertext links,
    1063-1064
  hypertext links, editing,
    1065
  hypertext links, graphic
    images, 1066
  marketing, 1070
  marketing, newsgroups,
    1070
  marketing, search
    engines, 1070
  placing on server,
    1068-1069
  publishing, 1067-1069
  publishing, Internet
    Service Providers
    (ISPs), 1069
  publishing, registering
    URLs, 1069
  special characters,
    1060-1061
  titles, 1049-1050
  viewing, 1068
Hypertext
  activating, 310
  designing, 1025-1026

importing, 570-572
  Convert feature,
    564-565
  Dynamic Data
    Exchange (DDE), 572
indexes
  defining, 862-864
  marking text, 859-862
initial codes style setting,
  199-200
initial font setting, 197-198
inserting
  drawings into, 716
  into other documents,
    85-86
  links, 1028-1029
interactive, 1021
intermediate format,
  converting, 569-570
length, 869
letters, creating, 59-60, 66
lines
  centering, 131-132
  copying to Clipboard, 85
  customizing with
    mouse, 252-253
  deleting, 88, 253-254
  flush right, 131-132
  formatting, 130
  graphics, 250-254
  height, 134-135
  horizontal, 250-251
  indentation, 58
  justification, 147-148
  spacing, 132-135
  vertical, 251-252
linking (Hypertext),
  1030-1033
lists
  creating, 834
  defining, 837
  generating, 886
  marking text, 835-837
looking up words in Spell
  Checker, 216-217
Make It Fit Expert
  command
  reformatting, 187
  removing (Undo
    command), 187

manual navigating, 1034
margins, 729-730
  setting, 135-136
  white space, 730
marking with bookmarks,
  1027
Master Document feature,
  870-871
master documents
  adding footers, 892
  adding headers, 892
  building, 872-876
  condensing, 882-884
  creating, 870-871
  creating endnotes, 893
  creating footnotes, 893
  creating template to
    contain styles, 888
  expanding, 878-881
  forcing page breaks,
    875-876
  inserting new page
    numbers, 891
  inserting page
    numbering codes, 890
  printing, 895
  printing selected pages,
    895-896
  saving, 881-882
  searching and
    replacing, 895
  spellchecking, 894-895
  styles, 887-888
measurements, 303
merge codes,
  displaying, 306
moving in, 61
  keyboard, 63-64
  mouse, 61-63
multiple, 43-44
  displaying, 43
  positioning on
    screen, 44
  tiling, 44
names, 71-72
  renaming, 76-77
navigating, 1034-1035
  automatic, 1034
  mouse, 16

scroll bars, 26
troubleshooting, 16
numbering
   automatically, 163
   default settings, 56
   inserting, 892
on-screen printing, 68-70
opening, 14, 82-86
   new, 78
   saved, 82-85
outlines, 461
page borders, adding, 258-259
page definition, 179
page numbers
   changing current page number, 168-169
   choosing format, 164-165
   counting, 172
   customizing appearance, 165-168
   incrementing, 169-170
   inserting, 170-172
   inserting number including formatting and text, 171-172
   inserting text, 167-168
   modifying, 165-168
   position, 163-164
   styles, 167
   suppressing, 172
page size
   choosing, 179-180
   default setting, 179
paired codes, 336
   character style, 337-338
   paragraph style, 337-338
paragraphs
   borders, 256
   borders, deleting, 261
   double indenting, 137
   ending, 59
   hanging indents, 138
   indenting, 137-138
   previewing, 73, 84
printer drivers
   formatting, 311
   troubleshooting, 312
printers, 180

printing, 280-281
   canceling print jobs, 281-282, 290
   controlling status of print jobs, 289-290
   current page, 283
   custom print options, 287-289
   displaying print jobs, 290
   double-sided, 285
   even-numbered pages, 285-286
   multiple copies, 281
   odd-numbered pages, 285-286
   previewing, 279-280
   removing print jobs from list, 290
   sorting print jobs, 290
   summaries, 287
   troubleshooting, 282
   troubleshooting font display, 652
   with color, 286-287
   with graphics, 286-287
proofreading, *see* proofreading documents
publishing, Envoy, 912-913
QuickMark, setting, 310
references
   creating, 842-843
   cross-references, 865-868
   indexes, 858
   marking, 866-867
   marking to footnotes/endnotes, 868
   Table of Authorities, 848
   Table of Contents, 843
   updating, 843
retrieving styles from other documents, 357
reveal codes, *see* reveal codes
revisions, 824
   automatically marking, 829

   highlighting, 824-826
   reviewing, 828
   routing documents for, 826-828
rows, subdividing, 184-185
saving
   file formats, 75-77
   file names, 71
   to disks, 70-74
scrolling, 61-62
sending e-mail, 295-296
Show options
   Comments features, 301-302
   Graphics features, 301-302
   Hidden Text feature, 302
   QuickSpots, 302
   Table Gridlines, 301-302
   Windows Systems Colors, 301-302
sound
   embedding, 1037
   linking, 1037-1038
   memory problems, 1037
   playing, 1040
spaces, displaying, 42
spell checking, 210
   double words, 213
   optimizing time, 221
   typos, 213
starting, QuickTasks, 913-914
styles
   activating, 353
   benefits 335
   chaining, 351-352
   copying, 347-348
   deleting , 346-347
   displaying, 345
   formatting your documents, 336
   nesting, 351
   overiding, 336
   saving, 356-357
   types, 336-338
subdocuments
   adding, 876
   creating, 871-872

documents

    deleting, 876
    editing styles, 888
    formatting, 871-872
    formatting styles, 888-889
    inserting chapter codes, 891-892
    moving within master documents, 877
    storing, 874-876
summaries
    Create Summary on Save/Exit, 320
    creating database, 201
    creating file names, 320
    customizing, 205-206, 319-320
    Default Descriptive Type, 319
    deleting, 204-205
    elements, 201
    extracting information, 204-205
    file naming rules, 320
    printing, 204-205
    saving, 205
    Subject Search Text, 319
switching between, 44
Table of Authorities
    defining, 854-858
    marking text, 850-854
Table of Contents
    defining, 845-849
    marking text, 843-845
    numbering, 847
tables
    copying, 507-508
    creating, 498
    cutting, 507-508
    defined, 496-498
    deleting, 507-508
    Edit Table QuickSpot, 507
    editing, 509
    moving in, 501-502
    printing, 508-509
    QuickMenus, 506
    saving, 508-509
    sizing, 513-514
    structure, 496
    *see also* tables
tabs, displaying, 42
templates, 368-369
    creating, 368
    *see also* templates
text
    adding, 67
    aligning, 132, 737-739
    borders, 255
    color, 751-753
    deleting, 87-88
    endnotes, 801-802
    endnotes, converting footnotes to, 820-821
    endnotes, converting to footnotes, 821
    endnotes, editing, 818
    endnotes, inserting, 818
    endnotes, manipulating, 818
    endnotes, options, 818-819
    endnotes, placing, 819-820
    entering, 56-60
    footnotes, converting endnotes to, 821
    footnotes, converting to endnotes, 820-821
    footnotes, copying, 809-810
    footnotes, cutting, 811
    footnotes, deleting, 811
    footnotes, editing, 808-809
    footnotes, inserting, 803
    footnotes, moving, 810-811
    footnotes, options, 812
    footnotes, pasting, 810
    footnotes, setting numbers, 811
    formatting, *see* text, formatting
    hidden, 128
    highlighting, 824-826
    hyphenation, 148
    inserting, 86-87
    justification, 147-148
    monospaced, 58
    overwriting, 86-87
    restoring, 88-89
    strikeout, 829
    word-wrap, 58
    *see also* text
troubleshooting
    converting to HTML, 1047
    navigating with scroll bars, 16
    printing with graphics, 288-289
    saving under different file names, 76
    viewing, 85
typing into WordPerfect, 58
updating, WP Draw, 685-686
user information, configuring, 307
viewing
    Hide Bars command, 30-31
    preview option, 73
    troubleshooting, 31
    View modes, 28-30
    zoom percentages, 279
window display, viewing, 304-305
word processing formats, Convert feature, 564
zooming, 30

**Documents command (Format menu), 123**

**Documents Display**
    measurements, 302-303
    scroll bars, 302
    Show options, 301-302

**[Dorm HRt] (dormant hard return), 156**

**dot leaders, 139**

**double curved arrows, drawing, 699**

double indenting paragraphs, 137
double vertical line (DLINE), 784
double words, 213
double-clicking (mouse operation), 15
double-sided documents, printing, 285
draft mode, 28-29, 874-876
Draft View mode
  editing footnotes, 808
  inserting footnotes, 804
Drag to Create command (Graphics menu), 682
dragging (mouse operation), 15
Draw command (Graphics menu), 684
drawing
  arcs, 695-697
  arrows, 698-699
    curved sweeping, 699
    double curves, 699
    line end, 698-699
    sweeping, 699
  circles, 697
  closed curves, 694-695
  curves, 694-695
  ellipses, 695-697
  freehand, 697
  lines, 693-695
  polygons, 694-695
  rectangles, 695-697
  shapes, 690-693
    adding text, 712-713
    attributes, 707
    attributes, color, 707, 708-709
    attributes, fills, 709
    attributes, line patterns, 710-712
    constraining, 693
    deleting, 692-693
    drawing tools, 691-692
    editing, 910
  inserting, 910
  inserting charts, 702-703
  inserting clip art, 700-701
  inserting into documents, 716
  keyboard, 692-693
  mouse, 692-693
  rectangles, 691
  removing after creating, 692
  text features, 713-714
  text wrap, 714-715
  WP Draw, 693
  squares, 697
drawing toolbar (WP Draw), 543
Drop Cap command (Format menu), 658
drop caps, adding to documents, 658
drop shadows, borders, 668-669
drop-down lists, 37
duplicating, *see* copying
Dynamic Data Exchange (DDE), 906
  documents, importing, 572
  linking data, 906
dynamic delimiters, 784

# E

e-mail, 295-296
E-mail dialog box, 612-613
Edit Box command (Graphics menu), 768
Edit Box dialog box, 671, 677, 768
Edit Box QuickSpot, 39
Edit button, 905
  Address Book dialog box, 905
  Hypertext Feature Bar, 1023-1024
Edit Checking Styles dialog box, 229
Edit command (Tools menu), 950
Edit Current Cell dialog box, 545
Edit Custom Format And Text text box, 166
Edit Data Link dialog box, 577-578
Edit Footnote dialog box, 805, 808
Edit Full Form dialog box, 853
Edit Graphics Line dialog box, 658, 660, 662
Edit Graphics Menu dialog box, 760
Edit Hypertext Link dialog box, 1030
Edit Label File dialog box, 196
Edit Labels dialog box, 194
Edit Line command (Graphics menu), 660, 662, 753
Edit Links command (Insert menu), 577-578
Edit List dialog box, 839
Edit menu commands
  Chapter, 896
  Chart Object, 544
  Clear, 545, 704
  Clear All, 545
  Convert, 561
  Copy, 506, 810, 918
  Cut, 506, 811, 918
  Delete, 547
  Equation Editor, 763
  Find and Replace, 152, 762
  Go To, 64
  Go To Cell, 542
  Insert, 547
  Paste, 542, 572, 810, 919
  Paste Link, 583

Paste Special, 584, 705
Preferences, 22, 74, 299, 372, 415, 774
Redo, 90
Rotate, 706
Select, 923
Select All, 703
Summary, 204
Undelete, 88
Undo, 89-90, 254, 692, 704, 880
Undo/Redo History, 90
WP Draw, 686

**Edit Named Settings dialog box, 288**

**Edit Outline Definition dialog box, 490-491**

**Edit Page Size dialog box, 181-182**

**Edit Printer/Document Font Mapping dialog box, 650**

**Edit Table of Authorities dialog box, 856**

**Edit Table QuickSpot, 40, 507**

**Edit Template command (Options menu), 374**

**editing**
Address Book entries, 904-905
addresses for envelopes, 189
Automatic Font Changes (AFCs), 650-651
charts
  axes, 552
  frames, 553
  grids, 553
  high/low data points, 557
  pie, 557
  in presentations, 909-910
  scatter, 557
  series changes, 554-556
  tick, 553
code page options for documents, 312
converted documents, 566-568
data file structure, 601-602
data links, 577-578
display font mapping, 651-653
Document Comments, 243-244
drawings in presentations, 910
endnotes, 818
equations, 768
fast searches, 943-944
footers in documents, 176
footnotes, 808-809
formulas, 1005
full form entries, 853
grammar problems, Grammatik, 226
graphics, starting WP Draw, 685
graphics images, 677
  brightness, 681
  color, 680
  contrast, 681
  fills, 681
  Image Settings dialog box, 682
  mirroring, 682
  moving images, 679
  rotating images, 678-679
  scaling images, 679-680
headers in documents, 176
hypertext links, 1030, 1065
initial style documents, 338
label definitions, 193
lists definition, 838
misspelled words, 214
new key assignments for keyboards, 327-331
outlines
  bullets and numbers style, 468
  definition, 489
  Outline Feature Bar, 477-478
  special keystrokes, 475
  text, 481
overstrikes, 647
page definitions for printers, 181-182
Redo feature, 89-91
separator lines (footnotes), 817
styles
  current document, 345
  definition, 349
  documents, 344-345
  system, 345
  template, 345
tables
  column width, 510-512
  creating header rows, 517-518
  joining cells, 514-515
  row height, 516-517
  sizing, 513-514
  splitting cells, 515-516
  tool selection, 509-510
template styles, 338-339
templates, 374-375
text
  in columns, 444-445
  inserting characters, 86-87
  in parallel columns, 451
  in text boxes, 34
  Typeover feature, 87
Undo feature, restoring deleted text, 88-91
user word lists, 223

**Editing Pane (Equation Editor), 762-763, 773**

**editing screen**
controls, 17-20
  Application Control menu, 18-19
  buttons, 17
  document controls, 19-20
Feature Bars, 27-28
guidelines, 25-26
Next Page button, 27

Power Bar
  customizing, 24
  hiding, 23
Previous Page button, 27
pull-down menus, 20-21
QuickMenus, 21
Ruler Bar, 25
scroll bars, 26-27
status bar, 24-25
title bar, WordPerfect
  window, 20
toolbar
  customizing, 23
  displaying, 23
  hiding, 23
  moving, 22
  positioning, 22
View modes, 28-30

**Editing the Numbering Style in Notes (Footnote Options dialog box), 814**

**Editing the Numbering Style in Text (Footnote Options dialog box), 813**

**electronic fill-in forms, 532**

**electronic mail,** *see* **e-mail**

**ellipses (...), 31**
  creating, 692
  drawing, 695-697

**elliptical arcs, creating, 692**

**ELSE command, 964-965**

**em dash (—), 642**

**embedding**
  data, 906
  equations in text, 794-795
  objects into templates, 380-381
    guidelines, 384
  sound in documents, 1037

**emphasis, designing documents for desktop publishing, 727**

**Empty option (Box Content dialog box), 672**

**emptying Recycle Bin, 921**

en dash (–), 642
**ENDFIELD code, 597**
**ENDFIELD command, 907**
**ENDIF commands, 964-965**
ending paragraphs, 59
**Endnote command (Insert menu), 818**
**Endnote dialog box, 805**
**Endnote Options dialog box, 818-819**
**Endnote Placement dialog box, 819, 894**
endnotes, 801-802
  converting footnotes to, 820-821
  converting to footnotes, 821
  creating, 893
  editing, 818
  fonts, 806
  format control
    note options, 893
    system style, 893
  inserting, 818
  manipulating, 818
  options, 818-819
  placing, 819-820
    documents, 893-894
  positioning, 802
  troubleshooting
    inserting, 820
    reference numbers, 819
  typing, 802
**ENDRECORD code, 597**
**ENDRECORD command, 907**
**ENDSWITCH command, 965-966**
entering, *see* inserting
**Envelope command (Format menu), 188-189, 617**
**Envelope Definitions drop-down list, 189**

**Envelope dialog box, 188-189, 594, 617**
**Envelope Options dialog box, 190**
envelopes
  addresses, 188-189
    changing position of, 190
    editing, 189
    font size, 189
  creating, 593-595, 617
  Envelope Definitions drop-down list, 189
  Print Return Address check box, 189
  printing, 289
  ZIP codes, 190
environment options
  Automatically Select Words options, 310
  confirmation deletion options, 309
  customizing, 306
  hyphenation formatting, 309
  languages, 307
  menu display, 308-309
  Save Workspace feature, 308
  user information, 307
**Environment Preferences dialog box, 306**
**Envoy 7**
  Corel WordPerfect Suite integrated applications, 1094
  documents
    publishing, 912-913
    viewing on networks, 912-913
**equation boxes, 264**
**Equation command**
  Font menu, 795
  Graphics menu, 761, 764
**Equation Editor, 759-760**
  commands, 770-771
    syntax, 772

components of, 762-764
creating equations, 764-768
    fractions, 766-767
    spacing, 764-765
    subscripts, 767-768
    superscripts, 767-768
Display Pane, 763, 776-777
editing equations, 768
Editing Pane, 762-763, 773
formatting equations
    functions, 781-782
    literals, 782-783
functions, 779-780
keyboard, 774
    layout types, 324-325
menu bar, 763-764
palettes, 763, 774-776
starting, 760-761
syntax of equations, 771-773
terms, 769-771
toolbar, 777-778

**Equation Font dialog box, 795**

**Equation Font Settings dialog box, 795**

**Equation Height option, 777**

**Equation Width option, 777**

**equations, 759**
    Arrows palette, 792
    characters, 776
        troubleshooting formatting, 797
    creating, 764-768
        fractions, 766-767
        spacing, 764-765
        subscripts, 767-768
        superscripts, 767-768
    diacritical marks (Other palette), 791
    displaying, 776-777
        troubleshooting, 763
    editing, 768
    embedding in text, 794-795
    Equation Editor, 760
        components of, 762-764
        functions, 779-780
        starting, 760-761
    files
        retrieving, 796-797
        saving, 796-797
    fonts
        changing, 795
        troubleshooting, 797
    formattig
        functions, 781-782
        literals, 782-783
    fractions, *see* fractions
    functions, troubleshooting, 797
    inserting characters into, 773
    integrals, creating, 785-786
    matrices, creating, 787-789
    multiline expressions, creating, 790-791
    numbering, 794
    palettes
        inserting commands, 775-776
        inserting symbols, 775-776
        viewing, 776
    roots, creating, 787
    saving files, 796-797
    spacing, troubleshooting, 778
    sums, creating, 785-786
    symbols (Large palette), 792
    Symbols palette, 792
    syntax, 771-773
    troubleshooting
        character formatting, 797
        fonts, 797
    verifying, 760-761
    viewing, 763, 776-777

**Error dialog box, 1082**

**ERROR: Incorrect Syntax message, 771**

**errors, *see* troubleshooting**

**Esc button, 68**
    deleting shapes, 692

**etiquette, Internet, 1071**

**even-numbered pages, printing, 285-286**

**events, triggering macros, 383**

**Exclude dialog box, 547**

**Exclude Row/Col. command (Data menu), 547**

**Exclude Row/Column feature, 547**

**Exit command**
    File menu, 12, 79
    Options menu, 54

**Exit Template option (Template Feature Bar), 370**

**exiting**
    help, 54
    WordPerfect 7, 12, 79
    *see also* closing

**exp function, 779**

**Expand Master command (File menu), 878-881**

**Expand Master Document dialog box, 878-881**

**expanding master documents, 878-881**

**Explode Slice dialog box, 557**

**Explode Slice option (Layout/Type dialog box), 557**

**Explorer, starting, 930**

**exporting**
    data to spreadsheets, 581
    documents with Convert feature, 568-569
    outlines for Presentations, 910-911

**expressions, multiline, 790-791**

Extended Characters check box, 947
extensions
    DAT file, merge data files, 590
    file names, 72
        TTF (TrueType fonts), 637
    viewing, 929
    WPD, 72
extracting information for document summaries, 204-205

# F

F1 (Help) command, 46
facing pages, 162
fast searches
    creating, 940-942
    custom, 942-943
    defined, 939
    editing, 943-944
    preferences, 945-947
    updating, 944
    viewing, 944-945
Favorites folder, 937-939
    opening, 937-938
    shortcuts
        adding, 938
        deleting, 938-939
        selecting, 938
        troubleshooting, 939
Favorites menu commands
    Add, 938
    Go To, 937
Fax Expert, 386
faxing documents, 294-295
Feature Bar, 27-28
    selecting buttons, 31
    templates, 369-370
        creating, 375-378
        editing, 374-375
Field Names option (Quick Data Entry dialog box), 599

fields, data files, 596
    names, 596, 598
figure boxes, 263
Figure tool, retrieving clip art, 702
File command (Insert menu), 82, 85-86, 701
file extensions
    DAT, merge data files, 590
    modifying documents, 315-316
    viewing, 929
file formats, saving documents, 75-77
File menu
    Equation Editor, 763
    WP Draw, 686
File menu commands
    Close, 71, 77
    Condense Master, 883
    Delete, 639, 920, 924
    Exit, 12, 79
    Expand Master, 878-881
    Insert File, 796
    Install New Font, 637
    Internet Publisher, 1045
    New, 78, 368
    New Folder, 923
    Open, 14, 82, 918, 950-951
    Page Range, 896
    Print, 69, 278, 280, 895, 923
    Properties, 203, 921
    Publish to Envoy, 912-913
    Restore, 924
    Save, 74, 796
    Save As, 72, 376, 720
    Send, 296
    Subdocument, 874-876
file name extension
    MD (master documents), 872-876
    SUB (subdocuments), 872-876
    TTF (TrueType fonts), 637
file names, 247-248, 929
    extensions, 72
    in folders, 72
    long, 930

MS-DOS, 929
saving documents, 71
    under different names, 75-77
    troubleshooting, 248
File On Disk option (Perform Merge dialog box), 612
File Open dialog box, 950-951
file preferences, customizing labels, 318
File Preferences dialog box, 74, 372
FileNew command, 976-977
FileOpenDlg command, 976-977
files
    ASCII Delimited Text Files, setting conversion preferences, 562
    attributes, 921-922
    backup options
        Original Document Backup, 316
        Timed Document Backup feature, 316
    concordance
        creating, 862
        marking text to create indexes, 861-862
    conversion options, customizing, 320
    copying, 918-919
    custom label definitions, creating, 195-196
    data
        arranging records, 624
        associating with form files, 605-606
        converting records, 622-623
        creating tables, 623-624
        data entry, in existing files, 600-601
        data entry, Quick Data Entry dialog box, 598-600

files

defining records
  selection, 615
editing structure,
  601-602
fields, 596
marking records,
  616-617
records, 596
selecting records,
  614-615
types, 597-598
user input information,
  capturing, 619-620
user input information,
  controlling, 621-622
user input information,
  creating, 619-622
deleting, 920-921
  macros, 412
displaying, 925
equation
  retrieving, 796-797
  saving, 796-797
finding, 928
  For Type option,
    929-930
  QuickFinder feature,
    931
  wildcards, 930-931
folders, *see* folders
forms, 604
  associating data files,
    605-606
  creating, 591-593
  envelopes, creating,
    593-595, 617
  keyboard codes,
    displaying, 609-611
  mailing labels,
    creating, 618
  merge codes, 607-608
  merge codes,
    displaying, 609
  merge codes,
    inserting, 608
  Merge Feature bar, 604
  performing merges,
    595-596
graphics, 702
icon vs. name, 920

importing, setting
  preferences, 561
macros
  accessing, 950-951
  printing, 951
Master Document types,
  870-871
merge data
  creating, 588-591
  DAT file extension, 590
moving, 918-919
multiple, 923
names, 920, 929
  long, 930
  MS-DOS, 929
  troubleshooting, 924
naming conventions, 873
opening as copies, 922-923
password-protected files,
  importing, 578-579
pasting, 919
preferences, customizing,
  312-315
printing, 923
printing to, 294
selecting
  contiguous, 923
  noncontiguous, 923
sorting, 926-927
  Arrange Icons by
    option, 927
  by icons, 926-927
STANDARD.QAD, 701
templates, *see* templates
troubleshooting
  deleting, 924
  finding, 937
  moving, 924
  selecting, 924
WP7US.WPT, 365
WPG, 701

**Files Preferences
  dialog box, 32-35,
  312-315, 401**

**FileSaveAsDlg command,
  976-977**

**Fill Attributes
  option (Series property
  sheet), 555**

**Fill Attributes palette, 711**
**Fill Attributes tab, 553**
**Fill Attributes tool, 709**
**Fill Color palette, 707**
**Fill Color tool
  (WP Draw), 697**
**fills**
  adding to paragraph
    borders, 257
  borders, 669
  color, 754-757
  graphics boxes, 675
  images, 681
  shapes, 709
    changing, 697
    troubleshooting, 712
  styles, charts, 555-556
  tables, 528-529
    alternating between
      rows and columns,
      988-990
    color, 990

**Find and Replace
  command (Edit menu),
  152, 713, 762**

**Find and Replace Text
  dialog box, 152**

**Find option (Quick Data
  Entry dialog box), 599**

**Find QuickMark command
  (Insert menu), 310**

**Find Setup Wizard, 50**

**Find tab (Help dialog box),
  50-53**

**finding**
  files, 928
    For Type option,
      929-930
    QuickFinder feature,
      931
    troubleshooting, 937
    wildcards, 930-931
  help with macros, macros
    online help, 955-956

macros
  folders, 410-411
  troubleshooting, 401
  templates, list of, 372-373

**Finish Document dialog box, 914**

**First option (Quick Data Entry dialog box), 600**

**FIRSTCAP (merge code), 621-622**

**flagging**
  correctly spelled words, troubleshooting, 232
  long sentences, 232

**floating cells**
  calendar math, 1015-1016
  creating, 1014-1015
  data entry, 1018

**flow charts, inserting, 911-912**

**flush right, lines, 131-132**

**Flush Right command (Quick menu), 176**

**Flush Right with Dot Leaders (WordPerfect), 1095**

**folders**
  creating, 923-924
    macros, 410
  defaults, 925
  displaying, 925
  Favorites, 937-939
    adding shortcuts, 938
    deleting shortcuts, 938-939
    opening, 937-938
    selecting shortcuts, 938
  file names in, 72
  finding macros, 410-411
  FONTS, 637-638
  MACROS, 820
  modifying files, 313-315
  moving macros, 410
  names, 923-924

  removing, 923-924
  selecting as defaults, 74
  sorting, 926-927
    Arrange Icons by option, 927
    by icons, 926-927
  storing additional templates, 317

**Followed by (..) operator, 934**

**Font command**
  Format menu, 127, 262, 650, 752, 953-954
  Options menu, 54
  Quick menu, 176

**Font dialog box, 32-33, 127, 198, 650, 752, 795, 1052**

**Font Face button (Power Bar), 130**

**Font Face list box, 36**

**Font Face option (Font dialog box), 127**

**Font Map dialog box, 833**

**Font menu commands**
  Character, 769, 776
  Equation Editor, 764, 795

**Font Properties feature, 713**

**Font Size button (Power Bar), 130**

**Font Size list box, 36, 198**

**Font Size option (Font dialog box), 127**

**Font Size text box, 37**

**Font Style list box, 36, 198**

**Font Style option (Font dialog box), 127**

**Font Style tool, 718**

**Font tool, 718**

**fonts**
  adding to printers, 292-293
  appearance, 128

  attributes, 741-742
  applying, 127
    applying to overstrikes, 646
    underlining, 742
  Automatic Font Changes (AFCs), 648
    attributes, 648-650
    editing, 650-651
  cartridge, 635
  colors, 129
  deleting from FONTS folder, 638
  display mapping, editing, 651-653
  endnotes, 806
  equations
    changing, 795
    troubleshooting, 797
  families, 740
  Font Size list box, 198
  Font Style list box, 198
  footnotes, 806
  graphic, 634
  initial font in documents, 197-198
  installing
    CD-ROM, 1087-1088
    from network drives, 638
    WordPerfect, 1087-1088
  internal, 635
  management, 634-636
  mapping, 648
  printer, 634, 741
  Redline, 200-201
  scalable, 635
  selecting, 740
  shading, 129
  size, 127, 130, 189
  smart quotes, 647
  soft, 635
  Strikeout, 200-201
  styles, 127, 130
  troubleshooting, 647, 750
    document creation from other computers, 652
    print display, 652

TrueType, 636, 741
    advantages, 636
    installing, 636-639
    installing in Windows
        95, 637-638
    installing, Word-
        Perfect 7, 639-640
    removing from
        Windows 95, 639
    TTF file name
        extension, 637
type sizes, 742-745
typefaces, 740-742
    changing, 833-834
typographical controls, 745
    kerning, 746-747
    leading, 745
    letterspacing, 747-748
    word spacing, 749-750

**Fonts dialog box, 1088**

**FONTS folder, 637-638**

**footers**
    adding graphics, 178-179
    adding to master
        documents, 892
    creating, 173-176
    discontinuing, 178
    editing, 176
    page numbers, 176-177
    replacing, 179
    searching, 179
    spellchecking, 178-179
    suppressing, 177

**Footnote command
(Insert menu), 803,
811, 817, 893**

**Footnote menu
commands, Options, 817**

**Footnote Number dialog
box, 811**

**Footnote Options dialog
box, 812**

**footnotes, 801-817**
    converting endnotes
        to, 821
    converting to endnotes,
        820-821

copying, 809-810
creating, 893
cutting, 811
deleting, 811
editing, 808-809
fonts, 806
format control
    note options, 893
    system style, 893
inserting, 803-808
moving, 810-811
navigating, 807
numbering options, 893
options, 812
    Changing Footnote
        Options for the
        Entire, 817
    Changing the Spacing
        Between Notes,
        814-815
    Choosing a Separator
        Line, 815-816
    Editing the Numbering
        Style in Notes, 814
    Editing the Numbering
        Style in Text, 813-814
    Insert (Continued…)
        Message, 815
    numbering style,
        812-813
    Restart Numbering
        On Each Page,
        813-814, 817
    Specifying the Position
        for Footnotes, 815
    Splitting Long
        Footnotes, 815
    Text under Edit
        Numbering Style,
        813-814
pasting, 810
positioning, 802
printing languages, 815
referencing numbers, 803
setting numbers, 811
spacing, 806
troubleshooting, 817
typing, 802

**For Type option, 929-930**

**Force Page command
(Format menu), 876**
    forcing a new page, 157

**Force Page dialog
box, 157**

**[Force: Even] code,
forcing an even page
number, 158**

**[Force: New] code, forcing
a new page, 157**

**[Force: Odd] code,
forcing an odd page
number, 158**

**foreign language versions
of WordPerfect 7,
653-656**
    character maps, 656
    inserting foreign language
        codes, 653-655
    keyboards, 655-656
    printing footnotes, 815

**form files, 604-611**
    associating data files,
        605-606
    creating, 591-593
    envelopes, creating,
        593-595, 617
    keyboard codes,
        displaying, 609-611
    mailing labels,
        creating, 618
    merge codes, 607-608
        displaying, 609
        inserting, 608
    Merge Feature Bar,
        604-605
    performing merges,
        595-596

**Format command**
    Data menu, 546
    QuickMenu, 516
    Table menu, 512, 516

**Format feature, 713**

**Format menu, 122**
    formatting text, 123
    WP Draw, 687

**Format menu commands**
Advance, 196-197
Border/Fill, 256-257, 259, 733
Color Palettes, 707-708
Columns, 731, 984
Count Pages, 172
Delay Codes, 186
Document, 656, 806
Documents, 123
Drop Cap, 658
Envelope, 188-189, 617
Font, 127, 262, 650, 752, 953-954
Force Page, 876
Headers/Footers, 174-176
Initial Font, 198
Initial Style, 199-200
Justification, 147
Justification All, 148
Labels, 191, 318, 618
Line, 131, 630, 739
Line Attributes, 694
Make It Fit Expert, 187
Margins, 135, 258, 730, 953-954
Object Properties, 694, 698, 711
Options, 190
Page Numbering, 170-171, 847, 892
Page Size, 180
Paragraph, 137, 740, 803
QuickFormat, 144
Redline Method, 200-201
Select, 163-164
Subdivide page, 184-185
Suppress, 172-173
Text/Background Colors, 1056
Title, 1049
Typesetting, 135, 646, 745
Watermark, 733

**formats,** *see* **file formats**

**formatting**
cells of tables, 521-522
paired codes, 336
columns, 731
codes, 444
of tables, 519-521
data, charts, 546
documents
displaying Toolbar, 156
Document styles, 336
for specific printer drivers, 311
equations
functions, 781-782
literals, 782-783
IF commands, 964-965
labels, 192
lines, 130
centering, 131-132
flush right, 131-132
height, 134-135
margins, 135-136
spacing, 132-134
numeric data in spreadsheets, 999-1001
styles, 334
subdocuments, 871-872
to ensure consistency, 888-889
styles, 889
symbols, 303-304
Table of Authority entries, 856-858
tables, 522-523
borders, 528
cell lines, 526
fills, 528-529
guidelines, 526
lines, 525
SpeedFormat, 524
troubleshooting, 523
text
appearance, 126-129
auto code placement, 126
character attributes, 130
characters, 126-130
customizing format options, 145-146
defaults, 122-123
Format menu, 123
in graphics boxes, 262
keyboard, 125
macros, 404-405
QuickMenu, 123
QuickFormat, 125-126, 144-145
QuickSpots, 125
setting changes, 124-125
size, 126-129
symbols, 146
tables, 518
tables, precedence, 518-519
tables, Table Format dialog box, 519

**formatting commands (Format menu), 155-206**

**forms, creating**
electronic fill-in, 532-533
phone message, 532
with irregular columns, 985

**formulas**
absolute references, 1008-1009
calculating, 1005
creating, letter grade formulas, 1010-1011
percent formulas, 1010
Quiz Points averages, 1009
reporting averages, 1008
total points formulas, 1009-1010
deleting, 1005
modifying, 1005
spreadsheets, 996
copying, 1003-1004
creating, 1001-1003
designing, 996-997
forcing text mode, 1001
formatting numeric data, 999-1001
functions, 1004-1005
pasting, 576
troubleshooting, 1018
updating, 1004

**forward slash (\), 935**

**fractions, 766-767**
   creating
      LEFT command, 783-785
      OVER command, 766-767, 783-785
      RIGHT command, 783-785

**Frame command (Chart menu), 553**

**frames (charts), editing, 553**

**freehand drawing, 697**
   mouse, 692

**FROM command, 770, 785**

**Front command (Graphics menu), 706**

**Full Equation option, 777**

**Full option**
   Alignment section of Table Format dialog box, 520
   Edit Graphics Line dialog box, 663, 665

**Full Page document display, 305**

**Full Page option (Zoom dialog box), 280**

**Full Page zoom value, 30**

**full justification, 739**

**FUNC command, 770**
   formatting equations, 782

**Function palette (Equation Editor), 775**

**functions, 1007-1008**
   defined, 769
   Equation Editor, 779-780
   equations
      formatting, 781-782
      troubleshooting, 797
   formulas, 1004-1005
   IF( ), creating letter grade formulas, 1010-1011
   PMT( ), calculating loan payments, 1016-1017
   SUM( ), creating total points formulas, 1009-1010

# G

**gcd function, 780**

**General tab (TextArt), 717-718**

**Generate command (Tools menu), 803, 887**

**Generate dialog box, 843, 887**

**Generate Lists command (Tools menu), 836**

**Generate toolbar, displaying, 829**

**generating**
   lists from marked text, 886
   table of contents, 887

**GETSTRING command, 960-962**

**GETSTRING dialog box, 961-962**

**glossary of terms, 52-53**

**GO command, 969**

**Go To Cell command (Edit menu), 542**

**Go To command**
   Edit menu, 64
   Favorites menu, 937

**Go To Data feature, 605**

**Go To dialog box, 24, 64, 1063**
   column movement, 443
   options, 64-66

**Go To feature, moving insertion point, 64-66**

**Go To Form feature, 606**

**gopher sites, creating links, 1034**

**grade-tracking tables, 1006-1007**
   creating report cards, 1011-1014
   form creation, 1011-1012
   formulas with absolute references, 1008-1009
   functions, 1007-1008
   letter grade formulas, 1010-1011
   names
      creating, 1012-1013
      navigating with, 1013-1014
   percent formulas, 1010
   Quick Points average, 1009
   total points formulas, 1009-1010

**Gradient Settings dialog box, 555, 711**

**gradients, troubleshooting, 711**
   fill style, charts, 555

**Grammatik, 207, 224-232**
   correcting grammar problems, 226
   customizing, 228-229
   disabling grammar rules, 227
   help, 227-228
   readability score, 231
   running, 225-228
   skipping errors, 226
   starting, 225
   statistics check, 231-232
   word replacement, 227
   writing styles, 229-230

**Grammatik command (Tools menu), 225**

**Grammatik dialog box, 225**

**graphic fonts, 634**

**graphic styles, 339-340**

**Graphic Styles dialog box, 994**

**graphics**
   aligning, 693
   brightness, 681

capturing with WP Draw, 715-716
clip art, importing, 582
color, 680, 753-756
contrast, 681
creating
  Drag To Create feature, 682
  WP Draw, 684-685
customizing toolbars, 424-427
editing, 677, 685
files, 702
fills, 681
formatting, 910
HTML documents, 1058-1061
importing, 581-582, 676-677
labels, applying, 192
as links, 1066
Metafiles, setting conversion preferences, 562-563
mirroring, 682
moving, 679
printing documents with, 286-288
rotating, 678-679
scaling, 679-680
scanning with WP Draw, 715-716
tables
  adding, 529
  troubleshooting, 532
troubleshooting
  formats, 1059
  printing, 757
see also images

**graphics borders, 255-261**
  color, 754
  columns, 259-260
  pages, 258-261
  paragraphs, 256
    adding fills, 257
    deleting, 261

**Graphics Box Edit Box palette, 793**

**graphics boxes, 262-272**
  adding to letters, 271-272
  creating, 268-269, 275
  customizing, 669
    borders, 675
    captions, 672-673
    contents, 671-672
    fills, 675
    positioning, 673-674
    size, 674-675
    styles, 670-671
    text wrap, 675
  default line styles, 262
  deleting, 271
  formatting text, 262
  lists, 841-842
  moving, 269
  positioning, 262
  selecting, 269
  sizing, 270
  styles, 262
  troubleshooting, 275
  watermarks, 272-275

**Graphics commands (View menu), 302**

**Graphics features, documents, 301-302**

**graphics lines, 250-254**
  color, 753
  horizontal, 250-253
  troubleshooting, 261
  vertical, 251-253

**Graphics menu commands**
  Chart, 541, 702
  Contour Text, 714
  Custom Box, 275
  Custom Line, 659, 753
  Drag to Create, 682
  Draw, 684
  Edit Box, 768
  Edit Line, 660-662, 753
  Equation, 761, 764
  Front, 706
  Graphics Styles, 670, 795
  Horizontal Line, 251, 1060
  Image, 268
  Inline Equation, 794
  Inline Equations, 778
  Insert, 677
  TextArt, 720
  Vertical Line, 252
  WP Draw, 687

**Graphics Styles command (Graphics menu), 670, 795**

**Graphics Styles dialog box, 795, 990**

**graphs,** *see* **charts**

**Greek character set (Set 8), 643**

**Greek palette (Equation Editor), 775**

**Grid/Snap command (View menu), 690**

**grids,**
  charts, 537, 553
  WP Draw, viewing, 689-691

**Grids command (Chart menu), 553**

**Group( ) operator, 934**

**Group option, 281**

**groups, creating, 378**

**guidelines, 25-26, 57**
  cells of tables, 526
  changing margins, 136
  desktop publishing, 724
  improved features of WordPerfect, 1095
  turning on/off, 26, 57

**Guidelines command (View menu), 26, 57, 526**

**Guidelines dialog box, 26, 57, 526**

**gutters, 440-441, 453-454, 735-736**

## H

**hanging indents, 138**

**hard disks**
defragmenting, 1078
installation consideration, 1077-1078

**hard hyphens, 149**

**hard page breaks, inserting into table of contents, 885**

**hard returns, 42, 59-60**

**Hard space code, 149**

**hard tabs, inserting, 143-144**

**HardReturn, macros, 954, 976-977**

**headers**
adding to master documents, 892
creating, 173-176
discontinuing, 178
editing, 176
graphics, adding, 178-179
page numbers, 176-177
replacing documents, 179
rows of tables, creating, 517-518
searching, 179
spellchecking, 178-179
suppressing, 177

**Headers/Footers command (Format menu), 174-176**

**headings, 744**
character styles, applying, 890
HTML documents, 1050-1053
paragraph styles, applying, 889-890
Table of Contents, troubleshooting, 848

**Headings option (QuickFormat dialog box), 145**

**Hebrew character set (Set 9), 643**

**height**
lines, 134-135
rows of tables, 516-517

**help, 45-54**
Coach feature, 54
exiting, 54
F1 (Help) command, 46
glossary of terms, 52-53
Grammatik, 227-228
Help dialog box, 48-52
Help menu, 47-48
navigating, 53-54

**Help button, accessing, 1082**

**Help dialog box, 47-52**
Contents tab, 48-49
Find tab, 50-51
Index section, 49-50
Show Me tab, 51-54

**Help menu commands**
About WordPerfect, 48
Ask the PerfectExpert, 47
Equation Editor, 764
Help Online, 47
Help Topics, 47-48, 955-956
Upgrade Expert, 48
WP Draw, 687

**Help, Online, WordPerfect, 1095**

**Help Online command (Help menu), 47**

**Help option (Quick Data Entry dialog box), 599**

**Help Topics**
button, 53
command (Help menu), 47-48, 955-956

**Hidden attribute (files), 922**

**Hidden Text, 208**

**hidden text, 244-245, 248**

**Hidden Text command (View menu), 128, 302**

**Hidden Text feature, documents, 302**

**Hide Bars command (View menu), 30-31, 415**

**Hide Bars Information dialog box, 415**

**Hide Codes option (Merge Feature bar), 603-605**

**Hide Completed Jobs command (Display menu), 290**

**hiding**
bars, 30-31, 57, 125
body text, 479-480
highlighting, 826
outlines, 478-480
Power Bar, 23, 427
Ruler Bar, 25
status bar, 25
text elements in outline, 478-480
toolbar, editing screen, 23
toolbars, 415

**high/low charts, 539**

**high/low data points, 557**

**Highlight command (Tools menu), 825**

**highlighting, 1095**
colors, 826
displaying, 826
hiding, 826
text, 824-826

**home pages, 1044**

**Horizontal Line command (Graphics menu), 251, 1060**

**horizontal lines, 250-251**
creating, HTML documents, 1060
customizing, 252-253, 662-664
inserting into documents, 251

**Horizontal Offset option (Gradient Settings dialog box), 555**
**horizontal scroll bars, 302**
**HORZ command, 770**
**HotSpots, 57**
**[HRt-SPg], 156**
**HTML (HyperText Markup Language) documents, 1044**
  address blocks, 1054-1058
  alignment, 1057-1058
  body text, 1050
  bookmarks, 1062-1063
  character formatting, 1053-1054
  color, 1056-1057
  converting WordPerfect documents into, 1047
  creating 1045
    bullets/lists, 1054-1056
    links, 1061
  graphics, 1058
  headings, 1050-1053
  hypertext links, 1063-1065
  marketing, 1070
  placing on server, 1068
  publishing, 1067-1068
    selecting Internet Service Providers (ISPs), 1069
    registering URLs, 1069
  special characters, 1060-1061
  tags, 1044
  titles, 1049-1050
  viewing, 1068
**hypertext, 1044**
  active documents, jumping, 1034-1035
  Bookmark, jumping within documents, 1022-1023
  buttons, modifying style, 1032-1033
  creating, 1063-1064
  defined, 1022-1023

  documents
    activating links, 1033
    automatic navigating, 1034
    connecting parts, 1022-1023
    designing, 1025-1026
    inserting links, 1028-1029
    linking, 1030-1031
    manual navigating, 1034
    marking with bookmarks, 1027
  editing, 1065
  graphics, 1066
  inactive documents, jumping, 1035
  jump maps, creating, 1025-1027
  links, editing, 1030
  loading, 1024
  macros
    linking, 1031-1032
    running, 1036
  setting, 310
  terms, 1022-1023
  text-switching capabilities, 1022-1023
**Hypertext Feature Bar, 1023-1024**
**hypertext links**
**HyperText Markup Language,** *see* **HTML (HyperText Markup Language)**
**Hypertext/Web Links command (Tools menu), 310, 1028-1029, 1064**
**Hyphen character code, 149**
**hyphenation, 148-153**
  automatic, 150
  environment options, 309
  inserting point of, 150-151
  preventing, 149
  removing from documents, 151-152

# I

**I-beam (mouse), 15**
**IBM Voice Type Control, special components, 1085-1086**
**Iconic Symbols character set (Set 5), 642**
**icons**
  displaying large, 926
  Power Bar, 416-417
  toolbars, 416-417
**IF command**
  accompanied always by ENDIF command, 964-965
  formatting structure, 964-965
  in macros, 963-965
  statement operators listed, 964
**IF( ) function, 1010-1011**
**Ignore Cell When Calculating option, 522**
**image boxes, 263**
**Image command (Graphics menu), 268**
**Image Editor dialog box, 425**
**Image menu commands, Text Box, 670**
**Image On Disk option (Box Content dialog box), 672**
**Image option (Box Content dialog box), 672**
**Image Settings dialog box, 682**
**Image Tools command (QuickMenu), 677**
**Image Tools palette, displaying, 677**
**Image Tools toolbox, closing, 678**

**images**
  brightness, 681
  color, 680
  contrast, 681
  editing, 677-682
  fills, 681
  Image Settings dialog
    box, 682
  mirroring, 682
  moving, 679
  rotating, 678-679
  scaling, 679-680
  watermarks, 273-275
  *see also* graphics

**Import command**
  Data menu, 541
  Insert menu, 574-576, 907

**Import Data dialog box,**
  **541, 566-568, 574-576,**
  **907, 987**

**importing**
  documents
    with Clipboard, 570-572
    to Convert feature,
      564-565
    with Dynamic Data
      Exchange (DDE), 572
  files
    password-protected
      files, 578-579
    setting preferences, 561
  graphics clip art, 581-582,
    676-677
  large spreadsheets, 579
  numerous database
    records, 579
  Quattro Pro spreadsheet
    data, 907
  spreadsheets
    with DDE link, 580
    with OLE link, 580-581
    to tables, 986-988

**In The Entire Document**
  **option, 936**

**Include For Search**
  **option, 946**

**Include Numbers in Fast**
  **Search check box, 947**

**Include Row/Col.**
  **command (Data**
  **menu), 547**

**increment arrows, 34**

**incrementing page**
  **numbers in documents,**
  **169-170**

**Indent command**
  **(Quick menu), 176**

**indentation, 58**
  creating indents with
    space bar, 138
  paragraphs, 137

**Index Feature Bar, 860**

**Index Style option, 864**

**Index tab (Help dialog**
  **box), 49-53**

**indexes**
  creating, 858-864
  customizing, 863-864
  defining, 862-864
  troubleshooting, 864, 868

**initial codes, creating, 123**

**initial codes style, setting,**
  **documents, 199-200**

**Initial Font button (Print**
  **dialog box), 292**

**Initial Font command**
  **(Format menu), 198**

**initial fonts, setting,**
  **197-198**

**initial styles, editing, 338**

**Initial Style command**
  **(Format menu), 199-200**

**inline equation boxes, 267**

**Inline Equation**
  **command (Graphics**
  **menu), 778, 794**

**inline text boxes, 268**

**Input File Code Page, 312**

**Insert (Continued...)**
  **Message option (Footnote**
  **Options dialog box), 815**

**Insert Bullet button, 464**

**Insert button, 234**

**Insert Character tool, 719**

**Insert Columns/Rows**
  **dialog box, 513**

**Insert command**
  Edit menu, 547
  Graphics menu, 677
  Table menu, 513

**Insert Field feature, 605**

**Insert Field Name or**
  **Number dialog box, 592**

**Insert File command**
  **(File menu), 796, 805**

**Insert File dialog box,**
  **86, 701**

**Insert File Name, 208**

**Insert Image dialog**
  **box, 268, 677, 910**

**Insert menu,**
  **(WP Draw) 687**

**Insert menu commands**
  Acquire Image, 716
  Bookmark, 1027, 1062
  Character, 644, 1061
  Create Link, 577-578
  Date, 66
  Edit Links, 577-578
  Endnote, 818
  File, 82, 85-86, 701
  Find QuickMark, 310
  Footnote, 803, 811,
    817, 893
  Import, 574-576, 907
  Link, 912
  Object, 911-912
  Other, 794
  Pages, 175-176
  Select Image Source, 716
  Sound, 1037-1038
  Spreadsheet/Database,
    623
  Update, 578

**Insert Merge Code dialog**
  **box, 608, 619-620**

**Insert Number in Text**
  **dialog box, 170-172**

**Insert Object dialog box, 584, 909-910**

**Insert Sound Clip Into Document dialog box, 1040**

**inserting**
- addresses into document, Address Book, 905
- blank lines, 59
- bookmarks into HTML documents, 1062-1063
- borders
  - around paragraphs, multiple, 256
  - into columns, 456-457
- chapter codes in subdocuments, 891-892
- chapter numbers in documents, 892
- characters into equations, 773
- charts
  - into drawings, 702-703
  - from Presentations, 909-910
- clip art, 700-701
- columns
  - borders in documents, 259-260
  - into charts, 547-548
- commands into equation palettes, 775-776
- dates into letters, 66
- delay codes into documents, 185-188
- diagrams from CorelFLOW, 911-912
- documents into documents, 85-86
- drawings
  - into documents, 716
  - from Presentations, 910
- drop caps into documents, 658
- drop shadows into borders, 668-669
- endnotes into documents, 818-820, 893-894
- fills to paragraph borders, 257
- flow charts from CorelFLOW, 911-912
- footnotes, 803-808
- foreign language codes, 653
- graphics
  - boxes into letters, 271-272
  - into HTML documents, 1059
  - into tables, 529
- hard page breaks into table of contents, 885
- headings into HTML documents, 1050-1053
- horizontal lines, 251
- hyphenation point, 150-151
- labels into charts, 550-551
- legends into charts, 549-550
- links, 1028-1029
- macros, Toolbar, 408-409
- main word lists into dictionaries, 220-221
- merge codes, 608
- objects into templates, 379-380
- page borders into documents, 258-259
- page numbers, 170-172
  - codes into master documents, 890
  - new numbers into documents, 891
- patterns into column borders, 457
- Power Bar buttons, 428-429
- programming commands into macros, 975
- rows
  - into charts, 547-548
  - into tables, 503, 513
- shortcuts into Favorites folder, 938
- subdocument codes into master documents, 873-876
- subtitles into charts, 548
- symbols into equation palettes, 775-776
- tabs, 138-144
  - hard, 143-144
  - QuickMenu, 143
  - Ruler Bar, 139-140
  - Tab Set dialog box, 142-143
- text
  - attributes into tables, 531
  - into Clipboard, 571
  - columnar text, 442
  - into documents, 67, 86-87
  - into page numbers, 167-168
  - into shapes, 712-713
  - into tables, 502-503
- time into letters, 66
- titles into charts, 548-549
- user input with Merge feature, 619-620
- words
  - into document user word lists, 215
  - into user word lists, 214-215, 223-224

**insertion point**
- keyboard commands, 443
- moving, 61-66
  - Go To feature, 64-66
  - keyboard, 63-64
  - mouse, 61-63
  - in tables, 502
  - to other columns, 442-443

**Install New Font command (File menu), 637**

**installation**
- AT&T WorldNet Service, 1086
- Autorun program, 1078
- backup files, 1077-1078
- CD-ROM, 1078-1082
- custom, 1084-1086
- choosing, 1082-1084
- compact, 1081-1082
- defragmenting, 1078

fonts, 638, 1087-1088
hard disk, 1077-1078
macro help options, 956
Netscape Navigator,
  1033-1034
network drives, 638
networks, 1081-1082
printer drivers, 1087
running from CD-ROM,
  1081-1082
typical, 1081

**Installation Progress dialog box, 1083**

**instant play macros, 397**

**INT operator, 785**

**integrals, creating, 785-786**

**interactive documents, advantages, 1021**

**interfaces**
keyboard, 14
mouse, 14-16
TextArt, 717
TWAIN, 716
WP Draw, 543-544

**internal fonts, 635**

**Internet**
access from link in
  WordPerfect documents,
  1036
etiquette, 1071
*see also* WWW (World
  Wide Web)

**Internet Publisher, 1044**
address blocks, 1054-1058
alignment, 1057-1058
color, 1056-1057
creating bullets/lists,
  1054-1056
graphics, 1058-1061
publishing HTML
  documents, 1067-1069
special characters,
  1060-1061
Web pages
  body text, 1050
    character formatting,
    1053-1054

converting WordPerfect
  documents into, 1047
creating, 1045-1054
headings, 1050-1053
titles, 1049-1050

**Internet Publisher command (File menu), 1045**

**inverting colors, 753**

**ISPs (Internet Service Providers), selecting, 1069**

**ITAL command, 771, 782**

**Italic feature, 713**

**italics, 713, 782**

# J

**Japanese character set (Set 10), 643**

**Join Cells command (Table menu), 514**

**Join command (Table menu), 985**

**joining**
cells of tables, 514-515
tables, 985

**jump maps**
creating, Hypertext,
  1025-1026
example illustrated,
  1026-1027

**jumping**
in active Hypertext
  documents, 1034-1035
in Hypertext via
  Bookmark, 1022-1023
in inactive Hypertext
  documents, 1035

**justification**
all, 739
center, 738
default settings, 56
full, 739
left, 737-738

lines, 147-148
right, 738
text, 147-148

**Justification All command (Format menu), 148**

**Justification command (Format menu), 147**

**Justification feature, 713**

**Justification menu commands**
Center, 530
Decimal Align, 521, 1000
Right, 520, 1001

**Justification tool, 718**

# K

**Keep Help on Top command (Options menu), 54**

**Keep Text Together dialog box, 160-161**

**kerning, 746-747**
troubleshooting, 757
typing, 747

**key words, 769**

**keyboard, 14**
asssignments, 327-331
closing dialog boxes, 41
codes, displaying, 609-611
definitions
  copying to another
    keyboard, 326
  customizing, 326
  deleting, 331
  storing in default
    template, 326
drawing shapes, 692-693
Equation Editor, 774
foreign, 655
formatting text, 125
functions, assigning, 327
keystrokes, assigning, 329
layout, customizing,
  324-325
macros, assigning, 330
minimizing windows, 18

mnemonics, 14
moving
  in documents, 63-64
  toolbars, 418
  windows, 19
programs, assigning, 330
sizing
  columns of tables, 511
  windows, 19
special characters, assigning, 329

**Keyboard Editor, creating keyboard definitions, 325-326**

**Keyboard Preferences dialog box, 325, 406-407, 774**

**Keyboard Shortcuts dialog box, 406-407**

**keys**
  Backspace, 87
  Delete, 63, 87
  Esc (Escape), 692
  moving insertion point, 63
  Shift, 693

**keystrokes commands, 1116-1117**

# L

**L?ST wildcard, 931**
**LABEL command, 967**
**label definitions, 193**
**Label description, 194**
**Label File dialog box, 195-196**
**Label Scale Factor option, 553**
**labels**
  adding to charts, 550-551
  file preferences, customizing, 318
  format selection, 191
  formatting, 192
  graphics, applying, 192
  label definitions, 192-193
  Label description, 194
  laser, 191
  mailing, creating, 618
  margins, 194-195
  personal file for custom creations, creating, 195-196
  sizes, changing, 194
  tractor-fed, 191
  troubleshooting, address spacing, 618

**Labels command (Format menu), 191, 318, 618**
**Labels dialog box, 318**
**Labels tab, 551**
**Language command**
  Customize menu, 228
  Tools menu, 654, 815

**Language dialog box, 228, 237, 654**
**Language feature, 236-237**
**Language Resource Database Properties dialog box, 237**
**Language Resource File, 237-238**
**languages, 208**
  foreign language versions of WordPerfect 7, 653-656
  printing footnotes, 815

**Large Icons command (View menu), 925-926**
**Large palette (Equation Editor), 775**
**Last option (Quick Data Entry dialog box), 600**
**Layout dialog box, chart styles, 552**
**Layout/Type command (Chart menu), 551**
**leading, 745**
**Left Align tab, 139**
**Left angle bracket (<), 784**
**left brace (\{), 784**
**left bracket ([), 784**
**LEFT command, 770**
  creating fractions, 783-785
  delimiters, 784

**Left option**
  Alignment section of Table Format dialog box, 520
  Edit Graphics Line dialog box, 663-664

**left parenthesis [ ( ], 784**
**left justification, 737-738**
**Legend command (Chart menu), 549**
**Legend Type option, 549**
**legends, 549-550**
**Letter Expert, 384-386**
  dialog box, 385

**Letterhead Document Style, 358-359**
**letters**
  adding graphics boxes to, 271-272
  creating, 59-60, 66
  inserting dates into, 66
  inserting time into, 66
  Letter Expert, 384-386

**letterspacing, 747-748**
**lim function, 779**
**liminf function, 780**
**limsup function, 780**
**Line (Sort feature), 625**
**Line Attributes command (Format menu), 694**
**line charts, 538**
**Line Color palette, 661, 707**
**Line command (Format menu), 131, 630, 739**
**line end arrows, drawing, 698-699**
**Line Height dialog box, 134**
**Line Hyphenation dialog box, 150**

**Line Separator dialog box, 815**

**Line Spacing dialog box, 133, 739**

**Line Style palette, 710**

**line styles, graphic boxes, 262-267**

**Line tool (WP Draw), 691**
    drawing lines, 694
    palette, Bezier Curve tool, 711

**Line Width/Style tab, 556**

**lines**
    blank, inserting, 59
    color, 753
    copying to Clipboard, 85
    creating, 692
    customizing, 658-665
        color, 661-662
        horizontal, 662-664
        styles, 659-660
        thickness, 660-661
        vertical, 664-666
    deleting, 88, 253-254
    drawing, 693-695
    formatting, 130-146
        centering, 131-132
        flushing right, 131-132
        height, 134-135
        margins, 135-136
        spacing, 132-134
    graphics, 250-254
    horizontal, 250-251
        creating in HTML documents, 1060
        customizing, 252, 662-664
    HTML documents, 1059-1060
    indentation, 58
    justification, 147-148
    patterns, shapes, 710-712
    shapes, color changes, 707
    spacing
        default, 739
        default settings, 56
        paragraphs, 740
        text alignment, 739-740
    tables
        cells, 526
        customizing, 990-991
        default style, 527
        styles, 525
        troubleshooting, 532
    troubleshooting, custom lines, 995
    vertical, 251-252
        customizing, 664-666
        customizing with mouse, 252-253

**Lines/Fill command**
    QuickMenu, 526
    Table menu, 525, 992

**LINESPACE command, 771**

**Link command (Insert menu), 912**

**Link Options dialog box, 578**

**linking**
    charts in Presentations, 909-910
    data, 906
    data with Spreadsheet Import/Link feature, 577-578
    documents with Hypertext, 1030-1031
    macros to Hypertext, 1031-1032
    Quattro Pro spreadsheets to WordPerfect, 906
    sound to documents, 1037-1038

**links, 1022-1023**
    bookmarks, creating, 1062-1063
    creating in HTML documents, 1061-1066
    editing
        data, 577-578
        Hypertext, 1030
    hypertext
        creating, 1063-1064
        editing, 1065
        graphic images, 1066
    setting options, data, 578
    updating data, 578

**Links dialog box, 583**

**List box, sorting files/folders, 926-927**

**list boxes, 36-37, 65**

**List command (View menu), 925, 927**

**List Feature Bar, 836**

**List view, 927**

**lists**
    bullets & numbers style, applying, 464-465
    creating, 834-843, 1056
        with Internet Publisher, 1054-1056
    defining, 837-842
        default styles, changing, 841
        graphics box options, 841-842
    defined, 1055-1056
    generating documents, 886
    multi-level bulleted, 1055
    numbered, 1055
    troubleshooting, 1056

**literals (\\), 771**
    formating, 782-783

**ln function, 779**

**loading hypertext document, 1024**

**loan payments, calculating, 1016-1017**

**locating,** see **finding**

**Location For Temporary Files text box, 947**

**Location of Files dialog box, 410**

**Lock option, 522**

**locking table cells, 1005-1006**

**log function, 779**

**logical pages, 162-163**

**logical states of True and False, 961**

long file names, 930
LONGDIV command, 771
LONGDIVS command, 771
lookup buttons, 35-36

# M

**M*.FRM wildcard, 931**
**Macro command (Tools menu), 647, 820**
**Macro Feature Bar, 952-953**
**Macro Location dialog box, 394**
**Macro menu, Equation Editor, 764**
   commands, 770-771
      syntax, 772
   components of, 762-764
   creating equations, 764-768
      fractions, 766-767
      spacing, 764-765
      subscripts, 767-768
      superscripts, 767-768
   Display Pane, 763, 776-777
   editing equations, 768
   Editing Pane, 762-763, 773
   formatting equations
      functions, 781-782
      literals, 782-783
   functions, 779-780
   keyboard, 774
      layout types, 324-325
   menu bar, 763-764
   palettes, 763, 774-776
   starting, 760-761
   syntax of equations, 771-773
   terms, 769-771
   toolbar, 777-778
**Macro Record indicator (status bar), 390-391**
**macros**
   ALLFONTS.WCM, playing, 647
   assigning
      to keyboards, 327-329
      to toolbar buttons, 423-424
   associating to triggers, 383-386
   benefits, 388
   commands
      // (Comment) Command, 971
      Applications, 954
      AttributeAppearanceToggle, 954
      BEEP command, 974
      comparing to older WordPerfect versions, 956-959
      conventions, 957
      decision making, 963-966
      DISPLAY command, 972-973
      HardReturn, 954
      help, 955-956
      IF, 963-965
      inserting programming, 975
      MacroStatusPrompt command, 973-974
      MarginsLeft, 954
      PauseKey command, 973
      running other macros within a macro, 969-971
      types, 955-956
      understanding syntax, 957-959
   descriptive names, managing library, 411-412
   dialog boxes, creating, 974
   files
      accessing, 950-951
      deleting, 412
      printing, 951
   flow control commands, 967-968
   folders, 410-411
   instant play, 397
   linking, 1031-1032
   locating, 401
   Macro Feature Bar, 952-953
   managing, 409-410
   memo writing, creating, 403-405
   naming conventions, 396
   online help, 955-956
   playback, stopping, 400
   practical applications, 391
   product function commands, 976-977
   programming skills, expanding, 977-979
   recording, 389, 953-954
      precautions, 389
      re-recording, 393-394
      stopping, 400
      troubleshooting, 407-408
   running, 1036
   sample recording, 954
   storage, 950
   syntax rules, 957-959
   system variables, 960-961
   templates, 366-367
      adding to toolbar buttons, 424
      current, 394
      default, 394
      opening, 950
   text
      applying for common uses, 391
      formatting, 404-405
      naming, 395
      playing, 392-393
      re-recording, 393-394
      recording, 389-391
   Toolbar, inserting, 408-409
   transposed characters, creating, 402-403
   variables, 959-960
   versus styles, 335
   WCM extension, 390-391
**MACROS folder, 820**
**Macros Help dialog box, 961**

**Macro Status Prompt command, 973-974**
**Magnifying Glass scaling option, 679**
**Mail To dialog box, 296**
**mailing labels, creating, 618-619**
**Main Word List Editor dialog box, 219**
**main word lists, 209, 220-224**
**Main Word Lists command (Customize menu), 220**
**Make It Fit Expert command (Format menu), 187**
**Make It Fit Expert dialog box, 187**
**Manual Kerning dialog box, 746**
**mapping fonts, 648-653**
**Margin dialog box, 730**
**Margin Left, 954**
**Margin Width, document display, 305**
**Margin Width option (Zoom dialog box), 280**
**Margin Width zoom value, 30**
**margins, 729-730**
   default settings, 56
   releasing, 138
   setting, 135-136
   white space, 730
**Margins command (Format menu), 135, 258, 730, 953-954**
**Margins dialog box, 34, 135, 953-954**
**Mark menu commands, 883**
**marketing HTML publications, 1070**

**marking**
   bookmarks in Hypertext, 1027
   data file records, merge feature, 616-617
   document revisions, 829-831
   text
      to create indexes, 859-862
      to create lists, 835-837
      to create table of contents, 843-845
      in table of contents, 884-885
   text to create table of authorities, 850-854
      full form, 851
      full form, editing, 853
      short form entries, 853-854
**Master Document feature, 870-871**
**master documents, 872-876**
   condensing, 882-884
   draft mode, 874-876
   endnotes, 893
   expanding, 878-881
   footnotes, 893
   forcing page breaks, 875-876
   footers, 892
   headers, 892
   inserting page numbers, 890-891
   name extension, MD, 872-876
   Page mode, 874-876
   printing, 895-896
   saving, 881-882
   searching and replacing, 895
   spellchecking, 894-895
   styles, 887-888
   styles take precedence over subdocument styles, 888

   subdocuments, 894
   codes, 873-876
   links, 872
   table of contents
      creating, 884-885
      marking text, 843-845
**Match Case option (Advanced Find dialog box), 933**
**Match menu commands, Codes, 152**
**MATFORM command, 770, 788**
**Math/Scientific character set (Set 6), 643**
**Math/Scientific Extensions character set (Set 7), 643**
**mathematical equations, 759**
   Arrows palette, 792
   characters, 776
   creating, 764-768
   diacritical marks (Other palette), 791
   displaying, 776-777
   editing, 768
   embedding in text, 794-795
   Equation Editor, 760
      components of, 762-764
      starting, 760-761
   fonts, changing, 795
   formatting, 781-783
   formulas
      absolute references, 1008-1009
      copying, 1003-1004
      creating, 1001-1003
      creating, letter grade formulas, 1010-1011
      creating, percent formulas, 1010
      creating, Quiz Points averages, 1009
      creating, reporting averages, 1008
      creating, total points formulas, 1009-1010
      deleting, 1005

functions, 1004-1005
  modifying, 1005
inserting characters
  into, 773
integrals, creating, 785-786
keyboard, 774
matrices, creating, 787-789
multiline expressions,
  creating, 790-791
numbering, 794
palettes, 774-776
retrieving files, 796-797
roots, creating, 787
saving files, 796-797
spreadsheets, 996-1006
  designing, 996-997
  forcing text mode, 1001
  formatting numeric
    data, 999-1001
sums, creating, 785-786
symbols (Large
  palette), 792
Symbols palette, 792
syntax, 771-773
verifying, 760-761
viewing, 763, 776-777

**matrices, creating, 787-789**

**MATRIX command, 770, 788**

**matrix commands, 787-789**

**max function, 780**

**Maximize button, 18**

**maximizing windows, 18, 44**

**measurements**
  columns, 512
  converting, 303
  default settings for
    columns, 439-440
  displaying, 303
  Documents Display,
    302-303
  modifying, 303

**Memo Expert, 385**

**memo writing, creating, macros, 403-405**

**memory requirements, 1087**

**Menu Bar Preferences dialog box, 324**

**Menu Editor, creating, menus, 324**

**MENULIST command, 962-963**

**MENULIST dialog box, 963**

**menus**
  Application Control,
    accessing, 18
  bars
    Equation Editor,
      763-764
    WP Draw, 543
  creating tables, 498
  **displays, 308-309**
    Document Control, 19-20
    Edit
      Equation Editor, 763
      WP Draw, 686
    File
      Equation Editor, 763
      WP Draw, 686
    Font, Equation Editor, 764
    Format, 122, 687
    Graphics, WP Draw, 687
    Help, 47-48
      Equation Editor, 764
      WP Draw, 687
    Insert, WP Draw, 687
    Macro, Equation
      Editor, 764
    Menu Editor, creating, 324
    pull-down menus, 20-21
      activating, 20
      modifying, 324-325
      WP Draw, 686-687
    QuickMenu, 21
      setting tabs, 143
      tables, 506
    Table, 509
    Tools, WP Draw, 687
    View
      Equation Editor, 764
      turning bars on/off, 57

  turning guidelines
    on/off, 57
  WP Draw, 686
Window
  Equation Editor, 764
  WP Draw, 687

**merge codes, 607-608**
  CAPS, 621-622
  displaying, 306, 609
  FIRSTCAP, 621-622
  inserting, 608
  text appearance,
    controlling, 621-622
  TOLOWER, 621
  TOUPPER, 621-622
  variables, 619

**Merge command (Tools menu), 588, 611**

**Merge dialog box, 588**

**Merge feature, 587-588, 602-603, 612-614**
  data files, 596-603, 616
    coverting, 622-623
    creating, 588-591
    creating tables, 623-624
    data entry, in existing
      files, 600-601
    data entry, Quick Data
      Entry dialog box,
      598-600
    editing, 601-602
    field names, 598
    types, 597-598
    user input information,
      619-622
    user input information,
      controlling, 621-622
  form files, 604-611
    associating data files,
      605-606
    creating, 591-593
    envelopes, 593-595, 617
    keyboard codes,
      displaying, 609-611
    mailing labels, 618
    merge codes, 607-608
    merge codes,
      displaying, 609

merge codes, inserting, 608
performing merges, 595-596
merging data, tables, 986
records, selecting range, 614-615
templates, 366-367
user input, inserting, 619-620

**Merge Form File Feature bar, controls, 604-605**

**Merge Message dialog box, 609-611**

**Merge Text (Sort feature), 625**

**Metafiles, setting conversion preferences, 562-563**

**min function, 780**

**Minimize button, 18, 210**
minimizing windows, 18, 44

**mirroring images, 682**

**misspelled words, editing, 214**

**Mixed option (Alignment section of Table Format dialog box), 520**

mnemonics, 14
defined, 644
special characters, 645

**mod function, 780**

**modifying**
addresses on envelopes, positioning, 190
beep options in documents, 308
Bullets & Numbers, outlines, 467-468
columns
appearance, 452
widths, 452-455
current page number in documents, 168-169
default folders for documents, 315-316
file extensions for documents, 315-316
folders for special files, 313-315
fonts in equations, 795
label sheet size, 194
measurements in documents, 303
outlines
definition, 485
levels, 481-482
pre-defined format for, 492
structure, 481
page numbers, 165-169
Power Bar, 322
pull-down menus, 324-325
space between rows, 450-451
Status Bar, 322-324
styles, 348-349, 356
Hypertext buttons, 1032-1033
toolbars, 321
writing styles, troubleshooting, 232
*see also* editing

**monospaced text, 58**

**mortgage loan letters, 1015-1017**

**mouse, 14-16**
drawing shapes, 692-693
moving
in documents, 61-63
shapes, 692
windows, 18
navigating documents, 16
positioning toolbars, 417
reversing button assignment, 63
sizing
graphics boxes, 270
windows, 18
troubleshooting button assignments, 62-63

**Move (Application Control menu), 19**

moving
between cells of tables, 501-502
between charts and documents, 544
clip art figures, 704-706
between documents, 44
in documents, 61-66
keyboard, 63-64
mouse, 61-63
files, 918-919, 924
between footnotes, 807
footnotes, 810-811
graphics boxes, 269
images, 679
insertion point, 61-66
Go To feature, 64-66
keyboard, 63-64
mouse, 61-63
in tables, 502
macros, folders, 410
in master documents, 877-884
Power Bar buttons, 428-429
rows in parallel columns, 451-452
shapes, mouse, 692
to text boxes, 34
toolbar, 22
buttons, 421
keyboard, 418
palette, 417
windows
keyboard, 19
mouse, 18

**MS-DOS file name, 929**

**multi-level bulleted lists, 1055**

**multiline expressions, creating, 790-791**

**Multinational cahracter set (Set 1), 641**

**Multiple Pages dialog box, 284**

# N

**Name text box, macros, naming, 390-391**

**names**
Address Book, 901
data file fields, 596, 598
documents, renaming, 76-77
files, 920, 929
    conventions, 873
    extensions, 72
    long, 930
    MS-DOS, 929
    troubleshooting, 924
folders, 72, 923-924
macros, 390-391, 395, 411-412
saving documents, 71
tables, 1012-1014
WCM extension, 396

**Names command (Table menu), 1012**

**narrowing columns, charts, 546**

**navigating**
datasheets, 545
dialog boxes, 32-33
between documents, 44
documents
    mouse, 16
    scroll bars, 26
    troubleshooting, 16
footnotes, 807
help system, 53-54
Hypertext documents automatically, 1034
Hypertext documents manually, 1034
Web pages
    bookmarks, 1062-1063
    graphic images, 1066
    hypertext links, 1063-1065

**NEST command, 971**

**nesting styles, 351**

**netiquette, Internet, 1071**

**Netscape, 1044**
HTML documents, viewing, 1068
installing, 1033-1034

**networks**
drives, installing fonts, 638
printers, adding to printer list, 293
printing on, 293
viewing Envoy documents, 912-913

**New command**
File menu, 78, 368
New Page Size dialog box, 181-182

**New Folder command (File menu), 923**

**New Group command (Options menu), 378**

**New Organization Properties dialog box, 902-903**

**New Page Size dialog box, 181**

**New Record option (Quick Data Entry dialog box), 599**

**New Slide Show dialog box, 911**

**New Template command (Options menu), 375**

**newsgroups, marketing Web pages, 1070-1071**

**Newsletter Expert, 386**

**newspaper columns**
building
    Columns Dialog box, 438-440
    Power Bar, 436-437
column type, 434-436
creating, 733
formatting text, troubleshooting, 736
turning off columns option, 446

**Next button, Hypertext Feature Bar, 1023-1024**

**Next Field option (Quick Data Entry dialog box), 599**

**Next option (Quick Data Entry dialog box), 600**

**Next Page button, 27, 62**

**No delimiter (.), 771**

**No Viewer Available messag, 85**

**non-standard page size, printers, 183-184**

**Normal (upright), paper orientation, 183**

**Normal feature, 713**

**normal space (~), 770**

**Not (!) operator, 933**

**Note Number button, 804**

**Novell GroupWise 4.1, e-mail, 295-296**

**NROOT command, 770**

**Num Lock feature, turning off, 63**

**Number of Columns text box (Columns Dialog box), 439-440**

**Number of Copies box, 281**

**Number Of Pages option (Spell Checker), 218**

**numbered lists, 1055**

**numbering**
default settings, 56
displaying page numbers, 62
equations, 794
footnotes, 893
logical pages, 162
outlines, 484-485
pages automatically, 163
physical pages, 162
position, lists, 839
table of contents, 847

**Numbering Position option**, 863
**numbering styles, 463-464**
 Arabic, 167
 footnotes, 812
 Roman, 167
**numbering types**
 chapter, 165-168
 secondary, 165-168
 standard page, 165-168
 volume, 165-168
**Numeric Format command (QuickMenu), 999, 1010**

# O

**Object command (Insert menu), 911-912**
**Object Linking and Embedding (OLE), 906**
**Object Properties command (Format menu), 694, 698, 711**
**Object Properties dialog box, 698, 712**
**objects**
 OLE, pasting clip art as, 705
 templates, 378-381
  adding, 379-380
  associating macros to triggers, 383-384
  associating to features, 382-383
  copying from other templates, 380-381
  embedding guidelines, 384
  removing, 381
 *see also* shapes
**odd numbered pages, printing, 285-286**
**Of Dimmed option (Quick Data Entry dialog box), 600**

**OLE 2.0, 693**
**OLE Close button (WP Draw Toolbar), 685**
**OLE Link, creating to another program, data, 583-585**
**OLE Server, 1097**
**OLE Update button (WP Draw Toolbar), 685**
**On The First Page option, 936**
**on-screen documents, 68-70**
**Open a File command (Options menu), 54**
**Open As Copy option, 922**
**Open command (File menu), 14, 82, 918, 950-951**
**Open dialog box, 14, 82, 220, 918**
**Open File dialog box, 86, 294, 397**
**[Open Style: InitialStyle], 199-200**
**opening**
 Chart Gallery, 551
 dialog boxes, 739
  Language, 228
  Open, 918
  Table Format, 512
  User Word List Editor, 228
 documents, 14, 82-86
  new, 78
  saved, 82-85
  FAVORITES folder, 937-938
 files as copies, 922-923
 macros stored in templates, 950
 menus, Document Control, 20
 Table Format dialog box, 519

**operators**
 finding files, 933-934
 INT, 785
 SUM, 785
**Options button, 53, 953**
**Options command**
 Footnote menu, 817
 Format menu, 190
 Toolbar menu, 22
 View menu, 930
**Options menu commands**
 Annotate, 53
 Copy, 53
 Define a Bookmark, 54
 Delete Group, 378
 Delete Template, 378
 Display a Bookmark, 54
 Exit, 54
 Font, 54
 Keep Help on Top, 54
 New Group, 378
 New Template, 375
 Open a File, 54
 Print Summary, 287
 Print Topic, 54
 Rename Group, 378
 Save As, 993
 Use System Colors, 54
 Version, 54
**Options tab (TextArt), 717-719**
**Or (|) operator, 933**
**orientation, fonts, 649-650**
**Original Document Backup, files, 316**
**orphan, 161**
**Other Codes dialog box, 149, 630**
**Other command (Insert menu), 794**
**Other option (Zoom dialog box), 280**
**Other palette (Equation Editor), 775**
**Out of Memory error, 721**

Outline Define dialog box, 339, 474, 493-494
Outline Definition Copy dialog box, 493-494
Outline Definition Duplicate dialog box, 493-494
Outline Definitions button (Outline Feature Bar), 485
Outline Feature Bar, 471-472, 477-478
Outline tool, 719
Outliner command (View menu), 911
outlines
    bullets, 463-464, 468, 476-477
    definitions
        changing, 485
        editing, 489
        saving, 494
    documents, 461
    families, cutting and pasting, 482-484
    features, 470-471
        hiding, 478-480
    hierarchical style, 469
    incrementing numbers, 477
    indentation, 470
    levels, adjusting, 481-482
    modifying
        Bullets & Numbers, 467-468
        Change To Body Text button (Outline Feature Bar), 482
    numbers, 468
        creating, 463-464
        renumbering, 484-485
    Outline Feature Bar, 471-472
    paragraphs, 469-471
    predefined formats
        creating, 473-474
        editing, 492
    presentations, exporting, 910-911
    special keystrokes, editing, 475
    structure, modifying, 481
    styles, creating, 339, 487
    text
        editing, 481
        hiding, 478-480
    theory, 469
Output File Code Page, 312
OVER command, 766-767, 770, 783-785
overiding document styles, 336
overlapping charts, 552
OVERLINE command, 770
OVERSM command, 771
Overstrike dialog box, 646-647
overstrikes, 645-647
Overwrite/New Name dialog box, 326, 420
overwriting text, 86-87

# P

Page Border/Fill dialog box, 259
Page command (View menu), 279
Page mode, 29, 874-876
Page Number Appearance option, 864
Page Number Format dialog box, 840
Page Number option, 65
Page numbering (Format menu), 170-171
page numbering codes, master documents, 890
Page Numbering command (Format menu), 847, 892
Page Numbering dialog box, 167-168
Page Numbering Font dialog box, 165-168
Page Numbering Format list box, 165-168
Page option (Spell Checker), 218
Page Range command (File menu), 896
Page Size command (Format menu), 180
Page Size dialog box, 180-181
Page View mode, 808-809
Page Width option (Zoom dialog box), 280
PAGEOFF code, 613
Pages command (Insert menu), 175-176
Pages dialog box, 175
pages
    breaks, 156-157
    borders, 258-261
    defaults, setting, 179
    definitions, 179
        creating, 180-181
        deleting, 182
        editing, 181-182
    numbers, 163-164
        changing, 168-169
        choosing format, 164-165
        counting, 172
        customizing appearance, 165-168
        formats, 840
        incrementing, 169-170
        inserting, 170-172, 891
        styles, 167
        suppressing, 172
        text, inserting , 167-168
    sizes, 183-184
        selecting, 179-180
    *see also* documents

paired codes, 336-338
paired styles, 337
palettes
  arrows, 792
  creating, 753
  Equation Editor, 763, 774-776
  equations, 775-776
  Fill Color, 707
  Graphics Box Edit Box, 793
  Large, 792
  Line Color, 707
  Line Style, 710
  Symbols, 792
  WP Draw, 689-691
paper
  feed, 183
  orientation, 183
  size, 56
  source, 183
Paper Feed button (Print dialog box), 292
paragraph (paired-auto) style, 337-338
Paragraph (Sort feature), 625
Paragraph Border/Fill dialog box, 256-257
Paragraph command (Format menu), 137, 740, 803
Paragraph dialog box, 39
Paragraph Number style, 467
Paragraph option (Add Compare Markings dialog box), 831
Paragraph option (Spell Checker), 218
Paragraph properties dialog box, 125
Paragraph-Auto text style, 887-888

paragraphs
  borders, 256
    customizing, 666-669
    fills, 257
    color, 754
    deleting, 261
    troubleshooting, 261
  Bullets & Numbers, automatic formatting, 466
  ending, 59
  fills, color, 754-757
  indenting, 137-144
  line spacing, 740
  styles
    headings, 889-890
    paired codes, 337-338
    paired styles, 337
    styles, 354-355, 887-888
parallel columns
  block protected parallel columns, 447
    creating, 449-450
  column breaks, 449-450
  creating, 448
  editing text, 451
  moving rows, 451-452
  spacing, adjusting between rows, 450-451
  standard parallel columns, 447
  types, 434-436, 446-447
  typing text into columns, 448-450
Parallel Columns (Sort feature), 625
Parse Tree, displaying, 230-231
parts of speech diagrams, displaying, 230-231
Password dialog box, 566
password-protected files, importing, 578-579
Paste command
  Edit menu, 542, 572, 810, 919
  Quick menu, 176

Paste Link commands (Edit menu), 583
Paste Special command (Edit menu), 584, 705
pasting
  clip art figures, 705
  data, 542, 571-572, 906
  files, 919
  footnotes, 810
  formulas to Clipboard, 576
  text from table cells, 505-506
path names, 247-248
Pattern fill style (charts), 555
Pattern tool, 719
patterns
  columns, adding, 457
  lines, shapes, 710-712
Pause button (Macro Feature Bar), 952-953
Pause Printing command (Document menu), 290
PauseKey command, 973
PerfectExpert, 46
  activating, 51
PerfectFit Conversions dialog box, 988
PerfectScript Commands dialog box, 960-961, 975
Perform button (Hypertext Feature Bar), 1023-1024
Perform Merge dialog box, 593, 611-617
performance, OLE 2.0, 693
Perspective command (Chart menu), 553
[Pg Num Fmt: format], 167-168
PHANTOM command, 771
phone message forms, 532

Phonetic character set (Set 2), 641
Phrase option (Add Compare Markings dialog box), 831
physical pages, 162-163
Picture fill style, charts, 556
Picture Settings dialog box, 556
pictures *see* graphics; images
pie charts, 540
   editing, 557
placing, *see* inserting; positioning
Play button (Macro Feature Bar), 952-953
Play Macro dialog box, 392-393, 820
playing
   macros
      ALLFONTS.WCM, 647
      stopping playback, 400
      text, 392-393
   sound clips in documents, 1040
PMT() function, calculating loan payments, 1016-1017
Polygon tool, creating rectangles, 696
polygons
   creating, 692
   defined, 694
   drawing, 694-695
pop-up lists, 37-38
Port option button, 294
PosCharNext, 976-977
PosCharPrevious, 976-977
Position Hyphen dialog box, 150, 566
Position list box, 65

Position option (Font dialog box), 128, 549
Position—Beginning of Selection option, 65
Position—Bottom of Current Page option, 65
Position—Next Table option, 65
Position—Previous Table option, 65
Position—Reselect Last Selection option, 65
Position—Reselect Text option, 65
Position—Top of Current Page option, 65
positioning
   clip art, 700-702
   endnotes, 802
   footnotes, 802
   graphics boxes, 262, 673-674
   multiple documents on screen, 44
   tables, 983-984
      pre-printed forms, 196-197
   Toolbars, 22, 417-418
Post Close event, 383
Post New event, 383
Post Open event, 383
Post Print event, 383
Post Startup event, 383
Post Switch Doc event, 383
Post Tables event, 383
Postscript printers, 294
Power Bar, 23-24, 56
   building columns, 436-437
   changing character attributes, 130
   creating tables, 499
   customizing, 24, 426-429
      buttons, 427-429
   hiding, 23, 427
   icons, 416-417

   modifying, 322
   reasons for using, 414
   styles, applying, 353-354
   text justification, 148
   troubleshooting, adding buttons, 429
   viewing, 427
Power Bar dialog box, 24
Power Bar Options dialog box, 427
Pre Close event, 383
Pre New event, 383
Pre Open event, 383
Pre Print event, 383
Pre Switch Doc event, 383
Pre Tables event, 383
precedence, formatting table text, 518-519
preferences
   improved features, 1098
   fast searches, 945-947
Preferences command (Edit menu), 22, 74, 299, 372, 415, 774
Preferences dialog box, 74, 300, 774
presentations, 908
   charts
      editing, 909-910
      inserting, 909-910
      linking, 909-910
   drawings
      editing, 910
      inserting, 910
   graphics, format saving, 910
   outlines exported from WordPerfect, 910-911
Presentations 7 (Corel WordPerfect Suite integrated applications), 1094
preventing hyphenation, 149
Preview command (View menu), 73

Preview, Content command (View menu), 84
Preview, No Preview command (View menu), 85
Preview, Page View command (View menu), 84
Preview, Use Separate Window command (View menu), 84
previewing
 documents, 73, 84, 279-280
 *see also* viewing
Previous button (Hypertext Feature Bar), 1023-1024
Previous Field option (Quick Data Entry dialog box), 599
Previous Level button (Outline Feature Bar), 481
Previous option (Quick Data Entry dialog box), 600
Previous Page button, 27, 62
Print As Booklet check box, 286
Print command (File menu), 69, 278, 280, 895, 923
Print dialog box, 69, 652, 896, 951
 closing, 278
 displaying, 278, 281
Print Graphics check box, 287
Print in Color check box, disabling, 287
Print Return Address check box, pre-printed addresses, 189
Print Summary command (Options menu), 287

Print To *Printer Name* dialog box, 179-180
Print Topic command (Options menu), 54
Printer command (Settings menu), 290
printer drivers
 default, troubleshooting documents, 312
 deleting, 292
 formatting documents, 311
 installing WordPerfect, 1087
Printer Initial Font dialog box, 292
Printer Name dialog box, 197-198
printers
 configuring, 291-292
 drivers, 291
  default, troubleshooting documents, 312
  deleting, 292
  formatting documents, 311
  installing WordPerfect, 1087
 fonts, 634, 741
  adding, 292-293
  orientation, 183
 name, 182-183
 network, adding to printer list, 293
 page definitions
  creating, 180-181
  customizing, 180
  deleting, 182
  editing, 181-182
  sizes, 183-184
 paper feed, 183
 paper source, 183
 Postscript, 294
 printing adjustments, 182-183
 selecting, 278-279, 291-292
 setting up, 290-293
 size, 182-183
 troubleshooting, 282

 types, 182
 viewing page definitions, 180
Printers dialog box, 290
printing
 adjustments, 182-183
 booklets, 286
 dialog boxes, 278, 281
 documents, 280-281
  canceling print jobs, 281-282, 290
  controlling status of print jobs, 289-290
  controlling status of print jobs with Windows 95, 290
  current page, 283
  custom print options, 287-289
  displaying print jobs, 290
  double-sided, 285
  even numbered pages, 285-286
  multiple copies, 281
  odd numbered pages, 285-286
  previewing, 279-280
  removing print jobs from list, 290
  sorting print jobs, 290
  summaries, 204-205, 287
  troubleshooting, 282
  troubleshooting font display, 652
  with color, 286-287
  with graphics, 286-287
 envelopes, 289
 files, 923
  to files, 294
 footnotes, languages, 815
 graphics, troubleshooting, 757
 help topics, 54
 macro files, 951
 master documents, 895
  selected pages from, 895-896
 on networks, 293
 on-screen documents, 68-70

printers
    configuring, 291-292
    drivers, 291-292, 311-312, 1087
    fonts, 183, 292-293, 634, 741
    name, 182-183
    network, adding to printer list, 293
    page definitions, 180-184
    paper feed, 183
    paper source, 183
    Postscript, 294
    printing adjustments, 182-183
    selecting, 278-279, 291-292
    setting up, 290-293
    size, 182-183
    troubleshooting, 282
    types, 182
    viewing page definitions, 180
    *see also* printers
soft fonts, 635
tables, 508-509
text
    selected blocks, 286
    troubleshooting font display, 652
TextArt images, troubleshooting, 721
ZIP codes on envelopes, 190

**product function commands, 955-956**
    Close macros, 976-977
    DeleteCharNext macros, 976-977
    DeleteCharPrevious macros, 976-977
    FileNew macros, 976-977
    FileOpenDlg macros, 976-977
    FileSaveAsDlg macros, 976-977
    HardReturn macros, 976-977
    PosCharNext macros, 976-977
    PosCharPrevious macros, 976-977
    SelectMode(On!) macros, 976-977
    Tab macros, 976-977
    Type(Text) macros, 976-977

**programming commands, macros, 955-956**

**programming skills, expanding macros, 977-979**

**Programs menu commands, Windows Explorer, 930**

**Prompt Before Auto Replacement command (Customize menu), 228**

**Prompt Before Auto Replacement option (Spell Checker), 219**

**prompt builder, creating templates, 376-378**

**Prompt Builder dialog box, 377**

**proofreading documents, 224-232**
    Grammatik
        correcting grammar problems, 226
        customizing, 228-229
        disabling grammar rules, 227
        help, 227-228
        running, 225-228
        skipping errors, 226
        word replacement, 227
        writing styles, 229-230
        writing styles, editing, 229-230
    Spell Checker, 208-224
        spell checking, optimizing time, 221

**Properties button (Print dialog box), 292**

**Properties command (File menu), 203, 921**

**Properties dialog box, 201-206, 240**

**Properties for New Entry dialog box, 903-914**

proportion, designing documents for desktop publishing, 727

**Publish to Envoy command (File menu), 912-913**

**publishing (desktop), 723**
    to Envoy, 912-913
    colors, 750-757
        graphics, 753-756
        text, 751-753
    design, 725-728
    guidelines, 724-725
    planning page presentation, 729-736
        columns, 731-737
        columns, custom widths, 732
        columns, gutter space, 735-736
        margins, 729-730
    refining page presentation, 736-740
        text alignment, 737-739
    selecting fonts, 740-750
        attributes, 741-742
        type sizes, 742-745
        typefaces, 741-742
        typographical controls, 745-750

**publishing (Web), 1067-1069**
    copyright law, 1071
    Internet Publisher, 1044
        creating Web pages, 1045-1054
    marketing, 1070
    placing HTML documents on servers, 1068
    registering URLs, 1069
    selecting Internet Service Providers (ISPs), 1069

**pull-down menus, 20-21**
  activating, 20
  WP Draw, 686-687

# Q

**Q&A Linked Paragraph Styles, 360**

**QuickCorrect command (Tools menu), 642**

**Quattro Pro 7, 1094**
  spreadsheets
    converting formulas, 908
    importing data, 907
    linking to WordPerfect, 906
    range of data imported, 907

**question mark (?) wildcard character, 216**

**Quick Data Entry dialog box, 589, 598-600**

**QuickMenu commands**
  Center, 176
  Flush Right, 176
  Font, 176
  Indent, 176
  Paste, 176
  SpellCheck, 176

**QuickArt, 691**
  tool, removing from STANDARD.QAD file, 701

**QuickCorrect, 208**
  adding words to, 215
  WordPerfect improved features, 1096-1097

**QuickCorrect feature, 238-239**
  command (Tools menu), 224
  dialog box, 224, 238-239, 647
  dictionary, troubleshooting, 224
  Options dialog box, 239

**QuickFill, 1019-1020**
  entering dates of months, 1020
  entering days of week, 1020

**QuickFinder feature**
  Custom Fast Search dialog box, 942
  dialog box, 931
  Fast Search Information dialog box, 944
  Fast Search Setup Expert dialog box, 931
  finding files, 931-937
    case-sensitive, 933-934
    expanding searches, 936
    name searches, 931-932
    operators, 933-934
    pattern searches, 932-933
    specifying where to search, 935-936
    wild cards, 934
    word closeness, 935
    word searches, 933-934

**QuickFinder Manager**
  dialog box, 940
  fast searches
    creating, 940-942
    custom, 942-943
    defined, 939
    editing, 943-944
    preferences, 945-947
    updating, 944
    viewing, 944-945
  Preferences dialog box, 946-947
  Select Subfolder dialog box, 932
  Standard Fast Search dialog box, 941
  starting, 939
  tab (Open dialog box), 940

**QuickFont button (Power Bar), 130**

**QuickFonts, 1097**

**QuickFormat, 125-126**
  button, 122
  changing margins, 136
  command (Format menu), 144
  dialog box, 144
  formatting text, 144-145

**QuickMark, 310**

**QuickMenus, 21**
  displaying, 123
  setting tabs, 143
  commands
    Calculate, 1003
    Format, 516
    Image Tools, 677
    Lines/Fill, 526
    Numeric Format, 999, 1010
    SpeedFormat, 524
    Split Cell, 515
    Style, 275
    Update Chart From Table, 546
  tables, 506

**QuickOpen, 1097**

**QuickSpot Paragraph properties dialog box, 137**

**QuickSpots, 39-41, 1097**
  documents, Show options, 302
  Edit Box, 39
  Edit Table, 40, 507
  formatting text, 125

**QuickStatus box, 57**

**QuickStyle**
  creating documents, 342-343
  ease of use in creating styles, 341-342

**QuickStyle dialog box, 342-343**

**QuickSum (Formula Bar), 1005**

**QuickTasks**
  documents, starting, 913-914
  financial, 913-914

publishing, 913-914
   templates from
      WordPerfect, 913-914
**QUIT command, 968**
**quiting**
   Spell Checker, 215
   WordPerfect 7, 12
   *see also* closing
**Quotation character style, 359**
**quotation marks, typographical, 642, 647**

# R

**radar charts, 539**
**radio buttons, 35**
**re-recording**
   macros, 393-394
   *see also* recording
**Read-Only attribute (files), 922**
**readability score (Grammatik), 231**
**reading text, troubleshooting, 261**
**Ready To Install dialog box, 1083**
**Recheck All Text option (Spell Checker), 219**
**Record button (Macro Feature Bar), 952-953**
**Record command (Tools menu), 953-954**
**Record Macro dialog box, 390-391, 953-954**
**recording**
   macros, 953-954
      keyboard, 390-391
      mouse, 390-391
      precautions, 389
      stopping, 400
      text, 389
      troubleshooting, 407-408

**records**
   data files, 596
   merge feature, selecting range, 614-617
**rectangles**
   creating, 692
      Polygon tool, 696
   drawing, 691, 695-697
**Recycle Bin**
   emptying, 921
   Properties dialog box, 921
**Redisplay command (View menu), 763**
**redisplaying,** *see* displaying
**Redline dialog box, 201, 832**
**redline enhancement (Compare Document feature), 832**
   changing display, 832-833
   removing display, 834
   marking methods, 200-201
   command (Format menu), 200-201
**Redo command (Edit menu), 89-91**
**Redraw command (View menu), 545**
**Reference Center, choosing WordPerfect setup options, 1079**
**references**
   creating, 842-843
   cross-references, 865-868
   indexes, 858-864
      marking text, 859-862
   marking, 866-867
      footnotes/endnotes, 868
   Table of Authorities, 848-858
      defining, 854-858
      indexes, 862-864
      marking text, 850-854
   Table of Contents, 843-848
      defining, 845-849
      marking text, 843-845
   updating, 843

**referencing numbers**
   endnotes, troubleshooting, 819
   footnotes, Cross Reference feature, 803
**reformatting**
   documents with Make It Fit Expert command, 187
   *see also* formatting
**registering URLs (Uniform Resource Locators), 1069**
**registration information, 1080**
**relative size attributes, fonts, 649**
**Relative Size option (Font dialog box), 128**
**Relative Size pop-up list, 37**
**releasing margins, 138**
**Remove command (Document menu), 290**
**Remove Merge Bar option**
   Merge Feature Bar, 603
   Merge Form File Feature Bar, 605
**removing**
   columns in charts, 547-548
   Compare Document markings, 834
   data from datasheets, 545
   folders, 923-924
   hyphenation from documents, 151-152
   objects from templates, 381
   print jobs from list, 290
   rows from charts, 547-548
   shapes after creating, 692
   tabs from Ruler Bar, 143
   TrueType fonts from Windows 95, 639
**Rename Address Book dialog box, 901**
**Rename command (Tool menu), 901**

**Rename Group command (Options menu), 378**
**renaming**
　documents, 76-77
　*see also* names
**replacing**
　footers in documents, 179
　headers in documents, 179
　text, 87
　in text boxes, 34
　words with Grammatik, 227
**replacing words**
　Thesaurus, 234
**report card tables**
　creating, 1011-1014
　　form creation, 1011-1012
　　names
　　　creating, 1012-1013
　　　navigating with, 1013-1014
**REPORT*.* wild card, 931**
**Reset Custom Installation dialog box, 1085-1086**
**resizing,** *see* sizing
**Restart Numbering On Each Page option**
　(Footnote Options dialog box), 813, 817
**Restore command (File menu), 924**
**restoring**
　default settings
　　tabs, 140
　deleted columns/rows of tables, 514
　deleted files, 924
　deleted tables, 508
　deleted text, 88-89
　minimized windows, 18, 44
　text deletions, 504
　Toolbar palette, 418
　*see also* undoing
**Retrieve Equation Text dialog box, 796**

**Retrieve Styles From dialog box, 357**
**retrieving**
　clip art, 700-702
　files equations, 796-797
**RETURN command, 967-968**
**Reveal Codes, 156**
**reveal codes, 41**
　auto placement, 126
　displaying, 837
　turning on/off, 122
　viewing, 41
**Reveal Codes check box, editing styles, 349**
**Reveal Codes command (View menu), 41, 122, 261**
**Reveal Codes window, 41**
**reverting line deletions, 254**
**revisions (documents), 824-834**
　highlighting text, 824-826
　routing documents for, 826-828
　　automatically marking, 829-833
　　reviewing, 828
**Rich Text Format (RTF)**
　documents
　　converting to intermediate format, 569-570
　　limitations, 569-570
**Right (Alignment section of Table Format dialog box), 520**
**Right Align tab, 139**
**Right angle bracket (>), 784**
**right brace (}), 784**
**right bracket (]), 784**
**RIGHT command, 770**
　creating fractions, 783-785
　delimiters, 784

**Right command (Justification menu), 520, 1001**
**Right option (Edit Graphics Line dialog box), 663, 665**
**right parenthesis [ ) ], 784**
**right justification, 738**
**roots, creating, 787**
**Rotate command (Edit menu), 706**
**Rotated (wide), paper orientation, 183**
**rotated text, tables, 530-531**
**Rotated Text option (Table Format dialog box), 530**
**rotating**
　clip art figures, 706
　display of charts, 553
**rotating images, 678-679**
**Rotation tool, 719**
**rounded borders, creating, 668**
**rounded rectangles, creating, 692**
**routing documents, 826-828**
　reviewing revisions, 828
**row separator (#), 770, 788**
**rows**
　charts
　　adding, 547-548
　　removing, 547-548
　matrices, *see* matrices
　subdividing documents, 184-185
　tables
　　adding, 503, 513
　　alternating fills, 988-990
　　creating headers, 517-518
　　cutting/copying, 506
　　deleting, 513
　　height, 516-517

**Ruler Bar, 25**
   adjusting column
      widths, 453
   changing margins, 136
   desktop publishing, 724
   displaying, 25, 140-141
   document display, 306
   hiding, 25
   selecting, 510
   tabs
      clearing, 143
      setting, 139

**Ruler command (View menu), 690**

**rulers (WP Draw), viewing, 689-691**

**rules for using macro variables, 960**

**RUN command, 970-971**
   playing second macro, 970-971

**running**
   Grammatik, 225-228
   macros with other macro commands, 969-971
   macros with hypertext, 1036

# S

**sans serif typeface, 741**

**Save & Compile button**
   Macro Feature Bar option buttons, 952-953

**Save All command (Mark menu), 883**

**Save As command (File menu), 72, 376, 720**

**Save As command (Options menu), 993**

**Save As dialog box, 37, 72, 568-569**

**Save command (File menu), 74, 796**

**Save Data File As dialog box, 590**

**Save Document Summary dialog box, 205**

**Save Equation As dialog box, 796**

**Save Rules command (Customize menu), 228**

**Save Styles To dialog box, 357**

**Save Template dialog box, 376**

**Save Workspace feature, 308**

**saving**
   converted documents, 568
   document summaries, 205
   documents
      file formats, 75-77
      file names, 71
      to disks, 70-74
   files
      equation, 796-797
   graphics to presentations, 910
   master documents, 881-882
   outline definitions, 494
   styles
      document, 356-357
   tables, 508-509
   templates, 376
   TextArt, 720

**scalable fonts, 635**

**SCALESYM command, 771**

**scaling images, 679-680**

**scaling method option, editing axes (charts), 552**

**scanning graphics**
   WP Draw, 715-716
      selecting image source, 715-716

**scatter charts, 539**
   editing, 557

**screens, copying documents to, 82**

**scroll bars, 26-27**
   disabling, 26
   Documents Display, 302
   equations, 777
   horizontal, 302
   navigating documents, 26
      troubleshooting, 16
   scrolling documents, 61-62
   viewing text in
      columns, 443
   vertical, 302

**scrolling documents, 61-62**

**Search Documents Only check box, 947**

**search engines, marketing Web pages, 1070**

**Search Level option, 946**

**Search Operators dialog box, 933**

**searching**
   footers in documents, 179
   headers in documents, 179
   help topics, 50-51
   subdocument files within master documents, 895

**sec function, 779**

**Secondary Location For Fast Search Information File text box, 947**

**Select All command (Edit menu), 703**

**Select Box to Edit dialog box, 768**

**Select command (Edit menu), 923**

**Select command (Format menu), 163-164**

**Select Default Template Folder dialog box, 316-317**

**Select File dialog box, 541**

Select Folder dialog box, 35
Select Image Source command (Insert menu), 716
Select Labels Location dialog box, 195-196
Select Macro dialog box, 330, 406-407, 423
Select New Document dialog box, 78, 368, 378, 862
Select Output File dialog box, 613
Select Page Numbering Format dialog box, 163-164
Select Printer dialog box, 24
Select Records dialog box, 614
Select Sound File dialog box, 1038
Select Source dialog box, 716
Select tool, 703
Selected Text option (Spell Checker), 218
selecting
  buttons from dialog boxes, 34
  cells of tables, 503-504
    all, 505
    troubleshooting, 509
  clip art figures, 703
  contiguous files, 923
  default folders for templates, 316-317
  drawing tools, 691
  Feature Bar buttons, 31
  files, troubleshooting, 924
  folders as defaults, 74
  fonts, 740-750
  glossary terms, 52
  graphics boxes, 269
  image sources, 715-716
  ISPs (Internet Service Providers), 1069
  keyboard preferences, 325
  label formats, 191
  Number of Columns text box (Columns Dialog box), 439-440
  page number position documents, 163-164
  page size for documents, 179-180
  noncontiguous files, 923
  printers, 278-279, 291-292
  records range, Merge feature, 614-615
  records to be imported with Access feature, 576
  shortcuts, 938
  text
    tables, 503-504
    troubleshooting, 16
  Toolbars
    Ruler Bar, 510
    Tables, 510
  WordPerfect installation options, 1078-1079
SelectMode(On!), 976-977
Send command (File menu), 296
sending
  e-mail documents, 295-296
  e-mail via Merge feature, 612-613
Sentence option (Add Compare Markings dialog box), 831
Sentence option (Spell Checker), 218
separator lines (footnotes)
  changing, 816
  troubleshooting, 817
Series command (Chart menu), 554
Series property sheet, 554-555

serif typeface, 741
servers
  placing HTML documents on, 1068
Set option (Edit Graphics Line dialog box), 663-665
Set Paragraph Number dialog box, 484-485
Sets palette (Equation Editor), 775
setting
  conversion preferences for ASCII delimited text, 562
  conversion preferences for Code Pages, 563
  conversion preferences for imported files, 561
  conversion preferences for Metafiles graphics, 562-563
  data link options, 578
  facing pages, 162
  Initial Codes style in documents, 199-200
  initial font in documents, 197-198
  merge options
    form files, 613-614
    QuickMark on Save on documents, 310
Settings command (Start menu), 66
Settings menu commands
  Control Panel, 63, 637
  Printer, 290
Setup program (WordPerfect 7), 1077
shading
  fonts, 129
  tables, customizing, 993-995
Shading option (Font dialog box), 129
shadow cursors, 57

**Shadow Pointer**
  improved features
      Preferences, 1098
  WordPerfect
      improved features, 1098

**Shadow tool, 719**

**shadows (TextArt),
  troubleshooting, 720**

**shapes**
  attributes, 707-712
      color, 707-709
      fills, 709
      line patterns, 710-712
  colors, changing, 697
  constraining, 693
  drawing, 690-693
      arcs, 695-697
      arrows, 698-699
      arrows, line end,
          698-699
      arrows, sweeping, 699
      circles, 697
      closed curves, 694-695
      curves, 694-695
      deleting, 692-693
      drawing tools, 691-692
      ellipses, 695-697
      freehand, 697
      inserting charts,
          702-703
      inserting clip art,
          700-701
      inserting into
          documents, 716
      keyboard, 692-693
      lines, 694-695
      mouse, 692-693
      polygons, 694-695
      rectangles, 691, 695-697
      squares, 697
      WP Draw, 693-699
  fills
      changing, 697
      troubleshooting, 712
  lines, color changes, 707
  moving mouse, 692
  removing after creating,
      692

  text
      adding, 712-713
      features, 713-714
      wrapping, 714-715
  *see also* objects

**Shapes Palette tool, 718**

**Shift key, constraining
  shapes, 693**

**short form entries,
  853-854**

**shortcuts, 14, 937-939**
  adding to FAVORITES
      folder, 938
  deleting from FAVORITES
      folder, 938-939
  selecting, 938
  text scripts, 423
  troubleshooting, 939

**Show command (View
  menu), 59, 146, 304**

**Show Me tab, 1098**

**Show Me tab (Help dialog
  box), 51-53**

**Show options**
  Comments features
      documents, 301-302
  Documents Display,
      301-302
  Graphics features
      documents, 301-302
  Hidden Text feature
      documents, 302
  QuickSpots
      documents, 302
  Table gridlines
      documents, 301-302
  Windows systems colors
      documents, 301-302

**Show Phonetic
  Suggestions option
  (Spell Checker), 219**

**Show QuickTips, menu
  displays, 309**

**Show Ruler Bar Guides
  option, 141**

**Showing a Hidden Outline
  Family option (outlines),
  479-480**

**Showing All HIdden
  Outline Families option
  (outlines), 479-480**

**Showing Hidden Body Text
  option (outlines), 480**

showing, *see* displaying;
  viewing

**Sidekick (Corel
  WordPerfect Suite
  integrated applications),
  1094**

**sin function, 779**

**single vertical line (|), 784**

**sinh function, 779**

**sites (Web), U.S.
  Copyright Office, 1071**

**size**
  fonts, 130
  paper, default settings, 56
  printer terms, 182-183
  text
      attributes, 129
      characters, 126-129
  *see also* sizing

**Size Column To Fit
  option, 1018**

**Size command
  (Application Control
  menu), 19**

**Size option (Layout/Type
  property sheet), 557**

**sizing**
  clip art figures, 706
  columns in charts, 546
  columns of tables, 510-512
  graphics boxes, 270,
      674-675
  tables, 513-514
  Toolbar palette, 417

windows
　keyboard, 19
　mouse, 18
**Small Icons command (View menu), 925**
smart quotes, 647
**SmartQuotes feature, 208, 239-240, 642**
**Smoothness tool, 719**
soft fonts, 635
soft hyphens, 149
soft page breaks, indicated by [SPg], 156
soft returns, 58, 60
　hyphens, 149
**Sort command (Tools menu), 626-628**
**Sort dialog box, 626-628**
**Sort feature, 588**
　data files, coverting, 624
　record types
　　Line, 625
　　Merge Text, 625
　　Paragraph, 625
　　Parallel Columns, 625
　　Table, 625
**Sort keys**
　data files
　　using, 626-628
　　using multiple sorts, 628-630
**Sort option (Merge Feature Bar), 603**
**Sort Slice option (Layout/ Type property dialog box), 557**
sorting
　data in tables, 986
　files, 926-927
　　Arrange Icons By option, 927
　　by icons, 926-927
　folders, 926-927
　　Arrange Icons By option, 927
　　by icons, 926-927

multi-word names, troubleshooting, 630
print jobs, 290
tabular lists, troubleshooting, 630
**sound**
　embedding in documents, 1037
　linking documents, 1037-1038
　memory problems in documents, 1037
**sound boards, WordPerfect compatibility, 1037**
**sound clips**
　insertion options, 1040
　　Link To File On Disk, 1038
　　Store In Document, 1038
　　Playback Controls buttons, 1039
　　Sound Clips In Document list, 1039
**Sound Clips dialog box, 1037-1039**
**Sound command (Insert menu), 1037-1038**
**spaces, displaying in documents, 42**
**spacing**
　borders, 666
　equations, 764-765
　　troubleshooting, 778
　footnotes, 806
　indentation, 58
　leading, 745
　lines, 132-134
　　default, 739
　　default settings, 56
　　paragraphs, 740
　　text alignment, 739-740
　rows (parallel columns), 450-451
**Spacing Between Columns text box, customizing column width, 441-442**

**special characters**
　accessing, 640-647
　as font attributes, 649
　Compose feature, 644-645
　HTML documents, 1060-1061
　mnemonics, 645
　overstrikes, 645-647
　　creating, 646
　　editing, 647
　types, 641-643
　viewing character sets, 642
**special components**
　Corel TrueType Fonts WordPerfect, 1085-1086
　custom installation WordPerfect, 1085-1086
　IBM Voice Type Control WordPerfect, 1085-1086
　WordPerfect SGML options, 1085-1086
**specifying conversion format for documents, 566-569**
**Specifying the Position for Footnotes option (Footnote Options dialog box), 815**
**SpeedFormat**
　command (QuickMenu), 524
　formatting tables, 524
　styles, creating, 988
**Spell As You Go feature, 1098**
**Spell Check command (Tools menu), 209**
**Spell Checker, 207-224, 1087**
　capitalization check, 212
　closing, 215
　customizing, 217
　dictionary, 211
　double words, 213
　editing misspelled words, 214
　looking up words in, 216-217

other languages, 236
QuickCorrect, adding words to, 215
spell checking documents, 210-216, 221
starting, 209-210
automatically, 219
stopping, 216
typos, 213

**Spell Checker dialog box, 209, 213, 238**

**Spell-As-You-Go, 217**

**Spell-As-You-Go command (Tools menu), 217**

**SpellCheck command (QuickMenu), 176**

**spellchecking**
documents, 894-895
footers in documents, 178-179
headers in documents, 178-179

**Speller feature, 714**

**[SPg] code, soft page break, 156**

**Split Cell command**
QuickMenu, 515
Table menu, 515

**Split Cell dialog box, 515**

**Split command (Table menu), 984**

**splitting**
cells of tables, 515-516
tables, 984-985

**Splitting Long Footnotes option (Footnote Options dialog box), 815**

**splitting words,** *see* **hyphenation**

**Spreadsheet Import/Link feature, data linking, 577-578**

**Spreadsheet/Database command (Insert menu), 623**

**Spreadsheet/Database Import feature**
advantages over Clipboard when importing, 573-576
spreadsheets
copying, 573-576

**spreadsheets, 996-1006**
ASCII file format, converting, 579-580
copying
Clipboard feature, 576
Spreadsheet/Database Import feature, 573-576
data entry
changing, 545
clearing, 545
QuickFill, 1019-1020
QuickFill, entering dates of months, 1020
QuickFill, entering days of week, 1020
troubleshooting, 1018
designing, 996-997
exporting data, 581
forcing text mode, 1001
formatting numeric data, 999-1001
formulas
absolute references, 1008-1009
calculating, 1005
converting, 908
copying, 1003-1004
creating, 1001-1003
creating, letter grade formulas, 1010-1011
creating, percent formulas, 1010
creating, Quiz Points averages, 1009
creating, reporting averages, 1008
creating, total points formulas, 1009-1010
deleting, 1005
functions in, 1004-1005
modifying, 1005
troubleshooting, 1018

importing
data, 580-581, 907
to tables, 986-988
large, importing, 579
linking to WordPerfect, 906
navigating, 545
range of data imported, 907
unknown formats, converting, 579-580

**SQRT command, 770**
creating roots, 787

**squares, drawing, 697**

**STACK command, 770**
creating multiline expressions, 790-791

**STACKALIGN command, 770**
creating multiline expressions, 790-791

**stacked 100% charts, 552**

**stacked bar charts, 538, 552**

**standard parallel columns, 447**

**STANDARD.QAD file, 701**

**Start menu commands, Settings, 66**

**starting**
blank documents, 366
Equation Editor, 760-761
Grammatik, 225
QuickFinder Manager, 939
QuickTasks, 913-914
Spell Checker, 209-210
automatically, 219
Windows Explorer, 930
WordPerfect 7, 12
WP Draw, 684-686
creating graphics, 684-685
editing graphics, 685
troubleshooting, 543, 693
*see also* accessing; activating

**startup options, adding to WordPerfect, 1088-1090**
**statement operators, IF commands, 964**
**statistics check (Grammatik), 231-232**
**status bar, 24-25, 56**
   displaying, 25
   hiding, 25
   modifying, 322-324
   Options dialog box, 323-324
   Preferences dialog box, 25, 322-324
   Preferences option, 62
**Stop button (Macro Feature Bar), 952-953**
**stopping**
   Spell Checker, 216
   *see also* closing; quitting
**storing**
   keyboard definitions in default templates, 326
   macros overview, 950
   subdocuments, 874-876
   templates in additional folders, 317
**strikeout (text), 829**
**Style button (Hypertext Feature Bar), 1023-1024**
**Style command (QuickMenu), 275**
**Style List dialog box, selecting styles for documents, 340**
**Style Name text box, naming styles, 342**
**Style Setup dialog box, 345-346**
**styles**
   applying (Power Bar), 353-354
   Border Text Paragraph Style, 360
   character styles, applying, 355-356
   current document, editing, 345-350
   defined, 1044
   definition, editing, 349
   documents
      activating, 353
      benefits, 335
      chaining, 351-352
      classifying, 336
      copying, 347-348
      creating, 340
      deleting, 346-347
      displaying, 345-346
      editing, 344-345
      nesting, 351
      retrieving from other documents, 357
      saving, 356-357
      system styles, 338
   fonts, 130
   formatting, 334
   codes
      copying, 348
      tools, 334-335
   graphics, copying, 348
   graphics boxes, 262-268, 670-671
   Letterhead Document Style, 358-359
   lines
      customizing, 659-660
      tables, 525
   modifying Styles Editor dialog box, 348-349
   naming Style Name text box, 342
   paragraph styles, applying, 354-355
   Q&A Linked Paragraph Styles, 360
   Quotation Character Style, 359
   SpeedFormats, creating, 988
   system
      editing, 345-350
      styles, modifying, 356
   templates, 366-367
      editing, 345-350
      creating, 340
      modifying, 356
   Toolbar buttons, 419-420
   troubleshooting location, 352
   types
      character, 336-338
      document, 336-338
      paragraph, 336-338
   versus macros, 335
   writing (Grammatik), 229-230
**Styles button (Power Bar), 130**
**Styles Copy dialog box, 347-348**
**Styles Editor, 814**
   dialog box, 344, 348-349, 468-469, 1032-1033
   editing Initial Style codes, 338
**SUB subdocuments name extension, 872-876**
**SUB command, 770**
   creating subscripts, 767-768
**Subdivide Page command (Format menu), 184-185**
**subdividing**
   pages into columns, 184-185
   pages into rows, 184-185
**Subdocument command (File menu), 874-876**
**Subdocument dialog box, 874-876**
**Subdocument Error dialog box, 879-881**
**subdocuments**
   adding, 876-884
   codes, inserting into master documents, 873-876
   creating, 871-872
   cross-referencing items, 894
   deleting, 876-884
   editing styles to permit managibility, 888

extension, SUB, 872-876
formatting, 871-872
styles, 888-889
inserting chapter codes, 891-892
links to master documents, 872
moving within master documents, 877-884
storing documents, 874-876

**subheads, 744**

**Subject Search Text, document summaries, 319**

**subscript text, 128**

**subscripts, 767-768**

**Subtitle command (Chart menu), 548**

**subtitles, inserting into charts, 548**

**Suggest Spelling Replacements command (Customize menu), 229**

**SUM operator, 785**

**SUM() function, creating total points formulas, 1009-1010**

**summaries of documents, printing, 287**

**Summary command (Edit menu), 204**

**sums, creating, 785-786**

**SUP command, 770**
creating superscripts, 767-768

**superscript text, 128**

**superscripts, 767-768**

**Suppress command (Format menu), 172-173**

**Suppress dialog box, 177**

**[Suppress: Header A], 177**

**[Suppress: Page Num], 172**

**suppressing**
footers in documents, 177
headers in documents, 177
page numbers in documents, 172

**sweeping arrows**
drawing, 699
troubleshooting, 711

**SWITCH command, 965-966**
accompanied always by ENDSWITCH command, 965-966
compared to IF command, 965-966
syntax rules, 966

**switching**
between documents, 44
between Toolbars, 415-416

**symbols**
defined, 769
formatting, 146
inserting into equation palettes, 775-776
Large palette, 792

**Symbols palette (Equation Editor), 775, 792**

**Symbols tab, 145**

**synonyms, searching documents, 936**

**Synonyms tab, 936**

**syntax**
DISPLAY command, 973
equations, 771-773
macros, 957-959
MENULIST commands, 962-963
SWITCH command, 966

**System attribute (files), 922**

**System Printers button (Print dialog box), 292**

**system styles**
changing default settings, 338
document, editing, 338
editing, 345-350
modifying, 356

**system variables**
actual values, 961
logocval states of True and False types of information, 961
macros overview, 960-961

# T

**Tab**
icons (WordPerfect), 1099
key, indentation, 58

**Tab Set dialog box, 142-143**
pre-exisiting macros (WordPerfect for Windows), 400-401

**Table (Sort feature), 625**

**Table Cut/Copy dialog box, 506**

**Table Format dialog box, 512, 516, 521**
formatting table text, 519
opening, 512, 519

**Table Gridlines (Show options), 301-302**

**Table Lines/Fill dialog box, 525, 528, 989**

**Table menu, 509**

**Table menu commands**
Calculate, 1003, 1005
Copy Formula, 1003
Create, 498
Format, 512, 516
Insert, 513
Join, 985
Join Cells, 514
Lines/Fill, 525, 992
Names, 1012
QuickFill, 1020
Split, 984
Split Cell, 515

**Table Names in Current Document dialog box, 1013**

**Table Numeric Format dialog box, 999**

**Table of Authorities**
  creating, 848-858
  defining, 854-858
  Feature Bar, 851
    defining, 845-849
    numbering, 847
    troubleshooting headings, 848
  marking text, 850-854
**table of contents**
  creating, 843-848
    with master documents, 884
  defining, 845-849
    with master documents, 885
  errors, fixing in body text, 887
  generating, 887
  hard page breaks, inserting, 885
  marking text in documents, 884-885
**Table option (Go To dialog box), 66**
**Table Position option (tables), 523**
**Table SpeedFormat dialog box, 524, 988**
**Tables features (WordPerfect), 1099**
**tables**
  as spreadsheets, 996-1006
    absolute references with formulas, 1008-1009
    calculating formulas, 1005
    copying formulas, 1003-1004
    creating formulas, 1001-1003
    deleting formulas, 1005
    designing, 996-997
    forcing text mode, 1001
    formatting numeric data, 999-1001
    functions in formulas, 1004-1005
    letter grade points formulas, 1010-1011
    modifying formulas, 1005
    percent points formulas, 1010
    Quiz Points averages formulas, 1009
    reporting averages formulas, 1008
    total points formulas, 1009-1010
  borders, 528
    customizing, 992-993
  boxes, 265
  cells
    customizing, 993-995
    deleting text from, 504-505
    floating, creating, 1014-1015
    formatting, 521-522
    guidelines, 526
    joining, 514-515
    lines, 526
    locking, 1005-1006
    moving between, 501-502
    selecting, 503-504
    selecting all, 505
    splitting, 515-516
  columns
    aligning, 520
    deleting, 513
    formatting, 519-521
    width, changing, 510-512
  converting tabular columns to, 500
  copying, 507-508
  creating, 498-509
    menus, 498
    from merged data, 623-624
    Power Bar, 499
  cutting, 507-508
  data
    merging, 986
    sorting, 986
  default settings, 509
  defined, 496-498
  deleting, 507-508
  Edit Table QuickSpot, 507
  editing, tool selection, 509-510
  fills, 528-529
    alternating between rows and columns, 988-990
    color, 990
  formatting, 522-523
    borders, 528
    cell lines, 526
    fills, 528-529
    guidelines, 526
    lines, 525
    SpeedFormat, 524
    troubleshooting, 523
  forms
    creating, electronic fill-in, 532-533
    creating, phone message, 532
    creating, with irregular columns, 985
  functions, 1007, 1008
  grade-tracking, 1006-1007
    creating report cards, 1011-1014
    formulas with absolute references, 1008-1009
    functions, 1007-1008
    letter grade formulas, 1010-1011
    percent formulas, 1010
    Quick Points average, 1009
    total points formulas, 1009-1010
  graphics
    adding, 529
    troubleshooting, 532
  joining, 985
  lines
    customizing, 990-991
    default style, 527
    styles, 525
    troubleshooting, 532, 995
  moving insertion point in, 502

names
    creating, 1012-1013
    navigating with,
        1013-1014
Outline Define dialog box,
    summary of controls,
    487-488
Outline Feature Bar
    summary, 471-472
positioning, 983-984
pre-exisiting macros
    (WordPerfect for
    Windows), 400-401
printing, 508-509
QuickMenus, 506
report cards
    creating, 1011-1014
    form creation,
        1011-1012
    names creation,
        1012-1013
    navigating with names,
        1013-1014
rows
    adding, 503, 513
    creating headers,
        517-518
    cutting/copying, 506
    deleting, 513
    height, 516-517
saving, 508-509
shading, customizing,
    993-995
sizing, 513-514
SpeedFormat styles,
    creating, 988
splitting, 984-985
spreadsheets, importing,
    986-988
structure, 496
Tables Toolbar,
    displaying, 982
text
    attributes, adding, 531
    copying, 505-506
    cutting, 505-506
    deleting from cells,
        504-505
    entering, 502-503
    formatting, 518-523

formatting, cells,
    521-522
formatting, columns,
    519-521
formatting, precedence,
    518-519
formatting, Table
    Format dialog
    box, 519
pasting, 505-506
rotated, 530-531
selecting, 503-504
troubleshooting, 995
troubleshooting
    creating, 508
    selecting cells, 509

**Tables Toolbar**
displaying, 982
selecting, 510

**tabs**
Advanced (Border/Fill
    dialog box), 755
Back, 138
Box Fill, 548-550
Box Type, 548
Center, 139
clearing from Ruler
    Bar, 143
Contents (Help dialog
    box), 48-49
creating with space
    bar, 138
Decimal, 144
Decimal Align, 139
default settings, 56
    restoring, 140
Display Options, 553
displaying, 42
dot leaders, 139
entering text into text
    boxes, 41
Fill Attributes, 553
Find (Help dialog box),
    50-53
General (TextArt), 717-718
indenting paragraphs, 139
Index (Help dialog box),
    49-53
Labels, 551

Left Align, 139
Line Width/Style, 556
Options (TextArt),
    717-719
QuickFinder (Open dialog
    box), 940
Right Align, 139
setting, 138-144
    hard, 143-144
    QuickMenu, 143
    Ruler Bar, 139-140
    Tab Set dialog box,
        142-143
Show Me (Help dialog
    box), 51-53
stops, 139
Symbols, 145
Synonyms, 936
Text Fill, 548
Text Outline, 548
Title Font, 548-550

**Tabs Snap To Ruler Bar
Grid option, 141**

**tabular columns,
converting to tables, 500**

**tags (HTML), defined,
1044**

**tan function, 779**

**tanh function, 779**

**TEMPLATE folder, 372**

**Template Feature Bar,
369-370**
    creating templates, 375-378
    editing templates, 374-375

**Template Information
dialog box, 377**

**Template Macro command
(Tools menu), 379**

**templates, 43, 364-370**
    associating macros to
        triggers, 383-384
        troubleshooting, 386
    Calendar Expert, 385
    creating, 375-378
        existing, 376-378
        new, 375
        styles, 340

## templates

default folders
  selecting, 316-317
defined, 364
deleting, 378
documents, 368-369
editing, 374-375
  associating, 382-383
Fax Expert, 386
Feature Bar, 369-370
  creating templates, 375-378
  editing templates, 374-375
folders, storing additional, 317
groups, creating, 378
Letter Expert, 384-385
  troubleshooting, 386
macros, 366-367
  adding to Toolbar buttons, 424
  opening, 950
Memo Expert, 385
merges, 366-367
Newsletter Expert, 386
objects, 378-381
  adding, 379-380
  associating macros to triggers, 383-384
  associating to features, 382-383
  copying from other templates, 380-381
  embedding guidelines, 384
  removing, 381
QuickTasks, 913-914
saving, 376
styles, 366-367
  editing, 338-339, 345-350
  modifying, 356
  style, 338-339
viewing list of, troubleshooting, 372-373
WordPerfect for Windows predefined, 370-372
WP7US.WPT file, 365

**text**
adding, 67
aligning, 132, 737-739
  all-justification, 739
  center-justification, 738
  columns, 444
  full-justification, 739
  left-justification, 737-738
  line spacing, 739-740
  right-justification, 738
appearance, controlling (merge codes), 621-622
ASCII delimited text files, setting conversion preferences, 562
blink, 1051
body in HTML documents, 1050
borders, 255-261
  paragraph, 256
  paragraph, adding fills, 257
  paragraph, deleting, 261
color, 751-753
columns
  displaying (scroll bar), 443
  editing, 444-445
  formatting advice, 442
  hyphenation, 442
  inserting, 442
  viewing (scroll bar), 443
converting into address blocks, 1054
customizing
  Redline method, 200-201
  Toolbars, 424-427
cutting and pasting in columns, 451
deleting, 87-88
  restoring, 88-89
  single characters, 87
displaying, hidden, 128
editing in text boxes, 34
embedding equations in, 794-795
endnotes, 801-802

converting footnotes to, 820-821
converting to footnotes, 821
editing, 818
fonts, 806
inserting, 818
manipulating, 818
options, 818-819
placing, 819-820
positioning, 802
typing, 802
entering into documents, 56-60
  creating letters, 59-60, 66
  inserting blank lines, 59
fonts
  appearance, 128
  attributes, applying, 127
  colors, 129
  shading, 129
  size, 127, 130
  styles, 127, 130
footnotes, 801-817
  Changing Footnote Options for the Entire option, 817-821
  Changing the Spacing Between Notes option, 814-815
  Choosing a Separator Line option, 815-816
  converting endnotes to, 821
  converting to endnotes, 820-821
  copying, 809-810
  cutting, 811
  deleting, 811
  editing, 808-809
  Editing the Numbering Style in Notes option, 814
  Editing the Numbering Style in Text option, 813-814
  fonts, 806
  Insert (Continued...) Message option, 815

inserting, 803-808
moving, 810-811
navigating, 807
Numbering Style
  option, 812-813
options, 812-817
pasting, 810
positioning, 802
Restart Numbering On
  Each Page option,
  813-814, 817-821
setting numbers, 811
spacing, 806
Specifying the Position
  for Footnotes
  option, 815
Splitting Long
  Footnotes option, 815
Text Under Edit
  Numbering Style
  option, 813-814
typing, 802
formatting
  auto code
    placement, 126
  character appearance,
    126-129
  character attributes, 130
  characters, 126-130
  customizing format
    options, 145-146
  default settings, 122-123
  Format menu, 123
  in graphics boxes, 262
  keyboard, 125
  QuickMenu, 123
  QuickFormat, 125-126,
    144-145
  QuickSpots, 125
  setting changes,
    124-125
  size, 126-129
  symbols, 146
hidden, 128, 244-245
highlighting, 824-826
hyphenation, 148-149
  automatic, 150
  inserting point of,
    150-151
  preventing, 149
  removing, 151-152

inserting, 86-87
justification, 147-148
macros
  applying for common
    uses, 391
  formatting, 404-405
  instant play, 397
  naming, 395
  playing, 392-393
  re-recording, 393-394
  recording, 389-391
marking
  to create indexes,
    859-862
  to create lists, 835-837
  to create Table of
    Authorities, 850-854
  to create Table of
    Contents, 843-845
monospaced, 58
outlines
  cutting and pasting,
    482-484
  editing, 481
  hiding elements, 478
  levels, 481-482
overwriting, 86-87
palette, 691
placing on Clipboard, 571
printing
  selected blocks, 286
  troubleshooting font
    display, 652
replacing in text boxes, 34
scripts, assigning to
  Toolbar buttons, 422-423
selecting, troubleshooting,
  16, 312
shapes
  adding, 712-713
  features, 713-714
  wrapping, 714-715
shortcut keys, 423
size attributes, 129
strikeout, 829
styles
  Character, 887-888
  Documents, 887-888

Paragraph, 887-888
Paragraph-Auto,
  887-888
subscript, 128
superscript, 128
tables
  attributes, adding, 531
  copying, 505-506
  cutting, 505-506
  deleting from cells,
    504-505
  entering, 502-503
  formatting, 518-523
  pasting, 505-506
  rotated, 530-531
  selecting, 503-504
TextArt, 717-721
  tools, 717-719
troubleshooting
  formatting in
    columns, 736
  legibility, 995
  reading, 261
  selection, 16
  typing, 148
typing over with Typeover
  feature, 67-68
watermarks, 272-273
word-wrap, 58
wrap in graphics
  boxes, 675

**Text Area, 713**

**Text Box command (Image
menu), 670**

**text boxes, 34, 263**
Desired Number Of Filled
  Pages, 187-188
editing text in, 34
entering text with Tab
  key, 41
Font Size, 37
Location For Temporary
  Files, 947
moving to, 34
replacing text in, 34
Secondary Location For
  Fast Search Information
  File, 947

Text Color tool, 718
Text Fill tab, 548
Text option (Box Content dialog box), 672
Text Outline tab, 548
Text under Edit Numbering Style option, (Footnote Options dialog box), 813
Text/Background Colors command (Format menu), 1056
Text/Background dialog box, 1056
TextArt, 717-721, 1087
  interface, 717
  printing, troubleshooting, 721
  saving, 720
  tools, 717-719
  troubleshooting, displaying shadows, 720
TextArt command (Graphics menu), 720
Texture fill style, charts, 555
Texture Settings dialog box, 555
Thesaurus, 207, 714
  looking up reference words, 235-236
  looking up words, 232-233
  replacing words, 234
  window, 233-234
Thesaurus Definition feature, 233
thickness, lines (customizing), 660-661
thin space (`), 770
[THPg] (temporary hard page break), 158
tick (charts), editing, 553
tilde (~) symbol, 765, 773
Tile Side By Side command (Window menu), 44

Tile Top To Bottom command (Window menu), 44
tiling documents, 44
Tilt option (Layout/Type dialog box), 557
time, inserting into letters, 66
Timed Document Backup feature (backup options), 316
title bar in WordPerfect window, 20
Title command
  Chart menu, 548
  Format menu, 1049
Title Font tab, 548-550
titles
  HTML documents, 1049-1050
  y-axis (charts), 556
TO command, 770, 785
To End Of Document option (Spell Checker), 218
ToA, *see* Table of Authorities
toggling features (check boxes), 35
TOLOWER (merge codes), 621
Tool palette (WP Draw), viewing, 689
Toolbar command (View menu), 57, 415, 687
Toolbar Editor dialog box, 421, 956
Toolbar Editor—Graphics dialog box, 421
Toolbar Editor—Power Bar dialog box, 428
Toolbar Options dialog box, 419

Toolbar Preferences dialog box, 321, 408-409, 415
Toolbars
  backups, 420
  buttons
    adding program features to, 421-422
    assigning macros to, 423-424
    assigning text script to, 422-423
    customizing appearance, 424-427
    moving, 421
    rows, 419
    styles, changing, 419-420
  customizing, 420-426
    assigning macros to, 423-424
    assigning program features to buttons, 421-422
    assigning text script to buttons, 422-423
    graphics, 424-427
    moving buttons, 421
    text, 424-427
  Equation Editor, 777-778
  Generate, displaying, 829
  hiding, 415
  icons, 416-417
  macros, inserting, 408-409
  modifying, 321
  moving, keyboard, 418
  positioning, 417-418
  reasons for using, 414
  Ruler Bar, selecting, 510
  switching between, 415-416
  Tables
    displaying, 982
    selecting, 510
  troubleshooting, displaying, 125
  viewing, 415
  WP Draw, 687-688
    cutomizing, 543
    viewing, 543, 687
  WP Draw drawing, 543

**Toolbars dialog box, 57, 125**

**Toolbars/Ruler command (View menu), 23**

**toolboxes (Image Tools), closing, 678**

**Tools dialog box, 507, 982**

**Tools menu commands**
Add, 902-903
Address Book, 900
Delete, 902
Edit, 950
Generate, 803, 887
Generate Lists, 836
Grammatik, 225
Highlight, 825
Hypertext/Web Links, 310, 1028-1029, 1064
Language, 654, 815
Macro, 647, 820
Merge, 588, 611
QuickCorrect, 224, 624
Record, 953-954
Rename, 901
Sort, 626-628
Spell Check, 209
Spell-As-You-Go, 217
Template Macro, 379

**Top option (Edit Graphics Line dialog box), 665**

**total points formulas, creating, 1009-1010**

**TOUPPER (merge codes), 621-622**

**transposed characters, creating with macros, 402-403**

**Tree view, 928**

**Tree View command (View menu), 928**

**triggering macros, events, 383**

**triggers**
associating macros to, 383-384
troubleshooting, 386

**troubleshooting**
address spacing on labels, 618
arrows, sweeping, 711
changing writing styles, 232
charts, 544
columns and formatting text, 736
cross-references, 868
data fields empty, 618
dialog boxes, closing, 41
documents
   converting to HTML, 1047
   navigating with scroll bars, 16
   printer driver default, 312
   printing, 282
   printing with graphics, 288-289
   saving under different file names, 76
   viewing, 31, 85
endnotes
   inserting, 820
   reference numbers, 819
equations
   character formatting, 797
   displaying, 763
   fonts, 797
   functions, 797
   spacing, 778
files
   deleting, 924
   finding, 937
   moving, 924
   names, 248, 924
   selecting, 924
fills, shapes, 712
flagging correctly spelled words, 232
flagging long sentences, 232
fonts, 647, 750
   document creation from other computers, 652
   print display, 652
footnotes
   deleting, 817
   numbering, 817
   separator lines, 817
formulas, 1018
gradients, 711
graphics
   aligning, 693
   formats, 1059
   positioning in tables, 532
   printing, 757
graphics lines, deleting, 261
hidden text, 248
indexes, 864
   defining, 868
Inline Equations command (Graphics menu), 778
kerning, 757
Letter Expert, 386
lines (custom), 995
lists, 1056
macros
   locating, 401
   recording, 407-408
mouse button assignments, 62-63
paragraph borders, 261
Power Bar, adding buttons, 429
printers, 282
QuickCorrect dictionary, 224
shortcuts, 939
sorting order on multi-word names, 630
sorting tabular lists, 630
spreadsheets
   data entry, 1018
   importing to tables, 988
styles, locating, 352
Table of Contents headings, 848

tables
- creating, 508
- formatting, 523
- lines, 532
- selecting cells, 509

templates, viewing list of, 372-373

text
- formatting in columns, 736
- legibility, 995
- reading, 261
- selection, 16
- typing, 148

text boxes, entering text, 41

text selection, 312

TextArt
- displaying shadows, 720
- printing, 721

toolbars, displaying, 125

typographical smart quotations, 647

user word lists, adding words, 224

WP Draw
- starting, 543, 693
- window, 693

**TrueType fonts, 636, 741**
- advantages, 636
- installing, 636-639
  - in Windows 95, 637-638
  - WordPerfect 7, 639-640
- removing from Windows 95, 639
- special components, 1085-1086

**TTF filename extension, 637**

**Turn On Rules command (Customize menu), 228**

**turning on/off**
- bars with View menu, 57
- Equation Editor Toolbar, 778
- guidelines, 26
- guidelines with View menu, 57

hyphenation, 150
irregular capitalization option, 213
Num Lock feature, 63
page borders, 260-261
reveal codes, 122
Spell-As-You-Go, 217
Typeover feature, 67
see also disabling

**TWAIN interface, 716**

**twisting arrows, 697**

**Two-Page mode (Document Display), 29, 304-305**

**Type (macros) commands, 954**

**type sizes, 742-745**

**Type(Text), macros, product function commands, 976-977**

**Type/Axis option (Series dialog box), 555**

**typefaces (fonts), 740-742**
- changing, 833-834

**Typeover feature, 68, 87**
- turning on/off, 67

**Typesetting command (Format menu), 135, 646, 745**

**typical installation, 956**

**typing**
- documents, 58
- endnotes, 802
- footnotes, 802
- kerning, 747
- text, 67
  - troubleshooting, 148
  - with Typeover feature, 67-68
- text into columns (parallel), 448-450

**Typographic Symbols character set (Set 4), 642**

**typographical**
- controls, 745-751
  - kerning, 746-747
  - leading, 745
  - letterspacing, 747-748
  - word spacing, 749-750
- errors, 213
- quotation marks, 642
- smart quotations, 647

# U

**U.S. Copyright Office Web site, 1071**

**Undelete command (Edit menu), 88**

**UNDERLINE command, 770**

**Underline Options (Font dialog box), 129**

**underlining attribute, 742**

**Undo command (Edit menu), 89-90, 254, 692, 704, 880**
- reformmating documents, 187

**Undo feature, in restoring deleted text, 88-91**

**Undo/Redo History**
- command (Edit menu), 90
- dialog box, 90
- feature, 90
- Options dialog box, 89-91

**undoing**
- line deletions, 254
- text deletions, 504
- see also restoring

**Uniform Resource Locators, see URLs (Uniform Resource Locators)**

**uninstalling WordPerfect, 1090**

**up/down arrows scaling option, 680**

Update Chart From Table command (QuickMenu), 546
Update command (Insert menu), 578
updating
  charts, 545
  data links, 578
  document references, 843
  documents in WP Draw, 685-686
  fast searches, 944
  formulas, 1004
Upgrade Expert command (Help menu), 48
URLs (Uniform Resource Locators)
  defined, 1044
  inserted in text boxes, 1034
  registering, 1069
Use Column Justification option, 522
Use System Colors command (Options menu), 54
user boxes, 266
User Defined character set (Set 12), 643
user information, configuring documents, 307
user input
  commands, 961-963
    GETSTRING, 961
    MENULIST, 961
  inserting with Merge feature, 619-620
User Word List Editor dialog box, 219, 223, 228
  closing, 222
user word lists, 209, 220-224
  adding words to, 214-215, 223
    QuickCorrect, 215
    troubleshooting, 224
  creating, 221-222
  editing, 223
User Word Lists command (Customize menu), 222, 228

# V

Value/Adjust Number dialog box, 171-172
Values dialog box, 168-169
variables
  assigning values to merge codes, 619
  defined, 769
  macros
    rules for using, 960
    understanding, 959
verifying equations, 760-761
Version command (Options menu), 54
VERT command, 770
Vertical Alignment option, 522
Vertical Line command (Graphics menu), 252
vertical lines, 251-252
  customizing, 664-666
    horizontal position, 664-665
    line length, 665
    with mouse, 252-253
    vertical position, 665
Vertical menu commands, Bottom, 530
vertical scroll bars, 302
vertical y-axis (charts), 536
View File Location Preferences dialog box, 314-315
View in Web Browser command (View menu), 1068

View menu
  Equation Editor, 764
  turning bars on/off, 57
  turning guidelines on/off, 57
  WP Draw, 686
View menu commands
  Arrange Icons By, 927
  Auto Redraw, 545
  Details, 925-927
  Graphics, 302
  Grid/Snap, 690
  Guidelines, 26, 57, 526
  Hidden Text, 128, 302
  Hide Bars, 30-31, 415
  Large Icons, 925-926
  List, 925, 927
  Options, 930
  Outliner, 911
  Page, 279
  Preview, 73
  Preview, Content, 84
  Preview, No Preview, 85
  Preview, Page View, 84
  Preview, Use Separate Window, 84
  Redisplay, 763
  Redraw, 545
  Reveal Codes, 41, 122, 261
  Ruler, 690
  Show, 59, 146, 304
  Small Icons, 925
  Toolbar, 57, 415, 687
  Toolbars/Ruler, 23
  Tree View, 928
  View in Web Browser, 1068
  Zoom, 30, 279
  Zoom Display, 777
View modes, 28-30
  changing, 28
  Draft, 28
  Page, 29
  Two Page mode, 29
  Zoom Draft, 30
viewing
  character sets, 642
  charts on monitors, 556

Hide Bars command, 30-31
preview option, 73
troubleshooting, 31, 85
View modes, 28-30
zoom percentages, 279
equations, 763, 776-777
extensions, 929
fast searches, 944-945
HTML documents, 1068
page definitions for printers, 180
palettes, 776
Power Bar, 427
reveal codes, 41
templates, list of, troubleshooting, 372-373
text columns (scroll bar), 443
Toolbars, 415
  WP Draw, 543
window display for documents, 304-305
WP Draw grid, 689-691
WP Draw ruler, 689-691
WP Draw Tool palette, 689
WP Draw Toolbar, 687
*see also* displaying; previewing

**views**
Details, 927
List, 927
Tree, 928

# W

**Watermark command (Format menu), 733**

**watermarks, 272-275**
asymmetric columns, 733-734
boxes, 267
creating, 275
desktop publishing, 724
images as, 273-275
text, 272-273

**WCM extension (WordPerfect Corp. Macro), naming, 396**

**Web browsers**
defined, 1044
Netscape, 1044
  viewing HTML documents, 1068

**Web pages**
address blocks, 1054-1058
alignment, 1057-1058
body text, 1050
bookmarks, 1062-1063
character formatting, 1053-1054
color, 1056-1057
creating, 1045-1054
creating bullets/lists, 1054-1056
creating links, 1061-1066
documents, 1033-1034
defined, 1042-1043
graphics, 1058-1061
  formats, 1058-1059
  lines, 1059-1060
headings, 1050-1053
hypertext links
  creating, 1063-1064
  editing, 1065
  graphic images, 1066
jumping from WordPerfect to Internet, 1036
navigating
  bookmarks, 1062-1063
  graphic images, 1066
  hypertext links, 1063-1065
special characters, 1060-1061
titles, 1049-1050

**Web publishing,** *see* **publishing (Web)**

**Web servers, placing HTML documents on, 1068**

**Web sites, U.S. Copyright Office, 1071**

**What You See Is What You Get (WYSIWYG), 278**

**white space**
designing documents for desktop publishing, 727
margins, 730

**[Wid/Orph: On], 161**

**widening columns for charts, 546**

**widow, 161**

**Widow/Orphan protection (Format menu)**
including in template, 162
Keep Text Together dialog box, 161

**widths**
altering column appearance, 452-454
table columns, 510-512

**wild cards, 216**
* (asterisk) character, 216
? (question mark) character, 216
finding files, 930-931, 934

**window display, viewing documents, 304-305**

**Window menu**
Equation Editor, 764
WP Draw, 687

**Window menu commands**
Cascade, 44
Tile Side By Side, 44
Tile Top To Bottom, 44

**Window Systems Color (Show options), 301-302**

**windows**
appearance, customizing, 321
cascading, 44
closing, 17
custom features
  Power Bar, 322
  pull-down menus, 324-325
  status bar, 322-324
  Toolbars, 321

maximizing, 18, 44
minimizing, 18, 44
moving
  keyboard, 19
  mouse, 18
Reveal Codes, 41
sizing
  keyboard, 19
  mouse, 18
tiling, 44
WordPerfect
  closing, 18
  title bar, 20
WP Draw,
  troubleshooting, 693

**Windows 95**
  controlling status of print jobs, 290
  installing TrueType fonts, 637-638
  removing TrueType fonts, 639
  setting date/time, 66
  WordPerfect 7 operating standards, 1092

**Windows Explorer, starting, 930**

**Windows Explorer command (Programs menu), 930**

**Windows Sound Recorder, 1037**

**wizards (Find Setup), 50**

**Word and Letter Spacing dialog box, 745, 748-749**

**word lists,** *see* **dictionaries**

**Word option (Add Compare Markings dialog box), 831**

**Word option (Spell Checker), 218**

**word processing formats (Convert feature), 564**

**word-wrap, 58**

**WordPerfect 5.2 features versus earlier versions, 1113-1116**

**WordPerfect 6.0 features versus earlier versions, 1104-1113**

**WordPerfect 6.1 features versus earlier versions, 1099-1104**

**WordPerfect 7**
  backup files, installation consideration, 1077-1078
  CD-ROM, installation procedures, 1078-1082
  customizing
    displays, 300-306
    Document display, 300-303
  exiting, 12, 79
  fonts, installing, 1087-1088
  foreign language versions of, 653-656
    character maps, 656
    inserting foreign language codes, 653-655
    keyboards, 655-656
  formatting features, 155
  hard disk
    defragmenting, 1078
    installation consideration, 1077-1078
  hardware minimum requirements, 1093
  help system, 45-54
    F1 (Help) command, 46
    glossary of terms, 52-53
    Help button, accessing, 1082
    Help dialog box, 48-52
    Help menu, 47-48
    navigating, 53-54
  improved features, 1094-1099
  installation options
    Autorun program, installation, 1078
    choosing, 1078-1079
    compact, 1081-1086
    custom, 1081-1082
    customizing warning, 1085-1086
    network, 1081-1082
    running from CD-ROM, 1081-1082
    typical, 1081-1084
  interface, 1037
  memory requirements, 1087
  printer drivers, installing, 1087
  registration information, entering, 1080
  setup options
    AT&T WorldNet Service installation, 1079
    bonus applications, 1079
    Demos, 1079
    Reference Center, 1079
    WordPerfect Setup (standalone installation), 1078-1079
    WordPerfect Suite Setup, 1078-1079
  Setup program, overview, 1077
  special components, custom installation, 1085-1086
  starting, 12
    startup options, adding, 1088-1090
  uninstalling, 1090
  upgrading issues
    hardware, 1092-1093
    training, 1092-1093

**WordPerfect 7 command (CorelOffice 7 menu), 12**

**WordPerfect Characters dialog box, 201, 644, 762, 776, 1061**

**WordPerfect Macro Help, CD installation, 956**

**WordPerfect SGML options, 1083-1084**

**WordPerfect window**
closing, 18
title bar, 20

**words**
adding to document user word lists, 215
adding to user word lists, 214-215
  QuickCorrect, 215
capitalization, 212
deleting, 88
duplicates, 213
finding files, closeness, 935
hyphenation, 148-149
  automatic, 150
  inserting point of, 150-151
  preventing, 149
  removing, 151-152
inserting into user word lists, 223
  troubleshooting, 224
misspelled, 214
replacing with Grammatik, 227
spacing, 749-750
typographical errors, 213

**Workflow (WordPerfect), 1099**

**working**
page numbers in footers, 176-177
page numbers in headers, 176-177

**World Wide Web, see WWW (World Wide Web)**

**WP Draw**
capturing graphics, 715-716
  selecting image source, 715-716
  TWAIN interface, 716
changing chart types, 551-552
drawing shapes, 690-699
  arcs, 695-697
  arrows, 698-699
  arrows, line end, 698-699
  arrows, sweeping, 699
  attributes, 707-712
  charts, 702-703
  circles, 697
  clip art, 700-702
  closed curves, 694-695
  curves, 694-695
  drawing tools, 691-692
  ellipses, 695-697
  freehand, 697
  keyboard, 692-693
  lines, 694-695
  mouse, 692-693
  polygons, 694-695
  rectangles, 695-697
  squares, 697
  text, 712-715
Drawing Toolbar, 543
grids, viewing, 689-691
interface, 543-544
pull-down menus, 686-687
rulers, viewing, 689-691
scanning graphics, 715-716
starting, 684-686
  creating graphics, 684-685
  editing graphics, 685
  troubleshooting, 693
Tool palette, viewing, 689
Toolbar, 687-688
  customizing, 543
  viewing, 543, 687
troubleshooting
  starting, 543
  window, 693
updating documents, 685-686

**WP7US.WPT file, 365**

**WPD file extension, 72**

**WPDOS 6.1 keyboard (layout types), 325**

**WPG files, 701**

**WPG image, 910**

**WPWin 7 keyboard (layout types), 324-325**

**WPWin dialog box, 961-962**

**wrapping text around shapes, 714-715**

**writing**
in other languages, 235-238
editing, 229-230
styles (Grammatik), 229-230
writing tools, 207-208, 1099

**WWW (World Wide Web)**
browsers
  defined, 1044
  Netscape, 1044
defined, 1042-1044
publishing, see publishing (Web)
  copyright law, 1071
  creating Web pages, 1045-1054
  Internet Publisher, 1044
  marketing, 1070
  newsgroups, 1070
  placing HTML documents on servers, 1068
  registering URLs, 1069
  search engines, 1070
  selecting Internet Service Providers (ISPs), 1069
servers, placing HTML documents on, 1068
Web pages, defined, 1042-1043

**WYSIWYG (What You See Is What You Get), 278, 724**

# X

**x-axis (charts), 536**
    adding titles, 549
    displaying labels, 550
    editing, 552

# Y

**y-axis (charts)**
    adding titles, 549
    displaying labels, 550
    editing, 552
    titles, 556

# Z

**ZIP codes, printing formats on envelopes, 190**

**Zoom, 279**
    button, 693
    command (View menu), 30, 279
    desktop publishing, 724
    dialog box, displaying, 279
    Display command (View menu), 777
    Draft mode, 30
    Equation Display dialog box, 777
    zooming, 30, 279-280
        in display for documents, 305

# GET CONNECTED
## to the ultimate source of computer information!

# The MCP Forum on CompuServe

Go online with the world's leading computer book publisher! Macmillan Computer Publishing offers everything you need for computer success!

Find the books that are right for you! A complete online catalog, plus sample chapters and tables of contents give you an in-depth look at all our books. The best way to shop or browse!

- Get fast answers and technical support for MCP books and software
- Join discussion groups on major computer subjects
- Interact with our expert authors via e-mail and conferences
- Download software from our immense library:
  - ▷ Source code from books
  - ▷ Demos of hot software
  - ▷ The best shareware and freeware
  - ▷ Graphics files

## Join now and get a free CompuServe Starter Kit!

To receive your free CompuServe Introductory Membership, call **1-800-848-8199** and ask for representative #597.

*The Starter Kit includes:*
- ➤ Personal ID number and password
- ➤ $15 credit on the system
- ➤ Subscription to *CompuServe Magazine*

*Once on the CompuServe System, type:*

## GO MACMILLAN

*for the most computer information anywhere!*

# Check out Que® Books on the World Wide Web
## http://www.mcp.com/que

As the biggest software release in computer history, Windows 95 continues to redefine the computer industry. Click here for the latest info on our Windows 95 books

Make computing quick and easy with these products designed exclusively for new and casual users

Examine the latest releases in word processing, spreadsheets, operating systems, and suites

The Internet, The World Wide Web, CompuServe®, America Online®, Prodigy® — it's a world of ever-changing information. Don't get left behind!

Find out about new additions to our site, new bestsellers and hot topics

In-depth information on high-end topics: find the best reference books for databases, programming, networking, and client/server technologies

A recent addition to Que, Ziff-Davis Press publishes the highly-successful *How It Works* and *How to Use* series of books, as well as *PC Learning Labs Teaches* and *PC Magazine* series of book/disk packages

Stay on the cutting edge of Macintosh® technologies and visual communications

Find out which titles are making headlines

---

With 6 separate publishing groups, Que develops products for many specific market segments and areas of computer technology. Explore our Web Site and you'll find information on best-selling titles, newly published titles, upcoming products, authors, and much more.

- Stay informed on the latest industry trends and products available
- Visit our online bookstore for the latest information and editions
- Download software from Que's library of the best shareware and freeware

Copyright © 1996, Macmillan Computer Publishing-USA, A Viacom Company

# QUE has the right choice for every computer user

From the new computer user to the advanced programmer, we've got the right computer book for you. Our user-friendly *Using* series offers just the information you need to perform specific tasks quickly and move onto other things. And, for computer users ready to advance to new levels, QUE *Special Edition Using* books, the perfect all-in-one resource—and recognized authority on detailed reference information.

## The *Using* series for casual users

### Who should use this book?
Everyday users who:
- Work with computers in the office or at home
- Are familiar with computers but not in love with technology
- Just want to "get the job done"
- Don't want to read a lot of material

### The user-friendly reference
- The fastest access to the one best way to get things done
- Bite-sized information for quick and easy reference
- Nontechnical approach in plain English
- Real-world analogies to explain new concepts
- Troubleshooting tips to help solve problems
- Visual elements and screen pictures that reinforce topics
- Expert authors who are experienced in training and instruction

## *Special Edition Using* for accomplished users

### Who should use this book?
Proficient computer users who:
- Have a more technical understanding of computers
- Are interested in technological trends
- Want in-depth reference information
- Prefer more detailed explanations and examples

### The most complete reference
- Thorough explanations of various ways to perform tasks
- In-depth coverage of all topics
- Technical information cross-referenced for easy access
- Professional tips, tricks, and shortcuts for experienced users
- Advanced troubleshooting information with alternative approaches
- Visual elements and screen pictures that reinforce topics
- Technically qualified authors who are experts in their fields
- "Techniques form the Pros" sections with advice from well-known computer professionals

# Complete and Return this Card for a *FREE* Computer Book Catalog

Thank you for purchasing this book! You have purchased a superior computer book written expressly for your needs. To continue to provide the kind of up-to-date, pertinent coverage you've come to expect from us, we need to hear from you. Please take a minute to complete and return this self-addressed, postage-paid form. In return, we'll send you a free catalog of all our computer books on topics ranging from word processing to programming and the internet.

Mrs. ☐   Ms. ☐   Dr. ☐

(t) ☐☐☐☐☐☐☐☐☐☐☐☐☐☐   (M.I.) ☐   (last) ☐☐☐☐☐☐☐☐☐☐☐☐☐☐☐☐

☐☐☐☐☐☐☐☐☐☐☐☐☐☐☐☐☐☐☐☐☐☐☐☐☐☐☐☐☐☐☐☐☐☐

☐☐☐☐☐☐☐☐☐☐☐☐☐☐☐☐☐☐☐☐☐☐☐☐☐☐☐☐☐☐☐☐☐☐

☐☐☐☐☐☐☐☐☐☐☐☐☐☐☐   State ☐☐   Zip ☐☐☐☐☐ ☐☐☐☐

☐☐ ☐☐☐ ☐☐☐ ☐☐☐☐   Fax ☐☐☐ ☐☐☐ ☐☐☐☐

Name ☐☐☐☐☐☐☐☐☐☐☐☐☐☐☐☐☐☐☐☐☐☐☐☐☐☐☐☐☐☐☐☐

dress ☐☐☐☐☐☐☐☐☐☐☐☐☐☐☐☐☐☐☐☐☐☐☐☐☐☐☐☐☐☐☐☐

## check at least (3) influencing factors for asing this book.

back cover information on book ............... ☐
pproach to the content ............................... ☐
ness of content ............................................ ☐
reputation ..................................................... ☐
's reputation ................................................. ☐
er design or layout ..................................... ☐
table of contents of book ......................... ☐
book ............................................................. ☐
ffects, graphics, illustrations .................... ☐
ease specify): _____ ☐

## did you first learn about this book?

Macmillan Computer Publishing catalog ...... ☐
ended by store personnel ............................... ☐
book on bookshelf at store ............................ ☐
ended by a friend ............................................ ☐
d advertisement in the mail .......................... ☐
advertisement in: _____ ☐
ok review in: _____ ☐
ease specify): _____ ☐

## many computer books have you chased in the last six months?

ok only ....... ☐   3 to 5 books .................... ☐
............ ☐   More than 5 ...................... ☐

## 4. Where did you purchase this book?

Bookstore ......................................................... ☐
Computer Store ............................................... ☐
Consumer Electronics Store .......................... ☐
Department Store ........................................... ☐
Office Club ...................................................... ☐
Warehouse Club ............................................. ☐
Mail Order ....................................................... ☐
Direct from Publisher .................................... ☐
Internet site ..................................................... ☐
Other (Please specify): _____ ☐

## 5. How long have you been using a computer?

☐ Less than 6 months    ☐ 6 months to a year
☐ 1 to 3 years          ☐ More than 3 years

## 6. What is your level of experience with personal computers and with the subject of this book?

| | With PCs | With subject of book |
|---|---|---|
| New | ☐ | ☐ |
| Casual | ☐ | ☐ |
| Accomplished | ☐ | ☐ |
| Expert | ☐ | ☐ |

Source Code ISBN: 0-7897-0140-5

## 7. Which of the following best describes your job title?

- Administrative Assistant ☐
- Coordinator ☐
- Manager/Supervisor ☐
- Director ☐
- Vice President ☐
- President/CEO/COO ☐
- Lawyer/Doctor/Medical Professional ☐
- Teacher/Educator/Trainer ☐
- Engineer/Technician ☐
- Consultant ☐
- Not employed/Student/Retired ☐
- Other (Please specify): _____ ☐

## 8. Which of the following best describes the area of the company your job title falls under?

- Accounting ☐
- Engineering ☐
- Manufacturing ☐
- Operations ☐
- Marketing ☐
- Sales ☐
- Other (Please specify): _____ ☐

## 9. What is your age?

- Under 20
- 21-29
- 30-39
- 40-49
- 50-59
- 60-over

## 10. Are you:

- Male
- Female

## 11. Which computer publications do you read regularly? (Please list)

_____
_____
_____
_____
_____
_____
_____
_____

**Comments**: _____

Fold here and scotch

---

BUSINESS REPLY MAIL
FIRST-CLASS MAIL PERMIT NO. 9918 INDIANAPOLIS IN

POSTAGE WILL BE PAID BY THE ADDRESSEE

ATTN MARKETING
MACMILLAN COMPUTER PUBLISHING
MACMILLAN PUBLISHING USA
201 W 103RD ST
INDIANAPOLIS IN 46290-9042

NO POSTAGE
NECESSARY
IF MAILED
IN THE
UNITED STATES